THE NEW INTERNATIONAL COMMENTARY
ON THE
OLD TESTAMENT

General Editors

R. K. HARRISON
(1968–1993)

ROBERT L. HUBBARD, JR.
(1994–   )

The Book of
EZEKIEL

Chapters 25–48

DANIEL I. BLOCK

WILLIAM B. EERDMANS PUBLISHING COMPANY
GRAND RAPIDS, MICHIGAN / CAMBRIDGE, U.K.

Publisher's Note

This commentary was planned and written as a single volume, but its length dictated the need to publish it in two volumes. The reader should note that the Introduction the entire book of Ezekiel is presented in volume 1; this second volume comprises only commentary on chapters 25–48 of Ezekiel.

For the reader's convenience, each volume has its own table of contents, abbreviation list, and indexes.

© 1998 Wm. B. Eerdmans Publishing Co.
255 Jefferson Ave. S.E., Grand Rapids, Michigan 49503 /
P.O. Box 163, Cambridge CB3 9PU U.K.

Printed in the United States of America

03 02 01 00 99 98   7 6 5 4 3 2 1

Library of Congress Cataloging-in-Publication Data

Block, Daniel Isaac, 1943-
The Book of Ezekiel: chapters 25-48 / Daniel I. Block.
p.   cm.
Includes bibliographical references and indexes.
ISBN 0-8028-2536-2 (cloth: alk. paper)
1. Bible.   O.T. Ezekiel XXV-XLVIII — Commentaries.   I. Title.
BS1545.3.B575   1997
224′.4077 — dc21   96-49758
CIP

In gratitude to

HENRY J. HARDER
WALTER C. KAISER
ALAN R. MILLARD

CONTENTS

INDEXES

GENERAL EDITOR'S PREFACE

Long ago St. Paul wrote: "I planted, Apollos watered, but God gave the growth" (1 Cor. 3:6, NRSV). He was right: ministry indeed requires a team effort — the collective labors of many skilled hands and minds. Someone digs up the dirt and drops in seed, while others water the ground to nourish seedlings to growth. The same team effort over time has brought this commentary series to its position of prominence today. Professor E. J. Young "planted" it forty years ago, enlisting its first contributors and himself writing its first published volume. Professor R. K. Harrison "watered" it, signing on other scholars and wisely editing everyone's finished products. As General Editor, my hands now tend their planting, and, true to Paul's words, through four decades God has indeed graciously "[given] the growth."

Today the New International Commentary on the Old Testament enjoys a wide readership of scholars, priests, pastors, rabbis, and other serious Bible students. Thousands of readers across the religious spectrum and in countless countries consult its volumes in their ongoing preaching, teaching, and research. They warmly welcome the publication of each new volume and eagerly await its eventual transformation from an emerging "series" into a complete commentary "set." But as humanity experiences a new century of history, an era commonly called "postmodern," what kind of commentary series is NICOT? What distinguishes it from other similarly well-established series?

Its volumes aim to publish biblical scholarship of the highest quality. Each contributor writes as an expert, both in the biblical text itself and in the relevant scholarly literature, and each commentary conveys the results of wide reading and careful, mature reflection. Ultimately, its spirit is eclectic, each contributor gleaning interpretive insights from any useful source, whatever its religious or philosophical viewpoint, and integrating them into his or her interpretation of a biblical book. The series draws on recent methodological innovations in biblical scholarship, e.g., canon criticism, the so-called "new literary criticism," reader-response theories, and sensitivity to gender-based and ethnic readings. NICOT volumes also aim to be irenic in tone, summarizing and critiquing influential views with fairness while defending their own. Its list of contributors includes male and female scholars from a number of Christian faith-groups. The diversity of contributors and their freedom to draw on all relevant methodologies give the entire series an exciting and enriching variety.

What truly distinguishes this series, however, is that it speaks from within that interpretive tradition known as evangelicalism. Evangelicalism is an informal movement within Protestantism that cuts across traditional denominational lines. Its heart and soul is the conviction that the Bible is God's inspired Word, written by gifted human writers, through which God calls humanity to enjoy a loving personal relationship with its Creator and Savior. True to that tradition, NICOT volumes do not treat the Old Testament as just an ancient literary artifact on a par with the *Iliad* or the Gilgamesh Epic. They are not literary autopsies of ancient parchment cadavers but rigorous, reverent wrestlings with wonderfully human writings through which the living God speaks his powerful Word. NICOT delicately balances "criticism" (i.e., the use of standard critical methodologies) with humble respect, admiration, and even affection for the biblical text. As an evangelical commentary, it pays particular attention to the text's literary features, theological themes, and implications for the life of faith today.

Ultimately, NICOT aims to serve women and men of faith who desire to hear God's voice afresh through the Old Testament. With gratitude to God for two marvelous gifts — the Scriptures themselves and keen-minded scholars to explain their message — I welcome readers of all kinds to savor the good fruit of this series.

ROBERT L. HUBBARD, JR.

AUTHOR'S PREFACE

The publication of this book completes the commentary whose first volume appeared in 1997. The entire manuscript was submitted in March of 1994. Because my energies have been consumed with other projects, I have been unable to incorporate the advances in our understanding of Ezekiel 25–48 that have been made since then. I regret especially not having had access to the second volume of Moshe Greenberg's Anchor Bible commentary on this most intriguing of biblical books. No scholar has had a greater influence on my understanding of and approach to the book than Professor Greenberg.

For clarification regarding the aims and procedures that have driven my work on Ezekiel the reader is referred to the preface of the first volume. But here I must reiterate my deepest gratitude to those who have made this work possible. Thanks are expressed to the administration and faculty colleagues of Bethel Theological Seminary (St. Paul, Minn.) for their encouragement during twelve years of research and composition of this commentary. More recently, the Southern Baptist Theological Seminary (Louisville, Ky.) has graciously provided financial assistance and support for a proofreader of the page proofs. I repeat my expression of indebtedness to the late R. K. Harrison and his successor Robert L. Hubbard, Jr. for their encouragement to me to participate in the NICOT commentary series. Special personal thanks are extended to Mr. Gary Lee for his scrupulous editing of my manuscript, to Rick Mansfield for checking all the biblical references, and to Gloria Metz for her extraordinary skill and assistance in translating ideas from my head to computer-generated hard copy, as reflected in the figures in this volume. Above all these, I repeat my thanks to my wife Ellen and my children Jonelle and Jason for their unwavering loyalty and support. Without their daily encouragement I should have grown weary and despaired of ever completing the project, and without Ellen's kind assistance in preparing the indexes this volume might never have appeared.

Finally, I declare my sincere gratitude to all who have invested their energies in my life and ministry, particularly the three men to whom this volume is dedicated. Just as Noah, Job, and Daniel, whom Ezekiel lists as paragons of virtue in chapter 14, inspired the ancient Israelites to lives of faith and service, so this trio of men has encouraged me in my spiritual and academic pilgrimage. I am grateful to Rev. Henry Harder, whose preaching ignited in my heart a love for the Scriptures, especially the Old Testament, when I was a university student in Saskatoon, Saskatchewan. I am indebted to Dr. Walter C. Kaiser, my seminary professor and advisor, whose inspiring instruction fanned that spark into flame. My sincerest thanks are expressed to Alan R. Millard, my mentor in doctoral studies, who ushered me into the fascinating cultural world from which the book of Ezekiel arose. I dedicate this volume to these three in deepest gratitude for the unique part each of them has played in my academic and ministerial service.

But even as I honor my mentors, I express my gratitude to God for the fourteen years I have spent with another of his servants, the prophet Ezekiel. My desire is that this commentary might assist all who read it to hear and understand the message of this extraordinary messenger of God. At the same time, I offer this work as a sacrifice of praise to Jesus Christ. May the Lord, who has graciously redeemed us, receive the honor and glory due to him alone.

DANIEL I. BLOCK

ABBREVIATIONS

AARSR	American Academy of Religion Studies in Religion
AB	Anchor Bible
ABD	D. N. Freedman, et al., eds. *Anchor Bible Dictionary.* 6 vols. New York: Doubleday, 1992
AfO	*Archiv für Orientforschung*
AHW	W. von Soden, *Akkadisches Handwörterbuch.* 3 vols. Wiesbaden: Harrassowitz, 1965-81
AJA	*American Journal of Archaeology*
AJBA	*Australian Journal of Biblical Archaeology*
AJSL	*American Journal of Semitic Languages*
Akk.	Akkadian
ALUOS	*Annual of Leeds Oriental Society*
AnBib	Analecta biblica
ANEP	J. B. Pritchard, ed. *Ancient Near Eastern Pictures Relating to the Old Testament.* 2nd ed. Princeton: Princeton University Press, 1969
ANET	J. B. Pritchard, ed. *Ancient Near Eastern Texts Relating to the Old Testament.* 3rd ed. Princeton: Princeton University Press, 1969
ANETS	Ancient Near Eastern Texts and Studies
AnOr	Analecta orientalia
AOAT	Alter Orient und Altes Testament
ARAB	D. D. Luckenbill, *Ancient Records of Assyria and Babylonia.* 2 vols. Chicago: University of Chicago Press, 1926-27
Arab.	Arabic
Aram.	Aramaic
ARM	Archives royales de Mari
ArOr	*Archiv orientalni*
ASTI	*Annual of the Swedish Theological Institute*

ATANT	Abhandlungen zur Theologie des Alten und Neuen Testaments
AusBR	*Australian Biblical Review*
AUSS	*Andrews University Seminary Studies*
AV	Authorized (King James) Version
BA	*Biblical Archaeologist*
Bab.	Babylonian
BAR	*Biblical Archaeologist Reader*
BARev	*Biblical Archaeology Review*
BASOR	*Bulletin of the American Schools of Oriental Research*
BBB	Bonner biblische Beiträge
BBET	Beiträge zur biblischen Exegese und Theologie
BBR	*Bulletin of Biblical Research*
BDB	F. Brown, S. R. Driver, and C. A. Briggs, *Hebrew and English Lexicon of the Old Testament.* Repr. Oxford: Clarendon, 1959
BeO	*Bibbia e oriente*
BETL	Bibliotheca ephermeridum theologicarum lovaniensium
BFCT	Beiträge zur Förderung christlicher Theologie
BHS	*Biblica hebraica stuttgartensia*
BHT	Beiträge zur historischen Theologie
Bib	*Biblica*
BibLeb	*Bibel und Leben*
BibOr	Biblica et orientalia
BJRL	*Bulletin of the John Rylands University Library of Manchester*
BKAT	Biblischer Kommentar: Altes Testament
BN	*Biblische Notizen*
BO	*Bibliotheca orientalis*
BR	*Biblical Research*
BSOAS	*Bulletin of the School of Oriental and African Studies*
BTB	*Biblical Theology Bulletin*
BUS	Brown University Studies
BWANT	Beiträge zur Wissenschaft vom Alten und Neuen Testament
BZ	*Biblische Zeitschrift*
BZAW	Beihefte zur *ZAW*
CAD	I. J. Gelb, et al., eds. *Assyrian Dictionary of the Oriental Institute of the University of Chicago.* Chicago: Oriental Institute, 1956-
CahRB	Cahiers de la Revue biblique
CB	Century Bible
CBC	Cambridge Bible Commentary

CBQ	*Catholic Biblical Quarterly*
CCSL	Corpus Christianorum Series Latina
CD	Cairo (Genizah text of the) Damascus Document
CIS	*Corpus inscriptionum semiticarum*
CML	J. C. L. Gibson, *Canaanite Myths and Legends*. Rev. ed. Edinburgh: T. & T. Clark, 1978
ConBOT	Coniectanea biblica, Old Testament
CRAIBL	*Comptes rendus de l'Académie des inscriptions et belles-lettres*
CTA	A. Herdner, ed. *Corpus des tablettes en cunéiformes alphabétiques*. 2 vols. Paris: Imprimerie Nationale, 1963
DBSup	*Dictionnaire de la Bible, Supplément*
DDD	K. van der Toorn, et al., eds. *Dictionary of Deities and Demons in the Bible*. Leiden: Brill, 1995
DISO	C.-F. Jean and J. Hoftijzer, *Dictionnaire des inscriptions sémitiques de l'ouest*. Leiden: Brill, 1965
DNWSI	J. Hoftijzer and K. Jongeling, *Dictionary of the North-west Semitic Inscriptions*. 2 vols. Handbook of Oriental Studies 2. Leiden: Brill, 1995
EAEHL	M. Avi-Yonah and E. Stern, eds. *Encyclopedia of Archaeological Excavations in the Holy Land*. 4 vols. Englewood Cliffs, N.J.: Prentice-Hall, 1975-78
EB	Echter Bibel
Egyp.	Egyptian
EM	*Encyclopedia Miqrait*
EncJud	*Encyclopedia Judaica*
ErFor	Erträge der Forschung
ErIsr	*Eretz Israel*
ETL	*Ephermerides theologicae lovanienses*
ETSMS	Evangelical Theological Society Monograph Series
ExpTim	*Expository Times*
FB	Forschung zur Bibel
FOTL	Forms of the Old Testament Literature
FRLANT	Forschungen zur Religion und Literatur des Alten und Neuen Testaments
Gk.	Greek
GKC	*Gesenius' Hebrew Grammar*. Ed. E. Kautzsch. Tr. A. E. Cowley. 2nd ed. Oxford: Clarendon, 1910
Greg	*Gregorianum*
GTJ	*Grace Theological Journal*
HALAT	W. Baumgartner, et al., eds. *Hebräisches und aramäisches Lexikon zum Alten Testament*. 4 vols. Leiden: Brill, 1967-90

HALOT	W. Baumgartner, et al., eds. *The Hebrew and Aramaic Lexicon of the Old Testament*. Tr. and ed. M. E. J. Richardson. Leiden: Brill, 1994
HAR	*Hebrew Annual Review*
HAT	Handbuch zum Alten Testament
HBC	J. L. Mays, et al., eds. *Harper's Bible Commentary*. San Francisco: Harper & Row, 1988
HBD	P. J. Achtemeier, et al., eds. *Harper's Bible Dictionary*. San Francisco: Harper & Row, 1985
Heb.	Hebrew
HS	*Hebrew Studies*
HSAT	Heilige Schrift des Alten Testaments
HSM	Harvard Semitic Monographs
HSS	Harvard Semitic Studies
HTR	*Harvard Theological Review*
HTS	*Hervormde Teologiese Studies*
HUCA	*Hebrew Union College Annual*
IB	G. A. Buttrick, et al., eds. *Interpreter's Bible*. 12 vols. Nashville: Abingdon, 1953-56
IBD	J. D. Douglas, et al., eds. *Illustrated Bible Dictionary*. 3 vols. Leicester: Tyndale; Wheaton, Ill.: InterVarsity, 1982
ICC	International Critical Commentary
IDB	G. A. Buttrick, et al., eds. *Interpreter's Dictionary of the Bible*. 4 vols. Nashville: Abingdon, 1962
IDBSup	K. Crim, et al., eds. *Interpreter's Dictionary of the Bible, Supplementary Volume*. Nashville: Abingdon, 1976
IEJ	*Israel Exploration Journal*
Int	*Interpretation*
IOS	*Israel Oriental Society*
ISBE	G. W. Bromiley, et al., eds. *International Standard Bible Encyclopedia*. Rev. ed. 4 vols. Grand Rapids: Eerdmans, 1979-88
JANES	*Journal of the Ancient Near Eastern Society*
JAOS	*Journal of the American Oriental Society*
JB	Jerusalem Bible
JBC	R. E. Brown, et al., eds. *Jerome Biblical Commentary*. Englewood Cliffs, N.J.: Prentice-Hall, 1968
JBL	*Journal of Biblical Literature*
JBLMS	JBL Monograph Series
JCS	*Journal of Cuneiform Studies*
JDS	Judean Desert Series
JESHU	*Journal of the Economic and Social History of the Orient*

JETS	*Journal of the Evangelical Theological Society*
JJS	*Journal of Jewish Studies*
JNSL	*Journal of Northwest Semitic Languages*
JQR	*Jewish Quarterly Review*
JSOT	*Journal for the Study of the Old Testament*
JSOTSup	*JSOT* Supplements
JSS	*Journal of Semitic Studies*
JSSEA	*Journal of the Society for the Study of Egyptian Antiquities*
JTS	*Journal of Theological Studies*
KAI	H. Donner and W. Röllig, eds. *Kanaanäische und aramäische Inschriften.* 3 vols. Wiesbaden: Harrassowitz, 1962-71
KAT	Kommentar zum Alten Testament
KB	L. Koehler and W. Baumgartner, *Lexicon in Veteris Testamenti libros.* 2nd ed. Leiden: Brill, 1958
KeH	Kurzgefasstes exegetisches Handbuch zum Alten Testament
KTU	M. Dietrich, et al., eds. *Die keilalphabetischen Texte aus Ugarit.* Vol. 1. AOAT 24. Neukirchen-Vluyn: Neukirchener, 1976
LÄ	W. Helck and E. Otto, eds. *Lexikon d'Ägyptologie.* Wiesbaden: 1972-
LD	Lectio divina
Leš	*Lešonénu*
LSJ	Liddell, Scott, Jones, *Greek-English Lexicon.* 9th ed. Repr. Oxford: Clarendon, 1961
LXX	Septuagint
MIO	*Mitteilungen des Instituts für Orientforschung*
ms(s).	manuscript(s)
MT	Masoretic Text
NASB	New American Standard Bible
NCBC	New Century Bible Commentary
NEB	New English Bible
NICOT	New International Commentary on the Old Testament
NIV	New International Version
NJPS	New Jewish Publication Society Version
NovTSup	*Novum Testamentum,* Supplements
NRSV	New Revised Standard Version
NTS	*New Testament Studies*
OBO	Orbis biblicus et orientalis
OBT	Overtures to Biblical Theology
Or	*Orientalia*
OTL	Old Testament Library

OTP	J. H. Charlesworth, ed. *Old Testament Pseudepigrapha*. 2 vols. Garden City, N.Y.: Doubleday, 1983-85
OTS	*Oudtestamentische Studiën*
par.	parallel
PEFQS	*Palestine Exploration Fund, Quarterly Statement*
PEQ	*Palestine Exploration Quarterly*
PG	J.-P. Migne, ed. *Patrologiae Graeca*. 162 vols. Paris: 1857-66
PJ	*Palästina-Jahrbuch*
PL	J.-P. Migne, ed. *Patrologiae Latina*. 221 vols. Paris: 1844-64
PRU	*Palais royal d'Ugarit*
PTMS	Pittsburgh Theological Monograph Series
Qad	*Qadmoniot*
RA	*Revue d'assyriologie*
RAI	Rencontre assyriologique internationale
RB	*Revue Biblique*
REB	Revised English Bible
REJ	*Revue des études juives*
RevQ	*Revue de Qumran*
RHR	*Revue de l'histoire des religions*
RivB	*Rivista biblica*
RLA	G. Ebeling, et al., eds. *Reallexikon der Assyriologie*. Berlin and New York: de Gruyter, 1932-
RS	Ras Shamra
RSP	*Ras Shamra Parallels*. 3 vols. AnOr 49-51. Vols. 1-2 ed. L. Fisher; vol. 3 ed. S. Rummel. Rome: Pontifical Biblical Institute, 1972-81
RSPT	*Revue des sciences philosophiques et théologiques*
RSV	Revised Standard Version
SANE	Sources from the Ancient Near East
SAOC	Studies in Ancient Oriental Civilizations
SBB	Stuttgarter biblische Beiträge
SBLDS	Society of Biblical Literature Dissertation Series
SBLMS	SBL Monograph Series
SBLSBS	SBL Sources for Biblical Study
SBLSCS	SBL Septuagint and Cognate Studies
SBS	Stuttgarter Bibelstudien
SBT	Studies in Biblical Theology
ScrHier	Scripta Hierosolymitana
SJLA	Studies in Judaism in Late Antiquity
SJOT	*Scandinavian Journal of Theology*
SNTSMS	Society for New Testament Studies Monograph Series
SOTSMS	Society for Old Testament Studies Monograph Series

SR	*Studies in Religion/Sciences religieuses*
ST	*Studia theologica*
Syr.	Syriac
TA	*Tel Aviv*
Targ.	Targum
TBT	*The Bible Today*
TCS	Texts from Cuneiform Sources
TDNT	G. Kittel and G. Friedrich, eds. *Theological Dictionary of the New Testament.* 10 vols. Tr. G. W. Bromiley. Grand Rapids: Eerdmans, 1964-76
TDOT	G. Botterweck and H. Ringgren, eds. *Theological Dictionary of the Old Testament.* Tr. D. Green, et al. Grand Rapids: Eerdmans, 1974-
TEV	Today's English Version
THAT	E. Jenni and C. Westermann, eds. *Theologisches Handwörterbuch zum Alten Testament.* 2 vols. Munich: Kaiser, 1971-76
TLZ	*Theologische Literaturzeitung*
TOTC	Tyndale Old Testament Commentary
TQ	*Theologische Quartalschrift*
TSK	*Theologische Studien und Kritiken*
TSSI	J. C. L. Gibson, ed. *Textbook of Syrian Semitic Inscriptions.* 3 vols. Oxford: Clarendon, 1971-82
TTZ	*Trierer theologische Zeitschrift*
TynBul	*Tyndale Bulletin*
TZ	*Theologische Zeitschrift*
UF	*Ugarit-Forschungen*
UT	C. Gordon, *Ugaritic Textbook.* AnOr 38. Rome: Pontifical Biblical Institute, 1965
UUÅ	Uppsala universitetsårsskrift
VAB	Vorderasiatische Bibliothek
VT	*Vetus Testamentum*
VTSup	*Vetus Testamentum,* Supplements
WBC	Word Biblical Commentary
WMANT	Wissenschaftliche Monographien zum Alten und Neuen Testament
WTJ	*Westminster Theological Journal*
WZKM	*Wiener Zeitschrift für die Kunde des Morgenlandes*
ZA	*Zeitschrift für Assyriologie*
ZAH	*Zeitschrift für Althebraistik*
ZAW	*Zeitschrift für die alttestamentliche Wissenschaft*
ZDMG	*Zeitschrift der deutschen morgenländischen Gesellschaft*

ZDPV	*Zeitschrift des deutschen Palästina-Vereins*
ZRGG	*Zeitschrift für Religions- und Geistesgeschichte*
ZThK	*Zeitschrift für Theologie und Kirche*
ZWT	*Zeitschrift für wissenschaftliche Theologie*

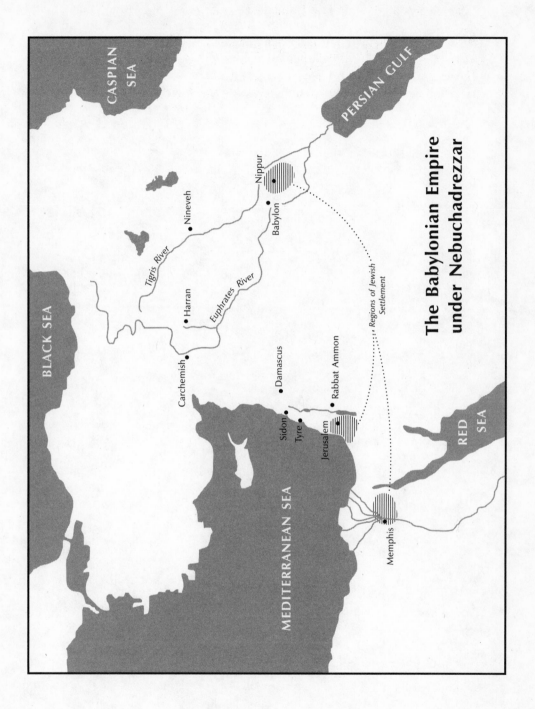

The Babylonian Empire under Nebuchadrezzar

PART 2

MESSAGES OF HOPE AND RESTORATION FOR JUDAH/ISRAEL (25:1–48:35)

I. NEGATIVE MESSAGES OF HOPE: THE ORACLES AGAINST FOREIGN NATIONS (25:1–32:32)

♦ *Nature and Design*

Ezekiel 25:1 marks a major break in the collection of Ezekiel's oracles. Until this point his prophecies had dealt with the fate of Jerusalem, climaxing in the specific prediction of the city's fall in 24:25-27. It is possible that the account of the fulfillment of this prophecy in ch. 33 followed immediately after the prediction in an earlier edition of these oracles. The editor(s) may have felt the need for a buffer between the prophet's harsh pronouncements of judgment in chs. 4–24 (i.e., chs. 4–24 plus ch. 33) and the hopeful oracles of chs. 34–48. One may view the genre of the oracles against the nations as transitional or hybrid forms. Like the preceding messages concerning Jerusalem, chs. 25–32 consist exclusively of judgment oracles. But no longer are they directed against Judah/Israel. Indeed, in anticipating the judgment of the enemies of God's people, they function as indirect messages of hope, a conclusion reinforced by the fragment separating the oracles against Tyre from those directed against Egypt (28:24-26). The resulting structure of the book (oracles of judgment — oracles against foreign nations — oracles of deliverance) bears a striking resemblance to other collections, specifically those of Isaiah, Zephaniah, and the LXX arrangement of Jeremiah. Oracles against foreign nations were apparently considered transitional, linking words of woe with proclamations of good news.

Nonetheless, to speak of the oracles against foreign nations as a distinctive genre is misleading.[1] Ezekiel's prophecies in this collection display no functional or formal differences from his oracles of judgment against Judah/Israel. The reasons for judgment are similar (social sins, hubris, etc.), the divine punishment is the same (the curses against Judah are turned against Judah's enemies), the vocabulary and tone are similar, and the forms are the same.[2] Ezekiel's audience would undoubtedly have

---

1. Contra Hals, *Ezekiel,* p. 351. For a study of oracles against froreign nations as a genre, see D. L. Christensen, *Transformations of the War Oracle in Old Testament Prophecy: Studies in the Oracles Against the Nations,* HDS 3 (Missoula, Mont.: Scholars Press, 1975).

2. Ezekiel's prophecies against foreign nations include proof oracles (most ending with the recognition formula; 25:1-7; 25:8-11; 25:12-14; 25:15-17; 26:1-6; 28:20-23; 29:1-16; 29:17-21; 30:1-19; 30:20-26), basic judgment oracles (25:1–26:21; 28:1-10; 28:20-26; 29:1-21; 30:16-26), prophetic laments (27:1-36; 28:11-19; 30:1-5; 32:1-32), and extended metaphors (27:1-36; 28:11-19; 29:1-9; 31:1-18). The overlapping reflects the paucity of "pure" forms of the genres.

welcomed these prophecies because they portrayed their enemies as the objects of Yahweh's judgment.[3]

Not all of Ezekiel's oracles against foreign nations are gathered in chs. 25–32. In ch. 35 an extended message concerning Edom interrupts his salvation oracles. Some scholars place the oracles against Gog in chs. 38–39 within this class as well.[4] The prophet may well have proclaimed additional oracles against the nations listed here, to say nothing of the nations not found in this collection. Conspicuously absent are messages addressed to the most powerful nation of the day, and the one most affecting Judean affairs, Babylon.[5] From 21:33-37 (Eng. 21:28-32) it is evident that Ezekiel occasionally drew Babylon into his judgmental pronouncements, but oracles of the type found in this part of the book are absent entirely. This absence may undoubtedly be attributed to the prophet's pro-Babylonian stance in political matters. To him Babylon was the sword in Yahweh's hand, executing his judgment on Judah. Indeed, the objects of divine wrath in these texts seem to have been selected deliberately, not only because they rejoiced over the demise of Judah but also because they stood in Nebuchadrezzar's divinely ordained path. This view would account for the inordinate attention given to Tyre and Egypt, who represented the principal obstacles to the fulfillment of the Babylonian's mission.

As already suggested, the function of these oracles is not simply to provide a transition between oracles of judgment against Judah and messages of hope for the nation. The nations addressed by Ezekiel all represented the enemies of Israel. Thus a divine pronouncement of judgment on them also served as a backhanded message of hope. Evidence for this understanding is found in the broad symmetrical structure of these oracles. Positioned at the center of this section is the key that unlocks the entire unit. The words of hope inserted in 28:24-26 function as a fulcrum, dividing Ezekiel's oracles against foreign nations into two sensitively balanced halves, virtually identical in length (see the diagram on p. 5).

This large section (chs. 25–32) displays other signs of deliberate structuring as well. It is dominated by the number seven.[6] Seven nations/states are

---

3. So also D. J. Reimer ("Political Prophets? Another Look at the Oracles Against Foreign Nations," paper read to the Society of Biblical Literature Annual Meeting, San Francisco, November, 1992), who rightly rejects Christensen's view of the writing prophets as political advisers on international affairs.

4. On the special form of these oracles see the commentary below.

5. Ezekiel's silence concerning Babylon contrasts with Jeremiah's utterances. Jeremiah devotes two chapters to Babylon (50:1–51:58), exceeding in length (104 verses) all of Ezekiel's oracles against Egypt.

6. On the significance of the number seven in the OT and the ancient Near East see A. S. Kapelrud, "The Number Seven in Ugaritic Texts," *VT* 18 (1968) 494-99; M. H. Pope, "Seven, Seventh, Seventy," *IDB*, 3:294-95.

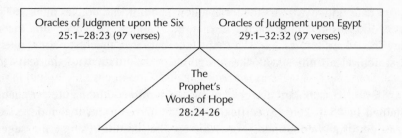

| Oracles of Judgment upon the Six
25:1–28:23 (97 verses) | Oracles of Judgment upon Egypt
29:1–32:32 (97 verses) |

The
Prophet's
Words of Hope
28:24-26

addressed: Bene Ammon (25:1-7), Moab (25:8-11), Edom (25:12-14), Philistia (25:15-17), Tyre (26:1–28:19), Sidon (28:20-23), and Egypt (29:1–32:32), a pattern reminiscent of Amos's proclamations against nations foreign to the northern kingdom in Amos 1:3–2:5.[7] But no effort is made to reduce these oracles to a common length. The prophecies against Egypt are equal in length to the sum of the previous six. Even among the latter there is great variation, from the short prophetic vignettes against Bene Ammon, Moab, Edom, Philistia, and Sidon, to almost three chapters devoted to Tyre. Seven mini-oracles are incorporated into the first half.[8] Seven oracles against Egypt are preserved in 29:1–32:32, signaled by the sevenfold occurrence of the word-event formula.[9] Seven date notices break up the oracles.[10]

Like Amos's oracles against the nations, Ezekiel's appear to be geographically arranged. In the first half (25:1–28:23) the prophet begins by gazing directly to the east (Bene Ammon), and, moving in a clockwise direction, he deals successively with Moab, Edom, Philistia, Tyre, and Sidon.[11] Structurally these prophecies divide into three major parts: (1) short oracles against the five nations (25:1–26:6); (2) additional Tyrian oracles (26:7–28:19); (3) a short oracle against Sidon. The classification of 26:1-6 among the oracles in ch. 25 may be questioned, especially since its intro-

7. The heptad of nations recalls Deut. 7:1, which lists the seven nations occupying the promised land. Garscha (*Studien,* p. 133) suggests that the prophet may be envisioning the eventual return of Judah as a new exodus. For a full discussion of Amos's oracles see J. Barton, *Amos's Oracles against the Nations, SOTSMS 6* (Cambridge: Cambridge University Press, 1980). For a comparison of Amos's and Ezekiel's oracles see J. B. Geyer, "Mythology and Culture in the Oracles Against the Nations," *VT* 36 (1986) 131-32.

8. The dropping of Egypt is compensated for by doubling the oracle(s) against Bene Ammon (25:1-5 and 6-7). See tables 1 and 2.

9. See 29:1, 17; 30:1, 20; 31:1; 32:1, 17.

10. See 26:1; 29:1, 17; 30:20; 31:1; 32:1, 17.

11. This arrangement may explain the placement of the oracle against Sidon (28:20-24) after Tyre, even though in length it resembles the first four (25:1-17). The oracles against Egypt (chs. 29–32) have their own distinctive style and structure, and may be treated separately.

ductory date notice appears to signal a new subunit, the oracles against Tyre that extend through most of the next three chapters. However, this discrepancy should not blind the reader to the fact that it has much stronger stylistic and structural affinities with the foregoing oracles than with the texts that follow.

Even so, scholars disagree about the number of separate prophecies contained in 25:1–26:6. Specifically, do 25:1-7 represent two independent oracles editorially combined,[12] or is the prophet issuing a single message in two parts? The latter is more likely, not only because the two segments are deliberately and uniquely connected by the particle *kî,* but also because the general nature of vv. 6-7 seems to presuppose vv. 3-5. Without vv. 3-5 a reason for Bene Ammon's joy "over the land of Israel" is missing. Furthermore, Yahweh's declaration of his determination to eliminate Bene Ammon as a nation in v. 7 is much more powerful if it is viewed against the backdrop of Bene Ammon's gloating over the annihilation of Israel in v. 3. Nevertheless, as the synopsis in table 1 (p. 7) indicates, both panels of this oracle preserve many of the formulaic features of the separate oracles that follow. With some variation, these mini-oracles tend to follow the standard structure of judgment oracles, each panel consisting of: (1) the introductory citation formula (26:1-6 being an exception); (2) the indictment introduced by *ya'an,* "because" (28:21-22 being an exception); (3) the punishment introduced by *lākēn,* "therefore," followed by two or more announcements of divine actions;[13] (4) the effect, described by means of the recognition formula. In view of the similarities already mentioned it is perhaps not surprising that this well-defined structure finds its closest parallel in Amos's oracles against the foreign nations (1:3–2:8), though Ezekiel's pronouncements lack Amos's second element, the proclamation of irreversible judgment.[14] Another common feature is the absence of mythological or religious motifs that characterize many of the other oracles against the nations that follow in Ezekiel (chs. 27–32) and those found in the other major prophets, Isaiah (chs. 13–23) and Jeremiah (chs. 46–51).

Stylistically and lexically the oracles display considerable overlapping (table 2, pp. 8-11). Each describes the judgment pronounced on the respective nations in broad terms, the emphasis being on Yahweh's personal initiative and involvement. But the pool of verbs and idioms used to describe his action,

---

12. So most scholars: Zimmerli, *Ezekiel 2,* pp. 12-14; Fohrer, *Ezechiel,* pp. 145-46; Wevers, *Ezekiel,* p. 196; van den Born, *Ezechiël,* pp. 159-60; Garscha, *Studien,* pp. 135-36.

13. Ezek. 28:20-23 lacks *lākēn,* but this is more than compensated for by the twofold statement of divine action, each of which ends with its own recognition formula.

14. "For three transgressions and for four I will not revoke the punishment." Cf. Geyer, *VT* 36 (1986) 131.

Table 1: Prophetic Formulas in Ezekiel's Short Oracles Against Nations

Formula	Ammon A 25:1-5	Ammon B 25:6-7	Moab 25:8-11	Edom 25:12-14	Philistia 25:15-17	Tyre 26:1-6	Sidon 28:20-24
Date Notice						X	
And the word of Yahweh came to me saying	X					X	X
Human (ben 'ādam)	X					X	X
Set your face to GN	X						X
Prophesy against GN and say . . .	X						X
Hear the word of the Lord Yahweh	X						
Thus has the Lord Yahweh declared	X	X	X	X	X		X
Because you ... (ya'an 'ăšer + verb)	X	X	X	X	X	X	
Therefore . . . (lākēn)	X	X	X	X	X	X	
Thus has the Lord Yahweh declared				X	X	X	
Behold I (hinĕnî) + participle	X		X		X		
Behold I + perfect		X					
Behold I + am against you						X	X
waw + perfect	X	X	X	X	X	X	X
For I have spoken						X	
The declaration of the Lord Yahweh						X	
waw + perfect	X	X	X	X	X	X	
And they/you will know that I am Yahweh	X	X	X	X(?)	X	X	X
The declaration of the Lord Yahweh				X			
waw + perfect							X
And they will know that I am Yahweh							X

7

Table 2. Ezekiel's Short Oracles Against the Nations: A Synopsis

25:1-5	25:6-7	25:8-11	25:12-14	25:15-17	26:1-6	28:21-24
hinĕnî	hinĕnî	hinĕnî		hinĕnî	hinĕnî	hinĕnî
					ʿālayik ṣōr	ʿalayik ṣidôn
nōtĕnāk	nāṭîtî ʾet-yādî	pōtēaḥ	wĕnāṭitî yādî	nōṭeh yādî	wĕhaʿălêtî ʿālayik	
libnê-qedem lĕmôrāšâ	ʾālêkā	ʾet-ketep môʾāb	ʾal-ʾĕdôm	ʾal-pĕlištîm	gôyim rabbîm	
wĕyiššĕbû		mēhe ʿārîm			kĕha ʿālôt	
		mēʿārāyw miqqāṣēhû			hayyām lĕgallāyw	
ṭirôtêhem bāk		ṣĕbî ʾereṣ			wĕšiḥătû	
wĕnātĕnû bāk miškĕnêhem		bêt hayĕšîmōt			ḥōmôt ṣōr	
hēmmâ yōʾkĕlû piryēk		baʿal mĕʿôn			wĕhārĕsû	
wĕhēmmâ yištû ḥălābēk		wĕqiryātāmâ			migdālêhā	
wĕnātattî	ûnĕtatîkā-	libnê-qedem	wĕhikrattî	wĕhikrattî	wĕsiḥetî	wĕnikbadtî

25:1-5	25:6-7	25:8-11	25:12-14	25:15-17	26:1-6	28:21-24
ʾet-rabbâ	lěbag laggôyim	ʿal-běnê ʿammôn	mimmennâ	ʾet-kěrētîm	ʾăpārāh mimmennâ	bětôkēk
linwēh gěmallîm		ûnětattîhā	ʾādām ûběhēmâ			
wěʾet-běnê ʿammôn		lěmôrāšâ				
lěmirbas-ṣōʾn		lěmaʿan lōʾ-tizzākēr				
		běnê-ʿammôn				
		baggôyim				
	wěhikrattîkā	ûběmôʾāb	ûnětattîhā	wěhaʾăbadtî	wěnātattî ʾōtāh	
	min-hāʿammîm	ʾeʿĕśeh	ḥorbâ mittêmān	ʾet-šěʾērît	lišḥaḥ sālaʿ	
		šěpāṭîm	ûdědāneh	hôp hayyām	miṣṭaḥ hărāmîm	
					tihyeh	
			baḥereb yippōlû		bětôk hayyām	
					kî ʾănî dibbartî	
					něʾum ʾădōnāy yhwh	

	25:1-5	25:6-7	25:8-11	25:12-14	25:15-17	26:1-6	28:21-24
						wĕhāyĕtā	
		wĕha'ăbadtîkā				*lēbaz laggôyim*	
		min-hā'ărāṣôt				*ûbĕnôtêhā*	
						'ăšer baśśādeh	
				wĕnātattî	*wĕ'āśîtî bām*	*baḥereb tēhārāgnā*	
				'et-niqmātî	*nĕqāmôt gĕdōlôt*		
				bĕ'ĕdōm	*bĕtôkĕḥōt ḥēmā*		
				bĕyad 'ammî yiśrā'ēl			
		'ašmîdĕkā		*wĕ'āśû bĕ'ĕdōm kĕ'appî wĕkaḥămātî*			*wĕyādĕ'û*
	wîda'tem	*wĕyāda'tā*	*wĕyādĕ'û*	*wĕyādĕ'û*	*wĕyādĕ'û*	*wĕyādĕ'û*	
				'et-niqmātî			
	kî-'ănî yhwh	*kî-'ănî yhwh*	*kî-'ănî yhwh*	*nĕ'um 'ădōnāy yhwh*	*kî-'ănî yhwh*	*kî-'ănî yhwh*	*kî-'ănî yhwh*

	28:21-24	26:1-6	25:15-17	25:12-14	25:8-11	25:6-7	25:1-5
	ba'ăśôtî bāh		bĕtittî				
	šĕpātîm		'et-niqmātî bām				
	wĕniqdaštî bāh						
	wĕšillaḥtî-bāh						
	deber wādām						
	bĕḥûṣôtêhā						
	wĕniplal ḥālāl						
	bĕtôkāh						
	bĕḥereb 'ālêhā						
	missābîb						
	wĕyādĕ'û						
	kî-'ănî yhwh						

particularly in the first six, is limited.[15] Indeed, of the twenty-one verbal forms only four occur once.[16] Numerous nominal links are also present,[17] creating the impression of a tightly knit, composite literary entity. This effect is strengthened by the features shared by the oracles against Bene Ammon and Tyre, which frame the entire unit: extended introductory statements involving the word-event formula and the direct address of the prophet as *ben-'ādām* ("human"), the reference to the addressee in the second person, and partic-ularly the quoted interjection *he'āḥ* ("Aha"), which occurs only in 25:3 and 26:2.

The recognition of these links between 26:1-6 and the foregoing should not obscure its connections with the following. In fact, this short section is transitional, 26:7-14 providing an exposition of the judgment pronounced on Tyre in vv. 3-6. Not only are the general comments found in vv. 3-6 replaced by specific details; but the focus also shifts from the divine activity to that of Nebuchadrezzar, Yahweh's agent. Vv. 15-21 describe the effects of the judg-ment of Tyre on the nations that witness the event. By contrast, 27:1-36 and 28:1-19 obviously represent independent oracles, each possessing its own introductory word-event formula.

The general nature of all these short oracles makes it impossible to date any of the oral pronouncements, except that the charges in each case presuppose the fall of Jerusalem in 586 B.C. Ezekiel's pronouncements of judgment on Israel's enemies would have excited the patriotic sensitivities of the Judean exiles. Although some have compared these prophecies with politi-cal pamphlets,[18] the recognition formula with which each ends suggests that the prophet's intention went far beyond merely satisfying nationalistic long-ings. These are proof sayings *(Erweisworte)*, whose aim is to announce each divine intervention in international affairs as a moment of self-disclosure for Yahweh.

---

15. The connections may be summarized as follows: *nātattî lě,* "I will impose," Ammon A, Ammon B, Moab, Tyre; *nāṭîtî yādî 'al,* "I will raise my hand against," Ammon B, Edom, Philistines; *hikrît (min),* "I will cut off from," Ammon B, Edom, Philistia; *'āśîtî,* "I will act," Moab, Edom, Philistia; *he'ěbîd,* "I will destroy," Ammon B, Philistia.

16. *hišmîd,* "to destroy," *pātaḥ,* "to open," *he'ěleh,* "to raise," *šāḥat,* "to be ruined."

17. *'admat yiśrā'ēl,* "the land of Israel," Ammon A, Ammon B; *šě'āṭ běnepeš,* "scorn of soul," Ammon B, Philistia (cf. also Sidon in 28:24); *běnê qedem,* "Qedemites," Ammon A, Moab; *môrāšâ,* "possession," Ammon A, Moab; *lěbaz laggôyim,* "for the plunder of nations," Ammon B, Tyre; *'ammîm,* "peoples," Ammon B, Tyre; *gôyim,* "na-tions," Ammon A, Moab, Tyre; *horbâ,* "waste," Edom, Tyre; *hereb,* "sword, Edom," Tyre; *bêt yěhûdâ,* "house of Judah," Ammon A, Moab, Edom.

18. See van den Born, *Ezechiël,* p. 158.

A. ORACLES OF JUDGMENT CONCERNING THE FIVE NATIONS (25:1–28:23)

1. Short Oracles Against Israel's Neighbors (25:1-17)

a. The Oracle(s) Against Bene Ammon (25:1-7)

1 *The following message of Yahweh came to me:* 2 *"Human, set your face toward Bene Ammon, and prophesy against them,* 3 *and say, 'O Bene Ammon![19] Hear the word of the Lord[20] Yahweh! Thus has the Lord Yahweh declared: Because you exclaimed,[21] "Aha!" against my sanctuary, when it was desecrated,[22] and against the land of Israel, when it was laid waste, and against the house of Judah, when they went off into exile —*

4 *Therefore I am handing you[23] over to the Qedemites, as dispossessed property.[24] They will set up[25] their encampments[26] and pitch their dwellings within you. They will devour your produce and drink your milk.* 5 *But I will transform Rabbah[27] into a pastureland for*

19. The vocative *lamed* is suggested by the fact that vv. 1-3a are formally virtually identical to 6:1-3, where the corresponding phrase *hārê yiśrā'ēl,* "O mountains of Israel," functions vocatively.

20. Many follow LXX in deleting *'ădōnāy* as anomalous in this formula. Cf. Allen, *Ezekiel 20–48,* p. 65.

21. MT's switch from masc. pl. (cf. "them," v. 2) to fem. sg. reflects *běnê 'ammôn*'s function as a territorial designation. See the commentary.

22. *niḥāl* is a Niphal perfect (cf. 7:24; 22:16); on the form see GKC, §67u.

23. The rare form of the fem. suffix on *nōtěnāk* (in place of expected *-ēk*) after *hiněnî* has occurred earlier in 23:28. LXX reads pl.

24. Although *môrāšâ* is rendered κληρονομίαν, "inheritance," by LXX, the root *yrš* has less to do with inheritance than with the simple transfer of property. The interpretation of Bene Ammon as a geographic designation, based on the fem. form of the suffix on *nōtēn,* is supported by the observation that *môrāšâ* is used elsewhere exclusively of land. Cf. 11:15; 25:10; 33:24; 36:2, 3 (contra BDB, p. 440), 5; Exod. 6:8; Deut. 33:4.

25. This is the only occurrence of *yiššēb* (Piel) in the OT, though it is common in Mishnaic Hebrew (Jastrow, *Dictionary,* p. 599). An analogous Yiphil form meaning "to cause to dwell" is attested in Phoenician (*KAI,* 14.17), on which see J. Friedrich and W. Röllig, *Phönizisch-punische Grammatik,* AnOr 46, rev. ed. (Rome: Pontifical Biblical Institute, 1970), §§158, 161, 187.

26. MT reads "within you" (*bāk*) after *ṭîrôt,* "encampments." In our translation "within you" at the end of the sentence does double duty. The latter, which is related to *ṭûr,* "row," refers not to cattle pens or sheepfolds, as is commonly thought, but to fortified nomadic settlements. Cf. A. Malamat, "*Ummatum* in Old Babylonian Texts and Its Ugaritic and Biblical Counterparts," *UF* 11 (1979) 533 n. 35. Num. 31:10 has the Midianites occupying such encampments.

27. The stereotypical compound phrase *rabbat běnê 'ammôn,* "Rabbah of Bene

13

camels,[28] *and Bene Ammon into a resting place*[29] *for flocks. Then you*[30]
will know that I am Yahweh.

6 *For thus has the Lord Yahweh declared: Because you clapped*[31]
your hand, and stamped your feet, and rejoiced with utter contempt[32]
over the land of Israel, 7 *therefore see,*[33] *I have stretched*[34] *out my hand
against you, and I will hand you over as booty*[35] *to the nations. I will
cut you off from among the peoples, and destroy you from the countries.
I will eliminate you.*[36] *Then you will know that I am Yahweh.' "*

1-3 The placement of the oracle against Bene Ammon at the head of the
oracles against foreign nations and the elaborate introduction[37] suggest that

---

Ammon" (Ezek. 21:25 [Eng. 20]; 2 Sam. 12:26, 27; 17:27; Deut. 3:11; Jer. 49:2) has been
broken up for the sake of the parallelism.

28. With *nĕwēh gĕmallîm* cf. *nĕwēh rō'îm,* "abode of shepherds" (Jer. 33:12); *nĕwēh
ṣō'n,* "abode of the flock" (Isa. 65:10); *nĕwēh tannîm,* "abode of jackals" (Isa. 34:13; 35:7);
nĕwôt midbār, "desert abode" (Jer. 9:9; 23:10; Ps. 65:13; Joel 1:19, 20; 2:22); *nĕ'ôt dеšе',*
"grassy pastures" (Ps. 23:2). On the Akkadian cognate *nawūm,* see A. Malamat, "Mari and
the Bible: Some Patterns of Tribal Organization and Institutions," *JAOS* 82 (1962) 146.

29. *mirbaṣ,* from *rābaṣ,* "to stretch out." Cf. *marbēṣ lĕḥayyâ,* "resting place of
wild animals," Zeph. 2:15. The term is cognate to Akk. *tarba/āṣum (*rabāṣu),* "sheepfold,
cattle fence, corral." See *AHW,* pp. 1327-28.

30. The switch to masc. pl. here and in vv. 6-7 reflects a shift in attention to the
inhabitants of Bene Ammon.

31. On the Aramaized form *maḥ'ĕkā,* "to clap," which occurs elsewhere only in
Isa. 55:12 and Ps. 98:8 (as expressions of joy), see Wagner, *Aramaismen,* p. 74, §158.

32. Failing to understand *bĕkol-šā'ṭĕkā,* LXX and Syr. omit the expression (cf. 16:57).
LXX's correct understanding of the term in 28:24, 26, and 36:5 is attributable to a different
translator. See McGregor, *Greek Text of Ezekiel,* pp. 197-99. On the form see GKC, §23c.

33. Wevers (*Ezekiel,* p. 196) deletes *hinĕnî* with LXX as a gloss. But see vv. 9, 16.

34. The first person (prophetic) perfect immediately after *hinnēh* occurs elsewhere
in the OT only in Jer. 44:26 (cf. *hinĕnî* plus *'ănî* plus converted perfect in 34:11, 20, and
hinĕnî plus two adverbial expressions plus perfect in 36:6). Isa. 28:16 contains the only
example of *hinĕnî* plus third person perfect, on which see J. J. M. Roberts, "Yahweh's
Foundation in Zion (Isa. 28:16)," *JBL* 106 (1987) 28.

35. Reading *lĕbaz* with Qere in place of Kethib's meaningless *lbg,* probably created
by a confusion of *g* with *z.* See J. Barr, *Comparative Philology and the Text of the Old
Testament,* with additions and corrections (Winona Lake, Ind.: Eisenbrauns, 1987), p. 322,
no. 46.

36. In view of the asyndetic construction of *'ašmîdĕkā* and its disruptive effect on
the parallelism, the word is often deleted as a variant gloss (cf. Zimmerli, *Ezekiel 2,* p. 8).
It is firmly attested, however, in the versions. For another explanation see Allen, *Ezekiel
20–48,* p. 65.

37. Only here does one find: (1) the direct charge to the prophet to set his face
toward Bene Ammon; (2) the direct command to speak, followed by the vocative, "O Bene
Ammon"; (3) an opening summons to hear the word of Yahweh; (4) the employment of
the second person of direct address instead of the more detached use of the third person.

among the community of nations Bene Ammon had a special fascination for Ezekiel. As in 21:23-37 (Eng. 18-32), the prophet refers to the hypothetical addressee by the long form of the name, *Bene Ammon*. Although most translate the expression with a gentilic, "Ammonites," on the analogy of *bĕnê yiśrā'ēl* (lit. "sons of Israel"), this practice is questionable for several reasons. First, of the following oracles only the Philistines are referred to by a gentilic.[38] Second, this compound form of the name is used consistently for the nation *and* the country throughout the OT.[39] Third, extrabiblical texts also prefer compound forms of the national name. The simple form *Am-ma-na* is attested twice, but the Akkadian sources display an overwhelming preference for *bît A-ma-na.* One text uses *ba-an Am-ma-na,* which seems to be a simple transliteration of West Semitic *bn 'mwn.*[40] But the most important evidence comes from the indigenous Tell Siran Bottle Inscription, which names three Ammonite rulers, each of whom is identified as *mlk bn 'mn,* "king of Bene Ammon."[41] The prefixed element was apparently an integral part of the national name.[42] Fourth, in the present context the gender of Bene Ammon alternates between masculine and feminine.[43] The feminine gender is seldom if ever used of a nation as such, unless the territory of the nation is in view. While many see in this inconsistency evidence of more than one editorial hand,[44] it is preferable to see here an alternation in focus between the nation and the land it occupies. In any case, if one does not adopt the transliteration of the full form Bene Ammon, the simple form "Ammon" is certainly preferable to the gentilic "Ammonites," unless of course one is speaking about the population.

It is not surprising that this collection of oracles begins with a message

---

38. The OT only rarely (and only in poetic texts) refers to a territory called "Philistia" *(pĕlešet).*

39. For a full discussion see Block, *AUSS* 22 (1984) 197-212. See also my *Ezekiel 1–24,* p. 684.

40. Ibid., pp. 207-8. For references see S. Parpola, *Neo-Assyrian Toponyms,* AOAT 6 (Neukirchen-Vluyn: Neukirchener, 1970), pp. 16, 76.

41. On the inscription see F. Zayadine and H. O. Thompson, "The Ammonite Inscription from Tell Siran," *Berytus* 22 (1973) 115-40. Cf. K. P. Jackson, *The Ammonite Language of the Iron Age,* HSM 27 (Chico, Calif.: Scholars Press, 1983), pp. 135-44; W. E. Aufrecht, *Corpus of Ammonite Inscriptions,* ANETS 4 (Lewiston: Mellen, 1989), pp. 203-11.

42. According to the biblical etymology in Gen. 19:30ff., the compound name derives from the eponymous ancestor of the nation, *ben-'ammî.*

43. (1) The introductory formulae, masc. (cf. *'ālêhem* and *šim'û,* vv. 2-3); (2) the first accusation, fem. (*'omrēk, nōtĕnāk, bāk, piryēk, ḥălābēk,* vv. 3b, 4); (3) the first recognition formula, masc. (*yāda'tem,* v. 5b); (4) the second panel, masc. (vv. 6-7); (5) the Moab oracle, fem. (*nĕtattîhā,* v. 10b).

44. Garscha, *Studien,* pp. 135-37.

concerning Bene Ammon. No doubt Nebuchadrezzar's earlier decision to attack Jerusalem rather than Rabbah (21:23-27 [Eng. 18-22]) had dismayed the exiles, and left them wondering whether Bene Ammon would remain untouched by the Babylonian emperor's western campaign. From their taunt over Jerusalem's calamity (21:33 [Eng. 28]) the Ammonites themselves seem to have thought they had escaped the disaster. But the following announcement of the sword had served notice of Yahweh's response to such smugness. Here the message first announced in the earlier context will be expanded.

According to biblical tradition, the Ammonites were distant relatives of the Israelites, being descended from Lot, the nephew of Abraham (Gen. 19:38). But in contrast to Moab, their national territory was not well defined geographically. The heartland consisted of the area around Rabbah (modern Amman), extending southward to the Arnon River, which served as a border with Moab. The land of Bene Ammon was bounded on the east by the vast desert of Arabia, on the north by the mountains of Gilead, and on the west by the territory occupied by the Transjordanian Israelite tribes.

Israelite relations with Bene Ammon were stormy from the beginning. While the Ammonites appear to have established themselves in this region shortly before the arrival of the Israelites, the lack of well-defined borders led to frequent clashes, particularly for the Transjordanian tribes (Judg. 10–11; 2 Sam. 10–12). When David's attempts at peaceful relations with King Hanun were rebuffed, David attacked Bene Ammon and added the country to his personal kingdom (2 Sam. 10–12). Sometime after the death of Solomon Bene Ammon regained its independence, but under Uzziah and Jotham they were paying tribute to Judah once again (2 Chr. 26:8; 27:5). The threat of the Assyrian hordes in the 9th century had led to a military alliance between Bene Ammon and Israel (under Ahab), along with several other Levantine states.[45] In the following centuries Tiglath-pileser III and Esarhaddon received tribute from Bene Ammon, and Ashurbanipal engaged Arab forces in Ammonite territory.[46] In 605, after the battle of Carchemish, Bene Ammon's fate was closely linked with that of Judah. Ammonites were among the forces of Nebuchadrezzar involved in the punishment of Jehoiakim for his rebellion in 598 (2 K. 24:1-2). Since early in his reign Zedekiah had joined an alliance against the Babylonians that included Bene Ammon,[47] however, one may imagine the Ammonites' relief over Nebuchadrezzar's decision to attack Jerusalem rather than their own capital.

---

45. See *ANET*, pp. 278-79.

46. See *ANET*, pp. 282, 291, 298, respectively. For a reconstruction of Ammonite history and the succession of her kings see J.-M. de Tarragon and G. J. Norton, *ABD*, 1:195.

47. See Jer. 27:3. This revolt seems to have precipitated the campaign of Nebuchadrezzar reflected in Ezek. 21:23-27 (Eng. 18-22).

In the light of the long-standing hostility between Judah and Bene Ammon, the schadenfreude expressed in this oracle is understandable. Bene Ammon's malicious delight is expressed verbally with the paralinguistic exclamation, he'āḥ, "Aha!"[48] By means of three deliberately constructed parallel clauses, the specific reasons for her scorn are cited: the desecration of Yahweh's sanctuary, the laying waste of the land of Israel, and the deportation of the population of Judah. These three actions strike at the heart of Judean national self-consciousness, disrupting the deity-land-people relationship. As far as Bene Ammon was concerned, the inveterate foe was destroyed and would surely never bother her again.

4-5   But the Ammonites failed to realize that contrary to appearance, Yahweh had not given up his patron status. He would not stand idly by while the world taunted his people and his land. Vv. 4-5 describe his reaction by means of a single verb used in two different senses: he will deliver *(nātan lĕ)* Bene Ammon into the hands of their own enemies to the east, and transform *(nātan lĕ)* her capital, Rabbah, into a habitation for livestock.[49] The Ammonites may have escaped the onslaught of the mighty Babylonians, but they will fall to the Qedemites. The expression *bĕnê qedem* (lit. "sons of the east, easterners") is not a proper name or a self-designation, but a vague label used by westerners to denote the nomadic groups that migrated about the Arabian desert, occasionally raiding the settled communities of the Transjordan and even Cisjordan itself.[50] Although Isaiah had envisioned Israel's ultimate conquest of the Qedemites along with Edom, Moab, and Bene Ammon, in the 6th and 5th centuries the Qedemites were still wreaking havoc in the area.[51] Situated on the edge of the desert, Bene Ammon was most vulnerable to the incursions of the Arab tribes.

---

48. Cf. the vivid description of the mockery over the fall of Jerusalem in Lam. 2:15-16. On *he'āḥ* see Ezek. 26:2; 36:2; Ps. 35:21, 25; 40:16; Isa. 44:16; Job 39:25 (of a horse in battle). For a discussion of the interjection see B. Gosse, "Le recueil d'oracles contre les nations d'Ezéchiel XXV–XXXII dans la rédaction du livre d'Ezéchiel," *RB* 93 (1986) 543-47.

49. Cf. Jeremiah's oracle against Bene Ammon (Jer. 49:1-6), which speaks of the exiles of Milkom, the Ammonite patron deity, the deportation of the population, and the devastation of the land.

50. See Gen. 29:1; Job 1:3; Judg. 6:3, 33; 7:12; 8:10. In contrast to *bĕnê 'ammôn*, *bĕnê qedem* may be legitimately rendered with the gentilic, Qedemites. Where the OT intends the gentilic sense "Ammonites," it always uses *'ammônî*. See Block, *AUSS* 22 (1984) 198-99.

51. Jer. 49:28 refers to an attack by Nebuchadrezzar on these people, a campaign that may be reflected in a report from Nebuchadrezzar's sixth year in the Babylonian Chronicle: "He dispatched his army from Hattu and they went off into the desert. They plundered extensively the possessions, animals, and gods of numerous Arabs." Thus A. K. Grayson, *Assyrian and Babylonian Chronicles,* TCS 5 (Locust Valley, N.Y.: J. J. Augustin, 1975), p. 101 (5:9-10).

According to this oracle, having received the land of Bene Ammon from Yahweh as their own property *(môrāšâ)*, the Qedemites will make themselves at home, erecting their own encampments, pitching their tents *(miškānîm)* right within the Ammonite heartland, and devouring the produce of land and livestock, a humiliating prospect for the nation. In v. 5 the emphasis returns to Yahweh's actions. He will turn the pride of Bene Ammon — their capital, Rabbah — into a city of animals, a place where Arabs rest their camels and bed their flocks.

6-7 Although opening with a new citation formula, this fragment is linked logically to v. 5 by the particle *kî (For)*. From here on the treatment of Bene Ammon as masculine reflects the shift in focus from the land of Bene Ammon to the human population; the gestures described in v. 6 are human actions, not the behavior of a country. Yahweh's second charge against Bene Ammon is essentially the same as in vv. 3-4, though the crime of malicious delight over the fall of Jerusalem is expressed by two nonverbal gestures, instead of the paralinguistic *he'āḥ*. The Ammonites were clapping their hands and stamping their feet with glee over Jerusalem's fall. Unlike 6:11 and 21:19, 22 (Eng. 14, 17), where the same gestures occur as expressions of anger, here the actions express intense scorn and malicious delight, an interpretation confirmed by the presence of *šā'ṭĕkā* (lit. "your contempt"), which is unique to Ezekiel.[52] Since no new cause of Bene Ammon's glee is specified, this may be supplied from the previous panel.

This time Yahweh's reaction is expressed in even more general terms. He will clap his own hands and stretch out his hand against her. Reiterating v. 4, Yahweh declares that he will seize Bene Ammon and hand over her population to enemy nations as spoils of war. While the aggressors are not identified, Yahweh's goal is announced with three devastatingly painful declarations: he will cut her off from the peoples *(hikrît)*, cause her to perish *(he'ĕbîd)*, and destroy her *(hišmîd)*. In short, he will personally eradicate the nation from history and wipe her off the map. With ironic justice, she who had rejoiced over the destruction of Judah (v. 3) would now suffer the same fate. The oracle ends abruptly with a concluding recognition formula. In this act of *damnatio memoriae,* the removal of the nation from the ancient Near Eastern political and ethnic scene, the mystery of the divine person would be revealed.[53] For those who rejoice over the demise of God's people and mock them, there is no mercy.

---

52. On the root, which occurs elsewhere only in Ezek. 16:57; 28:24, 26; and 36:6, see Bodi, *Ezekiel and the Poem of Erra,* pp. 69-81.

53. The finality of Ezekiel's word contrasts with the word of Jeremiah, who held out the hope of an eventual restoration of Bene Ammon's fortunes (49:6); Ezekiel offers no hint of this hope.

b. The Oracle Against Moab (25:8-11)

8 " 'Thus has the Lord Yahweh declared: Because Moab[54] is saying, "Look! The house of Judah[55] is just like all the nations."

9 Therefore, I will open up the flank of Moab, removing the cities, its cities[56] from all its territory,[57] the pride[58] of the land: Beth-jeshimoth, Baal-meon, and Kiriathaim. 10 And I will deliver it,[59] along with Bene Ammon,[60] to the Qedemites as dispossessed property, so that Bene Ammon might not be remembered[61] among the nations.[62] 11 Thus I will execute judgments in Moab, and they will know that I am Yahweh.' "

Now Ezekiel abandons the second person of direct address in favor of the third person. This mini-oracle is linked closely with the preceding by the reference to the Qedemites as agents of Yahweh's judgment, the deliverance of Moabite territory to them as "dispossessed property" *(nātan lĕmôrāšâ),*

---

54. This translation follows LXX. MT adds *wĕśēʿîr,* which is unlikely since (1) no other oracle identifies two addressees; (2) Seir is an Edomite site, not Moabite; and (3) Seir is out of the picture in the remainder of the oracle. Allen (*Ezekiel 20–48,* p. 65) plausibly suggests that a marginal note intending to draw the reader's attention to parallels with the oracles against Edom (vv. 12-14) and Seir (35:2-9) has mistakenly found its way into the text.

55. LXX reads "Israel and Judah." One Origen ms. reads "Israel" in place of "Judah."

56. *mēheʿārîm mēʿārāyw* is difficult, but it is reflected in Syr., Targ., and Vulg. LXX abbreviates by dropping *mēʿārāyw.* My translation treats *min* in each case privatively (cf. Isa. 23:1).

57. *miqqāṣēhû,* lit. "from its end, extremity."

58. On *ṣĕbî* see my *Ezekiel: Chapters 1–24,* pp. 264-65.

59. In MT *ûnĕtattîhā* appears after Bene Ammon, but the conjunction on the verb and the parallels (vv. 5, 7) call for a change in word order.

60. Lang (*VT* 29 [1979] 39) argues that the mention of Bene Ammon overloads the sentence, making it "clumsy and almost unreadable," and unnecessary because the Ammonites have their own judgment oracle in the preceding pericope. But this procedure is without manuscript or versional support and fails to account for the emphatic *ûbĕmôʾāb* in v. 11.

61. Syr. recognizes the problem of the third fem. form of *tizzākēr* and expands the subject to *rabbat bĕnê ʿammôn.* But Bene Ammon has already been used in a geographic sense in the preceding oracle. Cf. J. Reider, "Contributions to the Scriptural Text," *HUCA* 24 (1952-53) 91-92; G. R. Driver treats Bene Ammon as a fem. collective (*Aramaic Documents from the Fifth Century B.C.* [Oxford: Clarendon, 1954], p. 53 n. 2). In Late Biblical Hebrew *lĕmaʿan lōʾ* begins to be used in place of *pen* to express negative purpose. See M. F. Rooker, *Biblical Hebrew in Transition: The Language of the Book of Ezekiel,* JSOTSup 90 (Sheffield: JSOT Press, 1990), pp. 172-73.

62. LXX drops *baggôyim.*

and the reintroduction of Bene Ammon, which the prophet cannot seem to get out of his mind. The Moabites, descended from Lot in a line parallel to the Ammonites (Gen. 19:37), occupied the highland region east of the Dead Sea, from the Arnon River to the north and from Wadi Zered to the south.[63] The relationship between Moab and Israel was stormy from the beginning.[64] In recent times, the forces of Nebuchadrezzar attacking Jehoiakim of Jerusalem had included Moabites as well as Ammonites (2 K. 24:2). Although Zedekiah managed a brief alliance with these two states in common cause against Babylon (Jer. 27:3), when Jerusalem fell in 586 B.C. both countries stood by, taunting their devastated neighbor (see Jer. 48:27-35; Zeph. 2:8).

8 Compared to Jeremiah's oracle against Moab (Jer. 48:1-47), Ezekiel's prophecy is extremely short. Casting the charge in the form of a direct quotation, Yahweh accuses Moab of denying Judah's special status among the nations.[65] The comment is reminiscent of Israel's own self-depreciating remarks in Ezek. 20:32, in which Israel complained that since they were being treated like all of the other nations, they might as well serve gods of wood and stone. While one may speculate about the extent to which other nations were aware of Israel's theological claims to special status among them, this statement is certainly intended as a denial of her election. Consequently, the Moabite taunt is not only against her neighbor, but also a direct assault on Yahweh himself, who had granted this status to his people.

9 Yahweh could not tolerate such blasphemous assertions. In response he will personally turn the tables, making Moab go the way of all the nations: she will be destroyed like the rest. Her destruction will involve two divine acts. First, Yahweh will open her western frontier, the side opposite Judah, and deprive her of all her cities. Used geographically, *ketep* refers to a mountain ridge or slope, perhaps as seen from a neighboring region.[66] In

63. At one point they also claimed the Mishor north of the Arnon (Deut. 3:10), but it had been wrested from their control by the Amorite king Sihon of Heshbon (Num. 21:26). When the Israelites conquered him it was allocated to the Reubenites.

64. The former resisted the arrival of the latter in the 2nd millennium (Num. 22–25); once Israel had entered Canaan, Eglon of Moab even gained temporary hegemony over a segment of Israel (Judg. 3:12-20). During the reign of David, Moab was subdued and forced to pay tribute to him (2 Sam. 8:2). However, a renaissance of Moabite power occurred in the 9th century, enabling Mesha to regain control over the Mishor, an accomplishment memorialized on the famous Mesha Inscription (*ANET*, pp. 320-21; cf. 2 K. 3). Later Moab joined with Bene Ammon and Edom in an unsuccessful attack on Judah (2 Chr. 20:1-30). In the year that Elisha died bands of Moabites made incursions into Israel (2 K. 13:20). Along with the rest of the states in the area, in the 8th-7th centuries Moab became a vassal of the Assyrians, paying tribute successively to Tiglath-pileser III, Sargon II, Sennacherib, Esarhaddon, and Ashurbanipal (cf. *ANET*, pp. 282, 287, 291, 294, 298, 301).

65. Cf. Israel's self-depreciation in 1 Sam. 8:5.

66. See Num. 34:11; Josh. 15:8, 10-11; 18:12-13, 16, 18-19; Isa. 4:11.

this context the verb *pātaḥ,* "to open," evokes images of opening the gates of a city in conquest.[67] But the key to conquering a nation is found in gaining control of its principal cities, here described as *ṣĕbî 'ereṣ,* "the glory of the land." The ambiguous phrase *mē'ārāyw miqqāṣēhû,* "its towns, to its last one," or "its cities to its frontier," describes the extent of Moab's losses. Three representative cities are named: (1) Beth-jeshimoth, located at the site of modern Tell el-'Azeimeh, approximately 2½ kilometers northeast of the entrance of the Jordan into the Dead Sea; (2) Baal-meon, an abbreviation for the full form Beth-baal-meon (Josh. 13:17; cf. Num. 32:38; Jer. 48:23), preserved in modern day Ma'īn, 5 miles southwest of Medeba and about 8 miles east of the Dead Sea; (3) Kiriathaim, modern Khirbet el-Qureiyāt, about 6 miles west of Medeba.[68] These three sites lie on a line from the Jordan Valley (Beth-jeshimoth), southeastward via the ascent (Beth-baal-meon) to the top of the plateau (Kiriathaim). Remarkably, none of these cities is located in the Moabite heartland. Instead they represent Reubenite sites in the Mishor, the region north of the Arnon River, which raises the question of how their destruction can be a sign of the demise of Moab. Either Ezekiel concedes this region to Moab on historical grounds, or he rejects all Israelite claims to the Transjordan for theological reasons.[69] His vision of ideal Israel in 47:13–48:29 omits any reference to the Transjordan.

10 Second, Yahweh will deliver Moab into the hands of the Qedemites along with Bene Ammon. Although the reference is probably to a different occasion, Josephus recounts that five years after the fall of Jerusalem Nebuchadrezzar overran both of these countries (*Ant.* 10.9.7, §§181-82).

The pronouncement concludes awkwardly with a final word for Bene Ammon, whose anticipated fate is even worse than that of Moab. The assertion that she would not be remembered among the nations any more is equivalent to "being cut off from the peoples" (cf. v. 7), but echoes more closely the fate of Babylon announced in 21:37 (Eng. 32). This sentence did not mean merely being forgotten or relegated to political insignificance, "but utter

---

67. Cf. Nah. 3:13. The combination *pātaḥ 'et-ketep* represents an effective inverted assonantal sequence.

68. On Beth-jeshimoth see A. Kuschke, "Zweimal *ḳrjtn,*" *ZDPV* 77 (1961) 25. Cf. Num. 33:49; Josh. 12:3; 13:20. Only Beth-jeshimoth is rendered as a proper name by LXX: οἶκον Ασιμουθ. Baal-meon is listed on the Mesha Inscription (line 9) as one of the places rebuilt by Mesha. *qrytn* also occurs on the Mesha Inscription (line 10) as rebuilt by the Moabite king in the 9th century. Cf. Kuschke, *ZDPV* 77 (1961) 25-26. Kiriathaim appears elsewhere in Num. 32:37; Josh. 13:19; Jer. 48:1, 23.

69. Cf. 2 K. 13:20-21. It is unclear from 2 K. 14:25 whether Jeroboam II of Israel was able to recover this territory in the 8th century. Both Isaiah (15:1-9) and Jeremiah (48:1-47) assume Moabite ownership. The boundaries recognized in Deut. 3:12-17 were a concession to earlier Israelite demands (cf. Num. 32).

destruction of the population, so that there will be no one who may be called an Ammonite."[70]

11 As for Moab, her judgment is expressed in vague formulae.[71] When it has been carried out, however, Yahweh's goal of revealing the mystery of his person to this foreign nation will also have been served.

c. The Oracle Against Edom (25:12-14)

12 " 'Thus has the Lord Yahweh declared: Because Edom has treated the house of Judah with bitter vengeance, and incurred grievous guilt by taking revenge[72] against them —

13 Therefore, thus has the Lord Yahweh declared: I will stretch[73] out my hand against Edom, cutting off from it both human and beast and turning it into a wasteland. From Teman to Dedan[74] they will fall by the sword. 14 And I will inflict my vengeance upon Edom by the hand of my people Israel. And they will deal with Edom according to my wrath and according to my fury. Then they will know my vengeance. The declaration of the Lord Yahweh.' "

Like the prophecies against Bene Ammon and Moab, the oracles against Edom and the Philistines are closely connected in form but especially by the *Leitwort nāqam,* "to take vengeance." This oracle against Edom is a mere forty-seven words, but it will not be Ezekiel's last word against the nation. In ch. 35 he will come back with a much more fully developed attack.

Being descended from Esau, the older brother of Jacob, the Edomites were even more closely related to Israel than the Ammonites and Moabites. While Gen. 32 suggests that the clan of Esau had moved into the region of Seir soon after they had split off from the household of Isaac, the Israelites recognized the region of Mount Seir as Edom's divinely granted *yĕrûššâ,*

---

70. Lang, *VT* 29 (1979) 40. Related expressions occur in Exod. 17:14; Deut. 25:19; 32:26; Ezek. 21:37 (Eng. 32); Ps. 83:5.

71. On *ʿāśâ šĕpāṭîm,* "to execute punishments," see Ezek. 5:10, 15; 11:9; 16:41; 28:22, 26; 30:14, 19. Cf. *ʿāśâ mišpāṭ* in 18:8; 39:21.

72. The consecutive perfect bears a frequentative sense after the converted imperfect. See GKC, §112f; Joüon-Muraoka, *Grammar,* §119v. Zimmerli (*Ezekiel 2,* p. 9) suggests a hypotactical sense, describing "the nearer circumstances of the guilt."

73. A converted perfect after the citation formula occurs also in 35:10-11.

74. MT mistakenly links the phrase with the preceding. The combination *min . . . wĕ* replaces the more usual *min . . . ʿad.* Although the locative *hē* renders the conjunction superfluous, the present construction is attested elsewhere in Josh. 15:46. See G. R. Driver, *Bib* 35 (1954) 156. The *i*-class final vowel with the *he locale* is rare, but it is attested in 1 K. 2:36, 42; see GKC, §90i. Cf. also *sĕwēnēh* for *sĕwēnâ* in 29:10; 30:6.

"possession," just as Canaan belonged to them (Deut. 2:5). The Edomite heartland consisted of the mountainous region east of the Arabah, extending southward from the Brook Zered (Wadi el-Ḥaṣa) as far as the Gulf of Aqaba.[75] Since the Edomites have left us no written records, our reconstruction of their history depends primarily on Israelite records, which tend to be biased in the extreme, reflecting the hostility that existed between the two nations from the beginning.[76] The biblical emphasis on the kinship of Edom and Israel renders the former's persistent opposition to the latter even more poignant. In Num. 20:15 Moses' appeal for special consideration was based on a recognition of their "brotherhood." Deut. 23:7-8 warns the Israelites not to hold Edomites in contempt, "for he is your brother," and even permitted intermarriage in the third generation. In the 8th century, Amos had charged Edom with pursuing his brother with the sword and stifling his compassion toward him (1:11). Later Obadiah picked up this theme, accusing Esau of violence to his brother Jacob and gloating over the misfortune of the sons of Judah (Obad. 10-14).

12 In contrast to Jeremiah's detailed and often convoluted oracle against Edom (Jer. 49:7-22), Ezekiel's prophecy is cryptic and general, like the other oracles in this chapter. He opens with a charge of bitter vengeance toward the house of Judah, cast in the form of two typically Semitic cognate phrases. The first, ʿāśâ binqōm nāqām, "to act with vengeful vengeance," may be general in nature, but used here it highlights the malicious passion of the perpetrator. The second, ʾāšam ʾāšôm, "to incur grievous guilt," employs the infinitive absolute as a cognate accusative to intensify the idea of the verb.[77] While the crime is not specified, it undoubtedly relates to Edom's abandonment of his brother in the critical hour, and Edom's glee at the razing of Jerusalem (cf. Ps. 137:7).

13 The announcement of judgment consists of four declarations of divine intervention, highlighting the devastating effects of Yahweh's actions: the land will be laid waste and its entire population, human and animal, decimated by the sword. The scope of the disaster is defined by *From Teman to Dedan*. Teman signifies "south" in general; as a geographic designation it denotes either Edom as a whole, the southernmost Levantine state, or the part

75. See B. J. Beitzel, *The Moody Atlas of Bible Lands* (Chicago: Moody, 1985), pp. 23-24.

76. See Gen. 25:23. For a survey of the history of relations between Israel and Edom see J. R. Bartlett, *ABD*, 2:287-95.

77. Cooke (*Ezekiel*, p. 284) recognizes in the form "an irreparable injury." Ezekiel reverses the order of the infinitive and finite forms found in Lev. 5:19. The verb occurs elsewhere in Ezekiel in 6:6 (MT; see my *Ezekiel: Chapters 1–24*, pp. 221 n. 16, 225); 22:4; and perhaps 35:6 (with LXX). Cf. the nominal form of the same root used in the sense of "reparation offering" in 40:39; 42:13; 44:29; 46:20.

of the state surrounding the northern capital of Bozrah.[78] Dedan is identified with the modern town of al-ʿUla, situated at a major oasis, which was an important station on the "frankincense road" from Yemen to Palestine from ancient times.[79] In biblical genealogies Dedan appears as a descendant of Raamah son of Cush (Gen. 10:7; 1 Chr. 1:9) and as a grandson of Abraham by Keturah (Gen. 25:3; 1 Chr. 1:32). Dedan appears never to have been considered part of Edom, which raises questions about Ezekiel's (and Jeremiah's) association of Dedan with Edom. While differing slightly in form, the expression "from Teman and Dedan" is reminiscent of the common phrase "from Dan to Beer-sheba," which delimited the extremities of Israel.[80] Ezekiel's phrase functions merismically, like "human and animal," for "all Edom," from north to south, even beyond the nation's recognized borders.

14 The tables turn with poetic justice. First, the nation that had taken excessive vengeance on Judah should prepare for divine revenge in fullest measure. Yahweh's comment, *nātattî niqmātî*, "I will inflict my vengeance," recalls the divine epithet *ʾēl něqāmôt*, "God of vengeance" (Ps. 94:1), the phrase *niqmat yhwh*, "the vengeance of Yahweh" (Jer. 50:15, 28), and especially the declaration *lî nāqām wěšillēm*, "Vengeance and retribution are mine" (Deut. 32:35). The issue here is Yahweh's defense of his people. He will stand up on their behalf against the aggressor.

Second, in another ironical twist, the victims of Edomite vengeance are hereby identified as the agents of divine vengeance. Ezekiel's portrayal of the turning of the tables on Edom recalls a similar and even more explicit movement in the prophecy of Obadiah (vv. 15, 18):

> As you have acted, so it will be done to you;
> Your conduct will return on your own head. . . .
> The house of Jacob will be fire,
> And the house of Joseph a flame,
> But the house of Esau will be straw.
> They will burn it and devour it,
> Leaving no survivor of the house of Esau.

It is difficult to correlate the destruction envisaged by Ezekiel with the known course of history. By the 5th century (Mal. 1:3-4), Edom had been dislodged from its ancient homeland in Seir, presumably as a result of a series of events

---

78. In Jer. 49:7, 20, and Obad. 9 Teman functions as a synonym of Edom. Glueck's identification of Teman with Tawilan near Petra is untenable on philological and linguistic grounds. See E. A. Knauf, *ABD,* 6:347-48.

79. On the extensive ruins and history of ancient Dedan see D. F. Graf, *ABD,* 2:121-23.

80. See Saebø, *ZDPV* 90 (1974) 14-37.

set in motion by Nabonidus's monopoly over the trade routes in the mid-6th century B.C. A few decades later, however, in Ezra and Nehemiah's time, the Edomites had ceased to be a factor in Levantine affairs. Outside opposition to the new commonwealth of Jews in Jerusalem was spearheaded by the troika of Tobiah the Ammonite, Sanballat the Horonite, and Geshem the Arab (Neh. 2:18; 6:1-2). By the 4th century, Arabic Nabateans had taken over Petra, in the Edomite heartland. Under Nabatean pressure the last remnants of the Edomites appear to have moved across the Arabah to southern Judah, where the memory of their origins was preserved in the new name given to this region, Idumea.

Third, unlike earlier prophecies in which Israel was the object of Yahweh's fury, now the nation is portrayed as the agent of divine vengeance against the enemy. Unlike many other forms of the formula, which identify the goal of divine action as the recognition of the person of Yahweh in general, the concluding recognition formula declares Yahweh's aim as having the Edomites recognize in the actions of the Israelites his own vengeful judgment. The final signatory formula seals Edom's fate and guarantees the fulfillment of Yahweh's goals.

Ezekiel's vision of Edom's future transcends specific historical events, focusing on the divine causation and the ultimate effects of his action. As the patron of Israel, Yahweh assumes responsibility for punishing those who commit crimes against his people. Although the text offers no clues about the audience's response, Yahweh's warm designation of his people as *my people Israel* (ʿammî yiśrāʾēl) looks forward to a time when the suspended covenant will be in force again. The exiles should have welcomed this expression alone as a welcome message of hope.

d. The Oracle Against the Philistines (25:15-17)

15 " 'Thus has the Lord Yahweh declared: Because the Philistines have acted with vengeance, and taken bitter revenge[81] with utter contempt, destroying with everlasting enmity[82] —

16 Therefore, thus has the Lord Yahweh declared: Look! I will stretch out my hand against the Philistines, cutting off the Cherethites, and destroying the survivors of the seacoast.[83] 17 I will execute extreme

---

81. Cf. v. 12. The Niphal of nāqam followed by the cognate accusative resembles the construction in Judg. 16:28.

82. The final phrase, ʾēbat ʿôlām, "everlasting enmity," which functions as an adverbial accusative, resembles bĕrît ʿôlām, "everlasting covenant," in 37:26.

83. On ḥôp hayyām, "shore of the sea," as a common designation for the coastal region see Deut. 1:7; Josh. 9:1; Judg. 5:17; Jer. 47:7. Cf. also ḥôp yāmîm, "shore of seas," and ḥôp ʾŏnîyôt, "shore of ships" (Gen. 49:13).

vengeance upon them, with furious wrath.[84] *And they will know that I am Yahweh, when I have inflicted my vengeance upon them.'* "

15-17 Whereas 16:27, 57 had introduced the Philistines *(pĕlištîm)* as witnesses to Jerusalemite abominations, this oracle concerns them directly. The origins of the Philistines remain uncertain, but they are generally classified among the Sea Peoples who appeared in the eastern Mediterranean in the 13th century B.C. According to Israelite tradition (Amos 9:7) the Philistines arrived from Caphtor, usually identified with the Aegean island of Crete. However, the Table of Nations (Gen. 10:14; 1 Chr. 1:12) identifies them as Hamitic in descent, suggesting an earlier migration to Crete from the Delta region of Egypt.[85] When the Israelites arrived in Canaan from Egypt, the Philistines were firmly entrenched in the five major cities of Ashdod, Ashkelon, Ekron, Gath, and Gaza (Josh. 13:2-3), and conflicts between these two groups of newcomers were inevitable.[86] During David's time as a fugitive from Saul, he established good relations with the Philistine king of Gath (1 Sam. 27), and even after he became king he employed a contingent of Philistines in his personal service.[87] But the Philistines remained a menace in Israel's southwestern flank until, in response to Yahweh's charge, David delivered a decisive blow against them (2 Sam. 5:17-25).

Although their history was closely linked to the Judean state, the Philistines were able to maintain their separate identity over the centuries.[88] But like the rest of the Levant, in the 8th century they fell under the control of Assyria.[89] The role of the Philistines in Judah's final decades is unclear.

---

84. *bĕtôkĕḥôt ḥēmâ* is missing in LXX and often treated as a gloss. Cf. Wevers, *Ezekiel,* p. 199. On the expressions see my *Ezekiel: Chapters 1–24,* p. 212.

85. For a defense of this interpretation see G. A. Rendsburg, "Gen 10:13-14: An Authentic Hebrew Tradition Concerning the Origin of the Philistines," *JNSL* 13 (1987) 89-96. On Egyptian influence in Minoan Crete see A. Evans, *The Palace of Minos at Knossos,* 4 vols. (London: Macmillan, 1921-36), 2:21-28. For archeological evidence concerning the origin and culture of the Philistines see T. Dothan, *The Philistines and Their Material Culture* (New Haven: Yale University Press, 1982); idem, "Ekron of the Philistines. Part I: Where They Came from, How They Settled Down, and the Place They Worshiped In," *BARev* 16/1 (1990) 26-36; idem, *ABD,* 5:328-33.

86. See Judg. 3:31; 10:6-7; 13–16; 1 Sam. 4; 13:19-22.

87. Note his Cherethite and Pelethite bodyguards (2 Sam. 8:18; 20:23) and his core of Gittite troops (2 Sam. 15:18).

88. During the reigns of Baasha and Asa they seem to have enjoyed a measure of independence (2 K. 15:27; 16:15); under Jehoshaphat they were paying tribute (2 Chr. 17:11); in the late 8th century they, along with the Arameans, were causing trouble for Ahaz (Isa. 9:8-12).

89. For Philistine fortunes under the Assyrians see *ANET,* pp. 281 (Adadnirari III), 282-83 (Tiglath-pileser III), 286-87 (Sargon II), 287-88 (Sennacherib), 291 and 294 (Esar-

After the fall of Carchemish, Nebuchadrezzar responded to Ashkelon's refusal to pay homage to him by laying the city waste and carrying its king off into exile.[90] The last cuneiform reference to the Philistines occurs in Nebuchadrezzar's list of court officials, which includes among others the kings of Ashdod and Gaza.[91] In view of the long-standing feud between Judah and the Philistines, it is reasonable to suppose that the latter had joined the Edomites in vengeful actions against Judah at the time of its fall, though the specific occasion to which Ezekiel refers is nowhere recorded.[92]

Ezekiel's oracle against the Philistines divides into the customary three parts: the indictment (v. 15), the announcement of judgment (vv. 16-17a), and the effect of the judgment (v. 17b). The form of the opening charge of vengeful activity presents this oracle as a twin to the previous prophecy against the Edomites,[93] which probably also explains the absence of any reference to Judah as the object of the Philistine hostility (cf. v. 12). The phrase *běšě'āṭ běnepeš* (lit. "with scorn in the soul") links this oracle with the earlier Ammonite oracle as well (v. 6). The Philistines' sinister intentions are described in the last line of v. 15; finally they have an opportunity to give full vent to their long-standing hatred toward Judah.

Unlike the previous oracles, the announcement of judgment focuses exclusively on Yahweh's intervention, without reference to agents, and has the divine activity directed entirely against a population, not its land. The action is described in four pronouncements arranged in an ABBA pattern, two specific announcements being sandwiched between general statements. The combination of Yahweh's outstretched hand *(wěnāṭaṭṭî yādî)* and his cutting off *(wěhikrattî)* is familiar from the previous oracle. But *wěhikrattî 'et-kěrētîm,* which involves a sensitive wordplay, introduces the antagonists by a new name, *Cherethites.* Related to the name "Crete," this designation identifies another subgroup of the Sea Peoples.[94] The use of the verb *he'ěbîd,* "to destroy" (cf.

---

haddon). On the Philistines during the Assyrian hegemony see H. Tadmor, "Philistia under Assyrian Rule," *BA* 29 (1966) 86-102.

90. See Grayson, *Chronicles,* p. 100 (5:18-20).

91. See *ANET,* p. 308.

92. According to Neh. 13:23-24 the Philistines (Ashdodites) resurface as a problem for the postexilic community of Jerusalem.

93. The return to this theme in v. 17 creates an effective envelope structure.

94. The Cherethites may have been native Cretans, in contrast to the Pelethites/Philistines, who had lived on this island for only a limited period of time. Thus T. C. Mitchell, *IBD,* 1:264. M. Delcor attributes the absence of Cherethites from Rameses III's Medinet Habu list of Sea Peoples to the late arrival (in the Davidic era) of this group in Palestine ("Les Kéréthim et les Crétois," *VT* 28 [1978] 409-22). The expression "Negeb of the Cherethites" in 1 Sam. 30:14 suggests that they lived in the southeastern part of Philistia.

v. 7), and the reference to the survivors of the seacoast in the third statement highlight the intensity of Yahweh's actions. With true poetic justice, the offenses of the Philistines will return upon their own heads. Vengeance belongs to God, particularly when his people have been abused. With chastising fury Yahweh will break into the smug violence of the Philistines, and when he acts with his own vengeance, they will recognize him as the source of their demise.

Like the previous oracles, this message should have brought hope to Ezekiel's compatriots in exile. Although they have been abandoned by Yahweh and experienced the full force of his wrath themselves, the announcement that their divine protector would rise again to defend their cause was intended to instill new optimism about the future.

2. The Oracles Against Tyre (26:1–28:19)

♦ *Nature and Design*

As noted earlier, on the basis of its form and the general nature of its content, the short oracle against Tyre preserved in 26:2-6 belongs to the collection found in ch. 25. However, Ezekiel's particular interest in Tyre becomes apparent immediately. This mini-oracle is introduced by its own word-event formula, which had been absent since 25:1; and for the first time a prophecy against a foreign nation is introduced by a date notice (26:1). Even more impressive, in the remainder of the chapter the prophet offers a detailed exposition of the oracle in three parts. Furthermore, he will follow this oracle with two additional lengthy prophecies, the first cast in the form of a lament against the city (27:1-36), and the second as a two-part message for the king of Tyre (28:1-19).

A striking organizing feature of the oracles against Tyre as a block is the threefold occurrence of variations of the refrain *ballāhôt 'ettĕnēk (hāyît/hāyîtā) wĕ'ênĕkā 'ad-'ôlām/lĕ'ôlām*, "Terrors I will send you (you will become) and you will cease to be forever" (26:21; 27:36; 28:19), which serves both to unify the respective parts and to divide the block into three major segments. This division is reinforced by the appearance of the word-event formula, which follows the refrain in each instance. Several additional indications of intentional structuring are evident in the Tyrian oracles as a whole. The refrain itself is absent from 28:10, but the presence of the word-event formula in v. 11 divides 28:1-19 into two parts, each of which in turn bifurcates into two panels, creating the following ABAB pattern for the entire literary complex:

A Announcement of judgment upon Tyre (26:1-21)
B Lament over the fall of Tyre (27:1-36)
A Announcement of judgment upon the king of Tyre (28:1-10)
B Lament over the fall of the king of Tyre (28:11-19)

♦ *Historical Background*

All the oracles in ch. 25 had been hypothetically addressed toward the nation-states on Judah's eastern, southern, and southwestern doorsteps. Along with Israel and Judah, Ammon, Moab, Edom, and Philistia represented nation-states, entities whose ethnic boundaries tended to be coterminous with their geopolitical borders. The name of the state derived from the name of the people (*'am*) inhabiting the territory. But Tyre (and later Sidon) was different. This was a territorial state according to which a single ethnic group (*'am*) was divided into a series of political units (*gôyim*), each with its own capital city (from which the state usually received its name) and reigning monarch. The boundaries of territorial states fluctuated, depending on the strength and reach of a king. Like the Arameans, the Phoenicians were divided into a series of territorial states.[1] The ethnic composition of the Phoenician states provides a further contrast with their neighbors to the south. Whereas the latter were all relative newcomers to the Cisjordanian and Transjordanian scene, having dispossessed the native inhabitants in the last half of the 2nd millennium B.C., the Phoenicians represented the remnants of the original population that occupied Canaan when the Israelites arrived.

The name Tyre (Heb. *ṣûr, ṣūr*) derives from the rock (*ṣōr*) on which the city was built. In ancient times the rock formed an island about 600 yards off the coast of Phoenicia, approximately 25 miles south of Sidon and 28 miles north of Akko. Ezekiel's recognition of this insular state is reflected in his location of Tyre *bĕlēb/bĕtôk yammîm*, "in the heart/midst of the sea" (26:5; 27:4, 32). In 332 B.C. Alexander the Great conquered Tyre by connecting the island to the mainland by means of a massive mole, which, due to the buildup of alluvial deposits over the centuries, has broadened greatly so that present-day Tyre is situated on a peninsula.

While the history of Tyre has been traced to the early 3rd millennium B.C.,[2] the city's significant contacts with Israel began under the united monarchy. David and Solomon seem to have enjoyed friendly relations with Hiram I, consistently identified in the OT as *melek ṣôr,* "king of Tyre."[3] But the picture is complicated by other data. Although the 9th-century monarch, Ethbaal I, reigned in Tyre, he is identified as *melek ṣîdōnîm,* "king of the

---

1. On the distinctions between territorial states and nation-states see D. I. Block, *ISBE,* 3:492-94; idem, *The Foundations of National Identity: A Study in Ancient Northwest Semitic Perceptions* (Ann Arbor: University Microfilms, 1983), pp. 620-33; G. Buccellati, *Cities and Nations of Ancient Syria: An Essay on Political Institutions with Special Reference to the Israelite Kingdoms,* Studi Semitici 26 (Rome: University of Rome Press, 1967), pp. 13-15.

2. According to Herodotus (*Hist.* 2.44), the city was founded ca. 2700 B.C.

3. See 2 Sam. 5:11; 1 K. 5:15; 9:11; 1 Chr. 14:1; 2 Chr. 2:2, 10.

Sidonians."[4] According to the annals of Tiglath-pileser I (1116-1110) the Assyrians exacted tribute from Gebal (Byblos), Sidon, and Arvad, but there is no mention of Tyre.[5] Later documents speak of Elulaeus (Luli, ca. 700) "king of Sidon," ruling over Great Sidon, Little Sidon, Bit Zitti, Zaribtu, Mahalliba, Ushu (mainland Tyre), Akzib, and Akko.[6] Curiously, whereas *mlk ṣdnm*, "king of the Sidonians," appears repeatedly in native Phoenician inscriptions,[7] to date *mlk ṣr*, "king of Tyre," is unattested. In the OT the gentilic *ṣîdōnîm*, "Sidonian," serves broadly for "Phoenician."[8] This usage accords with Homer, who employs the terms interchangeably.[9] After the invasions of the Sea Peoples and the Philistines, "Sidonian" apparently served as the general designation for the remnant of the Canaanites, but the title "king of Tyre" reflected the political reality that the seat of rule had been transferred to that city.

This trend continues in the neo-Assyrian era. Although the royal annals from the 9th century speak of tribute received from both Tyre and Sidon,[10] never are contemporaneous kings of these cities named. When royal names finally appear in the annals of Tiglath-pileser III (744-727), Metennu and Hiram are ruling in Tyre.[11] The reign of Sennacherib (704-681) seems to have marked a turning point in Tyre's history. This Assyrian emperor responded to King Elulaeus's revolt by dividing southern Phoenicia into two kingdoms and installing Ethbaal as ruler in Sidon.[12] Under Esarhaddon (680-669), Abdi-milkutti and Baal I occupied the thrones of Sidon and Tyre, respectively. When the latter appealed to Tirhaqah, king of Egypt, for assistance in throwing off

---

4. See 1 K. 16:31. On this king see H. J. Katzenstein, *The History of Tyre: From the Beginning of the Second Millennium B.C.E. until the Fall of the Neo-Babylonian Empire in 538 B.C.E.* (Jerusalem: Schocken Institute for Jewish Research, 1973), pp. 129-66.

5. *ARAB,* 1:98, §302; cf. p. 103, §328; A. K. Grayson, *Assyrian Royal Inscriptions* (Wiesbaden: Harrassowitz, 1976), 2:26; *ANET,* p. 275.

6. *ARAB,* 2:118-19, §239; *ANET,* p. 287. Menander identified Elulaeus as the king of Tyre. See Josephus, *Ant.* 9.14.2, §283.

7. *KAI,* 13.1, 2; 14.1, 2 (bis), 13, 14 (bis), 15. Of particular interest is the Cypriot inscription of Hiram II (ca. 740 B.C.), in which the ruler identifies himself as "king of the Sidonians" (*KAI,* 31.1), even though Assyrian texts always refer to him as "king of Tyre" (*ARAB,* 1:292, 294, §§ 769, 772). Cf. his son Metanna II of Tyre, *ARAB,* 1:306-7, §803.

8. See Deut. 3:9; Josh. 13:4, 6; Judg. 3:3; 10:12; 18:7; 1 K. 5:20; 11:5; 16:31; 2 K. 23:13; Ezek. 32:20; Ezra 3:7; 1 Chr. 22:4.

9. Homer, *Il.* 6.290-91; 23.743-44; *Od.* 4.83-85, 618; 13.270ff.; 14.288-89; 15.118, 415ff., 473. Cf. J. D. Muhly, "Homer and the Phoenicians: The Relations between Greece and the Near East in the Late Bronze and Early Iron Ages," *Berytus* 19 (1970) 27; Katzenstein, *History of Tyre,* pp. 62-63.

10. The annals of Ashurnasirpal II (883-859): *ANET,* p. 276; of Shalmaneser III (858-824): *ANET,* p. 280; of Adad-nirari III (810-783): *ANET,* p. 281.

11. *ANET,* pp. 282-83.

12. *ANET,* p. 287. See Katzenstein, *History of Tyre,* p. 247, for discussion.

the Assyrian yoke, Esarhaddon forced the renegade ruler to submit by cutting off the supply lines to the island. Tyre's dependencies on the mainland were taken away and placed under more direct Assyrian administration.[13] But Baal I continued his rebellious ways under Ashurbanipal, provoking yet another campaign against the island kingdom.[14]

With the fall of Nineveh in 612 and the defeat of the Egyptians at Carchemish in 605, Babylonian hegemony in the ancient Near East was established. In his accession year (604), Nebuchadrezzar forced Tyre to submit to his rule and offer tribute, along with the rest of the small states of "Hatti-land."[15] According to Jer. 27:3, however, representatives from Tyre and Sidon were soon joining in a plot against the Babylonian overlord. The alliance itself disintegrated, but Tyre remained recalcitrant, looking for support from Egypt. Even so, Babylonian domination in some form seems to have been maintained. Administrative documents from Babylon from the late 590s record the presence in the city of 126 men, probably artisans and craftsmen like those removed from Jerusalem in 597 (2 K. 24:14). The precise dates are difficult to fix, but Josephus reports that under King Ethbaal III (ca. 591/590-573/572) Nebuchadrezzar besieged Tyre for thirteen years (*Ag. Ap.* 1.21, §156; *Ant.* 10.11.1, §228). The outcome of the siege is not described, but the appearance of "the king of Tyre" in Nebuchadrezzar's "Court Register" suggests that the city was forced to submit once more.[16] Since Josephus's sources indicate a new king Baal on the throne one year after the end of the siege, the king referred to in the "Court Register" was probably Ethbaal III himself, who seems to have been taken to Babylon in a manner and for reasons similar to the deportation of Jehoiachin of Jerusalem (2 K. 24:15).[17] If this reconstruction is correct, then the thirteen-year siege of Tyre would have begun shortly after the fall of Jerusalem in 587. At the end of the siege Baal was installed as king of Tyre. After a ten-year reign, the city was governed by a series of judges (δικαστής in Josephus, *Ag. Ap.* 1.21, §157), whose authority seems to have resembled that of Gedaliah in Jerusalem (2 K. 25:22-24). During this period, Babylonian interests in Tyre appear to have been guaranteed by the presence of a high commissioner, identified as a *šandabakku,* "keeper of the seal," on a tablet from Nebuchadrezzar's 41st year (564-563).[18] Under Baby-

---

13. *ANET,* pp. 291-92.

14. *ANET,* pp. 295, 297.

15. Grayson, *Chronicles,* p. 100, 5:12-19.

16. *ANET,* p. 308. On the "Court Register/List" see D. J. Wiseman, *Nebuchadrezzar and Babylon,* Schweich Lectures, 1983 (Oxford: Oxford University Press, 1985), pp. 73-75.

17. So Katzenstein, *History of Tyre,* p. 326.

18. On the title see E. Unger, *Babylon: Die heilige Stadt nach der Beschreibung der Babylonier,* 2nd ed. (Berlin: de Gruyter, 1970), p. 37; J. A. Brinkman, *Prelude to*

lonian rule, and into the Persian period, Tyre and Sidon rivaled for hegemony in Phoenician affairs. With the loss of control over Carthage, and Persian favoritism toward Sidon, the balances tipped in the latter's favor.[19] As mentioned above, Tyre was finally conquered by Alexander the Great in 332.

It is obvious from Ezek. 26–28 that the exilic prophet had a special interest in Tyre. He devotes more time to this city-state than to any of the nations addressed in ch. 25; further, he has more to say concerning Tyre than any other prophet.[20] Is this a case of perverted patriotism? Is Ezekiel showing himself a true son of his people, rejoicing over Tyre's doom with the same schadenfreude that the Tyrians had expressed over Jerusalem's fall?[21] Or does he fear the influence of Tyrian idolatry over his poor compatriots back home in Judah if Tyre should be successful in its anti-Babylonian adventures?[22] Neither suggestion satisfies. The first clue to Ezekiel's special fascination with Tyre is found in the oracle itself. The opening gleeful "Aha!" over the fall of Jerusalem (26:2) suggests that the Tyrians welcomed Judah's demise as an opportunity to expand their own commercial interests. Jerusalem could serve Tyre as an important trade center on the route from Phoenicia to the Red Sea and the southern Arabian peninsula. But for Ezekiel the significance of Tyre in God's scheme of things lay elsewhere. Like Jeremiah's, this prophet's underlying assumption was that Babylon had been appointed by Yahweh to fulfill a special role in the history of his people.[23] Because Yahweh had selected Nebuchadrezzar as his agent of judgment upon Judah, an attempt by any nation to thwart Babylonian activity in the Levant was perceived as defiance against the irrevocable divine decree. When Jerusalem finally fell in 586, the only states that were still resisting the Babylonians were Egypt and Tyre. It is not coincidental, therefore, that of the foreign nations addressed by Ezekiel, these two are singled out for the brunt of his oracular volleys.

Empire: Babylonian Society and Politics, 747-626 B.C. (Philadelphia: University Museum, 1984), p. 17.

19. Cf. H. J. Katzenstein, "Tyre in the Early Persian Period (539-486 B.C.E.)," *BA* 42 (1979) 23-34.

20. Prophecies concerning Tyre appear elsewhere in Amos 1:9-10; Isa. 23:1-18; Joel 4:4-8 (Eng. 3:3-8); Zech. 9:2-4. Ezekiel's contemporary, Jeremiah, has no message for Tyre at all.

21. See Kraetschmar, *Ezechiel*, p. 203.

22. See W. E. Barnes, "Ezekiel's Denunciation of Tyre (Ezek. xxvi-xxviii)," *JTS* 35 (1934) 50-54.

23. This accounts for the absence of oracles against this empire or its king in Ezekiel. The only text approaching an anti-Babylonian stance is found in 21:33-37 (Eng. 28-32).

a. Tyre Is No More! (26:1-21)

♦ *Nature and Design*

Ezekiel 26 divides formally into four segments, each of which begins with the citation formula, *kōh 'āmar 'ădōnāy yhwh,* "Thus has the Lord Yahweh declared": A (vv. 1-6), B (vv. 7-14), C (vv. 15-18), and D (vv. 19-21). However, the substantive links between A and B, on the one hand, and C and D, on the other, suggest two major bifurcated panels, an observation reinforced formally by the formulae employed to open and close the respective sections. First, the signatory formula, *nĕ'um 'ădōnāy yhwh,* "The declaration of the Lord Yahweh," occurs only twice in the chapter, but in both instances it concludes one of these major panels (vv. 14, 21). Second, although the citation formula appears four times (vv. 3, 7, 15, 19), twice it is preceded by the connective particle *kî* (vv. 7, 19), which links these segments logically with what has come before.

Scholarly attention has tended to focus on isolating the authentic prophetic core from secondary accretions.[24] A division of the text into four subsections is indeed warranted on grounds of content, form, and style, but the chapter contains enough indicators of cohesion to justify a more holistic approach. First, the pattern of "halving" evident here is typically Ezekielian and has been observed many times in previous oracles. Second, the respective panels are linked by lexical and stylistic ties scattered throughout the chapter. Not only does the fivefold recurrence of the root *ḥrb,* "sword" (vv. 6, 8, 11, 19, 20), provide a unifying thread; the positioning of keywords like *hārag,* "to kill" (vv. 8, 11, 16), and *yāšab,* "to dwell" (vv. 16, 17 [bis], 20 [bis]), highlights the pivotal role of the lament in vv. 15-18.[25] Third, the use of the first person and the emphasis on the role of Yahweh in sections A and D create a theological framework within which the prophet observes the demise of Tyre. The center sections employ the third person, highlighting the activity of the agent and the observers of the judgment upon the city, respectively. Fourth, and perhaps most important, the progression evident in the four parts is both logical and chronological. Section A deals in general terms with the ultimate cause of Tyre's demise, the judgment of Yahweh. Section B highlights the

---

24. Denying Ezekiel any hand in the chapter, Garscha (*Studien,* pp. 149-58, 292-93, 301-6) attributes the core (vv. 2-5a) to the 5th-century author of the prophetic book, vv. 5b-6 to a deutero-Ezekielian editor, and the remainder (vv. 1, 7-14, 15-18, 19-21) to a series of later accretions. Zimmerli (*Ezekiel 2,* p. 33) and Eichrodt (*Ezekiel,* p. 371) treat section B as an expository amplification of section A by a disciple or by the "school" of the prophet.

25. Cf. H. van Dyke Parunak, *Structural Studies in Ezekiel* (Ann Arbor: University Microfilms, 1983), pp. 358-60.

immediate cause and the human agency by focusing on Nebuchadrezzar and his forces. In view of Tyre's public role, section C deals appropriately with the response of the international observers to her fall. Section D completes the city's biography by describing her descent into Sheol. She has passed from the scene for good.

(1) The Announcement of Tyre's Demise (26:1-6)

1 Now[26] in the twelfth year, in the eleventh month[27] on the first day of the month, the following message of Yahweh came to me:

2 "Human, because Tyre[28] exclaims against Jerusalem, 'Aha! She is broken![29] The gateway of the peoples! She has been turned over to me![30] I will be satisfied![31] She has been laid waste!'

3 Therefore, thus has the Lord Yahweh declared: I am against you, O Tyre! As the sea hurls[32] its waves, so I will hurl against you many nations.[33] 4 They will destroy the walls of Tyre and tear down her towers. I will scrape her soil[34] off her, and transform her into a bare

26. A marginal note in MT identifies v. 1 as the midpoint in the book.

27. The text appears to be corrupt. W. F. Albright (*JBL* 51 [1932] 93) suggested that "eleventh" (month) dropped by haplography. Based on LXX[A] and the fact that Ezekiel renders "eleventh year" elsewhere as *'aḥat 'eśrēh šānâ* (30:20; 31:1), many emend *bĕ'aštê 'eśrēh šānâ* to *bĕ'aštê 'āśār šānâ*, "in the twelfth year." But the present form of "eleven" is well attested elsewhere (40:49; Jer. 1:3; 39:2; 52:5 [= 2 K. 25:2]; Zech. 1:7; Exod. 26:7, 8; 36:14, 15; Num. 7:72; 29:20; Deut. 1:3; 1 Chr. 12:13; 24:12; 25:18; 27:14). H. J. van Dijk considers the present form an archaism (*Ezekiel's Prophecy on Tyre (Ez. 26,1–28,19): A New Approach*, BibOr 20 [Rome: Pontifical Biblical Institute, 1968], p. 3). See further the commentary below.

28. LXX renders *ṣōr (ṣôr)* as *Sor* in chs. 26–27, and as *Tyros* in 28:2, 12 and 29:28, suggesting to Zimmerli (*Ezekiel 2*, p. 26) that another translator took over between 27:32 and 28:2.

29. The sg. verb, *nišbārâ*, seems awkward before pl. *dallĕtôt*. The speakers either assume Jerusalem as the subject or consider the city gates, which consisted of two doors, as a single entity. Either way emendation is unnecessary. Cf. Zimmerli, *Ezekiel 2*, p. 27. Van Dijk (*Ezekiel's Prophecy*, pp. 3-4) follows Mayer Lambert in treating the verb as a third fem. pl.

30. *nāsēbbâ* (from *sābab*) is a Niphal by-form of *nāsabbâ*. See GKC, §67t; Bauer-Leander, *Grammatik*, §431t.

31. *'immālĕ'â*, lit. "I will be filled." LXX and Targ. treat the form as a substantive, *hammĕlē'â*.

32. The versions read *ka'ălôt*, "as the sea comes up," instead of MT's causative form. Although some interpret the following *lĕgallāyw*, "with respect to its waves," as a nearer definition of *hayyām*, "the sea" (Allen, *Ezekiel 20–48*, p. 72), the comparison and Targ. support treating the *lamed* as an Aramaized sign of the accusative.

33. I reverse the Hebrew clause order for the sake of English style.

34. Here and in v. 12 *'āpār* refers to the debris of a ruined city. Cf. also 1 K. 20:10;

rock. 5 *She will be a place where nets are spread,*[35] *in the midst of the sea,*[36] *for I have spoken — the declaration of the Lord Yahweh. She will become plunder for the nations,* 6 *while her daughters who are on the mainland will be slaughtered with the sword. Then they will know that I am Yahweh."*

1-2 The word-event formula, which regularly announces the prophet's receipt of a divine message, is modified by the insertion of a date notice. This notice is problematic because it lacks the name of the month and the "eleventh year" is difficult to reconcile with 33:21, which has Ezekiel receiving news of the fall of Jerusalem (which this oracle seems to presuppose) in the tenth month of the twelfth year, that is, Jan. 8, 585 B.C.[37] To date no proposed solution is without problems.[38] My translation assumes that the ordinal "twelfth" has dropped out, perhaps by haplography, and "eleventh" has been mistakenly attached to *šānâ,* "year."[39] According to this reconstruction, the oracle may be dated Feb. 3, 585,[40] that is, within a month after the news of the fall of Jerusalem reached Ezekiel. This date has the additional attraction of coinciding with the commencement of Nebuchadrezzar's siege of Tyre, which, according to Josephus, lasted for thirteen years (*Ag. Ap.* 1.21, §156), dated by Katzenstein ca. 585-573/572.[41]

In form and content the introduction to this oracle bears the closest resemblance to the first prophecy in this series, the oracle against Ammon (25:3). Of the six (seven) oracles in this collection,[42] only these two commence with the word-event formula and the direct address of the prophet as *ben-'ādām,* "Human," and cast the charge in the form of a direct quotation. Here

---

Neh. 3:34; 4:4; Ps. 102:15 [Eng. 14]. For a study of the root see D. Hillers, "Dust: Some Aspects of Old Testament Imagery," in *Love and Death in the Ancient Near East: Essays in Honor of Marvin H. Pope,* ed. J. H. Marks and R. M. Good (Guilford, Conn.: Four Quarters Pub., 1987), pp. 105-10.

35. The noun form *mištah* occurs only here and in v. 14. On the construct vocalized with *a* theme vowel in place of *ô* (cf. 47:10) see Bauer-Leander, *Grammatik,* §69x.

36. *bĕtôk hayyām* is reminiscent of the common Akkadian expressions *ṣur-ru ša qabal tam-tim* and *ṣur-ri a-šib qabal tam-tim,* "Tyre which lies in the midst of the seas." Cf. *ANET,* pp. 291, 295, 297.

37. On this date see below on 33:21.

38. See Allen, *Ezekiel 20–48,* p. 71.

39. Cf. the similarity between the present *bĕ'aštê 'eśrēh,* "in the eleventh," and *bištê 'eśrēh,* "in the twelfth," in 33:21. The word for month is regularly omitted in Ezekiel's date notices.

40. So also Lang, *Ezechiel,* p. 36. Cf. Parker-Dubberstein, *Chronology,* p. 28.

41. Katzenstein, *ABD,* 6:690. On the siege see further Wiseman, *Nebuchadrezzar,* pp. 25-29.

42. See above, pp. 6-12.

again the introductory *he'āḥ*, "Aha!" accentuates Tyre's mockery of Jerusalem at her fall. But this is where the parallels end. Whereas the Ammonites, as well as the Moabites, Edomites, and Phoenicians, hoped to benefit from the demise of Judah by claiming shares of her territory, the present accusation reflects Tyre's trading interests. For Tyre the fall of Jerusalem meant the elimination of a commercial rival.

The quotation itself consists of four terse declarations, in the passive mood, arranged in a chiastic ABBA order. The outer statements focus on the recipients of the judgment, while the inner ones deal with the beneficiaries. The designation of the victims as *dalĕtôt hā'ammîm* (lit. "the doors/gates of the peoples") reflects the Tyrian perception of Jerusalem as the principal barrier to her own control of the overland trade routes between the Mediterranean in the west and the Transjordanian nations, the Arabian peninsula, and the Red Sea in the east and southeast.[43] The potential benefits for the Phoenician city are announced in the second and third clauses. Like *nišbārâ* in the first clause, the feminine verb *nāsēbbâ* (lit. "she is turned") assumes Jerusalem as the subject.[44] Her fall means the satisfaction of Tyre's voracious commercial appetite.[45] The last clause sums up the fate of Jerusalem: this foremost Levantine city will be turned into a wasteland.

3-6 Like all the preceding oracles against the nations, Yahweh's response to Tyre's glee at Jerusalem's destruction is introduced with *Therefore (lākēn)*. The announcement of judgment divides into two unequal parts, separated by the formulaic affirmation of the divine origin of the sentence in v. 5. Vv. 3-5a emphasize the direct intervention of Yahweh, beginning with a forthright declaration of his personal opposition to Tyre.[46] Tyre's fate is not merely the result of a conflict between two peoples. Yahweh, the divine patron of Judah, will stand up in defense of his own city.

Yahweh's agents of destruction, *many nations (gôyim rabbîm)*,[47] are appropriately compared with waves of the sea hurled up onto the shore, washing away Tyre's seemingly impregnable defensive walls and towers. The vivid imagery continues with the picture of Yahweh himself scraping

---

43. The political, if not economic, preeminence of Jerusalem in the region is confirmed by the Wiseman Chronicle. After the destruction of Ashkelon, "the city of Judah" is the only city of Hatti-land (the west) named explicitly. See Grayson, *Chronicles*, p. 100, 5: rev. 11-12.

44. Katzenstein (*History of Tyre*, p. 322) translates: "Her gates swing open to me."

45. *'immălĕ'â* may be interpreted as an abbreviated passive form of the full expression of *nimlā' hannepeš*, "the appetite is filled." Cf. Eccl. 6:7.

46. On the challenge formula, *hinĕnî 'ālayik*, see my *Ezekiel: Chapters 1–24*, pp. 201-2.

47. The expression occurs three additional times in Ezekiel: 31:6; 38:23; 39:27. Note also *'ammîm rabbîm*, "many peoples," in 3:6; 27:33; 32:3, 9-10; 38:6, 8-9, 15, 22.

away the soil and exposing bare rock. The magnificent structures of the commercial capital of the Mediterranean will be replaced by fishermen's nets, spread out on the bare rock to dry,[48] in the midst of the sea. With ironic justice Yahweh declares emphatically that she who had gloated over Jerusalem's fall and had exploited others will become the source of others' enrichment: she will become *plunder for the nations (lĕbaz laggôyim)*. Meanwhile, *her daughters who are on the mainland,* viz., the mainland villages under Tyrian jurisdiction, will be slaughtered.[49] This time it will be "like mother, like daughter"; the island fortress will offer no protection from the enemy for anyone. The final recognition formula affirms that Yahweh's motive for destroying Tyre is not only, or even primarily, retributive. His goal is that even this arrogant city will acknowledge him. He is the one who speaks and fulfills his declared word.

(2) The Agent of Tyre's Demise (26:7-14)

7 *"For thus has the Lord Yahweh declared: I am bringing against[50] Tyre from the north Nebuchadrezzar, the king of Babylon, the king of kings, with cavalry,[51] chariots,[52] and teams of horses; with a vast assembly of troops.[53]* 8 *Your daughters on the mainland he will slaughter with the sword. He will set up siege walls[54] against you, heap up a mound against you, and raise a protective shield against you.* 9 *He will direct the force[55] of his battering ram[56] against your*

---

48. On Tyre as a center of the fishing industry see *ANET,* p. 477; Strabo, *Geog.* 16.2.23. For brief discussion see Katzenstein, *History of Tyre,* p. 53. The image of fishermen spreading their nets will return in 47:10, but with a different significance.

49. The mainland village of Ušu (Gk. *Palaia Tyros*), situated opposite the island, figures prominently in the Assyrian annals. See *ANET,* pp. 287, 300.

50. LXX ἐπὶ σέ retains the second person of direct address.

51. Lit. "horses."

52. On *pārāšîm* see my *Ezekiel: Chapters 1–24,* pp. 739, 744, 750 n. 114, on 23:6, 12, 23.

53. LXX καὶ συναγωγῆς ἐθνῶν πολλῶν σφόδρα treats *wĕqāhāl wĕʿam rāb* as a hendiadys. The prefixed *bĕ,* "with," before the preceding word performs double duty. See van Dijk, *Ezekiel's Prophecy,* p. 15. In 16:40 *qāhāl,* lit. "assembly," had denoted an assembled mob. *qāhāl gādôl,* "a great assembly," is used militarily in 38:15 (parallel to *ḥayil rāb,* "a vast army").

54. Cf. *bānâ dāyēq* in 4:2; 17:17; 21:27.

55. *mĕḥî* is a hapax form from *māḥâ,* "to strike" (cf. Num. 34:11, and the Aramaized form *māḥā',* "to clap," in 25:6).

56. *qābollô* is cognate to Akk. *qablu,* "battle, warfare." See *CAD,* 13:12-16; *AHW,* p. 888. LXX treats *qābollô* as a preposition. On the MT vocalization in place of expected *qĕbollô* see Bauer-Leander, *Grammatik,* §79u.

walls, and your towers he will demolish with his axes.[57] 10 *The dust*[58] *raised by his hordes of horses will cover you, while your walls shake from the clatter of teams of horses,*[59] *wheels and chariots, when he enters your gates like people enter*[60] *a breached*[61] *city.* 11 *He will trample all your streets with the hooves of his horses,*[62] *slaughter your people with the sword, and your strong pillars*[63] *will topple*[64] *to the ground.* 12 *They will plunder*[65] *your wealth, and despoil your merchandise. They will demolish your walls, and tear down your luxurious mansions.*[66] *Your stones, your timbers, and your rubble they will hurl into the water.*[67] 13 *I will put an end*[68] *to the noise of your songs, so the sound of the lyre will no longer be heard.* 14 *I will transform you into a bare rock! She will be a place where they spread out nets, never to be rebuilt,*[69] *for I am Yahweh; I have spoken. The declaration of the Lord Yahweh."*

This subsection is framed by the citation formula at the beginning (v. 7) and the signatory formula at the end (v. 14). The expository function of the material

57. Although *ḥereb* usually denotes "sword" (cf. vv. 6, 8), it may refer to any cutting device (cf. knife, razor in 5:1). As in Exod. 20:25 and Jer. 5:17, here a tool of destruction is obviously involved.

58. *'ābāq,* a synonym for *'āpār,* "dust," occurs only here in Ezekiel. Elsewhere it denotes "fine dust, powder." Cf. Exod. 9:9; Deut. 28:24; Isa. 5:24; 29:5; Nah. 1:3.

59. On the vocalization of *pāraš* see GKC, §130b. On the meaning of the expression see my *Ezekiel: Chapters 1–24,* p. 739.

60. The masc. *měbô'ê* denotes acts of entrance, not entry places (cf. *měbô'ōt* in 27:3). The versions read sg., but cf. *mô'ṣā'ê* in 12:4.

61. *měbuqqā'â,* from *bāqa',* "to split."

62. Note the assonance of *parsôt sûsāyw yirmōs. pěrāśôt,* "hooves," from *pāras,* "to divide," refers fundamentally to split hooves of cattle and sheep, but is extended to include hooves in general.

63. *maṣṣěbôt 'uzzēk,* lit. "pillars of your strength," is intentionally ambiguous, referring fundamentally to the pillars supporting the magnificent buildings of the city, but also in an abstract sense to all the bases of Tyre's security.

64. The sg. form of *tērēd,* "it will come down," is influenced by the preceding genitive *'uzzēk,* "your strength." The causative rendering of the versions adapts the reading to the context.

65. The shift to the pl. is attributable to the expository nature of vv. 7-14. Cf. *gôyim rabbîm,* "many nations," in v. 5. This is missed by LXX, which harmonizes the forms by reading sg.

66. *bottê ḥemdātēk,* lit. "your desirable houses."

67. LXX and Syr. misread *mayim* as *hayyām,* "the sea."

68. LXX's third person is a harmonization.

69. Reading *tihyeh* and *tibneh* as third person fem. forms, assuming Tyre as the subject. Cf. v. 4. *BHS's* emendation to second fem. *(tihyî, tibnî)* is unnecessary.

within this framework is evident from the numerous links between these verses and the preceding vv. 3-6:

The description of Tyre's fate in terms of the city becoming a bare rock on which fishermen dry their nets (vv. 4-5, 14).

The reference to the rubble as ʿāpār, "dust" (vv. 4, 12).

The description of Tyre as bĕtôk hayyām, "in the midst of the sea" (v. 4), echoed in bĕtôk mayim, "in the midst of the water" (v. 12).

The self-identification formula, kî ʾănî yhwh (vv. 6, 14).

The signatory formula, nĕʾum ʾădōnāy yhwh (vv. 5, 14).

The references to "slaughtering your daughters on the mainland with the sword" (hārag bĕnôtayik baśśādeh bĕhereb, vv. 6, 8).

Beyond these explicit verbal connections, several statements in vv. 7-14 represent closer definitions of phrases in vv. 3-6:

The gôyim rabbîm portrayed as waves beating on the rock in v. 3 are identified as Nebuchadrezzar (with his title of melek mĕlākîm) and his hosts, referred to as qāhāl wĕʿam rāb.

The general announcement in v. 4 that the walls of Tyre will be destroyed is concretized with the reference to battering rams in v. 9.

The demolition of the towers in v. 4 is clarified in v. 9 as "breaking down your towers with axes."[70]

Even so, the exposition is free, adopting a more prosaic style and shifting the focus from the divine source of Tyre's punishment to the human agents. This is not to say the divine initiative has been forgotten. On the contrary, the core (vv. 8-12) is framed by strong theological affirmations of Yahweh's role, within the context of which the human activity is to be interpreted. This rhetorical strategy also highlights the conviction that, while Nebuchadrezzar may imagine himself to be operating sovereignly, and may appear to pursue his military tactics with impunity, his independence is more apparent than real. He is merely a tool in Yahweh's hands.

7 Yahweh's speech opens with an ominous announcement of an agent of destruction being brought in from the north. Although Babylon lies directly east of Jerusalem, the direction specified accords with the perspective of Jeremiah in Jer. 1:13-15 and the route always taken by Mesopotamian armies invading the Levant.[71] For the first time in the book the agent of Yahweh's

---

70. For further discussion of the correspondences see Parunak, *Structural Studies*, pp. 360-65.

71. Cf. Ezekiel's announcement of Gog's invasion of Israel from the north in 38:15.

judgment is identified by name: *Nebuchadrezzar.* The form *nĕbûkadre'ṣṣar*, which is found in the OT only in Ezekiel and Jeremiah, corresponds to the Babylonian *Nabû-kudurri-uṣur*, commonly interpreted as "O Nabu, protect my offspring."[72] The form *nĕbûkadne'ṣṣar*, "Nebuchadnezzar," more common in English, is a corruption of the Babylonian original, attested in the OT and in an Aramaic tablet.[73] Nebuchadrezzar is further identified by two titles. The first, *the king of Babylon (melek-bābel)*, is common in Ezekiel.[74] The second, *the king of kings (melek melākîm)*, corresponds to Akk. *šar-šarrāni*, a traditional Mesopotamian title, having been used in Assyria since the 13th century B.C., though to date neo-Babylonian texts attest the title only for the god Marduk.[75]

Although Nebuchadrezzar is Yahweh's primary agent, he will not come alone. Accompanying him will be a vast army consisting of cavalry *(sûsîm)*, chariotry *(rekeb ûpārāšîm)*, and troops *(qāhāl wĕ'am rāb)*.

8-12   These verses describe the strategy and impact of Nebuchadrezzar's attack on Tyre. The use of the second person of direct address creates the impression that Ezekiel is proclaiming this oracle to Tyre, but this is a rhetorical device in keeping with his posture of facing the subject of his messages (cf. 25:2). The description begins appropriately with the fate of the mainland Tyrian settlements, which must be the first to experience Nebuchadrezzar's attack, followed by a more detailed account of the assault on the island city itself.

8-9   The strategy described here reflects thorough knowledge of military tactics, containing all the elements normally associated with siege warfare:[76] (1) erecting siege mounds *(nātan dāyēq);* (2) constructing a ramp

---

When sweeping down into Palestine from Syria, invading armies had three choices: along the coast through Phoenicia; through the Beqa' Valley; through Damascus, east of the Anti-Lebanon range. See maps 52 and 58 in Beitzel, *Moody Atlas,* pp. 131, 137.

72. See Ezek. 29:18, 19; 30:10; Jer. 21:2, 7; etc. Cf. BDB, p. 613, for further references. Jer. 49:28 reads *nbwkdr'ṣwr.* On the Babylonian name see Wiseman, *Nebuchadrezzar,* pp. 2-5.

73. On the original form of the Babylonian name see Brinkman, *Post-Kassite Babylonia,* pp. 41-42. On the Aramaic tablet see Wiseman, *Nebuchadrezzar,* p. 2. LXX is consistent in reading *nun* for *resh.* This exchange of letters occurs elsewhere in the OT in the names Shenazzar (*šnṣr* for *šarra-uṣur,* 1 Chr. 3:18) and Osnappar ('*snpr* for *Aššur-ban-apli,* Ezra 4:10).

74. See 17:12; 19:9; 21:24, 26 (Eng. 19, 21); 24:2; 29:18-19; 30:10, 24-25; 32:11. Its use by Nebuchadrezzar himself is attested on an Aramaic clay tablet from Sefire (J. Starcky, "Une tablette araméene de l'an 34 de Nabuchodonosor [AO.21.063]," *Syria* 37 [1960] 100; cf. *KAI,* 227.5; *TSSI,* 2:22.5), and by a contemporary minor king Adon in a letter to Pharaoh Neco (*KAI,* 266.4; *TSSI,* 2:21.4).

75. See Seux, *Épithèts royales,* pp. 318-19. The title is popular with Persian kings as well. Cf. Ezra 7:12 (of Artaxerxes).

76. See my *Ezekiel: Chapters 1–24,* pp. 171-73.

(*šāpak sōlĕlâ);* (3) raising shields *(hēqîm ṣinnâ)* to protect the siege artillery and battering rams;[77] (4) pounding the walls with battering rams *(nātan mĕḥî qābollô);* (5) demolishing defensive towers with axes *(nātaṣ migdĕlōt bĕḥărābôt).*

10-12 It is apparent from these verses that the prophet envisions complete success for the invader. The scene of enemy forces rushing through the breach in the wall and stampeding through the city, destroying everything in sight, is painted in bold but realistic strokes. The last line in v. 10 is the key: the enemy will take the sea fortress by storm as if it were an ordinary walled city on the mainland. The dust raised by stampeding horses and racing chariots will darken the sky like a cloud. The din of neighing and snorting horses, the clatter of wheels on rocks, the noise of charioteers beating the sides of their vehicles, and the shouts of the invaders will cause the ground to tremble and the walls to shake. The scene of general devastation continues in v. 11 with the entire city crushed under the trampling horses' hooves, its population fallen to the sword, and the pillars of support toppled to the ground. Involved in the razing of the city are also the plundering of its wealth,[78] the smashing of its walls, and the demolition of its magnificent homes. The final act is to dump all the rubble, reduced here to stones, timbers, and debris *('āpār),* into the sea.

13-14 The prophet's attention returns to Yahweh's involvement in the transformation of this magnificent city into a bare rock out in the sea. First, he will bring an end to the festival atmosphere of the city, expressed in terms of silencing "the din of your songs," and "the sound of your lyres."[79] The present statement recalls Amos 5:23 and several Jeremianic declarations, but is especially reminiscent of ancient treaty curses that speak of the cessation of music as a punishment for covenantal infidelity.[80] V. 14 summarizes the

---

77. This usage of *ṣinnâ* is not to be confused with the long shield carried by soldiers (23:23; 38:4; 39:9).

78. The plundering is described in two perfectly parallel lines. The verbs *šalal* and *bāzaz* represent a standardized word pair (cf. 29:19; 38:12, 13; 39:10; Isa. 10:6). Elsewhere Ezekiel uses *ḥayil* of a military force (17:17; 23:14; 38:15), but the parallelism here requires the sense "wealth, property," as in 28:4-5. *rĕkullâ*, from *rākal*, "to go about (as a merchant)," denotes "merchandise," an appropriate expression for the booty found in Tyre.

79. Our knowledge of ancient Near Eastern music is limited. For an attempted reconstruction of ancient Canaanite music (with which Phoenician music would have had many affinities), see A. D. Kilmer, R. L. Crocker, and R. R. Brown, *Sounds from Silence: Recent Discoveries in Ancient Near Eastern Music* (Berkeley, 1976). Cf. also Kilmer, *IDBSup*, pp. 610-12; as well as D. A. Foxvog and Kilmer, "Music," *ISBE* (rev. ed.), 3.436-49. For illustrations and discussion of the *kinnôr*, "lyre" (not harp), see D. G. Stradling and K. A. Kitchen, *IBD*, 2:1031-40; I. H. Jones, *ABD*, 4:937.

80. See Jer. 7:34; 16:9; 25:10; 33:11; Lam. 5:14-15. Particularly striking is its similarity with Sefire I.A.29: "May the sound of the lyre be heard no more in Arpad and

effects of Yahweh's attack on Tyre, with a renewed announcement that the city will be transformed into a shining wind-swept rock, fit only for drying fishermen's nets. This phase of the oracle concludes with a solemn statement, guaranteed by the signature of Yahweh himself, that this great center of maritime commerce will never be rebuilt.

While Ezekiel is obviously aware of Tyre's position out in the Mediterranean (cf. the reference to dumping the debris into the sea), most aspects of Nebuchadrezzar's assault on the city are cast in stereotypical terms, as if the city were situated like any other mainland fortress.[81] The prophet's vision of a decisive victory resulting in the total destruction of the city is problematic, because it flies in the face of the actual course of events, at least according to a report by Philostratus preserved by Josephus: "This king [Nebuchadrezzar] besieged Tyre thirteen years, while Ethbaal was reigning in Tyre" (*Ant.* 10.11.1, §228). In reality Tyre was not destroyed until several centuries later when Alexander the Great finally succeeded in what no Asian emperor had been able to achieve. Ezekiel himself will acknowledge later that Nebuchadrezzar's efforts against Tyre were less successful than anticipated here (29:17-20), and that Yahweh would give him the land of Egypt as compensation for the disappointing results. But Nebuchadrezzar's campaign was not totally futile: the Babylonian sources referred to earlier certainly imply that Nebuchadrezzar exercised political control over Tyre in the following decades.

(3) The International Impact of Tyre's Demise (26:15-18)

15 *"Thus has the Lord Yahweh declared to Tyre:*[82] *How the coastlands will shake at the sound of your downfall,*[83] *when the victims*[84] *groan*[85] *and the slain are slaughtered*[86] *in your midst!* 16 *All the rulers*

---

among its people." See also the Ashurnirari Treaty: "Let the farmers of his land not sing the harvest-song in the fields" (*ANET*, p. 533). For discussion of these and related texts see Hillers, *Treaty-Curses*, pp. 57-58.

81. This language has led some (Eichrodt, *Ezekiel*, pp. 370-71; van den Born, *Ezechiël*, p. 165) to suggest that the prophet has drawn on an old battle song for his account.

82. Van Dijk (*Ezekiel's Prophecy*, p. 29) treats the *lamed* on *lĕṣôr* as a vocative particle. See below on 27:2.

83. *mappelet* occurs also in v. 18; 27:27; 31:13, 16; and 32:10. Outside Ezekiel it occurs only in Judg. 14:8 and Prov. 29:16.

84. On *ḥālāl*, lit. "pierced," see my *Ezekiel: Chapters 1–24*, pp. 227-28, and on 30:11, 24 below.

85. The verb *'ānaq* occurs elsewhere in Qal only in Jer. 51:52, and in Niphal in 9:4 and 24:17. Cf. the noun *'ănāqâ*, "crying, groaning," in Mal. 2:13; Ps. 12:6 (Eng. 5); 79:11; 102:21 (Eng. 20).

86. Many emend *bĕhārēg herreg* to *bĕhārîq ḥereb*, following LXX's free render-

of the sea will descend from their thrones. They will remove their robes,[87] and strip off their finely embroidered garments.[88] They will clothe themselves with trembling;[89] they will sit on the ground, and tremble horror-struck and appalled over you. 17 They will raise a dirge over you, saying to you:[90]

'How you have perished,[91] been wiped out[92] from the seas,
O city of renown,[93] once ruler[94] on the sea —
she and her inhabitants,[95] who spread their terror[96] —
all her inhabitants.[97]

---

ing, ἐν τῷ σπάσαι μάχαιραν (cf. BHS), though MT is supported by Syr., Targ., and Vulg., and the LXX rendering of hārag bahereb in vv. 6, 8, 11. On the pointing of the infinitive, with the elided h, instead of bahărōg, see GKC, §511; Bauer-Leander, Grammatik, §25z. The cognate accusative hereg occurs with the verb hārag also in Isa. 27:7.

87. mĕʿîlîm denotes robes worn by men of rank (1 Sam. 15:27; 18:4; 24:5, 12 [Eng. 4, 11]; 28:14; Job 1:20; 2:12; Ezra 9:3, 5). LXX "and they will remove their miters from their heads" either misreads the Hebrew or is based on a different Vorlage.

88. On bigdê riqmātām, "their variegated garments," see 16:18; 17:3 (of colorful plumage); and 27:7.

89. BHS proposes reading qadrût, "grief" (cf. Isa. 50:3), or hăgōrôt, "girdle," for hărādôt, but without support. Cf. lābēš šĕmāmâ, "to dress in horror," in 7:27. N. Lohfink (VT 12 [1962] 271 n. 3) interprets hărādôt as "mourning garments" (Trauerkleidung). The present sequence of actions recalls the behavior of the king of Nineveh upon hearing Jonah's message of doom for his city (Jon. 3:6).

90. lāk is missing in LXX, but it is present in 28:12; 32:2 has ʾēlāyw.

91. ʾābadt is missing in LXX and generally deleted on metrical grounds (see Zimmerli, Ezekiel 2, p. 30; Craigie, Ezekiel, p. 194). But the collocation of ʾābad and šābat is natural (cf. 30:13; van Dijk, Ezekiel's Prophecy, p. 35). Cf. the pairing of ʾābad with nišmad, "to be destroyed," in Jer. 48:8; with nikrat, "to be cut off," Jer. 7:28; with šibbēr, "to shatter," in Lam. 2:9.

92. MT nôšebet is a Niphal fem. participle from yāšab, "sit, dwell"; in Niphal, "be inhabited," which makes little sense in the context. I follow LXX κατελύθης = nišbat, from šābat, "to cease." So BHS, NRSV, REB, NAB, and most commentators.

93. hahullālâ is best treated as a Pual participle without the mem preformative, but with the article functioning as a relative pronoun. On the form see GKC, §§ 138k, 52s; Joüon-Muraoka, Grammar, §§ 158n, 145e.

94. hăzāqâ, lit. "strong one" (fem.).

95. The entire line is missing in LXX, probably due to homoeoarchton. Cf. the following line.

96. LXX ἡ δοῦσα τὸν φόβον αὐτῆς assumes nātĕnâ hătîtāh, "she produced her terror," an adjustment necessitated by the omission of the previous line. Elsewhere the idiom for inflicting terror upon someone is nātan hātît bĕ. . . (32:23-27, 32). hittît, from hātat, "to be shattered," used in the sense of "terror," is distinctively Ezekielian (see also 32:30).

97. Targ. expands to read "How have all her inhabitants been delivered to misfortune!" Syr. has bklhwn ʿmwryh dʾrʿ, which presupposes lĕkol-yôšĕbê hāʾāres, "to all

18 *Now the coastlands*[98] *will tremble,*
   on the day of your downfall.[99]
And the coastlands by the sea
   will be shocked at your demise.' "[100]

The citation formula in v. 15 signals the beginning of a new phase of the oracle. The piece has no formal closing, but it is evident from the new citation formula in v. 19 that a break is intended at the end of v. 18. Within the *inclusio* created by vv. 15 and 18, the structure follows the typical pattern of ancient Near Eastern expressions of grief.[101]

15 Phase 1. News of the collapse of Tyre is received across the seas. It is not clear whether the prophet intends v. 15 as a question or as a declarative or even exclamatory statement.[102] But the word order, with the predicate and subject at the end, preceded by three causal prepositional phrases, thrusts the reason for the reaction into the foreground. The respondents to Tyre's collapse are identified as the *coastlands ('iyyîm)*, a designation for the maritime lands, including islands and coastal cities, in this case the primary benefactors of and competitors to Tyre's mercantile ventures. Their reaction is expressed as "shuddering, shaking" *(rā'aš)*, which in v. 10 had been used of tottering city walls.[103] In this instance the shock is evoked by the sounds and sights of utter disaster: the city has come crashing down like a large building, the wounded lie groaning in the streets, and the signs of ruthless slaughter are everywhere.

16 Phase 2. All governmental activity is suspended. The prophet's

---

the inhabitants of the earth." But it is unlikely that a change of subject is envisioned for the two occurrences of *yôšĕbeyhā*. An emphatic *lamed* may be the best solution. See Lohfink, *VT* 12 (1962) 272.

98. On the Aramaized pl. *hā'iyyin* cf. *ḥiṭṭîn* in 4:9 (see my *Ezekiel: Chapters 1–24*, p. 181 n. 77). The normal form, *'iyyîm*, occurs in the next line. Cf. Lohfink, *VT* 12 (1962) 272 n. 3.

99. *yôm mappaltēk* functions as a temporal accusative (GKC, §118i). LXX reads "from the day"; Targ., "on the day your slain will fall."

100. Many delete this entire sentence as a gloss. Zimmerli (*Ezekiel 2,* p. 31) notes (1) its intolerable tautological nature after v. 18a; (2) its lack of metrical form; (3) its absence from LXX and a Latin version, L^CW. *miṣṣē'tēk* consists of a causative *min* plus a rare use of the infinitive of *yāṣā'*, "to go out." Van Dijk (*Ezekiel's Prophecy,* p. 39) proposes a root *nṣ'*, a by-form of *nṣh*, "to fall into ruin." Targ. expands, "by your departure into exile."

101. For a discussion of the structure of grief see Lohfink, *VT* 12 (1962) 269-73.

102. Thus NJPS; van Dijk, *Ezekiel's Prophecy,* pp. 29-30. On *hălō'* as an emphatic particle see M. L. Brown, " 'Is It Not?' or 'Indeed!': *HL* in Northwest Semitic," *Maarav* 4 (1987) 201-19. Cf. 24:15; 38:14.

103. Observers of Yahweh's judgment respond similarly in 27:28; 31:16; and 38:20.

attention focuses on "all the princes of the sea." They get off their thrones, descend *(yārad)* the steps leading up to it (cf. 1 K. 10:18-20), and exchange their royal robes and their colorful vestments for the garments of mourning. Ezekiel describes the reaction metaphorically with *lābēš ḥărādôt,* "to be clothed with trembling."

Phase 3. The kings sit on the ground and tremble with horror. A triad of expressions describes their reaction. Sitting on the ground was a customary way of showing grief in the ancient world (cf. Job 2:12-13). The verb *ḥārad,* "to tremble," is cognate to *ḥărādôt* in the previous line, but the modifier *lirgāʿîm* is difficult. Most understand the *lamed* distributively and derive the expression from *rgʿ,* "a moment," hence "every moment, continuously."[104] However, M. D. Goldman has proposed a second root for *rāgaʿ,* interpreting the present form (and 32:10) "with tremor."[105] The third verb, *šāmĕmû,* "they are appalled," recalls the usage of the term in 7:27.

17-18   Phase 4. A death lament *(qînâ)* is raised over the downfall of Tyre.[106] The use of the vocative suggests that the following lines represent an intentionally composed lament. Although some doubt the inclusion of v. 18 in the dirge,[107] it probably does double duty, providing the conclusion to the lament as well as answering to v. 15. Vv. 15 and 18 display a common primary interest in the maritime nations rather than in Tyre, and are linked lexically by "coastlands" *(ʾîyîm/ʾîyîn)* and "your downfall" *(mappalĕtēk).* Even if v. 18 is included in the lament, by Ezekielian standards this dirge is brief (cf. chs. 19, 27). In typical Ezekielian fashion, however, the subject is dropped temporarily, to be resumed at a later time for further development, in this instance in the very next chapter.

Pure forms of laments tend to display a 3:2 *qînâ* metrical pattern. Although some have tried to make this short dirge conform to this pattern, it can be achieved only with drastic surgery on three of the four lines (in Hebrew) of the text. The dirge is admittedly disjointed and somewhat incoherent in style, but MT offers a meaningful text. Rather than dismissing these difficulties as textual corruptions, they may reflect the heightened emotional state of those who chanted the dirge.[108]

104. For a survey of interpretations see Zimmerli, *Ezekiel 2,* p. 30.

105. M. D. Goldman, "The Meaning of *rgʿ,*" *AusBR* 4 (1954/55) 15. See also Dahood, *Psalms,* 1:182; and van Dijk, *Ezekiel's Prophecy,* pp. 32-33.

106. *nāśāʾ qînâ ʿal* occurs elsewhere in 27:2; 28:12; 32:2 (cf. v. 16). *ʾel* replaces *ʿal* in 19:1; 27:32, on which see 1:17. On the nature and forms of laments see my *Ezekiel: Chapters 1–24,* pp. 591ff. Garr does not discuss this dirge (*ZAW* 92 [1983] 54-75).

107. It does exhibit the 3:2 metrical pattern typical of laments in the first two lines, and the expression *ʿattâ* often introduces the "now" portion of the "once-now" pattern of laments.

108. See the discussion in my *Ezekiel: Chapters 1–24,* pp. 591ff.

This is the only lament in Ezekiel to open with the typical exclamation *'ēk* (or the longer form *'ēkâ*), "How!"[109] It apparently does double duty for both verbs in the opening line. The inclusion of v. 18 in the lament results in a now-then-now pattern. At the *present* time Tyre has disappeared from her place "in the seas," a fate expressed by two terms, *'ābad,* "to perish," and *šābat min,* "to cease from."[110] In the *past* she had been renowned *(hullālâ)* for her might on the seas *(ḥăzāqâ bayyām),* with which she as a city and her sailor-merchants individually had terrorized her rivals. Like modern day super-powers, motivated entirely by self-interest, Tyre and her merchants controlled the shipping lanes of the world, imposing their own conditions of commerce on their trading partners. But *now* she has fallen,[111] and the reverberations of the collapse of this seemingly invincible island fortress have spread throughout the Mediterranean basin. Given the terror she had spread all around, the maritime nations might have rejoiced over the demise of their rival and commercial overlord. Instead they express shock, trembling *(ḥārad),* and dismay *(nibhal).* For all her brutality, Tyre had represented stability, and places such as Carthage had flourished under her leadership. No doubt when they saw her go they realized not only that they too were vulnerable, but also that their continued prosperity depended on the establishment of entirely new trading patterns.

(4) The Role of Yahweh in Tyre's Demise (26:19-21)

19 *"For thus has the Lord Yahweh declared: When I make you into a desolate city, like cities that are uninhabited; when I bring up[112] the great deep over you, and the mighty waters cover you,* 20 *then I will bring you down to be with[113] those who go down to the Pit — to the people of old. I will make you dwell in the netherworld — like the ancient waste places[114] — with those who go down to the Pit, so you*

109. The word introduces dirges over deceased cities elsewhere in Isa. 1:21; Lam. 1:1; 2:1; and 4:1.

110. See n. 91 above. The phrase is common, but see esp. Isa. 17:3.

111. In place of "the day of Tyre" *(yôm ṣōr;* cf. "the day of Midian," Isa. 9:3 [Eng. 4]), Ezekiel employs the more colorful "day of your fall" *(yôm mappaltēk).*

112. Reading with the versions. Either the last two letters have been inadvertently transposed or the suffix on the previous *bĕtittî* does double duty. So van Dijk, *Ezekiel's Prophecy,* p. 40.

113. On the basis of LXX πρός many emend *'et* to *'el.* Here the preposition carries the sense "to be with."

114. *koḥŏrābôt mē'ôlām* is confirmed by LXX ὡς ἔρημον, and the emendation to *boḥŏrābôt* (on the basis of Targ. and Syr.) suggested by *BHS* is unnecessary.

will not be inhabited,[115] *nor radiate splendor*[116] *in the land of the living.* 21 *I will make you a horror,*[117] *and you will be no more. You will be sought, but you will never be found again.*[118] *The declaration of the Lord Yahweh."*

19   Like the first part of this prophecy against Tyre (vv. 1-6), the concluding segment highlights the role of Yahweh. Behind all the effort her human enemies have invested in the city's destruction stands the sovereign Lord of history, who ultimately determines this city's destiny as well. Two different images are used to describe Yahweh's devastating actions. First, he will transform the city into a desolate landscape, without any inhabitant.[119] Second, he will submerge her with the waters of a huge tidal wave. In view of v. 20, it is tempting to see in *těhôm* mythological allusions to the chaotic primeval waters, which constantly threaten the cosmic order.[120] But if there is any link at all, the notion of the chaotic primordial waters has been thoroughly demythologized. It is not the "great deep" as an independent force that threatens Tyre's existence. Like Nebuchadrezzar, *těhôm* is but a tool in the hand of Yahweh, executing his judgment on this city. At his command, the great flood, which had once destroyed the world (Gen. 6–8), will visit Tyre again.

20-21   The image shifts: Tyre is now personified, and her demise is presented as the departure of an individual into the dark realm of the dead, the netherworld. In typical Ezekielian style, the motif of the descent into the netherworld is raised and then immediately dropped, only to be picked up in

115. MT treats *tēšēbî* as a Qal form of *yāšab*. The present sense, "to be inhabited," occurs elsewhere in 29:11; 36:35; Jer. 17:6, 25; 50:13, 39; Isa. 13:20; Zech. 2:8 [Eng. 4]; 9:5; 14:11; etc. Donner and Röllig (*KAI*, 2:225-26) speak of a passive Qal underlying *yšbt* in the Aramaic Zenjirli inscription, *KAI*, 215.4. Repointing the word as if from *šûb*, "to return," is unnecessary (contra *BHS* and Zimmerli, *Ezekiel 2*, p. 32; N. J. Tromp, *Primitive Conceptions of Death and the Nether World in the Old Testament*, BibOr 21 [Rome: Pontifical Biblical Institute, 1969], p. 68 n. 215).

116. *wěnātattî ṣěbî* seems to read, "I will set glory . . ." But the verb is an archaic second fem. form as in 16:50. So also NJPS and van Dijk, *Ezekiel's Prophecy*, p. 46. The negative particle before the preceding *tēšēbî* does double duty. Many read *wětityaṣṣěbî* on the basis of LXX μηδὲ ἀνασταθῇς, "you will not rise again."

117. Vulg. *in nihilum* and Targ. *kdl' hwyt*, "as though you had never been," seem to reflect the III-*h* root *blh* and the negative particle *bly*.

118. Since *ûtěbuqšî wělō' timmāṣě'î* is missing in LXX and in similar contexts in 27:36 and 28:19, *BHS* and many commentators delete the line as a secondary expansion. Cf. Zimmerli, *Ezekiel 2*, p. 32. LXX harmonizes *'ôd lě'ôlām* with the simpler *'ad 'ôlām* in 27:36 and 28:19.

119. The verb *yāšab* (Niphal) deliberately plays on the root that had appeared twice in the previous verse.

120. See Zimmerli, *Ezekiel 2*, p. 39; van Dijk, *Ezekiel's Prophecy*, p. 42; Tromp, *Primitive Conceptions*, p. 61.

47

a later context and developed in greater detail (31:14-18; 32:17-32). While a fuller discussion of the Hebrew conception of the abode of the dead is reserved for the commentary on those sections,[121] several details call for brief comment.

20a-b The prophet uses several different designations for the abode of the dead. The first, *bôr,* is a by-form of *bĕ'ōr,* which refers primarily to a cistern in which rainwater is trapped and stored, but it was also applied to empty cisterns used as dungeons (Exod. 12:29; Jer. 37:16; 38:6-13), or convenient places in which to dump corpses (Jer. 41:7-9). Lam. 3:53 speaks of a pit as a hole in the ground in which one may be buried alive, which leads naturally to the denotation "grave" (Isa. 14:19; Prov. 28:17). Like Sheol, with which *bôr* is often paired (Ezek. 31:14-16; Isa. 14:15; Ps. 30:4 [Eng. 3]; cf. Ezek. 32:18, 21, 23-25, 27, 29, 30), once it had acquired this meaning, the application of this term to the subterranean abode of the dead was a small step. This is clearly its meaning here, as well as in 31:14, 16 and 32:17-32.[122]

Twice in this verse (and in 31:14) the occupants of this place are described as *those who go down to the Pit (yōrĕdê bôr).* That these are the dead is clear not only from the context, but also from the use of the related phrase, "to go down to the earth" (Jon. 2:7 [Eng. 6]), "to go down to the dust *('āpār)"* (Ps. 22:30 [Eng. 29]), and "to go down to Sheol" (Job 17:16).[123] Those who go down are identified further as *the people of old ('am 'ôlām,* lit. "eternal people").[124] On the one hand, the present context suggests a link with Ps. 143:3 and Lam. 3:6, which speak of the deceased as *mētê 'ôlām,* "the deceased of long ago," who dwell in dark places.[125] On the other hand, if one interprets *'ôlām* substantively, viz., as a designation for "eternity," or more specifically the netherworld, then the *'am 'ôlām* may be the inhabitants of the *bêt 'ôlām,* "eternal house," referred to in Eccl. 12:5, that is, "the people of the netherworld."[126] In any case, the modifier *'ōlam,* "of old, eternal," stresses

---

121. On the subject see D. I. Block, "Beyond the Grave: Ezekiel's Vision of Death and Afterlife," *BBR* 2 (1992) 113-42.

122. On the range of meanings of *bôr* see J.-G. Heintz, *TDOT,* 1:463-66. Cf. also Tromp, *Primitive Conceptions,* pp. 66-69.

123. A direct parallel to these expressions occurs in Ugar. *yrdm arṣ,* as in the following lines from *CTA,* 4.8.7-9; 6.5.14-17: *wrd bt ḥptt arṣ tspr byrdm arṣ,* "And go down (into) the house of 'freedom' (in) the earth, be counted with them that go down into the earth" (*CML,* pp. 66, 72).

124. The phrase occurs also in Isa. 44:7, but with a different sense.

125. Dahood (*Psalms,* 3:323) repoints *mētê* as *mĕtê,* and translates the phrase "men of the eternal home," which provides a nearer parallel to the present *'am 'ōlam.*

126. See A. Cooper, *"mlk 'lm:* 'Eternal King' or 'King of Eternity'?" in *Love and Death in the Ancient Near East,* pp. 1-8; and M. H. Pope, review of *Beatific Afterlife in Ancient Israel and in the Ancient Near East,* by K. Spronk, *UF* 19 (1987) 458, who interpret the Ugaritic expression *mlk 'lm,* "king of eternity," as "king of the underworld." According to Cooper (p. 2) and E. Jenni (*THAT,* 2:242), this spatial understanding of "eternity"

the irrevocable nature and finality of the departed's consignment to this realm of the dead.[127] A second expression for the abode of the dead used here, *the netherworld ('eres taḥtîyôt),* translates literally "the land of the depths," a distinctly Ezekielian variation of *'eres taḥtît,* "the lower world."[128] By itself *'eres* usually denotes the earth in contrast to the heavens, or the land in which people live, but it may also denote the abode of the dead.[129] The use of *'eres* suggests the perception of the netherworld as a self-contained country.[130] Yahweh adds that Tyre will become like *ancient waste places (ḥŏrābôt mēʿôlām,* lit. "waste places from eternity past"), which conjures up images of formerly flourishing cities now lying in ruins, whose inhabitants have been banished to the netherworld, never to return.

20c-21   The last statement of v. 20 and v. 21 underline the irrevocability of Tyre's judgment. Never again will the city be occupied, let alone achieve her past glory *in the land of the living. 'eres ḥayyîm* represents the sphere in which humans live, in contrast to the netherworld, the realm of the dead, and the heavens, the domain of God.[131] The meaning of Yahweh's announcement, *I will make you* [Tyre] *a horror* (v. 21), is not clear. On the one hand, the reference may be to the horrified response of observers who

---

derives from Egypt, where Osiris bore the title "Lord of Eternity" (Egyp. *ḥḳȝ ḏ.t* or *nb nḥḥ),* which alluded to his domain (the realm of the dead), as well as to the duration of his reign. The expression *byt 'lm,* signifying "grave," has surfaced in the Deir ʿAlla texts (II:6, on which see J. A. Hackett, *The Balaam Text from Deir ʿAllā,* HSM 31 [Chico, Calif.: Scholars Press, 1980], p. 59) and in other Northwest Semitic inscriptions (on which see E. Jenni, *ZAW* 64 [1952] 217; J. Hoftijzer and G. van der Kooij, eds., *Aramaic Texts from Deir ʿAlla,* Documenta et Monumenta Orientis Antiqui [Leiden: Brill, 1976], pp. 224-25), and is well known in the rabbinic writings (Jastrow, *Dictionary,* pp. 1084-85). H. Tawil ("A Note on the Aḥiram Inscription," *JANES* 3 [1970] 36) compares the expression to the Egyptian designation of a tomb as *nìwt nt nḥḥ,* "city of eternity." Heb. *bêt ʿôlām* finds a semantic equivalent in Akk. *šubat dārâti/dārât,* "the dwelling place of eternity," and *ēkal ṣalāli kimaḥ tapšuḥti šubat dārâti,* "a palace of sleeping, a resting tomb, a dwelling place of eternity."

127. So E. Jenni, "Das Wort *ʿôlām* im Alten Testament," *ZAW* 65 (1953) 14.

128. See 31:14, 16, 18. Cf. *šěʾôl taḥtît* in Deut. 32:33, and *taḥtîyôt 'eres,* "depths of the earth," in Isa. 44:23; Ps. 63:10 (Eng. 9); 139:15. *bôr taḥtîyôt* occurs in Ps. 88:7 (Eng. 6); Lam. 3:55.

129. *'eres ḥayyîm,* "land of the living," occurs later in this verse. For *'eres* as the abode of the dead see Isa. 26:19; Jon. 2:3, 7 (Eng. 2, 6); Ps. 22:30 (Eng. 29); 88:13 (Eng. 12); Job 10:21-22; 17:16. This usage resembles that of its cognate *ars* in Ugaritic (*CTA,* 4.8.5-14; 10.2.24-25; 19.3.111-12) and *ersetu* in Akkadian (*CAD,* 4:310; *AHW,* p. 245). On this usage see Tromp, *Primitive Conceptions,* pp. 23-46.

130. Elsewhere it is described as a land of gloom and deep darkness from which there is no return (Job 10:21-22), and a land of forgetfulness (Ps. 88:13 [Eng. 12]).

131. The phrase recurs in 32:23-27, 32, but is also common elsewhere in the OT (Isa. 38:11; 53:8; Jer. 11:19; Ps. 27:13; 52:7 [Eng. 5]; 116:9; 142:6 [Eng. 5]; Job 28:13).

witness her fall, or of those who will come and search for her after she is gone. On the other hand, from the construction *ballāhôt 'ettĕnēk,* "I will make you a horror," and its variants in 27:36 and 28:19, *ballāhôt* is something Tyre becomes. The abstract noun, which, except for Isa. 17:14, always occurs as an intensive plural, derives from a root *bālâ,* "to be terrified" (Ezra 4:4). Elsewhere the word always expresses the emotion felt at the experience of some form of disaster, whether it be caused by snares and traps (Job 18:11), flood waters (Job 27:20), tempests and storms (Job 30:15), darkness (Job 24:17), invading armies (Isa. 17:14), or the direct action of God (Ps. 73:19). Although *ballāhôt* frequently bears eschatological overtones, in Job 18:14 the connotations are clearly chthonic: "He is torn from the security of his tent, and marched off to the king of terrors" (NIV). The last phrase, *melek ballāhôt,* is especially telling, inasmuch as it refers to the ruler of the netherworld, known as Mot and Nergal in Canaan and Mesopotamia, respectively. The same chthonic connotations are present in our text. Yahweh is delivering Tyre over to the terrifying world of the dead.

As in 27:36 and 28:19 (also Isa. 17:14), to become this terror and to be banished to Sheol is equivalent to the termination of one's existence: *you will be no more ('ênēk).* Search parties may be sent out to find the lost city, but all such efforts will prove futile. The judgment of Tyre will be irreversible. No one ever returns from the realm of the dead. The concluding signatory formula drives the final nail into Tyre's coffin.

Some of Ezekiel's imagery is obviously influenced by the mythologies of surrounding peoples. However, his vision of the netherworld bears several fundamental differences. Whereas other ancient Near Easterners recognized the realm of the dead to be ruled by the god of the netherworld, the "King of Terrors," as far as Ezekiel and all orthodox Yahwists are concerned, Yahweh exercises full control over life and death. His sovereignty knows no bounds (Ps. 139:8). He opens and closes the doors of Sheol and he consigns his enemies to it. Unlike the surrounding nature religions, in which one of the deities (Baal in Canaan, Tammuz in Babylon) was thought to die each autumn and be banished to the netherworld, where he remained until his annual resurrection in the spring, when Yahweh banishes someone to Sheol and closes the door to the Pit, it is sealed. No one consigned to Sheol ever returns.[132] These notions will all be developed more fully in subsequent prophecies.

132. See further Tromp, *Primitive Conceptions,* pp. 196-210; G. von Rad, *Old Testament Theology,* tr. D. M. G. Stalker, 2 vols. (New York: Harper & Row, 1962-65), 1:387-91; W. Eichrodt, *Theology of the Old Testament,* tr. J. A. Baker, 2 vols., OTL (Philadelphia: Westminster, 1961-67), 2:210-23; H. Ringgren, *Israelite Religion,* tr. D. E. Green (Philadelphia: Fortress, 1966), pp. 239-47.

b. The Lament over the Shipwreck of Tyre (27:1-36)

♦ *Nature and Design*

Ezekiel's second oracle against Tyre raises his exploitation of metaphor to new heights.[1] The island city, renowned for maritime commercial enterprises, is imaged as a magnificent merchant ship loaded with the products of the world, only to be shipwrecked on the high seas. The introduction identifies the genre of the prophecy as a whole as a *qînâ,* which ordinarily signifies a dirge at the death of an individual, but which the prophets widely adapted to commemorate the demise of a city or nation. The prophecy actually involves two lamentations. While the entire chapter represents Ezekiel's prophetic lament over the fall of Tyre, embedded within the oracle is a second lament (vv. 32b-36), rising from the lips of the sailors of this great ship. In typical Ezekielian style, the latter particularly represents an expansion of the brief dirge found in 26:18-19.

The absence of obvious structural indicators (apart from the formal opening, vv. 1-3a) and of a formal division between metaphor and interpretation, which the reader has come to expect in Ezekiel's prophecies, gives this oracle a literary cohesion rare in the book.[2] It also forces the reader to search for more subtle rhetorical devices that signal the unit's movement and flow. Since this oracle is explicitly identified as a *qînâ,* one should not be surprised to discover a clear then-now sequence, as the prophet contrasts Tyre's glorious past (A: vv. 3b-25) with her tragic present (B: vv. 26-36). This break is reinforced by the shift from prose to poetic style at this point.

Ezekiel's habit of "halving" pronouncements is evident as each of these major segments divides further into two parts. A clear break occurs in the first between vv. 11 and 12 as the imagery changes from a metaphoric description of Tyre as a ship, magnificently constructed and handled by the nobility of surrounding nations (vv. 3b-11), to a trade list, apparently representing the ship's varied and substantial manifest (vv. 12-25). The former is demarcated by an *inclusio,* opening with Tyre's own assertion, *'ǎnî kělîlat yōpî,* "I am the perfection of beauty," and ending with the prophet's affirmation, *hēmâ kālělû yopyēk,* "They made perfect your beauty." This subdivision

---

1. Cf. C. A. Newsom, "A Maker of Metaphors — Ezekiel's Oracles Against Tyre," *Int* 38 (1984) 156-58; E. M. Good, "Ezekiel's Ship: Some Extended Metaphors in the Old Testament," *Semitics* 1 (1970) 79-103; J. A. Durlesser, "The Sinking of the Ship of Tyre (Ezek 27): A Study of Rhetoric in Hebrew Allegory," *Proceedings, Eastern Great Lakes and Midwest Biblical Societies* 7 (1987) 79-93.

2. Common structural indicators are *kî, lākēn, hinnēh,* etc. Even the commercial trade list (vv. 12-25), which is almost universally isolated as secondary, commences unannounced and concludes with hardly a punctuation mark.

is reinforced by the shift from a limping poetic *qînâ* meter[3] to a tedious prose in v. 12. Indeed, it is fashionable to isolate vv. 12-25 as a late non-Ezekielian insertion, interrupting what is otherwise a more or less uniformly poetic text.[4] While the "inspiration" for this segment may well have derived from an actual Tyrian trade list, the presentation is heavily influenced by ideological concerns, and considerable effort has been expended to link this "document" with both the preceding and succeeding parts.[5] Indeed, this section may represent the core of the entire oracle, especially if M. Liverani is correct in asserting that this text reflects Tyre's international trading position between the fall of Nineveh in 612 B.C. and the beginning of Nebuchadrezzar's siege of Tyre in 585.[6] In any case, the conclusion to the trade list is announced by the summary narrative statement in v. 25b, "You were filled and extremely heavily loaded in the heart of the seas," the last phrase of which creates an effective *inclusio* with the identical counterpart in v. 4.

Like the first major segment, the second subdivides into what looks like an original prophetic pronouncement (vv. 26-32a) and a purportedly external source, in this instance a lament heard from the lips of the sailors on board the sinking ship (vv. 32b-36). Both sections have stylistic and lexical links to the preceding section. The entire unit closes with the refrain announcing the end of Tyre, familiar from 26:21, and to be encountered again in 28:19.

This oracle poses numerous semantic and stylistic difficulties. Especially problematic is the series of technical expressions relating to commerce and products involved in trade, many of which are hapax forms. While these contribute to the impression of Ezekiel as a prophet with a breadth of expe-

---

3. An expression used by Durlesser, *Proceedings* 7 (1987) 80. Zimmerli's textual operations to restore a strict 3:2 *qînâ* meter (*Ezekiel 2,* pp. 53-56) are ill advised. Cf. E. S. Krantz, *Des Schiffes Weg Mitten im Meer,* ConBOT 19 (Lund: Gleerup, 1982), p. 29 n. 64; Garr, *ZAW* 95 (1983) 74; and my comments in *Ezekiel: Chapters 1–24,* pp. 591ff.

4. Zimmerli, *Ezekiel 2,* pp. 70-71. According to Allen (*Ezekiel 20–48,* p. 84) the basic poetic composition consisted of vv. 3-9a, 10, 25b, 26, 28-32, 34a, 35a, 36a. Similarly, with minor variations, G. Krinetzki, "Tiefenpsychologie im Dienste der alttestamentlichen Exegese: Zur Stil und Metaphorik von Ezechiel 27," *Tübinger Theologische Quartalschrift* 155 (1975) 133-35. See also J. Krašovec, *Antithetic Structure in Biblical Hebrew Poetry,* VTSup 35 (Leiden: Brill, 1984), pp. 104-5.

5. Regarding the preceding, vv. 9-11 introduce several technical commercial expressions that occur repeatedly in vv. 12-25: forms of *nātan,* "to give, offer, sell"; *'ārab,* "to receive, acquire"; cf. also *rākal,* "to trade" (v. 3). Regarding the following, vv. 26-36 include forms of *'ārab,* "to receive, acquire" (vv. 27 [3 times], 33, 34); *'āzab,* "to leave" (vv. 27, 33); *hôn,* "wealth" (vv. 27, 33); *sāḥar,* "to trade" (v. 36).

6. M. Liverani, "The Trade Network of Tyre According to Ezek. 27," in *Ah, Assyria . . . ! Studies in Assyrian History and Ancient Near Eastern Historiography Presented to Hayim Tadmor,* ed. M. Cogan and I. Eph'al, ScrHier 33 (Jerusalem: Hebrew University Press, 1991), p. 79.

rience, they frustrate the interpretation of the passage. Nevertheless, although some of the details may be obscure, the overall message of this oracle is beyond doubt. The prophecy is also remarkable for its secular tone and the absence of any homiletical focus. On the one hand, the lament itself lacks any direct references to God or allusions to his intervention in Tyrian affairs. The shipwreck of the vessel is attributed entirely to natural causes, a strong east wind (v. 26).[7] On the other, a convincing homiletical point seems to be missing. Unlike chs. 26 and 28, the oracle contains no denunciations of sin or overt announcements of judgment. The closest it comes to the former is quoting Tyre's boast that she is the perfection of beauty, but she is not castigated even for this claim. Expressions like "fall" (*nāpal,* vv. 27, 34) and the refrain of v. 36b evoke associations of judgment for the reader, especially since this oracle is sandwiched between two explicit oracles of judgment employing the same vocabulary, but two-thirds of the chapter is taken up with demonstrating the truthfulness of Tyre's claim. The lament has a wistful if somber quality, as if the prophet himself admired the city for her magnificence and is saddened by her demise. There is certainly no hint of indignation or schadenfreude.

As for the setting of the oracle, it seems to anticipate Tyre's demise as still in the future. There is no indication yet that the city has succumbed to the Babylonian pressure, nor of the disappointment reflected in 29:17-21. If this lament is indeed an expansion of 26:17-18, then it would probably have been raised shortly after the oracle in the previous chapter, which is dated to the eleventh year of Jehoiachin, that is, some time in late 587 or early 586. The reference to Judah and the land of Israel as trading partners and certain elements in the manifest suggest an earlier rather than later date. But the text offers no internal clues regarding the prophet's own situation or the condition of his exilic audience at the time of the oral delivery. In spite of the use of the second person of direct address, Tyre is clearly only

7. In the light of these and other considerations, the proposal of J. B. Geyer ("Ezekiel 27 and the Cosmic Ship," in *Among the Prophets: Language, Image and Structure in the Prophetic Writings,* ed. P. R. Davies and D. J. A. Clines, JSOTSup 144 [Sheffield: JSOT Press, 1993], pp. 105-27), that ch. 27 is modeled on the myth of the Egyptian cosmic ship, the Bark of Re, is not convincing. For example, rather than interpreting the high number of hapax legomena among the articles of trade as evidence that the author's mind is elsewhere, off on some cultic or mythological theme (p. 119), these strange words simply confirm that the Hebrew OT is but a linguistic fragment, missing many expressions from the everyday world of economic production, trade, and commerce. Lexical links with descriptions of the temple and tabernacle (pp. 119-25) need not suggest cultic influence; the common vocabulary derives from the attempts to design all of these structures as magnificently as possible. This is the language of affluence and luxury, not mythology.

a hypothetical addressee; and in spite of its relatively secular tone, the oracle was obviously intended to bolster the exiles' confidence in Yahweh's control of history.

(1) Preamble: The Call for Lamentation (27:1-3a)

1 *The following message of Yahweh came to me:*
2 *"As for you,*[8] *human, raise a lament over Tyre* 3a *and say:*
'O Tyre![9] *[You] who rule*[10] *the gateways of the sea,*[11] *broker of the peoples, to many coastal lands.'"*

1-3a The oracle begins predictably with the word-event formula, followed by Yahweh's direct address of the prophet as *ben-'ādām,* and a command to prophesy. While the occasion for the prophecy is not indicated, that it lacks a date notice, that v. 2 begins with *wĕ'attâ,* which elsewhere always signals a subdivision of a larger oracle, and that this command to raise a lament over Tyre recalls 26:17-18 suggest that this prophecy may have been linked to ch. 26. Indeed, the short lament embedded in the longer prophetic oracle (27:32b-36) seems to be an expansion of the lament in the previous chapter.

Yahweh charges Ezekiel to raise a lament over Tyre.[12] He is to address Tyre directly, but unlike previous oracles against the nations, which had commenced with formal charges of wrongdoing, the opening lines set a relatively neutral tone for the oracle. Instead of condemning the city for some offense, by means of two participial expressions the prophet acknowledges Tyre's position in the world of international commerce. First, Tyre is portrayed as the ruler of the seas, occupying the entrances of the seas. In this context the verb *yāšab,* which normally means "to sit, dwell," speaks of occupying with authority, that is, ruling.[13] This comment recognizes Tyre's maritime monopoly; she controls the harbors of the Mediterranean. But as

---

8. *wĕ'attâ* is missing in LXX.

9. With Gibson (*CML,* p. 149), treating the *lamed* on *lĕṣôr* as a vocative particle.

10. On the final *yod (hireq campaginis)* of Kethib, *hyšbty,* see GKC, §90i, m. The form appears elsewhere in Jer. 10:17; 22:23; Lam. 4:21. Cf. Qere *yšbt,* which reflects the normal form of the feminine participle.

11. LXX, Syr., and Vulg. assume sg. *mĕbô' hayyām,* instead of MT *mĕbô'ōt yām.* Since *mĕbô'* is masc. in 26:10, and *hayyām* is more natural in the context (cf. 25:16; 26:5, 16; 27:29), Zimmerli (*Ezekiel 2,* p. 42) assumes a *h/t* corruption and faulty word division in MT. But the versions may have deliberately smoothed out the reading.

12. The expression *nāśā' qînâ 'al/'el* is a standardized idiom. See 19:1; 26:17; 27:32; 28:12; 32:2; also Amos 5:1; Jer. 9:9.

13. Thus van Dijk, *Ezekiel's Prophecy,* pp. 50-55. Cf. also v. 8; Exod. 15:15; Mic. 6:12.

the second expression indicates, her authority is not political but commercial — she is the merchant of the peoples,[14] pursuing her trade in the far-flung coastal lands (*'iyyîm rabbîm*) of the Mediterranean. The term *rōkelet* and cognates occur eleven times in this oracle. Like *rĕkullâ* in 26:12, *rōkelet* derives from the root *rākal,* "to go about from one place to another." The present usage is similar to 17:4, where "city of peddlers" (*'îr rōkĕlîm*) had been paralleled with "land of traders" (*'ereṣ kĕna'an).*[15] Tyre's role as "peddler of the peoples *(hā'ammîm)"* will be demonstrated by the ship's commercial log in vv. 12-25.

(2) The Magnificence of Tyrian Glory (27:3b-11)

3b " *'Thus has the Lord Yahweh declared:*

O Tyre![16] *You have boasted, "I*[17] *am the perfection of beauty."*
4 *Your frontiers*[18] *are in the heart of the seas;*
your builders made your beauty perfect.
5 *Of juniper*[19] *from Senir they built for you the whole double deck.*[20]

14. Thus Good *(Semitics* 1 [1970] 82 n. 5), who recognizes a hint of sarcasm in the verb's link with *rākîl,* "slander." Cf. 22:4.

15. Liverani (in *Ah, Assyria,* pp. 75-76) suggests that the replacement of *mākar,* "to sell," by *rākal* and *sāḥar,* both meaning "to trade," in the 1st millennium B.C. reflects the shift from palace functionaries to independent merchants as the primary actors in trading activity.

16. LXX τῇ Σορ links the name to the citation formula.

17. Many emend *'ănî* to *'ŏnîyâ,* "ship" *(BHS)* or simply revocalize *'ŏnî,* citing *a-na-ji,* which glosses *eleppi,* a single ship, in Amarna Letter 245:28 (Zimmerli, *Ezekiel* 2, p. 42), and then either delete *'āmart* as intrusive to the normal 3:2 *qînâ* meter (Zimmerli), or repoint the verb as *'ummart,* "you are called" (van Dijk, *Ezekiel's Prophecy,* p. 56; M. Dahood, "Accadian-Ugaritic *dmt* in Ezekiel 27:32," *Bib* 45 [1964] 83; Allen, *Ezekiel 20–48,* p. 80). But MT yields a tolerable sense. Besides, Ezekiel seldom adheres rigidly to the *qînâ* meter.

18. G. R. Driver's derivation of *gĕbûlāyik* from a root *gbl,* "to fix, create" *(Bib* 19 [1938] 177; followed by Zimmerli, *Ezekiel 2,* pp. 42-43) is speculative and without parallel in the OT. On the appropriateness of assigning boundaries to the ship see Cooke, *Ezekiel,* p. 296.

19. *bĕrôšîm* (cognate to Akk. *burāšu;* see *CAD,* 2:326-28) identifies the tall Eastern savin *(Juniperus excelsa)* that still grows on Mt. Hermon (cf. Zohary, *Plants of the Bible,* pp. 106-7). Cf. LXX χέδρος, "cedar." According to Zohary, the Cilician fir *(Abies cilicica)* is also included under the designation. Solomon imported *bĕrôšîm* along with *'erez,* "cedar," from Lebanon for the construction of the temple of Yahweh (1 K. 5:22, 24 [Eng. 8, 10]; 6:34; 9:11).

20. *kol-luḥōtāyim,* lit. "all your two tablets/planks." On the preference for "decks" rather than "hulls" see Krantz, *Des Schiffes Weg,* pp. 85-91.

Of cedar[21] *from Lebanon they took to make a mast for you.*[22]

6 *Of oaks*[23] *from Bashan they made your oars.*

Your hull they built[24] *of cypresses*[25] *from the coasts of Cyprus.*[26]

7 *Your sail*[27] *was of finely embroidered linen from Egypt,*
serving as your banner.

Your deck coverings[28] *were of blue-violet and red-purple*
from the coasts of Elishah.

8 *The nobility*[29] *of Sidon and Arvad were your oarsmen;*[30]
your skilled men, O Tyre,[31] *were on board you —*
they were your helmsmen.[32]

21. *'erez* refers to the famed *Cedrud libani,* a large coniferous tree once abundant on the Lebanese ranges (Zohary, *Plants of the Bible,* pp. 104-5). Cf. LXX κυπαρίσσου, "cypress." The cedar often served as a figure for human grandeur. Cf. 31:3; Amos 2:9; Ps. 92:12; 2 K. 14:19.

22. *BHS* emends *'ālāyik* to *'elyônê* and links it to v. 6 to preserve the 3:2 meter, yielding "the tallest oaks." However, MT *'alāyik* provides a perfect parallel for *lāk* in the previous line. On *'al* in the sense of "for, on behalf of," see 1 K. 2:18; Dan. 12:1; etc.

23. On *'allôn* see Zohary, *Plants of the Bible,* pp. 108-9.

24. Although *šēn,* "ivory," after *'āšû* adds an exotic touch to this magnificent vessel, it is syntactically difficult. It looks suspiciously like dittography, destroying the chiasm in v. 6. Cf. Krantz, *Des Schiffes Weg,* p. 77.

25. *bat 'ăšurîm,* lit. "daughters of Assyrians," is nonsensical. Targ. correctly reads one word, the preposition *bĕ* plus *tĕ'aššurîm,* "cypresses." Cf. 31:3; Isa. 41:19; 60:13.

26. *kittîm* derives from Kition (modern Lanarka), a Phoenician colony on the southern shore of Cyprus.

27. *miprāš,* from *pāraš,* "to spread out."

28. The vocalization *mĕkassēk* occurs elsewhere only in Lev. 9:19; Isa. 14:11; and 23:18, with a different significance in each case. The word should be repointed *miksēk.* See Krantz, *Des Schiffes Weg,* pp. 137-38.

29. On the basis of LXX καὶ οἱ ἀρχοντές σου οἱ κατοικοῦντες Σιδῶνα, "your rulers and the governors of Sidon," *BHS* emends *yōšĕbê* to *ûnĕšî'ayik;* Zimmerli (*Ezekiel 2,* p. 45) to *wĕšārayik.* More attractive is Allen's reading, *śābê,* "elders," from *śîb,* "be grey, old." Cf. Aram. *śābê* in Ezra 5:5, 9; 6:7, 8, 14. Van Dijk's translation "kings" (*Ezekiel's Prophecy,* p. 66) goes too far. But there is no need to abandon MT, especially if *yōšĕbê* is linked with the same root in v. 3.

30. *šāṭîm,* "rowers," is related to *miššôṭîm* in v. 6.

31. NRSV and NEB accept Kraetchmar's emendation of *ṣwr* to *ṣmr* (*Ezechiel,* p. 209; cf. K. Elliger, "Ein Zeugnis aus der jüdischen Gemeinde im Alexanderjahr 332 v. Chr. Eine territorialgeschichtliche Studie zu Sach 9:1-8," *ZAW* 62 [1950] 71-72). For defense of MT see F. L. Moriarty, "The Lament over Tyre (Ez. 27)," *Greg* 46 (1965) 83-84.

32. On *hōbālîm,* from as yet unattested *ḥābal,* "to tie," but related to *ḥebel,* "rope," see Krantz, *Des Schiffes Weg,* pp. 184-88. In v. 28 and Jon. 1:6 the word denotes seamen in general. See also the figurative expression *nābôn taḥbulôt,* "to know the ropes," used of a wise or skillful person in Prov. 1:5.

9 *Skilled veterans of Byblos*[33] *were on board you —*
   serving as your repairmen.[34]
All the ships of the sea[35] *and their sailors*
   were in your harbor,[36] *to handle your merchandise.*
10 *Men of Paras, Lydia, and Put were in your army,*
   serving as your warriors.
They hung shields and helmets on you;
   they endowed you with your splendor.
11 *Men of Arvad and Helek manned your walls all around;*
   and Gammadites were stationed on your towers.
They hung their weapons[37] *on your walls all around —*
   they made your beauty perfect.'"

3b   Following the introductory citation formula, which highlights the oracle
as divine speech, the oracle proper opens with a quotation. Unlike the prophecies against Bene Ammon and Moab in ch. 25 and against Tyre in 26:2, which
begin with a quotation of contempt toward Jerusalem, the present citation
represents a self-confident, if not arrogant, boast by Tyre about her own beauty.
Although the phrase *kĕlîlat yōpî* also occurs in Lam. 2:15 (of Jerusalem), the
combination of terms seems to have been characteristically Ezekielian (cf.
16:14; 28:12). The verb *kālal*, "to make perfect," occurs only twice in the
entire OT, both times in this chapter and in association with *yōpî*, "beauty"
(vv. 4, 11). Ten of the latter noun's nineteen occurrences are in Ezekiel.[38]

---

33. Lit. "The elders of Gebal and her wise/skilled men." *waḥăkāmêhā* disrupts
the structure and is often deleted as dittography.

34. *maḥăzîqê bidqēk*, lit. "those who strengthen your leaks," viz., who caulk the
seams of the ship. The meaning of *maḥăzîqê bedeq* is illuminated by 2 K. 12:6-16, where
bedeq refers to unspecified damages in the temple and the Piel form of *ḥāzaq*, "to be
strong," is used for "repair." Krantz (*Des Schiffes Weg*, pp. 188-89) rightly argues that
"caulking the seams" is too specific a translation. Good's military interpretation, "manning
your openings" (*Semitics* 1 [1970] 84), is premature in the context.

35. *kol-'ŏnîyôt yām*, "all the ships of the sea," recalls Ugar. *anyt ym* (*UT*, 2061.13-
14).

36. *bāk*, lit. "in you," the same expression as "on board you," in vv. 8-9a.

37. The meaning of *šeleṭ* is unknown. Cant. 4:4 pairs it with *māgēn*, but its other
occurrences suggest that it may be simply a general term for arms. Cf. 2 Sam. 8:7 = 1 Chr.
18:7; 2 K. 11:10 = 2 Chr. 23:9; Jer. 51:11.

38. See 16:14, 15, 25; 27:3, 4, 11; 28:7, 12, 17; 31:8. Wagner (*Aramaismen*, p. 65)
follows G. R. Driver ("Hebrew Notes on 'Song of Songs' and 'Lamentations,'" in *Fest-
schrift Alfred Bertholet*, ed. W. Baumgartner, et al. [Tübingen: Mohr, 1950], pp. 144-45)
in seeing *kĕlîlat* as cognate to Aram. *kĕlîlā'*, "crown," and Akk. *kilīlum*, "circlet, headband"
(*AHW*, p. 476; *CAD*, 8:358). LXX renders this phrase in Lam. 2:15 accordingly as στέφανος
δόξης.

4a   Whereas in previous oracles boastful quotations by the addressees had been answered with denunciations of the disposition reflected in their assertions (as in the oracles against the nations) or refutations (as in earlier disputation speeches), here Ezekiel does neither. On the contrary, the prophet's own development of the thesis will take up a major part of the oracle. He will do so in vv. 4-11 by means of analogy, comparing Tyre with a stately ship sailing proudly on the high seas. The choice of metaphor is natural, given Tyre's geographical location and her commercial character. But the figure is not maintained consistently as brief glimpses of the real referent intrude into the allegory to remind the hearer that this is more than a fanciful tale. Indeed, unless one accepts the emendation of *'ănî* to *'ŏnîyâ* (noted above), the designation "ship" is nowhere applied expressly to Tyre. Instead the nautical subject is raised subtly through sound association.[39] Indeed, one could interpret all of v. 4 as a literal description of the city itself, situated on her island offshore and bordered by the seas all around.

4b-6   The anthropocentric perspective of the entire oracle is reflected in v. 4b. Tyre is a magnificent human achievement — a monument to her builders' ingenuity and energy. Without warning, Ezekiel shifts into a metaphorical mode, portraying the city as a glorious ship on the high seas. Three dimensions of her magnificence are highlighted: her superior construction (vv. 4b-6), her impressive decoration (v. 7), and her first-class personnel (vv. 8-11). Each facet of the description reflects a remarkable geographical and nautical awareness on the part of the prophet.[40]

(a) The Superior Construction of the Ship Tyre (27:4b-6)

4b-5a   The quality of the ship's construction is reflected in the materials used to build its various parts.[41] Four kinds of wood are listed, along with their geographic origin and their usage. First, *the decks* were made of juniper wood from Senir, the archaic Amorite name for Mount Hermon.[42] The dual form

---

39. The present indirect introduction of a figure of speech compares with 28:2 and reflects Ezekiel's evocation of images through the effective use of similarly sounding terms. Cf. Good, *Semitics* 1 (1970) 82 n. 6.

40. Liverani (in *Ah, Assyria . . .*, pp. 67-68) recognizes three realistic concentric belts in the description: (1) Phoenician cities (Sidon, Arvad, Byblos) provide the maritime personnel; (2) the inland mountains (Lebanon, Senir, Bashan), Cyprus (Elishah, Kittim), and Egypt provide the raw materials to construct the ship; (3) distant nations supply the troops.

41. On shipbuilding in the ancient Near East see Krantz, *Des Schiffes Weg;* S. Vinson, "Ships in the Ancient Mediterranean," *BA* 53 (1990) 13-18. This entire issue of *BA* is devoted to ancient nautical matters.

42. See Deut. 3:8. Senir (Akk. *saniru*), "facing the Lebanon," was the location of Shalmaneser III's decisive defeat of Hazael of Damascus (*ANET*, p. 280).

of the term for *decks, luḥōtāyim,* is difficult. *lûaḥ* is usually used of a writing "tablet," but also of wooden boards.[43] The connotations of flatness, the position of the term at the head of this list of the parts of the ship, which points to a prominent feature, and especially its immediate association with the mast, suggest that Ezekiel has the deck in mind. The dual form is intentional, referring to the double-decked design of the craft in which rowers occupied the lower deck and sailors the upper.[44]

5b   Second, *the mast* was made of cedar from Lebanon. Attaining a height of 290 ft. or more, cedars provided appropriate raw material for the mast. *tōren* occurs only three times in the OT. While Isa. 30:17 uses the term to denote a signal post on a hill (associated with *nēs*), a nautical sense is clear in Isa. 33:23, where reference is made to the base of the mast *(kēn tōren).* In Ezekiel's time ship's sails were held up by a single mast.[45]

6a   Third, *the oars* were made from oaks of Bashan.[46] The hardwood of the Tabor oak provided suitable material to withstand the stress to which the oars of large seagoing crafts were subjected. *miššôṭîm,* "oars," and its cognate *māšôṭ,* "rudder" (v. 29), which derive from *šûṭ,* "to move," occur only here in the OT. Large numbers of oarsmen were required to operate the merchant ships of the Mediterranean. According to Sennacherib's reliefs, Phoenician boats were biremes, having one row of oarsmen visible on the lower deck, and a second invisible row who plied the water from holes in the ship's hull.[47]

6b   Fourth, *the hull* was constructed of cypress lumber from Cyprus. The meaning of *tĕʾaššûr* is uncertain, but it is often equated with *Cupresus sempervirens,* which grows to a height of 40-65 ft. and provides excellent timber.[48] My rendering of *qereš* as "hull" is tentative. Appealing to Ugar. *qrš,* which is used of some sort of dwelling place or pavilion for El, some have seen here a reference to a fancy cabin decorated with ivory carvings.[49] Since

43. Tablets of stone (Exod. 24:12) or wood (Isa. 30:18; Hab. 2:2), but also in a metaphorical sense of *lēb,* "heart/mind" (Jer. 17:1; Prov. 3:3; 7:3); boards used to bar doors (Cant. 8:9) or construct altars (Exod. 27:8).

44. So also Krantz, *Des Schiffes Weg,* pp. 85-91. Two-decked Phoenician ships are portrayed on Sennacherib's palace reliefs from Nineveh. Cf. A. H. Layard, *The Monuments of Nineveh from Drawings Made on the Spot* (London: Putnam, 1849), vol. 1, plate 71; reproduced in Krantz, p. 36; *IBD,* 3:1441.

45. Cf. Krantz, *Des Schiffes Weg,* pp. 91-98.

46. On the Bashan, east of the upper Jordan and the Sea of Galilee, as a region renowned for its oaks, see Isa. 2:13 and Zech. 11:2.

47. See *ANEP,* no. 106.

48. Cf. Zohary, *Plants of the Bible,* pp. 106-7; Krantz, *Des Schiffes Weg,* pp. 160-62, 175.

49. See, e.g., *CTA,* 4.4.24. See also van Dijk, *Ezekiel's Prophecy,* pp. 63-65; Good, *Semitics* 1 (1970) 83 n. 8; M. H. Pope, *El in the Ugaritic Texts,* VTSup 2 (Leiden: Brill,

elsewhere *qereš* always refers to planks, especially those used to construct the portable tabernacle (Exod. 25–40; Num. 3:36; 4:31), some such usage is probably intended here. Having drawn his hearers' attention to the oars of this Tyrian ship, the second row of which emerged from holes in the hull, the prophet naturally turns to the construction of the hull itself. Accordingly, *qereš* is best understood as the planking of which the ship's sides were constructed, in which case an *abba* arrangement of the features of the vessel may be recognized: deck — mast — oars — hull. The outside members are constructed of numerous boards, the inner entries of single shafts.[50] The principal weakness of this interpretation revolves around the function of the ivory. But if *šēn* is indeed integral to the text, the term probably refers to expensive inlaid ivory decorations on the hull, an effect quite conceivable in the light of Phoenicia's known involvement in the ivory trade and craft.[51]

(b) The Magnificent Decoration of the Ship Tyre (27:7)

Ezekiel's attention shifts to the fabric used in crafting other prominent elements of the vessel. First, *the sail* was made of special linen from Egypt. The use of the term *šēš,* which had been used in 16:10 of the luxurious embroidered garments with which Yahweh had clothed the foundling Jerusalem, is intentional, reflecting the imported nature of this luxury item.[52] Ezekiel's reference to embroidered *(běriqmâ)* sails reflects an awareness of a common Egyptian custom of using patterned linen fabric for the sails of their vessels.[53] It is

---

1955), pp. 65-67. LXX reads τὰ ἱερά σου, "your holy place, temenos," probably misreading *qršk* as *qdšk.*

50. Similarly Krantz, *Des Schiffes Weg,* pp. 78-85.

51. See n. 24 above. S. Aḥituv interprets the *qereš* inlaid with ivory as some ornamented part of the ship, perhaps the prow beam (review of Krantz, *Des Schiffes Weg,* in *IEJ* 38 [1988] 95). On Phoenician involvement in the ivory industry see R. D. Barnett, *Ancient Ivories in the Middle East and Adjacent Countries,* Qedem 14 (Jerusalem: Institute of Archaeology, Hebrew University, 1982), esp. pp. 43-55. But cf. A. Cohen (*"Šēn," Beth Mikra* 23 [1978] 237-38), who argues that here, as in 1 K. 10:18, Amos 3:15, and 6:4, the word denotes a kind of wood, so named because its appearance resembled that of ivory.

52. On the term see M. Ellenbogen, *Foreign Words in the Old Testament: Their Origin and Etymology* (London: Luzac, 1962), p. 164; A. Brenner, " 'White' Textiles in Biblical Hebrew and Mishnaic Hebrew," *HAR* 4 (1980) 40; idem, *Colour Terms in the Old Testament,* JSOTSup 21 (Sheffield: JSOT Press, 1982), p. 148. Brenner notes that neither *šēš* nor *bûṣ* (v. 16) were ever dyed. On the production of linen (with its variations in quality and use) in Egypt see A. Lucas, *Ancient Egyptian Materials and Industries,* 4th ed. (London: Edward Arnold, 1962), pp. 142-46.

53. One may only speculate about the design on the sail. An Etruscan amphora from ca. 600 B.C. portrays a vessel with a bold geometric pattern. For illustration and discussion see Krantz, *Des Schiffes Weg,* pp. 126-37.

evident from v. 7aβ that the function of the sail on the magnificent ship Tyre was not just utilitarian, to propel the ship by catching the wind. It served also as a decorative and distinguishing ensign. Fundamentally, *nēs* denotes a standard or flag raised on a hill around which marshaled troops would rally.[54] Accordingly, this sail served as a symbol of Tyrian self-assurance and pride. Wherever the ship traveled observers would recognize her and marvel at her beauty.[55]

Second, *the deck coverings* were made of purple fabric from Elishah. The nature of the cloth is not specified, but its luxurious quality is highlighted by its royal colors, *blue-violet and red-purple*.[56] In the Table of Nations (Gen. 10:4 = 1 Chr. 1:7) Elishah identifies the eldest son of Javan, who occupied a coastal region. As a place-name, Elishah (Alashiya in extrabiblical sources) may denote all of Cyprus, or more likely part of the island, distinguishable from Kittim.[57] While the form of the term *mĕkassēk*, rendered "deck coverings," is problematic, the root *ksh* suggests some form of covering.[58] One should probably visualize awnings or a covering over the cabin of the ship to protect the passengers from the heat of the Mediterranean sun, features well attested in ancient art, particularly from Egypt.[59]

(c) The Special Crew of the Ship Tyre (27:8-11)

In describing the crew of the glorious ship Tyre, these verses offer the modern reader a window into the staffing of ancient merchant vessels. In v. 8 the list

---

54. See Isa. 13:2; 18:3; 30:17; Jer. 4:21; 51:27. In Num. 21:8 it identifies Moses' bronze serpent (Num. 21:8), indicating that such standards could be made of metal as well as fabric. It occurs in a nautical context also in Isa. 33:23. Num. 26:10 uses the term in a derived sense of "sign, warning."

55. On *nēs* see further B. Couroyer, "Le *nēs* biblique: signal ou enseigne?" *RB* 91 (1984) 1-29; Krantz, *Des Schiffes Weg,* pp. 122-26.

56. On the meaning of *tĕkēlet* and *'argāmān* see my *Ezekiel: Chapters 1-24,* p. 737 n. 36.

57. Some suggest that Elishah represented the non-Phoenician part of the island, Kittim the Phoenician segment. Alashiya is attested in texts from Egypt, Ugarit, el-Amarna, Alalakh, Mari, and Boghazköi. See further Cf. R. Dussaud, "Identification d'Enkomi avec Alasia," in C. F. A. Schaeffer, *Enkomi-Alasia: Nouvelles missions en Chypre, 1946-1950,* Publications de la mission archéologique française 1 (Paris: Librairie C. Klincksieck, 1952), pp. 1-10; Dussaud, "Ile ou rivage dans l'Ancien Testament," *Assemblées du Seigneur* 6 (1956) 63-65; M. C. Astour, "Second Millennium B.C. Cypriot and Cretan Onomastica Reconsidered," *JAOS* 84 (1964) 241-48.

58. See n. 28 above. In Gen. 8:13 a similar term identifies the roof of Noah's ark. In fifteen additional occurrences it denotes the covering over the ark of the covenant (Exod. 26:14 [bis]; 35:11; 36:19 [bis]; 39:34 [bis]; 40:19; Num. 3:25; 4:8-10; 12:25 [bis]).

59. See further Krantz, *Des Schiffes Weg,* pp. 137-47.

of personnel divides into two parts, dealing respectively with the classes of seamen on board the vessel and the military officers who defend it. While the style becomes more prosaic and the city returns to view in vv. 9-11, the entire section coheres through the effective sixfold repetition of *hāyû*, "they were," as well as the prophet's pervasive concern to identify the geographic origin of the men in the service of Tyre. It seems natural that the professional seamen on board the ship are all Phoenicians, coming from Sidon, Arvad, and Byblos. Sidon, 25 miles up the coast from Tyre, was the latter's chief competitor, and will be the object of her own prophecy in 28:20-23. Like Tyre, Arvad (modern Ruad), about 95 miles farther north, was an island city, situated less than 2 miles off the coast.[60] Gebal (Byblos, modern Jubeil) lay halfway between Tyre and Arvad. Its importance in Levantine affairs is demonstrated by the frequency with which the name surfaces in texts from all periods.[61]

8-9 Ezekiel's notice that the crew members came from the elite social classes of their cities of origin contributes to the majestic image of the Tyrian craft. The *yōšĕbîm* from Sidon and Arvad represent the citizens who count, probably officials who sit at the gate.[62] Tyre's own contributions are identified as *ḥăkāmayik*, "your wise/skilled men," in context probably a reference to her counselors and advisers. The crew members from Gebal were drawn from her elder class *(ziqnê gĕbal),* more closely defined as *ḥăkāmêhā,* "her wise men." Perhaps in the interests of efficiency, this heterogeneous crew was organized along city lines. The Sidonians and Arvadites were designated the rowers; the Tyrians, specialists in handling the ropes, manned the sails and maneuvered the tackle; and the Gebalites kept the ship in good repair by caulking holes in the hull and performing other maintenance duties to keep the vessel seaworthy.

The form of the expression *hāyû bāk,* "They were in you," links the last sentence of v. 9 to the preceding, but its meaning changes as the prophet's attention shifts from the figure of the ship to the city of Tyre itself. It had

---

60. Cf. Ashurbanipal's reference to "Arvad in the midst of the sea" (*ANET,* p. 276). The dominance of Tyre over these cities is substantiated by Nebuchadrezzar's Court Register, which lists the king of Tyre ahead of the rulers of Sidon and Arvad. Cf. *ANET,* p. 308. Wiseman (*Nebuchadrezzar,* p. 75) suggests that the document records the list of participants in a special procession. If *ṣwr* is to be emended to *ṣmr* (see n. 31 above), the reference would be to Ṣumur (Ṣamuru/Ṣimira, modern Sumra), which figures prominently in the Amarna Tablets but receives little attention in later documents. For a history of the region see S. Izre'el, *Amurru Akkadian: A Linguistic Study,* 2 vols., HSM 40-41 (Atlanta: Scholars Press, 1991), 2:135-79.

61. See R. L. Roth, *ABD,* 2:922-23.

62. Cf. the use of *yāšab* in Jer. 39:3, as well as in Ruth 4:1-2. In the latter those who sit at the gate are the elders *(zĕqēnîm),* a word that designates the nobility of Gebal in v. 9.

previously referred to the men on board the ship; now it applies to all the foreign ships gathered in Tyre's harbors. The personnel on these vessels are identified as *mallāḥîm,* a Sumerian loanword that found its way into many of the Semitic languages.[63] In each of its occurrences in Hebrew it denotes "seamen" in general, rather than a specific type of sailor (vv. 27, 29; Jon. 1:9).

The last phrase of v. 9 declares the ships' purpose in Tyre's harbors: they are there to pick up her wares. *laʿărōb maʿărābēk,* an expression that occurs only in this passage, introduces the reader to one of the key terms in the remainder of the oracle. *maʿărāb* obviously derives from a root ʿrb, but several homonyms are created by this combination of consonants. The present expression has traditionally been derived from a root meaning "to give a pledge," though more recently a root ʿrb, "to give," attested in Old South Arabic and Syriac, has been proposed.[64] More likely is a derivation from ʿrb, "to enter," hence the goods that come into one's hands, that is, that one acquires.[65]

10-11   In addition to the crew, on board the ship Tyre was a contingent of mercenary military personnel, referred to as *ḥêlēk,* "your army,"[66] and more closely defined as *'anšê milḥamtēk,* "your men of war." Their presence on board the merchant ship probably reflects Tyre's current war with Nebuchadrezzar, and the heightened need to protect her precious cargo from marauding pirates.[67] The distinction between the image of the ship and the reality of the island fortress blurs in v. 11 with the notice that these men were stationed on the *walls (ḥômōt)* and *towers (migdālôt).* While these may refer to defensive structures on the ship itself,[68] the description sounds more like fortifications used to defend cities.

Tyre's defensive forces are drawn from far and wide, as indicated by

63. Cf. Akk. *malāḫu (CAD,* 10/1:149-52; *AHW,* pp. 592-93); Aram. *mlḥ (DNWSI,* p. 632). See Wagner, *Aramaismen,* pp. 76-77.

64. For the former see BDB, p. 786. Cf. *ʿērābôn* (Gk. ἀρραβών), "pledge," in Gen. 38:17, 18; Job 17:3. For the latter see Zimmerli, *Ezekiel 2,* p. 45, following G. R. Driver, "Difficult Words in the Hebrew Prophets," in *Studies in Old Testament Prophecy,* Fest. T. H. Robinson, ed. H. H. Rowley (New York: Scribner's, 1950), pp. 64-66. NRSV reads "to barter wares."

65. Thus Liverani, in *Ah, Assyria . . . ,* p. 77; cf. E. Lipiński, "Products and Brokers of Tyre According to Ezekiel 27," in *Studia Phoenicia,* vol. 3: *Phoenicia and Its Neighbours,* ed. E. Lipiński and E. Gubel (Leuven: Peeters, 1985), pp. 216-17.

66. On this use of the word see 17:17. For discussion see H. Eising, *TDOT,* 4:351-52.

67. For the former see Zimmerli, *Ezekiel 2,* p. 59. For the latter see Good, *Semitics* 1 (1970) 84 n. 17; S. Smith, "The Ship Tyre," *PEQ* 85 (1953) 98.

68. Good, *Semitics* 1 (1970) 85; R. R. Stieglitz, *Maritime Activity in Ancient Israel* (Ann Arbor: University Microfilms, 1971), pp. 94-95.

two triads of place-names. Her close links with Egypt are reflected in the first group, which represents a traditional list of Egyptian allies: *Paras, Lydia* (Lud), *and Put.* The identity of *Put* (Libya) is reasonably certain.[69] Although the OT knows of two Luds, one Semitic, the other Hamitic, it is preferable to identify Ezekiel's *Lud* with the Lydians of Asia Minor.[70] Lydian mercenaries are known to have been operative in Egypt's armies since the reign of Ashurbanipal of Assyria in the mid-seventh century B.C.[71]

Paras is more difficult. The spelling is identical to the standard Hebrew form for Persia, and its place at the head of this list suggests a dominant position in international affairs. It is tempting to see in this triad references to different points of the compass, a reflection of the worldwide influence of Tyre. Whether vv. 9b-11 are original or a later addition, however, this interpretation creates enormous difficulties.[72] Unlike Jeremiah's oracles against Babylon, which involve people from the east (Jer. 51:11, 27-28), oracles referring to Paras are concerned with western Syro-Palestinian and Mediterranean alliances. Furthermore, it is highly unlikely that a text arising from the period of Persia's hegemony would portray Persia as subordinate to Egypt. Accordingly, one should seek a different identification for Paras.[73] Of the alternatives, it seems best to see in consonantal *prs* an alternative, perhaps Egyptian spelling for Pathros, corresponding to *pȝrśj,* a variant of *pȝtȝrśj,* which denotes "the southland."[74] A ration list from about this period contains the

---

69. On Put see D. W. Baker, *ABD,* 5:560. A fragmentary inscription of Nebuchadrezzar that refers to his Egyptian campaign mentions a city *Puṭu-yaman,* "Putu of Yawan (the Ionians)," perhaps a Greek colony in Cyrenaica. Cf. T. O. Lambdin, *IDB,* 3:971; Wiseman, *Nebuchadrezzar,* p. 40.

70. The Semitic Lud is a son of Shem, Gen. 10:22; 1 Chr. 1:17. The Hamitic Lud is a son of Mizraim (Egypt), Gen. 10:13; 1 Chr. 1:11. On the Lydian identification cf. Josephus, *Ant.* 1.16.4, §144. Thus Zimmerli, *Ezekiel 2,* p. 59; Liverani, in *Ah, Assyria . . . ,* p. 67.

71. See *ARAB,* 2:298, §785; cf. Zimmerli, *Ezekiel 2,* p. 59.

72. Since Persia did not achieve this position until the late 6th century, Zimmerli (*Ezekiel 2,* pp. 59-60) dates the prose insertion (vv. 9b-11) to the Persian period. Cf. M. S. Odell, "'Are you he of whom I spoke by my servants the prophets?' Ezekiel 38–39 and the Problem of History in the Neobabylonian Context" (Ph.D. diss., University of Pittsburgh, 1988), pp. 104-5.

73. Geyer's suggestion ("Ezekiel 27 and the Cosmic Ship," p. 118) that *prs* represents a late replacement for *kws* (cf. Ezek. 30:5) in an attempt to update the oracle is far-fetched.

74. Paras may refer to a power with strong links to Tyre and Egypt, but as yet unattested in extrabiblical records, or a scribal error for Pathros, named alongside Assyria, Egypt, Cush, Elam, Shinar, and Hamath in Isa. 11:11. The latter is preferred by M. C. Astour, "Ezekiel's Prophecy of Gog and the Cuthean Legend of Naram-Sin," *JBL* 95 (1976) 568 n. 5 and 576 n. 59. See further Odell, "Ezekiel 38–39," pp. 104-5. On the identification with Pathros see H. P. Rüger, "Das Tyrusorakel Ez 27" (Ph.D. diss., Tübingen, 1961), as cited by Zimmerli, *Ezekiel 2,* p. 60.

personal name Uhpar'asa, "the southerner," along with a series of other names, primarily Egyptian.[75] That this traditional list of Egypt's allies should appear in a list of Tyre's supporters attests to the close relationship between the African nation and this island state in the early 6th century.

Tyre's relations with her northern neighbors are reflected in the second triad of geographic names: Arvad, Helek, and Gammad. The first has been encountered earlier in v. 8.[76] The second plays on $\hbar\bar{e}l\bar{e}k$, "your army," in v. 10.[77] While Helek as a toponym is unattested elsewhere in the OT, an association with Ḥilakku (Cilicia) is widely accepted.[78] The last name represents the only gentilic form in this context. The location of Gammad is uncertain, but an equation with *Qumidi,* mentioned in the Amarna Tablets, is attractive in the present context.[79]

The final two lines in each of vv. 10 and 11 suggest that the prophet's primary interest in these mercenaries is not for their military prowess but for their contribution to the glorious image of Tyre. Rather than using their shields *(māgēn),* helmets *(kôbaʿ),* and other military gear in battle, the allies have hung them on Tyre's walls, where their value is purely decorative. The practice of hanging shields from walls and towers is attested in Cant. 4:4 and 1 Macc. 4:57, and illustrated clearly in Sennacherib's Nineveh relief of the storming of Lachish.[80] Indeed, one relief specifically links a tower decorated with shields to the Phoenician fleet.[81] These decorative weapons rounded out

75. Cf. Wiseman, *Nebuchadrezzar,* p. 83. For the text see E. F. Weidner, "Jojachin, König von Juda, in babylonischen Keilschrifttexten," in *Mélanges Syriens offerts à Monsieur René Dussaud par ses amis et ses éleves,* 2 vols. (Paris: Geuthner, 1939), 2:930-32.

76. *bĕnê 'arwād* is often taken as a gentilic in a broad sense (cf. van Dijk, *Ezekiel's Prophecy,* p. 73), but like "sons of Mizraim (16:26), "sons of Asshur" (16:28; 23:7, 9, 12, 23), and "sons of Babel" (23:15, 17, 23), here it applies more narrowly to the men of Arvad. Cf. Block, *SR* 13 (1984) 312.

77. Some interpret it accordingly as a common noun. Cf. J. Simons, *Geographical and Topographical Texts of the Old Testament* (Leiden: Brill, 1959), p. 455; Eichrodt, *Ezekiel,* p. 379.

78. The present military cooperation of Tyre, Arvad, and Cilicia finds a precedent in a temple inscription by Ashurbanipal. Cf. *ANET,* p. 297. See further S. P. Garfinkel, *Studies in Akkadian Influences in the Book of Ezekiel* (Ann Arbor: University Microfilms, 1983), pp. 73-74.

79. See Garfinkel, *Akkadian Influences,* pp. 62-63. Y. Aharoni (*The Land of the Bible,* tr. and ed. A. Rainey, rev. ed. [Philadelphia: Westminster, 1979], p. 178) and R. D. Barnett ("Ezekiel and Tyre," *ErIsr* 9 [1969] 7) propose a less likely equation with a *qmd,* probably located between Arvad and Gebal, mentioned in the texts of Seti I. Liverani (in *Ah, Assyria . . . ,* p. 68 n. 9) entertains the unnecessary emendation of *gammādîm* to *gōmērîm,* viz., Cimmerians.

80. See *ANEP,* nos. 372, 373.

81. See R. D. Barnett, "Phoenicia and the Ivory Trade," *Archaeology* 9 (1956) 93.

Ezekiel's image of Tyre's splendor (*hādār,* v. 10) and provided a finishing touch to the picture of her beauty (*kālĕlû yopyēk,* v. 11).

(3) The Source of Tyrian Glory (27:12-25)

12 " '*Tarshish was your agent, because of the abundance of all your wealth.*[82] *In exchange for silver,*[83] *iron, tin, and lead, they offered your wares.* 13 *Javan, Tubal, and Meshech — they were your brokers. In exchange for human beings*[84] *and copper utensils, they offered your merchandise.* 14 *From Beth-togarmah, [in exchange for] horses and chariot teams and mules, they offered your wares.* 15 *The people of Dedan*[85] *were your brokers; many coastal lands conducted trade on your behalf.*[86] *As your payment they brought back to you tusks of ivory and ebony.*[87] 16 *Aram*[88] *was your agent, because of the abundance of your products. In exchange for turquoise, purple products, embroidered cloth, fine linen, coral, and pearl,*[89] *they offered your wares.* 17 *Judah and the land of Israel — they were your brokers. In exchange for wheat of Minnith, resin, honey, oil, and balm, they offered your merchandise.* 18 *Damascus was your agent. In exchange for the abundance of your produce — because of the abundance of wealth,*[90] *in exchange for the*

82. Reading *hônēk,* with LXX in place of MT, which lacks the suffix. Cf. vv. 16, 27, 33.

83. The prefix on *bĕkesep* is a *bet pretii,* performing multiple duty in the context.

84. *nepeš 'ādām,* "human persons." On the use of *nepeš* for human chattel see Gen. 12:5 and Lev. 22:11.

85. *ddn* is generally read as "Rhodes" with LXX Ῥοδίων, on the basis of the commonly accepted confusion of *rēš* and *dalet* in Gen. 10:4. See E. Tov, *Textual Criticism of the Hebrew Bible* (Minneapolis: Fortress, 1992), pp. 12-13. But see the commentary for the identification of this place.

86. *sĕḥōrat yādēk,* lit. "trade agent of your hand." *sĕḥōrat* is a collective sg. The same phrase occurs in v. 21.

87. The versions all misunderstood *hāwbĕnîm,* a hapax, borrowed from Egyp. *hbnj.* Cf. Targ. "peacocks," Syr. "incense," LXX "to those who come in." On the term see H. R. Cohen, *Biblical Hapax Legomena in the Light of Akkadian and Ugaritic,* SBLDS 37 (Missoula, Mont.: Scholars Press, 1978), p. 118; Ellenbogen, *Foreign Words,* p. 63.

88. *BHS,* NAB, NRSV, REB, and most commentators read *'ĕdōm* with Syr., but LXX ἀνθρώπους read *'ādām.* However, Targ. supports MT. M. Haran argues that the products listed are more fitting for Aramaic (*IEJ* 18 [1968] 204). But as J. Lindsay observes, this position is not conclusive, given the "*transit* nature of the trade" ("The Babylonian Kings and Edom, 605-550 B.C.," *PEQ* 108 [1976] 30).

89. The meaning of some of these terms is uncertain. See the commentary.

90. LXX telescopes *bĕrōb ma'ăśayik mērōb kol-hôn* by reading only the second phrase. Though many delete the first as a gloss, Targ. supports MT. Is this a conscious conflation of alternative readings? Cf. Tov, *Textual Criticism,* pp. 241-43.

wine of Helbon, and wool from Suhru, 19 and casks of wine from Uzal[91]
— they offered your wares: wrought iron, cassia, and calamus were
among your merchandise. 20 Dedan was your broker. In exchange for
saddlecloths used for riding — [92] *21 Arabia, and all the sheikhs of*
Qedar, they conducted trade on your behalf. In exchange for lambs,
and rams, and goats, for these they were your agents. 22 The brokers
of Sheba and Raamah — they were your brokers. In exchange for the
choicest of perfumes,[93] *and for all kinds of precious stones, and gold,*
they offered your wares. 23 Haran, Canneh, Eden,[94] *Asshur, and Kil-*
mad[95] *were your brokers*[96] *— 24 they were your brokers. In exchange*
for the choicest of fabrics,[97] *for cloaks of blue-purple and embroidered*
cloth, for colorful carpets, and for tightly[98] *braided cords, for these*
they were your brokers.[99] *25 The ships of Tarshish transported your*
merchandise for you.[100] *So you were full and extremely heavily loaded*
in the heart of the seas.' "

91. MT *wĕdān wĕyāwān mĕʾûzzāl* bristles with difficulty. NIV follows Targ. in treating the first two words as proper names, but its "Danites and Greeks from Uzal" makes no sense in the context. The present translation follows the plausible but minor emendations suggested by A. R. Millard ("Ezekiel 27:19: The Wine Trade of Damascus," *JSS* 7 [1962] 201-3): *wĕdannê yayin mēʾîzāl.* Cf. Lipiński (in *Studia Phoenicia,* 3:219 n. 28), who reads the first two words (consonantal *wdn wywn*) as *wdnwywn,* "Danuna." M. Elat's defense of MT and his treatment of all three terms as proper names is not convincing ("The Iron Export from Uzal [Ezekiel XXVII 19]," *VT* 33 [1983] 323-30).

92. The ending to v. 20 seems to have fallen away.

93. *rōʾš kol-bōšem,* lit. "the head of all perfume." Since *bōšem* is associated with aromatic incense, perfumes, oils, and embalming substances (cf. Cant. 5:1, 13; 6:2; 8:14), but never with food, the common rendering of the term as "spices" is misleading. Cf. V. H. Matthews, *ABD,* 5:227-28.

94. MT adds *rōkĕlê šĕbāʾ,* "the brokers of Sheba," which is missing in LXX and seems to have mistakenly slipped into the text from v. 22.

95. The versions render *kilmad* differently: Syr. omits the term; LXX reads Χαρμαν; Vulg. *Melmad;* Targ. *kl mdy,* "all the Medes."

96. *rōkaltēk* is problematic here, and should perhaps be deleted as a mistaken insertion. The fem. form appears elsewhere only in v. 20, where it follows a single fem. toponym.

97. *bĕmaklûlîm* is missing in LXX and Syr.; Vulg. reads *multifariorum.*

98. The major versions read *ʾăruzîm* as "cedars."

99. MT *bĕmarkultēk,* often rendered "in your place of trade," is a hapax form. With BHS and Zimmerli (*Ezekiel 2,* p. 51) I think it more likely that this word should be divided and repointed as *bām rĕkullātēk.* Cf. v. 21.

100. The appositional construction with two suffixed nouns, *šārôtayik maʿărābēk,* is awkward, but see GKC, §128d; Zimmerli, *Ezekiel 2,* p. 51.

Without warning in v. 12 the interest turns from the magnificence of the ship to Tyre's trading links with the whole world. Adopting a more prosaic cataloguing style, Ezekiel presents a written report, what appears to be a manifest of goods that flowed in and out of Tyre's warehouses. The entries in this document tend to consist of four elements (see table 3, p. 69): (1) the name of Tyre's mercantile partner; (2) a statement of the nature of the relationship;[101] (3) a list of the products offered by this country to Tyre; (4) a summary statement of the role of Tyre's trading partner (in the form of a verbal clause). But the pattern was not rigidly followed. In three instances (vv. 12, 16, 18) vague reference is made to the volume of the trade. Indeed, each column deviates from the others in some form, suggesting that attempts to delete secondary elements on these exceptions are ill advised.

The second and fifth columns provide the keys to Ezekiel's perception of the commercial relationship between Tyre and her accomplices. The former defines their role; the latter records their fulfillment thereof. Five different expressions, all derived from the vocabulary of international trade and commerce, are used. (A sixth appears in v. 25.)

1. *sāḥar.* The finite verb is rare in the OT, but fundamentally it meant "to go about, minding one's business." Reflecting the mobility of its actors, in a derived sense it came to denote "trade," with the cognate noun, *sahar,* referring to "gain, profit."[102] The five occurrences of the participle in this context denote "trade agent."[103]

2. *rākal.* This root has a similar meaning, "to go about (for gossip or trade)," though the connection with gossip suggests less positive connotations.[104] Nine of the ten occurrences in the present text are participial forms,[105] rendered "broker" above. The exception, *rĕkullâ* in v. 24, is textually problematic, but probably means "brokerage, class of merchants."

---

101. In four instances (vv. 13, 17, 21, 22) the relationship is expressed by means of cleft sentences with pleonastic pronouns. S. Geller observes (*JANES* 20 [1991] 21 n. 24) that in each instance the subject is composed of two or more coordinated names (A + B PR Z); single subjects use nonclefted constructions (A Z). PR stands for pleonastic pronoun; Z for the predicate.

102. Cf. Liverani, in *Ah, Assyria . . . ,* p. 75. On *sāḥar* in the OT, particularly Genesis, see E. A. Speiser, "The Verb *sḥr* in Genesis and Early Hebrew Movements," *BASOR* 164 (1961) 23-28. The root is well attested in Akkadian. See B. Landsberger, "Akkadisch-hebräische Wortgleichungen," in *Hebräische Wortforschung,* Fest. W. Baumgartner, VTSup 16 (Leiden: Brill, 1967), pp. 176-90.

103. Vv. 12, 16, 18 (all fem.), v. 21 (twice masc.). Note the expanded forms, *sôḥar yādēk,* "trade agent of your hand," viz., operating on your account in vv. 15 and 21.

104. The same word is used in 17:4 of Babylon.

105. Except for v. 14 and the end of v. 23, which is textually problematic, all forms are masc. (vv. 13, 15, 17, 22a, 22b, 23, 24).

Table 3. The Commercial Records of Tyre (Ezekiel 27:12-24)

12	Tarshish	was your agent	because of the abundance of all your wealth.	In exchange for silver, iron, tin, and lead	they offered your wares.
13	Javan, Tubal, and Meschech —	they were your brokers.		In exchange for human beings and copper utensils	they offered your merchandise.
14	From Beth-togarmah			horses and chariot teams and mules, they offered your wares.	
15	The people of Dedan many coastal lands	were your brokers; conducted trade on your behalf		tusks of ivory and ebony	As your payment they brought back to you.
16	Aram	was your agent,	because of the abundance of your products.	In exchange for turquoise, purple products, embroidered cloth, fine linen, coral, and pearl,	they offered your wares.
17	Judah and the land of Israel —	they were your brokers.		In exchange for wheat of Minnith, resin, honey, oil, and balm,	they offered your merchandise.
18	Damascus	was your agent.	In exchange for the abundance of your produce — because of the abundance of wealth,	In exchange for the wine of Helbon, and wool from Suhru,	they offered your wares.
19				and casks of wine from Uzal, wrought iron, cassia, and calamus	were among your merchandise.
20	Dedan	was your broker.		In exchange for saddlecloths used for riding —	
21	Arabia, and all the sheikhs of Qedar	they conducted trade on your behalf.		In exchange for lambs, and rams, and goats,	for these were your agents.
22	The brokers of Sheba and Raamah —	they were your brokers.		In exchange for the choicest of perfumes, and for all kinds of precious stones, and gold,	they offered your wares.
23	Haran, Canneh, Eden, Asshur, and Kilmad	were your brokers —		In exchange for the choicest of fabrics, for cloaks of blue-purple and embroidered cloth, for colorful carpets,	
24		They were your brokers.		and for tightly braided cords,	for these they were your brokers.

3. *'ārab*. Apart from the ethnicon *'Arab* in v. 21, this root appears only in the noun form *ma'ărāb*, "merchandise, shipment."[106]

4. *'āzab*. In contrast to *ma'ărāb*, which refers fundamentally to "acquired" merchandise, with *'izābôn*, from *'āzab*, "to leave behind," the emphasis seems to be on goods delivered to someone else,[107] though these distinctions blur in the present context. The noun form, which appears only in this context, occurs five times (vv. 12, 14, 16, 19, 22).

5. *'eškār*. This is a rare loanword from Sum. ÉŠ.GAR, via Akk. *iškaru*, "payment, produce, tribute."[108] The word occurs only twice in Biblical Hebrew, but it has surfaced on a 6th-century-B.C. ostracon, suggesting that it may not have been uncommon in everyday speech.[109] Although "payment" offers a rather neutral interpretation of *'eškar* here, the context implies a stronger sense of obligation, as if to one's superior.[110]

6. *nātan*. This verb normally carries a general sense, "to give," but in this connection with *ma'ărāb* and *'izĕbônîm* it surely means "to offer, deliver," in a commercial sense.[111]

In addition to these mercantile expressions, several other related terms may be noted. *ma'ăśeh* (vv. 16, 18) designates the fruit of one's labor, the products put on the market. *hôn* (vv. 12, 18) speaks of the wealth one's work

---

106. See vv. 13, 17, 18, 25. Cf. the infinitive construct plus noun earlier in v. 9. On the meaning of the term see above on v. 9. Although Targ. tends to treat *ma'ărāb* and *'izbônîm* synonymously (both rendered *shwr'*), *m'rb* is confirmed as an authentic Aramaic term by an Elephantine papyrus (2:5; cf. A. E. Cowley, *Aramaic Papyri of the Fifth Century B.C.* [Oxford: Clarendon, 1923], pp. 4-5), which speaks of a "shipment" of lentils brought in by ship.

107. Thus Liverani, in *Ah, Assyria . . .* , p. 77. Cf. Akk. *ezēbu*, "to leave" (*CAD*, 4:416-26; *AHW*, pp. 267-69). The common derivation from *'āzab* II, "to prepare, make," hence "manufactured goods," is to be rejected (cf. Lipiński, in *Studia Phoenicia*, 3:214-15 [following Dahood, et al.], who suggests, on the basis of its absence from postbiblical Hebrew and Masoretic uncertainty regarding its vocalization, that it may have been borrowed from Phoenician). See O. Loretz, "Ugaritische und hebräische Lexikographie (II)," *UF* 13 (1981) 131-34; H. G. M. Williamson, "A Reconsideration of *'zb* II in Biblical Hebrew," *ZAW* 97 (1985) 74-85. Even less likely is van Dijk's proposal of *'āzab* III, "to convoy" (*Ezekiel's Prophecy*, pp. 75-76).

108. *CAD*, 7:246-48, "finished products, staples or materials, etc., to be delivered"; *AHW*, pp. 395-96. Cf. J. N. Postgate, *Taxation and Conscription in the Assyrian Empire*, Studia Pohl Series Maior 3 (Rome: Pontifical Biblical Institute, 1974), pp. 94-110, 205-11.

109. The broken inscription reads *'škr tb . . .* , "a good gift(?)" Cf. R. Cohen, *Kadesh-Barnea: A Fortress from the Time of the Judaean Kingdom* (Jerusalem: Israel Museum, 1983), pp. xix, 38, fig. 37.

110. As in Ps. 72:8-11, the only other OT occurrence of the expression, where it is paired with *minḥâ*.

111. Similarly *šûb* (Hiphil), "to bring back" (v. 15), and *hāyâ*, "to be," i.e., "to function as, represent" (v. 19), repeatedly in vv. 7-11.

and business ventures produce. Industry and finance provided the basis for Tyre's commercial success. Her trading partners provided Tyre with the raw materials and the exotic products; Tyre sent them out as manufactured products.[112] While her associates had much to gain from this mercantile relationship, this was hardly an egalitarian relationship. Tyre was the *rōkelet hā'ammîm*, "the broker of the peoples" (v. 3), and, as the ubiquitous suffixes on the expressions listed above indicate, the rest of the nations functioned as Tyre's agents.[113] Consequently, the capital of the world flowed into her treasuries, enabling this island city to establish a standard of living that was the envy of all.

Perusal of the list of traders and goods included in Tyre's manifest reveals the breadth of Tyre's influence and the variety of enterprises in which she was involved (see table 4, p. 72). The entries in the manifest will be examined in the order in which they appear.

1. *Tarshish.* The name seems to derive from a common Semitic root preserved in Akkadian as *rašāšu*, "to heat, melt, be smelted,"[114] which suits this and several other references that associate the name with metal industries (38:13; Jer. 10:9). The Table of Nations associates Tarshish with other Mediterranean names (Gen. 10:4; 1 Chr. 1:7), and Jon. 1:3 indicates that by boat one may reach it by heading west from Joppa. The annals of Esarhaddon associate a place called *Tar-si-si* with Cyprus (Iadanana) and other lands "amidst the sea."[115] While the place cannot be identified with certainty and the OT evidence is contradictory, an identification with the Tartessus of classical sources, a Phoenician colony in western Spain on the Guadalquivir River, seems most likely.[116] The present document does not necessarily affirm Tarshish as the source of the metals listed, but that she was Tyre's broker specializing in the exchange for her wares for silver, iron, tin, and lead. Tyre's

---

112. Cf. Liverani, in *Ah, Assyria . . .* , p. 77.

113. The expression compares with *sōḥărê hammelek,* "agents of the king," in 1 K. 10:28-29 (= 2 Chr. 1:16-17). Note esp. the expression *sĕḥōrat/sōḥărê/yādēk,* "agents of your hand," viz., "under obligation to you." G. Bunnens recognizes a corresponding phrase in Akk. *tamkāru ša qāti* in RS 17.145:4 (*PRU,* 4:172) (*L'expansion phénicienne en Méditerranée* [Brussels and Rome: Inst. Belge, 1979], p. 88). Cf. the suffixes: *sôḥărtēk/sōḥărāyik,* "your agents"; *rōkaltēk/rōkĕlāyik,* "your brokers"; *rĕkullātēk,* "your brokerage"; *'izĕbônāyik,* "your wares"; *ma'ărābēk,* "your merchandise."

114. *AHW,* p. 960-61. Cf. W. F. Albright, "The Role of the Canaanites in the History of Civilization," in *The Bible and the Ancient Near East,* Fest. W. F. Albright, ed. G. E. Wright (Garden City, N.Y.: Doubleday, 1961), p. 347 n. 96.

115. *ANET,* p. 290.

116. Strabo, *Geog.* 3.2.1, 14; Herodotus, *Hist.* 1.163; 4.152. See D. W. Baker, *ABD,* 6:331-33, for a discussion of the problems. Also M. Görg, "Ophir, Tarschisch und Atlantis: Einiger Gedanken zur symbolischen Topographie," *BN* 15 (1981) 79-82.

Table 4. Tyre's International Trade Record (Ezek. 27:12-25)			
Agents	Agents' Contributions	Tyre's Contributions	Record of Deal
Tarshish	silver, iron, tin, lead	manufactured wares	X
Javan, Tubal, Meshech	slaves, copper vessels	merchandise	X
Beth-togarmah	horses, chariot teams, mules	manufactured wares	X
Rhodes, coastal lands	tusks of ivory, ebony	produce	X
Edom	tourquoise, purple products, embroidered cloth, fine linen, coral, pearl	manufactured wares	X
Judah, land of Israel	wheat, resin, honey, oil, balm	merchandise	X
Damascus	wine of Helbon, wool of Suhru,	manufactured wares	X
	wine from Uzal, wrought iron, cassia, calamus	merchandise	X
Dedan	saddlecloths		
Arabia, Qedar	lambs, rams, goats		
Sheba, Raamah	choice perfumes, precious stones, gold	manufactured wares	X
Haran, Canneh, Eden, Assyria, Kilmad	choice fabrics, blue-purple cloaks, purple-colored cloaks, colorful carpets, tightly braided cords	merchandise	X

prosperity (*rōb kol-hôn*, lit. "abundance of all wealth") is expressly linked to the activity of Tarshish.

2. *Javan, Tubal, and Meshech. Javan*, the standard OT designation for the Greek world, is related etymologically to "Ionians."[117] *Tubal* or Tabal was the territorial designation of the interior Anatolian kingdom know to the Assyrians as Bīt Buritash.[118] This landlocked kingdom, between the Halys River and the Taurus River in Asia Minor, was bounded on the west by

117. Cf. Akk. *Jawan/Jaman*. Parpola, *Neo-Assyrian Toponyms*, 186-87. LXX reads Ἑλλάς.

118. M. Dietrich and O. Loretz argue that the name derives from a root meaning "to pour," and that the name Tabal/Tubal means "Metalcaster-land" ("Hurritisch-ugaritisch-hebräisch *tbl* 'Schmied,'" *UF* 22 [1990] 87-88).

Meshech, on the south by Hilakku, on the east by Melidu and Til-garimmu (Beth-togarmah), and on the north by Kasku. While there is no evidence that Lydia/Phrygia ever ruled over Tubal, Sargon II's annals report that he squelched an Anatolian revolt in which Mitâ of Mushki was allied with Tabalu.[119] *Meshech,* to be identified with Mushku/Mušku in neo-Assyrian sources, was also located in central Anatolia. Ancient records attest to contact with the Assyrians as early as the reign of Tiglath-pileser I in the 12th-11th century. During the reign of Sargon II, Meshek was ruled by Mitas of Phrygia (probably the legendary King Midas of Greek tradition), who posed a major problem for Sargon II.[120] Herodotus (*Hist.* 3.94) has both Tubal and Meshek belonging to the nineteenth satrapy of Darius I. While Tubal and Meshech formed a standard pair in biblical writings,[121] their present association with Javan accords with Gen. 10:2 (= 1 Chr. 1:5), which presents all three as sons of Japheth, and Isa. 66:19, which includes this trio among the distant nations to whom the glory of Yahweh will be declared.

Our text has these three nations engaged in the slave trade and the transportation of copper/bronze vessels. Information on the former is scanty, but the cooperation of Greece and Tyre in the trading of human merchandise is attested in Joel 4:6 (Eng. 3:6; cf. Amos 1:6, 9). Evidence for the latter may be found in Sargon II's report of seizing booty consisting of bowls with gold handles and other vessels from the land of Tabalu, and Ashurnasirpal II's reference to "vessels of copper, cattle, sheep, and wine," taken in Mushku.[122]

3. *Beth-togarmah.* Gen. 10:3 identifies Togarmah (along with Ashkenaz and Riphath) as the son of Gomer and the nephew of Javan, Meshech, and Tubal. Most scholars equate the name with the capital of Kammanu

---

119. See *ARAB,* 2:40-41, §80; on Tubal/Tabal see further M. Wäfler, "Zu Status und Lage von Tabal," *Or* 52 (1983) 181-93; J. N. Postgate, "Assyrian Texts and Fragments," *Iraq* 35 (1973) 30-31; E. M. Yamauchi, *Foes from the Northern Frontier: Invading Hordes from the Russian Steppes* (Grand Rapids: Baker, 1982), pp. 24-27; idem, "Meshech, Tubal, and Company: A Review Article," *JETS* 19 (1976) 243-45. The popular identification of Tubal with Tobolsk in Russia (H. Lindsey, *The Late Great Planet Earth* [Grand Rapids: Zondervan, 1970], p. 53) is ludicrous.

120. For further data on Meshech see Postgate, *Iraq* 35 (1973) 27-28; Yamauchi, *Foes,* pp. 24-27. The popular identification of Meshech with Moscow (cf. Lindsey, *Late Great Planet,* p. 53) is absurd.

121. See 32:26; 38:2-3; 39:1. On these identifications see also Astour, *JBL* 95 (1976) 569. Josephus preserves the following tradition of the origins of these peoples: "Theobel founded the Theobelians, nowadays called Iberians. The Meschenians, founded by Meschos, are to-day called Cappadocians, but a clear trace of their ancient designation survives; for they still have a city of the name of Mazaca, indicating to the expert that such was formerly the name of the whole race" (*Ant.* 1.6.1, §124).

122. For Sargon II see *ARAB,* 2:95, §172. For Ashurnasirpal II see *ARAB,* 1:144, §442.

(Kummanni), known in Hittite texts as *Tegarama,* in Akkadian as *Til-garimmu,* and in classical sources as Gauraena (modern Gurun).[123] Located "in the remotest part of the north" (Ezek. 38:6), on the border of Tubal, this region was renowned for its horse breeding.[124]

4. *Dedan and the coastal lands.* An identification of MT Dedan with the central Arabian site is excluded by the name's association with the Mediterranean and the reappearance of Dedan in v. 20. Most read Rhodes with LXX, but an association of the name with the land of Danuna, a region north of Tyre, mentioned in the Amarna Letters, is preferable.[125] Accordingly *many coastal lands ('iyyîm rabbîm)* refers to the Anatolian coastlands, perhaps, but not necessarily, inclusive of the Aegean islands. This interpretation is supported by the products these lands contribute to the Tyrian economy: ivory and ebony. *qarnôt šēn* (lit. "horns of ivory") refers to the tusks of an elephant, which must have come from Asia, either Syria or India. The former is less likely since the animal had become an endangered species by the time of Ezekiel.[126] The latter accords with the present association of ivory and ebony, which originated in India and Ceylon.[127]

5. *Aram.* Though generally emended to "Edom," MT *Aram* refers to the Syrian hinterland from upper Mesopotamia in the northeast to Damascus in the southwest.[128] Tyre's Syrian agents contributed a variety of products to her economy, particularly luxury items like gem stones and specialty fabrics.

123. For the Hittite see *ANET,* p. 318. For the Akkadian see Yamauchi, *Foes,* p. 26 n. 28. For both see J. Garstang and O. R. Gurney, *Geography of the Hittite Empire* (London: British Institute of Archaeology at Ankara, 1959), pp. 46-48. For the classical sources see A. Goetze, *Kleinasien* (Munich: Beck, 1957), p. 46. Atypically Lipiński identifies Togarmah with Tugdamme, the name of a 7th-century Cimmerian chief (in *Studia Phoenicia,* 3:218 n. 20).

124. Cf. Ashurbanipal's receipt as tribute from King Mugallu of Tabal of "large horses" (*ARAB,* 2:297, §781), and Sargon II's report that "horses there (neighbouring Urartu) are so numerous that they could not all be broken in" (*ARAB,* 2:352, §848; p. 352, §911). Cf. Goetze, *Kleinasien,* p. 196. On the role of mules *(pĕrādîm)* in the ancient world see G. S. Cansdale, *All the Animals of the Bible Lands* (Grand Rapids: Zondervan, 1970), pp. 79-80.

125. So also Liverani (in *Ah, Assyria . . . ,* p. 69) and G. J. Wenham on Gen. 10:4 (*Genesis 1–15,* WBC 1 [Waco: Word, 1987], p. 219). Lipiński (in *Studia Phoenicia,* 3:219) prefers an identification with the Cilician *dnnym,* "Danunites," mentioned in the Phoenician inscriptions from Karatepe and Zinjirli. See *ANET,* pp. 73-74.

126. On the elephant in ancient Syria and Anatolia see Barnett, *Ancient Ivories,* pp. 5-7. On Phoenicia's trade in ivory and production of ivory luxury goods see ibid., pp. 43-55; I. J. Winter, "Phoenician and North Syrian Ivory Carving in Historical Context: Questions of Style and Distribution," *Iraq* 38 (1976) 1-22.

127. On ebony in the ancient Near East see M. Stol, *On Trees, Mountains, and Millstones in the Ancient Near East* (Leiden: Ex Oriente Lux, 1979), pp. 36-38.

128. See n. 88 above. Similarly Liverani, in *Ah, Assyria . . . ,* p. 69.

The meaning of *nōpek* is uncertain, but its inclusion in the lists of jewels in the king of Tyre's pectoral (28:13) and in the Israelite high priest's chest piece (Exod. 28:18; 39:11) suggests a precious gem of some sort. Turquoise or some form of green feldspar is likely.[129] *'argāmān* is always used of purple cloth (cf. v. 7), which links well with the following *riqmâ*, "embroidered cloth." *bûṣ*, "fine linen," occurs elsewhere only in Esther and Chronicles. This is a Semitic expression that replaced the Egyptian loanword *šēš*.[130] *rā'mōt*, occurring elsewhere only in Job 28:18, is commonly interpreted as "coral," but this is admittedly speculative.[131] *kadkōd*, "pearl," occurs also in Isa. 54:12. Neither context offers much help in clarifying the meaning. "Pearl" is suggested by Targ. *mrglyn*.[132]

6. *Judah, the land of Israel.* Ezekiel names his own country, Judah, and the sister nation to the north as the middle entries in this catalogue of Tyrian commercial connections. The reference to *'ereṣ yiśrā'ēl*, "the land of Israel," is remarkable, not only because of Ezekiel's reluctance to use the phrase but also because Israel had ceased to exist more than a century earlier.[133] All that remains of the northern kingdom is the *land* called "Israel." Three of the five commodities listed here are traditional Cisjordanian agricultural products: wheat, honey, and olive oil. The designation of the grain as *ḥiṭṭê minnît* suggests a special variety, unless Judah and Israel functioned as brokers for wheat grown in the Transjordanian region of Minnith, a place named in Judg. 11:33.[134] The second

129. See *HALOT*, p. 709, "a green coloured semi-precious stone, found at Sinai," following T. O. Lambdin ("Egyptian Loan Words in the Old Testament," *JAOS* 73 [1953] 152), who suggests a derivation from Egyp. *mfkʒkt*. Cf. P. L. Garber and R. W. Funk, *IDB*, 2:902; I. H. Marshall, *IBD*, 2:783. Others prefer "garnet." Cf. H. Quiring, "Die Edelsteine im Amtsschild des jüdischen Hohenpriesters und die Herkunft ihrer Namen," *Sudhoffs Archiv für Geschichte der Medizin und der Naturwissenschaften* 38 (1954) 199-200; G. R. Driver, *Bib* 35 (1954) 156; followed by Zimmerli, *Ezekiel 2*, p. 66.

130. Rooker, *Biblical Hebrew in Transition*, pp. 159-61; Lambdin, *JAOS* 73 (1953) 155. On the linen industry and trade in the ancient world see H. Waetzoldt, *RLA*, 6:583-94.

131. So also M. H. Pope, *Job*, 3rd ed., AB 15 (Garden City, N.Y.: Doubleday, 1973), p. 204; cf. Harris, *ALUOS* 41 (1962/63) 60-61. The root appears in Ugaritic as *rimt* (*CTA*, 3.3.1-2).

132. From which Gk. μαργαρίτης derives. The common rendering "rubies" is based on a supposed derivation from **kdd*, "to strike fire." Cf. *HALOT*, pp. 460-61. However, Brenner (*Colour Terms*, p. 166) questions a color significance.

133. It occurs elsewhere only in 40:2 and 47:18, where it refers to the entire region west of the Jordan. On Ezekiel's preference for *'admat yiśrā'ēl* see my *Ezekiel: Chapters 1–24*, pp. 248, 352 n. 39. With Ezekiel's geographic use of the name cf. 2 Chr. 30:25 and 34:7. The inclusive use occurs also in 1 Chr. 22:2 and 2 Chr. 2:16 (Eng. 17).

134. But see C. Rabin ("Rice in the Bible," *JSS* 11 [1966] 2-9), who reintroduces a rabbinic interpretation in arguing for *minnît* as an Indian loanword for "rice." M. Kislev equates the species with *ḥiṭṭîm makkôt*, referred to in 2 Chr. 2:9 ("Towards the Identity of Some Species of Wheat in Antiquity," *Leš* 42 [1977] 64-72).

term, *pannag,* is a hapax of uncertain meaning. The most likely explanation argues for a medicinal plant, opopanax, from which galbanum may derive, though the more common identification with some sort of flour remains a possibility.[135] The last item, *ṣŏrî,* was a balm derived from the balsam tree.[136] The OT identifies its source as Gilead and confirms its medicinal use (Gen. 37:25; Jer. 8:22; 46:11; 51:8).

7. *Damascus.* The importance of Tyre's trade with Damascus, in earlier times the foremost of the Aramean city-states, is highlighted by the redundant insertion, "In exchange for the abundance of your produce — because of the abundance of wealth," in v. 18. According to this list Damascus provided Tyre with a variety of specialty commodities. (a) Wines from Helbon and Uzal. The former is to be identified with Akk. *Ḫilbunu,* modern Ḫalbun, 10 miles north of Damascus. The interpretation of the latter depends on a reconstruction of the beginning of v. 19. Accordingly *wĕdān* is treated as a common noun, related to Ugar. *dn,* "jar, cask," and Akk. *dannu,* a large vat used for storing wine, beer, and so on.[137] While Uzal occurs elsewhere in Gen. 10:27, in association with the Joktanite tribes of southern Arabia, it is preferable to equate the name with Izalla, a site in the Anatolian foothills.[138] (b) Wool of Suhru. *ṣemer ṣāḥar* is also problematic. Following wine of Helbon, one expects a geographic name, perhaps Zuhru, named in the Amarna Letters, or aṣ-Ṣaḥra, northwest of Damascus.[139] LXX ἔρια ἐκ Μιλήτου, "wool from

135. Gk. πάναχες (from which our word *panacea* derives) and its product, χαλβάνη, are loanwords from Semitic. Cf. Stol, *Trees,* pp. 68-71. On galbanum see Zohary, *Plants of the Bible,* p. 201. For the meaning "flour" *pannag* is treated as a loanword from Akk. *pannigu/pannegu,* "a small bread" or "type of flour." Cf. the conjunction of *pannigu* and *dišpu,* "honey," as in our text, in Esarhaddon's tribute list (R. Borger, *Die Inschriften Asarhaddons, Königs von Assyrien,* AfO 9 [Graz: 1956], no. 94:26-27). For defense of this interpretation see Garfinkel, *Akkadian Influences,* pp. 118-19. Cf. REB "meal," NRSV "millet," NASB "cakes." NIV translates ambiguously "confections," which may refer to a delicacy or a sweetened medicinal preparation.

136. Cf. Stol, *Trees,* pp. 50-53.

137. On Ugar. *dn* see *CTA,* 16.3.14, as a container for bread; 4.1.12 (as read by Gibson, *CML,* p. 46), where it occurs alongside *ks,* "cup," *krpn,* "flagon," *bk rb,* "large jar," and *kd,* "pitcher." For Akk. *dannu* see *CAD,* 4:98; Millard, *JSS* 7 (1962) 202; Cohen, *Biblical Hapax Legomena,* pp. 135-36.

138. A region in which iron has been found. See R. J. Forbes, *Studies in Ancient Technology,* 2nd ed. (Leiden: Brill, 1972), 9:194. The fame of both these regions as a source of wine is attested in an inscription of Nebuchadrezzar that mentions "pure wine, wine of Izallu, Tu'immu, Ṣimminu, and Helbon" (VAB, 4:90, lines 22-23). On this text see Millard, *JSS* 7 (1962) 201-3. Seeing in *dĕdān* at the beginning of v. 19 a reference to the *dnnym,* "Danunites," of Cilicia, M. Elat equates Uzal with the Anatolian town *Ušawalaš* ("The Iron Export from Uzal [Ezekiel XXVII 19]," *VT* 33 [1983] 323-30).

139. On the former see J. A. Knudtzon, *Die El-Amarna-Tafeln,* 2 vols. (repr. Aalen: Zeller, 1964), 145:22; 334:3; 335:3; but cf. W. L. Moran, *Amarna Letters* [Baltimore: Johns

Milit," a town on the coast of Asia Minor, suggests another possibility. The rendering appears speculative, but the name is echoed in Targ. *w'mr mylt kbyn'*, "soft fluffy wool of fine sheep."[140] (c) Wrought iron. The hapax phrase *barzel 'āšôt* (lit. "smooth iron") refers to a malleable grade of iron produced at relatively low temperatures, in contrast to cast iron, which requires a much more intense heat.[141] (d) Cassia. That Damascus traded in *qiddâ*, a costly perfume native to east Asia,[142] reflects how well established the trade routes between the Levant and the Far East were in ancient times. (e) Calamus. *qāneh* identifies an aromatic grass used in perfume, cosmetics, flavoring, and medicine. Although one type of calamus grows wild in Israel, India was probably the source of Damascus's supply.[143]

8. *Dedan.* This central Arabian oasis served as Tyre's broker for special riding gear.[144] The phrase *ḥopeš lĕrikbâ* involves two hapax forms, though the root of the second, *rkb*, "to ride," is familiar. The meaning of the first word is uncertain, though most translations read "saddlecloths." Many associate *ḥōpeš* with Akk. *ḥabšu*, "chopped straw," in which case the saddlecloths were probably stuffed with straw.[145] However, a derivation from Akk. *taḥapšu*, "a covering for a horse," viz., a saddle blanket, is more likely.[146]

9. *Arabia and all the sheikhs of Qedar.* *'ărab*, "steppe dweller," is a general term for bedouin people that came to denote also a mode of life (Isa. 13:20; Jer. 3:2). The earliest OT attestation of Arabs by name occurs in the textually uncertain 1 K. 10:15. Although the name seems not to have been widely used of the desert peoples until several centuries later, it appears to have become a generic designation for desert tribes, including Ishmaelites, Amalekites, and Midianites.[147] The second phrase, *nĕśî'ê qēdār*, is more

---

Hopkins University Press, 1992], who reads the first and last references differently [pp. 231, 357]). On the latter see Rüger, "Tyrusorakel," p. 22; Zimmerli, *Ezekiel 2*, p. 67. Less likely is G. R. Driver's equation with Ṣuḥar in Yemen (*Bib* 35 [1954] 157).

140. Thus Levey, *Ezekiel*, p. 80. NRSV, NJPS, and NASB translate "white wool." For discussion see M. Dietrich and O. Loretz, "Zur ugaritischen Lexikographie I," *BO* 23 (1966) 132, who propose "brilliant white wool."

141. See Forbes, *Studies in Ancient Technology*, 9:206.

142. Zohary, *Plants of the Bible*, p. 203. This perfume was used in preparing the anointing oil used in the tabernacle ritual (Exod. 30:24).

143. See ibid., p. 196.

144. On Dedan see above on 25:13.

145. Cf. Zimmerli (*Ezekiel 2*, p. 68), "stuff for saddle-cloths."

146. *AHW*, p. 1301. For discussion see Garfinkel, *Akkadian Influences*, pp. 79-80.

147. Cf. Isa. 13:20, and Isaiah's prophecy against the Arabs, including Dedanites, Tema, and the sons of Qedar, Isa. 21:13-17. On the historical development of the term see I. Eph'al, " 'Ishmael' and 'Arab(s)': A Transformation of Ethnological Terms," *JNES* 35 (1976) 227-31; idem, *The Ancient Arabs: Nomads of the Borders of the Fertile Crescent, 9th-5th Centuries B.C.*, rev. ed. (Jerusalem: Magnes and Hebrew University Press, 1984),

specific. From both biblical and extrabiblical evidence, Qedar, a tribe associated with the oasis at Dumah, seems to have been preeminent in Arabian contacts with the outside world.[148] These desert folk are appropriately said to have traded in small livestock: male lambs *(kārîm)*, rams *('êlîm)*, and goats *('attûdîm)*.[149]

10. *Sheba and Raamah.* Sheba *(šĕbā')* identifies a kingdom in southwestern Arabia.[150] Although the Sabeans were probably originally camel nomads, by the time of the visit of the queen of Sheba to Solomon (1 K. 10:1-13), they had settled down in what is now eastern Yemen, establishing their capital city at Mārib.[151] Situated strategically where overland Arabian caravan routes converged with trade routes from Ethiopia and Somaliland across the narrow Red Sea strait, and the maritime routes on the Indian Ocean, Sheba gained a monopoly on the Arabian caravan trade. Raamah is mentioned in the OT only in association with Sheba. The name resembles that of ancient *Rgmt,* a city in the district of Najrān, but the identification is uncertain.[152] According to the present trade list, the wares Sheba and Raamah contributed to Tyre's trade were all luxury items: choice perfume, jewels, and gold.[153] The source of these items is not indicated, but the gold probably came from Ophir, a site yet to be positively identified.[154] The gemstones *('eben yĕqārâ)* could have been mined locally or imported from Africa.

---

pp. 60-63. For Assyrian problems with the Arabs see *ANET,* pp. 279 (Shalmaneser III), 291-92 (Esarhaddon), and 297 (Ashurbanipal).

148. Isa. 21:13-17 associates Dumah with Tema and Dedan. In Jer. 2:10 Kittim and Qedar represent "west" and "east," respectively; 49:28 pairs Qedar with *bĕnê qedem,* "sons of the east." On Ashurbanipal's problems with Ammuladi, "king of Qedar," see *ANET,* pp. 298-99. On the Arabs see further A. K. Irvine, "The Arabs and Ethiopians," in *Peoples of Old Testament Times,* ed. D. J. Wiseman (Oxford: Clarendon, 1973), pp. 287-311; R. H. Smith, *ABD,* 1:324-27.

149. The same triad (in different order), with the addition of *pārîm,* "bulls," occurs in 39:18.

150. Genesis presents two lines of descent for Sheba (referred to in native sources as Saba, hence Sabeans, but not to be confused with Seba [*sĕbā'*], Gen. 10:7), reflecting convergence of African and Asian lines: brother of Dedan and son of Raamah, descendant of Hamitic Cush (Gen. 10:7; 1 Chr. 1:9); brother of Dedan and son of Jokshan, descendants of Abraham and Keturah, hence Semitic (Gen. 25:3), Sheba and Dedan appear as sons of Jokshan, and descendants of Abraham and Keturah. See Block, "Table of Nations," *ISBE,* 4:710.

151. G. van Beek, *IDB,* 4:145; F. V. Winnett, "The Arabian Genealogies in the Book of Genesis," in *Translating and Understanding the Old Testament,* Fest. H. G. May, ed. H. T. Frank and W. L. Reed (Nashville: Abingdon, 1970), p. 184.

152. Cf. Winnett, in *Translating and Understanding the Old Testament,* pp. 179-80.

153. These same three elements occur also in 1 K. 10:10, suggesting Sheba's typical stock-in-trade.

154. See D. W. Baker, *ABD,* 5:26-27.

11. *Haran, Canneh, Eden, Asshur, Kilmad.* In v. 23 the prophet's vision shifts to Tyre's north and east. Haran, from Akk. *ḫarrānu,* "road," was situated on the Balikh River, about 60 miles north of its confluence with the Euphrates in upper Mesopotamia.[155] Canneh is probably to be identified with *Kannu',* whose precise location is unknown but which appears in Assyrian texts from the 8th-7th century B.C. as the home of several individuals involved in economic transactions, including slave sales.[156] Eden represents an abbreviated form of Beth-eden, Assyrian Bīt Adini, an Aramean state situated west of the Balikh and incorporated into the Assyrian empire by Shalmaneser III in 856.[157] Asshur identified a deity (god of the Assyrians), the Assyrian nation, and at times its capital city.[158] Kilmad is unknown and looks suspiciously corrupt.[159]

These cities located northeast of Tyre provided her with more luxury goods, especially cloths. Some of the terminology is as rare as the goods themselves. *maklûlîm,* a hapax form, denotes a specially crafted garment of some type.[160] These are accompanied by expensive blue-purple *(tĕkēlat)* and embroidered *(riqmâ)* cloaks. The garment is identified with another hapax, here *gĕlômê,* cognate to Aram. *glym',* "mantle," and Akk. *gulēnu,* "coat."[161] *ginzê bĕrōmîm* (lit. "carpets of color") involves two additional hapax forms. The meaning of the first is suggested by the targumic rendering of Est. 1:3, *gnzy mylt',* "fine woolen garments.[162] The second is a loanword from Akk. *birmu,* "multicolored."[163] It is difficult to tell from the syntax whether *ḥăbālîm ḥăbušîm,* "wound cords," represents separate luxury items or if they were simply used to tie goods.[164] The issue is complicated by the addition of

155. The city figures prominently in the patriarchal narratives (Gen. 11:31-32; 12:5; 27:43).

156. See S. A. Meier, *ABD,* 1:837.

157. See Amos 1:5; cf. "sons of Eden" in 2 K. 19:12; Isa. 37:12. On the Assyrian information see *ANET,* pp. 277-78.

158. At other times the capital was located in Nineveh, Calah, and Dur Sharrukin.

159. Zimmerli (*Ezekiel 2,* p. 50) reads *kol madai,* "the whole of Media," with Targ. Lipiński (in *Studia Phoenicia,* 3:219 n. 29) reads *Klmr,* viz., Kulmer or Kullimer, a city known from neo-Assyrian and later sources and located northeast of Diyarbakir. Cf. Garfinkel, *Akkadian Influences,* pp. 90-91.

160. Thus M. Görg, " 'Prachtgewänder' für Tyrus: Ein Hapax in Ez 27,24," *BN* 17 (1982) 35-36. See the related *miklôl,* in 23:12. Cf. the Akkadian cognate *kilīlu,* "circlet, headband," *CAD,* 8:358.

161. Cf. Cohen, *Biblical Hapax Legomena,* p. 93 n. 253; Garfinkel, *Akkadian Influences,* p. 61.

162. To be distinguished from the homonymous root *gnz,* "to hide." See Cohen, *Biblical Hapax Legomena,* p. 93 n. 254; *HALOT,* p. 199.

163. Garfinkel, *Akkadian Influences,* pp. 54-55; Brenner, *Colour Terms,* pp. 149-50.

164. NRSV, NIV, NJPS; Lipiński, in *Studia Phoenicia,* 3:219.

wa'ăruzîm, which was understood by the versions as "cedars," presumably a reference to the containers used to store and transport these luxury goods. But the Masoretic vocalization points in a different direction. This is probably another hapax, cognate to an Arabic root meaning "to be firm."[165]

With this exotic catalogue of merchandise from the northeast, Tyre's trade list closes. V. 25 is transitional. The first sentence, which glances back at the trade list, serves a double rhetorical function. On the one hand, although it is more cryptic, it provides a narrative echo of v. 9b,[166] linking the present catalogue of merchants and merchandise with the previous description of the ship, particularly the register of its personnel, and highlighting the purpose of the preceding manifest. Just as the products and men from around the world contributed to the magnificence of the ship Tyre, so the fleets of the world serve the purposes of the city.[167] On the other hand, the reference to Tarshish creates an effective *inclusio* with the beginning of the manifest in v. 12. Even so, one recognizes in these occurrences of *taršîš* a typically Ezekielian shift in meaning. Whereas in v. 12 Tarshish had denoted a specific Iberian locale, the present *'ŏniyyôt taršîš,* "ships of Tarshish," should not be restricted to ships carrying merchandise back and forth between Tyre and Spain, or to ships owned by Iberians. This point is confirmed by the usage of the phrase elsewhere. In Isa. 2:16 Tarshish ships are magnificent vessels, symbols of pride. According to 1 K. 10:22 Tarshish ships bring luxury items to Solomon from Africa and the Orient, and 1 K. 22:4 has them based in Ezion-geber on the Red Sea and heading for Ophir in quest of gold. *'ŏniyyôt taršîš* seems originally to have been a technical designation for large, high-quality freighters designed to sail on the high seas.[168] An original Phoenician provenance for the ships of Tarshish is suggested not only by our text but particularly by Isaiah's oracle against Tyre (Isa. 23:1-18).[169]

The function of these ships is described in the following phrase, *šārôtayik ma'ărābēk,* which is difficult syntactically and lexically. While the meaning of *šārôtayik* is uncertain, it is best understood as a feminine participle with a dative suffix, derived from *šûr,* "to descend, incline," cognate to Akk. *šurru.*[170] The predication of "ships of Tarshish" with a verb meaning "to go

<hr/>

165. Thus Zimmerli, *Ezekiel 2,* p. 51.

166. *'ŏniyyôt taršîš,* "the ships of Tarshish," answers to *'ŏniyyôt hayyām,* "the ships of the sea"; and *šārôtayik ma'ărābēk,* "your carriers, your merchandise," answers to *la'ărōb ma'ărābēk,* "to handle your merchandise."

167. This observation requires that the metaphor and the trade list be interpreted in relation to each other, and not in isolation.

168. Ps. 48:8 (Eng. 7) highlights Yahweh's power to destroy the "ships of Tarshish" with the east wind.

169. For further study of the phrase see Krantz, *Des Schiffes Weg,* pp. 48-51.

170. Cf. P. Xella, "Fenico *mšr* (Tabnit, 5) ed ebraico *tšwrh* (1 Samuele 9:7)," *UF*

down" is reminiscent of Ps. 107:23, which speaks of merchants going down to the sea in ships.[171]

The second sentence of v. 25 sets the stage for the final segment of the oracle by returning to the image of the ship Tyre. With delightful ambiguity,[172] he describes the scene: the pride of the high seas is fully laden, ready to set sail, to tour the world, imposing her mercantile power and advertising her grandeur. In the words of Isa. 23:8, "Her merchants were princes; the most honored men on earth." She who controls the economy rules the world and accumulates vast quantities of wealth.

The arrangement of entries in Ezekiel's version of Tyre's trade list deserves reflection. As an early 6th-century-B.C. document,[173] this text offers an important window into Tyrian trade relations. The list is not exhaustive, nor is there an obvious pattern in the arrangement of the names and products.[174] The prophet's gaze moves successively from Tarshish in the farthest west, to Greece and Anatolia, down the coast to Syria-Palestine, then on to Arabia, and finally to the cities and nations of Mesopotamia. While the monotonous style adds realism to the map, the text has been highly influenced by ideological concerns. The connections with the Table of Nations (Gen. 10) are obvious, particularly the Japhetic names in vv. 10-15 and the South Arabian names of v. 22. As already mentioned, the reference to the land of Israel in v. 17 is anachronistic. The placement of Judah and Israel in the center of a

---

14 (1982) 299-301, though Xella treats *šārôt* as a substantive, "caravans." On the basis of LXX ἐν τῷ πλήθη, P. Wernberg-Møller ("Two Notes," *VT* 8 [1958] 307-8) proposes a derivation from *šrh*, "to multiply," hence "riches, wealth." But most derive the form from *šûr*, "to travel" (cf. M. V. Fox, *The Song of Songs and the Ancient Egyptian Love Songs* [Madison: University of Wisconsin Press, 1985], p. 135, on Cant. 4:8).

171. *yôrĕdê hayyām boʾŏnîyyôt ʿōśê mĕlāʾkâ bĕmayim rabbîm*, "Those who go down to the sea in ships, who conduct business on many waters."

172. The verb *wattikbĕdî* (from *kābēd*, lit. "to be heavy," but in a derived sense "to be heavy with majesty, glorious") refers to either the weight of the ship's cargo or to its magnificence, or both. In the end both precipitate the sinking of the ship.

173. See the introductory comments above.

174. Some of Tyre's most important partners are absent: Egypt, Cyprus, Carthage, Philistia, even Babylon. Liverani's recognition of four concentric belts is forced (in *Ah, Assyria . . .*, pp. 73-74). Rüger finds here a reflection of four major trade routes: the Persian royal route (vv. 12-15; cf. Herodotus, *Hist.* 5.53); north-south routes between the Euphrates and Egypt (vv. 16-18), with a branch on the western side of the Jordan (v. 17), and "the King's Highway" (*derek hammelek*) east of the river (cf. Num. 20:17; 21:22); the incense route from southern Arabia (vv. 19-22); and the *ḥarrān šarri*, "road of kings," in upper Mesopotamia from Asshur to Bit-Adini (vv. 23-24; see Rüger, "Tyrusorakel," as cited by Zimmerli, *Ezekiel 2*, p. 71). While geographically sensitive, his dating of the list to the time of Xerxes in 484 and 482 B.C. overlooks that Persian control never extended as far west as Tarshish, and the system of roads used by the Persians existed long before the rise of Persia (cf. Liverani, in *Ah, Assyria . . .*, pp. 74-75 n. 30).

list of eleven entries (see table 4) reflects the bias of the author. But his agenda is to highlight the power and magnificence of Tyre, not only by describing the geographical scope of her commercial ventures but also by cataloguing the goods for which her agents plied the seas. While some of the commodities were common, most were luxury wares: precious metals, jewels, special woods, ivory, choice cloth, fine carpets, perfumes, and foodstuffs. Even the wheat is special Minnith wheat. As a ship and as a city, Tyre is filled to the brim, basking in luxury, and capitalizing on the political power that attends her economic hegemony, a picture that plays directly into the prophet's theological concern.

(4) The Imminent End of Tyrian Glory (27:26-36)

26 " 'Out into the high seas your oarsmen have brought you.
An easterly gale has shipwrecked you in the heart of the seas.
27 Your wealth, your wares, and your merchandise;
your sailors, your helmsmen, and your repairmen;
the merchants of your merchandise,
    and all your warriors on board you,
    along with your entire crew[175] in your midst —
they will sink into the heart of the seas,
    on the day of your fall.
28 Amid the loud outcry[176] of your helmsmen,
the mainland suburbs[177] will heave.
29 All who handle the rudder[178] will come down from their ships.
The sailors and all the mariners[179] will stand on the land.
30 They will shout loudly over you,
and cry out bitterly.

175. qāhāl, lit. "assembly."

176. On the preference for zāʿaq over ṣāʿaq in Late Biblical Hebrew see Rooker, *Biblical Hebrew in Transition*, pp. 134-38.

177. The phrase yirʿăšû migrōšôt is awkward. While migrāš usually denotes the common pastureland outside a walled settlement (Num. 35:2ff.; Josh. 21:11ff.), here the mainland opposite the island, including the villages and the open countryside, seems to be in view. See J. Barr, "*Migraš* in the Old Testament," *JSS* 29 (1984) 15-31, esp. 28-29. REB "troubled waters" follows G. R. Driver's "driven waves" (*Bib* 35 [1954] 157), but it ill suits the context. LXX "they shake in fear" reads yirʿăšû migrōšôt as yirʿăšû marʿeset, perhaps by mistake, perhaps reflecting a different *Vorlage*. Targ. prwry', "port-cities" (thus Levey, *Ezekiel*, p. 81), and Syr. dhdryky, "that which surrounds you," are closer.

178. See Krantz, *Des Schiffes Weg*, pp. 110-22. tōpĕśê māšôṭ may also be interpreted as "rowers of oars." See the commentary.

179. ḥōbĕlê hayyām, "helmsmen of the sea." Cf. ḥōbĕlîm alone in vv. 8, 27, 28.

They will throw dust on their heads,
and wallow[180] in the ashes.
31 On account of your plight they will shave their heads,
and don sackcloth.
They will weep bitterly[181] over you,
with bitter mourning.
32 And in their wailing[182] they will raise a lament over you.
They will lament over you:
"Who is like Tyre,
when she was moaning[183] in the midst of the seas?
33 When your wares were unloaded[184] from the seas
you met the needs of many peoples.
With your bountiful wealth and your merchandise,
you enriched the kings of the earth.
34 Now[185] that you have been shipwrecked[186] by the seas,[187]
in the deepest waters your merchandise,
and your entire crew in your midst have gone down.
35 All who live on the coastal lands are appalled over you,
and the hair of their kings bristles[188] with horror;
their faces are contorted.[189]

180. Or "sprinkle themselves." Thus REB, following G. R. Driver, *Bib* 35 (1954) 157-58.

181. *běmar nepeš,* lit. "with bitterness of soul."

182. LXX and Syr. misread *běnîhem* as *běnêhem,* "their sons." Cf. Targ. *b'ynyhwn,* translated by Levey (*Ezekiel,* p. 82) "in their affliction." J. Reider assumes an inadvertently dropped *aleph,* reconstructing *bo'ŏnîhem,* "in their ships" ("Contributions to the Scriptural Text," *HUCA* 24 [1952-53] 92). It is preferable to regard MT as the preposition *bě* plus *nî,* an abbeviation of *něhî,* "lament," plus suffix. See GKC, §23k.

183. *BHS*'s reconstruction, *nidmâ* (after Vulg. and Theodotion) may be interpreted "destroyed" (NRSV) or "compared" (thus Barthélemy, et al., *Preliminary and Interim Report,* 5:93). Targ. reads affirmatively, *lyt ddmy lh,* "There is none compared to her." LXX evades the problem by omitting the question altogether. See the commentary below.

184. *běṣē't* from *yāṣā',* "to go out," refers not to exporting goods but to removing them from ships. Cf. REB.

185. Reading *'ēt* in the sense of *'attâ,* with LXX, Targ., Vulg., but contra Syr. *bzbn',* "at the time." For the defective spelling cf. Ps. 4:8 (Eng. 7); 74:6.

186. The context seems to require a finite verb, *nišbart,* in place of the participle *nišberet.*

187. Thus NRSV. On the agentive use of *min* with the passive verb see Waltke-O'Connor, *Syntax,* §11.2.11d.

188. *śā'ar śa'ar,* lit. "to hair with hair," involves a denominative verb (found elsewhere only in 32:10 and Jer. 2:12, both times paired with *śāmam),* and a cognate substantive used in an abstract sense of "horror."

189. *rā'am* is a rare homonym of a similar root meaning "to thunder." Its meaning

36 *The agents among the peoples hiss*[190] *over you;*
you have become a horror,
and you will be no more forever." ' "

Having described in prose style the loading of Tyre (vv. 12-25), the prophet resumes the poetic narrative. As noted earlier, vv. 26-36 divide into two uneven parts: the announcement of the shipwreck of Tyre (vv. 26-27), and a description of the onlookers' response (vv. 29-36). The disproportionate attention given to the latter reflects Ezekiel's primary concern. This is implicitly not simply a report of a major maritime disaster but a warning to all nations of the world to avoid the error of her ways.

(a) The Wreck of the Tyrian Ship (27:26-32a)

Everything seems under control as the crew of the magnificent ship Tyre guide her out to sea. But suddenly the tables turn. An eastern gale attacks the stately vessel and smashes her in the open seas. In comparison with the description of a near shipwreck of a Phoenician vessel in Jon. 1, Ezekiel's word is blunt, lacking any explicit reference to human[191] or divine causation, and little if any indication of the sailors' response. Harking back to vv. 8-11, v. 27 heightens the scope and economic significance of the disaster by repeating the triad of special terms for her cargo *(hôn, 'izĕbônayik, ma'ărābēk)* and taking the roll of the various classifications of seamen on board. All of Tyre's wealth and all her noble sailors will sink with her. The prophet makes only passing reference to the response of the sailors themselves to the wreck of their craft (v. 28a), preferring instead to concentrate on external reaction. The people on the mainland are aghast, and the sailors on board other ships are horrified at the sinking of this Tyrian *Titanic*. Lesser vessels might be expected to perish in a Mediterranean squall, but surely not this proud monarch of the seas!

The intensity of the sailors' shock at the demise of Tyre is highlighted in several ways. First, Ezekiel repeats the prepositional expression *'ālayik/ 'ēlayik,* "over you," seven times in vv. 30-36.[192] Second, he describes in detail

---

is suggested by the subject, *pānîm,* "faces." Targ. reads "Their faces are drawn." LXX and Syr. misread *rā'ămû* as *dāmĕ'û,* "to run [with tears]," but this verb is used of eyes, not faces.

190. Although *šāraq* usually involves derisive hissing (cf. Isa. 5:26), here it represents an expression of intense grief.

191. The destructive force of the east wind on the open sea obviates the need for a veiled reference to Nebuchadrezzar or any other military power here (cf. Ps. 48:8 [Eng. 7]).

192. On the interchangeability of *'el* and *'al* in Ezekiel see Rooker, *Biblical Hebrew in Transition,* pp. 125-31.

the verbal and nonverbal gestures of mourning (cf. 26:16) by the seamen: a loud and bitter outcry, throwing dust on their heads (cf. Josh. 7:6; Job 2:12; Lam. 2:10), wallowing in ashes (Mic. 1:10; Jer. 6:26; 25:34), plucking out hair (cf. Ezek. 7:18; Lev. 21:5; Mic. 1:16), donning sackcloth (cf. Ezek. 7:18), bitter weeping, ritual wailing,[193] and raising a formal lament. Third, he repeats the word *mar/mārâ*, "bitter, bitterness," three times in vv. 30-31. Fourth, he allows the literary flow to break down. The approach of the lament proper (for which the reader has been waiting since v. 1) is signaled by an awkward and repetitious announcement in v. 32a.

The grief of Tyre's partners over the city's demise is genuine, without a hint of the schadenfreude felt by the witnesses to Jerusalem's fall (25:3, 8, 12, 15; 26:2). As the lament will suggest (vv. 33-34), they too had profited from her success. Tyre's collapse casts a dreadful shadow over the economy of the entire world.

(b) The Lament over the Tyrian Ship (27:32b-36)

Following the narrative announcement, the lament proper divides into five parts: (1) an introductory rhetorical question (v. 32b); (2) a statement of Tyre's past glory (v. 33); (3) a statement of Tyre's present demise (v. 34); (4) a description of the response of the nations (vv. 35-36a); (5) a concluding refrain (v. 36b).

32b   The opening *mî kĕṣôr*, "Who is like Tyre?" constitutes a call for reflection on the fate of Tyre, similar in form to the personal names Michael (*mî kā'ēl*, lit. "Who is like God?") and Micaiah (*mî kāyāhû*, lit. "Who is like Yahweh?").[194] Like the prophet Micah's challenge (Mic. 7:18), the rhetorical question expects a negative answer: Tyre is without equal![195] The problematic hapax *kĕdumâ* renders the meaning of the last line far from certain. While various etymologies have been suggested, the most satisfactory in the context links the word with Akk. *damāmu*, "to moan."[196] Not only is this root used

193. On the pairing *bākâ*, "to weep," and *sāpad*, "to lament, wail," see 23:16, 23; Gen. 23:2; Est. 4:3; Eccl. 3:4; Joel 2:12. Cf. also the Ugaritic text *CTA*, 19.4.171-72: *'rb bkyt bhklh mšspdt bḥzrh*, "The weeping women entered his palace, the wailing women his house."

194. On these names see J. D. Fowler, *Theophoric Personal Names in Ancient Hebrew: A Comparative Study*, JSOTSup 49 (Sheffield: JSOT Press, 1988), pp. 128-29.

195. Cf. the opening question in the oracle against Pharaoh, 31:2, and elsewhere Isa. 44:7; Rev. 18:18.

196. Thus J. P. van der Westhuizen, "A Proposed Possible Solution to KTU 1.12 II 7 Based on Babylonian and Biblical Evidence," *UF* 17 (1986) 359; Garfinkel, *Akkadian Influences*, pp. 66-67. Cf. *CAD*, 4:59. Other etymologies are: (1) *dāmâ*, "to compare" (Targ.); (2) *dāmam*, "to be dumb, silent," viz., silenced by destruction (NJPS, NASB,

in another oracle against Tyre,[197] but Ezek. 24:17 also indicates that our prophet was familiar with it. Whatever its derivation, this line announces that Tyre, once so smug in her security "in the midst of the seas," has sunk like the *Titanic.*

33-34 These verses follow the then-now pattern typical of laments. Returning to the vocabulary of the commercial register, v. 33 emphasizes that in the past the kings of the earth have profited from Tyre's commercial successes, which explains the intensity of their reaction at her fall. But now, all that has changed. Resuming the motif of the shipwreck,[198] v. 34 announces the disappearance of the vessel, and with it the loss of both merchandise and crew.

35-36a These lines continue the portrayal of the observers' shock over the fall of Tyre by expanding on 26:18 with more vivid description. Four expressions highlight the intensity of their reaction: the nations are appalled *(šāmam);* the hair of their kings bristles; their faces are contorted; they hiss over Tyre.

36b Instead of the customary ending, with a signatory or recognition formula, this chapter closes with a modified version of the refrain found in 26:21 and 28:19. The final line of v. 36 reflects the irony of the situation: she who had been number one in the world of international commerce has disappeared from the scene.

♦ *Theological Implications*

Although this chapter lacks a clear homiletical trajectory, the lessons to be learned from the magnificent ship Tyre are obvious.

First, hubris carries within itself the seeds of one's own destruction. This parable is one of the most imaginative of Ezekiel's extended metaphors. Its effectiveness derives not only from the propriety of the figure but especially from the ironies in the story. The sea, the source of Tyre's power and protection, turns its back on her and becomes Yahweh's agent of doom. For Ezekiel Tyre is the supreme illustration that "pride goes before destruction, and a haughty spirit before a fall" (Prov. 16:18). However, this oracle is not intended

---

NIV); (3) *kādam,* cognate to Arab. *kadama,* "to hold fast" (A. Guillaume, "The Meaning of *kdmh* in Ezek. XXVII.32," *JTS* 13 [1962] 324-25; cf. Barr, *Comparative Philology,* p. 329, no. 172); (4) cognate to Akk. *dimtu,* "tower," and Ugar. *dmt* (M. Dahood, "Accadian-Ugaritic *dmt* in Ezekiel 27:32," *Bib* 45 [1964] 83-84, followed by Allen, *Ezekiel 20–48,* p. 83); (5) cognate to Akk. *karāmu,* "to throw down, destroy," the *resh* having been misread as a *daleth* (G. R. Driver, "Hebrew Notes on Prophets and Proverbs," *JTS* 41 [1940] 169).

197. See Isa. 23:1-2, together with *hêlîl,* "to wail."
198. Note the root *šbr* here and in v. 26.

only as a warning for the city, once so proud. The emphasis on eyewitnesses and the detailed description of their responses highlights the paradigmatic value of her experience. Let all the high and mighty of this world beware, lest they share the fate of Tyre.

Second, the fates of all nations are in the hands of the Lord. Within the collection of Ezekiel's oracles, this oracle is remarkable for its apparent disinterest in divine involvement in human affairs. In the crassly materialistic world of commerce, the glory of Tyre is presented as the legitimate and desirable reward for enterprise, diligence, and business acumen. The "trickle down" effect of her success renders her achievements all the more admirable. Indeed, the reader is tempted to join the nations in mourning the tragic demise of this model of free enterprise and this benefactor of humankind. In the arena of human history, however, neither the magnificence of a civilization nor its contributions to the material well-being of others serves as an accurate measure of quality. For all her fiscal accomplishments, Tyre had dared to oppose Babylon, and in so doing had taken her stand against Yahweh and his inexorable purposes for the nations. Inasmuch as this dirge is presented as the very oracle of God, his silence is more apparent than real. His hand may be hidden, but it is present in the east wind that blows upon that ship. Indeed, the east wind is his breath, blowing on the high and mighty, reducing them to nothing (cf. Isa. 40:24). In her apparent invincibility, Tyre represented the glory of human achievement. Because her successes were driven by avarice and pursued in defiance of God, however, she could not stand. The Lord of history always has the last word.

c. The Oracle(s) Against the Prince of Tyre (28:1-19)

♦ Nature and Design

Chapter 28 is at the same time one of Ezekiel's most intriguing artistic creations and one of the most difficult texts in the entire book. The problems, many of which defy satisfactory scholarly solution, include the identification of the limits of the unit, the relationship between vv. 1-10 and 11-19, the relationship between these oracles concerning the king of Tyre and the foregoing messages about the city, numerous textual difficulties, perplexing hapax legomena and phrases, the source of the prophet's ideological notions, the relationship between this text and biblical traditions (esp. the narratives of Gen. 1–3, as well as the Priestly material in Exod. 28, and the wisdom writings), the message the prophet is attempting to convey to his own people. While some of these questions will be answered in the course of the exposition, several relate to the entire section, vv. 1-19, and call for a response before the analysis of the separate parts begins.

87

Table 5. A Comparison of Ezekiel 28:1-10 and 28:11-19		
	vv. 1-10	vv. 11-19
Genre	judgment speech	lament *(qînâ)*
Literary style	standard narrative prose	elevated prose
Addressee	*nĕgîd ṣōr,* "prince of Tyre"	*melek ṣōr,* "king of Tyre"
Issue	the arrogant claim	the glorious reality
Manner of punishment	through agents	by Yahweh himself
The role of the nations	agents of judgment	witnesses of judgment

The text of 28:1-19 poses as many nagging questions as any section in the book. Were vv. 1-10 and 11-19 originally two separate oracles? Does a preexistent document (oral or literary) underlie either of these segments or both? Or did the prophet merely utilize a commonly shared tradition of human origins? How were the prophet's pronouncements adjusted and shaped to create the present text? If the variety of scholarly responses to these questions is not discouraging, it certainly cautions against dogmatism in the interpretation of many details. But the reader need not despair because the central message of the chapter is clear: Human hubris must be answered by divine judgment.

On the surface vv. 1-10 and 11-19 appear to contain two originally separate oracles editorially conjoined. The concentration of a series of prophetic formulae in vv. 10-11 provides an obvious hinge in the literary unit. The combination of a signatory formula, which often concludes Ezekielian oracles,[1] in v. 10, with a new word-event formula (cf. v. 1), a new direct address of the prophet as *ben-'ādām*, a command to engage in prophetic activity, followed by the citation formula, in vv. 11-12a, obviously points to two distinct literary panels, if not two distinct original prophetic utterances. This suspicion is reinforced by the divergences in genre, style, and content of the two parts, as reflected in table 5, above. But the significance of these differences should not be exaggerated. While formally distinct, a series of stylistic features combine to create the impression of an intentional overall unitary composition:

1. It does not always conclude them. See S. A. Meier, *Speaking of Speaking: Marking Direct Discourse in the Hebrew Bible,* VTSup 46 (Leiden: Brill, 1992), pp. 230-42.

1. Addressee. In contrast to all the foregoing oracles against the nations, including those against Tyre, as well as the following prophecy concerning Sidon, in both panels the addressee is the leader of a city or nation.
2. General theme. The primary issue in both units is hubris.
3. Subthemes. The panels are linked by several lexical links: "lifting up the heart" (*gābah lēb*, vv. 2, 5, 17), wisdom (*ḥokmâ*, vv. 3, 4, 5, 12, 17), trade (*rĕkullâ*, vv. 5, 16), beauty (*yōpî*, vv. 7, 12, 17), splendor (*yip'â*, vv. 7, 17).[2]
4. Other lexical connections. Several homonymous roots occur: *ḥālal*, "to bore, pierce" (vv. 8, 9), is answered with *ḥillēl*, "to desecrate" (vv. 7, 16, 18); *šaḥat*, "the Pit, grave" (v. 8), is echoed by *šiḥat*, "to be shattered, appalled" (v. 17).
5. Complementarity of genre. Within the canonical context, ch. 28 is placed after two oracles against Tyre, both of which also consist of oracles of doom plus lament. This text exploits this division most fully.
6. Formulaic punctuation. The refrain of inevitable and permanent doom that breaks up the oracles against Tyre into three parts (26:21; 27:36; 28:19) reflects the disposition of the editors toward these oracles. The fact that this refrain occurs only at the end (v. 19) suggests that the formulae in vv. 10-11 should be understood as transitional signals rather than markers of separate prophecies.

A holistic approach to the text may yield further dividends if one recognizes beneath the surface of the oracle a preprophetic tradition that has been utilized and reshaped for Ezekiel's polemical purposes. Hints of the underlying story may be recognized in the five-dimensional announcement: *'attâ 'ādām*, "You are merely a human being" (v. 2); *ḥākām 'attâ*, "You are wise" (v. 3); *'attâ ḥôtēm*, "You are the signet" (v. 12); *'attâ kĕrûb*, "You are

---

2. On this root, which occurs only here in the OT, see the commentary below. In the past scholars have tended to attribute the subthematic connections in particular to later editorial activity. This applies esp. to the references to Tyre's trade (vv. 5, 18) and the ruler's wisdom (vv. 3-5, 12, 17a-b), which, if deleted, eliminate the major connections. See Hossfeld, *Untersuchungen,* pp. 153-83, esp. 181; Garscha, *Studien,* pp. 160-64, who credits these segments to the same hand that inserted the commercial list in ch. 27. However, Tyre's trade and the manner in which she pursued it constitute the major thematic link with the prophet's words against the city. The pairing of *rĕkullâ* and *ḥayil* in 28:5 echoes 26:12 and summarizes the long commercial list in 27:12-25. Since the king of Tyre embodies the collective spirit of the city, the references to his commercial ventures are not as unexpected in this chapter as some would imagine. On the contrary, his hubris is fed by his mercantile success. Cf. A. J. Williams, "The Mythological Background of Ezekiel 28:12-19?" *BTB* 6 (1976) 49-61.

a cherub" (v. 14); *tāmîm 'attâ,* "You were blameless," followed by *miyyôm hibbārĕ'āk,* "from the day you were created" (v. 15). Ezekiel has apparently taken a preexistent tradition of a primeval royal figure, divinely endowed with special status and nobility, and recast it into an oracle of judgment because a historical figure (the king of Tyre) has perverted what was his by divine gift into an occasion for hubris.[3]

A holistic approach to the chapter may also be defended from a generic point of view. Although the two subsections bear the marks of different genres, if one treats 28:1-19 as a unit, one observes the prophetic exploitation of the motif of reversal at its best: because of hubris, a colossal figure is reduced to nothing. Ezekiel achieves this rhetorical effect by skillfully incorporating the features typical of biblical satire: (1) It contrasts the sinner's inflated self-esteem, expressed through direct quotation (v. 2), with the humiliation awaiting him (v. 19); (2) it recognizes the qualities in the sinner that have made his rise possible, and paints them in positive strokes (vv. 3-4, 12, 14-15, 17); (3) it describes the sinner's wealth and power by cataloguing articles he cherishes (symbolized by the king's pectoral, v. 13); (4) it employs metaphorical imagery to intensify the reversal (v. 14).[4] But the prophet does not simply tell the story *about* the sinner; it is addressed *to* him. Furthermore, through direct quotation of the addressee's thoughts and detailed description of his wisdom and wealth, the prophet draws the audience into the mind and values of the king. But this is a rhetorical ploy, exposing the hedonism of the audience, and warning them of their own destiny if they persist in their egotistical ways.

(1) The Announcement of Doom for the Prince of Tyre (28:1-10)

1 *The following message of Yahweh came to me:*
2 *"Human, say to the prince of Tyre: 'Thus has the Lord Yahweh declared: Because you have become arrogant, and have said, "I am a god, and I occupy the seat of gods in the heart of the seas" — though you are merely a human being, and no god at all — and you have*

---

3. For a fuller development of this thesis see K. Jeppesen, "You are a Cherub, but no God!" *SJOT* 1 (1991) 83-94. Cf. J. Van Seters, "The Creation of Man and the Creation of the King," *ZAW* 101 (1989) 335-39. For a contrasting stichometric approach see O. Loretz ("Der Sturz des Fürsten von Tyrus [Ez 28,1-19]," *UF* 8 [1976] 455-58; idem, "Der Wohnort Els nach ugaritischen Texten und Ez 28,1-2.6-10," *UF* 21 [1989] 259-67).

4. The rhetorical use of reversal usually involves reductive use of animal imagery (cf. Pharaoh as a sea monster in 29:3). Here the king is portrayed as a cherub, generally perceived as composite animal figures, on which see ch. 1. For a discussion of prophetic satire and the role of these features therein see D. Fishelov, "The Prophet as Satirist," *Prooftext* 9 (1989) 195-211.

claimed[5] the intelligence of gods. 3 *Look, you are indeed wiser than Daniel.[6] No secret[7] baffles you.[8] 4 By your wisdom and your understanding you have gained wealth for yourself and you have accumulated gold and silver in your treasuries. 5 By your superior wisdom through your trade you have increased your riches, but on account of your wealth you have become arrogant.*

6 *Therefore, thus has the Lord Yahweh declared: Because you claimed the intelligence of gods,[9] 7 therefore, look! I am bringing strangers[10] against you — the most ruthless nations.[11] They will unsheathe their swords[12] against the magnificence of your wisdom,[13] and they will desecrate your splendor. 8 They will send you down to the Pit, and in the heart of the seas you will die the death[14] of the slain. 9 Will you insist on claiming, "I am a god," even in the presence of your killers?[15] But you are merely a human being, and no god at all, in the hands of those who strike you down?[16] 10 You will die the death of the uncircumcised at the hands of strangers, for I have spoken! The declaration of the Lord Yahweh.' "*

5. On *nātan* meaning "to treat, regard as," see Gen. 42:30; 2 K. 9:9.

6. Kethib *dn'l;* Qere *dny'l*. LXX Δανιηλ and Akkadian counterparts *(Da-ni-èl* at 18th-century-B.C. Mari; Bab. *Dan-i-là)* demonstrate that the Semitic pronunciation was Daniel, not Danel. Cf. E. Lipiński, *VT* 28 (1978) 233.

7. LXX ἤ σοφοί reads *kol sātûm* as *ḥăkāmîm,* apparently under the influence of the following verses.

8. *'ămāmûkā* is an unusual pl. form. The pl. suggests that *sātûm* was considered a collective.

9. Lit. "You regarded your heart/mind like the heart/mind of gods/God." See the comment on v. 2.

10. The term normally refers simply to foreigners (cf. Ezek. 11:9), but religious overtones are evident here. See the commentary.

11. Cf. 30:11; 31:12; 32:12. *'ārîṣîm* is also associated with *gôyim* in Isa. 25:3. On the superlative significance of the present construction see GKC, §133k.

12. On the idiom *hērîq ḥereb,* lit. "to empty the sword," see 30:11. In contrast to 5:2, 12, and 12:14, the subject here is human rather than Yahweh himself.

13. LXX ἐπὶ σὲ καὶ ἐπὶ τὸ κάλλος τῆς ἐπιστήμης σου, "against you and your fine understanding," expands on MT's odd *yĕpî ḥokmātekā. yĕpî* forms an attractive assonantal pair with *yip'â* in the next line. P. Joüon emends *yĕpî* to *pĕrî,* hence "fruit of your wisdom" ("Notes philologiques sur le texte hébreu d'Ezéchiel," *Bib* 10 [1929] 307).

14. The cognate accusative *māmôt,* "death," with *mût,* "to die," occurs elsewhere only in Jer. 16:4. Cf. the more conventional *māwet* in v. 10 and Num. 23:10 (sg.). On *ḥālāl* as a designation for those who have been murdered or executed see my *Ezekiel: Chapters 1–24,* pp. 227-29.

15. For MT *hōrĕgekā* read pl. *hōrĕgêkā* with LXX, Vulg., Syr.

16. *bĕyad mĕḥalĕlêkā* is unattested in LXX. *mĕḥalĕlêkā* translates "who desecrate you," and should be repointed *mĕḥōlĕlêkā* with LXX[G], Vulg., Targ., Syr.

♦ *Nature and Design*

The boundaries of the first panel of this oracle are set by Ezekiel's customary introductory formulae (vv. 1-2a) and a concluding declaration that Yahweh has spoken, followed by the signatory formula (v. 10b). The message itself follows Ezekiel's common pattern of "halving," each of the parts being signaled by the citation formula (vv. 2, 6). Although many scholars have dismissed the entire oracle as non-Ezekielian, Zimmerli recognizes the authentic prophetic text in vv. 1-2, 6, and most of 7, 8-10.[17] By excluding vv. 3-5, however, he eliminates the link with the previous oracles and destroys the perfect balance between the two parts. The text is admittedly somewhat disjointed, but remarkably, apart from introductory and concluding formulae, the number of words in each is identical: forty-four. Modern standards of stylistic consistency should not be imposed on ancient texts, especially prophetic writings, the shapes of which are determined more by rhetorical and homiletical considerations than by Western rules of literary composition.

The manner in which the addressee is introduced and the employment of the sequence *ya'an . . . lākēn,* "Because . . . therefore," establishes this oracle clearly as a judgment speech to an individual.[18] The first part (vv. 2-5) functions as the accusation, the second (vv. 6-10) as the pronouncement of judgment. Most oracles of this type display a well-defined structure, but in this instance the prophet rambles, beginning with a quotation of the prince's thoughts, then refuting his words, and finally repeating the *ya'an . . . lākēn* pattern.[19] As in 26:3, the first "Because" is answered in v. 6 not by a divine act of judgment but by a further statement of Yahweh, introduced by *lākēn*

---

17. Zimmerli, *Ezekiel 2,* p. 76. D. E. Gowan opines, "These oracles are almost certainly the work of the prophet Ezekiel" (*When Man Becomes God: Humanism and Hybris in the Old Testament,* PTMS 6 [Pittsburgh: Pickwick, 1975], p. 71). Although he leaves aside the issue of Ezekielian involvement, Loretz (*UF* 21 [1989] 259-67) isolates vv. 3-5 as a secondary prosaic expansion. So also R. R. Wilson, "The Death of the King of Tyre: The Editorial History of Ezekiel 28," in *Love and Death in the the Ancient Near East,* p. 212. Among those who dismiss the oracle, see Hölscher, *Hesekiel,* p. 140. Garscha (*Studien,* pp. 160-61, 306-7) attributes 28:1, 6a, 7-10 to the same editorial hand that produced the accounts of the descent into Hades in 26:19-21; 30:10-12; 31:2b, 14b-18; 32:11-14, 17-28. Vv. 3-5, 6b, 7ba derive from a subsequent wisdom reworking. Hossfeld (*Untersuchungen,* pp. 179) credits the basic text, 28:1-2, 6a, 7-10, to one of the prophet's disciples, with the remainder deriving from a later redactor.

18. The form has been encountered earlier in 17:11-21. See C. Westermann, *Basic Forms of Prophetic Speech,* tr. H. C. White (Philadelphia: Westminster, 1967), pp. 129-68.

19. This irregular style, sounding more like a diatribe than the concisely formulated accusations one expects in such contexts, is reflected in the translation by the anacoluthon. See D. E. Gowan, "The Use of *ya'an* in Biblical Hebrew," *VT* 21 (1971) 168-85, esp. p. 173 n. 1. Cf. the diatribe style in Malachi.

plus the citation formula, "Therefore, thus has the Lord Yahweh declared." Accordingly the second half consists of a summary of the charges against the prince, followed by the anticipated *lākēn* and the detailed announcement of Yahweh's intervention in the life of the prince of Tyre.

(a) Preamble and Accusation (28:1-5)

1-2 Following the usual formulae alerting the reader to a new prophetic event, Yahweh charges Ezekiel to speak directly to the *prince of Tyre*. Although the title *nāgîd* is common elsewhere in the OT, this is its only occurrence in Ezekiel, and the reason for its use here is not clear. Etymologically the expression is related to the verb *nāgad,* which is common in the Hiphil and Hophal stems, meaning "to make known" and "to be made known," respectively. Combining this usage with the employment of *neged* either as a substantive, "what is in front," or a preposition, "before, in front of," suggests that a "*nāgîd* was perceived as one who goes before, a conspicuous person."[20] Outside our text, the title is applied to foreigners only three times: Dan. 9:6; 2 Chr. 32:21; Ps. 76:13. The last reference is especially significant because it pairs *nāgîd* with *malkê 'eres,* "kings of the earth," suggesting that in common usage *nāgîd* could function equivalently to *melek* (or *nāśî'*), hence the easy switch to *melek* in v. 12. But *nāgîd* may have been preferred in this initial position to prevent misunderstanding. In contrast to *melek,* which was used of both earthly and divine rulers, this expression is attested only for humans.[21] At the same time, since the term is loaded theologically, referring primarily

---

20. Cf. BDB, pp. 616-18; *HALAT,* pp. 630-31. Finding a cognate in Arab. *nagada* I, J. van der Ploeg defines *nāgîd* as "the eminent man, the prince" ("Les chefs du people Israël et leur titres," *RB* 57 [1950] 45-47). Cf. A. Alt, who explained *nāgîd* as a charismatic leader "made known, announced, designated" by Yahweh ("The Formation of the Israelite State in Palestine," in *Essays on Old Testament History and Religion,* tr. R. A. Wilson [Garden City, N.Y.: Doubleday, 1968], p. 254). W. Richter identifies five stages in the usage of the term in Israel ("Die *nāgîd*-Formel: Ein Beitrag zur Erhellung des *nāgîd*-Problems," *BZ* 9 [1965] 71-84): (1) In the premonarchic era it applies to persons bound to Yahweh and installed by a prophet for the purpose of delivering Israel. (2) King David claimed the title and bound it to the royal office. By installing his son Solomon as the *nāgîd* an originally religious title was transformed into a political label. (3) After the division of the kingdom, the term was used in northern Israel, but without its military overtones, and with a renewed religious significance. (4) In preexilic Judah the term was used more generally of leaders, including priestly functionaries (cf. Jer. 10:1). (5) In postexilic Judah it was used in both the Davidic (particularly in Chronicles and in messianic prophecies; Dan. 9:25, 26; 11:22; cf. Isa. 55:4) and the more general significance. In the wisdom writings it denotes simply "the nobility."

21. Cf. N. Wyatt, "The Hollow Crown: Ambivalent Elements in West Semitic Royal Ideology," *UF* 18 (1986) 425.

to one designated by God,[22] it anticipates the divine appointment described in the second panel (vv. 12-14).

The charge leveled against the prince of Tyre is simple and direct: *you have become arrogant* (gābah libbĕkā, lit. "your heart has been lifted up"). The phrase gābah lēb appears again in v. 5, creating an effective envelope structure for the accusation, and in v. 17, providing an important link between the two panels of this oracle.[23] Like the previous oracles against Ammon (25:1-7), Moab (25:8-11), and Tyre (26:1-3), the prophet presents the point of view of the target of this satire through direct speech. The prince's statement expresses three fantastic dimensions of his hubris.

First, the king claims to be divine. Scholars are not agreed on whether the declaration 'ēl 'ānî signifies identification with the God El, or serves as an appellation for deity. Those who understand the oracle to have been influenced heavily by Canaanite mythology tend to argue that the king is not merely arrogating to himself the status of divinity; he is identifying with El, known from the Ugaritic texts as the high god of the Canaanites.[24] Support for this view is found in that this is the only occurrence of 'ēl in the book, and in his position on "the seat of the gods in the heart of the seas," in the following line.[25] A more generic interpretation is preferable, however, for several reasons: (1) The following clause, "I occupy the seat of gods ('ĕlōhîm)," employs the generic designation for divinity as the correlative for 'ēl. (2) When the statement is repeated in v. 9, the prophet quotes, 'ĕlōhîm 'ānî, "I am a god." (3) In the present context, the antithesis is not between a lesser god, Baal, or

---

22. S. Shaviv supports Alt in concluding: "the term nāgîd originated not in 'secular' usage ('designated by the ruling king') but in the 'theological' one ('announced by God'), the secular usage being later" ("nābî' and nāgîd in 1 Samuel IX 1–X 16," VT 34 [1984] 111-13).

23. The idiom, which is part of an extensive Hebrew vocabulary of pride, occurs elsewhere in Ps. 131:1; Prov. 18:12; 2 Chr. 26:16; 32:25. Related noun forms of gbh occur in genitive constructions with lēb (Prov. 16:5; 2 Chr. 32:26). Other phrases from the same semantic field include gĕbah 'ênayim, "haughtiness of eyes," paralleled with rĕhab lēbāb, "arrogant heart" (Ps. 101:5); 'ênê gabĕhût (Isa. 2:11) and 'ênê gĕbōhîm (Isa. 5:15), "eyes of haughtiness"; gōbah rûah, "haughtiness of spirit," contrasted with šĕpal rûah, "lowliness of spirit" (Prov. 16:18-19); gĕbah rûah, "haughtiness of spirit," contrasted with 'erek rûah, "length of spirit" (Eccl. 7:8); gōbah 'ap, "haughtiness of nose" (Ps. 10:4). See further Gowan, When Man Becomes God, pp. 20-21; R. Hentschke, TDOT, 2:359; H.-P. Stähli, THAT, 1:396.

24. Cf. Pope, El in the Ugaritic Texts, pp. 98-99; R. J. Clifford, The Cosmic Mountain in Canaan and the Old Testament, HSM 4 (Cambridge: Harvard University Press, 1972), pp. 168-70; Wyatt, UF 18 (1986) 428; Loretz, UF 8 (1976) 456-57; K. Yaron, "The Dirge over the King of Tyre," ASTI 3 (1964) 48.

25. Elsewhere Ezekiel always speaks of God as 'ĕlōhîm. Cf. Isaiah's use of El as a divine name and his identification of El with Yahweh in Isa. 43:12; 45:22; 46:9. Cf. the residence of El in the Ugaritic texts "at the source(s) of the rivers, amid the springs of the two oceans" (CTA, 4.4.21-22; 6.1.33-34; 17.6.47-48). See Clifford, Cosmic Mountain, p. 170.

any other deity claiming the status of El, and the high god, but between a human *('ādām)* and deity.[26] (4) Although El may have been the head of the pantheon in 2nd-millennium-B.C. Ugarit, the patron deity of Tyre was Melkart, also known as Baal Shamem.[27] (5) The syntax argues for a generic interpretation. The predicate-subject word order of *'ēl 'ānî* contrasts with Yahweh's oft-repeated self-introduction, *'ănî yhwh,* "I am Yahweh."[28] Perhaps the prophet uses *'ēl* to heighten the sense of hubris. This prince is not merely claiming the status of the patron Melkart; he is also claiming equality with the head of the pantheon.

To Ezekiel and all orthodox Yahwists, to claim divinity is to identify oneself with Yahweh. But this claim might even have shocked Phoenicians. Whereas the notion of divine kingship was common in Egypt, this was not the case in either Mesopotamia or the Levant.[29] The claim may also allude intentionally to the name of the king at this time, Ethbaal III, whose name meant "Baal is with him" (*'etba'al,* at least according to Hebrew vocalization), or to his successor, known from Josephus as Baal.[30]

Second, the king claims divine authority. From his position in the heart of the seas, he imagines himself to be seated on the throne of gods. The term *môšāb* refers not to a dwelling place but to the object on which one sits, viz., a throne.[31] The location of this throne *in the heart of the seas (bĕlēb yammîm)* has no connection with El's dwelling place at the source of the two rivers,[32] but refers simply to the city's insular situation (cf. 27:4, 25-26, 32). Since the

26. A similar contrast is evident in Isa. 31:3 and Hos. 11:9.

27. So also J. Morgenstern, "The King-God Among the Western Semites and the Meaning of Epiphanes," *VT* 10 (1960) 141-42.

28. A close analogue to the present statement occurs in Hos. 11:9, *kî 'ēl 'ānōkî wĕlō' 'îš,* "For I am a god, not a man." Cf. Andersen, *Hebrew Verbless Clause,* pp. 39-45, rules 1 and 3. Zimmerli's reference (*Ezekiel 2,* p. 78) to Yahweh's self-introductory declarations in Isaiah (41:4; 42:6; 43:11; 45:22; 46:9) overlooks this distinction. Cf. the comments of Hossfeld, *Untersuchungen,* p. 166.

29. On the subject of divine kingship in Egypt and Babylon see H. Frankfort, *Kingship and the Gods* (repr. Chicago: University of Chicago Press, 1978); on kingship in Canaan see J. Gray, "Canaanite Kingship in Theory and Practice," *VT* 2 (1952) 193-220.

30. See *Ag. Ap.* 1.21, §156. The latter was actually Baal II, who ruled Tyre after Nebuchadrezzar's siege from 573 to 564. See Katzenstein, *History of Tyre,* pp. 332-34. A predecessor by the same name ruled Tyre in the days of Esarhaddon (*ANET,* pp. 302-3). Ethbaal III ruled Tyre from 591 until the end of Nebuchadrezzar's siege of the city in 573. See Katzenstein, *History of Tyre,* pp. 324-32. Ethbaal I was the Sidonian father of Jezebel (1 K. 16:31). On the form *'etba'al* see Fowler, *Theophoric Personal Names,* p. 127. Ethbaal is transliterated Ιθώβαλος by Josephus, *Ag. Ap.* 1.18, 21, §§123, 156. Akkadian sources render the name Tuba'lu. See *ANET,* p. 287.

31. With *môšab 'ĕlōhîm* cf. Ugar. *m[ṯ]b il (CTA,* 4.1.13). This is the only OT occurrence of this cognate accusative with *yāšab.*

32. See n. 25 above.

dwelling places of gods were generally perceived to be located on prominent mountains (cf. Ps. 48:2-3 [Eng. 1-2]), the prince of Tyre imagines his island fortress rising out of the seas and becoming some such mountain, which might have justified his arrogation to himself of authority belonging to deity. How this illusion of divine power was exercised we are not told, though v. 5 hints at high-handed mercantile practices. But the arrogant claim is interrupted by Yahweh's direct rejoinder, *though you are merely a human being, and no god at all,* viz., of the genus *'ādām,* not *'ēl.*[33] The king may imagine himself enthroned among the gods, but God sees reality for what it is, not what egomaniacs perceive it to be.

Third, the king claims divine intelligence. Unlike the previous statements, this claim is cast in the form of a charge by the prophet. *wattittēn libbĕkā kĕlēb 'ĕlōhîm* translates literally, "you regarded your heart/mind[34] like the heart of gods."

3-5 The train of thought is interrupted with a second rejoinder, which does indeed concede superior intelligence to the prince. He may not have the "heart" of deity, but he is *wiser than Daniel.* While some view this person as a legendary extrabiblical character, as in 14:14, Ezekiel hereby refers to his fellow Hebrew exile, who has distinguished himself in the court of Nebuchadrezzar, and whose reputation for wisdom as well as piety has spread among the exiles.[35] There is no reason why a person could not have established a reputation for excellence in both areas.[36] The book of Daniel portrays this young Hebrew as an exceptionally gifted man from whom no secrets are hidden (Dan. 2:19-23; 4:7-8; 5:13-14; etc.). In any case, the term *ḥokmâ* was multinuanced,[37] and to ancient Near Easterners wisdom, the key to success,

33. Cf. Isaiah's characterization of the Egyptians, who had made similar boasts in Isa. 31:3.

34. The context requires that *lēb* be treated primarily as the seat of thought rather than the emotions. On this use of *lēb* see Eichrodt, *Theology,* 2:142-44; P. Joyce, *Divine Initiative and Human Response in Ezekiel,* JSOTSup 51 (Sheffield: JSOT Press, 1989), p. 108. Hossfeld (*Untersuchungen,* p. 169) sees *lēb* as reduced almost to a personal pronoun.

35. See my *Ezekiel: Chapters 1–24,* pp. 447-49, for discussion and literature on the subject. So also Alexander, "Ezekiel," pp. 880-81. H. G. May ("Ezekiel," p. 137) proposes a revision of an original Ezekielian allusion to Danel in the light of the Hebrew Daniel tradition ("The King in the Garden of Eden: A Study of Ezekiel 28:12-19," in *Israel's Prophetic Heritage,* Fest. J. Muilenburg, ed. B. W. Anderson and W. Harrelson [New York: Harper & Bros., 1962], pp. 167-68).

36. Cf. H.-P. Müller, "Magisch-mantische Weisheit und die Gestalt Daniels," *UF* 1 (1969) 79-93.

37. The term could denote skill in a craft (cf. Exod. 35:30-35), academic understanding (1 K. 5:9-14 [Eng. 4:29-34]), shrewdness (1 K. 3:16-28), administrative ability (Deut. 34:9), and ethical and religious wisdom (Prov. 1:2-7; 2:2).

involved both intellectual power and prudence. Daniel had risen to the top in the Babylonian court because of his wisdom. According to vv. 4-5, the prince of Tyre had the same gift in superior measure, but he was not satisfied with being at the top of a human court; he needed to rule over the gods as well.

The Tyrian king's wisdom is described in extravagant terms. On the one hand, he possesses special insight into the secrets and mysteries hidden from ordinary humans.[38] But what impresses the prophet about the prince's wisdom is the material success it brought him. The present pairing of *ḥokmâ* with *tĕbûnâ*, "understanding," is typical of the wisdom writings (cf. Prov. 8:1; 21:30; etc.), confirming *lēb*'s function here as the seat of mental activity. A wise man is clever, able to govern his life in such a way that desired goals are met. The gold and silver accumulated in the prince of Tyre's treasuries provide concrete proof of his administrative and commercial acumen. Indeed, we now learn that the prosperity that had been such a prominent motif in the foregoing oracles was the result of deliberate and official royal policy.[39] Significantly, the prophet castigates him neither for his shrewdness nor for his amassed wealth. Neither brilliance nor riches is reprehensible; the problem arises in his response. The wisdom that had brought him his wealth led to hubris. It was this inordinate pride that provoked Yahweh's ire.

(b) The Sentence (28:6-10)

6 The textual and conceptual distance from the original accusation (v. 2) to the announcement of the sentence requires a recapitulation of the basic charge before the divine response is pronounced: the prince has claimed the status of deity. The prophet focuses the audience's attention on Yahweh's reaction by opening with *hinĕnî,* "Behold me!" If the prince has the audacity to claim prerogatives of deity, then let him prepare for a direct confrontation with the divine Lord of history, who commissions his agents to carry out a sentence most appropriate for the offense. But first the executioners must be introduced.

7-8 In contrast to the previous oracle, where Nebuchadrezzar was named, here the agents are referred to vaguely as *strangers (zārîm)* and

---

38. *sātûm* derives from a root meaning "to stop up, to close off," hence something undisclosed (2 K. 3:19, 25; Dan. 8:26; 12:4). Targ. renders the term *rāz,* "mystery." *ʿāmam* is a rare verb, occurring elsewhere only in Ezek. 31:8 and Lam. 4:1. It means lit. "to be dark," but it is used here in the sense of "to be concealed." The root occurs in Judean Aramaic and is cognate to Arab. *ğamma,* "to be covered, concealed." Cf. G. R. Driver, *Bib* 19 (1938) 177.

39. Cf. Solomon's appointment by Yahweh as *nāgîd* over Israel (1 K. 1:35), and the traditional association of his wisdom with trade and wealth (1 K. 10). R. R. Wilson (in *Love and Death,* pp. 216-17) argues that the editor responsible for inserting vv. 3-5 had Solomon in mind.

ominously as *the most ruthless of nations* (*'ārîṣê gôyim*). The verb *'āraṣ* denotes "to cause to tremble, to strike terror."[40] Although the vocabulary is slightly different, this expression may be understood as a shorthand description of Deut. 28:49-52, which spells out in great detail the barbaric treatment of a conquered people.

The assault on the prince involves three actions, which, while directed at a human monarch, reflect the treatment that images of a deity in the temple would receive from an attacking army. If the king of Tyre would claim the status of a god, then let him put up with the treatment of a god at the hands of invaders. First, the nations will attack the source of the prince's pride, the symbols of his wealth and glory. *yĕpî ḥokmātĕkā* (lit. "the beauty of your wisdom") refers to the magnificence of Tyre with its beautiful buildings and other treasures, made possible through the prince's shrewd commercial enterprises. Second, the invaders will *desecrate* the prince's radiant splendor. The choice of *ḥillēl*, "to profane, desecrate," ascribes to the action a fundamentally religious quality. Ezekiel coins a new word to identify the object of desecration, *yip'â*, "splendor," which occurs elsewhere only in v. 17. The expression refers to the radiance, the awe-inspiring glow, inherent in divine and royal items.[41] Third, the strangers will send the prince *down to the Pit*. The use of *šaḥat* for the realm of departed dead substitutes here for its synonym, the more common *bôr*.[42] The last comment in v. 8 clarifies his fate: the prince will exchange his falsely secure position "in the heart of the seas" for the world of the dead. The one who dares to claim the status of deity and demands to live among the gods must join the dead in Sheol. For this man the way up led down.

9-10 The religious allusions continue with the portrayal of the invaders as enemies encroaching upon sacred space and storming the residence of the king/god. But this prince clings desperately to his claims of divinity.

40. See BDB, pp. 791-92; *HALOT*, p. 888.

41. Expressed by Akk. *melemmu* (cf. *AHW*, p. 643; *CAD*, 10/2:9-12). The verb *yāpa'* derives from a root *wp'*, "to shine forth, to send out beams." In religious contexts it was used particularly of theophanic manifestations (Deut. 33:2; Ps. 50:2; 80:3-4 [Eng. 2-3]; 94:1). Cf. Akk. *(w)apū*, "to be visible" (*AHW*, pp. 1459-60; *CAD*, 1/2:201-4), which is distinguished from Ugar. *yp'* and Arab. *yapa'a*, "to rise, grow up," and Old South Arab. *yp'*, "to raise oneself." Cf. E. Jenni, *THAT*, 1:753-55; O. Loretz, "Ugaritische und hebräische Lexikographie," *UF* 12 (1980) 284-85.

42. For *bôr* see 26:20; 31:14, 16; 32:18-30. *šaḥat* occurs with this meaning in Isa. 38:17; 51:14; Jon. 2:7; Ps. 16:10; 30:10 (Eng. 9); 49:10 (Eng. 9); 55:24 (Eng. 23); 103:4; Job 18:30; 33:22, 24. For discussion see Tromp, *Primitive Conceptions*, pp. 69ff.; L. J. Stadelmann, *The Hebrew Conception of the World*, AnBib 39 (Rome: Biblical Institute Press, 1970), pp. 167-68; M. H. Pope, "The Word *šaḥat* in Job 9:31," *JBL* 83 (1964) 269-78; idem, "A Little Soul-Searching," *Maarav* 1 (1978) 25-31. In 19:4, 8 Ezekiel had used *šaḥat* of a trap for game. Cf. Held (*JANES* 5 [1973] 173-90), who distinguishes between *šaḥat* I, "pit, netherworld," and *šaḥat* II, "net."

He is a god; no enemy may challenge him in his sanctuary. However, the delusion is negated by Yahweh's own rebuttal: the king of Tyre is a mere mortal, and will not escape the ultimate indignity: desecration and death at the hands of strangers. Indeed, in his disgraceful death he will join the ranks of *the uncircumcised (ʿărēlîm)*. This expression recurs in 31:18 and is given more attention in 32:17-32. Since Phoenicians, like most other ancient Near Easterners, practiced circumcision,[43] Ezekiel's usage of the term is metaphorical. In Israel circumcision was the sign and seal of membership in the covenant community (Gen. 17), which in time became a symbol of cultural superiority. To call anyone "uncircumcised" was an insult. As far as Ezekiel is concerned, for this man to be sentenced to join the uncircumcised meant being consigned to the most undesirable compartment of the netherworld, along with other vile and unclean persons.[44] The concluding declaration and signatory formula seal the prince's fate.

(2) The Lament over the King of Tyre (28:11-19)

11 *The following message of Yahweh came to me:* 12 *"Human, raise a lament over the king of Tyre, and say to him:*
'Thus has the Lord Yahweh declared: You are the signet[45] of perfection,[46] full of wisdom,[47] and the ultimate in beauty.[48] 13 *You were in Eden, the garden of God. Every kind of precious stone adorned you[49]*

---

43. J. M. Sasson, "Circumcision in the Ancient Near East," *JBL* 85 (1966) 473-76; T. Lewis and C. Armerding, *ISBE*, 1:700-702.

44. On the subject see A. Lods, "La 'mort des incirconcis,' " *CRAIBL* (1943) 271-83; Block, *BBR* 2 (1992) 123-24.

45. I follow the versions and most scholars in repointing MT's participle *ḥôtēm*, "sealing," as *ḥôtam*, "seal, signet." So also NRSV, NJPS, etc. REB "You set the seal on perfection" follows G. R. Driver, *Bib* 35 (1954) 159.

46. The versions appear to have read *toknît* as *tabnît*, "pattern." Yaron (*ASTI* 3 [1964] 35) follows Hölscher (*Hesekiel*, p. 141) in deleting the expression entirely. Driver (*Bib* 35 [1954] 158-59) revocalizes as *taknît* on the basis of Akk. *taknû, taknîtu*, "careful preparation, correctness, perfection." Cf. von Soden's "loving care" (*AHW*, p. 1344b); *CAD*, 8:540. For discussion of the Akkadian connection see Garfinkel, *Akkadian Influences*, p. 135.

47. *mālēʾ ḥokmâ* is missing in LXX, perhaps because the translators found it incomprehensible in the context. Zimmerli (*Ezekiel 2*, p. 82) deletes the phrase as one of many secondary insertions in the chapter.

48. As in Lam. 2:15, LXX καὶ στέφανος κάλλους, "and a crown of beauty," and Syr. *klylh* concretize MT *ûkĕlîl yōpî*.

49. *mĕsukātekā*, from *skk*, "to cover." Cf. LXX ἐνδέδεσαι, "you bound on"; Vulg. *operimentum*, "covering." Symmachus περιεφρασε σε may support a derivation from *sûk*, "to hedge about." Both *sukkâ* in Gen. 33:10 and *mĕsûkâ* in Mic. 7:4 mean "fence." MT's strange vocalization suggests that the Masoretes also had difficulty with the word.

*— carnelian, peridot, and moonstone; topaz, onyx, and jasper; lapis
lazuli, turquoise, and emerald*[50] *— along with gold,*[51] *the craftsmanship of your beauty,*[52] *and your mountings in you.*[53] *They were firmly
set*[54] *on the day that you were created.* 14 *You*[55] *are the anointed*[56]
cherub; as the guardian I had appointed you.[57] *You were on the holy*[58]
mountain of God. You walked back and forth[59] *among stones of fire.*

Yaron's suggestion of a miswriting of *msktk* for *bkstk* (*ASTI* 3 [1964] 37-38) remains a
possibility.

50. MT takes *ûzāhāb* with the preceding (so also Targ. *mšq'n bdhb,* "set in gold").
The remainder of the verse is extremely obscure, and any rendering is provisional.

51. Because the enumeration destroys the parallelism of *kol-'eben yĕqārâ
mĕsukātekā,* "Of precious stones of every kind was your garment," and *wĕzāhāb mĕle'ket
tuppêkā,* "and of gold was it woven," Zimmerli (*Ezekiel 2,* pp. 82-84) removes the list as
a late gloss, but this deletion is unwarranted.

52. The inconsistency in the versional renderings of *mĕle'ket tuppêkā* reflects the
phrase's difficulty: LXX καὶ χρυσίου ἐνέπλησας τοὺς θησαυρούς σου, "you filled your
treasuries"; Syr. *wdhb' mlyt byt gzyk,* "and gold filled your storehouses"; Targ. expands
freely. Yaron (*ASTI* 3 [1964] 34) transposes *t* and *k,* reading *ml't twk whms,* "you were
filled with oppression and violence." Cf. the pairing of *tôk* and *hāmās* in Ps. 72:14. AV
"thy tabrets" assumes a derivation from *tāpap,* "to beat." Cf. Fohrer (*Ezechiel,* p. 161),
"hand drum." REB "jingling beads" follows G. R. Driver ("Uncertain Hebrew Words,"
JTS 45 [1944] 14). My translation derives *tuppêkā* from *ypy/wpy,* "to be beautiful." Cf.
Vulg. *opus decorus tui.* See further the commentary.

53. *BHS* treats *bāk* as dittography. The Hebrew is difficult.

54. On the basis of meter and its absence from LXX and Syr., Zimmerli deletes
kônānû as a secondary expansion; but, as Allen suggests (*Ezekiel 20–48,* p. 91), one hears
here an echo of *toknît* in v. 12.

55. MT's fem. form *'att* is an orthographic error for *'attâ* (cf. Targ.). *BHS* and
many commentators (cf. NRSV) follow LXX μετά and Syr. *'m* in reading *'att* as *'et,* "with."
Out of more than 740 cases of the second masc. sg. pronoun, the present defective form
occurs elsewhere only in Num. 11:15 and Deut. 5:24. For a full discussion of the present
textual problem see J. Barr, " 'Thou art the Cherub': Ezekiel 28.14 and the Post-Ezekiel
Understanding of Genesis 2–3," in *Priests, Prophets and Scribes,* Fest. J. Blenkinsopp,
ed. E. Ulrich, et al., JSOTSup 149 (Sheffield: JSOT Press, 1992), pp. 213-17.

56. LXX omits *mimšah hassôkēk.* Vulg. *extentus et protegens* derives the first
word from *māšah,* "to measure." Cf. Symmachus, καταμετρημένος. Syr. *dmšyh wmtl* and
several Greek mss. (cf. Ziegler, *Ezechiel,* p. 223) reflect *māšah,* "to anoint." Targ. paraphrases, "You are a king anointed for the kingdom."

57. Interpreting the *waw* on *ûnĕtattîkā* as an emphatic *waw* with the verb in the
postposition, as in the remainder of this verse; see Dahood, *Psalms,* 3:400-401; van Dijk,
Ezekiel's Prophecy, p. 120. On LXX's omission of the *waw* see Barr, in *Priests, Prophets,*
p. 219.

58. Zimmerli (*Ezekiel 2,* p. 85) deletes *qōdeš* in spite of its unanimous attestation
in the versions.

59. LXX omits *hithallākĕtā.* Zimmerli (*Ezekiel 2,* p. 86) follows Syr. in attaching
the verb to v. 15.

15 You[60] were blameless in your behavior, from the day you were created, until misconduct[61] was found in you. 16 In the abundance of your trade you were filled[62] to the core[63] with violence,[64] and you sinned. So I banished you[65] from the mountain of God and destroyed you,[66] O guardian[67] cherub, from the midst of the stones of fire. 17 You became arrogant because of your beauty, and corrupted your wisdom for the sake of your splendor. So I cast you to the ground, and made a spectacle of you before kings,[68] that they might stare at you.

18 By the magnitude of your iniquities[69] in your unscrupulous trade you have desecrated your sanctuaries.[70] So I sent fire out from your midst, and it consumed you. I reduced you to ashes on the ground, in the sight of all who gazed on you. 19 All who know you among the peoples are appalled over you. You have become a horror; you will be no more forever.' "[71]

60. Zimmerli (*Ezekiel 2,* p. 86) deletes *'attâ* with Syr. and links *hithallēk* from the previous verse with *tāmîm.*

61. On the archaic accusative case ending on *'awlātâ* see GKC, §90g; Bauer-Leander, *Grammatik,* §§65t, 75g. Cf. Hos. 10:13; Ps. 125:3; 92:16 Qere. *'awlātâ* is a variation of *'āwel* (v. 18), a favorite word in Ezekiel. See 3:20; 18:8, 24, 26 (bis); 33:13 (bis), 15, 18.

62. On MT *mālû* for *mālě'û* see GKC, §75qq. Cf. 39:26. The pl. form calls for interpreting *tôkěkā* as a pl., "all who are in you." LXX and Syr. read Piel, "you filled." Zimmerli (*Ezekiel 2,* p. 86) suggests that the original *t* fell out through haplography.

63. Lit. "your midst."

64. On *ḥāmās* see 7:23; 8:17; 12:19.

65. LXX καὶ ἐτραυματίσθης assumes *wattěḥullal,* "and you were pierced/killed." In keeping with its reading of v. 14, LXX attempts to harmonize Ezekiel's account with Gen. 2–3 by distinguishing between the king and the guardian cherub. The following *min* would be partitive.

66. LXX καὶ ἤγαγέ σε reads MT *wā'abbeděkā* as *wě'ibbaděkā,* assuming a third party as the subject (a second cherub?). Thus REB, NRSV. On the elided *aleph* in MT see GKC, §68k; BDB, p. 2a. On the textual problems see Barr, in *Priests, Prophets,* pp. 217-18.

67. *hassōkēk* is missing in LXX.

68. Targ. adds *'zhr',* "as a warning."

69. The masc. pl. form of *'āwōn,* which occurs nowhere else in Ezekiel, looks suspicious. Reading sg. has considerable mss support. Cf. *BHS;* Zimmerli, *Ezekiel 2,* p. 86. Van Dijk (*Ezekiel's Prophecy,* p. 122) reads the *yod* as an old genitive case ending.

70. Like *'ăwōnêkā* earlier in the verse, *miqdāšêkā* may be erroneously written as a pl.; Syr., Targ., and several Cairo Geniza fragments read sg. If MT is correct, the pl. reflects all the elements that make up the sacred precinct on God's holy mountain, which normally included the temple itself, the walls, and the gardens.

71. Lit. "You shall not be forever."

♦ *Nature and Design*

The interpretive problems posed by Ezekiel 28:11-19 begin with Yahweh's opening command to Ezekiel to raise a lament over the king of Tyre. Following the pronouncement of the death sentence on him in vv. 6-11, a funeral song *(qînâ)* would indeed be appropriate. But even though Ezekiel has shown himself a master of the dirge form, the present oracle deviates markedly from the expected patterns.[72] First, overt expressions of grief are lacking entirely (cf. 2 Sam. 1:26; 1 K. 13:30; Jer. 22:18). Far from grieving the death of the king of Tyre, the concern of this text is to vindicate Yahweh in his judgment upon the man. Indeed, the oracle sounds more like a divine judgment speech than a lament. Second, the style of this panel is so irregular that it is difficult to decide whether to classify it as prose or poetry. It displays some of the standard components of poetry, but many expected features are missing: the lines are inconsistent in length, balanced parallelism is rare, *waw*-consecutives are common.[73] Third, only a few lines adhere to the so-called 3:2 *qînâ* meter. Efforts to reconstruct a poem on the basis of metrics involve such massive changes that the approach appears fundamentally flawed.[74] Fourth, although hints of the "once-now" scheme are evident,[75] the entire panel is cast in the past tense. Some see here a disintegration of the original lament form,[76] but to consider this a loose usage of the term *qînâ* is preferable.

Although formal structural indicators are absent from vv. 11-19, on the basis of style and content following the preamble (vv. 11-12a) the prophecy proper divides into three parts:

---

72. For the dirge see ch. 19; 26:15-18; 27. See esp. my *Ezekiel: Chapters 1–24*, pp. 591ff. Garr (*ZAW* 95 [1983] 54-75) omits this text in his discussion of the *qînâ* genre.

73. The standard components include heavy use of figurative language, unusual vocabulary (see the textual notes), archaisms (*'awlātâ*, v. 15; *'ăwōnêkā*, v. 18), parallelism (vv. 14c, 16b, 17), the absence of prose elements (*'ăšer, 'et* as *nota accusativi* [though many treat *'et* in v. 14 thus; cf. n. 55 above]), unusual word order (no fewer than nine sentences begin with adverbial modifiers, some with more than one adverbial phrase [v. 18]), and breakup of sterotyped phrases (*gan 'ēden*, v. 13). For further discussion of poetry-prose distinctions see W. G. E. Watson, *Classical Hebrew Poetry: A Guide to Its Techniques*, JSOTSup 26 (Sheffield: JSOT Press, 1984), pp. 44-60.

74. So also G. Widengren, *The Ascension of the Apostle and the Heavenly Book: King and Savior III*, UUÅ 7 (Uppsala: Lundequistska Bokhandeln, 1950), p. 94; Yaron, *ASTI* 3 (1964) 55 n. 1; Gowan, *When Man Becomes God*, pp. 70-71. Cf. H. Jahnow (*Das hebräische Leichenlied*, pp. 222-23) and Zimmerli (*Ezekiel 2*, pp. 87-89) for two different approaches.

75. Note the king's glorious past (vv. 12b-14) and his subsequent demise (vv. 16b-18).

76. Jahnow, *Leichenlied*, pp. 222-23; Zimmerli, *Ezekiel 2*, pp. 87-89.

(a) The king of Tyre's superlative wealth and exalted status (vv. 12b-14). The description is imaginative, drawing heavily on mythological traditions.

(b) The king of Tyre's hubris and Yahweh's response (vv. 15-18). The text is irregular but not chaotic as it alternates accusations and declarations of judgment:

    i. Accusation   (vv. 15-16a)
    ii. Declaration of judgment   (v. 16b)
    iii. Accusation   (v. 17a)
    iv. Declaration of judgment   (v. 17b)
    v. Accusation   (v. 18a)
    vi. Declaration of judgment   (v. 18b)

(c) The impact of the king's demise (v. 19)

(a) Preamble and the King's Superlative Wealth and Exalted Status
(28:11-14)

11-12a   After opening with the customary word-event formula, Yahweh commands Ezekiel to prophesy by raising a lament *(qînâ)* over the king of Tyre.[77] Instead of addressing the king as *nāgîd,* as he had in v. 2, Yahweh now identifies him as *the king of Tyre (melek ṣôr).* Although some see in the change a shift in focus from the human ruler of the city to its divine patron,[78] a divine addressee is unlikely for several reasons. First, the links between vv. 11-19 and the previous panel, particularly the references to the ruler's trade (vv. 16, 18), point to an identification of this *melek* with the previous *nāgîd.* Second, the present figurative portrayal of the king followed by reasoned divine announcements of judgment finds analogues in chs. 29 (Pharaoh is compared to a dragon) and 31 (Pharaoh is spoken of as a giant tree).[79] Third, in Ezekiel *melek* always refers to an earthly king.[80]

    12b   Ezekiel's portrayal of the king of Tyre's superlative status and wealth involves highly imaginative and colorful imagery. But interpretive problems abound, beginning with the opening announcement: *'attâ ḥôtām toknît.*[81] The king is being compared to a seal or signet. The seals used in the

77. Cf. the similar charge in 27:1.
78. The name of the divine patron of Tyre, Melkart, translates "king of the city." C. M. Mackay, "The King of Tyre," *Church Quarterly Review* 117 (1934) 239-58; J. Dus, "Melek Ṣōr-Melqart," *ArOr* 26 (1948) 179-85.
79. So also Gowan, *When Man Becomes God,* p. 71.
80. See 17:12; 19:9 (Babylon); 29:2-3 (Egypt); 27:33; 28:17 (kings of the earth); 34:24; 37:25 (Davidic ruler).
81. See n. 45 above for *ḥôtēm.* The present word order resembles 27:3, *'ănî kĕlîlat*

ancient world varied greatly in form and design. In Mesopotamia cylinder seals decorated with mythological scenes prevailed,[82] but scarab and stamp seals were more common in Egypt and Palestine. Levantine seals in particular were generally made of precious or semiprecious stones and often featured a skillfully engraved insignia of the owner.[83] Some exemplars that have been discovered have holes bored through them, presumably for a string to wear around the neck; others were fastened on finger rings.[84]

Seals were used for a variety of purposes: as pledges (Gen. 38:18) and adornment (Exod. 28:11, 21, 36), but especially to seal letters (1 K. 21:8) and legal documents (Jer. 32:11-14; Neh. 9:38; 10:1). Seals functioned as insignias of authority and authenticity. Possession of the seal of a superior was a mark of great honor, signifying that one had been deputized to sign documents on his or her behalf.[85] The present portrayal of a human as a seal is odd but not unprecedented.[86] V. 14b suggests that this signet was deputized to represent divinity in paradise.

The exceptional quality of this seal, the king of Tyre, is highlighted by the three modifying expressions, though each poses its own interpretive problems. First, he is a perfectly proportioned and designed seal. *toknît* appears to derive from a root *tkn,* "to measure, regulate."[87] The present form occurs elsewhere only in 43:10, where it denotes the perfect proportions of the temple in Ezekiel's final vision. Royal seals in the ancient world not only were made

---

yōpî, "I am the perfection of beauty." For similar departures from the standard predicate-subject order in verbless clauses of classification see F. I. Andersen, *The Hebrew Verbless Clause in the Pentateuch,* JBLMS 14 (Nashville: Abingdon, 1970), nos. 26, 36, 56, 66, 67.

82. For a study of Mesopotamian seals see D. Collon, *First Impressions: Cylinder Seals in the Ancient Near East* (Chicago: University of Chicago Press, 1987).

83. P. Bordreuil, *Catalogue des sceaux ouest-sémitiques inscrits* (Paris, 1986). For color illustrations see R. Hestrin and M. Dayagi-Mendels, *Inscribed Seals: First Temple Period* (Jerusalem: Israel Museum, 1979).

84. Joseph's ring (Gen. 41:42) probably contained an engraved scarab. Cf. also Est. 3:10, 12; 8:2, 8, 10. On royal seals in the ancient Near East see A. R. Millard, *RLA,* 6:135-38; M. Gibson and R. D. Biggs, *Seals and Sealing in the Ancient Near East* (Malibu: Undena, 1977).

85. See Gen. 41:42; Est. 3:10; 8:8-10. Only the owner of a seal or one deputized by the owner had the right to open documents by breaking a seal. See Rev. 5:1-2.

86. Jer. 22:24 and Hag. 2:23 designate Jehoiachin and Zerubbabel, respectively, as the signets of Yahweh.

87. On the root see my *Ezekiel: Chapters 1–24,* p. 585 (it also occurs in 18:29), and below on 33:17, 20. The proposed Akkadian cognate *taknîtu* is generally derived from *kunnû,* "to treat (a person) with tender care," and is used to describe temples, shrines, and furniture. Accordingly Garfinkel (*Akkadian Influences,* p. 135) renders the present phrase "the tenderly cared for signet."

of precious stones but also, with their exquisitely crafted designs, were themselves works of art. Second, he is *full of wisdom.* Unless *mālē' ḥokmâ* is an abbreviation for "the work of one full of skill,"[88] the description of this seal is awkward. Now Ezekiel's attention seems to have shifted from the signet to the person whom it represents. The emphasis on the king's wisdom provides a clear link with the preceding panel, in which the prince's wealth (and ultimately pride) is credited to his *ḥokmâ.* Third, the seal is *the ultimate in beauty.*[89] Although the versions tend to concretize *kělîl,* Ezekiel's use of the term may reflect further Mesopotamian influence: in Akkadian *kilīlu* was used of gold headbands that were often inlaid with precious stones.[90]

Taken together, this triad of special phrases highlights the status, magnificence, and beauty of the king of Tyre. All three descriptors derive from the realm of metalworking and gemstone cutting. The description leaves no hint of illicit conduct or wrongful attitudes. On the contrary, the king is portrayed as the height of nobility. His identification as a seal hints at a special status, conferred by one higher than himself.

13a The first line compares the domain of the king of Tyre with Eden, the garden of God.[91] In spite of LXX, which translates *gan* as παραδείσος, "paradise," and *'ēden* as τρυφή, "luxury, splendor," in the past scholars have generally explained "Eden" as a loanword from Sum. *eden,* "plain, steppe," via Akk. *edinu.*[92] However, the name is now known to derive from an indigenous West Semitic root, *'dn,* "to enrich, make abundant."[93] Ezekiel, an Israelite, would probably have preferred to describe this garden as "the garden of Yahweh" (Gen. 13:10; Isa. 51:3), but *gan 'ĕlōhîm* avoids the incongruity of associating an alien ruler with the divine patron of Israel.[94] In placing the

---

88. The root *ḥkm* fundamentally denotes skill in a craft, such as was needed in the designing and construction of the tabernacle, its furnishings, and the vestments of the priests (Exod. 25–31; 35–40). Note the description in Exod. 35:30-35 of Bezalel as one filled *(mālē')* with the divine Spirit *(rûaḥ 'ĕlōhîm),* wisdom *(ḥokmâ),* understanding *(tĕbûnâ),* knowledge *(da'at),* and all craftsmanship *(kol-mĕlā'kâ).* The sequel highlights his craftsmanship in precious metals and the engraving and setting of gemstones.

89. Cf. 27:3, where Tyre had claimed to be *kělîlat yōpî,* "perfect in beauty."

90. See *CAD,* 8:358; *AHW,* p. 476.

91. The prophet has broken up a stereotyped phrase, *gan 'ēden,* "garden of Eden" (cf. 36:35; Joel 2:3; as well as Gen. 2:15; 3:23-24).

92. See, e.g., E. A. Speiser, *Genesis,* 2nd ed., AB 1 (repr. Garden City, N.Y.: Doubleday, 1978), pp. 16, 19; C. Schultz, *Theological Wordbook of the Old Testament,* ed. R. L. Harris, et al., 2 vols. (Chicago: Moody, 1980), 2:646.

93. A verbal cognate, *m'dn,* appears in the 9th-century-B.C. bilingual Tell Fekheriyeh inscription opposite Akk. *muṭaḥḥidu kibrāti,* which clearly means "who enriches the regions." See A. R. Millard, "The Etymology of Eden," *VT* 34 (1984) 103-6.

94. Similarly 31:8-9, where both "Eden" and "garden of God" recur in an oracle against the king of Egypt.

king of Tyre in Eden Ezekiel is adapting a well-known biblical tradition of the garden of God as a utopian realm of prosperity and joy.[95]

13b But the prophet's primary concern is the occupant of the garden, so his gaze quickly returns to the figure, magnificently bedecked in gold and jewels. The syntactical construction of the second sentence in v. 13 is complex. The principal clause commences with the reference to every kind of precious stone, but the subject is suspended momentarily in favor of a catalogue of precious stones, after which it is resumed with the reference to the gold bases on which the jewels were mounted. Ezekiel is now obviously mixing his metaphors. The king of Tyre is not only a beautifully crafted jeweled seal himself; he is adorned with a series of gemstones, many of which were exploited by ancient jewelers in the crafting of signets.

This interpretation assumes that the *precious stones* (*'eben yĕqārâ;* cf. 27:22) function as decorations for the king's garments, analogous to the jewels adorning the chestpiece of Israel's high priest.[96] Indeed, a comparison between Ezekiel's list of gemstones and those of the high priest suggests that his catalogue was inspired by this chestpiece (see table 6, p. 107): (1) Both lists group the stones in triads, probably reflecting their arrangement in rows. (2) They start out identically with *'ōdem* and *piṭĕdâ.* (3) Ezekiel's second triad is identical to the fourth triad in Exodus. (4) Although the order is reversed, in both texts *sappîr* and *nōpek* appear together. The most obvious difference is the deletion of one entire triad in Ezekiel.[97] While the identification of some of the gemstones in Ezekiel's list remains problematic, the following equations may be proposed, with varying degrees of certainty.[98]

95. Ezekiel expands on this imagery in 36:33-35. See also the prophetic vision of Zion's future in Isa. 51:3. For a discussion of the garden as a utopian symbol see W. Berg, "Israels Land, der Garten Gottes: Der Garten als Bild des Heiles im Alten Testament," *BZ* 32 (1988) 35-51.

96. See Exod. 28:17-20 and 39:10-13. Not all agree. Deriving *mĕsukāteka* from *sûk,* "to hedge about" (cf. n. 49 above), van Dijk (*Ezekiel's Prophecy,* pp. 116-18) sees here a reference to a protective hedge or fence, analogous to the walls surrounding ancient royal gardens and temple grounds. In 2 Sam. 17:19 the cognate noun *māsāk* denotes a cloth spread over a well (cf. BDB, p. 697). Cf. Ezekiel's own reference to some sort of nautical covering in 27:7 with *mĕkassēk,* a word that refers to a garment in Isa. 23:18.

97. Whether this gap is original or an accidental omission cannot be determined. LXX not only corrected the problem by restoring the the full complement of stones, but also the order of Exod. 28:17-20 and 39:10-13. The translators also added "silver" and "gold" in the very middle.

98. The difficulty is reflected in the inconsistency with which modern translations render the terms. See table 7, p. 108. Of the nine gemstones common to the high priest's and Ezekiel's lists, RSV rendered only two consistently: *piṭĕdâ,* "topaz"; *sappîr,* "sapphire." For further discussion see H. Quiring, "Die Edelsteine im Amtsschild des jüdischen Hohenpriesters und die Herkunft ihrer Namen," *Sudhoffs Archiv für Geschichte der Medizin*

Table 6. A Comparison of the Gemstones in Exodus 28:17-20; 39:10-13; and Ezekiel 28:13		
Exod. 28:17-20 Exod 39:10-13	Ezek. 28:13	Ezek. 28:13 (LXX)
'ōdem	'ōdem	σάρδιον
piṭĕdâ	piṭĕdâ	τοπάζιον
bāreqet	yāhălōm	σμάραγδον
nōpēk	taršîš	ἄνθρακα
sappîr	šōham	σάπφειρον
yāhălōm	yāšĕpēh	ἴασριν
		ἀργύριον
		χρυσίον
lešem	sappîr	λιγύριον
šĕbô	nōpek	ἀχάτην
'aḥlāmâ	bārĕqat	ἀμέθυστον
taršîš		χρυσόλιθον
šōham		βηρύλλιον
yāšĕpēh		ὀνύχιον

1. *'ōdem.* The root alone suggests some red gemstone, probably dark red carnelian (cf. NAB, NJPS, NRSV).[99] Ruby (NASB, NIV) appears not to have been known in the ancient Near East before the Ptolemaic era. Even if it was known, it was too hard to use for engraved stones (Exod. 28:17-20).

2. *piṭĕdâ.* Most translations follow LXX τοπάζιον, "topaz," but this term was used too loosely to be very helpful. Pale green peridot is more

---

und der Naturwissenschaften 38 (1954) 193-213; Lucas, *Ancient Egyptian Materials,* pp. 386-405; J. S. Harris, "The Stones of the High Priest's Breastplate," *ALUOS* 5 (1963-65) 40-62; idem, *Lexicographical Studies in Ancient Egyptian Minerals,* Deutsche Akademie der Wissenschaften zu Berlin Institut für Orientforschung 54 (Berlin: Akademie Verlag, 1961), pp. 95-140; P. L. Garber and R. W. Funk, *IDB,* 2:898-905.

99. Cf. LXX σάρδιον, "sard," a deep orange-red chalcedony, which some view as a variety of carnelian.

Table 7. A Comparison of Modern Versional Renderings of Ezekiel's Jewels

Gems	JB	NAB	NASB	NIV	NJPS	NRSV	REB
ʾōdem	sard	carnelian	ruby	ruby	carnelian	carnelian	sardin
piṭĕdâ	topaz	topaz	topaz	topaz	chrysolite	chrysolite	chrysolite
yohălōm	diamond	beryl	diamond	emerald	amethyst	moonstone	jade
taršîš	chrysolite	chrysolite	beryl	chrysolite	beryl	beryl	topaz
šōham	onyx	onyx	onyx	onyx	lapis lazuli	onyx	carnelian
yāšĕpēh	jasper	jasper	jasper	jasper	jasper	jasper	green jasper
sappîr	sapphire	sapphire	lapis lazuli	sapphire	sapphire	sapphire	sapphire
nōpek	carbuncle	garnet	turquoise	turquoise	turquoise	turquoise	purple garnet
bārĕqat	emerald	emerald	emerald	beryl	emerald	emerald	green feldspar

likely, an interpretation supported by Targ. *yrqn,* the Aramaic word for green.

3. *yāhǎlōm.* The derivation from *hālam,* "to strike hard," suggests a hard stone.[100] Because the priest's stones were engraved, diamond (AV, NASB, JB) is ruled out. Perhaps the whitish moonstone (cf. NRSV) is meant.[101]

4. *taršîš.* LXX χρυσόλιθος, "golden stone," in the Exodus passages points to a yellow stone of some type, probably Spanish gold topaz (cf. REB). The common rendering, beryl (NASB, NJPS, NRSV), which is ordinarily green in color, is influenced by Targ. *krwm ym',* "beryl of the sea."

5. *šōham.* This was probably onyx (so most translations), a translucent chalcedony with alternating bands of black or gray and white. The word itself means "fingernail."

6. *yāšěpēh.* Probably opaque red, brown, or yellow jasper.[102]

7. *sappîr.* This is undoubtedly the dark blue lapis lazuli, used frequently in jewelry. The modern sapphire (so most translations) or blue corundum was scarcely known to the ancients, and in any case was too hard for engraving.

8. *nōpēk.* This uncertain gem was mentioned in 27:16, where it was tentatively identified with turquoise or green feldspar. Based on LXX ἄνθρακα, "burning coal," in the Exodus passages, some suggest a deep red carbuncle (cf. JB) or purple garnet (cf. NAB, REB).

9. *bārěqat.* A derivation from *bāraq,* "to flash, shine," connects the word with "lightning." In Exod. 28:17 LXX renders it σμάραγδος, which is probably to be identified with emerald.

According to the Masoretic punctuation, the list of gemstones concludes with *zāhāb,* "gold," but most interpreters follow LXX and Syr. in linking this term to the following phrase. Although any attempt to interpret *mělě'ket tuppêkā ûněqābêkā bāk* is provisional, the most satisfactory explanation recognizes in *mělě'ket* a reference to the special craftsmanship of a goldsmith.[103] *tuppêkā* is even more puzzling. Like the common noun *yāpâ,*

---

100. Cf. *šāmîr,* "adamant," in 3:9.

101. LXX reads σμάραγδον, a green precious stone.

102. LXX ἴασπιν, "jasper," transliterates *yāšěpēh.* In Exod. 28:1 ἴασπι [wrongly] translates *yāhǎlom,* perhaps under the influence of this verse. Jasper is known to have been used for engraving in Egypt. But since ἴασπι is described as "clear as crystal" in Rev. 21:11, modern jasper, an opaque form of chalcedony, is unlikely.

103. See n. 52 above. *mělā'kâ,* "work, workmanship," is well attested, esp. in descriptions of the construction of the tabernacle and the temple (Exod. 31:3, 5; 35:29-35; 1 K. 7:14; 1 Chr. 22:15; 28:21; 29:5).

"beauty," *tuppîm* seems to derive from a root *wpy*, a by-form of *yāpâ*, "to be beautiful."[104] Accordingly the entire phrase means "the craftsmanship of your beauty." *nĕqābêkā* is equally enigmatic. The derivation from *nāqab*, "to pierce," suggests some aspect of a jeweler's work, perhaps the perforations in the gold for the gemstone mountings.[105]

13c The last clause of v. 13 points back to the origin of the figure. Far from being equal to deity (as claimed in vv. 1-10), the king of Tyre is a product of God's creative work, a conclusion suggested by the verb *hibbārā'ăkā*.[106] The verb *bārā'* always has God as its subject, and it recalls the creation of the first human in Gen. 1:26-28. The final verb, *kônānû*, cast in the plural, assumes the jewels as its subject, completing the picture of the primeval man in paradise, deliberately created and beautifully decorated.

How is the modern reader to envisage the king of Tyre, portrayed in this imaginative fashion? Are these jewels actually part of his costume, like the pectoral worn by the Israelite high priest?[107] Widengren observes that Mesopotamian and Phoenician rulers were equipped with pectorals, and claims a similar chestpiece, square in shape and inlaid with twelve (?) stones, was found in the excavations at Byblos. He suggests that the Davidic rulers of Jerusalem took over the practice from the Palestinian princelets after the conquest of Canaan.[108] But the present pectoral seems to have been inspired

104. The sg. should probably be vocalized *tôpî*, from *tawpay*. In the Ugaritic text RS 22.225, *tp* is paired with *n'm*, "delight, charm." Thus W. F. Albright, *Yahweh and the Gods of Canaan* (repr. Garden City, N.Y.: Doubleday, 1969), pp. 131-32 n. 54. Cf. M. Dahood in *RSP*, 2:375-76. E. Lipiński understands *tp* as a euphemism for penis, the masc. counterpart to the following *nĕqābêkā*, which he relates to *nĕqēbâ*, "female," and metonymically "vulva" ("Les conceptions et couches merveilleuses de 'Anath," *Syria* 42 [1965] 49-50). This anatomical interpretation is present already in Targ.; cf. the quotation from Codex Reuchlinianus (as translated by Levey, *Ezekiel*, p. 84 n. d): "You were in Eden, the garden of the Lord. All kinds of jewels adorned your robe. You saw with your own eyes the ten canopies which I made for the Primal Adam, made of carnelian, topaz, and diamonds; beryl of the Mediterranean Sea and spotted stone, sapphire, emerald, smaragd, and fine gold. They showed him at his wedding all the works of Creation, and the angels were running before him with timbrels and with flutes. So, on the day when Adam was created they were prepared to honor him, but after that he went astray and was expelled from there. You, too, did not take a lesson from him but rather your heart became haughty and you did not reflect wisely on your body, that you are made of orifices and organs which you need for excretion, and it is impossible for you to survive without them. They were designed for you from the day on which you were created."

105. So also Zimmerli, *Ezekiel 2*, p. 85. May's proposed association with Akk. *nakibu* ("Ezekiel," p. 220) is rejected by Garfinkel (*Akkadian Influences*, p. 116).

106. Contra Morgenstern (*VT* 10 [1960] 154), who interprets the Niphal reflexively, i.e., as self-generated.

107. For a reconstruction of this chestpiece see *IBD*, 1:207.

108. Widengren, *Ascension*, p. 95; idem, "Early Hebrew Myths and Their Inter-

by the one that the Israelite high priest wore, suggesting that this king is somehow identified with him. This point raises a different and perhaps more serious question. How could a pagan monarch be dressed in the most sacred garment of the highest Israelite religious official? Surely Ezekiel, of priestly background himself, and many of his hearers would have revolted at the idea. Some have proposed that this part of the oracle was originally directed at the high priest, and only secondarily incorporated into an oracle against the king of Tyre; that is, this is a veiled oracle against Israel's priest.[109]

Ezekiel did indeed often deliver his messages obliquely (e.g., chs. 16, 17, 19, 20, 23), but this interpretation is unlikely for several reasons. First, although others have recognized the cultic context of some of the allusions,[110] the association of "the mountain of God," "the cherub," and "the stones of fire" with Jerusalem is strained. Second, the text does not refer directly to the chestpiece. *měsukâ* is too vague an expression to make this identification; this priestly prophet may have used this word deliberately to prevent identification with the *ḥōšen mišpāṭ,* "breastpiece of judgment" (cf. Exod. 28:15). Third, apart from the list of gemstones, the allusions in the oracle are all either to Gen. 1–3 or to extrabiblical mythologies.[111] The designation of the king as the *ḥôtēm toknît* recalls the creation of the first man as the representative and deputy of God,[112] not the high priest. Eden and the "garden of God" designate the paradisiacal context in which he was placed. Even the appearance of gold and precious stones harmonizes with the primeval antecedent (cf. Gen. 2:12).

---

pretation," in *Myth, Ritual and Kingship,* ed. S. H. Hooke (Oxford: Clarendon, 1958), pp. 166-68. Cf. Yaron, *ASTI* 3 (1964) 39-40. For an illustration of a beautifully designed gold pectoral from ancient Iranian Kurdistan see Amiet, *Art,* fig. 136.

109. Thus Wilson (in *Love and Death,* pp. 214-18), who identifies the "garden of God," and later the "holy mountain of God," with the temple in Jerusalem. The cherub mentioned in v. 14 is viewed as a collective designation for the cherubim in the temple. The firestones (v. 14) are coals of fire on the altar. Vv. 12-14 deal with the installation of the high priest in the temple; v. 15 describes his perfection until his sin; vv. 16-18 announce his punishment. Thus, while being ostensibly directed at the king of Tyre, this dirge was so laced with allusions to the Israelite high priest that his exilic audience, consisting largely of upper-class bureaucrats and priests, could not have missed the real thrust of his prophecy. Even more farfetched is P.-M. Bogaert's view that this oracle, originally applied to the temple and high priest, has been reapplied to Tyre after Alexander captured Tyre because of the resemblance between the cherub and the sea horse ("Le Chérub de Tyr (Ez 28, 14.16) et l'hippocampe de ses monnaies," in *Prophetie und geschichtliche Wirklichkeit im alten Israel,* Fest. S. Herrmann, ed. R. Liwak and S. Wagner (Stuttgart: Kohlhammer, 1991), pp. 29-38.

110. A. A. Bevan sees here the Tyrian sanctuary ("The King of Tyre in Ezekiel XVIII," *JTS* 4 [1903] 500-505). Cf. also Morgenstern, *VT* 10 (1960) 152-54.

111. See below.

112. On this interpretation of the *imago dei* see D. J. A. Clines, "The Image of God in Man," *TynBul* 19 (1968) 53-103.

Fourth, if Ezekiel's audience would recognize the primary target to be the priest, how is it that the editors of Ezekiel's prophecies either failed to do so or twisted the oracle almost beyond recognition? By this interpretation, 28:11-19 belongs more naturally after ch. 11, if not within ch. 8, rather than within the oracles against the foreign nations. Furthermore, the oracles against Judah/Israel concluded in ch. 24; the final verses of the present chapter intend the prophecies against the nations to be interpreted as positive messages for Israel/Judah. Fifth, it is doubtful that either Ezekiel or his audience would have tolerated the image of a pagan king dressed in the most sacred of all Israelite garb. If the prophet resists speaking of Eden as "the garden of Yahweh" (v. 13) to avoid incongruencies, as a priest he would have been even more sensitive about treating a Tyrian king as if he were an Israelite priest.

Even if the link between Ezekiel's list of gemstones and the high priest's chestpiece is strong, the significance of this connection should not be exaggerated, nor blind the reader to the prophet's special adaptation of the imagery for his own rhetorical purposes. The correspondences may indeed have been influenced by the prophet's heritage, but his deviations from the official *Vorlage* make it evident that he has taken the motif in a new and creative direction. He has no interest in identifying the king of Tyre with the high priest of Israel. In this satirical context, the catalogue of gemstones is intended to clarify the phrase *kol-'eben yĕqārâ,* "every precious stone," and to offer concrete evidence of the wealth and splendor of the king of Tyre.[113] The monarch is adorned *(mĕsukâ)* by a dazzling collection of precious stones, perhaps even from head to toe.[114] The jewels were probably not attached to any priestly chestpiece at all, but, like ancient images, inlaid in the figure itself.[115] In this case the stones were firmly fixed in their settings the day this person was created.

14a The status enjoyed by the signet is described by means of three vivid, if enigmatic, statements, each of which is loaded with mythological allusions. First he is identified as a guardian cherub, with wings outstretched. Every one of the four words in this verbless clause is problematic. As already

---

113. On this function of catalogue structure in prophetic satire see Fishelov, *Prooftext* 9 (1989) 201-2. Cf. also T. Jemielity, *Satire and the Hebrew Prophets* (Louisville: Westminster/John Knox, 1992), pp. 96-97.

114. See the winged Egyptian figure covered from top to bottom with eyes/gemstones in O. Keel, *Jahwe-Visionen und Siegelkunst,* SBS 84/85 (Stuttgart: Katholisches Bibelwerk, 1977), figs. 193-94. In Akk. *īnu,* "eye," served also for "jewels." See *CAD,* 7:158; *AHW,* p. 383. Cf. my *Ezekiel: Chapters 1–24,* pp. 100-101.

115. This view assumes that the beautifully crafted gold mentioned in v. 13 refers to the overlay of an image, and that the *nĕqābîm* represent the perforations in the gold in which these stones were set. This interpretation has the added advantage of making sense of the following *bāk,* too readily deleted as a superfluous dittograph.

noted, the first word, *'t*, was misvocalized by the Masoretes as a feminine pronoun because of the absence of the final vowel letter. According to the word order (subject-predicate), *kĕrûb* is construed as definite.[116] The king was not simply one cherub among many; he was *the* cherub par excellence. But what has inspired this vision of the king of Tyre as a cherub in Eden? There seems to be no connection with the cherubim Ezekiel had witnessed earlier transporting the glory out of the temple, nor with the cherubim atop the ark of the covenant in the temple.[117] Even if *mimšaḥ* means "to stretch out,"[118] by using this enigmatic expression, instead of some form of *pāraś,* usually employed to describe the outstretched wings of the temple cherubim (Exod. 25:20; 1 K. 8:7), Ezekiel appears to have deliberately dissociated this figure from those that protected the ark of the covenant. But both Targ. and Syr. support a derivation of *mimšaḥ* from *māšaḥ,* "to anoint,"[119] in which case *hassôkēk* describes his function in the garden, "to cover, screen," that is, to protect or guard it. This interpretation accords with the sense of Gen. 3:24, which has Yahweh strategically stationing sword-wielding cherubim to guard *(šāmar)* the way to the tree of life. Even so, the equation is not total; Ezekiel's cherub is singular, not a plurality, and he walks about *in* the garden, rather than being stationed at the entrance east of the garden.[120]

116. Note the article on the following modifier, *hassôkēk,* as well as in v. 16. Zimmerli (*Ezekiel 2,* p. 85) opines that here *krwb* may have the quality of a proper name.

117. Regarding the former, the vision in ch. 10 involved a plurality of cherubim with a totally different function, and must have resembled the sphinxlike figures commonly carved in the bases of ancient Near Eastern thrones. As for the latter, Wilson (in *Love and Death,* pp. 215-16) finds a link in the root *skk.* Cf. Exod. 25:20; 37:9; 1 K. 8:7; 1 Chr. 28:18; also Yaron, *ASTI* 3 (1964) 31-32. However, the root *skk,* "to cover, screen," is too general to point specifically in this direction. Wilson's interpretation also depends on reading *'t* as a preposition, "with," i.e., the cherub is with the high priest; but see Jeppesen, *SJOT* 1 (1991) 90-92.

118. Thus van Dijk, *Ezekiel's Prophecy,* p. 119; Yaron, *ASTI* 3 (1964) 32.

119. So also Jeppesen, *ASTI* 3 (1964) 91-92; Widengren, *Ascension,* pp. 94-97; T. N. D. Mettinger, *King and Messiah: The Civil and Sacred Legitimation of the Israelite King,* ConBOT 8 (Lund: Gleerup, 1976), p. 271 n. 14. Garfinkel (*Akkadian Influences,* pp. 100-101) treats as plausible a third possibility, viz., to derive *mimšaḥ* from *mšḥ* III, "to shine brightly," hence "cherub of luminosity." Cf. *CAD,* 10/1:354, on Akk. *mašāḫu.*

120. Those familiar with Tyrian art will recognize how natural is Ezekiel's association of a cherubic figure with Tyre. As early as the 10th century Tyrian-style cherubim decorated Solomon's temple (1 K. 6:23-36). The growing collection of Phoenician ivories attests to the prominence of the cherub in Phoenician iconography. Many of these carvings were richly decorated with gemstones. Note esp. the carving of a king-cherub, whose face appears to be the portrait of the king, and under whose feet are seen alternating patterns of stylized tulip flower gardens and mountains, in M. E. L. Mallowan, *Nimrud and Its Remains,* 3 vols. (London: Collins, 1966), vol. 2, figs. 504, 506, 538; Barnett, *Ancient Ivories,* fig. 51. For disussion, see idem, "Ezekiel and Tyre," *ErIsr* 9 (1969) 9.

14b   The second half of v. 14 locates this cherub on *the holy mountain of God (bĕhar qōdeš 'ĕlōhîm)*. The expression "mountain of God" is familiar from the Sinai and Zion traditions,[121] but Ezekiel has neither of these in mind. This statement bears a closer resemblance to Isa. 14:13, which speaks of Helel presumptuously grasping for the throne on *har mō'ēd*, "the mount of the assembly," that is, of the gods. But here our prophet seems again to be mixing his metaphors. How can the cherub be in the garden of God and on the mountain of God at the same time? Two possibilities exist. Either the garden is on the mountain, or the former highlights the paradisiacal aspect of his home while the latter reflects his status, viz., he had direct access to God, the head of the divine assembly. This privilege was necessitated by his role as anointed agent of God, guarding the garden.[122]

The final line depicts the cherub *walking back and forth among stones of fire*. Although some interpret the verb *hithallēk* negatively,[123] this is unlikely. Unlike the carved stationary cherubim that decorated ancient hallways or guarded the entrances of buildings and grounds, this figure walks back and forth, expressing his freedom and especially his supervisory role within this environment.[124] While numerous interpretations have been proposed for the phrase *among stones of fire (bĕtôk 'abnê-'ēš)*, these stones are best understood as decorative, contributing to the magnificence and brilliance of the picture.[125]

---

121. On Sinai traditions see Exod. 3:1; 18:5; 24:13; cf. Exod. 19:3-4, which has Yahweh bringing the people to himself on this mountain. Ps. 48:2-3 (Eng. 1-2) describes Zion as *har qodšô*, "his holy mountain," at *yarkĕtê ṣāpōn*, "the far north," an obvious borrowing from Canaanite. On this text see B. C. Ollenburger, *Zion, the City of the Great King: A Theological Symbol of the Jerusalem Cult*, JSOTSup 41 (Sheffield: JSOT Press, 1987), pp. 45-46. On Zion as the mountain of God see T. E. Mullen Jr., *The Assembly of the Gods: The Divine Council in Canaanite and Early Hebrew Literature*, HSM 24 (Chico, Calif.: Scholars Press, 1980), pp. 154-58.

122. Zimmerli's contention (*Ezekiel 2*, p. 93) that this refers to paradise as a universal mountain in the north (from a Mesopotamian perspective) is impossible, since the paradise motif is unattested in Akkadian literature. On this issue see B. Batto, "Paradise Reexamined," in *Scripture in Context*, vol. 4: *The Biblical Canon in Comparative Perspective*, ed. K. L. Younger, et al., ANETS 11 (Lewiston: Mellen, 1991), pp. 33-66.

123. REB "you walked proudly" follows G. R. Driver's unlikely suggestion (*Bib* 35 [1954] 159), "you strutted proudly, swaggered about." The Hithpael is also used in Gen. 3:8, of God walking up and down in the garden.

124. The same form of the verb is used in Gen. 13:17 of Abraham walking up and down the land, in effect staking his claim to it. See also the surveyors of the land of Canaan in Josh. 18:4 and the satan in Job 1:7.

125. See Gowan, *When Man Becomes God*, p. 82. Some other interpretations are: (1) a palace of fused gemstones, like the one described in *CTA*, 4.6.22-35 (Pope, *El in the Ugaritic Texts*, pp. 99-102); (2) "thunderstones," viz., flint, used to make fire (cf. Ugar. *'abn brq*, on which see F. C. Fensham, "Thunderstones in Ugarit," *JNES* 18 [1959] 173-74); (3) coals of fire *(gaḥĕlê 'ēš)*, associated with the throne chariot in 1:13 and 10:2

If this interpretation is correct, this passage is illuminated by a remarkable analogue in a fragment of the Gilgamesh Epic that describes the arrival of the hero in the garden of the gods:

> He went directly to the [ ] of the garden [*Ḫiṣṣu* enclosure] of the Gods in order to admire (it), as its fruit it carries carnelians, vines are climbing (there) — beautiful to look at — (with a) foliage (made) of lapis lazuli. The(ir) grapes (lit. fruits) — a pleasure to behold — [are made of . . . -stones].

[Break of about 23 lines]

> [ ] cedar [ ] its [. . . are made of] white ston[es] . . . The sea-*laruš* [its . . . are made of] *sâsu*-stones. Instead of thistles (?) and thorny shrubs [their . . . are made of] (red) AN.GUG-stones, (and) the *ḫarubu*-thorns [their . . . are made of] *abarummu*-stones. *Sabû*-stones and haematite [are], [ ]-*ri-e* and pearls (?) [are]. Instead of [are made of] agate (?), of the [ ] sea [ ] While/when Gilgamesh was walking [through the . . . of] this [garden?] he looked up [and] this [ ].[126]

Whatever the origin of Ezekiel's image of the king of Tyre in all his glory, the announcement that Yahweh had appointed *(nātattî)* him to his position in the garden is orthodox.[127] The sovereign Lord of history is also behind the throne of Tyre. The king is Yahweh's officially designated signet, his guardian cherub, his gardener.[128]

(b) The King's Hubris and Yahweh's Response (28:15-19)

Beginning with v. 15, this prophecy sounds more and more like a judgment oracle. Having gone to extravagant lengths to explain the original divinely sanctioned or appointed status of the king, Ezekiel describes his response. In short, his glory went to his head; his soul rotted within him. Vv. 15-18 divide into three parts, each of which consists of an accusation and an announcement

(Yaron, *ASTI* 3 [1964] 38-39); (4) hail and fire as instruments of divine wrath, which Garfinkel (*Akkadian Influences,* pp. 23-27) compares with Akk. *abnū u išāti;* (5) the coals on the altar (Wilson, in *Love and Death,* p. 216). For discussion see Garfinkel, *Akkadian Influences,* pp. 23-27.

126. As translated by A. L. Oppenheim, "Mesopotamian Mythology II," *Or* 17 (1948) 47-48. Cf. *ANET,* p. 89.

127. On *nātan* in the sense of "to appoint," see 33:7 and Num. 14:4; 2 K. 23:5; Jer. 1:5.

128. Cf. M. Hutter, "Adam als Gärtner und König (Gen 2, 8, 15)," *BZ* 30 (1986) 258-62, who compares the king's role with that of Adam in the garden of Eden.

of judgment. The verbs in the latter are all cast as prophetic perfects, imminent future events being treated as already accomplished.

15-16a The first accusation contrasts the king of Tyre's original blamelessness with his latter-day corruption. The use of *tāmîm* immediately after *hithallēk* invites comparison with Noah, who also was "blameless" and "walked with God" (Gen. 6:9), and Abraham, who was charged by God: "Walk *(hithallēk)* before me and be blameless *(tāmîm)*" (Gen. 17:1). But the primary inspiration for Ezekiel's description of the king clearly derives from Israel's creation traditions. The influence of Gen. 1:1–2:4a is evident in the underlying royal ideology and the reuse of the verb *bārā'*, "to create" (cf. v. 13); the motif of the garden and the king's guardianship over it derives from Gen. 2–3.[129] It is also from the latter that Ezekiel draws his image of expulsion because of sin. The success of the king's trading ventures had brought with it a transformation in his character. Instead of fulfilling his charge under God, he practiced misconduct or unrighteousness, was filled with violence, and committed sin *(ḥāṭā')*, notions that will be expanded in the following verses.

16b Yahweh announces his response with two parallel clauses. Although the root *ḥll*, "to pierce, stab," appears in the next verses, the traditional reading of the first verb, *wā'eḥallelĕkā*, "I banished you," is preferable.[130] That *ḥillēl*, "to profane, desecrate," tends to be used in cultic contexts is no objection, since the sanctity of this garden and its keeper have been implicit throughout the preceding description. By his sin, however, the king has violated the sanctity of the garden and rendered himself unfit for his role.[131] Therefore Yahweh (who is the speaker in this oracle) has every right to treat him as profane and to banish him from the garden, and remove him from this glorious environment.

17 In the second accusation, in which Ezekiel identifies the king's fundamental defect, he brings his audience back to the primary notion of the first panel (cf. vv. 2, 7). The king's beauty *(yōpî)* has produced hubris in his heart, and the brilliance of his visage *(yip'â)* has corrupted his rational powers *(ḥokmâ)*. Neither beauty nor wisdom itself is to be disparaged. After all, these

---

129. Van Seters (*ZAW* 101 [1989] 341) reverses the order, proposing that the Yahwist has combined the tradition of the creation of humankind to do the work of the gods (as in the Atraḫasis Epic) with that of Ezekiel's king in the garden of God, who is banished on account of his sin. Regarding the royal ideology, as *imago dei*, *'ādām* was created to represent God and deputized to rule the world for him (Gen. 1:26-28; cf. Ps. 8). Cf. Clines, *TynBul* 19 (1968) 53-103; C. Westermann, *Genesis 1–11*, tr. J. J. Scullion, Continental Commentary (Minneapolis: Augsburg, 1984), pp. 147-55.

130. So also NRSV. Cf. NJPS, "I struck you down."

131. Cf. Israel's defiling of the land with their sin (36:17-18), for which Yahweh expels them.

are qualities with which he was endowed that he might rule the garden for God. Imagining himself to be the lord of this holy mountain, however, he strutted his splendor before the rulers of the world. How appropriate, therefore, that he should also be cast down in their sight (v. 17b; cf. 26:15-18).

The image of Yahweh hurling *(hišlîk)* the king down to the ground is ambiguous. On the one hand, it evokes an iconoclastic picture of an idol being hurled down and lying in ruins on the ground.[132] On the other hand, since *'ereṣ* is also used of the netherworld (26:19-20), the word may function as a variant of *šaḥat,* "Pit," in v. 8.[133] But how far the mighty have fallen! The one who had been appointed by God to be his signet, the guardian and gardener of the divine estate, is banished and consigned to Sheol.

18   In the third accusation the prophet returns to the iniquitous manner *('āwōn)* with which the king pursued his commercial ventures. With the increase in trade[134] had come increased iniquity and unrighteousness, and the consequent defiling of the sacred place. The nature of Yahweh's final judgment is not clear. The syntax suggests that the fire sent by God bursts forth from within the cherub himself and consumes him from the inside out, perhaps implying that sin brings with it its own punishment. Or one may understand *mittôkēkā* more generally as from within the sacred complex, again highlighting the appropriateness of the judgment. Because his responsible walk (v. 14) had turned into an arrogant swagger, the "stones of fire" (v. 14) previously symbols of glory, will flare up and consume him in a final conflagration.

19   The refrain with which the oracle against the king of Tyre concludes bears a horrifying note of finality. The proud ruler, the envy of the nations is gone — forever, leaving the bystanders paralyzed with shock.

♦ Theological Implications

The theological implications drawn from this pair of oracles depend to some extent on one's view of the traditions that underlie them. From where did Ezekiel derive the imagery for these oracles? Discussions of this issue tend to go in several directions. First, the numerous allusions to Gen. 1–3 link this cherub with the first man, Adam of Gen. 2–3. This is most obvious in the setting of the second oracle in Eden, the garden of God. But echoes of the original Adam are evident in the characterization of the prince of Tyre in the first panel and the description of the cherub in the second. Like the king of Tyre, the first man (1) was created by God, (2) was divinely authorized to

132. See the image of Dagon in 1 Sam. 5.
133. This theme will be picked up and developed much more fully in 32:17-32, with reference to the king of Egypt.
134. Cf. *běrōb rěkullātěkā* in v. 16.

rule over the garden as king, (3) not being satisfied with the status of 'ādām, sought or claimed divinity, (4) was punished for this hubris by humiliation and death.

But Ezekiel does not have only Gen. 2–3 in mind. The twofold reference to creation, using the verb bārā' (vv. 13, 15), also links the second panel at least with the first creation account, which is framed by the same verb (Gen. 1:1; 2:4a).[135] Although they play slightly different roles, Ezekiel's cherub is also naturally linked with the sword-wielding cherubim stationed by Yahweh at the entrance of the garden when Adam and Eve are expelled (Gen. 3:24). The LXX reading of v. 14 here suggests that when the man was placed in the garden, a cherub was present as a guardian. Accordingly, Ezekiel may be basing his description of the cherub on a memory of a primeval event in which, when the man was expelled from the garden, the cherub was left in charge. But this reading of Ezekiel is speculative.[136]

Second, during the second temple period, the view developed that Ezek. 28 was based on a tradition of an angelic "fall," closely associated with the "fall" of humanity. Since the time of Origen many conservative Christians in particular have equated the king of Tyre with Lucifer (= Satan), "Brilliant One, son of the morning" (hêlēl ben-šāḥar), mentioned in Isa. 14:12.[137] Accordingly, Ezekiel's prophecy is thought to recount the circumstances of the original fall of Satan, who had previously been one of the cherubim attending the throne of God.[138] But those who interpret the oracle historically

135. The verb is absent from Gen. 2:4b-5, the so-called Yahwist account of creation. Ezekiel's linkage of Gen. 1:1–2:4a with Gen. 2–3 suggests that in his time these two accounts were already conjoined, challenging prevailing scholarly opinion, which identifies Gen. 1:1–2:4a as the Priestly account of creation, and dates this document as post-Ezekielian. According to Albertz (History of Israelite Religion, 2:481-82) the persons behind the Priestly source represented a branch of the reform priesthood that had emerged in the Babylonian exile from the disciples of Ezekiel and had returned to Jerusalem in 520 B.C.

136. So also Barr, in Priests, Prophets, p. 222.

137. For discussion and citations see J. B. Russell, Satan: The Early Christian Tradition (Ithaca: Cornell University Press, 1981), pp. 130-33. This interpretation is evident already in Tertullian (Against Marcion 5.11, 17; cf. Russell, pp. 92-95) and 2 (Slavonic Apocalypse of) Enoch 29:4-5. Although the provenance of the latter is disputed, F. I. Andersen attributes its core at least to a Jewish writer of the 1st century A.D. For the text see OTP, 1:91-97.

138. L. S. Chafer, Systematic Theology (Dallas: Dallas Seminary Press, 1947), 2:33-50; M. F. Unger, Biblical Demonology: A Study of the Spiritual Forces Behind the Present World Unrest (Wheaton, Ill.: Scripture Press, 1952), pp. 15-16; J. D. Pentecost, Your Adversary, the Devil (Grand Rapids, 1969), pp. 11-19; H. C. Lindsey, with C. C. Carlson, Satan Is Alive and Well on Planet Earth (Grand Rapids: Zondervan, 1972), pp. 41-50; M. Green, I Believe in Satan's Downfall (Grand Rapids: Eerdmans, 1981), pp. 36-39; H. Lockyer, Satan: His Person and Power (Waco: Word, 1980), pp. 14-16.

reject this approach.[139] Ezekiel's prophecy is indeed couched in extravagant terms, but the primary referent within the context is clearly the human king of Tyre.[140] In any case, for this prophet and his professional colleagues, as well as for the Hebrew historiographic narrators, human rebellion is problem enough. A detailed treatment of the origin of the demonic is not to be expected from the OT.[141]

Third, scholars have tended to interpret this text mythologically, finding here traditions that have their origins outside mainstream Israelite Yahwism. It is appropriate that external influence should be most apparent in oracles against the foreign nations, and perhaps one should even expect that an oracle against Tyre should draw on Canaanite traditions.[142] Many have also recognized Mesopotamian influences in this text. A Neo-Babylonian account contains a description of human origins with remarkable conceptual links to Ezekiel's account:

> Ea began to speak, he directed his word to Belet-ili, "Belet-ili, Mistress of the great gods, are you. You have created the common people, now construct the king, distinctively superior persons. With goodness envelop his entire being. Form his features harmoniously; make his body beautiful!" Thus did Belet-ili construct the king, distinctively superior persons. The great gods gave the king the task of warfare. Anu gave him the crown; Enlil gave him the throne. Nergal gave him weapons; Ninurta gave him

139. Had he got this far in his commentary on Ezekiel, John Calvin's response to the diabolical interpretation would probably have sounded like his comments on Isa. 14 (*Commentary on the Book of the Prophet Isaiah,* tr. W. Pringle [Grand Rapids: Eerdmans, 1948], 1:442): "The exposition of this passage, which some have given, as if it referred to Satan, has arisen from ignorance; for the context plainly shows that these statements must be understood in reference to the king of the Babylonians [Tyre in our case]. But when passages of Scripture are taken up at random, and no attention is paid to the context, we need not wonder that mistakes of this kind frequently arise. Yet it was an instance of very gross ignorance, to imagine that Lucifer [prince/king of Tyre in our case] was the king of devils, and that the Prophet gave him this name. But as these inventions have no probability whatever, let us pass by them as useless.

140. B. S. Childs observes that the mythological motifs are employed for illustrative purposes only, as extended figures of speech (*Myth and Reality in the Old Testament,* SBT 27 [London: SCM, 1960], pp. 70-71).

141. Not only is the OT remarkably disinterested in demonology (in stark contrast to the extrabiblical world); there is no connection between the OT figure of Satan and such figures as may be considered demonic. See J. K. Kuemmerlin-McLean, "Demons," *ABD* 2:138-40; G. J. Riley, "Demon," *DDD,* 445-55.

142. The efforts to relate this passage to the Ugaritic materials are ubiquitous. Among many cf. Pope, *El in the Ugaritic Texts,* pp. 97ff.; van Dijk, *Ezekiel's Prophecy,* pp. 92-122.

glistening splendor. Belet-ili gave him a beautiful appearance. Nusku gave him instruction and counsel and stands at his service.[143]

Given their syncretistic bent, one should not be surprised if traditions like this circulated even among the Israelites, or that the prophets should draw on prevailing notions in the communication of their message. Both aspects feature prominently in Ezekiel's prophecies. Here the prophet has apparently drawn elements from more than one source. Nevertheless, one should not exaggerate the influence of extrabiblical traditions. Ezekiel's theology is informed primarily by his Yahwistic heritage, and most of the features in the present oracle can be accounted for within the biblical tradition. Indeed, Batto has argued that the paradise motif is a distinctly Israelite development, and J. Van Seters that Ezekiel's introduction of the theme of judgment for hubris into the myth of primeval royalty represents a prophetic transformation.[144] This prophet's concern is not primarily to transmit ancient traditions, but to challenge the arrogance of the Tyrian state in the face of Yahweh's purposes. In communicating this prophetic word to his fellow exiles, he challenges all subsequent readers to hear the message of God, which has several points.

First, pride goes before a fall. Taking a leaf out of Isaiah's notebook (Isa. 14), Ezekiel has delivered a powerful lesson on the self-destructive danger of hubris. His satirical story is cast in the classical form of a tragedy. Divinely endowed with beauty, status, wisdom, and wealth, the prince was offered every opportunity for genuine greatness. But, as in the case of the wife of Yahweh in Ezek. 16, the gracious gifts of God became the occasion for perversion. Like 'ādām in the original garden of Eden, the king of Tyre was not satisfied with signet-deputy-gardener status; he arrogated to himself the status of divine lord. But the biography of this ruler is repeated every day. None is so vulnerable to the judgment of God as the one preoccupied with his or her divinely endowed beauty, wisdom, prosperity, status.

Second, Yahweh is the Lord of all history. He appoints rulers (even over pagan nations and states) to manage his estate with equity, justice, and humility. The exploitation of a divinely bestowed privilege to satisfy one's personal greed and ambition calls for divine intervention. In Yahweh's ability to humble the proud lay the hope of Israel. The remnant of God's people may be languishing in exile, but that does not mean he has conceded his throne to other deities, let alone to mortals. Even the king of Tyre, the envy of the nations, must answer to him. This point, which will be greatly expanded in

143. As translated by Van Seters, *ZAW* 101 (1989) 337. For the original publication see W. R. Mayer, "Ein Mythos von der Erschaffung des Menschen und des Königs," *Or* 56 (1987) 55-68.

144. Batto, in *Scripture in Context,* 4:33-66; Van Seters, *ZAW* 101 (1989) 339.

the oracles against the Egyptians, offers a timely lesson for Ezekiel's compatriots at the personal and national level.

Third, forceful communicators of divine truth martial every conceivable means for the clear and effective delivery of the message. Ezekiel's adaptation of ancient traditions offers a striking paradigm for the modern communicator. When dealing with people outside one's own traditions, one tells stories with which they can identify. The communicator does not thereby accord them the same truth value he recognizes in the words he receives from God; these are merely homiletical and literary devices. But both credibility and rhetoric are served when the messenger understands his or her audience as well as subject.

B. YAHWEH'S AGENDA FOR THE NATIONS (28:20-26)

♦ *Nature and Design*

This literary piece is set off as a separate unit by a series of introductory formulae that actually have more in common with 35:1-4 than with the preceding oracles.[1] Ostensibly directed at Sidon, in comparison with earlier prophecies against the foreign nations, this passage lacks vibrancy and luster.[2] The reader learns nothing of Yahweh's real complaint against the city, only that he is against her. Except for the naming of Sidon as the addressee, the oracle could have been pronounced against any of the nations addressed earlier, as well as many that receive no attention in the book. But herein lies the key to its significance in the present context. The general pronouncements in vv. 22-23 and the specific concern for the fate of Israel in vv. 24-26 summarize Yahweh's purposes in dealing with the nations (the display of Yahweh's glory and holiness).[3]

The fourfold repetition of the recognition formula within five verses (vv. 22b, 23b, 24b, 26b) leaves no doubt about this unit's genre and intention: it is a proof saying announcing the intervention of Yahweh with the goal that the nations and Israel acknowledge him as Yahweh. While these verses are linked by a common goal, the distribution of the formula has a disruptive effect on the oracle, breaking it up into a series of small proof sayings. This

---

1. Note the absence of a specific accusation, the introduction of Yahweh's intervention with *hinĕnî 'ālayik,* "I am against you," and reference only to Yahweh's role in the judgment.

2. Hölscher (*Hesekiel,* p. 143) describes this oracle as "the emptiest piece in the entire book."

3. Klein (*Ezekiel,* pp. 130, 141) finds in v. 22 the theological key to Ezekiel's oracles against the nations.

impression is reinforced by shifts in style and content. Whereas vv. 24-26 are quite prosaic, the style of vv. 22-23 is more elevated, making ample use of parallelism. As for content, the preamble leads one to expect a unitary prophecy addressed to Sidon, but less than half concerns this city directly (vv. 22-23). Indeed, based on the form of direct address, the actual oracle is reduced to one distich in v. 22. The remainder of this verse and v. 23 are cast in the third person, reflecting the prophet's primary concern with his rhetorical audience. The rest of the oracle (vv. 24-26) forgets about Sidon altogether, focusing instead on Ezekiel's own people and the effect that Yahweh's judgment of the nations will have on Israel's welfare.

Although the entire unit is held together by typically Ezekielian formulae and phrases,[4] the present text raises several questions. First, in the face of the general nature of vv. 20-23, why was an oracle addressed to Sidon included at all. Is Ezekiel responding to the king's participation in the anti-Babylonian alliance at the beginning of Zedekiah's reign (Jer. 27:3)? Or has Sidon been randomly chosen to complete the complement of seven nations in the present assemblage of oracles addressed to Israel's enemies?[5] Unfortunately we know little about Ezekiel's international prophetic agenda. However, if Jeremiah had messages for Damascus, Hamath, and Arpad (Jer. 49:23), Qedar and Hazor (49:28), Elam (49:34), and particularly Babylon (50:1), it is conceivable that Ezekiel might have done the same.[6] It is also conceivable that Sidon's inclusion here was dictated by a quota of seven nations in the present collection, support for which interpretation is found in that chs. 29–32 contain seven oracles against Egypt.[7]

The desire for balance may also have played a role in the inclusion of the oracle against Sidon. It is curious that vv. 24-26, in which the prophet focuses his attention on his own people for the first time since ch. 24, divide

---

4. The challenge formula, *hinĕnî 'ālayik,* "I am against you" (cf. 5:8; 35:3); *nikbadtî,* "I will display my glory" (cf. 39:13); *'āśâ šĕpāṭîm,* "to execute judgments" (cf. 5:10, 15; 11:9; 16:41; 23:10; 25:11; 30:14, 19); *niqdaštî,* "I will display my holiness" (cf. 20:41; 36:23; 38:16, 23 [Hithpael]; 39:27); *deber wādām,* "pestilence and blood" (cf. 14:12ff.; also 5:12; 6:12); *nāpal ḥālāl,* "a victim fell" (cf. 6:4, 7; 26:15); *bêt yiśrā'ēl,* "house of Israel" (cf. on 3:1); *šā'aṭ/šûṭ,* "to treat with contempt" (16:57; 25:6, 15; 36:5); *qābaṣ,* "to gather" (the people of Israel from the peoples where they have been scattered [*pûṣ*]; cf. on 11:17; 20:34, 41; 36:24; 37:21; 39:27); *yāšab 'al 'admātām,* "to live on their own soil" that was given to Jacob (cf. 37:25); *yāšab lābeṭaḥ,* "to live securely" (cf. 34:25-28); in addition to the fourfold occurrence of the recognition formula.

5. See Eichrodt, *Ezekiel,* p. 396.

6. Cf. the oracle against Mount Seir (Edom), which is placed later in ch. 35.

7. Perhaps the grouping in Ezekiel was intended to match the list of seven Canaanite nations in Deut. 7:1. Cf. also the Table of Nations (whose influence has been witnessed in ch. 27), which was governed by the number seventy. Cf. Block, *ISBE,* 4:708-10.

the complex of oracles against the nations into two halves, almost equal in length.[8] Perhaps the oracle against Sidon was added to bring chs. 25–28 into balance with chs. 29–32. Those responsible for the versification of the text seems to have recognized this symmetry, for the number of verses on each side of vv. 24-26 is identical: ninety-seven.

There is no reason to deny the prophet any of the segments making up this collage of Ezekielian pronouncements. Nevertheless, the complexity of its structure probably reflects the editorial process more than the nature of prophetic preaching. While any reconstruction of the growth of a biblical book is speculative, 28:24 was apparently added to the preexistent collection of Ezekielian oracles against the nations (25:1–26:6 [plus its expansion, vv. 7-21]). After the first oracle against Egypt (29:1-9a [plus its expansion, vv. 9b-21]) had been added to the collection (because of its stylistic links), the prophecy against Sidon (28:20-23) was added, to become the seventh nation in this series. Instead of preserving the distinctly Sidonian details of the oracle, its message was reduced to theological motive statements, which in their present position perform a retrospective paradigmatic function. Meanwhile additional oracles against Tyre (27:1–28:19) were appended to ch. 26, and six oracles against Egypt were added to 29:1-21, creating a sevenfold grouping, and were placed after the oracle against Tyre. With 28:24 now situated at the approximate midpoint of the oracles against the nations, vv. 25-26 were added to highlight the significance of these oracles for Israel. Finally the entire corpus of oracles against the nations was inserted between chs. 24 and 33 to soften the harsh transition between these two major collections.[9]

1. Yahweh's Theological Goal (28:20-23)

20 *The following word of Yahweh came to me:*

21 *"Human, direct your face*[10] *toward Sidon, and prophesy against her.*

22 *Say, 'Thus has the Lord Yahweh declared: Look! I am against you, O Sidon. I will display my glory in your midst, and they will know*[11] *that I am Yahweh when I inflict punishments on her and display my holiness in her midst.* 23 *I will send pestilence against her and*

---

8. The former consists of about 1270 words; the latter, about 1480 words.

9. Analogous summary statements occur in 36:24-32; 37:24b-28; 39:25-29.

10. On the formula *śîm pānêka 'el/ʿal* see my *Ezekiel: Chapters 1–24*, p. 221.

11. LXX smooths out the text by reading a second sg. verb, and adjusting the third person suffixes in vv. 22b-23 accordingly. Contra Fohrer (*Ezechiel*, p. 163), "correction" of MT after LXX is unnecessary. Cf. Joüon-Muraoka, *Grammar,* §158n. The third person reflects the rhetorical situation, Ezekiel's primary audience being the exiles, not Sidon.

bloodshed into her streets. And the slain will fall[12] in her midst, [cut down] by the sword attacking her from all sides. Then they will know that I am Yahweh.' "

20-21 A new prophetic event is signaled by Yahweh's command to his prophet to set his face toward Sidon and prophesy against her. Although in earlier times Sidon was the premier Phoenician city,[13] since the time of Solomon Sidon had lived in Tyre's shadow. After the Babylonian conquests, however, Sidon was able to recover more quickly than Tyre, and regained her superior position among Phoenician cities.[14] Given the strength of Ezekiel's feelings toward any who would stand in the way of the Babylonians, the present oracle may have been provoked by Sidon's involvement in the revolt against Babylon during Zedekiah's reign in Jerusalem (Jer. 27:3).

22 The oracle proper opens abruptly with an announcement of Yahweh's fundamentally hostile orientation toward the city. However, perhaps because of its paradigmatic function at the end of a series of oracles against the nations, unlike most judgment oracles this one omits the charges (against Sidon). Instead, it immediately moves into a clarification of Yahweh's intentions in his actions against the city. First, he is determined to manifest his glory in the midst of the city. The Niphal form, *nikbadtî,* which occurs elsewhere in Ezekiel only in 39:13, is to be interpreted not passively, "I will be glorified," but reflexively, "I will show myself glorious."[15] Its meaning is illustrated by Exod. 14:4, 17-18, where the crossing of the Red Sea and the drowning of the Egyptians were deliberately planned by Yahweh that he might manifest his glory to Pharaoh. But Yahweh's actions should not be interpreted as the tantrums of an egomaniac. They represent punitive actions,[16] provoked by Sidonian guilt. On the basis of 25:1–26:6 and the statement in v. 24, the offenses must have included derision toward Judah at the time of its fall.

---

12. Kethib *wnpll* involves a dittography of *l;* it should read *wnpl.*

13. The Table of Nations, which omits Tyre altogether, lists Sidon as the firstborn of Canaan (Gen. 10:15). In the OT the gentilic "Sidonians" stands for "the Phoenicians" (Deut. 3:9; Josh. 13:4, 6; Judg. 3:3; 10:12; 18:7; 1 K. 5:20 [Eng. 6]; 11:5; 16:31; 2 K. 23:13; Ezek. 32:30; Ezra 3:7; 1 Chr. 22:4). In Homer "Sidonian" and "Phoenician" are interchanged, suggesting that the Greeks considered this city representative of the entire region. Cf. *Il.* 6.290, 291; 23.743-44; *Od.* 4.83-85, 618; 13.270ff.; 14.288-91; 15.118, 415-17, 473. See further J. D. Muhly, "Homer and the Phoenicians," *Berytus* 19 (1970) 27; Katzenstein, *History of Tyre,* pp. 62-63.

14. On the demise of Tyre and the ascendancy of Sidon in the 6th century see H. J. Katzenstein, "Tyre in the Early Persian Period (539-486 B.C.)," *BA* 42 (1979) 23-34.

15. So also *niqdaštî* later in the verse. On this use of the Niphal see Hurvitz, *Linguistic Study,* pp. 39-43; C. Westermann, *THAT,* 1:801.

16. On this meaning of *'āśâ šĕpāṭîm,* see my *Ezekiel: Chapters 1–24,* p. 204.

Since in the Ancient Near East the reputation of a patron deity was always implicated in the demise of his/her people, it is not surprising that Yahweh should be concerned about his glory. Here too the proof of Yahweh's majesty will be seen in his intervention in human affairs to destroy the enemies of his people. When this occurs the Sidonians will recognize Yahweh. The switch to the third person in the recognition formula, a feature that continues to the end of v. 23, indicates that Sidon is not the prophet's primary audience; the oracle is for his own people's consumption.

Second, Yahweh is determined to manifest his holiness.[17] The present text does not elaborate, but it will presumably involve the vindication of his sacred name, which has been desecrated among the nations to which the Israelites have been scattered.[18] Whereas everywhere else in the book this objective is played out before "all the nations,"[19] here the display of Yahweh's holiness is localized in a single city.

23 Yahweh will inflict his punishment on Sidon by dispatching (*šillah*) his agents of death: *pestilence (deber), bloodshed (dām),* and *sword (hereb)*. As in other similar lists,[20] the emphasis is entirely on the divine causation, without reference to human agency, so that when the slaughter has been completed, the Sidonians too will acknowledge Yahweh as the sovereign Lord of their own history.

While the circumstances of Sidon's fall are unknown, it is reasonable to suppose that Sidon succumbed to Nebuchadrezzar with the rest of the Phoenician mainland sometime before the collapse of Tyre.[21] In any case, the fulfillment of this prophetic word is confirmed by Nebuchadrezzar's Court Register, which mentions the king of Sidon along with other notables from conquered states.[22]

2. Yahweh's Design for Israel (28:24-26)

24 " 'The family of Israel will never again suffer from prickling briars or painful thorns inflicted by any of their neighbors who have treated them with contempt. And they will know that I am the Lord[23] Yahweh.

---

17. In 38:23 the Hithpael carries the same meaning as the present Niphal, *niqdaštî*.

18. In typical Ezekielian style the subject is suspended to be resumed and developed more fully at a later time. See 36:16-32.

19. See 20:41; 28:25; 36:23; 38:16, 23; 39:27.

20. Pestilence, famine, and sword (5:12; 6:12; 7:15; 12:16); famine, wild animals, sword, pestilence (14:12-22). On Yahweh's agents of death see Block, *BBR* 2 (1992) 116-19.

21. So Katzenstein, *History of Tyre,* p. 324.

22. See *ANET,* p. 308; Unger, *Babylon,* p. 193.

23. The compound form of the divine name occurs in recognition formulae of a proof saying four other times: 13:9; 23:49; 24:24; 29:16. *BHS* and most commentators

25 *Thus has the Lord Yahweh declared: When I regather the house*[24]
of Israel from the peoples among whom they have been dispersed, I
will display my holiness through them in the sight of the nations. Then
they will live on their own land, which I gave to my servant Jacob.
26 *And they will live on it securely; they will build houses and plant*
vineyards. They will live on it securely when I have inflicted punish-
ments upon all from the surrounding peoples who have treated them
with contempt. Then they will know that I am Yahweh their God.' "[25]

Literarily vv. 24-26 function as a hinge between two remarkably balanced
complexes of oracles directed against the six nations (25:1–28:23) and Egypt
(29:1–32:32), respectively.[26] But theologically they provide the key to the
significance of these oracles for Ezekiel's rhetorical audience, his fellow
exiles. In announcing the doom of Israel's enemies the prophet has been
offering hope to his own people. All is not lost. Yahweh, the Lord of history,
remains firmly committed to their well-being and their restoration.

24 Judging by its content and style, this verse offers a fitting conclusion to the five oracles against the nations (25:1–26:21), and may originally
have been placed there. Sidon seems out of the picture, and no allusion is
made to the previous oracles denouncing Tyrian hubris (chs. 27–28). Instead,
the verse announces the end to the pain caused by the derision (*haššāṭîm*) of
all Israel's neighbors *(kol sĕbîbōtām)*. While the term *šĕ'āṭ* has not been
encountered since 25:6, it aptly describes the scornful comments found in
25:3, 8, and 26:2, and that underlie 25:15.[27] V. 24 is artificially linked to the
preceding, but the copula at the beginning may originally have tied the verse
to 26:6, if not to v. 21.

Verse 24 is gospel for Ezekiel's people because it announces the end
of the insults they have endured from their enemies. Two parallel figures of
speech describe the pain. First, the derision is compared to the jabs of a
prickling briar. sillôn, "briar," is a distinctively Ezekielian term, being found
elsewhere only in 2:6.[28] The modifier, *mam'îr*, from *mā'ar*, "to prick, wound,"
occurs elsewhere only in Lev. 13:51-52 and 14:44, where it describes a
malignant leprous wound. The second image, *painful thorns*, is more common.
qôṣ is a generic term for a noxious thorny weed, here modified by *mak'ib*,

delete it accordingly, with support from LXX and several Hebrew mss. Cf. Zimmerli,
Ezekiel 2, p. 556.

24. LXX drops *bêt;* Targ. reads *bĕnê*, "sons of."

25. LXX adds "and the God of their ancestors."

26. See the introductory comments to oracles against foreign nations above, pp. 4-5.

27. On the meaning see above on 25:6.

28. The term is cognate to Arab. *silla*, a spiny perennial herb. Cf. Zohary, *Plants*
of the Bible, p. 166.

from *kā'ēb,* "to be in pain."[29] The recognition formula reminds the audience that, although Yahweh's intervention on behalf of his people reaffirms their special status, he does so for his own name's sake. They may take hope in the announcement of the end of abuse, but Yahweh's ultimate goal is the recognition of his person and the confession of his involvement in human affairs.

25 The presence of the citation formula at the beginning of vv. 25-26 suggests that they are a fragment of Ezekielian proclamation editorially inserted here to expand on the good news for his people. First the prophet announces the reconstitution of the nation of Israel, an event that will transpire in two phases: the dispersed population will be gathered,[30] and the nation will be returned to its homeland. Only one land qualifies as *their own land* (*'admātām*): the territory Yahweh had given to his servant Jacob. In a restricted sense the prophet is referring to the patriarchal promise, specifically Gen. 28:13 and 35:12, where title to the land of Canaan is transferred proleptically from Abraham to Jacob. However, the phrase *my servant Jacob ('abdî ya'qōb)* also carries a national sense. Although the expression occurs elsewhere in Ezekiel only in 37:25, it appears often in restoration oracles as a designation for Israel.[31] Coming from the mouth of Yahweh, "my servant Jacob" announces the restoration of a broken relationship. The people of Yahweh will be serving him again in the land they received as their grant from him.

Second, picking up on v. 22, Ezekiel announces the public manifestation of Yahweh's holiness. The divine patron of Israel, whose name had been brought into disrepute through the rebellion and calamity of his people, will be vindicated. How this will be accomplished will be developed at length in 36:16-32.

26 This verse summarizes the significance of Yahweh's intervention on Israel's behalf. Instead of suffering the insults of the nations, among whom they are scattered, Yahweh's people will dwell securely in their own land. This point is emphasized rhetorically by the repetition of *they will live securely* (*wĕyāšĕbû lābeṭaḥ*) and the presentation of concrete symbols of security: the construction of houses and planting of vineyards.[32] The concluding statements reaffirm the role of Yahweh in the restoration of Israel. The reconstituted nation will be a work of God, and God alone. When he resumes his patron

---

29. In 13:22 the verb had applied to mental anguish, a heart in pain. On *qôṣ,* note its connection with tilled soil (Gen. 3:18; Hos. 10:8 [both parallel to *dardar*]; Isa. 32:13) and the desert (Judg. 8:7, 16). See Zohary, *Plants of the Bible,* p. 159.

30. On this theme see 11:17; 20:24, 41; 34:13; 36:24; 37:21; 38:8; 39:27.

31. See Isa. 44:1, 2; 45:4; 48:20; Jer. 30:10; 46:27-28.

32. This imagery is probably borrowed from Jeremiah. Cf. Jer. 29:5, 28. The theme of dwelling in safety will be resumed and developed in 34:25-31. Cf. 38:8, 11, 14; 39:26.

role the people will be impressed not with their own achievements but with Yahweh, who has intervened on their behalf again.

♦ *Theological Implications*

Like many of Ezekiel's previous oracles, this collage of prophetic statements affirms several basic theological principles.

First, no nation stands outside the scope of divine sovereignty. Like the nations in previous oracles, Sidon too must submit to the Lord of history.

Second, when the Lord intervenes in human affairs, he does so to manifest his own glory and holiness. A recognition of this principle (which will be developed much more fully later) delivers one from an undue anthropocentrism, which views the world as revolving around oneself. As affirmed by our Lord's own prayer, the agenda that drives God and that should motivate his people is the sanctity of his name and the recognition of his sovereignty. Both are affected by the well-being of his people.

Third, God keeps his covenant. Ezekiel's people may be languishing in exile, but God has not forgotten his promises to the patriarchs. Accordingly, a holistic vision of Israel's future must involve both a restoration of the people's status as Yahweh's servant, and a return to the land promised centuries ago.

C. ORACLES OF JUDGMENT CONCERNING EGYPT
(29:1–32:32)

♦ *Nature and Design*

In 29:1 Ezekiel's attention turns toward Egypt, where it will remain for the next four chapters. Nowhere in the book does the arrangement of prophecies follow such a clearly sevenfold pattern as in 29:1–32:32. Egypt, the seventh nation to be dealt with, is addressed in seven separate oracles:

1. The oracle against Pharaoh, the crocodile of the Nile   (29:1-16)
2. The land of Egypt: Nebuchadrezzar's consolation prize   (29:17-21)
3. The day of Yahweh in Egypt   (30:1-19)
4. Breaking the arms of Pharaoh   (30:20-26)
5. The doom of the pharaonic tree   (31:1-18)
6. The doom of the pharaonic monster   (32:1-16)
7. Egypt's descent into Sheol   (32:17-32)

With the exception of the third oracle, all are introduced with a date notice, producing the highest concentration of such notices in the book. Although the significance of this imbalance in their distribution is debated, it lends authenticity to the date notices in the book as a whole. Had the editors inserted these dates secondarily they would surely have fashioned a more consistent product, in both distribution and form.[1] According to these notices, the first and last four prophecies in this series have been chronologically ordered. Inserted between the first and fourth are two anomalous oracles. The date given for 29:17-21 suggests that this was the latest of Ezekiel's recorded utterances. Why it was inserted here one may only speculate. Perhaps the interest in Tyre in this oracle moved the editor to advance it within the book nearer the oracles against the island nation that have ended in ch. 28. Having created a breach in the chronological arrangement with this insertion, the editor added immediately thereafter the only undated oracle. This remarkable sevenfold series divides into two major segments, 29:1–31:18 and 32:1-32, each of which presents the destruction of Egypt at the hands of the Babylonians, followed by the descent of Pharaoh into Sheol. Particularly striking are the correspondences between the introductions to the respective parts, viz., 29:1-5 and 32:1-4.[2]

Like his contemporary Jeremiah, Ezekiel appears to have been more interested in Egypt than in any other foreign nation. This is undoubtedly attributable to Egypt's position in the international community, particularly its involvement in Judean affairs in the latter's final years. In Ezekiel's mind, Nebuchadrezzar was Yahweh's instrument of judgment upon Israel for their persistent revolt against him. Thus Ezekiel interpreted any outside interference in Nebuchadrezzar's Palestinian campaign as a challenge to the plan of God. Instead of heeding prophetic admonitions to return to their divine patron, however, the Judeans had appealed to Egypt for help in resisting the Babylonians.

But Egypt had been involved in Israelite affairs for more than a millennium. A thousand years earlier the ancestors of the nation had languished in slavery in this African land.[3] In the process of delivering these Asiatics from Egyptian bondage Yahweh had revealed himself to his people with unprecedented clarity and force, climaxing this revelation with the establishment of his covenant with them at Sinai. The OT is silent on any further contacts between Israel and the Egyptians until the 10th century. However, a stela erected by Pharaoh Merneptah (1213-1203 B.C.) commemorates a Palestinian campaign in which among other conquests he claims to have "laid Israel waste" and destroyed her grain.[4] Egyptian influence in Israel was secured in

---

1. So also L. Boadt, *Ezekiel's Oracles Against Egypt: A Literary and Philological Study of Ezekiel 29–32*, BibOr 37 (Rome: Pontifical Biblical Institute, 1980), p. 11.

2. See Parunak (*Structural Studies*, pp. 381-82) for a tabulation of the motifs and expressions that link these parts.

3. See Ezekiel's recollection of this period in 20:5-8.

4. Lit. "seed." For the text of the stela see *ANET*, pp. 376-78. This document provides the earliest extrabiblical attestation of the Israelites. The dates are according to K. A. Kitchen, *ABD*, 2:329.

the early monarchic period by the marriage alliance between Solomon and the king of Egypt (1 K. 3:1; 7:8; 9:16; 11:1). However, this relationship was short-lived, and within five years of Solomon's death, Pharaoh Sheshonq I (Shishak) invaded Judah, making off with many of the royal and temple treasures that Solomon had accumulated (1 K. 14:25-26). In the 8th century Egypt was taken over by an "Ethiopian" dynasty, which, anxious to enhance its influence in the Levant, encouraged resistance against the neo-Assyrians. However, the prophet Isaiah warned Judah of the futility of going down to Egypt for assistance, when they should have found security in Yahweh alone (2 K. 18:21; Isa. 36:6). In the end, Egypt itself was conquered by Esarhaddon and Ashurbanipal, and Assyrian control extended as far south as Thebes.[5]

In the latter part of the 7th century, under a new Saite dynasty, Egypt regained its independence. When Ashurbanipal was forced to loosen his grip on Egypt because of troubles in the east, Psammetichus I (664-610) extricated his country from Assyrian control without a fight. Egyptian foreign policy during this period tended to be pragmatic. With keen historical sense, Psammetichus's successor, Necho II (610-596), recognized that Assyria was no longer the principal threat to his ambitions in Palestine. In a complete about-face in foreign policy, he led his army northward through Palestine to lend support to the tottering Assyrians against an emerging Babylonian power headed by Nabopolassar. For some unknown reason, the Judean king, Josiah, attempted to stop him at Megiddo, but this act of foolishness cost Josiah his life (2 K. 23:29-30; 2 Chr. 35:20-24). Capitalizing on the resultant dynastic turmoil in Jerusalem, Necho placed on the throne of Judah his own puppet Eliakim, whom he renamed Jehoiakim (2 K. 23:35). At the battles of Carchemish and Hamath, however, the Babylonians shattered Egyptian dreams of control over Palestine, and by the turn of the century Nebuchadrezzar was in firm control of Judah.

But this did not end Egypt's ambitions in Judah. As in the days of the Assyrians, Egypt's rulers encouraged Palestinian resistance to the Babylonians. The weak-willed king Zedekiah vacillated between obedience to Nebuchadrezzar and reliance on the Egyptian kings, first Psammetichus II (595-589; see Ezek. 19:2-4), then Hophra (Apries, 589-570). While Nebuchadrezzar was pitching his forces against Jerusalem, Hophra sent an army against the Babylonians (Jer. 37:5-8). Back in Jerusalem the prophet Jeremiah insisted that the Egyptians would be of no help for the Judeans against Nebuchadrezzar. On the contrary, Hophra would be given into Nebuchadrezzar's hand, just as Zedekiah had been (Jer. 44:30), a prediction whose apparent fulfillment is suggested by Josephus's report (*Ant.* 10.11.1, §227) that Nebuchadrezzar eventually conducted campaigns against the Libyans,

5. *ANET,* pp. 294-95.

implying that Egypt had also been overrun. Nebuchadrezzar's role in the demise of Hophra is not clear. Josephus comments that Nebuchadrezzar slew him (*Ant.* 10.9.7, §182), but this contradicts Herodotus, who reports that he was slain by his successor Amasis (*Hist.* 2.163ff.). Whatever the case, Nebuchadrezzar's incursions into Egypt undoubtedly contributed to his weakening position on his own throne.[6]

1. The Oracle Against Pharaoh, the Crocodile of the Nile (29:1-16)

♦ *Nature and Design*

The limits of the first oracle against Egypt are set by the date notice at the beginning, and a new notice in v. 17. If one assumes that the opening notice and the charge to the prophet to address Egypt (vv. 1-2) apply to the entire prophecy, the oracle itself is structurally complex and the formulaic indicators inconsistent. On the one hand, on first sight this prophecy seems to consist of three semi-independent oracles, each introduced by the citation formula: *kōh-'āmar 'ădōnāy yhwh,* "Thus has the Lord Yahweh declared": vv. 3-7, 8-12, 13-16. The first two consist of twelve lines/cola apiece, and the third seven. On the other hand, these segments appear to be deliberately linked not only by common motifs and vocabulary but also by connecting particles. *lākēn,* "therefore," in v. 8 ties the second logically to the first, suggesting that vv. 8-12 are intended as an explanation of vv. 3-7. Similar comments may be made of *kî,* "For," in v. 13.[7] But this evidence in turn is contradicted by the threefold occurrence of the recognition formula, "Then they will know that I am (the Lord) Yahweh" (vv. 6a, 9a, 16). Since this formula usually signals the end of a demonstration oracle/proof saying in Ezekiel, a tripartite division is evident: A, 29:3-6a; B, 29:6b-9a; C, 29:9b-16. Dividing the text this way has the added advantage of keeping cause and effect together, particularly in the second and third subdivisions, where *ya'an,* "because," introduces a protasis, to be followed by the apodosis signaled by *lākēn,* "therefore." Each segment contains features found in the earlier oracles against the foreign nations in 25:1–26:6,[8] the formal similarities increasing as one moves from A to B to C. But the *order* of shared elements is reversed, so that A has the closest affinity to the oracles against Tyre (26:1-6) and Sidon (28:20-23), B

---

6. For discussion of the historical context of Ezekiel's oracles against Egypt see K. S. Freedy and D. B. Redford, "The Dates of Ezekiel in Relation to Biblical, Babylonian and Egyptian Sources," *JAOS* 90 (1970) 462-85.

7. This structure is recognized by H. F. van Rooy, "Parallelism, Metre and Rhetoric in Ezekiel 29:1-6," *Semitics* 8 (1982) 90-105.

8. Cf. Boadt, *Ezekiel's Oracles,* pp. 15-16; Zimmerli, *Ezekiel 2,* p. 109.

to the oracles against Edom (25:12-14) and Philistia (25:15-17), and C to the oracles against Ammon (25:2-7) and Moab (25:8-11).

The most obvious link between A and the oracles against Tyre and Sidon is the declaration of Yahweh's disposition by means of the challenge formula *hinĕnî 'ālyik/'ālêkā,* "I am against you," followed by the identification of the addressee with the vocative. Beyond this, although no specific offense is cited in the Sidonian pronouncement, like the accusation against Tyre, here the charge is cast in the form of a direct quotation that reflects the disposition of the nation. Structurally, however, they are different. Segment A, 29:3-6a, not only lacks the formulaic signals, *ya'an,* "because," and *lākēn,* "therefore," but also reverses the order of cause and effect. Yahweh's disposition toward Pharaoh is announced before the charge is laid. Segment B displays several resemblances with the oracles against Edom and the Philistines. First, the charge is cast not in the form of an offensive quotation but as an announcement of offensive action. Second, both contain the *ya'an . . . lākēn* elements, preserving the logical cause-effect order. Third, the direct effect is cast as a divine pronouncement, introduced with *lākēn* plus the citation formula, "Therefore, thus has the Lord Yahweh declared," after which will come a prediction of Yahweh's judgmental actions. The adherence of segment C to the pattern of the oracles against Ammon and Moab is also most obvious in the usage of *ya'an* and *lākēn.* In each the former introduces a direct quotation thus: "Because X has declared . . . therefore . . ." In each the consequence is the direct intervention of Yahweh, announced without a preceding formal citation of the charges.

Although some find three separate oracles in vv. 1-19,[9] most tend to look for an authentic core, and then to view the remainder as interpretive accretions. Hölscher, who led the way by looking for an original poetic core that concerned only Pharaoh, reduced the primary text to vv. 3b-4.[10] To this day it is commonly held that much of the remainder of 29:1-16 derives from later editorial and interpretive hands.[11]

However, this approach is unnecessarily limited. First, the distinction between a pharaonic core and general Egyptian expansions overlooks the sense of corporate solidarity that ancients recognized between rulers and their subjects.[12] Second, the entire unit is replete with typical Ezekielian vocabulary

9. See Fohrer, *Ezechiel,* pp. 165-66. Wevers (*Ezekiel,* pp. 221-22) recognizes four oracles in vv. 1-16.

10. Hölscher, *Hesekiel,* pp. 144-45. Cf. the slightly different original proposed by Irwin, *Problem of Ezekiel,* pp. 186-87.

11. See Zimmerli, *Ezekiel 2,* pp. 115-16; Garscha, *Studien,* p. 168; May, "Ezekiel," p. 223.

12. On the relationship of a king to his people and the role of the former in the development of national self-consciousness, see Block, *Foundations of National Identity,* pp. 556-87.

and diction.[13] Third, since the forms of prophetic oracles varied greatly, it is inadvisable to force them into molds shaped by modern Western standards of consistency and smoothness. Fourth, on the basis of their natures and content, the present arrangement displays an effective ABA pattern, in which the first and third segments focus on Pharaoh's hubris, with a concern for Egypt's relationship with Israel sandwiched between. A division based on the placement of the citation formula creates unnecessary confusion. Finally, as the exposition will show, the present organization is logical, with the movement from A to B to C deliberately heightening the force of the entire oracle.

On the basis of these thematic and structural considerations I propose the following outline for the first oracle against Egypt:

a. Preamble (29:1-2)
b. Yahweh's Disposition toward Pharaoh (29:3-9a)
  (1) The First Statement (29:3-6a)
    (a) The Charge of Hubris (29:3)
    (b) The Divine Response (29:4-6a)
  (2) The Second Statement (29:6b-9a)
    (a) The Charge of Treachery (29:6b-7)
    (b) The Divine Response (29:8-9a)
c. Yahweh's Intentions concerning Egypt (29:9b-16)
  (1) His Immediate Plans (29:9b-12)
  (2) His Long-range Plans (29:13-16)

a. Preamble (29:1-2)

1 *In the tenth year,*[14] *in the tenth [month], on the twelfth [day] of the month,*[15] *the following message of Yahweh came to me:* 2 *"Human, direct your face toward*[16] *Pharaoh, king of Egypt, and prophesy against him and against all Egypt."*

The opening date notice fixes the time of Ezekiel's first prophecy against Egypt at Jan. 7, 587 B.C., almost one year after the commencement of Nebuchadrezzar's siege of Jerusalem (Ezek. 24:1; 2 K. 25:1; Jer. 29:1), and two

13. Cf. the tabulation of motifs found here and the earlier oracles against Judah by L. Boadt, "Rhetorical Strategies in Ezekiel's Oracles of Judgment," in *Ezekiel and His Book,* ed. J. Lust, BETL 74 (Leuven: Leuven University Press, 1986), p. 198.

14. Only here and in 40:1 does a date notice lack an opening *wayĕhî,* perhaps signaling a new movement/section in the overall plan of the book.

15. LXX μιᾷ reads *b'ḥd* for MT *bšnym 'śr,* perhaps a pseudo-dittograph from the following *laḥōdeš.* Vulg. *undecima die,* "eleventh day," appears to have reinserted '*śr.*

16. Here and in 35:2 the idiom replaces *'el* with *'al.*

years before the fugitive brings news of the fall of the city to the exiles (Ezek. 33:21).[17] The oracle therefore represents the prophet's response to political and military developments in Judah, or more accurately, his reaction to the exiles' response to those events. As in the previous prophecy against Sidon, Ezekiel, addressed as *ben-'ādām,* is commanded to turn toward his addressee. As in ch. 28, this time the addressee is an individual, here identified as "Pharaoh." The word "pharaoh" derives from Egyp. *pr-ʾ* (lit. "great house").[18] Originally designating the royal living quarters of the palace complex in Memphis, by extension it came to signify royal authority and the king himself, perhaps synonymous with "His Majesty." Here the title is defined in Hebrew terms, *melek miṣrayim,* "king of Egypt." Ezekiel never identifies the pharaoh by name, but from Jer. 44:30 we learn that Hophra is in view.[19] At the turn of the century the restrained policy of his predecessor, Psammetichus II, had enabled Nebuchadrezzar to capture Jerusalem unmolested. But Hophra's foreign policy was opportunistic and ambitious. Responding to Zedekiah's call for aid, he challenged the Babylonians by sending troops into Palestine,[20] which forced Nebuchadrezzar to lift briefly the siege of Jerusalem. But the efforts proved futile for Zedekiah, as the Egyptians were quickly driven from Judean soil.[21] According to v. 2b the scope of this oracle extends beyond the Egyptian royal house to all Egypt. On the principle of corporate solidarity, v. 2b indicates that the fate of nation is inextricably bound to the fate of the king, though the first phase of the oracle will focus on the pharaoh himself.

b. Yahweh's Disposition toward Pharaoh (29:3-9a)

3 *"Speak,[22] and declare: 'Thus has the Lord Yahweh declared:*

17. This also makes this oracle the earliest of Ezekiel's prophecies against the foreign nations (cf. 26:1). For the date see Parker-Dubberstein, *Chronology,* pp. 27-28. So also Malamat, *IEJ* 3 (1968) 152; Lang, *Ezechiel,* p. 37; Hayes and Hooker, *New Chronology,* p. 97.

18. See D. B. Redford, *ABD,* 5:288-89.

19. Greek Apries. Hophra derives from Egyp. *ḥ'-ib-r',* "happy-hearted is Re." On Hophra see J. K. Hoffmeier, "A New Insight on Pharaoh Apries from Herodotus, Diodorus and Jeremiah 46:17," *JSSEA* 11 (1981) 165-70.

20. The land expedition appears to have been matched by a maritime mission up the Phoenician coast, which seems to have been more successful. Cf. Herodotus, *Hist.* 2.161; *Diodorus of Sicily* 1.68.1.

21. See Ezek. 17:11-21; Jer. 37; Josephus, *Ant.* 10.7.3, §§108-10.

22. *dabbēr* is missing from LXX and often deleted as an otiose gloss (cf. *BHS*). But the combination *dabbēr wĕ'āmartā* occurs elsewhere in 14:14; 20:3; 33:2, as well as in Lev. 1:2; 18:2; 23:2; Num. 5:12; 6:2. For a defense of its integrity see Boadt, *Ezekiel's Oracles,* pp. 21-23.

Look, I am against you, O Pharaoh, king of Egypt,[23] *the great monster,*[24] *sprawled out*[25] *in the midst of his channels, who says, "My Nile*[26] *belongs to me; I made [it] for myself."*[27] 4 *But I will place hooks in your jaws, and make the fish of your channels*[28] *stick to your scales. I will haul you up from your channels, with*[29] *all the fish of your channels sticking to your scales.*

5 *I will hurl you out into the wilderness —*
You and all the fish of your channels.[30]
On the open field you will fall;
You will not be gathered,
And you will not be collected.[31]
To wild animals of the earth
And birds of the heavens
I have consigned you as food.

6 *Then all who live in Egypt will know that I am Yahweh.*

23. *melek miṣrayim* is missing in LXX and considered by Freedy and Redford (*JAOS* 90 [1970] 471 n. 37) as a late scribal gloss influenced by 30:21.

24. Targ. and Syr. correctly read *tnyn* for *htnym* here and in 32:2. Cf. Jer. 51:34.

25. *rābaṣ* means "to lie," in this instance securely, at ease. See Ps. 23:2; Isa. 17:2; Zeph. 3:13; Job 11:19.

26. The sg. *yĕʾōr* suggests a shift in meaning. The name *yĕʾōr* is commonly thought to derive from Egyp. *i(t)rw*, "river, Nile" (Lambdin, *JAOS* 73 [1953] 151). In this context the sg. denotes the Nile as a whole; the pl., *yĕʾōrîm*, refers to the channels of the Delta and the irrigation canals. Ezekiel's use of the crocodile as a figure for Pharaoh recalls a statement of Amon-Re in a hymn to Thutmose III: "I cause them [Thutmose's enemies] to see thy majesty as a crocodile, the lord of fear in the water, who cannot be approached" (*ANET*, p. 374). The prophet's orientation toward the Delta reflects an appreciation for this area as the base of Saite dynastic power. See A. Spalinger, *ABD*, 2:360-61.

27. *ʾăśîtinî*. On the datival use of the pronominal suffix on verbs see Joüon-Muraoka, *Grammar*, §125ba. For other examples in Ezekiel see Boadt, *Ezekiel's Oracles*, p. 30.

28. LXX and Syr. read sg.

29. Treating *wĕʾet* as the beginning of a circumstantial clause with *ʾet* functioning as an emphatic particle before a nominative case. T. Muraoka suggests influence from the previous transitive construction (*Emphatic Words and Structures in Biblical Hebrew* [Leiden: Brill, 1985], p. 153).

30. LXX, Syr., Vulg. read sg.

31. Many emend *tqbṣ* to *tqbr* with several Hebrew mss. and Targ. (NRSV, REB, NJPS, *BHS*). Cf. Watson, *ZAW* 96 (1984) 429. But the emendation is unnecessary if *qbṣ* is understood as conceptual shorthand for "gathering a person's remains and treasured artifacts for burial." Cf. the idiom "to be gathered to one's fathers/people," i.e., buried (Gen. 25:8; etc.). LXX reads περιστέλλω, which describes the preparation and burial of a corpse. See Tob. 12:13; Sir. 38:16.

Because you are[32] *a reed crutch to the house of Israel —*

7 *When they grasp you, you splinter in their hand,*[33]
And tear up their entire[34] *armpits;*[35]
When they lean on you, you shatter,
Causing their hips to collapse — [36]

8 *Therefore, thus has the Lord Yahweh declared:*
I will bring a sword[37] *against you, and cut off from you both human*
and animal.[38] 9a *Then the land of Egypt will be a desolate wasteland,*[39]
and they will know that I am Yahweh.' "

(1) The End of the Great Sea Monster (29:3-6a)

As in ch. 28, the rhetorical force of Ezekiel's attack on the pharaoh derives
from its satirical form, specifically his use of animal imagery to tell a story
of intensified reversal — a gargantuan figure is reduced to nothing.[40] The
prophet employs several effective strategies to create the self-inflated image
of colossal Pharaoh.

3 First, he highlights his status by using his full title, "Pharaoh, king
of Egypt." This is no ordinary person. He is the monarch of the great nation
on the Nile.

Second, he identifies him as a *the great monster (hattannîn haggādôl)*.

32. MT *hĕyôtām*, "their being," mistakenly views "all who live in Egypt" in the
previous line as the subject. The requirement of a cause for judgment after *ya'an* suggests
an original *hĕyôtĕkā*, the form reflected in LXX, Syr., Vulg.

33. Read *bkpm* with LXX (cf. Qere *bkp*) in place of Kethib *bkpk*. Although LXX
and Syr. presuppose *kp*, many (*BHS;* Allen, *Ezekiel 20–48,* p. 102) delete the word as a
gloss.

34. *kol*, lit. "all, the whole of," used here to denote the entirety. See GKC, §127c.

35. Hebrew *ktp*, lit. "shoulder." See the commentary. LXX and Syr. mistakenly
read *kp*, perhaps under the influence of 2 K. 18:21 = Isa. 36:6. MT is preferred on the
basis of *lectio difficilior.* Cf. G. R. Driver, *Bib* 35 (1954) 299.

36. *wĕha'ămadtā*, "you caused to stand," is the exact opposite of the required
meaning. LXX, Syr., and Vulg. suggest a metathetical error for *wĕhim'adtā.* Cf. Ps. 69:24
(Eng. 23). Driver (*Bib* 35 [1954] 299) defends MT on the basis of Akkadian and Arabic
cognates meaning "to cause something to be knocked together, bruised."

37. *hinĕnî mēbî' ḥereb* occurs elsewhere in Ezek. 6:3; 11:8; 14:17; 33:2; and Lev.
26:25.

38. On *kārat 'ādām ûbĕhēmâ*, "to cut off human and beast," cf. Ezek. 14:13, 17,
19, 21.

39. *ḥorbâ*, "waste," occurs elsewhere in 5:14; 25:13; 30:12; 35:4; 38:8. See also
ḥōreb, v. 10, and its pl. counterparts in 13:4; 26:20; 33:24, 27; 36:4, 10, 33, 35, 38; 38:12.
ḥorĕbôt occurs with *šĕmāmâ* in 29:10 and 36:4.

40. Cf. Fishelov's discussion of this oracle in *Prooftext* 9 (1989) 204-5.

The term refers concretely to a marine creature,[41] in this instance a crocodile, the ruler of the Nile, sprawled out in the channels of the river. However, the term also carries mythological overtones. Elsewhere *tannîn* refers to the mythical sea monster, the chaos god, known elsewhere as Rahab and Leviathan.[42] In the OT this figure appears especially in poetic contexts celebrating Yahweh's victory over the forces of evil.[43] However, Ezekiel's *tannîn* has been thoroughly historicized,[44] being identified with the king of Egypt, but who, like the ruler of Tyre in ch. 28, dares to defy Yahweh. As in the previous oracle against Sidon, Yahweh's hostile response is expressed in the opening challenge formula.[45]

Third, the ground for Ezekiel's satirical attack is an arrogant claim, cast in the form of direct speech, a rhetorical device designed to assist the audience in assuming the addressee's point of view. Pharaoh's assertion consists of two parts. The first declares his sovereignty over the Nile, the implication being that, like the crocodile, he will tolerate no challenges. The second is not as clear. On the surface the construction of *wa'ănî 'ăśîtinî* looks like an affirmation of self-creation, "I have made myself."[46] As already noted, however, a datival interpretation of the suffix is preferable. But this leaves open the question of what Pharaoh has made. Is it the Nile? While more subtle than the claims of the prince of Tyre (28:2), the image of Pharaoh as owner and creator of the Nile fits perfectly with Egyptian doctrines of divine kingship.[47]

41. See Gen. 1:21. Cf. the references to serpents as *tannîn* in Exod. 7:9, 10, 12; Deut. 32:23.

42. On Rahab see Ps. 87:4; 89:11 (Eng. 10); Job 9:13; 26:12; Isa. 30:7; 51:9; see also J. Day, *ABD,* 5:610-11. On Leviathan see Ps. 74:14; 89:11 (Eng. 10); 104:26; Isa. 27:1. Cf. *ltn,* the name of the seven-headed monster defeated by Baal in Ugaritic mythological texts. In Job 40:25–41:26 (Eng. 41:1-34) Leviathan functions as a naturalized designation for some fantastic creature (with features resembling tyrannosaurus rex). For citations and discussion see J. Day, *ABD,* 4:295-96; also E. L. Greenstein, "The Snaring of the Sea in the Baal Epic," *Maarav* 3 (1982) 195-216.

43. See M. K. Wakeman, *God's Battle with the Monster: A Study in Biblical Imagery* (Leiden: Brill, 1973); J. Day, *God's Conflict with the Dragon and the Sea: Echoes of a Canaanite Myth in the Old Testament,* University of Cambridge Oriental Publications 35 (Cambridge: Cambridge University Press, 1985).

44. It is still tempting to see here an allusion to the Egyptian crocodile god Sobek, whose veneration was particularly important in the Nile Delta region. See E. Brovarski, "Sobek," *LÄ,* 5:995-1031, esp. 999-1000.

45. On this formula see my *Ezekiel: Chapters 1–24,* pp. 201-2.

46. Cf. the Egyptian god Atum's claim of being self-created, on which see J. Černý, *Ancient Egyptian Religion* (London: Hutchin's University Press, 1952), p. 43.

47. On the deity of kings in Egypt see Frankfort, *Kingship and the Gods,* pp. 24-47. The importance of the Nile for the well-being of Egypt — its annual inundation of the agricultural land with fresh fertile silt from upstream and its channels from which water is drawn to water the growing crops — is universally recognized. See Herodotus's reference to Egypt as "the gift of the Nile" (*Hist.* 2.4).

However, one should perhaps understand the verb more generally, "I have acted for my own sake." Or is this simply an affirmation of independent action? The ambiguity is probably intentional, inviting the audience to interpret this boast against the background of Yahweh's self-introduction, "I am Yahweh; I have spoken; and I will perform *(waʿăśîtî)*." Either way the statement reflects Pharaoh's inordinate hubris; he acts with independence and effect. No one will stand in his way.

4-6a But Yahweh cannot let such arrogance go unanswered. In his description of Yahweh's response, Ezekiel's style shifts into a semipoetic mode, but the product is a grotesque literary cartoon. The announcement of judgment is not restricted to the king, however. In keeping with the opening charge to the prophet (v. 2), the focus of Yahweh's actions alternates between the pharaoh and his people in an AA'BB'CC' pattern.[48] Adopting the strategy of intensified reversal, the prophet describes the collapse of the myth of pharaonic and Egyptian greatness. By a series of divine actions, the great sea monster *(hattannîn haggdôl)* is reduced to an ordinary fish *(dāg)*, not only incapable of delivering himself but also dragging down to their death other fish caught in his scales. Yahweh's threatened actions may be summarized as follows:

A Yahweh will catch the monster (Pharaoh) with hooks in his jaws, nullifying his claims to independence.[49]

A′ Yahweh will capture the fish of the Nile (the citizens of Egypt) by causing them to stick (Hiphil of *dābaq*) to the scales of the reptile.

B Yahweh will haul the monster (Pharaoh) up out of his channels, nullifying his claim to the Nile.

B′ Yahweh will bring the fish of the channels (citizens) up with him in his scales.

C Yahweh will cast the monster onto the arid desert sand, away from his natural habitat.

C′ Yahweh will cast all the fish of his channels out on the sand with him.

The divine objective is spelled out in v. 5b. Intent on destroying the monster, Yahweh delivers him and the fish clinging to him to the hyenas and vultures, the scavengers of the desert. The picture is grotesque and macabre.

48. Note *kol-dĕgat yĕʾōrêkā,* "all the fish of your channels."

49. Note the identical expression in 38:4. Perhaps because the crocodile was venerated in some regions of Egypt, hunting scenes involving this creature are rare in Egyptian art (cf. H. Kees, *Ägypten* [Munich: Beck, 1933], p. 53). When the reptile was hunted, the instruments tended to be ropes and harpoons (cf. A. Erman and H. Ranke, *Ägypten und ägyptisches Leben im Altertum* [Tübingen: Mohr, 1922-23], p. 271 n. 4), though Herodotus speaks of a hook baited with pork (*Hist.* 2.70).

So far the oracle offers no specific hint of Hophra's Palestinian adventures, or his interference with Nebuchadrezzar as agent of Yahweh. The issue is one of principle. For all his arrogant pretensions, the glorious lord of the Nile is no match for Yahweh, who toys with him as a fisherman plays with his catch, then throws him away as carrion, unfit for human consumption. In the end the decisive action is performed not by Hophra but by Yahweh, and when he is through all boastful claims will be silenced; even the Egyptians will acknowledge him as supreme.

(2) The End of the Broken Reed (29:6b-9a)

The judgment of Egypt moves into a second phase in v. 6b. The metaphor changes, the charges against Pharaoh become specific, and his interference in Israelite affairs becomes the critical issue. Vv. 6b-7 are taken up with the accusation, and like the previous segment, these verses divide into two parts: the accusation (vv. 6b-7) and an announcement of judgment (vv. 8-9a).

6b-7 The accusation is cast in metaphorical form: as a crutch Pharaoh is worse than useless. By definition a *crutch* is an instrument designed to assist a person, especially one who is feeble, in standing or walking. *miš'enet* derives from *šā'an,* "to lean, support oneself," but the verb is often utilized in a derived sense of trusting another person for support.[50] The sarcastic identification of Pharaoh as a *reed crutch (miš'enet qāneh)* employs what must have been a widely circulated image of the Egyptians.[51] Once again Egypt's support would prove worthless for the house of Israel.[52] In fact, instead of aiding the nation, Israel's southern neighbor would maim them.

The problems of a reed staff are cited in two parallel lines. Beyond failing to offer any support, it splinters the hands of those who use it as a cane, and tears the armpits of those who use it like a crutch. In other words, Judah will collapse with or without Egypt's aid, which means the Egyptians have the most to lose by even offering help. For persisting in his Levantine enterprises and trying to ward off the Babylonians, Hophra will find himself and his people the target of the same covenant curses that Yahweh is about

---

50. See Isa. 10:20; 2 Chr. 16:7. It is also applied to reliance on horses (Isa. 31:1), gods (Isa. 50:10), and Yahweh (Mic. 3:11; Isa. 10:20; 2 Chr. 13:18; 14:10; 16:7-8; Ps. 23:4). Cf. F. Stolz, *THAT,* 2:161.

51. Cf. the Assyrian Rabshakeh's comment to Hezekiah more than a century earlier: "Look, you rely on the crutch of this crushed reed, Egypt, on which, if a man leans, it will enter his hand and pierce it. Such is Pharaoh to all who rely on him" (Isa. 36:6 = 2 K. 18:21).

52. The reed as a picture of fragility is also known outside Israel, as the following Hittite treaty curse demonstrates: "May the oath sworn in the presence of these gods break you like reeds, you, Kurtiwaza, together with your country" (*ANET,* p. 206).

to inflict on his people. He will attack Egypt with the sword, cut off all life, and turn the land of Egypt into a wasteland. Under the ensuing duress they will acknowledge Yahweh.

In isolation Ezekiel's development of the metaphor could have been interpreted as condemnation of Egypt for not having lent enough support to Judah and for failing to rescue Judah from the Babylonians. But in the broader context this is clearly not his intention. Egypt's guilt stems from its agreement to assist Zedekiah in his resistance to Nebuchadrezzar. In so doing Egypt placed itself in the way of Yahweh's agent, rendering itself an enemy not only of the Babylonian but also of God. Accordingly, this oracle represents the obverse of ch. 17, which reflects the Judean king's appeal to Egypt for help instead of submitting to Babylon. By resisting Yahweh's agent Hophra was interfering in Yahweh's inexorable divine plan for Israel. For that he would pay dearly.

c. Yahweh's Intentions Concerning Egypt (29:9b-16)

9b " 'Because you said,[53] "The Nile[54] belongs to me; I made it."[55]

10 Therefore I am against you and against your river channels. I will turn the land of Egypt into an utterly desolate wasteland,[56] from Migdol to Syene,[57] as far as the Nubian frontier. 11 No foot, human or animal, will pass through it.[58] It will remain uninhabited for forty years. 12 I will turn the land of Egypt into the most desolate of all desolate lands,[59] and her cities will be the most desolate among ruined[60] cities — for forty years. And I will scatter the Egyptians among the nations, and disperse them among the lands.

13 That is[61] — thus has the Lord Yahweh declared — at the end of

---

53. Reading second person with LXX, Syr., Vulg., in place of MT third person, which seems to have been influenced by v. 3.

54. LXX has pl., Οἱ ποταμοί, harmonizing with its pl. rendering of v. 3.

55. LXX provides a plural object which harmonizes with its rendering of v. 3.

56. lĕḥorĕbôt ḥōreb šĕmāmâ, lit. "to wastes, waste, desolation." LXX reads the second term as ḥereb, "sword," but the occurrence of the present triad of expressions in Isa. 61:4 and Jer. 49:13 supports MT.

57. Vocalizing sĕwēnēh as sĕwēnāh. LXX adds the copula.

58. Note the chiastic structure of the Hebrew: lō' ta'ăbār-bāh regel 'ādām wĕregel bĕhēmâ lō' ta'ăbār-bāh.

59. On bĕtôk used with a superlative force see Joüon-Muraoka, Grammar, §141j (1).

60. Some Hebrew mss. substitute a Niphal participle, naḥărābôt, for MT Hophal mohŏrābôt. Cf. 30:7. Joüon's suggestion (Bib 10 [1929] 308) that the initial mem is a dittograph from preceding 'ārîm is possible.

61. kî functions deictically (cf. W. T. Claassen, "Speaker-Oriented Functions of

forty years, I will gather Egypt from among the peoples where they have been scattered. 14 *I will restore the fortunes of Egypt, and bring them back*[62] *to the land of Pathros, the land of their origin. There*[63] *they will be a lowly kingdom.* 15 *It will be the lowliest of kingdoms,*[64] *and will never again assert itself over the nations. I will keep them small so they never again lord it over the nations.* 16 *Never again will they*[65] *serve as an object of trust*[66] *for the house of Israel — a reminder*[67] *of guilt they incurred when they turned toward them. Then they will know that I am the Lord Yahweh.' "*

(1) Yahweh's Immediate Plans (29:9b-12)

Verses 9b-12 consist of two parts typical of judgment speeches, the accusation and the announcement of judgment, introduced by *ya'an* and *lākēn,* respectively.

9b-10a   These lines deliberately echo v. 3, though the order of the two principal parts is reversed. The accusation is brief, repeating the presumptuous boast of Pharaoh in v. 3, with some minor variations.[68] The announcement of divine action opens by repeating Yahweh's fundamental opposition to Pharaoh by means of the challenge formula. Although the echo strategy is obvious, several striking modifications from v. 3 are introduced. First, the great sea monster has been reduced to nothing. Ezekiel (on Yahweh's behalf) refuses to honor him with either his Egyptian or his Hebrew title, "Pharaoh" or "king of Egypt," respectively. He makes no explicit reference to Pharaoh at all. Second, instead of focusing on the king, Yahweh's opposition is extended to the channels of the Nile. In fact, the sentence is concerned only about the fate of the land of Egypt. Pharaoh has become irrelevant.

Kî in Biblical Hebrew," *JNSL* 11 [1983] 32), pointing forward to an epexegetical clause, clarifying the meaning of the preceding reference to forty years.

62. LXX καὶ κατοικιῶ mistakenly treats *wahăšibōtî* as if from *yāšab,* "to dwell," rather than *šûb,* "to return."

63. LXX omits *šām.*

64. LXX telescopes the transition from v. 14 to v. 15 by omitting *tihyeh šĕpālâ.*

65. Read pl. with the versions in place of MT masc. sg., which is awkward in the context of masc. pls. and fem. sgs. But MT might be defended on the grounds of *lectio difficilior* and the interchangeability of king and nation in the context. However, see the commentary on v. 10a.

66. On *lamed* plus *mibṭāḥ* meaning "an object of trust," see Jer. 17:7 (cf. also 2:37).

67. *mazkîr,* from *zākar,* "to remember," is used elsewhere of "herald, spokesman." In Ezek. 21:28 the term denotes an official prosecutor, who accuses Israel of perjury and violating her vassal oath.

68. V. 3: *lî yĕʾōrî waʾănî ʿăśîtinî;* v. 9b: *yĕʾōr lî waʾănî ʿăśîtî.*

10b-12 Verse 10b functions as a thesis statement for vv. 11-12: Yahweh will transform the land into an utter wasteland. Ezekiel employs a series of rhetorical devices to highlight the thoroughness of the devastation. First, he heaps up terms for desolation, using the plural of intensity *lĕḥorĕbôt* (lit. "into wastes"), and conjoining the cognate nouns *ḥorĕbôt* and *ḥōreb* (lit. "wastes and waste"). Second, he proclaims the ruination of all Egypt. Like Israelite "from Dan to Beer-sheba,"[69] the expression "from Migdol to Syene as far as the border of Cush" defines the borders of the country. Migdol, "Fortress Tower," treated as the northernmost military outpost, is probably to be identified with the remains discovered one kilometer north of Tell el-Kheir, east of the Suez Canal.[70] Syene (modern Aswan), on the First Cataract of the Nile, was the site from which campaigns into Nubia were launched, a fact reflected in the explanatory *Nubian frontier (gĕbûl kûš)*. Third, he announces the cessation of all normal creaturely activity in Egypt. The feet of neither humans *('ādām)* nor animals *(bĕhēmâ)* will pass over or traverse *('ābar)* the land.[71] Fourth, with twin superlatives, he declares the unprecedented scope of the disaster (v. 12). Among ruined cities and countries, Egypt will set a new standard of devastation. Fifth, twice he announces that the ruination will last *forty years*. The figure recalls 4:4-8, according to which Ezekiel was to lie on his right side, one day for every year that Judah was to be exiled, but the number is also reminiscent of the duration of Israel's wilderness wanderings, the purpose of which was to eliminate a faithless generation (Num. 14:20-35). Yahweh's goal here is presumably similar — to punish a generation that had dared to interfere with Yahweh's plans for Judah and the Babylonians. Sixth, in terms reminiscent of earlier warnings of the deportation of Judah's population,[72] Ezekiel predicts the exile of Egypt's population among the nations and countries of the earth. The prophet's vagueness and hyperbolic style contrast sharply with the detail and realism with which Jeremiah describes the same events. In Jer. 43–44 the senior prophet speaks specifically of Nebuchadrezzar attacking Pharaoh's palace at Tahpanhes, burning the temples of the Egyptian gods, shattering the obelisks of Heliopolis, and bringing disaster to the Jewish exiles in that land.[73]

---

69. On which see M. Sæbø, "Grenzbeschreibung und Landideal: Mit besonderer Berücksichtigung der *min-'ad*-Formel," *ZDPV* 90 (1974) 14-37.

70. So E. Oren, " 'Migdol' Fortress in North-Western Sinai," *Qad* 10 (1977) 71-76. According to Jer. 44:1 and 46:14, a colony of Jews was located at Migdol, as well as at Tahpanhes and Memphis.

71. On the merismic phrase *'ādām ûbĕhēmâ*, see Ezek. 5:14; 14:15; 33:28; 36:34; as well as 32:14.

72. See 11:16; 12:15; 20:23; 22:15; cf. also 36:19. The warning will resurface in 30:23, 26.

73. Ezekiel's style bears a closer resemblance to Jer. 46:13-26, which predicts the

(2) Yahweh's Long-Range Plans (29:13-16)

13 The introductory *kî* followed by the citation formula catches the reader by surprise, but it is intentional, drawing attention to a dramatic new development in the oracle. The earlier references to a forty-year devastation contributed to the image of Egypt's total destruction. Now Ezekiel offers the Egyptians a ray of hope by giving the number a positive spin. Unlike the oracles against Tyre, which had announced the absolute termination of the city's existence (cf. 26:21; 27:36; 28:19), the forty-year figure sets a chronological limitation on the divine fury. Yahweh will not be angry with Egypt forever; on the contrary, when this generation has been punished he will be roused to action on the nation's behalf.

14-15 In stereotypical terms reminiscent of Ezekiel's promises of restoration for his own people, the prophet announces that the God of Israel will reverse his judgment of Egypt and correct its causes: *I will restore the fortunes of Egypt (wĕšabtî 'et-šĕbût miṣrayim).*[74] In the context this expression means gathering the dispersed population and reuniting land and people by bringing them home to the land of Pathros, "the land of their origin."[75] The name Pathros *(patrôs),* Egyp. *p'-t'-rs(y),* "the south land," refers to Upper Egypt, the territory along the Nile between the Delta *(miṣrayim)* and Ethiopia *(kûš).*[76] The reference to Pathros as *the land of their origins* reflects the anti-Delta and anti-Saite stance of this oracle. When the nation is restored it will not be under the present conditions, a fact reinforced by the last line of v. 14 and by v. 15. The people may be regathered and the kingdom reestablished, but Yahweh will ensure that they never regain their past glory; Egypt will remain a "low kingdom." The great nation that had held ruled over others will itself become a vassal state.[77] To whom Egypt will be subject is not indicated, but it cannot be Nebuchadrezzar since he will be gone long before

---

invasion of the land, the punishment of Pharaoh, the land, and its gods, and the exile of Egypt's population; but Jeremiah's picture of devastation does not appear as thorough as Ezekiel's.

74. On the expression "to restore the fortunes," see J. M. Bracke, "*šûb šᵉbût:* A Reappraisal," *ZAW* 97 (1985) 233-44, esp. 240. Ezekiel uses the expression elsewhere in 16:53 and 39:25.

75. Cf. promises of regathering *(qibbēṣ)* Israel and bringing them back to their land: 11:17; 20:41, 42; 28:25; 34:13, 27; 36:24; 37:21; 39:27. On the uniquely Ezekielian expression *'ereṣ mĕkûrātām* see 16:3 and 21:35.

76. The order of names in Isa. 11:11, *miṣrayim, patrôs, kûš,* is found in Esarhaddon's self-designation as "king of kings of Egypt, Pathros, and Cush" *(māt muṣur māt paturisi u māt kusi).* Cf. *ANET*, p. 290. Gen. 10:14 (= 1 Chr. 1:12) treats the Pathrusim as descendants of Mizraim (Lower Egypt).

77. In Ezek. 17:14 *mamlākâ šĕpālâ* had referred to Zedekiah's vassal status. On the expression see M. Tsevat, *JBL* 78 (1959) 201.

the forty-year limitation has expired. Perhaps Ezekiel already anticipates the rise of Persia, whose domination over Egypt was succeeded by Greek and Roman empires. But he probably thinks only of Yahweh as Egypt's suzerain. He is the subject of the actions in vv. 13-15; he will keep the nation small (*šĕpālâ*) so it never again imposes its power over the nations (or indulges in the hollow boasting of vv. 3, 9).

16 Ezekiel returns to Yahweh's specific complaint against Egypt. They had encouraged the house of Israel to trust them for relief against Nebuchadrezzar, his agent. But rather than providing Israel with another opportunity for help, Egypt's restoration will serve as a reminder to Yahweh's own people of their perfidy (*'āwōn*) in trusting anyone other than himself. Ever since Isaiah, the prophets had condemned reliance on Egypt as a sure ticket to disaster.[78] This prophecy concludes with a final reminder that when Egypt's punishment and restoration are complete, the Egyptians will recognize the One behind all these events as the sovereign Yahweh.

The genre of vv. 13-16 is a modified restoration oracle. But the question arises why Ezekiel should have held out such hope for Egypt, when none appears to have been offered the other nations. Yahweh had previously spoken of cutting Ammon off from the peoples, making it perish from the lands, and destroying it (25:7); erasing the memory of the Ammonites (and presumably of Moab) from among the nations (25:10); cutting off all life and laying the entire land of Edom waste (25:13); cutting off the Cherethites (Philistines) and destroying the remnant of the Sea Peoples (25:16); and eliminating Tyre altogether (26:21; 27:36; 28:19). Why should Egypt be singled out for preferential treatment? A hint may be found in the correspondence between 28:24 and 29:16, whose common features may be highlighted by juxtaposing them as follows:[79]

28:24	29:16
wĕlō'-yihyeh 'ôd lĕbêt yiśrā'ēl	*wĕlō' yihyeh-'ôd lĕbêt yiśrā'ēl*
sillôn mam'îr wĕqôṣ mak'ib	*lĕmibṭāḥ*
mikkol sĕbîbōtām haššā'ṭîm 'ōtām	*mazkîr 'āwōn bipĕnôtām 'aḥărêhem*
And there will be no more	And there will be no more
for the house of Israel	for the house of Israel
a prickling briar or painful thorn	an object of trust —
from any of their neighbors	a reminder of iniquity
who treated them with contempt.	because they turned to them [Egypt].

78. See Isa. 20:5; 30:7; 36:6; Jer. 37:5-10; 43:8-10; 44:29-30; 46:25-26.
79. The translation is necessarily wooden and literal.

The dissimilarities between these two purpose statements reflect the differences in the charges Ezekiel had leveled against the six neighbor states on the one hand and against Egypt on the other. The other nations were condemned because they gloated over the destruction of Israel and saw in its demise an opportunity to take over its land. Yahweh's answer was to eliminate these enemies. With Egypt the problem was the reverse. Whatever its motives, Egypt had tried to prevent the collapse of Judah, leaving Yahweh free to pursue a different course with Egypt to ensure that this would never happen again.[80] This could be accomplished by merely reducing Egypt to vassal status and neutralizing its imperialistic ambitions.[81]

♦ *Theological Implications*

This text reinforces several principles familiar from previous oracles. First, Yahweh is the divine Lord of history. In their hubris nations (and individuals), particularly superpowers, may perceive themselves as independent and in control of their destinies, but Yahweh is able to change this illusion overnight. Indeed, he times the rise and fall of nations according to his purposes. The forty-year devastation of Egypt and the exile of its population serve as a reminder of his lordship over the specifics as well as the generalities of history.

Second, whether they realize it or not, those who stand in the way of Yahweh's plans render themselves his enemies. Since Nebuchadrezzar arrived in Palestine as an agent of Yahweh, Egypt's efforts to stop him represented a challenge to the divine power behind the Babylonian throne.[82]

2. The Land of Egypt: Nebuchadrezzar's Consolation Prize (29:17-21)

> 17 *In the twenty-seventh year, in the first [month], on the first day of the month, the following message of Yahweh came to me:*

---

80. Cf. P. Höffken, "Zu den Heilszusätzen in der Völkerorakelsammlung des Jeremiabuches," *VT* 27 (1977) 409.

81. Isaiah goes much farther in his oracles against Egypt (Isa. 18–19), announcing that "in that day" Judah will occupy a hegemonic position over Egypt, the Egyptians will worship Yahweh, and they, along with Assyria, will be fully incorporated into the people of Yahweh. See esp. 19:16-25.

82. Herein may also lie the solution to the problem of Josiah's premature death, in which ironically the roles were reversed. The author of 2 K. 23:28-30 offers no theological reflection on the event, but the Chronicler (2 Chr. 35:20-27) seems aware of Egypt's historical role. By Necho's own confession and the author's editorial comment, the pharaoh had an appointment with destiny in Syria, being called on to play a role in the providential transfer of power in Asia from the neo-Assyrians to the neo-Babylonians. Josiah foolishly stepped in the path of God's activity.

18 *"Human, Nebuchadrezzar,*[1] *the king of Babylon, forced his army to expend extreme effort against Tyre. Every head is worn bald, and every shoulder rubbed bare. Still neither he nor his army has received any compensation from Tyre for the energy he expended against her.*

19 *Therefore,*[2] *thus has the Lord Yahweh declared: 'Look! I am presenting the land of Egypt to Nebuchadrezzar, the king of Babylon. He will carry off her wealth,*[3] *take her spoil, and seize her loot. And she will be compensation for his army.* 20 *As his reward for which*[4] *he labored, I have given him the land of Egypt, because they were acting on my behalf*[5] *— the declaration of the Lord Yahweh.* 21 *In that day I will cause a horn*[6] *to sprout*[7] *for the house of Israel,*[8] *and I will grant to you fluency of speech in their midst. Then they will know that I am Yahweh.' "*

♦ Nature and Design

Taking up only five verses, 29:17-21 constitutes the shortest of Ezekiel's oracles against Egypt and one of the shortest in the book. Except for a few parallelistic lines, this unit is cast in prose rather than poetic style. In spite of its brevity, it incorporates most of the formulaic elements found in Ezekiel's oracles: an opening date notice; the address of the prophet as *ben-'ādām,* "human"; a bipartite division into a declaration of the issue and the divine response, respectively; the use of *lākēn,* "therefore," followed by the citation formula, to signal the latter (cf. v. 8); a signatory formula; and a concluding recognition formula. The tacked-on appearance of the last verse need not be taken as a sign of inauthenticity; the prophet is merely and rather naturally reflecting on the implications of the oracle for his people. The ideas expressed here would have been even more intrusive prior to the signatory formula.

Conspicuous for their absence are the identification of an addressee,

1. On the spelling of the name see above on 26:7.
2. LXX omits *lākēn.*
3. Since *wĕnāśā' hămōnāh* is missing in LXX it is commonly deleted as a gloss *(BHS).* Zimmerli *(Ezekiel 2,* p. 117) suggests that this is an interpretive element involving the catchword *hāmôn.* Cf. 30:10, 15; 31:2, 18; 32:12, 16; etc.
4. *'ăšer 'ābad bāh,* the suffix on *bāh,* "in/with it," referring to *pĕ'ullātô,* his reward." Vulg. *adversus eam* follows LXX and Syr., which read "against Tyre."
5. Interpreting *'ăšer* causally. See BDB, p. 83, 8.c; Waltke-O'Connor, *Syntax,* §38.4a. Since MT *'ăšer 'āśû lî* is unattested in LXX, Syr., and several minor versions, it is usually deleted as a gloss. Targ.'s paraphrase, "thus exacting payment from them," goes another direction.
6. Targ. *pwrqn,* "liberation," interprets rather than translates *qeren.*
7. LXX ἀνατελεῖ reads *tiṣmaḥ,* "it will sprout," in place of MT *'aṣmîaḥ.*
8. LXX reads "to all the house of Israel."

146

as well as the command to prophesy or to declare this message publicly. Does this mean that this revelation was intended primarily for the prophet's own consumption? Perhaps the problem of the nonfulfillment of his earlier oracle against Tyre[9] was more perplexing to him than to his exilic audience. The concluding reference to the opening of the prophet's mouth and the use of the third person plural in the recognition formula might support this conclusion. The oracle's structure is simple, yielding the following outline:

a. Preamble   (29:17)
b. Nebuchadrezzar's Labors   (29:18)
c. Nebuchadrezzar's Reward   (29:19-20)
d. Concluding Apologia   (29:21)

17 According to the opening date notice Ezekiel received this oracle from Yahweh on New Year's Day in the twenty-seventh year of Jehoiachin's (and his own) exile (April 26, 571 B.C.).[10] Thus this is the latest of his dated prophecies, two years after the vision of chs. 40–48 (cf. 40:1), almost seventeen years later than the previous oracle (29:1-19), and almost sixteen years later than the next dated oracle in the book (30:20). However, this oracle presents a major hermeneutical dilemma. Whereas chs. 26–28 had consistently envisaged a total and permanent destruction of Tyre at the hands of Nebuchadrezzar, delivered some fifteen years later, this prophecy seems to admit the failure of that campaign. Cambyses was the first to conquer this city, though incompletely; not until Alexander the Great did Tyre pass definitively into the hands of a conqueror. How is this apparent failure of Ezekiel's prophecy to be explained? Several solutions have been proposed.

First, the contradiction has been denied. Older scholars have maintained that the oracles against Tyre were fulfilled, and that Nebuchadrezzar did conquer Tyre.[11] However, few if any contemporary proponents of this view may be found. Even if Tyre was subdued, it was not destroyed as had been predicted.

Second, some have claimed that the city was conquered, but when Nebuchadrezzar's troops finally entered they found the island fortress abandoned and its treasures transported safely overseas.[12] This older view has been abaondoned for lack of evidence.

Third, some view the difficulty as an editorial issue, this oracle having been inserted at a relatively late date by a redactor aware of the futile siege

---

9. See 26:1–28:19.

10. See Parker-Dubberstein, *Chronology*, p. 28.

11. E. W. Hengstenberg, *The Prophecies of the Prophet Ezekiel Elucidated*, Clark's Foreign Theological Library, 4th series, 21 (Edinburgh: T. & T. Clark, 1869), pp. 260-61.

12. G. H. A. von Ewald, *Hézeqiél, "Yesaya," XL–LXVI*, tr. J. F. Smith (London: Williams and Norgate, 1880), p. 154, following Jerome.

and concerned to correct the error of the earlier prophecies. In Ezekiel's name he announced the plundering of the Egyptians as a substitute for the taking of spoils from Tyre.[13]

Fourth, the prophet had been mistaken in his original pronouncement, but he is to be commended for honestly intimating that a word from Yahweh had not been fulfilled.[14] Zimmerli observes correctly, however, that the issue here is not the honesty of the prophet but the earlier Egyptian prophecies (29:1-16; 30:1-32:32), whose fulfillment he now announces as imminent.[15]

Fifth, by drawing attention to the fact that the divine word had not been fulfilled (unparalleled in prophetic literature), the prophet calls for the opposite to occur. Van den Born characterizes the fact that Nebuchadrezzar should receive Egypt as payment for his failed efforts against Tyre as a "cynical performance," presumably unworthy of Ezekiel. For him the real tragedy was Nebuchadrezzar's failure to receive Egypt as well.[16]

Sixth, a new situation may call for the adaptation of an unfulfilled prophecy. According to Carroll, "If the first expectation did not measure up fully to the prediction then a further oracle could be produced to incorporate the failure into it." He sees in this oracle clear evidence of prophetic awareness of nonfulfillment and the phenomenon of prediction after the event (*vaticinium ex eventu*).[17]

Seventh, though preserved literary forms of oracles may contain no hint of conditionality, the outcomes announced were often contingent. Prophetic pronouncements did not possess inherent power so that the mere utterance of the word set in motion the events that they predicted, thus leading to an inevitable and mechanical fulfillment. The efficaciousness of the word lay not in the word itself but in the power of the divine speaker to carry out what he had predicted.[18] Nor should one pity prophets for being captive to their utterances. Although the prophets never questioned Yahweh's power to fulfill what he had predicted, they often left room for a different outcome, especially if the conditions that had provoked the prophecy in the first place should change.[19] The oracles against Tyre had been provoked by Tyrian resistance

---

13. Garscha, *Studien,* p. 173.

14. Kraetzschmar comments (*Ezechiel,* p. 222), "Ezekiel was great enough to admit frankly the failure of his prediction, and to draw further consequences from the same. He is fully aware his prophetic status does not depend on the fulfillment or nonfulfillment of an isolated prediction."

15. Zimmerli, *Ezekiel 2,* p. 120.

16. Van den Born, *Ezechiël,* p. 183. But see the response of Eichrodt, *Ezekiel,* p. 409.

17. Carroll, *When Prophecy Failed,* p. 175.

18. Cf. Friebel, "Sign-Acts," p. 167.

19. Note the cynicism of the apostate community in 13:21-25. Note also the

to Nebuchadrezzar, the divinely appointed agent of punishment for Judah who had labored for thirteen years to capture the island fortress.[20] But in the end, Nebuchadrezzar withdrew without capturing the city, let alone totally devastating it, as envisioned in Ezekiel's oracles. While the circumstances surrounding the lifting of the siege are not clear, it is plausible that Baal II finally bowed to Babylonian pressure, accepting vassal status under Nebuchadrezzar,[21] thereby eliminating the need for any further action against the city. The Tyrians would hardly have realized the theological ramifications of their change in policy. From the divine perspective, however, their submission to Babylon constituted a resignation to the will and plan of Yahweh. Now Yahweh could suspend the threats that he had pronounced upon the city, and indeed delay the actual fulfillment of the oracle for 250 years, until the time of Alexander the Great.[22]

But the present prophecy seems to look on these developments as a failure. To be sure, Nebuchadrezzar would have made off with the tribute payments of Tyre jingling in his pockets, but this is a far cry from having conquered the city and confiscated all the precious loot that the merchant state had gathered into its treasure-houses. Furthermore, the lifting of the siege of Tyre after thirteen difficult years put in question the prophet's credibility. Whether these developments (or lack thereof) had overshadowed the remarkable fulfillment of Ezekiel's repeated predictions of the fall of the exiles' own city and had thrown into question his authenticity as a spokesman for Yahweh cannot be determined. Nor are we clear on the effect of the lifting of the siege on Ezekiel himself. Yahweh's intrusion with another prophetic message so soon after the apparent fiasco suggests that the prophet may have been agonizing over his prophetic status. After all, had not Yahweh himself commissioned him to declare the sure word of God?

18 This verse describes the occasion for the oracle. Yahweh is exercised because Nebuchadrezzar came away from Tyre with little or nothing to show for his labors. The verse emphasizes both the pressure the king had placed on his army *(he'ĕbîd 'et-ḥêlô)* to conquer the city, and the great efforts *('ăbōdâ gĕdōlâ)* they had expended in the campaign. Yahweh expands on the latter by mentioning: *every head is worn bald (muqrāḥ), and every shoulder*

---

obvious though undeclared conditionality of Jonah's announcement of doom for Nineveh in Jon. 3:4, and the change in the divine action in v. 10. For the conditional interpretation of this text see Cody, *Ezekiel,* p. 144.

20. See Josephus, *Ag. Ap.* 1.4, §21, on which see Katzenstein, *History of Tyre,* pp. 328-30; Wiseman, *Nebuchadrezzar,* p. 27.

21. See above on ch. 26.

22. This understanding differs from that of Eichrodt (*Ezekiel,* p. 410), who insists on "the sovereign freedom of God to fulfill a prediction of a prophet in whatever way seems good to him," which from the human perspective looks capricious.

worn bare (*mĕrûṭâ*). These expressions could refer to the chafing effects of helmets and armor,[23] but since the Babylonian strategies involved a siege rather than a battle, it is preferable to think in terms of the backbreaking work involved in carrying out a siege. The baldness and raw shoulders were the effects of carrying the vast amounts of dirt required to construct siege mounds and ramps, and probably also an unsuccessful attempt to build a causeway to the island fortress.[24]

The verse speaks of the futility of the effort in terms of unpaid wages. Normally *śākār* applies to the payment a person receives for services rendered on another's behalf,[25] which alone suggests that Nebuchadrezzar is the agent of a third party. The portrayal of Yahweh as a superior who has engaged mercenaries to carry out his agenda is remarkable by itself. Since the task for which Nebuchadrezzar had been hired had not been completed, one could argue that Yahweh was not legally bound to pay him for his work. But he seems morally obligated to compensate the Babylonian for the efforts expended on his behalf, even if they were less than successful.

But how is this verse to be interpreted? Is Yahweh so concerned about material compensation for mortals engaged in his service? Did Ezekiel believe that Yahweh had actually incurred a debt to the king of Babylon? Where is Isaiah's vision of Yahweh of hosts, who leads the stars in martial array and has power to dispose of rulers and nations with a mere breath (Isa. 40:21-26)? Does he not have full freedom to deal with humans as he wants, without being subject to earthly standards of equity and justice? Or is the issue of compensation, which Yahweh himself raises, a foil for the real problem raised by the Tyrian fiasco — that Ezekiel's prophecy has failed? He who had repeatedly declared, "I am Yahweh! I have spoken! I will act!" has not kept his word. The lifting of the siege raised questions of Yahweh's ability and challenged the veracity of his prophetic spokesman. It made Ezekiel look like one of the false prophets whom he had criticized so severely in ch. 13 for seeing false visions. Or is the problem more apparent than real? Perhaps the prophet has forgotten the conditional nature of his own original utterances. Perhaps the discrepancy between this oracle and the original messages against Tyre merely demonstrates Yahweh's absolute freedom of movement. He will be coerced by no one; nor will he be held hostage by his own word.

---

23. See Taylor, *Ezekiel*, p. 201.

24. Cf. the image of Ashurbanipal carrying a basket of building materials (soil?) on his head, *ANEP*, no. 450; *IBD*, 1:135.

25. E.g., of mercenaries (2 Sam. 10:6; 2 K. 7:6; 1 Chr. 19:6; 2 Chr. 25:6); skilled workers (2 Chr. 24:12; Isa. 46:6); advisers (Ezra 4:5). Balaam is hired to curse Israel for Balak (Deut. 23:5; Neh. 13:2); Leah pays Rachel mandrakes for the privilege of sleeping with Jacob (Gen. 30:16). Elsehwere the king of Ya'udi-Sam'al "hires" the king of Assyria against the king of the Danunites (*ANET*, p. 654).

19-20   These verses reaffirm that even if Yahweh's plans have been altered, he has forgotten neither his word nor his agent. The announced settlement of the account is framed by two statements that the land of Egypt is being given to Nebuchadrezzar as a compensation prize.[26] The payment offered by Yahweh is defined concretely as *wealth (hāmôn),*[27] *spoil (šālāl),* and *loot* or booty *(baz),* the normal prizes of conquest, the plundered treasures of defeated cities. Some of the loot may have consisted of Tyrian goods that had been shipped to Egypt for safekeeping during the siege, but the text emphasizes that Nebuchadrezzar is being handed the land of Egypt and *its* treasures. However, Egypt and its treasures are not to be hoarded by the king; they are to be distributed among his troops as well. Whereas the previous oracle had presented the devastation of Egypt as punishment for hubris and its efforts to frustrate the plan of God, here Yahweh's motive is more materialistic. Egypt was to provide the compensation to the Babylonian forces for operating on his behalf, a decision sealed with the signatory formula.

This prophecy envisions a military campaign into Egypt by Nebuchadrezzar. While external evidence for such a campaign is scant, a fragmentary cuneiform text refers to Nebuchadrezzar's thirty-seventh year (568 B.C.) when the king of Babylon marched against Egypt *(Miṣir),* that is, within three years of this prophecy.[28] The occasion for the invasion is unclear, but the apparent reference to Amasis *([Am]asu)* as the reigning king may be correlated with the last years of Hophra's (Apries's) reign. According to Herodotus (*Hist.* 2.161-62), in 570 civil war broke out in Egypt, the end result of which was the death of Hophra and the succession of Amasis (570-526). Nebuchadrezzar may have timed his invasion to take advantage of these troubled political conditions in Egypt.

21   Instead of concluding the oracle with the signatory formula in v. 20, an apologia announcing its significance for Ezekiel's audience and the prophet himself is appended.[29] The statement consists of two parts. First,

---

26. Here "compensation" is *pĕʿullâ,* from *pāʿal,* "to do, make." The noun refers fundamentally to work or deeds performed: Isa. 65:7; 2 Chr. 15:7; Ps. 17:4; Prov. 11:18 (all of humans); 28:5 (of Yahweh). In a derived sense, however, *pĕʿullâ* also denotes the results of one's work, such as the pain it produces (Jer. 31:16) or, as in this instance, the wages paid for work performed. Cf. Lev. 19:13; Isa. 40:10; 62:11 (both parallel to *śākār*); 49:4; 61:8; Prov. 10:16. In Ps. 109:20 it refers to deserved punishment.

27. This term carries undertones of pride. See Bodi, *Ezekiel and the Poem of Erra,* pp. 119-29.

28. See Parker-Dubberstein, *Chronology,* p. 28. For the text see *ANET,* p. 308b; D. J. Wiseman, *Chronicles of the Chaldaean Kings (626-556 B.C.) in the British Museum* (London: British Museum, 1956), p. 94. For a more recent discussion of the text see idem, *Nebuchadrezzar,* pp. 39-40.

29. Cf. the apologia after the oracles against Tyre and Sidon in 28:24-26.

Yahweh announces he *will cause a horn (qeren) to sprout (ṣāmaḥ) for the house of Israel*. Because *qeren* is used in several different metaphors, this statement is ambiguous. The noun denotes literally an animal's horn, and is often used synonymously with *šôpār* (e.g., Josh. 6:5ff.), though the latter usually refers more specifically to a ram's horn. Since horns are the focus of many creatures' power, *qeren* naturally functions figuratively for "strength."[30] Understood in this way, Yahweh hereby offers hope to the exiles. Just because the fulfillment of the prophecies against Tyre has been delayed for more than a decade does not mean he has had second thoughts. He had not forgotten his promises to Israel any more than he had forgotten his debt to Nebuchadrezzar. When the prophet and his people see him settling this outstanding account, they may take heart that Yahweh's long-standing account with Israel (albeit of a different nature) will also be settled.

But the issue has another side. The mixed metaphor, *ṣāmaḥ qeren*, occurs in one other text, Ps. 132:17, where Yahweh promises to "cause a horn to sprout for David" (cf. Dan. 7:7-8, 24; 8:5). This link provides the basis for the long-standing messianic understanding of this text.[31] But most scholars reject the messianic interpretation, on the grounds that the idea of a royal messianic deliverance is not important in Ezekiel, and the notion would in any case be intrusive in this context. But neither argument is entirely convincing. Ezekiel does in fact make several clear messianic pronouncements (34:24; 37:24; cf. 17:22), and the resurfacing of earlier ideas is not unusual in this book.

The second part of v. 21 relates to the prophet personally. Yahweh promises to give Ezekiel *fluency of speech (pithôn-peh*, lit. "openness of mouth") among his compatriots. The audience's first reaction to this statement is to recognize here an allusion to the prophet's previous dumbness (3:26-27; 24:25-27; 33:21-22). But that problem had been resolved long ago, and the unusual construction, *lěkā 'ettēn pithôn-peh bětôkām* (lit. "to you I will grant

---

30. See Deut. 33:17; 2 Sam. 22:3 (= Ps. 18:3 [Eng. 2]); Ps. 92:3 (Eng. 2); 148:14. Cf. also 1 Sam. 2:1, 10; Lam. 2:17; Ps. 75:11 (Eng. 10); 89:18, 25 (Eng. 17, 24); 92:11 (Eng. 10); 112:9. The horn may also connote "arrogance, haughtiness" (Ps. 75:5-6 [Eng. 4-5]), so that one may speak of humiliation as "the hewing off of the horns" (*gāda' qeren*, Lam. 2:3; Ps. 75:11 [Eng. 10]; Jer. 48:25).

31. See *b. Sanh.* 98a. Cf. Herrmann, *Ezechiel*, p. 200; Fohrer, *Ezechiel*, p. 170. Keil (*Ezekiel*, 2:14) recognizes a reference to "Messianic salvation," but not to the Messiah as an individual figure. Levey (*Ezekiel*, p. 87 n. 10) notes that the designation *māšîaḥ* "would have been in order here." The Targ.'s rendering, *pwrqn*, "liberation," is not a strong argument against this interpretation since, in contrast to their treatment of other prophets, the targumists studiously avoided the term "Messiah" (ibid., pp. 4-5; idem, *The Messiah: An Aramaic Interpretation. The Messianic Exegesis of the Targum* [Cincinnati: Hebrew Union College–Jewish Institute of Religion, 1974], pp. 78-79, 85-87).

opening of mouth in their midst''), rather than the simpler, *'eptaḥ pîkā* ("I will open your mouth"; cf. 24:27; 33:21), suggests a more technical usage. As in 16:53, the expression *pithôn-peh* may be associated with Akk. *pît pî,* the ritual by which sacred images are consecrated. Whereas in the earlier iconoclastic context the issue had been the final failure of idolatry,[32] here the idiom is applied to a human being as the authenticated image of God. Ezekiel is hereby reconstituted a living idol,[33] viz., his prophetic status is unequivocally reaffirmed by Yahweh himself. Therefore he need not be embarrassed at the apparent nonfulfillment of previous oracles against Tyre. In any case, the fulfillment is near. When it occurs, that is, when Egypt has been delivered to Nebuchadrezzar and when the horn has sprouted, his status will be acknowledged, and Israel will recognize Yahweh. This, after all, is his principal goal.

♦ Theological Implications

The use of human agents for the achievement of the divine agenda is a common theme in the prophetical books. Now we learn that Yahweh's employment of such agents is neither arbitrary nor callous. His servants may despair, feeling that the only rewards for their toil are grief and pain. As the Servant expresses it in Isa. 49:4:

> I thought, "I have labored in vain,
>> I have spent my strength for empty breath."
> But my case rested with Yahweh,
>> My compensation was in the hands of God.

But God is sensitive to the feelings of his agents. He does not merely call them to do his dirty work and then discard them like some worn-out utensil when it is done. Whether the agents realize it, God leaves no accounts unsettled.

But in spite of appearances to the contrary, this oracle is not primarily about God settling accounts with humans. The mystery of divine providence and the question of God's faithfulness to his word are greater concerns than the reward of human agents. In Ezekiel's audience were literalists who, even though they accepted the empty pronouncements of false prophets, demanded complete fulfillment of Ezekiel's predictions.[34] But this demand robs both

---

32. See my *Ezekiel: Chapters 1–24,* pp. 519-20.

33. Cf. J. Kennedy, *VT* 41 (1991) 233-35; idem, "O Human Being: The Rhetoric of Iconoclasm in the Book of Ezekiel," paper read at the Society of Biblical Literature Annual Meeting, New Orleans, November, 1990.

34. Cf. D. E. Gowan, *Ezekiel,* Knox Preaching Guides (Atlanta: John Knox, 1985), p. 103.

Yahweh and his prophet of vitality and freedom, and renders them impervious to human response. This oracle may not justify Yahweh's apparent change of mind concerning the fate of Tyre, but it reassures the prophet and reminds his audience that this was not a mark of divine impotence or amnesia. God is aware that the oracles against the island fortress have not been fulfilled as originally delivered. But he will not be held captive even by his own word. In the meantime the hearers and readers are challenged with the mystery of providence. In their concern for the literal fulfillment of Ezekiel's predictions, his audience had overlooked the primary function of his preaching: to persuade them to repent of their sins and to acknowledge Yahweh, and to submit to his claims on their lives. Prophetic proclamation is more than fortune-telling; it is rhetorically charged with exuberance, passion, hyperbole, figurative language, abstraction, whatever means it will take to evoke a response in the hearer.[35] But preoccupation with the fulfillment of predictions has a tendency to deafen hearers to the primary message of God and his agent in any age. The enigmas of providence and human history may challenge the observer's faith, but the hearer is warned not to respond with the cynicism or skepticism of unbelief.

This oracle not only reaffirms Yahweh's sovereignty over historical affairs but also declares his personal concern for those he engages as his mouthpieces. In addition to the external charges of incompetence and inauthenticity that the nonfulfillment of Ezekiel's oracles provoked, it must also have created considerable internal stress in the prophet's own mind, perhaps even raising doubts about his role in Yahweh's service. But it is reassuring to messengers of God to read an oracle like this concluding with a personal word for the prophet. Nebuchadrezzar was not the only one who would discover his compensation in the generosity of God; the prophet too may rest in the knowledge that his cause is in the Lord's hands.[36] The knowledge of his presence and the promise of his self-revelation liberate his messengers to confident and cheerful proclamation of his truth.

3. The Day of Yahweh in Egypt (30:1-19)

◆ Nature and Design

Scholarly opinion on the authenticity of 30:1-19 tends to be extremely skeptical. The absence of a date notice (unique in the Egyptian collection), the

---

35. Cf. J. J. M. Roberts, "A Christian Perspective on Prophetic Prediction," *Int* 33 (1979) 240-53, esp. p. 251.

36. See Isa. 49:4; 1 Cor. 4:1-5. Cf. Allen, *Ezekiel 20–48,* p. 111.

poverty of language, and the haphazard enumeration of Egyptian cities are considered unworthy of Ezekiel.[1] The numerous discrepancies between the LXX and MT do not help the prophet's cause. This literary unit has the appearance of a series of footnotes, completing the picture of Egypt's doom as outlined in ch. 29: vv. 1-4, 6-8 link with 29:8-16; vv. 10-12 with 29:17-21; vv. 13-19 with 29:10-11. V. 5 looks like a marginal note that has found its way into the text; v. 9, an exegetical note inspired by Isa. 18. Although the forms of expression sound Ezekielian, they are considered imitative rather than original with the prophet.[2] However, such conclusions not only assume a consistently high literary standard (by Western definitions) as a mark of authenticity, but they also deny the prophet the freedom to expand on his own oracles.

Following the customary word-event formula and the formal address of the prophet in vv. 1-2a, the prophetic utterance proper breaks up into four segments, each introduced with its own citation formula:

a. The Announcement of the Day of Yahweh in Egypt   (vv. 2b-5)
b. The Effects of the Day of Yahweh on Egypt's Allies   (vv. 6-9)
c. The Agent of the Day of Yahweh in Egypt   (vv. 10-12)
d. The Scope of the Judgment on the Day of Yahweh
   in Egypt   (vv. 13-19)[3]

This quartet of subunits is held together thematically by a common interest in the intervention of Yahweh. Stylistically and formally, however, each goes its own way. A, a highly charged announcement of the imminence of the day, reminiscent of ch. 7, lacks a formal conclusion. B is the most complex, being broken up into two halves by the signatory formula at the end of v. 6, and framed by prosaic comments (vv. 5, 9). C is the most tightly knit unit, concluding with the divine self-introduction formula. D incorporates a catalogue of toponyms intended rhetorically to highlight the comprehensiveness of Yahweh's judgment of Egypt. This section concludes with the recognition formula, which gives the entire literary unit the flavor of a proof saying.

---

1. Cf. Cooke, *Ezekiel*, p. 331, and the negative comment of G. Jahn, *Das Buch Ezechiel auf Grund der Septuaginta hergestellt, übersetzt und kritisch erklärt* (Leipzig: Pfeiffer, 1905), p. 213, also cited and translated in Zimmerli, *Ezekiel 2*, p. 127.

2. Zimmerli, *Ezekiel 2*, pp. 127-28; Garscha, *Studien*, pp. 175-78. Eichrodt (*Ezekiel*, p. 415) charitably credits the prophet with vv. 1-8.

3. Blenkinsopp (*Ezekiel*, p. 133) speaks of four oracular sayings. The first two are linked by an AB . . . BA inverted inclusion, featuring "the day of Yahweh" and a cluster of terms (Ethiopia, Egypt, "anguish" [*ḥalḥālâ*]), which leads some to treat them as a single subunit. Cf. Allen, *Ezekiel 20–48*, p. 114; Boadt, *Ezekiel's Oracles*, p. 71.

The absence of a date notice makes it difficult to determine the historical setting for this prophecy. The new word-event formula in 30:1 and the marked change in style argue against treating 30:1-19 as a continuation of 29:17-21.[4] Since the oracles against Egypt are arranged chronologically, with the exception of 29:17-21, it seems reasonable to date the present utterances sometime within the three-month period, Jan. 7 (29:1) to April 29, 587 B.C. (30:20), again in response to the exiles' hopes in Zedekiah's flirtations with Egypt.

a. The Announcement of the Day of Yahweh in Egypt (30:1-5)

1 *The following message of Yahweh came to me:*

2 *"Human, prophesy, saying, 'Thus has the Lord Yahweh declared:*
Howl![5] Alas,[6] O day![7]
3 *For the day[8] is near!*
Near is the day of Yahweh![9]
A day of clouds,[10]
A time for the nations, it will be.
4 *A sword will enter Egypt,*
And anguish will grip Ethiopia,
When the slain fall in Egypt,
And they take away her pomp,[11]
And her foundations are razed.

---

4. Contra Becker, *Der priesterliche Prophet*, pp. 72-73.

5. Targ. adds *w'mrw* (= Heb. *wĕ'āmartā*), "and say," to connect *hêlîlû* with the following. LXX and Vulg. omit the word, but compensate by duplicating *hāh*, viz., ὦ ὦ and *vae vae*, respectively.

6. *hāh*, a hapax variation of the paralinguistic interjection *'ăhâ*. Cf. *'ăhâ layyôm* in Joel 1:15. Elsewhere in Ezekiel the interjection takes other forms: *'āh*, 6:11; 21:20; *he'āh*, 25:3; 26:2 (reflecting malicious delight); *'ôy*, 26:4.

7. Since *hāh/'ăhāh* tends to be followed by the direct address (cf. 4:14; 9:8; 11:13; 21:5), the *lamed* on *layyôm* should perhaps be interpreted as a vocative or at least as an emphatic particle. Thus Boadt, *Ezekiel's Oracles*, pp. 58-59.

8. LXX correctly treats *yôm* as definite.

9. Although most delete *wĕqārôb yôm* with LXX as dittography (cf. *BHS*), the LXX omission may just as well be due to haplography.

10. LXX ἡμέρα πέρας (= *yôm qēṣ*) for *yôm 'ānān* has been influenced by ch. 7.

11. Since *wĕlāqĕhû hămônāh* is missing in LXX and disturbs the rhythm, many (e.g., Zimmerli, *Ezekiel 2*, p. 123) delete the phrase as a gloss. However, Bodi (*Ezekiel and the Poem of Erra*, pp. 120, 128) rightly rejects as arbitrary Fohrer's dismissal of 60 percent of the occurrences of this catchword in Ezekiel.

5 *Ethiopia,*[12] *Put, Lud, all the mixed horde, Libya,*[13] *and the warriors*[14] *of the covenant land with them will fall victims of the sword.'* "

1-2a Following the expected opening sequence of word-event formula, the divine address of the prophet as *Human (ben-'ādām),* the command to prophesy, and the citation formula, the divine word opens with a shrill alarm, reminiscent in diction and tone of ch. 7. The threat originally pronounced upon Israel has been transferred to Egypt. Although the exiles represent Ezekiel's immediate audience, the call to *howl (hêlîlû)* leaves the impression that Ezekiel is addressing Egypt directly,[15] the rhetorical addressee of this message of woe.

2b-3a The prophet's excited words blurt from his lips in short disjointed exclamations whose increasing length and specificity create an ascending climax:

hāh layyôm	Alas, O day!
kî qārôb yôm	For the day is near!
wĕqārôb yôm layhwh	Near is the day of Yahweh!

As in ch. 7, and elsewhere in the prophets, the day of Yahweh identifies the frightening day of his visitation in judgment, though in this opening strophe Yahweh's direct involvement is veiled.

3b-4 The ominous tone is maintained. First, the event is described as a dismal *day of clouds (yôm 'ānān),* which abbreviates Joel's version (Joel 2:1-2).[16] Second, Ezekiel calls it *a time for the nations.* On first sight this ambiguous expression seems to refer to the invasion of Egypt by foreign nations as agents of Yahweh. However, from vv. 5-9, which may be interpreted as an exposition of the last line in v. 3, it is evident that the nations are targets of divine wrath as well. The "day of Egypt" (*yôm miṣrayim,* v. 9) is also the "time for the nations" (*'ēt gôyim,* lit. "day of nations," v. 3a). Ezekiel's primary interest is in Egypt, however, so he must first focus on the effects of the day of Yahweh on this nation itself. Third, the day will be marked by the

---

12. LXX mistakenly reads Πέρσαι, probably under the influence of 27:10.

13. Following LXX Λίβυες (viz., *lûb*) for MT's incomprehensible *kûb*.

14. *bĕnê 'ereṣ habberît,* lit. "sons of the land of the covenant." Contextually, warriors are in view.

15. *hêlîl* appeared previously in a different context in 21:17. The present association of the term with the day of Yahweh is reminiscent of Isa. 13:6; Joel 1:5, 13; Zeph. 1:11.

16. Joel's version reads: *kî bā' yôm yhwh kî qārôb yôm ḥōšek wa'ăpēlâ yôm 'ānān wa'ărāpel,* "For the day of Yahweh is coming! Indeed it is near! A day of darkness and gloom! A day of clouds and thick darkness." Cf. Zephaniah's more detailed description in Zeph. 1:15.

sword — a metonymic expression for war in general — entering Egypt. Whose sword is involved, whether Yahweh's own or that of his agent, is not yet specified. But the effects of the sword are clear. Fourth, it will be a day of terror spilling over into Ethiopia (Cush).[17] Fifth, it is a moment of judgment. The identification of those who fall as *the slain (ḥālāl)* intimates that the victims of the catastrophe are not simply casualties of war; they will be executed for their crimes.[18] Sixth, it is a day of humiliation: Egypt's *hămôn* will be taken away. The choice of this ambiguous expression is deliberate. It means basically "noise, murmur, uproar," but it may also denote "multitude, horde, troops, wealth," and in a metaphorical sense, "pomp, pride, hubris."[19] This is a keyword in Ezekiel.[20] Many treat the expression militarily in this context, viz., as a reference to the hordes of Egyptian and allied soldiers insolently opposing Yahweh, or economically, that is, "wealth, a horde of possessions."[21] Both are possible, but Ezekiel's concern for hubris in general in the oracles against the nations, especially Tyre and Egypt, and the specific reference to *gĕʾôn ʿuzzâ*, "the pride of her strength," in this context (vv. 6, 18), point in a metaphorical direction.[22]

5 While v. 5, constructed in prose, may well be a later addition, there is no reason why Ezekiel could not have glossed his own oral pronouncements with explanatory comments.[23] In any case, the pattern of prophetic exclamations followed by a prose conclusion is repeated in vv. 6-9. In its present context v. 5 serves a transitional function, expanding the vision of vv. 2b-3 and laying the foundation for vv. 6-9 by announcing the fall of nations allied with Egypt. The catalogue of supporters consists of six entries, the first three of which are easily identified; the last three are obscure.

Ethiopia or Cush is Nubia, Egypt's southern neighbor on the Upper Nile. Whereas in the 8th-7th centuries Nubia had provided Egypt with its 25th

17. Note the sensitive assonance between *halḥālâ*, from *ḥûl*, "to writhe in pain," esp. of a woman in childbirth, and *ḥālāl*, "the slain," in the next line.

18. On this meaning of *ḥālāl* see Eissfeldt, in *Studies in Old Testament Prophecy*, pp. 73-81.

19. See Bodi, *Ezekiel and the Poem of Erra*, pp. 118-19, for references.

20. Of its 85 occurrences in the OT 27 occur in this book, 16 in the oracles against Egypt.

21. For the military contexts see 7:11-14; 39:11, 15-16. For the economic, see Eccl. 5:9; 1 Chr. 29:10; Ps. 37:16.

22. So also Zimmerli, *Ezekiel 2*, p. 131.

23. Scholars generally delete the verse as a marginal gloss by a secondary hand, but they cannot agree on the referent. Proposed candidates include Cush in v. 4 (Eichrodt, *Ezekiel*, p. 414), *hămônāh*, "her troops," in v. 4b (Boadt, *Ezekiel's Oracles*, p. 65), "Egypt's allies" in v. 6 (Wevers, *Ezekiel*, p. 227; Zimmerli, *Ezekiel 2*, p. 129; Garscha, *Studien*, p. 175). But this verse is linked with the preceding lexically by *baḥereb yippōlû*, "by the sword they will fall."

Dynasty, in Ezekiel's time Egypt and Ethiopia were sovereign neighbors.[24] *Put* is identified with Libya, located on the North African coast west of Egypt.[25] *Lud* is Lydia in Asia Minor. In the 7th century already, during Ashurbanipal's reign in Assyria, Gyges of Lydia had sent troops to support Psammetichus I against the Assyrians.[26] Herodotus reports an alliance between Croesus and Amasis against Cyrus.[27]

Whom Ezekiel has in mind with *all the mixed horde (kol-hā'ereb)* is unknown. Many modern versions read "all Arabia, all the Arabs," with Syr., but this interpretation is anachronistic. Ezekiel's gaze is on North Africa, a region the Arabs did not overrun until the 6th-7th centuries A.D. His usage of *'ereb* is probably similar to Jeremiah's, who applies the term to the "mixture of foreign mercenaries" in the Babylonian army (Jer. 25:20; 50:37).

Libya (kûb) presents an even greater mystery. Either *kûb* represents an alternative name for another North African nation, preferred here for assonantal reasons, alongside Cush, Put, and Lud, or the form is the result of a scribal error. LXX Λίβυες suggests that *kûb* is a mistake for an original *lûb,* "Libya."[28] This interpretation is weakened by the fact that elsewhere Λίβυες translates *pûṭ* (Ezek. 27:10; 38:5; Jer. 46:9), a name already included in this list. However, the separate listing of Put and Lubim as allies of Egypt in Nah. 3:9 may suggest greater precision in these names, two regions of Libya that occupied the territory between Cyrene and Egypt.

The phrase *běnê 'ereṣ habběrît 'ittām* (lit. "the sons of the land of the covenant with them") is equally strange. Targ. and Vulg. interpret "the people of the land with whom they have a covenant," presumably more mercenaries of a nation allied with Egypt. However, LXX "my covenant" points in a more likely direction, viz., Yahweh's covenant people. Evidence of Jewish mercenaries in Egyptian campaigns is found in several sources. The Letter of Aristeas 13 speaks of Psammetichus I having dispatched confederate (Jewish) troops to fight against the king of the Ethiopians.[29] It is possible that Jews also participated in the campaign of Psammetichus II against Nubia (591 B.C.). Carian, Ionian, Rhodian, and Phoenician soldiers commemorated their involvement in this event by inscribing their names on the colossus of Ramesses II at Abu Simbel.[30] Jeremiah knew the Jewish colonies in Egypt

---

24. On Cush see D. B. Redford, *ABD,* 4:109-11.

25. Cf. above on 27:10.

26. Rassam Cylinder II:95-96, 111-15. See *ARAB,* 2:297-98, §§784-85.

27. Herodotus, *Hist.* 1.77. Cf. above on 27:10.

28. The pl. *lûbîm* occurs in Nah. 3:9 (with Put, Egypt, and Ethiopia or Cush), 2 Chr. 12:3 (with Sukkiim and Ethiopians or Cushim), 16:8 (with Ethiopians or Cushim), and Dan. 11:43 (with Egypt and Ethiopians or Cushim).

29. Cf. *OTP,* 2:13.

30. Cf. Freedy and Redford, *JAOS* 90 (1970) 476-77.

from personal experience, and one of his oracles is addressed to "all the Jews living in Egypt, those living in Migdol, Tahpanhes, Memphis, and the land of Pathros" (Jer. 44:1). Indeed, Jer. 24:8 suggests that the Jewish community in Egypt was sizable enough to be juxtaposed with the remnant remaining in Jerusalem and Judah, which would certainly have contributed to the attractiveness of Egypt as a haven for fugitives from Nebuchadrezzar in 586 (Jer. 43:5-7).[31] Accordingly, "the sons of the land of the covenant" contains a veiled reference to Jewish mercenaries from the land of Israel in Pharaoh's forces, whom the prophet was not willing simply to lump together with the "mixed rabble." The prophet predicts that these troops, who had prostituted themselves by serving in Egypt's armies, would fall to the sword along with the rest of Egypt's allies.

b. The Effects of the Day of Yahweh on Egypt's Allies (30:6-9)

> 6 " 'Thus has Yahweh[32] declared:
> Egypt's supporters[33] will fall and her own arrogant might will collapse. From Migdol to Syene[34] they will fall victims of the sword within her — the declaration of the Lord Yahweh. 7 She[35] will be the most devastated among devastated lands, and her cities[36] will be the most desolate of cities. 8 But they will know that I am Yahweh, when I have set fire to Egypt, and all her allies[37] are crushed. 9 In that day envoys will go out from my presence[38] in ships[39] to terrorize self-

31. For further discussion of the Jewish presence in Egypt during this period see B. Porten, *Archives from Elephantine: The Life of an Ancient Jewish Military Colony* (Berkeley: University of California Press, 1968), pp. 3-16.

32. *'ădōnāy* is absent from the citation formula only here and in 21:8. Some minor versions add it.

33. On *sāmak*, "to lean, support," see BDB, pp. 701-2; *HALOT*, 3:759.

34. Repointing *sĕwēnēh* as *sĕwēnâ* as in 29:10.

35. With LXX and 29:12, reading sg. *wĕnāšammâ*, where MT (as well as Targ. and Vulg.) reads pl. *wĕnāšammû*.

36. Since the land of Egypt is considered feminine, the masc. suffix on *wĕ'ārāyw* is awkward. Read *wĕ'ārêhā*, as in 29:12.

37. For the politico-military use of *'āzar* see Nah. 3:9. P. D. Miller Jr. (*UF* 2 [1970] 167) cites the present text, along with 12:14 and 32:31, as evidence for a root *'zr* II, related to Ugar. *ġzr*, "to be strong, mighty, valiant," hence "warriors" here. But see Rainey, *RSP*, 2:75.

38. Perhaps not knowing what to make of *millĕpānay*, LXX dropped the word.

39. LXX σπεύδοντες and Syr. *msrhb'yt* misread *baṣṣîm* as *'āṣîm*, from *'ûṣ*, "to hurry" (GKC, §93y; Cooke, *Ezekiel*, p. 336) or as *rāṣîm*, from *rûṣ*, "to run" (Ellenbogen, *Foreign Words*, p. 145). G. R. Driver (*Bib* 35 [1954] 300) relates *baṣṣîm* to Arab. *bāṣa*, "to run away." But Ezekiel is probably echoing Isa. 18:2, which would argue for retaining MT.

reliant[40] *Ethiopia. Anguish will seize them in the day of Egypt. Watch out!*[41] *It is at hand!'* "

Verses 6-9 elaborate on v. 5 by describing the context of the allies' demise. The exposition is cast in the form of a modified proof saying, announcing the acknowledgment of Yahweh by Egypt's allies, here identified as *sōmĕkê miṣrayim* (lit. "those who support Egypt," v. 6) and *'ōzĕrêhā* (lit. "her helpers," v. 8). Ezekiel emphasizes that when the props are pulled out from Egypt, the supports themselves will be smashed.

6-8   First, their fall *(nāpal)* will occur in association with the collapse *(yārad)* of *her own arrogant might,* a typically Ezekielian expression for hubris.[42] Second, their fall will occur by the sword *within* the land of Egypt. From Migdol in the north to Syene in the south,[43] the land of Egypt will be filled with the slain of her allies. Third, they will share in Egypt's desolation, a point highlighted by the parallelistic and superlative construction of v. 7.[44] Fourth, their demise is a divine act, an intended consequence of Yahweh's torching of Egypt.[45] The construction suggests that the fire finally convinces them of Yahweh's involvement.

9   Like v. 5, v. 9 offers a prose clarification of *that day (hayyôm hahû')* to the oral presentation. Now Ethiopia is singled out as a representative of the nations that will experience the terror of the day of Yahweh in Egypt. While the phrase *Anguish will seize them (wĕhāyĕtâ ḥalḥālâ bāhem)* ties the statement to v. 4a, the style of the verse reflects Isaianic influence. The only analogue to *day of Egypt (yôm miṣrayim)* found in the OT is *yôm midyān,* "the day of Midian," in Isa. 9:3.[46] However, Ezekiel's interpretation of the collapse of Ethiopia seems to be inspired by Isaiah's oracle against this nation, specifically Isa. 18:2.[47] But

---

40. LXX drops *beṭaḥ;* many delete accordingly.

41. Interpreting *kî* emphatically, heightening the force of *hinnēh,* "behold."

42. With *gĕ'ôn 'uzzāh* cf. *gĕ'ôn 'azzîm* in 7:24.

43. On *mimmigdôl sĕwēnâ* see above on 29:8.

44. *wĕnāšammû bĕtôk 'arṣôt nĕšammôt*
    wĕ'ārāyw bĕtôk 'ārîm naḥărābôt tihyĕnâ

> They will be devastated in the midst of devastated lands,
> and her cities will be in the midst of desolated cities.

On the use of this form to express the superlative degree see above on 29:12.

45. Fire as an agent of Yahweh's judgment is traditional. Cf. Amos 1:4, 7, 10, 12; 2:2, 5. The present construction, *nātan 'ēš bĕ,* "to set fire in," is a stylistic variant of *šillaḥ 'ēš bĕ,* "to send fire in," in 39:6, on which see Block, *BBR* 2 (1992) 118-19.

46. Cf. *yôm hillāḥămô,* "the day of his fighting," in Zech. 14:3.

47. Cf. *haššōlēaḥ bayyām ṣîrîm ûbiklê gōme' 'al pĕnê mayim,* "who sends envoys by the sea, papyrus boats on the surface of the waters," with Ezekiel's *yēṣĕ'û mal'ākîm [millĕpānay] baṣṣîm,* "messengers will go out [from me] in ships."

rather than simply imitating his predecessor, this prophet reconstructs his statement. (1) The direction is reversed; these envoys go upstream, not down. (2) The envoys *(mal'ākîm)* come from the divine court of Yahweh *(millĕpānay),* not simply some earthly capital. (3) Although they also come in ships, these are not flimsy papyrus crafts, but war vessels. Local coloring is added by employing an Egyptian loanword, *ṣîm,* from Egyp. *ḏj,* a type of river ship.[48] The word occurs elsewhere only in Num. 24:24; Isa. 33:21; and Dan. 11:30. The last two texts suggest some large and sturdy vessel, suitable for military duty.[49] (4) The feared become the terrorized. The message of the envoys is summarized in the last line, *kî hinnēh bā'â, Watch out! It is at hand!* As in ch. 7 (cf. v. 14), the announcement functions rhetorically like a sentry's trumpet blast, warning residents and the military to prepare for an attack. On the day that Egypt falls, secure, carefree *(beṭaḥ)* Ethiopia will find no safety in her isolation.[50] Coming after the recognition formula in v. 8, this verse highlights the role of Yahweh in the judgment of Egypt's allies. Although this is Egypt's day, Yahweh extends its effects as far as Egypt's military tentacles had reached.

c. The Agent of the Day of Yahweh in Egypt (30:10-12)

10 " 'Thus has the Lord Yahweh declared:
I will bring an end to the pomp of Egypt by the hand of Nebuchadrezzar,[51] the king of Babylon. 11 He, together with[52] his forces,[53] the most barbarous of nations, will be brought in to ruin the land. They will draw their swords[54] against Egypt, and fill the land with victims. 12 I will dry up[55] the channels of the Nile, and sell the land into the hands of evil men.[56] I will devastate the land and everything in it by the hand of foreigners. I am Yahweh. I have spoken.' "

48. Cf. Ellenbogen, *Foreign Words,* p. 145; Krantz, *Des Schiffes Weg,* pp. 66-69; Lambdin, *JAOS* 73 (1953) 153-54.

49. See C. J. Davies, *IBD,* 3:1442.

50. Elsewhere Ezekiel uses the root only in the phrase *yāšab lĕbeṭaḥ,* "to dwell, live securely" (28:26; 34:25, 27, 28; 38:8, 11, 14; 39:9, 26). Gen. 34:25 also uses *beṭaḥ* in an adjectival sense.

51. On the orthography of the name see above on 26:7.

52. *'ittām* is not reflected in LXX. Boadt (*Ezekiel's Oracles,* pp. 72-73) repoints as *'ātû,* "they have come," from *'ātâ.* But the present use of *'et* occurs also in 38:6, 9, 22; 39:4.

53. *'ammô.* On *'am,* lit. "people," as a military term see 17:9, 15.

54. On *hērîq ḥarbôt,* lit. "to empty the swords," i.e., to unsheathe them, see 5:2, 12; 12:14; 28:7; also Exod. 15:9; Lev. 26:33.

55. The use of *ḥorābâ,* "dry," which occurs only here in Ezekiel (cf. Gen. 7:22; Exod. 14:21; Josh. 3:17; Hag. 2:6), produces an effective wordplay with *ḥarbôt,* "swords," in v. 11. Cf. the Niphal participle of the verb *ḥāreb,* "be desolate," in v. 7.

56. LXX omits this clause, perhaps by homoioteleuton, the scribe's eye having skipped from *yĕ'ōrîm* to *rā'îm.*

In the present context this fragment performs the same function as 26:7-14 did after 26:1-6. The sound of alarm for Egypt and her allies is followed by an announcement of Yahweh's agent of doom, Nebuchadrezzar. His task is to bring to an end the arrogance and insolence of Egypt.[57] But Nebuchadrezzar will not come alone. He will be accompanied by his troops and a host of alien forces described as *'ārîṣê gôyim,* "the most barbarous of nations,"[58] an expression that struck terror in the heart of anyone. These Yahweh will bring in wielding their swords, "to destroy *(lĕšaḥēt)* the land" and fill it with slain *(ḥālāl).* V. 12 focuses on Yahweh's personal intervention. Drawing on a traditional and ancient motif,[59] he declares first of all that while the invaders are slaughtering the Egyptians and their allies in battle, he will dry up the channels of the Nile, a threat reminiscent of Assyrian's boast in Isa. 37:25. For river economies like Egypt and Mesopotamia, the drying up of water supplies was the most disastrous event imaginable.[60] Second, Yahweh threatens to sell the land into the hands of evil enemies, Ezekiel's version of the committal formula.[61] Third, he will devastate the land and its contents through the agency of foreigners *(zārîm).*[62] The concluding self-introduction formula reflects the divine determination. For Yahweh to announce the event is for him to carry it out.

d. The Scope of the Judgment of the Day of Yahweh in Egypt (30:13-19)

13 " *'Thus has the Lord Yahweh declared:*

I will destroy the idols;[63]

---

57. *hišbît hămôn* represents a specific link with 26:13. Cf. Ezekiel's use of *hišbît,* "to put an end to," in 7:24; 12:23; 16:41; 23:27, 48; 30:13; 34:10; 34:25. As in v. 4, the ambiguity of *hămôn,* "boisterous multitude, troops, wealth, pride," must be respected.

58. The expression seems also to have been borrowed from Isaiah. Cf. *gôyim 'ārîṣîm* in Isa. 25:3, 5. The present expression has been encountered earlier in Ezek. 28:7. See also 31:12 and 32:12 below.

59. See the 12th-century-B.C. prophecy of Nefer-Rohu, who spoke of the rivers of Egypt being so empty that they could be crossed on foot (*ANET,* p. 445), and the Sumerian "Lamentation over Sumer and Ur," which describes Enki depriving the Tigris and Euphrates of water (*ANET,* p. 613, line 61).

60. Cf. the description of its effects in Isa. 19:5-10.

61. *mākar bĕyad rā'îm* is equivalent to *mākar bĕyad 'ôyĕbîm* in Judg. 2:14; 3:8; 4:2, 9; 10:7; 1 Sam. 12:9. Cf. the slightly milder and more common form, *nātan bĕyad . . . ,* "to give into the hand of. . ." (Deut. 1:27; Josh. 6:2; 7:7; Judg. 2:14; 13:1; 15:12; 1 K. 22:6; 2 K. 18:30; 19:10).

62. The juxtaposing of *rā'îm* and *zārîm* provides another link with ch. 7. Cf. *rā'ê gôyim,* "the most wicked of nations," in 7:24; *zārîm* in 7:21. See also 28:7, 10; 31:12.

63. *wĕha'ăbadtî gillûlîm* is missing from LXX. Some suggest that the phrase was added to MT after the following *'êlîm* was corrupted to *'ĕlîlîm* (Zimmerli, *Ezekiel 2,* p. 125;

I will put an end to the empty gods[64] from Noph.
Never again will a prince[65] rise from the land[66] of Egypt.
And I will instill fear in the land of Egypt.[67]
14 *I will devastate Pathros and set Zoan on fire;*
I will execute punishments on No.[68]
15 *I will pour out my fury on Sin, the stronghold of Egypt;*
I will cut off the pomp of No.[69]
16 *I will set fire to Egypt,*
And Sin[70] will writhe in anguish;[71]
No will be breached,
And Noph will face enemies in broad daylight.[72]
17 *The young men of On[73] and Pi-beseth will fall by the sword,*
And her cities[74] will go into captivity.
18 *And in Tehaphnehes the day will be dark,[75]*

Hossfeld, *Untersuchungen*, p. 198), but this involves one speculative decision based on another. For defense of MT see Boadt, *Ezekiel's Oracles*, p. 77. On *gillûlîm* see my *Ezekiel: Chapters 1–24*, pp. 226-27.

64. This is the only occurrence of *'ĕlîlîm* in Ezekiel. LXX μεγιστᾶνας (followed by many commentators) eliminates the deity-king association by misreading *'ĕlîlîm* as *'êlîm*. See n. 62 above. On *'êlîm*, "rams," as "rulers," see Miller, *UF* 2 (1970) 181.

65. LXX reads pl., but the sg. predicate supports MT.

66. LXX reads "in the land."

67. This line is often deleted as secondary, because it is missing in LXX and Syr., it interrupts the sequence of Egyptian toponyms, and it employs *yir'â* in a novel way in Ezekiel.

68. Targ. *b'lksndry'* and Vulg. *in Alexandriam* are anachronistic.

69. LXX reads "Memphis," assuming *nōp* in place of *nō'*.

70. REB "Syene" follows LXX Συήνη in place of MT *sîn*.

71. The infinitive absolute *ḥôl* is misvocalized as *ḥûl*, perhaps under the influence of the Qere reading of the following *tāḥûl*. Cf. Kethib *tḥyl*.

72. LXX καὶ διαχυθήσεται ὕδατα reflects *wĕnāpôṣû mayim*, "and water will spread." REB "and floodwaters will burst into it" follows G. R. Driver's rearrangement of the consonants, *wmym nprṣwn* (*Bib* 19 [1938] 177). RSV "and its walls broken down" assumes emendation to *wnprṣw ḥwmtyh* (cf. *BHS*), but this operation is rejected in NRSV: "and Memphis face adversaries by day." MT *wĕnōp ṣarê yômām* translates literally as "and Nop, enemies by day."

73. *'ôn* is misvocalized in MT as *'āwen*, "iniquity." LXX and Vulg. correctly reflect Heliopolis.

74. I assume that the previously named cities represent the antecedent to *wĕhēnnâ*, "and they." LXX supplies καὶ αἱ γυναῖκες, "and the women," which offers a suitable counterpart to *baḥûrîm*. REB "her daughters" assumes that *whnh* is a textual error for *bnwtyh*.

75. Either *ḥāśak*, lit. "he will withhold," represents a mispointing of *ḥāšak*, "to be dark" (cf. the versions), or one must assume an ellipsis of a natural object, viz., "its light."

When I smash there the yoke[76] of Egypt.
Then her arrogant might will be brought to an end in her.
She herself will be covered with a cloud,
And her daughters will go into captivity.
19 I will execute punishments in Egypt,
And they will know that I am Yahweh.' "

That Ezekiel follows up the announcement of the judgment upon Egypt, specifically the drying up of the Nile, with a treatment of the cities affected by the disaster offers further evidence of the influence of Isa. 19 on this literary unit. The apparently random arrangement of the names in the present catalogue does not reflect limited literary skill on the part of the writer. At least three factors may have contributed to the present shape of the text. First, unlike Jeremiah, who resided for a time in Egypt, Ezekiel, living far away in Babylon, had to depend on secondary sources and/or on divine inspiration for his geographical information. Second, the absence of a discernible pattern in the entries may be intentional, reflecting the chaos in Egypt envisioned by the prophet. Third, in spite of the lack of organization, this catalogue of toponyms reflects a keen geographical and historical sense. All the cities listed have had their proud moments. Brought together, the assemblage of names highlights the (apparently) eternal glory and inexhaustible wealth of the kingdom on the Nile.[77] Since the association of particular punitive actions with specific places seems to be random, an understanding of the text is best gained by examining separately the punitive actions inflicted on Egypt and the place-names listed.

Verses 13-19 examine the disastrous day of Yahweh in Egypt from two perspectives. On the one hand, Ezekiel highlights Yahweh's personal involvement in the punishment of the land. Speaking of Yahweh's intervention in the first person, the prophet lists the following actions, most of which are familiar from previous oracles: "to execute punishments" (*ʿāśâ šĕpāṭîm*, vv. 14, 19; cf. 5:10, 15; 11:9; 14:21; 16:41; 25:11; 28:22, 26); "to pour out my fury" (*šāpak ḥămātî*, v. 15; cf. 7:8; 9:8; 14:19; 16:38; 20:8, 13, 21; 22:22; 36:18); "to destroy" (*heʾĕbîd*, v. 13; cf. 26:7, 16; 32:13); "to terminate" (*hišbît*, v. 13; cf. 16:41; 23:27, 48; 34:10, 25; also cf. 7:24); "to devastate" (*hēšîm*, v. 14; cf. 20:26; 30:12); "to break, smash" (*šābar*, v. 18; cf. 27:26; 30:21, 22, 24); "to set fire to" (*nātan ʾēš bĕ*, vv. 14, 16; cf. 30:8, 26); "to cut off" (*hikrît*, v. 15; cf. 14:13, 17, 19, 21; 21:8, 9; 25:7, 13, 16; 29:8); "to put fear into" (*nātan yirʾâ bĕ*, v. 13). On the other hand, statements cast in the third person describe the experience from the perspective of the victims: "be no longer" (*lōʾ yihyeh ʿôd*, v. 13; cf. 12:24); "writhe in pain" (*ḥûl tāḥûl*, v. 16; cf. *ḥalḥālâ*,

76. MT *mōṭôt* speaks of liberation; LXX, Vulg., and Syr. read *māṭṭôt*, "scepters."
77. Cf. Eichrodt, *Ezekiel*, p. 417.

vv. 4, 9); "to be breached" (*nibqaʿ*, v. 16; cf. 13:11; 26:10); "to fall by the sword" (*nāpal baḥereb*, v. 17; cf. 5:12; 6:11, 12; 7:15; 11:10; 17:21; 23:25; 24:21; 25:13; 30:5, 6; 32:22, 23, 24; 33:27; 39:23); "to go into captivity" (*hālak baššĕbî*, vv. 17, 18; cf. 12:11); "to be terminated" (*nišbat*, v. 18; cf. 6:6; 33:28); "to be covered with a cloud" (*kissâ ʿānān*, v. 18; cf. 30:3; 32:7; 38:9, 16); "the day be dark in" (*ḥāšak hayyôm bĕ*, v. 18; cf. 32:8). The cumulative effect of this assemblage of expressions should have put the fear of God into anyone who heard the oracle.

Ezekiel's geography of destruction contains eight toponyms (see map 1, p. 167). The repetition of some entries reflects the relative importance of specific names. I will deal with each one separately.

Mizraim (Egypt). Ezekiel's national interest is evident in the sixfold occurrence of the name of the nation. In biblical times the land of Egypt proper consisted of two parts: the narrow ribbon of green along both sides of the Nile from the First Cataract northward to the apex of the Nile Delta near modern Cairo, and the Delta region as far north as the Mediterranean. The Egyptians themselves referred to their country either as *tȝwy*, "Two Lands," reflecting the duality of Upper and Lower Egypt, or *kmt*, "The Black Land," referring to the Nile riverbed in contrast to the red desert sands. As noted earlier, the English name *Egypt* derives from the sacred name of Memphis, which is unrelated to the Hebrew designation *miṣrayim*. But this name seems to have been common Semitic, being attested in the 14th-century-B.C. Amarna Letters as *miṣri*, in the Ugaritic tablets as *mṣrm,* and in the Assyro-Babylonian texts as *Muṣur*. The last name, however, was used ambiguously, referring sometimes to Egypt, at other times to areas in northern Syria or Asia Minor. The etymology of the name is uncertain, but many derive it from a root meaning "marshlands, borders."[78] Whether the dual form of Heb. *miṣrayim* reflects the duality of Egypt is not certain.

Noph (Memphis). The name Noph, which appears twice in this oracle (vv. 13, 16), and its variant Moph (Hos. 9:6) derive from Egyp. *mn-nfr,* itself an abbreviation for *pepy-mn-nfr,* "Pepy is firm and fair," from which is also derived Gk. *Menophreōs,* Memphis.[79] The sacred name of the city, *Ḥwt-kȝ-ptḥ,* "*Ka* mansion of Ptah," which underlies Gk. Αἰγυπτος, "Egypt," reflects the importance of Memphis as the center of the Ptah cult. Located 15 miles south of the southern apex of the Nile Delta, Memphis was the capital and principal residence of the pharaohs during much of Egypt's history. Even when her political position was eclipsed by Thebes, Memphis remained an important religious and cultural center. In the 1st millennium Memphis fell with the rest of Egypt successively to the Nubians, and Assyrians, and later the Persians

---

78. See J. A. Wilson, *IDB,* 2:39-40; K. A. Kitchen, "Egypt," *IBD,* 1:414-15.
79. Cf. D. B. Redford, *ABD,* 4:689.

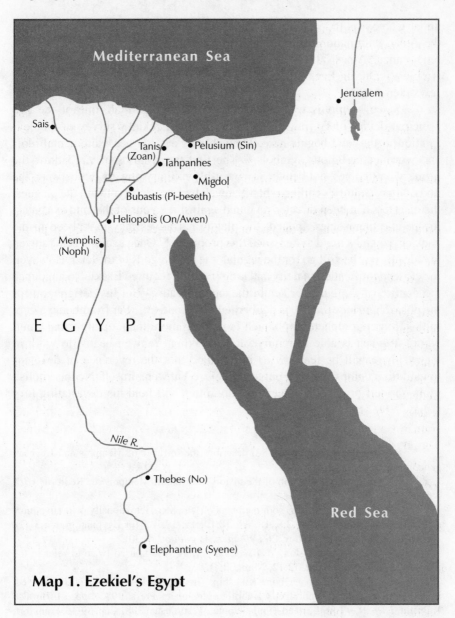

Map 1. Ezekiel's Egypt

under Cambyses (525). With the Saite Psammetichus I (664-610), however, the Asian domination of Egypt was shaken off and Memphis experienced a renaissance. Amasis (569-526) paid particular attention to refurbishing its temples.[80] During Ezekiel's time, the city contained a significant colony of Jews (Jer. 44:1).[81]

Since Memphis was the center of the cult of Ptah, one of the two principal deities of Egypt, it is appropriate that Ezekiel's survey of the devastation in the land begins here. Yahweh will destroy her excremental idols and worthless religious symbols.[82] The first two clauses of v. 13 draw the primary battle lines, not between two earthly military powers but between the gods. Many centuries earlier, when Yahweh had struck Egypt with the plagues, the disasters had been directed as much against the gods of the land as against the people themselves. Indeed, the plague narratives may have been in the back of Ezekiel's mind as he issued this prophecy.[83] Once again, when Yahweh invades Egypt, he will go for the jugular, the patron gods of the land. However, the close identification of deity and king in Egypt required Ezekiel to announce the demise of the human ruler in the same breath.[84] But his designation for the pharaoh, *prince (nāśî'),* is deliberately diminutive.[85] Far from being a god, to the Hebrew prophet the pharaoh is nothing more than a petty tribal chief, whom Yahweh is able to remove at will. When Yahweh begins to work in Egypt, there will be fear *(yir'â)* in the land, not the reverence of devotees toward their deities or kings, but terror before Yahweh himself. Neither foolish idols nor self-proclaimed pharaonic divinities will hold his devastating fury at bay.[86]

---

80. Herodotus (*Hist.* 2.150-82) describes the fortunes of Memphis and Egypt in general under the Saites.

81. For further discussion of the history and role of Memphis see Redford, *ABD,* 4:689-91.

82. The assonantal pair, both members of which are intentionally pejorative, may reflect Isaianic influence (Isa. 2:8, 18, 20; 10:10, 11; 19:1, 3 [of Egyptian gods]; 31:7), though both terms appear in Lev. 26 (*'ĕlîlîm,* v. 1; *gillûlîm,* v. 30).

83. Ezekiel's expression, *'āśâ šĕpāṭîm* (vv. 14, 19) is used twice to refer to the judgment of the gods (Exod. 12:12; Num. 33:4).

84. See B. J. Kemp, "Divine Kingship," in *Ancient Egypt: A Social History,* ed. B. G. Trigger, et al. (Cambridge: Cambridge University Press, 1983), pp. 71-76; also J. Bright, *History of Israel,* 3rd ed. (Philadelphia: Westminster, 1981), pp. 39-40; Frankfort, *Kingship and the Gods,* pp. 148-61.

85. Cf. F. Raurell, "The Polemical Role of the ΑΡΧΟΝΤΕΣ and ΑΦΗΓΟΥΜΕΝΟΙ in Ez LXX," in *Ezekiel and His Book,* p. 88.

86. The notion of instilling fear in Yahweh's enemies as an offensive strategy would have been well understood by an Egyptian audience. In a Karnak text Thutmose III had written, "I [Amon-Re] give thee [Thutmose III, identified with Horus] valor and victory over all foreign countries; I set the glory of thee and the fear of thee in all lands,

Pathros. Like "Egypt," "Pathros" (v. 14) identifies not a city but a region, viz., Upper Egypt, the region from the apex of the Nile southward to the First Cataract at modern Aswan.[87]

Zoan (Tanis). Heb. *ṣōʿan,* from Egyp. *ḏʿnt,* identifies a major city of the 1st millennium B.C. on the Tanitic branch of the eastern Nile Delta, 29 miles from the Mediterranean.[88] The city served as the official royal residence under the 21st and 22nd Dynasties (1069-745), even during the reigns of the priest-kings of Thebes.[89] Although Tanis was eclipsed in political importance by Napata and Sais under succeeding dynasties, the city continued to prosper until Roman times.

No (Thebes). Next to Memphis (Noph), Thebes was the most important and most populous city in Egypt. While there is some question of the origin of Heb. *nō',* many assume a derivation from Egyp. *niwt,* "the city," an etymology that seems to be reflected in Nahum's reference to *nō' 'āmôn,* "the city of Amon" (Nah. 3:8). This expression also recognizes the theological significance of Thebes, the center of the cult of Amon, the state god of Egypt in the New Kingdom (1550-1069). During this time the wealth of the world poured into the royal and temple coffers of this city straddling the Nile some 440 miles south of the Mediterranean. These glory days are memorialized in the magnificent temples whose remains still stand in Karnak and Luxor on the east shore of the Nile, and the Valley of the Kings on the west side.[90] Ezekiel's threefold reference to Thebes reflects the city's historical and cultural significance. Indeed, his announcement of Yahweh's judgment upon Thebes deliberately echoes Exod. 12:12 and Num. 33:4, set historically in a context when Amon was supreme.[91]

Sin (Pelusium). Sin (vv. 15 and 16), derived from Egyp. *swn,* "fortress," resembles *sʾin,* "mud," hence Pelusium, "mud city," in Greek sources. Ezekiel's description of the city as *the stronghold of Egypt (māʿôz miṣrayim)* reflects its strategic location. Situated on "the way of the land

---

the terror of thee as far as the four supports of heaven. I magnify the awe of thee in all bodies. I set the battle cry of thy majesty throughout the Nine Bows" (*ANET,* p. 374). For discussion see J. K. Hoffmeier, "Some Egyptian Motifs Related to Warfare and Enemies and their Old Testament Counterparts," in *Egyptological Miscellanies: A Tribute to Professor Ronald J. Williams,* ed. J. K. Hoffmeier and E. S. Meltzer, Ancient World 6 (Chicago: Ares, 1983), p. 66.

87. See further on 29:14 above.

88. Num. 13:22 has Zoan established seven years after Hebron.

89. The city's importance in the 8th century is reflected in Isaiah's reference to the nobility of Egypt as "the princes of Zoan" (19:11).

90. On ancient Thebes see D. B. Redford, *ABD,* 6:442-43.

91. Cf. Jeremiah's specific announcement of the punishment of Amon of Thebes (*'āmôn minnō'),* along with the pharaoh of Egypt, in Jer. 46:25.

of the Philistines" (Exod. 13:17), east of the Delta near the Mediterranean coast (modern Tell Farama), Sin served as an important point of entry and first line of defense against potential invasions from Asia.[92] Ezekiel associates Yahweh's outpouring of wrath on Sin with his torching of Egypt as a whole.

Awen (On, Heliopolis). Ezekiel's *'āwen* (lit. "wickedness") represents a deliberately pejorative vocalization of *'ôn*, which has its origin in Egyp. *iwnw*, "city of the pillar."[93] Known in Greek sources as Heliopolis (lit. "sun city"), this site, 10 miles north of Cairo, served as the center of the worship of Re and Atum, the Egyptian sun deities.[94] During the New Kingdom, Heliopolis played an important role in Egyptian theology of kingship, inasmuch as kings were viewed as images of the sun god on earth.[95]

Pi-beseth (Bubastis). The Hebrew name, *pî-beset,* deriving from Egyp. *pr-bȝstt,* "house of Bastet," the cat/lion goddess,[96] is preserved in modern Tell Basta, located 35 miles northeast of Cairo on the Tanitic branch of the Nile. The city enjoyed its zenith during the 22nd Dynasty, when it served as a residence for Sheshonq I (Shishak I, 945-924). Ezekiel's reference to her women going into captivity may reflect the prominence of the women in the elaborate festivals held in Bastet's honor.

Tehaphnehes (Daphnai). *tĕhapnĕḥēs,* a variant of *taḥpanḥēs,* answers to Egyp. *tȝ-ḥ(t)-n.t-pȝ-nḥsy,* "the fortress of Penhase." The city was located 15 miles southwest of Pelusium and 5 miles west of el-Qantara. According to Herodotus, Psammetichus I had established a garrison of Greek mercenaries at this fortress to protect Egypt from Asian invaders.[97] However, the fortress will not protect the country on the day of Yahweh when he covers Egypt with a dark cloud and smashes the yoke or staff *(maṭṭôt)* of the nation.

While the day of Yahweh holds out nothing but doom and gloom for Egypt, for Yahweh it offers a ray of light, for on that day even the Egyptians will acknowledge him as the divine sovereign of history.

---

92. In 525 B.C. Cambyses's defeat of Psammetichus III at Pelusium gave the Persians entrance into Egypt. Cf. Herodotus, *Hist.* 3.10-17.

93. Note Jeremiah's reference to the "obelisks of Heliopolis" (43:13).

94. Note the marriage of Joseph to Asenath, a daughter of Potiphera, the priest of On (Gen. 41:45, 50; 46:20).

95. See further Redford, *ABD,* 3:122-23.

96. Herodotus describes the temple of Bastet in *Hist.* 2.138. On the veneration of the cat in Egypt see H. te Velde, "The Cat as Sacred Animal of the Goddess Mut," in *Studies in Egyptian Religion* (Leiden: Brill, 1982), pp. 127-37.

97. See Herodotus, *Hist.* 2.30, 107. This was the destination of Gedaliah's assassins, who took Jeremiah with them against his will (Jer. 43:1-7).

♦ *Theological Implications*

This oracle paints a powerful picture of Yahweh's absolute sovereignty. The day of Egypt belongs to him. He, not Amon or Re or Ptah, is Lord of history, a point he will prove by invading Egypt a second time. On the day of his appointment with this great nation, neither gods, nor kings who perceived themselves to be divine, nor the assembled forces of this vast alliance would prevent his triumphant march through the land. All nations, even mighty Egypt, and all the forces of nature are subject to him. At his command the Nile dries up, fire passes through the land, and daylight turns to darkness. Nor is there hope for "the people of the land of the covenant" who look to Egypt for security. By joining with the neighbor to the south they cast their vote against Yahweh and sentence themselves to the same fate.

While this oracle lacks a direct indictment of Egypt, in it Ezekiel presents a warning for all who are guilty of hubris (cf. *hămôn*, vv. 4, 10, 15) and who worship worthless idols (v. 13). However, it also offers hope to Ezekiel's immediate audience. Although they are in exile, far from the land of the covenant, they may take comfort in the knowledge that Yahweh reigns supreme over all. He who is able to dispose of Egypt in a day can surely eliminate all other obstacles to their restoration as his people.

4. Breaking the Arms of Pharaoh (30:20-26)

20 *In the eleventh year,*[1] *in the first month, on the seventh day, the following message of Yahweh came to me:*
21 *"Human, thus has the Lord Yahweh declared:*
'I have broken the arm of Pharaoh, the king of Egypt. Now look! It has not been bound[2] *so it might heal,*[3] *nor firmly bandaged*[4] *to bind it, to strengthen it*[5] *so it might grasp a sword.*
22 *Therefore, thus has the Lord Yahweh declared:*

---

1. LXX[967, 62, 763] read "tenth year."
2. *ḥābaš*, "to bind," occurred previously in 16:10, of donning clothes, and in 24:7, of binding a turban.
3. *lātēt rĕpu'ôt* may denote either "to give healing" in the abstract sense, or "to administer medicines." See Zimmerli, *Ezekiel 2*, p. 136. Cf. Jer. 30:13; 46:11; and Sir. 3:28, the only other occurrences of *rĕpu'â*.
4. *ḥittûl* is a hapax. The meaning of *lāśûm ḥittûl* can be determined only from the context and from two other occurrences of the root. In 16:4 the verb *ḥātal* denotes "to wrap in swaddling clothes"; in Job 38:9 the noun *ḥătullâ* is used of a "swaddling band." Some soft bandage material seems to be involved.
5. MT *lĕḥābĕšāh* is unattested in LXX*, perhaps by pseudo-haplography, though most delete it as a gloss on *lāśûm ḥittûl* (cf. Zimmerli, *Ezekiel 2*, p. 136).

I am against Pharaoh, the king of Egypt! I will break his arms, both the healthy one and the injured one,[6] and the sword will fall from his hand. 23 I will scatter Egypt among the nations, and disperse them among the countries. 24 I will strengthen the arms of the king of Babylon, and place my sword in his hand. Then I will break the arms of Pharaoh, and he will groan before him like one slain.[7] 25 I will strengthen the arms of the king of Babylon, but the arms of the pharaoh will fall. And they will know that I am Yahweh, when I place my sword in the hand of the king of Babylon, and he extends it against the land of Egypt. 26 I will scatter Egypt among the nations, and disperse them among the countries, and they[8] will know that I am Yahweh.'"

♦ Nature and Design

This oracle is to 30:1-19 what 29:17-21 had been to 29:1-16. A general pronouncement of the imminent devastation of the land of Egypt is followed by a specific introduction of the agent of judgment. This time, however, the agent Nebuchadrezzar is not named (cf. 29:18-19); he is referred to by title three times (30:24-25). These two short oracles share several additional features. Both address the subjects indirectly in the third person, and both have similar structures including the following elements: a date notice, the word-event formula *(wayĕhî dĕbar-yhwh 'ēlay lē'mōr);* the direct address of the prophet *(ben-'ādām);* a divine word to the prophet (cast in the perfect tense); the introduction of the divine response with *lākēn* plus citation formula *(kōh-'āmar 'ădōnāy yhwh);* the announcement of the divine response, begun with *hinnēh,* "Take note!";[9] the recognition formula.

In terms of genre this oracle may be classified as a demonstration oracle, whose goal is to proclaim the presence and character of Yahweh. The style of the oracle is somewhat disjointed and repetitious, leading many to

6. Most scholars delete *'et-haḥăzāqâ wĕ'et-hannišbāret* as a gloss because "arm" is sg. in v. 21, and the expression clumsily breaks the flow. Cf. *BHS.* LXX smooths the difficulty by reading pl., "his strong and weak arms." Targ. paraphrases, "I will break his auxiliaries and his mighty rulers who are in them" (Levey, *Ezekiel,* p. 88). For a defense of MT see Freedy and Redford, *JAOS* 90 (1970) 471 n. 39.

7. LXX reads quite differently: καὶ ἐπάξει αὐτὴν ἐπ' Αἴγυπτον καὶ προνομεύσει τὴν προνομὴν αὐτῆς καὶ σκιλεύσει τὰ σκῦλα αὐτῆς, "and he will bring the sword on Egypt and capture her spoil and seize her plunder," probably a harmonization with 29:19. Cf. Allen's complex reconstruction of the history of MT (*Ezekiel 20–48,* p. 118).

8. LXX strengthens the statement by adding "all."

9. The present announcement is complex, incorporating redundant declarations and an expanded version of the recognition formula. These are probably to be understood as signs of later expansion by the prophet, a phenomenon that was also witnessed in 29:21, although in slightly different form.

question its integrity and authenticity.[10] However, repetition is a weak mark of inauthenticity, and the text contains no certain signs of secondariness: historical anachronisms, hopeless syntactical incoherencies beyond mere textual corruptions, internal contradictions.[11] Furthermore, terms like "inauthentic" and "secondary" should not be confused. An inauthentic text is non-Ezekielian, from a different hand, usually viewed as a member of the prophet's "school" or an external editor, whereas "secondary" is a primarily chronological expression, identifying a segment as an addition to an earlier basic text, without reference to authorship. The prophet may himself have supplemented an earlier oracle with later expansions. This seems to have been the case with 30:5, 9, and may well be the case here. If one assumes that prophetic predictions were made only immediately prior to the events foretold, those elements in this oracle relating to the last phase of the siege of Jerusalem and those dealing with Nebuchadrezzar's invasion of Egypt may have been delivered at least seventeen years apart. But if one allows a prophet the ability to see farther into the future, the problems with Ezekiel adding his own comments almost immediately evaporate. In any case, although one may distinguish primary and secondary elements, the present oracle may be attributed to the prophet in its entirety.

The problems of redundancy and secondariness are acute in the material following the citation formula in vv. 22-26. The pattern of pronouncements, particularly the use of the principal motifs, may be highlighted as follows:

A   1   breaking the arms of Pharaoh
    2   the sword falling from his hands
B   1   scattering the Egyptians
    2   dispersing them
C   1   strengthening the arms of the king of Babylon

10. The stylistic matters include: "I will break his/Pharaoh's arms" (vv. 22b, 24c); "I will scatter Egypt among the nations and disperse them among the lands" (vv. 23a, 26a); "I will strengthen the arms of the king of Babylon" (vv. 24a, 25a); "I will put my sword into his/the king of Babylon's hands" (vv. 24b, 25d); "And they will know that I am Yahweh" (vv. 25c, 26c). Zimmerli (Ezekiel 2, p. 139) proposes three phases in the growth of this prophecy: (1) The core (vv. 20-21) was delivered during the last phase of the siege of Jerusalem. (2) Since vv. 22, 24 assume that Pharaoh already has a broken arm, these verses must derive from a slightly later period (after 587 B.C.). (3) Vv. 25-26 envisage the devastation of all Egypt and the dispersal of its population, which suggests a date near 570, the time of Nebuchadrezzar's invasion of Egypt. Only v. 23 is deleted as inauthentic. See also Cooke, Ezekiel, p. 335; Wevers, Ezekiel, p. 233. Garscha (Studien, pp. 178-81) denies the prophet any hand in this oracle.

11. On repetition see Boadt, Ezekiel's Oracles, p. 85. On the rest of these criteria see Greenberg, in Ezekiel and His Book, pp. 133-34.

    2 putting the sword in his hands
A′ 1 breaking the arms of Pharaoh
C′ 1 strengthening the arms of the king of Babylon
A′ 2 the arms of Pharaoh falling
D   knowing that I am Yahweh
C′ 2 putting the sword in the king of Babylon's hands
E   raising the sword against Egypt
B′ 1 scattering the Egyptians
    2 dispersing them
D′   knowing that I am Yahweh.

The pattern of statements is logical and ordered from the beginning to the midpoint of v. 24. Three bicola are employed to describe three successive stages in the destruction of Egypt: A, the removal of power from Pharaoh; B, the effect on the nation; C, the transfer of power to the king of Babylon. From v. 24b to the end the sequence is confused. While every element in the first section finds a counterpart in the second, the progression is less logical and is disturbed by several interruptions. The only bicolon that remains intact is B, but it is transferred to the end, immediately preceding the recognition formula. Nevertheless, the effect is impressive, bringing three statements involving "arms" together. The interruption of A′1 — A′2 with C′1 highlights the transfer of power from Pharaoh to the king of Babylon. After the first recognition formula (D), the sword itself becomes the focus of attention.

    The core of the oracle is represented by vv. 21-24a, followed by the simple form of the recognition formula (v. 26c). These statements contain all the essential ingredients of the prophecy and present them in a logical, deliberately constructed sequence, while focusing in vv. 22-24a entirely on the divine activity. The intervening material, vv. 24b-26b, represents an explanatory expansion on the core, involving several statements in which the subject is no longer Yahweh but Pharaoh or the king of Babylon.[12] But the style throughout is genuinely Ezekielian, and given the rhetorical function of his oracles (even if a command to prophesy is absent; cf. 30:2), there is no obvious reason why it could not have been part of the original presentation. Repetition is often the key to effective communication.

    Structurally this oracle breaks down into three uneven parts as follows:

    a. Preamble   (30:20)
    b. Yahweh's Past Actions against Pharaoh   (30:21)
    c. Yahweh's Future Plans for Pharaoh   (30:22-26)

12. Pharaoh will groan, his arms will fall; the king of Babylon will raise the sword placed in his hand.

20   The opening notice dates the oracle in the eleventh year of Jehoiachin's exile, on the seventh day of the first month, which translates into April 29, 587 B.C.,[13] three months after the oracle preserved in 29:1-16 was delivered. This prophecy also represents a response to Pharaoh Hophra's (Apries's) interference in Nebuchadrezzar's siege of Jerusalem (Jer. 37:5-11).[14] The residents of Jerusalem would have greeted the news of the lifting of the siege with celebration and new confidence that their claim to being the true people of Yahweh had been vindicated. Although it may have taken several months for the news to reach Babylon (cf. 2 K. 24:8; Ezek. 33:21), Ezekiel's fellow exiles may also have interpreted this turn of events as a sign of Babylon's imminent demise and their soon return.

21   The keyword is obviously *zĕrōaʿ/zĕrōʿôt*, "arm/arms," which appears six times in this short text. The "arm of a king" represents the instrument through which he conquers his enemies. *zĕrōaʿ nĕṭûyâ*, "outstretched arm" (cf. 20:33, 34), is closely related and often associated with *yād ḥăzāqâ*, "strong hand" (see Deut. 4:34; 5:15; 7:19). Indeed, our text refers to the hand (which grasps a sword) three times (vv. 22, 23, 25). Within the OT these expressions tend to cluster in texts involving Egypt, particularly the Exodus narratives.[15] Corresponding expressions occur occasionally in Mesopotamian sources, but the prominence of these phrases in texts concerning Egypt provides effective local coloring. The figure of the flexed arm of the king wielding a sword or club is common in Egyptian iconography. A scene from the reign of Amenhotep II depicts the king holding the locks of his enemy in one hand and the other hand poised to bludgeon the man. The accompanying inscription reads: "Amenhotep . . . who smites the rulers of the foreign lands of the far north, he is a god whose arm is great."[16] But the imagery persists in Egyptian art until Ezekiel's time.[17] Since the days of the Hyksos rulers, the expression *ḫpš*, "arm, power," appears in pharaonic titles.[18] The present Pharaoh, Hophra,

13. See Parker-Dubberstein, *Chronology,* p. 28.

14. On which see J. K. Hoffmeier, "A New Insight on Pharaoh Apries from Herodotus, Diodorus and Jeremiah 46:17," *JSSEA* 11 (1981) 165-70.

15. In addition to the above references, cf. "the greatness of your arm" (*gĕdōl zĕrōʿăkā*), Exod. 15:16; "outstretched arm" (*zĕrôaʿ nĕṭûyâ*), Exod. 6:6; Deut. 9:29; 26:8. On *yād* employed this way see Exod. 3:19; 13:3, 14, 16; 32:11; Deut. 3:14; 6:21; 9:26. See also *yĕmînĕkā,* "your right hand," Exod. 15:6a, 6b, 12.

16. Thus Hoffmeier, in *Egyptological Miscellanies,* p. 57. See figs. 1, 4, 5 there; also O. Keel, *The Symbolism of the Biblical World,* tr. T. J. Hallett (New York: Seabury, 1978), figs. 395, 397-401.

17. See the elaborately decorated 7th-century bronze bowl from the Bernardi tomb at Palestrina, pictured and discussed in H. Frankfort, *The Art and Architecture of the Ancient Orient,* 4th ed., Pelican History of Art (New Haven: Yale University Press, 1970), pp. 329-31.

18. Pharaoh Apophis calls himself *nb ḫpš rʿ,* "Re is Lord/Possessor of a Strong

identifies himself as *nb ḥpš,* "Possessor of a Strong Arm," in both his Golden Horus and Two Ladies names.[19] Indeed, Yahweh's opening declarations in this oracle, "I have broken the arm of Pharaoh," in v. 21, and "I will break the arms of Pharaoh," in vv. 22 and 24, appear to represent a deliberate wordplay on his *nbty* name,[20] which Ezekiel's audience would have had no difficulty appreciating. Freedy and Redford recognize the irony: "the 'strong-armed' king had suffered a broken arm, and Yahweh, not Amun-re, had offered his own *ḥpš*-sword to Nebuchadrezzar, not to Apries [Hophra]!"[21]

In the opening statement Yahweh declares that he is responsible for the deprivation of the Egyptian's power.[22] The particle *wĕhinnēh, Now look* (lit. "behold"), draws the hearers' attention to the following announcement: the pharaoh's arm will not be healed. The syntax of v. 21b is difficult, but the sense is clear. Medical attention has been deliberately withheld from the king. The arm has been left unbound and unbandaged that it might not heal or regain its strength to seize the sword again. Yahweh's aim in smashing Pharaoh's arm is therefore twofold: to punish him for daring to interfere with his plans and his agent, and to crush all hopes of the Judeans, who were looking to the Egyptians for deliverance from the Babylonians.

22-23 The shift in tense of the verbs from the past to the future announces the imminent defeat of Egypt. As noted earlier, the link between vv. 21 and 22 is awkward. In judgment speeches the formulation *lākēn* plus citation formula usually marks the transition from the indictment to the announcement of the sentence. Since the present oracle contains no charges against the Egyptians, the formulae must be interpreted rhetorically, linking two parts of an oracle to prevent the reader from stopping prematurely.[23] Here

---

Arm"; the Golden Horus name of Thutmose IV was *wsr ḥpš dr psḏt,* "Mighty of Arm Who Subdues the Nine Bows." Of Amenhotep II it is written, "Amenhotep . . . who smites foreign rulers of the far north, he is a god whose arm *(ḥpš)* is great." For a discussion of these and similar names see J. K. Hoffmeier, "The Arm of God Versus the Arm of Pharaoh in the Exodus Narratives," *Bib* 67 (1986) 378-87.

19. On the use of multiple names and titles reflecting a pharaoh's divine and earthly roles, see D. B. Redford, "Pharaoh," *ABD,* 5:288-89.

20. On which see A. Gardiner, *Egypt of the Pharaohs: An Introduction* (repr. London: Oxford University Press, 1966), pp. 51-52.

21. Freedy and Redford, *JAOS* 90 (1970) 482-83. So also Hoffmeier, *JSSEA* 11 (1981) 168; idem, *Bib* 67 (1986) 384.

22. Cf. other forms of the idiom: *gāda' zĕrôa',* "to cut off the arm" (1 Sam. 2:31), and *dikē' zĕrō'ôt,* "to crush the arms" (Job 22:9).

23. Cf. W. E. March, *"Lākēn: Its Functions and Meanings,"* in *Rhetorical Criticism,* Fest. J. Muilenburg, ed. J. J. Jackson and M. Kessler, PTMS 1 (Pittsburgh: Pickwick, 1974), p. 260. It is also possible, but less likely, that vv. 22-26 represent fragments of what was originally a more complete prophecy, or that the prophet assumes general familiarity with the offenses of which Egypt is guilty.

the construction highlights the fact that Yahweh is not yet finished with Egypt. Not only will the wounded arm not heal, but the other arm will be broken as well.

Yahweh's fundamental disposition is expressed in the challenge formula, *I am against Pharaoh, the king of Egypt!" (hinĕnî 'el-par'ōh melek-miṣrayim).*[24] This opposition will be demonstrated by Yahweh's breaking both of Pharaoh's arms. The imagery suggests that Pharaoh has transferred the sword to his left hand. Indeed, some see here an allusion to Egypt's two-pronged attack on Nebuchadrezzar's forces. The broken arm represents Hophra's land force, which has already been defeated, and the sound arm his navy, which is still actively engaged in the defense of Tyre. It seems Egyptian naval aid had made it possible for Tyre to withstand Nebuchadrezzar's siege for thirteen years. But when this arm is destroyed chaos will fill the land of Egypt and its population will be dispersed throughout the world (cf. 29:12).

24 With the announcement of the transfer of power, it becomes evident that the sword being wielded is in fact Yahweh's sword. Having seized it from Pharaoh's hand, Yahweh will deliver it to the king of Babylon. Egypt has had its day in Palestine; the time has come for Nebuchadrezzar to play his role in the divine scheme of things without interference. V. 24 reiterates Yahweh's determination to break Pharaoh's arm. But now we learn that the effects of Yahweh's action against the pharaoh go beyond neutralizing his power. The prediction that *he will groan* [*nā'aq na'ăqôt,* lit. "groan groanings"] *before him like one slain* implies that Pharaoh himself will be killed.

25 The themes of the preceding verses are reiterated. The strengthening *(heḥĕzîq)* previously denied Pharaoh's crushed arm (v. 21) will be granted to the king of Babylon's healthy arm, into which Yahweh will then place his sword. After the manner of the Egyptian rulers, the king of Babylon will flex his arm and brandish the sword of Yahweh over the entire land of Egypt. In the meantime Yahweh will scatter the population throughout the world. In an impressive affirmation of corporate solidarity, king, people, and land will all succumb to the fury of God's wrath. In the end Yahweh's purposes will have been served: even the Egyptians will acknowledge him.

♦ *Theological Implications*

To "enlightened" Westerners, with their secular view of reality, the course of human history is determined by the Machiavellian politics of power. Whoever amasses the most powerful military force wins. So it appeared to the people of Jerusalem. Forgetting they were under the divine patronage of Yahweh,

---

24. On the form and significance of the challenge formula see my *Ezekiel: Chapters 1–24,* pp. 201-2.

they turned to Egypt, a formidable ally, for help, expecting its military might to turn back the enemy forces of Nebuchadrezzar. However, they overlooked one important fact. Their God was at the same time the universal Sovereign who alone determines the course of history. By God's decision Nebuchadrezzar's forces are besieging Jerusalem, and by God's determination they will succeed. Anyone who opposes the Babylonian opposes God. The arms of the strongest nation in the world crumble before God's mighty power.

But a second drama is being played out on another plane. The primary conflict in this oracle is not between Judah and Nebuchadrezzar, or even between Egyptian and Babylonian imperial forces. It is being waged in the heavens. Hophra has come as Horus, the divine king of Egypt, to thwart the plans of the divine King of Israel. As in the days of the exodus, when Yahweh announces his opposition to Pharaoh, he is challenging the gods of Egypt to a duel. This time, however, instead of standing by as spectators to Yahweh's rout of the Egyptians, outsiders (Nebuchadrezzar and the Babylonians) will serve as his agents. Instead of seeking to deliver his people from the bondage of the Egyptians, Yahweh is determined to destroy the remnant who have relied on the Egyptians for support. But the outcome of the battle on the heavenly plane will be the same: the gods of Egypt will be humbled, and the strong arm of Yahweh will prevail. His will shall be done on earth as it is in heaven.

5. The Doom of the Pharaonic Tree (31:1-18)

◆ *Nature and Design*

The boundaries of Ezekiel's fifth oracle against Egypt are marked by the date notice and word-event formula in 31:1 and the divine signatory formula in v. 18. After the preamble (vv. 1-2a) the oracle proper divides structurally into three parts: a poetic allegory of the magnificent cosmic tree (vv. 2b-9), an announcement of judgment concerning the cosmic tree (vv. 10-14), and an announcement of the descent of the cosmic tree to Sheol (vv. 15-18). Both the second and third segments are set off by initial citation formulae.

The text is obviously composite, and most scholars deny the exilic prophet major portions.[1] The arrangement of the three primary divisions is

---

1. On the assumption of a poetic original, Hölscher (*Hesekiel,* pp. 152-55) limited the authentic core to vv. 3-4, 6-8. Supposedly vv. 10-18 have nothing to do with the poem. Because v. 5 opens oddly with *'al-kēn,* "Therefore," and contains two Aramaic forms (*gābĕhā',* "height," and *sar'appōtāyw,* "boughs"), and v. 9 introduces a new theological dimension, his deletion of these two verses is widely accepted. Cf. Wevers, *Ezekiel,* p. 234; Zimmerli, *Ezekiel 2,* pp. 142-46, 150. Cf. the complex reconstruction of the text's evolution with radically different results by Garscha (*Studien,* pp. 184-85) and H. Schweizer ("Der

logical, however, and the parts display strong signs of coherence. The entire oracle is enveloped in a double frame containing references to Pharaoh and his hordes *(parʿōh wahămônô)* and the critical question, *ʾel-mî dāmîtā*, "To whom do you compare?" Parts A and B are deliberately conjoined with *lākēn*, "Therefore," in v. 10. V. 14 is a hinge verse, tying the downfall of the tree, dealt with in vv. 10-13, to the descent into Sheol, described more fully in vv. 15-18. The lexical links among the three are also strong, and may be portrayed diagrammatically as follows:

Feature	A	B	C
tower high *(gĕbah qômâ)*	3, 5	10, 14 (cf. 10b, 14b)	
shade *(ṣēl)*	3, 6	12	17
crown among the clouds *(ṣamartô ʾel-bên ʿăbōtîm)*	3	10, 14	
waters/deep/streams *(mayim/tĕhôm/nahărôtêhā)*	4		15
trees of the field *(ʿăṣê haśśādeh)*	4, 5		16
boughs *(pōʾrōt)*	5, 6, 8	12, 13	
branches *(dālîyôt)*	7, 9	12	
mighty waters *(mayim rabbîm)*	5, 7		15
birds of the sky *(ʿôp haššāmayim)*	6	13	
wild animals *(ḥayyat haśśādeh)*	6	13	
trees of Eden *(ʿăṣê ʿēden)*	9		16, 18a, 18b
all well-watered trees *(kol-ʿăṣê-/šōtê-mayim)*		14	16
the netherworld *(ʾereṣ taḥtît)*		14	16, 18
those who go down to the pit *(yôrĕdê bôr)*		14	16, 18

Generically the oracle is amorphous, not conforming neatly to the patterns Ezekiel has used elsewhere. Unlike all his other oracles against Egypt, this text lacks the recognition formula, excluding its classification as a proof saying. Based on Yahweh's causation of lamentation *(heʾĕbaltî)* and mourning *(ʾaqdir)* in v. 15, some have recognized a metaphorical lament.[2] The initial recitation of past glory in vv. 2b-9, followed by a portrayal of the calamity and reaction thereto, follows the then-now pattern typical of laments. However,

---

Sturz des Weltenbaumes [Ez 31] — literarisch betrachtet," *TQ* 165 [1985] 197-213; idem, "Die vorhergesehene Katastrophe: Der Sturz des Weltenbaumes [Ez 31]," in " . . . *Bäume braucht man doch!" Das Symbol des Baumes zwischen Hoffnung und Zerstörung,* ed. H. Schweizer [Thorbecke: Sigmaringen, 1986], pp. 89-108).

2. See Fohrer, *Ezechiel*, pp. 174-78; Parunak, *Structural Studies*, p. 400; van den Born, *Ezechiël*, pp. 187-89.

nowhere is this oracle identified as a *qînâ* lament,[3] nor is it possible to restore the characteristic 3:2 *qînâ* meter without drastic reconstruction of the text.

Although most discussions of the genre of this text begin with vv. 2-9, if one considers vv. 10-15 the rhetorical core then this oracle is best classified as a prophetic announcement of judgment.[4] Admittedly, when an announcement of punishment is introduced by *lākēn* plus citation formula, it has usually been preceded by a presentation of charges against the accused. In this case, however, the preceding poem lacks any hint of condemnation. Indeed, one could interpret vv. 2b-9 in isolation as a genuinely positive song of praise for the pharaoh.[5] Not until v. 10 does the reader discover that the poem is to be interpreted negatively. Either the prophet has composed the allegorical poem to provide background for a judgment oracle, or he has adapted a preexistent piece.[6] In either case, the genre of vv. 10-14 is suggested by *ya'an 'ăšer . . . ,* "Because . . . ," which typically introduces a formal indictment. Indeed, the accusation in v. 10 recalls the oracle against the prince of Tyre in 28:1-10 in both content and form.[7] The formal links extend to 28:6-7, where *lākēn* plus citation formula plus *ya'an* introduces an expanded version of the indictment, followed by the announcement of punishment in the first person, with Yahweh as the subject, though in the present case the transition to the latter is marked simply by the *waw*-consecutive plus imperfect (v. 11).[8] The function of vv. 15-18 is to describe the effect of the judgment of Pharaoh on the surrounding nations.[9]

The formal links with ch. 28 suggest that this oracle also be interpreted as prophetic satire. Here too Ezekiel employs the technique of intensified reversal to tell a story of a colossal fall. Like the king of Tyre, the pharaoh,

---

3. Cf. 19:1, 14; 26:17; 28:12; 32:2.

4. See Hals, *Ezekiel,* p. 220.

5. Cf. Gowan, *When Man Becomes God,* p. 94.

6. See Schweizer, *TQ* 165 (1981) 197-213; idem, in *Bäume braucht man doch,* pp. 90-92.

7. Cf. the following synopsis (with literal translations):

28:2	31:10
	lākēn
kōh-'āmar 'ădōnāy yhwh	*kōh 'āmar 'ădōnāy yhwh*
ya'an gābah libbĕkā	*ya'an 'ăšer gābahtā bĕqômâ*
Thus has the Lord Yahweh declared,	Thus has the Lord Yahweh declared,
"Because your heart is high . . ."	"Because you have been high in height . . ."

8. See the more formal *lākēn* plus *hinĕnî* plus participle in 28:7.

9. This pattern of accusation — announcement of judgment — public reaction (signaled by the citation formula) has been witnessed in earlier oracles against Tyre. Vv. 15-18 display clear affinities of both form and substance to 26:15-21. See also the notices of public reaction in 27:28-36; 28:19; 32:9-10, 16.

plagued by bloated self-esteem and hubris, is not merely brought down to the ground but consigned to the farthest reaches of the netherworld, where the most despicable sorts of people reside. The oracle contains most of the principal rhetorical features of prophetic satire: an initial positive portrayal of the accused, a catalogue of evidences of status, the reductive use of natural imagery.[10] The only major element that may be missing is a quotation put in the mouth of the accused to clarify the grounds for the satirical attack. On form-critical grounds, however, vv. 3-8, introduced by *hinnēh* (lit. "behold"), may be construed as Pharaoh's verbal response to the opening question.

a. Preamble and the Allegory of the Pharaonic Tree (31:1-9)

1 *In the eleventh year, in the third month, on the first [day] of the month, the following message of Yahweh came to me:*
2 *"Human, say to Pharaoh, the king of Egypt, and to his pomp:*

'To whom[11] *do you compare*[12] *in your greatness?*
3 *"Look, Assyria!*[13]
A cedar in Lebanon,
With beautiful branches,[14]
Giving protective shade,[15]
Towering high,
With its crown[16] *among the clouds.*[17]

10. See Fishelov, *Prooftext* 9 (1989) 195-211. He speaks only of animal imagery (pp. 203-5).

11. Many follow G. R. Driver (*Bib* 35 [1954] 300) in interpreting *mî* impersonally, "what?" Thus Boadt, *Ezekiel's Oracles*, p. 95; Allen, *Ezekiel 20–48*, p. 122. See the commentary.

12. LXX strengthens the statement by reading the reflexive, "To whom do you compare yourself?"

13. In spite of the unanimous support for MT in the versions, *BHS* and many commentators emend *'šwr* to *t'šwr*, "cypress" (cf. 27:6). See Allen, *Ezekiel 20–48*, pp. 122-23; and the commentary below.

14. The construction of *yĕpēh 'ānāp* is similar to the description of the great eagle in 17:3.

15. Boadt (*Ezekiel's Oracles*, p. 103) repoints *wĕḥōreš mēṣal*, "shading forest"(?), as *ḥārāš mēṣal*, "skilled in shade-giving." Cf. *horošê māšḥît*, "skilled destroyers," in 21:36. Since the phrase is missing in the major LXX mss. and interrupts the parallelism of *yĕpēh 'ānāp* and *ûgĕbēh qômâ*, many scholars delete it as a marginal gloss on *'ăbōtîm*, interpreted as "interwoven foliage" (BDB, p. 721b). But the phrase serves an important thematic function in the context. See the commentary.

16. *ṣemer* as in 17:3, 22.

17. Ezekiel is consistent in his use of *'ăbōtîm*, a mixed form, which incorporates both fem. (*'ăbôt*) and masc. (*'ăbîm*) pl. endings of *'āb*, "cloud," from *'ûb*, "to weave, wind."

4 *Waters nourished it;*
The deep caused it to grow tall,
Sending[18] *its streams around its bed*[19]
And causing its channels to flow
To all the trees of the field.[20]
5 *So it towered*[21] *over all the trees of the field.*
Its branches[22] *multiplied,*
And its boughs grew long,[23]
Because of the abundant waters in its conduits.[24]
6 *In its branches all the birds of the sky made their nests;*
And under its boughs all the wild animals bore their young,
While in its shadow lived[25] *all the great nations.*[26]
7 *It was beautiful*[27] *with its height —*
With the length[28] *of its branches,*

18. LXX ἤγαγε seems to read fem. *hōlîkâ*, assuming *tĕhôm* to be the subject, instead of MT's masc. *hōlēk*. MT should be construed as a Hiphil infinitive absolute (thus J. B. Curtis, "On the Hiphil Infinitive Absolute of *hālak*," *ZAH* 1 [1988] 22-31), though some treat it as a *verbum copiae* (cf. GKC, §117z; thus M. Dijkstra and J. C. de Moor, "Problematic Passages in the Legend of Aqhâtu," *UF* 7 [1975] 193).

19. *maṭṭā'* also occurs in 17:7; 34:29. The fem. suffix on MT *maṭṭā'āh* has apparently been mispointed for *maṭṭā'ōh*, since the antecedent is either *'aššûr* or *'erez*, both of which are masc. The final *hē* represents an archaizing *mater lectionis* for *-ô*. See Boadt, *Oracles against Egypt*, p. 107.

20. MT *'el kol-'ăṣê haśśādeh* looks suspiciously like a vertical dittograph (cf. v. 5). One might have expected a parallel to *maṭṭā'ōh* such as *mĕqômô*, "its place." Cf. Zimmerli, *Ezekiel 2*, p. 142. BHS emends to *'el kol-śĕdēhû*, "to its entire field."

21. *gābĕhā' qōmātô mikkol*, lit. "its height was higher than all." On the Aramaized form of *gābĕhā'* see GKC, §44f. Cf. 27:31; 36:5; 41:15.

22. The *r* in *sar'appōtāyw* is an Aramaic feature (cf. v. 6), inserted to facilitate pronunciation, on which see Wagner, *Aramaismen*, p. 89. Cf. *kārsē'* for *kissē'*, "throne" (Dan. 5:20; 7:9); *darmāšeq* for *dammešeq*, "Damascus" (2 Chr. 24:23; 28:5); *šarbîṭ*, presumably for *šabbîṭ* (cf. Akk. *šabbitu*), "scepter" (Est. 4:11; 5:2; 8:4).

23. LXX καὶ ἐπληθύνθησαν οἱ κλάδοι αὐτοῦ may represent a conflation of these parallel lines.

24. *bĕšallĕhô*, lit. "in its sending," makes little sense in the context, which may be why LXX dropped the word. The context requires a noun of some sort, suggesting repointing to *bišlāhô* or *bišlahāyw*, "in its channel/s." Cf. *šelah*, Neh. 3:15; *šilōah*, Isa. 8:6.

25. The contextual pattern of perfect verbs suggests that MT's imperfect *yēšĕbû* should probably be repointed as *yāšĕbû*. The verb *yāšab*, "to sit, dwell," denotes much more than simply "sitting" in the shade of a tree. As in 1 K. 5:5 and Mic. 4:4, it speaks of tranquility, security, the absence of war.

26. *gôyim rabbîm* occurs elsewhere in 26:3; 37:27; 38:23; 39:27.

27. On the odd vocalization, *wayyĕyip*, see GKC, §76f.

28. LXX διὰ τὸ πλῆθος (= Heb. *bĕrōb*) harmonizes the reading with v. 9.

Because its roots were beside abundant waters.
8 *Cedars in the garden of God cannot compare[29] with it;*
Cypresses[30] cannot match its branches,
Nor can plane trees[31] rival its boughs.
No tree in the garden of God was its equal in beauty.
9 *I made it a beautiful thing[32] in the profusion of its branches.*
All the trees of Eden were envious,
Those that were in the garden of God." ' "

1 The opening date notice fixes this oracle on the first day of the third month of the eleventh year of Jehoiachin's exile, that is, June 21, 587 B.C.,[33] two months after the previous oracle (30:20). Some have speculated that the oracle was triggered by the arrival in Babylon of news that Nebuchadrezzar had routed a second relief column sent by Pharaoh Hophra/Apries to relieve the pressure on Jerusalem.[34] However, external evidence for such a battle at this time is lacking; further, in assuming the defeat of Pharaoh as an accomplished event, this interpretation fails to recognize the past tense verbs in vv. 3-17 as prophetic perfects. This rhetorical device is based on the conviction that prophetically foretold events have been decreed by Yahweh, and their fulfillment is certain.

2 The prophecy is prefaced with a command to Ezekiel to speak to Pharaoh and his hubris. In the oracles against Egypt, *hămônô* is usually interpreted as "his people," that is, the military forces, or the wealth of Pharaoh.[35] While both will undoubtedly be implicated in the king's demise, in contexts like this, with the attention focused on the persona of the pharaoh, and the central issue being his pride, the term refers primarily to his "pomp, arrogance, insolence."[36] This prophetic agenda is suggested by the opening rhetorical question, "To whom do you [sg.] compare in your greatness?" but overtly expressed in the charges in v. 10.

The opening question, *To whom do you compare in greatness?* ('*el-mî*

---

29. On '*āmam*, "to compare," as a synonym of *dāmâ* see 28:3.

30. On *běrôšîm* see 27:5.

31. '*armônîm* occurs elsewhere only in Gen. 30:37. The name, related to '*ērōm*, "naked," reflects the ease with which the tree's bark may be peeled off. See Zohary, *Plants of the Bible*, p. 129.

32. *yāpeh 'ăśîtîw* is missing in LXX and often deleted as a theological gloss. Cf. Zimmerli, *Ezekiel 2*, p. 143. But the note sets the stage for the sequel. Cf. vv. 11, 15.

33. See Parker-Dubberstein, *Chronology*, p. 28.

34. Freedy and Redford, *JAOS* 90 (1970) 472.

35. Cf. 29:19; 30:10, 15; 31:2, 18; 32:12, 12, 16, 18, 20, 25, 31, 32. The term is also associated with Elam (32:24), Meshech and Tubal (32:26), and Gog (39:11).

36. See Bodi, *Ezekiel and the Poem of Erra*, pp. 119-25.

dāmîtā běgodlekā), seems innocent enough. However, scholars have stumbled over the use of the interrogative pronoun *mî*. The word is normally used personally, referring either to an individual or to a group of persons.[37] Since the allegorical sequel involves a stately cedar, however, an impersonal significance, "To what do you compare in your greatness?" is thought to be required. While this sense is generally covered by *mâ*, scholars appeal to poetic license (i.e., the desire to personify the tree) and several OT precedents in support of this exceptional usage.[38] As will be seen below, however, such rationalizations are unnecessary, and the interrogative is best allowed its normal sense.

3-6 The question receives an immediate answer, *hinnēh 'aššûr*, "Look, Assyria." Based on the abruptness of the appeal, Ezekiel seems not to allow the pharaoh a chance to respond but to propose his own comparison. However, this comment has the form of a direct answer, and it occurs where prophetic satires tend to put words into the accused's mouth (cf. 28:2; 29:3). Accordingly, the pharaoh is hereby offering the Assyrians as his paradigm of greatness, the content of which will be filled out in the following verses.

My translation assumes the originality of MT, against the flow of scholarly opinion. Most commentators cannot accept MT's reference to Assyria in an oracle directed against Egypt. A simple textual operation, the restoration of an initial *taw* on *'šwr*, which has supposedly been dropped by pseudo-haplography after the final *hē* of the preceding word,[39] yields *tě'aššûr*, "cypress," a suitable parallel to *'erez*, "cedar," in the following phrase.[40] However, the unanimity of the versions, the generally personal use of *mî*, and the fact that Ezekiel never identifies the pharaoh with a cedar (cf. 29:3; 32:25) caution against emending MT.[41] Furthermore, the reference to Assyria is not as out of place as is often imagined. The context requires a symbol of imperial greatness with which Egypt could be compared. No standard would have been more suitable than Assyria, whose memory would surely still have been alive in the minds of Ezekiel and his hearers. After all, this great cedar had been

---

37. The question is reminiscent of other prophetic challenges to comparisons with Yahweh. Cf. Isa. 40:18, 25; 46:5. Abbreviated versions are reflected in the personal names *mîkā'ēl*, "Who is like God," and *mîkāyāhû*, "Who is like Yahweh?"

38. See Gen. 33:8; Judg. 13:17; 1 Sam. 18:18; Mic. 1:5; 1 Chr. 29:14. On poetic license see Boadt, *Ezekiel's Oracles*, p. 95.

39. In contrast to simple haplography, which preserves only one of repeated elements, pseudohaplography preserves only one of similar elements. In the square script *taw* and *hē* are easily confused.

40. On "cypress" see above on 27:6. On the pairing of cedar and cypress elsewhere, including extrabiblical texts, see Boadt, *Ezekiel's Oracles*, pp. 98-99; idem, "Textual Problems in Ezekiel and Poetic Analysis of Paired Words," *JBL* 97 (1978) 492-94.

41. So also M. Fishbane, *Biblical Interpretation in Ancient Israel* (New York: Oxford University Press, 1985), p. 46 n. 6.

felled within their lifetime.[42] That Ezekiel viewed Assyria as the imperial power par excellence is confirmed in the next oracle, which places Assyria at the head of the list of those who welcome the pharaoh to Sheol (32:22-32).

Viewed in this light, vv. 3-16 describe primarily the glory and fall of Assyria.[43] Indeed, in contrast to the previous oracles, which keep Egypt in center stage throughout, only the framework (vv. 2, 18b) links this oracle with Egypt at all. Some go so far as to suggest that the basic text of vv. 3-9 circulated originally as an independent hymn to Assyria, celebrating its role during the 8th-7th centuries B.C. as the axis and guardian of an ideal and harmonious world.[44] The framework introduces Egypt as the imperial successor to Assyria. While the entire oracle is ostensibly addressed to the arrogant pharaoh, Ezekiel subtly draws his hearers and readers into the mind-set, the value system, of the accused by cataloguing the evidences of his greatness. Indeed, vv. 3-9 present the king in an entirely positive light; there is no hint of guilt at all. This strategy is fundamental to prophetic satire. The addressee is deliberately painted in the most glowing terms possible, setting the stage for his colossal fall.

Ezekiel's description of Assyria as *a cedar in Lebanon* is remarkable, especially since ancient reliefs usually associate Assyrian kings with the date palm.[45] But the cedar was a well-known ancient Near Eastern symbol of majesty. Referred to as "the glory of Lebanon" (Isa. 35:2), from the 2nd millennium the cedar was especially valued for the construction of palaces and temples.[46] Vv. 3c-9 provide a description of this fantastic tree. The first

42. Ezekiel was not the only prophet to conjoin Egypt and Assyria as two symbols of imperial oppression. Cf. Isa. 19:23; Hos. 7:11; Zech. 10:11.

43. So also P. Joüon, "Notes philologiques sur le texte hébreu d'Ezékiel," *Bib* 10 (1929) 309-10; B. Gosse, "Le recueil d'oracles contre les nations d'Ezéchiel XXV-XXXII dans la rédaction du livre d'Ezéchiel," *RB* 93 (1986) 559.

44. According to Schweizer (in *Bäume braucht man doch!* pp. 90-100; *TQ* 165 [1985] 210-12) the basic text consists of vv. 3b-4, 6. V. 7, along with vv. 10, 11a, 12a-d, 13, represents a prophetic correction of the image of Assyria, looking back on the fall of Assyria in 612 B.C.

45. Cf. B. N. Porter, "Sacred Trees, Date Palms, and the Royal Persona of Ashurnasirpal II," *JNES* 52 (1993) 129-39; U. Magen, *Assyrische Königsdarstellungen — Aspekte der Herrschaft,* Baghdader Forschung 9 (Mainz am Rhein: Phillip von Zabern, 1986).

46. The Karnak reliefs of Seti I (1318-1304 B.C.) depict chiefs of Lebanon felling tall cedars in submission to him (*ANEP*, no. 327). In his autobiography Wen-Amon (ca. 1100) speaks of being sent to Lebanon to procure lumber for the ceremonial barge of Amon-Re, king of the gods (*ANET*, pp. 25-29). From Assyria Tiglath-pileser I (1114-1076) recounts how he cut down the cedars and transported the beams home for the temples of his gods (A. K. Grayson, *Assyrian Royal Inscriptions* [Wiesbaden: Harrassowitz, 1976], 2:26, et passim). Nebuchadrezzar identifies Lebanon as "the [Cedar] Mountain, the luxurious forest of Marduk" (*ANET*, p. 307).

three phrases, "with beautiful branches, giving protective shade, towering high," function as a thesis statement for the remainder of this first segment, introducing the audience to three dimensions of the tree's magnificence. These notions are developed in reverse order.

First, the account explains what is meant by *gĕbah qômâ*, "it towered high" (vv. 3f-5a). Nourished by abundant subterranaean waters *(tĕhôm)* the tree's crown rose above all the trees of the field and disappeared in the clouds. The prophet creates a sympathetic feeling toward the plant by deflecting credit for its magnificence away from the tree itself. The verb forms *giddēl*, "to make big," *rōmēm*, "to thrust upward," *hōlîk*, "to issue forth," and *šillēaḥ*, "to send out," highlight the agentive, life-giving role of the waters. They possess the energy, the impulse, from which the tree drew its life.

The reference to *tĕhôm* and its pairing with *mayim* are reminiscent of Gen. 1:2, and many have found mythological overtones in these expressions.[47] However, since the present description contains no hints of hostility between Yahweh and the sea, one should not exaggerate the mythological implications. Indeed, Ezekiel's account bears a closer resemblance to Gen. 7:11 and 8:2, where *tĕhôm* represents the nether source (along with "the windows of heaven") of the waters that inundated the world.[48] Sending its waters through streams *(nĕhārôt)*, channels *(tĕʿālôt)*,[49] and conduits *(šĕlāḥîm*, v. 5d), the great deep provided an unlimited source of nourishment for the tree in the bed where it was planted.

Second, offering a horizontal view of the cedar's magnificence, vv. 5b-6 expound on the enigmatic phrase *ḥōreš mēṣal* in v. 3. In addition to causing the crown to reach upward, the waters of *tĕhôm* energized the tree to send out its branches in great profusion in all directions. But these branches have more than aesthetic significance; like the cedar of 17:23, this tree offers shelter for animals.[50] All kinds of birds nest in its boughs, and all the land creatures bear their young beneath it. The last line of v. 6 betrays the political agenda of the allegory. All the great nations also congregate in its shadow. The picture of the tree is obviously being drawn from the idealized perspective of the Assyrian emperors themselves. In reality the nations incorporated into the Assyrian empire were annexed by force. Those who had experienced the brutality of the Assyrian hordes would scarcely have portrayed them this way.

47. See Boadt, *Ezekiel's Oracles*, pp. 106-7.

48. In 26:19 *tĕhôm* had denoted the deep sea that flooded Tyre.

49. *nĕhārôt* refers to natural streams; *tĕlāʿôt* denotes artificial irrigation ditches. Cf. 1 K. 18:32-38; 2 K. 18:17 (= Isa. 36:2); 20:20; Isa. 7:3.

50. On *ṣēl*, "shade," used in the derived sense of "shelter, protection," see I. H. Eybers, "The Root *ṣ-l* in Hebrew Words," *JNSL* 2 (1972) 26; B. A. Levine and J.-M. de Tarragon, O.P., "Dead Kings and Rephaim: The Patrons of the Ugaritic Dynasty," *JAOS* 104 (1984) 651-52.

But anything is possible in art, particularly in self-description. In this imaginative literary cartoon, Assyria (Egypt) may view itself as the benevolent patron of the entire world.

7-9 Finally, Ezekiel expands on *yĕpēh ʿānāp* (lit. "beautiful of branch," v. 3). With its roots sunk down to the limitless supply of water, the magnificence of the Assyrian cedar, specifically the length and profusion of its branches, exceeded even the cedars, cypresses, and plane trees in the paradisiacal garden of God. Its incomparable beauty evokes images of Eden, described in Gen. 2:9 as a garden filled with trees renowned for their beauty, their fruit, their life-giving power, and the knowledge they offer. The present description draws a comparison only with the first category, trees renowned for their appearance. V. 9 reminds the hearer that, like the trees in the garden, the great cedar's glory is not of its own making; Yahweh has endowed it with the kind of superlative beauty that would evoke jealousy *(qinnē')* among all the other trees in the garden. This theological comment is often considered intrusive, but it serves an important rhetorical function in assuring the hearer of the divine imprimatur on the cedar's grandeur and eliminating any hint of wrongdoing on the part of the tree. Assyria (Egypt) draws its vitality and glory immediately from the subterranaean waters, but they derive ultimately from God.

The source of Ezekiel's dendritic imagery has evoked a great deal of discussion. The resemblance to the majestic *mēsu* tree described in the Babylonian Erra Epic is striking:

> Where is the *mēsu* tree, the flesh of the gods, the ornament of the king of the univ[erse]? That pure tree, that august youngster suited to supremacy, whose roots reached as deep down as the bottom of the underwor[ld]: a hundred double hours through the vast sea waters; whose top reached as high as the sky of [Anum].[51]

However, the vagueness of the context precludes a determination of this tree's precise significance. The motif of a magnificent tree offering shelter to animals is found in the Sumerian account of Gilgamesh and the *ḫuluppu* tree. Inanna discovers the tree on the banks of the Euphrates and transplants it in her sacred garden in Erech. Growing profusely, it attracts the mythical Zu-bird, the evil Lilith, and the snake, which reside in the crown, the middle, and the base, respectively.[52] But the myth of the cosmic tree is attested in other parts of the world as well. The best-known example is Yggdrasill, a tree in Norse mythology whose roots reached down to Niflheimr, the netherworld where lived

---

51. Erra I:150-53, as translated by L. Cagni, *The Poem of Erra,* SANE 1/3 (Malibu: Undena, 1977), p. 32.

52. See D. Wolkstein and S. N. Kramer, *Inanna, Queen of Heaven and Earth* (New York: Harper & Row, 1983), pp. 2-9.

the giants and demons, whose trunk, wound around by the ocean snake, was in Midgard, the realm of humans, and whose crown extended to Asgaror, the residence of the gods.[53]

These comparisons are attractive on the surface, but the differences in the accounts are much more important than the similarities. Foremost, Ezekiel's allegory is a political rather than mythological statement. Allusions to the gods are missing entirely, and the appeal to the garden of God/Eden carries little if any mythological baggage. Because the tradition of Gen. 2 would have been familiar to Ezekiel's audience, it provides a useful standard by which the glory of Assyria (Egypt) could be measured. For Ezekiel the superlative cedar of Lebanon represents simply the foremost political force of the day, in whose shade the creatures and the nations found protection, and whose magnificence evokes jealousy among rival powers. Indeed, Ezekiel's allegory finds its closest analogue in another biblical story, Dan. 4:7-9 (Eng. 10-12):

> I saw a tree of great height in the midst of the earth;
> The tree grew and became mighty;
> Its top reached heaven,
> And it was visible to the end of the earth.
> Its foliage was beautiful
> And its fruit abundant;
> There was food for all in it.
> Beneath it the beasts of the field found shade,
> And the birds of the sky dwelt on its branches;
> All creatures fed on it.

Daniel's portrayal of the tree has probably been influenced by Ezekiel, but he gives it his own stamp.[54] He does not identify the species of tree, but a cedar is ruled out by his emphasis on the tree as a source of food for all the creatures. For Ezekiel this issue is irrelevant, which probably eliminates comparison with the tree of life in the garden of God, or the sacred tree in ancient mythology that was thought to nourished humans and animals.[55] The tree

53. For further examples and discussion see M. Eliade, *A History of Religious Ideas,* vol. 2, *From Gautama Buddha to the Triumph of Christianity,* tr. W. R. Trask (Chicago: University of Chicago Press, 1982), pp. 154-61; P. R. Frese and S. J. M. Gray, "Trees," *The Encyclopedia of Religion,* ed. M. Eliade (New York: Macmillan, 1987), 15:27-28. B. Margulis finds in *'ṣ brqy['] rišh,* "a tree (with) its 'head' in the firma[ment]" (RS 24.245), a Ugaritic reference to the cosmic tree ("A Weltbaum in Ugaritic Literature?" *JBL* 90 [1971] 481-82).

54. For a discussion of both these texts see Gowan, *When Man Becomes God,* pp. 93-116.

55. Cf. the Egyptian goddess Hathor (occasionally alternated with Isis or Nut), who

represented one of the most common iconographic and mythological symbols, and could be exploited for a variety of purposes — as a symbol of deity, as a protective cosmic symbol, as a symbol of life and prosperity, as a symbol of the divine-human relationship.[56] Ezekiel's cedar bears his own distinctive stamp.

b. The Judgment of the Pharaonic Tree (31:10-14)

> 10 " 'Therefore, thus has the Lord Yahweh declared:
> Because you[57] towered high — it[58] sent its shoots up to the clouds, and its heart became proud because of its height. 11 Therefore, I will deliver[59] it into the hand of a chief of nations.[60] He will certainly act toward it according to its wickedness.[61] I have banished it![62] 12 Foreigners, the most barbaric of nations, have cut it down; they left it

was portrayed as a gigantic sycamore tree with roots sunk down to the subterranean waters, and whose top reached heaven. She afforded the dead not only protection and shade but also daily nourishment. Cf. I. Gamer-Wallert, "Baum, heliger," *LÄ*, 1:656-57; idem, "Nut," *LÄ*, 4:535-41; R. Moftah, "Die uralte Sykomore und andere Erscheinungen des Hathor," *Zeitschrift für Ägyptische Sprache und Altertumskunde* 92 (1966) 40-47. In fact, in Thutmose III's grave a tree goddess, identified as Isis, offers her son Horus her breast (Moftah, p. 44, fig. 6; Keel, *Symbolism*, p. 186, fig. 253). See also U. Winter, "Der Lebensbaum in der Altorientalischen Bildsymbolik," in *Bäume braucht man doch!* pp. 57-88. On the sacred tree in Semitic art see H. York, "Heiliger Baum," *RLA*, 4:269-82; C. Kempinski, *L'arbre stylisé en Asie occidentiale au 2e millénaire avant J.-C.*, 3 vols. (Paris: 1982). Especially widespread is the stylized tree flanked by goats/ibexes feeding on it.

56. For the tree as a symbol of life and prosperity, see W. G. Lambert, "Trees, Snakes and Gods in Ancient Syria and Anatolia," *BSOAS* 48 (1985) 435-51. As a symbol of the divine-human relationship, see the tree of the knowledge of good and evil, Gen. 2:9.

57. Most read third person *gābah* for MT second person of direct address (*gābahtā bĕqômâ*) with Syr. and Vulg., but this reading may be a later harmonization.

58. The antecedent is the tree/Pharaoh in the previous section. The inconsistency of pronouns should be retained as *lectio difficilior*. It reflects the shifts in the prophet's mind from the Pharaoh as addressee to subject about whom he is speaking.

59. MT *wĕʾetnēhû*, "I will deliver him," harmonizes with the incompleted sense of *ʾāśô yaʿăśeh lô*, "he will certainly treat him," but it flies in the face of the following *gēraštihû*, "I have banished it." NRSV follows LXX in smoothing out the reading by rendering all as past action. But these harmonizing solutions seem too facile; the principle of *lectio difficilior* argues for the originality of MT. Targ. preserves the incongruity.

60. Ezekiel uses *ʾayil*, lit. "ram," for "leader" elsewhere (cf. on 17:13), but the phrase *ʾêl gôyim*, which highlights the agent's international stature, is unique.

61. Many simplify *ʾāśô yaʿăśeh* to *wayaʿaś*. Cf. *BHS*; Zimmerli, *Ezekiel 2*, p. 144.

62. Many delete *gēraštihû* at the end of the verse as a dittograph on *kĕrišʿû*. See *BHS*; Zimmerli, *Ezekiel 2*, p. 144; Freedy and Redford, *JAOS* 90 (1970) 472 n. 40. But it is best linked with v. 12. So also Boadt, *Ezekiel's Oracles*, p. 115.

lying[63] *on the mountains. In all the valleys its branches have fallen;
its boughs were broken off in every ravine of the earth. All the peoples
of the earth*[64] *went down*[65] *from its shade and left it lying.*[66] 13 *On its
fallen trunk all the birds of the sky lodge,*[67] *and on its branches dwell
all the wild animals —*[68] 14 *that no well-watered trees might grow tall
in stature,*[69] *nor send their tops up into the clouds. Nor shall any
watered tree stand next to them*[70] *in height. Indeed, all of them have
been consigned to death, to the netherworld,*[71] *in the company of
humans,*[72] *who descend to the pit.' "*[73]

10 *Therefore (lākēn),* followed by the citation formula, signals a new movement in the oracle, cast in the form of divine speech. The prophet's switch in
the first statement from the second person of direct address to the third person
reflects his tension over the primary significance of the allegory, viz., its
portrayal of the glory of Assyria, and its secondary application in this context,
as a picture of the fall of Egypt. It also contributes to the striking change in
tone. Ezekiel's literary portrait of the cedar was painted with totally positive
strokes. The great tree Assyria was impressive in its height, magnificent in

63. With *BHS,* linking *wayyiṭṭĕšuhû* with what follows. On the Late Biblical
Hebrew practice of attaching the third masc. sg. suffix directly to the verb ending in *-û*
(*plene* or defective) see Rooker, *Biblical Hebrew in Transition,* pp. 86-87. On *nāṭaš,* which
occurs twice in this verse, see above on 29:5.

64. *kol-ʿammê hāʾāreṣ* is a stylistic variant of *kol gôyim rabbîm,* "all the mighty
nations," in v. 6.

65. So MT *wayyērĕdû* and the versions. *BHS* emends to *wayyiddĕdû,* "and they
fled." But the verb assumes a tree at the top of the mountain.

66. *wayyiṭṭĕšuhû* appears redundant, but like the inconsistency in person (third/sec-
ond) may reflect the prophet's heightened emotional state.

67. The prefixed *yod* on *yšknw* is often dropped as a pseudo-dittograph on the
preceding *waw* (cf. Allen, *Ezekiel 20–48,* p. 123), but Boadt (*Ezekiel's Oracles,* p. 115)
suggests that the *yqtl-qtl* sequence is a conscious stylistic variation. Cf. the following *hāyû.*

68. Although linked by *lĕmaʿan ʾăšer,* "in order that," there does not seem to be
a logical connection between these verses. See the commentary.

69. The proleptic suffix, as on *bĕqômātām,* is a feature of Late Biblical Hebrew,
occurring elsewhere in Ezekiel in 10:3 and 42:14. Cf. Rooker, *Biblical Hebrew in Transition,* pp. 91-93.

70. MT points *ʾēlêhem* as if from *ʾayil,* "ram, chieftain."

71. The sg. form of *ʾereṣ taḥtît* here and in vv. 16, 18 compares with *ʾereṣ taḥtîyôt*
in 26:20; 32:18, 24, on which see below. Cf. also *taḥtîyôt hāʾāreṣ,* Isa. 44:23; Ps. 63:10
(Eng. 9); 139:15. On these expressions see Tromp, *Primitive Conceptions,* pp. 180-83.

72. This is the only occurrence of the pl., *bĕnê ʾādām,* lit. "sons of man," in
Ezekiel.

73. On *yôrĕdê bôr* see above on 26:20. The expression recurs in v. 16; 32:18,
24-25, 29-30.

its beauty, and beneficent in the protection it offered to the creatures and the nations. In fact it had been planted in the garden by Yahweh himself. If the allegory contained any negative hint at all, it was the jealousy of the rest of the trees in the garden over this cedar's grandeur. But this was their problem, not the cedar's. Thus Ezekiel has toyed with his audience, drawing them into the mind of the rhetorical addressee and impressing them with his virtues. Suddenly, without warning, he jolts them with a radical reinterpretation of the scene. This cedar is not to be admired but condemned. The purpose of the hymn of praise was not to entertain but to prepare the stage for the divine woodcutter.

Cast in the form of a judgment speech, the denunciation of the tree commences with a direct accusation, introduced formally by *ya'an 'ăšer,* "Because . . ." The song may credit the tree's glory to the subterranean waters and Yahweh, but this is not the response of the tree. Instead of acknowledging this debt, the cedar prides itself on its magnificence. Like the cherub on the mountain of God (28:17), the tree succumbed to the temptation of hubris. *wĕrām lĕbābô bĕgābĕhô,* "and its heart was lifted up in its height," represents an effective play on the roots *rwm* and *gbh* that had been used in vv. 3-5 to describe the physical stature of the tree. But the words have taken on a sinister meaning. To be high of height and heart means "to be haughty."[74]

11   The divine response to this hubris is announced. The inconsistency in the tense of the verbs is perplexing, but it apparently reflects the prophet's continued tension between the primary referent of the allegory, whose past demise is well known, and the new application to Egypt, whose fall he is predicting. Yahweh declares that Pharaoh will be handed over to *a chief* ['*êl,* lit. "ram"] *of nations.* In Ezekiel's mind the "ram" is undoubtedly Nebuchadrezzar, the emperor over many nations. As the agent of divine justice, he will punish Egypt in a manner commensurate with its arrogance. The last verb of v. 11, *banished,* returns the prophet's gaze to the paradigmatic tree, Assyria, whom Yahweh has already driven away. If Pharaoh wants to compare his greatness with that of Assyria, let him do the same with his demise.

12-14   The divine action recedes into the background while the actions of third parties against the tree take center stage. The agents of divine punishment are identified as *Foreigners (zārîm),* and described as "the most barbarous of nations."[75] They are portrayed as rough lumberjacks, who chop the tree down and leave it lying on the mountains, its broken branches strewn up

---

74. Cf. Deut. 8:14; 17:20; Hos. 13:6; Jer. 48:29. On the Hebrew vocabulary of pride see above on 28:2.

75. *zārîm* and *'ārîṣê gôyim* were linked earlier in 28:7 and 30:11-12. On *zārîm* see 7:21; 11:9; 28:10.

and down the mountains, valleys, and ravines of the land.[76] The fall of the cedar also means the end of its beneficent protective role. "All the peoples of the earth" abandon it. Instead of building their nests in its branches and bearing their young under its boughs, the birds and the animals sit exposed on its fallen remains.[77]

14 Because of its unexpected parenetic nature and the absence of an antecedent for *lĕmaʿan ʾăšer,* "in order that," this verse is often deleted as inauthentic. One can make sense of it, however, if one interprets it as a resumption of the divine reaction to the tree's hubris announced in v. 11, the description of the actions of the third parties (vv. 12-13) having momentarily interrupted the flow of thought. Accordingly, rather than being a secondary addition, v. 14 captures the spirit of the entire oracle. The scope of Ezekiel's vision is expanded beyond the Assyrian cedar by means of two strange expressions, *kol-ʿăṣê-mayim* (lit. "all trees of water") and *kol-šōtê mayim* (lit. "all drinkers of water"). These expressions include any tree that has found nourishment from the subterranean depths, as described in v. 4, and for whom the fall of the cedar should serve as a warning against haughtiness on account of one's height and against an arrogant reaching for the heavens. "All the well-watered trees" generalizes on the lesson that Egypt in particular is to learn.

The last line of v. 14 functions rhetorically to correct all who are tempted in their greatness to forget their mortal humanity. In consigning *(nātan)* them to death and the netherworld Yahweh reaffirms that he always has the last word. The sentence for the proud is simple: death. Far from symbolizing life and offering shelter to living creatures, such trees go down to the netherworld, where they will join the *bĕnê ʾādām* (lit. "sons of man") and all those who descend to the Pit. In other words, the depths to which the arrogant are cast will be commensurate with the heights to which they have aspired.

c. The Demise of the Pharaonic Tree (31:15-18)

15 "'Thus has the Lord Yahweh declared:
On the day it went down to Sheol, I shut off [the water supply],[78]
and I covered it[79] *with the deep. I dammed up its streams, and the*

---

76. The triad of *hārîm, gēʾyôt,* and *ʾăpîqê hāʾāreṣ* compares with the quartet that adds *gĕbāʿôt,* "hills," in 6:3; 32:6; 35:8; 36:4, 6. In 32:4 and 34:13 only the pair, mountains and ravines, occurs.

77. Contra Boadt (*Ezekiel's Oracles,* p. 116), who sees the animals as preying on the tree.

78. On *heʾĕbaltî* see the commentary.

79. LXX does not reflect *kissētî,* either through an oversight or because of a different *Vorlage.* Targ. and Syr. support MT.

mighty waters were held in check. I made Lebanon mourn on account of it, and all the wild trees wilted[80] on its account. 16 At the sound of its fall I made nations quake. When I sent it down to Sheol with those who go down to the pit, then all the trees of Eden, all the choice and best[81] of Lebanon, all that drink water, found relief[82] in the netherworld.[83] 17 They also descended to Sheol with it, to the victims of the sword,[84] that is its arm,[85] those who had dwelt[86] in its shade in the midst of the nations.[87] 18 To whom do you compare like this[88] in glory and magnificence, among the trees of Eden? Still you will be brought down to the netherworld with the trees of Eden. In the midst of the uncircumcised you will lie along with the victims of the sword. This applies to Pharaoh and all his pomp. The declaration of the Lord Yahweh.'"

Set off by the citation formula, and borrowing the sequence of judgment-descent into the netherworld from the oracle against Tyre (26:19-20), these verses describe the final phase of the colossal tree's fall. Ezekiel uses a variety of designations for the realm of the dead: *bôr*, "pit, cistern" (vv. 14, 16; 26:20; 32:18, 23-25, 29-30); *šaḥat*, "pit, trap" (28:8); *'ereṣ taḥtît*, "the lower land/world" (31:14, 15, 18), and his own distinctive variation, *'ereṣ taḥtîyôt*, "the land of the depths" (26:20; 32:18, 24). For the first time the term *šě'ôl*, *Sheol*, appears. The expression is distinctively Hebrew, appearing elsewhere as a loanword in Syriac, Ethiopic, and Elephantine Aramaic.[89] The aim of this

---

80. MT *'ulpeh* is pointed as an adjective, "languishing," or a noun, "faintness, languor," but both seem impossible in the context. LXX ἐξελύθησαν reflects a Pual verb, *'ullāpû*, a stem that occurs elsewhere in Cant. 5:14 and Isa. 51:20.

81. *wěṭôb* is missing in LXX.

82. On *nāḥam* (Niphal) meaning "to breathe easier, to be quieted, relieved," see my *Ezekiel: Chapters 1–24*, pp. 451-53, 514 n. 296.

83. *taḥtît* is missing in LXX, but should be retained. Cf. v. 17.

84. On *ḥalělê ḥereb* cf. 6:4, 13; 9:7; 11:6. On the sword as Yahweh's instrument see 21:6-11.

85. MT *ûzrō'ô*, "and his arm," is obscure. LXX καὶ τὸ σπέρμα αὐτοῦ and Syr. read *wězar'ô*, "and his seed." Appealing to Syr. *zr'*, G. R. Driver (*Bib* 19 [1938] 179) recognizes a root meaning "to disperse" (cf. *zārâ*), though Ezekiel never uses this root in this sense elsewhere. *BHS* suggests emendation either to *wě'ōzěrāyw*, "and its helpers," or *wěgāwě'û*, "and they perished." The reference seems to be to the arm that wields the sword.

86. Following LXX, read *yōšěbê* in place of MT's *yāšěbû*, the subject being the victims of the sword, not "its arm."

87. *bětôk gôyim* is missing in LXX.

88. MT *kākâ* is difficult, but it functions rhetorically to highlight the comparative question. Several minor LXX witnesses try to make sense of it by reading *běkōaḥ*, "in strength." Cf. *BHS*.

89. While the lack of an article suggests a proper name, the etymology of *šě'ôl*

account of the colossal tree's descent into the netherworld is not to offer a full dissertation on Sheol. Ezekiel assumes his audience's familiarity with his own beliefs in death and afterlife. This segment offers another example of the typically Ezekielian habit of suspension-resumption. Vv. 15-18 present the motif of the descent only in summary form. Since this theme will be picked up and developed much more fully in 32:17-32, discussion of Sheol is reserved for the commentary on that oracle.

The emphasis in the present text is on Yahweh's total control, not only over the fate of the cedar (Assyria, and secondarily Egypt), but also on the reactions of the nations. While the prophet clearly begins by describing the divinely induced reaction to the tree's descent, the first verb raises questions concerning the nature of that response. The versions and most modern translations (cf. NASB, NIV, JB, RSV) derive *he'ĕbaltî* from *'ābal,* "to mourn," which makes good sense following the description of the cedar's fate but is awkward in the light of what comes next. How is the mourning to be associated with covering the tree with the great deep *(tĕhôm)*? As already noted, LXX smooths out the difficulty by deleting *kissētî,* in which case the great deep takes on the role of the divinely induced mourner. Some interpret MT as a hendiadys: "I make mourn, I cover," means "I cover *tĕhôm* with mourning garments," whereby *tĕhôm* becomes a mythical figure engaged in mourning rites over the fall of the tree.[90] However, the imagery is without parallel, and it is difficult to understand why or how the great

---

remains unclear. Several possibilities have been suggested: (1) From *šā'al,* "to ask," viewing Sheol as a place of inquiry, with reference to necromancy (BDB, p. 982). However, it is unlikely that orthodox Hebrews, who were otherwise opposed to the practice of consulting the dead, would have adopted such an expression as their distinctive name for the place of the departed dead. (2) From *šu'āla,* an as yet unattested Akkadian ghost word (W. von Soden, "Assyriologische Erwägungen zu einem neuen Buch über die Toten-reichvorstellungen im Alten Testament," *UF* 2 [1970] 331-32). (3) A Sumerian loanword from *šu'āra,* the netherworldly residence of Tammuz (W. Baumgartner [following W. F. Albright], "Zur Etymologie von *schĕ'ōl," TZ* 2 [1946] 233-35). (4) A combination of Egyp. *š* and Heb. *'l,* "El," viz., "lake of El" (W. Wifall, "The Sea of Reeds as Sheol," *ZAW* 92 [1980] 325-32). (5) From Egyp. *še-'il,* an expression used in the mortuary texts for the epitome of perfection in the hereafter, a sort of Champs-Élysées (M. Görg, " 'Scheol' — Israels Unterweltsbegriff und seine Herkunft," *BN* 17 [1982] 26-33). (6) From a root *š'h,* "to be desolate," plus epenthetic final consonant *l,* according to which Sheol is a "No-land" *(Unland),* a world "where are found shadowiness, decay, remoteness from God (Isa. xxxviii.18, Ps. vi.6): Nothingness" (L. Köhler, "Problems in the Study of the Language of the Old Testament," *JSS* 1 [1956] 19-20; idem, "Alttestamentliche Wortforschung," *TZ* 2 [1946] 71-74). On Sheol see further *HALAT,* pp. 1274-75; G. Gerleman, *THAT,* 2:837-41; T. J. Lewis, *ABD,* 2:101-5.

90. Thus Boadt, *Ezekiel's Oracles,* p. 118, following Dahood. Cf. Zimmerli, *Ezekiel 2,* p. 152.

deep should be covered.[91] Others propose a homonym of 'ābal, "to mourn," viz., 'ābal II, "to dry up."[92]

It seems best, however, to recognize here a denominative verb meaning "to close [a gate]," cognate to Aram. 'ibbûl and Akk. abullu, "gate."[93] Accordingly, the imagery is that of shutting off the flow of water in a stream or irrigation ditch, which harmonizes well with holding back the river channels (mānaʿ nĕhārôt) and damming up the mighty waters (kālā' mayim rabbîm), and offers an appropriate attendant action to the felling of the tree. The weakness of this interpretation is that kissētî ʿālāyw 'et-tĕhôm, "I covered it with the deep," is intrusive. Nonetheless, the comment is conceivable, since tĕhôm and kāsâ occur together elsewhere. It seems Yahweh not only cuts off the source of nourishment but also transforms it into a destructive deluge.

The motif of mourning is introduced for the first time at the end of v. 15, which describes how the cedar's fall affects the observers. On the one hand, Yahweh clothes the trees of Lebanon with mourning garb. wā'akdir ʿālāyw lĕbānôn (lit. "I brought darkness on Lebanon") functions idiomatically for dressing the mountains in black.[94] On the other hand, the sight of the demise causes wilting among the rest of the trees of the forest.[95] The first line of v. 16 extends the horror to the nations, as Yahweh causes the din of the majestic cedar's collapse to reverberate around the world.[96]

In v. 16b attention returns to cedar's fate. It has arrived in Sheol, where

---

91. Contra Zimmerli (Ezekiel 2, p. 152), the covering of the heavens and the sun and the darkening of the stars and moon in 32:7 is quite different. The verbs associated with the great deep include bāqaʿ, "to burst open" (Gen. 7:11; Prov. 3:20); sākar, "to stop up" (Gen. 8:2), heḥĕrîb, "to dry up" (Isa. 51:10; cf. Ps. 106:9), ḥûq ḥûq ʿal-pĕnê tĕhôm, "to inscribe the circle on the surface of the deep" (Prov. 8:27), ʿāzaz, "to prevail" (Prov. 8:28), qāpā', "to congeal" (Exod. 15:8), 'ākal, "to consume" (Amos 7:4). The great deep may "cover" (kāsâ) objects (Exod. 15:5; Ps. 104:6), "engulf" them (sōbēb, Jon. 2:6), or "be brought over" them (heʿĕlâ, Ezek. 26:19), but never is tĕhôm itself covered.

92. P. Skehan, as cited by Boadt, Ezekiel's Oracles, p. 118 n. 70. HALOT, p. 7, cites Amos 1:2; Jer. 12:4; 23:10 as other examples of this root. Cf. REB "I dried up the deep."

93. On the Aramaic see Jastrow, Dictionary, p. 4. G. R. Driver and J. C. Miles delete kissētî as a gloss on heʿĕbaltî, which they render "to shut (like a door)" (The Babylonian Laws, 2 vols. [Oxford: Clarendon, 1955], 2:181 n. 1). Cf. NJPS and NRSV, "I closed the deep over it and covered it." On the Akkadian see CAD, 1:82-88. Cf. also Palmyrene 'bl, "vestibule" (DISO, p. 2); DNWSI, p. 5.

94. The Hiphil forms occurs elsewhere only in 32:7, 8. The Qal, "to be dark," is used in connection with mourning in 2 Sam. 19:5 (Eng. 4); Jer. 8:21; 14:2; Job 5:11; 30:28; Ps. 35:14 (Eng. 13); 38:7 (Eng. 6); 42:10 (Eng. 9); 43:2.

95. Cf. the pairing of ʿālap and qādar in Isa. 24:7; 33:9; Jer. 14:2.

96. qôl, "sound," and rāʿaš, "to quake," are also combined in 27:28.

it joins many other magnificent trees, including those from Eden and the finest specimens of the Lebanon, who have preceded it. These now find relief, knowing that no matter how high and mighty a tree may have been during its earthly existence, in death all are equal. The glorious cedar may have evoked jealousy in its earthly life (v. 9), but in Sheol it has nothing to be envied; all are on the same level.[97] V. 17 declares that Sheol contains not only trees felled by the divine woodcutter but also the victims of Yahweh's punishing sword, further identified as *its arm (zĕrōʿô)*, apparently a reference to Assyria's allies.[98] Those nations that had previously found refuge in the shade of the cedar have preceded the tree in the netherworld and are there to welcome it when it arrives.

18 With the direct address of the pharaoh and the restatement of the opening question here, Ezekiel jolts his hearers back to reality. He has not been simply presenting a satirical allegory of the Assyrians whose might had once terrorized the world. Pharaoh is the problem. If he perceives himself as the heir of the Assyrians' imperial might, then let him also share in their fate and the fate of all other glorious trees, including those of Eden. As the Assyrians had experienced, so the netherworld will reduce him to the lowest common denominator — rather, the lowest uncommon level. Pharaoh will be consigned a place to lie *(šākab)* in Sheol among the uncircumcised and the criminal victims of the sword.[99] The final statement declares unequivocally the prophet's intent in this oracle. While the satirical tale may have described the fate of the Assyrians, it is directed at Pharaoh and his hubris. Yahweh's concluding signature seals not only the oracle but also the pharaoh's fate. In so doing Ezekiel seeks to undermine his fellow exiles' hopes in all Egyptian enterprises against the Babylonians in Judah.

♦ *Theological Implications*

This satirical tale of the magnificent cedar of Lebanon reiterates many themes familiar from previous oracles against the nations.

First, Yahweh is the sovereign Lord of history. Nations are not self-made; they draw their vitality from resources built into the universe and they derive their place by divine appointment. Yahweh has planted this cedar in Eden, and endowed it with unsurpassed magnificence and beauty. But when such gifts become occasions for pride, like a lumberjack he brings down the

---

97. Ezekiel's vision, esp. vv. 10 and 17, may have been inspired by the picturesque portrayal of the netherworld in Isa. 14:10-17.

98. Unless *zĕrōʿô* alludes to the Egyptians. Cf. the development of the motif of Pharaoh's strong arm in 30:20-26.

99. For further discussion of the significance of this statement see below on 32:26.

tree and consigns it to the netherworld. He therefore holds the keys not only to one's place in history but also to one's position among the dead. This message needs to be affirmed in every age. Like Ezekiel's fellow exiles, the church must recognize the futility of reliance on any secular power. Its confidence must be in God alone.

Second, pride in human accomplishments draws the fury of God. This lesson applies not only to the secular world of the nations, but especially to those who lead in the kingdom of God. Many centuries earlier Moses had warned Israel of the devastating consequences of claiming: "My power and the might of my own hand have gotten me this wealth" (Deut. 8:17-20). The need for a warning against hubris in the Western church has seldom if ever been more urgent than today. Churches and their leaders may not gloat over their influence or achievements without suffering divine fury, just as the pharaohs and emperors of the world did.

6. The Doom of the Pharaonic Monster (32:1-16)

♦ *Nature and Design*

The boundaries of the present oracle are clearly marked by the date and word-event formulae in v. 1 and the colophonic conclusion and signatory formula in v. 16. Within these borders the unit is fragmented by a series of formulae, often surprisingly situated. Instead of appearing at the head of the oracle (v. 2), following the command to Ezekiel to speak, the citation formula, "Thus has the Lord Yahweh declared," appears twice (vv. 3 and 11). The signatory formula appears at the end (v. 16), but also twice in between (vv. 8, 14), in neither instance correlated with the citation formula, though the latter separates a direct description of the effects of Yahweh's sword from an expanded version of the recognition formula in v. 15.

The effect of these formulae is to break up the oracle into a series of fragments, consisting of vv. 1, 2, 3-8, 9-10, 11-14, 15, 16, loosely joined together.[1] However, one should not too readily dismiss the prophet's own involvement in the literary form of the oracle, for several reasons. First, from start to finish the vocabulary is thoroughly Ezekielian.[2] Second, the text

---

1. Scholars have tended to find in these prophetic formulae evidence for textual layers. For example, Garscha (*Studien,* pp. 185-92) recognizes four stages in the text's evolution, none of which he credits to Ezekiel. Zimmerli (*Ezekiel 2,* pp. 157-58) identifies v. 2 as the kernel of the oracle, which has grown through four expansions in vv. 3-8, 9-10, 11-14, and 15, but he leaves open the possibility that these might have come from the prophet himself.

2. The oracle draws on many motifs that were encountered in earlier prophecies

contains no historical, syntactical, or substantive contradictions that demand more than one author.³ Third, each of the fragments builds on what has come before. Vv. 3-8 provide a commentary, giving point to the lament in v. 2.⁴ The description of the onlookers' reaction to the demise of Egypt (vv. 9-10) in the context of a lament is familiar from earlier oracles (26:15-18; 27:28-36; 28:19). The reference to Yahweh's sword in v. 11 triggers an extended exposition of the manner in which that sword will operate in vv. 11-15. Fourth, the oracle displays what appears to be a deliberate if loose chiastic structure: vv. 13-14 echo v. 2b; vv. 11-12 echo v. 4b; v. 9b echoes vv. 5-6; vv. 9a, 10 echo vv. 7-8.⁵ Fifth, the entire unit is held together by the keyword gôyim, "nations," which occurs in vv. 2, 9, 12, 16. The intrusive prophetic formulae should not, therefore, be taken as signs of secondary stitching, but as interjected affirmations by the prophet concerning the origin, authority, and integrity of his word.⁶ In keeping with his status as Yahweh's specially commissioned spokesman (cf. chs. 2–3), the message he declares is an official divine proclamation.

But the issue of genre remains. The opening command to the prophet to raise a lament (nāśā' qînâ, v. 2) and the concluding colophon, with its fourfold use of qînâ/qônēn (v. 16), identify this oracle as a dirge. Indeed, the framework is strongly reminiscent of ch. 19, where a similar *inclusio* had enveloped the lament over the kings of Judah. However, the absence of the

---

and that will be picked up later: the lion (kĕpîr, v. 2; cf. 19:2), the monster (tannîm, v. 2; cf. 29:3 [MT tannîn]), the rivers (nĕhārôt, v. 2; cf. 31:4, 15), fouling water with the feet (rāpas, v. 2; cf. 34:18-19 [rāpaś]), Yahweh spreading the net over someone (pāraś rešet 'al, v. 3; cf. 12:13; 17:20), the company of many peoples (qĕhal 'ammîm rabbîm, v. 3; cf. qāhāl wĕ'am rāb, 26:7; qĕhal 'ammîm, 23:24), to hurl the monster onto the open field (nāṭa' 'al-pĕnê haśśādeh, v. 4; cf. 29:5 [to the desert; the following line mentions 'al-pĕnê haśśādeh]), all the birds of the heavens sitting on (the victim) (šākēn kol-'ôp haśśāmayim, v. 4; cf. 31:13), mountains, valleys, ravines (hārîm, gē'āyôt, 'ăpiqîm, vv. 5, 6; cf. 6:3; 31:12; 34:13; 35:8; 36:4, 6), many peoples ('ammîm rabbîm, vv. 3, 9, 10; cf. 3:6; 27:33; 38:6, 8, 9, 15, 22), observers being appalled (šāmam, v. 10; cf. 26:16; 27:35; 28:19), observers bristle with horror (śā'ar, v. 10; cf. 27:35), Yahweh's sword (harbî, v. 10; cf. 21:8, 9, 10; 30:24, 25), to tremble continually (hārad lirgā'îm, v. 10; cf. 26:16), collapse, downfall (noun, mappelet, v. 10; cf. 26:15, 18; 27:27; 31:13), most barbarous of nations ('ārîṣê gôyim, v. 12; cf. 28:7; 30:11; 31:12), many waters (mayim rabbîm, v. 13; cf. 1:24; 17:5, 8; 19:10; 27:26; 31:5, 7, 15; 43:2), clear water (hišqîa' mayim, v. 14; cf. 34:18), make the land a desolation (nātan 'ereṣ šĕmāmâ, v. 15; cf. 6:14; 15:8; 29:12; 33:28, 29; 35:7), multitude, horde, pomp (hāmôn, vv. 12a, 12b, 16; cf. 7:11, 12, 13, 14; 23:42; 29:19; 30:4, 10, 15; 32:18-32; 39:11, 15).

3. See M. Greenberg, in *Ezekiel and His Book*, pp. 133-34.

4. So also Wevers, *Ezekiel*, p. 240.

5. Cf. Allen, *Ezekiel 20–48*, p. 130.

6. Cf. Meier's conclusions (*Speaking of Speaking*, pp. 238-42) regarding the distribution and significance of divine speech markers in Ezekiel.

3:2 lament meter (except in v. 2, and perhaps v. 8a) makes it difficult to imagine how this oracle as a unit would have been chanted. Furthermore, the unit does not follow the expected "once-now" pattern, according to which the doom of the present is contrasted with the good fortune of the past.[7] The oracle is in fact a hybrid. Insofar as it commemorates a death, viz., of the Egyptian monster, one may construe it as a lament. If one judges by the content, however, this is not a serious dirge but a parodic adaptation of the genre.[8] Further, the recognition formula at the end of v. 15 points in the direction of a proof saying: the divine action announced is intended to produce in the witnesses to that activity a recognition of Yahweh as both the sovereign Lord of history and the one who issues an effective word. But the oracle also displays characteristics of the prophetic judgment speech. Although the approach is indirect, the lament segment in v. 2 actually functions as a formal accusation. As v. 12 will confirm, the monster's snorting about in the seas and muddying the waters are expressions of pride. The remainder, vv. 3-14, for the most part cast in the future tense, constitutes the divine announcement of judgment. The focus is entirely on Yahweh's impending punitive reaction to the monster's behavior.

a. The Delusion of the Monster (32:1-2)

1 *In the twelfth*[9] *year, in the twelfth month, on the first day of the month, the following message of Yahweh came to me:* 2 *"Human, raise a lament over Pharaoh, king of Egypt, and say to him:*

'You compare yourself[10] *to the lion of the nations;*
But you are like a sea monster;[11]

7. On the nature of laments see my *Ezekiel: Chapters 1-24,* pp. 591ff.

8. Cf. the study of dirge parodies by G. A. Yee, "The Anatomy of Biblical Parody: The Dirge Form in 2 Samuel 1 and Isaiah 14," *CBQ* 50 (1988) 565-86.

9. Many follow numerous Hebrew mss., LXX^A, and Syr. in reading *bĕʿaštê šānâ,* "in the eleventh year." Cf. *BHS;* Zimmerli, *Ezekiel 2,* p. 154; Freedy and Redford, *JAOS* 90 (1970) 468 n. 30. But this reading arose from a desire to date the oracle before the fall of Jerusalem and the report of the event to the prophet as described in 33:1. Cf. Cooke, *Ezekiel,* p. 346; Boadt, *Ezekiel's Oracles,* p. 129.

10. Since *dāmâ,* "to be like," never occurs in the Niphal, many (e.g., REB, NJPS) read its homonoym, "to be silence, destroyed" (cf. 27:32). However, not only does the word appear too infrequently to make such a judgment; but this etymology also flies in the face of consistent versional evidence and neutralizes the contrast called for by the opening of the following line, *wĕʾattâ,* "But you," whose function is to rebut Pharaoh's exalted claims. The traditional reading also accords better with the use of the comparative *dāmâ* in 31:2, 8, 18.

11. On Ezekiel's spelling, *htnym,* instead of the usual *htnyn,* see 29:3.

You have snorted[12] about in your rivers;[13]
You have stirred up the waters with your feet;[14]
You have muddied their[15] rivers.' "

1 The opening notice dates the oracle against the pharaonic monster on the first day of the twelfth month of the twelfth year of Jehoiachin's exile, which translates into March 3, 585 B.C.,[16] almost two years later than the previous oracle against Egypt (31:1). Because of the vagueness of the oracle it is difficult to determine the historical circumstances that might have provoked it.[17] Ezekiel is apparently more concerned with the relationship between Yahweh and Egyptian kings in principle than with a specific monarch. In any case, this prophetic event occurred two months after he had received word that Jerusalem had fallen to Babylon (33:21). Perhaps Ezekiel had been reflecting on those fateful days, or his compatriots may have still been hoping that somehow Egypt would recover and deliver their land from Babylonian power, permitting them to return home.

2 While the opening command charges the prophet to raise a lament over the pharaoh, the king of Egypt, only a fragment, consisting of an opening three-stress line followed by two 3:2 cola, remain. The use of the second person of direct address creates the impression that it was delivered in person to the pharaoh. This is a purely rhetorical device, however, Ezekiel's real audience being his fellow exiles. The prophet raises the central issue of the oracle with a simple announcement: Pharaoh views himself as a lion. While ch. 19 had applied the metaphor to the Judean royal house, the lion was a widely recognized symbol of royalty, especially in Egypt.[18] The Saite kings,

12. *wattāgaḥ*, from *gîaḥ*, "to burst forth."

13. Since *běnahărôtêkā* clashes with *nahărôtām* in the following line, it is commonly emended to *běnahărātěkā*, "with your nostrils" (cf. *BHS*), though without versional support.

14. The expression *dālaḥ mayim*, "to stir up water," is paralleled in Akkadian by *mê dalāḫu*, which is used in both the concrete sense and as a metaphor for "confusing the political order." See Garfinkel, *Akkadian Influences*, p. 65.

15. LXX reads "your," in agreement with the form two lines above. I retain MT as *lectio difficilior*.

16. See Parker-Dubberstein, *Chronology*, p. 28.

17. Freedy and Redford (*JAOS* 90 [1970] 473-74) propose an allusion to the defeat of Egypt in 588, but recognize that "it has now been transmuted into a cosmic concept."

18. See the self-descriptions of Ramesses II as "the living lion . . . slayer of his enemies" (A. Gardiner, *The Kadesh Inscriptions of Ramesses II* [Oxford: Oxford University Press, 1960], no. R 2), and his successor, Ramesses III as "the lion who rages when he sees his assailant." A portrait of the pharaoh, giving him the head of a lion, is labeled, "The Lion, the lord of victory, concealed, going forward, and making a conquest — his heart is full of might." Cf. E. R. Goodenough, *Jewish Symbols in the Greco-Roman Period,*

particularly Amasis, seem to have had a special interest in depicting themselves as sphinxes, according to which the recumbent leonine body symbolized the king's role as the invincible protector of the people.[19] By referring to himself as *kĕpîr gôyim,* "the lion of the nations,"[20] he is placing himself alongside the great emperors of the past.

How different from the pharaoh's self-perception is the view of the prophet, to whom the latter is more like a sea monster than a lion. Although the present portrayal of the king as a *tannîm* (Gk. δράχων, "dragon") shares some features with 29:3, where the same motif had been used to describe the pharaoh as a crocodile, the present description of the monster is more vague and ambiguous. On the one hand, since crocodiles do not inhabit the seas, the phrase *hattannîm bayyammîm,* "the monster in the seas," invites an association with the mythical sea divinity.[21] In Egypt the crocodile was considered a royal creature,[22] but in the world of myth the animal represented darkness and the netherworld. Like other OT poets and prophets, who employed the sea monster motif to describe Yahweh's primeval or eschatological conflicts, Ezekiel does not hesitate to use mythological language.[23] On the other hand, though the vocabulary is mythological, the monster painted in the remainder of the verse looks more like a crocodile thrashing about in the Nile than the cosmic monster. Whether the metaphor derives from myth or nature, in Ezekiel

---

vol. 7, *Pagan Symbols in Judaism,* Bollingen Series 37 (New York: Pantheon, 1958), pp. 46-50.

19. A. B. Lloyd, "The Late Period, 664-323 B.C.," in *Ancient Egypt: A Social History,* ed. B. G. Trigger, et al. (Cambridge: Cambridge University Press, 1983), p. 286. The lion also served as a symbol of divinity, the lion-headed goddess Sekhmet being perceived as the bloodthirsty wife of Ptah. See J. Yoyotte, "Sekhmet," *Dictionary of Egyptian Civilization,* ed. G. Posener, tr. A. Macfarlane (London: Methuen, 1962), p. 256; *ANEP,* no. 558.

20. Cf. *'êl gôyim,* "ram of the nations," in 31:11, on which see P. D. Miller Jr., *UF* 2 (1970) 183.

21. The presence of the *tannîm* in the Nile *(yĕ'ōr)* and its channels *(nĕhārôt)* is more realistic. This sea god was known in Canaan as Yamm. According to the Ugaritic texts, Baal challenges the divine royal status of Yamm, apparently bestowed on him by El, in a fierce battle that ends with Baal smashing the head of the sea monster. See *CTA,* 2, esp. 4.24ff. Cf. Wakeman, *God's Battle,* pp. 37-38.

22. Cf. Kees, *Ancient Egypt,* p. 32.

23. On the primeval conflict see Ps. 74:12-14; 89:9-11 (Eng. 8-10). Cf. the references to Leviathan, the multiheaded monster, in *CTA,* 5.1.1-3, on which see Wakeman, *God's Battle,* pp. 64-65; and esp. J. Day, *God's Conflict,* pp. 1-61. On the eschatological conflict see esp. Isa. 27:1, whose pairing of *nāḥāš bāriaḥ,* "slippery serpent," and *nāḥāš 'ăqallātôn,* "wriggling serpent," also echoes *CTA,* 5.1.1-3. See Day, *God's Conflict,* pp. 141-78. On the mythological language see P. D. Hanson, "Rebellion in Heaven, Azazel, and Euhemeristic Heroes in 1 Enoch 6-11," *JBL* 96 (1977) 209-10.

the sea monster motif is thoroughly historicized;[24] the prophet has the pharaoh in mind.

The actions of this monster are both rebellious and chaotic. He snorts with his nostrils and flails his feet, stirring up the waters. The verb *muddied (rāpas)* links this text with 34:18-19, in which pugnacious rams and male goats foul the drinking waters by trampling in it with their feet, preventing the rest of the flock from drinking. While Ezekiel might have portrayed Pharaoh as a royal shepherd, in keeping with common ancient Near Eastern custom, the present picture is anything but pastoral. Here the concrete actions represent defiance against Yahweh. The prophet's lament represents a rejection of the noble leonine imagery for the Egyptian king in favor of the sinister and repugnant figure of the crocodile.[25]

b. The Capture and Slaughter of the Monster (32:3-10)

> 3 *"Thus has the Lord Yahweh declared:*
> *'But I will spread my net over you*
> *In the company of many nations.*[26]

24. Ezekiel's identification of the pharaoh with the monster is esp. reminiscent of Isa. 51:9-10:

> Awake! Clothe yourself with strength!
> O arm of Yahweh!
> Awake as in days of old,
> The generations of long ago!
> Were you not the one who hacked Rahab in pieces,
> That pierced the monster *(tannîn)?*
> Were you not the one that dried up Yam,
> The waters of the Great Deep *(tĕhôm rabbâ)?*
> Were you not the one who transformed the abysses of Yam
> Into a road for the redeemed to pass over?

"Rahab" occurs as a nickname for Egypt also in Isa. 30:7 (so Day, *God's Conflict*, p. 89) and Ps. 87:4. Elsewhere the figure of the monster as Yahweh's enemy is applied to Assyria (Isa. 8:5-8; 17:12-14), to Babylon (Jer. 51:34; Hab. 3:8-10, 15), and to unspecified enemies (Ps. 44:19-20 [Eng. 18-19]). In Ps. 18:5-18 (Eng. 4-17); 46:3-6 (Eng. 2-5), and 144:5-7, the nations are referred to as the cosmic waters. On this text within the context of prophetic metaphorical representations of the great powers see R. Liwak, "Die altorientalischen Grossmächte in den Metaphorik der Prophetie," in *Prophetie und Geschichtliche Wirklichkeit im alten Israel*, Fest. S. Herrmann, ed. Liwak and S. Wagner (Stuttgart: Kohlhammer, 1991), pp. 214-15.

25. At the same time, this may be an intentional allusion to indigeneous Israelite traditions, esp. those poetic texts which speak of the salvation of Israel from Egypt in terms of Yahweh's victory over the sea (Exod. 15:1-18; Isa. 51:9-11; Ps. 77:17-21 [Eng. 16-20]).

26. LXX's omission of *biqhal* yields "the nets of many nations," which leads

And they will haul you up[27] in my dragnet.[28]
4 I will hurl you to the ground;
Out onto the open field[29] I will fling you.
I will cause all of the birds of the heavens to sit on you;
And have the creatures of the whole world[30] gorge on you.
5 I will strew your carcass upon the mountains;
I will fill the valleys with your corpse.[31]
6 I will drench the land with your gore —
With your blood[32] up to the mountains —
And the ravines will be filled from you.
7 When I snuff you out,[33]
I will cover the sky,
And darken[34] their[35] stars.
I will cover the sun with a cloud,
And the moon will not give its light.
8 All the lights that shine in the sky
I will darken over you.
I will impose darkness on your land.

The declaration of the Lord Yahweh.

---

many to see the entire phrase as an unfortunate interpretive addition, disrupting the parallelism (Allen, *Ezekiel 20–48*, p. 129; Zimmerli, *Ezekiel 2*, p. 154). But the vocabulary is typically Ezekielian (cf. *wĕqāhāl wĕʿam rab*, 26:7; *biqhal ʿammîm*, 23:24), and without it the pl. verb *wĕheʿĕlûkā* lacks an appropriate subject.

27. LXX and Vulg. treat Yahweh as the subject. Those who delete the previous line emend accordingly. Cf. Allen, *Ezekiel 20–48*, p. 129.

28. *hērem* suits the present marine context of the capture better than *rešet*. Cf. 26:5, 14; also 47:10; Mic. 7:2; Hab. 1:15, 16, 17; Eccl. 7:26. For discussion and illustrations of ancient Egyptian use of the net see Keel, *Symbolism*, pp. 89-94, esp. figs. 111 and 115; *ANEP*, nos. 112, 189.

29. LXX πεδία πλησθήσεταί σου, "plains will be full of you," reads *ʾăṭîlekā* as *yimmālĕʾûkā mimmekā*, perhaps influenced by the next line.

30. *ḥayyat kol-hāʾāreṣ* is a hapax modification of the more common *kol ḥayyat hāʾāreṣ* (thus Targ.). Cf. 31:6, 13; 34:5, 8; 39:17.

31. Reading *rimmôt*, lit. "maggots," with Symmachus, Syr., and Vulg., in place of MT *rāmûtekā*, "your heap." LXX ἀπὸ τοῦ αἵματός σου read the word as *middāmekā*, "from your blood," and then added πᾶσαν τὴν γῆν (= *kol hāʾāreṣ*), "all the earth," as a counterpart to "all the creatures of the earth" in v. 4. A different *Vorlage* is also possible.

32. *middāmĕkā* is usually deleted as a gloss on the hapax *ṣāpātĕkā*. Though misread as *mērabbĕkā*, "from your abundance," it is attested in LXX.

33. MT *bĕkabbôtĕkā*, lit. "in your snuffing out," lacks a subject. I follow LXX and Targ. by treating Yahweh as the subject of the Piel verb.

34. On *hiqdîr* see 31:15.

35. The pronominal suffix is odd. The nearest antecedents are "ravines" and "mountains." The association heightens the cosmic implications of Pharaoh's fall.

9 *I will trouble the minds of many peoples,*
When I bring your shattered remains[36] *among the nations,*
To countries unknown to you.
10 *I will make many peoples appalled over you,*
And their kings will bristle with terror[37] *because of you,*
When I brandish[38] *my sword in front of them.*
They will tremble continually,[39]
Each person for his own life,
On the day of your collapse.' "

3 The citation formula interrupts the lament before it can be developed by signaling Yahweh's response to the turbulent sea monster. By casting his reaction in the form of a modified judgment speech, Ezekiel invites his audience to interpret the foregoing description as an accusation, a charge of hubris, of insolence against Yahweh. The speech may be analyzed by summarizing his specific actions against the pharaoh.

First, Yahweh will capture the monster. Echoing earlier announcements of the capture of Zedekiah (12:13; 17:20), Ezekiel identifies the instrument of capture as a *net (rešet)* that Yahweh *spreads (pāraš)* over the victim.[40] Ezekiel's image is reminiscent of Job 26:13: "With his wind he [God] placed Yam in his net *(šiprâ);* his hand pierced the wriggling serpent *(nāḥāš bārîaḥ).*" But the scene is also familiar from extrabiblical traditions, especially of Marduk's capture of his arch-rival Tiamat and Baal's snaring of Yamm.[41]

36. LXX misread *šibrĕkā* as *šibyĕkā,* "your captivity." Targ. reads "those broken by your war."

37. *yiš'ărû 'ālêkā śa'ar,* involving a denominative verb from *śa'ar,* "hair," with cognate accusative, refers to hair standing on end, a physiological symptom of fright or shock. Cf. 27:35; Jer. 2:12; Deut. 32:17.

38. *bĕ'ôpĕpî,* from *'ûp,* "to fly," the Polel signifying "to fly back and forth." See *HALOT,* pp. 800-801. *BHS* suggests emending *b'wppy* to *bnwppy,* as if from *nûp,* "to move to and fro"; Joüon (*Bib* 10 [1929] 311) proposes *b'wrry,* "when I rouse." G. R. Driver derives the word from *'āpap,* "to double" ("Studies in the Vocabulary of the Old Testament VI," *JTS* 32 [1931] 376-77), but for this meaning Ezekiel uses *kāpal.* Cf. 21:19.

39. On *wĕḥārĕdû lirgā'îm,* see 26:16, which displays other links with this text as well.

40. In 29:4 the crocodile was captured with hooks in his jaws.

41. On Marduk and Tiamat see *ANET,* p. 67. The Akkadian term *saparrum,* "net," is a Sumerian loanword, cognate to *šiprâ* in Job 26:13, quoted above. On the expression and the motif see P. Steinkeller, "A Note on sa-bar = sa-par₄/par 'Casting Net,' " *ZA* 75 (1985) 39-46; J. B. Geyer, "Twisting Tiamat's Tail: A Mythological Interpretation of Isaiah XIII 5 and 8," *VT* 37 (1987) 171. For Baal and Yamm see *CTA,* 2.4.27: *yqt b'l wyšt ym ykly ṭpṭ nhr,* "Baal ensnares and places Yamm [in the snare]; he would destroy Ruler Nahar." For a discussion of the relationship of these texts see E. L. Greenstein, "The Snaring of the Sea in the Baal Epic," *Maarav* 3/2 (1982) 195-216.

According to our text, Yahweh's capture of the *tannîm* is a public affair, accomplished in the company of many nations; moreover, they are actively involved in hauling the captive out of the water in Yahweh's dragnet.

4   Second, Yahweh will hurl the monster out onto the open field. This language is reminiscent of 29:5, particularly Ezekiel's use of *nāṭaš*, "to hurl." The sense of the parallel expression *fling (hēṭîl)* is illustrated by Isa. 22:17 (cf. Jer. 16:13; 22:26 [Eng. 28]). The sea monster may throw his weight around in the water where he is at home, but on land he is out of his element. Under the hot desert sun he will quickly perish and become food for scavenging buzzards and jackals. Ezekiel highlights the magnitude of their banquet with the unique expression, *the creatures of the whole world.*

5-6   Third, Yahweh will scatter the remains of the monster's body all over the land. The primary action here is described in terms reminiscent of the portrayal of the felling of the tree in 31:12-13. The reference to the creature's remains filling the mountains, ravines, and valleys is obviously stereotypical, derived from the landscape of Palestine, or perhaps Lebanon. Two expressions are used for the monster's dead body, whose remains are strewn over the land. I have translated *bāśār*, the common word for "flesh" (cf. 39:17), as *carcass* in this context. The obscurity of *rāmût* has resulted in a variety of interpretations. The word derives either from *rûm*, "to be high," hence "heap [of corpses, rubble?]," or from *rmm*, "to rot, decay," in which case Ezekiel uses it metonymically for dead flesh eaten by worms. The latter provides a better parallel for *bāśār* here.

Verse 6 is also obscure. MT's hapax form, *ṣāpātĕkā*, seems to be corrupt. Many assume a derivation from *ṣûp*, "to flow, overflow,"[42] which agrees roughly with LXX ἀπὸ τῶν προχωρημάτων σου, "from your excrement." However, LXX could also have had before it *ṣō'ātĕkā*, which is used of human feces in 2 K. 18:27 (= Isa. 36:12) and which would also explain Targ. *dwhnyt'*, "manure."[43] In either case, combined with the following *middāmĕkā*, the prophet has painted a disgusting if vivid picture of the earth drinking the excrement, blood, and other body fluids that are discharged when an animal is slain. One can scarcely imagine a more ignominious death.

7-8   Fourth, Yahweh will turn the lights out on the monster. The imagery takes on an apocalyptic flavor, as the prophet contemplates the sea

---

42. See BDB, p. 847; Boadt, *Ezekiel's Oracles*, p. 139; Zimmerli, *Ezekiel 2*, p. 155. The same root underlies *ṣapṣāpâ*, "willow," in 17:7.

43. On the LXX see Day, *God's Conflict*, p. 94 and n. 27. For the Targ. see Levey, *Ezekiel*, p. 93; *HALOT*, p. 992. Less likely is S. Talmon's proposal of a miswritten *yĕpātĕkā*, "your splendor" ("The Ancient Alphabet and Biblical Text Criticism," in *Mélanges bibliques et orientaux en l'honneur de M. Mathias Delcor*, ed. A. Caquot, S. Legasse, and M. Tardieu, AOAT 215 [Neukirchen-Vluyn: Neukirchener, 1985], p. 400).

monster's "extinction." The term *kābâ,* which is used concretely of snuffing out a wick or a lamp, is occasionally used figuratively of death.[44] Ezekiel's application of the expression to Yahweh's enemy recalls Isa. 43:17: "They lay down, never to rise again; they have been extinguished, snuffed out like a wick *(pîštâ)*." But the defeat of this monster has cosmic implications. When he is snuffed out, the heavenly luminaries that light the earth will also be extinguished. Echoing Joel's portrayal of the eschatological day of Yahweh (2:10; 4:15 [Eng. 3:15]), the prophet opens with a general statement, announcing the covering *(kissâ)* of the heavens *(šāmayim)* by darkening the stars, covering *(kissâ)* the sun with a cloud *('ānān),* and stopping the light of the moon *(yārēaḥ).* These heavenly luminaries are all gathered together in v. 8 under the phrase *kol-mĕ'ôrê 'ôr baššāmayim* (lit. "all the lamps of light in the heavens"). Yahweh's announcement that he will impose darkness on Pharaoh's land carries a double meaning. On the one hand, reminiscent of the plague of darkness in Exod. 10:21-24, the sun, moon, and stars will cease to shine on Egypt. On the other, just as David was perceived as the *nēr yiśrā'el,* "lamp of Israel" (2 Sam. 21:17), so the pharaoh, the monster of the seas, was viewed as the light of Egypt. With his death darkness will strike the entire land.[45] The signatory formula at the end of v. 8 puts Yahweh's own imprimatur on the announcement.

9-10 Fifth, Yahweh will impose great fear on all who witness the monster's fall. The mythological overtones give way to historical reality as the prophet describes the international effect of Pharaoh's defeat. Changing the metaphor from "snuffing out" (v. 7) to "falling," the last line of v. 10 summarizes the issue in a sentence. On the day of Pharaoh's collapse,[46] Yahweh will deliberately *trouble,* or instill consternation *(hik'astî),* in the *minds of many peoples (lēb 'ammîm rabbîm,* lit. "heart of many peoples"); he *will make many peoples appalled (hăšimmôtî 'ammîm rabbîm),* resulting in their kings bristling with terror and the people trembling perpetually over the monster's demise. This effect will be guaranteed by distributing the frag-

---

44. Concrete references include Prov. 31:18; also the extinguishing of altar fire, Lev. 6:5-6. 1 Sam. 3:3 speaks of extinguishing the "the lamp of God" *(nēr 'ĕlōhîm).* Examples of figurative references are 2 Sam. 21:17, where David's men determine not to let their king accompany them in battle any more lest "the lamp of Israel *(nēr yiśrā'ēl)* be snuffed out; earlier, in 2 Sam. 14:7, the widow of Tekoa had complained to David that her coal *(gaḥelet),* viz., her family's future, would be extinguished if her son would be slain.

45. Isa. 50:2-3 associates the defeat of the dragon with the drying up of the seas and clothing the heavens with garments of mourning.

46. *mappelet* has been applied previously to the demise of the king of Tyre (Ezek. 26:15, 18; 27:27) and to the felling of the tree, which represents Assyria/Egypt (31:13, 16).

ments of his body among the nations, including those whom even the pharaoh knows nothing about, and brandishing his sword in their faces.

If one interprets the abstraction *šibrĕkā, your shattered remains,* concretely, Yahweh's action is illuminated by two events recorded in narrative texts. According to 1 Sam. 11:7, in an effort to marshal the forces of Israel against the Ammonites, the newly crowned King Saul took a yoke of oxen and, having cut them in pieces, sent them throughout the land, with the ultimatum that similar treatment would be afforded anyone who did not fall in line. As a result the dread *(pahad)* of Yahweh fell on all the people, and they came out in full force. Much more shocking, Judg. 19:29 recounts how a Levite dismembered his concubine's body into twelve pieces and distributed the fragments throughout the territory of Israel, intent on galvanizing the population to action against the neo-Sodomites of Benjaminite Gibeah.[47] When the peoples receive the fragments of the monster and see the flashing sword of Yahweh they will recognize the warning and all will fear for their own lives *(napšô).* The parenetic insertion at this point is not objectionable. Yahweh's acts of judgment are not performed in a corner. On the contrary, just as the felling of the magnificent cedar of Lebanon served as a warning to all trees (31:14), so the destruction of the Egyptian monster reminds all nations that they too are subject to the sovereign Yahweh.

c. The Lesson of the Monster (32:11-15)

> 11 *"For thus has the Lord Yahweh declared:*
> *'The king of Babylon's sword will come against you!*[48]
> 12 *With the swords of heroes,*
> *From the most barbarous of nations,*[49] *all of them,*

47. Cf. my discussion of the text in *WTJ* 52 (1990) 325-41. The action finds an extrabiblical analogue in a 2nd-millennium letter from Bahdi-Lim to Zimri-Lim king of Mari: "To my lord, speak. Bahdi-Lim, your servant, speaks as follows: For five full days I have waited for the Hanaeans, but the people do not gather. The Hanaeans have arrived from the steppe and established themselves among the settlements. Once, twice, I have sent (word) to the settlements and the appeal has been made. But they have not gathered together, and for the third day they have not gathered. Now, if I had my way, a prisoner in jail should be killed, his body dismembered, and transported to the area between the villages as far as Hudnum and Appan, in order that the people would fear and gather quickly, and I could make an attempt in accordance with the command which my lord has given to carry out the campaign quickly" (ARM, II:48). For discussion see G. Wallis, "Eine Parallele zu Richter 29ff. und 1 Sam. 11 5ff. aus dem Briefarchiv von Mari," *ZAW* 64 (1952) 57-61.

48. The suffix on *tĕbô'ekā* is datival. Cf. Joüon-Muraoka, *Grammar,* §125ba.

49. On *'ārîṣê gôyim* see above on 28:7; 30:11; 31:12.

I will bring down your pomp.
They[50] will ravage the pride of Egypt,
And all its pomp will be destroyed.
13 I will destroy all its cattle
From beside abundant waters.
No human feet will ever muddy them again,
Nor will the hooves of cattle muddy them.
14 Then I will let the waters settle,[51]
And make their rivers flow like oil.
                    The declaration of the Lord Yahweh.

15 When I lay the land of Egypt[52] waste,
And the land is stripped[53] of its contents[54] —
When I strike down[55] all its inhabitants,
Then they will know that I am Yahweh.' "

11a The citation formula marks a transition in the oracle. Triggered perhaps by the reference to Yahweh's sword in v. 10, Ezekiel offers an excursus on the manner in which Yahweh's sword is wielded. In the process the figure of the mythical monster disappears from view, and the crisis of the present, viz., the Babylonian threat to Egypt, is thrust into the foreground.

11b-12a The segment opens with a laconic introduction of the Babylonian sword. As in 21:24 (Eng. 19), the weapon appears to take on a life and power of its own. In keeping with 30:24-25, however, it is Yahweh's, not the king's, sword that will be wielded against Egypt; it is as Yahweh's agent that the Babylonian comes. And he does not come alone. *The king of Babylon's sword (ḥereb melek bābel)* is a collective designation for a whole host of swords, *the swords of heroes,* wielded by warriors from the most brutal of nations. While LXX γιγάητων is not a precise translation of *gibbôrîm,* "heroic men," it captures the frightening prospect.[56] Like the Vikings and Vandals who overran Europe, these ruthless barbarians will leave behind a path of devastation, destroying the *pride (gā'ôn)* and the *pomp (hāmôn)* of Egypt.

50. On the sudden change of person (from second to third) see Joüon-Muraoka, *Grammar,* §158n (1).
51. On the basis of Targ. *šqyṭ,* "I will make quiet," and LXX ἡσυχάσει, *BHS* suggests emendation to *'ašqîṭ,* but see the commentary.
52. *'eṭ-'ereṣ* is missing in LXX. Zimmerli (*Ezekiel 2,* p. 156) suggests that *'ereṣ* and *miṣrayim* may originally have been distributed over two parallel lines.
53. The syntax requires a finite verb, *wěnāšammâ* in place of MT's participle, *ûněšammâ.* Cf. Joüon-Muraoka, *Grammar,* §119o.
54. *mělō'āh,* lit. "its fulness," refers to the land's plant and animal life.
55. LXX interprets Heb. *hikkâ* as "scatter."
56. *gibbôrîm* will resurface in vv. 21, 27, and 39:18, 20.

Both terms are ambiguous,[57] but together they highlight the fundamental problem of the pharaoh and his land: hubris. The onrushing barbarians will make quick work of the magnificence and the military might of the nation.

12b-13 But Ezekiel deliberately highlights the role of Yahweh in destroying the pride of Egypt. He brings about the fall (*'appîl*) of Egypt's pomp (v. 12); he destroys the livestock of Egypt (v. 13). The devastation in the land is described in terms of putting an end to anyone *muddying* waters. The verb *dālaḥ* provides an obvious link with v. 2, but in typical Ezekielian fashion the significance of the stirring up of the waters has changed. Whereas earlier the muddy waters were the result of the monster's (Pharaoh's) arrogant and chaotic activity, here they are a sign of life, of people and their livestock going down to the irrigation ditch or river channel to drink. But Yahweh will bring an end to this kind of activity. When he causes the pride of Egypt to fall and destroys the livestock, there will be no feet or hooves to disturb the water. On the contrary, the water will have a chance to rest and rejuvenate itself.

14 The archaizing opening *'āz, Then,* which occurs only here in Ezekiel, alerts the hearer to a new word picture. The muddy waters give way to clear, smoothly flowing rivers, as the soil and dirt suspended in the water settle to the bottom.[58] The reference to rivers running like *oil (šemen)* is puzzling in this context. In biblical and Jewish tradition the motif of streams running with oil usually speaks of paradisiacal peace and prosperity.[59] The Targ. interprets accordingly, "Then I will bring tranquility to the nations and lead their kings with gentleness." But such a picture of bliss seems out of place, unless we have here a hyperbolic declaration of Yahweh, that an Egypt

---

57. On *gā'ôn*, "pride," see 7:20 and 16:49, 56, though Ezekiel often links the word with *'ōz*, "strength," as in the construct phrase *gĕ'ôn 'ōz*, "the pride of strength" (37:24; 24:21; 30:6, 8; 33:28), perhaps under the inspiration of Lev. 26:19. *hāmôn*, a key term in the oracles against Egypt, denotes also "wealth, power, people, army."

58. *šāqa'*, translated "settle," denotes lit. "to sink." The present text may reflect local coloring, alluding to the muddy state of the Nile, particularly at flood stage, and its annual deposit of silt, a phenomenon well known in the ancient world. Cf. Herodotus, *Hist.* 2.1-25. Ezekiel was undoubtedly aware of this behavior of the river, though his explanation for its turbidity is quite different.

59. Cf. Gen. 27:28; Job 29:6. Also in *2 Enoch* 8:5 it is written of paradise, "Two streams come forth, one a source of honey and milk, and a source which produces oil and wine" (*OTP,* 1:116). In *b. Sanh.* 98a, Rabbi Hanina interprets the present text (in conjunction with 29:21) as a sign of the imminent appearance of the Messiah: "The Son of David will not come until a fish is sought for an invalid and cannot be procured, as it is written, 'Then I will make their waters deep, and cause their rivers to run like oil'; whilst it is written, 'In that day will I cause the horn of the house of Israel to bud forth.' " Similar associations are attested in the Ugaritic literature. *CTA,* 3.2.38ff. (= 4.86ff.), describes Anat washing "with the dew of heaven, the oil of earth, the rain of the Rider of the Clouds." *CTA,* 6.3.6-7, observes, "the heavens rain down oil; the wadis run with honey."

wasted and without inhabitant means peace and hope for the nations. This interpretation seems to be suggested by the next verse.

15 Following the divine signature at the end of v. 14, the prophecy arrives at a formal conclusion with an expanded version of the recognition formula. Now we learn Yahweh's ultimate goal in humiliating Egypt: the universal acknowledgment of his person and his involvement in human affairs. Three aspects of the divine activity are reviewed: desolating the land *(nātan šēmāmâ)*, emptying it of its contents, and striking down its inhabitants (presumably human). With this intensification of divine judgment, Egyptian history will run its course, causing its remaining inhabitants and the people of the world to recognize the hand and person of Yahweh.

d. Colophonic Conclusion (32:16)

16 *"This is a dirge to be chanted. The women of the nations*[60] *will chant it. Over Egypt and all its pomp they will chant it. The declaration of the Lord Yahweh."*

The text concludes with a colophon that provides four kinds of information concerning the foregoing oracle.[61] (1) Its genre. This is a *qînâ* lament composition, reflecting its central concern: death. The superscription had identified the victim as "Pharaoh, king of Egypt" (v. 2); now, by the principle of corporate solidarity, the reference is expanded to Egypt as a whole. (2) Its use. The composition was not written primarily as literature to entertain or to be stored in the archives of the exilic community, but to be chanted, suggesting public oral group activity. (3) Its chanters. The women of the nations are to mourn the death of Egypt by chanting this lament. Ancient funeral rites often involved professional mourners, usually women, who chanted the dirge over the deceased.[62] (4) Its referents. The last line identifies the deceased as Egypt

60. Targ. interprets these *bĕnôt haggôyim*, lit. "daughters of the nations," as villages *(kpyrn)*, perhaps the settlements surrounding the "mothers," the capitals of city-states. Cf. above on 26:6.

61. On the nature and function of biblical colophons see H. M. I. Gevaryahu, "Biblical Colophons: A Source for the 'Biography' of Authors, Texts and Books," in *Congress Volume: Edinburgh 1974*, VTSup 28 (Leiden: Brill, 1975), pp. 42-59.

62. Referred to in the OT as "the singing women" *(šārôt,* 2 Chr. 35:25), "mourning women" *(mĕqônĕnôt)*, or "skillful women" *(ḥăkāmôt,* Jer. 9:16 [Eng. 17]). Cf. also Isa. 22:12; Jer. 7:29. The 11th-century sarcophagus of Ahiram of Byblos contains a carving of four Canaanite professional women, the two on the left beating their breasts, and the right pair with hands raised, perhaps tearing their hair. See *ANEP,* no. 459. Cf. also the picture from the tomb of Ramose at Thebes (ca. 1400) of a group of female Egyptian mourners with hands raised in *IBD,* 1:210.

and its entire *pomp* or horde or wealth *(hāmôn)*. With the concluding signatory formula Yahweh pounds the final nail into the nation's coffin.

The oracle proper seems to end with the recognition formula in v. 15, suggesting that v. 16 represents a later addition, after the oracle had been committed to writing. While most scholars attribute the verse to another hand,[63] the reasons for doing so are not convincing. It is evident from Jer. 36 that prophecies were often transcribed shortly after their oral presentation, either by the prophet himself or by a secretary (Baruch). Accordingly, if Ezekiel was involved in the literary adaptation of his oral pronouncements, he may well have attached this colophon himself. The need for the addition may have arisen from the internal generic tensions created by the oracle as a whole. Having abandoned the lament form almost immediately (v. 2), he probably added this note to remind the reader of the oracle's central issue, the death of the pharaoh, and to provide guidance for the later use of the prophecy.[64] In the process Ezekiel expresses his own self-consciousness as a literary prophet; further, by attaching the signatory formula to the colophon he also affirms its divine origin and authority.[65] For another to claim these prophetic formulae was the height of presumption, the kind of plagiarism false prophets were guilty of (cf. ch. 13). It is best, therefore, to attribute the concluding colophon to the prophet's own hand, though it belongs to the transcriptional phase of his prophecy rather than to the original oral occasion. By appending the signatory formula, however, God invests the subscription with the same authority as the oracle proper, for it too bears Yahweh's own seal of approval.

♦ *Theological Implications*

The oracle against the pharaonic monster contains few new theological lessons. Like the previous oracle, and the oracles against Tyre, it warns the readers in every age against hubris, the pride *(gā'ôn)* and pomp *(hāmôn)* with which humans celebrate their own magnificence. Humans who imagine themselves as noble masters of their own destiny (the lion) are monsters *(tannîm)* in the eyes of God. If he was able to vanquish the mythical monster, surely no human can evade his judgment. He who turned the lights on in the heavens in the first place is able to turn them off at will. And if he exercises such

---

63. Wevers (*Ezekiel,* p. 244) attributes it to a traditionist for whom "lament" was no longer a technical term; Fohrer (*Ezechiel,* p. 179) deletes it as a "spätere Unterschrift," "later postscript."

64. See Davis, *Swallowing the Scroll,* p. 63.

65. Cf. Yahweh's explicit authorization of Ezekiel to use the citation formula in 2:4; 3:11.

control over the great luminaries in the sky, surely he is able, at the snap of his finger, to snuff out the light of mortals.

The oracle affirms that Yahweh is the Lord not only of individuals but also of history. The rise and fall of nations may appear attributable to charismatic and gifted leaders, but behind all international movements one must acknowledge the supreme hand of Yahweh, who alone fixes the times and seasons of their lives, sets the limits to their conduct, determines the nature of their downfall, appoints the agents of judgment, and in the process accomplishes his goal: the universal recognition of his power and his person.

7. Egypt's Descent into Sheol (32:17-32)

♦ Nature and Design

The boundaries of Ezekiel's last oracle against Egypt are clearly marked by the date notice, followed by the word-event formula in v. 17 and the signatory formula in v. 32. The greatest difficulty posed by this literary unit is probably the text itself. Seldom since Ezekiel's opening vision has a unit been plagued by such a concentration of truncated sentences, grammatical inconsistencies, and redundancy, yielding a literary/rhetorical style some consider ill befitting the prophet so renowned for his creativity. The plethora of deviations from the MT in the LXX suggest that the Alexandrian translators, who were removed from the prophet himself by several centuries, were as frustrated with the text as modern interpreters are. On the one hand, this early Greek version omits 15-18 percent of the material found in MT; on the other hand, it fills in several lacunae.[1] It also simply changes the reading where it is deemed appropriate.[2] Some of these readings improve the sense and are probably

---

1. Examples of the former: "The sword has been appointed" (v. 20); "mightiest of" (v. 21); "with his allies" (v. 21); "They have gone down; they have lain down, the uncircumcised" (v. 21); "Her graves are round about" (v. 22); "having fallen by the sword" (v. 22); all but the first three words, "in the midst of the victims, they have been appointed," of v. 25; "and not" (v. 23); "You shall be shattered and" (v. 28); "and" before *'et* (v. 29); "in shame" (v. 30); "Pharaoh and his entire army are victims of the sword" (v. 31); "Lord" (vv. 31, 32). Examples of the latter: "In the first month" (v. 17); "with him" (v. 19); "in the midst of" (v. 21); "and" (v. 26, before "Tubal").

2. "Dead" for "mighty" (v. 18); v. 19 is placed after "Sheol" in v. 21, displacing the MT readings; "and all their horde will be made to lie down" replaces "They have dragged her and all her horde off" (v. 20); "to you" for "to him" (v. 21); "in the remotest recesses of the pit," for "from the midst of Sheol" (v. 21); "there" for "whose" (v. 23); "they were given," which follows "in the midst of the victims," at the beginning of v. 25 in MT is placed after "there" (v. 26); "their horde" for "her horde" (v. 26); "round about his grave" for "round about her graves" (v. 26); "who" for "although" (v. 26); "from of old" for "apart from the uncircumcised" (v. 27); "whom the princes of Assyria have given"

correct; others are confusing.[3] Stylistically, the oracle lacks color, being composed from a limited pool of expressions, drawn mostly from the vocabulary of death, and crafted in morbidly repetitious fashion.[4]

Structurally, the text is complex. After the customary introductory formulas, Ezekiel is commanded to wail the descent of Egypt to the netherworld (vv. 17-18a). V. 18b functions as a thesis statement, to be developed in the remainder of the oracle. Vv. 19-21 constitute a general announcement of judgment upon the nation, emphasizing the depths to which this loveliest of all nations will fall. The second person of direct address in v. 19 gives way to the third person in v. 20, a form maintained to the end. The bulk of the oracle (vv. 22-30) represents a formal roll call of nations already in Sheol that welcome the arrival of Egypt. The text concludes with a declaration of the significance of the previous scenes for Pharaoh, followed by the signatory formula (v. 31), and a theological interpretation of the descent of the king of Egypt into Sheol (v. 32). A second signatory formula brings the oracle to a close.

Since the nature and structure is unlike anything we have encountered before in Ezekiel, the genre of the oracle is difficult to classify. The opening charge to the prophet to "wail, lament" *(nāhâ)* invites the reader to interpret what follows as a formal expression of grief,[5] an impression strengthened by the involvement of the "women of the mighty nations," a class of professional mourners. But the oracle proper is neither formally identified as a *qînâ*, nor does it bear the distinctive marks of a lament: a 3:2 meter and a "then-now"

---

for "Edom, her kings and her princes" (v. 29); "all the lords of Assyria" for "all of them, every Sidonian who . . ." (v. 30); "and their might" for "from their might" (v. 30); "he gave" for "I gave" (v. 32).

3. An example of the former is "from of old," rather than "apart from the uncircumcised," in v. 27. An example of the latter is νεκρός in v. 18.

4. Expressions occurring more than once include: *hāmôn,* "horde, pomp" (7 times); *yārad,* "to go down" (11 times); *'ereṣ taḥtîyôt,* "netherworld" (twice); *yôrĕdê bôr,* "those who go down to the Pit" (5 times); *šākab,* "to lie" (8 times); *'ărēlîm,* "uncircumcised" (9 or 10 times); *ḥereb,* "sword" (14 times); *ḥălālîm,* "victims" (5 times); *ḥalĕlê ḥereb,* "victims of the sword" (9 times); *nāpal,* "to fall" (5 times); *nātān,* "to give, appoint, hand over" (11 times); *kol,* "all, every" (17 times); *gibbôr,* "mighty," and related forms (4 times); *qāhāl,* "assembly, company" (twice); *qeber,* "graves/tombs" (6 times); *sĕbîbôt,* "around, surrounding" (5 times); *ḥittît,* "terror" (7 times); *'ereṣ ḥayyîm,* "land of the living" (6 times); *šām/mâ,* "there" (5 times); *kĕlimmâ,* "disgrace" (3 times).

5. The verb occurs elsewhere only in Mic. 2:4 and 1 Sam. 7:2(?), both in the context of a lament. The noun *nĕhî,* "mourning, mourning song," is more common. Amos 5:16 identifies professional mourners as *yôdĕ'ê nĕhî,* "those who know how to mourn." In Jer. 9:9, 19 *nĕhî* is used synonymously with *qînâ,* which recalls Ezekiel's similar employment of hapax forms of the root, *hî* (2:10) and *nî* (27:32).

structure. Indeed, neither the prophet nor Yahweh seems to be saddened by the descent of Egypt to the netherworld. If anything, the oracle parodies the lament form.[6] To be sure, it is preoccupied with death, and for those Judeans who were looking to Egypt for a last-minute rescue, Egypt's demise represented a tragedy of the first order. But the description of Egypt's arrival in Sheol and consignment to the farthest recesses of the netherworld has a triumphant ring. In effect, the prophet is taunting the high and mighty nation of Egypt.

In the present oracle we witness another example of typically Ezekielian resumptive exposition. While the motif of the descent into the netherworld had been raised in 28:17, the present prophecy may be interpreted as an exposition or expansion of 31:14-18. The links in vocabulary are obvious,[7] but the earlier notice that nations (gôyim) would quake (ra'aš) over the fall of the tree and find relief (niḥam) at its descent into Sheol (31:16) is especially intriguing. This prophecy introduces a representative sampling of those nations and describes in detail their relationship to the Egyptian newcomer. In a typically Ezekielian twist, however, the shoe of comfort is placed on the other foot. Instead of the nations being relieved at learning that even the great and mighty Egypt has joined them, Egypt may take comfort in knowing that it is not alone in the netherworld; other nations, great and small, have experienced the same fate (32:31).

More will be said later about the source of Ezekiel's notions of the realm of the dead. For the moment it is sufficient to observe that Ezekiel seems to have borrowed many of his ideas of death from Isa. 14, another prophetic parody of the dirge form, and van den Born's suggestion of Isaianic influence is quite plausible.[8]

---

6. Cf. Yee, *CBQ* 50 (1988) 565-86.

7. *nātan*, "to hand over, deliver" to death (*lammāwet*, 31:14); *'ereṣ taḥtît*, "netherworld" (31:14, 16, 18); *yôrĕdê bôr*, "those who go down to the Pit" (31:14, 16); *yārad šĕ'ôlâ*, "to go down to Sheol" (31:15-17); *ḥalĕlê ḥereb*, "victims of the sword" (31:17); *'ărēlîm*, "uncircumcised" (31:18); *šākab bĕtôk*, "to lie with/among" (31:18); *hāmôn*, "pomp, horde" (31:18).

8. See van den Born, *Ezechiël*, p. 193. B. Gosse's reversal of the direction of borrowing ("Un texte pré-apocalyptique du règne de Darius: Isaïe XIII,1–XIV,23," *RB* 92 [1985] 200-22, esp. 208-10) relies on a questionable dating of the Isaiah text to the reign of Darius. Borrowed ideas include: (1) a nation being greeted in Sheol by other nations (Isa. 14:9-10, 16); (2) heroes of long ago in Sheol (Isa. 14:9 speaks of *rĕpā'îm*, "shades"; Ezekiel of *gibbôrîm mē'ôlām*, "mighty men of old," but cf. Isa. 13:3); (3) the motif of comparison (Isa. 14:10; cf. Ezek. 32:19); (4) bringing "pomp" down to Sheol (Isa. 14:11 uses *gā'ôn;* Ezekiel *hāmôn*, but cf. Isa. 13:4); (5) falling (*nāpal*, Isa. 14:12); (6) "the remotest parts of the Pit" (*yarkĕtê bôr*, Isa. 14:15); (7) "lying in tombs" (*šākab bĕbayit/qeber*, Isa. 14:18, 19); (8) "to be pierced with the sword" (*ṭā'an* in Isa. 14:19, *ḥālal* in Ezekiel).

a. Preamble and the Lament over Egypt's Descent into Sheol (32:17-21)

17 *In the twelfth[9] year, on the fifteenth day of the month,[10] the following message of Yahweh came to me:* 18 *"Human, wail[11] — you[12] and the women[13] of the majestic nations — over the pomp of Egypt:*

> *'Send it[14] down to the netherworld,*
> *to those who have gone down to the Pit.*
> 19 *"Whom do you surpass in loveliness?[15]*
> *Go on down and make your bed[16] with the uncircumcised!"[17]*
> 20 *Amid the victims of the sword they will fall.[18]*
> *The sword has been appointed![19]*

9. As in v. 1, several Hebrew mss. and Syr. read *bĕ'aštê,* "in the eleventh year."

10. MT lacks a month (cf. 26:1). Many follow LXX in filling in the lacuna with "in the first month" (e.g., Freedy and Redford, *JAOS* 90 [1970] 468; Kutsch, *Chronologischen Daten,* p. 67).

11. On *nāhâ* see the introductory comments to this oracle.

12. MT places *'ôtāh* and the following phrase after *wĕhôridēhû,* "and send her down," suggesting that *'ôtâ* be interpreted as a duplicated object after the suffix on the verb. However, the inconsistency of gender in the suffixes renders this reading unlikely. MT appears to have misvocalized *'attâ,* a resumptive subject for the imperative verbs.

13. *ûbĕnôt* is often treated as a corruption of *bĕtôk* under the influence of *bĕnôt haggôyim* in v. 16. See Zimmerli, *Ezekiel 2,* p. 164, following Heinisch and Bewer, *ZAW* 63 (1951) 200-201. Cf. Allen, *Ezekiel 20–48,* p. 134, for additional explanation.

14. LXX reads a pl. verb, perhaps assuming *gôyim* as the subject. The suffix should probably be read as fem., after *hāmôn.*

15. *nā'ēm,* "to be delightful, lovely," is used in a variety of contexts: of a country (Gen. 49:15), friend (2 Sam. 1:26), one's beloved (Cant. 7:7 [Eng. 6]), words (Ps. 141:6), knowledge (Prov. 2:10), bread (9:17), a blessing (24:25). Cf. the name Naomi (Ruth 1:20, the opposite of *mārâ,* "bitterness"), and the noun *nō'am,* "pleasantness, delightfulness," Zech. 11:7, 10; Ps. 27:4; 90:17; Prov. 3:17; 15:26; 16:24. *n'm* is equivalent to *ṭb,* "good, beautiful," in Phoenician and Ugaritic, the latter of which favors the word in descriptions of the gods (cf. *n'm ilm,* "the gracious gods," *CTA,* 5.3.15; *n'm 'nt,* "the grace of Anat," 14.3.145; 16.3.7 refers to the rain of Baal as a delight [*n'm*] to the earth) and human heroes (Keret, *n'mn,* "the gracious one," 14.1.40; Aqhat, *n'mn 'mq nšm,* "charming one, strongest of men," 17.6.45; 18.4.14. Cf. the maiden Huray, 14.3.144; also Zaphon, the residence of Baal, 3.3.28; *n'my arṣ,* "the pleasant land," 5.6.6; etc.

16. *wĕhoškĕbâ* is a literary creation, one of only two Hophal imperatives in the OT (cf. Jer. 49:2). Waltke and O'Connor (*Syntax,* p. 452 n. 6) compare it to the English passive imperative, "Drop dead!" On the reflexive use of the Hophal, i.e., "bed yourself," cf. H. Dahan, "Reflexivity," *Leš* 44 (1980) 219-23.

17. LXX has v. 19 after *šĕ'ôl* in v. 21, supplying the direct speech required.

18. LXX assumes *'ōtô,* "with him," after the verb.

19. *ḥereb nittānâ,* "a sword was given," is missing in LXX, perhaps because of its awkwardness. Targ. makes the reading more reasonable with *lḥrb' ytmsrwn,* "They shall be delivered to the sword."

They have dragged her off,
  along with her entire horde.[20]
21 *The mightiest of the heroes*[21] *will speak to him,*
  and to his allies,[22] *from the midst of Sheol.*[23]
They have gone down;
They have lain down,
  the uncircumcised,
  the victims of the sword.' "[24]

17 Ezekiel's final oracle against Egypt and last against a foreign nation is dated to the twelfth year on the fifteenth day of the month of Jehoiachin's exile. The absence of an identification of the month invites the reader to fill in "the twelfth," based on v. 1.[25] Accordingly, this prophetic event may be dated March 18, 585 B.C.,[26] two weeks later than the previous oracle. Perhaps Ezekiel had been wondering what would become of the captured monster. In any case, in its present literary context, this oracle functions as a belated conclusion to the previous one, analogous to 31:14b-18, which had provided an ending for 31:1-14a, albeit within the same prophecy.

18 Following the customary word-event formula and the divine address of the prophet as *Human (ben-'ādām)*, Ezekiel is commanded to wail

20. LXX καὶ κοιμηθήσεται πᾶσα ἡ ἰσχὺς αὐτοῦ, reflecting Heb. *wĕhoškab kol-hămônām*, harmonizes the reading with later expressions. But MT is filled with inconsistencies: (1) Feminine suffixes on *'ôtāh* and *hămônêhā* clash with the masc. *yippōlû* and the suffixes in v. 21. (2) The perfect verb *māšĕkû* clashes with the previous imperfect *yippōlû*. (3) *māšĕkû*, "They have dragged off," lacks a subject (Boadt [*Ezekiel's Oracles*, p. 154], suggests that the nations, referred to impersonally, are in mind). (4) The pl. form *hămônêhā* is impossible (read *hămônāh*). Allen ("Annotation Clusters in Ezekiel," *ZAW* 102 [1990] 408-9) suggests that a cluster of marginal notes have been combined and inserted in the wrong place.

21. MT *'ēlê* is defectively written for *'êlê*. Cf. Vulg., Targ., and Syr.; LXX omits the word.

22. MT *'et-'ōzĕrāyw* is missing in LXX and Syr. The sg. suffix here and on the previous *lô* are unexpected after the last line of v. 20. *'et* functions as a preposition, parallel to *lĕ*. Cf. v. 18. On *'ōzĕrāyw*, "helpers, allies," see my *Ezekiel: Chapters 1–24*, p. 378, and above on 30:8.

23. This is the first occurrence of *šĕ'ôl* in this context. On the term see above on 31:15. LXX harmonizes *mittôk šĕ'ôl* with v. 23 by reading *bĕyarkĕtê bôr*.

24. LXX omits *yārĕdû šākĕbû hā'ĕrēlîm* and inserts κατάβηθι καὶ κοιμήθητι μετὰ ἀπεριτμήτων ἐν μέσῳ τραυματῶν μαχαίρος, which is precisely what was expected in v. 19. Allen (*ZAW* 102 [1990] 409-10) treats these four lines as another cluster of annotations that has found its way into the text.

25. So also Boadt, *Ezekiel's Oracles*, p. 152; Greenberg, *Ezekiel 1–20*, p. 11.

26. See Parker-Dubberstein, *Chronology*, p. 28; Lang, *Ezechiel*, p. 39, though Lang is open to the reading in LXX.

over *the pomp (hāmôn) of Egypt.* In the light of the previous oracles, the word *hāmôn* raises expectations of another challenge to the nation's hubris. While this notion is not excluded, the immediate contextual requirements, particularly the clarification in v. 31, thrust the military nuance of the term into the foreground. The content of the lament is not specified. Instead the divine word moves immediately to a new charge, to bring Egypt down to the underworld. This command reintroduces the verb *yārad,* "to go down," one of the keywords in this text and in the foregoing oracles against both Tyre and Egypt.[27] The use of the Hiphil, with Ezekiel as the subject,[28] is intentional, reflecting the prophet's vocational self-awareness and his recognition of the force of his official utterances. This is not to say that the prophetic word possessed an independent, inherent effacaciousness,[29] but to acknowledge Yahweh as the agent behind the prophetic pronouncement. Yahweh hereby calls on Ezekiel to send Egypt down to the netherworld, announcing Egypt's doom, the content of which announcement is recorded in the very next verse.

But Ezekiel is not to wail alone. Yahweh calls on the *women of the majestic nations* to join him in lamenting the fall of Egypt. The phrase *běnôt gôyim* (lit. "daughters of the nations") provides an obvious link with the previous oracle, which had ended with "the daughters of the nations" *(běnôt haggôyim)* mourning the passing of Pharaoh (32:16), and thus suggests that this oracle represents an intentional sequel to 32:1-16. By characterizing these nations as *majestic ('addirim),* the prophet acknowledges these women's countries of origin to be more than third-rate states; they are significant powers.[30] But who are these daughters? On the one hand, in the light of the common involvement of women as professional mourners, the reference could be to the female populations of the nations. On the other hand, *běnôt gôyim* should probably be treated as an epexegetical genitive, "the daughters who are the nations."[31] These will be identified in the course of the oracle as Assyria, Elam, Meshech-Tubal, Edom, and Sidon, the first four of which are treated as feminine according to normal Hebrew usage.[32] Inasmuch as these nations are "those who have gone down to the Pit" *(yôrĕdê bôr),* in effect, their

27. Zimmerli (*Ezekiel 2,* p. 172) observes that of the twenty-nine occurrences of the word in Ezekiel, twenty-six are in these oracles.

28. Earlier texts had Yahweh (26:20; 31:16) or the nations (28:8) as the subjects of the Hiphil.

29. See Friebel, "Sign-Acts," pp. 117-24.

30. Cf. 17:8, 23, where the same word describes the stately vine and cedar, respectively.

31. Like *ṣō'n 'ādām,* "flock of humans," 36:18. Cf. GKC, §128k-q; Waltke-O'Connor, *Syntax,* §9.5.3i (genitive of genus).

32. The masc. gender of Sidon is determined by the references to the "princes of Sidon" and the use of the gentilic, "the Sidonian(s)," in v. 30.

greeting to the newcomers from the land of the living substitutes for the death wail.

19 The actual words of greeting are taunting and harsh, challenging Egypt's self-esteem as the most delightful nation on earth. While the language is different, the rhetorical function of the question is similar to the prophet's earlier challenges to name anyone equal to Egypt with reference to greatness (31:2) and glory (31:18). But now Egypt is mocked. What good does unsurpassed beauty do in the netherworld, especially when one is ordered to make one's bed with *the uncircumcised?* Ezekiel's inclusion of the Egyptians among the uncircumcised is remarkable, given the fact that they (like the Edomites and Sidonians from this list) practiced the rite of circumcision.[33] Ezekiel's usage of the term is obviously metaphorical and determined by his own culture. In Israel, circumcision was the sign and seal of membership in the covenant community (Gen. 17), which in time became a symbol of cultural superiority. To be uncircumcised meant exclusion from the family grave, hence consignment to the most undesirable compartment of the netherworld along with other unclean and vile persons.[34] The Egyptians would have found this announcement of their fate shocking. The nation that perceived itself as the epitome of culture, greatness, and glory is hereby sentenced to the most ignominious fate in the netherworld.

20 Borrowing a leaf from Isaiah's notebook, though with different vocabulary,[35] Ezekiel identifies other "dishonorable" members of the netherworld among whom Egypt will lie as *the victims of the sword (ḥalĕlê ḥereb).* As already observed repeatedly, and as will be confirmed in v. 27, those pierced by the sword are not simply soldiers who have died on the battlefield, but murderers and evildoers who have been executed, and who, instead of being given an honorable burial, are tossed in a heap in a separate disposal place.[36] Consequently, in the netherworld they are separated from those who have died honorable deaths and been given proper burials. To join such as these, Egypt and her entire horde will be dragged off *(māšak)* to their doom.

21 This verse introduces a new group of inhabitants in the netherworld, *the mightiest of the heroes (ʾêlê gibbôrîm,* lit. "the rams of the mighty men").[37]

---

33. On circumcision see J. M. Sasson, "Circumcision in the Ancient Near East," *JBL* 85 (1966) 473-76. See the illustration in *ANEP,* no. 629, and the inscription dealing with the rite, *ANET,* p. 326; also Herodotus, *Hist.* 2.104; Josephus, *Ant.* 8.10.3.

34. Cf. A. Lods, "La 'mort des incirconcis,'" *CRAIBL* (1943): 271-83.

35. Isa. 14:19 speaks of *mĕṭōm ʿănê ḥereb.*

36. See Eissfeldt, in *Studies in Old Testament Prophecy,* pp. 73-81, esp. 81. See above on 31:17, 18; also 6:7; 26:15; 30:11. Isaiah uses the expression in 22:2.

37. Ezekiel's metaphorical usage of *ʾayil* accounts for one-half of its occurrences in the OT. Cf. 17:13; 30:13; 31:11, 14; 39:18. For discussion see Miller, *UF* 2 (1970) 181-82.

While their exact identity cannot be determined from this verse,[38] their participation in the drama is remarkable: they speak to Egypt and her allies *from the
midst of Sheol.* Presumably *bĕtôk šĕʾôl* refers to the heart of the netherworld,
perhaps more honorable quarters than *yarkĕtê bôr,* "the remotest recesses of the
Pit," to which Egypt is consigned with the uncircumcised and the victims of the
sword. Accordingly, these mighty men seem to be individuals who have been
buried honorably.

The last half of the verse is textually problematic, and the syntactical
relationships among the phrases are unclear. Either these are parenthetical
additions, that is, "Egypt, and her allies, the uncircumcised, the victims of
the sword, have gone down . . . ," or they are adverbial accusatives: "Egypt
and her allies have gone down, as the uncircumcised and as victims of the
sword." Either way, they reiterate the inevitable doom of Egypt.

b. The "Dishonor Role": Egypt's Company in Sheol (32:22-32)

22   " 'Assyria is there with her entire company, with her graves round
about her.[39] All of them are victims, those who have fallen by the
sword,[40] 23 whose graves have been appointed in the remotest recesses
of the Pit.[41] Her company is round about her tomb, all of them victims,
having fallen[42] by the sword — the ones who had struck[43] terror[44] in
the land of the living.
24 Elam is there with her entire horde, with her tomb round about.

---

38. But see below on v. 27.

39. MT *sĕbîbôtāyw qibrōtāyw* is missing in LXX. Although the phrase occurs in
various forms in this context, most emend to *sĕbîbôt qĕburātāh,* as in v. 23, and with Syr.
The suffixes vary, some being fem., others masc. Cf. *BHS;* Zimmerli, *Ezekiel 2,* p. 165.

40. *hannōpĕlîm* is not reflected in LXX. Most delete the unexpected article with
v. 23 (cf. *BHS*), even though it recurs in v. 24. S. R. Driver interprets it explicatively,
"namely, those who have fallen" (*A Treatise on the Use of Tenses in Hebrew,* 3rd ed.
[Oxford: Clarendon, 1892], §209).

41. Outside Ezekiel, *yarkĕtê bôr* occurs only in Isa. 14:15. *yĕrākâ,* which denotes
the farthest and most inaccessible corner, is used elsewhere in Ezekiel of the remotest parts
of the north (*ṣāpôn,* 38:6, 15; 39:2; cf. also Isa. 14:13; Ps. 48:3 [Eng. 2]), and of the temple
(Ezek. 46:19). Elsewhere it applies to the innermost recesses of a cave (1 Sam. 24:4), a
house (Amos 6:10), a ship (Jon. 1:5), the earth (Jer. 6:22; 25:32; 31:8; 50:41).

42. G. R. Driver (*Bib* 19 [1938] 179) adds a resumptive article, viz., "who fell by
the sword." Zimmerli (*Ezekiel 2,* p. 165) performs the reverse operation, deleting the article
in vv. 22 and 24 on the basis of v. 23.

43. LXX omits, perhaps by homoioteleuton, the material between "appointed . . ."
and "who had spread . . . ," which are quite similar in Hebrew: *ʾăšer nittĕnû* vs. *ʾăšer
nātĕnû.*

44. LXX τὸν φόβον αὐτῶν (= Heb. *hittîtām*) harmonizes MT *hittît* with vv. 24,
26, 30.

All of them are victims, those who have fallen[45] *by the sword, who went down uncircumcised to the netherworld. They are the ones who had struck terror in the land of the living. They have borne their disgrace with those who have gone down to the Pit.* 25 *In the midst of the victims they have appointed a bed for her, along with her entire horde. Her graves are round about.*[46] *All of them are uncircumcised, victims of the sword. Although their terror was struck on the land of the living, they have borne their disgrace with those who have gone down to the Pit. In the midst of the victims [a bed] has been appointed.*[47]

26 *Meshech-Tubal*[48] *is there with her entire horde,*[49] *with her graves round about.*[50] *All of them are uncircumcised, having been slain*[51] *by the sword, although*[52] *they had struck their terror in the land of the living.* 27 *But they do not lie*[53] *with the fallen heroes of old,*[54] *who went down to Sheol with their weapons of war, who placed their swords beneath their heads, and whose shields*[55] *were on top of their bones, although the heroes had terrorized*[56] *the land of the living.* 28 *But you*

45. MT *hannōpĕlîm,* as in v. 22.

46. MT *sĕbîbôtāyw qibrōtehā* should probably be read *sĕbîbôt qĕburātāh* (so *BHS*). Cf. Syr. and v. 22. LXX reflects only *bĕtôk ḥălālîm,* the remainder having been dropped by homoioteleuton.

47. This line is problematic. Along with *BHS* and most commentators, I read pl. *nātĕnû* with Vulg., Syr., Targ., as at the beginning of the verse, instead of MT Niphal participle *nittān,* lit. "being given/appointed." I also supply an object, *miškāb,* for the verb, again as earlier in the verse. Perhaps by homoioteleuton, LXX omits the entire verse, except for *bĕtôk ḥălālîm,* "in the midst of the victims," which appears at the beginning and end of the verse in MT. Allen (*Ezekiel 20–48,* p. 135) proposes a series of annotations that have found their way into the text.

48. LXX, Syr., Vulg., and many Hebrew mss. separate these names with the copula, overlooking the sg. suffixes on the following *hămônāh* and *qibrôtêhā.*

49. LXX reads a pl. suffix, consistent with its rendering of the previous line.

50. Reading *sĕbîbôt qĕburātāh* for MT *sĕbîbôtāyw qibrôtêhā.* Cf. v. 24.

51. Although the Pual participle *mĕḥulĕlê* makes good sense, most treat the *mem* prefix as a dittograph, since it departs from *ḥalĕlê* used elsewhere in the context.

52. The particle *kî* subordinates this clause to the preceding. Cf. GKC, §111d.

53. LXX (as well as REB, NIV) misses the point by omitting the negations and translating as a rhetorical question, "Do they not lie . . . ?" anticipating a positive answer.

54. Reading *mē'ôlām* with LXX ἀπ' αἰῶνος, the *waw* having been mistaken for a *rēš.* On the term *'ôlām,* "eternity, antiquity," see Jenni, *ZAW* 64 (1952 [1953]) 197-248; 65 (1953 [1954]) 1-35, esp. 28-30; idem, *THAT,* 2:228-43.

55. Although MT *'ăwōnōtām,* "their iniquity, guilt," is supported by all the versions, it makes no sense in the context. A slight emendation yields *ṣinnôtām.* Thus NRSV, JB, REB.

56. LXX and Syr. capture the sense by treating *ḥittît,* "terror," as a verb, perhaps *ḥiṭṭĕtû.*

will be broken[57] *and lie among the uncircumcised, with the victims of the sword.*

29 *Edom is there,*[58] *her kings and all her chieftains,*[59] *who, in spite of their heroism,*[60] *are assigned [a bed]*[61] *with the victims of the sword. They too will lie with the uncircumcised, with those who have gone down to the Pit.*

30 *The northern princes are there, all of them, along with every Sidonian,*[62] *who went down in shame*[63] *with the victims in spite of the terror*[64] *of their might. They lie uncircumcised with the victims of the sword, and bear their disgrace with those who have gone down to the Pit.' "*

♦ *Nature and Design*

Egypt will not be alone in the dishonorable compartment of Sheol. Vv. 22-30 represent a roll call of other nations that have preceded her. This segment breaks down into five or six panels.[65] Table 8 (p. 222) summarizes the pattern of common elements (with some variation in vocabulary), and table 9 (p. 223) juxtaposes them. The adherence to a precast structure is obviously not slavish. The tightest pattern is evident between Elam A and Elam B, the relationship of which presents a special problem.[66] V. 23 contains redundant

57. LXX omits *tiššābar* and the following conjunction, probably by homoioteleuton. For defense of MT see Boadt, *Ezekiel's Oracles,* p. 166.

58. *šāmmâ,* "there," here and in v. 30 is a stylistic variant of *šām.*

59. LXX reads *mĕlākêhā wĕkol-nĕśî'êhā 'ăšer-nittĕnû* as *nittĕnû nĕśî'ê 'aššur hannōtēn,* "the rulers of Assyria who gave were given...," either because of a different *Vorlage* or a mistake.

60. *BHS* proposes emendation of MT *bigbûrātām* to *biqburātām* ("their grave"), but that is unnecessary. On the preposition *bĕ,* meaning "in spite of," see Lev. 26:27; Num. 14:11; Isa. 5:25; etc. *gĕbûrâ* occurs in Ezekiel only here and in v. 30.

61. As in v. 25, MT lacks an object after the passive verb *nittĕnû,* "they are given/appointed." *miškāb* is supplied on the basis of *nātĕnû miškāb* in v. 25.

62. LXX reads *wĕkol-ṣidōnî 'ăšer* as *kol-nĕśî'ê 'aššûr,* perhaps under the influence of v. 9. See n. 59 above.

63. Many delete *bôšîm* with LXX. Cf. *BHS.* The word occurs elsewhere in Ezekiel only in 16:52, 63; 36:32.

64. Treating *bĕ* as in v. 29 (so Boadt, *Ezekiel's Oracles,* p. 167). The suffix is a subjective genitive.

65. Allen (*Ezekiel 20–48,* p. 136) recognizes three stylized parallel strophes of increasing length: Assyria, three lines; Elam, six lines; Meshech-Tubal, nine lines.

66. Except for the opening "Elam is there," the middle clause, "who have gone down, uncircumcised, to the land of the deepest depths," and several minor changes, Elam B represents a virtual quotation of Elam A. Four explanations for this phenomenon are possible. (1) Elam B (missing in LXX) may have been added by dittography. However,

Table 8. The Structural Pattern of Ezekiel 32:22-30						
Element	Assyria	Elam A	Elam B	Meshech-Tubal	Edom	Phoenicia
šām, "There"	X	X		X	X	X
name of resident	X	X		X	X	X
"all" her company	X	X	X	X	X	X
surrounding graves	X	X	X	X		
kullām, "all of them"	X	X	X	X		
twofold description of victims	X	X	X	X		
subordinate conjunction + verb	X	X		X	X	X
reference to netherworld	X	X		X		
adverbial modifier		X		X	X	X
subordinate conjunction + verb	X	X	X	X		X
reference to terror	X	X	X	X		X
"in the land of the living"	X	X	X	X		X
reference to lying down				X	X	X
twofold reference to state/company				X	X	X
"bearing their disgrace"		X	X			X
reference to company		X	X			X

an undetected dittograph of such length is unlikely (cf. Parunak, *Structural Studies*, p. 417), and the second version would have been copied with uncharacteristic scribal carelessness. (2) Elam B is authentic, but the name of the nation at the head has inadvertently fallen out. Perhaps it applied originally to Meshech, whose name is anomalously conjoined with Tubal in v. 26 (under the influence of chs. 38–39?). Perhaps the panel concerns a southern land like Cush or Libya. (3) Some of the repetitious elements in Elam B are secondary. Wevers (*Ezekiel,* p. 247) retains only "They have made their bed with the slain, all of them uncircumcised, slain by the sword," which has been deleted in LXX by parablepsis. But such decisions regarding authentic and secondary elements are often made on subjective grounds and overlook the close correspondence between Elam A and B. (4) The omission in LXX was intentional or inadvertent, the result of haplography. In the case of the former the translators may have purposely abbreviated the text, a common tendency in Ezekiel. In the case of the latter, the similarities between these two panels, esp. their endings, may have caused the omission.

Table 9. Synoptic Chart of Ezekiel 32:22-30					
Assyria	**Elam A**	**Elam B**	**Meshech-Tubal**	**Edom**	**Northern Princes**
Assyria is there	Elam is there		Meshech-Tubal is there	Edom is there,	The northern princes are there
with her entire company,	with her entire horde,	with her entire horde,	with her entire horde,	her king and all her chieftains,	all of them, along with every Sidonian,
with her graves round about her.	with her tomb round about.	with her graves round about.	with her graves round about.		
All of them are victims, those who have fallen by the sword	All of them are victims, those who have fallen by the sword	All of them are uncircumcised, victims of the sword.	All of them are uncircumcised, having been slain by the sword,		
			although they had struck terror in the land of the living.		
			But they do not lie with the fallen heroes of old,		
whose graves have been appointed in the remotest recesses of the Pit.	who went down uncircumcised to the netherworld,	who went down to Sheol	who, in spite of their heroism, are assigned [a bed]	who went down in shame	
			with their weapons of war, who placed their swords beneath their heads, and whose shields were on top of their bones,		
Her company is round about her tomb,					
all of them victims, having fallen by the sword —				with the victims of the sword	with the victims
the ones who had struck terror in the land of the living.	the ones who had struck terror in the land of the living.	Although their terror was struck in the land of the living	although the heroes had terrorized the land of the living		in spite of the terror of their might.
			But you will be broken and lie amoung the uncircumcised, with the victims of the sword	They too will lie with the uncircumcised	They lie uncircumcised with the victims of the sword,
	They have borne their disgrace with those who hav gone down to the Pit.	They have borne their disgrace with those who hav gone down to the Pit.		with those have have gone down to the Pit.	and bear their disgrace with those who have gone down to the Pit.
	In the midst of the victims they have appointed a bed for her.	In the midst of the victims [a bed] has been appointed.			

references to "Her [Assyria's] company is round about her tomb. All of them are victims, having fallen by the sword," which looks suspiciously ditto-graphic.[67] The effect of the addition is to highlight the status of Assyria among the nations listed. While the Meshech-Tubal panel adheres closely to the basic structure, distinctive additions facilitate new emphases. The motifs of "spreading terror in the land of the living" and "lying with the great ones" are inserted early in the panel, and then, after resuming the expected pattern, picked up again at the end. The second half of v. 27 offers an excursus on the manner of burial of long-ago heroes. Addressing Egypt directly in the second person, the final statement (v. 28) draws an intentional contrast with these ancient figures. The Edom and Phoenicia panels are relatively short and free, though certain aspects of the basic structure are still recognizable. Their conclusions display direct links not only with the ending of the Meshech-Tubal panel (the references to the uncircumcised and lying down), but also with Elam A and Elam B (the references to "those who go down to the Pit").

In contrast to masculine Egypt,[68] each entry (except for Sidon, which is anomalous in other regards as well) is portrayed as feminine, which accords with the cultural requirements of female mourners (cf. v. 18). Each is sur-rounded by its host, referred to as *qāhāl,* "assembly," in the case of Assyria, and *hāmôn,* "horde," for the rest. The arrangement of grave complexes re-sembles that of a royal tomb, with the king's or queen's crypt (sarcophagus?) in the center, and his or her nobles all around. With this image the oracle displays effective local coloring. The pyramid complexes, in which the pharaoh's tomb (the pyramid itself) was surrounded by the tombs of his princes, courtiers, and other high officials, provides the closest analogue to Ezekiel's portrayal of Sheol.[69]

The bases for the entries in this international dishonor roll are not clear. One may recognize in the names Ezekiel's inclination toward the number seven, symbolic perhaps of all nations,[70] but this feature is muted by the combination of Meshech and Tubal as a single entry, the vague reference to "the princes of the north," and the structural division of this subunit into five (or six) panels. The names divide formally and geographically into two groups of three and two, respectively. The entries in the first triad identify great powers to the north of the Fertile Crescent, counterparts to the southern empire

67. But redundancy alone is not sufficient grounds for deletion. Cf. Zimmerli, *Ezekiel 2,* p. 16.

68. In MT Egypt is consistently portrayed as both feminine (vv. 17, 20b) and masculine (vv. 19, 21).

69. On Egyptian royal burial patterns see P. Montet, *Eternal Egypt,* tr. D. Weight-man (New York: Mentor, 1964), pp. 199-234, esp. 212-23; C. Aldred, *LÄ,* 2:859-62.

70. Cf. the nations named as objects of divine judgment in Deut. 7:1.

addressed in the oracle.[71] The final pair are both nearer neighbors of Israel and Egypt. Edom represents the nation-states of Palestine and the Transjordan, and Sidon the city-states of Phoenicia and perhaps Aram. Except for Sidon, which was addressed briefly in 28:20-23, none has been the focus of its own prophecy in this corpus of oracles against the nations.

While the prophet does not offer a full explanation why these nations have been consigned to the dishonorable area of Sheol, a clue may be found in the word *ḥittît, terror,* a uniquely Ezekielian expression that occurs seven times in vv. 22-32 (cf. 26:17, of Tyre). Only Edom escapes the charge. The context in which these nations spread their terror *(nātan ḥittît)* is defined as *the land of the living ('ereṣ ḥayyîm),* the middle sphere in Ezekiel's three-tiered universe:

Heaven *(šāmayim):* The realm of deity[72]

Earth *('ereṣ ḥayyîm):* The realm of the living

Sheol *('ereṣ taḥtît/taḥtîyôt):* The realm of the dead[73]

Within this structure, *'ereṣ ḥayyîm* denotes the sphere in which animals and humans live and in which, according to this text, they impose terror on each other. This charge reflects the conviction that a person's status in the hereafter is determined by one's conduct during one's lifetime.

22-23   In Ezekiel's dishonor role of nations, *Assyria* occupies first place. In the light of ch. 31, this is not surprising, but it becomes even more understandable when the charge of "spreading terror in the land of the living" is tested in the Assyrian records. From early times the neo-Assyrian emperors gloated over their ruthless ferocity. The following excerpt from Shalmaneser III's (858-824 B.C.) Monolith Inscription is typical:

> I fought with them [a western alliance] (assisted) by the mighty power of Nergal [god of the netherworld], my leader, by the ferocious weapons which Ashur, my lord, has presented to me, (and) I inflicted a defeat upon

---

71. The omission of Babylon reflects Ezekiel's generally positive disposition toward the agent of Yahweh and wielder of his sword.

72. *šāmayim* occurs eight times in the book, but only in 1:1 does it denote the realm of deity.

73. On the three-tiered universe see B. Lang, "Life after Death in the Prophetic Promise," in *Congress Volume: Jerusalem 1986,* VTSup 40 (Leiden: Brill, 1989), pp. 145-48; idem, "Afterlife: Ancient Israel's Changing Vision of the World Beyond," *BR* 4 (1988) 12-23, esp. 16-17.

them. I slew their warriors with the sword, descending upon them like Adad when he makes a rainstorm pour down. In the moat (of the town) I piled them up, I covered the wide plain with the corpses of their fighting men, I dyed the mountains with their blood like red wool. I took away from him many chariots (and) horses broken to the yoke. I erected pillars of skulls in front of his town, destroyed his (other) towns, tore down (their walls) and burnt (them) down.[74]

But according to Ezekiel, those who live by the sword shall die by the sword and find themselves among the residents of the ignominious "remotest recesses of the Pit." The prophet probably has 605 in mind, when Nebuchadrezzar defeated a joint Egyptian-Assyrian force at Carchemish, putting an end to the Assyrian Empire. These momentous events would still have been prominent in the prophet's memory at the time of this oracle.

24-25 Second on Ezekiel's list is *Elam*. This ancient nation, with its capital of Susa, was situated in the modern Iranian province of Khuzestan. The Elamites appear in biblical writings only rarely. The Table of Nations identifies Elam as a son of Shem, alongside Ashur, Arpachsad, Lud, and Aram (Gen. 10:22). The most notable Elamite in the OT is King Chedarlaomer, whose military exploits carried him as far west as the Dead Sea region (Gen. 14:1-16). The nation appears several times in the prophetic writings. Isaiah portrays Elam as a fierce nation, skilled in archery and chariotry. When Assyria was attacking Judah, Elamite contingents were found in the imperial army (Isa. 22:6; cf. 21:2), and some of the Israelite captives were taken to this eastern land.[75] Of all the prophets, only Jeremiah contains an entire oracle against the Elamites (Jer. 49:35-39).

The history of Elam is obscure, most of what is known deriving from Mesopotamian sources. During much of their history the Elamites were dominated by Mesopotamian overlords, though on numerous occasions they swept in from the Zagros Mountains like Vikings, destroying the cities of the lower Mesopotamian plain and everything in their path.[76] Hittite and Elamite forces were instrumental in bringing down the Amorite dynasty of Babylon in 1595.[77] Elamite civilization reached its brief zenith in the 13th century. Thereafter the nation's history is still largely unknown, until the 8th century, when Elam was

---

74. *ANET,* p. 277.

75. See Isa. 11:11. This is confirmed by the records of returnees from the Babylonian captivity, which included Jews from Elam (Ezra 2:7, 31; 8:7), and Acts 2:9, which notes the presence of Elamite Jews in Jerusalem at the time of Pentecost.

76. See the "Lamentation over the Destruction of Sumer and Ur," at the hands of the Elamites and Gutians, *ANET,* pp. 611-19; the destruction of Naram-Sin's Agade, ibid., pp. 646-51.

77. Hammurabi was the most notable member of the Amorite dynasty.

incorporated into the Assyrian Empire. Little is know of Elam under the Babylonians, but the city of Susa was revitalized under the Persian Achaemenids, when Darius made it one of his principal capitals.[78]

What historical event triggered Ezekiel's reference to Elam is unknown, but the fact that her status in Sheol is described in two panels (vv. 24-25) reflects a measure of importance in his mind. These panels deviate from the Assyrian predecessor (vv. 22-23) by noting Elam's presence among the uncircumcised, explicitly announcing their fate,[79] and referring to the beds on which they lie among the victims *(hălālîm)*. The imagery of this *miškāb* (lit. "place to lie") derives from the pattern of ancient Near Eastern tombs in which the place where the corpse was laid was designed as a bed, often complete with headrest.[80]

26-28 The *Meshech-Tubal* panel of this international dishonor roll consists of a basic text, vv. 26, 28, and an intrusive disclaimer. Both names have appeared earlier (in reverse order) in 27:13, and will recur in 38:2 as allies of Gog, but they are now combined as if they represent a single entity (cf. the sg. pronouns), which they may well have been in the minds of the Israelites. Again the historical events underlying this reference cannot be recovered. The tenses of the verbs in v. 28 seem to point to a "shattering" *(tiššābar wĕtiškab)* some time in the future.[81] If chs. 38–39 are to be dated later than the present prophecy, then a national resurrection seems envisaged for these fearful foes from the north. But for the moment Meshech-Tubal is sentenced to take her place of shame with the slain and the uncircumcised.

27 This verse is intrusive not only for its style but particularly for its content. The prophet shifts his attention unexpectedly from the company with which Meshech-Tubal shall lie to those from whose company she is excluded: *gibbôrîm nōpĕlîm mēʿôlām* (lit. "the fallen heroes from ancient times"). Unlike Meshech-Tubal and the rest in this list, these persons had been afforded noble burials. They lie there with their weapons of war *(kĕlê*

---

78. For a survey and bibliography on the history of Elam see F. Vallat, *ABD*, 2:424-29.

79. They have borne their disgrace. On *nāśāʾ kĕlimmâ* see my *Ezekiel: Chapters 1–24*, p. 505 n. 248.

80. Cf. Jeremiah's reference to a perpetual sleep *(yāšēn šĕnat ʿôlām)*, from which there is no awaking (51:39, 57), and the psalmist's "the sleep of death" *(ʾîšan hammāwet*, 13:4 [Eng. 3]). On Judahite bench tombs see E. Bloch-Smith, *Judahite Burial Practices and Beliefs about the Dead*, JSOTSup 123 (Sheffield: JSOT Press, 1992), pp. 41-52. See the superbly illustrated discussion of a complex family tomb in Jerusalem by G. Barkay and A. Kloner, "Jerusalem Tombs from the Days of the First Temple," *BARev* 12/2 (1986) 22-39.

81. Herodotus (*Hist.* 3.94) observes these states were incorporated into Darius's nineteenth satrapy.

milḥāmâ), their swords laid under their heads and their shields placed on their bones. This image accords with ancient burial customs according to which personal items and symbols of status were buried with the corpses of the deceased.[82]

But who are these heroes? The phrase *gibbôrîm nōpĕlîm mēʿôlām* seems to be inspired by Gen. 6:4, which labels the antediluvian progeny of the "sons of God" *(bĕnê ʾĕlōhîm)* and "human daughters" *(bĕnôt hāʾādām)* Nephilim,[83] and describes them more closely as *haggibbôrîm ʾăšer mēʿôlām ʾanšê haššēm,* "the heroes who were from ancient times, the men of renown." But such use of ancient traditions is shocking. How could the prophet hold up the antediluvians as honorable residents of Sheol, when his own religious tradition presents them as the epitome of wickedness, corruption, and violence?[84] Ezekiel himself recognizes that they too had terrorized the land of the living, but why should these mighty men of hoary antiquity be granted special status in the netherworld?

Three explanations may be considered. First, Ezekiel's picture may be inspired by some independent Israelite traditions that actually perceived the antediluvians as noble figures, à la Gilgamesh of Mesopotamia, the hero of the great deluge, who was said to be two-thirds god and one-third human.[85] But this hypothesis founders for lack of evidence. Second, the present image may derive from extra-Israelite traditions in which departed kings were viewed as divinized heroes.[86] However, this explanation overlooks the link with Gen. 6:4; moreover, according to the picture of the netherworld painted in vv. 22-26, the kings are surrounded by their courtiers in "the farthest recesses of the Pit." Third, this description may represent another example of Ezekielian revisionism, according to which authentic traditions are reinterpreted for rhetorical effect. The present aim is to highlight the ignominy of Meshech-Tubal. No matter how negatively the tradition might have considered the antediluvians, they were noble com-

82. On the Judahite practice see Bloch-Smith, *Judahite Burial Practices,* pp. 72-93, esp. 90-92.

83. Many repoint the present *nōpĕlîm* accordingly. Cf. Eichrodt, *Ezekiel,* p. 436.

84. See Gen. 6:5, 11-12. For a discussion of the relationship between these texts see Hanson, *JBL* 96 (1977) 208-9.

85. See *ANET,* p. 73.

86. Often identified as *rĕpāʾîm,* "Rephaim" or "shades." The literature on this subject is vast. See J. F. Healey, "The Ugaritic Dead: Some Live Issues," *UF* 18 (1986) 27-32; idem, "*MLKYM/RPʾUM* and the *KISPUM,*" *UF* 10 (1978) 89-91; B. A. Levine and J.-M. de Tarragon, "Dead Kings and Rephaim: The Patrons of the Ugaritic Dynasty," *JAOS* 104 (1984) 649-59. For a fuller study on these beliefs, which underlay ancient mortuary cult practices, see T. J. Lewis, *Cults of the Dead in Ancient Israel and Ugarit,* HSM 39 (Atlanta: Scholars Press, 1989).

pared to these nations, and by extension the Egyptians, who will join them in the netherworldly recesses.[87]

29 In the fourth panel the prophet's attention focuses on Edom, a representative nation-state from Judah and Egypt's own neighborhood. The Edomite panel differs from the preceding in several respects. First, the prophet anticipates a future event, further details of which will be given in an oracle directed specifically at this nation (ch. 35). Second, Ezekiel offers a nearer definition of Edom's assembly *(qāhāl)* or horde *(hāmôn)* by referring specifically to her kings *(mělākîm)* and chieftains *(něśî'îm)* in the Pit. Third, instead of charging Edom with "spreading terror in the land of the living," the prophet almost apologizes that the lot of the Edomites is with those who have been shamefully slain and the uncircumcised. His reference to their heroic quality *(gěbûrâ)* invites the audience to associate this nation with the mighty men of old. But Edom's heroism is insufficient to gain her the right to a more honorable compartment in Sheol.

30 The dishonor roll concludes with *the northern princes* and *every Sidonian,* who represent Judah's northern neighbors. The expression *něśîkê ṣāpôn* involves one of only four instances in the OT where the root *nsk* is applied to leaders.[88] This usage resembles that of the Akkadian cognate, *nasīku,* used to designate Aramean "princes, sheikhs."[89] Since the other panels had consistently identified the dishonorable residents of Sheol precisely, *the northern princes, all of them,* represents an intentional variation. This designation obviously includes the Sidonians, who are named probably because of their hegemonic position in Phoenicia, but it is broad enough to include other Phoenicians and even the Arameans.[90] Like *něśîkîm, mělākîm,* and *něśî'îm, kol-ṣidōnî,* "every Sidonian," offers a closer definition of *hāmôn.* This verse

---

87. Cf. 16:44-59, where Jerusalem is shamed not only for being more wicked than her sister but for abominations that exceeded those of Sodom; 20:25, according to which Yahweh had given Israel "not-good" statutes and ordinances by which they could not live; 20:32 (Eng. 27), which reinterprets Gen. 49:10 as a reference to Nebuchadrezzar.

88. Josh. 13:21 (the princes of Sihon, who are lower in status than the king [*melek*], alongside *něśî'îm,* "princes of Midian"); Mic. 5:4 (Eng. 5) (parallel to *rō'îm,* "shepherds"); Ps. 83:12 (Eng. 11) (parallel to *nādîb,* "nobleman"). The relation of *něśîkîm* to Ezek. 20:28 and 45:17, where the root is associated with liquid libations, seems remote, unless one views a leader as a person who has been consecrated by anointing. Cf. P. Collini, "Il 'contributo' dei profeti alla formazione del lessico Biblico della metallurgia," *RivB* 32 (1984) 316.

89. On which see J. A. Brinkman, *A Political History of Post-Kassite Babylonia 1158-722 B.C.,* AnOr 43 (Rome: Pontifical Biblical Institute, 1968), pp. 273-75. J. van der Ploeg proposes an Akkadian loanword ("Les chefs du people Israël et leur titres," *RB* 57 [1950] 51). Zimmerli (*Ezekiel 2,* p. 177) suggests a connection with Arab. *nasaka,* "to sacrifice," in which case the term *nāsîk* denoted originally a tribal chief as priest.

90. Confirmation of *nāsîk* as a loanword from Akk. *nasīku* would strengthen this hypothesis.

envisions all these northerners going down in shame (*bôš*). Since their might, demonstrated by terrorizing their subjects, has not saved them, they too must bear their disgrace in the remotest part of Sheol, along with the rest of the despicable victims of the sword and the uncircumcised.

c. The Final Word Concerning Egypt (32:31-32)

31 *" 'Those Pharaoh will see and be relieved[91] for [the loss of] his entire horde,[92] Pharaoh and his entire army, victims of the sword[93] — the declaration of the Lord Yahweh — 32 for I will inflict[94] my terror[95] in the land of the living, and he will be laid in the midst of the uncircumcised with the victims of the sword, Pharaoh and his entire horde! The declaration of the Lord Yahweh.' "*

Ezekiel brings the oracle to a close with a reminder of its relevance for Pharaoh, who has been all but forgotten for nine verses. Upon his own arrival in Sheol, he will look around and find relief from what he sees. The response is remarkable. One might have expected him, as the representative of Egypt, to react to his fate with hostility and anger. The greatest, most glorious and beautiful king(dom) in all the world is sentenced to spend his (its) afterlife with this despicable crowd of uncircumcised and ignominious victims of the sword! What is there to breathe more easily about here? An important clue is found in 31:16, according to which the well-watered trees of the garden of Eden found comfort in Sheol knowing that the greatest of their number, the cedar of Lebanon, was also there. But the audience should realize by now the rhetorical games that the prophet plays. In typical Ezekielian fashion, the motif of consolation in the netherworld is given a new twist. Instead of the lesser finding consolation in their solidarity with the suffering of the greater, the roles are reversed. The fate of the king of Egypt may be humiliating, but he is not alone. Other nations have lost their hordes as well; they will commiserate with him.

Verse 31 functions rhetorically like the last nail in Pharaoh's coffin by

---

91. On *niḥam*, "to breathe easier, to find relief, to be consoled," see my *Ezekiel: Chapters 1–24*, pp. 451-53, and above on 31:16. Based on an original connection of the root with mourning, some interpret *niḥam* metonymically for "to express grief," perhaps even "to perform rites of mourning," in this case over the loss of his *hāmôn*, viz., his army, wealth, and pomp. See Boadt, *Ezekiel's Oracles*, p. 168.

92. Kethib *hmnwnh;* cf. Qere *hmwnw*.

93. This sentence is missing in LXX.

94. LXX, Syr., and Vulg. support MT in reading first person. Targ. reads third person.

95. Read *ḥtyty* with Qere; cf. Kethib *ḥtytw*.

summarizing the primary issue in this oracle: the treatment that awaits Pharaoh in Sheol will be as degrading as that offered any other victims of the sword who have died dishonorable deaths and been refused an honorable burial. The divine imprimatur guarantees it. However, this verse also brings the oracle to a theological conclusion. In contrast to the secularity of the dishonor role (vv. 22-30), which drew a simple correlation between the nations' conduct "in the land of the living" and their sentence in Sheol, this verse affirms the divine hand in Pharaoh's fate. Yahweh will have the last word. Borrowing vocabulary from the dishonor role, he announces his intentions. First, as the nations have inflicted their terror on their victims, so Yahweh will terrorize Egypt. Although the manner of action is not specified, Ezekiel is undoubtedly thinking of Nebuchadrezzar as the divine agent (cf. 30:20-26). Second, Pharaoh and all his hosts are sentenced to lie in disgrace among the uncircumcised and victims of dishonorable slaughter. The immutable word of Yahweh, reaffirmed by a new signatory formula, has sealed Egypt's fate.

♦ *Theological Implications*

Even though Ezekiel has as much, if not more, to say on death and the afterlife as any other biblical author, Christian theologians tend to ignore him, even in discussions of Sheol/Hades.[96] While questions regarding the normativeness of Ezekiel's vision of the afterlife arise,[97] several summary observations may be made.

First, Sheol represents the lowest level in Ezekiel's three-tiered universe. This arrangement is reflected most clearly in ch. 31, which describes the great cedar planted on "the land of the living" and offering shade to the beasts of the field and all the peoples of the earth. But in its hubris the tree sends its top into "the heavens," presumably to enter the realm of the gods. As punishment, the tree is cut down, consigned to death, and sent down to "Sheol," the realm of the dead. The location of Sheol at the lowest level is emphasized by Ezekiel's repeated use of verbs like *yārad,* "to go down" (20 times in chs. 31–32), his use of designations like *bôr* and *šaḥat,* "Pit," for the place of the dead, and the qualification of *'ereṣ,* "land, world," with *taḥtît/taḥtîyôt,* yielding "netherworld."

96. For a full discussion of the subject see D. I. Block, "Beyond the Grave: Ezekiel's Vision of Death and Afterlife," *BBR* 2 (1992) 113-41; for representative bibliography see p. 114 n. 4.

97. Cf. ibid., pp. 134-36. For a full study on Israelite views of the afterlife in the context of their ancient Near Eastern environment see K. Spronk, *Beatific Afterlife in Ancient Israel and in the Ancient Near East,* AOAT 219 (Neukirchen-Vluyn: Neukirchener, 1985).

Second, Sheol is perceived as a massive communal cemetery, in which graves are arranged by nationality, with the principal grave in the center, surrounded by the graves of attendants. But Sheol is also subdivided into compartments by class, so that the uncircumcised and those dishonorably buried are consigned to *yarkĕtê bôr,* "the remotest parts of the Pit" (32:23), separated from "heroes of old" who are buried with honor, their weapons of war at their sides. Whether these compartments are to be viewed horizontally or vertically is not clear, though the plural form *'ereṣ taḥtîyôt,* "land of the depths," may suggest the latter.

Third, Sheol is a place to which the wicked are consigned. This text has focused on wicked nations and their collective ruling/military classes *(hāmôn, qāhāl),* though Ezekiel's interest in "the heroes of old" (v. 27), the uncircumcised, and those criminals executed by the sword points toward an interest in individual destinies as well. Nowhere does Ezekiel contemplate the fate of the righteous dead; for such information one must consult other sources.[98] But he emphasizes that in death injustices perpetrated in "the land of the living" are repaid. Those who practice oppression and demonstrate hubris meet their due reward in the hereafter.

Fourth, in Sheol the deceased live on as "living corpses."[99] Ancient Mesopotamians perceived the netherworld as an inhospitable place, dark and dingy, especially for those who had been killed in battle or who had not been afforded a proper burial.[100] Ezekiel must have been familiar with such tradi-

---

98. For example, Jesus' parabolic reference to the impenetrable barrier between "Abraham's Bosom" and "Hades," both of which appear to be located in the netherworld (Luke 16:19-31).

99. Thus R. Cooley, "Gathered to His People: A Study of a Dothan Family Tomb," in *The Living and Active Word of God: Studies in Honor of Samuel J. Schultz,* ed. M. Inch, et al. (Winona Lake, Ind.: Eisenbrauns, 1983), pp. 47-58. Elsewhere Ezekiel describes death phenomenologically as the termination of existence (26:21; 27:36; 28:19).

100. Note the following extract from "The Descent of Ishtar to the Underworld":

To Kurnugi, land of [no return],
Ishtar daughter of Sin was [determined] to go. . . .
To the dark house, dwelling of Erkalla's god,
To the house which those who enter cannot leave,
On the road where travelling is one-way only,
To the house where those who enter are deprived of light,
Where dust is their food, clay their bread.
They see no light, they dwell in darkness,
They are clothed like birds, with feathers.
Over the door and the bolt dust has settled.

As translated by Dalley, *Myths from Mesopotamia,* p. 155. This account recurs almost verbatim in "Nergal and Ereshkigal" (Sultantepe version) and the standard Babylonian version of the Gilgamesh Epic, VII.iv (ibid., p. 89). The absence of peace or joy is also

tions, but he offers his own portrait of "life" in the netherworld, several details of which deserve notice. (1) That which survives of the deceased is not simply the spiritual component of the human being but a shadowy image of the whole person, complete with head and skeleton. (2) The deceased lie *(šākab)* on beds *(miškāb)* in their respective wards, arranged by nationality. (3) The inhabitants of Sheol are not asleep but fully conscious.[101] They are aware of one another and their relative positions; they also know that their assignment was determined by their conduct during their tenure "in the land of the living." Those who were high and mighty on earth express grief over their loss and power (32:31). They consciously bear the disgrace *(nāśā' kĕlimmātām)* of those who have been dishonorably buried. Thus the tomb was not considered a deceased person's permanent resting place. While the physical flesh decomposed, the person was thought to descend to the vast subterranean mausoleum in which the dead continued to live in a remarkably real sense as "living corpses."[102]

Fifth, Ezekiel deliberately demythologizes life after death. Whereas Israel's neighbors envisaged the netherworld on the model of a city-state under the tyrannical rule of a divine king and queen,[103] according to Ezekiel, Yahweh alone holds the key to death and Sheol. He determines both the time

---

reflected in the following excerpt from a dialogue between Gilgamesh and his friend Enkidu (Gilgamesh Epic XII.v-vi):

> I saw him, whom you saw [die] a sudden death:
> He lies in bed and drinks pure water.
> I saw him, whom you saw killed in battle:
> His father and mother honour him and his wife weeps over him.
> I saw him, whose corpse you saw abandoned in the open country:
> His ghost does not sleep in the Earth.
> I saw him whom you saw, whose ghost has nobody to supply it:
> He feeds on dregs from dishes,
>   and bits of bread that lie abandoned in the streets.

As translated by Dalley, ibid., pp. 124-25.

101. Contrast Job's desire expressed in 3:8, 13; 7:9, and the phenomenological language of Dan. 12:2; Matt. 9:24; John 11:11; 1 Cor. 11:30; 15:51; 1 Thess. 4:14; 5:10.

102. Cf. the imaginative portrayal of the realm of the dead by Fyodor Dostoyevsky in *Bobok,* in *The Gambler/Bobok/A Nasty Story,* tr. J. Coulson (New York: Penguin, 1966), pp. 161-81.

103. Known in Mesopotamia as Nergal and Ereshkigal, respectively; in Canaan as Mot (from the same root as the word for "death") or Resheph, the god of pestilence. See M. Hutter, *Altorientalische Vorstellungen von der Unterwelt: Literar- und religionsgeschichtliche Überlegungen zu Nergal und Ereškigal,* OBO 63 (Freiburg: Universitätsverlag; Göttingen: Vandenhoeck & Ruprecht, 1985). For a comparison of Israelite and extra-Israelite conceptions of the netherworld see L. Wächter, "Unterweltsvorstellungen in Babylonien, Israel und Ugarit," *MIO* 15 (1969) 327-36.

and the circumstances of one's arrival there, and the fate of the deceased in Sheol. This historicizing tendency may also explain the prophet's avoidance of the term *rĕpā'îm,* a designation for the "chthonic shades."[104] Perhaps the word was too loaded with pagan associations, too closely associated with the cult of the dead.[105] For Ezekiel the occupants of Sheol are real people: Assyrians, Elamites, Sidonians, Egyptians, antediluvians, the uncircumcised, those who have been executed by the sword. By avoiding mythopoeic vocabulary he discourages his audience from imposing on his prophecy meanings derived from the pagan notions of the people among whom they are living.[106]

In contemplating the relevance of Ezekiel's vision of the netherworld for Christian doctrine, the reader must keep in mind that the primary aim of this oracle is not doctrinal but rhetorical — to inspire hope in the hearts of his fellow exiles by announcing the eventual demise of their prideful foreign enemies. The caricatured and contrary-to-fact features of this prophecy suggest that one should interpret the passage as a literary cartoon rather than a literary photograph.[107] Nor should the reader be surprised by the gaps in Ezekiel's presentation. His occasional use of the term *'ôlām,* "eternity," creates the impression of an enduring stay, but he provides no clear indication of how permanent the assignments in Sheol are. Furthermore, his Sheol is not to be confused with Gehenna or hell. This prophet leaves no hints yet of a final eschatological judgment, or of eternal fiery punishment of the wicked. All of these developments must await a later day.[108]

II. THE END OF AN ERA (33:1-33)

♦ Nature and Design

The present arrangement of the book of Ezekiel invites the reader to interpret ch. 33 as the beginning of the positive messages of hope that make up

---

104. See Isa. 14:9; 26:14, 19; Job 26:5; Ps. 88:11 (Eng. 10); Prov. 2:18.

105. Cf. Levine and Tarragon, *JAOS* 104 (1984) 653-59; A. Caquot, "Rephaim," *DBSup,* 10:344-58; J. C. de Moor, "Rāpi'ūma-Rephaim," *ZAW* 88 (1976): 323-45. S. Talmon, "Biblical *repā'îm* and Ugaritic *rpu/i(m),*" *HAR* 7 (1983) 241-49.

106. For further discussion of the Israelite view of Sheol and the afterlife see Eichrodt, *Theology,* 2:210-28; Ringgren, *Israelite Religion,* pp. 239-47.

107. E.g., Egypt, Sidon, and Edom lie among the uncircumcised.

108. On which see R. Bauckham, "Early Jewish Visions of Hell," *JTS* 41 (1990) 355-85; also S. J. Fox, *Hell in Jewish Literature* (Northbrook: Whitehall, 1972); G. W. Bromiley, "Hell, History of the Doctrine of," *ISBE,* 2:677-79.

chs. 34–48. Accordingly some interpret vv. 1-20 as something of a second call to the prophetic office, preparatory for the prophet's second phase of ministry.[1] As vv. 21-22 indicate, this phase is signaled by the arrival in Babylon of a fugitive from Jerusalem with the news that the city has fallen. With the report of the fulfillment of his judgment oracles against Jerusalem, the nature of Ezekiel's messages will shift dramatically. To borrow the imagery of his contemporary, Jeremiah (1:10), having uprooted and torn down, destroyed and overthrown, he may now turn toward the reconstructive tasks of building and planting. The turning point is marked in Ezekiel's personal life by the opening of his mouth and a recommissioning to his prophetic office.

However, this interpretation is complicated by several factors. First, vv. 1-20 are not cast as a call narrative or as a report of a prophetic recommissioning, but as a divine speech for public consumption. Second, the motifs and style of ch. 33 display a closer resemblance to chs. 4–24 than to chs. 34–48. All the allusions are retrospective: 33:1-9 echoes 3:19-21, but with a new urgency; 33:10-20 summarizes 18:1-32; 33:21-22 fulfills 24:25-27 and ends the prophet's silence reported in 3:22-27; 33:23-29 summarizes the same charges of idolatry and abominations and announces the same judgment proclaimed in chs. 5–6, while also alluding to 11:14-21; 33:30-33 reflects 20:1-3, 31 and announces the fulfillment of the prediction of his audience's hardened hearts (2:3-7; 3:4-11).[2] The chapter contains no hint at all that a new era in Ezekiel's preaching is about to begin.

The three-part division of the book of Ezekiel appears to follow the general pattern of sandwiching oracles against foreign nations (chs. 25–32) between oracles of judgment against Israel (chs. 1–24) and oracles of hope and salvation (chs. 33–48), a pattern evident also in Isaiah and Jeremiah. But logically this chapter belongs immediately after ch. 24, underscoring the effectiveness of the divine word. The insertion of the oracles against the nations (chs. 25–32) before, rather than after, ch. 33 has put textual distance between these chapters and artificially linked the latter with the following salvation messages. One may speculate that a buffer was desirable between the prediction of the imminent fall of Jerusalem (ch. 24) and the report of its occurrence (33:21-22), but the effect of this editorial decision on the interpretation of the chapter is drastic. Not only does an oracle of judgment (33:1-9) now look like a recommissioning of the prophet, but the moral and spiritual foundation of the new order is also laid. While the salvation oracles (chs. 24–48) will highlight the involvement of Yahweh in restoring the nation, the

---

1. See Zimmerli, *Ezekiel 2,* p. 183.
2. Thus L. Boadt, "The Function of the Salvation Oracles in Ezekiel 33 to 37," *HAR* 12 (1990) 7-8.

present arrangement affirms the continuity of the old covenant, whose violation had led to the disaster of 586 B.C. The exilic community is hereby informed that the doors to a glorious future will be thrust wide open if they heed Lev. 26:40-45, abandon their evil ways, acknowledge the justice of Yahweh in their judgment, and commit themselves to him.

As just noted, the chapter is composite. Scholars generally recognize five individual units, but the first two (vv. 1-20) are literarily conjoined and the last two (vv. 23-33) present two sides of a single coin of persistent hardness on the part of the people, viz., the remnant in Jerusalem and the exiles in Babylon. Sandwiched between these divine speeches is the narrative announcement (vv. 21-22). Nevertheless, it is clear that the editors have intended for the reader to treat this entire section as one larger composition. An important unifying thread is provided by the fourfold occurrence of the phrase *bĕnê ʿammĕkā* (lit. "sons of your people," vv. 2, 12, 17, 30), which replaces the common *bêt yiśrāʾēl* ("house of Israel") and the occasional *bĕnê yiśrāʾēl* (lit. "sons of Israel"). *bĕnê ʿammĕkā* occurs elsewhere in the book only twice; as a closer definition of *haggôlâ,* "the exiles," in 3:11, and in 37:18. It finds a feminine counterpart in *bĕnôt ʿammĕkā* (lit. "daughters of your people," i.e., "your countrywomen," 13:17). The suffixed form of *ʿam,* itself a kinship term, highlights not only the prophet's identification with his audience but also their sense of ethnic kinship, particularly vis-à-vis their Babylonian hosts.[3]

A. THE FINAL SUMMONS (33:1-20)

♦ *Nature and Design*

The first major literary block, vv. 1-20, is introduced by the customary word-event formula, but it lacks a formal conclusion;[4] v. 20 leaves the oracle hanging in midair. The larger unit is punctuated by Yahweh's repeated direct address to Ezekiel, *(wĕʾattâ) ben-ʾādām* (lit. "[as for you] son of man," vv. 2, 7, 10, 12), dividing it into four subunits of unequal length. Vv. 1-6 and 7-9 are linked by the common watchman motif, and vv. 10-11 are tied to vv. 12-20

---

3. In Lev. 19:17-18 *ʿammĕkā* is associated with *ʾāhîkā,* "your brothers, *ʾămîtekā,* "your neighbor," and *rēʿăkā,* "your friend." Within a hostile environment security is found in "the sons of one's people and one's native land" (cf. Isa. 13:14, Jer. 46:16, and 50:16). Gen. 23:11 and Judg. 14:16-17 juxtapose "the sons of one's people" with people of alien ethnic and national stock. Num. 22:5 is to be interpreted differently. See further Block, "People," *ISBE,* 3:760.

4. The signatory formula, *nĕʾum ʾădōnay yhwh,* "the declaration of the Lord Yahweh," in v. 11 functions more emphatically than disjunctively.

by their common ties to ch. 18. Thus this section has two major panels, each of which subdivides into two subunits. But the second is clearly to be interpreted in the light of the first. Taking these verses as a unit, then, one hears the prophet delivering a final appeal for his fellow exiles to respond to his message. In so doing he vindicates both his own prophetic status (hence the importance of their paying heed to his warning, vv. 1-9) and the justice of Yahweh in his judgment. But he leaves the door open for a positive response, and invites his people to find life in the grace of God.

1. The Charge for the Prophetic Watchman (33:1-9)

1 *Now[5] the following message of Yahweh came to me:*
2 *"Human, speak to your compatriots and say to them: 'Suppose[6] I bring a sword[7] against a country, and the country's citizens pick one man from among them[8] and appoint him to be their watchman.[9] 3 Suppose he sees the sword advancing against the country, and warns the people by blowing the horn. 4 If anybody heard[10] the sound of the horn but ignored the warning,[11] and the sword[12] came and took him away, then his blood[13] would be upon his own head.[14] 5 He heard the sound of the horn, but he ignored the warning,[15] thus his blood is upon*

5. Syr. adds the superscription to the chapter: *zwhr' wlwbb',* "Admonition and Consolation."

6. The complex protasis of this hypothetical sentence carries on to v. 4b.

7. Throughout this paragraph Targ. expands with *dqtlyn bhrb',* "those who slay by the sword." Here LXX[A] adds κρίμα αἵματος, "judgment of blood."

8. *miqṣêhem,* lit. "from their extremities," viz., within the entire circumference. Cf. 25:9. The generalized sense of "within their midst" is reflected in LXX ἐξ αὐτῶν; Vulg. *de novissimis suis.*

9. Targ. renders *lĕṣōpeh* inconsistently: *lmzhr',* "as one who gives warning," here harmonizes with the following charge to *hizhîr* (v. 3), but *mlyp* in v. 7 follows 3:17.

10. The indefiniteness of the subject is stressed by *wĕšāmaʿ haššōmēaʿ,* rendered lit. by LXX, καὶ ἀκούσῃ ὁ ἀκούσας. Cf. A. B. Davidson, *Hebrew Syntax,* 3rd ed. (Edinburgh: T. & T. Clark, 1912), §108, Rem. 1; Joüon-Muraoka, *Grammar,* §155d; though, as Allen (*Ezekiel 20–48,* p. 141) observes, the switch to the perfect suggests a real case is now envisaged.

11. After *nizhār* the customary perfect gives way to the customary imperfect.

12. LXX smooths the reading by adding the article, hence ἡ ῥομφαῖα (= Heb. *haḥereb*), here and in v. 6, but cf. the anarthrous *rāšāʿ* in vv. 8, 9, 11.

13. Targ. *hwbt qtwlyh,* "the guilt of his death," makes explicit MT *dāmô,* "his blood."

14. On *dāmô bĕrōʾšô yihyeh* see my *Ezekiel: Chapters 1–24,* p. 535 n. 79. Cf. ibid., p. 577, on the weaker expression *dāmô bô yihyeh,* "his blood shall be upon himself." On the formula see K. Koch, *VT* 12 (1962) 396-416; G. Matties, *Ezekiel 18,* pp. 77-78.

15. Syr. omits this repetitious statement.

himself. Now suppose he had heeded the warning;[16] *then he would have saved his life. 6 As for the watchman, if he sees the sword advancing, and the people are not warned because he fails to blow the horn, and the sword arrives and takes one person away from them, that person was taken away on account of his own guilt, but I will hold the watchman responsible for his death.'*[17]

7 Now you, human, are the one I have appointed as watchman for the house of Israel. Whenever you hear a message from my mouth,[18] *then you are to warn*[19] *them about me.*[20] *8 If I say to the wicked, 'O wicked person,*[21] *you shall surely die!'*[22] *and you do not issue a warning*[23] *to the wicked person to abandon his course,*[24] *that wicked person*[25] *shall die for his iniquity, but I will hold you accountable for his death. 9 But if you have warned the wicked person to turn from his course,*[26] *and he has refused to do so,*[27] *he, on account of his iniquity, shall die, but you will have saved your life.'*

16. *BHS* and many commentators emend *nizhār* to *hizhîr,* supposing the statement to refer to the watchman. However, Ezekiel tends to use *hiṣṣîl,* "to save," when the watchman is in view (cf. Zimmerli, *Ezekiel 1,* p. 180). Furthermore, the watchman has been out of the picture since v. 3 (cf. Allen, *Ezekiel 20–48,* p. 141).

17. An idiomatic rendering of *wĕdāmô miyyad haṣōpeh 'edrōš,* lit. "but his blood I will seek from the hand of the watchman." The more common *biqqēš dām,* "to seek the blood of" (cf. v. 8; 3:18), is replaced by the synonymous *dāraš dām.*

18. Targ. softens the anthropomorphism with *mmymry,* "My Memra," on which see Levey, *Targum of Ezekiel,* pp. 15-16.

19. Even if the verb *hizhîr* means "to teach," rather than "to warn," as Simian-Yofre has argued (*Künder des Wortes,* pp. 151-62), the watchman's task is much more urgent than that of a teacher lecturing pupils on right and wrong.

20. *wĕhizhartā 'ōtām mimmennî* is dropped in LXX, either as an oversight or because of a different *Vorlage.* As in 3:17, the preposition is not the *min* of source, but denotes motion away from, implying an infinitive like "to flee, hide, escape from." Cf. GKC, §119z.

21. The second *rāšā',* missing in several Hebrew mss., LXX, Syr., etc., looks like a dittographic error. Cf. v. 14 below and 3:18.

22. *môt tāmût,* "You shall surely die," is an apodictic legal declaration, patterned after sentences kings pronounced over subjects who had fallen out of their favor (1 Sam. 14:44; 22:16; 1 K. 2:37, 42), and priests pronounced on those who disparaged the temple (Jer. 26:8). Cf. Matties, *Ezekiel 18,* pp. 71-77.

23. *wĕlō' dibbartā lĕhazhîr,* lit. "and you do not speak to warn."

24. *middarkô.* Here the *min* functions as in v. 7, *mimmennî.* The verb *šûb* is implied. Cf. v. 9; 3:19-20.

25. On the difficult phrase *hû' rāšā',* see on 3:18.

26. *maddarkô lāšûb mimmennâ* is missing in 3:19, but nothing is gained by deleting it as is commonly done.

27. Smoothing out the repetitious *wĕlō' šāb middarkô,* lit. "and he has not turned from his way," for the sake of English style alone.

a. The Metaphor of the Watchman (33:1-6)

The renewed charge to Ezekiel opens with a parable cast in casuistic legal style. A hypothetical condition is proposed by means of a classic *casus pendens, 'ereṣ kî,* "As for a land, if . . . ," reminiscent of the style of 14:13ff. Although the prophet's own philosophy/history is reflected in the theological assertions that frame the parable, within these borders the metaphor is totally secular. As in 14:13, the story opens by contemplating Yahweh bringing a sword against a country; it concludes by declaring that in such an event, he will hold a negligent watchman responsible for the death of citizens who die in the attack. An alert listener should have caught the significance of the parable from these notices, but the sequel suggests that the hardened exiles were carried away with the story itself.

The prophet describes two realistic wartime scenarios, each with its own simple plot. In the first (vv. 2b-5), (a) news reaches a country of an enemy invasion, (b) a man is appointed to serve as their lookout to observe carefully the movements of the enemy, (c) the enemy is sighted, (d) the citizens are alerted by the sound of the watchman's horn, (e) the people ignore the warning, (f) they are slain, and (g) they are held accountable for their own deaths. V. 5b offers an alternative ending to the first scenario: (e) the people respond to the warning, and (f) they are delivered. The second scenario (v. 6) commences with stage (c'), the enemy is sighted, and continues as follows: (d') the sentry fails to sound the alarm; (e') a single person is captured; (f') the person is held responsible for his own guilt; (g') the watchman is held accountable for the man's death.

Both scenes would have been familiar to most of Ezekiel's audience, and he leaves it to them to fill in the details. The means by which the watchman was selected is not indicated, but the verb *lāqaḥ* (lit. "take") suggests that he is a conscript rather than a volunteer (hence the translation *pick*). Nor does the passage describe the qualifications for sentry duty, though he would naturally be selected from the people themselves *(miqṣêhem)*. More important even than keen eyesight and skill with the horn would have been a reputation for integrity and reliability. From other texts we learn that watchmen were stationed at the highest lookout post in a town: the roof of the city gate (2 Sam. 18:24) or towers constructed specially for that purpose (2 K. 9:17). The manner in which the people were warned varies. In smaller communities a strong voice was adequate to report enemy movements, but where the distances were too great other means were devised. The Lachish Letters speak of messages sent from one lookout post to another by means of smoke signals, a method especially suited to contexts involving invasions of a land rather than a city.[28] Our text identifies *the horn* as the instrument of warning. The

---

28. See Lachish Letter 4:9-10 (*ANET*, p. 322). *mśʾt* is a technical term, abbreviated

šôpār is the most frequently named musical instrument in the OT.[29] Because the number of notes that could be produced on the *šôpār* was limited, it was used primarily as a signaling instrument for cultic observances, and especially in military contexts to call troops to arms (Judg. 3:27; 6:34; Neh. 4:18-20), signal retreat (2 Sam. 8:16), proclaim victory (1 Sam. 13:3), announce the disbanding of the army (2 Sam. 20:1, 22), even terrify the enemy (Judg. 7:8, 16-22). Indeed, the *šôpār* became a symbol of war itself, being used, as in our text, to signal impending attack or doom.[30]

A responsible watchman would blow the trumpet at first sight of danger, calling the warriors to take up defensive positions at strategic points on the walls, while the women and children retreated to refuges within the city. If the citizens failed to respond to his warning and were slaughtered in the attack, the watchman was absolved of responsibility for the lives of the victims. He had fulfilled his duty; their blood would be upon their own heads. But if they heeded the warning, they would escape with their lives. V. 6 reverses the situation. Failure on the part of the watchman to sound the warning renders him liable for the deaths of those who fall to the enemy.

The meaning of the parable is clear, but Ezekiel veils its significance by mentioning no names, employing the third rather than the second person, using a hypothetical casuistic style, and focusing on the watchman rather than on the residents of the city. But he undoubtedly maintained his reputation as an entertainer (cf. 33:30-33), perhaps even winning his audience's support with the sound moral of his story. Nonetheless, the manner in which the story is told raises several questions. Isn't it too late for the exiles to be lectured on a negligent watchman's responsibility? Why does the prophet raise the parable to the theological plane by highlighting the involvement of Yahweh, who brings on the sword? Why does Ezekiel commence with, "As for a land, if . . . ," and not "As for a watchman, if . . ."? Why does he insert in v. 6, "That person will be taken away on account of his own guilt *('āwōn)*"? What guilt? These unanswered questions suggest a deliberate rhetorical strategy challenging the audience to look beyond the watchman. While a sentry is held accountable for his negligence, guilty residents are responsible for their own sins. Could their own guilt have precipitated the emergency itself by bringing on the sword of Yahweh?

---

from *mś't 'šn*, "rising cloud [of smoke]." The practice is also attested in Judg. 20:38-40, and in numerous letters from Mari. Cf. G. Dossin, "Signaux lumineux au pays de Mari," *RA* 35 (1938) 174-86.

29. The word seems to be related to Akk. *šappāru,* which in turn derives from Sum. *šegbar,* "wild goat, ibex." On the instrument see D. A. Foxvog and A. D. Kilmer, *ISBE,* 3:439.

30. See Jer. 4:19-21. Cf. also Jer. 6:1; Amos 3:6; Hos. 5:8. Cf. ch. 7, where Ezekiel had developed Zephaniah's notion (Zeph. 1:16) of the horn heralding the arrival of the dreaded day of Yahweh.

b. The Charge to Ezekiel (33:7-9)

Ezekiel's audience undoubtedly expected him to follow up the parable with an interpretation, but the explanation takes a surprising turn, as he draws on an episode from his own call to the prophetic ministry.[31] The influence of 3:16-21 on the present account is obvious, as a juxtaposing of these texts demonstrates (see table 10, p. 242; material not included in both texts is italicized).

In vv. 7-9 the hypothetical charge of the parable is translated into real life. V. 7 identifies the principal characters in the drama. First, Yahweh seizes the authority from the citizens and commissions the sentry himself. Indeed, his control over the scene is total: he determines the crisis (the sword); he appoints the watchman (Ezekiel); he identifies the enemy (house of Israel); he pronounces the sentence (death); he calls all to account.

Second, the sentry commissioned is the prophet, Ezekiel. Ezekiel's portrayal of himself as a watchman for Yahweh may have been inspired by his contemporary, Jeremiah, who declared: "I have raised up watchmen (*ṣōpîm*) over you; pay attention to the sound of the horn (*šōpār)!* But they responded, 'We will not pay attention' " (6:17). But the notion is much older. More than a hundred years earlier Isaiah had expressed his prophetic self-consciousness with bold strokes (21:6-9):

> For thus the Lord said to me:
> Go! Post a lookout (*hamĕṣappeh),*
> Let him announce what he sees.
> When he sees chariotry, teams of horses,
> Riders on donkeys, riders on camels,
> He must be on the alert,
> Fully on the alert.
> The watcher cried out,
> "On the watchtower (*miṣpeh),* O Lord,
> I stand, day in and day out.
> At my post (*mišmartî)*
> I am stationed all night long.
> Look! There he comes!
> Men on chariots,
> Teams of horses!"
> He answered back,
> "She has fallen! Babylon has fallen!

---

31. Contra Zimmerli (*Ezekiel 1,* pp. 143-46; *Ezekiel 2,* pp. 183-84) and many others, I assume the originality of 3:16-21. Cf. W. E. Lemke, "Life in the Present and Hope for the Future," *Int* 38 (1984) 168 n. 4; Klein, *Ezekiel,* pp. 28-30.

Table 10. Synopsis of Ezekiel 3:17-19 and 33:7-9

3:17-19	33:7-9
	As for you,
Son of man,	son of man,
I have appointed you	I have appointed you
as a watchman	as a watchman
for the house of Israel.	for the house of Israel.
Whenever you hear a message	Whenever you hear a message
from my mouth,	from my mouth,
then you are to warn them from me.	then you are to warn them from me.
If I say to the wicked,	If I say to the wicked,
	"O wicked person,
"You shall surely die!"	you shall surely die!"
and you do not warn him,	
and you do not speak up	and you do not speak up
to warn the wicked person	to warn the wicked person
from his *wicked* way	from his way,
that he may live,	
that wicked person shall die	that wicked person shall die
for his iniquity,	for his iniquity,
but his blood I will require	but his blood I will require
from your hand.	from your hand.
But you,	But you,
if you have warned the wicked person	if you have warned the wicked person
	to turn from his way,
and he has not turned	and he has not turned
from his wickedness and	
from his *wicked* way	from his way,
he, on account of his iniquity,	he, on account of his iniquity,
he shall die,	he shall die,
but you,	but you,
you will have saved your life.	you will have saved your life.

> And all the images of her gods,
> Have crashed to the ground!"[32]

In the present instance, Ezekiel is charged to look out for danger, here identified as *the message,* the word or event *(dābār),* that issues forth from

32. For discussion of this obscure text see J. N. Oswalt, *The Book of Isaiah, Chapters 1–39,* NICOT (Grand Rapids: Eerdmans, 1986), pp. 388-97. See also Hab. 2:1, which portrays Habakkuk standing on the watchtower *(ʿal-mišmartî).*

Yahweh's mouth, viz., his divine decree. Having been alerted to it, he is to sound the alarm: Yahweh is the enemy poised for attack! This watchman is indeed from the exiles' midst (*miqṣêhem*, v. 2), but he is probably not the kind of person the community would have chosen.

Third, the nation in danger is *the house of Israel,* which in this case refers primarily to the exilic community.[33] The characterization of the nation in vv. 8-9 as *rāšāʿ* and *ʿāwôn* (wicked, criminal, villainous) leaves no doubt about the divine disposition.[34] The prophet's alarm, cast in the form of ancient law, pronounces the death sentence on those who had repudiated the covenant, thereby bringing on themselves its curses as spelled out in Lev. 26 and Deut. 28.[35] Like Ahaziah in 2 K. 1:4, 6, 16, Ezekiel has been charged to communicate the sentence. This oracle is his *šôpār* blast, his appeal from Yahweh to the wicked *(rāšāʿ)* to turn *(šûb)* from rebellion to the path of righteousness, or fall under Yahweh's sentence of death. If Ezekiel failed to issue this warning, he would be guilty of a capital offense himself. But the wicked are still responsible for their own fate. If they die, having disregarded the prophetic *šôpār,* the prophet is absolved of all guilt.

The manner in which the motifs found in 3:16-21 have been exploited and recast in 33:1-9 renders it unlikely that these texts deal with the same event, or that the former was originally at home in this context.[36] The chronological notice in 3:16 specifically links the earlier watchman encounter with Ezekiel's call and commission (1:1–3:15), and it was in this capacity that he had functioned from 593 to 586. Furthermore, since the message in 3:16-21 had been private, designed to impress on the prophet the awesome burden attending the privilege of divine service, that text could deal with hypothetical cases involving both the wicked and the backslider. But here the issues are different. This message is public.[37] It has the nature of an apologia, whose aim is to clarify once and for all Ezekiel's prophetic self-consciousness before his people. If he has denounced them as wicked, this has been Yahweh's evaluation. If he has pronounced the death sentence on them, this is the divine verdict. His role has been to alert the community to the peril of their ways, and to call them back to the path of righteousness. He has taken his charge seriously; now let them do the same.

---

33. A fact reinforced by the placement of vv. 10-20 immediately after this sentry text.

34. On Ezekiel's use of *rāšāʿ* and *ʿāwōn* see my *Ezekiel: Chapters 1–24,* pp. 144ff.

35. See Reventlow, *Wächter,* pp. 116-34, specifically pp. 127-30, on this text; also W. Eichrodt, "Das prophetische Wächteramt: Zur Exegese von Hesekiel 33," in *Tradition und Situation: Studien zur alttestamentlichen Prophetie,* ed. E. Würthwein and O. Kaiser (Göttingen: Vandenhoeck & Ruprecht, 1963), pp. 31-41; idem, *Ezekiel,* pp. 442-52.

36. Cf. above, p. 235 and n. 1.

37. So also Klein, *Ezekiel,* pp. 28-29.

2. The Appeal of the Prophetic Watchman (33:10-20)

♦ *Nature and Design*

Whether or not vv. 10-20 were delivered at the same time as the preceding material, the absence of introductory formulae demands that one interpret them together. These verses provide an illustration of how the watchman went about his duty. Far from simply sounding the alarm, Ezekiel showed his compatriots how the sentence of death might still be avoided. The window of hope and life was still open. Borrowing the form and style of ch. 18, Ezekiel crafts this unit as a complex disputation speech.[38] The structure is clear, the respective parts of the people and the prophet for the most part being signaled by speech markers. The oracle consists of two disputations, each of which is structured according to standard disputational patterns:

a. The first disputation	(vv. 10-16)
(1) The popular quotation	(v. 10)
(2) The prophet's response	(vv. 11-16)
(a) The dispute	(v. 11)
(b) The counterthesis	(vv. 12-16)
b. The second disputation	(vv. 17-20)
(1) The popular quotation	(v. 17a-b)
(2) The prophet's response	(vv. 17c-20)
(a) The counterthesis	(vv. 17c-19)
(b) The dispute	(v. 20)

a. The First Disputation (33:10-16)

10 *"Now you, human, say to the house of Israel as follows:*[39] *'This is what you have said,*[40] *"Certainly*[41] *our crimes and our sins are upon us, and because of them we are wasting away. How then shall we survive?"*

11 *Say to them, 'As I live — the declaration of the Lord Yahweh —*

---

38. On the form and nature of disputation speeches see my *Ezekiel: Chapters 1–24,* pp. 330ff.

39. *'ĕmōr . . . lē'mōr,* lit. "Say . . . saying," occurs elsewhere in Ezekiel only in v. 24 and 37:18, on which see Meier, *Speaking of Speaking,* pp. 85-86, 88, 332. LXX presupposes simply *'ĕmōr* or *dabbēr.*

40. Elsewhere quotations of popular sayings are preceded by the participle. See 9:9; 11:15; 35:12.

41. *kî* seems redundant after *lē'mōr,* unless it is treated as an emphatic particle. See Boadt, *Ezekiel's Oracles,* p. 37.

I find no pleasure in the death of the wicked, but in the wicked per-
son's[42] *turning from his way so he may live. Turn back, turn back from*
your evil[43] *ways, for why should you die, O house of Israel?'*

12 *Now you human,*[44] *say to your compatriots, 'The righteousness*
of the righteous person will not save him at the time he commits a
crime. Nor will the wickedness of the wicked trip him up[45] *at the time*
he turns away from his wickedness. As for the righteous person, he
will not survive on account of it at the time he sins.[46] 13 *Suppose I say*
of the righteous, "He shall certainly live,"[47] *and he, counting on his*
righteousness, commits evil. Then none of his righteous actions[48] *will*
be credited [to him]. As for the evil he has perpetrated, for it he will
die. 14 *But suppose I say to the wicked, "You shall surely die," and he*
turns from his sin and practices justice and righteousness. 15 *The*
wicked person[49] *returns a pledge; he makes restitution for his robbery;*
he pursues the statutes of life; he refuses to practice evil — he shall
surely live; he shall not die! 16 *None of the sins*[50] *that he has per-*
petrated will be charged against him.[51] *Since he has done that which*
is just and right, he shall certainly live.' "

10   The section opens with a command to the prophet to quote a comment
circulating among the exiles. While this quotation lacks the proverbial quality

---

42. MT lacks the article. Cf. n. 12 above.

43. Perhaps under the influence of v. 9, LXX omits *hārā'îm*, "evil," and renders
darkêkem as sg. The presence of *darkêkem hārā'îm* in 20:44 and 36:31 supports MT.

44. LXX omits *wĕ'attâ ben-'ādām*, but the phrase is attested in Vulg., Targ., Syr.,
etc., and functions here as a rhetorical signal of a change of focus.

45. Lit. "as for the wickedness of the wicked, he will not be tripped/trip himself
up *(yikkāšel)* in it."

46. Many delete this statement as a gloss disturbing the parallelism and leaving
the suffix on *bāh* without a near antecedent (Zimmerli, *Ezekiel 1,* p. 181; Graffy, *Prophet
Confronts His People,* p. 75). LXX abbreviates: καὶ δίκαιος οὐ μὴ δύνηται σωθῆναι. But
ṣĕdaqâ is probably an assumed antecedent (cf. Vulg. *in justitia*), based on the construction
of *riš'at hārāšā'* in the previous sentence.

47. Some LXX mss. harmonize *yiḥyeh* by reading second person, *tiḥyeh*, but the
emendation (contra *BHS*) is unnecessary. Cf. vv. 15, 16; also 3:21; 18:9, 13, 17, 19, 21,
28.

48. Reading pl. *ṣdqtyw* with Qere, though Kethib *ṣdqtw* reflects an older spelling
(F. I. Andersen and A. D. Forbes, *Spelling in the Hebrew Bible,* BibOr 41 [Rome: Pontifical
Biblical Institute, 1986], pp. 325-26). Cf. also 3:20; 18:24.

49. Many delete *rāšā'* with LXX as an otiose annotation (cf. *BHS*), but this is
unnecessary.

50. The verb requires reading pl. *ḥṭ'tyw* with Qere and the versions in place of
Kethib *ḥṭ'tw*, but see n. 48 above.

51. LXX drops *lô*, as in the parallel text, 18:22.

we have come to expect in a disputation, the tripartite statement is cast in effective rhetorical style:

> Our rebellious and sinful acts haunt us.
> On account of them we are wasting away.
> How then shall we survive?

The tone is depressing, the rhythm and rhyme of the quotation being characteristic of laments.[52] The first part of the verse describes the problem: the people's sinfulness. The keyword of vv. 2-9, *rāšā'*, is replaced by two semantically related expressions, *peša'*, crime or "rebellion," and *ḥaṭṭā't*, sin. The former, which first appeared in 14:11, derives from suzerainty covenantal contexts and denotes primarily rebellion, revolt against one's overlord.[53] The latter signifies a missing of the mark established by Yahweh's covenantal stipulations. Ezekiel had been aware of Israel's guilt for a long time (see chs. 16, 20, 23); now the people are finally feeling the burden.

The second part of the verse highlights the painful effect of the people's revolt: they *are wasting away*. The verb *māqaq* is used elsewhere of putrefying gangrenous flesh.[54] The present usage derives from the covenant curse found in Lev. 26:39, which describes this very circumstance: the people of Yahweh in exile among enemy nations far from home. Ezekiel's compatriots have apparently finally recognized their fate to be a fulfillment of this covenant curse. The question in the final part of the verse highlights the people's despair.[55] They have escaped the sword, but that fate might have been preferable to this slow death.

The quotation reflects the demoralized state of the exiles. All hope is gone; their faith has been crushed; the darkness is overwhelming. For the first time they admit their own guilt as the cause of their suffering. But is this confession repentance? In view of the prophet's response, it seems to be little more than a cry of pain. As in Judg. 10:10, 15, this is an appeal for relief; a plea for the release of pressure. This is an empty cry for songs in the night; there is still no desire for the One who gives the songs (cf. Job 35:9-13). But the last clause is the key to the entire text. The question is rhetorical, assuming a negative answer, "Survival is impossible." But Yahweh seizes the opportu-

---

52. Note the triple *-ēnû* ending in the first line: *pěšā'ênû wěḥaṭṭō'tênû 'ālênû*. Cf. Isa. 59:12; Jer. 14:7, 9, 20. Thus Zimmerli, *Ezekiel 2*, p. 187; Graffy, *Prophet Confronts His People*, p. 73.

53. See R. Knierim, *THAT*, 2:488-95. See also 18:22, 28, 30-31; 21:29; 37:23; 39:24.

54. See Ps. 38:6 (Eng. 5); Zech. 14:12. Cf. its earlier occurrences in Ezek. 4:17 and 24:23.

55. The tone is even more pathetic than Isaiah's "How shall we escape?" (20:6).

nity for a response. The people have raised the issue of life; perhaps a teachable moment has finally arrived.

11 Ezekiel's divinely dictated answer consists of two parts. First, he disputes their logic. Appropriately Yahweh strengthens the force of the response to the question of life with an oath that affirms his own: *As I live.*[56] The oath is followed up with an unequivocal affirmation that he is not a sadistic ogre, who finds pleasure *(ḥāpēṣ)* in watching the wicked die.[57] Yahweh's pleasure is found in life even for the wicked. His impassioned twofold appeal emphasizes that all they need to do is *turn* or repent *(šûb)* from their evil course of life. He ends the dispute with a question of his own. Since a way of survival has been announced, why then should the people die? Quoting 18:31 verbatim,[58] he highlights how needless their death is. Yahweh's plea for repentance is a call to life! Death is not inevitable.

12-16 In these verses Ezekiel presents his counterthesis. Shifting abruptly from his appeal for repentance, which should have consoled despairing sinners, to the respective fates or fortunes of the apostasized righteous person and the repentant wicked, he establishes the principle on which the appeal in v. 11 could be made in the first place. It is Yahweh's delight in life that causes him to acknowledge the repentance of the wicked and to replace the death sentence with the sentence of life. V. 12, which has no counterpart in ch. 18, functions as a prefatory statement of principle, explaining the modus operandi of divine justice.[59] Speaking for Yahweh in the first person, Ezekiel

---

56. M. Greenberg translates "By my life" (*JBL* 76 [1957] 34-39), but cf. my *Ezekiel: Chapters 1–24*, pp. 207-8.

57. V. 11 turns the earlier rhetorical question (18:23; cf. v. 32) into an emphatic disavowal. The following synopsis highlights the relationship between these texts (modified slightly for the sake of comparison:

18:23	33:11
	As I live —
	the declaration of the Lord Yahweh —
Do I really find pleasure	I find no pleasure
in the death of the wicked?	in the death of the wicked
the declaration of the Lord Yahweh —	
Is it not rather in his turning	but in the turning
	of the wicked
from his ways	from his way
that he may live?	so he may live.

58. Including the hypothetical deprecatory interrogative *lāmmâ,* "Why?" Cf. Barr, *JTS* 36 (1985) 19-21.

59. The vocabulary of v. 12 displays several interesting departures from both ch. 18 and the context in which it is embedded. Along with *ḥāyâ,* "to live," we now read of "saving" *(hiṣṣîl)* the righteous (cf. v. 9; also 14:14, 16, 18, 20); *mût* "to die," is replaced by paraphrastic *nikšal,* "to be tripped up," from *kāšal,* "to stumble" (cf. *mikšôl ʿāwōn,*

affirms that one's end is not determined by how one begins a race, but how one ends it. A person's past does not determine his or her future. Neither may the righteous presume on the favor of Yahweh if they turn from their righteousness, nor need the wicked fear him if they abandon their wicked ways and adopt a righteous manner of life.

Having announced the thesis, the prophet's exposition follows the pattern set in ch. 18 by presenting several hypothetical cases. Indeed, the similarities between these two texts are remarkable, as table 11 (p. 249) demonstrates. It is unnecessary to repeat the interpretation offered on 18:21-24, but some of the adaptations to the new situation deserve notice. First, sentences of life and death are now cast in the form of direct speech, prefaced with *bĕ'ŏmĕrî laṣṣaddîq,* "Suppose I say of the righteous" (v. 13), and *bĕ'ŏmĕrî lārāšā',* "Suppose I say of the wicked" (v. 14). The latter presents the repentance as a response to the sentence addressed directly to the criminal in the second person, "You shall surely die."

Second, the sequence of cases is rearranged. Whereas 18:21-24 had begun with the repentant wicked (vv. 21-23) and then moved to the apostatized righteous (v. 24), now Ezekiel begins with the apostatized righteous (33:13) and ends with the repentant wicked (33:14-16). This arrangement harmonizes with 33:7-9, which had dealt only with the wicked (cf. 3:20-21), and affirms the correctness of the people's admission of guilt in vv. 10-11. Ezekiel hereby expresses willingness to treat his audience not as apostatized righteous persons but as wicked persons, for whom repentance can change the disposition of Yahweh.

Third, while some explanatory comments are dropped,[60] significant new material is added. The general statement *does what is right and just* (v. 14) is concretized with a threefold elaboration (v. 15), borrowed from 18:7, though with some modification. The first two statements are probably intended as a shorthand expression for the entire list of just behaviors in the Decalogue, affirming that the commitment to righteousness is more than a good idea: faith without works is dead. The third expression is unique: *he pursues the statutes of life (bĕḥuqqôt haḥayyîm hālak,* lit. "in the statutes of life he walks") functions as a rough equivalent of "he keeps all my statutes" in 18:21.[61] Pursuing the statutes of life involves that course of conduct that earns for the

---

"the stumbling block of iniquity," in 18:30, as well as 14:3, 4, 7; 44:12); the phrases *yôm pišʿô,* "day of his rebellion," *yôm šûbô,* "day of his repentance," and *yôm ḥăṭōʾtô,* "day of his sin," are all unique, *bĕyôm* denoting "at the time of."

60. E.g., the comparative comment in 18:24, and the expansionistic "which he has done and he keeps all of my statutes" in 18:21.

61. Cf. *ḥuqqôtay ûmišpāṭay 'ăšer ya'ăśeh 'ōtām hā'ādām wāḥay bāhem,* "my statutes and judgments by which a man shall live if he does them," in 20:11, 13, 23.

Table 11. Synopsis of Ezekiel 18:21-22, 24, and 33:14-16, 13

18:21-22, 24	33:14-16, 13
	14 But suppose I say to the wicked, "You shall die,"
21 Now if the wicked person	
turns from all his sins, that he has committed, and observes all my decrees, and practices justice and righteousness,	and he turns from his sin, and practices justice and righteousness.
	15 The wicked person returns a pledge, he makes restitution for his robbery; he pursues the statutes of life; he refuses to practice evil;
He shall certainly live! He shall not die!	He shall surely live; He shall not die!
22 None of his rebellious acts that he has perpetrated will be charged against him. On account of his righteousness that he has practiced he shall live.	16 None of the sins that he has perpetrated will be charged against him. That which is just and right he has practiced. He shall certainly live.
	13 Suppose I say of the righteous, "He shall certainly live!" and he,
24 But if a righteous man turns from his righteousness and practices evil,	counting on his righteousness, practices evil.
like all the abominable actions that the wicked practice, shall he behave this way and live? None of his righteous actions that he has performed	
will be credited [to him]. On account of his treachery that he has perpetrated, and on account of the sins that he has committed, on their account he shall die.	Then none of his righteous actions will be credited [to him]. As for the evil that he has perpetrated — on account of it he shall die.

individual the divine declaration, "He is righteous[62] — he shall certainly live; he shall not die."

Fourth, the present text makes some significant changes in vocabulary. Negative phrases, "to turn from one's righteousness" and "to commit treachery" (*māʿal maʿal*), in 18:24 are replaced with positive affirmations, "to trust (*bāṭaḥ*) in one's righteousness" and "to commit evil" (*ʿāśâ ʿāwel*), respectively, in 33:13.

In sum, while the borrowing is heavy it is not slavish. The changes reflect the new situation: in ch. 33 the prophet is facing a real audience in a real crisis; the people are despairing over their hopeless condition. Vv. 12-16 offer a consoling message of the freedom that Yahweh offers to the penitent evildoer. The death sentence of the exiles may yet be altered. Their destiny will change if they turn from their rebellion against Yahweh to a life of righteousness and justice. Yahweh's commitment to life, declared many years earlier, still stands.

b. The Second Disputation (33:17-20)

17 "*But your compatriots say, 'The action[63] of the Lord[64] is unscrupulous!'[65]*

But they are the ones whose action is unscrupulous.[66] 18 *If a righteous person turns from his righteousness and practices evil, on account of it[67] he shall die.* 19 *But if a wicked person turns from his wickedness and practices justice and righteousness, on account of these deeds he shall live.* 20 *But you insist,[68] 'The action of the Lord is unscrupulous.' I will judge each person on the basis of his actions, O house of Israel!*"

The rejoinder and reply to the offer of life are cast in the form of a second disputation speech. Table 12 (p. 251) indicates that, like the previous response, the links with ch. 18 are strong. Except for the addition of an opening reference

---

62. Cf. 18:9. On the form see Matties, *Ezekiel 18*, pp. 66-70.

63. As in 18:25-30, "action" translates *derek*, lit. "way."

64. Many Hebrew mss. read *yhwh* for *ʾădōnāy*, here and in v. 20. However, the same reading occurs in 18:25, and MT should be retained on the basis of *lectio difficilior*.

65. On the meaning of *tākēn* see my *Ezekiel: Chapters 1–24*, p. 585.

66. *wĕhēmmâ darkām lōʾ-yittākēn*, lit. "But they, their action is without principle." On this emphatic adnominal *casus pendens* construction see Muraoka, *Emphatic Words*, pp. 94-95.

67. The pl. *bāhem* corresponds to *ʾălêhem* in v. 19, and the parallel text in 18:26. Cf. LXX ἐν αὐταῖς. The pl. suggests a collective sense for *ʿāwel*.

68. LXX expands, καὶ τοῦτό ἐστιν, ὃ εἴπατε, "and this is what you say."

Table 12: Synopsis of Ezekiel 18:25-30 and 33:17-20

18:25-30	33:17-20
25 But you say, "The Lord's action is unscrupulous!" Hear now, O house of Israel! Is my action unscrupulous? Is it not your own actions that are unscrupulous?	17 But your compatriots say, "The Lord's action is unscrupulous!" But they are the ones whose action is unscrupulous.
26 If a righteous person turns from his righteousness, and practices evil, he dies for his actions. On account of his evil, that he has committed, he shall die.	18 If a righteous person turns from his righteousness and practices evil, on account of it he will die.
27 But if a wicked person turns from his wickedness, that he has committed, and he practices justice and righteousness, he shall preserve his own life.	19 But if a wicked person turns from his wickedness and he practices justice and righteousness, on account of these deeds he shall live.
28 He has taken heed, and repented of all his wicked acts, that he had committed. He shall surely live! He shall not die!	
29 But the house of Israel insists: "The Lord's action is unscrupulous." Are my actions unscrupulous, O house of Israel? Is it not your actions that are unscrupulous?	20 But you insist, "The Lord's action is unscrupulous."
30 Therefore, I will judge you, O house of Israel, each one on the basis of his actions — The declaration of the Lord Yahweh.	I will judge each person on the basis of his actions, O house of Israel!

251

to "your compatriots," and a minor "on account of them" in v. 19, and a few stylistic variations, the changes involve mostly deletions whose effects on the meaning of the text are minor.

17a Like the previous disputation, this segment opens on a bitter note. But instead of continuing their lament over their inevitable doom, the Israelites complain about being at the mercy of God, whose ways are arbitrary, nonsensical, and without principle.[69]

17b-19 Yahweh counters the people's protest with a thesis of his own. It is not Yahweh's ways that lack a standard or sense; it is their own. Yahweh has just reminded them that if a person abandons a righteous lifestyle in favor of wickedness, this is grounds for the death sentence. But the reverse is equally true. When a wicked person repents and adopts a righteous manner of life, the latter ensures his life. This is the rule by which Yahweh's justice is administered. The illogic and absence of principle rests with the audience, if they fail to repent in the face of the divine offer of life.

20 Yahweh disputes rather than counters their thesis by reiterating the divine modus operandi, the logic of which is apparent: each person will be judged according to his or her conduct. The oracle concludes with a final impassioned appeal, "O house of Israel!" The text closes abruptly without a concluding formula and with no hint of the people's reaction.

♦ Theological Implications

This passage reiterates the lessons of ch. 18, but the present placement of the prophecy renders the theme all the more urgent. The parable of the watchman in vv. 1-9 highlights the imminence of the impending crisis. Although some view the quotation in v. 10 as a symptom of the exiles' despair after the judgment had taken place,[70] it is preferable to date this oracle at the conclusion of Ezekiel's first phase of prophetic service, immediately prior to the fall of Jerusalem. The prophecy affirms that the recalcitrance and stubbornness of Ezekiel's audience, predicted at the time of his commissioning (2:1–3:15), persisted to the very end. Ezekiel has dutifully performed his responsibilities as a watchman, sounding the alarm, but no one has listened. The hearts of his hearers remain fossilized.

This text reaffirms the inability of a hardened human heart to comprehend the things of God. For almost a decade the exiles had heard Ezekiel defending and explaining his actions. Still they cannot grasp the simple logic of divine justice. They have admitted they are sinners, and they realize that their sin has brought on their present grief. But when the prophet reminds

69. Cf. note 65 above.
70. See Zimmerli, *Ezekiel 2,* p. 189.

252

them that their death is not inevitable, and that it may be averted by a simple act of repentance, instead of hearing the message of hope, they continue to get hung up on the incomprehensibility of divine justice. But herein lies a lesson for the contemporary reader as well. The call of the gospel is simple. It offers life to all who will turn from sin and commit themselves to the divine way of righteousness. However, instead of acting on the good news of this invitation, the hardened heart still stumbles on theological issues, so that ultimately God is blamed for one's fate: he has not communicated clearly.

Finally, this oracle presents an important dimension of the divine character. God does not desire death, not even for the wicked. He appeals for all to repent and find life in his grace. For this reason he had sent the watchman, and for this reason the prophet had appealed for repentance, even at this late date. This message offers hope to the modern reader as well. 2 Pet. 3:9 will express this truth in another way: The Lord is patient, not desiring that any should perish, but that all should repent and find life in his grace.

B. THE FINAL WORD (33:21-22)

21 *Now in the twelfth year*[71] *of our exile, in the tenth month,*[72] *on the fifth day of the month, a certain survivor*[73] *from Jerusalem came to me and announced, "The city has fallen!"* 22 *Now the hand of Yahweh had come upon me*[74] *the previous evening, before the arrival of the survivor, and he*[75] *had opened my mouth prior to*[76] *his coming*[77] *to me in the morning. Thus my mouth was opened and I was no longer dumb.*

Without warning a narrative fragment interrupts the prophetic messages. This historical note reports two events of great consequence for both the exiles and

---

71. Some emend *bištê* to *bĕʿaštê*, "eleventh," with 8 mss. of the Lucianic recension of LXX and Syr. Cf. LXX[88] and Syr., which read "tenth." See Ziegler, *Ezechiel*, p. 249.

72. The word for month is missing in MT. LXX ἐν τῷ δωδεκάτῳ μηνί, "in the twelfth month," assimilates the number to that of the year.

73. On the use of the article before indeterminate nouns in contexts that give the person determination see Joüon-Muraoka, *Grammar*, §137n; GKC, §126r.

74. The anthropomorphic idiom speaks of the overwhelming force with which Yahweh exercises his mastery over his prophet. Cf. 3:14-15, 22; 8:1 (with *napal*, "to fall"); 37:1; 40:1.

75. The subject of the masc. verb is obviously Yahweh, rather than "hand," which would have required a fem. form.

76. On *ʿad* meaning "before" see Waltke-O'Connor, *Syntax*, §11.2.12.b.

77. The infinitive *bôʾ* requires a subject. It appears that the *aleph* and *waw* have been transposed.

Ezekiel. First, it reports the arrival of a survivor from Jerusalem at Ezekiel's house with the announcement *The city has fallen* (*hukkĕtâ hāʿîr,* lit. "the city has been smitten"). Although the bearer of the tidings is not named, to Ezekiel this anonymous *pālîṭ,* "survivor," is no ordinary escapee, who has spent five or six months on the fly. Had he been fleeing from the Babylonians he would have headed in the opposite direction, to Egypt, like Gedaliah's assassins and Jeremiah's kidnappers would do (Jer. 43–44), or to the mountains of Judah (cf. 7:16), not to the land of his conquerors. This man was probably a member of the first wave of prisoners deported to Babylon after Nebuzaradan, the captain of Nebuchadrezzar's army, had burned the city (2 K. 25:11). As such he represents the confirmation of the divine word, the fulfillment of the prediction made in 24:25-27 that such a person would arrive at the prophet's house to announce that Yahweh had taken away the people's stronghold, their pride and joy, and the delight of their eyes. While to the rest of the exiles the message of Jerusalem's fall represented the worst news imaginable, and for Ezekiel it undoubtedly caused intense anguish, it did mean his vindication as a true prophet of Yahweh.

The timing of the man's arrival on 5 Tebet of the twelfth year of the exile (= Jan. 8, 585) is difficult to reconcile with 24:1, which seems to have announced the beginning of the siege approximately three years earlier, a period that all agree is much too long.[78] Some resolve the issue by emending "twelfth" to "eleventh" year, but the textual evidence for this operation is weak and looks like a secondary rationalization.[79] A more satisfactory solution recognizes different points of reference in these two texts. The form of the date notice in Ezek. 24:1 and its links with 2 K. 25:1 suggest that it was based on the official Jewish calendar, which dated events according to a king's regnal year, viz., his first full year in office. The present date, like all others in the book, reflects Ezekiel's idiosyncratic dating of events on the basis of the exile.[80] Accordingly, the time it took for the bearer of the news to reach Ezekiel

78. See Parker-Dubberstein, *Chronology,* p. 28. See also Edwards, *ZAW* 102 (1992) 105.

79. Those emending include Zimmerli, *Ezekiel 2,* p. 191; Eichrodt, *Ezekiel,* pp. 457-58; Fohrer, *Ezechiel,* p. 187; D. J. A. Clines, "Regnal Year Reckoning in the Last Years of the Kingdom of Judah," *AJBA* 2 (1972) 20 n. 40. Critics of this emendation include Kutsch, *Chronologischen Daten,* p. 44; Allen, *Ezekiel 20–48,* p. 152.

80. For further discussion see my *Ezekiel: Chapters 1–24,* pp. 772-74. Some follow the lead of the 17th-century Jewish commentator David Altschul in suggesting that 2 K. 25 and Jeremiah reflect a Jewish calendar that computed regnal years on the basis of an autumnal (1 Tishri) calendar, whereas Ezekiel's date is based on the Babylonian spring (1 Nisan) New Year. By a quirk of chronology, in either system the date for the razing of Jerusalem may be fixed at July 14, 586. Cf. A. Malamat, "The Last Kings of Judah and the Fall of Jerusalem: An Historical-Chronological Study," *IEJ* 18 (1968) 137-55; idem, "The Twilight of Judah: In the Egyptian-Babylonian Maelstrom," in *Congress Volume:*

was slightly less than five months, a reasonable figure in the light of Ezra 7:9, which notes that an entire company of returning exiles made the return journey in five months.

Second, this narrative note reports that on the day he learned of the fall of Jerusalem Ezekiel regained his normal speech. Contrary to the expectations raised by 14:22, the text is completely disinterested in the impact of the herald's coming on the exiles, or even the messenger's own emotion. The attention is focused entirely on the prophet, for whom this moment had great symbolic significance.[81] Indeed, v. 22 creates the impression that Yahweh had carefully orchestrated the entire scenario. The sequence of events had actually begun the previous evening, when "the hand of Yahweh had come upon" Ezekiel. How the divine hand manifested itself this time is not disclosed, but the results are dramatic. The style is redundant and the vocabulary deliberately chosen to capture Ezekiel's sense of release, and to echo the prediction in 24:25-27.[82] Even if there is no mention of loosing the prophet's tongue, which Yahweh had stuck to the roof of his mouth (3:26), the comment *and I was no longer dumb* celebrates the lifting of the restriction that had been imposed on him more than a decade earlier.

Ezekiel seems to have felt the effects of his liberation at two levels. On the surface, he was freed to engage in ordinary speech as a private individual again. His decade of enforced nonverbal communication was over. At a deeper level, this event would signal a dramatic shift in his ministry. He could finally assume the normal role of a prophet, interceding on the people's behalf before Yahweh and offering messages of hope for the future. So long as the temple and the city had stood, these basic functions had been denied him. But hereafter, though he would continue to issue diatribes (cf., e.g., 33:24-29; 34:1-10), he could begin to focus on a new day when the corrupt tenets of official theology would be replaced by authentic spirituality and Yahweh would reconstitute the nation as his covenant people. But this change

---

Edinburgh 1974, VTSup 28 (Leiden: Brill, 1975) 123-45; idem, "The Last Years of the Kingdom of Judah," in *World History of the Jewish People,* vol. 4: *The Age of the Monarchies: Part 1, Political History* (Jerusalem: Masada Press, 1979), pp. 205-21, esp. 218-20. Also Greenberg, *Ezekiel 1–20,* p. 11; Freedy and Redford, *JAOS* 90 (1970) 462-85. However, if the autumnal New Year was ever celebrated in Judah (for my critical evaluation see *ISBE,* 3:529-32), it had been replaced by the spring New Year by Zedekiah's time. Cf. Hayes and Hooker, *New Chronology,* pp. 86-92; Galil, *ZAW* 102 (1992) 103.

81. According to *b. Roš Haš.* 18b, Rabbi Simon maintained that the fast of the tenth month (Zech. 8:19) had its origin in this event.

82. Cf. *wîyippātaḥ pî wĕlō' ne'ĕlamtî 'ôd,* "Thus my mouth was opened and I was no longer dumb," here with *yippātaḥ pîkā 'et-happālîṭ ûtĕdabbēr wĕlō' tē'ālēm 'ôd,* "Then your mouth will be opened toward the survivor and you will speak; you will be dumb no longer," in 24:27.

does not result from the people's greater receptivity. Like his dumbness, and everything else about his ministry, it proceeds entirely from Yahweh's initiative.[83] But for him the burden has been lifted; the future may be anticipated with liberated tongue and spirit.

The precise moment of liberation is unclear, but it seems to have coincided with the coming of the hand of Yahweh upon him the night before.[84] In any case, overnight both Ezekiel and Yahweh are vindicated. The liberated prophet stands before his people as a *môpēt,* a "sign," living proof of the veracity of the divine word. It took only two short words from the lips of the *pālîṭ: hukkĕtâ hāʿîr,* "The city has fallen!" to silence the charges of falsehood and empty pronouncements from Ezekiel's opponents (12:21-28). Yahweh has confirmed the word of his servant; let the exiles acknowledge the true prophet in their midst (Jer. 28:9).

But Yahweh is vindicated as well. He is not, as some imagined, an impotent deity, superseded by the god of the mighty Babylonians. He is in firm control of all events, even the destruction of his own city and temple. He, not Marduk, declares events before they transpire.[85] It is not that the word itself has any inherent or independent power that "moves the world and itself become history,"[86] but that Yahweh, the sovereign Lord of history, speaks and performs. Above the mockery, skepticism, and unbelief of the audience, through his prophet's liberation he shouts from heaven, "I am Yahweh! I have spoken! I have acted!"

C. THE FINAL DISPUTATION: STAKING OUR CLAIMS (33:23-29)

23 *Now the following message of Yahweh came to me:*

24 *"Human, this is how the people living in these*[87] *ruins in the land of Israel are arguing:*[88] *'Even though Abraham was only one person,*[89] *still he had claim to the land. However, we are many; surely the land has been handed over to us as a possession.'*

---

83. Cf. Davis, *Swallowing the Scroll,* p. 57.

84. Interpreting the verb *wayyiptak* as a pluperfect, and the prepositional phrase *ʿad bôʾô ʾēlay* as "by the time he had come to me." Cf. textual note 77.

85. This theme is prominent in Isaiah. Cf. 37:26; 40:8; 41:26-27; 42:9; 44:7; 45:21; 46:8-11; 48:3; 55:10-11.

86. Contra Zimmerli, *Ezekiel 2,* p. 194.

87. *hāʾēlleh,* "these," is missing in LXX, perhaps because it was deemed inappropriate for the context in which the prophet and his fellow exiles live.

88. LXX removes an apparent redundancy in MT by omitting *lēʾmōr.*

89. Targ. expands by adding *yḥydʾy bʿlmʾ,* "unique in the world."

25 *Therefore say to them, 'Thus has the Lord Yahweh declared:*[90]
You eat [flesh] that contains blood;[91] *you raise your eyes*[92] *toward
your worthless idols; you shed blood — still you claim the land?*[93] 26 *You
have relied*[94] *on the sword;*[95] *you have committed*[96] *abominations;*[97] *you
have defiled one another's wives — still you claim the land?'*

27 *This is what you shall say to them:*[98] *'Thus has the Lord Yahweh
declared: As I live, whoever is found in the ruins will fall by the sword;
whoever is found out in the open field I have handed over as food*[99]
*for the animals; whoever is found in the strongholds and in the caves
will die of the plague.* 28 *I will turn the land into an utter desolation.*[100]
Her pride in her power[101] *will cease, and the mountains of Israel will
be desolate, without any one passing through.* 29 *And they will know
that I am Yahweh when I turn the land into an utter desolation on
account of all the abominable acts that they have committed.'*"

◆ *Nature and Design*

Although a single word-event formula heads 33:23-33, this section consists
of two separate oracles, vv. 23-29 and 30-33. Each begins with its own direct
address of the prophet (vv. 23, 30), and they differ in form, audience, and

---

90. LXX drops the remainder of v. 25 and v. 26 in its entirety by homoioteleuton,
the scribe's eye having skipped to the next occurrence of the citation formula in v. 27.

91. A paraphrastic rendering of *'al-haddām tō'kēlû*, the construction of which is
borrowed from Lev. 19:26. On *'al* used in the sense of "accompanied by, in addition to,"
see Cooke, *Ezekiel*, p. 371. *BHS* and many commentators emend unnecessarily to *'al-
hehārîm*, after 18:6.

92. MT *wě'ēnēkem* represents a defective spelling for *wě'ênêkem*. Cf. Andersen
and Forbes, *Spelling*, p. 138.

93. On the *waw* conjunction used interrogatively see S. R. Driver, *Tenses*, §119g.

94. On *'āmad 'al'el* as "to rely on, to resort to," see 31:14.

95. Under the influence of *hehŏrābôt*, "the ruins," Syr. and Vulg. interpret
ḥarběkem, "your sword," as "on your ruins." Targ. paraphrases "You have endured
because of your might."

96. *'ăśîten* looks like a simple scribal error for *'ăśîtem*. But Cooke (*Ezekiel*, p. 371)
proposes that the final *nun* may have been preferred over the *mem* to ease pronunciation
before *t*. Cf. 44:8 and Mic. 3:12.

97. Interpreting *tô'ēbâ* collectively.

98. Reading *'ălêhem* with numerous Hebrew mss. instead of MT *'ălēhem*.

99. *lě'okělô*, lit. "to eat him," is difficult but not impossible. *nātan lě'oklâ*, reflected
in numerous Hebrew mss., LXX, Syr., and Vulg., may be an intentional harmonization
with 15:4, 6; 29:5; 35:12; 39:4.

100. Treating *šěmāmâ ûměšammâ* as a hendiadys, as in 6:14. The phrase recurs
in v. 29 and 35:3.

101. *gě'ôn 'uzzāh*, lit. "the pride of her power."

concern. Their conjunction here is natural, however, since both pertain to the period immediately following the fall of Jerusalem. Following the narrative note of vv. 21-22, these oracles orient the reader to the mentality prevailing among two remnant Judean populations after the national tragedy: those who remained in the homeland after the destruction of the city and the deportation, and the exilic population in Babylon. In demonstrating the hardened condition of the people, both segments function more naturally as conclusions to the first phase of Ezekiel's preaching than as preludes to the second. Like the loosing of the prophet's tongue and the announcement of Jerusalem's fall, the people's persistent recalcitrance confirms the veracity of the divine word (see 2:1–3:15). On the other hand, by placing these prophecies immediately before the salvation oracles, the editor(s) affirms that Ezekiel's messages of hope are not preconditioned by a repentant people; it required only the external fulfillment of his word of judgment.

The genre of vv. 24-29 represents a remarkable hybrid form, fully integrating two different genres without neutralizing the rhetorical structures of either. On the one hand, this unit contains the three elements of a classic prophetic proof oracle: the motivation (*Begründung*, vv. 24-26), the pronouncement of judgment (*Gerichtswort*, vv. 27-28), and the recognition formula (*Erkenntnisformel*, v. 29).[102] Accordingly its aim is to demonstrate the character of Yahweh. On the other hand, it also bears the structural marks of a classic disputation oracle: thesis, expressed as a quotation of a popular saying (v. 24); dispute (vv. 25-26); counterthesis (vv. 27-29). As such its aim is to refute popular opinion.[103]

1. The Popular Quotation (33:23-24)

As in other disputation addresses, the oracle proper begins with a direct quotation of an opinion circulating among the people. The links between this citation and that found in an oracle delivered more than six years earlier (11:14-21) are striking. First, while the rhetorical audience is the exilic community, the focus is on the population left behind in the homeland. In 11:15 that residue, designated *yōšĕbê yĕrûšālaim*, "the inhabitants of Jerusalem," consisted of those who had been spared the deportation of 597. The post-586 situation is reflected in a new designation, *the people living in these ruins in the land of Israel* (*yōšĕbê hehŏrābôt hā'ēlleh 'al-'admat yiśrā'ēl*). For Ezekiel

---

102. So also Murray, *JSOT* 38 (1987) 103. On the form of the proof oracle see Zimmerli, *Ezekiel 1,* pp. 36-40; idem, "The Word of Divine Self-Manifestation (Proof-Saying): A Prophetic Genre," in *I Am Yahweh,* pp. 99-110.

103. Combinations of demonstration and disputation oracles occur also in 11:2-12 and 37:11-14.

the place no longer deserves the name Jerusalem, and the name Judah is avoided. According to 2 K. 25:12, Nebuchadrezzar's field commander, Nebuzaradan, had left the poorest of the land behind to try to maintain the Judean agricultural economy. Some have estimated the surviving remnant in Judah after the deportation and the migration to Egypt that followed the assassination of Gedaliah at under 20,000.[104] Although many of the outlying villages would have been pillaged by the Babylonian troops, the land was obviously not totally emptied of inhabitants. Indeed, the destruction and deportation probably involved primarily the major towns and the military strongholds.[105] Unlike the Assyrians (2 K. 17), the Babylonians did not transplant people from other lands to replace the population of conquered territories.

Second, as in 11:15, the prophet's knowledge of the Judean scene is attributed to Yahweh himself.[106] Like the rest of his pronouncements, this oracle represents not Ezekiel's personal response to the crisis, but Yahweh's. He is the one offended by the territorial claims being made.

Third, in both oracles the issue addressed concerns illegitimate claims to the real estate of Judah. Indeed, the last clause of v. 24, *lānû nittĕnâ hā'āreṣ lĕmôrāšâ, surely the land has been handed over to us as a possession,* echoes *lānû hî' nittĕnâ hā'āreṣ lĕmôrāšâ* in 11:15. The earlier claimants to the land had based their demands on theological grounds. Assuming the integrity of the deity-people-land association, they had argued that since the exiles found themselves outside the land of Israel, they had been rejected by Yahweh, the divine landlord, and their property had now been transferred to them as their possession. Now the people's reasoning takes the form of a totally secular a fortiori argument:

> Abraham was an individual *('eḥād hāyâ 'abrāhām);*
> Still he possessed the land *(wayyîraš 'et-hā'āreṣ).*
> But we are many *(wa'ănaḥănû rabbîm);*
> The land has been given to us as a possession.

There is no acknowledgment of the ancient tradition of Yahweh's oath to Abraham, or that the Israelite occupation of the land was the fulfillment of that promise.[107] Nor is there any recollection of Yahweh's covenant with Abraham,

---

104. Bright estimates that even after the return from exile the population was no more than 20,000 (*History of Israel,* p. 344, following W. F. Albright, *The Biblical Period from Abraham to Ezra,* rev. ed. [New York: Harper & Row, 1963], pp. 87, 105-6, 110-11).

105. Cf. B. Oded, in *Israelite and Judaean History,* pp. 476-80.

106. Since the quotation reflects a situation much later than the departure of the survivor referred to in vv. 21-22, he could not have been the source of the information.

107. On the former see Gen. 13:14-17 and throughout Genesis. On the latter see Exod. 6:2-8; Deut. 1:8; 6:10; 9:5; 30:20; 34:4.

to be God to him and to his descendants (Gen. 17:1-7).[108] After the destruction of the temple, for the surviving remnant the theological argument had become irrelevant. Since Yahweh no longer resides in the land, his authority to determine who should own it is annulled. The reference to the insignificance of Abraham, specifically his being only "one," is reminiscent of Isa. 51:2 (*kî 'eḥād qĕrā'tîw*, "as one I called him"), but the tone is different. Contrary to Graffy, this claim is not based on the faith of the fathers.[109] The use of the verb *nātan*, "to give," is insufficient grounds for interpreting the last line of the argument as a theological statement. The role of Yahweh is overlooked completely, and the patriarch is being exploited for purely pragmatic purposes. If he could possess *(yāraš)* the land, even though he was only a single person, how much more should not they possess it, since they are numerous?[110]

The popular citation is patently inaccurate, if not perverse. On the one hand, they are underestimating the patriarch's significance and overestimating their own. Abraham had indeed entered the land as the only male in the family, but by the time he broke up the Mesopotamian alliance (Gen. 14), he was head of a large household and, according to Genesis 14, had established himself as a significant force in the region. By contrast, although their own population certainly exceeded the patriarch's clan, it was hardly numerous even by ancient national standards, let alone the standard set by Yahweh's promise to Abraham, that his descendants would be as innumerable as the stars in the sky and the grains of sand on the seashore.[111] On the other hand, they are overestimating the patriarch's territorial rights. Although Abraham had lived in the land, he never actually possessed it. Indeed, had he not encountered congenial Hittites at Hebron, he would not even have had a place to bury his wife (Gen. 23). Tradition portrays him as a sojourner *(gēr)* in an alien land (cf. Heb. 11:13-16). Actual possession of the land was delayed four centuries, until his descendants had become a numerous people (cf. Gen. 15:12-21).

The lack of spiritual sensitivity and the smug self-interest evident in the quotation contrast with Abraham's total dependence on God. Ironically, those whom others describe as "the poorest of the land" (2 K. 25:12) have succumbed to the temptation of hubris. The faith of Abraham has been replaced by Darwinian materialism — the fittest have survived. This reorientation is evident also in the survivors' disposition toward the exiles. Whereas 11:14-21 had portrayed the Jerusalemites looking down their noses on their deported kin, now the latter are

---

108. Cf. Isa. 41:8, where Yahweh speaks endearingly of his people as "Israel my servant, Jacob my chosen, seed of Abraham my friend."

109. See Graffy, *Prophet Confronts His People*, p. 79.

110. Cf. the exploitation of the patriarchal connection without the theological basis or the pietistic implications in Matt. 3:9; Luke 3:8; 8:33, 39.

111. See Gen. 13:16; 15:5; 22:17; 26:4; 32:12.

out of the picture entirely. There is no thought for the welfare of their compatriots nor any anticipation of their return. The survivors' world has shrunk to the physical property on which they are trying to scrounge a living.

2. The Prophet's Response (33:25-29)

The transition from thesis to refutation is signaled formally by *lākēn,* "Therefore," followed by the divine injunction to the prophet to speak and the citation formula in v. 25. The refutation subdivides into a dispute of their claim (vv. 25-26) and a counterthesis (vv. 27-29). The dispute addresses the impious logic of the claimants to the territory of Judah by raising the debate to the theological plane. Far from being the deserving possessors of the land, the survivors have disqualified themselves by their wanton disregard for the responsibilities associated with being true heirs of the Abrahamic promise. By means of a series of formal charges, each of which is familiar from earlier prophecies,[112] Yahweh presents his case. The six specific accusations are broken up into two groups of three, each of which ends with the rhetorical question, "Should you then possess the land?":

a. They eat meat from which the blood has not been drained.[113]
b. They pay homage to worthless idols.[114]
c. They commit murder.[115]
d. They depend on violence.[116]
e. They commit abominations.[117]
f. They defile one another's wives.[118]

112. Vv. 23-29 repeat the general charges of chs. 5–6, but the specific charges here derive from chs. 18 and 22.

113. Tradition dates this taboo back to the time of Noah (Gen. 9:4-6), but it was built into Israel's constitution (Lev. 17:10-16; 19:26), and recognized as operative by later generations (1 Sam. 14:32-34). The Council of Jerusalem determined that the taboo remained in force for Christians as well (Acts 15:20). Ezekiel had dealt with the problem earlier in 24:7.

114. On *nāśā' 'ênayim 'el-gillûlîm,* "to raise the eyes to dung pellets," see 18:6, 12, 15 (linked with social ills of all sorts, including violence, oppression, and the defilement of menstruant women), and 20:24.

115. On *šāpak dām,* "to pour out blood," as a euphemism for murder see ch. 22, where Ezekiel had associated the crime with all sorts of abominable deeds.

116. The idiom *'āmad 'al-ḥereb,* "to stand on one's sword," occurs nowhere else. Specific evidence of the lawlessness in the land is provided by the assassination of Gedaliah (Jer. 41) and the need for another deportation by Nebuchadrezzar in 582/581 (Jer. 52:30).

117. On *tô'ēbâ* as a general expression for all kinds of offensive acts see Ezek. 6:9. In 18:6-7 and 12-13 both social and religious crimes had been involved.

118. On *ṭimmē' 'et-'ēšet rē'ēhû,* see 18:6, 15 and 22:11.

Ezekiel's strategy is deliberate. The "inhabitants of the ruins" are presented as the antithesis to the patriarch, for whom the promise of the land was accompanied by the injunction to walk before God (El Shaddai) and to be blameless (*tāmam;* Gen. 17:1-8). With their greed, violence, and unrighteousness, the survivors have demonstrated that they possessed neither morality nor faith. The specific nature of the prophet's accusations deflects the attention away from the patriarch, to the stipulations of Yahweh's covenant with the nation of Israel (Leviticus and Deuteronomy). But the integrity of the tripartite deity-people-land relationship depended on covenantal fidelity. The moral degeneracy exhibited by these ritual and social ills has disqualified this generation from any legitimate claims to the promised land.

A second command to the prophet to speak, followed by the citation formula in v. 27, signals the commencement of the counterthesis. The statement is cast in the form of a strongly worded sentence, typical of judgment speeches, followed by an expanded version of the recognition formula.

The opening oath formula reflects the divine passion with which the judgment is pronounced upon the surviving remnant in the homeland. As if the horrors of the past are not enough, Yahweh explodes all false claims to security by summoning his three great agents of wrath. The sword will smite those found among the ruins of the city; wild animals will devour those out in the open field; the plague *(deber)* will strike down those who have sought refuge in the strongholds and the caves.[119] The effects of these further acts of judgment listed in v. 28 are not new in kind, only in degree: total desolation, utter humiliation, and ruthless depopulation.[120] After the devastation of 586 it is remarkable that further destruction is even possible. But the lessons of that tragedy have obviously been lost to the handful of survivors, and their conduct continued to provoke the wrath of Yahweh. Consequently, no privilege, let alone refuge, was to be found in their Abrahamic connection.

The concluding recognition formula expresses the divine aim in his harsh treatment of the "inhabitants of the ruins": Yahweh continues to seek acknowledgment of his action and his person. The expansion summarizes both the divine involvement and the human causation behind these devastating historical events.

♦ Theological Implications

The oracle holds out several surprises for those who reduce divine activity to simplistic formulae.

---

119. Cf. Judg. 6:2. For earlier variation of this triad see Ezek. 5:1-2, 12; 6:11-17; 7:15; 14:12-23.

120. On the first cf. 6:14; 15:8; 29:10, 12; 32:15. On the second, 7:24; 30:6, 18. On the third, 14:15.

First, Yahweh may have abandoned his temple, but he is still present. He stands above the earth, and the land of Israel in particular, as a witness to the deeds of humans. When they refuse to conduct their affairs according to his standards of righteousness and morality, he acts in judgment. When the survivors of the destruction retain the old values and simply rebuild the old ways of life, God remains the enemy. For those who persist in rebellion there is no escape. The tentacles of divine judgment reach to the farthest corners of the earth as well as into the homes of those who claim to be the heirs of his promises.

Second, this oracle serves as a warning to those who claim to be the people of God not to miss or pervert the lessons of history. It is tempting for survivors of disaster to interpret their fortune as a sign of personal merit instead of an act of divine grace. But apart from a commitment to the divine Lord and a spiritual sensitivity to his will, expressed in ready obedience, their is no title to the land or to any other blessings of God. The privilege of being a son or daughter of Abraham must be accompanied by a commitment to walk before the Lord and to be blameless in one's conduct.

Third, God's disposition toward his land and his people is not determined by soft sentimentality. As human observers we feel sorry for the miserable remnant, trying to establish itself among the ruins of Jerusalem after the devastation of 586. We may even admire them for their determination to make the best of a deplorable situation. But God does not react this way; nor does people's pain excuse them from covenantal fidelity. Claims to the birthright must be accompanied by devotion to his will.

D. THE FINAL VINDICATION (33:30-33)

30 *"As for you, human, your compatriots are talking*[121] *about you near the walls and in the doorways of the houses. Each person proposes*[122] *to his fellow*[123] *as follows: 'Come and hear what the mes-*

---

121. Targ. and Syr. delete the article on *hannidbārîm*, which is strange, but LXX reflects MT. The reciprocal use of the Niphal of *dābar*, "to speak to one another," occurs elsewhere only in Mal. 3:13, 16 and Ps. 119:23. It has the force of *wĕdibbēr 'îš 'et-'āḥîw*. See the following line.

122. *BHS* follows LXX, Vulg., and Syr. in reading pl. in place of the sg. of MT and Targ.

123. *BHS* and many commentators follow LXX in simplifying the redundant reciprocal expressions *ḥad 'et-'aḥad 'îš 'et-'āḥîw* (lit. "one to one each to his brother") by deleting the former as an expansionistic gloss. *ḥad*, an Aramaized variant of *'eḥad* (Joüon-Muraoka, *Grammar*, §100b; Wagner, *Aramaismen*, p. 51) occurs elsewhere in the OT only in Ezra 4:8 and Dan. 2:31.

sage[124] *is that issues forth from Yahweh.'* 31 *So my people*[125] *come*[126] *to you in droves*[127] *and sit before you. They hear your words, but they refuse to act on them, because*[128] *they act*[129] *only with lust in their mouths,*[130] *and their hearts pursue*[131] *nothing but ill-gotten wealth.*[132] 32 *Look, to them you are like a singer of sensual songs,*[133] *with a beautiful voice and a fine musical touch.*[134] *They hear your words, but they refuse to comply with them.* 33 *But when it comes*[135] *— and come it certainly will — then they will know that a prophet has been in their midst."*

124. LXX abbreviates by omitting *mâ haddābār.*

125. LXX and Syr. drop *'ammî,* not recognizing the delayed subject, awkwardly placed at the end of the sentence. See G. R. Driver, *Bib* 35 (1954) 301-2.

126. In MT *wĕyābô'û* begins the apodosis after a lengthy protasis describing the state of the people in v. 30. Cf. GKC, §143d; Brockelmann, *Syntax,* §123f.

127. An interpretive rendering of the idiomatic phrase *kimĕbô' 'ām,* lit. "like the coming of people." Cf. LXX ὡς συμπορεύεται λαός, "as people gathering together"; Targ. paraphrases *kmyty gbryn tlmydyn,* "as students might come."

128. The construction from here to the end of the verse is awkward, leading many to delete this segment as a series of annotations. Cf. Allen, *Ezekiel 20–48,* p. 150.

129. LXX and Syr. omit *hēmmâ 'ōśîm,* "they are doing." Zimmerli (*Ezekiel 2,* p. 196) deletes the phrase as a clarifying gloss, inserted after the sense of v. 31a was no longer clear.

130. *'ăgābîm bĕpîhem. 'ăgābîm,* from *'āgab,* "to lust, to have inordinate affection," is an Ezekielianism. The verb occurs in 23:7, 9, 12, and the abstract noun *'ăgābâ,* used of lustfulness, in 23:11. The present intensive masc. pl. finds a semantic analogue in *dôdîm* (16:8). LXX ψεῦδος ἐν τῷ στόματι αὐτῶν and Syr. *dglwt'* read *kĕzābîm,* "falsehoods." *BHS* emends accordingly. But the sg. reading of LXX is suspicious, and looks like a harmonization with 13:6-9, 19; 21:34; 22:28. Targ. *twl'b' bpwmhwn,* "with scorn in their mouths," goes a different direction.

131. LXX and Syr. smooth out MT by adding the copula before *'ăḥărê.*

132. LXX μιασμάτων reads *biṣ'ām* as *'ăzabbâm.* Since MT is comprehensible and *beṣa'* is attested elsewhere in Ezekiel (22:13, 27), there is no need to emend the text.

133. *šîr 'ăgābîm* is rendered variously in the versions: LXX φωνὴ ψαλτηρίου; Vulg. *carmen musicum;* Targ. *zmr 'bwbyn;* Syr. *zmyrt'.* The awkwardness of comparing the prophet himself with a song in each of these (and MT) is resolved by revocalizing *šîr 'ăgābîm* as *šar 'ăgābîm,* "a singer of sensual songs."

134. The verb *nāgan* denotes "to play on a stringed instrument," presumably a lyre. The root is familiar from *nĕgînôt,* a designation appearing in the headings of several psalms (4, 6, 54, 55, 67, 76: Hab. 3:19; Ps. 61 reads sg.) and *nĕgînâ,* a term applied to music in general (Isa. 38:20; Lam. 5:14), and to taunt (Job 30:9) or drunkard's songs (Ps. 69:13 [Eng. 12]) in particular. Cf. Akk. *nigûtu,* "music," from *nagû,* "to sing joyfully" (*AHW,* p. 712; *CAD,* 11/1:123-24; 11/2:217-18, 313). For a brief discussion see Foxvog and Kilmer, *ISBE,* 3:448.

135. The implicit expression, *ûbĕbō'āh,* "and when it comes," is made explicit by Vulg. *quod praedictum est* and Syr. *ptgmyk hydyn,* "your prediction occurs."

The opening *As for you, human (wĕ'attâ ben-'ādām)* refocuses the audience's attention on the exilic situation, specifically the prophet and his relationship to his people. The genre of this fragment is unique, being cast as a report, presented by a superior to his officially designated spokesman.[136] On the surface, that Yahweh should describe for Ezekiel the disposition of the exiles toward his ministry seems superfluous. Surely he cannot have been oblivious to their rejection of his ministry. But the aim of this report is clear: to offer the prophet encouragement at the conclusion of the first phase of his ministry. Ezekiel had been forewarned of public opposition at the time of his call and commissioning, but he had also been promised that faithfulness in fulfilling the prophetic charge would be rewarded with a recognition of his prophetic status. Now, at the end of the most difficult phase of his service, Yahweh returns with a personal word for his spokesman, reassuring him of his aware-ness of all he has endured and reminding him that his status as prophet has been vindicated. While the account leaves no hint of the timing of the event, its editorial placement at the end of ch. 33 creates an effective *inclusio* with his call and commission (2:1–3:15), framing his oracles of judgment against his own people.

This literary fragment, unique in the prophetic writings, provides a rare glimpse into Ezekiel's personal contacts with his compatriots in Babylon, although the reader is not totally ignorant of their reaction. From 14:3 and 20:3 we learn that the elders sought to exploit his presence for revelatory purposes, but Ezekiel's response to these overtures had been harsh. According to 8:1, the vision of the abominations in the temple and the departure of the divine glory had been precipitated by the appearance of the elders before the prophet in his house. When the vision had ended, Ezekiel reported all that he had seen to his visitors (11:25), but how they reacted is not indicated. Ac-cording to 12:21-28, they had rejected his predictions as empty and irrelevant; in 21:5 (Eng. 20:49) he is dismissed disparagingly as a spinner of parables. However hostile they might have been in the past, this text leaves the impres-sion that by the time Jerusalem fell the relationship between prophet and audience had become casual, if not friendly. His compatriots *(bĕnê 'ammĕkā)* seem free to enter and leave his house (and his life) at will.

30 After opening with the characteristic direct address of the prophet, Yahweh begins with a thesis statement: the whole community of exiles is talking about Ezekiel. The reference to the *walls* and the *doorways* has a merismic function, suggesting that wherever people find shade from the

---

136. The text exhibits some structural similarities to the lament–divine response passages in the confessions of Jeremiah (12:1-6; 15:15-21; also Isa. 49:1-6; so Zimmerli, *Ezekiel 2,* p. 200), but the differences in literary form, style, and tone are much greater than the resemblances.

scorching Mesopotamian sun, and whenever they have time for a quick chat, Ezekiel's name surfaces as the subject of discussion. Specifically, the members of the community encourage each other to go to his house to receive a message from Yahweh. Their true disposition is reflected in the direct quotation in v. 30b, whose overtly theological nature contrasts sharply with the secular claims of the inhabitants of Jerusalem's ruins quoted in 33:24. On the surface, the statement reflects three important assumptions: (1) Yahweh exists, even after the debacle of 586; (2) Yahweh speaks, even on the foreign soil of Babylon; and (3) Ezekiel is his spokesman. There is evidently no need for the prophet to summon his audience to attention any more.

31-32 To a casual observer the response to Ezekiel's ministry is impressive. V. 31a presents the exiles as disciples, eager to learn all they can from some great teacher. So they come in droves, crowding his house and sitting before him, eager to hear him.[137] The scene exhibits all the signs of success. Even the reference to the "disciples" as *'ammî,* "my [Yahweh's] people," suggests that all is normal in the relationship between the people, on the one hand, and the prophet and deity on the other. But the vast difference between the reality and the facade is described in vv. 31b-32. The people's apparent eagerness for a word from Yahweh is belied by a blatant refusal to take that word seriously.

Two symptoms of their attitude are cited. First, the people's presence before the prophet is motivated by a craving for the sensuous and sensational. Erotic speech is on their lips, and he has become for them a singer of erotic songs. Ezekiel's oracles titillate his hearers, offering temporary satisfaction, but like any other addiction, they drive the audience back for more. Second, they are motivated by greed. Their heart commitment (*'aḥărê biṣ'ām libbām hōlēk*) is to gain, and any means, violent or unjust, is to be used to satisfy their avarice (cf. 22:13, 27). These then are the twin sins of insincerity: sensuality and greed. The former explains the people's interest in Ezekiel's message; the latter their refusal to heed it.

32 This verse elaborates only on the former, perhaps because Ezekiel has dealt with the problem of greed in earlier oracles. The prophet himself is compared to a singer of love songs. He is an entertainer renowned for his beautiful voice (*yĕpēh qôl*) and skill in playing the instrument (*mēṭîb naggēn*). This observation goes far beyond Isa. 5:1-7, which illustrates prophetic use of the love song as a medium of communication. Ezekiel is perversely treated as a pop star, the hottest ticket in town. His announcements of judgment and appeals for repentance are treated as entertainment. Instead of dealing with the truth to which his messages call attention, his utterances have facilitated

---

137. Cf. 8:1; 14:1; 20:1. The elders are apparently not the only ones coming to him.

escape from reality. Rhetorical form has overshadowed rhetorical function; artistry has interfered with communication.[138] The blame lies not with the prophet, carried away by his own rhetorical genius, or concerned primarily with the medium of communication rather than the message. The responsibility is placed squarely on his audience; they refuse to act on his words. Their reaction affirms Ezekiel's artistic genius, but the sacred message, crafted for life-changing effect, is reduced to an erotic diversion. The prophet, deadly serious in his proclamation, is frivolously acclaimed as a showman. By their attendance at his "performances" they sustain the illusion that they are a spiritual congregation, eager to hear a word from Yahweh.[139]

33 The message of this verse is ominous for the audience, even if it is reassuring for the prophet. When the predicted events occur, and there is no doubt that they will, then the people will realize that Ezekiel is much more than an entertainer. The text does not specify which further actions of Yahweh, after the events of 586, are envisioned. Since many of his oracles against the foreign nations are dated after the fall of Jerusalem, Ezekiel probably continued to address his hardened fellow exiles, calling for repentance on the one hand, and warning of further judgment on the other. In any case, the modified recognition formula assures the prophet of ultimate public vindication. Yahweh had not ceased to speak or work; nor would he cease to stand behind his spokesman.

♦ Theological Implications

The theological significance of this literary fragment for the contemporary church, particularly for understanding its prophetic mission, is profound.

First, messengers of God are not called to success but to faithfulness. At the time of this prophetic event Ezekiel had been preaching among his fellow exiles for more than a decade. Although his oracles of judgment upon the city of Jerusalem and Judah had all been fulfilled, few if any of his rhetorical aims had been achieved. But the prophet is undaunted, having learned not to base his security or sense of effectiveness on the response of his audience. This text warns against confusing success with skill as a communicator or ability to charm large crowds. The preacher is not called to entertain, but is charged to speak for God.

---

138. Cf. M. V. Fox, "The Rhetoric of Ezekiel's Vision of the Dry Bones," *HUCA* 51 (1980) 2 n. 4; L. Alonso-Schökel, "Hermeneutical Problems of a Literary Study of the Bible," in *Congress Volume: Edinburgh 1974,* VTSup 28 (Leiden: Brill, 1975), p. 3.

139. For further discussion see S. Lasine, "Fiction, Falsehood, and Reality in Hebrew Scripture," *HS* 25 (1984) 32-33; G. Quell, *Wahre und falsche Propheten: Versuch einer Interpretation,* BFCT 46/1 (Gütersloh: Bertelsmann, 1952), p. 184.

Second, appreciation for literary flair and rhetorical skill may camouflage a hardened heart. Like the survivors back in the homeland, the exiles had failed to grasp the theological significance of the arrival of the latest band of deportees.[140] They should have recognized the work of God and paid heed to the pronouncements of his messenger. But where hearts have fossilized, the pleas of a prophet become entertaining skits; divine passion is reduced to artistic enthusiasm. A cynical church evaluates the divine word for its aesthetic qualities, and the messenger for his ability to hold an audience.

Third, those who are called by God as his spokespersons may find security in him. The challenge for the communicator of divine truth is to be as gripped by the message as is the divine commissioner himself, to cast that message in as effective a form as possible, and then to commit the results to God.[141]

III. POSITIVE MESSAGES OF HOPE FOR ISRAEL: THE GOSPEL ACCORDING TO EZEKIEL (34:1–48:35)

♦ *Nature and Design*

In ch. 34 the denunciatory oracles of the previous chapter, as well as the judgments announced in chs. 1–24, give way to glorious messages of renewal and hope. With the fall of Jerusalem, Ezekiel's prophecies of doom have been fulfilled, and he may begin to contemplate in earnest the new day that will dawn after the midnight of divine wrath. While glimpses of a glorious future for Israel have been witnessed in earlier oracles (6:8-10; 11:14-21; 16:60-63; 17:22-24), now the storm clouds of fury will give way to the rainbow of divine grace and covenant recommitment.

Although the individual oracles in this larger section represent different prophetic genres, the entire assemblage falls under the general rubric of "salvation oracles" (German *Heilsworte*).[1] A salvation oracle is a prophetic pronouncement of deliverance from a stressful situation and the restoration

---

140. The survivor represented the third wave, after Nebuchadrezzar's initial visit in 605 B.C. (Dan. 1:1-2) and the subjugation of Jerusalem in 597 (the time of Ezekiel's own deportation).

141. Cf. the Pauline affirmation, "Faithful is he who calls you, and he will also bring it to pass" (1 Thess. 5:24).

1. On "salvation oracles" as a genre see C. Westermann, "Zur Erforschung und zum Verständnis der prophetischen Heilsworte," *ZAW* 98 (1986) 1-13; idem, *Prophetic Oracles of Salvation in the Old Testament,* tr. K. Crim (Louisville: Westminster/John Knox, 1991).

of total peace and harmony. Like laments, these oracles often envision the rescue of an individual or of a group.[2] However, laments and salvation oracles differ in that laments represent pleas for rescue; salvation oracles are prophetic announcements of deliverance. Furthermore, laments arise out of a distressed human heart; salvation oracles originate in God. The frequency of salvation oracles in the prophetic books indicates the strength of the hope of Israel's restoration in prophetic preaching. The vast majority of those that have been preserved were precipitated by the catastrophe of 586 B.C., which had left the land of Israel devastated, Jerusalem lying in ruins, and the population scattered among the nations. Four categories of oracles announcing the end of critical situations have been recognized:[3]

1. Unilateral announcements of deliverance and restoration. These sub-divide into two types: independent announcements of salvation, and announcements of deliverance followed by promises of blessing or restoration after deliverance. A tripartite structure (liberation-regathering-return to the land) is particularly common.
2. Bilateral announcements of the destruction of the enemy (sometimes involving their defeat at the hands of Judah-Israel; sometimes the occupation of their land by Judah-Israel).
3. Conditional announcements of salvation reminiscent of parenetic Deuteronomistic preaching (esp. common in Jeremiah).
4. Announcements of salvation associated with the motif of pious wisdom (the fate of the fool vs. the fortune of the wise).

According to Westermann, these categories are distributed among the writing prophets as in table 13 (p. 270). In Ezekiel the first category is represented by brief notices of deliverance scattered here and there in the prophet's earlier pronouncements of judgment, but especially in the lengthy oracles of restoration assembled in chs. 34–48.[4] Included in the second category, announcing the defeat of Israel's enemies, are 35:1-15 (in conjunction with 36:1-13 Edom/Seir) and 38:1–39:29 (Gog and Magog). The third category is represented in chs. 18 and 33, but the fourth is unattested in Ezekiel.

2. For oracles of individual salvation see 1 K. 17:8-16; 2 K. 2:19-22; 4:8-17; 4:42-43; 20:1-76. For oracles of community salvation see 1 Sam. 7:3-15; 2 K. 19:1-7; 19:14-34.

3. Westermann's method of counting is not always clear, nor is it consistent. My survey is based largely on his later work.

4. For the former see 11:14-21; 14:21-23; 16:53-63; 17:22-24; 20:34-44; 28:24-26; 29:21; segments of chs. 18 and 33. Westermann (*Prophetic Oracles,* pp. 169-77) includes the following among the latter: 34:1-31; 36:1-15; 36:17-31; 37:1-14; 37:15-28; chs. 40–48; also the conclusion to the Gog-Magog oracle in 39:21-29.

Table 13: Oracle Categories among the Prophets

Prophetic Section	Category I	Category II	Category III	Category IV
Isaiah 1–39	29	14	5	7
Isaiah 40–55	35	—	2	—
Isaiah 56–66	6	4	4	3
Jeremiah	38	3	10	—
Ezekiel	15	2	2	—
The Twelve	34	19	13	6
Totals	157	42	36	16

The shape and content of Ezekiel's restoration oracles in chs. 34–48 are influenced by several factors. First, although their tone contrasts sharply with his earlier messages of judgment, familiar judgmental elements persist. The woe oracle against the leaders of Israel preceding the promise of a restored flock in 34:1-10 is reminiscent of the oracles against the false prophets and prophetesses in ch. 13. The oracle against Mount Seir/Edom before the promise of a restored land in 35:1-15 recalls the prophecies against the foreign nations in chs. 25–26. The lengthy Gog-Magog prophecy in chs. 38–39 shares many of these features as well.

Second, these extended salvation oracles provide further examples of typically Ezekielian resumptive exposition. Notions briefly introduced in the context of earlier judgment oracles are picked up and expounded in great detail.[5] There is no reason to depreciate these fragments as later additions inserted under the influence of these fully developed oracles.[6] The covenant curses in Lev. 26:40-45 held out the prospect of such a renewal after judgment, and the compassionate character of Yahweh and his fidelity to his covenant necessitated it (cf. Deut. 4:25-31). Furthermore, Ezekiel's predecessor and contemporary, Jeremiah, envisioned just such an event within seventy years.[7]

5. See 11:14-21; 16:53-63; 17:22-24; 20:39-44; 28:24-26.

6. So also Boadt, *HAR* 12 (1990) 3.

7. Jer. 29:10-14, on which see G. Larsson, "When did the Babylonian Captivity Begin?" *JTS* 18 (1967) 417-23. Fishbane has rightly maintained (*Biblical Interpretation*, p. 480) that this passage is not to be dismissed as an *ex eventu* prophecy: (1) *Ex eventu* proclamations could afford to be more precise. (2) In Israel's *Umwelt* the figure 70 was a commonly accepted typological number for the duration of exile. Cf. Borger, *Die Inschriften Asarhaddons,* episode 15. On this text see D. D. Luckenbill, "The Black Stone of Esarhaddon," *AJSL* 41 (1925) 167-68; J. Nougayrol, "Textes hépatoscopiques d'époque ancienne conservée au Musée du Louvre II," *RA* 40 (1946) 65; Block, *Gods of the Nations,*

It is preferable, therefore, to interpret the earlier statements as pre-586 pre-monitions of Israel's ultimate restoration.[8]

Third, theologically, the salvation oracles represent the inverse of Ezekiel's earlier judgment oracles upon Judah. Prior to 586 his aim had been to demolish Judah's false sense of security by undermining the theological premises on which it was based: Yahweh's irrevocable covenant with his people, his immutable promise of the land to the ancestors and their descendants, his eternal covenant with David and his royal house, and the inviolability of Jerusalem and the temple as the seats of his residence. The razing of Jerusalem confirmed the prophet's analysis of the nation's spiritual rot and dashed their false hopes, leaving many disillusioned, questioning divine competence and integrity in the face of Marduk's apparent victory. But Ezekiel's salvation oracles challenge depressed and cynical exiles with the glorious news that all is not lost! Ironically, the very notions Ezekiel had discredited as false bases of security with such vigor are resurrected in the salvation oracles and presented as the certain and only reasons for hope for the future.[9] The nation's earlier problem had been not its theology but the misapplication of its theology. Divine patronage was not to be viewed as an unconditional privilege, but as a gracious favor to be responded to with gratitude and submission. In chs. 34–48 the prophet announces that the dashed humpty-dumpty will be put together again, but not by king's horses or any king's men; only the gracious intervention of Yahweh can accomplish this.

Fourth, the facets of Ezekiel's vision of Israel's future were determined by common Near Eastern understandings of nationhood. These perceptions demanded that Israel's national restoration involve: (1) the participation of the entire house; (2) the renewal of the relationship between people and deity; (3) the return of the population to the homeland; (4) the installation of an indigenous (Davidic) monarchy. That Ezekiel should have addressed all these issues in his oracles is hardly coincidental.[10]

Fifth, Ezekiel's understanding of the sequence of events involved in Israel's restoration was conventional, being patterned after common ancient Near Eastern judgment-restoration traditions. Since the sequence of human sin–divine wrath–divine abandonment–disaster–exile in the prophet's earlier

---

pp. 142-43. (3) The text fails to mention the reconstruction of the temple, an element that would certainly have been expected in an oracle after the fact.

8. D. Baltzer acknowledges that at least 11:14-21 dates to a time when the temple was still standing ("Literarkritische und Literarhistorische Anmerkungen zur Heils-prophetie im Ezechiel-Buch," in *Ezekiel and His Book*, p. 171).

9. See my *Ezekiel: Chapters 1–24*, pp. 15-16 and table 1 there.

10. See D. I. Block, "Nations," *ISBE*, 3:492-95.

oracles of judgment followed established patterns,[11] this observation should not surprise one. On the contrary, Ezekiel's structure of reconstruction finds numerous analogues in ancient literature that include the following succession of motifs: (1) a change in the disposition of the deity; (2) the appointment of a new ruler; (3) the reconstruction of the temple; (4) the return of the deity; (5) the regathering of the scattered population; (6) the establishment of peace and prosperity.[12] Ezekiel's restoration oracles are evidently cast in an idiom familiar not only to his audience but even to the Babylonians among whom he lived — they would have expected his message of hope and renewal to follow this general form. The hope for the future depended on deliverance from foreign control, and the return of shalom required the full restoration of relationships among deity, nation, and land. For the prophet, and for those responsible for collecting and arranging his oracles, the fateful year of 586 did not mark the end but the center of the nation's history and Yahweh's dealing with his people.[13]

In the light of these factors, the shape of the gospel according to Ezekiel in particular and the arrangement of his salvation oracles in general are both logical and traditional. Although they divide generically into two major blocks, the first (chs. 34–39) concerned with proclaiming the good news, and the second (chs. 40–48) with envisioning the good news, the focus is on Yahweh's restorative actions, for the glory of his name, according to the following grand apologetic scheme:

1. Restoring Yahweh's role as divine shepherd/king of Israel (34:1-31)
2. Restoring Yahweh's land (35:1–36:15)
3. Restoring Yahweh's honor (36:16-38)
4. Restoring Yahweh's people (37:1-14)
5. Restoring Yahweh's covenant (37:15-28)
6. Restoring Yahweh's supremacy (38:1–39:29)
7. Restoring Yahweh's presence among his people (40:1–46:24)
8. Restoring Yahweh's presence in the land (47:1–48:35)

---

11. See my *Ezekiel: Chapters 1–24,* pp. 272ff., on chs. 8–11; Bodi, *Ezekiel and the Poem of Erra,* pp. 183-218.

12. For details see my discussion in *Gods of the Nations,* pp. 133-48.

13. Cf. D. Baltzer, in *Ezekiel and His Book,* p. 181.

A. PROCLAIMING THE GOOD NEWS:
"STAND BY AND SEE THE SALVATION OF YAHWEH!"
(34:1–39:29)

1. The Salvation of Yahweh's Flock (34:1-31)

♦ *Nature and Design*

Chapter 34 is a self-contained literary unit bounded by the word-event formula in v. 1 and a modified version of the recognition formula in vv. 30-31, followed by a thematic conclusion and sealed with the divine signatory formula. Although the material within these borders is united by a common pastoral theme, the content and formal rhetorical signals reflect a complex structure. The citation formula, *kōh 'āmar 'ădōnāy yhwh,* "Thus has the Lord Yahweh declared," appears five times (vv. 2, 10, 11, 17, 20); the signatory formula, *ně'um 'ădōnāy yhwh,* "the declaration of the Lord Yahweh," four times (vv. 8, 15, 30, 31); the summons to listen, *šim'û 'et-děbar yhwh,* "Hear the word of Yahweh," twice (vv. 7, 9); the recognition formula, *wěyādě'û kî 'ănî 'ădōnāy yhwh,* "And they will know that I am Yahweh," twice (vv. 27, 30); the divine self-introduction formula, *'ănî yhwh,* "I am Yahweh," once (v. 24). The oath formula *ḥay 'ānî,* "As I live," followed by the sequence *ya'an . . . lākēn,* "Because . . . therefore," in vv. 7-8, and *lākēn* in vv. 20 and 22, constitute additional disjunctive/conjunctive signals. While these formulae are important in highlighting this unit as divine speech and in focusing the audience on the speaker, they are not entirely reliable bases for structuring the chapter, let alone reconstructing its literary evolution.[14] Since the text contains no historical anachronisms demanding a later context, no syntactically incoherent elements that cannot be attributed to textual corruption or ancient literary practice, and no blatant internal contradictions, there is no a priori reason for considering the chapter as inauthentic. While this does not mean the present product is a transcript of

---

14. Cf. Meier, *Speaking of Speaking,* pp. 230-39, esp. p. 238. The lack of scholarly consensus reflects the uncertainty of the enterprise and the subjective bases on which such hypotheses are constructed. For the most thorough critical investigation of the chapter see B. Willmes, *Die sogenannte Hirtenanalogie Ez 34: Studien zum Bild des Hirten im Alten Testament,* BBET 19 (Frankfurt: Peter Lang, 1984), pp. 235-37, 466-71; more briefly, idem, "Differenzierende Prophezeiungen in Ez 34," in *Ezekiel and His Book,* pp. 248-54. Allen (*Ezekiel 20–48,* pp. 158-61) recognizes a nucleus of two authentically Ezekielian oracles (vv. 1-16, 17-22), rounded out with three supplements (vv. 23-24, 25-30, 31), the first of which is denied Ezekiel because of its dependence on 37:24-25, itself a late addition. The second obviously betrays another hand, and the third is a redactional conclusion wrapping up the entire chapter.

the original oral communication, it respects the present text as a deliberate literary composition, probably by the prophet himself.

Nonetheless, one need not exclude an original rhetorical unity. The aural quality of the passage suggests some correspondence between the written form and the original presentation. The use of the second person of direct address (vv. 3-4, 17-22, 31), the vocative case (vv. 2, 7, 9), the call to hear the word of Yahweh (vv. 7, 9), the redundancy (vv. 7-8 and 9-10; 11-15 and 16; 17-19 and 20-22; 23a and 23b; 30 and 31), the emphasis on the authority of the proclaimed word (reflected in the citation and signatory formulae, as well as in "I am Yahweh, I have spoken," v. 24), the evocative diction (vv. 2, 8, 10, 17), and the opening rhetorical declaration,[15] all contribute to the oracle's homiletical flavor. Furthermore, it seems more logical to attribute the inconsistency (not contradiction) of person, the repetition and recapitulation, the interjected citation and signatory formulae, and so on, to an oral stage of the prophecy, rather than to a series of late editorial revisions, in which scribal editors should have eliminated, rather than added, such discordant elements.

In identifying the structure of the text, one must coordinate formulaic features with shifts in tone and content. Accordingly, after the preamble (v. 1), the oracle proper divides into three parts approximately equal in length: (a) the announcement of deliverance (vv. 2-10); (b) the nature of the deliverance (vv. 11-22); (c) the goal of the deliverance (vv. 23-31). Most scholars recognize in the first panel a more or less independent woe oracle directed against the rulers of Israel. This segment divides naturally into two parts, which in style and tone represent a formal accusation (vv. 2-6) and an announcement of judgment (vv. 7-10), respectively, elements typical of woe oracles. However, its location forces the reader to interpret this segment within its present literary framework. The second panel focuses entirely on Yahweh and his salvific activity on behalf of his flock. The statements of deliverance, employing the verbs *hiṣṣîl* (v. 12) and *hôšîaʿ* (v. 22), form an *inclusio* around this section. Within this framework two dimensions of deliverance are described: rescue from external enemies (vv. 11-16) and rescue from internal exploiters (vv. 17-22). The last panel (vv. 23-31) is framed by allusions to Yahweh's covenant with his people (vv. 24, 30-31). Now that he has freed them from all forms of oppression, the focus shifts to positively reconstructing the shalom that Yahweh has intended from the beginning. But this panel also divides into three subsections. The first, consisting only of vv. 23-24, focuses on David, reinstalled as under-shepherd over the flock; the second (vv. 25-29), different in style and tone from the first, develops a new theme, the covenant of peace which Yahweh establishes with his people. Vv. 30-31 give the entire subunit (vv. 11-31) the stamp of a proof oracle.

15. Usually translated as a question. See the textual note on v. 2.

Although this chapter is complex literarily, the linkages among the parts are strong. The sentence pronounced upon the evil rulers in vv. 7-10 is tied to the preceding accusation with the twofold *lākēn*, "Therefore," as is the divine response to internal injustices in vv. 20-22. Although the citation formula in v. 11 introduces the second major division of the chapter, the two parts are tied together by the connective *kî*, "for." V. 16 consciously echoes vv. 4-6, albeit in reverse (but logical order). The last line of this verse, with its otherwise superfluous *běmišpāṭ*, functions as a link between the foregoing portrayal of divine care and the succeeding administration of divine justice. The concluding verse ties in with the covenantal affirmations in vv. 24 and 30, and the expression *ṣō'nî*, "my flock," draws attention to the *Leitwort* of the entire passage.[16]

Since ancient Near Eastern literature often portrays civil authorities as shepherds, Ezekiel may simply have drawn on a common motif. However, this text also displays strong semantic and formal links with Jer. 23:1-6, as the following translation of the Jeremianic passage illustrates (the common elements are in italics):

> *O shepherds,* who are *destroying and scattering the flock of my pasture! The declaration of Yahweh. Therefore, thus has Yahweh* the God of Israel *declared* concerning *the shepherds, who are tending my* people: "You have *scattered my flock, and driven* them away. You have not attended to them. *Take note!* I am about to attend to you for the evil of your misdemeanors. *The declaration of Yahweh. I myself shall gather* the remnant of *my flock out of all the countries* where I have driven them; *I shall bring them back to their pasture,* and they will be fruitful and multiply. *I shall also install over them shepherds,* who will tend them. *They will be afraid no longer,* nor will they be terrified, nor will they be unaccounted for. *The declaration of Yahweh. Take note!* Days are coming — *the declaration of Yahweh* — when *I shall install* for *David* a Righteous Branch. He will reign as king, and he will act wisely. *He will exercise justice* and righteousness in the land. In his days Judah *will be delivered,* and Israel *will dwell securely.* This is his name by which he shall be called: "Yahweh Our Righteousness" *(yhwh ṣidqēnû).*

The linkages in theme and structure, style, and diction are too numerous and too specific to be accidental, and their distribution throughout Ezek. 34 may support the unitary interpretation of the latter.[17] Ezekiel seems to have had

---

16. Cf. vv. 6 (bis), 8 (4 times), 10 (3 times), 11, 12, 15, 17, 19, 22.

17. On theme and structure: (1) the opening pronouncement of woe (Jer. 23:1; Ezek. 34:2); (2) the formal accusation, which serves at the same time as a description of the crisis facing the flock (Jer. 23:1b-2; Ezek. 34: 3-6); (3) the judgment on the shepherds, which signifies salvation for the flock (Jer. 23:2c; Ezek. 34:7-10); (4) Yahweh's personal intervention on behalf of the flock (Jer. 23:3; Ezek. 34:10-22); (5) the appointment of caring human shepherd(s) (Jer. 23:4; Ezek. 34:23a); (6) the identification of the human

Jeremiah's oracle before him and presented his "Shepherd Address" as an exposition of his contemporary's prophecy.[18] But his adherence to Jeremiah is not slavish. Signs of adaptation and reinterpretation are evident in his downplaying the status of David while highlighting the role of Yahweh, and in his incorporation of elements from Lev. 26.[19]

---

shepherd as a Davidide (Jer. 23:5; Ezek. 34:23b-24); (7) the concluding peace and security in the land (Jer. 23:6; Ezek. 34:25-29).

On style: (1) the punctuation of the oracles with the citation and signatory formulae; (2) the emphatic use of the first person pronoun (*'ānî*) to highlight Yahweh's personal involvement in the rescue of the flock (Jer. 23:3; Ezek. 34:11); (3) the emphatic use of *hinĕnî*, "Behold," to draw attention to Yahweh's activity (Jer. 23:2; Ezek. 34:10, 11, 17, 21); (4) the rhetorical (as opposed to logical) use of *lākēn*, "therefore" (cf. March, in *Rhetorical Criticism*, pp. 259-62).

On diction: (1) the dominant *Leitwörter*, *ṣō'nî*, "my flock" (2 times in Jeremiah; 15 times in Ezekiel), and *rā'â*, "to tend, shepherd" (various forms 6 times in Jer. 23:1-6; 32 times in Ezek. 34); (2) key verbs: *'ābad*, "to destroy" (Jer. 23:1; Ezek. 34:4, 16), *pûṣ*, "to scatter" (Jer. 23:1; Ezek. 34:5, 21), *niddaḥ*, "to drive away" (Jer. 23:2, 3; Ezek. 34:4, 16), *qābaṣ*, "to gather" (Jer. 23:3; Ezek. 34:13, 16), *hēšîb*, "to bring back" (Jer. 23:3; Ezek. 34:16), *hēqîm*, "to raise up, install" (Jer. 23:4, 5; Ezek. 34:23, 29); (3) other key expressions: *ṣō'n mar'îtî*, "the sheep of my pasturage" (Jer. 23:1; Ezek. 34:31); *mišpāṭ*, "justice" (Jer. 23:5; Ezek. 34:16; cf. the verb *šāpaṭ*, in vv. 17-22); *lābeṭaḥ*, "securely" (Jer. 23:6; Ezek. 34:25, 27, 28); *nāweh*, "pastureland" (Jer. 23:3; Ezek. 34:14 [2x]); *'ammî*, "my people" (Jer. 23:2; Ezek. 34:30); also *'admātām*, "their own land" (Jer. 23:8; Ezek. 34:27); (4) motifs referred to by synonyms: "to save" (*yāša'*, Jer. 23:6, vs. *hiṣṣîl*, Ezek. 34:10:12, 27); the absence of fear (*wĕlō'-yîr'û 'ôd wĕlō'-yēḥattû*, Jer. 23:4, vs. *wĕ'ên maḥărîd*, Ezek. 34:28); "to dwell [in the land]" (*šākan*, Jer. 23:6, vs. *yāšab*, Ezek. 34:25, 28, and *hāyâ 'al*, v. 27).

For further discussion of these links see J. W. Miller, *Das Verhältnis Jeremias und Hesekiels sprachlich und theologisch untersucht* (Assen: Van Gorcum, 1955), p. 106.

18. See also Miller, ibid., although some argue for Ezekielian independence (cf. W. Brownlee, "Ezekiel's Poetic Indictment of the Shepherds," *HTR* 51 [1958] 191-203), and others for Ezekielian influence on the Jeremiah text. Hossfeld (*Untersuchungen*, pp. 255-57) assumes that Jer. 23:1-4, 7-8 derive from a later Deuteronomistic reworking of Jeremiah; similarly E. W. Nicholson, *The Book of the Prophet Jeremiah, Chapters 1-25*, CBC (Cambridge: Cambridge University Press, 1973), pp. 191-92; R. W. Klein, "Jeremiah 23:1-8," *Int* 34 (1980) 167-72; N. Mendecki, "Die Sammlung und die Hineinführung in das Land in Jer 23,3," *Kairos* 25 (1983) 99-103; idem, "Ezekielische Redaktion des Buches Jeremia?" *BZ* 35 (1991) 242-47. W. L. Holladay credits vv. 1-4 and 5-6 to Jeremiah, but he considers vv. 7-8 to be 5th century (*A Commentary on the Book of the Prophet Jeremiah*, 2 vols., Hermeneia [Philadelphia and Minneapolis: Fortress, 1979-86], 1:613-23). Noting the *Stichwörter* and the ABBA structure of vv. 3-8, Fishbane (*Biblical Interpretation*, p. 472) treats the entire Jeremianic block as a unit and dates the oracle firmly to 597, the year of the exile of Jehoiachin and the nobility, and the year of the enthronement of Zedekiah, whose name is alluded to in the designation of the future Davidic line as "YHWH is our righteousness (*ṣidqēnû*)."

19. So also Boadt, *HAR* 12 (1990) 9. Cf. W. Gross, "Israel's Hope for the Renewal of the State," *JNSL* 14 (1988) 124-27, who focuses on the differences between Jeremiah's text and Ezek. 34:23-24.

Because this oracle lacks specific clues regarding its occasion, any suggestions regarding its date and context are speculative. Was Ezekiel responding to a written form of Jeremiah's prophecy circulating among the exiles?[20] Was his promise of just divine and Davidic rule a reaction to the oppressive style of the last members of the Judean monarchy and the rest of ruling class prior to the fall of Jerusalem? Or was he attacking exploitative government within the exilic community — the "rams" of v. 21? Whatever the context, in pronouncing woe upon oppressive leaders, this oracle promises glorious deliverance for the downtrodden and hope to those in despair. Ironically, the rescue desired is not from the grip of the Babylonians or from any other enemy of Judah, but from internal captivity. Indeed, as the concluding thematic statement affirms, the primary concern of the chapter is not wicked shepherds but the relationship of the Good Shepherd and his flock. Placed at the beginning of this corpus of salvation oracles, this chapter serves a paradigmatic function, announcing the reestablishment of Yahweh's kingship over his people[21] and highlighting his role in Israel's restoration. A clearer picture of his involvement in this agenda emerges in subsequent oracles.

a. Preamble and the Announcement of Deliverance (34:1-10)

1 *The following message of Yahweh came to me:*

2 *"Human, prophesy against the shepherds of Israel. Prophesy and say*[22] *to them: 'O shepherds!*[23] *Thus has the Lord Yahweh declared: Hey!*[24] *Shepherds*[25] *of Israel, who have been tending*[26] *themselves*[27]

---

20. Cf. the report in Dan. 9:2 of Jeremiah's letter (Jer. 29) in Daniel's hands.

21. Boadt (*HAR* 12 [1990] 11) concludes that a major purpose of chap. 34 is to establish God's kingship over a restored Israel according to the program of ch. 20, esp. 20:32-33.

22. The versions preserve the duplication of *hinnābē'* after *wĕ'āmartā* (as in 13:2; 37:9; cf. 11:4).

23. The *lamed* prefixed to *rō'îm* appears redundant after *'ălêhem*, unless it is treated as a vocative particle with Syr. Cf. G. R. Driver, *Bib* 35 (1954) 302; *CML*, p. 149; *TSSI*, 3:84.

24. *hôy*, usually rendered "Woe!" See the commentary.

25. Contra NJPS and NIV, there is no need to harmonize the third person opening with the following verses by inserting "you," since the switch from third to second person is common in woe oracles. Cf. D. R. Hillers, "*Hôy* and *Hôy*-Oracles: A Neglected Syntactical Aspect," in *The Word of the Lord Shall Go Forth*, pp. 185-88.

26. LXX μὴ βόσκουσιν οἱ ποιμένες ἑαυτούς reflects an original *hăyir'û hārō'îm*, "Should the shepherds tend themselves?" but there is no need to depart from MT. Exact sg. equivalents to the present construction *(hāyâ rō'eh)* occur in Gen. 4:17; 37:2.

27. On *'et* with suffix used reflexively see GKC, §135k.

alone. Surely[28] *it is the flock that shepherds ought to tend.*[29] 3 *The milk,*[30] *you consume; the wool, you wear; and the fatlings,*[31] *you butcher. But*[32] *the flock you do not tend,* 4 *the weak*[33] *you have not strengthened, the sick you have not healed, the injured you have not bound up, the stray*[34] *you have not fetched, and the lost*[35] *you have not sought. With harshness*[36] *and ruthlessness*[37] *you have mistreated*[38] *them.*[39] 5 *They*[40] *have been scattered for want of a shepherd; they have become prey for every wild animal.* 6 *My flock wander about*[41] *among*

28. MT *hălô'*, usually interpreted as *hā* plus *lô'*, "Should not . . . ?" should perhaps be repointed as *hălû'* or *hallû'* and treated as an emphatic particle, cognate to Ugar. *hl*, Amarna Akk. *allū*, and Aram. *hlw*, *'ălū*. See M. L. Brown, " 'Is It Not?' or 'Indeed!': *HL* in Northwest Semitic," *Maarav* 4/2 (1987) 201-19; also Greenberg, *Ezekiel 1–20*, p. 211, on 12:9.

29. Preserving the emphatic object-verb-subject order, found here and in many of the following statements.

30. Consonantal *hḥlb* is ambiguous. Although MT may be defended as the *lectio difficilior*, I read *heḥālāb* with LXX and Vulg. in place of MT (and Syr.) *haḥēleb*, "the fat," since the latter is subsumed under the third charge.

31. MT lacks the copula, but see the versions and many Hebrew mss.

32. LXX, Syr., and Vulg. recognize the adversative sense by adding the copula.

33. Reading sg. *hannaḥĕlâ* with LXX, Syr., and Vulg. Stylistic monotony is avoided by varying the stem, here Niphal and Qal. Such alternation is common in Ezekiel. Cf. Qal and Niphal in vv. 5, 6; 12:11, 25; 20:3; 38:23; Qal and Hophal in 32:19, 21; Piel and Pual in 36:23; Qal and Hiphil in 14:6; 18:30.

34. Whereas Jer. 23:3 has Yahweh as the subject of *niddaḥ*, Ezekiel avoids reference to divine causality. The term may denote a simple stray (Deut. 22:1), or one that has been expelled by other members of the flock (cf. vv. 20-22).

35. *'ābad*, lit. "to perish," here means "to be/go lost."

36. LXX assumes a noun (perhaps *bahăzāqâ*, "and the strong") for MT's abstract noun, *ûbĕḥāzĕqâ*, "and with strength." With *rādâ*, "to rule, dominate," the object is frequently introduced by *bĕ*. Cf. 29:19; BDB, p. 922a. But see n. 38 below.

37. In Exod. 1:13-14 *perek* refers to the Egyptian oppression of Israelite slaves. See Lev. 25:43, 46, 53 for warnings against such treatment of a fellow Israelite.

38. The difficulty of this clause is reflected in the versions. LXX deletes *'ōtām û-* after *rĕdîtem;* Syr. deletes the last word. G. R. Driver (*Bib* 19 [1938] 180) repoints *'ōtām* as *'attem*, "you," and deletes the conjunction from the following *ûbĕpārek*. Zimmerli (*Ezekiel 2*, p. 205) deletes the word as dittography after *rĕdîtem*. NJPS treats the pair as a hendiadys, "with harsh rigor." *rādâ bĕ* occurs elsewhere in Ezekiel only in 29:15.

39. LXX, Syr., and Vulg. assume an original *ṣō'nî*, "my flock." Cf. v. 6.

40. MT ends the verse with a second *wattĕpûṣênâ*, but this looks like dittography and should be deleted with Syr. LXX attaches the word to v. 6.

41. *yiśgû* is problematic for many reasons: (1) it is absent from LXX; (2) the masc. form clashes with the fem. nouns around it; (3) the consecutive *waw* is missing; (4) the verb is never used of a flock, only of erring humans; (5) it disrupts *wattĕpûṣênâ* of v. 5 and *ṣō'nî*, which belong together; (6) this form of the verb is not found in Ezekiel. Nevertheless, the word may be defended: (1) Targ. translates it with the common expression

all the mountains and on every high hill.[42] *My flock*[43] *have been scattered over the entire face of the earth,*[44] *with no one to search, and no one to look for them.*

7 *Therefore, O shepherds,*[45] *hear the word of Yahweh!*

8 *As I live — the declaration of the Lord Yahweh — surely. . . .*[46] *Because my flock has become spoil, and my flock has become prey for every wild animal, for want of a shepherd, and my shepherds*[47] *have not searched for my flock, and the shepherds have tended themselves instead of tending my flock —*

9 *therefore, O shepherds, hear the word of Yahweh!*[48] 10 *Thus has the Lord Yahweh declared: Look, I am against the shepherds! I will hold them responsible for my flock, and terminate their tending my flock.*[49] *The shepherds will not tend themselves any longer. I will rescue my flock from their jaws, so they will no longer be prey for them.' "*

(1) The Indictment of the Shepherds of Israel (34:1-6)

1-2 Following the customary opening word-event formula and the direct address of the prophet as *Human (ben-'ādām)*, Ezekiel receives the double command to prophesy against *the shepherds of Israel (rō'ê yiśrā'ēl)*. The designation *shepherds* for leaders is traditional in ancient Near Eastern usage,

---

t'h, "to go astray"; (2) the word is too infrequent for no. 4 above to be convincing; (3) cognates meaning "to go astray" are attested in Aram. *šg'* (*Ahiqar* 137; cf. *DISO*, p. 291; *DNWSI*, p. 1108; contra H. L. Ginsberg, *ANET*, p. 429) and Akk. *šagû* (*AHW*, p. 1127); (4) the principle of *lectio difficilior*. The advertent addition of so difficult an expression contradicts scribal concern for clarity and would have been caught before it became fixed in the text. Targ. offers the most likely solution, changing the verb to a perfect form. So G. R. Driver, *Bib* 19 (1938) 181. But see Allen, *Ezekiel 20–48*, p. 157.

42. *bĕkol-hehārîm* and *'al kol-gib'â rāmâ* reflect the Canaanite landscape (cf. 6:13; 20:28, on which see Holladay, *VT* 11 [1961] 170-76), but the following *'al kol-pĕnê hā'āres*, "over the whole face of the earth," includes Babylon, where the exiles now reside.

43. *sō'nî* is missing from LXX. Zimmerli (*Ezekiel 2*, p. 206) suggests that it has been mistakenly dropped from v. 5a and inserted here.

44. Although many read *'al pĕnê kol-hā'ares* with LXX, in place of the unusual *'al kol-pĕnê hā'āres*, precedents for MT are attested in Gen. 19:28 and 41:26.

45. The vocative is possible without the article, but most add it as in v. 9. Cf. GKC, §126e.

46. The oath formula, *'im-lō'*, follows *hay-'ānî*, but instead of completing the oath (is v. 10 the continuation?), a motive clause introduced by *ya'an* is added. On such anacolouthic constructions see GKC, §167b.

47. LXX and Syr. drop the suffix, probably as a harmonization with the context.

48. LXX drops *šim'û dĕbar yhwh*.

49. MT has dropped the suffix from *sō'n* by pseudo-haplography. Cf. Zimmerli, *Ezekiel 2*, p. 205.

dating back to Sumerian times.[50] An Old Babylonian version of the Etana legend suggests that the association of kingship with shepherding dates back to the very founding of the monarchic institution:

> The great Anunnaki who decree destinies
> Sat and conferred their counsel on the land.
> They were creating the four quarters (of the world)
>   and establishing the form (of it).
> The Igigi [ ] decreed names (?) for them all.
> They had not established a king over all the teeming people.
> At that time the headband and crown had not been put together,
> And the lapis lazuli sceptre had not been brandished (?),
> At the same time (?) the throne-dais had not been made.
> The Sebitti barred the gates against armies (?),
> [The] barred them against (other) settled peoples.
> The Igigi would patrol the city [ ].
> Ishtar [was looking for] a shepherd
> And searching high and low for a king.[51]

The ancient Babylonian self-perception of kings as shepherds of the people, specially chosen by the gods, is reflected in the prologue to the Code of Hammurabi:

> When lofty Anum, king of the Anunnaki,
> (and) Enlil, lord of heaven and earth,
> the determiner of the destinies of the land,
> determined for Marduk, the first-born of Enki,
> the Enlil functions over all mankind,
> made him great among the Igigi,
> called Babylon by its exalted name,
> made it supreme in the world,
> established for him in its midst an enduring kingship,
> whose foundations are as firm as heaven and earth —
> at that time Anum and Enlil named me
> to promote the welfare of the people,
> me, Hammurabi, the devout, god-fearing prince,
> to cause justice to prevail in the land,

50. The Sumerian King List describes the divinized Dumuzu as "a shepherd" (*sipa*) who reigned 36,000 years. See T. Jacobsen, *Sumerian King List*, pp. 72-73; *ANET*, p. 265. Of Etana, a postdiluvian ruler of Kish, the same document records, "Etana, a shepherd, the one who ascended to heaven, who consolidated all countries, became king [*lugal*] and reigned 1,560 years." See *Sumerian King List*, pp. 80-81; *ANET*, p. 265.

51. As translated by Dalley, *Myths from Mesopotamia*, p. 190; cf. *ANET*, p. 114.

to destroy the wicked and the evil,
that the strong might not oppress the weak,
to rise like the sun over the black-headed (people),
and to light up the land.
Hammurabi, the shepherd, called by Enlil, am I;
the one who makes affluence and plenty abound;
who provides in abundance all sorts of things for Nippur-Duranki;
the devout patron of Ekur;
the efficient king, who restored Eridu to its place.[52]

Hammurabi's Assyrian and neo-Babylonian successors defined their role with a series of pastoral titles, and a Babylonian proverb had it that "A people without a king (is like) sheep without a shepherd."[53] Indeed, the verb *re'û*, "to graze, to shepherd," often functions as a technical term for "to rule."[54] The motif is known in Egyptian writings as well, where the typical formula claimed: "the god has chosen the king to be the shepherd of Egypt and the defender of the people."[55] Reminiscent of the Babylonian proverb cited above is this observation on a papyrus text: in the absence of a ruler, the people are "like a flock gone astray without a shepherd."[56]

In Israel the designation of rulers as shepherds had a long-standing tradition as well. According to Num. 27:17, Moses prayed that Yahweh would appoint a man over the congregation so they might not be like sheep without a shepherd. This statement compares with Micaiah ben Imlah's prophetic observation, "I saw all Israel scattered on the mountains, like sheep without

52. *ANET,* p. 164.

53. Lambert, *Babylonian Wisdom Literature,* pp. 229, 232, lines 14-15. The titles include "faithful shepherd," "beloved shepherd of Marduk/Ninurta," "shepherd, favorite of Enlil, Shamash, and Marduk," "shepherd, protector of the regions," "shepherd of the land of Assyria," "shepherd of the great people," "marvelous shepherd," "shepherd of the black-headed." Cf. M. J. Seux, *Épithèts royales,* pp. 244-50; L. Dürr, *Ursprung und Ausbau der israelitisch-jüdischen Heilandserwartung: Ein Beitrag zur Theologie des Alten Testaments* (Berlin: C. A. Schwetschke und Sohn, 1925), pp. 116-20. See more recently I. Seibert, *Hirt-Herde-König: Zur Herausbildung des Königtums in Mesopotamien* (Berlin: Akademie Verlag, 1969); U. Magen, *Assyrische Königsdarstellungen,* pp. 18-21.

54. Like its Akkadian cognate *re'û,* Heb. *rā'â* means lit. "to pasture, tend, graze," but it also functions as a technical term for "to rule." See J. A. Soggin, *THAT,* 2:791-94. Although the nuance shifts slightly, this verb replaces *pāqad,* "to attend to," used by Jeremiah in 23:2.

55. A. Erman and H. Ranke, *Ägypten und ägyptisches Leben im Altertum* (Tübingen: Mohr, 1922-23), p. 73. Cf. also D. Müller, "Der gute Hirte: Ein Beitrag zur Geschichte ägyptischer Bildrede," *Zeitschrift für ägyptische Sprache und Altertumskunde* 86 (1961) 126-44.

56. Leiden I, 344 rev. ix:2. Cf. A. Erman, *The Literature of the Ancient Egyptians,* tr. A. M. Blackman (London: Methuen, 1927), p. 83.

a shepherd" (1 K. 22:17). Our text does not specifically identify the persons whom Ezekiel refers to as "shepherds." In the light of his dependence on Jer. 23:1-6 in particular, and Jeremianic use of the expression in general,[57] it is tempting to interpret "shepherds" here as a general reference to the noblemen around Zedekiah, including the elders in Jerusalem whom he has observed pursuing their idolatrous ways in the vision of ch. 8; and the officers of 22:27, who tear their prey like wolves; and perhaps even the false prophets of ch. 13, who announce "Peace, Peace!" when there is no peace; and the leaders of the exilic community. However, two considerations point to a more limited application to the former kings of Judah. First, later in this chapter Ezekiel will deal with fat members of the flock who bully their fellow sheep (vv. 16-19). This refers apparently to the entire ruling class, who are guilty of abusing their power within the flock. Ezekiel maintains the distinction between shepherds and sheep, even powerful sheep. Second, according to vv. 23-24, the appointment of a single, good shepherd, David, who acts on behalf of the divine Shepherd, represents the solution to the present problem of a series of bad shepherds.[58] Ezekiel's use of the name "Israel" coheres with his conviction that the exiles, this remnant of the kingdom of Judah, also represented the nation of Israel. In so doing, however, he modifies the Jeremianic *Vorlage*, which had employed the more personal expression *'ammî*, "my people" (Jer. 23:2).

On the surface the opening pronouncement *hôy rōʿê yiśrāʾēl*, followed by the accusation in participial form, resembles the opening of Ezekiel's earlier message against the false prophets (13:2), creating in the reader an anticipation of a normal woe oracle. However, the common rendering, "Woe to the shepherds of Israel," overlooks a small but important syntactical difference between the two texts — the absence of *lamed* after *hôy*. Without the *lamed*, *hôy* may either function simply as a vocative particle, without any overtones of woe,[59] or even introduce a positive message (Isa. 55:1). As in Amos 6:1, it is best understood here simply as a call for attention: *Hey!*[60] The present form signals a shift in rhetorical function from 13:2. Whereas 13:1-16 is

---

57. Jeremiah uses only the pl. form, *rōʿîm*, always with reference to leaders in general, but never of a specific member of the Davidic house (Jer. 3:15; 10:21; 22:22; 23:1-4; 25:34-37; 50:6). In Jer. 2:8 the word occurs alongside priests, lawyers, and prophets. Note also Zechariah's similar reference to incompetent and worthless shepherds in 10:3 and 11:4-17, and Jesus' reference to thieves and robbers in John 10:1.

58. So also Duguid, *Ezekiel and the Leaders*, pp. 39-40.

59. The difference is reflected in LXX, which renders *hôy* as Οὐαί in 13:2 but as Ὦ in this text.

60. See J. J. M. Roberts, "Amos 6:1-7," in *Understanding the Word*, Fest. B. W. Anderson, ed. J. T. Butler, et al., JSOTSup 37 (Sheffield: JSOT Press, 1985), p. 156. He provides further bibliography.

construed as a woe oracle from start to finish, this is not the case here. Admittedly, the opening accusation (vv. 2-6), followed by an announcement of judgment (vv. 7-10), is typical of woe oracles. Within the context of vv. 1-10, however, as well as the rest of the chapter, these verses provide the background for what will emerge as a genuine salvation oracle. Indeed, the primary focus is not on the shepherds but on the flock. The leaders are introduced mainly because their actions have precipitated the crisis and created the need for divine intervention on behalf of the sheep.

According to vv. 2-6, the flock has been jeopardized because of gross malpractice by the leaders, who have been tending *(rō'eh)* themselves instead of caring for *(rō'eh)* the sheep. This may be acceptable in real life, where shepherds are justifiably motivated by self-interest, but when the image is used metaphorically of humans tending humans, the shepherd holds office for the sake of the ruled.[61]

3-4 Shifting to the second person of direct address, these verses concretize the general indictment with a series of specific charges. Cast in inverted word order for emphasis, the charges break down into two categories, crimes of commission and crimes of omission. Each group ends with a general statement of principle.

3 Ezekiel charges the rulers with three crimes of commission. First, they *consume* the milk of their flock. The verb *'ākal* (lit. "to eat") suggests a solid milk product, perhaps curds or cheese. Again in real life, consuming the milk of the sheep is not an exploitative act, but here it is made to look like robbery. Second, the shepherds fleece the flock: *the wool you wear.* This too is natural in a pastoral economy, but Ezekiel's figure assumes the forceful removal of wool, making it look like the sheep are left naked before the elements. Third, they *butcher the fatlings (habběrî'â).* The verb *zābaḥ* often denotes the slaughter of a sacrificial animal, especially for the *zebaḥ,* "sacrificial" meal. But here the verb functions simply as a synonym for *ṭābaḥ,*[62] without any religious overtones. Shepherds do raise sheep for their mutton, but in this metaphorical context, such slaughter represents the most blatant violation of the shepherd's role, presumably judicial murder (cf. 7:23; 9:9; etc.). The triad of accusations concludes with a reiteration of the general charge in v. 2. The rulers have taken excellent care of themselves, but they have not cared for the flock.

4 The crimes of omission reflect a stratum of Israelite "pastors"

---

61. Cf. Zimmerli, *Ezekiel 2,* pp. 214-15; Hossfeld, *Untersuchungen,* p. 259. On this Deuteronomic theology of leadership see Deut. 17:14-20. But the theory of "servant leadership" was not distinctly Israelite. See "The Advice to a Prince," in Lambert, *Babylonian Wisdom Literature,* pp. 110-15.

62. Deut. 12:15, 21; 1 Sam. 28:24; 2 K. 19:21; 2 Chr. 18:2.

representing the antithesis of responsible shepherds. First, they have shown no concern for the physical health of the flock. They have not strengthened *(ḥizzēq)* the weak *(naḥĕlôt),* healed *(rippē')* the sick *(ḥôlâ),* or bound up *(ḥābaš)* the injured *(nišberet).* Second, they have shown no concern for the sheep that have left the flock. They have neither gone after the strays nor sought the lost. Instead of caring *(rā'â)* for the flock, the shepherds have ruled over them with harshness *(ḥāzĕqâ)* and brutality *(perek).*

5-6 These verses describe the disastrous effects of the irresponsible conduct of the rulers. To have leaders like this is worse than being shepherdless. Scattered, the sheep roam about the mountains and high hills, defenseless prey for all the wild animals *(ḥayat haśśādeh).* The parallelism of the final two lines summarizes the bitter fate of the nation: there is no one to seek the scattered sheep.

Whereas the opening lines of this oracle lead the reader to expect a regular woe oracle directed against the rulers of Israel, the unexpected insertion of *my flock (ṣō'nî)* in v. 6 betrays Yahweh's and the prophet's primary concern. The abused sheep are Yahweh's flock, not the rulers'. Theirs was a delegated authority and they would answer to him for the manner in which they have exercised leadership. But *my flock* is more than an expression of ownership; it is a term of endearment. Finally, after what seems to have been an endless series of judgmental pronouncements against his own nation, a change in the divine disposition is evident. Jerusalem has fallen and her population is dispersed, but Yahweh, the divine shepherd, has not forgotten his people.

Ezekiel's portrayal of Yahweh in the role of shepherd follows another common Near Eastern notion of deities functioning as shepherds over humans. The perception is reflected in divine epithets like Marduk's *re-e'-i tenišêti,* "the shepherd of the people," and Akkadian personal names like *Ir-a-ni* ^dMarduk, "Marduk has shepherded me," and ^dŠamaš-ri-ú-a, "Shamash is my shepherd," which is strikingly similar to *yhwh rō'î,* "Yahweh is my shepherd," in Ps. 23:1.[63] Ezekiel's characterization of Yahweh as the shepherd of Israel

---

63. See Erra Epic, I:3; cf. *AHW,* p. 978. On these names see Stamm, *Akkadische Namengebung,* p. 189. The role of Shamash, the sun god, is celebrated in the concluding line of "The Babylonian Theodicy": "The shepherd Shamash guides the people like a god" (Lambert, *Babylonian Wisdom Literature,* pp. 88-89, line 297) and the following excerpt from a hymn in his honor:

O Shamash . . .
Thou art holding the ends of the earth suspended
   from the midst of heaven.
The people of the world, all of them, thou dost watch over.
Whatever Ea, the counselor-king, has willed to create,
   thou art guarding altogether.

draws on a long-standing Israelite tradition, dating back to the patriarch Jacob, who acknowledged God as "my shepherd all my days" (Gen. 48:15) and identified Yahweh by the title *rō'eh*, "shepherd," alongside other epithets.[64] With his present identification of Israel as "my flock," Yahweh reaffirms his divine kingship over the nation.[65] The manner in which he will exercise his kingship is explained in the remainder of the chapter.

(2) The Sentencing of the Shepherds of Israel (34:7-10)

These verses describe Yahweh's response to the crisis faced by his flock. A twofold appeal to hear the divine declaration (vv. 7, 9) leads the reader to expect an announcement of judgment upon the irresponsible rulers. But his primary interest obviously remains the flock. First, the shepherds are never directly addressed, but referred to in the third person. Second, vv. 8-10 are dominated by the sixfold occurrence of the *Leitwort ṣō'nî*, "my flock." Third, the pronouncements are framed by references to the present fate of the flock as food (*'oklâ*) for predators. The attention paid the shepherds serves as a foil for this principal concern.

On formal and substantive grounds this subunit divides into two segments of roughly equal length, each opened with an appeal to hear the word of Yahweh. But the declarations are quite different.

7-8 The first, which begins with an oath formula that is never completed, reiterates the crisis of the people. The divine patron bemoans the desperate condition of his flock; they have become spoil (*baz*) and prey (*'oklâ*) for all the wild animals. Responsibility for this state of affairs is placed squarely on the shoulders of the shepherds, who, having been appointed by Yahweh to care for his flock, have exploited the office for personal gain.

9-10 Yahweh announces his fundamental opposition to the shepherds.[66] He will rescue his flock from the hands of the shepherds by removing the shepherds from office and putting an end to their parasitism. The first

---

Those endowed with life, thou likewise dost tend;
Thou indeed art their shepherd both above and below.
Faithfully thou dost continue to pass through the heavens;
The broad earth thou dost visit daily. (*ANET*, pp. 387-88)

On the divine shepherd motif see further Dürr, *Ursprung und Ausbau*, pp. 121-22; Seibert, *Hirt-Herde-König*, pp. 15-16.

64. *'ăbîr ya'ăqōb*, "Mighty One of Jacob," *'eben yiśrā'ēl*, "Stone of Israel," *'ēl 'ăbîkā*, "God of your Father," and *šadday*, "Almighty." Gen. 49:24-25.

65. Cf. Ps. 80:2-4 (Eng. 1-3); 95:3-7; Mic. 2:12-13; 7:14. For further discussion see Block, *Gods of the Nations*, pp. 56-60.

66. On the challenge formula *hinĕnî 'al/'el*, see my *Ezekiel: Chapters 1–24*, pp. 201-2.

statement, *I will hold them responsible,* involves a typically Ezekielian shift in verb meaning. Whereas in v. 6 *dāraš* had meant simply "to look for," now, followed by *mîyyādām* (lit. "from their hand"), it expresses the legal disposition of calling an evildoer to account, in this case holding the criminal shepherds accountable for the fate of the flock.[67] The imagery of v. 10b borders on caricature. Since the shepherds, who had been appointed by Yahweh to care for his sheep, have not only neglected their duty but turned into ravenous wolves themselves, Yahweh is compelled to intervene and rescue *(hiṣṣîl)* his sheep from their jaws. For the rulers this is an announcement of judgment, but for the flock it is a message of hope.

b. The Nature of the Deliverance (34:11-22)

11 " '*For thus has the Lord Yahweh declared:*

Here I am![68] *I will seek the welfare of my flock, and examine them carefully.* 12 *Just as a shepherd examines*[69] *his herd, when*[70] *he is present among his scattered flock,*[71] *so I will examine my flock. I will rescue them from all the places where they have been scattered on a day of dark clouds.*[72] 13 *I will lead them out from the peoples, gather them from the countries, and bring them to their own land.*[73] *I will*

67. S. Wagner, *TDOT,* 3:297; G. Gerleman, *THAT,* 1:461.

68. *hinĕnî 'ānî,* with disjunctive accent and followed by *waw*-consecutive perfect, occurs only here and in v. 20 (cf. 6:3, which has the participle). The construction expresses firm determination. See Muraoka, *Emphatic Words,* p. 139; Joüon-Muraoka, *Grammar,* §146d.

69. On the Aramaized form of *baqqāret,* see Wagner, *Aramaismen,* p. 133.

70. Lit. "on the day."

71. *bĕyôm hĕyôtô bĕtôk ṣō'nô niprāšôt* is difficult but not incomprehensible. LXX borrows expressions from the latter part of the verse in describing the day ("in a day in which there is gloom and cloud"), dropping the suffix, and reading *niprāšôt,* from *pāraš,* "to be separated, made distinct" (Niphal), as *niprāśôt,* from *pāraś,* "to be scattered." Syr. omits the last part of the phrase and characterizes the day as "in the day of storm" *(bywm' dzyq').* Cooke *(Ezekiel,* p. 380) suggests *btwk,* which ill suits the context, is dittography of *hywt[w].*

72. The conjoined pair, lit. "day of cloud and deep gloom," represents a stock hendiadys for "dark clouds" (cf. Brongers, *OTS* 14 [1965] 108-9), elsewhere associated with the Sinai theophany (Deut. 4:11; Ps. 97:2; occurring disjunctively in Exod. 19:16; 20:21), or the coming day of Yahweh (Joel 2:2; Zeph. 1:15). Ezekiel's "day of dark clouds" is a euphemism for the latter, which identifies the fall of Jerusalem (13:5; 22:24; also ch. 7).

73. The triad of expressions here represents standard prophetic new exodus terminology (cf. 20:34-35, 41-42; 36:24; 37:12, 21). Whereas Ezekiel often refers to "the land of Israel" *('admat yiśrā'ēl,* 7:2; 11:17; 12:19, 22; 13:9; 20:38, 42; 21:7, 8; 25:3; 33:24; 36:6; 37:12; 38:18, 19), suffixed forms occur only in the restoration oracles *('admatĕkem,* "your land," 36:24; 37:14; *'admātām,* "their land," 28:25; 34:27; 37:21; 39:26, 28).

tend them on the mountains of Israel, in the valleys, and in all of the inhabited places[74] *of the land.*[75] 14 *In lush meadows*[76] *I will tend them, and on the lofty mountains of Israel*[77] *will be their pasture.*[78] *There they will lie down*[79] *in lush pasture, and feed on rich meadows on the mountains of Israel.* 15 *I myself will tend my flock, and I myself will let them lie down*[80] *— the declaration of the Lord Yahweh.*[81] 16 *The lost I will seek; the strays I will fetch; the injured I will bind up; and the sick I will strengthen. But the fat*[82] *and the healthy ones*[83] *I will police;*[84] *I will tend them*[85] *with justice.*

17 *Now as for you, my sheep,*[86] *thus has the Lord Yahweh declared: Look, I will judge between one sheep and another, that is, between*

74. *môšĕbê* is a hapax masc. form replacing *môšĕbôt* (cf. 6:6, 14 and elsewhere in the OT). G. R. Driver (*Bib* 19 [1938] 181) recognizes a root cognate to Arab. *wasaba*, "to be lush with grass."

75. *hārîm*, "mountains," and *'ăpîqîm*, "valleys," have appeared in other quatrads (with *gĕbā'ôt*, "hills," and *gē'āyōt*, "ravines," in 6:3; 35:8; 36:4, 6) and triads (31:12; 32:5-6; cf. the pairs *hārîm* and *gib'â* in 34:6; *hārîm* and *gē'āyôt* in 7:16). In place of the expected *gĕbā'ôt* or *gē'āyôt* is *môšĕbê hā'āreṣ*, "the habitable places of the land," which hints at the rebuilding of the population centers (cf. my *Ezekiel: Chapters 1-24*, pp. 221ff.).

76. *mir'eh*, a noun from the same root as *rā'â*, "to tend, graze," and *rō'eh*, "shepherd."

77. Two Hebrew mss., Targ., and LXX read sg. "mountain," as in the messianic and cultic contexts of 17:23 and 20:40.

78. *nāweh* is cognate to Akk. *nawûm*, used in the Mari texts of seminomadic encampments. Cf. A. Malamat, "Mari and the Bible: Some Patterns of Tribal Organization and Institutions," *JAOS* 82 (1962) 147; idem, "Aspects of Tribal Societies in Mari and Israel," RAI, 15:135-37.

79. LXX ἐκεῖ καὶ κοιμηθήσονται καὶ ἐκεῖ ἀναπαύσονται provides a double translation of *šām tarbaṣnâ bĕnāweh*. Cf. 16:14; 17:23; 20:18; etc.

80. LXX adds the recognition formula after this statement.

81. LXX τάδε λέγει κύριος replaces the signatory formula with the citation formula, introducing a new section.

82. With support from LXX, many delete *wĕ'et-haššĕmēnâ* as a gloss, but LXX may have harmonized the reading with v. 4. Cf. Allen, *Ezekiel 20-48*, p. 157. *haššēmānâ* plays on the same root as *šāmēn*, "rich, fertile," in v. 14.

83. Note Targ.'s interpretive rendering, *wyt ḥṭ'y' wyt ḥyyby'*, "sinners and guilty ones."

84. Reading *'ešmōr* for MT *'ašmîd*, "to destroy," with LXX, Vulg., and Syr., though many delete the word as a gloss. The Hebrew letters *d* and *r* were easily confused in both the archaic and square scripts. Cf. Allen, *Ezekiel 20-48*, p. 157.

85. LXX, Syr., and Vulg. add the copula to *'er'ennâ*. The sg. suffix continues the objects of the previous verbs, all of which have been sg.

86. LXX reads *wĕ'attēn haṣṣō'n*, "As for you, O sheep"; Targ. interprets *w'twn 'my*, "but you my people." On the vocalization of *'attēnâ* see 13:11, 20; also Gen. 31:6.

the rams and the bucks.[87] 18 *Is it not enough for you*[88] *to feed on the lush pasture, that you must trample the rest of your pastures with your feet? And is it not enough for you to drink the clear water,*[89] *that you must foul that which is left with your feet?*[90] 19 *Meanwhile my flock must feed on what your feet have trampled, and drink what your feet have fouled.*

20 *Therefore, thus has the Lord Yahweh declared to them:*[91]

Look! I myself will judge between the fat[92] *and the scrawny sheep.* 21 *Because you throw your weight around*[93] *with flank and shoulder, and you butt all the weak with your horns, until you have scattered them abroad,* 22 *therefore*[94] *I will rescue my flock, so they will no longer be prey; and I will judge between one sheep and another.'* "[95]

As noted earlier, the references to deliverance in vv. 12 and 22 form an *inclusio* around the second panel of this chapter. This section subdivides into two parts, however, each of which develops a unique aspect of the salvation effected by Yahweh.

(1) Deliverance from External Threats (34:11-16)

11 The particle *kî* serves a transitional function, linking the citation formula with the preceding and introducing an explanation of the way Yahweh intends to rescue (*hiṣṣaltî*, v. 10) the sheep. Meanwhile the evil shepherds disappear from view completely, and the exilic situation is more clearly reflected in vv. 12-13. The divine savior begins his glorious message of deliverance by announcing his presence among the oppressed: "Here I

87. Targ. interprets, "sinners and guilty persons."

88. LXX ὅτι reads *kî*. Cf. Num. 16:9, 13. Without this particle an infinitive is expected, as in Isa. 7:13.

89. *mišqaʿ mayim*, "clear water," is a hapax from *šāqaʿ*, "to sink," the reference being to water in which the sediments and dirt have settled to the bottom.

90. The accusation in v. 18 is cast in the form of two parallel rhetorical questions:

hameʿaṭ mikkem hammirʿeh haṭ ṭôbtirʿû wĕyeter mirʿêkem tirmĕsû bĕraglêkem ûmišqaʿ mayim tištû wĕʾēt hannôtārîm bĕraglêkem tirpōšûn.

91. *ʾălêhem* is missing in several Hebrew mss., LXX, and Syr., but reflected in Targ. and Vulg.

92. *biryâ* should be repointed either as *bĕrîʾâ* or as *bĕrîyâ*. Cf. Bauer-Leander, *Grammatik*, §74h′.

93. *tehdōpû*, lit. "thrust, push."

94. The conjunction on *wĕhôšaʿtî* functions for *lākēn*, which normally follows *yaʿan* in a judgment oracle. Cf. S. R. Driver, *Tenses*, §123γ.

95. Under the influence of v. 17, Syr. adds *wbyt dkrʾ ldkrʾ*.

am!"[96] This is followed in vv. 11-16 by a long chain of verbs with Yahweh as their subject, highlighting this event as an act of Yahweh himself.

The last half of v. 11 functions as a thesis statement. The first verb, *dāraš*, is borrowed from v. 10, but in typical Ezekielian fashion, its meaning shifts again from the basic "seek, look for" (v. 6), to "demand, hold accountable" (v. 10), to "pursue," whose judicial sense is clarified by the following semantic correlative *examine (biqqēr)*. Ezekiel uses this root only here and twice in v. 12. It is a priestly expression whose meaning is illustrated by Leviticus, where it refers to the physical examination of a leper (13:36), and in cultic contexts, to examination of a potential sacrificial animal (27:33).[97] Here *biqqēr* denotes a careful examination of the sheep's condition, in which case the previous "to seek my flock" may either mean "to examine carefully" or, more likely, serve as an abbreviation for "to seek the welfare of."[98]

12-15   These verses outline Yahweh's procedure by listing a series of divine actions whose textual arrangement is both logical and chronological. (a) Having arrived at the scene of his scattered flock, Yahweh will examine their physical condition.[99] (b) Yahweh will rescue the flock from the clutches of the enemy. Now the jaws of the predators are no longer the evil rulers (v. 10) but the geographic locations (*měqômôt*) where the exiles are found,[100] the event of their dispersion being characterized as *běyôm 'ānān wa'ărāpel* (lit. "on a day of cloud and deep gloom"). (c) He will bring the flock out

96. Targ. *h'n' mtgly,* "Behold, I will reveal myself," highlights the revelatory nature of the event.

97. Cf. also Ps. 27:4 (thus H.- J. Kraus, *Psalms 1–59,* tr. H. C. Oswald, Continental Commentary [Minneapolis: Augsburg, 1988], p. 334; but Dahood [*Psalms,* 1:167] sees here a denominative verb from *bōqer,* "morning") and 2 K. 16:15 (cf. M. Cogan and H. Tadmor, *II Kings,* AB [Garden City, N.Y.: Doubleday, 1988], p. 189). Nabataean *mbqr'* denotes a temple official in charge of examining sacrifices (*DISO,* p. 41). The Qumran Manual of Discipline (1QS 6:12, 20) identifies the overseer of the community as a *mbqr* (thus A. Dupont-Sommer, *The Essene Writings from Qumran,* tr. G. Vermes [Cleveland and New York: World, 1961], p. 86, though J. Jeremias sees here a prototype of the NT *episkopos; see Jerusalem in the Time of Jesus,* tr. F. H. and C. H. Cave [Philadelphia: Fortress, 1969], pp. 260-61). The Damascus Document (CD 13:7-10) describes the overseer's duties thus: "He shall have pity on them as a father of his children and shall carry them in all their dependency as a shepherd his flock. He shall unloose all the bonds which bind them that there may no more be any oppressed or broken among the congregation" (ibid., p. 157; cf. C. Rabin, *Zadokite Documents* (Oxford: Clarendon, 1958), pp. 64-65.

98. For the former see Zimmerli, *Ezekiel 2,* p. 216. Variations of *dāraš šālôm,* "to seek the peace," of someone occur in Deut. 23:7 (Eng. 6); Jer. 29:7; 38:4; Ezra 9:12; Est. 10:3.

99. Unlike Jer. 23:3, Ezekiel does not attribute the scattering of the sheep to the same person who gathers them.

100. Cf. Ezekiel's identification of the region of the diaspora as "the lands" (*hā'ărāṣôt,* 11:17; 20:34, 41; 34:6) or "the nations" (*haggôyim,* 28:25; 29:13).

(hôṣî') of their places of exile. (d) He will gather *(qibbēṣ)* the flock from the countries that hold them. (e) He will bring *(hēbî')* them to their own land. (f) He will tend *(rā'â)* the flock on Israelite soil.

14-15 These verses elaborate on Yahweh's shepherding style. In contrast to the self-serving rulers of Israel, he promises to graze the flock in fine meadows *(mir'eh ṭôb)* and on the lofty mountains of Israel *(hārîm mĕrôm yiśrā'ēl)*. The effects of his care are described from the sheep's perspective: they will lie down, viz., be secure, in good pasture *(nāweh ṭôb)* and graze in fertile meadows *(mir'eh šāmēn)*. The same ideas are reiterated in v. 15, though the addition of emphatic *I myself* highlights Yahweh's personal role in providing rest and provender. The promise is sealed with the divine signatory formula.

The present picture of Yahweh the good shepherd expands on 11:17 but is reminiscent of several other OT texts as well, including Jer. 23:3 and the familiar Ps. 23, and two texts in Micah:

> I will surely assemble *('āsap)* Jacob, all of you;
> I will surely gather *(qibbēṣ)* the remnant of Israel;
> I will make them all like sheep in the fold;
> Like a flock in the midst of its pen,
> They will be noisy with people. (2:12)

> In that day — the declaration of Yahweh —
> I will gather *('āsap)* the lame,
> And gather *(qibbēṣ)* the outcast *(hannidaḥ),*
> And those I have treated harshly.
> I will transform the lame into a remnant,
> And the expelled into a mighty nation.
> And Yahweh will reign over them on Mount Zion,
> Now and evermore. (Mic. 4:6-8)

While texts involving the regathering of Israel are often considered postexilic interpolations,[101] this imagery has a long history in the ancient Near East. After identifying himself as "the shepherd, called by Enlil," Hammurabi speaks of having "collected the scattered people of Isin."[102] Elsewhere in a self-laudatory text he declares: "The scattered population of Sumer and Akkad I gathered; I offered them bread and drink; with blessing and prosperity I pastured them."[103] Similarly, at the election of Merodach-baladan, Marduk is

---

101. Cf. L. C. Allen, *The Books of Joel, Amos, Obadiah, Jonah and Micah,* NICOT (Grand Rapids: Eerdmans, 1976), pp. 245-46; Mendecki, *BZ* 27 (1983) 218-21.

102. *ANET,* p. 164.

103. Cf. Dürr, *Ursprung und Ausbau,* p. 120.

supposed to have pronounced, "This man is indeed the shepherd who once again gathers the dispersed." The Babylonian king himself declares that he has gathered and restored them.[104] The "Prophetic Speech of Marduk" lacks the terms "shepherd" and "flock," but after announcing the appearance of a king/prince, the divine patron of Babylon declares: "This prince will be mighty and without rival. The city he will rule. The dispersed he will gather. . . . The scattered land he will gather and its foundations he will establish."[105] In Esarhaddon's account of the reconstruction of Babylon, the Assyrian king portrays himself as the divinely chosen king who, after rebuilding the city, regathered the Babylonians who had been taken off as slaves and prisoners, and restored them to full Babylonian citizenship.[106]

These texts follow a common pattern: the divine patron names a human shepherd-king, who functions as the agent of the actual regathering. The closest biblical analogue occurs in Isa. 44:28, where, following a description of his own redemption of Israel and the rebuilding and repopulation of Jerusalem, Yahweh announces that he has chosen Cyrus as his shepherd. The unique feature of this text is that Yahweh the divine patron regathers the sheep himself.

16 This verse is transitional, reviewing Yahweh's salvific activity on the one hand, and preparing the way for vv. 17-22 on the other. The summary consists of six short sentences exhibiting a modified mirror image of v. 4:

V. 4 A   The weak (*naḥĕlôt*) you have not strengthened (*ḥizzeq*).
     B   The sick (*ḥôlâ*) you have not healed (*rippē'*).
     C   The injured (*nišberet*) you have not bound up (*ḥābaš*).
     D   The stray (*niddaḥat*) you have not fetched (*hēšîb*).
     E   The lost (*'ōbedet*) you have not sought (*biqqēš*).
V. 16 E' The lost (*'ōbedet*) I will seek (*biqqēš*).
     D' The stray (*niddaḥat*) I will fetch (*hēšîb*).
     C' The injured (*nišberet*) I will bind up (*ḥābaš*).
     B' The sick (*ḥôlâ*)
     A' I will strengthen (*ḥizzēq*).

Except for B' and A', which telescope A and B of v. 4, the elements are identical. By inverting the sequence Ezekiel emphasizes that with Israel's restoration the tragedies of the past will be reversed. By recasting negative statements as positive affirmations, he deliberately portrays Yahweh as a good shepherd, the antithesis of the earlier evil shepherds.

104. Ibid.
105. Aššur IV:4-5, 21-22. Cf. Block, *Gods of the Nations,* p. 174; T. Longman III, *Fictional Akkadian Autobiography* (Winona Lake, Ind.: Eisenbrauns, 1991), pp. 234-35.
106. Borger, *Asarhaddon,* pp. 25-26, episode 37.

The last two statements in v. 16 are difficult, but it seems that the rulers were not the only ones exploiting the weak. The *fat (haššĕmēnâ)* and the *healthy* or strong *(hăzāqâ)*, that is, the bullies within the population, are hereby forewarned that Yahweh *will police* them and *tend them with justice.*[107] On the basis of vv. 17-22, with which the term *mišpāṭ* provides an obvious link, Yahweh's action involves imposing restraints on the healthier members of the flock to prevent them from misusing their superior strength against the weaker sheep.

(2) Deliverance from Internal Threats (34:17-22)

Although the shift in style and content sets vv. 17-22 off literarily from its textual environment,[108] this block plays a vital role in the progression of the oracle by offering an exposition of the theme of internal judgment *(šāpaṭ)* announced in v. 16. An additional link with the preceding is provided by the notion of deliverance *(hôšîaʿ, v. 22)*, even if the nature of the deliverance shifts slightly. The absence of a formal conclusion and the commencement of v. 23 with the *waw*-consecutive as if there were no break at all caution against deleting this segment or treating it in isolation. Though linked rhetorically by *lākēn,* "therefore," in v. 20, these verses divide into two halves (vv. 17-19, 20-22), each of which begins with the citation formula, followed by *hinnēh* plus the threat of divine judgment upon particular sheep. Whereas the first half does not move beyond the accusation, the second takes the form of an independent judgment speech, with its own formal indictment beginning with *yaʿan,* "Because," in v. 21, followed by the announcement of judgment in v. 22.

17 The first half opens with a direct appeal to the flock to observe the activity of Yahweh: he will judge *(šāpaṭ)* between one sheep and another and between the *rams (ʾêlîm)* and the *bucks* or male goats *(ʿattûdîm)*. While the collective terms *ṣōʾn* and *śeh* refer to flocks of both sheep and/or goats,[109] here these expressions identify the males of the respective species. The former

---

107. Note the ironical use of *šāmar* (with the versions) and *rāʿâ*, which elsewhere mean "to guard, watch," and "to tend, feed," respectively.

108. (1) The section begins with its own formulae: *wĕʾattēnâ* followed by a vocative, and the citation formula. (2) It is dominated by its own keyword, *šāpaṭ*, "to judge." (3) It is framed by "I will judge between one sheep and another," which occurs at the beginning and at the end (in slightly different forms). (4) The sheep are addressed directly in the second person; elsewhere they are treated as a third party. (5) Only here is the relationship between members of the flock the central issue; elsewhere the issue is their relationship with superiors or external enemies. (6) For the first time the flock is referred to as *śeh*, rather than *ṣōʾn*.

109. See Cansdale, *Animals of Bible Lands*, pp. 44-56.

is the most common animal designation for human leaders in the OT; the latter will recur in 39:18, referring to animals/leaders who have been sacrificed or judged.[110] In the present context these terms designate individuals within the flock at the top of the butting order, the *zĕqēnîm*, "elders," and *śārîm*, "officers," of earlier texts, but not to be confused with the *rōʿîm*, "shepherds," dealt with in vv. 2-10, who represent the last kings of Judah. The "fat sheep" of vv. 16 and 20 would refer to the same class of rapacious and self-serving lay leaders of the community.[111]

18-19   Yahweh's deliverance of his flock from their leaders and from the enemies among whom they are exiled will obviously not solve all the community's problems. Now the weaker members are being victimized by aggressive and robust males. Not satisfied with filling their own stomachs, they trample the grass that remains and foul the drinking water with their feet, denying their colleagues this nourishment. Such bullying calls for a response.

20   Instead of introducing an anticipated announcement of judgment upon the greedy animals, *Therefore (lākēn)* here functions rhetorically to signal an afterwave, announcing divine intervention in the troubled situation. *I myself will judge.* Unlike 20:32-38, where the verb *šāpaṭ* had referred to legal activity involved in establishing guilt and purging wickedness, in this context, where both the crime and the offender are known, the word speaks of establishing justice, removing the cause of relational dysfunction, and restoring shalom. As the divine shepherd, Yahweh intervenes to rescue the weak from the strong and to reestablish order in the community.[112]

21-22   Yahweh reiterates that he himself will mediate because the robust animals have not only denied weaker victims access to food and water but also pushed them around, scattering them in all directions, another allusion to the exiles in Babylon. He offers hope to the oppressed by taking his stand on their side. Like the *šōpĕṭîm* in the book of Judges, the divine "judge" functions as the deliverer for his people.[113]

---

110. For the former see 17:13; 30:13; 31:11, 14; 32:20; 39:18. Elsewhere Exod. 15:15; 2 K. 24:15; Jer. 4:22; Ps. 2:5; 58:2 (Eng. 1); Job 41:17. For a discussion see Miller, *UF* 2 (1970) 181-82. Cf. the use of the latter term for rulers in Isa. 14:9; 34:6-7; Zech. 10:3. On this use of the term see Miller, ibid., p. 184.

111. So also Duguid, *Ezekiel and the Leaders,* pp. 121-22.

112. See Hossfeld, *Untersuchungen,* pp. 266-67.

113. Cf. Zimmerli, *Ezekiel 2,* p. 218. Consistent with the foregoing, v. 22 highlights the deliverance of the flock, not the punishment of the wicked, as the primary concern of the oracle.

c. The Goal of the Deliverance: Yahweh's Covenant of Peace (34:23-31)

23 " 'Then I will appoint a single[114] shepherd over them[115] to tend them — my servant David.[116] He will tend them,[117] and be their shepherd. 24 Then I, Yahweh, will be their God, and my servant[118] David will be ruler among them. I am Yahweh; I have spoken.[119]

25 Then I will make a covenant of peace for them.[120] I will eliminate vicious animals from the land so they may dwell securely[121] in the desert, and sleep[122] in the forest. 26 I will make them and the environs about my hill a blessing.[123] I will send down the shower in its season. They will be[124] showers of blessing. 27 The trees of the field will yield their fruit, and the land will yield its produce.[125] Then they will live securely[126] on their land. And they will know that I am Yahweh, when

114. LXX ἕτερον misreads 'ēḥād, "one," as 'aḥēr, "another."

115. The broader context calls for 'ălêhen (fem.) instead of MT masc. 'ălêhem. The inconsistency within this verse (cf. 'ethen, 'ōtām, lāhen) is attributable to the lack of a clear distinction between the figure (the sheep) and the reality (the people).

116. The present *plene* orthography of *dwyd* contrasts with the preference for the defective spelling *dwd* elsewhere (v. 24; 37:24-25). On the spelling of the name and its chronological significance for the development of the Hebrew language see Andersen and Forbes, *Spelling in the Hebrew Bible*, pp. 4-9; Rooker, *Biblical Hebrew in Transition*, pp. 68-70. The object marker 'ēt introduces a definite object in apposition to indefinite rō'eh, from which it is separated by wěrā'â 'ethen. On this use of 'et see Muraoka, *Emphatic Words*, p. 153.

117. This clause, missing in LXX, is often deleted as an intrusive explanatory gloss.

118. 'abdî is missing in LXX.

119. Syr. lacks the concluding formula.

120. LXX reads lĕdāwid, "for David."

121. LXX mistakenly drops lěbeṭaḥ.

122. Targ. "grow old" misreads MT yāšēn, "to sleep," as yāšan.

123. The difficulties posed by wěnātattî 'ôtām ûsěbîbôt gib'ātî běrākâ are reflected in the variations in the versions. As it stands, MT requires wě'et before sěbîbôt unless the sign of the direct object on 'ōtām is viewed as doing double duty. Zimmerli (*Ezekiel 2*, p. 210) follows LXX in deleting běrākâ. Targ. paraphrases gib'ātî, "my hill," as bêt miqdāšî, "my holy temple," and ends the line with wyhwn mbrkyn, "and they will be blessed," or "they will offer blessing." See Levey, *Ezekiel*, pp. 98-99. Some assume consonantal gb'ty is a corruption of b'tw, "in its time," perhaps under the influence of v. 6 (Allen, *Ezekiel 20-48*, p. 158), yielding an appropriate parallel to v. 26b, and then drop the copula on ûsěbîbôt with the the versions. 'ōtām sěbîbôt means "them in their environment." No solution so far proposed is convincing.

124. LXX omits yihyû.

125. yěbûlâ, from yābal, "to flow," suggests well-watered land.

126. LXX interprets lābeṭaḥ, "in hope of peace." Cf. Symmachus "without being afraid."

I break the bars of their yoke and rescue them from the power of those
who enslave them. 28 They will no longer be booty for the nations; nor
will the wild animals[127] *devour them. They will dwell securely, with*
no one terrorizing them. 29 I will provide them with a peaceful plan-
tation.[128] *No more will there be victims of famine in the land, nor will*
they suffer the derision of the nations. 30 They will know[129] *that I am*
Yahweh their God with them,[130] *and that they, the house of Israel, are*
my people. The declaration of the Lord Yahweh.

31 Now you[131] *are my flock; you are the human*[132] *flock of my*
pasture,[133] *and I*[134] *am your God.*[135]

The declaration of the Lord Yahweh.' "

127. Targ. interprets "the kings of the earth."

128. MT *lšm,* "for a name/renown," is followed by Vulg., but LXX, Targ., and Syr. appear to have read *šlm.* MT has been corrupted by metathesis. Thus *maṭṭaʿ šālôm,* which answers to *wĕnātattî šālôm bāʾāreṣ* in Lev. 26:6, is commonly interpreted, "And I will grant peace in the land," but a translation "I will plant/sow peace in the land" is also possible. Cf. Jesus' comment in Matt. 10:34, "Do not think that I have come to cast peace on the earth (βαλεῖν εἰρήνην ἐπὶ τὴν γῆν); I have not come to cast peace, but a sword." βάλλω is used of scattering seed in Mark 4:26 and Luke 13:19. B. F. Batto suggests that Jesus' announcement intentionally reverses Lev. 26:6 ("The Covenant of Peace: A Neglected Ancient Near Eastern Motif," *CBQ* 49 [1987] 205).

129. Numerous Hebrew mss. add *haggôyim,* "the nations," as the subject of the recognition formula.

130. Three Hebrew mss., LXX, and Syr. omit *ʾōtām,* "with them." Targ. paraphrases, "I am Yahweh their God and my Memra comes to their aid," on which see Levey, *Ezekiel,* p. 98.

131. LXX omits *wĕʾattēn* (fem.), which is difficult in any case, because masc. forms have predominated since v. 23. Nonetheless, these two lines may reflect the ambivalence of the entire paragraph, line 1 speaking more directly of the flock, hence the fem. form, and line 2 moving from the image to the reality, hence the masc. *ʾattem.*

132. *ʾādām* appears intrusive in the formulaic statement, and absent from 3 Hebrew mss., LXX, Syr., and Targ. The word may be a dittograph of the following *ʾattem* (Wevers, *Ezekiel,* p. 264) or a secondary interpretive insertion, perhaps under the influence of 36:37-38 (Allen, *Ezekiel 20–48,* p. 158). But G. R. Driver (*Bib* 35 [1954] 264) defends MT, arguing for a qualifying noun in the accusative case, "the sheep of my pasturage in men." Cf. 16:27.

133. *marʿîtî,* "my pasture," occurs elsewhere in Jer. 23:1; Ps. 74:1; 79:13; 95:7; 100:3.

134. Inserting the copula with LXX, Vulg., and Syr.

135. Several Hebrew mss., LXX, Vulg., and Syr. have harmonized the recognition formula with the conventional Ezekielian form by inserting *yhwh* before *ʾĕlōhêkem.* But Zimmerli (*Ezekiel 2,* p. 211) has defended MT by noting that the present statement involves the covenant formula that does not contain the divine name.

♦ Nature and Design

The attention moves abruptly from Yahweh's negative activity, viz., resolving problems within the flock, to exciting new positive actions on Israel's behalf. Although the opening *waw*-consecutive in v. 23 links this section to the preceding one, the dramatic shift in content alerts the reader to a new and climactic movement in the oracle. As noted earlier, this section divides into three segments, a larger midsection (vv. 25-30) sandwiched between two shorter pieces (vv. 23-24, 31). The divisions are formally marked by a modified form of the divine self-introduction formula in v. 24 and the recognition and signatory formulae in v. 30. Although each segment is distinctive in style and content, the grounds for interpreting them in relation to one another and to the chapter as a whole are strong. First, in contrast to the preceding focus on the removal of barriers to shalom, these parts share a common interest in Yahweh's affirmative actions in administering peace. Second, the association of Yahweh's appointment of a just ruler with the restoration of peace and security is consistent with other texts, both within Ezekiel and in other prophets.[136] Third, the third person pronouns in vv. 23-24 and 25-29 are dependent on an external source, viz., *ṣō'nî,* "my flock," in v. 22, for their antecedent. Fourth, the covenant formula, which summarizes the goal of Yahweh's salvific actions, appears at the beginning (v. 24) and at the end (v. 31), providing a framework for interpreting the intervening material. Consequently, although one may separate vv. 23-24 from the rest for the sake of convenience, the coherence among the parts is strong. In any case, the two principal motifs dealt with here, the appointment of David as under-shepherd of Yahweh's flock and the covenant of peace, are fundamental to the Jewish messianism that flourished in the intertestamental period.[137]

---

136. See Ezek. 17:22-24; 37:21-28; Jer. 23:1-8; 30:8-11; 33:12-26.

137. See S. H. Levey's definition of "messianism" (*The Messiah: An Aramaic Interpretation: The Messianic Exegesis of the Targum* [Cincinnati: Hebrew Union College–Jewish Institute of Religion, 1974], p. XIX): "the predication of a future Golden Age in which the central figure is a king primarily of Davidic lineage appointed by God. . . . It was believed that during the time of the Messiah the Hebrew people will be vindicated, its wrongs righted, the wicked purged from its midst, and its rightful place in the world secured. The Messiah will pronounce doom upon the enemies of Israel, will mete out reward and punishment in truth and in justice, and will serve as an ideal king ruling the entire world. The Messiah may not always be the active agent in these future events, but his personality must always be present, at least as the symbol of the glorious age which will be ushered in." Although the Hebrew eschatological vision shares many of these features, the involvement of the messianic figure distinguishes messianism from eschatology in general. In spite of Targ.'s refusal to recognize the Messiah in this text (or anywhere else in Ezekiel), the centrality of the Davidic personage, and the absence of any reference to fulfillment at the end of the age (cf. *bĕ'aḥărît hayyāmîm,* "in the latter days,"

(1) The Human Agent of Peace (34:23-24)

The repetitious and staccato style of vv. 23-24 reflects Ezekiel's increasing excitement as he approaches the climax of the oracle. The prophet begins his positive description of Israel's new day by announcing Yahweh's appointment of a new shepherd for Israel. These verses are packed with information on the new shepherd's status within Israel.

First, this ruler will be neither self-appointed nor elected by the people, but chosen by Yahweh himself.[138] Like his contemporary Jeremiah, Ezekiel perceives Israel as a theocracy.

Second, the shepherd will be alone, singular. The reference to *a single shepherd (rō'eh 'eḥād)* goes beyond Jer. 23:4, which has Yahweh installing responsible shepherds (pl.) to replace the present exploitative and irresponsible rulers. In announcing a single ruler Yahweh seeks a reversal of the division of Israel into northern and southern kingdoms that occurred after the death of Solomon (1 K. 11–12), as well as an end to the inconsistency of standards by which the last kings of Israel, from Josiah onward, had ruled. Like the rest of the prophets, Ezekiel perceived the nation as one and recognized as legitimate only the dynasty reigning from Jerusalem.[139]

Third, the shepherd will be *David*. Although this ruler is explicitly identified as David only twice outside this book,[140] Ezekiel's identification of the divinely installed king as David is based on a long-standing prophetic tradition. On the one hand, the 8th-century prophet Hosea had looked forward to the day when the children of Israel would "return and seek Yahweh their

---

38:16; *bĕ'aḥărît haššānîm,* "in the latter years," 38:8), this text, along with 37:21-28, is better classified as messianic rather than eschatological. A messianic interpretation is implied in LXX and Syr., and overt in Vulg. and in *Gen. Rab.* 97.

138. A principle established already in the "Mosaic charter for kingship," Deut. 17:14-20. *hēqîm,* "to raise up," in the sense of "to install in office," with Yahweh as the subject, is applied in the OT to the appointment of prophets (Deut. 18:15, 18; Jer. 29:15; Amos 2:11), judges (Judg. 2:16, 18), priests (1 Sam. 2:35), kings (1 K. 14:14; Jer. 30:9), watchmen (Jer. 6:17), deliverers (Judg. 3:9, 15), shepherds (Jer. 23:4, 5; Zech. 11:16), and even adversaries (1 K. 11:14).

139. He will expand on this notion in 37:15-24, where the term *'eḥād* occurs eleven times.

140. Jer. 23:5 speaks of raising up *for* David "a righteous Branch" (*ṣemaḥ ṣaddîq;* cf. 33:15); Amos 9:11 of restoring (*hēqîm*) "the fallen hut *of* David" (*sukkat dāwîd hannōpelet*). Cf. Isa. 9:5-6 (Eng. 6-7), which speaks of the child (*yeled*) on the throne of David (*kissē' dāwid*), Isa. 11:1 of "a shoot from the stump of Jesse" (*ḥōṭer miggēza' yišāy;* cf. "the root of Jesse," *šōreš yišay,* in v. 10). W. Gross ("Israel's Hope for the Renewal of the State," *JNSL* 14 [1988] 125-26) follows F. Hossfeld (*Untersuchungen zu Komposition und Theologie des Ezekielbuches,* FB 20 [Würzburg: Echter, 1977], pp. 230ff. and 284ff.) in deleting the reference to David as a late intrusion, dependent on Ezek. 37:24-25.

God and David their king."[141] On the other hand, Ezekiel's diction is closer to Jer. 30:8-10, which also combines the appointment of David with the anticipated restoration of the nation. There is no thought in these prophecies of the resurrection of the historical king, as some kind of David *redivivus*. Ezekiel's use of the singular "shepherd," and his emphasis on *'eḥād*, "one," also preclude the restoration of the dynasty in the abstract, that is, simply a series of kings. He envisions a single person, who may embody the dynasty but who occupies the throne himself.

Although Ezekiel's hope of a divinely appointed shepherd-king in the context of national restoration agrees with common Near Eastern thinking, his specific prediction of a revival of the nation's original royal house (excluding the failed Saulide experiment) contrasts with the general nature of extra-Israelite expectations.[142] Having earlier foretold and witnessed the fall of the Davidic house (ch. 17), Ezekiel now declares its restoration. His pronouncement is based on Yahweh's covenant with David, announced by Nathan the prophet (2 Sam. 7:8 = 1 Chr. 17:7). Significantly for our discussion, David's divine election had earlier been described as a call from the "pasture" *(nāweh),* from following the flock, to be "ruler" *(nāgîd)* of Yahweh's people Israel.[143] Yahweh's affirmation of the eternality of the Davidic covenant had provided the basis for all the prophetic hopes, a fact reflected most clearly in Jer. 33:17, 20-21, 25-26:

> David will never lack a man to occupy the throne of Israel. . . . If you could break my covenant with the day and my covenant with the night,

---

141. The statement is commonly deleted as a late Judean insertion. Cf. Zimmerli, *Ezekiel 2,* p. 219; H. W. Wolff, *A Commentary on the Book of the Prophet Hosea,* tr. G. Stansell, Hermeneia (Philadelphia: Fortress, 1974), p. 63. For a contrary opinion see F. I. Andersen and D. N. Freedman, *Hosea,* AB 24 (Garden City, N.Y.: Doubleday, 1980), p. 307.

142. The *ex eventu* reference to Cyrus with the archaic title "King of Elam" in the "Dynastic Prophecy" provides the nearest analogue. Cf. A. K. Grayson, *Babylonian Historical-Literary Texts* (Toronto: University of Toronto Press, 1975), pp. 24-37. The "Prophetic Speech of Marduk" (II:19-34) refers to the promised king simply as "a king of Babylon." For the text see Block, *Gods of the Nations,* p. 172; Longman, *Fictional Akkadian Autobiography,* p. 234. Other Akkadian prophecies define the tenures of a series of kings, but refer to them generically as *šarru.* Cf. A. K. Grayson and W. G. Lambert, "Akkadian Prophecies," *JCS* 18 (1964) 12-14.

143. Note the popular awareness of David's divine election reflected in 2 Sam. 5:2: "Yahweh said to you, 'You will shepherd *(tir'eh)* my people Israel, and you will be a ruler *(nāgîd)* over Israel.' " Cf. the psalmist's celebration of the same notion in Ps. 78:70-72: "He chose David, his servant, and took him from the sheepfolds. From caring for the nursing ewes he brought him to tend *(lir'ôt)* Jacob, his people, Israel his own possession. He tended *(rā'â)* them with integrity of heart; with his skillful hands he led them."

so that day and night should cease to appear at the proper time, then my covenant with David could also be broken with the result that he would cease to have a son reigning upon his throne. . . . As surely as I have established my covenant with night and day — the fixed laws of the universe — so surely I will never reject the descendants of Jacob and of my servant David; I will never fail to take rulers for the descendants of Abraham, Isaac, and Jacob from his descendants.[144]

But the capture of Zedekiah, and with it the collapse of the Davidic house in 586 B.C., must be viewed against the backdrop of this covenant. If Yahweh appeared to have revoked the covenant in allowing this collapse to happen, Ezekiel hereby announces that the ancient promise has not been forgotten. Yahweh would fulfill his irrevocable promise and his unfailing covenant to the house of David as the sole legitimate dynasty in Israel.

Fourth, the shepherd will be the *servant* of Yahweh. Ezekiel's repetition of *'abdî,* "my servant," simultaneously presents an intentional contrast with the self-seeking shepherds of vv. 1-10 and recalls the traditional view of David's willing subordination to Yahweh.[145] Moreover, in the OT *'ebed yhwh,* "servant of Yahweh," also functioned as an honorific title for those who stood in an official relationship to God, often with the implication of a special election to a task.[146] David's own standing is expressed most clearly by Yahweh himself, who identifies him as "David my servant, whom I have chosen" (1 K. 11:34).

Fifth, the shepherd will be a *ruler (nāśî',* usually "prince") in the midst of his people. Ezekiel's use of the archaic title *nāśî'* contrasts with Hosea and

144. The word *'ôlām* appears eight times in 2 Sam. 7:13, 16, 24-29. See esp. v. 13, "I will establish the throne of his kingdom forever," and v. 16, "Your dynasty *(bayit)* and your kingdom will endure before me forever; your kingdom will be established forever." The psalmist celebrates David's eternal title to the throne of Jerusalem even more enthusiastically in Ps. 89:29-30, 34-37 (Eng. 28-29, 33-36).

145. *'abdî* is used of David 31 times in the OT. See 2 Sam. 3:18; 7:5, 8, 26; etc. (further references in BDB, p. 714). The title is also applied to Hezekiah (2 Chr. 32:16), Zerubbabel (Hag. 2:23), and "my servant the Branch" (Zech. 3:8; cf. 6:12).

146. Accordingly the patriarchs served as the bearers of the divine revelation, promise, and blessing (Abraham, Gen. 26:24 and Ps. 105:6, 42; Isaac, Gen. 24:14 and 1 Chr. 16:13; Jacob, Exod. 32:13 and Deut. 9:27); Moses served as Yahweh's agent of deliverance and the mediator of the divine covenant (so designated 40 times: Exod. 14:31; Josh. 1:2, 3, 13, 15; Num. 12:7-8; etc.); the Levitical singers performed as official benedictors for Yahweh (Ps. 113:1; 134:1; 135:1); and the prophets functioned as Yahweh's officially commissioned spokespersons (Ezek. 38:17; 2 K. 17:13; Dan. 9:6 plus more than 20 times). For references see BDB, p. 714. Even the non-Israelite Job was a servant of Yahweh, modeling the divine ideals of piety and (unwittingly) functioning as a vehicle through whom the pattern of divine-human relationships was vindicated before Satan (Job 1:8; 2:3; 42:7-8).

Jeremiah, who had both spoken explicitly of "David their king." It is consistent, however, with his efforts elsewhere to downplay the roles of Israel's monarchs,[147] and harks back to 1 K. 11:34, which says of Solomon, "I will make him *nāśî'* all the days of his life for the sake of David my servant." In chs. 40–48 Ezekiel will apply the title to the official sponsor and patron of the cult, but the term usually functions primarily as a political designation. Ezekiel's preference for *nāśî'* over *melek,* the normal designation for Israel's rulers, is not intended to deny this person's true kingship but to highlight the distinction between him and the recent occupants of the office.

among them. The prophet emphasizes the ruler's identification with the people by noting that he will be not only "prince over Israel" (v. 23; cf. 19:1, etc.) but "prince in their midst." The *nāśî'* may officially be "the promoted one," but in view of his presence in the midst *(bĕtôk)* of Israel, some see him simply as primus inter pares.[148] One may perhaps recognize here an ironical allusion to Deut. 17:19-20, which had prescribed for Israel's kings the reading of the Torah "to prevent their hearts from being exalted above their kinfolk." However, both his status as shepherd among sheep and the expression "prince among them" suggest authority as well as identification.[149] In this arrangement, Yahweh is the divine patron of the people; David is his representative and deputy.

Ezekiel's announcement of the appointment of a new David for Israel was intended to instill new hope in the hearts of the exiles. Contrary to appearance, the demise of the Davidic house in 586 did not reflect divine impotence or indifference to previous commitments. These events had not only fulfilled previous prophetic utterances (12:1-16; 17; 19) but had also set the stage for a dramatic and new act of Yahweh. The decadence of the old order had been removed; now the people are challenged to look forward to a new day when Yahweh's Davidic servant would be reinstated in accordance with his eternal and irrevocable covenant.

The texts from Hosea and Jeremiah cited above hinted at an inseparable link between the election of David and the status of Israel as the people of Yahweh.[150] A similar development is evident in 34:24, which ties Yahweh's national covenant with Israel to the dynastic covenant with David. Indeed, a comparison of the national covenant formula and Ezekiel's statement suggests

147. Cf. the use of the term in 7:27; 12:10, 12; 19:1; 21:17, 30 (Eng. 12, 25); 22:6; 26:16; 27:21; 30:13; 32:29; 37:25; 38:2, 3; 39:1, 18. Except for the reference to Jehoiachin as *melek* in 17:12, and David in 37:22-24, Ezekiel reserves this title for the foreign kings of Egypt, Babylon, and Tyre.

148. So Hossfeld, *Untersuchungen,* p. 272.

149. So also Duguid, *Ezekiel and the Leaders,* p. 49.

150. Both Hos. 3:5 and Jer. 30:9-10 speak of "Yahweh their God and David their king."

that the prophet perceives the appointment of David as *nāśîʾ* as an aspect of the fulfillment of the national pledge, "I will be your God, and you shall be my people." The echo of the first line of this covenant formula is obvious in the first statement of v. 24.[151] Reminiscence of the second line will be delayed until v. 30.

But how is Ezekiel's assertion, "My servant David will be prince among them," related to this formula? The answer is found in the prepositional expression *among them* (*bĕtôkām*, lit. "in their midst"), which reminds the reader of an auxiliary affirmation often viewed as a part of the covenant formula, "I will dwell in your midst" (cf. Gen. 17:7; Exod. 29:45-46; Lev. 26:12-13; etc.). For Ezekiel, the prince is more than a political or military functionary, effecting the restoration; his role begins after the restoration has been achieved by God, at his initiative, and in his time.[152] In short, he symbolizes the presence of Yahweh in the midst of his people.

The messianic promise of David the prince taking his place among the people of Israel is sealed with an expanded version of the divine self-introductory formula. The formula has been deliberately inserted to reinforce confidence in the present prophetic pronouncement *and* in Yahweh's irrevocable commitment to David, the promise celebrated in Ps. 89:34-38 (Eng. 33-37). Accordingly, the primary motivation behind the restoration of Yahweh's flock arises not out of pity for the bruised and battered sheep of Israel, but out of his covenant with his people (cf. Deut. 4:31). The goal of the restoration is the reestablishment of that covenant in its full force and scope.

(2) The Nature of the Peace (34:25-30)

25-29 These verses announce that at the time Yahweh appoints the Davidic shepherd he will also establish a covenant of peace for Israel. The first statement, which functions as a thesis statement for the entire section, recalls 16:60, in which Yahweh had promised that after the judgment of Jerusalem he would remember his covenant made with her (as representative of the nation) in the days of her youth, and establish *(hēqîm)* an eternal covenant *(bĕrît ʿôlām)* for them. Now, the subject is resumed and expounded under the title *covenant of peace (bĕrît šālôm)*.[153] Variations of the expression occur in

---

151. Cf. *waʾănî yhwh ʾehyeh lāhem lēʾlōhîm*, "And I, Yahweh, shall be their God," with Ezekiel's version of the covenant formula: *waʾănî/ʾānōkî ʾehyeh lāhem lēʾlōhîm* (14:11; 36:28; 37:23, 27).

152. Cf. A. Caquot, "Le messianisme d'Ézéchiel," *Semitica* 14 (1964) 18-19.

153. Although political connotations are lacking in the biblical occurrences of the phrase, it is semantically similar to Akk. *ri-kàl-ta ša-la-ma*, a designation for a peace treaty in Ugaritic Akkadian (RS 17:340.14), on which see Baltzer, *Covenant Formulary*, p. 13; F. B. Knutson, "Literary Phrases and Formulae," in K. Baltzer, *RSP*, 2:407-9.

three other places in the OT, two outside Ezekiel. Num. 25:12 has Yahweh rewarding Phinehas for his zeal by granting *(nātan)* him "my covenant of peace" *(běrîtî šālôm)*, by which he guaranteed the priesthood to him and his descendants in perpetuity for having averted the wrath of God.[154] While the links of this covenant with the present text are remote, this is not the case with respect to Isa. 54:7-10:

> For a brief moment I abandoned you,
> But with deep compassion I will regather you.
> In overflowing wrath for a moment
> I hid my face from you.
> Nevertheless with everlasting kindness *(ḥesed ʿôlām)*
> I will have compassion on you,
>   has your redeemer Yahweh declared.
> For this is like the days of Noah to me:
> As I swore that the waters of Noah
> Would never again flood the earth,
> So I have now sworn not to be angry with you,
> Nor to rebuke you again.
> Though the mountains may shake,
> And the hills may move,
> My kindness *(ḥesed)* for you will never be shaken;
> Nor will the covenant of my peace *(běrît šělômî)* be moved,
>   has your compassionate one Yahweh declared.

Like our text, this passage associates the covenant of peace with the cessation of divine wrath, expressed by Yahweh's abandonment of his people and the hiding of his face.[155] The paradigm for "the covenant of my peace" is found in the postdiluvian covenant with Noah, according to which Yahweh swore never again to destroy all living beings by a flood (Gen. 9:8-17).[156] Beyond

---

154. Cf. Batto, *CBQ* 49 (1987) 188 n. 3. Mal. 2:4-8 seems to extend the scope of the covenant to the Levites as a whole.

155. See Ezekiel's own description in chs. 8–11. This idea will surface in Ezek. 39:29. On the motif see S. E. Balentine, *The Hidden God: The Hiding of the Face of God in the Old Testament* (Oxford: Oxford University Press, 1983).

156. The form *běrît šělômî*, lit. "the covenant of my peace," compares with *šēm qodšî*, "the name of my holiness," viz., "my holy name." See Ezek. 36:22-23. For Noah the sign was the rainbow *(qešet);* for Isaiah it seems to have been the mountains and hills. For discussion of these and related extrabiblical texts see Batto, *CBQ* 49 (1987) 187-211. Atraḫasis (on the sign cf. III v:46-vi:4) and Gilgamesh (on the sign cf. XI:163-65) present extrabiblical analogues to the pattern of (1) the deluge as an expression of divine wrath; (2) an oath/covenant never again to destroy all life with a flood; (3) the identification of a sign guaranteeing the divine oath.

these texts, the phrase occurs only in Ezek. 37:26, which represents a summary version of the present passage. Although neither of these passages mentions the aversion of divine wrath, one may assume it, based on the pattern set by 16:60 and the general transformation of Ezekiel's previous oracles of judgment into oracles of deliverance.[157]

Yahweh's promise of peace for his people is presented as a treaty oath, freely promised and unilateral. While the use of *kārat lĕ*, "to cut for," rather than the more conventional *kārat 'et*, "to cut with," highlights the monergistic nature of this covenant *(I will make . . . for them)*, the remainder of the oracle elaborates on the benefactions for Israel of this *bĕrît šālôm*, "covenant of peace." The description offers one of the fullest explications of the Hebrew notion of *šālôm*. The term obviously signifies much more than the absence of hostility or tension. It speaks of wholeness, harmony, fulfillment, humans at peace with their environment and with God.[158] It is evident from the synopsis in table 14 (p. 304) that the inspiration for Ezekiel's description of *šālôm* derives from the ancient covenant blessings as recorded in Lev. 26:4-13 (common elements are italicized).

Given Ezekiel's heavy dependence on the covenant curses for his pronouncements of doom against Judah, one would probably expect him to rely on the covenant blessings in this restoration oracle. But his dependence is not slavish. He freely rearranges the elements, modifies expressions, expands on some, and abbreviates others. Lev. 26:5 has no counterpart in Ezekiel; the references to the sword are dropped completely and the attention to human enemies is minimized. However, the most striking modification of the covenant blessings is found in the unconditional nature of his prophecy. The earlier document had been prefaced with stern prohibitions on idolatry and commands to observe Yahweh's Sabbaths and to revere his sanctuary, and then cast the blessings in the form of clear conditional clauses. Ezekiel drops all hints of contingency, citing no qualifications or human preconditions and making no appeal for repentance. In fact, the picture of Israel's restoration is painted entirely from the divine perspective. Just as the original exodus from Egypt had been accomplished by Yahweh's own will and for his own purposes, so he would initiate and effect this new chapter in the history of his relationship with his people. The complete destruction of the old order had freed him from the burdens of the nation's past infidelity and allowed him to begin anew.[159]

157. For a discussion of this transformation see Raitt, *Theology of Exile*, pp. 106-27.

158. For a study of the term see J. I. Durham, "*šālôm* and the Presence of God," in *Proclamation and Presence*, Fest. G. H. Davies, ed. J. I. Durham and J. R. Porter (London: SCM, 1970), pp. 272-93; von Rad, *Old Testament Theology*, 1:130; idem, *TDNT*, 2:402-6.

159. See Raitt, *Theology of Exile*, p. 108.

Table 14. Synopsis of Leviticus 26:4-13 and Ezekiel 34:25-30

Leviticus 26:4-13	Ezekiel 34:25-30
4 *Then I will give you rains in their season,* *and the land will yield her produce,* *and the wild trees will yield their fruit.* 5 Your threshing will last until the vintage, and your vintage will last until sowing time. You will eat your fruit to the full, *and you will dwell securely in the land.* 6 *And I will grant peace in the land* So you may lie down *with none to frighten you.* *I will remove dangerous animals from the land;* Nor will the sword pass through your land. 7 But you will pursue your enemies, And they will fall before you to the sword. 8 Five of you will chase a hundred, And a hundred of you will chase ten thousand, And your enemies will fall before the sword. 9 Thus I will turn toward you; I will make you fruitful; I will multiply you; *I will confirm my covenant with you.* 10 You will eat the old supply, And clear out the old because of the new. 11 I will make my dwelling among you, And my person will not reject you. 12 I will walk about in your midst; *I will be your God;* *And you will be my people.* 13 I am Yahweh your God, Who brought you out of the land of Egypt, to end *your slavery.* *I broke the bars of your yoke,* *And I made you walk erect.*	25 *I will make a covenant of peace for them;* *I will remove dangerous animals from the land.* *They will dwell securely in the desert;* They will sleep in the forest. 26 I will make them a blessing round about my hill. *I will send down the rain in its season;* They will be showers of blessing. 27 *The wild trees will yield their fruit;* *And the land will yield her produce.* *They will live securely on their own land.* And they will know that I am Yahweh, *when I break the bars of their yoke,* And rescue them for the hand of those *who enslave them.* 28 They will no longer be booty for the nations; Nor will the wild animals devour them. *They will dwell securely with none to frighten them.* 29 *I will establish for them a peaceful plantation;* No more will there be victims of famine in the land; No more will they suffer the derision of the nations. 30 They will know that *I am Yahweh their God with them,* And that *they the house of Israel are my people.* The declaration of the Lord Yahweh.

The description of the effects of Yahweh's covenant of peace is intentionally repetitious. Security is purposely highlighted as the central issue by the keyword *lābeṭaḥ*, "in safety, securely" (vv. 25c, 27c, 28c), an ambiguous expression that may denote both freedom from fear and casual smugness.[160] The association of *beṭaḥ* with the absence of terror *('ên maḥrîd)* in v. 28 argues for the former in this context.[161] Ezekiel envisions Israel's security being guaranteed by six specific actions by Yahweh, cited in an ABCA'B'C' order as follows:

A   peace with the animals (vv. 25b-d)
B   blessing of the vegetation (vv. 26-27c)
C   deliverance from oppression (vv. 27d-28a)
A' peace with the animals (vv. 28b-d)
B' blessing of the vegetation (vv. 29a-b)
C' deliverance from oppression (v. 29c)

Three types of divine activity are involved. First, Yahweh will restore security by eliminating predatory animals from the land.[162] This promise reverses Ezekiel's earlier pronouncements identifying wild animals as agents of divine judgment (cf. 5:17; 14:15, 21; 33:27). V. 25 describes an environment so secure the people will be able to sleep out in the open anywhere they please.[163]

Second, Yahweh will restore security by blessing the land with great fruitfulness. The first line of v. 26 is difficult, but it may be interpreted as a theme statement for the following lines, announcing Yahweh's special touch on the physical land of Israel. The word *blessing (bĕrākâ)* occurs twice in v. 26. The root *brk* is absent from Lev. 26:4-13, but occurs ten times in the Deuteronomic counterpart (Deut. 28:2-14), suggesting Deuteronomic influence in this description. The significance of *my hill (gib'ātî)* is uncertain, but Ezekiel's studious avoidance of any reference to Zion precludes the temple mount. The reference seems to be to the land of Israel itself (cf. v. 6), perceived as the property of Yahweh. The means by which Yahweh's blessing is communicated to the land is identified with the unique expression *gašmê bĕrākâ*, "showers of blessing."[164] Whether or not the plural, borrowed from Lev. 26:4,

160. See Judg. 18:7, 27. The word occurs elsewhere in Ezekiel in 28:26; 38:8, 11, 14; 39:26.
161. Cf. the pairing of *beṭaḥ* with *lō' yārē'* in Isa. 12:2; Ps. 27:3; 56:5, 12 (Eng. 4, 11); 78:53; 112:7, on which see M. Held, *JBL* 84 (1965) 282.
162. Ezekiel designates the creatures as *ḥayyâ rā'â*, "fierce animals," in v. 25, and *ḥayyat hā'āreṣ*, "animals of the land," in v. 28. The former derives from Lev. 26:6.
163. *midbār*, "desert," and *yĕ'ārîm*, "forests," constitute a merism for all regions, from territories devoid of vegetation to areas of lush growth.
164. To be distinguished from the destructive *gešem šōṭēp*, "flooding rains," of 13:11, 13.

refers to the former and latter rains,[165] the showers have an invigorating effect on the vegetation, causing the wild trees (*'ēṣ haśśādeh*) and the earth itself to yield an abundance of fruit (*pĕrî*) and crops, respectively, and holding off the drought, a fundamental element in the covenant curses.[166] In v. 29 Ezekiel describes this renewal with another new phrase: Yahweh will *provide* or establish (*hēqîm*) for his people a *peaceful plantation* (lit. "planting of peace"). The following line promises that the famine will never again ravish the land, as it had during the days of the nation's judgment.[167]

Third, Yahweh will restore security to Israel by removing the oppression of foreign enemies. Employing a modified version of the recognition formula (v. 27b), Ezekiel declares that Yahweh will break the bars of their yoke of bondage and rescue them from the hand of those who enslave them.[168] The language intentionally casts the restoration of Israel as a new exodus, reminiscent of the nation's earlier deliverance from Egyptian bondage.[169] The promise to end the taunts of the nations represents a reversal of 16:52, 54.

30 These external demonstrations of the messianic gift of shalom are welcome, but Ezekiel's portrayal of the new day climaxes with his announcement of the new covenant. Casting this promise in another modified form of the recognition formula, Ezekiel declares Yahweh's true goal in his salvific activity: that the family of Israel might realize the presence of God among them, and the reestablishment of the covenant relationship between them and their God. The tragedy of 586 will finally be reversed. The signatory formula seals Ezekiel's glorious promise with the divine imprimatur.

Ezekiel's idyllic picture of the messianic age as a time of universal peace, involving even the animal world, recalls Isa. 11:6-9. But his association of covenant renewal with the taming of the wild animals and the rejuvenation of the vegetation bears even closer resemblance to Hos. 2:20-25 (Eng. 18-23), which portrays Yahweh not as a principal to the covenant but as a covenant mediator, establishing peace between feuding parties:

---

165. So Cooke, *Ezekiel*, p. 378. Cf. Deut. 11:14; 28:12; Zech. 10:1; Job 38:26-27.

166. Cf. the threat of making the sky like iron and the earth like bronze in Lev. 26:19-20 and Deut. 28:23-24 (metals reversed). On the withholding of rain as a feature of ancient Near Eastern treaty curses see Hillers, *Treaty-Curses*, pp. 38, 41-42.

167. On *rā'āb* as an agent of divine judgment see my *Ezekiel: Chapters 1–24*, pp. 210, 212-14, etc.

168. These expressions appear in Lev. 26:13 in reverse order.

169. Allusions to the exodus are recognizable in two expressions in v. 27c that derive from the explicit statement in Lev. 26:13. First, "the bars of their yoke" (*mōṭôt 'ullām*) recalls *mōṭôt miṣrayim*, "the bars of Egypt," which in 30:18 had referred to Egypt's hold on its subjects. Second, the idiom "those who enslave them" (*hā'ōbĕdîm bāhem*) is similar to the use of *'ābad bĕ* in Exod. 1:14; Lev. 25:39, 46; Jer. 22:13.

On that day, I will make a covenant for them with the wild animals, the birds of the air, and the creeping creatures of the ground. I will also abolish the bow, the sword, and war from the land. Thus I will permit them to lie down in safety. I will betroth you to me forever; indeed, I will betroth you to me with righteousness and justice, with goodness and compassion. I will betroth you to me with faithfulness. Then you will know Yahweh. In that day I will respond — the declaration of Yahweh — I will respond to the sky, and it will respond to the earth. Then the earth will respond with new grain, wine, and oil, and they will respond to Jezreel. And I will sow it[170] for myself in the land. I will show mercy toward Lo-ruhamah, and say to Lo-ammi, "You are my people." And he will say, "[You are] my God."[171]

Some such covenant also underlies Job 5:23, which describes divine deliverance from a series of disasters:

> From six calamities he will deliver you;
> In seven no harm will touch you:
> In famine he will ransom you from death;
> In battle from the stroke of the sword.
> You will be protected from the lash of the tongue,
> And need not fear when destruction comes.
> You will laugh at violence and starvation,
> And have no fear of the wild animals.
> For you will have a covenant with the stones of the field,
> And the wild animals will be at peace with you.

Remarkably, this list is framed by the two elements found in Ezekiel's picture of peace, suggesting that famine and dangerous animals function as shorthand for the full range of calamities.

e. Epilogue: The Significance of the Peace (34:31)

Ezekiel's vision of the messianic age (vv. 25-30) has temporarily suspended the shepherd-flock imagery that has dominated the oracle to this point. No attempt has been made to relate the wild animals to creatures that prey on the flock, nor is the rejuvenation of vegetation connected with the renewal of pasture land. Even the evil shepherds have disappeared. It is fitting, therefore,

---

170. The suffix on *ûzra'tîhā*, pointed in MT as fem., is commonly repointed as masc., i.e., as a reference to Jezreel. However, the reference may be to the fertility of the land, which by extension represents *šālôm*. "Sowing fertility" then corresponds to Ezekiel's "planting peace." Cf. Batto, *CBQ* 49 (1987) 202.

171. On this text see Wolff, *Hosea,* pp. 53-54.

for the prophecy to be wrapped up by returning to the central issue. V. 31 reaffirms that the flock of which the prophet had spoken earlier represents the nation of Israel by reversing the order of the bipartite form of the covenant formula. In place of *'attem 'ammî,* "You are my people," the prophet declares, *'attēn ṣō'nî,* "You are my flock." The issue is clarified with Yahweh's reiteration that Israel is the flock of his pasture, and the inserted affirmation that the flock he is talking about is indeed a human *('ādām)* flock. The obverse of Yahweh's taking Israel as his flock is represented in Yahweh's renewed commitment of himself to be their God. Once again the signatory formula guarantees the veracity of the divine word.

♦ *Theological Implications*

The theological implications of Ezek. 34 are both profound and exhilarating. First, when Yahweh extends his grace to Israel again, the disintegrated deity-nation-land triangle is restored. Ezekiel's vision of the messianic age recognizes a measure of truth in his contemporaries' theological formulations. Yahweh had indeed entered into an eternal marriage covenant with them. Yahweh has an enduring interest in his land. His promise to David of eternal title to the throne of Jerusalem still stands. These covenant hopes will all be fulfilled in the messianic age. At that time, when Yahweh's people live securely in their land, are ruled by a divinely appointed David, and enjoy the shalom of God's presence and grace, they will finally acknowledge him as their Savior and covenant Lord.

Second, the true shepherd of God's people is the Lord himself. Whereas human leaders capitalize on positions of power and privilege for personal gain, Yahweh has the interests of his people at heart. He gathers the strays, nurtures the sick, feeds the flock from the finest of pastures, offers them his personal presence, and protects them from enemies, whether inside or out. Looking back on this text from the perspective of the NT, the reaction of the Jewish leaders to Jesus' characterization of them as "thieves and robbers" and his own assumption of the title "Good Shepherd" become understandable. This was not merely an attack on them or simply the statement of a lunatic (John 10:19-21); it was a blasphemous identification with deity, worthy of death (vv. 31-33).

Third, the Messiah, who will function as a servant of Yahweh, must come from the house of David, a theme to be developed more fully in 37:15-28.

Fourth, like the newly appointed David, ministers serve their congregations as shepherds under God. They are neither self-appointed nor engaged primarily by the flock; ministers are first and foremost servants of God, called to divine, not personal, service. The flock they serve is God's flock, not theirs.

For the sake of the ministry they may be viewed as *primi inter pares,* especially in their responsibility to nurture and care for the people. But the exploitation of the congregation for personal advantage provokes the ire of the divine Shepherd. Even the Messiah comes to serve, to seek and to save that which was lost. In this eminently "pastoral" text, Ezekiel has offered the OT paradigm for NT ministerial ideals.[172]

2. The Restoration of Yahweh's Land (35:1–36:15)

♦ *Nature and Design*

Despite the chapter division, there are many indications that the editors of the book intended 35:1-15 and 36:1-15 to be treated as two panels of a single literary unit. First, a single word-event formula in 35:1 governs the entire section.[1] Second, Edom, the addressee of 35:1-15, is still in view in 36:5 as a representative of Israel's enemies. Third, the focus throughout is on the land of Israel, referred to as *hārê yiśrā'ēl,* "the mountains of Israel." The preference for this expression over *'admat yiśrā'ēl,* "the land of Israel," is probably determined by the references to *har śē'îr,* "the mountain of Seir," in 35:2, 3, 7, 15. Fourth, the panels are linked by the description of the land as *šĕmāmâ ûmĕšammâ,* "desolation and waste," on the one hand, and *môrāšâ* and *nahălâ,* "a possession," on the other.[2] Fifth, they open with stylistically parallel formulae: "Human . . . prophesy and say" (35:1; 36:1). Sixth, the prophet cleverly employs two virtually identical expressions with opposite meanings: *hinĕnî 'ēlêkā har-śē'îr,* "Behold, I am against you, O Mount Seir," in 35:3, and *hinĕnî 'ălêkem,* "Behold, I am for you" (i.e., the mountains of Israel), in 36:9. Seventh, the terrain of both Edom and Israel is described with the stereotypical combination of "mountains" *(hārîm),* "hills" *(gib'ôt),* "valleys" *(gē'ôt),* and "ravines" *('ăpîqîm)* (35:8; 36:4, 6). Eighth, both panels speak of zeal/passion *(qin'â)* as a motive for divine action (35:11; 36:5, 6), and both mention the verbal abuse of the nations against Israel (35:10; 36:2, 3, 13). Ninth, both associate the cities *('ārîm)* with waste places *(horbâ)* (35:4; 36:10). Tenth, both employ *kullāh/kullā'* after "Edom" to emphasize totality.[3] Elev-

---

172. Cf. 1 Pet. 5:1-5; Acts 20:28ff.; John 21:15-17. On the pastoral implications of this text see M. T. Winstanley, "The Shepherd Image in the Scriptures: A Paradigm for Christian Ministry," *Clergy Review* 71 (1986) 197-206.

1. The next occurrence is in 36:16.

2. On the first see 35:3, 7, 9, 14, 15; 36:3, 4. On the second, for *môrāšâ* see 35:10; 36:2, 3, 5, 12; for *nahălâ* see 35:15; 36:12.

3. See 35:15; 36:5; cf. 36:10, "the whole house of Israel." This construction occurs elsewhere in Ezekiel in 29:2 with reference to Egypt.

enth, both panels rely heavily on the *ya'an . . . lākēn,* "Because . . . therefore," sequence of clauses.[4]

Taken together, 35:1–36:15 provide one of the most impressive examples of "halving" in the book of Ezekiel. Whether the present diptych derives from the original rhetorical situation or is an editorial creation is unclear (see further below). Together the panels present two sides of a single divine concern: the restoration of the land of Israel. 35:1-15 focuses on the cause of the land's desolation and the removal of those who stand in the way of the restoration; 36:1-15 on the reversal of the land's fate. The first is cast in the form of a modified judgment oracle against a foreign nation; the second as a restoration prophecy. In so doing a close structural parallel to ch. 34 has been achieved, as the following synopsis illustrates:

	New leadership for the people of Israel	New prosperity for the land of Israel
Judgment oracle: removal of hindrances of the old order	34:1-11	35:1-15
Restoration oracle: establishment of the new order	34:12-31	36:1-15

In both cases the restoration phase subdivides further into descriptions of the nature of the restoration (34:11-22; 36:1-7) and Yahweh's ultimate goals (34:23-31; 36:8-15). This synopsis also reflects the thematic editorial strategy. The attention has shifted from the first pillar of hope, viz., Yahweh's commitment to his people, to the second, his commitment to the land of Canaan as Israel's feudal estate *(naḥălâ).* This oracle answers earlier warnings of the nation's imminent removal from the land, which many would have interpreted as a breach of Yahweh's eternal promise made already to the patriarchs (cf. Gen. 17:8).

A comparison of the preambles to chs. 35 and 36 on the one hand and ch. 6 on the other also suggests an intentional reversal of the earlier prophecy against the mountains of Israel in particular.[5] The opening command to "set

---

4. See 35:5-6, 10-11; 36:2-3a, 3b-4, 5, 6, 7, 13-14.

5. The parallels may be highlighted by juxtaposing the texts as follows:

6:1-4	35:1-4; 36:1
The following message of Yahweh came to me: Human, direct your face against the mountains of Israel and prophesy against them,	The following message of Yahweh came to me: Human, direct your face toward the mountain of Seir, and prophesy against it,

your face toward" the addressee followed by the double command to "prophesy and say" in 6:2-3 is echoed in 35:1-2; and in 36:1 the opening vocative,
"O mountains of Israel," the call to attention, "Hear the word of [the Lord]
Yahweh," and the citation formula, "Thus has the Lord Yahweh declared,"
are picked up virtually verbatim from 6:3. Furthermore, the strange identification of the addressee in 35:2 as har-śēʿîr, "mountain of Seir," rather than
the national name Edom obviously answers to "mountains of Israel" in the
earlier oracle. This impression of intentional reversal is reinforced by the
repetition of the four geographical terms of 6:3 in 35:8 and 36:4, 6,[6] and the
reference to bāmôt, "high places," in 36:2, which recalls 6:3, 6. Moreover,
the announcement of judgment in 35:3b-4 derives its diction from 6:6 (heʿārîm
teḥĕrabnâ, "the towns lie desolate"), 6:7b (recognition formula), and 6:14a.
     Although 35:1–36:15 represents a single logical literary unit, dealing
with the subject of the restoration of Yahweh's land, for closer discussion of
generic and stylistic issues, the two panels are best considered separately.

a. The Prerequisite to Restoration: The Judgment of Seir (35:1-15)

1 *The following message of Yahweh came to me:*

2 *"Human, set your face toward Mount Seir and prophesy against
it.* 3 *Say to it*[7]*: 'Thus has the Lord Yahweh declared: I am against you,
O Mount Seir! I will raise my hand against you, and transform you
into utter desolation.* 4 *Your towns I will turn to ruin, and you yourself
will become a wasteland. Then you will know that I am Yahweh.*

5 *Because you have harbored long-standing enmity, and handed the
people of Israel*[8] *over to the sword at the time of their calamity, the
time of their final punishment*[9] *—* 6 *therefore, by my life — the decla-*

---

and say:	and say to it:
	. . . .
	But you human, prophesy
	to the mountains of Israel
	and say:
O mountains of Israel,	O mountains of Israel,
Hear the word of the Lord Yahweh!	Hear the word of Yahweh!
Thus has the Lord Yahweh declared:	Thus has the Lord Yahweh declared:

6. This grouping occurs also in 31:12 and 34:13.

7. LXX[B] harmonizes the text with 13:18; 28:22; 29:3; and 38:3 by omitting lô.

8. In keeping with Ezekiel's usage elsewhere, LXX reads bêt yiśrāʾēl, "house of
Israel," in place of MT bĕnê yiśrāʾēl.

9. LXX ἐν καιρῷ ἀδικίας ἐπ᾽ ἐσχάτῳ, "in an evil time of the end," conflates MT
bĕʿēt ʾêdām bĕʿēt ʿāwōn qēṣ. Targ.'s expansion, "at the time of the retribution for their
sins, when their doom had come," recalls this version's reading of 21:30.

ration of the Lord Yahweh[10] *— surely, [it was] the blood of hatred,*[11] *so blood will pursue you.* 7 *I will transform Mount Seir into an utter desolation,*[12] *and terminate all traffic*[13] *from it.* 8 *I will fill its mountains*[14] *with its victims.*[15] *The victims of the sword will fall on your hills and in your valleys and all your ravines.*[16] 9 *I will transform you into a permanent wasteland,*[17] *leaving your towns uninhabited.*[18] *Then you*[19] *will know that I am Yahweh.*

10 *Because you have said, "These two nations and these two lands*[20] *will belong to me, and we will possess them"*[21] *— even though Yahweh was there —* 11 *therefore, by my life — the declaration of the Lord*

---

10. *kî lĕdām 'e'esĕkā wĕdām yirdăpēkā*, which is missing in LXX, appears to be a dittographic insertion before the similar *'im-lō' dām śānē'tā wĕdām yirdăpēkā*. Cf. Allen, *Ezekiel 20–48*, p. 167. The presence of the gloss in Targ. attests to the aniquity of the insertion.

11. *dām śānē'tî*, "you hated blood," is meaningless, if not the opposite of what is required by the context. My rendering assumes a scribal error for *dam śin'â*, treating the *nomen rectum* attributively, viz., "hateful bloodshed." Cf. GKC, §128p. This interpretation finds support in Targ.'s interpretation: "Indeed, you have hated with a bloody hatred, therefore those who shed blood will pursue you." Cf. Codex Reuchlinianus, "You have hated the blood of circumcision." *BHS* emends to *lĕdām 'āšamtā*, "with reference to blood you have incurred guilt," based on LXX εἰς αἷμα ἥμαρτες. REB follows G. R. Driver's suggestion (*Bib* 19 [1938] 181) of reading *dām nāśā'tā*, "you bear [the guilt] of blood." For a similar ellipsis see Num. 14:33, "They will bear [the guilt] of your harlotries."

12. MT *lĕšimĕmâ ûšĕmāmâ* misvocalizes the first word, which should be pointed as *lišmāmâ*. Cf. v. 3; 6:14; 33:28. See *BHS*.

13. Interpreting *'ōbēr wāšāb*, lit. "who passes by and returns," as a merism.

14. Since the order differs, *gē'ôt* is spelled differently, the second masc. suffixes agree more with vv. 3-6, 9a than vv. 7-8, and the word is missing in LXX, many treat *'et-hārāyw* as a secondary addition. Cf. H. Simian-Yofre, *Nachgeschichte*, p. 106.

15. LXX reads "your slain." NRSV "the slain" follows *BHS* to read *ḥălālîm*.

16. Targ. smooths out the text by reading the third person suffix throughout. Wevers (*Ezekiel*, p. 266) treats the second person suffix as a sign of a later expansion.

17. The pl. form *šimĕmôt* occurs only here in Ezekiel, but is found elsewhere in Jer. 25:12; 51:26, 62, and finds support in the phrase *bāmôt 'ôlām* in Ezek. 36:2. LXX, Targ., and Syr. all read sg.

18. Contra Qere, which reads the verb *šûb*, "to return," Kethib correctly derives *tāyšōbnâ* from *yāšab*, "to inhabit, dwell." MT's unusual orthography (in place of anticipated *tēšabnâ*) may reflect a determination to prevent the error in Qere. Cf. Cooke, *Ezekiel*, p. 384. *yāšab*, in the sense of "to be inhabited," has occurred earlier in 29:11.

19. LXX and Syr. read MT pl. as sg. in keeping with the context.

20. The object sign before the subject anticipates the following verb. See further Joüon-Muraoka, *Grammar*, §125j; Muraoka, *Emphatic Words*, pp. 146-58.

21. LXX, Targ., and Syr. smooth out MT *wîrašnûhâ*, "and we shall possess it," to *wîraštîn*, "and I shall possess them," but MT is preferred on the basis of *lectio difficilior*.

Yahweh — I will respond[22] *with the same anger and passion with which you in your hatred*[23] *treated them. I will make myself known through them*[24] *when I punish you.* 12 *Then you will know that I am Yahweh.*

12b *I have heard all*[25] *the taunts*[26] *you shouted against the mountains of Israel: "It has been laid waste!*[27] *They have been handed over to us for food!" 13 With your speech you have challenged me! With your words you have defied*[28] *me! I have heard [you] myself! 14 Thus has the Lord Yahweh declared: While the whole world celebrates, I will make you a desolation.*[29] *15 Just as you rejoiced over the possession of the house of Israel, because it was laid waste, so I will deal with you:*[30] *You, Mount Seir, will become a wasteland, along*

---

22. For the perfect with *waw*-consecutive after the oath formula cf. 17:22. LXX and Syr. fill out the sense by adding "to you."

23. Many Hebrew mss. read MT's pl. form, *miśśin'ātêkā,* as sg., *miśśin'ātĕkā.* MT may have been influenced by v. 12.

24. Many follow LXX in reading "you," changing the focus from agency to locus. Targ. expands, "and I will reveal myself by being good to them."

25. LXX misreads *kol* as *qôl,* "voice, sound."

26. *nā'ṣôt* derives from *nā'āṣ,* "to belittle, despise, insult." Cf. H. Wildberger, *THAT,* 2:3-6. Jer. 33:24 offers the clearest illustration of its sense: "You observe what this people has said: 'The two families which Yahweh chose have now been rejected by him.' Thus they despise *(nā'āṣ)* my people, no longer regarding them as a nation." Cf. Hezekiah's similar complaint that the Assyrian siege of Jerusalem has brought on the city a day of distress, chastisement, and disgrace *(nĕ'āṣâ),* for Rabshakeh asserted that the Judeans' God was no more able to deliver them from his power than were the gods of the other nations that had fallen to Sennacherib (2 K. 18:33-35). The Akkadian cognate, *na'āṣu,* bears the same meaning in Amarna tablet 137:14, 23, according to which Rib-Addi, the ruler of Byblos, complains to the pharaoh that even the members of his own household are belittling him for his apparent incompetence. See *ANET,* p. 483. Cf. *AHW,* p. 578.

27. Kethib's fem. sg. *šmmh* treats Israel as the subject, though Israel is normally masc. Cf. Qere's third masc. pl., *šmmw,* which assumes "the mountains of Israel" as the subject. The treatment of Israel as fem. in Kethib may be intentional, highlighting the role of the land, rather than the population of Israel. See the commentary.

28. Not knowing how to interpret *wĕha'tartem,* LXX dropped the entire clause. Many follow *BHS*'s conjectural emendation to *wh'tqtm,* "you were arrogant," but this is unnecessary.

29. Even though LXX and Targ. support MT, many treat v. 14 as corrupt, and v. 15a as a later theological paraphrastic clarification. Cf. Zimmerli, *Ezekiel 2,* p. 227. *BHS* reconstructs *kiśmōaḥ kol-hā'āreṣ šĕmāmâ 'e'ĕśeh-lāk* as *kĕśimḥātĕkā lĕ'arṣî 'al-'ăšer šāmēmâ kēn,* "Just as you rejoiced over my land, because it was desolate." Allen (*Ezekiel 20–48,* p. 168) deletes *kol-hā'āreṣ* as an original gloss on *šmmh* (Kethib) in v. 12, mistakenly inserted here and then reinterpreted as an alternative to v. 15a.

30. Although some treat v. 15a as dittography (cf. Fohrer, *Ezechiel,* p. 199), its omission by LXX is better interpreted as homoioteleuton. See Parunak, *Structural Studies,* p. 463.

with all Edom, the whole land.[31] *Then they will know*[32] *that I am Yahweh.' "*[33]

♦ Nature and Design

Following the customary word event formula (v. 1), the limits of the first panel are set by the divine address of the prophet in v. 2 and the recognition formula in v. 15. The citation formula in v. 3 sets the formal pronouncement off from the opening charge to the prophet. With regard to aesthetics this is one of the least satisfying oracles in the book. The excessive reliance on old themes robs it of color, and its fragmentary nature prevents the establishment of a clear rhetorical rhythm. But the tone is set by the root *šmm,* "desolation," which appears ten times. The oracle has a complex structure, being divided into four segments each of which ends with its own recognition formula (vv. 3-4, 5-9, 10-12aα, 12aβ-15). An ABBA pattern is evident in the arrangement of these segments: two mini-judgment oracles, governed by the *yaʿan* . . . *lākēn,* "Because . . . therefore," sequence, are sandwiched between pronouncements highlighting Yahweh's fundamental opposition to Seir. These parts may represent the cores of separate oracles delivered in different contexts. In comparison with the rest of Ezekiel's prophecies, by themselves these pronouncements might all be considered lightweight. By bringing them together in this fashion, however, their force is strengthened like four successive volleys of a cannon.

Although it is longer and more complex, by itself this oracle would have been more at home in the corpus of Ezekiel's earlier oracles against the foreign nations. The schadenfreude expressed in the direct quotation in v. 10 in particular suits the pattern of 25:1–26:6. Perhaps vv. 5-9 and 10-12aα were originally included in this earlier collection. That 25:12-14 already contains a prophecy against Edom does not preclude this possibility since 25:1-7 appears to have incorporated two oracles against the Ammonites, and chs. 26–28 contain three against Tyre. It seems that earlier pronouncements against Edom have been retrieved and reworked for new purposes, thereby providing concrete illustration of the principle announced in 28:24-28: the restoration of the nation of Israel will occur within the context of the judgment of her international enemies. Edom is selected as a representative of those nations (cf. 36:3-7), probably because of her proximity to Judah as well as her long-standing enmity toward Judah. The judgment of a foreign nation is hereby explicitly linked with the salvation of Israel by appealing to an earlier prophecy

---

31. The fem. suffix on *kullāh* refers to the territory of Edom. See n. 27 above.
32. LXX reads second person sg.
33. LXX adds ὁ θεὸς αὐτῶν, "their God."

of judgment upon Israel. In the present oracle Ezekiel lifts the maledictions predicted in ch. 6 from Israel and transfers them to the enemy.[34]

It is impossible to identify the original context in which these utterances were delivered. The claims of Seir to the territory of Israel suggest a context different from that of the oracles preserved in ch. 25, which are issued against the backdrop of the fall of Jerusalem. Nor can one demonstrate that ch. 35 was presented orally as a unit. But there are no convincing reasons for denying each of the segments to the prophet himself; in diction and style they are certainly Ezekielian. While I prefer to attribute the literary product to the prophet, it is possible that the present structure was achieved by the editors of his work. In either case, the exiles are presented with a glorious message of hope: Yahweh himself will deal with those who have rejoiced at their extinction.

(1) Preamble and the First Volley: Yahweh's Disposition toward Seir (35:1-4)

After the opening word-event formula, the occasion for a new prophecy is signaled by Yahweh's command to Ezekiel to set his face toward Mount Seir, to prophesy against it, and to speak to it.[35] The identification of the hypothetical addressee as *Mount Seir,* rather than "Edom," the national designation, alerts the reader immediately to the geographic focus of this oracle. This is the first certain occurrence in the book of the name, which derives etymologically from a root meaning "hairy," apparently a reference originally to the wooded slopes descending from the Transjordanian plateau between Wadi al-Ḥasâ and Wadi Râs en-Naqb down to the Wadi al-ʿArabah.[36] The name is well attested in extrabiblical sources.[37] It occurs thirty-eight times in the OT, thirty of which employ Seir as a toponym,[38] the name of the mountainous

---

34. This point is argued convincingly by B. Gosse, "Ézéchiel 35–36,1-15 et Ézéchiel 6: La désolation de la montagne de Séir et le renouveau des montagnes d'Israël," *RB* 96 (1989) 511-17.

35. The triad of verbs recalls 6:1 and 25:2.

36. The reference to *har-śēʿîr* in 25:8 (MT) is textually dubious. On Seir see E. A. Knauf, *ADB,* 5:1072-73; M. Weippert, "Edom: Studien und Materialien zur Geschichte der Edomiten auf Grund schriftlicher und archäologischer Quellen" (Ph.D. diss., Tübingen, 1971), p. 391.

37. See the 14th-century Amarna Letter 288:26 (*mâtāti še-e-riki, ANET,* p. 488); several Rameses II texts (*dw n ś-ʿ-r-ï,* e.g., Papyrus Harris I, *ANET,* p. 262); and neo-Assyrian texts (URU*sa-ʾ-ar-ri,* e.g., *ANET,* p. 298).

38. Cf. "land of Seir," Gen. 32:4 [Eng. 3]; 36:30; "Mount Seir," Gen. 14:6; 36:8; Deut. 1:2; 2:1, 5; Josh. 15:10; 24:4; Ezek. 35:2, 3, 7, 15; 1 Chr. 4:42; 2 Chr. 20:10, 22; 20:23; *śēʿîr* with *hē*-directive, Gen. 33:14, 16; Josh. 12:7 (cf. 11:17); "in Seir," Deut. 1:44; 2:4, 8, 12, 22, 29; "from Seir," Deut. 33:2; Judg. 5:4; Isa. 21:11.

region originally inhabited by Horites (Gen. 14:6) but taken over by the descendants of Esau (Gen. 33:14, 16; 36:8-9; 42:4). According to Deut. 2:1-7, Yahweh had designated Seir as Esau's grant (yĕruššâ) in the same way that Moab, Ammon, and the Israelites had been given their respective territories. In our text Mount Seir serves as an alternative territorial name for Edom, appropriate for the prophet's present interest and his need for a correlative to hārê yiśrā'ēl in 6:2-3, on which this oracle is based.

The oracle proper is cast in the form of a modified proof saying, using the second person of direct address. It opens abruptly with the challenge formula, hinĕnî 'ēlêkā har-śē'îr, "I am against you, O Mount Seir," which sets the tone for the prophecy.[39] The introduction offers no reason for Yahweh's fundamental opposition to Seir, only his hostile reaction, which is described in four balanced lines of three beats each. The diction is formulaic and typically Ezekielian. The precise nature of the divine action is not disclosed — only that he will strike the land with his outstretched hand. The ruinous effects of his actions are reflected in the hendiadys šĕmāmâ ûmĕšammâ, which involves two words from the same root, šmm, "to be wasted, desolated."[40] If the reference to ruined cities adds concreteness to the picture, the last line reiterates that Mount Seir itself will be totally transformed. The borrowing of diction from earlier oracles of judgment against Judah is intentional; the nation that had gloated over the devastation of the land of Israel will suffer the same fate; and when they experience Judah's calamity, they too will acknowledge this as a revelatory encounter with Yahweh.

(2) The Second Volley: Yahweh's First Case Against Seir (35:5-9)

Having set the stage by declaring Yahweh's fundamentally hostile stance toward Seir and his determination to destroy her, the prophet justifies this decision with two modified judgment speeches, each consisting of a formal accusation (introduced by ya'an) and an announcement of judgment (introduced by lākēn). The concluding recognition formula identifies these mini-oracles as proof sayings as well.

5 The formal indictment of Mount Seir begins with a charge of long-standing enmity ('êbat 'ôlām, lit. "enmity of eternity"). The accusation is familiar from 25:15, but it is much more understandably applied to the Edomites than to the Philistines. Israelite tradition dates the history of sour relations between Israel and Edom to their respective ancestors' rivalry, begun already in the womb of Rebekah (Gen. 25:22-23) and continued during Jacob

---

39. See my Ezekiel: Chapters 1–24, pp. 201-2.

40. The phrase is borrowed from 6:4. It recurs in v. 7, and has appeared earlier in 33:28-29.

and Esau's adult lives (Gen. 27:41-45; 32:4-22; 33:1-16). Although centuries later the Israelites were enjoined to show special consideration to the Edomites because of their kinship (Deut. 23:8 [Eng. 7]), no love seems to have been lost between these two nations. The 8th-century prophet Amos inveighed against Edom for stifling natural brotherly compassion and pursuing Israel with the sword (Amos 1:11-12), and Isaiah viewed the nation as the archenemy of Israel (Isa. 34; cf. 63:1-6). Edom's expressions of hatred toward Judah apparently intensified in the latter's darkest hours. When Nebuchadrezzar razed Jerusalem, the Edomites had stood by clapping their hands with glee.[41] Our text suggests that they played an active part in Judah's calamity, delivering her population over to the sword. The idiom *higgîr ʿal-yĕdê-ḥereb* (lit. "to pour into the hands of the sword") combines the notions of violence and betrayal.[42]

Verse 5 refers to Judah's calamity with two special expressions. For the Edomites the ring of the first, *at the time of their calamity, bĕʿēt ʾêdām,* is ominous. While the etymology of *ʾêd,* "calamity," is uncertain,[43] the prophets capitalized on its sound to play on the name "Edom" *(ʾĕdôm).* Of the four occurrences relating to the fall of Jerusalem, three are found in oracles against Edom.[44] Ezekiel will maintain the play in the following verse with his fourfold reference to blood, *dām.* The second expression refers to Judah's fall as *the time of their final punishment. bĕʿēt ʿāwôn qēṣ* is a typically Ezekielian expression (cf. 21:30, 34 [Eng. 25, 29]), employing *ʿāwōn* not in the common sense of "iniquity, guilt," but as "punishment" for guilt.

6 The remainder of this mini-oracle (vv. 6-9) is taken up with Yahweh's frightening response to Seir's crimes. Force and solemnity are added to the announcement of divine intervention by prefacing it with the oath formula, the inelegantly placed signatory formula,[45] and a pair of impassioned if enigmatic allusions to the "bad blood" between these ethnically related nations. If *ʾêbat ʿôlām* in v. 5 highlights the long-standing duration of Edom's enmity toward Israel, *the blood of hatred (dam śinʾâ)* reflects its intensity; the relationship was poisoned by murderous hatred demonstrated by delivering the Israelites over to the sword (v. 5). The victims are not merely Judeans who may have fallen to Edomite soldiers participating in Nebuchadrezzar's campaign; the bloodguilt was incurred by searching out and slaughtering

41. Cf. Ps. 137; Joel 4:19 (Eng. 3:19); Obad. 1-14; Mal. 1:2-5; Lam. 4:21.

42. The idiom occurs elsewhere in Jer. 18:21 and Ps. 63:11 (Eng. 10).

43. *ʾêd* occurs 24 times in the OT. In Jeremiah it expresses Yahweh's judgmental activity (Jer. 18:17; 46:21; 48:16; cf. Deut. 32:35); in Ps. 18:19 (Eng. 18) (= 2 Sam. 22:19) it represents the antithesis to divine aid and salvation.

44. See Obad. 13; Jer. 49:8; Ezek. 35:5; cf. Jer. 49:32, to Damascus.

45. *ḥay ʾānî,* "By my life," is normally followed immediately by *ʾim-lōʾ,* "assuredly," which in turn precedes the announcement of divine action. Cf. 5:11; 17:19; etc.

fugitives. These were murderous actions.[46] Where the blood of Abel had cried out to Yahweh to avenge Cain's murder (Gen. 4:10), here the blood of Edom's victims takes on a life of its own, like a near kinsman relentlessly pursuing the criminal and demanding full retribution.[47]

7 As if to remind the reader of the primarily geographic interest of the oracle, Ezekiel returns to the theme of the devastating effects of Yahweh's judgment on the Seirite landscape. He will render it totally desolate and wipe out all signs of life. The merismic phrase ʿōbēr wāšāb refers primarily to human *traffic,* but the scope may be extended to all life.[48] In contrast to 5:14 and 36:34, where ʿōbēr identifies passersby who witness the divine activity, here they are the victims, eliminated from *(hikrît min)* the land.[49]

8-9 The results of Yahweh's actions described here are familiar from previous judgment pronouncements against Judah. The filling of the region with the slain *(millēʾ ḥălālîm)* recalls 9:7; 11:6; 30:11. The quartet of mountains, hills, valleys, and ravines derives from 6:3, but recalls also 31:12 and 32:5-6. The reference to *the victims of the sword will fall (ḥalĕlê-ḥereb yippĕlû)* is reminiscent of 6:4, 7; 31:17-32; and 32:20. The notice of the transformation of the Seirite landscape into a permanent wasteland and her towns into uninhabited ruins echoes 29:12 and 30:7. The concluding recognition formula emphasizes, however, that Yahweh's ultimate goal is not the destruction of Seir; the nation is to recognize that the patron defender of Israel is also the Lord of their own history.

(3) The Third Volley: Yahweh's Second Case Against Seir (35:10-12a)

The structure of this mini-oracle resembles the previous segment. Vitality is added to the accusation, however, by casting it in the form of a direct quotation, reminiscent of the minor oracles in ch. 25. In the citation, the prophet has included all the elements needed for synonymously parallel lines, but he has avoided composing them as poetry.[50] The announcement expresses the Edomites' desire to fill the vacuum in Palestine created by Nebuchadrezzar's

---

46. Fuhs, *Ezechiel 25–48,* p. 197.

47. On the role of the near kinsman (gōʾēl) in avenging the death of a relative, see Num. 35:16-34; Deut. 19:6; Josh. 20:5.

48. LXX reads "human and beast," though this may reflect harmonization with 14:13, 17, 19, 21; 25:13; 29:8, where ʾādām ûbĕhēmā follows the verb hikrît. The present phrase occurs elsewhere in Exod. 32:27 and Zech. 7:14; 9:8.

49. In Ezek. 21:8 (Eng. 3) hikrît min occurs with "the righteous and the wicked."

50. A poet might have constructed the lines as follows: ʾet-šĕnî haggoyîm lî tihyênā / wĕʾet štê hāʾărāṣôt yîrašnûhā, "These two nations shall belong to us, / and these two lands we shall possess."

deportation of the population of Judah. Now both kingdoms, north and south, have been depopulated. This is the time for Edom to stake its claims *(yāraš)* on the territories of Judah and the northern kingdom of Israel. How realistic this claim was is uncertain, but those who lived across the Arabah would have envied the fertility of Palestine. Perhaps they perceived this land as the reward owed by Nebuchadrezzar for their assistance in the Palestinian campaign. In any case only the poor were left in Judah, and these would be easy prey for the Edomites, who had the good fortune of siding with the winner in the conflagration of 586.

Archeological evidence for Edomite encroachment into Judean territory is available from several sources. Arad Letter 24 refers to the pressure of the Edomites at this southern military outpost even before the fall of Jerusalem.[51] An Edomite seal, whose nationality is established by the name Qaus, discovered at Aroer, 12 miles southeast of Beer-sheba, suggests Edomite presence at this place a short time later.[52] The remains of what appears to have been an Edomite temple have been discovered at Ḥorvat Qitmit, south of Tel Arad. But the most direct evidence of Edomite presence in southern Judah comes from an ostracon unearthed at Ḥorvat ʿUza southeast of Arad, dated near the time of the fall of Jerusalem. Of special interest in the six-line inscription is a blessing in the name of Qaus wished by Lumalak upon someone named *Blbl*.[53] However, to date there is no evidence for Edomite penetration north of Jerusalem. The prophet is speaking of Edomite aspirations rather than historical reality.

10 For Ezekiel the Edomite seizure of Israelite territory represented more than opportunistic grabbing of another nation's territory. The last line of v. 10 highlights the theological significance of the crime. The Edomites failed to recognize one crucial fact: Yahweh's continued presence in the land. With their typical ancient Near Eastern perspective they assumed that a land whose population had been deported and whose cities lay in ruins must have been abandoned by its god. Yahweh may indeed have left the temple and the city, allowing Nebuchadrezzar, his agent of judgment on his own people, to raze Jerusalem; but this did not mean he had abandoned all interest in the place, nor did it authorize any other nation to seize his land. If he would rise against any Israelite making illicit land claims (11:15; 33:24), how much more would he defend it against invaders. This land was his grant to Jacob/Israel (28:25; 37:25); Edom must be content with its own allotment (Deut. 2:1-7).

51. See Aharoni, *Arad Inscriptions,* pp. 46-49, 150.

52. See A. Biran and R. Cohen, "Notes and News: Aroer," *IEJ* 26 (1976) 139, plate 28:B.

53. I. Beit-Arieh and B. Cresson, "An Edomite Ostracon from Ḥorvat ʿUza," *TA* 12 (1985) 96-101. Aharoni (*Arad Inscriptions,* p. 150) maintains that Edomite occupation of this region occurred some three or four years after the conquest of Jerusalem in 598/597.

11-12a In response, Yahweh announces on oath his determination to give full vent to his fury. The anger *('ap),* passion *(qin'â),* and hatred *(śin'â)* that Edom vented on Israel will be the measure of Yahweh's action against Edom. His own land may lie in ruins and its population languish in exile, but the divine patron's passion has been aroused. Through his acts of judgment he will vindicate himself, and even the devotees of Qaus will acknowledge him.[54]

(4) The Fourth Volley: Yahweh's Disposition Toward Seir (35:12b-15)

Without warning the formal proceedings against Edom are dropped and a new phase is begun. Vv. 12b-15, which clarify the last clause in v. 10, constitute a divine apologia, explaining why Yahweh has taken Seir's presumptuous claims to the mountains of Israel so personally. The segment divides into two parts, separated by the citation formula.

12b-13 The first part is framed by the verb *šāma'tî, I have heard.* After Yahweh's earlier asseveration that no matter how loudly his people would cry he would not listen (8:18), to learn that Yahweh hears should have been music to the ears of the exiles. But it is not the cries of his own people that reach him in this instance; it is the *taunts* of the enemy. Yahweh hears the taunts of Seir directed at the mountains of Israel. Like vultures they look on the ruins of Judah as prey delivered into their talons. The phrase *they have been handed over for food (nittěnû lě'oklâ)* recalls 29:5, where Yahweh hands Pharaoh to the beasts of the earth as their prey; and 34:5, 8, 10, which portray the people of Israel like scattered sheep, at the mercy of the wild animals. The passive verb may even imply divine permission for seizing the land. But Yahweh will have none of this. In fact, he takes the revilings personally: *I have heard [you] myself.* To deride the land of Israel is to taunt the true owner of the land. His tenants may have been expelled, but Yahweh remains the divine landlord, and he will not tolerate such belittling of the mountains of Israel.

Two expressions characterize the Edomite derision. The first, *with your speech you have challenged me (higdîl 'ālay běpîkem,* lit. "to act great against me with your mouth"), is equivalent to "to talk big" in our parlance.[55] The second term, *defied (ha'tartem),* is less clear. A derivation from an Aramaized root, *'tr* (cf. Heb. *'šr),* "to be abundant," seems most likely, in which case the hiphil verb means something like "to speak arrogantly."[56] A semantic

54. The motif of Yahweh making himself known through his judgment of the nations will return in 38:23 and 39:21-23.

55. On the inwardly transitive use of the Hiphil see Waltke-O'Connor, *Syntax,* §27.2f.

56. See *DISO,* p. 224; *DNWSI,* p. 898; *Ahiqar* 207. N. S. Doniach's suggestion of

parallel is found in Akk. *(w)atartu*, "excessive, exaggerated."[57] Yahweh interprets Seir's claim to the mountains of Israel as a blasphemous and presumptuous challenge against himself, the patron deity.

14-15 An unexpected citation formula announces the conclusion to this oracular fragment and to the first panel as a whole. In this final speech Yahweh summarizes the basic problem with Edom. V. 14 is problematic textually, but it appears to announce a turning of the tables. Seir's turn to experience the punishment of Yahweh, while the whole world looks on with glee, has arrived. As in v. 11, v. 15 states that this nation that had rejoiced over the desolation of Israel will be forced to take some of her own medicine. She is about to become the object of the same Schadenfreude with which she had observed and participated in the wasting of Israel. Not only Mount Seir but the entire land of Edom will become a wasteland just like the mountains of Israel.

The first line of v. 15 is the key not only to this oracle but to the special relationship existing between *bêt yiśrā'ēl,* "the house of Israel," and *hārê yiśrā'ēl,* "the mountains of Israel," here designated as her *possession (naḥălâ).* Given Ezekiel's special interest in the land, it is remarkable that this is the first occurrence of the word in the book.[58] The word has traditionally been translated with inheritance terminology. For example, von Rad interpreted it as denoting the hereditary possession of a clan or tribe.[59] As Forshey has demonstrated, however, the expression is better associated with landed property, pointing to "the practice of giving loyal servants the utilization of land as a reward for past service — fundamentally military service is involved — and in expectation of future service."[60] The phrase *naḥălat bêt yiśrā'ēl* expresses the underlying

---

a connection with Arab. *'aṯara,* "to push," hence, "You have caused me to stumble," is unlikely ("Studies in Hebrew Philology: *'tr,'" AJSL* 50 [1934] 178). M. Baldacci proposes an infixed *t* stem from *'ûr* I, which with *'al* denotes "to rouse oneself against" ("Alcuni novi esempi di *taw* infisso nell'ebraico biblico," *BeO* 24 [1982] 107-14).

57. See *CAD,* 1/2:485-86; *AHW,* pp. 1489-90. For a discussion of this and related texts see N. M. Waldman, "A Note on Excessive Speech and Falsehood," *JQR* 67 (1976-77) 142-45.

58. The word recurs in 36:12 and appears frequently in chs. 44, 46, and 47. It is fundamental to the theology of Numbers, Deuteronomy, and Joshua.

59. G. von Rad, "The Promised Land and Yahweh's Land in the Hexateuch," in *The Problem of the Hexateuch and Other Essays,* tr. E. W. Trueman Dicken (New York: McGraw-Hill, 1966), p. 80.

60. H. O. Forshey, "The Hebrew Root *NḤL* and Its Semitic Cognates" (Th.D. diss., Harvard, 1973), p. 233. For further discussion of national territory as a divine estate and as a grant placed in the charge of human vassals see Block, *Gods of the Nations,* pp. 74-124. The traditional "inheritance" interpretation is defended by C. J. H. Wright, *God's People in God's Land: Family, Land, and Property in the Old Testament* (Grand Rapids: Eerdmans, 1990), pp. 19-23.

presupposition in this entire oracle. The land of Israel is her *naḥalâ,* her fiefdom to be managed on the landowner's behalf. The vassal tenant has been temporarily removed, but Yahweh remains its rightful owner. Any encroachment on the land by another nation is a direct challenge to him.

In her claims to Israel's territory Seir failed to recognize its owner. She treated the devastation of Yahweh's land and the deportation of its population either as a sign that like his people Yahweh had abandoned his land, or as simply the natural consequences of shifting political circumstances. She could not see the judgment of Yahweh upon his own people in the demise of the nation and the ruination of the land, let alone his concern to cleanse his land of its defilement. Consequently, the mountains of Israel were hers for the taking, like a carcass for vultures. But the first panel of this oracle reminds Edom and the audience that perceptions and reality may indeed be worlds apart.

b. The Nature of the Restoration: The Transformation of the Land (36:1-15)

♦ Nature and Design

If ch. 35 seems disjointed, 36:1-15 is even more so. Numerous repetitive and disruptive prophetic formulae appear to chop it up into little fragments.[1] Indeed, it is difficult to determine when Yahweh is addressing his messenger and when he is addressing the mountains. The result looks like a patchwork quilt, except that quilts usually reflect more deliberate design. Wevers describes this as "a hodge-podge" of materials.[2] Recent scholarship has tended to explain the text in terms of an authentic core, to which a series of interpretive additions have been added.[3] However, to attribute such a disjointed text to late editors not only places too heavy a burden on their shoulders but also contradicts logic. Later editors would have been concerned to create a smoother and clearer text, not one that was more confused. Since the language and style are thoroughly Ezekielian, there may be no need to attribute any of the present text (other than inadvertent scribal lapses) to later traditionists.

---

1. Repetitive material: (1) three times Ezekiel is commanded to prophesy (*hinnābē'* ... *wĕʾāmartā,* "Prophesy ... and say," vv. 1, 3, 6); twice the mountains of Israel are summoned to attention (vv. 1, 4); the citation formula occurs seven times (vv. 2, 3, 4, 5, 6, 7, 13); thrice the logical *yaʿan* ... *lākēn,* "Because ... therefore," sequence appears (cf. *yaʿan* in vv. 2, 3, 13; *lākēn* in vv. 3, 4, 5, 6, 7, 14). Disruptive formulae: "But as for you, mountains of Israel," in v. 8, and the recognition formula in v. 11, long before the end of the unit.

2. Wevers, *Ezekiel,* p. 267.

3. See Garscha, *Studien,* pp. 211-19; Simian, *Theologische Nachgeschichte,* pp. 67-87, 129-56; Fuhs, *Ezechiel 25–48,* pp. 199-200.

But this need not suggest that the oracle was originally delivered by Ezekiel in its present form. The present literary shape may well be the result of (his own?) editorial activity. Ezekiel undoubtedly spoke of the restoration of the land of Israel on numerous occasions. 36:1-15 appears to consist of one basic message, to which excerpts from other oracles that dealt with the same subject have been added. The basic oracle, complete with proper introduction, argumentation, and conclusion, must lurk somewhere in this maze, but any conclusion is tentative. I propose the following reconstruction of the history of the text.

Verses 1-2 seem certainly to have represented the introduction of the basic oracle. Since vv. 6-7 offer a reassuring declaration that Yahweh is on the side of the land of Israel, and that the harassment of the nations will be stopped, Zimmerli's suggestion that vv. 6-7 continue the core has merit: the resultant *ya'an . . . lākēn* linkage is typical of Ezekiel's oracles.[4] The formal conclusion may be located in the recognition formula at the end of v. 11, except that the verb is cast in the second person, with the mountains of Israel as the subject (see v. 8). After the announcement of judgment against the nations in v. 7, one would have expected them to be the ones recognizing Yahweh. But since this is not the case, the formula must have been preceded by a promise directed to the land of Israel, which is precisely what one finds in vv. 8-9. The opening *wě'attem hārê yiśrā'ê*, "But you, O mountains of Israel," in v. 8 provides a rhetorical signal of this shift in gears. The conjunction plus second person pronoun followed by the vocative of direct address occurs frequently in Ezekiel at transitional junctures.[5] While the content of vv. 10-11 provides a fitting sequel to vv. 8-9, the blatant redundancy leads most scholars to delete at least v. 10 as secondary. But since it is characteristic of Ezekielian style, redundancy alone is insufficient grounds for deletion.

The remaining segments of text, vv. 3-6 and 12-15, may have been incorporated secondarily into the written document, but this alone does not render them inauthentic. They probably represent excerpts from oracles delivered by the prophet on different occasions, but since they display affinities to the core, the editor probably inserted them at this point. Vv. 3-4 consist of four fragments, each signaled by its own prophetic formulae. Although vv. 12-15 are not formally introduced as a new piece, the new motif of childlessness suggests that these verses could derive from another prophecy.[6]

---

4. Zimmerli, *Ezekiel 2*, 231-32.

5. *wě'attâ ben-'ādām*, lit. "As for you, son of man," 2:6, 8; 3:25; 4:1; 5:1; 7:2; 12:3; 13:17; 21:11, 19, 33 (Eng. 6, 14, 28); 22:2; 24:25; 33:7, 10, 12, 30; 36:1; 39:1, 17; *wě'attem bêt yiśrā'ēl*, "As for you, O house of Israel," in 20:39; *wě'attâ ḥālāl rāšā*, "As for you, O wicked victim," 21:30 (Eng. 25); cf. *wě'attâ* without the vocative, 3:19, 21; 4:3, 4, 9; 12:4; 32:28; 33:9.

6. Cf. Jeremiah's use of the motif in 15:7.

In spite of these tensions in the text, the arrangement of the segments that make up 36:1-15 is not as random or arbitrary as scholars often maintain. Parunak finds in the unit a formal inversion of the chiasm found in ch. 35,[7] illustrated as follows:

35:1-15	**36:1-15**
heading, vv. 1-2	heading, v. 1a
absolute announcement of judgment, vv. 3-4	motivated announcement of judgment, vv. 1b-7
motivated announcements of judgment, vv. 5-9, 10-13	absolute announcement of judgment, vv. 8-12
absolute announcement of judgment, vv. 14-15	motivated announcement of judgment, vv. 13-14

But the logic of the arrangement extends beyond mere form to substance. The formal opening to v. 8 divides the second panel into two halves. The first (vv. 1b-7) highlights the judgment on the nations as the prerequisite to the salvation of Israel. The second (vv. 8-15) focuses entirely on the restoration of the land of Israel. This "halving strategy" is further substantiated by the fact that both segments conclude with a reference to the insults of the nations. The editor of Ezekiel's prophecies obviously intended this entire section to be interpreted as a unit, and the signatory formula at the end of v. 15 puts the divine imprimatur on the whole.

(1) Yahweh's Answer for the Nations (36:1-7)

1 "*As for you, human, prophesy to the mountains of Israel and say: 'O mountains of Israel! Hear the word of Yahweh!* 2 *Thus has the Lord Yahweh declared: Because the enemy has declared concerning you: "Aha! The ancient heights[8] have become[9] our possession!"'*"

---

7. Parunak, *Structural Studies,* pp. 456, 464-70.

8. Syr. smooths out the awkward copula on *ûbāmôt* by inserting a second *'āmar.* LXX ἔρημα αἰώνια (= *šimĕmat 'ôlām*) looks suspiciously harmonistic; cf. 35:9. MT is preferred by H. Haag, *Was lehrt die literarische Untersuchung des Ezechiel-Textes?* (Freiburg: Paulusdruckerei, 1943), pp. 19-20.

9. Although the sg. verb *hāyĕtâ* does not seem to fit its pl. subject *(bāmôt),* it may be understood in several ways, without recourse to emendation: the "heights" may be a collective sg. (Simian, *Nachgeschichte,* p. 130); one may understand *'ereṣ* as its subject (cf. 11:15; 33:24; 36:5); or it may reflect the influence of the adjacent *môrāšâ.*

3 *Therefore, prophesy and say, 'Thus has the Lord Yahweh declared: Assuredly, because[10] they have devastated and crushed you[11] from all sides, that you might become the possession of the rest of the nations, you have become[12] the subject of popular gossip and calumny.*

4 *Therefore, O mountains of Israel, hear the word of the Lord[13] Yahweh! Thus has the Lord Yahweh declared to the mountains and hills, the ravines and valleys, the desolate wastes and abandoned cities, which have become targets of plunder[14] and the object of scorn[15] to the remaining nations round about.*

5 *Therefore, thus has the Lord Yahweh declared: Surely, I have spoken[16] in the fire of my passion[17] against the rest of the nations, and against Edom,[18] all who have claimed my land as their own possession*

10. On *yaʿan bĕyaʿan* see Joüon-Muraoka, *Grammar,* §170f (2). Cf. Targ.'s expansion, "Because they vaunted their superiority, and because they thought to ruin you." LXX, Syr., and Vulg. telescope *yaʿan bĕyaʿan* into a single expression. Several Hebrew mss. harmonize with 13:10 and Lev. 26:43 by adding the copula to the asyndetic construction. Was it mistakenly attached to *bāmôt* in v. 2?

11. The variety among versional renderings reflects the extreme difficulty of *šammôt wĕšāʾōp:* LXX "Because they have insulted and hated you"; Targ. "They thought to ruin you and to make you desolate"; Vulg. "Because you are desolate and crushed." Syr. renders the phrase with three expressions. The emendation of *šmwt* to *śmwt,* cognate to Arab. *šamita,* "to treat with malice" (G. R. Driver, *Bib* 19 [1838] 181-82), or to *śmwḥ,* "to rejoice" (Fohrer, *Ezechiel,* p. 199), are ill advised, given the frequency of the root *šmm* in the context. After *yaʿan, šammôt* represents a rare form of the Qal infinitive (GKC, §67r; Bauer-Leander, *Grammatik,* §58pʹ). *šāʾōp* is an infinitive absolute of *šāʾap,* a by-form of *šûp,* "to trample on, crush." On the infinitive absolute functioning like a preceding infinitive construct see GKC, §113e; Joüon-Muraoka, *Grammar,* §§123x, 124r.

12. *tēʿālû* is a hybrid form combining Qal *(taʿālû)* and Niphal *(tēʿālû)* features. Cf. Bauer-Leander, *Grammatik,* §57tʺ.

13. Cf. Zimmerli (*Ezekiel 2,* pp. 228, 556-62). The presence of *ʾădōnāy* in two other occurrences of this formula (6:3; 25:3) cautions against deletion.

14. *BHS* revocalizes *lĕbaz* as *lĕbuz,* from *bûz,* "to despise," which forms a better parallel with the following *laʿag.* Thus apparently Targ., *lhyk wllʿyb,* "an object of derision and mockery." LXX supports MT.

15. The root *lʿg,* "to mock, deride," occurs elsewhere in the book only in 23:32, parallel to *ṣāḥaq,* "to laugh."

16. Cooke (*Ezekiel,* p. 394) notes that the perfect is rare after *ʾim-lōʾ;* cf. the more common *hinĕnî dibbartî* in v. 6. Since *dibbartî* often occurs with the self-identification formula, *ʾănî yhwh,* at the conclusion of oracles, its presence may allude to a previously delivered oracle.

17. *ʾēš qinʾâ,* "the fire of jealousy/passion," occurs elsewhere only in Zeph. 1:8 amd 3:18, but *ʾēš* and *qinʾâ* are also conjoined in Isa. 26:11 and Ps. 79:5.

18. The syntax of *wĕʿal ʾĕdôm kullāʾ,* "and against Edom, all of it," resembles 11:15 and esp. 35:15, which suggests that *kullāʾ* is an Aramaized form of *killāh.* However, before *ʾăšer* the final aleph is probably dittography.

with wholehearted delight and utter contempt,[19] *as their adjoining territory,*[20] *as booty.'*[21]

6 *Therefore, prophesy about the land of Israel, and say to the mountains and the hills, the ravines and valleys: 'Thus has the Lord Yahweh declared: Look! In my passionate fury*[22] *have I spoken,*[23] *because you have borne the taunting*[24] *of the nations.* 7 *Therefore, thus has the Lord Yahweh declared:*[25] *I hereby solemnly swear*[26] *that the nations all around you will themselves bear their own disgrace.'"*

As in most of Ezekiel's restoration oracles, the prospects for a new day for Israel depend on the resolution of problems of the past. This is the aim of the first half of ch. 36, as Yahweh outlines his response to the nations who have insulted the land of Israel.

19. *biš'āṭ nepeš*, lit. "scorn of soul/person," recalls *bĕkol-šā'ṭĕkā bĕnepeš* in 25:6, and *biš'āṭ bĕnepeš* in 25:15.

20. In Leviticus and Numbers *migrāš* denotes the territory adjoining the walls of a city given to the Levites as "pastureland," and this is how many understand it here. However, the sense of "pastureland" derives from the contexts in which the expression occurs, not from the word itself. See J. Barr, "*Migraš* in the Old Testament," *JSS* 29 (1984) 15-31. In the present context, Edom is portrayed as the city, and the mountains of Israel are the territory that the nation is claiming as its own.

21. It is difficult to make sense of *lĕma'an migrāšāh lābaz*. What is the antecedent of the suffix on *migrāšāh*, "her adjoining territory"? If *migrāš* is treated as an Aramaized infinitive construct (cf. GKC, §45e), with an object suffix, "my land" seems likely (cf. NASB, JB), except that "land" is an inappropriate object for the verb *gāraš*, commonly interpreted as "to drive (cattle)." More likely are the NJPS and NRSV treatment of *migrāš* as "pasture(land)," but this meaning of the noun in this context is strange. But if Edom is the antecedent, *migrāš* may be allowed its common meaning, "territory adjoining a city." See further the commentary. Many despair and delete the phrase as a gloss. Cf. Allen, *Ezekiel 20–48*, p. 168.

22. *bĕqin'ātî ûbahămātî*, "in my passion and in my wrath," is a hendiadys for "in my passionate fury."

23. The separation of *hinĕnî* from the verb (cf. 25:7; Jer. 44:26) and the use of the perfect after *hinnēh* add force to the statement.

24. The idiom *nāśā' kĕlimmâ*, "to bear the taunt," occurs frequently in Ezekiel: 16:52, 54; 32:24-25, 30; 34:29; 39:26; 44:13.

25. LXX retains *lākēn* but drops the citation formula, perhaps because of its perceived superfluity after v. 6.

26. Lit. "I have raised my hand." On the nonverbal gesture of raising the hand, see 20:5-6, 15, 23, 28, 42; 44:12.

(a) The Indictment of the Nations (36:1-2)

The emphatic opening *wě'attâ* signals a new command for the prophet and a new movement within the context of 35:1–36:15. Picking up on the phrase introduced earlier in 35:12, but drawn ultimately from 6:2, Ezekiel is charged to address the *mountains of Israel*. The expression *hārê yiśrā'ēl* not only reflects the hilly nature of the landscape of Ezekiel's homeland, perhaps in contrast to the alluvial plains of southern Mesopotamia where the exiles were residing, but also answers to *har-śē'îr,* "Mount Seir," in ch. 35. While the Israelites could identify the heartland of Edom with a single mountain, this was not true of their own country, whose topography was dominated by a series of ranges.[27] As in ch. 6, for which this oracle offers a restorative reflex, the direct address of the mountains of Israel highlights the prophet's current geographic focus. This prophecy concerns primarily the land of Israel, not the people.

In form vv. 1-2 resemble the introduction to the mini-oracles against foreign nations gathered in 25:1–26:6.[28] Although addressed to the mountains of Israel, the opening lines represent a modified third person indictment of Israel's enemies,[29] whose identity is withheld until v. 5, which refers to "the remnant of the nations and all Edom." The expression of glee is problematic, particularly the reference to *the ancient heights (bāmôt 'ôlām)*. Elsewhere in Ezekiel *bāmôt* denotes idolatrous high places (6:3, 6; 16:16; 20:29). But the root *bmh* refers fundamentally to the back or center of the body of an animal, a usage attested in both Akkadian and Ugaritic, and reflected in Deut. 33:29, where it refers to the back of a man.[30] Here it seems to be used in a derived geographic sense of "outbacks," ridges, or high places in the landscape.[31]

---

27. See Beitzel, *Moody Atlas,* pp. 25-42.

28. Note the dual command to "Prophesy and say to X," the summons to the addressee to "Hear the word of the Lord Yahweh," the emphatic placement of the vocative subject at the head of the verse (on which see J. C. de Moor, "The Art of Versification on Ugarit and Israel," *UF* 12 [1980] 314), the form of a motivated judgment speech governed by the *ya'an . . . lākēn,* "Because . . . therefore," structure (though the function of *lākēn* is slightly different in v. 3 and Yahweh's response is delayed until v. 4), and the casting of the indictment in the form of a direct taunting quotation (cf. 25:2, 8; 26:1). Indeed, the opening interjection, *he'āḥ,* is identical to the exclamations of the Ammonites (25:2) and Tyrians (26:2).

29. The root *'yb* occurs only four times in Ezekiel: *'ôyēb/'ôyēbîm,* "enemy/enemies," here and in 39:27; *'êbâ,* "enmity," in 25:15 and 35:5.

30. See Akk. *bāmtu(m)* (*AHW,* p. 101); Ugar. *bmt* (*UT,* p. 373, no. 480). See also the figurative adaptation of *bāmâ* to the back of clouds in Isa. 14:14 and Job 9:8.

31. Cf. 2 Sam. 1:19, 25; Amos 4:13; Mic. 1:3; 3:12; Isa. 58:14; Ps. 18:34 (Eng. 33). For further discussion see K.-D. Schunck, *TDOT,* 2:139-40.

Ezekiel's *ancient heights* is therefore a poetic designation for the mountains of Israel.[32]

The indictment generalizes to the nations Edom's specific claim to the mountains of Israel as their *possession. môrāšâ* derives from *yāraš,* which refers fundamentally to the transfer of property and may signify either "to possess" or "to dispossess."[33] Plöger views the word as technical war terminology, representing the human activity, the act of taking possession involved in the transfer of territory, as opposed to the divine action, that is, the granting *(nātan)* of the land.[34] The present characteristically Ezekielian form, *môrāšâ,* contrasts with *yĕruššâ,* the common designation for territorial possession in Deuteronomic writings. Similar claims to the same land had been made by those Judeans who had escaped the deportation in 11:15 and 33:24. The present claimants will soon discover that the true owner of the land is Yahweh, and in his eyes there is only one nationality that may rightfully claim this territory as their *môrāšâ,* their fiefdom.

(b) Yahweh's Disposition Toward the Nations (36:3-5)

Yahweh's disposition toward the nations who have railed on the mountains of Israel is described in a triad of fragments (vv. 3, 4, 5) that have been inserted into the basic oracle. The combination of the opening word-event formula, with the particle *lākēn,* a new command to prophesy, the citation formula, and the absence of an announcement of judgment after *ya῾an bĕya῾an,* "because," in v. 3 in particular create the impression of a secondary insertion. But v. 3 continues the indictment of Israel's enemies begun in v. 2, though in an indirect manner, with the crimes being described from the perspective of the victims. This divine word summarizes the actions of the enemies toward the mountains of Israel, their intention, and the results.

Two words describe the treatment the enemies have afforded the mountains of Israel. The form of the first, *šammôt, devastated,* is new, but its meaning is clear.[35] The second verb, *šā᾽ōp, crushed,* is less common, and may have been chosen for assonantal reasons. *šā᾽ap* is used in two different senses,

---

32. On mountains as symbols of eternality and stability see Deut. 33:15; Hab. 3:6; Isa. 54:10; Job 15:7; Ps. 90:2; Prov. 8:25.

33. See F. Dreyfus, "La théme de l'héritage dans l'Ancien Testament," *RSPT* 42 (1958) 5-8.

34. J. G. Plöger, *Literarische, formgeschichtliche und stilkritische Untersuchungen zum Deuteronomium,* BBB 26 (Bonn: Hanstein, 1967), p. 83. Similar usage is evident in the Moabite Stone or Mesha Inscription, *KAI,* 181.7; *TSSI,* 1:16.7. On the term see further H. H. Schmid, *THAT,* 1:778-81.

35. The infinitive *šammôt* is cognate to the oft-repeated *šĕmāmâ* and *mĕšammâ* (35:3, 4, 7, 14, 15; 36:4).

"to pant, to gasp for air,"[36] and "to trample, crush." Whether these are homonyms or one is derivative from the other is difficult to determine, but the present usage is illumined by Ps. 56:2-3 (Eng. 1-2) and 57:4 (Eng. 3), where the psalmist pleads for deliverance from his enemies who are trampling on him all day long. In Amos 2:7 and 8:4 the verb describes the exploitation of the poor. This had been the experience of the mountains of Israel in the wake of the Babylonian conquest. From all sides the enemies had come, taking advantage of them in their destitution.

According to the second clause, the aim of the enemies was to claim the mountains of Israel as their *possession (môrāšâ)*. The statement offers the first clue concerning the identity of the foes; here and in v. 4 they are referred to as *the rest of the nations (šĕʾērît haggôyim)*. *šĕʾērît* denotes fundamentally "residue, remainder" (cf. 25:16), but Ezekiel uses it of those who have survived divine judgment (5:10; 9:8; 11:13). Here it must refer to those people that survive after the Babylonian campaigns in the Levant. Conquerors deliberately attempted to crush the national spirit of defeated nations by deporting whole populations. By the time the Persians and the Greeks under Alexander had had their turns in the region, many nationalities had disappeared from the map. Earlier we witnessed Ezekiel's compatriots, the survivors of Nebuchadrezzar's Judean campaign, claiming the national territory as their *môrāšâ* (11:15; 33:24); now outsiders are doing the same.

As a result of the enemies' actions, like the prophet himself in 33:30-33, the mountains have become the subject of popular gossip. Two expressions describe this gossip (v. 3b). The first, *wĕtēʿălû ʿal-śĕpat lāšôn* (lit. "they have been taken up on the lip of the tongue"), sounds redundant to our ears[37] but its meaning is clear. The second, *dibbat-ʿām,* is rare. *dibbâ* is used elsewhere of the "bad report" about his brothers that Joseph brought to his father (Gen. 37:2), of slanderous stories of plots against the righteous (Prov. 10:18; 25:10; Ps. 31:14 [Eng. 13]; Jer. 20:10), and of unfavorable (and faithless) reports resulting from an investigation (Num. 13:32; 14:36-37). In this context the gossip involves the land of Israel's failure to fulfill its part in the deity-nation-land relationship. Instead of providing security and prosperity for its inhabitants, the mountains of Israel are known as devourers of their population.

4 As in v. 3, the introductory particle *lākēn* is rhetorical, calling the audience's attention to the divine speech to follow. The combination of a vocative address to the mountains of Israel, the summons to hear the word of Yahweh, and the citation formula may suggest that this verse once stood at the beginning of an independent oracle, and that like v. 3 it has been second-

---

36. Jer. 2:24; 14:6. Cf. to pant after shade, Job 7:2; to long for the night, Job 36:20.
37. One expects either "on the lips" or "on the tongue."

arily inserted here. This conclusion is supported by the topographical list of addressees, which is strangely redundant before v. 6. But the presence of the list confirms that *hārê yiśrā'ēl*, "mountains of Israel," in this entire literary unit functions as a general designation for the territory of Israel rather than as a restricted reference to the highlands. The quartet of topographical expressions — mountains *(hārîm)*, hills *(gĕbā'ôt)*, ravines *('ăpîqîm)*, and valleys *(gē'āyôt)* — may help explain the insertion. The list, obviously borrowed from 6:3, alerts the audience to interpret this message of salvation as a reversal of the earlier judgment oracle. This intention is strengthened with the addition of "the desolate wastes" *(hŏrābôt haššōmĕmôt)* and "the abandoned cities" *('ārîm hanne'ĕzābôt)*.[38] Because of the ruination of the land it has been seized as booty *(baz)* and become the object of derision *(la'ag)* to the remaining nations *(šĕ'ērît haggôyim)* surrounding Israel.

5 A third insertion is signaled by another *lākēn*, followed by the citation formula. The reference to Yahweh's passion *(qin'â)* ties this verse to v. 6; the references to "the remaining nations" *(šĕ'rît haggôyim)* and "for booty" *(lĕbaz)* link this verse with v. 4. The reference to Edom provides the key to the purpose of this insertion. Since Edom is named nowhere else in 36:1-15, this addition forges a connection to the oracle against this nation in 35:1-15. Now we learn that Edom functions representatively for those nations that have seized Israelite territory for themselves.

Yahweh's excitement is hinted at in the asseverative particle *'im-lō'*, "Assuredly, by all means,"[39] but explicitly expressed in his own admission that his declarations against the nations and Edom have been uttered *in the fire of my passion,* that is, in zeal for his honor. Three dimensions of the enemies' conduct had brought his reputation into question. First, the actions of Edom and the nations involved staking claims on Yahweh's land *('arṣî)*. To a casual observer this might have appeared simply as a historical event, a case of opportunists moving in and grabbing the territory of their crushed neighbors. However, these enemies have overlooked the divine implications of their actions. Their seizure of the land of Israel was an insult to Yahweh, the true owner of the land. He could not sit idly by. Second, their attitude was an affront to Yahweh. They had seized the land with unrestrained delight and utter contempt. Finally, their intentions demanded a divine response. Their claim to the mountains of Israel as their own possession *(môrāšâ)*, adjoining territory *(migrāš)*, and booty *(bāz)*, represented a direct challenge to Yahweh. His inflamed passion over the actions of Edom and the nations against the land of Israel as a whole recalls in particular the psalmist's lament over the destruction of Jerusalem in Ps. 79:1-8:

38. These expressions also provide a link with vv. 10, 22, 38.
39. See GKC, §149.

O God, the nations have entered your domain (naḥălâ).
> They have defiled your holy temple,
> and laid Jerusalem in ruins.
They have left the corpses of your servants
> as food for the fowl of heaven,
and the flesh of your faithful for the wild beasts.
Their blood was spilled like water around Jerusalem,
> with none to bury them.
We have become the butt of our neighbors' jokes,
> the scorn (la'ag) and derision of those around us.
How long, O Yahweh, will you be angry forever,
> will your indignation blaze like fire?
Pour out your fury on the nations that do not know you,
> upon the kingdoms that do not invoke your name.
For they have devoured Jacob,
> and desolated his homeland.

(c) The Sentencing of the Nations (36:6-7)

After the interruption of vv. 3-5, v. 6 resumes the basic oracle. Although the addressee is identified as *the land of Israel ('admat yiśrā'ēl),* which is defined more specifically as the mountains, hills, ravines, and valleys,[40] these verses announce Yahweh's response to the crimes of the nations cited in the indictment in v. 2.

Functioning as an indirect oracle of salvation, the proclamation makes three important affirmations. First, Yahweh announces his presence. For the beleaguered land, one simple word, *hinĕnî* (lit. "behold me!"), represented the best news imaginable. Yahweh has appeared to defend his land. Second, Yahweh speaks. The land has borne the insults of the nations long enough, and Yahweh's own passion has been ignited. He will have the last word, the content of which is recorded in the following verses. Third, Yahweh swears that the nations will take their own medicine. With raised hand he pronounces the sentence. The nature of the nations' punishment is not specified, but for Israel to hear that the tables will be turned and that the nations will bear their own disgrace *(nāśā' kĕlimmâ)* is enough.

(2) Yahweh's Answer for the Land (36:8-15)

8 "'As for you, O mountains of Israel, you will grow your branches[41] and bear your fruit for my people Israel,[42] for their return

40. See the comments on v. 4 above.
41. LXX "grapes" misreads 'npkm as 'nbkm. On 'ānāp see 17:23; 31:3.
42. LXX drops "Israel."

331

is imminent.[43] 9 *For see now, I am on your side, and I will turn to you, and you will be tilled and sown.* 10 *I will multiply people on you, the entire house of Israel, all of it! The cities will be resettled, and the ruined sites rebuilt.* 11 *I will multiply people and animals on you. They will increase and be fruitful.*[44] *I will resettle you the way you once were,*[45] *and I will make you more prosperous than ever before. Then you will know that I am Yahweh.*

12 *I will cause humans, my people Israel, to walk on you!*[46] *They will take possession of you, and you will become their domain. You will never again rob them of their children.*[47]

13 *Thus has the Lord Yahweh declared: Because people are saying*[48] *to you,*[49] *"You*[50] *are a [land] that devours humans and robs your nation*[51] *of children,"* 14 *therefore [hear],*[52] *you will never again devour humans, nor will you ever rob*[53] *your nation again of children. The*

43. *kî qĕrĕbû lābô'*, lit. "for they are near to come." Targ. reads "the day of my redemption draws near."

44. Many delete *wĕrābû ûpārû* with LXX because it interrupts the sequence of first person statements. Cf. Allen, *Ezekiel 20–48*, p. 169. However, the third person also occurs in v. 12.

45. *kqdmwtykm*, "as in your former times," compares with the sg. in 16:55.

46. LXX καὶ γεννήσω reads *whwlkty* as *whwldty*, "I shall cause you to give birth," perhaps an inadvertent mistake or reflective of a different *Vorlage*. Targ. *w'sgy*, "I will multiply," has been influenced by v. 11.

47. The switch to second masc. sg. suffixes in this line leads many (e.g., Zimmerli, *Ezekiel 2*, p. 231) to delete it as secondary. But the suffixes should probably be repointed as fem., since the reference is to land. The sg. shifts the attention from the mountains of Israel to the land as a whole. The pl. forms in LXX and Syr. are secondary attempts to smooth out the grammar.

48. Since *ya'an* usually precedes an infinitive construct, *BHS* emends *'ōmĕrîm* to *'omrām*. Cf. 25:3, 6, 8. But the indefinite pl. before a quotation is encountered elsewhere in 8:12; 13:7; 37:11.

49. The versions read sg., *lāk*, but this is surely a secondary smoothing out of the text. The *lākem/lāk* interchange reflects an alternation of vision between the mountains of Israel (masc.) and the land as a whole (fem.).

50. Kethib's archaic form of the fem. pronoun *'ty* occurs elsewhere in Judg. 17:2; 1 K. 11:2; 2 K. 4:16, 23; 8:1; Jer. 4:30. Qere commends the more conventional *'t*. See GKC, §32h.

51. Qere reads pl., *gwyyk*, but the versions support the sg. of Kethib. Syr. recognizes the unusual nature of *gwy* with a suffix and reads *'m* in its place. See the commentary.

52. Normally *lākēn* follows *ya'an*, introducing a description of Yahweh's response to previously cited crimes, usually preceded by the citation formula. As in Isa. 30:18, here *lākēn* has approximately the force of *hinnēh*, "Behold," at the beginning of a promise. See March, in *Rhetorical Criticism*, p. 280.

53. Kethib reads *tkšly*, an obvious metathesis for *tškly*. Cf. Qere, numerous Hebrew mss., and the versions, viz., "you will not stumble."

declaration of the Lord Yahweh. 15 *I will never allow the insults of the nations against you to be heard again. Nor will you ever again bear the taunting of the peoples. And you will never again rob your nation*[54] *of children.*[55] *The declaration of the Lord Yahweh.'"*

(a) The Promise of a New Day for the Land (36:8-11)

8 *As for you (wĕ'attem)* followed by the vocative address of the mountains of Israel signals a turning point in the oracle. What follows is an exciting and excited announcement of the reversal of the land's humiliation. The description of the new day envisions the complete restoration of the deity-nation-land relationship. The sign of the new day will be the renewed fruitfulness of the land, described according to the ancient covenant blessings (Lev. 26:1-13). The mountains of Israel are portrayed as a tree whose boughs are filled once more with branches and fruit. However, the transformation presupposes two momentous events. First, the covenant relationship between Yahweh and his people Israel will have been reestablished. What a welcome sound it should have been for Ezekiel's audience to hear Yahweh referring to Israel endearingly as *'ammî,* "my people," once again. The benefactors of the new fertility of the land will be the nation whom Yahweh had chosen for himself, and to whom he had originally given this land. Second, the nation of Israel will have come back home from its exile. In terms reminiscent of earlier predictions of the day of Yahweh (7:7; 30:3) and of the judgment of Israel (9:1; 12:23), Yahweh announces the imminent return of the people to their homeland. The divorce of 586 B.C. will finally be reversed as people and land are brought together once again.

9-11 The focus shifts from the land to Yahweh, the agent behind these exciting developments. The recitation of divine benefactions is prefaced with an announcement of his new disposition toward the land. By a clever and unique wordplay, the hostile orientation formula *hinĕnî 'ălêkem,* usually "I am against you," is transformed into a declaration of commitment: *I am on your side.* The first sign of Yahweh's new attitude is expressed in *and I will turn to you (ûpānîtî 'ălêkem),* which recalls Yahweh's covenant promise in Lev. 26:9, "I will turn to you *(ûpānîtî 'ălêkem)* and make you fruitful and multiply you, and I will confirm my covenant with you." As a consequence, land formerly wasted will be cultivated once again.

10 Yahweh's new commitment to the land will be evidenced con-

---

54. As in v. 14 Qere reads pl. *gwyyk* for sg. *gwyk* of Kethib. This entire line is missing in LXX (except LXX[B]) and Syr.

55. On the basis of *lectio difficilior* one might retain Kethib's *tkšly* (see NRSV, NASV, etc.), but as in v. 14 this appears to be a metathetical error for *tškly.*

cretely by his multiplication of its population. V. 10 specifies that this new population will not consist of Edomites or any other foreign nation, but the entire house of Israel. With *the entire house of Israel (bêt yiśrā'ēl kullâ),* Yahweh stresses that this will not be simply a partial restoration with a few people or clans trickling back. Although he does not elaborate, by "the house of Israel" the prophet is undoubtedly thinking of the twelve tribes that had originally constituted the nation, not just Judah alone.[56] As a result of the burgeoning population, the desolate ruins will be rebuilt and the abandoned cities reoccupied.

11 Ezekiel drives this point home even more emphatically by extending the scope of the land's transformation. The multiplication will affect all life, human and animal alike. The phrase *they will increase and be fruitful* is an obvious echo of the divine blessing of beasts in Gen. 1:22 and humans in 1:28 as well as 9:1, 7. This new fertility will exceed anything the land has experienced in history; the land will be like paradise itself, and thus proclaim the mystery and presence of the divine person.

(b) The Promise of a New Day for the People (36:12-15)

12 After the recognition formula in v. 11, v. 12 is striking for its unannounced shift in focus from the land to its occupants, and for its introduction of a new theme of a land cutting off the children of its population. This is undoubtedly an authentic Ezekielian saying, but probably another secondary addition to the core oracle, intended to elaborate on the subject of *'ammî yiśrā'ēl,* "my people Israel," who will once more occupy the mountains of Israel.[57] The note specifies four stages in the reoccupation of the land. First, the empty cities and ruin heaps will bustle with life as Yahweh causes people *to walk* on the land once more. The use of *hôlaktî* presents a contrast with 35:7, which spoke of the elimination of all who go to and fro on Mount Seir. But the population will not be simply whichever people happen to migrate into the land or stake their claim on it. These are none other than "my people Israel." Second, this population *will take possession* of the land. The verb *yāraš* intentionally answers to claims of the nations to the mountains of Israel as their *môrāšâ* (cf. 35:10; 36:3, 5). Third, the divine suzerain will return the land to Israel as their *domain* or official grant *(naḥălâ),* ending the insults of the Edomites over its desolation (35:15). Fourth, the land will never again cut off the progeny of its population. The imagery seems odd, but the promise reverses 5:17, in which Ezekiel had warned of the divine agents — famine, wild beasts, the plague, bloodshed, and the sword — bereaving Judah of her

---

56. This notion will be resumed and developed more fully in ch. 37.
57. As suggested by the continuation of the masc. pl.

children. But here the land is personified as having stifled natural maternal feelings for the nation that inhabits it and having robbed the nation of its children. Yahweh hereby promises that this will never happen again.

13-15   Although the *Because . . . therefore (ya'an . . . lākēn)* here suggests another addition, this excerpt from another oracle has been thoroughly integrated into the present context.[58] After the opening citation formula, as in 35:10 and 36:12, the occasion for this utterance is given in the form of a direct quotation, which summarizes the taunts of the nations. Again the imagery is grotesque. The land of Israel is portrayed as a vicious beast, with a rapacious appetite for humans, *devouring ('ākal)* her own population and leaving her nation bereft of any progeny. While the allusion is most directly to 5:13-17, the figure of speech also recalls the early Israelite surveyors' description of the land of Canaan as "a land that devours its inhabitants" (*'ereṣ 'ōkelet yôšĕbêhā hiw'*, Num. 13:32).[59] Contributing to the remarkable nature of the imagery is Ezekiel's use of the expression *gôyayik, your nation.* In contrast to *'am,* "people," which is a warm, relational expression, *gôy* is a cold and rigid designation for a group of people as a political entity. Whereas suffixed forms of the former appear hundreds of times in the OT, pronominal suffixes are attached to *gôy* only nine times and in only four contexts.[60] Only twice is Israel referred to as "Yahweh's nation."[61] Inverting the normal roles, Ezekiel personifies the land of Israel as the owner of the nation that inhabits it. The preference for *your nation* over "your people" or the national name "Israel" highlights the prophet's conviction that the devastation of the land signified not only its depopulation but also the loss of a political entity, the legitimate national tenants of a territory.

The opening *lākēn (therefore)* in v. 14 is difficult, but it appears to function rhetorically, heightening the hearer's anticipation and highlighting the ensuing declaration. Accordingly, vv. 14-15 announce a fundamental transformation in the disposition of the land of Israel toward its inhabitants. The segment is structured on an ABA pattern. The first and last components consist

---

58. The absence of a subject for the participle *'ōmĕrîm,* "saying," assumes continuity with the foregoing; the masc. pl. form of the indirect object, *lākem,* "to you," refers to the previously mentioned mountains of Israel; the reference to the bereaved nation continues the thought of v. 12; the phrase *kĕlimmat haggôyim,* "the insults of the nations," provides a lexical link with v. 6.

59. Note also the contrast with the metaphor of a land, whose inhabitants have been sent off into exile, "spewing out its population" in Lev. 18:25, 28.

60. Outside our text: (1) of self-consciously political entities in the colophonic summaries of the Table of Nations, Gen. 10:5, 20, 31, 32; (2) parallel to *'ammî,* "my people," in Zeph. 2:9; (3) parallel to *bĕḥîrêkā,* "my chosen ones," and *naḥălātĕkā,* your possession," in Ps. 106:5. For a study of the term and its relationship to *'am* see Block, "Foundations of National Identity," pp. 84-127; also idem, *ISBE,* 3:492-93.

61. Zeph. 2:9; Ps. 106:5, on which see A. Cody, "When is the Chosen People Called a *Gôy?*" *VT* 145 (1964) 1-6.

of promissory statements, describing the effects of the restoration on the land and her nation, between which is sandwiched Yahweh's affirmation of his own personal involvement in the event (v. 15a). He hereby announces that he will terminate forever the insults of the nations against the land of Israel by altering fundamentally the relationship between territory and nation and putting an end to the land's appetite for human flesh. The double signatory formula guarantees the promise.

♦ *Theological Implications*

Many themes represented in this oracle are familiar from previous prophecies, but several are afforded a new slant and a new emphasis. First, the promises of Yahweh are sure. This oracle addresses the heart of Israel's theology and one of the primary issues behind the spiritual crisis of the exiles: Had Yahweh forgotten his ancient promises to Abraham to give to him and his descendants the land of Canaan as an eternal possession?[62] This promise had been fulfilled under Joshua, when Yahweh dispossessed the Canaanites and delivered the land to his people as their fiefdom (*naḥălâ*). But the devastation of the land and the deportation of its population had cast serious doubt on Yahweh's willingness or ability to keep his word. The rupture of the deity-nation-land relationship was complete and apparently permanent. The present oracle addresses this theological and national crisis.

But there is a mysterious logic in Ezekiel's message. The same promises he seems to have repudiated in his earlier announcements of woe have now become the basis for his prophecies of hope. In the immediate past, the people's rebellion had disqualified them from benefiting from the ancient promises, but these same pledges provide the basis for Ezekiel's vision for the future. Yahweh had not forgotten his land or the fundamental relationship existing between it and his people, Israel. He would personally answer the Edomite claim to their territory and bring the taunts of the nations over the desolated landscape to an end. And he would restore the fiefdom and transform the relationship between the land and its people.[63] In the divine word the exiles could find new hope for their future.

Second, those who position themselves in opposition to the people of Yahweh render themselves his enemies. Taunts against the kingdom of God are ultimately insults against God himself. He must therefore come to their aid for his own name's sake. He will build his church; neither the gates of

---

62. *'ăḥuzzat 'ôlām*. Cf. Gen. 17:8; 13:14-17; 15:18-21.
63. On the "land" motif in Ezekiel see further W. Zimmerli, "The 'Land' in the Pre-exilic and Early Post-exilic Prophets," in *Understanding the Word*, Fest. B. W. Anderson, ed. J. T. Butler, et al., JSOTSup 37 (Sheffield: JSOT Press, 1985), pp. 255-58.

Edom and the nations nor hell itself shall prevail against it. The peoples of this earth may arrogantly seek to carve out for themselves a place under the sun. In the end, however, God determines the boundaries and the places of the nations in history. This was true of those who professed to be the people of Qaus (Edom); it remains true of all who bow down to any other god today.

3. The Restoration of Yahweh's Honor (36:16-38)

♦ Nature and Design

The word-event formula in 36:16, followed by the divine address of Ezekiel with "human," signals the commencement of a new oracle, which carries on until the recognition formula in v. 38. But the intervening material is extremely complex, being punctuated by numerous typical Ezekielian prophetic formulae: the citation formula, "Thus has the Lord Yahweh declared" (vv. 22, 33, 37), the signatory formula, "the declaration of the Lord Yahweh" (vv. 23b, 32), and variations of the recognition formula (vv. 23b, 36). Vv. 33-36 and 37-38 are most readily isolated as subunits, if not actually independent fragments. The issue in vv. 17-32 is not so clear. Scholars do not agree on whether this section should be interpreted as a coherent whole or as a composite. On the basis of style, vv. 17-21 are readily distinguishable from vv. 22-32. The former section is cast in the form of a divine speech addressed to Ezekiel himself, with the nation of Israel referred to in the third person. But vv. 22-32 are cast as a divine speech to be relayed by the prophet to his audience. It opens with a charge to the prophet to speak to the "house of Israel," concludes with a hortatory appeal to the "house of Israel," and refers to Israel throughout with the second person of direct address. Furthermore, the presence of the declaration "Not for your sakes have I acted" in vv. 22 and 32 creates an effective *inclusio* for the prophetic speech. Nevertheless, the opening *lākēn*, "Therefore," in v. 22 recognizes a logical connection between the two parts. But this apparent cohesiveness of vv. 22-32 is disturbed by several disjunctive features. In addition to the recognition and signatory formulae in v. 23b, to be noted are the shifts in subject matter as one proceeds through this section, particularly the intrusive reference to the new heart and new spirit that Yahweh will implant within the nation (vv. 26-28); this reference breaks up the discussion of the cleansing of the nation from its uncleanness.

    Scholars have responded to these features in a variety of ways, usually with complex theories of the text's evolution.[1] The issue is complicated by

---

1. See most recently S. Ohnesorge, *Jahwe gestaltet sein Volk neu: Zur Sicht der Zukunft Israels nach Ez 11,14-21; 20,1-44; 36,16-38; 37,1-14.15-28*, FB 64 (Würzburg:

divergences in vv. 23-38 from the rest of the translational block consisting of chs. 26–39 in the extant Greek manuscripts, and the omission of vv. 23bβ-30 in Papyrus 967 and in the Old Latin Codex Wirceburgensis.[2] The former, dated from the 2nd or early 3rd century A.D., represents our earliest witness of the pre-Hexaplaric LXX of Ezekiel. In addition to omitting this segment, this papyrus rearranges chs. 36–39 as follows: 36:1-23b; 38–39; 37; 40–48. The 6th-century Codex Wirceburgensis represents one of the two earliest and best preserved Vetus Latina manuscripts of Ezekiel.[3] That this codex does not follow Papyrus 967 in many of its omissions suggests that it represents an independent textual witness.[4]

Echter, 1991), pp. 203-82. The simplest explanation recognizes three oracles: vv. 22-32, 33-36, 37-38 (Allen, *Ezekiel 20–48*, p. 176). Others identify four stages in the growth of the text: (1) Vv. 17-23bα contain the original core, accounting for Yahweh's determination to restore Israel to its homeland. Vv. 17-21 describe the dilemma the exile has created for Yahweh's reputation; vv. 22-23bα, his actions to vindicate his name. (2) Vv. 23bβ-32 were added by a later traditionist, a conclusion confirmed by the "somewhat lame recapitulation of the theme of the original oracle" in v. 32 (Wevers, *Ezekiel*, p. 271). (3) Another traditionist added vv. 33-36, distinguishable by the stereotypical phrases used to describe the restoration. (4) The opening citation formula followed by '*ôd zō't* in v. 37 identifies vv. 37-38 as a final accretion. Since even the first stage seems to expect an imminent return from the exile, and appears to have borrowed its key ideas from so-called Deutero-Isaiah, many deny the prophet Ezekiel any hand in this text at all. For variations of this approach see Wevers, *Ezekiel*, p. 272; Zimmerli, *Ezekiel 2*, pp. 22-23; Garscha, *Studien*, pp. 216-19. For different but even more pessimistic results, esp. relating to the prophet's involvement, see Simian, *Theologische Nachgeschichte*, pp. 89-103; and Hossfeld, *Untersuchungen*, pp. 329-40.

2. On the Greek mss. see McGregor, *Greek Text of Ezekiel*, pp. 190-91. On Papyrus 967 cf. F. V. Filson, "The Omission of Ezek. 12 26-28 and 36 23b-38 in Codex 967," *JBL* 62 (1943) 27-32. Segments of Papyrus 967 have been published by F. G. Kenyon, *The Chester Beatty Papyri: Ezekiel*, Fasc. 7 (London, 1937), and A. C. Johnson, H. S. Gehman, and E. H. Kase, Jr., *The John H. Scheide Biblical Papyri* (Princeton, 1938); L. G. Jahn, *Der griechischer Text des Buches Ezechiel nach dem Kölner Teil des Papyrus 967*, Papyrologische Texte und Abhandlungen 15 (Bonn, 1972); M. Fernandez Galiano, "Nuevas páginas del códice 967 del A.T. griego (Ez 28,19–43,9) (PMatr. bibl. 1)," *Studia Papyrologica* 10 (1971) 7-76. Most of 11:25–48:35 is now available, though for his work Ziegler had only the Chester Beatty and Scheide papyri, which did not include our text (*Ezechiel*, p. 28; idem, "Die Bedeutung des Chester Beatty-Scheide Papyrus 967 für die Text Überlieferung der Ezechiel-Septuaginta," *ZAW* 61 [1945/48] 76-94). These were found later in Cologne and Madrid, and have been discussed by D. Fraenkel, "Nachtrag zur 1. Auflage von 1952," in Ziegler, *Ezechiel*, 2nd ed. (1977), pp. 332-52. On Vetus Latina see P.-M. Bogaert, "Le témoignage de la Vetus Latina dans l'étude de la tradition des Septante Ézéchiel et Daniel dans le Papyrus 967," *Bib* 59 (1978) 387-92.

3. The ms. was published by E. Ranke, *Par palimpsestorum Wirceburgensium* (Vienna: G. Braumüller, 1871).

4. So J. Lust, "Ezekiel 36–40 in the Oldest Greek Manuscript," *CBQ* 43 (1981) 518.

Because scholars have tended to treat this omission as parablepsis,[5] this factor has until relatively recently received little attention in discussions of the history of the text. But this interpretation has come under increasing criticism.[6] An omission of 1,451 letters is too long for an accidental skip of the scribe's eye; an omission of this length is unprecedented in the papyrus.[7] Not even the most absentminded scribe would have overlooked a passage so rich in theological meaning.[8] Furthermore, if this were an accidental omission, v. 23b should be followed by 37:1, not by 38:1, with ch. 37 being inserted between chs. 39 and 40.

Having rejected the parableptic explanation, Lust offers his own creative interpretation. He proposes that Papyrus 967 preserves the earlier form of the book of Ezekiel and that MT's arrangement is secondary and late, perhaps an anti-Christian Pharisaic reaction, with 36:23c-38 composed to provide a transition between 36:16-23b and ch. 37.[9] In addition to the omission of this text from Papyrus 967 (and Codex Wirceburgensis), and its numerous deviations from the Greek style elsewhere in the book, Lust is impressed with (1) the fact that 36:23b concludes with the recognition formula, usually the mark of the end of an oracle or text unit; and (2) the unusually high number of stylistic anomalies in the Hebrew of 36:23c-38,[10] which point to an editorial hand other than the one(s) responsible for the rest of the book. Some of the forms reflect postbiblical developments in the language itself.[11]

However, several factors caution against a too hasty rejection of MT

5. The scribe's eye having skipped from the recognition formula in v. 23 to v. 38. Cf. Filson, *JBL* 62 (1943) 31; Wevers, *Ezekiel*, p. 273.

6. Cf. Lust, *CBQ* 43 (1981) 517-33; Bogaert, *Bib* 59 (1978) 384-95.

7. So also M. V. Spottorno, "La omisión de Ez. 36,23b-38 y la transposición de capitulos en el papiro 967," *Emerita* 50 (1982) 93-98. The problem was already noted by Irwin, *Problem of Ezekiel*, p. 62 n. 3.

8. Lust, *CBQ* 43 (1981) 520.

9. Ibid., pp. 525-28.

10. Lust (ibid., pp. 521-24) cites the following: (1) *zāraq* to denote pouring clean water over people (v. 25; only here in the OT); (2) the pl. of *ṭum'â* for the people's defilement (vv. 25, 29); (3) *wa'āśîtî 'et 'ăšer* followed by a purpose clause (v. 27); (4) *'ānōkî* for *'ănî*, "I" (v. 28); (5) "The land which I gave to your fathers" (v. 28), (6) *nātan* plus *rā'āb*, "to give famine" (v. 29; cf. *šillaḥ*, "to send," in 5:15, 16; 14:13); (7) *ma'alĕlîm*, "wanton deeds," for *'ălîlâ* (v. 31); (8) *ṭihar*, "to cleanse," with "iniquity" as the object (v. 33); (9) the conjunctive phrase *taḥat 'ăšer* (v. 34); (10) the emphatic particle *hallēzû* (v. 35; only here in the OT); (11) *ḥārēb*, "desolate," as an adjective, in place of *ḥorbâ* (v. 35); (12) the combination of *bānâ*, "to build," *nāṭa'*, "to plant," *hāras*, "to destroy" (v. 36); (13) *nidraš lĕ* of God permitting his people to inquire of him.

11. E.g., the emphatic particle *hallēzû* (v. 35), which seems to belong to postbiblical Hebrew.

in favor of the papyrus. First, the appearance of the recognition formula within an oracle rather than at the end is not uncommon in Ezekiel.[12]

Second, the distinctive style in this section may be attributed to the special content and need not argue against Ezekielian authorship. In 36:16-38 the theology of the book reaches its zenith. Although the diction borrows heavily from previous oracles and from Jeremiah,[13] the special characteristics of the present statement may reflect authorial awareness of its significance. A lofty subject deserves an exalted literary style.[14]

Third, the LXX evidence is not conclusive. In the first instance, the reliability of Papyrus 967 for reconstructing the Hebrew *Vorlage* to the Greek translation is not without question. A. C. Johnson has identified seventeen significant omissions by parablepsis or homoioteleuton in this papyrus.[15] Although none is as long as 36:23c-38, in several instances whole columns (as many as 24 lines) seem to have been lost. While such scribal errors seem to account for most of these lapses,[16] the length of the present omission and its theological content seem to preclude a scribal lapse. An accidental loss of a leaf or two seems more likely.[17] Furthermore, if the absence of this section were original, it is remarkable that it is preserved in only one Greek manuscript and an obscure Latin text. In any case, those responsible for the transmission of the LXX recognized the gap and filled it in with a reading that bears remarkable resemblance to Theodotion's text-form.[18] Moreover, as Greenberg observes, the reconstruction of a Hebrew *Vorlage* on the basis of LXX, or any other early version for that matter, even when the manuscripts agree, is a highly subjective task and full of pitfalls.[19]

Fourth, Lust's proposal flies in the face of recent form-critical scholarship; he eliminates evidence that runs counter to his theory. V. 23c, "when

---

12. See 28:22; 35:12; 37:13; 38:23; 39:28; etc. See Meier's discussion and conclusion (*Speaking of Speaking,* pp. 230-42).

13. Lust recognizes this point (*CBQ* 43 [1981] 525).

14. Simian (*Theologische Nachgeschichte,* p. 159) speaks of a "formal" (*formelhaft*) and "dignified" (*feierlich*) style, in contrast to the figurative portrayal of the sins of Israel in ch. 16.

15. Johnson, *Scheide Papyri: Ezekiel,* pp. 7-8.

16. So also Lust, in *Ezekiel and His Book,* pp. 14-15.

17. A. C. Johnson, *Scheide Papyri: Ezekiel,* pp. 8-9; more recently, Spottorno, *Emerita* 50 (1981) 93-99.

18. Cf. H. St. J. Thackeray, "The Greek Translators of Ezekiel," *JTS* 4 (1903) 408; idem, *The Septuagint and Jewish Worship,* 2nd ed. (London: Milford, 1921), pp. 125-26. It is possible, however, that the original translators intentionally tried to preserve the elevated style by introducing special features of their own.

19. Greenberg, *Ezekiel 1-20,* pp. 19-20; idem, "The Use of Ancient Versions for Interpreting the Hebrew Text: A Sampling from Ezek ii 1-iii 11," in *Congress Volume: Göttingen 1977,* VTSup 29 (Leiden: Brill, 1978), pp. 131-48.

through you I vindicate my holiness before their eyes," is discounted as a secondary correction of 38:16, even though this expansion of the recognition formula, involving *bě* plus an infinitive construct and summarizing the effects or content of Yahweh's action, is quite Ezekielian.[20] Further, deleting "It is not for your sakes" in v. 32 neutralizes an effective *inclusio* with the same expression in v. 22.[21]

Fifth, by itself the section in vv. 16-23bβ appears fragmentary.[22] On the one hand, in contrast to the rest of Ezekiel's restoration oracles, which average twenty-seven verses,[23] deleting 36:23c-38 reduces the present oracle to less than eight verses. Furthermore, removing vv. 23c-38 reduces this text to a bland and truncated two-part pronouncement, lacking any explanation of how Yahweh intends to vindicate his holiness. On the other hand, in assuming a late en bloc addition, Lust overlooks other signs of disjunction within the text. Since vv. 33-36 and 37-38 each have their own introductory citation and concluding recognition formulae, these look more like separate oracular fragments than vv. 23c-38 as a unit.

Sixth, Lust's reconstruction of the history of the LXX text is speculative, lacking any objective evidential basis for a Pharisaic reaction to the sequence of events suggested by the arrangement of Papyrus 967. Indeed, one could argue with equal if not greater force that the growth of apocalypticism in the late intertestamental period stimulated the rearrangement of oracles in this text-form, so that the resurrection of the dead is seen as the final eschatological event prior to the reestablishment of a spiritual Israel, rather than simply a metaphor for the restoration of the nation from exile.

Seventh, Lust's understanding of 36:23c-38 as a composition intentionally crafted to serve as a bridge between 36:16-23bβ and ch. 37, after these chapters had been brought together, is not convincing. The evidence of lexical and thematic links cuts both ways. The ties between vv. 23c-32 and 16-23bβ argue for unitary treatment.[24] The oracle fragments represented by vv. 33-36 and 37-38 appear authentically Ezekielian, and may have been inserted in their present positions precisely because of their connections with ch. 34 and 36:1-15.[25] Furthermore, the present arrangement of 36:23c-38 and

---

20. See 5:13; 6:13; 12:15; 15:7; 20:42, 44; 25:17; 28:22; 30:8, 25; 33:29; 34:27; 37:13; 38:16; 39:28. The construction appears before the formula in 24:24; 32:15; 33:33. For discussion see Zimmerli, *I Am Yahweh,* pp. 37-39.

21. Zimmerli (*Ezekiel 2,* p. 245) cites 20:1-31 as a parallel.

22. Thus Zimmerli, *Ezekiel 2,* p. 245.

23. Inclusive of the word-event formula. See 34:1-31 (31); 35:1–36:15 (30); 36:16-38 (23); 37:1-14 (14); 37:15-24 (14); 38:1–39:29 (52).

24. Parunak, *Structural Studies,* pp. 471-77. See further the commentary below.

25. Cf. U. Cassuto, "The Arrangement of the Book of Ezekiel," in *Biblical and Oriental Studies,* vol. 1: *Bible,* tr. I. Abrahams (Jerusalem: Magnes, 1973), pp. 227-28.

ch. 37 follows a typical Ezekielian pattern of raising a subject, only to drop it immediately, and then returning to it for fuller development in a subsequent oracle. Accordingly, the editors of MT intend 37:1-14 as an explication of 36:27. 37:15-28 not only portrays a reversal of 36:16-23 but also expands on 34:23-31.

In the centuries preceding the birth of Christ a standardized text-form of Ezekiel had evidently not yet been accepted in all circles.[26] The closing of the Hebrew canon undoubtedly gave impetus to the standardization of text-forms, but divergent forms continued in use for several centuries, especially in hellenized circles.[27] Moreover, variant text-forms of the prophetic books may have emerged early, perhaps within a century or two after the prophet's works had been collated, and Papyrus 967 may still represent an old text-form. The text-critical task of retroverting the translated text to a supposed Hebrew *Vorlage* remains an imprecise science.[28] In many instances LXX reflects an older stage in the development of a biblical book than MT,[29] but a text's antiquity is not necessarily a sign of either originality or superiority. A reconstructed Hebrew reading may be preferred if MT is unintelligible or obviously corrupt. But the MT of 36:16-38 is quite sensible; few textual units in Ezekiel have called for fewer textual notes in *BHS*. There is no need, therefore, to abandon MT in favor of a hypothetical archetypal "original" based on Papyrus 967 that might then serve as the basis for exegesis.[30] MT represents the standardized form, a fact recognized by the LXX scribes who, in the case of 36:23c-38, brought their own traditions into

26. Note the differences between MT and LXX in the arrangement and content of Jeremiah, as well as the NT, which often cites readings diverging from MT. The fragments from Qumran tend to correspond to MT (cf. Lust, in *Ezekiel and His Book,* pp. 90-100), despite the probability that sectarian groups tended to develop their own canons (cf. S. Z. Leiman, *The Canonization of Hebrew Scripture: The Talmudic and Midrashic Evidence,* Transactions of the Connecticut Academy of Arts and Sciences 47 [Hamden: Archon, 1976], p. 37; also E. Tov, "Recensional Differences between the MT and LXX of Ezekiel," *ETL* 62 [1986] 89-101).

27. Leiman concludes (*Canonization,* p. 132) that the standardization of the text presupposes a fixed canon. He also suggests (ibid., pp. 36-37) that the stabilization of the Masoretic Hebrew text was a fait accompli by the First Jewish Revolt, and that the Proto-Lucianic recension of the Greek Bible indicates efforts were being made already in the 2nd-1st centuries B.C. to bring the LXX into conformity with the Hebrew Bible.

28. For guidelines for dealing with LXX see E. Tov, "Septuagint: Contribution to OT Scholarship," *IDBSup,* pp. 807-11; cf. also idem, *Textual Criticism,* pp. 129-33.

29. So also Tov, "Textual Criticism (OT)," *ABD,* 6:403-4.

30. Tov (*ETL* 62 [1986] 100-101) agrees with Lust that the textual witnesses represent different stages in the literary growth of the book of Ezekiel, but asserts that "*none* of the readings should be preferred *textually* to another one." Cf. Tov, *The Text-Crtitical Use of the Septuagint in Biblical Research,* Jerusalem Biblical Studies 3 (Jerusalem: Simor, 1981), pp. 307-11.

conformity with the received Hebrew text. My exposition assumes the integrity of MT and attempts to interpret each segment of this textual unit in the light of its canonical literary environment. Although the distinct literary style and compendious nature of the passage may point to the hand of a redactor who sought to place a summary of the prophet's message of hope in the middle of the collection of restoration oracles, Ezekiel should not be prematurely eliminated as a candidate for that redactor. In any case, the content of 36:16-38 is thoroughly Ezekielian.

Despite its disjointed style and the variety of topics introduced in the unit, 36:16-38 represents a clearly demarcated textual unit. It has been characterized as a disputative stylized salvation oracle,[31] though according to the key v. 20, the central issue is not the deliverance of Israel but the vindication of the reputation of Yahweh. The text is deliberately crafted so that each segment contributes significantly to the development of the theme, as reflected in the following outline:

The Formulaic Introduction	(v. 16)
a. The Crisis for Yahweh's Honor	(vv. 17-21)
b. The Recovery of Yahweh's Honor	(vv. 22-32)
(1) Yahweh's Name-Sanctifying Goal	(vv. 22-23)
(2) A Catalogue of Yahweh's Name-Sanctifying Actions	(vv. 24-30)
(3) Yahweh's Name-Sanctifying Goal	(vv. 31-32)
c. The Vindication of Yahweh's Honor	(vv. 33-38a)
(1) Among the Nations	(vv. 33-36)
(2) In Israel	(vv. 37-38a)
The Formulaic Conclusion	(v. 38b)

a. Introduction; the Crisis for Yahweh's Honor (36:16-21)

16 *The following message of Yahweh came to me:* 17 *"Human, concerning the house of Israel, at the time they were occupying[32] their land, they defiled it with their conduct and their unrestrained behavior.[33] In my view their conduct was like the impurity of menstruation.* 18 *So I poured out my fury on them, on account of the blood they had poured out on the land and for their pellets of dung with which*

---

31. D. Baltzer, in *Ezekiel and His Book,* p. 175.

32. On the circumstantial use of the participle see Cooke, *Ezekiel,* p. 395.

33. LXX translates *ûbaʿălîlôtām* with two concepts: καὶ ἐν τοῖς εἰδώλοις αὐτῶν καὶ ἐν ταῖς ἀκαθαρσίαις αὐτῶν, "and with their idols and with their uncleanness," probably reflecting either a different *Vorlage* or a misreading as *ûgillûlêhem* and the addition of *ûbĕṭumʾātām. derek* and *ʿălîlôt* are juxtaposed elsewhere in v. 19; 14:22-23; 20:43-44.

they had defiled it.[34] 19 *I scattered them among the nations, and they were dispersed*[35] *among the countries. I punished them in accordance with their conduct and their unrestrained behavior.*[36] 20 *But when they arrived*[37] *among those nations,*[38] *they caused my holy name*[39] *to be desecrated, inasmuch as it was said of them, 'These are the people of Yahweh? How is it then that they have had to leave his land?'*[40] 21 *Then I was concerned about my holy name, which the house of Israel had desecrated among the nations to which they had come."*

Based on formal structural indicators, the first segment of this literary unit encompasses vv. 16-32. But, as already noted, the shift in content and style suggests a subdivision into two parts, vv. 17-21 and 22-32. The absence of a command to prophesy and the failure to name a target audience after *ben-'ādām,* along with the use of the third person of indirect address, suggest that this text represents a divine monologue to the prophet, rather than an oracle to be communicated to a third party. In this segment Ezekiel appears to function as Yahweh's confidant and friend,[41] to whom he discloses the rationale for his judgment of his own people (v. 17) and confesses the harshness of his treatment (vv. 18-19), and with whom he shares his personal grief over their lot (vv. 20-21). Like Abraham, to whom Yahweh had disclosed his plans for Sodom and Gomorrah, and Moses, with whom he had shared his ways (*děrākîm*) and his character (Exod. 33:12–34:9), as a prophet Ezekiel has been admitted to Yahweh's inner circle.

17-18 The reason for the absence of an addressee becomes apparent immediately. For Yahweh the fundamental issue in this oracle is not the restoration of Israel but the defilement of *the land.*[42] The rupture in the

34. Because the motive clauses are missing in LXX and awkwardly constructed, Allen (*Ezekiel 20–48*, p. 176) considers these misplaced explanatory comments on v. 17a. Cf. Zimmerli, *Ezekiel 2*, p. 241.

35. LXX and Syr. harmonize MT *wayyizzārû* with the previous verb by rendering it actively. Cf. also 22:15; 29:12; 30:23, 26.

36. Targ. interprets *derek* and *'ălîlôt* theologically: "their evil ways" and "their corrupt deeds."

37. LXX and Targ. correctly read MT *wybw'* as pl. *wyb'w*. MT represents a metathetical error.

38. MT *'el-haggôyim 'ăšer-bā'û šām,* lit. "to the nations to which they had come."

39. The same expression occurs in vv. 20-22. The form compares with *har qodšî,* "my holy mountain," in Ps. 2:6; and with *'îr qodšî,* "my holy city," in Dan 9:24. On the construction see GKC, §135n.

40. Targ. correctly recognizes the contextual need for a question.

41. Cf. Jesus' definition of a "friend" as a person to whom one discloses his secret thoughts (John 15:15).

42. The use of *bêt yiśrā'ēl* highlights the corporate nature of the guilt.

deity-nation-land relationship had been precipitated by the pollution of the land by *the house of Israel*.[43] A land could be defiled in two ways: by a pagan foreigner invading it (cf. Ps. 79:1), or by the native population violating the will of the divine sovereign (Num. 35:33-34; Jer. 2:7). The latter is obviously the case here. The land that Yahweh had graciously given to the family of Israel as their grant *(naḥălâ)* and as their possession *(môrāšâ)* had been defiled with their unrestrained evil.

Given the prominence of the land in Ezekiel's oracles, it is remarkable that this is the only time he speaks of the land as *defiled*.[44] In the OT the root *ṭm'* is used of two kinds of pollution: ceremonial and moral. Whereas the former resulted from nonmoral actions or experiences, not associated with guilt or shame,[45] the latter was incurred by violating the will of the deity. In Israel most morally defiling actions were classified under one of three headings: murder, sexual abominations, and idolatry. The pollution incurred by such conduct was not considered contagious, but its effects were much more dangerous than those produced by ritual defilement. Such behavior incurred guilt and demanded divine sanction.[46] This condition could not be altered merely by performing purification rites. The pollution could be removed only by a divine act of cleansing, achieved through repentance and sacrifice.[47]

The notion of polluting the land has a long history. The rationale cited for delivering the land of Canaan into Israel's hands was the land's defilement through the inhabitants' wicked conduct (Deut. 9:4-5). Deut. 18:9-12 warned Israel that if they adopted the moral and spiritual standards of the Canaanites, they would cause the same kind of pollution and should be prepared for the same fate as the original population. Lev. 18 and 20 specify sexual crimes, necromancy, and Molech worship as defiling actions that would result in the

---

43. The typically Ezekielian preference for *'ădāmâ*, rather than *'ereṣ*, values national territory not just as real estate over which the nation exercises political jurisdiction but as a home, which, in an agricultural economy, provided the basis for national well-being and prosperity.

44. Elsewhere he speaks of defiling the temple (5:11; 9:7; 23:38), Yahweh's holy name (43:7, 8), one's neighbor's wife (18:6, 11, 15; 22:11; 23:17; 33:26).

45. E.g., touching a carcass or experiencing a bodily discharge. Such pollutions were considered contagious, but no harm came to the person affected, other than temporary isolation from the community and alienation from all things sacred during the period of uncleanness. When the period of uncleanness was past, the individual could be restored to a state of purity by participating in ceremonial purification rites. See T. Frymer-Kensky, in *The Word of the Lord Shall Go Forth*, 401-4.

46. Cf. the pairing of *'āšam* and *ṭāmē'* in 22:4.

47. Cf. Frymer-Kensky, in *The Word of the Lord Shall Go Forth*, pp. 404-6, who also observes (p. 408) that repentance was to be seen as a privilege, not as an automatic right.

land disgorging its inhabitants (20:22-25).[48] By the 6th century the pollution of the land of Israel had reached the saturation point, beyond repentance or sacrifice. In Ezekielian terms it was full of "lawlessness" (*ḥāmās,* 8:17; 12:19) and bloody crimes (*dāmîm,* 7:23; 9:9), and the exile of the population remained the only way of purgation.[49]

17 The terms used for Israel's misconduct are vague, but *conduct* or "ways" *(děrākîm)* and *unrestrained behavior* or "wanton deeds" *(ʿălîlôt)* categorize their behavior as land-defiling crimes.[50] In the face of the nation's crimes Yahweh compares the land's condition with *the impurity of menstruation.*[51] Given the feminine gender of *ʾădāmâ,* and especially Ezekiel's characterization of Jerusalem/Judah as a woman in chs. 16 and 23, menstrual defilement seems an appropriate figure for the land's state. However, it is somewhat incongruous in the present context, inasmuch as defilement caused by voluntary bloodshed (murder) is of a fundamentally different order from the involuntary pollution of menstruation. Nevertheless, the land is not considered culpable for its defilement in this context, any more than a menstruant is rendered morally guilty by her discharge.

18 Although the focus remains on the human cause of the defilement, in describing his response to the land's pollution Yahweh adopts a new metaphor, taken from the realm of metallurgy (cf. 22:22): *I poured out my fury.*[52] Two specific crimes had polluted the land, one moral (murder), the other cultic (idolatry). The former is referred to by the common Ezekielian idiom *the blood they had poured out (šāpak dām),* which, according to Num. 35:29-34, polluted the land beyond expiation, except for the life of the murderer himself.[53] The latter is identified appropriately by Ezekiel's favorite term for idols,

---

48. These notions surface repeatedly in the prophetical books. See esp. Jeremiah's contrast between Yahweh's gracious gift of land to Israel with the nation's ungrateful response: "I brought you to a fruitful land, to eat its fruit and its good things, but you came and defiled *(ṭimmēʾ)* my land, and my property *(naḥălātî)* you made an abomination" (2:7).

49. See Frymer-Kensky, in *The Word of the Lord Shall Go Forth,* pp. 406-12, for further discussion.

50. The pair appears again in v. 19. Cf. 14:22, 23; 20:43, 44; 24:14; 36:3; and outside Ezekiel, Jer. 7:3, 5; 17:10; 18:11; 23:22; 26:13; 32:19; Zech. 1:4, 6. Cf. Ezek. 20:43-44 and 36:31, which characterize the actions represented by these expressions as "evil" *(rāʿâ)* and "not good" *(lōʾ-ṭôbîm),* evoking intense self-loathing *(qûṭ,* Niphal) in perpetrators when they come to their senses.

51. The expression *kěṭumʾat hanniddâ,* "like the menstrual defilement," occurs elsewhere only in Lev. 15:26, where it is used in its normal hygienic sense. Ezekiel uses the figure elsewhere in 7:19-20; 18:6; 22:10.

52. Cf. 7:8; 9:8; 14:19; 20:8, 13, 21, 33, 34; 22:22; 30:15. The phrase occurs elsewhere only in Jer. 10:25 and Ps. 79:6.

53. Cf. 16:38; 22:4, 6, 9, 12, 27; 23:45; 33:25. For an illustration of the defiling effect of murder on the land see Cain's murder of Abel in Gen. 4:1-15.

gillûlîm, pellets of dung, for that is what idols are in Yahweh's sight.[54] The combination of murderous and idolatrous motifs alludes to the child sacrifices mentioned in 20:26 and 23:36-38 as the ultimate crime and the reason for Yahweh's intervention.[55]

19 The next verse shifts to more straightforward language: *I scattered them . . . and they were dispersed.*[56] Yahweh punished *(šāpaṭ)* them *in accordance with their conduct and their unrestrained behavior (kĕdarkām ûka'ălîlôtām),* that is, in keeping with their offenses (cf. v. 17; also 24:14). Israel's violence is met with divine fury, and her treachery toward him with dispersion to pagan lands, where the people could pursue their idolatrous ways to their hearts' content (cf. Deut. 4:27-28; 28:64; Amos 7:17).

But there is more to this comment than merely meting out punishment according to the crime. Behind the statement lies the ancient covenant curse threatening the population with exile so the land might finally enjoy its divinely ordained sabbatical rest (Lev. 26:33-45; cf. 2 Chr. 36:21). Now the appropriateness of the analogy of the menstruous woman also becomes apparent. The Priestly legislation had fixed her period of impurity at seven days (Lev. 15:19-30), after which she would be considered clean and fit to return to the house of Yahweh. For the land the period of uncleanness would be calculated on the basis of unobserved Sabbaths while the people were living on the land.[57]

20-21 The covenant curse had intimated that Israel's deportation and the desolation of her land would cause consternation among her enemies (Lev. 26:32-33). But the term *šāmam* in Leviticus is vague and the manner of the desecration is unspecified. Yahweh offers his interpretation here in Ezekiel, and in so doing reveals that the principal issue is neither demographic nor geographic — it is theological. Among foreign observers, the removal of Israel from their land has led to a disturbing conclusion concerning the character of Yahweh. Their radically theocentric reaction is described by means of two direct quotations (v. 20b), both constructed as declarative sentences but in context requiring an interrogative interpretation. According to ancient Near Eastern theological perceptions, the reasoning is logical, capturing in a nutshell popular perceptions of deity-nation-land relationships. As the God of Israel, Yahweh was obligated to defend his land and his people, and to prevent the divorce of the two. But the divorce has occurred, throwing into question both

---

54. Cf. my *Ezekiel: Chapters 1–24,* pp. 185-86. See also Bodi, *RB* 100 (1993) 481-510.

55. See also the references to Jerusalem as "the bloody city" in 22:3-4 and 24:6-7.

56. The conventional pair *pûṣ* and *zārâ* occurs elsewhere in 12:15; 20:23; 22:15; 29:12; 30:23, 26. In 11:16 *hirḥîq* replaces *zārâ.*

57. A specific link between these texts is provided by *bĕšibtĕkem 'ālêhā* in Lev. 26:35, which is echoed in *yōšĕbîm 'al-'admātām* in Ezek. 36:17.

Yahweh's and the people's claims. Outsiders were left to conclude that either Yahweh had willingly abandoned his people,[58] or that he was incapable of defending them against the superior might of Marduk, the god of Babylon. The first option challenges Yahweh's credibility and integrity; the second, his sovereignty. In either case, his reputation has been profaned among the nations. Thus the defilement of the land had led ultimately to the defilement of Yahweh's *name*.

In this context *šēm* means more than a mark of identification; it stands for the character and reputation of Yahweh. The expression *šēm qodšî* (lit. "name of my holiness") derives from the cultic law of Lev. 20:2-3, which associates the defiling of Yahweh's holy name with the desecration of the sanctuary through cultic abuses.[59] However, Ezekiel tends to attribute the desecration (*hillēl*) of Yahweh's holy name to historical events.[60] In his earlier revisionist portrayal of Israel's history (ch. 20), at three critical moments the motive for Yahweh's gracious treatment of his people had been "that my name be not profaned in the sight of the nations" (vv. 9, 14, 22). In each instance that profanation would have resulted from the nations' drawing negative and false conclusions about Yahweh from Israel's misfortune.[61] Similarly here, the exile of Israel from the land has made a mockery of his character and reputation. Reiterating the central issue of this first part of the oracle, v. 21 raises the hope that *concern* or "pity" for his sacred name will move Yahweh to action.[62] The emotion Yahweh had earlier denied his people is now roused to defend his reputation.[63]

The present concern for Yahweh's reputation is not new to Ezekiel. Twice Moses had moved Yahweh to withdraw his threat to destroy Israel by arguing that the nations would draw the wrong conclusions concerning his motivation and his character if he carried out his plan (Exod. 32:12; Num. 14:15-16). As in the present text, in both cases the failure of outside observers

---

58. Cf. the Judeans' own assertions in 8:12 and 9:9.

59. Yahweh's name is desecrated also through priestly mishandling of sacred objects/gifts (Lev. 22:2), and the incorrect presentation of sacrifices (Lev. 22:32).

60. On this text see G. Bettenzoli, *Geist der Heiligkeit: Traditionsgeschichtliche Untersuchung des qdš-Begriffes im Buch Ezechiel*, Quaderni di semitistica 8 (Florence: Univ. Ist. di Linguistica e Lingue Orientali, 1979), pp. 189-95. In 43:7-8 *timmē'* replaces *hillēl* as the verb of defilement in conjunction with Yahweh's holy name.

61. 39:25 attributes Yahweh's restoration of Israel's fortunes to his "passion" (*qin'â*) for his holy name.

62. On the idiom *ḥāmal 'al*, see M. Tsevat, *TDOT*, 4:470-72; H. J. Stoebe, *THAT*, 2:764. Cf. the repeated pairing of *ḥāmal* with *ḥûs* ("show/have pity") in the judgment oracles to express Yahweh's repression of any pity toward his people: 5:11; 7:4, 9; 8:18; 9:5, 10.

63. In 16:5 the term describes Yahweh's response to the foundling abandoned by its mother. The present use of the prophetic perfect treats Yahweh's future action for his name's sake as if it had already occurred.

to distinguish between ultimate human causation and the immediate divine action could lead to false views of God, hence the profanation of his name.

b. The Recovery of Yahweh's Honor (36:22-32)

> 22 "Therefore, say to the house of Israel, 'Thus has the Lord Yahweh declared: It is not[64] for your sake that I will act,[65] O house of Israel, but for the sake of my holy name, which you have desecrated among the nations wherever you have gone. 23 I will sanctify my great name, which has been desecrated among the nations — which you have desecrated in their midst. And the nations will know that I am Yahweh — the declaration of Yahweh[66] — when I manifest my holiness through you[67] before their very eyes.

> 24 I will take you from the nations;
> I will gather you from all the lands;
> I will bring you to your own land.
> 25 I will sprinkle clean water on you,
> and you will be clean.
> From all your defilements and from all your idols
> I will cleanse you.[68]
> 26 I will give you a new heart;
> I will implant a new spirit[69] within you.[70]
> I will remove the stone heart from your body;
> I will give you a heart[71] of flesh.[72]

64. The negation of a noun clause with *lō'* rather than *'ên* is emphatic, the force of the negation falling on a particular word rather than the clause. Cf. GKC, §152d; Joüon-Muraoka, *Grammar,* §160c.

65. *'āśâ* occurs without object also in 20:9, 14, 22, 44. Cf. the expanded form of the self-introduction formula: "I am Yahweh; I have spoken, and I will act" (17:24; 22:14; 24:14; 36:36; 37:14).

66. LXX and 2 Hebrew mss. drop the intrusive signatory formula. On the omission of vv. 23bβ-38 in LXX[967] see above, "Nature and Design."

67. Some Hebrew mss. read third person, emphasizing Yahweh's work among the nations.

68. LXX καὶ καθαριῶ ὑμᾶς creates an independent clause of the last line and links the foregoing prepositional phrases to the previous verb.

69. Targ. interprets theologically, "a fearful heart and a fearful spirit."

70. Targ. intensifies the reading with "in your intestines."

71. On the sg. for a body part common to a plurality see Davidson, *Syntax,* §17, Rem. 4.

72. Targ. again interprets theologically: "And I will demolish the wicked heart, which is as hard as stone, from your flesh, and I will give you a heart that is faithful before me to do my will."

27 *I will implant my Spirit within you.*
I will cause you to walk in my decrees,[73]
  so you will diligently observe my laws.
28 *You will occupy the land that I gave to your fathers;*
You will be my people,
And I[74] *will be your God.*
29 *I will deliver you from all your defilements;*
I will summon the grain;
I will make it abundant.
I will not impose famine on you.
30 *I will increase the fruit of the tree and the crops of the field,*[75]
  so you will never again[76] *suffer*[77] *the abuse among the nations*
  that famine causes.

31 *Then you will recall your evil conduct and your improper be-*
havior, and loathe yourselves[78] *on account of your iniquities and on*
account of your abominations. 32 *It is not for your sake*[79] *that I will*
act — the declaration of the Lord Yahweh — be informed![80] *You should*
be ashamed and humiliated[81] *on account of your ways, O house of*
Israel!'"

73. On the increasing use of *'ăšer* in the sense of "that" to introduce subordinate clauses in Late Biblical Hebrew see Rooker, *Biblical Hebrew in Transition*, p. 111. Cf. also GKC, §157c; Brockelmann, *Syntax*, §161bβ. Cooke (*Ezekiel*, p. 395) observes that the only parallel occurrence of *'āśâ* meaning "to cause" is found in Eccl. 3:14, but without the sign of the accusative following. Cf. GKC, §157c.

74. This is the only occurrence of *'ānōkî* in Ezekiel. Several Hebrew mss. harmonize with his usage elsewhere by reading *'ănî*. On the significance of the form see the commentary.

75. The expression *tĕnûbat haśśādeh* occurs elsewhere only in Deut. 32:13 and Lam. 4:9. *tĕnûbâ*, from *nûb*, "to grow," is used in Judg. 9:11 of the produce of the olive tree, in Isa. 27:6 of Israel in a metaphorical sense.

76. *lō' 'ôd*, "never again," is common in the restoration oracles of Jeremiah and Ezekiel (cf. Ezek. 16:42; 34:10, 22, 28-29; 36:14-15, 30; 37:22-23; Jer. 16:14; 23:4, 36; 30:8; 31:11, 28, 33), underscoring an important theological-psychological concern of the times. Cf. Fishbane, *Biblical Interpretation*, pp. 374-75.

77. This use of *lāqaḥ*, meaning "to take upon oneself, to experience," is attested elsewhere only in Hos. 10:6.

78. On the phrase *nĕqōtōtem bipnêkem*, "to feel intense revulsion in your face," see 6:9 and 20:43. In the former, the feeling arises out of remembering Yahweh, whose heart their idolatry, evils, and abominations have broken.

79. On the negation of a substantive with *lō'* see n. 64 above.

80. On *nôda lĕ* see 20:5; 1 Sam. 6:3; Neh. 4:9.

81. MT *wĕhikkālĕmû* is imperative. Cf. the noun *kĕlimmâ*, from the same root, used elsewhere in connection with "bearing insults" (16:52, 54, 63; 32:24, 25, 30; 34:29; 36:6-7, 15; 39:26; 44:13). The frequency with which *bôš* and *kĕlimmâ* are conjoined

♦ *Nature and Design*

Though linked logically to the preceding by *lākēn,* "Therefore," the command to Ezekiel to speak, followed by the citation formula in v. 22, signals the beginning of a new movement in this literary unit. Accordingly, the genre shifts from personal reflections by Yahweh (in Ezekiel's hearing) on the dilemma that the exile of his people has created for his reputation, to an oracle for Ezekiel to communicate to his people. Thus vv. 22-32 are cast in the second person of direct address. Whether or not the background information found in vv. 17-21 was shared with the audience, Yahweh's disclosure of his plans for the exiles should have been interpreted as a sign that he had not forgotten them; the last chapter of their lives and their relationship with their God had not yet been written. The declaration "It is not for your sakes that I am about to act," which appears at the beginning and the end of this subunit, functions as an effective framework for the pronouncement and points to the central theme of the oracle. Despite the signs of cohesion, the oracle itself subdivides into three sections: a declaration of Yahweh's motive in restoring Israel (vv. 22-23); a catalogue of actions to be performed on their behalf (vv. 24-30); and a description of the appropriate response from Israel (vv. 31-32). We will deal with each in turn.

(1) Yahweh's Name-Sanctifying Goal (36:22-23)

The oracle proper opens on a vague note, intimating a new phase in divine activity but without specifying the nature of Yahweh's actions. Ironically, although this prophecy turns out to be a salvation oracle, the tone of the opening statements is more accusatory than sympathetic, and more polemical than conciliatory. The assertion that the Israelites have desecrated the name of Yahweh wherever they have gone might have led Ezekiel's audience to expect another wave of judgment. Ezekiel will delay the positive news momentarily so he may highlight his radically theocentric perspective from the outset, which he does by adopting a repetitive rhetorical style. As if to dismiss any hint of merit on Israel's part, he announces that when Yahweh begins to act he will do so with a single object in mind: the vindication of his sacred name.[82]

The use of the verb *qiddēš,* "to sanctify," highlights the fact that his activity is designed to resolve the present theological crisis. That which was once holy, but has been desecrated, must be reconsecrated. Because the name

---

suggests a standardized pair. Note also Isa. 30:3; 45:16; 61:7; Jer. 20:11; 51:51; Ezek. 16:52; Ps. 35:26; 44:16 (Eng. 15); 69:20 (Eng. 19); 71:13.

82. Note the emphatic inverted word order: *lō' lĕmaʿanĕkem 'ănî-ʿōśeh.*

has been desecrated, the expression *šēm qodšî, my holy name,* seems anachronistic and must be replaced by *šěmî haggādôl, my great name.*[83] The use of the passive modifier *hamĕhullāl, which has been desecrated,* seems to lessen Israel's responsibility for the moment. But no! Yahweh cannot allow this thought to take root. The speech is interrupted by another affirmation of Israel's guilt.

This segment closes with an expanded version of the recognition formula, announcing that the very nations among whom the house of Israel has desecrated Yahweh's name will witness the manifestation of his holiness. His name will be cleared. Those who are presently wondering about his ability or willingness to rise in defense of his people (v. 20) will have their questions answered. For the moment the manner in which this will be accomplished remains a mystery. Ezekiel's audience has been reminded of their own guilt; they have been assured of Yahweh's jealousy for his holiness; and they have been made aware of the problem their presence among the nations has created for Yahweh.

The modern reader may find Yahweh's apparent heartlessness at this point disturbing, if not offensive. Yahweh looks like a stuffy egotistical monarch, upset that his subjects have not given him the honor he demands. His response hardly enhances his image. Absent is any compassion toward a bleeding nation, any mercy, or any hint of forgiveness. Absent also is any reference to the covenant promises. Indeed, as Zimmerli has observed, a whole class of terms is missing from Ezekiel: *hesed,* "covenant loyalty," *rǎhāmîm,* "compassion," *'ǎmûnâ,* "faithfulness," *yěšû'â,* "salvation," *'ahǎbâ,* "love."[84] Unlike Isa. 40:1ff., this announcement is not intended primarily as a message of comfort for a broken people; nor is the issue for Yahweh their humiliation and pain huddled in a foreign land. Because they have shamefully trampled underfoot the grace of God, they have forfeited all rights to compassion. When Yahweh begins to work, his concern will be the vindication of his own name, not theirs, among the nations.

(2) A Catalogue of Yahweh's Name-Sanctifying Actions (36:24-30)

The questions raised by the vague reference to Yahweh's action in v. 22 are answered in remarkable detail in vv. 24-30. This passage, which expands on 11:17-20,[85] contains the most systematic and detailed summary of Yahweh's

---

83. Cf. the use of this expression in Josh. 7:9; 1 Sam. 12:22; Ps. 76:2 (Eng. 1); Mal. 1:11.

84. The root *'hb* occurs in chs. 16 and 23, but only of human lovers. Cf. Zimmerli, *Ezekiel 2,* pp. 248-49.

85. See Hossfeld, *Untersuchungen,* p. 336.

restorative agenda in Ezekiel, if not in all the prophetical books. Although the catalogue is cast in prose form, I have formatted it to reflect its catalogic nature and its focus on the activity of Yahweh. With the exception of a few notices of the effects of the divine work (vv. 25b, 27c, 28a, b, 30), the prominence of Yahweh as the subject of the verbs requires that these verses be interpreted as an exposition of *'ănî 'ōśeh,* "I am about to act," in v. 22.

The list arranges the divine actions in an ABA pattern, with the central core (vv. 25-28) dealing with the internal spiritual dimension to Israel's restoration, framed by external promises for the return of the nation from exile (v. 24) and the rejuvenation of their hereditary homeland (vv. 29-30). Since the issues dealt with in the framework have already received considerable attention in Ezekiel's salvation oracles, the commentary on these may be brief. The new or hitherto underdeveloped issues raised in the central core call for more detailed analysis. The influence of Deut. 30:1-10 is apparent and will be highlighted below.

(a) The Regathering of Israel (36:24)

Yahweh's restorative actions begin where they must, with the regathering of his people from all the countries to which they have been scattered. The promise, which conceives the event as a new exodus, envisions three phases, described in three parallel lines:

> *wĕlāqaḥtî 'etkem min-haggôyim*
> *wĕqibbaṣtî 'etkem mikkol-hā'ărāṣôt,*
> *wĕhēbē'tî 'etkem 'el-'admatĕkem.*

> I will take you from the nations,
> I will gather you from all the lands,
> I will bring you to your own land.

The new exodus motif occurs ten times in Ezekiel, but it gains increasing prominence in the restoration oracles.[86] Although Exod. 6:6-7 may also have been in Ezekiel's mind, his diction has been influenced more directly by Deut. 30:4: "Though your outcasts be at the ends of the heavens, from there Yahweh your God will gather (*qibbēṣ*) you, and from there he will take (*lāqaḥ*) you, and Yahweh your God will bring (*hēbî'*) you to the land that your ancestors

---

86. See 11:17; 20:34-35; 20:41-42; 28:25; 29:13; 34:13; 36:24; 37:12; 37:21; 39:27. The present terminology recalls 34:13, except for the novel replacement of *hôṣî'* with *lāqaḥ* (cf. also 37:21) and *'ammîm* with *gôyim*. For discussion of Ezekiel's use of exodus terminology see Hossfeld, *Untersuchungen*, pp. 309-14, who provides additional bibliography.

possessed." Directly addressing the mocking taunt of the observers to Israel's exile (v. 20), this promise declares that Yahweh will prove himself both faithful to his people and land, and competent to fulfill his patron responsibilities as understood by the nations.

(b) The Transformation of Israel (36:25-28)

But Yahweh's efforts to rehabilitate his reputation will go far beyond merely reuniting people and land; he will also revitalize the relationship between himself and his people. Coming immediately after the announcement of the new exodus, vv. 25-28 offer an exposition of Deut. 30:6-8, particularly the following statement: "Then Yahweh your God will circumcise your heart and the heart of your descendants to love Yahweh your God with your whole heart and your whole being in order that you may live. . . . Then you will again heed Yahweh and obey all his commandments with which I am charging you today." This promise envisions a wholesale transformation of the nation, surpassing even Yahweh's actions on behalf of his name in Ezek. 20:9, 14, 22. Three dimensions of revitalization are announced.

25 First, Yahweh will purify Israel of its defilement, an action highlighted by the threefold occurrence of *ṭhr,* "to be clean." Yahweh will cleanse *(ṭihar)* the regathered people with clean water *(mayim ṭĕhôrîm),* as a result of which they will be clean *(ṭihar)* from their defilements *(ṭum'ôt)* and idols *(gillûlîm).* The description mixes the metaphors of priestly cleansing rituals and blood sprinkling ceremonies.[87] Although some interpret this as a divine ritual cleansing act upon the newly constituted nation, it is preferable to see here Yahweh's direct cathartic actions, removing the defilement caused by the people's idolatry and other violations of Yahweh's covenant.[88] In the present context, the issue is not simply an external ceremonial cleansing

---

87. The rituals include the use of water in the consecration of priests (Exod. 29:4) and Levites (Num. 8:7), the ablutions of the chief priest on the Day of Atonement (Lev. 16:4, 24, 26), the heifer ashes ceremony (Num. 19:11-19; cf. v. 21); and the ceremonial washing of garments (Exod. 19:10). The pollution involved in each of these cases was contagious but not dangerous and incurred no guilt. Cf. the tabulation and discussion of these texts by Frymer-Kensky, in *The Word of the Lord Shall Go Forth,* pp. 420-23. Some see in this text a connection with later proselyte baptism at Qumran and Christian baptism. Cf. O. Betz, "Die Proselytentaufe der Qumransekte und die Taufe im Neuen Testament," *RevQ* 1 (1958/59) 213-34. On the use of *zāraq* in the blood sprinkling ceremonies see BDB, p. 284; *HALOT,* p. 283.

88. For the former see Fuhs, *Ezechiel 25–48,* p. 205; Zimmerli, *Ezekiel 2,* p. 249. Cf. Isa. 1:15-16 and Jer. 4:14, which challenge the hearers to "wash themselves" as a ritual sign of repentance. For the latter see Hossfeld, *Untersuchungen,* pp. 316-17. Cf. this text with other references to Yahweh's cleansing action on his people: Isa. 1:15-16; 4:3-5; Ps. 51:4, 9 (Eng. 2, 7), though with different verbs.

accompanying the internal renewal described in vv. 26-27, but a wholesale cleansing from sin performed by Yahweh, a necessary precondition to normalizing the spiritual relationship between Yahweh and his people.

26-27 Second, Yahweh will remove Israel's fossilized heart and replace it with a sensitive fleshly organ. V. 26 is a virtual quotation of 11:19, as the following synopsis demonstrates:[89]

11:19	36:26
wĕnātattî lāhem lēb 'eḥād	*wĕnātattî lākem lēb ḥādāš*
wĕrûaḥ ḥădāšâ 'ettēn bĕqirbam	*wĕrûaḥ ḥădāšâ 'ettēn bĕqirbĕkem*
wahăsirōtî lēb hā'eben	*wahăsirōtî 'et-lēb hā'eben*
mibbĕšarām	*mibbĕšarĕkem*
wĕnātattî lāhem lēb bāśār	*wĕnātattî lākem lēb bāśār*

I will give them a single heart;	I will give you a new heart;
And a new spirit I will put within them;	And a new spirit I will put within you;
I will remove the heart of stone from their body;	I will remove the heart of stone from your body;
I will give them a heart of flesh.	I will give you a heart of flesh.

As in the antecedent texts, *lēb* and *rûaḥ* represent the person's internal locus of emotion, will, and thought.[90] Like Jesus, centuries later (Matt. 15:17-20), Ezekiel recognized the problem of rebellion and sin against Yahweh to be more deeply ingrained than mere external acts. Ezekiel concretizes the metaphor by describing the heart as *stone,* which speaks of coldness, insensitivity, incorrigibility, and even lifelessness (cf. 1 Sam. 25:37). Ezekiel knew whereof he spoke, having had to deal with the obduracy of his people from the time of his call.[91] But God has been struggling with the problem for centuries. The present solution is more radical even than the circumcision of the heart prescribed by Deut. 30:6-8. The only answer is the removal of the petrified organ and its replacement with a warm, sensitive, and responsive heart of flesh *(bāśār).*

Concomitant with the heart transplant, Yahweh will infuse his people with a new spirit, his Spirit. On first sight, the present juxtaposing of *rûaḥ* and *lēb* in such precise, if chiastic, parallelism suggests that "spirit" and "mind/heart" should be treated as virtual synonyms. However, the synonymity

---

89. Translated more literally than above to preserve the parallelism. See also the reference to a new heart and a new spirit in 18:31, though the challenge there is for the people to make for themselves a new heart and a new spirit, in keeping with the contextual emphasis on personal human responsibility.

90. Cf. Joyce, *Divine Initiative,* pp. 108-9.

91. Expressed in their refusal to listen to him. Cf. 2:4-11; 3:4-11.

is seldom exact in Hebrew parallelism,[92] and here the terms are associated with different prepositions. The new heart is given *to (nātan lĕ)* the Israelites, but the spirit is placed *within (nātan bĕqereb)* them. This distinction is confirmed by the manner in which vv. 26b-27 elaborate on the two statements. The provision of the new heart involves a removal of the petrified organ and its replacement with a heart of flesh, the source of which is unspecified. But the new spirit placed inside Israel is identified as Yahweh's *rûaḥ* (v. 27), which animates and vivifies the recipients.[93] In customary Ezekielian style, the subject is not developed here, but will be picked up and afforded full-blown exposition in 37:1-14.

Third, Yahweh will cause his people to be obedient to himself. The construction of v. 27b is unique, highlighting the divine coercion: *I will cause you to walk in my decrees, so you will diligently observe my laws* (lit. "I will make [*wĕʿāśîtî*] that you walk in my statutes [*ḥuqqîm*] and observe my covenant standards [*mišpāṭîm*] and act [accordingly]").[94] According to M. Greenberg, "God will no longer gamble with Israel as he did in old times, and Israel rebelled against him; in the future — no more experiments! God will put his spirit into them, he will alter their hearts (their minds) and make it impossible for them to be anything but obedient to his rules and his commandments."[95] The declaration abandons all hope that Israel, in her present condition, can achieve the ideals of covenant relationship originally intended by Yahweh. The status quo can be altered only by direct divine intervention.[96]

28 Fourth, Yahweh will renew his covenant with his people. Ezekiel's recital of Yahweh's restorative acts climaxes with the announcement of the fulfillment of Yahweh's ancient ideal: a transformed people living in their hereditary homeland, covenantally related to their divine Lord. A comparison of these verses with Jer. 31:33 suggests Jeremianic influence.[97] Jeremiah and

---

92. See R. Alter, *The Art of Biblical Poetry* (New York: Basic Books, 1985), pp. 13-26.

93. See Block, *JETS* 32 (1989) 34-38.

94. Cf. this construction with Deut. 30:6, *wĕʾattâ tāšûb wĕšāmaʿtā bĕqôl yhwh*, lit. "And you will return and heed the voice of Yahweh." See also 30:2.

95. M. Greenberg, "Three Conceptions of the Torah in Hebrew Scriptures," in *Die Hebräische Bibel und ihre zweifache Nachgeschichte*, Fest. R. Rendtorff, ed. E. Blum, et al. (Neukirchen-Vluyn: Neukirchener, 1990), p. 375.

96. Cf. the earlier allusion to this new reality in 11:20, though without any mention of the spirit (literally translated for the sake of comparison):

97.   **Jer. 31:33**   **Ezek. 36:27-28**

nātattî ʾet-tôrātî bĕqirbām   *wĕʾet-rûḥî ʾettēn bĕqirbĕkem*

wĕʿal-libbām ʾektăbennâ   . . . .

wĕhāyîtî lāhem lēʾlōhîm   *wihyîtem lî lĕʿām*

wĕhemmâ yihyû-lî lĕʿām   *wĕʾānōkî ʾehyâ lākem lēʾlōhîm*

Ezekiel obviously have the same covenant renewal in mind, but what Jeremiah attributes to the divine Torah, Ezekiel ascribes to the infusion of the divine *rûaḥ*. This verse more than any other answers the charge of the nations in v. 20. With the restoration of these relationships, not only have ancient Near Eastern perceptions of normal relations among deity, people, and land been satisfied; but Yahweh's name has also been sanctified and his own ancient ideal for the nation is finally achieved.[98]

(c) The Blessing of Israel (36:29-30)

These verses carry the restorative activity of Yahweh to their logical conclusion. Yahweh's reputation is not rehabilitated simply through Israel's occupation of their homeland; it depends also on the quality of their life in the land. Before the prophet elaborates on this issue, however, he reminds his audience once more of the psychosomatic nature of the current problem. The productivity of the land is contingent on the cleansing of the nation, here described remarkably as salvation from defilements *(ṭum'ôt)*. The root *yš'*, "to save, rescue," is rare in Ezekiel, occurring only here and in 34:22 and 37:23. The expression *hôšîa' min*, "to save from," normally denotes rescue from trouble, especially deliverance from a person or power in whose hands one is held captive or under whose authority one is oppressed.[99] However, the present context considers Israel to be held captive not by human enemies but by their own uncleanness.

The people's salvation is accompanied by the rejuvenation of their land. Yahweh will cause it to yield its bounty for the welfare of the people once again. Although some delete vv. 26-28 as secondary,[100] these verses

---

I will have put my Torah within them,	And my spirit I will put within you.
And on their hearts I will inscribe it,	. . . .
And I will be their God	And you will be my people,
And they will be my people.	And I will be your God.

98. Deut. 8:1. The use of the long form *'ānōkî* instead *'ănî*, which occurs consistently elsewhere in Ezekiel, is better interpreted as a conscious archaism in the covenant formula (Rooker, *Biblical Hebrew in Transition*, p. 74) than evidence of a non-Ezekielian hand or of Jeremianic influence (Zimmerli, *Ezekiel 2*, p. 249; cf. Jer. 11:4; 24:7; 30:22). Jeremiah himself is inconsistent: in 32:38 he uses *'ănî;* in 7:23; 13:11; and 31:33 he omits the pronoun.

99. See Judg. 2:16; 8:22; 12:2; 13:12; 1 Sam. 9:16; Neh. 9:27.

100. Based on the resumption of the theme of deliverance from defilement, Simian (*Theologische Nachgeschichte*, p. 93), claims that vv. 29b-30 have nothing to do with the preceding text as it stands in vv. 16-25. The repetition of *mikkol ṭum'ôtêkem*, "from all your defilements," which is found also in v. 25, suggests that the intervening material is secondary. On this procedure see C. Kuhl, "Die 'Wiederaufnahme' — ein literar-kritisches Prinzip?" *ZAW* 64 (1952) 1-11.

are crucial within the present literary context. According to prevailing ancient Near Eastern perceptions, and specifically according to the terms of Yahweh's covenant with his people, the productivity of the land is a natural outgrowth of the normalization of relationships among God, people, and land.[101] Vv. 29b-30 expand on the description of the rejuvenated land found earlier in 34:25-29. Yahweh's involvement in the people's new prosperity is highlighted with three simple declarations. First, he will *summon the grain* and cause it to yield abundant harvests. The expression *qārā' 'el-haddāgān* is striking, evoking images of a general summoning his troops to battle (Judg. 8:1), or a person inviting friends to a celebration (Judg. 14:15).[102] Second, he will withdraw the *famine (rā'āb),* his fearful agent of death.[103] Third, he will increase the productivity of the fruit trees *(pĕrî hā'ēṣ)* and plants of the field.

The significance of this new productivity is spelled out in v. 30b. Never again will the nation experience the reproach *(ḥerpâ)* of infertility among the nations. Instead, they will realize that the curse has been lifted and that their God has visited them with his favor once more, thereby stopping the mouths of those who mock them. Furthermore, instead of the land devouring its inhabitants (cf. v. 13), it will now provide them with food in abundance.

(3) Yahweh's Name-Sanctifying Goal (36:31-32)

The focus shifts from Yahweh's salvific work to Israel's response. In contrast to the salvation oracles of other prophets, which brought comfort and inspired celebration,[104] even Ezekiel's messages of hope are affected by the somber tone of his ministry. The parallels between this text and 20:43 are obvious.[105]

---

101. See Deut. 30:8-9; also 28:1-14. For discussion of the role of the land in this relationship see Block, *Gods of the Nations,* pp. 101-6.

102. This expression answers to Yahweh's summoning *(qārā')* the famine *(rā'āb)* in 2 K. 8:1 and Ps. 105:16.

103. Unlike the earlier judgment oracles (Ezek. 5:16-17; 14:13, 21; cf. also Jer. 24:10; 29:17; Amos 8:11), Ezekiel here speaks not of sending *(šillaḥ)* a famine, but of placing *(nātan)* it upon his people.

104. See Isa. 40:1-2; 51:3, 12; 52:9; 61:2; 66:13; Jer. 31:10-14; Zech. 1:13.

105. The resemblances between v. 31 and 20:43 suggest that this restoration oracle serves as a reflex of ch. 20 (literally translated to preserve the parallelism):

20:43	36:31
ûzĕkartem-šām 'et-darkêkem	*ûzĕkartem 'et-darkêkem hārā'îm*
wĕ'ēt kol-'ălîlôtêkem	*ûma'alĕlêkem*
'ăšer niṭmē'tem bām	*'ăšer lō'-ṭôbîm*
ûnĕqōṭōtem bipnêkem	*ûnĕqōṭōtem bipnêkem*
bĕkol-rā'ôtêkem 'ăšer 'ăśîtem	*'al 'ăwōnōtêkem wĕ'al tô'ăbôtêkem*

Both maintain a serious mood through several emotionally charged verbs. Both describe the human reaction after assertions of Yahweh's concern for his holy name profaned by the people's behavior, Yahweh's promise to re-gather Israel in the sight of the nations (20:41), and the promise of restoration to the ancestral homeland (20:42). Both are followed by affirmations that this restorative activity was motivated by Yahweh's concern for his name (40:44). Both emphasize that when Yahweh begins to act favorably toward his people it has nothing to do with their initiative or merit. On the contrary, in their salvation they will wake up to the remarkable grace of God, who has taken wretched sinners and restored them to full covenant relationship with himself.

When Yahweh has completed his salvific work on Israel's behalf, the people will look back and remember *(zākar)* their past conduct, characterized here as *evil conduct (dĕrākîm rā'îm)* and *improper behavior (maʿalĕlîm 'ăšer lō'-ṭôbîm,* lit. "deeds that are not good"). The first expression is familiar from previous oracles, but the second is new. This is the only occurrence of *maʿălāl,* "deed," in Ezekiel, and Jeremianic influence is suspected.[106] The modifying clause, "that are not good," echoes 20:25, where it had described Yahweh's decrees that are not good. The present statement indicates that for those who have experienced divine grace, the memory of guilt deserving of judgment should not be suppressed. On the contrary, recalling 6:9 and 20:43, Ezekiel declares that Israel's experience of divine grace will produce intense disgust over her perverted ways *(ʿāwōn)* and abominations *(tôʿăbôt).* The indicative mood in v. 31 suggests spontaneity in these responses, but the switch to imperatives in v. 32b confirms the propriety of this reaction. Israel is com-manded to be ashamed *(bôš)* and humiliated (Niphal of *klm)* on account of her conduct. As if to heighten the shame, the text adds a final reminder: Israel's restoration is not motivated by their repentance or merit; Yahweh acts for the sake of his sacred name.

And there you will remember	And there you will remember
your ways	your wicked ways
and all your wanton behaviors	And your wantonness
with which you defiled yourself	which were not good
and you will loathe yourselves	and you will loathe yourselves
on account of all your wickednesses	because of your iniquities
which you have committed.	and because of your abominations.

Rendtorff (in *Ezekiel and His Book,* pp. 260-65) argues that 36:16ff. represents an inten-tional advancement on ch. 20. This interpretation is preferable to that of T. Krüger (*Geschichtskonzepte,* pp. 441-49), who argues that 36:16ff. represents an earlier stage in the conceptual development of Ezekiel's restitution prophecies.

106. The present form occurs 17 times in Jeremiah, but the stylistic variant *'ălîlâ* is absent. See *'ălîlâ* in vv. 17 and 19, which in 20:44 had also been juxtaposed with *dĕrākîm rā'îm.*

EXCURSUS:
THE INFUSION OF THE SPIRIT OF YAHWEH
UNDER THE OLD COVENANT

Many believe that the role of the Spirit of Yahweh in the life of the Old Covenant believer differed fundamentally from the operation of the Holy Spirit in the NT and in the present. Especially common is the view that in ancient Israel the Holy Spirit came upon persons for specific tasks, but in the church he indwells the believer.[107] However, this interpretation is questionable for several reasons.

First, this view fails to distinguish between spiritual endowment and spiritual infusion. In both OT and NT the Spirit comes upon persons to authorize and empower them for divine service,[108] sometimes, as in the book of Judges, irrespective of the spiritual condition of the individual.

Second, this view fails to recognize the ecclesiological continuity between the Testaments. Believing that ancient Israelites were accepted into the community of faith through adherence to the Torah, keeping the law, many overlook the important fact that Israelite religion was from the outset a religion of the heart. Jeremiah's call for circumcision of the heart (Jer. 4:4) was not an innovation but a recollection of Deut. 10:16 and especially 30:6, whose influence on our text is considerable. But Gen. 2:7 provides the paradigm for Ezekiel's understanding of the animating power of the Spirit of Yahweh. The term *rûaḥ* is admittedly absent from this text, but the life-giving power of the divine breath *(nĕšāmâ)* is evident in transforming the lump of earth into a living being *(nepeš ḥayyâ)*. As under the New Covenant, under the Old Covenant regeneration was achieved not by works of righteousness but by Yahweh's infusion of the individual with his Spirit. Ezekiel's present anticipation of a fundamental internal transformation, effected by Yahweh putting his Spirit within the believer, rests on ancient foundations.

Third, this view misunderstands or disregards the witness of Ps. 51:12-13 (Eng. 10-11), which, aside from Isa. 63:10-11, is the only other OT passage in which the expression *rûaḥ qodšĕkā*, "your holy Spirit," occurs. In the context, the psalmist stands before God fearing rejection, the loss of his salvation *(yĕšûʿâ)* and the sentence of death *(dāmîm)*. His continued acceptance in the divine presence and the divine presence within him through his *rûaḥ* represent his only hope.

Fourth, this view ignores important evidence in the NT. When Nico-

107. For references cf. Block, *JETS* 32 (1989) 40.
108. As in Ezekiel's own experience. Cf. the role of the Spirit in the empowerment of the disciples in Acts 1:8.

demus requests of Jesus an explanation for his ministry, the discussion quickly digresses to a lecture on the role of the Spirit in the life of one who would enter the kingdom of God (John 3:5-8). Jesus' explanation of the vitalizing work of the Spirit could be interpreted as an innovation characteristic of the new dispensation, except that he rebukes Nicodemus for being ignorant of these matters, even though he was a trained theologian. Rather than introducing a new idea, Jesus' comments appear to be based on Ezek. 36:25-29, a text with which any rabbi would have been familiar.

Perceptions of radical discontinuity between the Testaments have desensitized many interpreters to the point of the present text. Ezekiel's understanding of the animating power of the Spirit of Yahweh is neither new nor distinctly eschatological. He was certainly aware of the theology underlying texts like Ps. 51; moreover, his present pronouncement reflects the fundamental incongruity between the idealistic designation of his own people as "the people of Yahweh," and the reality he observes among his compatriots. The problem for him was not dispensational, viz., the absence of the Holy Spirit in that era to transform lives, but ecclesiological — this transformation was not occurring on a national scale. The issue was one of scope. In 36:25-29 Ezekiel anticipates the day when the boundaries of physical Israel will finally be coterminous with the borders of the spiritual people of God. But, as 37:1-14 will demonstrate, this can be achieved only through direct divine intervention, Yahweh's infusion of his people with life.

c. The Vindication of Yahweh's Honor (36:33-38)

33 "'Thus has the Lord Yahweh declared: At the same time as I cleanse you from all your iniquities, I will cause your cities to be inhabited and the ruined places to be rebuilt. 34 The wasteland will be cultivated, instead of[109] lying desolate before all passersby. 35 Then they will say, "This very[110] land, once desolate, has become like the garden of Eden;[111] the cities, once waste,[112] and desolate, and

109. taḥat 'ăšer occurs only here in Ezekiel. Cf. Deut. 28:62.

110. hallēzû is a hapax fem. form. Cf. hallāzeh, Gen. 24:65; 37:19; hallāz, with masc., Judg. 6:20; 1 Sam. 17:26; 2 K. 23:17; Zech. 2:8; Dan. 8:16; with fem., 2 K. 4:25; cf. 1 Sam. 14:1. The rare particle functions as a reinforced demonstrative. See GKC, §34f; Joüon-Muraoka, Grammar, §36b.

111. LXX renders kĕgan 'ēden uniquely here as ὡς κῆπος τρυφῆς, "like a luxurious garden," which compares with ἐν τῇ τρυφῇ τοῦ παραδείσου τοῦ θεοῦ (28:13); ἐν τῷ παραδείσῳ τοῦ θεοῦ (31:8); τὰ ξύλα τοῦ παραδείσου τοῦ θεοῦ (31:9); τὰ ξύλα τῆς τρυφῆς (31:16); μετὰ τῶν ξύλων τῆς τρυφῆς (31:18).

112. The pl. form, ḥŏrēbôt, from the sg. ḥāreb, which occurs only here and in v. 38, compares with ḥōreb and ḥorbâ elsewhere.

ruined,[113] *are now fortified and inhabited."*[114] 36 *Then the nations that are left round about you*[115] *will know that I am Yahweh;*[116] *I have rebuilt the ruins; I have replanted*[117] *the wasteland. I am Yahweh; I have spoken;*[118] *I will act.*

37 *Thus has the Lord Yahweh declared: Furthermore,*[119] *I will respond to the request*[120] *of the house of Israel to act on their behalf. I will cause their population to increase like a human flock.* 38 *Like a consecrated flock, like the flock in Jerusalem*[121] *at the time of her appointed feasts, so will the ruined cities be filled with human flocks.*[122] *Then they will know that I am Yahweh.' "*

(1) Among the Nations (36:33-36)

33a A new citation formula in v. 33 sets off vv. 33-36 as a new section, if not a fragment of another oracle secondarily added here to fill what the editor considered a gap in the presentation of the restoration. But there is no reason to deny the content to the prophet himself. This segment consists of three parts, each with a slightly different focus: Yahweh's action toward his people (v. 33b), his actions toward the land (vv. 33c-34), and the public response (vv. 35-36). The last item has particular relevance for the preceding because of its concern for Yahweh's reputation among the nations. Although the key expression "my holy name" is absent, the issue continues to be addressed. When Yahweh is through with his salvific actions, the surrounding nations will be forced to acknowledge his special relationship with his people and his land. The restoration of the deity-nation-land triad will vindicate the holy name of Yahweh.

113. The triad of modifiers, *ḥŏrēbôt, nĕšammôt,* and *nehĕrāsôt,* expresses the superlative degree of devastation. See GKC, §133l.

114. *bĕṣûrôt yāšābû,* lit. "as fortified they are inhabited."

115. The expression *haggôyim 'ăšer yiššā'ărû sĕbîbôtêkem* clarifies *šĕ'ērît haggôyim,* "the remnant of the nations," in vv. 3-5.

116. The interpretation of *'ănî yhwh* as a self-contained recognition formula is supported by LXX[A], which inserts εἰμι, which itself conforms to the more common rendering of the formula in 28:22–45:35. See on v. 38 below.

117. The versions and 2 Hebrew mss. soften the abruptness of MT by adding the copula.

118. Targ. strengthens the statement with "I have decreed it by my Memra."

119. *'ôd zō't* introduces a secondary segment, as in 20:27.

120. On the tolerative Niphal, *'iddārēš,* which may be translated "I will let myself be sought," see my *Ezekiel: Chapters 1–24,* pp. 420 n. 6, 645 n. 163.

121. Targ. paraphrases, "Like the holy people, like the people who are cleansed and come to Jerusalem at the time of the Passover festivals."

122. *'ādām* functions appositionally to *ṣō'n,* "flock." See GKC, §131d, k. Targ. interprets the metaphor, "the people of the house of Israel."

33b-34 The first statement in v. 33 after the opening citation formula provides an important link with the foregoing. The most significant feature of the new day for Israel will not be her restored prosperity but her cleansing. Whereas previously Yahweh had spoken of cleansing the people of their uncleanness *(ṭum'â)* and their idolatry *(gillûlîm,* v. 25), here a more general, but still characteristically Ezekielian term, *'ăwōnōt, iniquities* or "guilt," is used. Contextually, the implantation of the new heart and the infusion of the new Spirit referred to earlier imply that the people's wicked behavior has stopped and their guilt has been removed. The account has been closed. As long as the land lies devastated, however, the name of Yahweh is slandered. Shalom must exist not only between deity and people but also between deity and land, and between people and land. Vv. 33b-34 address this territorial issue in overtly materialistic terms. Not only will the land become fertile again (vv. 29-30) but also the cultural signs of human occupation will return: the cities will be occupied *(yāšab),* the ruin heaps *(ḥŏrēbôt)* rebuilt, and the devastated land *('ereṣ nĕšammâ)* cultivated *('ābad).*[123] All who pass by will be amazed at the transformation of the landscape.

35 Like the reaction of the observers to Israel's destruction (v. 20), so their response to the nation's restoration is cast in the form of direct speech. The passersby do not mention the return of the people or their spiritual regeneration; what impresses them is the physical transformation of the environment. First, with obvious hyperbole, they speak of a wasteland being transformed into an Edenic paradise. Although references to Eden are common in Ezekiel (28:13; 31:9, 16, 18), the present description is particularly reminiscent of Isa. 51:3:

> Yahweh will surely comfort Zion,
>> He will look with compassion on all her ruins *(ḥorbōtêhā);*
> He will make her deserts *(midbārāh)* like Eden;
>> Her wastelands *('arbātāh)* like the garden of Yahweh.

Second, they notice that the ruined cities have been totally rebuilt. The description of rebuilt settlements as *fortified and inhabited (bĕṣûrôt yāšābû)* reflects a complete return to normalcy. In this cultural context a *city ('îr)* is by definition a permanent settlement surrounded by defensive walls.

36 The segment concludes with an expanded version of the recognition formula, the subjects being *the nations that are left round about you.* These are presumably those that have survived Yahweh's judgments, that is, Nebuchadrezzar's campaigns. Yahweh had apparently spared some that they

---

123. These promises provide an important link with the previous oracle, esp. vv. 9-10.

might serve as outside witnesses to his saving action and give testimony to his renewed commitment to Israel. The concluding self-introduction formula identifies the guarantor of the promise. Yahweh, the God of Israel, whose name has been desecrated, is the source of this oracle, and he will fulfill it.

But there is more to this statement than guaranteeing the prophetic word. As the covenant Lord, Yahweh had spoken long ago. The original covenant curses had warned Israel of the consequences of persistent rebellion (Lev. 26:14-39; Deut. 28:15-68). The present devastation of the land and the exile of its population attest to the truthfulness of that divine word. But those same covenant curses had left open the possibility of the nation's restoration. Indeed, Yahweh had promised that he would not reject his people forever. When the land has rested long enough to make up for the missed Sabbaths, and the people have borne the consequences of their iniquity, then he will remember the covenant. After all, he is Yahweh (Lev. 26:40-45). He does not utter vain promises; for him to speak is for him to execute (Isa. 42:5-9; 48; 55:6-13).

(2) In Israel (36:37-38)

The citation formula signals the start of a second addendum with a dramatic shift in tone. For more than twenty verses Yahweh has appeared as a cold, almost heartless divinity, preoccupied with the holiness of his name. Indeed, the audience may have wondered if Yahweh, rather than Israel, has a heart of stone. Unwilling to end the text on this note, the prophet has added a positive prophetic word. Finally we recognize the personal, sensitive side of Yahweh, who permits himself to be entreated, and even seems excited about the prospect of his people coming home. Although the original rhetorical context of this segment cannot be determined, the language is consistent with Ezekielian style, and the opening ʿôd zōʾt, "This also, . . ." deliberately integrates this piece with the preceding. The fragment consists of three parts: a description of Yahweh's disposition and action, a statement of the effects of his action, and the recognition formula.

37 The opening statement indicates how dramatically the relationship between Yahweh and his people has changed. For the first time in the book he permits himself to be entreated by the house of Israel. Twice before we have observed him slam the door on any appeals because of the nation's iniquities (14:3; 20:3; cf. also 8:18). The reopening of his ear to human inquiries symbolizes the radical transformation in his disposition. What the people might have approached him for we may only speculate. Would they still be plagued by doubts concerning Yahweh's commitment to his covenant promises? Would they come to him for support against external threats, or to settle internal disputes? Or would they come with pleas to replenish the population? The promise in v. 37b suggests that the last may be the case.

Why the size of the population would be an issue for the returning exiles is obvious. As a result of Yahweh's judgment, their numbers had been decimated through battle, famine, disease, and dispersion. Thus Yahweh anticipates a question that would arise among the exiles: How can the restoration be complete if they remain just a handful of people? After all, in both the Abrahamic (Gen. 17:2) and Mosaic covenants (Lev. 26:9) Yahweh had promised to multiply the population. Whereas the previous oracle had raised the subject from the land's perspective (36:11), here the people's disposition is the issue. But like every other aspect of the restoration, Yahweh holds the key; he alone can make it happen.

38 To describe the effects of Yahweh's action, the prophet compares the population of the land with flocks of sheep, jamming the streets of Jerusalem at festival time. Having grown up in a priestly family, Ezekiel would have remembered the scene well. While the expression *consecrated flock (ṣō'n qādāšîm)* refers primarily to the sacrificial animals, it also hints at the new sanctification of the people. Yahweh acts on behalf of his holy name by creating for himself a numerous holy people. But the reference to Jerusalem is illustrative only. The final clause asserts that this population explosion will occur in all the ruined cities, and the *human flocks* will fill the entire land.[124] While the emphasis differs, Ezekiel's picture of the human flock back in the ancestral homeland links this oracle with ch. 34. The flock of Yahweh's pasture (*ṣō'n mar'îtî*, 34:31) is indeed a human flock. When the nation of Israel fills the ancestral homeland, then they will recognize Yahweh, and his name will have been vindicated within the borders of his own land and among his own people.

♦ Theological and Practical Implications

Perhaps because this literary unit brings together so many strands in Ezekiel's preaching, it is unmatched for its theological intensity and spiritual depth. Several motifs are especially impressive.

First, although the Lord's ways may be mysterious, they are not hidden. His activity is played out in the public arena for the world to observe and to draw their conclusions. Sometimes the inferences about the character of God drawn from human experience are incorrect. This had been Israel's problem. For them the exile created an intense crisis of faith. They had come to look on God as a sentimental dispenser of gifts, whose primary role was to cater to their needs. When he failed to defend them against the Babylonians, they perceived him as unfaithful to his covenant. Even though their disaster was

---

124. For the Isaianic vision of a burgeoning population within the rejuvenated land see Isa. 49:19 and 54:1-3.

the result of their own sin, Yahweh took their doubts seriously. Concern for his reputation drove him to act soteriologically on their behalf. For outsiders, with their simplistic perceptions of patron deities as resident landlords defending turf and home, and their inability often to distinguish between divine and human causation, this oracle affirms the morality of all Yahweh's actions. The mockery of the nations over his apparent incompetence or betrayal of his people could have been resolved simply by reuniting land and people. But the taunting world must witness his transforming power in recreating a people intent on serving him.

Second, God's actions in human history are driven by revelatory aims: that his people and the world may know that he is Yahweh. The recipients of divine grace are easily deluded into thinking that they are the center of the universe, that their desires determine God's agenda. They may even be offended that sentimental pity toward a person in need takes second place to his concern for his own reputation. But the universal Lord is concerned that all may see his glory and his grace. He acts to preserve the sanctity of his reputation.

Third, the only solution for the fallen human race is a fundamental cleansing, a heart transplant, an infusion of the divine Spirit. It is tempting in our context in particular to imagine that social ills can be healed by economic, social, and educational programs. But Ezekiel's radical theocentricity finds the answer in God alone. While efforts to advance the social conditions of all humankind must be lauded, to propose these as the answer for a person's needs without reference to the fundamental problem, the depravity of the human soul, is to continue the idolatry of the Israelites. What is needed in our day is a dramatic reversal and return to the biblical heart imagery,[125] and to a recognition that the required transformation can be achieved only by the gracious act of God. Only God can remove our hearts of stone and give us hearts of flesh; new life comes only by the infusion of his Spirit.

Fourth, the future of Israel rests in the eternal, immutable promises of God. In 586 B.C. the nation saw all their hopes and aspirations dashed. To the exiles all God's promises regarding their status as his covenant people, their title to the ancestral homeland, the right of the Davidic dynasty to rule, and the residence of God in Zion seemed in vain. But Ezekiel reassures his people that God has not forgotten his covenant; the ancient promises still stand. Therefore the population must be regathered, their hearts transformed, and their community returned to the homeland, there to enjoy the blessings of God. After all, his honor is at stake.

125. So also J. A. Grassi, "The Transforming Power of Biblical Heart Imagery," *Review for Religious* 43 (1984) 714-23.

How these prophetic promises will be fulfilled remains an open question. Nevertheless, to reduce these oracles to symbolic language and to restrict their fulfillment to the NT church is to annul the hope that the prophet was attempting to restore. But Ezekiel does not assume that access to the benefits promised here is automatic. The principle operative in 586 still applies. Apart from personal and national spiritual renewal, those who claim to be heirs of Abraham have no right to the blessings that Yahweh promises to his covenant people.

4. The Resurrection of Yahweh's People (37:1-14)

> 1 *The hand of Yahweh came upon me.*[1] *He carried me away*[2] *by the Spirit of Yahweh and set me down*[3] *in the middle of the valley. It was full of bones.*[4] 2 *As he led me*[5] *around among them,*[6] *I was surprised to see*[7] *how exceedingly numerous they were there on the surface of the valley, and astonished*[8] *at how extremely dry they were.*
>
> 3 *Then he asked me, "Human, can these bones live again?"*[9] *I replied, "O Lord Yahweh, that only you know."*

1. Syr. adds a superscription, *'l ḥyt myt'*, "Concerning the life to come."

2. Masc. *wayyôṣi'ēnî* is striking after the fem. subject, "hand." As in 3:15 and 40:1, the form is determined by the genitive, Yahweh, who, as the following phrase indicates, is perceived as the real actor in the event.

3. As in 40:2, MT misvocalizes *wayĕnîḥēnî* for *wayyannîḥēnî*.

4. LXX and Targ. clarify with "human bones."

5. The *waw* plus perfect construction recurs in vv. 7, 8, 10, as well as elsewhere in the book (13:6, 8; 17:18; 19:12; 40:24, 35; 41:3, 8, 13, 15; 42:15). Though commonly explained as a weak *waw*, under the influence of Aramaic (GKC, §112pp; Joüon-Muraoka, *Grammar*, §119z), Late Biblical Hebrew features the diminished use of the *waw*-consecutive and its replacement with the perfect plus *waw* conjunction. See Rooker, *Biblical Hebrew in Transition*, pp. 100-102. R. Bartelmus identified this as an iterative case ("Ez 37,1-14, die Verbform *wĕqal* und die Anfänge der Auferstehungshoffnung," *ZAW* 97 [1985] 370). Cf. GKC, §112e.

6. The duplication of *sābîb sābîb* is characteristically Ezekielian style, occurring frequently in chs. 40–41, but elsewhere only in 2 Chr. 4:3. That the duplication is stylistic rather than emphatic is confirmed by Targumic Aramaic, which renders the single *sbyb* of Lev. 8:15 as *sḥwr sḥwr* (Onqelos) or *ḥzwr ḥzwr* (Pseudo-Jonathan). For discussion see Hurvitz, *Linguistic Study*, pp. 84-87.

7. *wĕhinnēh* functions elliptically for *wā'er'e['] wĕhinnēh*, "And I looked and behold," which is common in Ezekiel's vision reports (1:4, 15; 2:9; 8:2, 7, 10; 10:1, 9). V. 8 has the variant *wĕrā'îtî wĕhinnēh*. Similar ellipses occur in 3:23; 8:14, 16; 11:1; 40:3; 43:5; 44:4.

8. The duplication of *hinnēh* heightens the surprise, a point missed by LXX and Syr., which drop the second occurrence.

9. *hătiḥyênâ* carries an ingressive sense. Cf. Hossfeld, *Untersuchungen*, pp. 376-77. On the modal use of the imperfect see Joüon-Muraoka, *Grammar*, §113l.

4 *Then he said to me, "Prophesy over these bones. Declare to them,* *'O dry bones, hear the message of Yahweh.* 5 *Thus has the Lord Yahweh declared to these bones: Look! I will infuse you with breath,*[10] *and you will come to life.* 6 *I will attach sinews*[11] *to you, cover you with flesh, and overlay*[12] *you with skin. I will infuse you with breath;*[13] *then you will come to life. Then you will know that I am Yahweh.'"*

7 *So I prophesied as I had been commanded. While I was prophesying, there was a noise,*[14] *a rattling sound!*[15] *The bones*[16] *came together,*[17] *each in its proper place.*[18] 8 *I stared in amazement*[19] *as sinews appeared on them, flesh grew, and skin overlaid them.*[20] *But there was no breath in them.*

10. The substitution of *nātan bākem* for *hēbî' bākem* is stylistic.

11. *giddîm* occurs elsewhere in the OT only in Gen. 32:33; Jer. 48:4; Job 10:11; 40:1.

12. The verb *qāram*, which occurs only here and in v. 8 in the OT, is cognate to Akk. *qarāmu*, "to pull over, cover." See *AHW*, p. 902. In the Mishnah the word denotes the membrane of an egg, the film over wine, or the crust of loaf of bread. See Jastrow, *Dictionary*, p. 1421.

13. LXX reads "my breath," under the influence of 36:27 and 37:14.

14. This is one of only six occurrences of *wayĕhî* plus *kĕ/bĕ* plus infinitive construct in Ezekiel. See Rooker, *Biblical Hebrew in Transition*, pp. 103-5.

15. *wĕhinnēh ra'aš*, lit. "behold a rattling." *wayĕhî qôl kĕhinnābĕ'î wĕhinnēh ra'aš* is awkward but not unintelligible, nor is the construction unprecedented. *wayĕhî* plus verb or temporal note plus *wĕhinnēh* occurs elsewhere in Gen. 15:17; 29:25; 42:35; etc. Cf. S. R. Driver, *Tenses*, §78.2. Many follow LXX by dropping *qôl*. In 3:12 *qôl* and *ra'aš* are conjoined in a construct relation. Elsewhere in Ezekiel *rā'aš* denotes trembling (12:18) and quaking (38:19).

16. Anarthrous *'ăṣāmôt* is missing in 2 Hebrew mss. Two others, LXX, and Targ. have the definite article. Allen (*Ezekiel 20–48*, p. 182) suggests either an uncorrected miswriting of the following *'eṣem* or a marginal notice of the subject.

17. GKC, §60a n. 1, suggests that MT *wattiqrĕbû* is a clumsy correction of original *wayyiqrĕbû*, intended to agree in gender with *'ăṣāmôt*. This interpretation may find support in 4Q385 Second Ezekiel 2:5, which, according to E. Puech, reads *wyqrbw* (cited by R. Bauckham, "A Quotation from *4Q Second Ezekiel* in the *Apocalypse of Peter*," *RevQ* 15 [1992] 441 n. 14). J. Strugnell and D. Dimant, the original editors of the fragment, recognized only an initial *h* and reconstructed the verb as *hqrbw* ("*4Q* Second Ezekiel," *RevQ* 13 [1988] 53). G. R. Driver (*Bib* 35 [1954] 303) treats MT as a dialectical or colloquial variation.

18. *'eṣem 'el-'aṣmô*, lit. "a bone to its bone," expressing reciprocity and order. Cf. the common idiom *'îš 'el-rē'ēhû*, "a man to his neighbor." LXX reads "the bones approached each one to its joint." 4Q385 Second Ezekiel 2:5-6 takes the LXX reading one step farther, reading *'ṣm 'l 'ṣmw wprq ['l prqw]*, "bone to its bone and joint to its joint," on which see R. Bauckham, "A Quotation from 4Q Second Ezekiel," *RevQ* 15 (1992) 441-42.

19. *rā'îtî wĕhinnēh*, lit. "And I looked and behold."

20. *BHS* and many commentators read Niphal *wayyiqqārēm* with LXX, Syr., and Vulg., in place of MT *wayyiqram*. But the Qal may be either stative or transitive. So Wevers, *Ezekiel*, p. 279.

9 *Then he said to me, "Prophesy to the breath.*[21] *Prophesy, human! Declare to the breath, 'Thus has the Lord Yahweh declared: Come from the four winds, O breath!*[22] *Blow into these slain corpses, so they may come to life.' "*

10 *So I prophesied*[23] *as he commanded me. The breath entered them, and they stood up on their feet, an exceedingly vast host.*[24]

11 *Then he said to me, "Human, as for these bones, they represent the entire house of Israel.*[25] *Look!*[26] *They are saying: 'Our bones are dried up; our hope has vanished;*[27] *we are doomed.'*[28] 12 *Therefore, prophesy and say to them,*[29] *'Thus has the Lord Yahweh declared: Look! I will open your graves, and I will raise you up from your graves,*[30] *O*

21. *rûaḥ* may be translated "spirit" or "breath" in vv. 9-10.

22. LXX mistakenly drops *hārûaḥ*.

23. Like *wĕhinnehāmtî* in 5:13, *wĕhinnabē'tî* is pointed in MT as a Hithpael with an assimilated *taw.* See GKC, §54c; Bauer-Leander, *Grammatik,* §59c (p. 400). Since the Hithpael of this verb appears elsewhere in Ezekiel only in 13:17, some suggest a scribal error for the Niphal. Cf. Zimmerli, *Ezekiel 2,* p. 256.

24. Note the effusive expression *ḥayil gādôl mĕ'ōd mĕ'ōd. ḥayil,* "host, army," continues the military imagery. Cf. 17:17; 27:10.

25. The retraction of the athnach (accent mark) from *hēmmâ* to *yiśrā'ēl* (so Hossfeld, *Untersuchungen,* pp. 361-62; D. Baltzer, *Ezechiel und Deuterojesaja,* pp. 101-2) is unnecessary (cf. R. Bartelmus, "Textkritik, Literaturkritik und Syntax: Anmerkungen zur neueren Diskussion um Ez 37,11," *BN* 25 [1984] 55-64). *hā'ăṣāmôt hā'ēlleh kol-bêt yiśrā'ēl hēmmâ* is a normally constructed verbless clause of classification with a final pleonastic pronoun. Cf. Andersen, *Hebrew Verbless Clause,* p. 45, Rule 4, and pp. 68-69, nos. 162-72, for analogues. As in 45:1, the masc. gender of *hēmmâ* is determined by the nearest word.

26. LXX*, Vulg., and Targ. clarify by adding a pronominal subject, "they," viz., *hinnām,* but a suffix is not required on *hinnēh* when it precedes a participle. See Amos 7:4.

27. The copula on *wĕ'ābĕdâ* looks like dittography. Cf. LXX and Targ.

28. *BHS* recommends emending *nigzarnû lānû* to *nigzar nawĕlēnû,* "our thread [of life] is cut off," which provides a better parallel with the preceding phrase. But the preposition on *lānû* is best construed as a "centripetal *lamed,*" which focuses the attention on subject/actor represented by the suffix and isolating it from the surrounding world. See T. Muraoka, "On the So-called dativus ethicus in Hebrew," *JTS* 29 (1978) 495-98; idem, *Emphatic Words,* p. 122; Joüon-Muraoka, *Grammar,* §133d; Waltke-O'Connor, *Syntax,* §11.2.10d. The verb *gāzar,* "to cut off," is used in 2 K. 6:4 of cutting down trees; in Isa. 9:19 of cutting off a piece of meat. The Niphal is used occasionally in a derived sense of persons being cut off from the rest of humanity. Cf. Isa. 53:8: "He was cut off from the land of the living."

29. *'ălêhem* is missing in LXX.

30. "I will raise *(wĕha'ălîtî)* you from your graves" is reminiscent of declarations of thanksgiving for deliverance from the Pit or Sheol in the Psalms; see C. Barth, *Die Errettung vom Tode in den individuellen Klage- und Dankliedern des Alten Testaments* (Zurich: Zollikon, 1947), pp. 67-91. Cf. Ps. 30:4 (Eng. 3); 40:3 (Eng. 2); 71:20; Jon. 2:7 (Eng. 6).

my people,[31] *and I will bring you into the land of Israel.* 13 *And you will know that I am Yahweh, when I have opened up your graves, and raised you up from your graves, O my people.*[32] 14 *Then I will infuse you with my Spirit and you will come to life. I will set you down on your own land, and you will know that I am Yahweh. I have spoken and I will act. The declaration of Yahweh.' "*[33]

◆ *Nature and Design*

With the possible exception of the opening vision, no prophecy in the book of Ezekiel is as well known as 37:1-14. Although C. Barth has argued for the unity of the entire chapter,[34] most agree that vv. 1-14 should be isolated as a separate literary unit, marked off by the opening announcement of the arresting hand of Yahweh in v. 1 and the concluding signatory formula in v. 14. Within these borders an obvious break occurs at v. 11, as the prophet's visionary experience gives way to a series of interpretive comments.

As with most of the literary units in the book of Ezekiel, scholarly treatment of this text has varied greatly. Some have excised vv. 12aβ-13 as a gloss, offended that the image of the dry bones scattered about the plain could be succeeded by a scene of resurrected bodies emerging from graves.[35] Others treat vv. 11b-13 as an originally independent disputation oracle, with "These bones are the whole house of Israel" in v. 11aβ concluding the vision of vv. 1-10. The disputation speech consists of vv. 11aα, b-13, with v. 14 representing a later interpretive comment by a member of the Ezekielian school who, in his reflection on 37:6b and 37:12-13, recalls 36:26-28.[36] Some go an entirely different direction, attributing the final shape of the text to a Maccabean redaction.[37]

---

31. *'ammî,* missing in LXX and Syr., is often treated as a gloss. Cf. Allen, *Ezekiel 20–48,* p. 183; Lang, in *Ezekiel and His Book,* p. 312.

32. Although LXX preserves this *'ammî,* Syr. omits it again.

33. Vulg. and Syr. double the divine name in the signatory formula.

34. See C. Barth, "Ezechiel 37 als Einheit," in *Beiträge zur alttestamentlichen Theologie,* Fest. W. Zimmerli, ed. H. Donner, et al. (Göttingen: Vandenhoeck & Ruprecht, 1977), pp. 39-52.

35. See Fohrer, *Ezechiel,* p. 206; Wevers, *Ezekiel,* p. 277.

36. For variations of this approach see D. Baltzer, *Ezechiel und Deuterojesaja,* BZAW 121 (Berlin: de Gruyter, 1971), pp. 100-118; Hossfeld, *Untersuchungen,* pp. 341-401; Graffy, *Prophet Confronts His People,* pp. 83-86; Fuhs, *Ezechiel 25–48,* pp. 206-7.

37. P. Höffken ("Beobachtungen zu Ezechiel XXXVII 1-10," *VT* 31 [1981] 307-8) has noted a series of inconsistencies in vv. 1-10: (1) between the prophet's charge (vv. 5-6) and the two-phased fulfillment (vv. 7-10); (2) the ways in which *rûaḥ* is used; (3) reference to the *hărûgîm,* "the slain" (v. 9), in a context that spoke only of "bones"; (4) other tensions between vv. 4-6 and 7-10. He concludes that an original single-phase execution, corresponding to the basic command in vv. 5-6, has been secondarily transformed into a

Although R. Bartelmus recognizes the problem of imposing modern Western standards of logic on ancient oriental literature,[38] he appears to have succumbed to this temptation in this conclusion. Rigid adherents to form- or source-critical standards may assume that prophets could or would never mix their forms, but we have seen Ezekiel do so repeatedly (cf. ch. 34). The present literary unit incorporates at least three different prophetic forms: a vision report (vv. 1-10), a disputation address (vv. 11-14), and two proof sayings with this address (vv. 12-13, 14) in the refutation of the circulating quotation. Adhering too rigidly to form-critical structures, or to any other hermeneutical approach, may negate rhetorical strategies employed deliberately by the prophet.[39]

Zimmerli recognizes the relationship between vv. 1-10 and 11-14 as that of image and interpretation, analogous to the patterns found in chs. 17 and 21, with v. 11 playing a pivotal role. This verse explains the occasion for the oracle and marks the turning point in the narrative. Glancing backward, it interprets the imagery of the vision; looking forward, it introduces the disputation between God and the people that follows.[40] Despite several literary tensions inherent in the text, vv. 1-14 as a whole display strong signs of intentional composition. Allen recognizes a double movement in the vision account. The first movement consists of a negative picture of Israel's condition (vv. 1b-3), followed by a positive, transforming event (vv. 4-8a). The second movement is briefer, echoing and telescoping elements found in the preceding verses (vv. 8b-10). The vision account is followed by an oracular pronouncement of salvation (vv. 9-14), which reinforces the message of hope.[41] Others observe an artful chiastic arrangement of subjects that confirms the pivotal role of v. 11:

A   Ezekiel is inspired by the divine Spirit *(rûaḥ)* and relocated *(wayĕnîḥēnî)* in a death valley (vv. 1-2).

B   Ezekiel is instructed to prophesy over the bones so that they may revive; he does so and the predicted revival occurs (vv. 3-10).

---

two-phased recreative act. Taking Höffken's work a step farther, Bartelmus isolates vv. 7a, 8b-10a as a much later Maccabean insertion, which has transformed a prophecy, originally concerned with Yahweh's power to restore the exiled nation of Israel, into a message of hope for the Jews of the 2nd century B.C. (*ZAW* 97 [1985] 366-89; cf. his earlier response to Hossfeld and Garscha in *BN* 25 [1984] 55-64).

38. R. Bartelmus, "Ez. 37,1-14," *ZAW* 97 (1985) 368.

39. Cf. M. Fox, "The Rhetoric of Ezekiel's Vision of the Valley of the Bones," *HUCA* 51 (1980) 1-15.

40. Zimmerli, *Ezekiel 2,* pp. 256-58.

41. L. C. Allen, "Structure, Tradition and Redaction in Ezekiel's Death Valley Vision," in *Among the Prophets: Language, Image and Structure in the Prophetic Writings,* ed. P. R. Davies and D. J. A. Clines, JSOTSup 144 (Sheffield: JSOT Press, 1993), pp. 126-34.

C   The preceding vision is interpreted and the following explanation anticipated (v. 11a).

C′ The following explication is anticipated ("behold . . . therefore"), and the preceding vision is given idiomatic focus (v. 11b).

B′ The national meaning of the miraculous resurrection is divinely explained (vv. 12-13).

A′ Israel is resuscitated through the divine Spirit *(rûaḥ)* and relocated *(wĕhinnaḥtî)* in its ancestral homeland (v. 14).[42]

Since 37:1-14 contains no glaring grammatical impossibilities, no demonstrable historical anachronisms, and no real theological contradictions, a holistic approach to the prophetic and literary product is commended.[43] The literary unit is cast in the form of a dramatic autobiographical narrative. Even so it is difficult to establish precisely the nature of Ezekiel's experience. Is this a vision account, or does it describe a moment of prophetic ecstasy? The absence of the verb *rā'â*, "to see" (cf. 1:1; 8:2),[44] or the derived noun *mar'eh*, "vision," and the seizure by the hand/Spirit of Yahweh point to the latter. Nonetheless, the particle *hinnēh* (v. 2), common in dream and vision reports, implies a visual experience. It is probably unnecessary to vote for one or the other. In none of the other visionary reports in the book (1:1–3:15; 8:1–11:25; 40:1–48:35) is the prophet a detached observer. Each example portrays him being physically led around the visionary scene by Yahweh (or by his representative). In this vision his involvement is even more dramatic as his own activity and speech actually affect the events envisioned. The nearest parallel is the vision of Pelatiah's death (11:13), but only here does the prophet's activity have a direct bearing on the outcome. Vv. 1-14 represent an autobiographical account of Ezekiel's seizure and commissioning by Yahweh. As the narrative proceeds, however, the reader learns gradually that this is a salvation oracle for the exiles. The occasion for the prophecy is indicated by v. 11: they have lost all hope in their future and all hope in God. The nation obviously needs deliverance not only from their exile in Babylon but also from their own despondency. In promising this deliverance, Ezekiel's salvation oracles reach a new and dramatic height.

---

42. Thus Fishbane, *Biblical Interpretation,* pp. 451-52.

43. Too little is known of ancient standards of oral and literary communication; moreover, Ezekiel's linguistic style is transitional, displaying numerous features that become entrenched in postbiblical Hebrew. See the studies of Hurvitz, *Linguistic Study;* Rooker, *Biblical Hebrew in Transition.* Furthermore, Ezekiel often varies the usage of a single root or word within a given context to heighten the rhetorical force of his pronouncements. On the variation in the use of *rûaḥ* in this context see S. Wagner, "Geist und Leben nach Ezechiel 37,1-14," *Theologische Versuche* 10 (1979) 53-65; Fox, *HUCA* 51 (1980) 14-15.

44. *rā'â* occurs for the first time in v. 8. Cf. 1:1; 8:2; 40:2.

a. The Vision of the Dry Bones (37:1-2)

These verses are cast in simple narrative style, opening abruptly with a perfect verb form, *hāyĕtâ*. Since the opening line, *The hand of Yahweh came upon me (hāyĕtâ 'ālay yad-yhwh)*, is identical to 40:1, except that it lacks the latter's date notice, many have harmonized this introduction to other vision accounts (cf. 1:1-3; 8:1) by filling in the missing element. What that date might have been one can only speculate,[45] but if some such note was present, it seems to have been dropped intentionally to tie ch. 37 more closely to ch. 36. As elsewhere in the book, the arrival of the hand of Yahweh upon the prophet speaks of the overwhelming force with which the prophet perceives himself to have been seized by God, and in this instance carried away.[46]

The manner of Ezekiel's translocation is described as *by the Spirit of Yahweh (bĕrûaḥ yhwh)*.[47] The statement introduces the reader to the *Leitwort*, *rûaḥ*, which occurs ten times in vv. 1-14. In characteristic Ezekielian style, however, *rûaḥ* bears at least three different nuances within this unit: agency of conveyance (v. 1), direction (v. 9c), and agency of animation (vv. 5-6).[48] The present phrase, *Spirit of Yahweh*, occurs elsewhere in the book only in 11:5, where the falling of the Spirit of Yahweh upon Ezekiel is followed by a command to prophesy. But one should distinguish the role of the *rûaḥ* as agency of prophetic inspiration from its role as agency of conveyance.[49] The present activity bears a closer resemblance to 11:24, according to which *bĕrûaḥ 'ĕlōhîm*, "by the Spirit of God," explains *bĕmar'eh*, "by a vision," as the transporting agency.[50] Both are technical expressions associated with trancelike prophetic experiences, and there is no need to suppose a literal physical journey in any of these instances.

In the vision the prophet finds himself carried away and deposited in a valley *(habbiq'â)*, unidentified but presumably well known to Ezekiel, if not to his audience.[51] From God's perspective this was certainly not just any valley, randomly chosen. More important than its location is the sight that greeted the prophet there: a massive collection of bleached bones glistening in the sun. As if to ensure the full impact of the vision on the prophet, Yahweh leads him back and forth all around the bones.

The scene is striking in three respects. First, the circumstantial clause

45. Brownlee (*Ezekiel 1–19*, pp. xxxi-xxxii) ill advisedly claims that 1:1 (the 30th year) originally prefaced this prophecy.

46. Cf. 1:3; 3:14, 22; 8:1; 33:22; 40:1.

47. Scholars often discount the comment. Cf. Hossfeld, *Untersuchungen*, pp. 345-47.

48. Cf. S. Wagner, "Geist und Leben," *Theologische Versuche* 10 (1979) 53-65.

49. Cf. Block, *JETS* 32 (1989) 33-34, 41-43.

50. These expressions are condensed in 40:2: *bĕmarôt 'ĕlōhîm*, lit. "by visions of God."

51. As in 3:22, the article on *habbiq'â* suggests a specific, well-known valley.

at the end of v. 1 and the phrase *wĕhinnēh rabbôt mĕʾōd* highlight Ezekiel's amazement at the exceedingly high number of bones.[52] The significance of their number will not become apparent until later (v. 10), but the sight suggests the remains of a major catastrophe. Second, the bones lay on the surface of the valley, like the remains of corpses denied a proper burial and left for scavenging buzzards. As an Israelite and especially as a priest, Ezekiel knew how important was the proper treatment of human corpses,[53] and the altered image of graves in the interpretive comments of v. 12 would certainly have been more welcome for the prophet. Third, the prophet is surprised at the bones' extreme dryness, which indicates that the people whose remains they represent have been dead for a long time. The image concretizes the hopelessness expressed in v. 11; no life force remains in them at all. The narrative leaves no hint regarding whose bones these might be,[54] but the picture is one of death in all its horror, intensity, and finality.

b. The Resuscitation of the Dry Bones (37:3-10)

In v. 3 the literary style changes as direct speech takes over from simple narration. But this conversation can hardly be described as dialogue. Ezekiel's own words are quoted only at the end of v. 3. Otherwise the quoted speech belongs entirely to Yahweh. Twice the prophet is said to have prophesied as he had been commanded, but the failure to record his own speech reflects the nature of the prophetic office. His speech is subordinated entirely to the words of God. He may respond to God when invited (in v. 3), but otherwise what God says is more important than what he says.

3 While Ezekiel is contemplating the sight of the dry bones, he is addressed directly by Yahweh, *ben-ʾādām,* (lit. "son of man"), and asked a curious question, *Can these bones live again?* The question is ridiculous. Ezekiel's own tradition knows of people coming back to life, but only in cases of recent death.[55] *these bones (hāʿăṣāmôt hāʾēlleh,* which occurs 3 times in

---

52. In dreams and visions *wĕhinnēh* expresses a strong emotional reaction to an awesome sight. See D. J. McCarthy, "The Uses of *wĕhinnēh* in Biblical Hebrew," *Bib* 61 (1980) 332-33; Andersen, *Sentence in Biblical Hebrew,* p. 95.

53. Cf. the care with which the corpses are disposed of in 39:12-16 to prevent the contamination of the land. On Israelite customs concerning the dead see Spronk, *Beatific Afterlife,* pp. 238-44; Bloch-Smith, *Judahite Burial Practices,* pp. 110-21.

54. Rashi identified them as the bones of slain Israelites who had left Egypt before the appointed time. *b. Sanh.* 92b speculates they were the bones of Jews who had worshiped Nebuchadrezzar's image on the plain of Dura (Dan. 3). For additional citations see Levey, *Ezekiel,* p. 103.

55. See the resuscitative miracles of Elijah (1 K. 17:17-24) and Elisha (2 K. 4:18-37), and the effect of the latter's bones touching a corpse (2 K. 13:21).

vv. 3-5) represent the deceased of long ago. Any hope for them would need to be tied to belief in a general eschatological resurrection (cf. Dan. 12:1-2). The prophet's response suggests that such notions had not yet matured in Israel.[56] People had begun to grasp for the idea, as Job 14:14 seems to imply (though in the end Job's hope aborts). Ezekiel's answer to Yahweh's question is cautious. With "O Lord Yahweh, that only you know," he tosses the ball back into Yahweh's court. He neither rules out the possibility — after all, with God all things are possible (Gen. 18:14; Jer. 32:17), and Yahweh exercises control over life and death (Job 34:14-15; Ps. 104:29-30) — nor betrays the hopelessness of his contemporaries (v. 11). Instead he casts himself entirely upon the will and the power of God. Yahweh responds by returning the ball, demanding that the prophet be personally involved in providing the answer.

4-10   In these verses we witness another typically Ezekielian example of literary "halving." Despite some significant differences in the two parts, the parallelism between vv. 4-8 and 9-10 is obvious.[57] The two halves appear to be constructed as separate oracles, each with its own prophetic formulae and structure. In the first segment, Ezekiel is summoned to call the dry bones

---

56. Cf. E. Haag, "Ez 37 und die Glaube an die Auferstehung der Toten," *TTZ* 82 (1973) 78-92.

57. Note the following synopsis:

37:4–7	37:9-10
wayyō'mer 'ēlay	*wayyō'mer 'ēlay*
hinnābē' 'al-hā'ăṣāmôt hā'ēlleh	*hinnābē' 'el-hārûaḥ*
	hinnābē' ben-'ādām
wĕ'āmartā 'ălêhem	*wĕ'āmartā 'el-hārûaḥ*
hā'ăṣāmôt hayĕbēšôt	
šim'û dĕbar yhwh	
kōh 'āmar 'ădōnāy yhwh	*kōh 'āmar 'ădōnāy yhwh*
. . . . . .	. . . . . .
wîda'tem kî 'ănî yhwh	.
wĕnibbē'tî ka'ăšer ṣuwwêtî	*wĕhinnabbē'tî ka'ăšer ṣiwwānî*
Then he said to me,	Then he said to me,
"Prophesy over these bones.	"Prophesy to the breath.
	Prophesy, human!
Declare to them,	Declare to the breath,
'O dry bones,	
hear the message of Yahweh!	
Thus has the Lord Yahweh declared	Thus has the Lord Yahweh declared
. . . . . .	. . . . . .
Then you will know that I am Yahweh.' "	
So I prophesied	So I prophesied
as I had been commanded.	as he commanded me.

to attention on Yahweh's behalf. It may seem absurd to speak to "dry bones," but Ezekiel is famous for his disregard for convention. Beginning with the citation formula, Ezekiel issues a prophecy to the bones as if they were a living audience. His message consists of a general thesis statement (v. 5b), a fourfold explication, and a concluding statement of the goal or result (v. 6).

5 Anticipation is created in both the hypothetical audience (the bones) and the prophet's real audience (his fellow exiles) by alerting them to the impending activity of Yahweh with *hinnēh 'ănî* . . . (lit. "Behold I . . ."). The promised action is cast in simplest form: Yahweh will put breath into the bones, with their revivification as the stated goal. In spite of its simplicity, the use of the term *rûaḥ* creates ambiguity. The shift in meaning from v. 1 is obvious, but it is difficult to decide whether *rûaḥ* should be interpreted as "spirit" or "breath." In any case, *rûaḥ* represents the divine animating force without which no life is possible (Judg. 15:19).[58] Only God, from whom all life derives (Eccl. 12:7), can revive these bones.

6 As developed here, the process by which Yahweh will fulfill his promise involves four discrete stages: He will reconnect the bones with sinews, cover the bones with flesh, overlay the flesh with skin, and infuse them with breath. The sequence involving bones, sinews, flesh, and skin reflects an understanding of anatomy available to anyone who had witnessed the slaughter of an animal;[59] it also reverses the decomposition process. The concluding recognition formula gives this segment the quality of a proof saying, highlighting that Yahweh's goal in reviving these bones is not simply the biological-chemical reconstitution of the body or even the restoration of physical life. He desires spiritual revival: a new recognition of and relationship with himself.

7-8 These verses describe the prophet's compliance with the divine order and its effects. The syntax of *While I was prophesying, there was a noise, a rattling sound,* is awkward, but it emphasizes the connection between the prophetic word and the event. The declaration, announced as the word of Yahweh (v. 4), signals him to action. The construction also creates the impression that the reconstruction proceeded rapidly; bone knocked on bone until each was in its proper place. The prophet is filled with amazement as he watches Yahweh's promise being fulfilled before his eyes. At the critical moment, however, the process appears to abort. The circumstantial clause at the end of v. 8 identifies the problem — *there was no breath (rûaḥ)* in the bones — and prepares the way for the second phase of divine activity.

---

58. Cf. Block, *JETS* 32 (1989) 34-41; R. Koch, *Der Geist Gottes im Alten Testament* (Frankfurt: Lang, 1991), pp. 19-34; on this text, pp. 124-25.

59. Zimmerli (*Ezekiel 2,* p. 260) suggests that this reflects Ezekiel's experience as a priest dissecting sacrificial animals.

9   The repetition here heightens anticipation. The prophet now has a new addressee, the *rûaḥ* itself. But the word carries two different meanings within this verse. Whereas previously *rûaḥ* had denoted "breath" in general, now *the breath* (*hārûaḥ*, with the definite article) is clearly the breath that will blow (*nāpaḥ*) on these bones and bring them to life. But the source of *hārûaḥ*, "the breath," is *'arba' rûḥôt*, "the four winds," meaning "the four directions." This usage of *rûaḥ* occurs more than one hundred times in the OT. In 27:26 *rûaḥ haqqādîm*, "the east wind," designated a violent gale that destroyed the Tyrian galleys. In 17:10 and 19:12 the word referred to the scorching sirocco wind that blows off the desert, causing the vegetation to wither and die. In the expression *'arba' rûḥôt*, *rûaḥ* may denote "direction," a sense familiar from previous texts.[60] Or the winds may represent the divine breath that blows in every corner of the earth, giving life to all creatures. Here Yahweh, the sovereign of the universe, is summoning the winds from around the world to direct their life-giving energy to these corpses lying in the valley.[61]

The identification of the lifeless corpses as the *slain corpses* (*haḥărûgîm*) offers the first clue to the identity of the deceased. The bones are the remains of victims of some enormous battle.[62] While the oracle expresses no interest in which battle they might have fallen, Ezekiel would naturally have thought of his compatriots, casualties to Nebuchadrezzar's conquest of Judah and Jerusalem (cf. v. 11).

But why have they not been properly buried? The answer is to be found in the covenant curses.[63] The practice of throwing bodies out into the open to be eaten by wild animals is well attested in ancient Near Eastern sources. The treatment was applied especially to those who had broken contracts and treaty oaths, as illustrated by a curse in Esarhaddon's vassal treaty with Ramataya of Urakazabanu: "May Ninurta, leader of the gods, fell you with his fierce arrow, and fill the plain with your corpses, give your

---

60. In 5:10-12 Ezekiel scatters his hair *lĕkol-rûaḥ*, "in every direction." Cf. also 17:21. Forms of the expression occur elsewhere in 42:20; Zech. 2:10 (Eng. 6); 6:5; 1 Chr. 9:24; Dan. 7:2 (Aramaic); 8:8; 11:4. Cf. also Matt. 24:31. This usage of *rûaḥ* is best illustrated by Jer. 49:36: "I shall bring upon Elam the four winds (*'arba' rûḥôt*), from the four ends of heaven, and I shall scatter them in all these directions (*lĕkol hārûḥôt hā'ēlleh*)." In the NT, Rev. 7:1 speaks even more picturesquely of four angels holding back the four winds of the earth. *'arba' rûḥôt* is semantically cognate to Akk. *šari erbetti*, also "four winds." Both expressions reflect the hypothetical division of the earth into four quadrants. Cf. *AHW*, p. 1192; *CAD*, 4:256.

61. Cf. S. Wagner, *Theologische Versuche* 10 (1979) 59-60.

62. Hence W. Baumgartner's designation of this text as a "Schlachtfeld-sage," in *Zum Alten Testament und seiner Umwelt: Ausgewählte Aufsätze* (Leiden: Brill, 1959), p. 361.

63. See F. C. Fensham, "The Curse of the Dry Bones in Ezekiel 37:1-14 Changed to a Blessing of Resurrection," *JNSL* 13 (1987) 59-60.

flesh to eagles and vultures to feed upon."[64] Israelite familiarity with this cursed treatment of corpses is evident in 2 Sam. 21, according to which David authorizes the Gibeonites to avenge Saul's treachery against their people by slaying several of his sons and exposing their corpses on a hilltop. But Rizpah, their mother, stationed herself among the bodies to keep away the birds and wild animals.[65]

Ezekiel probably viewed the present scene as evidence of the fulfillment of Yahweh's own covenant curse in Deut. 28:25-26: "Yahweh will put you to rout before your enemies. You will march out against them by a single road, but flee from them by many roads. You will become a horror to all the kingdoms of the earth. Your carcasses will become food for all the birds of the sky and all the beasts of the earth, with none to frighten them off." Indeed, his contemporary, Jeremiah, had predicted its fulfillment in 34:17-20: "I will make you a horror to all the kingdoms of the earth. I will make the men who violated my covenant, who did not fulfill the terms of the covenant which they made before me, like the calf which they cut in two so as to pass between the halves: the officers of Judah and Jerusalem, the officials, the priests, and all the people of the land who passed between the halves of the calf will be handed over to their enemies, to those who seek to kill them. Their carcasses will become food for the birds of the sky and the beasts of the earth."[66] While Ezekiel would undoubtedly have been reminded of this curse, the command to prophesy to the breath to enter these corpses that they might live offers hope. Yahweh is hereby announcing the lifting of the curse!

10 After the prophet has complied with Yahweh's order, he witnesses a most remarkable sight. The breath entered the bodies, and they came to life and stood up on their feet.[67] The scope of the miracle is highlighted by noting that the exceedingly numerous bones (*rabbôt mě'ōd*, v. 2) were transformed into an exceedingly vast host. Although the command to Ezekiel in vv. 5-6 seemed to envisage a single-stage revivification, the bifurcation of events into two phases serves a rhetorical purpose of creating suspense and strengthening

---

64. See *ANET*, p. 538. Fensham (*JNSL* 13 [1987] 60) translates "vulture" as "jackal." Cf. a mid-7th-century-B.C. neo-Assyrian contract in which the violator of the oath is threatened with: "May the dogs tear his corpse which is not buried." See J. Kohler and A. Ungnad, *Assyrische Rechtsurkunden* (1913), pp. 16, 19, as quoted by Fensham, p. 60.

65. See 2 Sam. 21:9-10, on which see Fensham, "The Treaty Between Israel and the Gibeonites," *BA* 27 (1964) 100 (repr. in *BAR* 3 [Garden City, N.Y.: Doubleday, 1970], p. 126).

66. See Hillers's discussion of this curse in *Treaty-Curses*, pp. 68-69.

67. Cf. Ezekiel's analogous experience in 2:1-2 and 3:24. The present scene is also reminiscent of 2 K. 13:21, according to which contact with the bones of Elisha causes a dead man to revive (*wayyěḥî*) and stand up (*wayyāqām*).

the force of the imagery.[68] The last statement in v. 8 had forced the hearer to pause, wondering if, after all this, the curse would continue to hang on the bones. In so doing it focused attention on the climactic resolution. Only by a specific act of God do these bodies come to life; and when that divine breath comes, every single corpse is revived. But the dead rise not because they are reconstituted biologically, nor because of some internal force, but because Yahweh has infused them with breath. The two-phased process of resuscitation also serves a theologico-anthropological function, emulating the paradigm of Yahweh's creation of *'ādām*. According to Gen. 2:7, the lump of soil that Yahweh had molded into the form of a man did not become a living being (*nepeš ḥayyâ*) until he had breathed into it his own breath.[69]

c. Interpretation (37:11-14)

Verses 11-14 are cast as a continuous divine speech, framed by a new address of the prophet, *Human (ben-'ādām),* at the beginning, and the signatory formula at the end. V. 11 serves a transitional function. The absence of an identified subject for *wayyō'mer,* "And he said," and the need for an antecedent to "These bones" suggest that this verse explains the preceding vision. Furthermore, vv. 12-14 involve a significant shift in the visual metaphor. The bones strewn about the valley have disappeared and been replaced by bodies buried in graves. However, form-critical considerations also link v. 11 with vv. 12-14. Whereas vv. 1-10 are cast as a vision, incorporating the prophet within the visionary experience, vv. 11b-14 are composed as a modified disputation speech, opening with a quotation of popular opinion (v. 11b), followed by a refutation (vv. 12-14). The refutation itself is complex, subdividing into two parts (vv. 12-13 and 14), each of which contains a promise of divine action and an expanded form of the recognition formula. The signatory formula at the end seals the oracle.

11   As already intimated, the opening declaration is expository, offering the first clear interpretive statement on the vision.[70] The bones on the surface of the valley do not represent just any victims of Nebuchadrezzar's wars who have been denied a proper burial; *they represent the entire house of Israel,* including even those who had been exiled by the Assyrians more than 130 years earlier. The scope of Yahweh's restorative activity, which had

---

68. See Fox, *HUCA* 51 (1980) 10-13.

69. On the Hebrew view of the constitution of humankind see Eichrodt, *Theology,* 2:515-26.

70. For similarly constructed interpretive statements see 5:5; 10:15, 20, 22; 11:2, 7; 31:18; 39:8. Cf. also 40:46; 41:4, 22; 43:12, 18; 45:13; 46:20, 24; 47:13, 15; 48:1, 16, 29, 30. *qînâ hî',* "It is a lament," in 19:14 and 32:16 is a classificatory rather than identificatory interpretation.

been affirmed earlier in 36:10, and will be reiterated in 39:25 and 45:6, reflects the consistent prophetic picture of the people of Yahweh as encompassing the entire twelve-tribe house of Israel.[71] Indeed, the sequel to this oracle (37:15-28) will elaborate on Yahweh's design for the nation as a whole.

But Yahweh interrupts his own exposition of the nature of the nation's revivification to inform his prophet of a quotation circulating among the exiles, even though Ezekiel would surely have been aware of the conversations among his compatriots. After all, the prophet's house had become a focal point of exilic communal activity (cf. 33:30-33). Although the present pattern, with Yahweh reminding the prophet of the people's words, occurs in each of the disputation speeches found in the book,[72] this is the only instance in which the quotation is introduced with *hinnēh, Look.* The particle serves two functions in this context. Rhetorically, it represents a quasi-imperative attention-getter. With this *hinnēh* Ezekiel is jolted back into reality, away from the excitement of this visionary world, in which dry bones have come to life before his eyes. Logically, it provides a link, teaming up with *lākēn* in v. 12 to create an occasion-response, if not cause-effect, sequence of clauses.[73]

The people's comment is a lament, cast in rhythmic tripartite form, each statement consisting of two words and concluding with the rhyming sounds *-ēnû/-ānû.* (1) *yābĕšû 'aṣmôtēnû, Our bones are dried up,* is a metaphorical statement, conjoining two common elements in expressions of lament in the Psalms.[74] (2) *wĕ'ābĕdâ tiqwātēnû, our hope has vanished,* interprets the metaphor. The same expression of hopelessness was used of the lioness in 19:5 at the loss of her cub.[75] (3) *nigzarnû lānû, we are doomed,* reflects

71. On the significance of the expression *bêt yiśrā'ēl* see Block, *JETS* 28 (1985) 257-75.

72. See my *Ezekiel: Chapters 1–24,* pp. 330ff.; and for comment, Graffy, *Prophet Confronts His People,* p. 108.

73. In Ezekiel cause and effect clauses are usually introduced with *ya'an* and *lākēn,* respectively. See the discussion of causal and occasional uses of *wĕhinnēh* plus participle by McCarthy, *Bib* 61 (1980) 333-37.

74. References to ailing bones appear in Ps. 22:15 (Eng. 14), "All my bones are out of joint"; 31:11 (Eng. 10), "My bones have wasted away"; 102:4 (Eng. 3), "My bones have been scorched like a hearth." Two of these Psalm texts also refer to "drying up": 22:16 (Eng. 15), "My strength is dried up like a potsherd"; 102:5 (Eng. 4), "My heart has been stricken and dried up like grass"; 102:12 (Eng. 11), "I dry up like grass." Cf. also Num. 11:6, "Now our appetite [energy?] has dried up."

75. Cf. Job's desperate conclusion in Job 14:19 (a context in which he has toyed with the idea of resurrection), "You destroy a human being's hope *(tiqwâ)*." The "cord," which served as a symbol of hope in Josh. 2:18, 21, is identified by the homonym. For a discussion of the root *qwh* see C. Westermann, *THAT,* 2:619-29.

their pessimism. The emotional impact of being cut off is poignantly expressed in Ps. 88:6-15 (Eng. 3-12).[76] The despondency of the Israelites is obvious in the present quotation. They had counted on Yahweh's immutable promises for their security, but he had abandoned them. The successive calamities of 732, 722, 597, and 586 had destroyed any remnant of hope.

12-14   Although Ezekiel never betrays his own feelings about the despondency of the exiles, the vision of vv. 1-10 represents Yahweh's response. V. 12 intimates for the first time that this message of hope is for Ezekiel's compatriots. He had faithfully prophesied to the bones and to the breath; now he is commanded to deliver to his fellow exiles a message of hope from Yahweh. Yahweh's reaction to the lament divides into two parts, corresponding to the refutation and counterthesis of other disputation speeches.[77] Although there is some overlapping of ideas, v. 14 advances the notions raised in vv. 12-13. But the focus throughout remains on Yahweh, who alone is able to bring hope to a despairing people.

12   The deictic particle *hinnēh, Look,* arouses the audience's attention, pointing to the good news announced in a triad of promises that correspond to the tripartite lament. First, Yahweh announces that he will open Israel's graves. For the upper classes this meant pushing aside the stones that blocked the entrance to the rock-cut family tombs. For the majority of the population, who were of more modest means, this meant removing the soil that covered those who had been buried in shallow holes in the ground.[78] If the prophet had shared with his audience the earlier vision of the dry bones, this mixing of metaphors would probably have caught them off guard, just as it does the modern reader of the literary account. But the scene of a vast host of white bones glistening under the Mesopotamian sun has given way to the image of a cemetery in which the corpses have been dutifully buried. Given his personal involvement in vv. 1-10, however, this vision may have been intended for Ezekiel's own benefit, offering him tangible assurance of the veracity of Yahweh's promises.

Second, Yahweh declares that he will raise Israel from the graves. The first statement had left no hint of Yahweh's intention in opening the tombs. He might have had another secondary burial in mind. Family tombs, particularly the rock-cut variety, were reopened every time another family member

---

76. Cf. the similar usage of *gzl*, the Phoenician cognate of Heb. *gzr*, in a lament by Eshmunazar, king of Sidon (early 5th century B.C.), inscribed on his sarcophagus: "I have been snatched away *(gzl)* before my time, just a few days old, smitten, an orphan, the son of a widow. I am lying in this casket and in this grave, in the place I myself have built" (*KAI*, 14.2-3; *ANET*, p. 662). For commentary see *TSSI*, 3:108-9.

77. See D. F. Murray, *JSOT* 38 (1987) 98-99.

78. See Spronk, *Beatific Afterlife*, pp. 238-44; Bloch-Smith, *Judahite Burial Practices*, pp. 25-62.

died, so the person could be "gathered to the people/ancestors."[79] Cynics in Ezekiel's audience might have assumed a sinister motive, perhaps to rob the tombs or to desecrate the remains, both common practices in the ancient Near East. But now Yahweh poses as a tomb robber like no other. The treasure he is after is the bodies of his people, whom he will raise from the grave. Since the verb he'ĕlâ belongs to exodus terminology,[80] however, the choice of this word prepares for Yahweh's third promise.

Third, Yahweh will bring them into the land of Israel. Now the cemetery imagery is abandoned altogether and new exodus language, which lies at the heart of Ezekiel's restoration oracles (20:42; 34:13; 36:24; 37:21), leaves no doubt about Yahweh's intentions. Although many delete 'ammî, "my people," as an intrusive gloss, this operation robs the promises in vv. 12-13 of a crucial theme. The exiles' despondency arose from the conviction that with the fall of Jerusalem in 586 the deity-nation-land relationship had been ruined forever. With this statement, however, Yahweh promises to restore the tripartite relationship. He will take them back as his people, and return them to their hereditary homeland.

13 As in most of Ezekiel's oracles, the concluding recognition formula announces Yahweh's actual goal, the acknowledgment of his person and his claims on the restored people. For too long the nation had presumed upon their relationship with Yahweh by virtue of their presence in the land.[81] Now Yahweh announces the good news that his physical revivification of the nation will be accompanied by a spiritual revival as well. In the end they will be reconstituted not only as a nation in their hereditary homeland but also as the people of Yahweh.

14 The oracle might have ended here, but a final word is added to dispel any further despair. V. 14 breaks up into two parts, each of which consists of an announcement of a divine action followed by a human response. First reiterating 36:27, Yahweh declares that he will put his own Spirit within the house of Israel. This announcement answers the questions concerning the identity of the Spirit that gives life to the bones in the vision and the manner in which the corpses in the graves will be resuscitated; the forms of expression also deliberately link this oracle with the preceding prophecy.[82] Having infused the corpses with his life-breath, Yahweh will take them and deposit them in

---

79. A common idiom for burial in a family tomb. Cf. Gen. 25:8, 17; Judg. 2:10; etc. For additional references see *HALOT*, p. 74,

80. See Exod. 3:17 plus 41 times. For discussion see G. Wehmeier, *THAT*, 2:287-90. Wehmeier observes (p. 284) that with reference to death and the grave he'ĕlâ is the antithesis to yārad, "to go down" to the netherworld. See Ezek. 26:20; 31:14-17; 32:18-30.

81. Cf. the claims of those who remained in the land in 33:24.

82. Cf. the combination of wĕnātattî rûḥî bākem and wiḥyîtem with wĕrûaḥ ḥădāšâ 'ettēn bĕqirbĕkem in 36:26-27.

their own land.[83] As in 36:36, the addition of *dibbartî waʿāśîtî, I have spoken and I will act,* reminds the audience about the veracity of the divine word. Israel's only hope rests in her God, who is at the same time the sovereign Lord of history and the source of life. The restoration of his people will be his climactic moment of self-revelation. The final signatory formula seals or guarantees this message.

EXCURSUS:
THE BACKGROUND TO EZEKIEL'S
NOTIONS OF RESURRECTION

Ezekiel's vision of the dry bones raises numerous questions, one of the most difficult of which concerns the origin of his ideas and the implication of this chapter for the Christian doctrine of resurrection. The primary concern of this vision is obviously the revival of the nation of Israel, but the manner in which the subject is presented is remarkable. While the people's comment in v. 11 seems to express utter hopelessness for life after death, it sets the stage for the extremely graphic and concrete portrayal in v. 12 of graves opening and revived people emerging. But does the prophet hereby imply a belief in individual resurrection? In addressing this issue one may consider two types of evidence: the witness of comparative ancient Near Eastern religions, and inner-biblical data.

Some have found the roots of Ezekiel's ideas in Egyptian beliefs about the deceased rising as stars and taking their place in the heavens.[84] Others have recognized a belief in personal resurrection in ancient Mesopotamian and Syrian festivals celebrating the annual revivification of the storm god, or

---

83. The verb *wĕhinnaḥtî* creates an effective *inclusio* with the same root in v. 1.

84. On which see H. Frankfort, *Ancient Egyptian Religion: An Interpretation* (New York: Columbia University Press, 1948), pp. 100-123; cf. Spronk, *Beatific Afterlife,* 86-95; S. Morenz, *Egyptian Religion* (Ithaca: Cornell University Press, 1973), pp. 204-13. In some Old Kingdom texts hope for a beatific afterlife was held out only for the king, who in his identification with a star, or later the sun god Re, crossed the heavens each day and entered the netherworld at night. Some texts identify the king with Osiris, the ruler of the dead, but this role offered him no possibility of leaving that realm. Later these two notions merged, and Osiris took his place in the heavens, being associated with Orion or the moon as a nightly counterpart to Re. The custom of mummification was designed to enable the deceased to live on as a "living corpse" and to protect him on his nightly journey to the world of the dead and the daily journey through heaven. With the decline of the Egyptian kingdom, some democratization of the hope of beatific afterlife made possible by identification with Osiris after death becomes apparent. On the role of Osiris see H. Kees, *Totenglauben und Jenseitsvorstellungen der alten Ägypter* (Berlin: Akademie, 1980), pp. 132-59.

the annual New Year Festival that commemorated the storm god's victory over death (Mot).[85] K. Spronk argues that the hope for a beatific afterlife, which he defines as "being forever with God (or the gods) in heaven (cf. 1 Thess. 4:17)," was an important element in Israelite "folk religion" (as opposed to "official Yahwistic religion").[86] He concludes, "The Israelites were clearly familiar with the Canaanite belief in Baal rising from the nether-world every year and taking the deified spirits of the royal dead with him."[87] These royal dead, known as Rephaim, are thereby entitled to celebrate with Baal at the New Year Festival, and as "divine ancestors" (*'il 'ab*).[88]

However, neither the Egyptian nor the New Year Festival theory is convincing.[89] Also, Ezekiel's vision of the resuscitation of the dead has nothing to do with a beatific afterlife "forever with God in heaven," as Spronk defines it.[90] The theory of Zoroastrian influence seems more likely; B. Lang is especially impressed by the sight of the dry bones lying exposed on the surface of the ground, which he relates to the Zoroastrian practice of exposing human corpses to the elements, rather than burying them.[91] He surmises that Ezekiel

85. Cf. Spronk, *Beatific Afterlife,* pp. 195-96. On the issue of the Ugaritic New Year Festival see D. Marcus in a review of J. C. de Moor, "New Year with Canaanites and Israelites," *JAOS* 93 (1973) 589-91; L. L. Grabbe, "The Seasonal Pattern and the Baal Cycle," *UF* 8 (1976) 57-63. On the New Year Festival background to Ezekielian ideas see H. Riesenfeld, *The Resurrection in Ezekiel XXXVII and in the Dura-Europas Paintings,* UUÅ 11 (Uppsala: Lundesquist, 1948). But cf. H. Birkeland, "The Belief in the Resurrection of the Dead in the Old Testament," *ST* 3 (1949) 60-78; Zimmerli, *Ezekiel 2,* p. 264.

86. See Spronk, *Beatific Afterlife,* p. 85.

87. Ibid., p. 344.

88. See *CTA,* 17.1.27.

89. There are no hints of Egyptian influence in Ezek. 37. The resuscitation of the dry bones is presented as a one-time event; the graves actually open and return their occupants to the land of the living (not to heaven); and Yahweh, at once the patron of Israel and sovereign Lord of life and death, imbues the corpses with his breath. It is doubtful that a New Year Festival based on the Mesopotamian or Canaanite model was ever part of the Yahwist cult (Block, "New Year," *ISBE,* 3:529-32); further, orthodox Yahwism viewed notions of fertility deities and their conflicts with the god of death as pagan, and tended to react against them, rather than to incorporate them into its cult. See Birkeland, *ST* 3 (1949) 60-78; and Zimmerli, *Ezekiel 2,* p. 264, for rejection of this connection.

90. See the critique of Spronk by M. S. Smith and E. Bloch-Smith, "Death and Afterlife in Ugarit and Israel," *JAOS* 108 (1988) 277-84.

91. See B. Lang, in *Ezekiel and His Book,* pp. 307-16; idem, "Life after Death in the Prophetic Promise," in *Congress Volume: Jerusalem 1986,* VTSup 40, ed. J. A. Emerton (Leiden: Brill, 1988), pp. 144-56, esp. 154-55; idem, "Afterlife: Ancient Israel's Changing Vision of the World Beyond," *BR* 4 (1988) 12-23, esp. 19-20 (a popular treatment); C. McDannell and B. Lang, *Heaven: A History* (New Haven: Yale University Press, 1988), pp. 12-13. M. Nobile relates the motif of resurrection in Ezek. 37 to the annual Iranian festival of *Farvardigān* ("Influssi Iranici nel Libro di Ezechiele?" *Antonianum* 63 [1988] 449-57). For a survey of the history of this view and a more cautious understanding of the

may have visited or heard of funeral grounds such as these, and that the prophet's vision echoes the Zoroastrian belief that one day the bones will be reassembled and revived.

There is no a priori reason why Ezekiel could not have incorporated Iranian notions into his message for rhetorical effect, even as he makes use of Mesopotamian, Syrian, and Phoenician ideas elsewhere. Indeed, the monotheism and ethical character of this religion render it much more compatible with Yahwism than the other pagan ideologies. However, Lang does not answer the chronological and conceptual objections to the theory of Iranian influence that have been raised previously;[92] and his suggestion that Ezekiel may have been familiar with and may even have visited Zoroastrian funeral grounds is speculative. This speculation would require visionary translocation far to the northeast of the exilic community to the land of Persia, a land that no other Israelite is known to have visited. Furthermore, the description of "the slain," in v. 9 rules out the possibility of Ezekiel's valley of dry bones being a cemetery of any kind, Israelite, Babylonian, or Persian. What Ezekiel sees in the bones is a graphic portrayal of the effects of the covenant curse on his people. If there is any connection with Persian notions at all, rather

---

relationship see R. Martin-Achard, *From Death to Life: A Study of the Development of the Doctrine of the Resurrection in the Old Testament,* tr. J. P. Smith (Edinburgh and London: Oliver and Boyd, 1960), pp. 186-95; Spronk, *Beatific Afterlife,* pp. 57-59. See also G. Widengren, "Israelite-Jewish Religion," in *Historia Religionum,* 2 vols., ed. C. J. Bleeker and G. Widengren (Leiden: Brill, 1969-71), 1:311-12; Birkeland, *ST* 3 (1949) 60-78. See also Herodotus, *Hist.* 1.140. For a description of Zoroastrian funeral practices see Mary Boyce, *A History of Zoroastrianism,* Handbuch der Orientalistik 1/8/1 (Leiden and Cologne: Brill, 1975), pp. 325-30. Cf. also J. R. Russell, "Burial iii. In Zoroastrianism," *Encyclopaedia Iranica,* ed. E. Yarshater (London and New York: Routledge and Kegan Paul, 1982), 4:561-63.

92. Concerning the chronological objections, it is unclear when the doctrine of the resurrection of the dead was developed in Persian religion. The earliest certain reference derives from the Greek Theopompus (born ca. 380 B.C.). The citation by Aeneas of Gaza in Theophrastus 77 reads as follows: "And yet even Plato brings back Armenius in bodily form from Hades to the land of the living. And Zoroaster prophesies that some day there will be a resurrection of all dead. Theopompus knows of this and is himself the source of information concerning it for the other writers." No explicit contemporary Persian attestation is known. On the conceptual objections: Whereas the OT concentrates on life before death, the Persian attention is focused on life after death. The OT has no counterpart to the Persian view of the separation of body and soul. The Persian focus on judgment immediately after death contrasts with the Israelite, and specifically Ezekielian, view of Sheol as a place of shadowy existence. When the doctrine of judgment emerges it is seen as an eschatological event. Perhaps the most important difference is the Israelite interest in reconciliation with God and the remission of sins, notions that have no parallel in Persian thought. See the critique of F. König, *Zarathustras Jenseitsvorstellungen und das Alte Testament* (Vienna, 1964), pp. 271-85. Cf. also Spronk, *Beatific Afterlife,* p. 58.

than adopting Zoroastrian ideas, in vv. 11-14 in particular, Ezekiel has presented a powerful polemic against them.[93]

Native Israelite soil provides a more likely seedbed for Ezekiel's notions of resurrection. First, the doctrine of resurrection would have developed as a natural corollary to Israelite anthropological views. The Hebrews looked on the human as a unity, a *nepeš ḥayyâ*, constituted by the infusion of divine life-breath into the physical form (Gen. 2:7).[94] At death, which was viewed as the divine sentence for sin (Gen. 2:17; 3:19), the physical matter and life-giving breath are divorced and the *nepeš* dissolves (Job 34:14-15; Ps. 104:29; Eccl. 3:18-21; 12:7). It follows then that any hope of victory over death and a beatific afterlife would require a reunion of the divorced components, which is exactly what happens in Ezek. 37.[95]

Second, the revivification of the dry bones is reminiscent of the life-giving power of Ezekiel's predecessors, Elijah and Elisha (1 K. 17:17-24; 2 K. 4:18-37; 13:20-21). One could interpret these cases simply as postmortem healings, inasmuch as the raised persons had recently died and their flesh was certainly still on the bones. Nonetheless, as in the case of Ezekiel, through the involvement of a prophet the dead come to life.

Third, as a figure of speech the psalmists regarded having one's life threatened as being in the grip of Sheol, and to be delivered as being brought back to life.[96] Admittedly, the concern is for an early, if not immediate rescue, rather than an eschatological deliverance from Sheol, but the language of resurrection is obvious.

Fourth, earlier prophets anticipated Ezekiel's vision of a national res-

---

93. This Zoroastrian connection is also rejected by A. A. di Lella, in L. F. Hartman and A. A. di Lella, *The Book of Daniel,* AB 23 (Garden City, N.Y.: Doubleday, 1978), p. 308.

94. Cf. *nepeš mēt,* Num. 6:6; Lev. 21:11. On the expression see A. Johnson, *The Vitality of the Individual in the Thought of Ancient Israel* (Cardiff: University of Wales Press, 1964), p. 19; H. W. Wolff, *Anthropology of the Old Testament,* tr. M. Kohl (Philadelphia: Fortress, 1974), p. 22; Eichrodt, *Theology,* 2:134-42.

95. See the discussion of L. J. Greenspoon, "The Origin of the Idea of Resurrection," in *Traditions in Transformation: Turning Points in Biblical Faith,* Fest. F. M. Cross, ed. B. Halpern and J. D. Levenson (Winona Lake, Ind.: Eisenbrauns, 1981), pp. 249-53 (Greenspoon argues that the doctrine arises out of the image of Yahweh as a divine warrior); L. Rost, "Alttestamentliche Wurzeln der Ersten Auferstehung," in *In Memoriam Ernst Lohmeyer,* ed. W. Schmauch (Stuttgart: Evangelisches Verlagswerk, 1951), pp. 66-72. But this interpretation is rejected by di Lella, *Daniel,* p. 308.

96. E.g., Ps. 16:11-12 (Eng. 10-11); 49:15-16 (Eng. 14-15). Cf. Andersen and Freedman, *Hosea,* p. 421. For discussion of the relevant texts in the Psalms, as well as several from Proverbs, see Dahood, *Psalms,* 3:xlii-lii. Dahood's recognition of this "obvious meaning" (p. xlv) contrasts with that of earlier scholars like C. Barth, who maintained that the belief in Yahweh's ability to rescue one from death has nothing to do with a belief in a beatific afterlife (*Die Errettung vom Tode,* p. 166).

urrection. That Hosea (6:1-3) and Isaiah (26:19) had already toyed with the idea suggests that in ch. 37 an idea that had germinated at least one and one-half centuries earlier has begun to bud.[97] Moreover, although scholars are reluctant to acknowledge the creative contributions of any prophet, one should not overlook the significance of internal evidence. This message comes to Ezekiel as a direct revelation from God. In a new and dramatic way, the conviction that the grave need not be the end provided a powerful vehicle for announcing the full restoration of Israel. The curse would be lifted. Yahweh would bring his people back to life. To be sure, the form of Ezekiel's message is striking, but his concept of resurrection need not have caught his audience by surprise.[98] Even so, it remained for his successors to develop a clearer picture of an eschatological individualized revivification.[99]

97. Note the resurrection language in the verbs in Hos. 6:2: *ḥîyâ,* "to make alive," and *hēqîm,* "to raise up," with which may be compared Ezekiel's *ḥāyâ,* "to live," and *'āmad,* "to stand" (37:10). Recent scholars have tended to view this penitential song as a reflex of the Canaanite myth of Baal, whose death and resurrection are celebrated annually in the cult. Wolff (*Hosea,* p. 117) speaks of "the Canaanization of the Yahweh cult." Cf. Martin-Achard, *From Death to Life,* pp. 74-86; Spronk, *Beatific Afterlife,* pp. 62-63. Since it is doubtful that Hosea himself would have composed such a song, it has become fashionable to see here the words of Hosea's opponents, perhaps the priests, who found in the pagan myth cheap grounds for hope. Cf. Eichrodt, *Theology,* 2:504-5; Wolff, *Hosea,* pp. 109, 117. But the style of the text is genuinely Hoseanic and its placement in the context follows the doom-hope alternation characteristic of the book as a whole. Cf. Andersen and Freedman, *Hosea,* pp. 417-25; D. Stuart, *Hosea–Jonah,* WBC 31 (Waco: Word, 1987), pp. 106-9.

The other text, Isa. 26:19, provides one of the clearest statements of resurrection in the OT, whether one interprets it as a prayer (Martin-Achard, *From Death to Life,* p. 131; NJPS; etc.) or as an affirmation of certainty (O. Kaiser, *Isaiah 13–39,* tr. R. A. Wilson, OTL [Philadelphia: Westminster, 1974], p. 215; J. D. W. Watts, *Isaiah 1–33,* WBC 24 [Waco: Word, 1985], p. 337; Spronk, *Beatific Afterlife,* p. 299; etc.). On the passage see G. F. Hasel, "Resurrection in the Theology of Old Testament Apocalyptic," *ZAW* 92 (1980) 268 n. 8; G. Stemberger, "Das Problem der Auferstehung im Alten Testament," *Kairos* 14 (1972) 279-80. For defense of an early date for this text see J. N. Oswalt, *Isaiah 1–39,* NICOT (Grand Rapids: Eerdmans, 1986), p. 441; idem, "Recent Studies in Old Testament Eschatology and Apocalyptic," *JETS* 24 (1981) 289-302. Cf. also R. J. Coggins, "The Problem of Isa. 24–27," *ExpTim* 90 (1978-79) 329-33.

Other texts that have been drawn into the discussion of resurrection include Deut. 32:39; Hos. 13:4; Isa. 53:10-12; Jer. 51:39, 57.

98. M. Fox's comment applies to his rhetorical strategy, but not to his theology: "Ezekiel's primary strategy is boldly to affirm the absurd. . . . He will seek to make them expect the unexpectable" (*HUCA* 51 [1980] 10). While Ezek. 37 may represent *one* determinative moment for the OT belief in the resurrection of the dead (cf. Haag, *TTZ* 82 [1973] 78-92), contra many (e.g., D. S. Russell, *The Method and Message of Jewish Apocalyptic,* OTL [Philadelphia: Westminster, 1964], p. 368), in view of the foregoing discussion, it is unlikely that this passage provides the first reference to the resurrection of the dead in Hebrew literature.

99. Cf. R. A. Muller, "Resurrection," *ISBE,* 4:145-50.

EXCURSUS:
THE AFTERLIFE OF EZEKIEL'S
VISION OF DRY BONES

The drama and force of Ezekiel's vision of the revivification of the dry bones in 37:1-14 has few equals in Scripture. But what influence did it have in Jewish and Christian tradition? Specifically, what influence did Ezek. 37 have on the growth of the belief in a general eschatological resurrection for all humankind? The answers to this question have varied.

Within the OT the notion of a general resurrection surfaces in only a single text, Dan. 12:2.[100] However, it is impossible to confirm a direct link between this statement and Ezek. 37. In the intertestamental period, interest in life after death seems to have increased, though few of the intertestamental notions found their way into either the Jewish or Christian canons.[101] By NT times a sharp debate had arisen within Judaism whether there would be a resurrection. Whereas the Pharisees answered the question in the affirmative, the Sadducees denied any resurrection at all.[102] However, no direct evidence connects the Pharisaic position and Ezek. 37. The rabbinic witness is inconsistent. Some maintained that Ezekiel was referring to a historical event in his own lifetime. The following represent excerpts from an interesting interchange recorded in *b. Sanh.* 92b.

> R. Eliezer said: The dead whom Ezekiel resurrected stood up, uttered song, and [immediately] died. What song did they utter? — *The Lord slayeth in righteousness and reviveth in mercy* (1 Sam. 2:6). R. Joshua said: They sang thus, *The Lord maketh alive: he bringeth down to the grave and bringeth up.* R. Judah said: It was truth; it was a parable. . . .
>
> R. Eliezer the son of R. Jose the Galilean said: "The dead whom Ezekiel revived went up to Palestine, married wives and begat sons and daughters." R. Judah b. Bathyra rose up and said: I am one of their descendants, and these are the *tefillin* which my grandfather left me [as an heirloom] from them."
>
> Now who were they whom Ezekiel revived? — Rab said: "They were the Ephraimites, who counted [the years] to the end [of the Egyptian bondage], but erred therein."

100. Some do deny a general resurrection in this text. According to di Lella (*Daniel,* p. 308) the resurrection envisaged is a free gift bestowed only on the faithful Jew.

101. Cf. 1 Enoch, 2 (Syriac) Baruch, Psalms of Solomon, Qumran writings. On the subject see E. Schuller, "Ideas of Resurrection in Intertestamental Sources," *TBT* 27 (1989) 140-45. On the echoes of v. 7 in 4Q385 Second Ezekiel, *Sib. Or.* 2, the Apocalypse of Peter, Justin, and Tertullian, see Bauckham, *RevQ* 15 (1992) 437-45.

102. See Mark 12:18; Acts 4:12; 23:80; Josephus, *Ant.* 18.1.4, §16.

This last comment is reminiscent of a Palestinian Targum fragment, in which, in response to Ezekiel's wondering what would happen to those who die in the exile, the answer is given that those who are revived are 30,000 Ephraimites who left Egypt thirty years "before the end" and were slaughtered by the Philistines. Later, the Haggadah referred to in the Mahzor Vitry would speak of 200,000 Ephraimites. The use of the name Ephraim suggests that the house of Israel is restricted to the northern kingdom.[103]

A different picture is presented in *Pirqe R. Eliezer.* At one point the rabbi makes the sweeping assertion, "All the dead will arise at the resurrection of the dead, dressed in shrouds."[104] The fullest treatment of the resurrection is presented in chs. 33–34, but without direct reference to Ezek. 37.[105] The rabbinic commentaries frequently interpreted this passage as a prophecy of the eschatological resurrection in the messianic age.[106]

Allusions to Ezekiel's vision of the dry bones are rare in the NT. The comment in Rev. 11:11 that "the spirit of life [πνεῦμα ζωῆς; cf. Ezek. 37:5 LXX] entered them [the two witnesses] and they stood on their feet" echoes Ezek. 37:11, and Paul's reference to God, "who gives his Holy Spirit to you," in 1 Thess. 4:8 seems to be based on Ezek. 37:14. J. Grassi has found other allusions in the Gospels as well.[107] The description of the resurrection scene after the death of Jesus in Matt. 27:51-54 suggests that this event may have been interpreted in the light of Ezek. 37:1-14.[108] In v. 51 the Lord himself goes before a band of folk who have risen from their tombs into the holy city.[109] In John 20:22, the risen Christ breathed on his disciples, saying

---

103. So Zimmerli, *Ezekiel 2,* p. 264. On the Targum fragment see A. Diez-Macho, "Un segundo fragmento del Targum Palestinense a los Profetas," *Bib* 39 (1958) 198-205, esp. 201.

104. *Pirqe de Rabbi Eliezer,* tr. G. Friedlander (1916; repr. New York, 1971), p. 245. Rabbi Joshua ben Qorchah has Yahweh saying to Ezekiel, "As I live, I will cause you to stand at the resurrection of the dead in the future that is to come, and I will gather you with all Israel to the land." Resurrection and regathering are united, but both seem to be pushed back into the eschaton. For further references see Levey, *Ezekiel,* p. 103.

105. The motif of the new exodus no doubt contributed to the tradition in the liturgy of the synagogue to read Ezek. 37:1-14 as the *haphtara* on the Sabbath of the Passover, corresponding to the *sidroth* Exod. 33:12–34:26 and Num. 28:19-25.

106. *Midrash Rabbah: Gen. Rab.* 13.6; 14.5; *Deut. Rab.* 7.7; *Lev. Rab.* 14.9.

107. J. Grassi, "Ezekiel XXXVII.1-14 and the New Testament," *NTS* 11 (1964-65) 162-64.

108. Is this an interpretation of "their land" in Ezek. 37:13-14?

109. Cf. W. Neuss, *Das Buch Ezechiel in Theologie und Kunst bis zum Ende des XII. Jahrhunderts,* Beiträge zur Geschichte des Alten Mönchtums und des Benediktinerordens (Münster: Aschendorff, 1912), pp. 25 (Justin Martyr), 26 (Irenaeus), 32 (Tertullian, Cyprian), 43 (Cyril of Jerusalem), 47 (Epiphanius of Constantine), 85 (Severus and John of Damascus), 89 (Ambrose). But Augustine broke ranks on this score (cf. p. 89).

"Receive the Holy Spirit." Although John may have Gen. 2:7 in mind, he could also be thinking of Ezek. 37, in which case this vision was being interpreted eschatologically and messianically. By breathing on the disciples he was constituting them the new people of God. The early church fathers were less ambiguous in their interpretation of this text. References to Ezekiel's vision of the dry bones appear frequently in their discussions of the eschatological resurrection.[110]

Given the vividness and power of Ezekiel's vision, it is not surprising that it has captured the imagination of Jewish and Christian artists alike. The most impressive example of the former is found on the lower frieze of the north wall of the 3rd-century-A.D. synagogue of Dura Europos, located on the right bank of the Euphrates River midway between Aleppo and Baghdad. While the meaning of many of the details of the work remains uncertain, the main features seem to be clear. The action seems to move from left to right. A series of hands, undoubtedly representative of the hand of Yahweh, appears at the top of the frieze, but three discrete scenes seem to be presented. In the first, the left part of the panel, the ground is strewn about with fully fleshed body parts, heads, hands, feet (not simply the bones). Among these stand three men dressed in identical Parthian garb, but in three different poses. That the first is pictured with a hand above his head grabbing a tuft of hair suggests that the three figures represent the prophet's own experience of being seized by the hand of God and deposited among the dry bones. In the middle of the center scene stands another man, also dressed in Parthian clothing, with his right hand raised toward and almost touching a divine hand coming down from the top, and his left hand extended more horizontally toward a winged humanoid figure. If the latter represents the *rûaḥ* that comes from the four winds, the man must also be Ezekiel, receiving his instructions from Yahweh and actually addressing the "breath." The space to the prophet's right is dominated by a large mountain. The cleavage that splits the mountain in half and the figure of a crumbling house on the right suggest that the term *rāʿaš*, "rattling sound," in v. 7 is understood as the sound of an earthquake.[111] At the foot of the right half of the mountain are three lifeless bodies, presumably representing the first phase of the revivification. Why there are three is not clear. Perhaps they represent the tribes of Judah, Benjamin, and Levi, which made up the southern kingdom.

---

110. The bibliography on this synagogue is extensive. For the most comprehensive discussion and color plates of the friezes see C. H. Kraeling, *The Synagogue: The Yale University Excavations at Dura-Europos,* final report, part 1 (New Haven: Yale University Press, 1956), pp. 178-207, and plates LXIX-LXXI.

111. Cf. Rabbi Phineas's comment on this verse, "Immediately the Holy One, blessed be He, caused His voice to be heard, and the earth shook, as it is said, 'And as I prophesied there was a thundering, and behold an earthquake" (*Pirqe R. El.,* p. 249).

The second phase in the revival of the bodies is depicted to the prophet's left. In response to his prophesying to the breath, three long-skirted and winged Psyche-like figures appear, apparently one for each of the bodies. The moment of resuscitation, however, is depicted below the prophet's left hand. Here the three dead bodies reappear, but the head of one is being raised by another larger Psyche-like figure, who seems to stand for the one divine breath that enlivens humanity. One more enigmatic person appears to the right of these figures, with right hand outstretched to the three Psyches. His coiffure and face resemble the prophet figures in the previous scenes, but his clothing differs; this man wears the χιτών and ἱμάτιον characteristic of prophets. He represents either Ezekiel again, this time in a different role, or a Davidic Messiah. If the latter is the case, then the frieze has now moved into Ezek. 37:15-28. The man returns at the extreme right of the third scene. This time his right hand is extended toward a crowd of ten men, four in the front row and three in each of two rows behind. The number ten is hardly accidental. These represent the ten tribes that had made up the northern kingdom prior to its collapse in the 8th century. The message is clear. The miracle envisioned by the prophet will involve *kol-bêt yiśrā'ēl,* "the whole house of Israel."

The use of the motifs of Ezek. 37:1-14 has been uneven in Christian art. The disappearance of Ezekiel's dry bones in the West contrasts sharply with the continued Eastern fascination with the theme.[112] Unlike the creators of the Dura Europos synagogue frieze, however, Christian artists have tended to interpret the vision in terms of an eschatological general resurrection. One recently discovered example comes from the 6th-century quarries at Dara in northern Syria.[113] At the entrance to one of the tomb chambers is a large stone-cut relief depicting several scenes. Not all have been identified, but in one scene Ezekiel is portrayed as striding down toward a pile of skulls, his clothing flowing out behind him. Above him one can see the hand of God, along with the four winds who, according to Ezek. 37:9, hold the key to life. In front of the prophet two small figures may be recognized, emerging from a sarcophagus. According to O. Nicholson, the relief expresses the hope of this Byzantine community that their members who had fallen to the Persians in a battle in 573, and whose bodies had been left out in the open in typical Persian manner, would rise again.[114]

112. For a discussion of 37:1-14 in the history of Christian art see Neuss, *Ezechiel,* pp. 141-53, 180-87, 261-62.

113. For a description of the site see O. Nicholson, "A Newly Discovered Quarry at Dara," *AJA* 89 (1985) 663-67.

114. Idem, "Shall These Bones Live? A Dakhma at Dara?" *AJA* 89 (1985) 667-71, esp. 669.

♦ *Theological Implications*

It is remarkable that as recently as 1985 biblical scholars were still maintaining that "in ancient Israel there was no belief in a life after death."[115] Many believe that the Pharisaic acceptance of the doctrine (see Acts 23:6-9) derives from a limited number of late texts that reflect Persian influence, and that the Sadducees, who rejected the notion, were the true heirs of OT belief. That some scholars have recently reversed the roles of these two parties is welcome: many now insist that the Sadducean position represented a conscious departure from both Hebrew and common Semitic beliefs.[116]

As in his earlier representations of the netherworld, Ezekiel's vision of the resuscitated dry bones offers his compatriots powerful declarations of hope. The gospel according to Ezekiel affirms that there is life after death, and there is hope beyond the grave. Yahweh remains the incontestable Lord not only of the living but also of the dead. He alone determines the moment and nature of a person's decease. He alone has the keys to the gates of Sheol, and he faces no challenge from Mot or any other chthonic power. In this regard Ezekiel, like all orthodox Yahwists, distances himself from the prevailing notions of his day.

But this vision of the resuscitation of dry bones is not only for the nation of Israel. The valley represents the whole world, and the bones the entire human race under the curse of death for its rebellion against God. Accordingly, this text holds out hope for all who accept the grace of God in Christ (Eph. 2:1-10). With good reason, we who are heirs of the glorious message of the prophets and apostles may find in this text a dramatic affirmation that the sting of death will be overcome by the animating power of Yahweh's Spirit. It also holds out hope for a defeated and moribund church. Revival cannot be worked up from within; it will occur only as God, by his grace, breathes on us again and brings us back to life. After all, as Ezekiel had witnessed, and as he had heard on dozens of occasions, the Lord is Yahweh. He has spoken. He will make good his word.

---

115. See J. H. Neyrey, "Eternal Life," in *Harper's Bible Dictionary,* ed. P. J. Achtemeier (San Francisco: Harper & Row, 1985), p. 282. See the reaction to this statement by Lang, in *Congress Volume,* p. 144.

116. See B. Lang, *Monotheism and the Prophetic Minority,* Social World of Biblical Antiquity 1 (Sheffield: Almond, 1983), p. 25; idem, in *Congress Volume,* pp. 144-45, with citations of other scholars who have come to similar conclusions.

5. Yahweh's Eternal Covenant with Israel (37:15-28)

♦ Nature and Design

Although the word-event formula in v. 15 and an expanded version of the recognition formula in v. 28 set this passage off as a separate literary unit, the intervening material contains several significant links with the preceding vision of the dry bones, especially the interpretation, vv. 11-14. The motifs of Yahweh "bringing out" his people (vv. 12a, 21a) and "bringing them in" to their hereditary homeland (vv. 12b, 21b) are obvious,[1] but not to be overlooked is the common interest in the nation of Israel as a whole. Ezekiel's exilic audience may have been puzzled by his reference to kol-bêt yiśrā'ēl, "the whole house of Israel," in v. 11. The prophet had consistently used the name Israel to refer to both northern and southern kingdoms, but how could the remnants of the northern kingdom participate in Yahweh's salvation when they had been dispersed among the nations for one and a half centuries? Whether or not these prophecies were originally delivered in their present literary order, the purpose of the present oracle is to answer that question.[2]

The appearance of the citation formula, "Thus has the Lord Yahweh declared," in vv. 19 and 21 suggests a division of the literary unit into two unequal parts. However, form-critical considerations provide better clues to its structure. From the opening instructions for Ezekiel it is apparent that this prophecy will take the form of a sign-act, the last one in the book, and the only one in the corpus of salvation oracles.[3] Sign-acts typically break down into two principal parts: the description of the prophetic action, followed by a verbal interpretation. In this case, however, the pattern is more complex. The unit opens as expected with Yahweh's directives for Ezekiel (vv. 16-17), followed by a brief interpretation (vv. 18-19). But the latter is interrupted in v. 20 with further instructions, as if the sign-act were not yet completed. The new orders are simple, but they are succeeded by a lengthy divine speech, which begins ostensibly as an interpretation of the sign-action. The longer Yahweh speaks, however, the farther removed is the subject matter from the issue that initially inspired the sign-act.

The speech itself makes effective rhetorical use of repetition not only of major theological themes[4] but also of significant Leitwörter. The threefold

---

1. Cf. C. Barth, in Beiträge zur alttestamentlichen Theologie, pp. 47-48.
2. Ezek. 37:15-28 expounds on v. 11 just as 37:1-14 explicates 36:26.
3. The other sign-acts in the book are in chs. 4–5; 6:11-12; 12:1-16, 17-20; 21:11-12, 13-22, 23-29; 24:15-24. For a discussion of the genre see my Ezekiel: Chapters 1–24, pp. 164ff.
4. (1) The restoration of Israel to its hereditary homeland (vv. 20, 25); (2) the appointment of a single ruler over the nation (vv. 22, 24); (3) the spiritual renewal of the

occurrence of *'eḥād*, "one," in the first half of the speech (vv. 22a, 22b, 24a) answers vv. 16-19, where the word occurs eight times. Yahweh highlights the end of Israel's past divisiveness by declaring three times *lō' 'ôd*, "never again."[5] However, the shift in thematic and chronological focus in vv. 24b-28 is reflected by the absence of *'eḥād* and its replacement by *'ôlām*, which occurs five times. Because of the formal signals, stylistic changes, shifts in perspective, repetition, and other points of tension in the text, scholars have expended a great deal of energy attempting to reconstruct the history of the text.[6] However, the lack of agreement in details and the subjectivity of the criteria used to identify the stages in the growth of the text raise serious methodological questions. There are no convincing reasons, historical or otherwise, to deny Ezekiel credit for both the visual and the oral presentation of this prophecy. In a text that affirms his literacy, he may even have been responsible for its transcription. Far from minimizing formal, syntactical, and logical disjunctions, a holistic approach to 37:15-28 asks what rhetorical purposes are served by the apparent tensions. Indeed, the progression in thought is deliberate and logical, inviting the audience to look beyond the sign-action to Yahweh's original and ultimate designs for his people. In the process, the text leads one up at least four levels of significance, which may be illustrated as follows:

---

nation, expressed negatively (v. 23a), and positively (v. 24b); (4) the renewal of Yahweh's covenant with his people (vv. 23b, 27); (5) the designation of David as Yahweh's appointed ruler (vv. 24a, 25).

5. *'ôd* appears a fourth time at the end of v. 22, but see n. 73 below.

6. Leaving aside the glosses, many attribute the directions for the sign-act and its interpretation in vv. 15-19 to the prophet Ezekiel himself. Cf. D. Baltzer, "Literarkritische und literarhistorische Anmerkungen zur Heilsprophetie im Ezechiel-Buch," in *Ezekiel and His Book*, p. 179; Zimmerli, *Ezechiel 2*, pp. 271-75; Fuhs, *Ezechiel 25–48*, p. 211 (with the addition of v. 22aβ-b). Even as radical a scholar as Irwin conceded the actual sign-act in v. 16 to Ezekiel (*Problem of Ezekiel*, p. 248), but the original interpretation is found in vv. 21, 22b. Scholars cannot agree on who was responsible for vv. 20-28, though most recognize more than one hand. Zimmerli (*Ezekiel 2*, pp. 275-76) finds in vv. 20-24a a new attempt by the prophet himself, or perhaps a member of his school, to provide a fuller interpretation of the sign-act, while vv. 25-28, which bring together many Ezekielian salvation themes, were added at a later stage. Recognizing in vv. 21-28 a reflection of exilic or early postexilic theological history, Fuhs (*Ezechiel 25–48*, pp. 211-13) identifies two stages of later interpretation: stage I, vv. 20-21, 22aα, 23a, b, 24b, 25a; stage II, vv. 26-28. Wevers (*Ezekiel*, p. 280) describes vv. 21-28 as "a verbose amalgam of restoration hopes representing the later hopes of the Ezekiel school," of which vv. 21-22 are the earliest. Baltzer (in *Ezekiel and His Book*, pp. 178-79) finds in vv. 20-28 a series of additions: vv. 20-23, 24a, 24b, 25-28.

> Yahweh unites the unified nation
> with himself in a permanent
> covenant relationship

> Yahweh unites two kingdoms in
> a political and spiritual union

> Yahweh unites two sticks
> in a physical union

> Ezekiel unites two sticks
> in a physical union

The details of this scheme will be developed in the commentary. In the meantime, one may observe that the twofold repetition of the covenant formula in vv. 23b and 27 highlights the center of gravity. The object lesson at the beginning serves as a rhetorical device to capture the people's attention and to promote comprehension of the central message. The sign-action zeros in on one aspect of the theme, viz., the participation of all twelve original tribes in the fulfillment of Yahweh's ancient but eternal promises to Israel (specified in vv. 24b-28). In the divine speech, the rhetorical strategy involves a greater-to-lesser method of argumentation. The previous prophecy had addressed the utter despondency of the Judeans in Babylon, and their failed hopes of ever returning home as a viable nation. The present prophecy addresses an even greater difficulty. If the restoration of Judah represented a major problem in the people's minds, how much more would they have stumbled over the idea of the restoration of the northern kingdom. This is the very issue that the nonverbal action addresses. It affirms that by a special divine act four hundred years of divided history will be reversed. If Yahweh is able to perform such an incredible feat, there is reason to hope that the other elements involved in their own (the Judean exiles') restoration — their survival, regathering and return to the land, the restoration of the Davidic monarchy, the renewal of the covenant, and Yahweh's reestablishment of his residence in their midst — could also be fulfilled.[7]

---

7. For a discussion of this and other rhetorical strategies involved in the oracle see Friebel, "Sign-Acts," pp. 840-55.

a. Dramatizing the New National Reality (37:15-20)

15 *The following message of Yahweh came to me:* 16 *"As for you, human, take*[8] *a single*[9] *piece of wood and write on it, 'Pertaining to Judah*[10] *and to the descendants of Israel who are associated with him.'*[11] *Then take*[12] *a second*[13] *piece of wood and write on it, [the Ephraimite wood]*[14] *'Pertaining to Joseph and to the entire*[15] *family of Israel*[16] *associated with him.'* 17 *Set them side by side for yourself to create*[17] *a single piece of wood. They shall form a single entity*[18] *in your hand.* 18 *Now when*[19] *your compatriots*[20] *ask you,*[21] *'Will you not explain to us*

8. The introductory *qaḥ lĕkā* is identical to the opening commands in previous sign-actions (4:1, 9; 5:1), and formally similar to *'ăśēh lĕkā*, "Make for yourself," in 12:3.

9. LXX omits *'eḥād*, "one," used here to express indetermination (cf. Joüon-Muraoka, *Grammar*, §137u), but the contrast with the following speaks for its preservation.

10. The *lamed* in *lyhwdh* is commonly understood as a *lamed inscriptionis*, in which case it would not have been included in the inscription and is not to be translated (GKC, §119u). Zimmerli (*Ezekiel 2*, p. 274) interprets it as a possessive *lamed;* F. Nötscher suggests a datival sense ("Zum emphatischen Lamed," *VT* 3 [1953] 378). A *lamed* of reference is preferable. See the commentary.

11. Here, in the next line, and in v. 19, reading pl. *ḥbryw* with Qere, rather than Kethib *ḥbrw.*

12. With the unusual triliteral imperatival form *ûlĕqaḥ* (instead of *qaḥ*) cf. Exod. 29:1; 1 K. 17:11; Prov. 20:16. Many repoint as an infinitive absolute (cf. Allen, *Ezekiel 20–48*, p. 190), or emend to *qḥ lk* or *lqḥt*. See Friebel, "Sign-Acts," p. 837 n. 13.

13. LXX captures the sense of *'eḥād* with δευτέραν, "second"; cf. Vulg. *alterum* and Syr. *'ḥrn'*, which misread *'eḥād* as *'aḥēr,* "another." Contra R. Martin-Achard ("Quelques remarques sur la réunification du peuple de Dieu d'après Ezéchiel 37,15ss," in *Wort-Gebot-Glaube: Beiträge zur Theologie des Alten Testaments,* Fest. W. Eichrodt, ed. H. Stoebe [Zurich: Zwingli, 1970], pp. 67-68), there is no need to emend MT.

14. *'ēṣ 'eprayim* lacks a counterpart in the first inscription and is to be taken as explanatory.

15. Whether MT *wĕkol* or *ûlĕkol* (thus Rossi ms. 892), called for by the parallelism, is original, the sense is clear.

16. LXX and Syr. read "descendants of Israel," a harmonization with the previous inscription.

17. An idiomatic rendering of *wĕqārab . . . lĕ,* lit. "and bring near . . . to." *lĕkā* is an ethical dative. *qārab* recalls v. 7, in which the separated bones had been reassembled, eventually to be joined by sinews and flesh.

18. *la'ăḥādîm* is unusual but not unprecedented (Gen. 11:1). The form reflects simultaneously the unity and composite nature of the wood.

19. MT opens the temporal clause abruptly with *ka'ăšer,* which LXX smooths by adding καὶ ἔσται ὅταν λέγωσι = *wayĕhî ka'ăšer yō'mĕrû.*

20. *bĕnê 'ammĕkā,* lit. "sons of your people."

21. MT reads *lē'mōr,* "saying," which is not reflected in LXX or Syr., and is absent before similar queries elsewhere (12:9; 21:5, 12), but it is not ungrammatical.

what these things mean to you?' 19 *then you shall respond,*[22] *'Thus has the Lord Yahweh has declared: Look! I am taking*[23] *the wood*[24] *of Joseph — which is in Ephraim's hand*[25] *— along with the tribes of Israel, which are associated with him, and placing them upon it, that is on the wood of Judah,*[26] *and I will make them into a single piece of wood.*[27] *And they will form a single entity in my hand.'*[28] 20 *Let the pieces of wood, on which you write, lie in your hand for them to see."*[29]

Following the customary word-event formula and the divine address of the Ezekiel, the prophet receives orders for a final sign-action. On the surface Yahweh's instructions seem simple enough: Ezekiel is to take two pieces of wood, inscribe on them the names of Judah and Joseph, respectively, bring them together to create a single piece, and hold the product up for all to see. But the simplicity of the plot camouflages the pervasive ambiguity in the account. Each phase is capable of more than one interpretation.

(1) The prophet is commanded by Yahweh to procure two pieces of wood. But what kind of wood is this? The question cannot be answered simply by appealing to the expression for wood used here. *'ēṣ* is a general term capable of a variety of meanings. Ezekiel himself uses it at least four different ways: trees in general (6:13; 17:24), fruit trees in particular (34:27), a piece of wood from a vine or a forest tree from which a skilled craftsperson may make an object (15:2-3), fuel for fire (15:4-5; 24:10; 39:10). Several possibilities have been proposed for the present context.

22. *dabbēr* is abrupt (cf. *wĕdabbēr* in v. 21). LXX assumes a smoother reading, *wĕdibbartā*. The employment of this word (instead of *'ĕmōr*) in the command to speak is relatively rare in Ezekiel. In 14:4; 20:27; and 33:2 it seems to have replaced *hinnābē'*. Cf. also 3:1; 12:23; 20:3.

23. *qaḥ lĕkā* of v. 16 is here rephrased as *hinnēh 'ănî lōqēaḥ*.

24. Twice in this verse LXX renders *'ēṣ* as φυλήν/φυλάς, "tribe," interpreting the expression in accordance with *šēbeṭ*, which also appears, rather than translating it.

25. *'ăšer bĕyad 'eprayim* is often deleted as a secondary gloss (cf. Allen, *Ezekiel 20–48*, p. 190), but it represents a natural explanation, given the anachronistic reference to Joseph, probably added by the prophet himself.

26. LXX καὶ δώσω αὐτοὺς ἐπὶ τὴν φυλήν Ιουδα captures the intended sense of *wĕnātattî 'ōtām 'ālāyw 'et-'ēṣ yĕhûdâ*, presumably reading *'ālāyw 'et* as *'al* (= ἐπί). BHS suggests deleting *'ōtām*, but this results in an unlikely reversal of roles for the respective tribes. MT is awkward but not ungrammatical if the pl. suffix on *'ōtām* is understood to refer to the tribes that the piece of wood represents, whereas the sg. suffix on *'ālāyw* refers to the piece of wood that represents primarily Judah. *'et-'ēṣ yĕhûdâ* is then simply an appositional explanation for the suffix.

27. Like LXX's previous treatment of *'ēṣ*, Targ. *l'm ḥd*, "to one people," interprets rather than translates the metaphor.

28. LXX ἐν τῇ χειρὶ Ιουδα reads the suffix on *bĕyādî* as an abbreviation for *yĕhûdâ*.

29. Lit. "be before their eyes."

Trees. Some have viewed the two houses of Judah and Israel "apart like two palms standing solitary and apart on the great Euphratean plain, but they are to be brought near to one another by Ezekiel's ministry, so they will become again as 'one tree.' "[30]

Shepherds' staves, ready-made. Support for this interpretation may be drawn from the reference to the *rō'eh,* "shepherd," in v. 24, and the manner in which the motif of the union of two staves is developed by Zechariah, who envisages the conjoining of staves labeled "Grace" and "Union," respectively (Zech. 11:4-17). It seems odd, however, that Ezekiel would have referred to shepherds' instruments as *'ēṣîm* when he could have used the more common and certainly more specific terms *maṭṭeh* (cf. 4:16; 5:16), *maqqēl* (39:9), or *miš'enet* (29:6), all of which are used elsewhere in the OT of shepherds' staves or clubs.[31]

Rulers' scepters, ready-made.[32] This meaning suits the present royal context (cf. vv. 21-24) and accords with Ezekiel's use of *maṭṭôt 'ōz,* "strong branches," and *šibṭê môšĕlîm,* "rulers' scepters," in 19:11. It also appears to have been the LXX understanding. Departing from convention, the Greek translators rendered the term ῥάβδος, which elsewhere translates *šēbeṭ* and *maṭṭeh.* Perhaps this passage reminded them of Num. 17:16-26 (Eng. 1-11), which has Moses procuring twelve staves *(maṭṭôt),* one for each of the tribes, and inscribing on each the name of the prince *(nāśî'),* that is, the leader *(rō'š)* of the respective tribes.[33] This seems also to have been the understanding of Ben Sirach, whose reflections on the breakup of the kingdom and the implications of the division for the eternality of the Davidic covenant in Sir. 47:20-22 seem to have been inspired by the present text.

Although this is probably the majority view, the strength of its support is illusory. First, LXX ῥάβδος is an extremely general term, varying in significance from "stick, twig," through "club, rod," and "shepherd's staff" to "royal scepter." This is admittedly the only place where it translates *'ēṣ,* but this alone does not rule out the simple meaning "stick, piece of wood."[34] Second, that Yahweh interrupts his instructions for Ezekiel in v. 18 with an advance warning that his observers will ask for clarification of his actions

---

30. Thus W. E. Barnes, "Two Trees Become One: Ezek. xxxvii 16-17," *JTS* 39 (1938) 391-93.

31. Cf. Ps. 23:4; Zech. 11:7; 1 Sam. 17:43. For discussion of these texts see E. Power, "The Shepherd's Two Rods in Modern Palestine and in Some Passages of the Old Testament," *Bib* 9 (1928) 434-42.

32. Cf. Friebel, "Sign-Actions," p. 844; Eichrodt, *Ezekiel,* p. 512; Fohrer, *Ezechiel,* p. 210. Zimmerli (*Ezekiel 2,* p. 274) hesitates to commit himself.

33. Here LXX renders *maṭṭeh* as ῥάβδος. The staff of Levi is to be inscribed with Aaron's name.

34. Cf. C. Schneider, *TDNT,* 6:966-71.

suggests a strange or incomprehensible action. The meaning of joining two royal scepters would have been obvious. Third, if the two pieces of wood represented two royal houses, their unification flies in the face of the consistent witness not only of Ezekiel but of all the prophets that, while historically Israel was divided into two kingdoms, there was only one legitimate dynasty, the house of David. Nowhere is the union of the northern dynasty with the Davidic house contemplated; on the contrary, the northern kingdom was considered an aberration from the beginning and all its kings illegitimate. Furthermore, the identification of the kingdom of Israel with any dynasty is studiously avoided.[35] Ezekiel does not envision the unification of northern and southern dynasties, but the reunion of the kingdoms themselves. Here he takes extra pains to link these wooden objects with their respective nations rather than their kings,[36] and in the interpretation to follow he will highlight Yahweh's activity of bringing the "descendants of Israel" to their own land and making them one nation. Furthermore, as already noted, it is difficult to imagine why Ezekiel would have used a term as general as ʿēṣ when specific expressions like šēbaṭ and maṭṭeh were readily available.

Common pieces of wood. Given Ezekiel's penchant for manipulating ordinary objects in his sign-actions, these ʿēṣîm may have been simple pieces of wood, perhaps even sticks.[37] This sense accords with Ezekiel's use of ordinary objects for symbolic purposes,[38] and would certainly heighten the ambiguity of his actions, evoking in his audience a demand for interpretation (v. 18).

Special pieces of wood, writing tablets. REB's rendering, "wooden tablet," reflects an ancient if uncommon interpretation of Ezekiel's ʿēṣîm.[39]

---

35. The comment by A. Biran and J. Naveh: " 'House of David' is the dynastic name of the kingdom of Judah," requires qualification ("An Aramaic Stele Fragment from Tel Dan," *IEJ* 43 [1993] 93). This may be how non-Israelites perceived the situation, but biblical authors never referred to the united kingdom as "the house of Saul," or "the house of David," nor to the northern kingdom as "the house of Jeroboam," or "the house of Omri." See further Block, *JETS* 28 (1985) 274-75.

36. The first ʿēṣ is for Judah and the descendants of Israel, not for David; the second is for Joseph, the stick of Ephraim and all the house of Israel, his companions (v. 16; cf. v. 19).

37. Cf. NRSV, NASB, NIV, JB; Alexander, "Ezekiel," p. 927. Thus also B. E. Keck ("Ezekiel 37, Sticks, and Babylonian Writing Boards: A Critical Reappraisal," *Dialogue: A Journal of Mormon Thought* 23 [1990] 126-38), who errs, however, in interpreting the "sticks" as metaphorical representations of ruling scepters.

38. Other common objects used in his sign-acts include a brick, 4:1; an iron griddle, 4:5; and a knapsack, 12:3.

39. Zimmerli (*Ezekiel 2,* p. 274) entertained the notion momentarily, but appears quickly to have returned to the standard "royal scepter" view. J. P. Hyatt confesses that it is unclear whether the wood refers to wooden tablets or sticks ("The Writing of an Old Testament Book," *BA* 6 [1943] 75).

Targ. translates *ʿēṣ* as *lwḥ'*, "tablet," the same word that is used of *gillāyôn* in Isa. 8:1. *lwḥ* (Heb. *lûaḥ*) is cognate to Akk. *lêʾu*, a generic designation for "(wax-covered) writing board," or sets of writing boards consisting of two or more "leaves."[40] These boards were made of flat pieces of wood, and occasionally ivory or metal, covered on the writing surface with a compound of beeswax and 25 percent orpiment, into which a message would be etched.[41] But some have argued that such writing boards were too luxurious for Ezekiel, a deported Hebrew living away from the urban center of Nippur. Papyrus, potsherds, and perhaps clay tablets would have been available to him, but not expensive writing boards, let alone the required beeswax compound.[42] One may answer this challenge with two kinds of evidence.

First, extrabiblical sources point to a remarkable antiquity and breadth of distribution of writing boards. To the east, their use in Mesopotamia is attested as early as the Sumerian and Old Babylonian periods.[43] In the west, they are mentioned by the 5th-century-B.C. Greek historian Herodotus, who recounts an occasion on which Greeks passed along secret messages inscribed on a pair of folding tablets (δελτίον δίπτχον) covered with wax.[44] Ugaritic and Hittite sources hint at the use of writing tablets in these cultures, and an 8th-century-B.C. north Syrian relief depicts such an object in the hand of a scribe.[45] Until recently the oldest known exemplars were several writing boards found in Sargon II's palace at Nimrud. However, the discovery of a diptych (two-leaved board) in the cargo of a 14th-century-B.C. Canaanite ship that sank at Ulu Butun off the coast of southwestern Turkey has pushed the evidence for such boards back six hundred years.[46]

40. See D. J. Wiseman, "Assyrian Writing Boards," *Iraq* 17 (1955) 7; cf. S. Parpola, "Assyrian Library Records," *JNES* 42 (1983) 2.

41. In addition to the articles cited in n. 39 above see J. N. Postgate, "Middle Assyrian Tablets: The Instruments of Bureaucracy," *Altorientalische Forschungen* 13 (1986) 10-39; G. R. Driver, *Semitic Writing from Pictograph to Alphabet,* rev. and ed. S. A. Hopkins (London: Oxford University Press, 1976), pp. 16, 79-80. Note esp. Hopkins's comments on pp. 225-26. For illustrations see plates 24, 25; also *IBD,* 3:1663.

42. Cf. Keck, *Dialogue* 23 (1990) 133.

43. See *CAD,* 8:157.

44. Herodotus, *Hist.* 7.239. Cf. also 8.135, on which see below. Homer must have had some such object in mind when he wrote of "a folded tablet (πίναχι πτυκτῷ) on which he had traced a number of devices with a deadly meaning" (*Il.* 6.169). For additional references see Hopkins, in *Semitic Writing,* p. 226. δέλτος is a loanword from Semitic *dlt,* "door." Cf. A. Baumann, *TDOT,* 3:231; K. Galling, "Tafel, Buch und Blatt," in *Near Eastern Studies in Honor of William Foxwell Albright,* ed. H. Goedicke (Baltimore: Johns Hopkins University Press, 1971), pp. 210-11.

45. Cf. Ugar. *lwḥ, lḥ; UT,* p. 427, no. 1358. For Hittite, see S. A. Hopkins, *Semitic Writing,* p. 226. For the relief see *ANEP,* no. 460; cf. Hyatt, *BA* 6 (1943) 75.

46. For the official publication see G. F. Bass and C. Pulak, "Excavations at Ulu

Second, several OT texts suggest familiarity with writing tablets. In Isa. 30:8 Yahweh instructs the prophet,

> Go, write *(kātab)* it down on a tablet *(lûaḥ);*
> Inscribe *(ḥāqaq)* it on a writing object *(sēper),*
> That it may be with them in the future,
> As an eternal witness.

This text compares with Hab. 2:2:

> Record *(kātab)* the vision;
> Transcribe it clearly *(bēʾēr)* on the tablets *(hallûḥôt),*
> So a herald may run with it.[47]

While these passages do not identify the materials on which the prophets were to transcribe their texts, wooden tablets are plausible.[48] Writing boards were more expensive than other materials, but given the antiquity and widespread distribution of the evidence, Ezekiel must have been familiar with them, and may even have possessed some of his own leaves. The present royal message presents a worthy subject to be recorded on these special objects.

(2) The prophet is commanded to write *(kātab)* a message on each piece of wood. The content of the inscriptions is dictated by Yahweh and comes in the form of two almost perfectly parallel phrases:

> *lyhwdh wlbny yśrʾl ḥbryw*
> *lywsp wkl byt yśrʾl ḥbryw*
> Pertaining to Judah and the descendants of Israel, his associates
> Pertaining to Joseph and all the house of Israel, his associates.

Burun in 1986," *AJA* 93 (1987) 10-11. For a more popular treatment see G. F. Bass, "Splendors of the Bronze Age," *National Geographic* 172/6 (1987) 730-31.

47. On this text see Floyd, *ZAW* 105 (1993) 462-81.

48. Ps. 69:29 (Eng. 28) refers to *sēper ḥayyîm,* "the register of life," on which H. Gevaryahu comments, though perhaps with some overstatement, "most of the psalms and the writings of the prophets were originally written on wooden tablets. . . . The papyrus that could be used as writing material was expensive, had to be imported, and is almost never mentioned in the Bible. So wooden tablets and animal skins appear to be the main writing materials of the day" ("Tehilim," *Dor le-dor* 16 [1987/88] 240). Further possibilities are opened by considering the use of the word *delet.* Fundamentally the word denotes "door" (BDB, p. 195; *HALOT,* pp. 223-24; Baumann, *TDOT,* 3:23-33). In Lachish Letter 4:3 *dlt* refers to a writing object that could be held in the hand and delivered to another person (*KAI,* 2:194). *dlt* is used for writing boards in Ugaritic (*UT,* 142:5) and Phoenician (*KAI* 32.12 refers to a tablet of bronze, *hdlt nḥšt*). Jer. 36:23 refers to *dĕlātôt* of a *mĕgillat sēper,* presumably "columns" of a written scroll, which are comparable to individual tablets of a polyptych. On the use of writing boards in the ancient world see further A. Lemaire, *ABD,* 6:1002-3.

The reasons for inscribing Judah's name are obvious. This was the dominant tribe in the south, the source of the Davidic dynasty, and the name for the southern state. But the unconventionality of Joseph was recognized already in the transcription of the oral message by the addition of ʿēṣ ʾeprayim, "the wood of Ephraim." Joseph was the father of Ephraim and Manasseh, the two dominant tribes in the northern kingdom.[49] Of these two, Ephraim, the younger son,[50] dominated northern politics from the beginning. From Jeroboam I to the fall of the northern kingdom, the state was ruled by Ephraimite kings from Ephraimite capitals.[51] But "Joseph" as a designation for the northern kingdom is less common,[52] a fact that necessitated the clarifying comment. Ezekiel's preference for "Joseph" may have been determined by the same disparaging considerations as his designation of Israel's rulers as nĕśîʾîm, "princes," instead of mĕlākîm, "kings." For him the northern state headed by Ephraim was illegitimate from the beginning. Unlike Judah, the tribe did not impose its name on the nation.

The expansions to the inscriptions, "and to the descendants of Israel," "and to the whole house of Israel," respectively, highlight the inclusive nature of the oracle. The presence of the name "Israel" in both accords with Ezekiel's consistent usage: "Israel" denotes the covenant nation as a whole.[53] bĕnê yiśrāʾēl in the first refers to those descendants of the eponymous ancestor that joined Judah in making up the southern kingdom, including the Simeonites, whose allotted territory had consisted of pockets within the land of Judah (Josh. 19:1-9); many Benjaminites, whose territory alternated between Judean and north Israelite domination; and Levites who served the southern kingdom; along with the descendants of those faithful northerners who had defected to the south at the time of the schism (2 Chr. 11:13-17). kol-bêt yiśrāʾēl in the second represents the tribes which, along with Ephraim, made up the northern state of Israel. Ezekiel introduces a special word, ḥbr, "compatriots, associates," to describe their relationship to the dominant tribes.[54]

49. Cf. the predicted ascendancy of Joseph in Jacob's (Gen. 49:22-26) and Moses' (Deut. 33:13-17) blessings.

50. See the predicted ascendancy of Ephraim over Manasseh in Gen. 48:8-20.

51. "Ephraim" is Hosea's favorite designation for the northern kingdom (over 30 times); the name is also common in Isaiah (7:2; plus 13 times), occasional in Jeremiah (7:15; 31:9, 18, 20), the Psalter (78:9; cf. 60:9 [Eng. 7] and 108:9 [Eng. 8], with Manasseh), and Chronicles (2 Chr. 25:7, 10; cf. 30:1, with Manasseh).

52. Amos 5:15; 6:6; Obad. 18; Zech. 10:6; Ps. 77:16 (Eng. 15) (parallel to Jacob); 78:67 (parallel to Ephraim); 80:2 (Eng. 1) (parallel to Israel); 81:6 (Eng. 5) (parallel to Israel, Jacob). Ezekiel uses the name elsewhere only in a tribal sense (47:13; 48:32).

53. Cf. Zimmerli, Ezekiel 2, pp. 563-65.

54. The word occurs only here in Ezekiel. Elsewhere it is used of military confederates (Judg. 20:11), accomplices in crime (Isa. 1:23), peers and colleagues (Cant. 1:7; 8:13). On the meaning of the term see M. O'Connor, "Northwest Semitic Designations for Elective Social Affinities," JANES 18 (1986) 67-80.

While the content of the inscriptions is clear, their interpretation depends on the meaning ascribed to the introductory *lamed*. Based on the form, *lamed* plus name (or title), it could be interpreted as a mark of ownership, similar to the form found on hundreds of seals,[55] and illustrated in Isa. 44:5:

> One shall say, "I belong to Yahweh *(lyhwh)*,"
> And another shall be called by the name of Jacob;
> One shall write on his hand, "Belonging to Yahweh" *(lyhwh)*,
> And another shall claim the name of Israel.

If the staves represent royal scepters, the inscriptions identify them as symbols of rule claimed by the southern and northern kingdoms, respectively, and the joining of the two staves would signal the unification of the two kingdoms (cf. *mamlĕkôt*, v. 22). But staves are not usually the property of collective groups. Even in Num. 17:16-26 (Eng. 1-11), cited earlier, the twelve staves are inscribed with the names of the heads of each tribe, not the tribal name. Had Ezekiel envisioned the unification of dynasties, the inscription should have read *ldwd*, "to David," and *l'mry*, "to Omri," or *lyhw*, "to Jehu." To democratize the ownership to the entire tribes is both anachronistic and absurd.

It is preferable to interpret the introductory *lamed* as a *lamed* of reference, whose form is best known from the Psalter but also familiar from Ugaritic texts.[56] Accordingly, these inscriptions translate, "Pertaining to Judah and to the descendants of Israel who are associated with him," and "Pertaining to Joseph and to the entire family of Israel associated with him," respectively. If this is all that was inscribed on the pieces of wood, these headings are purely symbolic, the reunification of northern and southern kingdoms being reflected in the union of two pieces of wood. But the writing board hypothesis

---

55. Virtually all of the 51 stamped bullae found in the 586 B.C. ruins of the City of David begin with this *lamed* (Shiloh, *IEJ* 36 [1986] 29). The same is true of the vast majority of the over 180 bullae published by Avigad, *Hebrew Bullae from the Time of Jeremiah*. See also the *lmlk* jar handle stamps from the same period (on which see N. Avigad, *Bullae and Seals from a Post-Exilic Judean Archive,* Qedem 4 (Jerusalem: Institute of Archaeology, Hebrew University, 1976). On the semantic issue involved in the form see A. Rainey, "Private Seal Impressions: A Note on Semantics," *IEJ* 16 (1966) 187-90.

56. Note the references in the Psalm titles: *ldwd*, "to David," occurs 73 times; *lšlmh*, "to Solomon," twice; *lmšh*, "to Moses," once; *l'sp*, "to Asaph," 12 times; *lhymn,* "to Heman," once; *l'ytn*, "to Ethan," once; *lmnṣh,* "to the choirmaster," over 50 times; *lbny qrḥ,* "to the sons of Qorah," 11 times. On these titles see N. H. Ridderbos and P. C. Craigie, *ISBE,* 3:1032-33. For Ugaritic see *lb'l,* "Pertaining to Baal" (*CTA,* 6.1.1; *ANET,* p. 139); *[la]q[h]t,* "Pertaining to Aqhat" (as reconstructed by Herdner, *CTA,* 19.1.1; and Gibson, *CML,* p. 113); probably *[lk]rt,* "Pertaining to Keret" (as reconstructed by Gordon, *UT,* Krt 1; also Herdner, *CTA,* 14.1.1; and Gibson, *CML,* p. 82; cf. *ANET,* p. 143).

opens the question whether their texts were limited to the quoted inscriptions, or whether these were merely headings for longer documents. Support for this interpretation may be drawn from neo-Assyrian exemplars, on which the obverse of the first tablet carried the titles of the texts that followed, as well as the owner's name and the library to which it belonged.[57] But what would Ezekiel's documents have been? We are now in the realm of speculation, but several possibilities arise.

First, Ezekiel may be manipulating two registers, real or hypothetical lists of names of citizens of Judah and Joseph. This would accord with the function of the *seper ḥayyîm* in Ps. 69:29 (Eng. 28),[58] as well as with neo-Assyrian practice. In the cache of tablets discovered in Calah (Nimrud), clay was used for insignificant private records, while important documents, such as royal edicts and religious and astronomical texts, were recorded on wood, lapis lazuli, gold, and silver tablets.[59] If Ezekiel's tablets represented some type of royal register, the boards offer visual affirmation of the truth declared in the following promises that *all* Israel would participate in the envisioned restoration. No tribe or clan would be missing.

Second, one may speculate that these tablets contained an oracle from Yahweh, specifically the interpretation of the sign-action that follows in vv. 21-28. OT evidence for divine messages transcribed on tablets has already been recognized in Isa. 30:8 and Hab. 2:2, and analogues may be found outside Israel as well.[60] It is reasonable to suppose, therefore, that once Ezekiel had presented his interpretation of the sign-action (vv. 21-28), he would have used

57. The title tablet of one sixteen-leaved polyptych, inscribed with an Assyrian version of the *Enuma Anu Enlil* ("When the gods Anu and Enlil") omen series, reads as follows: "Palace of Sargon, king of the world, king of Assyria. The text series (beginning) Enuma Anu Enlil he had written on an ivory tablet and deposited it in his palace at Dur-Sarukkun." Thus Wiseman, *Iraq* 7 (1955) 7; cf. Hopkins, *Semitic Writing*, p. 226.

58. See n. 48 above.

59. See Hopkins, *Semitic Writing*, p. 225.

60. Most of the writing boards listed on published administrative records from Ashurbanipal's library contained omen texts; cf. Parpola, *JNES* 42 (1983) 5-7. Especially significant are the recorded prophecies from Mari and the revelations of Ishtar to Ashurbanipal. These are discussed by Millard, *RHR* 202/2 (1985) 125-45. A remarkable analogue appears in Herodotus's report of the experience of Mys, a Carian, who had been dispatched by Mardonius to consult as many oracles as he was able concerning the course of an imminent battle with the Persians. His visit to the Theban shrine of Apollo Ptoüs is recorded as follows: "Mys entered the shrine accompanied by three men from Thebes, who had been officially appointed to take down whatever answer the god might give. The prophet through whom the god spoke at once delivered his oracle — in a foreign language. The three Thebans were astonished at hearing a strange tongue instead of Greek, and did not know what to do about it; Mys, however, snatched the tablet (δέλτος) they had brought to write on, and, declaring that the god's response had been delivered in Carian, wrote it down himself and hurried back to Thessaly" (*Hist.* 8.136).

these tablets to record the oracle. Indeed, the twofold division of the interpretation itself (vv. 21-24a, 24b-28) corresponds to the two pieces of wood
making up the final unitary product.

(3) The prophet is commanded to bring the two pieces of wood together,
thereby creating a single entity in his hands. If these were plain sticks, they could
have been laid end to end and spliced, or side by side and tied together. However,
if these *'ēṣîm* were writing boards, the method of joining is probably like that of
Assyrian diptychs and polyptychs, which were created by linking two or more
tablets in series edge to edge by means of hinge pins or leather cords.[61] If the
tablets contained registers of Judah and Joseph, this act provided a powerful
visual portrayal of the unification of the two populations. If they contained the
interpretive oracle that follows, the action demonstrates visually that the promises contained in the explanation apply to the entire house of Israel.

The enigmatic nature of Ezekiel's prescribed actions causes Yahweh
to interrupt his own instructions to give advance notice of the people's puzzled
response to the prophet's performance.[62] Had Ezekiel been dealing with royal
staves, such a request would have been unnecessary, since the meaning would
have been obvious. But Ezekiel maintains his reputation as a spinner of
enigmas, both verbal and pantomimic.[63] His present actions are a riddle,
calling for clarification. The explanation Ezekiel is to offer is cryptic, as if
Yahweh is impatient with the interruption and anxious to have the prophet
complete the sign-action so he may get on with a full-scale interpretation. He
says no more than necessary. But from the opening *hinnēh,* "Look," to the
concluding reference to "my hand," the audience's attention is drawn away
from the prophet to the divine agent in the events. The shift from second to
first person pronouns highlights the fact that as in earlier sign-actions, Ezekiel
himself has become a metaphor for God.[64] His manipulation of the pieces of
wood represents an action to be performed by Yahweh.

In addition to this shift in pronouns, one may observe several other small
but significant changes from the instructions in vv. 16-17. First, the order in
which the inscribed pieces of wood are mentioned is reversed — Joseph now
precedes Judah. Second, Judah appears without his associates (*ḥăbērāyw*).
Third, in emphasizing the hegemonic position of Ephraim, the parenthetical *'ēṣ*

61. See Wiseman, *Iraq* 7 (1955) 3-5, 10-12; Hopkins, *Semitic Writing,* pp. 225-26.
For a photograph of the ivory-hinged diptych from Ulu Burun see *National Geographic*
172/6 (1987) 731.

62. This anticipated reaction offers modern scholars much farther removed from
the event some consolation in not being able to solve all the enigmas of the sign-action
satisfactorily.

63. See the people's reaction to verbal pronouncements in 17:12 and 21:5 (Eng.
20:49); to pantomimic actions in 12:9 and 24:19.

64. Thus Keck, *Dialogue* 23 (1990) 136. Cf. 4:3; 21:19-22 (Eng. 14-17); 24:16-27.

'eprayim, "the Ephraimite wood," is expanded into a subordinate clause, *'ăšer běyad-'eprayim,* "which is in the hand of Ephraim." Fourth, the *kol-bêt yiśrā'ēl,* "the entire house of Israel," is replaced with *šibtê yiśrā'ēl,* "the tribes of Israel." Fifth, instead of simply being brought near to each other *(qārab)* so that they become one *(hāyâ la'ăḥādîm)* in the prophet's hand, the Josephite piece of wood is placed on *(nātan 'al)* the Judahite counterpart, hinting at the superiority of the southern tribe. Finally, the two pieces of wood are made *('āśâ)* one in Yahweh's hand. Beyond declaring that the prophet's actions mirror the divine intentions, with these alterations the prophet drops hints of the fuller explanation to come. But v. 19 stops short of explaining what these divine actions represent or what their effects will be. There is no hint yet of the new covenant, a theme that will dominate the interpretation.

(4) The prophet is commanded to let the two pieces of wood rest in his hands and to hold them up for all to see. V. 20 returns the audience's attention to the sticks. The statement reaffirms that the prophet is dealing with real pieces of wood, which he holds in his hands, and that these pieces are the same ones that he had inscribed earlier. Furthermore, it reminds the prophet and the audience that, like Ezekiel's previous sign-actions, this is to be a public performance. The united pieces of wood are to be carried about as a visual reminder of Yahweh's promise.[65] Meanwhile, he is to accompany these actions with verbal pronouncements of hope, summarized in vv. 22-28.

b. Proclaiming the New National Reality (37:21-28)

21 *"Now declare to them, 'Thus has the Lord Yahweh declared: Look! I will take the descendants of Israel*[66] *from the nations among which they have gone. I will gather them from around;*[67] *I will bring them to their own land.*[68] 22 *I will make them into a single nation within the land,*[69] *on the mountains of Israel.*[70] *Then a single king*[71] *will be*

---

65. Friebel recognizes correctly the durative significance of the construction of *wěhāyû . . . běyāděkā lě'ênêhem,* "They shall be . . . in your hands before their eyes" ("Jeremiah's and Ezekiel's Sign-Actions," pp. 847-48).

66. MT *běnê yiśrā'ēl;* LXX presupposes *kol bêt yiśrā'ēl,* "the whole house of Israel."

67. MT *missābîb;* LXX presupposes *mikkol sěbîbōtām,* "from all that surround them."

68. MT *'el-'admātām;* LXX presupposes *'el 'admat yiśrā'ēl,* "to the land of Israel." Syr. drops the entire phrase.

69. MT *bā'āreṣ;* LXX presupposes *bě'arṣî,* "within my land."

70. MT *běhārê yiśrā'ēl;* LXX presupposes *ûběhārê yiśrā'ēl,* "and on the mountains of Israel."

71. Many emend *melek* to *nāśî',* following LXX ἄρχων, "prince, ruler," here and

king[72] *for all of them. Never again will they be*[73] *two nations, and never again will they be divided into two kingdoms.*[74] 23 *Never again will they defile themselves*[75] *with their pellets of dung,*[76] *with their disgusting practices,*[77] *or with their rebellious actions.*[78] *I will rescue them from all their apostasies,*[79] *by which they sinned, and I will cleanse them. Then they will be my people, and I will be their God.* 24 *And my servant David*[80] *will be king*[81] *over them, and there will be a single shepherd for all of them.*

They will follow my laws and observe my decrees; they will put them into practice. 25 *They will occupy the land I gave to my servant Jacob, and in which your ancestors*[82] *lived. They, their children, and their grandchildren will occupy it forever.*[83] *And David my servant will*

---

in v. 24. Cf. K.-D. Schunck, "Die Attribute des eschatologischen Messias," *TLZ* 111 (1986) 651 n. 23. Rofé (*Textus* 14 [1988] 173) attributes LXX to a theological revision in the *Vorlage*. But *melek* provides a better correlative with *gôy*, esp. in the face of the following association of *mamlākôt* and *gôyim* (cf. Zimmerli, *Ezekiel 2*, p. 269). For additional contextual support for MT see the commentary.

72. Many delete *lĕmelek* with LXX and Syr. But the absence of the word in the latter may reflect haplography after *lklm*, which involves the same consonants, albeit reversed.

73. Recognizing the error in Kethib, *yhyh*, "he will be," Qere commends *yhyw*, "they will be." So also the versions.

74. LXX and Vulg. drop the final '*ôd*, either recognizing its superfluity or reflecting a different *Vorlage*. Syr. retains it but transfers it to the next verse after the initial copula. Allen (*Ezekiel 20–48*, p. 190) sees in MT a conflation of two readings.

75. Repointing MT *yiṭammĕ'û* as *yiṭṭammĕ'û*.

76. On idols as *gillûlîm*, "dung pellets," see my *Ezekiel: Chapters 1–24*, p. 226.

77. On *šiqqûṣîm* see ibid., p. 208.

78. Many (cf., e.g., Zimmerli, *Ezekiel 2*, p. 270) delete *ûbĕšiqqûṣêhem ûbĕkol piš'êhem* after LXX. 14:11 supports MT. On *pĕšā'îm* see my *Ezekiel: Chapters 1–24*, p. 436.

79. Reading *mikkol mĕšûbōtêhem*, lit. "from all their turnings," in place of MT *mikkol môšĕbôtêhem*, "from all their settlements," with support from LXX (ἀνομιῶν) and Symmachus (ἀσεβειῶν). The masc. form of the latter is attested in 34:13, but this sense is clearly out of place here. MT represents a metathetical error involving *w* and *š*. On the unusual form of the pl. ending (cf. *môšĕbôtām* in Gen. 36:43; Num. 31:10) see Hurvitz, *Linguistic Study*, pp. 24-27. The noun *mĕšûbâ* occurs frequently in Jeremiah (2:19; 3:6, 8, 11, 12, 22; 5:6; 8:5; 14:7) as well as in Hos. 3:22; 14:5; Prov. 1:32. Ezekiel's usage reflects Jeremianic influence. Cf. Miller, *Das Verhältnis Jeremias und Hesekiels*, pp. 114-15.

80. The addition of "David" seems awkward, but the occurrence of a similar phenomenon in 34:23 cautions against its deletion.

81. LXX again reads ἄρχων, "rulers." See n. 71 on v. 22.

82. LXX and Syr. assimilate the word to the context by reading '*ăbôtêhem*, "their fathers."

83. LXX drops *ûbĕnêhem ûbĕnê bĕnêhem 'ad 'ôlām*.

be their prince forever. 26 *I will make with them a covenant of peace;
it will be an eternal covenant with them.*[84] *I will give to them [the land
of Israel]*[85] *and multiply them.*[86] *I will place my sanctuary in their
midst forever.* 27 *My residence will be over them,*[87] *and I will be their
God and they will be my people.* 28 *And when my sanctuary is in their
midst forever, then the nations will know that I am Yahweh, the one
who sanctifies Israel.'* "

♦ Nature and Design

The interpretation proper is signaled in v. 21 by a new command to Ezekiel to
explain to his audience the meaning of his sign-action. However, the interpretation quickly departs from an exposition of the performance to an anthology of
Ezekielian restoration ideas,[88] thereby bringing his salvation oracles to a fitting
conclusion. Although English translations tend to divide vv. 21-28 into two parts
with the break appearing between vv. 23 and 24, a good case can be made for
dividing the interpretation in the middle of v. 24.[89] The twofold appearance of
the covenant formula (vv. 23, 27) offers the first clue to the bipartite division.
Elsewhere in the book this formula stands at the end of oracles or segments
thereof (11:20; 14:11; 34:30, 31; 36:38). Vv. 21-23 are preoccupied with the
reunification of the nation under one king, a theme totally absent from vv.

84. 'ôtām is difficult. My translation follows LXX μετ' αὐτῶν, which assumes
'ittām in the *Vorlage.* But the existence of the same problem in a similar context in 16:60
may suggest a dialectical variation.

85. "The land of Israel" is inserted to make explicit what is implicit in the verb
ûnĕtatîm. See the following note.

86. ûnĕtattîm wĕhirbêtî 'ôtām is missing in LXX, the scribe's eye probably having
skipped from one 'ôtām to the other. Herrmann (*Ezechiel*, p. 234) suggested that 'wtm
wnttym is a slight corruption of a marginal note that found its way into the text, creating
a doublet of the following 'wtm ntty. NRSV follows Targ. in reading w'bryknwn, "and I
will bless them." It may be preferable to interpret the final *mem* on nātattîm as a datival
suffix (on this syntactical feature see M. Bogaert, "Les suffixes verbaux non accusatifs
dans le sémitique nord-occidental et particulièrement en hébreu," *Bib* 45 [1964] 220-47;
Dahood, *Psalms,* 3:377-79) and to see here an abbreviation for the land grant formula,
wĕnātattî lāhem 'et-'admat yiśrā'ēl (cf. 11:17). See further the commentary. Alternatively
MT may represent a scribal error of hearing for nĕṭa'tîm, "I will plant them," which would
suit the context well. The figure of Yahweh planting his people in the land occurs in Jer.
24:6, 32:41 (both in connection with the covenant formula), and 42:10 (linked with the
promise of Yahweh's presence), and has been hinted at by Ezekiel in 34:29 and 36:36.

87. Lit. "over them."

88. For summaries see Lust, *CBQ* 43 (1981) 526-27; Friebel, "Sign-Actions," pp.
848-49.

89. So also Zimmerli, *Ezekiel 2,* pp. 275-76. NRSV, NASB, NIV, and NJPS break
between vv. 23 and 24; JB and REB do not break the text at all.

24b-28, which are dominated by the eternality of Yahweh's restorative acts. Accordingly, the specification of one shepherd over all Israel in v. 24a links this segment to the foregoing, rather than to that which follows. Furthermore, the identification of David as *melek* in v. 24a ties in with the use of the same word in v. 22, but contrasts with Ezekiel's preferred designation for Israel's rulers, *nāśî'*, "prince," in v. 25. Finally, on the analogy of 34:24, the reference to David in v. 24a should be linked to the preceding covenant formula.

This division of vv. 21-28 results in two panels of almost equal length.[90] If it is correct to view the *'ēṣîm* of the sign-action as writing boards, it is plausible that once the prophet had received the interpretation he recorded it on these tablets. One may suppose further that the first panel represents the inscription on the Josephite tablet, and the second the text of the Judahite board. This supposition accords with the order in which the names appear in v. 19, and it corresponds to the positioning of the Ephraimite tablet on the Judahite (so MT). If a reader were perusing the entire document, this one would therefore be read first. Most importantly, the first panel stresses the reunification of the nation, a subject that has greater significance for the future of the northern kingdom than for the southern kingdom, since Judah had no need to learn of her incorporation into the future envisaged by Ezekiel — he had already made numerous pronouncements of her restoration, independent of any reunification with the north. This approach may help resolve, among other problems, the anomalous reference to an Israelite ruler as *melek* in the first panel (see below). But this is not to suggest that either panel had relevance for only one kingdom — both represent messages of hope for both kingdoms. Rather, this analysis recognizes the differences in emphases in the two parts.

(1) The First Tablet (37:21-24a)

The formal interpretation of the sign-action opens with a second command to Ezekiel to address his audience (cf. v. 19) and to offer them Yahweh's own interpretation. The prophet begins with an attention-arousing *hinnēh,* "Look!" and then launches directly into the explanation. The first part of his speech follows an ABAB structure, with the first and third sections focusing on Yahweh's restorative activity and the second and fourth on his agent, the king, who serves as a symbol of the glorious new realities. In this first panel, Ezekiel extends the substitution begun in v. 19. Whereas he had previously drawn attention to the theological significance of his performance by substituting the subjects of the actions (Yahweh for himself), now he replaces the objects. His interest is not really in creating an *'ēṣ 'eḥād,* "a single piece of wood," from two pieces (*'ēṣîm*), but a *gôy 'eḥād,* "a single nation," from two nations (*šěnê*

---

90. In MT the first panel consists of 72 words; the second 68.

gôyim, v. 22). The preference for the term *gôy* over *'am,* "people," is deliberate. The latter, a warm relational term, with undertones of kinship, would have been appropriate in another context, but here the concern is the restoration of Israel as a nation, which requires the use of *gôy.*[91] Within the ancient Near Eastern cultural context, the achievement of this status involved a combination of ethnic, political, territorial, religious, and linguistic factors.[92] By touching on four of these factors within this paragraph, Ezekiel paints a remarkably comprehensive picture of a mature nation. If any one of these elements were missing, ancient Near Easterners would have considered the restoration process abortive. The commentary below highlights the elements that make up the prophet's comprehensive vision of a nation restored.

(a) The Restoration of Israel's Ethnic Integrity (37:21a)

Ezekiel's verbal presentation opens with a quartet of promises summarizing the process whereby Yahweh will restore the ethnic unity of Israel. The prophet's ethnic focus is highlighted by the expression *běnê yiśrā'ēl,* "descendants of Israel." Not only does he hereby abandon the tribal names, Judah and Joseph (Ephraim), in vv. 15-20, but he also deliberately eschews *bêt yiśrā'ēl,* "house of Israel," which is overwhelmingly preferred elsewhere in the book. Although these phrases may occur as stylistic variations of one another, as perhaps in v. 16, they are not synonymous. Ethnic overtones are present in "house of Israel,"[93] but they are much stronger in "descendants of Israel." The latter preserves a memory of the origins of the nation in a single eponymous ancestor, Israel/Jacob. One expects the expression to be applied to the immediate offspring of Jacob in the patriarchal narratives (Gen. 48:8-27; Exod. 1:1-6), but the long form identified the nation as long as the memory of the eponymous ancestor survived, and as long as the tribal entities, named after Jacob's twelve sons, retained their significance in national life. The rapid decrease in tribal influence in the wake of Solomon's administrative reforms is reflected in the decline in the use of "descendants of Israel" as the national designation.[94] However, the prophets never forgot the nation's ancestral roots. For describing Israel's restoration as a new exodus, the long form of the name is particularly appropriate. After all, Ezekiel's concern is the reunification of the eponymous ancestor's vast extended family, "the

---

91. See Block, *ISBE,* 3:492, 759-60. For a fuller study of these terms see idem, *Foundations of National Identity,* pp. 12-127.

92. See idem, *ISBE,* 3:492-94.

93. See idem, "Israel's House: Reflections on the Use of *byt yśr'l* in the Old Testament in the Light of Its Ancient Near Eastern Environment," *JETS* 28 (1985) 257-75.

94. See idem, "'Israel'-'sons of Israel': A Study in Hebrew Eponymic Usage," *SR* 13 (1984) 301-26.

whole household of Israel" (v. 11), which included the "tribes of Israel" *(šibṭê yiśrā'ēl)* associated with Joseph/Ephraim (v. 19).

In Ezekiel's fourfold promise of ethnic reunification the reader may hear a clear echo of 36:24,[95] particularly in the use of the verb *lāqaḥ,* "to take," to describe Yahweh's initial action. However, the preference for this term over the more common *hôṣî',* "to bring out,"[96] derives more immediately from Yahweh's previous instructions for Ezekiel to "take" *(lāqaḥ)* the sticks (v. 16), which are followed by his announcement that he will take *(lāqaḥ)* the wood of Joseph and the tribes of Israel (v. 19). Indeed, the structure of the present statement parallels the previous one precisely,[97] suggesting perhaps that just as 37:1-14 presented a visionary exposition of 36:27, so 37:15-24a offers a dramatic and verbal exposition of 36:24. In the process Ezekiel's Judean audience learns that the scope of the anticipated restoration extends far beyond their own exilic situation in Babylon; Yahweh will regather the descendants of Israel from all around *(missābîb).*

From a human perspective, Ezekiel's vision of remnants of the original twelve-tribe nation streaming back to their hereditary homeland seems impossible. The northern population had been dispersed in upper Mesopotamia

95. Note the common features in the following synopsis:

36:24	37:21-22a
wĕlāqaḥtî 'etkem min-haggôyim	*'ănî lōqēaḥ 'et-bĕnê yiśrā'ēl mibbên haggôyim 'ăšer hālĕkû-šām*
wĕqibbaṣtî 'etkem mikkol-hā'ărāṣôt	*wĕqibbaṣtî 'ōtām missābîb*
wĕhēbē'tî 'etkem 'el-'ādmatām	*wĕhēbē'tî 'ōtām 'el-'admātām*
	wĕ'āśîtî 'ōtām lĕgôy 'eḥād bā'āreṣ bĕhārê yiśrā'ēl
I will take you from the nations;	I will take the descendants of Israel from the nations among which they have gone.
I will gather you from all the lands;	I will gather them from around;
I will bring you to your own land.	I will bring them back to their own land;
	I will make them into a single nation within the land, on the mountains of Israel.

Except for the abbreviation of the third statement, "from all the lands," to "from around," the present text tends to be expansionistic. The canon of textual criticism that the shorter version is probably original may argue against Lust's view that 36:24 was inserted under the influence of 37:21 *(CBQ* 43 [1981] 526-27).

96. See Exod. 6:6-7. For discussion see the commentary above on 36:24. In 39:29 Ezekiel will use *šôbēb,* from *šûb,* "to return."

97. Note the largely verbatim repetition: v. 19: *dabbēr 'ălēhem kōh-'āmar 'ădōnāy yhwh hinnēh 'ănî lōqēaḥ 'et-'ēṣ yôsēp . . . wĕšibṭê yiśrā'ēl ḥăbārāyw;* v. 21: *dabbēr 'ălêhem kōh-'āmar 'ădōnāy yhwh hinnēh 'ănî lōqēaḥ 'et-bĕnê yiśrā'ēl.*

by an entirely different regime, the Assyrians, one and one-half centuries earlier; further, Assyrian imperial policy deliberately aimed to assimilate them into the population.[98] However, the presence of distinctly Israelite names in documents from their exilic settlements generations after the collapse of Samaria suggests that many retained a distinctive ethnic self-consciousness.[99] Nevertheless, religious and political jealousies were too deeply entrenched to contemplate rapprochement between the northern Israelite exiles and their southern Judean counterparts.[100] The reconciliation envisioned by Ezekiel could no more be achieved by their own initiative than the Judeans could perform their own heart transplant (36:26-27), or the dead bones could of themselves come back to life (37:1-14). Every phase of the restoration required direct and miraculous divine intervention.

(b) The Restoration of Israel's Territorial Integrity (37:21b)

Recognizing that ethnic reunion alone was insufficient to restore the national integrity of Israel, the second pair of promises announces Yahweh's determination to return the exiles to their ancestral homeland. The mass deportations of the Assyrians and Babylonians had to be reversed. In view of Yahweh's promise of the land of Canaan to the ancestors as their hereditary possession forever (e.g., Gen. 13:15), the people had to be brought back to their own land (*'admātām*). In an intentional reversal of ch. 6, Yahweh would make them one *gôy* "within the land" (*bā'āreṣ*), on the mountains of Israel (*bĕhārê yiśrā'ēl*). The conjunction of this triad of designations for the land of Israel highlights how inconceivable any land other than the original homeland could be.

(c) The Restoration of Israel's Political Integrity (37:22)

The elders' request to Samuel to install over them a king "like all the nations" (1 Sam. 8:5, 19-20) reflects the importance of the monarchy for Israel's

---

98. 2 K. 17:6 and 18:11 name these lands: Halah (Ḫalaḫḫu, a district northeast of Nineveh), Gozan on the river Khabur, and the cities of Media. See B. Oded, *Mass Deportations and Deportees in the Neo-Assyrian Empire* (Wiesbaden: Reichert, 1979).

99. Names like *Neriyau* and *Palṭiyau* in Assyrian documents from Gozan have been identified as Israelite. See I. Eph'al, "On the Identification of the Israelite Exiles in the Assyrian Empire," in *Excavations and Studies,* Fest. S. Yeivin (Tel Aviv: University of Tel Aviv, 1973), pp. 201-4; R. Zadok, *The Jews in Babylonia During the Chaldean and Achaemenian Periods* (Haifa: University of Haifa Press, 1979), pp. 7-22, 97-106; idem, "Notes on the Early History of the Israelites and Judaeans," *Or* 51 (1982) 391-93.

100. Contra B.-Z. Luria, "The Exile From Samaria," *ErIsr* 17 (1984) 212-25 (Eng. summary, p. 10*), who argues that Samarian exiles integrated eventually with their Judean counterparts to form the vast Jewish diaspora of the East.

national self-consciousness.[101] With the division of the monarchy in 931 B.C. a single people had de facto become two nations. The removal of Hoshea from the throne of Samaria in 722 and Zedekiah from the throne of Jerusalem in 586 signaled the end of the nations of Israel and Judah, respectively. Contrary to the opinion of many, Ezekiel was not fundamentally opposed to monarchic social structures. If he appears to denigrate the dynasty ruling in Jerusalem, the problem was not the institution itself, but the manner in which kingship operated in Israel. For him a restored nation without a restored kingdom was inconceivable.

Verse 22b addresses the problem of the missing monarch. Shifting the attention momentarily away from Yahweh and his role in the installation of the king, Ezekiel assumed that his audience either was familiar with 34:23 or was driven by a different objective. Omitting any reference to Yahweh or David, this factual statement was called for by the previous notice that Israel would be constituted a single nation *(gôy 'ehād)*. Accordingly, the emphasis is on the singularity of the monarchy: a single king will rule over all the tribes; never again should there be two nations *(gôyim)*, that is, two kingdoms *(mĕlākîm)*. Scholars have long stumbled over the present choice of *melek*, when throughout the book Ezekiel has demonstrated a decided preference for *nāśî'*, "chieftain, prince," especially in reference to Israel's kings.[102] *melek* and derivatives occurs thirty-seven times in the book, twenty-five of which refer to foreign kings.[103] Ezekiel's reluctance to designate Israelite kings as *mĕlākîm* supposedly reflects an antimonarchic stance, which the LXX translators perpetuated by rendering *melek* here as ἄρχων.[104] But this interpretation

---

101. In ancient times kings fulfilled three primary functions: (a) to provide leadership in the administration of justice, the conduct of war, and the maintenance of the national cult; (b) to serve as an ideal of courage, dignity, justice, and piety for the citizens; (c) to embody the collective aspirations of the people. Cf. Block, *Foundation of National Identity*, p. 587.

102. Cf. J. Boehmer, "*mlk* und *nśy'* bei Ezechiel," *TSK* 79 (1900) 112-17; E. Hammershaimb, "Ezekiel's View of the Monarchy," in *Some Aspects of Old Testament Prophecy from Isaiah to Malachi*, Teologiske Skrifter 4 (Copenhagen: Rosenkinde og Bagger, 1966), pp. 51-63. See n. 71 above.

103. E.g., the kings of Babylon (17:12; 19:9; 21:23-25; 26:7), Egypt (29:2-3), Tyre (28:12), Edom (32:29), the earth (28:17), the coastlands (27:35).

104. Exceptions, outside this context, are 1:2 (of Jehoiachin); 7:27 (unnamed and parallel to *nāśî'*); 17:12 (of Jehoiachin, removed by the king of Babylon; 43:7, 7, 9 (3 times, of Israel's past paganized kings). LXX renderings of *melek* vary. Only 1:2 and 17:12 translate βασιλεύς; 7:27 drops the reference; 43:7, 7, 9 read ἡγούμενος; the present context (37:22, 22, 24) reads ἄρχων. Cf. the discussions of the problem by J. Lust, "Exegesis and Theology in the Septuagint of Ezekiel: The Longer 'Pluses' and Ezekiel 43:1-9," *VI Congress of the International Organization for Septuagint and Cognate Studies, Jerusalem 1986*, ed. C. E. Cox, SBLSCS 23 (Atlanta: Scholars Press, 1987), pp. 217-21; Rofé, *Textus* 14 (1988) 171-73.

overlooks a fundamental dimension in Israelite perceptions of national self-consciousness. If the reference to "one king" symbolizes the nation's new unity, the present choice of *melek* highlights the restoration of Israel to full nationhood. To the prophet's audience, the use of *nāśî'* would have signified less than complete restoration. For the moment Ezekiel offers no hints of the king's identity. He deals only with the issue of principle: a nation *(gôy)* is by definition a monarchy *(mamlākâ)*, which must be ruled by a royal figure, a *melek*.[105] This promise assures the exiles that full-fledged and unitary nationhood is included in Yahweh's plan for Israel.

(d) The Restoration of Israel's Spiritual Integrity (37:23-24a)

23 This verse addresses the fourth dimension of ancient perceptions of national identity — a healthy relationship between Israel and her patron deity. The departure of Yahweh's glory from the temple and the subsequent fall of Jerusalem to Nebuchadrezzar reflected the rupture in the relationship in 586. But Ezekiel's vision of a restored Israel must also include righting this wrong. After all, true Israel was first and foremost a spiritual entity united in covenant with their God. Arguing from effect to cause, the prophet begins by announcing the symptoms of the new spiritual reality: the nation will be rid of the defilement *(ṭum'â)* resulting from the people's idolatry and other disgusting practices, and from her acts of rebellion.

The process of purification envisioned involves two actions, in both of which Yahweh functions as the agent. First, Yahweh *will rescue* the Israelites from their *apostasies*. The verb *hôšîa'*, "to save," usually envisions deliverance from external enemies (cf. 34:22), but like 36:29, the present usage envisions the people's sin as the enslaving power. Second, Yahweh *will cleanse* or "purify" them. The verb *ṭihar* recalls 36:25-28, which, in offering a fuller description of the cleansing process, had associated the experience with a heart transplant and an infusion of Yahweh's Spirit. The link is confirmed by the reference to covenant renewal, expressed in both instances by citing the covenant formula. The declaration, "They will be my people, and I will be their God," signals the full restoration of Israel's relationship with Yahweh. The present association of covenant renewal with the termination of idolatry, disgusting conduct, and rebellion is reminiscent of 14:11, and it intentionally announces the reversal of 5:11. Provoked by their defiling and abominable acts, Yahweh had abandoned his people. Now that he has purified them, he may return and normalize the covenant relationship with them.

24a Yahweh's expansion of the covenant formula concretizes the

105. Cf. Duguid, *Ezekiel and the Leaders,* pp. 24-25; Laato, *Josiah and David Redivivus,* p. 186.

spiritual renewal by announcing his appointment of David as *king* in Israel. By naming the *melek,* Yahweh not only affirms the eternality of his original promise to David (2 Sam. 7:16) but also discredits all past rulers who have claimed the title "king of Israel," particularly the Josephite/Ephraimite rulers of the northern kingdom. The king's special relationship with Yahweh is reflected in the designation *my servant ('abdî).*[106] Whereas all the northern kings and many of their Judean counterparts, especially Ezekiel's contemporaries, had been driven by self-service, this new ruler will embody the ideals established in Deut. 17:14-20, submitting to the overlordship of Yahweh. As shepherd-king, he will function as the agent of Yahweh's reign and the symbol of the nation's unity, exercising watch care after the model set out in ch. 34.

With this note the first (Josephite?) tablet concludes. In reversing the judgment announced in earlier oracles against Judah, this segment obviously offered new hope for the Judean exiles. However, its special significance lies in its extension of the restoration to the remnant of the northern kingdom scattered about the former Assyrian Empire. Ezekiel hereby announces that they too would benefit from Yahweh's great work of salvation. They would be reunited with the southern tribes and restored to their land, be spiritually renewed and reconstituted Yahweh's special covenant people, and be cared for by David, the reappointed agent of Yahweh's reign. For clarification of their incorporation into the reconstituted people of Yahweh, the reader must await the prophet's final vision (47:13–48:35).

(2) The Second Tablet (37:24b-28)

No formal break separates the two panels of this oracle. Perhaps none should be expected, since, as vv. 17 and 19 had suggested, the product is to have the appearance of a single piece of wood. On thematic grounds many interpret vv. 24b-28 as a later, secondary addition to vv. 21-24a,[107] but the style and syntax appear genuinely Ezekielian. The absence of a subject for the first verb, *yēlēkû* (lit. "they will walk"), suggests that "the descendants of Israel" in v. 21 must be the antecedent. Even so, the theme shifts dramatically from the unification of the nation to the permanence of the restored deity-nation-land relationships, highlighted by the fivefold occurrence of *'ôlām.* As E. Jenni has argued, this word denotes fundamentally "the remotest time,"[108] either the

---

106. On the expression see above on 34:23-24.

107. Cf. Zimmerli, *Ezekiel 2,* p. 276. B. Gosse interprets the association of the "new David" and "new covenant" themes as a postexilic development ("La nouvelle alliance et les promesses d'avenir se référant à David dans les livres de Jérémie, Ezéchiel et Isaïe," *VT* 41 [1991] 419-28).

108. Jenni, *THAT,* 2:228-30; cf. idem, *IDB,* 4:642-49, esp. 644. For a full study see idem, "Das Wort *'ôlām* im Alten Testament," *ZAW* 64 (1952) 197-248; 65 (1953) 1-35.

remote past or the distant future. Since in practice the word could also refer to more recent time (Deut. 32:7; Job 22:15), however, "a kind of range between 'remotest time' and 'perpetuity' " is more accurate.[109] In this context the meaning "forever, to eternity," is assured by prefixing *'ôlām* with the separable preposition *'ad* and the inseparable preposition *lĕ*.[110] Along with the sense of duration, the word bears nuances of permanence, durability, inviolability, irrevocability, and immutability, and in so doing serves as the designation of the definitive nature of the coming salvation.[111]

With his fivefold affirmation of the eternality of the restoration, Yahweh transforms this oracle into a powerful eschatological statement, envisaging an entirely new existence, where the old historical realities are considered null and void, and the new salvific work of God is perceived as final.[112] For Ezekiel eschatological events are neither ahistorical nor suprahistorical; they are based on Yahweh's past actions in history and represent a final solution to the present historical crisis. But the scope of his eschatological hope extends beyond a new exodus and a renewal of Yahweh's covenant with his people; it incorporates all the other promises on which the Israelites had based their security: Yahweh's covenant with David, his establishment of Jerusalem as the place for his name to dwell, and his special interest in the land of Canaan as his land, offered as a gracious fiefdom to Israel to administer on his behalf. In contrast to the following prophecy against Gog, which fixes the time of the battle with this northern foe in the distant future with a variety of temporal phrases,[113] no hints concerning the time of fulfillment are given. Accordingly, these events are deemed eschatological not because they are

109. See J. Barr, *Biblical Words for Time,* 2nd ed., SBT 1/33 (Naperville, Ill.: Allenson, 1969), p. 73 n. 1.

110. If a distinction is to be made between these constructions, it is a matter of degree. *'ad 'ôlām* is slightly stronger, perhaps reflecting successive progress into the future, whereas *lĕ'ôlām* seems to stress more the future state. See Jenni, *THAT,* 2:234. 1 Chr. 23:25 and 28:6-7 use the doubly emphatic *'ad lĕ'ôlām.*

111. Jenni, *THAT,* 2:239.

112. The nearest Hebrew equivalent to Gk. ἔσχατος, "last" (cf. G. Kittel, *TDNT,* 2:697-98), is *'aḥărît.* This word combines nuances of finality and newness, as evidenced by Jeremiah's characterization of the eschatological covenant as both "everlasting" (*bĕrît 'ôlām,* 32:40) and "new" (*bĕrît ḥădāšâ,* 31:31). See further K.-D. Schunck, "Die Eschatologie der Propheten des Alten Testaments und ihre Wandlung in exilisch-nachexilischer Zeit," in *Studies on Prophecy,* VTSup 26 (Leiden: Brill, 1974), p. 119; von Rad, *Old Testament Theology,* 2:112-19.

113. "Many days hence" (*mîyyāmîm rabbîm,* 38:8), "on that day" (*bayyôm hahû',* 38:10, 14, 18, 19; 39:11), "in the future years" (*bĕ'aḥărît haššānîm,* 38:8), "in the future days" (*bĕ'aḥărît hayyāmîm,* 38:16), "the coming day" (*bā'â hayôm,* 39:8), "the day when I manifest my glory" (*yôm hikkābĕdî,* 39:13), "from that day onward" (*min-hayyôm hahû',* 39:22).

expected to transpire at the end of history but because they are new and they are final — their effects are guaranteed to continue forever. The prophet's vision concerns not so much the consummation, the end of history, as its climax.

The present description of Israel's glorious hope breaks down on the basis of subjects of the verbs into three parts as follows:

(a) The Evidence of Israel's Renaissance (vv. 24b-25)
(b) The Source/Cause of Israel's Renaissance (vv. 26-27)
(c) The Impact of Israel's Renaissance (v. 28)

Here the discussion is elevated completely to the theological plane; no more hints, not even lexical, of the sign-action remain.

(a) The Evidence of Israel's Renaissance (37:24b-25)

24b This tablet opens with the prediction of three new realities for Israel. First, the nation will have a new commitment to the will of Yahweh, the divine patron. The triad of expressions, *follow my laws (hālak běmišpāṭay), observe my decrees (šāmar ḥuqqōtay),* and *put them into practice ('āśâ 'ôtām),* captures the essence of the response of faith to the privilege of being Yahweh's people (cf. 20:19). The phrases, all borrowed from the language of the original covenant itself,[114] have been heard before in the book. In 11:19-20 and 36:26-28, this response was identified as the goal and effect of the transplantation of Israel's heart of stone with a heart of flesh. In both, this new covenant loyalty is associated with a return to the hereditary homeland, and followed by Yahweh's reaffirmation of his covenant commitment. V. 24b represents a shorthand announcement of the inner transformation to be experienced by the Israelites, resolving forever the issue of the rebellion that had originally brought on their judgment and deportation (see 5:6-7). The restoration must begin here. Apart from obedience all claims to the land and to the special covenant relationship with Yahweh are vain.

25 Second, the Israelites will occupy their hereditary homeland forever. The land is identified *theologically* as the territory Yahweh gave originally to his servant Jacob. Echoing 28:25, this statement finds its antecedents in Gen. 28:13-15 and 35:9-15. Why Ezekiel should have associated the promise of land with Jacob rather than Abraham is not clear, especially since the Abrahamic versions highlight the eternality of this aspect of the patriarchal promises (Gen. 13:14-17; 17:1-8). However, it accords with his

114. See Lev. 26:3 (cf. vv. 24-25); Deut. 4:1, 5, 14, 40; 5:1, 31-33; 7:11-12; etc. Cf. Weinfeld, *Deuteronomy and the Deuteronomic School,* pp. 336-37.

general reluctance to name Abraham at all,[115] and with the fact that Jacob was the true eponymous ancestor of Israel; the national name was derived from him, and the tribal ancestors were his immediate sons. But the land is also defined *historically* as the same land the nation occupied in the past. Thus the people-land divorce effected by the exile will be reversed. The eternality of the new territorial hope is emphasized by repeating *they will occupy the land,* and identifying the beneficiaries of the promise as *they, their children, and their grandchildren* in perpetuity. Yahweh hereby commits himself never again to threaten the nation with exile.

Third, Israel will enjoy the rule of David, Yahweh's servant, forever. Shifting attention away from political reunification in the first panel, Ezekiel reverts to his preferred designation for Israel's kings, *nāśî', prince* (cf. vv. 22, 24a), and defines David's role spiritually as Yahweh's *servant* and *their* "prince," rather than politically as "king over them" (v. 24). The term *nāśî'* alludes to the prince's ties with the people and his function as regent under Yahweh, and prepares the way for chs. 40–48, where the person with this title functions primarily as religious leader. Just as Israel's title to the hereditary homeland is based on Yahweh's gift to "his servant" Jacob, so the pledge of a new ruler is based on his promise to another servant, David. The language obviously depends on 2 Sam. 7, where David is twice identified by Yahweh as *'abdî,* "my servant" (vv. 5, 8), and where he acknowledges this role no fewer than ten times.[116] This link is strengthened by the description of the new David's tenure as *forever ('ôlām),* a word that occurs eight times in 2 Sam. 7.[117] Yahweh's covenant with the dynasty may have been suspended, but it has not been forgotten. He hereby dismisses unequivocally the past conditionality of occupancy of the throne.[118] What happened to Zedekiah in 586 will never happen again.

115. In the only occurrence of the name in the book, it is on the lips of apostate Judeans (33:24).

116. See 2 Sam. 7:19, 20, 21, 25, 26, 27 (bis), 28, 29 (bis).

117. See 2 Sam. 7:13, 16 (bis), 24, 25, 26 — all *'ad 'ôlām;* 29 (bis), *lĕ'ôlām.* David expresses his consciousness of the eternality of this covenant in his charge to his subjects and to his son Solomon in 1 Chr. 28:4, 7, 8, 9.

118. D. Bloesch's description of the new covenant (Jer. 31:31-34; Ezek. 34:25) applies to the Davidic as well: "It is unconditional in that it proceeds out of the free grace and mercy of God, but its efficacy is contingent on faith and obedience" ("'All Israel Will Be Saved': Supersessionism and the Biblical Witness," *Int* 43 [1989] 132). While David recognized an element of contingency in his charge to Solomon (1 K. 2:4; cf. also Ps. 132:13 [Eng. 12]; cf. 1 Chr. 28:9), Yahweh's threat of discipline in 2 Sam. 7 does not suggest cancellation of title to the throne. Ps. 89:4-5, 29-38 (Eng. 3-4, 28-37) speak specifically of an eternal and irretractable covenant.

(b) The Source of Israel's Renaissance (37:26-27)

Now the attention returns to Yahweh, the source of Israel's renewal, who hereby promises to make a new (renewed) covenant with Israel. The declaration modifies the standard formula for covenant making with two significant if familiar qualifiers.[119] The first, *covenant of peace (běrît šālôm)*, derives from 34:25-31, where Ezekiel had expounded on the gloriously harmonious relations it effects among all parties in the deity-nation-land association. The second, *eternal covenant (běrît 'ôlām)*, stems from Lev. 26:4. This expression, which is found in other prophets as well,[120] speaks of both the chronological durability of Yahweh's commitment and its inviolability. The latter places the "covenant of peace" into the same category as other eternal covenants: Noachian (Gen. 9:12), Abrahamic (Gen. 17:7), Mosaic (Exod. 31:16; Lev. 24:8), Davidic.[121] Does Ezekiel envision a new covenant, or the renewal of one of these? If the latter is correct, which of these covenants is restored? Ezekiel provides his own clues to the answer.

First, the content of the covenant is defined by the familiar covenant formula, "I will be their God, and they will be my people."[122] Second, as a corollary to the covenant Yahweh *will give to them* [*the land of Israel*] *(ûnětattîm)*. Without an adverbial modifier *ûnětattîm* appears to be a truncated form of the land-grant formula, forms of which appear in connection with the Abrahamic and Mosaic covenants.[123] Significantly, in three of the four occurrences of the covenant formula in Ezekiel it is accompanied by Yahweh's promise to restore the nation-land tie.[124] Third, Yahweh will *multiply* the

119. On *kārat lāhem běrît*, lit. "I will cut for them a covenant," cf. above on 34:25. For discussion see Weinfeld, *TDOT*, 2:259-63.

120. See Isa. 24:5; 55:3; 61:8; Jer. 32:40; 50:5.

121. The Noachian is also referred to as the covenant of peace in Isa. 54:10, on which see Batto, *CBQ* 49 (1987) 190-92. The eternality of the Davidic covenant is repeatedly affirmed in 2 Sam. 7, though it is never technically designated a *běrît 'ôlām*.

122. This formula, taken from legal marriage terminology (cf. my *Ezekiel: Chapters 1–24*, pp. 354, 626) provides a unifying thread through the Abrahamic covenant (Gen. 17:7-8), the Mosaic covenant (Exod. 6:7; Lev. 26:12; Deut. 27:9; 29:11-12 [Eng. 12-13]; cf. Jer. 7:23; 11:4; 13:11), the future covenant with Israel (cf. 11:20; 14:11; 36:28; 37:23; Zech. 8:8), the Christian covenant (2 Cor. 6:16), and the final eschatological covenant made between God and his people in the context of the new heaven and the new earth (Rev. 21:3). The formula is replaced in the Davidic covenant with the adoption formula, "I shall be his father, and he will be my son" (2 Sam. 7:14; cf. Ps. 89:27-28 [Eng. 26-27]).

123. For the Abrahamic see Gen. 15:18; 17:8. For the Mosaic see Exod. 6:8; Deut. 27:2-3. Note the connection with the covenant formula in v. 9. A. E. Hill argues that Deut. 27:1-26 represents an adaptation of an official land grant ceremony ("The Ebal Ceremony as Hebrew Land Grant?" *JETS* 31 [1988] 399-406).

124. Ezek. 11:17 actually uses a version of the land grant formula; 36:28 declares

nation, an expression that alludes to the promise to Abraham to multiply his descendants as the stars of the sky, the grains of sand on the seashore, and the dust of the earth.[125] Fourth, Yahweh will establish his own *residence* in the midst of the nation. That this statement represents the climax of Ezekiel's vision of Israel's great new day is evident from: (1) the semipoetic parallelistic construction;[126] (2) the assurance of the promise's durability and irrevocability with the key word *ʿôlām*; (3) the repetition of the theme in the expanded recognition formula in v. 28; (4) the later resumption of this subject with the most detailed discussion in the entire book (chs. 40–48). Fifth, in a previous reference to the "everlasting covenant" (16:60-63), Yahweh had spoken of "remembering" *(zākar)* his covenant made with his people in their youth; this reference suggests a preexistent entity. Sixth, Ezekiel's vision of the restoration is always presented in terms of past realities and past experiences.[127] The original exodus from Egypt provides the paradigm for the new exodus from among the nations.

The terms of the covenant made at Sinai thus provide the background not only for Israel's judgment but also for the hope of restoration. Built into the original Mosaic covenant was the prospect that Yahweh would not forever reject his people. Indeed, the present complex of promises bears a striking resemblance to Lev. 26:1-13, a text that has figured often in Ezekiel's oracles. Here the prophet also anticipates nothing less than the fulfillment of Deut. 4:30. From the context of dispersion among the nations, the Israelites will learn that Yahweh, their God, is a compassionate God. He will neither fail them nor destroy them utterly. The basis of the nation's eternal hope is Yahweh's eternal, immutable covenant with the ancestors.

---

explicitly that the nation will live in the land which Yahweh granted to the ancestors; in 37:21-22 Yahweh had promised to bring the sons of Israel back to their own land, and making them one nation in it.

125. See Gen. 15:5; 22:17; 26:4; 28:14; 32:12 (also 17:2, 6). See Ezekiel's earlier use of this theme in 36:10-12 and 36:37.

126. Note the construction of vv. 26b-27a:

wĕnātattî ʾet-miqdāšî bĕtôkām lĕʿôlām
wĕhāyâ miškānî ʿălêhem

I shall place my sanctuary in their midst forever.
My residence will be over them.

127. This is also true of Jeremiah's "new covenant" (31:31-34), which is linked to the Mosaic by references to Yahweh's Torah and the covenant formula, and the elaboration on this covenant in 32:37-44, which refers specifically to restoring ancient deity-nation-land relationships. The same divine will will characterize both, but in the new the commitment will have been internalized by a specific act of Yahweh himself. The persons in whom the will of God is implanted are transformed in their natures so the covenant will never be broken.

Yahweh's residence is identified by two expressions, which reflect opposite dimensions of the divine character. *miqdāš*, Ezekiel's favorite designation for the *sanctuary* (5:11; 8:6; 9:6), from *qdš*, "to be holy," highlights the holiness of the residence and reflects the transcendent nature of the one who dwells within.[128] *miškān, residence,* from *šākan*, "to reside, dwell," occurs only here in the book with reference to the house of God (cf. 25:4, used of human dwellings). This expression reflects the immanence, the condescending presence, of God. In Exodus it is often associated with the *'ōhel mô'ēd*, "tent of appointments," which symbolized Yahweh's desire for regular contact with his people.[129] Ezekiel's combination of nouns and prepositions is paradoxical. The sanctuary is *in their midst,* among *(bĕtôk)* the people; the residence or dwelling place is *over ('al)* them. The latter may have been influenced by the image of the *kābôd* of Yahweh, which resided over *(šākan 'al)* the tent of meeting (Exod. 40:35). Like the promise of land, so the promise of the divine presence among his people is often associated with the ancient covenant formula (cf. Exod. 29:45-46). Ezekiel's statement expresses Yahweh's definitive rejection of any threat ever to abandon his people again, as he had in 586 B.C., and as was so graphically portrayed in the temple vision of chs. 8–11.

(c) The Impact of Israel's Renaissance (37:28)

The oracle concludes with an expanded form of the recognition formula, highlighting the effect of Israel's renewal on the nations among whom the Israelites are scattered. Ezekiel hereby reiterates that Yahweh's salvific activity on Israel's behalf is driven primarily not by pity for his people but by a concern for his reputation.[130] Of the four *'ōlām* gifts (renewed obedience, title to the land, Davidic rule, divine presence), the last is climactic. Yahweh's sanctuary in the midst of his people will finally convince the nations of his sanctifying power. The concluding statement answers to the two elements of the covenant formula. The presence of his sanctuary *(miqdāš)* in the midst of the people will be the ultimate demonstration of his commitment to them ("I will be your God"). His sanctification *(qiddēš)* of Israel will be the final proof of his election of them as his holy nation, consecrated to himself for his glory ("You will be my people"). This brief statement represents only the tip of the iceberg of Ezekiel's understanding of Yahweh's sanctuary among his people. Indeed,

---

128. See M. Haran, *Temples and Temple-Service in Ancient Israel: An Inquiry into Biblical Cult Phenomena and the Historical Setting of the Priestly School* (repr. Winona Lake, Ind.: Eisenbrauns, 1985), pp. 14-15.

129. Ibid., pp. 195-96.

130. Cf. above on 36:16-32.

the subject looms so large in his mind and ministry that it receives extended treatment in his final vision (chs. 40–48).

♦ *Theological Implications*

In bringing Ezekiel's restoration oracles to a climax, this prophecy collects numerous themes found in earlier pronouncements. The following represents a summary of the prophet's views on specific aspects of theology, ecclesiology, and messianism.

1. This oracle reinforces Ezekiel's exalted view of God. First, the designation of his renewed commitment to his people as *bĕrît 'ôlām,* "the eternal covenant," and the fivefold repetition of *'ôlām* symbolize Yahweh's fidelity to his word. Israel's hope for the future rests in his immutable covenants with the ancestors, the nation of Israel at Sinai, and his servant David in Jerusalem. The devastation of 586 had cast doubts in everyone's mind about his ability or willingness to act on his people's behalf. But his ancient pronouncement and his new promise guarantee the permanence and finality of Yahweh's eschatological work of grace.

Second, the designation of his renewed commitment as *bĕrît šālôm,* "covenant of peace," symbolizes the goal of Yahweh's salvific activity. This shalom represents much more than merely the absence of war. It denotes a state of harmony and equilibrium among all participants in the divine-human-territorial relationships. The renewal of covenant vows, the cleansing of the population, the restoration of the people to their hereditary homeland, and the establishment of his residence among his people are prerequisites and evidences of this peace.

Third, the concluding recognition formula reiterates that Yahweh's restoration of Israel is motivated above all by a concern for his reputation. So long as the Israelites remained in exile the nations would stumble over questions concerning his fidelity and competence to function as the divine patron of the nation. But his salvific actions demonstrate his grace and mercy toward his people. Although they have rebelled against him, he remains their patron. As in the days of old (Exod. 40), the climactic revelatory moment will occur when he takes up residence among them once again. This event will not transpire in the back corners of the desert, but in the sight of all the nations, that they may acknowledge his presence, action, and character.

2. This oracle reinforces Ezekiel's realistic view of God's people. God's people were formed by a divine act of grace. The Israelites had nothing to commend them for divine election when he rescued them from the bondage of Egypt, and they certainly have no merit now (cf. 36:31). On the contrary, throughout their history the nation has demonstrated its bent toward rebellion against the divine Lord, seduction to idolatry, and the disgusting practices of

the pagans. But in his grace God removes their defilement, delivers them from their apostasy, and cleanses them from their sin. What is more, by his own initiative he offers to be their God and calls them to be his people.

Especially significant for the Israelites was Yahweh's unequivocal declaration that all the descendants of Jacob were heirs of the covenant. Against the grain of centuries of history and deep-seated prejudices, Yahweh extends his grace to the whole house of Israel — not only Judah but Joseph and his confederates as well. He rescues them from sin as well as from their divisive past. By establishing his residence in the midst of the nation, all tribes enjoy equal access to the divine patron and participate in the benefactions that emanate from him.

3. This oracle reinforces Ezekiel's complex view of the Messiah.[131] In spite of the prophet's avoidance of specifically messianic designations, the messianic significance of this oracle is obvious.[132] The principal features of Ezekiel's Messiah are reflected in the titles and role designations he bears. As *David* he is heir to the eternal dynastic promises made by Yahweh through the prophet Samuel to Israel's greatest king.[133] As *'abdî,* "my servant," he enjoys a special relationship with Yahweh. In this fundamentally religious role, he derives his authority by divine appointment rather than by personal acumen or democratic election. As *naśî',* "prince, chieftain," he stands at the head of his people, not as a tyrannical ruler but as one who has been called from their ranks to represent them. As *melek* he is a royal figure, symbolizing the nation's new unity. All other pretenders to the throne have been dismissed that Israel may be "one nation" *(gôy 'eḥād)* under "one king" *(melek 'eḥād)* occupying the land of Israel. As *rô'eh 'eḥād,* "one shepherd," a title added by the prophet in v. 24 to remind his audience of the new dynastic disposition, he will seek the welfare of the flock, protecting and nurturing them after the pattern of Yahweh himself (ch. 34) and in fulfillment of the ancient Mosaic charter for kingship (Deut. 17:14-20).

In all these roles, Ezekiel's Messiah symbolizes the realities of the new age. Remarkably, he plays no part in the restoration of the nation. He neither gathers the people nor leads them back to their homeland. Furthermore, unlike other prophets, Ezekiel makes no mention of the Messiah as an agent of peace

---

131. For a fuller discussion of Ezekiel's vision of the Messiah, see D. I. Block, "Bringing Back David: Ezekiel's Messianic Hope," in *The Lord's Anointed: Interpretation of Old Testament Messianic Texts,* ed. P. E. Satterthwaite, et al. (Grand Rapids: Baker, 1995), pp. 167-88.

132. So also Targ., on which see S. H. Levey, *Ezekiel,* pp. 4-5; idem, *Messiah,* pp. 83-87.

133. See 2 Sam. 7. In this regard Ezekiel follows long-standing prophetic tradition: Amos 9:11; Hos. 3:5; Isa. 8:23–9:6 (Eng. 9:1-7); 11:1-5; Mic. 4:14–5:5 (Eng. 5:1-4); Jer. 23:5-6.

or righteousness.[134] These effects he attributes to the direct activity of God. But the Messiah's personal presence symbolizes the reign of Yahweh in the glorious new age.[135]

6. The Guarantee of Yahweh's Protection over Israel (38:1–39:29)

♦ Nature and Design

The boundaries of the Gog oracle are clearly defined. The word-event formula in 38:1, followed by Yahweh's direct address of the prophet and the command to set his face toward Gog and prophesy against him in v. 2, sets this text off from the preceding. The signatory formula in 39:29 forms an appropriate closing, a conclusion confirmed by 40:1, which commences a new visionary account with a date notice. The intervening text is presented as a single oracle describing first the invasion of the land of Israel by Gog and his hordes, and then Yahweh's utter annihilation of these forces. But this does not mean that the plot is smoothly developed, or that the literary style of the unit is consistent. In addition to frequent and abrupt shifts of focus, the plethora of disjunctive formulae creates the impression of a series of episodes often only loosely strung together.

   This text provides one of the most impressive examples of typically Ezekielian literary "halving," the panels consisting of 38:1-23 and 29:1-29.[1] The intentionality of this division is confirmed by a remarkable correspondence between the respective introductions to each part, as the following synopsis illustrates:

38:1-4aα	39:1-2aα
wayĕhî dĕbar yhwh ʾēlay lēʾmōr	
	wĕʾattâ
ben ʾādām	*ben ʾādām*
śîm pānêkā ʾel gôg ʾereṣ hammāgôg	
nĕśîʾ rōʾš mešek wĕtubāl	
wĕhinnābēʾ ʿālāyw wĕʾāmartā	*hinnābēʾ ʿāl gôg wĕʾāmartā*

---

134. For peace see Isa. 9:5-6 (Eng. 9:6-7); 11:6-9; Mic. 5:5; Jer. 23:6; Zech. 9:9-10. For righteousness see Isa. 5–6; 11:2-5; Jer. 23:5-6. On the relationship of Ezekiel's Messiah with other biblical portraits see A. Moenikes, "Messianismus im Alten Testament (vorapokalyptische Zeit)," *ZRGG* 40 (1988) 289-306.

135. For a critique of Laato's forced thesis that the model of kingship of Ezekiel's new David derives from the royal ideology prevailing in Josiah's time (*Josiah and David Redivivus,* pp. 177-89), see J. Becker's review in *Bib* 75 (1994) 250-55.

1. Panel A (38:2-23) consists of 365 words; panel B (39:1-29) 357 words.

kōh 'āmar 'ădōnāy yhwh
hinĕnî 'ēlêkā gôg
nĕśî'
rō'š mešek ûtubāl
wĕšôbabtîkā

The following message of Yahweh
came to me.

"Human,
set your face toward Gog,
of the land of the Magog,
the prince,
chief of Meshech and Tubal.
Prophesy against him and say:
'Thus has the Lord Yahweh declared:
Look! I am against you, O Gog,
prince,
chief of Meshech and Tubal,
I will turn you around. . . .' "

kōh 'āmar 'ădōnāy yhwh
hinĕnî 'ēlêkā gôg
nĕśî'
rō'š mešek ûtubāl
wĕšôbabtîkā

"As for you,
human,

prophesy against Gog and say:
'Thus has the Lord Yahweh declared,
Look! I am against you, O Gog,
prince,
chief of Meshech and Tubal,
I will turn you around. . . .' "

The opening word-event formula serves as a general heading for both chapters, but the echo strategy thereafter suggests that chs. 38 and 39 function as a diptych, two leaves of a single document. However, each of these leaves is broken down further by a series of rhetorical formulae, most of which highlight this text as divine speech or emphasize the divine objective in the proclamation and the event: (1) new charges to the prophet to speak, which subdivide each of the major panels into two subsections;[2] (2) the citation formula (38:3, 14; 39:1, 17); (3) the signatory formula;[3] (4) variations of the recognition formula;[4] (5) the logical particle *lākēn*, "Therefore" (38:14; 39:25); (6) time notices.[5] Combined with dramatic shifts in content, and sometimes in style, these features create the impression of an extremely complex oracle.

2. Ezek. 38:14; 39:17, yielding the following subsections: A[1] 38:2-13; A[2] 38:14-23; B[1] 39:1-16; B[2] 39:17-29.

3. Three of the eight occurrences signal the conclusion of a paragraph (39:10, 20, 29); the remainder appear within segments and function more as rhetorical punctuation marks than as literary dividers (38:18, 21; 39:5, 8, 13).

4. Only two of the six occurrences signal the conclusions of paragraphs, 38:16 (cf. the following citation formula) and 38:23 (the end of panel A). The remainder are incorporated into the divine speeches (39:6, 7, 22, 28).

5. *wĕhāyâ bayyôm hahû'*, "and it will happen in that day," 38:18; 39:11. *mîyyāmîm rabbîm*, "after many days," and *bĕ'ăhărît haššānîm*, "in the latter years," in 38:8 are chronological markers.

425

In the past, scholarly investigation of the Gog oracle has exploited the disjunctions in the text to recapture its literary evolution.[6] But disenchantment with this basic methodology has been growing in recent years, and many are adopting a more holistic approach.[7] M. S. Odell, who offers a comprehensive treatment of chs. 38–39 as a coherent whole, criticizes previous form critics' work on two counts. First, they have severed the Gog oracle from the rest of the book of Ezekiel, often interpreting it as a postexilic modification of the prophet's restoration oracles. Second, they have artificially and arbitrarily divorced prophecy, which represents a response to historical events, and theological reflection on prophecy, which is supposedly less tied to events; this divorce results in an inadequate interpretation of the final form of the text.[8] Odell offers a welcome alternative that respects the historical context out of which it has arisen,[9] the position of this oracle within the context of Ezekiel's salvation oracles, viz., chs. 34–37, and the final form of the text itself.

A holistic approach does not demand that the present literary shape of the Gog oracle reflects the original oral presentation by the prophet. Further

6. Often these studies end by identifying an Ezekielian core and attributing the rest to a series of interpretive additions (*Nachinterpretation*) by the "School of Ezekiel." Zimmerli's (*Ezekiel 2*, pp. 296-99) reduction of the basic text to 38:1-9 (minus significant glosses), 39:1-5, 17-20, is more generous than some, but he ascribes the remainder to a series of interpretive expansions, each addition commenting on the preexistent text. For evaluations of Zimmerli's treatment of these chapters see Scalise, *From Prophet's Word to Prophetic Book*, pp. 114-34; M. S. Odell, " 'Are You He of Whom I Spoke by My Servants the Prophets?' Ezekiel 38–39 and the Problem of History in the Neobabylonian Context" (Ph.D. diss., University of Pittsburgh, 1988), pp. 1-42. Hossfeld (*Untersuchungen*, pp. 402-508) limits the original core to 38:1-3a and 39:1b-5, the rest representing six stages of expansion: (1) 38:3b-9; (2) 39:17-20; (3) 38:10-16; 39:6-7, 21-22; (4) 38:17; 39:8-10; (5) 38:18-23; 39:11-13 (14-16?); (6) 39:23-29.

7. M. C. Astour admits that the oracle contains doublets and glosses that betray subsequent elaboration, but he argues that "the style and imagery of its basic parts are not different from those of the chapters which are generally accepted as genuine writings of Ezekiel" ("Ezekiel's Prophecy of Gog and the Cuthean Legend of Naram-Sin," *JBL* 95 [1976] 567). Hals (*Ezekiel*, p. 285) comments, "The efforts of Zimmerli and Hossfeld here are welcome as speculative attempts of considerable heuristic value in enabling the discovery of even further complexities, but they are not at all convincing as actual literary reconstructions." Klein (*Ezekiel*, p. 158) maintains that these chapters antedate 539, and if such an early date can be accepted for all or part of the oracle, then the possibility remains that the prophet himself is responsible for the text. Contrast the approach of R. Ahroni ("The Gog Prophecy and the Book of Ezekiel," *HAR* 1 [1977] 1-27), who, while defending the unity of the oracle, particularly 38:1–39:24, argues for a late, postexilic date, hence a late intrusion into the book of Ezekiel.

8. Note Odell's conclusions, "Ezekiel 38–39," pp. 181-85.

9. She views the context as the failure of the restoration of Israel after Nebuchadrezzar's execution of judgment on Yahweh's enemies (cf. 28:25-26; 29:21).

reflection may well have led to secondary additions.[10] But this does not mean that we dismiss them as inauthentic or non-Ezekielian. To deny segments (e.g., 38:18-23) to the prophet because they are not structured as a direct address to Gog, or because they abandon the focus on Yahweh's conflict with Gog in favor of a more cosmic, even apocalyptic, perspective, is highly subjective, forcing ancient writers to conform to modern standards of style and plot. As Klein has shown, even these verses make excellent sense within the present context, providing a third reason for the defeat of Gog, viz., the wrath of Yahweh.[11]

Scholars continue to dispute the genre of the Gog pericope. Ever since F. Hitzig first applied the term "apocalyptic" to the prophecies of Ezekiel,[12] it has been fashionable to interpret the Gog oracle as an example of this genre. Technically, the notion of "apocalyptic" has less to do with the form of a text than with its content and style. According to Hitzig, the distinguishing features of apocalyptic texts were a heightened use of symbol and imagery, and visionary experiences by the prophet/apocalypticist. Accordingly, from "the scale of the events, the vague outlines, the loosely-strung sequence of ideas," along with the nature of the language, Cooke concluded that chs. 38–39 were apocalyptic, rising from unfulfilled prophecy.[13] More recently Ahroni has opined that its "totally unrealistic and imaginative" style, along with its hyperbole and fantasy, contrasts sharply with the historical roots and the realism of the rest of the book. Furthermore, the cosmic dualism, represented by the conflict between Yahweh and Gog, the obscurities, the symbolic language, the prominence of the number seven, and the enigmatic nature of the names of peoples all point to an apocalyptic genre, and the references to previous prophecy (38:17) and the expression "the navel of the earth" (38:12) give supporting evidence for a late date.[14]

Although scholars continue to recognize apocalyptic features in the Gog oracle, they are increasingly reluctant to place it within this genre. It certainly does not fit the standard definition of "apocalyptic" offered by J. J. Collins:

> "Apocalypse" is a genre of revelatory literature with a narrative framework, in which a revelation is mediated by an otherworldly being to a

---

10. Ezek. 39:25-29 looks like it was composed to integrate the oracle with its present context within the book.

11. Klein, *Ezekiel,* p. 161.

12. F. Hitzig, *Der Prophet Ezechiel,* KeH 8 (Leipzig: Weidmann'sche Buchhandlung, 1847), pp. xiv-xv.

13. Cooke, *Ezekiel,* p. 407.

14. Ahroni, *HAR* 1 (1977) 11-18, esp. 11-13. Becker (*Künder des Wortes,* pp. 137-49) interprets the entire book of Ezekiel as a late pseudonymous apocalyptic work.

human recipient, disclosing a transcendent reality which is both temporal, insofar as it envisages eschatological salvation, and spatial insofar as it involves another, supernatural world.[15]

Collins's preceding paradigm of apocalyptic characteristics demonstrates the weakness of the links between Ezek. 38–39 and other apocalyptic writings.[16] Not only is none of the revelatory features of apocalyptic present;[17] many substantive and stylistic characteristics shared with true apocalypses are common in ordinary prophecies: conflict between Yahweh and the enemies of Israel, the deliverance of his people, Yahweh's sovereignty over the universe. Furthermore, the claim that this text transcends temporal structures and is divorced from a real historical situation derives from inadequate attention to the social environment from which the prophecy derives and to which it speaks.[18] Expressions like "after many days/years" (38:8) and "in that day" (38:18; 39:11) thrust some of the developments in this prophecy into the distant future, and 38:18-23 introduces the notion of a cosmic shaking, but neither serves as a precursor to an ultimate eschatological salvation or a true consummation.[19] The focus remains on Israel's own salvation, which, like Ezekiel's previous restoration oracles, results in the vindication of Yahweh's holiness and the nation's recognition of him. At issue is the local problem: Gog and his hordes invading the land of Israel. The name Gog and the dominance of the number seven may be symbolic, but this is a far cry from the elaborate symbolism of Daniel or of the NT book of Revelation. On these bases, the apocalyptic approach to the Gog oracle should be abandoned.

Some have interpreted the Gog oracle along the lines of Ezekiel's

---

15. J. J. Collins, "Towards the Morphology of a Genre," in *Apocalypse: The Morphology of a Genre*, ed. Collins, Semeia 14 (Missoula, Mont.: Scholars Press, 1979), p. 9. According to P. D. Hanson (*IDBSup*, p. 27; cf. idem, *The Dawn of Apocalyptic* [Philadelphia: Fortress, 1975], for a fuller study), apocalyptic involves a revelation given by God through a mediator (usually an angel, but cf. Jesus Christ in Rev. 1:1-2) to a seer concerning future events, expressed in terms either of a cosmic drama or elaborate symbolism. Cf. also D. S. Russell, *Method and Message,* esp. pp. 104-39; L. Morris, *Apocalyptic* (Grand Rapids: Eerdmans, 1972); G. E. Ladd, "Apocalyptic," *ISBE,* 1:151-61.

16. Collins, *Apocalypse,* pp. 5-9. See his fuller discussion of apocalyptic texts in ibid., "The Jewish Apocalyses," pp. 21-59.

17. Ibid., p. 28.

18. One of the primary criticisms leveled by Odell ("Ezekiel 39-39," pp. 43-60) at many contemporary approaches.

19. So also Hals, *Ezekiel,* p. 284, contra B. S. Childs ("The Enemy from the North and the Chaos Tradition," *JBL* 78 [1959] 187-98) and B. F. Batto (*Slaying the Dragon: Mythmaking in the Biblical Tradition* [Louisville: Westminster/John Knox, 1992], pp. 157-62). The latter characterizes the Gog oracle as "proto-apocalyptic," a metahistorical portrayal of the cosmic conflict between Yahweh and chaos, symbolized by Gog.

oracles against foreign nations in chs. 25–32. Having isolated 38:1-3a and 39:1b-5 as the original *Grundtext,* Hossfeld recognizes a structure similar to that of the first oracle against Egypt (29:1-6 +) and Seir (35:1-4),[20] and dates the prophecy prior to the oracles of ch. 32, which were delivered in 587-586 B.C.[21] However, this interpretation is problematic for several reasons. First, the methodology disregards the final shape of the text. Even if one could demonstrate that 38:1-3a, 39:1b-5 represent the basic text, the meaning of the oracle is determined by its present literary context, not by some hypothetical

20. Using my structure and translation, Hossfeld's text breaks down like this (*Untersuchungen,* pp. 494-501):

Introduction (38:1-3a)

Word-Event Formula	The following message of Yahweh came to me:
Address of the Prophet	Human,
Hostile Orientation Formula	Set your face toward Gog, prince of Meshech and Tubal,
Commissioning Formula	Prophesy against him and say,
Citation Formula	Thus has the Lord Yahweh declared:

The Message (39:1b-5a)

Challenge Formula	Look, I am against you, O Gog, prince of Meshech and Tubal!
Announcement	I shall turn you around, drive you on, lead you up from the remotest parts of the north, bring you to the mountains of Israel, only to strike your bow from your left hand, and knock your arrows out of your right hand. On the mountains of Israel you will fall — you and all your hordes, and the peoples accompanying you — I will hand you over as food to every kind of scavenging bird and wild animal. On the open field you will fall —

Conclusion (39:5b)

Conclusion of Divine Speech Formula	For I have spoken,
Signatory Formula	— the declaration of the Lord Yahweh.

21. M. Nobile argues that the redactor of ch. 32 had the Gog oracle in front of him, and that the Gog pericope appeared as the continuation and climax of the oracles against the foreign nations ("Beziehung zwischen Ez 32,17-32 und der Gog-Perikope [Ez 38–39] im Lichte der Endredaktion," in *Ezekiel and His Book,* pp. 255-59). In fact, the Gog oracle radicalizes the conflict between Yahweh and the nations. But it was separated from the oracles against the nations because its fulfillment lies in the more remote future. Its placement before the temple vision (chs. 40–48) was determined by literary-liturgical considerations. The new temple cannot be described without first accounting for the basis of its construction, viz., Yahweh's final victory over the cosmic forces of chaos (represented by the nations).

reconstruction. Second, assuming that the basic oracle antedates ch. 32 creates a major chronological problem. Since ch. 32 announces the demise of Meshech and Tubal, it is unlikely they could have risen to greatness so quickly after the defeat announced here.[22] Third, although the form and structure of the *Grundtext* bear some resemblance to 32:1-6 + and 35:1-4, the pronouncements in 25:1–26:6 show that the basic structure of Ezekiel's oracles against the foreign nations follows that of typical judgment speeches: accusation (introduced by *ya'an,* "because"), followed by the announcement of judgment (introduced with *lākēn,* "therefore").[23] Fourth, an oracle against an enigmatic entity like Gog would be out of place in the context of the rest of the prophecies against the foreign nations, all of whom are Israel's immediate neighbors, and whose own history had touched Israel's at many points. This has never been true of any nation called Gog. Fifth, it fails to respect the editor's evaluation of the Gog prophecy as a salvation oracle, evidenced by his placement of this text.

The form critics' identification of the basic text may indeed be correct, but the prophet himself could have been responsible for the expansions. Since Gog and his forces represent foreign nations in opposition to Yahweh, it is not surprising that this text should bear some, if not many, resemblances to the former. But the differences in the final products are so pervasive that it is unwise to force the present oracle into that grid. The literary unit is not only much longer than any of these but also much more complex.

In its broad outline the oracle proper (38:1–39:20) displays some features of a judgment speech, especially the description of an action deemed worthy of punishment and the divine response. But its complexity of style and content precludes formal classification on the basis of structure alone. The most obvious clue concerning its genre and intention may be found in the sevenfold occurrence of the recognition formula,[24] which represents a denser concentration than anywhere else in the book. In the mind of the compiler of Ezekiel's prophecies, his pronouncements have apparently reached their climax. Only two of these formulae occur in their simplest form (38:23; 39:6). The remainder vary greatly from the simple modification of Yahweh with "the Holy One in Israel" in 39:7 to the elaborate additions in 39:23 and 39:28. The subject of the verb shifts in the course of the oracle, from the nations in the first four and the sixth, to Israel in the fifth and seventh. Significantly, nowhere is the divine aim declared to be Gog's acknowledgment

22. Noted by Odell, "Ezekiel 38–39," p. 37.

23. See the discussion above on 25:1–26:6. But this evidence is neutralized by the premature termination of the oracle at v. 4.

24. See 38:16, 23; 39:6, 7, 22, 23, 28. For a fuller discussion of these see Odell ("Ezekiel 38–39," pp. 126-63), who dubiously includes 39:24.

of Yahweh, which highlights his role as agent through whom Yahweh achieves his goal, rather than the primary concern of his activity.

All in all, the Gog pericope consists of a series of fragmentary proof sayings that, when brought together in this fashion, result in a single powerful proof oracle. Above all else, this complex divine speech expresses Yahweh's determination once and for all to reveal to the nations his holiness, and to his own people his covenant loyalty. Both notions had appeared in an earlier fragment of theological reflection at the end of the oracle against Tyre (28:25-26). Indeed, since so many of the ideas raised there will be resumed and expanded here,[25] the Gog pericope appears to offer another example of typically Ezekielian resumptive exposition. Whereas the earlier text had referred to the objects of Yahweh's judgment vaguely as *kol haššā'tîm 'ōtām missĕbîbôtām,* "all who scorn them [viz., Israel] round about," these are now identified specifically as Gog and his allies. The offense, expressed by the verb *šā'aṭ,* "to scorn," is now described in detail as showing contempt for Israel dwelling at peace within her own land, and taking advantage of her defenseless state to satisfy their greed (38:10-14). But as exposition, the Gog oracle is not slavishly bound to the antecedent fragment. Nor does it offer a phrase-by-phrase commentary or adhere to Western canons of logic and progression. The demand for the latter in particular has led astray many interpreters, who, by dissecting the text into a series of fragments, rob the oracle of its force.

For sheer vividness, imagery, and hyperbole, this oracle has few equals, which cautions against overliteralism in interpretation. One may best appreciate the intention of this text by approaching it as a satirical literary cartoon strip consisting of eight frames. As the unit progresses the images become increasingly caricatured, climaxing in a bizarre picture of predatory birds and wild animals seated around a table, gorging themselves on human flesh (39:17-20). Following the opening formulae, the sequence of events reflected in the frames may be outlined as follows:

Panel A: The Defeat of Gog	(38:2c-23)
Frame 1: The Conscription of Gog	(38:2c-9)
Frame 2: The Motives of Gog	(38:10-13)
Frame 3: The Advance of Gog	(38:14-16)
Frame 4: The Judgment of Gog	(38:17-22)
Interpretive Conclusion	(38:23)

---

25. The regathering of the nation (*qibbēṣ;* cf. 38:8); the manifestation of Yahweh's holiness (*niqdaš,* cf. 38:16; 39:7, 25, 27); "in the sight of the nations" (cf. 38:16); Israel living securely in the land (*yāšab lābeṭaḥ;* cf. 38:8, 11; 39:26); Yahweh executing judgments (*'āśâ šĕpāṭîm,* 28:26; *'āśâ mišpāṭîm,* 39:21); Israel recognizing Yahweh as their God (cf. 39:21, 28).

As will be seen in the commentary, many of these frames subdivide further on stylistic and substantive grounds into separate subsections. While each subunit has an identity and character of its own, the subunits are thoroughly integrated to create a sequence of events whose total impact is much greater than the sum of its parts.

a. Preamble (38:1-2b)

> 1 *The following message of Yahweh came to me:*[26] 2 *"Human, set your face toward Gog, of the land of Magog,*[27] *the prince, chief of Meshech and Tubal."*[28]

The Gog oracle opens in customary Ezekielian fashion with the word-event formula, followed by the direct address of the prophet as *ben-'ādām*, "Human," and an order to the prophet to orient himself toward Gog.[29] The hypothetical audience is identified enigmatically as *Gog, of the land of Magog*. Since this person is never mentioned elsewhere in the OT, we are dependent entirely on this oracle for his identity.[30]

---

26. Syr. introduces the oracle with a superscription: "Against those of the house of Gog and Magog who came up against those who had come back from Babylon."

27. Vulg. and Targ. follow MT, but LXX and Syr. add the copula, suggesting Magog was treated as a name of a people. Magog occurs with the article only here (cf. 39:6; Gen. 10:2; 1 Chr. 1:5), perhaps representing an error in word division. Cooke (*Ezekiel*, p. 415) and Zimmerli (*Ezekiel 2*, p. 284) read *'arṣâ hammāgôg*, with *hē-* directive. Cf. Ezek. 21:2, where *śîm pānêkā*, "Set your face," is followed by *derek têmānâ*, "in the direction of Teman." But most treat the phrase as a gloss. Cf. Allen, *Ezekiel 20–48*, p. 199. It is omitted in LXX[62], probably a case of homoioteleuton.

28. The versions are inconsistent in their renderings of *nĕśî' rō'š mešek wĕtubāl*. LXX Ρως treats *rō'š* as a proper name. Targ. apparently follows MT's pointing as an extended construct chain with two genitives. Syr. understands the first two terms as a coordinate pair. Vulg. *principem capitis* sees in *rō'š* an intensification of the title *nāśî'*. Many delete *nĕśî'* as a secondary interpretation of *rō'š*, though the present construction recurs in v. 3 and 39:2. For further discussion see the commentary.

29. This is the last of six occurrences of the hostile orientation formula. Cf. 6:2; 13:17; 21:7; 25:2; 28:21.

30. Cf. the Reubenite Gog named in 1 Chr. 5:4. But LXX reads Γωγ for Agag in Num. 24:7; for Og in Deut. 3:1, 13; 4:47 (all LXX[B*]); for *gzy*, "locust," in Amos 7:1.

If there is no consensus on the interpretation of the name *Gog,* it is not for lack of effort.[31] The most likely explanation derives Gog from Gyges, the name of the king of Lydia, mentioned in six inscriptions of Ashurbanipal (668-631 B.C.), and known for his invention of coinage.[32] Since the 7th-century dates of Gyges preclude an actual identification with Gog, some treat Gog/Gyges as a dynastic name, applying it to his great grandson, Alyattes, under whom Lydia had once again become the dominant power in western Anatolia.[33] While this interpretation has the advantage of identifying the historical background of the Gog oracle with known events during Ezekiel's lifetime, there is no hint that Lydia ever posed a real threat to Judah. Nor did the prophet envision any miraculous deliverance from the northern invader. Indeed, at this time he consistently identified Babylon as his nation's only threat and held out no hope at all for deliverance.[34]

Gog's homeland is identified simply as *the land of Magog.* The name, which recurs in 39:6, though apparently as the name of a people, is found elsewhere in the OT only in Gen. 10:2 and its parallel 1 Chr. 1:5, where Magog is identified as the second son of Japheth, alongside Gomer, Madai, Javan, Tubal, Meshech, and Tiras. LXX adheres to this personal interpretation in the present context as well, preparing the way for later writings in which Gog and Magog become a fixed pair of names of persons involved in the final

31. Proposed explanations include: (1) a mythological "locust giant," analogous to the scorpion man in the Gilgamesh Epic (*ANET,* p. 88); cf. Amos 7:1, which LXX read as *gzy,* "locust" (H. Gressmann, *Der Messias,* FRLANT 6 [Göttingen: Vandenhoeck & Ruprecht, 1929], p. 129 n. 1); (2) a personification of darkness; cf. Sum. *gûg,* "darkness" (P. Heinisch, *Das Buch Ezechiel übersetzt und erklärt,* HSAT 8 [Bonn: Hanstein, 1923], p. 183); (3) *Gaga,* a name that appears in Amarna Letter 1:36-40, alongside Hanigalbat and Ugarit (W. F. Albright, "Gog and Magog," *JBL* 43 [1924] 381-82); (4) Gaga, a deity mentioned in the Ugaritic sources (cf. K. H. Cuffey, *ABD,* 2:1056).

32. On his legendary reputation see Herodotus, *Hist.* 1.8-13. See M. Cogan and H. Tadmor, "Gyges and Ashurbanipal: A Study in Literary Transmission," *Or* 46 (1977) 65 n. 1. The most important reference is in *ARAB,* 2:351-52, §§909-10. I am grateful to Alan R. Millard for reminding me that the name *Gugu* has been identified on a sixth-century-B.C. ashlar inscription found at Bin Tepe, thought to be the mound of Gyges in the heart of ancient Lydia. See D. G. Mitten, "The Synagogue and the 'Byzantine Shops,'" BASOR 177 (1965) 34-35; M. J. Mellink, "Archaeology in Asia Minor," *AJA* 69 (1965) 148 and plate 38, fig. 11.

33. J. L. Myres suggested that this oracle was prompted by the "Battle of the Eclipse" between Lydia and Media in 585 B.C. ("Gog and the Danger from the North in Ezekiel," *PEFQS* 64 [1932] 213-19). Cf. more recently, I. M. Diakonoff, *Predystorija armjanskogo naroda [Protohistory of the Armenian People]* (Erevan: AN Armjanskoj SSR, 1968), p. 179 (as cited by Astour, *JBL* 95 [1976] 569-70).

34. See the critique of Diakonoff by Astour, *JBL* 95 (1976) 571-72. For a critique of Astour's thesis that this oracle was inspired by the legend of Naram-Sin see Longman, *Fictional Akkadian Autobiography,* pp. 125-26.

eschatological battle.[35] Like the location of Gog itself, that of Magog is uncertain. Although both names may turn out to be artificial creations,[36] it seems best to interpret Magog as a contraction of an original *māt Gūgi*, "land of Gog,"[37] and to see here a reference to the territory of Lydia in western Anatolia.[38]

Verse 2b appears to place Gog at the head of Meshech and Tubal, though the syntax of *něśî' rō'š mešek wětubāl* is problematic. The issue revolves around whether *rō'š* is the name of an ethnic group or a common noun. Both LXX ἄρχοντα Ρως and the construct pointing of the Masoretes argue for the former.[39] But who then is this Rosh? The popular identification of Rosh with Russia is impossibly anachronistic and based on a faulty etymology, the assonantal similarities between Russia and Rosh being purely accidental.[40] In the 19th century some scholars associated Rosh with *Rûs*, a

35. Rev. 20:8; *Sib. Or.* 3:319-20, 512; a fragment of Targ. Pseudo-Jonathan to the Pentateuch on Num. 11:26 (cf. Levey, *Messiah,* pp. 105-7); 5th-century *3 Enoch* 45:5. On the treatment of Gog and Magog in later Jewish and Christian tradition see below.

36. Many have seen in the names a cipher for Babylon: Ewald, *Commentary on the Prophets,* pp. 192-93; Cooke, *Ezekiel,* p. 480. J. Boehmer ("Wer ist Gog von Magog? Ein Beitrag zur Auslegung des Buches Ezechiel," *ZWT* 40 [1897] 321-55) saw in *mgg* a cryptogram for Babylon, a reverse kind of "athbash" (cf. Jeremiah's *ššk,* "Sheshach" [25:26; 51:41], which, by replacing the first letter of the alphabet with the last, the second with the penultimate letter, etc., yields *bbl*). Ezekiel's method is more complex. Replacing each letter in *bbl* by its successor yields *ggm,* which, when reversed, produces *mgg.* Unfortunately, like all interpretations that see in the Gog oracle a message directed at Babylon, this understanding flies in the face of Ezekiel's consistent perception of the Babylonians as agents, not enemies, of God.

37. So Astour, *JBL* 95 (1976) 569; Yamauchi, *Foes,* p. 23.

38. Josephus (*Ant.* 1.6.1, §123, followed by Gressmann, *Messias,* pp. 123-24) identified Magog with the Scythians: "Magog founded the Magogians, thus named after him, but who by the Greeks are called Scythians." A. van den Born assumes a scribal error for *'rṣ hmg',* an ancient abbreviation for *'rṣ hmgdn,* "the land of the Macedonian," from which he deduces Gog to be a pseudonym for Alexander the Great ("Études sur quelques toponyms bibliques," *OTS* 10 [1954] 197-201; idem, *Ezechiël,* p. 223). The name has no geographic or ethnographic analogues in ancient Near Eastern literature, though Albright (*JBL* 43 [1924] 383) proposed a blend with Manda, an abbreviation of Umman Manda, the common Mesopotamian designation for "barbarian."

39. So REB, JB, NASB, "the prince of Rosh, Meshech, and Tubal." For a recent defense of this rendering see J. D. Price, "Rosh: An Ancient Land Known to Ezekiel," *GTJ* 6 (1985) 67-89.

40. The name Russia, of northern Viking derivation, was first used for the region of the Ukraine in the Middle Ages. See Yamauchi, *Foes,* pp. 20-21. Cf. the note in the Scofield Reference Bible, ad loc.: "That the primary reference is to the northern European powers, headed up by Russia, all agree." H. Lindsey (*Late Great Planet,* p. 54) comments, "Long before Russia rose to its present state of power [men] foresaw its role in history." In a later work Lindsey interpreted Ezek. 38:5 as a prediction of an imminent Russian

Scythian tribe inhabiting the northern Taurus Mountains,[41] according to Byzantine and Arabic writings. Recent attempts to equate Rosh with Râshu/Rêshu/Arashi in neo-Assyrian annals are more credible,[42] except that the place so named was located far to the east on the border between Babylon and Elam, and would have had nothing to do with Meshech and Tubal.[43] This interpretation is also difficult (though not impossible) from a grammatical point of view. If Rosh is to be read as the first in a series of names, the conjunction should precede "Meshech."[44] *rōʾš* is therefore best understood as a common noun, appositional to and offering a closer definition of *nāśîʾ*.[45] Accordingly, *the prince, chief of Meshech and Tubal,* combines Ezekiel's preferred title for kings with a hierarchical designation, the addition serving to clarify the preceding archaic term.[46] Ezekiel's point is that Gog is not just one of many Anatolian princely figures, but the leader among princes and over several tribal/national groups.

Gog's confederates are identified as *Meshech and Tubal.* These names have appeared earlier in the trade list of Tyre (27:13, in reverse order) and among the slain in Sheol (32:26). Both Meshech (Musku/Mušku) and Tubal (Tabal) are well attested in neo-Assyrian sources. Ancient records affirm the former's contacts with Assyria as early as the 12th-11th century B.C. During Sargon II's reign Meshech (Mushki) was ruled by King Mitas

---

invasion of Persia (idem, *The 1980's: Countdown to Armageddon* [New York: Bantam Books, 1980], pp. 67-68). See also J. Van Impe and R. F. Campbell, *Israel's Final Holocaust* (Nashville: Nelson, 1979), pp. 130-39.

41. Keil, *Ezekiel,* pp. 159-60; C. von Orelli, "Gog und Magog," in *Realencyklopädie für protestantische Theologie und Kirche,* 3rd ed. (Leipzig: Hinrichs, 1896-1913), 6:761-63C.

42. J. D. Price, "Rosh: An Ancient Land Known to Ezekiel," *GTJ* 6 (1985) 69-73. His appeal to Ugaritic references to the Reshites is less convincing.

43. So also Astour, *JBL* 95 (1976) 567 n. 4. For a catalogue of references to these names see Parpola, *Neo-Assyrian Toponyms,* pp. 23-24.

44. Simons, *Geographical Texts,* p. 81.

45. Cf. Alexander, "Ezekiel," p. 930. The MT evidence is ambivalent. Although *nĕśîʾ* is vocalized as a construct linked to the following word, the accent mark is a strongly disjunctive *zāqēp magnum,* while *rōʾš* has a conjunctive accent *(mâjĕlā)* tying it to the following Meshech.

46. E. A. Speiser translates Ezekiel's phrase "*nāśîʾ*-in-chief" ("Background and Function of the Biblical *nāśîʾ*," *CBQ* 25 [1963] 113). The common deletion of *nśyʾ* as a secondary clarification of *rōʾš* is ill advised, esp. since the present form recurs in v. 3 and 39:1. Furthermore, it is inconceivable that a common term like *rōʾš* would have been glossed with an archaic expression (contra Cooke, *Ezekiel,* p. 415; Wevers, *Ezekiel,* p. 287). Cf. Hossfeld, *Untersuchungen,* p. 434. The construction is similar to "Pharaoh, the king of Egypt," in 29:2-3; 30:21-22; 31:2; 32:2. Note also the variations in the designation of the chief priest in Israel as *kōhēn hārōʾš* (2 K. 25:18; 2 Chr. 19:11), *hakkōhēn hārōʾš* (Ezra 7:5), and *hakkōhēn rōʾš* (1 Chr. 27:5; 2 Chr. 31:10).

of Phrygia.[47] The present association of Meshech with Gog is supported by Ps. 120:5-7, which portrays the former as a barbaric enemy. According to Herodotus, later Meshech was part of Darius's nineteenth satrapy.[48] Tubal/Tabal was the territorial designation of the interior Anatolian kingdom known to the Assyrians as Bit Buritash. This landlocked kingdom was bounded on the west by Meshech, on the south by Hilakku, on the east by Melidu and Til-garimmu (Beth-Togarmah), and on the north by Kasku. While we have no evidence that Lydia/Phrygia ever ruled over Tubal, Sargon II's annals report that he squelched an Anatolian revolt in which Mitâ of Mushki (probably Mitas of Phrygia) was allied with Tabalu.[49]

The order of Ezekiel's triad of names reflects an awareness of geographic and recent political realities in Anatolia. Gog (Lydia), situated farthest west, is at the head of an alliance with Meshech on her eastern border, and Tubal east of Meshech. Why the prophet's gaze should have focused on these particular nations is unclear. Informed citizens of Judah were probably aware of the existence of these peoples in the far north, but their knowledge of them must have been based on second- and thirdhand reports. Perhaps the fame of Gyges and Midas had spread as far as Jerusalem, and if not to Jerusalem, then certainly to Babylon, whose imperial tentacles reached out into the Anatolian heartland. However, unlike the Egyptians, Assyrians, and Babylonians, with whom Judah had frequent contact, the peoples in the distant north were shrouded in mystery. The reports of these mysterious people groups that filtered down spoke of wild peoples, brutal and barbaric. This combination of mystery and brutality made Gog and his confederates perfect symbols of the archetypal enemy, rising against God and his people.

b. The Defeat of Gog (38:2c-23)

(1) Frame 1: Yahweh's Conscription of Gog (38:2c-9)

2c *"Prophesy against him* 3 *and say: 'Thus has the Lord Yahweh declared:*
Look, I am against you, O Gog, prince, chief of Meshech and Tubal.
4 *I will turn you around,*[50] *and put hooks into your jaws; I will take*

---

47. Probably the legendary King Midas of Greek tradition.
48. Herodotus *Hist.* 3.94. For further information on Meshech see above on 27:13.
49. *ARAB*, 2:40-41, §80. For further information on Tubal/Tabal see above on 27:13.
50. The Polel of *šûb* recurs in 39:2 and 39:27.

you out[51] *and all your army, horsemen, and charioteers,*[52] *all magnif-icently dressed,*[53] *a vast assembly,*[54] *armed with body shields and hand shields,*[55] *all of them brandishing swords.*[56] 5 *Paras, Cush, and Put accompany them, all armed with shields and helmets;*[57] 6 *Gomer and all its hordes,*[58] *Beth-Togarmah from the remotest parts of the north, and all its hordes*[59] — *vast armies accompany you.*

7 *Be prepared! Get ready*[60] — *you and your entire assembly that have been mobilized*[61] *about you. You will serve as their*[62] *guard.* 8 *After a long time you will be summoned;*[63] *in the distant future you will*

51. LXX condenses MT's three verbs, *wĕšôbabtîkā wĕnātattî . . . wĕhôṣē'tî*, into one, συνάξω, "I will gather," which translates *wĕšōbabtîkā* in 39:2. Since the reference to hooks in the jaws is missing in LXX, many delete the first two verbs and the object as a misplaced gloss, influenced by 29:4, but introducing a notion foreign to the present context. For a possible reconstruction of the growth of MT see Allen, *Ezekiel 20–48*, p. 200. For the first verb Syr. reads *w'knšk*, "and I will lead you out"; Targ. *w'šdlynk*, "and I will persuade you."

52. On the word pair *sûsîm* and *pārāšîm*, see above on 26:7. Cf. also 23:6, 12, where *pārāšîm* was followed by *rōkĕbê sûsîm*, "riders of horses."

53. LXX ἐνδεδυμένους θώρακας πάντας, "dressed in breastplates," and Syr. *zyn'*, "weapon," for *miklôl* render the military imagery more explicit.

54. Cf. *qāhāl gādôl wĕḥayil rāb* in v. 15. *qāhāl rāb* also occurs in 17:17; 26:7; 32:3.

55. The translation reflects the difference between *ṣinnâ*, "buckler," and *māgēn*, "shield."

56. Without a connective particle *ṣinnâ ûmāgēn tōpĕśê ḥărābôt kullām* is cryptic and intrusive. Syr. smooths the text, reading *bnyzk' wbskn'*, "with lances and shields," and linking the following *klhwn* (MT *kullām*) to v. 5. Targ. clarifies by inserting the participle *dmzyynyn*, "who are armed," to go with the added preposition *b*. LXX appears to read *māgēn wĕqôbā'*, "hand shield and helmet," while dropping *tōpĕśê*. Most commentators delete the whole line as a gloss. Cf. Zimmerli, *Ezekiel 2*, p. 285; Allen, *Ezekiel 20–48*, p. 200. Note the parallel construction in *lĕbušê miklôl kullām* and *tōpĕśê ḥărābôt kullām*.

57. Many delete *kullām māgēn wĕqôbāʿ* as a cue word gloss on *kullām* in v. 4. See Zimmerli, *Ezekiel 2*, p. 285; Allen, *Ezekiel 20–48*, p. 200.

58. *'ăgappîm* is a genuinely Ezekielian word, occurring outside this context (cf. vv. 9, 22; 39:4) only in 12:14 and 17:21.

59. The particle *'et* and the masc. suffix in *wĕ'et kol 'ăgāpāyw* conflict with the form of the phrase at the beginning of the verse, but this may be a stylistic variation.

60. Note the assonance of *hikkōn wĕhākēn lĕkā*, a combination of Niphal and Hiphil imperatives of the same root. Cf. the coordination of Qal and Hiphil forms of *šûb* in 14:6; 18:30.

61. *hanniqhālîm* defines the collective *qāhāl*. Cf. GKC, §145c. Num. 10:7 and 20:10 contain similar constructions. The coordination of nominal and verbal forms of *qāhāl* recurs in v. 13.

62. MT *lāhem*, "for them" (also Targ. and Syr.) is difficult, but is preferable to *lî*, "for me," reflected in LXX (cf. REB), on the principle of *lectio difficilior*.

63. On *pāqad* meaning "to summon, muster," in military contexts, see 23:21.

*march against a land that has been reclaimed[64] from the sword, and
[whose population] has been regathered[65] from many peoples on the
mountains[66] of Israel, which had lain desolate for such a long time.
Now they [its inhabitants] have been liberated from the peoples;[67] they
are living securely, all of them.* 9 *You will advance like a thunderstorm;
you will come[68] like the storm cloud, covering the land[69] — you and
all your allies and many peoples with you.'* "[70]

2c-3 Following an exceptionally lengthy introduction, the challenge formula
leaves no doubt about where the lines are drawn in this oracle.[71] The conflict
will inevitably touch Israel, but what Ezekiel envisages is essentially a duel
between Yahweh and Gog. Unlike most of the previous occurrences of the
challenge formula, which had generally been followed up with threats of
severe divine punishment,[72] the opening frame sounds more like a summons
to battle. Indeed, the emphasis is on Yahweh's direct and deliberate manipulation of Gog, calling him into the fray (vv. 4-6), and announcing the military
strategy he is to pursue (vv. 7-9). These two phases are reflected in the two
subsections that constitute this frame.

4-6 The lines are drawn. These verses create the impression that Gog

---

64. MT *měšôbebet* is a Polal fem. participle of *šûb*. Cf. W. L. Holladay, *The Root
šûb in the Old Testament with Particular Reference to Its Usages in Covenantal Texts*
(Leiden: Brill, 1958), pp. 106-7.

65. Following Syr. and Vulg., which smooth out MT by adding the copula before
měqubbeṣet. Elsewhere in Ezekiel the verb *qibbēṣ,* "to gather," is associated only with
living objects: the house of Israel, 22:19-20; the entire people of Israel or portions thereof,
11:17; 20:34, 41; 28:25; 34:13; 36:24; 37:21; 39:27; Jerusalem's lovers, 16:37; the Egyptians, 29:13; animals, 29:5; 39:17.

66. LXX reads "land" instead of "mountains."

67. The fem. forms of *wěhî'* . . . *hûṣā'â* assume the land as the subject, but the
following *killām,* "all of them," has the people in mind. Contra *BHS,* the Syr. omission
of these two clauses looks like homoioteleuton. So Zimmerli, *Ezekiel 2,* p. 286.

68. LXX and Syr. add the copula, but the latter drops the verb *tābô'.* Targ. "You
shall rise like a cloud and cover the earth" offers a free stylistic variation.

69. Syr. and Vulg. drop what appears to be a superfluous *tihyeh.*

70. On MT *'ôtāk,* as a stylistic variant of *'ittāk,* see my *Ezekiel: Chapters 1–24,*
p. 114 n. 7.

71. The introduction consists of (1) the word-event formula; (2) the address of the
prophet as "human"; (3) the double command to "prophesy against X and say"; (4) the
citation formula; (5) the challenge formula. The closest parallel occurs in 21:6-8 (Eng.
1-3), but see also 15:7. In previous oracles Yahweh had challenged Judah/Israel (5:8; 21:8
[Eng. 3]), the false prophets (13:8), Pharaoh (29:3; 30:22), and Edom (35:3); this time the
duel will be between himself and Gog and his confederates.

72. An exception is 36:9, which uses the formula (with *'el*) in a positive sense
preceding a glorious announcement of salvation.

is an imperial power with vast military resources. The expression *kol-ḥêlekā,* which may be translated "all your wealth" (26:12; 28:4-5) or "your entire army" (cf. 17:17; 27:10; 32:31), functions as a thesis statement, encompassing both the inventory of military hardware provided in v. 4 and the catalogue of Gog's allies in vv. 5-6. According to v. 4b Gog's forces are not only well dressed but also well armed. They will sweep through the land mounted on steeds *(sûsîm)* and driving teams of chariots *(pārāšîm),* armed with defensive (buckler and shield) and offensive weapons (swords). V. 5 adds helmets *(qôbāʿ)* to the list. The portrait is that of a superbly equipped force, fearfully efficient against unsuspecting targets.[73]

But Gog does not come alone. The phrase *qāhāl rāb,* "a great assembly," in v. 4 prepares for the enumeration of forces that join Meshech and Tubal in vv. 5-6. The text names five allies, but because of the unlikelihood of the African nations Cush (Ethiopia) and Put (Libya) joining forces with Anatolians in a Syrian campaign, and the premature reference to Paras (Persia), the triad in v. 5 is often deleted as a late, unrealistic gloss.[74] But Odell rightly warns against removing the verse too readily.[75] First, in Ezekiel's time the Persians were still a relatively unknown people on the fringes of Israelite consciousness, hence qualifying for the present mysterious context. Second, the conjunction of Paras, Cush, and Put elsewhere in the book[76] suggests that this triad derives from a traditional list of allies of Egypt. As an imperial power, Egypt is known to have engaged the aid of Anatolian forces in its conflicts with Assyria.[77] Third, the presence of Persia in a list of subordinates to Gog here and in 27:10 would have been unrealistic in any post-539 B.C. situation. Fourth, in contrast to Jeremiah (e.g., 51:11, 27, 28), Ezekiel never shows the slightest concern for peoples to the north and east of Babylon. His interest is in the Mediterranean rim. Fifth, the identification of Paras with Persia is probably mistaken, the resemblance of names being purely coincidental.[78] One should rather see here a reference to

---

73. For an illustration of Urartian forces alternating cavalry armed with swords, helmets, round shields, and chariotry, see the bronze belt in Yamauchi, *Foes,* p. 38.

74. See Zimmerli, *Ezekiel 2,* p. 306; Wevers, *Ezekiel,* p. 287; H.-M. Lutz, *Jahweh, Jerusalem und die Völker,* WMANT 27 (Neukirchen-Vluyn: Neukirchener, 1968), p. 75. At this time the Persians were just beginning to emerge as a force in ancient Near Eastern affairs. Cf. Zimmerli, *Ezekiel 2,* p. 60.

75. Odell, "Ezekiel 38–39," pp. 103-6; idem, "From Egypt to Meshech and Tubal: The Extent of Rebellion Against Yahweh in Ezekiel 38–39," paper read at the Society of Biblical Literature Annual Meeting, November, 1989.

76. In 27:10 Paras, Lud (Lydia), and Put are military partners of Tyre; 30:5 lists Cush, Put, and Lud among allies of Egypt.

77. See Ashurbanipal's reference to Gyges of Lydia sending troops to aid Tush-amilki of Egypt in throwing off the Assyrian yoke (*ARAB,* 2:297-98, §§784-85).

78. Though the references to Persia in Dan. 10:1; Ezra 1:1-2; Est. 1:3; 2 Chr. 36:20; etc., are undisputed.

some commercial or military power with strong links to Tyre and Egypt, but which is to date unattested in extrabiblical records, or an alternative, perhaps Egyptian, spelling for Pathros, "Southland."[79] By either interpretation, what is commonly dismissed as an unrealistic gloss becomes evidence for a remarkable awareness of Egypt's traditional allies.

Verse 6 names two more allies, *Gomer* and *Beth-Togarmah*. The former appears here for the first time in Ezekiel, but its presence is supported by the identification of Gomer as a brother of Meshech, Tubal, and Magog, and father of Togarmah in Gen. 10:2-3. Rendered Gimmiraia in Akkadian and Cimmerian in Greek, Gomer identified a wild tribe living in the fog-bound region north of the Black Sea, perhaps as far west as the Crimean Peninsula.[80] Beth-Togarmah is familiar from an earlier list of Tyre's trading partners.[81]

Whereas the military might of the southern armies had been described in terms of armaments (all armed with shields and helmets), these northern allies are impressive for their military hordes and for their association with the remotest part of the north. Basing their views on 38:17 and 39:8, many interpret the Gog invasion as the fulfillment of earlier prophetic proclamation. The expression *yarkĕtê ṣāpôn,* particularly its application to Gog in the doublet in 39:2, provides evidence that the Gog oracle is intended as a reinterpretation of unfulfilled prophecies of Jeremiah and Isaiah concerning "the foe from the

---

79. Thus H. P. Rüger, "Das Tyrusorakel Ezek 27" (Ph.D. diss., Tübingen, 1961), as cited by Zimmerli, *Ezekiel 2,* p. 60. Isaiah lists Pathros alongside Assyria, Egypt, Cush, Elam, Shinar, and Hamath (11:11); Jeremiah views the place as a region within Egypt (44:15), and Ezekiel himself recognizes it as the original homeland of the Egyptians (29:14; cf. 30:14). The unlikelihood of the same mistake having been made twice in the book (cf. 27:10) diminishes the plausibility of a scribal error for Pathros. Cf. Odell, "Ezekiel 38–39," p. 105. See further the comments above on 27:10.

80. According to Homer (*Od.* 11.12-19) the Cimmerians lived at the entrance of Hades, unreached by any rays of the sun. Later writers use the names Cimmerian and Scythian interchangeably (cf. Strabo 1.3.21; the Akkadian column of Darius's Behistun Inscription, which renders Persian *Saka* [Scythian] with *Gimairaia;* cf. R. G. Kent, *Old Persian: Grammar, Texts, Lexicon,* rev. ed. [New Haven: American Oriental Society, 1953], p. 134), but neo-Assyrian annals distinguish them. It may indeed have been Scythian pressure from the northeast that caused the Cimmerians to irrupt into Anatolia in the 8th century B.C., eventually conquering Urartu and creating havoc for the Assyrians in the northern fringes of their empire. During Ashurbanipal's reign their pressure on Gyges of Phrygia/Lydia was so great that, inspired by a dream, he appealed to Ashurbanipal for support (*ARAB,* 2:297-98, 326, 351-52, §§784-85, 849, 909-10). According to Strabo (1.61), despair over the Cimmerian destruction of the Phrygian capital Gordion led King Midas to commit suicide. The Cimmerians were finally subdued by the Assyrians, and their people melted into the native Anatolian populations. On the Cimmerians see Yamauchi, *Foes,* pp. 49-61; M. Chahin, *The Kingdom of Armenia* (New York: Dorset, 1987), pp. 99-100, et passim.

81. See further the comments above on 27:14.

north," if not the personification of this foe.[82] This interpretation is problematic, however, not only because of the questionable text-critical grounds on which it is based, but also because it applies the expression to Beth-Togarmah, not to Gog.[83] Furthermore, as we will see below, the references to previous prophecies in 38:17 and 39:8 are too vague to be restricted to oracles concerning "the foe from the north."[84]

Finally, and perhaps most critically, this understanding fails to recognize the significance of the list of nations in alliance with Gog. First, in contrast to the addressees in Ezekiel's oracles against the foreign nations, the names listed all represent distant peoples, from the fringes of Israelite awareness. Second, the number of allies totals seven, exactly the same number as had been addressed in the collection of oracles against the nations (chs. 25–32), and those who accompany Egypt in Sheol (37:17-32).[85] Given the prominence of the number seven in the present oracle,[86] this must be intentional. The reference to seven nations, which symbolize totality, completeness,[87] raises the conspiracy against Israel from a minor opportunistic incursion into her territory to a universal conspiracy. Third, the names in Ezekiel's list form a merismic pattern: Meshech, Tubal, Gomer, and Beth-Togarmah represent the northern extreme of the world known to Israel; Paras, Cush, and Put the southern extreme, again suggesting that the whole world is involved in this attack. Similar rhetorical strategies have been recognized in ancient neo-Assyrian sources, particularly the following boast of Sargon II: "In the might and power of the great gods, my lords, who sent forth my weapons, I cut down all of my foes from Iatnana (Cyprus), which is in the sea of the setting

---

82. Ahroni, *HAR* 1 (1977) 14-15. The texts most often cited are Jer. 1:13-14; 4:6-17; 6:1-30. Cf. Zimmerli, *Ezekiel 2,* pp. 299-300; Wevers, *Ezekiel,* pp. 283-87. For a recent study of this motif see D. J. Reimer, "The 'Foe' and the 'North' in Jeremiah," *ZAW* 10 (1989) 223-32.

83. Even Zimmerli accepts this statement as part of the *Grundtext*. See Odell, "Ezekiel 38–39," p. 107. Odell (p. 36) points out the text-critical problem in response to Zimmerli, who first removes 38:17 from the basic text but then uses it as the basis for his interpretation.

84. Batto (*Slaying the Dragon,* pp. 159-62) interprets the expression *yarkĕtê ṣāpôn* as the antithesis of creation and evidence for Gog as a mythical symbol of chaos. M. Dietrich and O. Loretz attribute these references to "the remotest parts of the north" to a redactor who attempted to impose mythical qualities on Gog, the king of Lydia ("Ugaritisch *ṣrrt ḥpn, ṣrry* und hebräisch *jrkyj ṣpwn,*" *UF* 22 [1990] 85).

85. Nobile (in *Ezekiel and His Book,* pp. 256-57) sees here evidence that the redactor of this text had the Gog pericope in front of him.

86. Note the enemies' seven weapons (39:9), the seven years' worth of fuel these provide (39:9), the seven months needed to bury the enemies' remains (39:12). Ahroni (*HAR* 1 [1977] 17) even identifies seven sections in the composition.

87. See M. H. Pope, *IDB,* 4:294-95.

sun, as far as the border of Egypt and the land of the Muski [Meshech], — the wide land of Amurru, the Hittite-land in its entirety."[88]

This combination of features suggests that Ezekiel envisions a universal conspiracy against Israel.[89] The description creates the impression of a formidable foe, able to attack whenever and wherever he pleases. But how different is the appearance from the reality. Vv. 4-6 are emphatic in affirming Yahweh's total control over the movements of Gog. This truth is announced in three short declarations.

First, Yahweh says to Gog: *I will turn you around.* The verb *wĕšôbab-tîkā* suggests the image of horsemen turning their steeds around (cf. v. 4b), a metaphor well chosen for peoples who come from a region renowned in antiquity for its horses.[90] While the statement connotes a change of direction, which way is not yet specified. The threat of foes from the north was a well-established motif in Israelite prophecy. Hittites, Assyrians, and Babylonians had all taken their turns invading Palestine; now Yahweh will bring on Gog and his hordes. Second, Yahweh says: *I will put hooks into your jaws.* The figure is reminiscent of Ezekiel's earlier portrayals of the lion of Judah being captured and deported to Egypt (19:4, 9), and of Yahweh's own capture of the pharaonic monster (29:4). Indeed, Yahweh not only drives Gog and his hordes; the hunting metaphor (*ḥaḥîm*) portrays Gog as his captive.[91] Third, Yahweh says: *I will take you out.* The expression *wĕhôṣē'tî 'ôtĕkā* conjures up ideas of exodus and liberation, but this is hardly the sense intended. Here the mysterious region beyond the Taurus Mountains is portrayed as the lair from which Yahweh will lead Gog out like an animal on a leash.

7-9 Verse 7 represents Yahweh's formal summons to Gog, cast in the form of a double command.[92] Although the singular form of the imperative

88. *ARAB,* 2:25-26, §54. Cf. p. 41, §82; pp. 48-52, §§96, 97, 99; and pp. 101-2, §183, which uses the expression "from Egypt to Mushki." See the discussion by Odell, "Ezekiel 38–39," pp. 101-2; idem, "From Egypt to Meshech and Tubal."

89. Odell's thesis that Gog's campaign represents a rebellion against Nebuchadrezzar, incurring the wrath of Yahweh (as Gyges's revolt against Ashurbanipal had incurred the wrath of Ashur), is unlikely because: (1) Nebuchadrezzar is entirely out of the picture in this oracle; (2) the Gog invasion is thrust into the distant future; and (3) the relationship between Ashurbanipal and Ashur is not really parallel to Yahweh's relationship with Nebuchadrezzar. Whereas Ashur was indeed the divine patron of Ashurbanipal and his Assyrians, Yahweh is the patron of Israel, not Nebuchadrezzar.

90. See Yamauchi, *Foes,* pp. 66-68.

91. One might have expected a reference to bits or bridles (*meteg*) in their mouths. Cf. 2 K. 19:28; Isa. 37:27; Ps. 32:9; Prov. 26:3. On *ḥaḥîm* see my *Ezekiel: Chapters 1–24,* p. 601; it also occurs in 19:9.

92. With the opening imperative (*hikkōn* [*wĕhākēn lĕkā*]) plus a purpose clause constructed of *lamed* plus noun/infinitive construct, cf. *hikkôn liqra't 'ĕlōhêka,* "Prepare to meet your God," in Amos 4:12. According to K. Koch ("Die Rolle der hymnischen

reflects the oracle's primary preoccupation with Gog, the following phrase extends the charge to his allies: *your entire assembly that have been mobilized about you* (lit. "the assembly that has been assembled to you"). The meaning of the final clause in the verse is unclear, but in the context *mišmār* must carry a military nuance.[93] Yahweh appears to be charging Gog to assume leadership over the vast forces allied with him by serving as their guardian, in keeping with his role as their leader.[94] But Ezekiel's audience may have taken comfort in v. 8, which explains that the summoning of Gog and his forces is not to be expected in the near future, but after a considerable period of time, a point highlighted by two expressions. *mîyyāmîm rabbîm,* "after a long time," occurs elsewhere only in Josh. 23:1, where it defines the period between Israel's entrance into the land of Canaan and Joshua's farewell address.[95] *bĕ'ahărît haššānîm* (lit. "in later years"), which occurs only here in the OT, functions as a stylistic variant of *bĕ'ahărît hayyāmîm* in v. 16.[96] In isolation the latter means "in the course of time, in the future."[97] Unlike Dan. 2:28 and 10:14, where it serves technically for the eschaton, here both expressions refer simply to a later time, when the historical phase of the exiles is over and the new period of settlement in the land has arrived.

The rest of v. 8 offers further clarification of the timing of the summons for Gog. The focus is on Gog's invasions of the land of Israel, but the choice of verbs (*šûb,* "to return," and *qubbaṣ,* "to be gathered") and the alternation of subject reflect a concomitant interest in its population. Two conditions will antedate Gog's invasion. First, the land itself will have recovered from *the sword,* a metonymic expression for the destruction and slaughter of an invading army. *the mountains of Israel* identifies Gog's target for the first time. This is the homeland of Ezekiel and his fellow exiles, the land that Nebuchadrezzar's forces had devastated, and which will have lain desolate for a long time.[98] Second, the population will have been regathered from many peoples

---

Abschnitte des Amos-Buches," *ZAW* 86 [1974] 504-37) Amos's more cryptic form represents a liturgical summons.

93. But not necessarily associated with siege warfare, contra Odell, "Ezekiel 38–39," p. 111.

94. Davidson (*Ezekiel,* p. 276) interprets *mišmār* as "something to be kept or observed, a rallying point." Cf. G. R. Driver, *Bib* 35 (1954) 303.

95. Cf. this expression with partitive *min* with the abbreviated *mîyyāmîm,* "after (some) days," in Judg. 11:4; 14:8; 15:1.

96. The expression occurs elsewhere in Gen. 49:1; Num. 24:14; Deut. 4:30; 31:29; Hos. 3:5; Isa. 2:2 = Mic. 4:1; Jer. 23:20 = 30:24; 48:47; 49:39; Dan. 2:28; 10:14. An exact counterpart is found in Akk. *ina/ana ah-ri-a-at ūmī.* See *AHW,* p. 21; *CAD,* I/1:194.

97. H. Seebass, *TDOT,* 1:210-12; E. Jenni, *THAT,* 1:116-17.

98. Note the play on *hereb,* "sword," and *horbâ,* "desolation." The adverb *tāmîd,* which occurs elsewhere in the book only in 39:14 and 46:14-15, usually connotes con-

of the diaspora *('ammîm rabbîm)* and resettled securely within it. The metonymic use of "land" for "people" continues in the last line of v. 8 with the verb *hûṣā'â,* "it will be brought out," which recalls the exodus terminology of the foregoing restoration oracles.

they are living securely. The state of the population at the time of the invasion is reflected in *yāšab lābeṭaḥ.* Derived from the Holiness Code, this phrase serves as a minor key word in the oracle (see vv. 11, 14; 39:26), describing the security offered by Yahweh when the blessings of the covenant are operative and the divine patron stands guard over them (cf. Lev. 26:5b-6). Indeed, v. 8 may be interpreted as a shorthand version of Ezekiel's salvation oracles, especially 36:1-15, addressed to the mountains of Israel and highlighting the restoration of its population. Moreover, in 36:24, 33-36 he had spoken of regathering the people and rebuilding the ruins, and in 34:25-29 he had described the scene of perfect peace and tranquility. Obviously Gog's invasion presupposes the fulfillment of the salvation oracles in chs. 34–37.

9 Yahweh's marching orders for Gog are spelled out. Although Jeremiah had also spoken of the enemy advancing from the north like storm clouds *(ka'ănānîm)* at Yahweh's command (4:12-13), Ezekiel's use of *šō'â,* "storm," points to inspiration from Isa. 10:3: "What will you do on the day of punishment *(pĕquddâ),* in the storm *(šô'â)* that will cover the land?" *šō'â* means literally "devastation," but its pairing with *'ānān* suggests a destructive "storm cloud,"[99] a metaphor for a sudden invasion by vast numbers of troops.

The opening frame portrays Yahweh as a general mobilizing the forces of Gog and his allies for his own military agenda. In so doing it raises several questions. How can Gog, whom vv. 3-6 had portrayed as the enemy of Yahweh, simultaneously play the role of Yahweh's agent? How can Yahweh employ foreign nations against his people after the reestablishment of the eternal covenant relationship and the restoration of the people to the land? In raising these questions this frame sets the rhetorical agenda for the following frames of the prophecy against Gog. Meanwhile, the audience has been informed that Gog's invasion of the land represents part of the calculated plan of God for his people.

---

tinuous action, but here it carries a durative sense, "for a long time," complementing "many days hence" and "in later years," and highlighting the chronological distance between the events described here and Yahweh's salvific activity as described in chs. 34–37.

99. Cf. 30:3; Zeph. 1:3 (both of the day of Yahweh). For discussion of the metaphor in Ugaritic and Hebrew (including this text) see J. C. de Moor and H. F. de Vries, "Hebrew *hēdād* 'Thunder-Storm,' " *UF* 20 (1988) 176-77.

(2) Frame 2: The Motives of Gog (38:10-13)

10 *"Thus has the Lord Yahweh declared: On that day, ideas will rise in your mind,*[100] *and you will conceive a wicked scheme.*[101] 11 *You will think, 'I will invade an undefended country;*[102] *I will attack*[103] *the tranquil*[104] *people, who live securely,*[105] *all of them living in unwalled towns without bars or gates,* 12 *to seize spoil and to carry off booty'* *— to turn your hand*[106] *against the repopulated ruins and against a people regathered from the nations, who have acquired*[107] *livestock and possessions,*[108] *and living on top of the world.* 13 *Sheba and Dedan and the merchants of Tarshish, and all its magnates,*[109] *will ask you, 'Is it to seize spoil that you have come? Is it to carry off booty that*

---

100. On the idiom *'ālâ 'al-lēb* see my *Ezekiel: Chapters 1–24*, p. 425 n. 35; a similar idiom occurs in 11:5 and 20:32, with *rûaḥ* instead of *lēb*. *děbārîm*, usually "words," here means "thoughts," viz., unspoken words. For an Aramaic version of this idiom, reflecting the relationship between internal and external speech, see Sefire Inscription iii:14: *whn ysq 'l lbbk wtś' 'l śptk*, "If the idea comes to your mind and you take it upon your lips." See *TSSI*, 2:48-49, 54.

101. *ḥāšab maḥšebet*, "to scheme schemes," is a standard Hebrew idiom (2 Sam. 14:14; Jer. 11:19; 18:11, 18; 29:11; 49:20, 30; 50:45; Dan. 11:24, 25; Est. 8:3; 9:25). In Exod. 31:4; 35:32, 33, 35; 2 Chr. 2:13; 26:16, the idiom has a positive sense, "to be expert in a craft."

102. The versions are inconsistent in their renderings of *'ereṣ pěrāzôt:* LXX, "a rejected land"; Syr., "a prosperous land"; Targ., "the land that abides tranquilly in open cities"; Vulg., "a land concealed by walls."

103. The anticipated cohortative after *'e'ĕleh* may be achieved by redividing *'bw' hšqtym* as *'bw'h šqtym* (Zimmerli, *Ezekiel 2*, p. 287), but *bô'*, in the sense "to attack," may tolerate a direct object. See 32:11. The pairing of *'ālâ*, "to go up against," and *bô'*, "to enter," provides an intentional link with v. 9. On the military usage of *'ālâ* see G. Wehmeier, *THAT*, 2:277.

104. In 16:42 the root *šqṭ* referred to Yahweh's pacific disposition toward his people after his anger had been vented; in 16:49 the Hiphil described Sodom's presumptuous and illusory tranquility.

105. The construct state followed by a prepositional phrase occurs also in the next verse *(yôšěbê 'al ṭabbûr)*. On this construction see Waltke-O'Connor, *Syntax*, §9.6.

106. LXX "my hand" continues the internal monologue.

107. The sg. form *'ōśeh* is influenced by the preceding collective *'am*. The following *yōšěbê* calls for a pl. form. So Syr., Targ.

108. LXX telescopes *miqneh wěqinyān* into one word. On the Aramaized form of the latter see Wagner, *Aramaismen*, p. 101, §266.

109. LXX, Syr., and Vulg. mistranslate *kěpirêhā*, "young lions," as if from *kāpār*, "village." So also RSV (but not NRSV), NASB, NIV. Cf. Josh. 18:24; 1 Sam. 6:18; Cant. 7:12; 1 Chr. 27:25. But MT's vocalization and Targ. *wkl mlkh'*, "and all her kings," point in a different direction. *BHS*, Zimmerli (*Ezekiel 2*, p. 287), and others see here a corruption for *rklyh*, "its traders." Cf. *šḥr* parallel to *rkl* in 27:12-13, 15-16, 17-18, 20-21a, 21b-22.

you have assembled your allies? To make off with silver and gold? To take away livestock and property? To seize vast amounts of booty?' "[110]

10 A new citation formula signals the beginning of the second frame. Although *bayyôm hahû'*, "in that day," links this frame with the preceding, the focus shifts from Yahweh's initiative to the private motivations of Gog, here described as "ideas" that rise in his mind, and evil *(rā'â)* schemes he devises. Whereas the first expression is ethically neutral, the negative connotations of the second set the tone for this frame. The first frame had not specified what Gog would do once he reached the mountains of Israel, but now it becomes clear: his aim is to bring calamity *(rā'â)* on the land. The image is rendered more forceful by letting Gog express his intentions through direct if internal speech. His aim is to attack an unsuspecting country. The target land is not named, but Gog's opportunistic and aggressive attitude is highlighted by portraying the land and its population as innocent and tranquil (v. 11).

11 The country itself is described as a land of *pĕrāzôt*. The word appears elsewhere only in Zech. 2:8 (Eng. 4) and Est. 9:19, but its significance is not in doubt — *pĕrāzôt* are defined as rural settlements without walls, bars, or gates, in contrast to fortified cities.[111] As for the residents of these villages, Gog recognizes them all as undisturbed and secure. The combination of the aggressor's scheming and the target's (false) sense of security recalls Nebuchadrezzar's designs on the isolated Arabian desert town of Qedar in Jer. 49:30-31:

> Nebuchadrezzar, king of Babylon, has devised a plan against you;
> he has conceived a scheme against you *(ḥāšab 'ālêkem maḥăšābâ).*
> Arise, attack *('ălû)* a nation at ease *(gôy šĕlēyw),*
> that lives securely *(yôšēb lābeṭaḥ)* —
> the declaration of Yahweh —

110. LXX omits *gādôl*, probably by pseudohaplography after the previous *lišlōl šālāl*.

111. Walls, bars, and gates represent a standardized triad. Cf. Deut. 3:5; 2 Chr. 8:5; 14:6. According to Ezekiel's own vision of the reconstituted community, even the future Jerusalem will have gates (48:30-35), though their function need not have been military. Cf. the gentilic, *pĕrāzî*, for residents of rural unwalled villages (Deut. 3:5; 1 Sam. 6:18; Est. 9:19). The enigmatic *pĕrāzôn*, mentioned in Judg. 5:7, 11, refers either to the villages themselves or their residents. For further discussion see N. Na'aman, "Amarna *ālāni pu-ru-zi* (EA 137) and Biblical *'ry hprzy/hprzwt* ('rural settlements')," *ZAH* 4 (1991) 72-75; L. E. Stager, "Archaeology, Ecology, and Social History: Background Themes to the Song of Deborah," in *Congress Volume: Jerusalem 1986*, VTSup 40, ed. J. A. Emerton (Leiden: Brill, 1988), pp. 224-25. For discussion and illustrations of Israelite defensive fortifications see Yadin, *Art of Warfare*, 1:22-23.

that has no gates or bars;
that dwells in isolation.

Why the inhabitants of the mountains of Israel have taken no defensive
precautions is not indicated; they have apparently put their confidence in
Yahweh's promises of eternal peace and prosperity as spelled out in the
previous restoration oracles. They have finally cast themselves on their divine
patron for security.

12 According to v. 12a, by his own confession Gog is motivated by
a single passion: the lust for loot and booty. His speech reflects no consciousness of the divine commission; all that drives him is greed. But with this
statement the direct quotation breaks off, and the oracle reverts to the divine
address of Gog in the second person. The remainder of the verse resumes the
description of the tranquility in the target land. (1) Its ruins have been repopulated in fulfillment of 36:10, 33. (2) The people are regathered from their
dispersion among the nations. (3) The population is prospering with abundant
livestock and other movable goods, in fulfillment of 34:26-27.[112] (4) Her
people live on top of the world.

The meaning of *ṭabbûr hā'āreṣ* continues to engage scholars. The
common rendering "navel of the earth," which derives from LXX ὀμφαλόν,
is perpetuated in the Vulg. *umbilici terrae,* as well as in pseudepigraphic and
rabbinic writings, and is reflected in several renowned medieval maps.[113] But
many modern interpreters have abandoned the literal "navel" explanation,
preferring to see here a figure of speech for "the center of the earth." By this
understanding the land of Israel/Zion is viewed as a cosmic midpoint, which
accords better with later Hebrew;[114] moreover, our prophet himself declared
earlier that Yahweh had placed Jerusalem in the middle of the nations (5:5).
The expression *ṭabbûr hā'āreṣ* occurs elsewhere only in Judg. 9:37, where it
describes Mount Gerizim overlooking Shechem, which some contend the
Canaanites considered as the navel, viz., center, of the land of Canaan.[115]

112. *miqneh wĕqinyān* represents a standardized pair of cognate terms from *qānâ,*
"to acquire, purchase" (cf. v. 13; also Gen. 34:23; 36:6; Josh. 14:4. *qinyān* is an Aramaized
form (Wagner, *Aramaismen,* p. 101, §266).

113. For Pseudepigrapha see *Jub.* 8:19 reads, "Mount Sinai (was) in the midst of
the desert and Mount Zion (was) in the midst of the navel of the earth." Cf. also *1 Enoch*
26:1. Josephus (*J.W.* 3.3.5, §52) notes that some called Jerusalem the navel of the country.
For rabbinic writings see *b. Yoma* 54b, "The world was created from Zion"; *Midrash
Tanḥuma Qedoshim* 10, "As the navel is situated in the center of a person, so is the land
of Israel — in the center of the world." See also *b. Sanhedrin* 37a. For maps see particularly
the 13th-century Latin ms. of the book of Psalms and the 16th-century "clover leaf" map,
reproduced and discussed by Beitzel, *Moody Atlas,* pp. 201-3.

114. Cf. NRSV, NJPS, REB, NASB, NIV, JB. See also Jastrow, *Dictionary,* p. 529.

115. B. W. Anderson, "The Place of Shechem in the Bible," *BA* 20 (1957) 10-11.

Support for this understanding is also drawn from extra-Israelite attestation to the notion of a navel or center of the earth.[116]

Nonetheless, this interpretation suffers from several major weaknesses and should probably be abandoned.[117] First, the etymology of *ṭabbûr* is uncertain. Admittedly, it is used of the umbilical cord in Mishnaic Hebrew and later Aramaic, but the OT itself provides no support for this interpretation.[118] Furthermore, Biblical Hebrew possesses a word for "navel" or "umbilical cord," *šōr*, which Ezekiel himself has used in 16:4 (see also Cant. 7:3 [Eng. 2]; Prov. 3:8). Second, Ezek. 5:5 refers not to a cosmic center but to Jerusalem's position in the context of her neighbors. Third, the context of Judg. 9:37, specifically the previous verse, suggests a simple denotation "elevated ground."[119] Fourth, there is no obvious need for a reference to either the navel or the center of the earth in the present context. In fact, its juxtaposition with "unwalled villages" points to some safe and secure location. This requirement is fully met if *ṭabbûr hā'āreṣ* is interpreted as an elevated plateau without external fortifications, as in Judg. 9:37. Fifth, this interpretation finds early support in the Targ., which translates the word as *twqp'*, "stronghold."[120]

13 The attention turns to outside witnesses to Gog's preparation for his campaign. The interested parties represent merchant peoples who conduct their trade via the overland routes across the Arabian Desert to the east of Israel (Sheba and Dedan), and the maritime Mediterranean route to the west (Tarshish).[121] Like the list of Gog's allies, who come from the northern and southern extremes of the world known to Israel, these names constitute a merism, from east to west, connoting all nations involved in international commerce.

---

116. (1) A circular 6th-century-B.C. map of the world from Babylon locates this city in the center surrounded by neighbors, some positioned irrespective of their actual location (cf. Beitzel, *Moody Atlas,* pp. 197-98; Unger, *Babylon,* pp. 20-24). (2) In Greece, Homer saw the navel in the geographic midpoint of the sea (*Od.* 1.50). (3) Major Greek oracle sanctuaries, such as those at Didyma, Miletus, and Delphi, were viewed as the navel of the earth. (4) According to Aristides the Eleusinian mystery cults reserved this honor for Athens. (5) Islam ascribes this status to Mecca. For discussion and bibliography see S. Terrien, "The Omphalos Myth and Hebrew Religion," *VT* 20 (1970) 315-38; cf. Zimmerli, *Ezekiel 2,* p. 311.

117. So also S. Talmon, *TDOT,* 3:437-38.

118. Ahroni (*HAR* 1 [1977] 12-13) accepts the omphalic interpretation here, but sees in the presence of the phrase an argument for the late date of the Gog prophecy.

119. So also D. Winton Thomas, "Mount Tabor: The Meaning of the Name," *VT* 1 (1951) 230.

120. Kimchi explains this translation geographically, as a reference to the territory of Israel being elevated higher than the rest of the countries. See Levey, *Ezekiel,* p. 107.

121. On Sheba see above on 27:22-23; on Dedan see on 25:13; 27:15, 20. On Tarshish see the comments on 27:12 above.

Two words highlight the character of these nations. *sōḥărîm,* "traders," recalls Tyre's trade list in ch. 27 and identifies them as mercantile peoples. *kĕpirîm,* commonly interpreted "villages," translates literally "lions," another animal name used as a designation for a class of people, here presumably the leading merchants.[122] These traders' reaction to Gog's designs is expressed in the form of a series of rhetorical questions, but their motive is not entirely clear. Are these decent nations challenging Gog's greed, or are they wishing to capitalize on the opportunity themselves? Since their questions echo many of the expressions found in the previous verse, it seems Gog's disposition is mirrored in their own covetousness. They too have their eyes on spoil *(šālāl),* booty *(baz),* silver *(kesep),* gold *(zāhāb),* livestock *(miqneh),* and the movable property *(qinyān).* These merchants are vultures, hoping to take advantage of the spoils of this war.

(3) Frame 3: Yahweh's Counterplan: His Goal (38:14-16)

14 *"Therefore, prophesy, human, and declare to Gog:*[123] *'Thus has the Lord Yahweh declared: Surely,*[124] *on that day, when my people, Israel, are dwelling securely, you will take note!*[125] 15 *You will come from your homeland in the remotest parts of the north — you and many peoples with you, all of them mounted on horses, a vast horde, a mighty army.* 16 *You will advance upon my people, Israel, like a storm cloud covering the land. In the distant future, when it happens, I will bring you against my land in order that the nations may know me,*[126] *when I display my holiness among you, before their eyes, O Gog!' "*[127]

122. So REB. JB translates lit., "young lions." On this designation for nobility see Miller, *UF* 2 (1970) 183. In 32:2 *kĕpîr gôyim,* "lion of nations," had served as a royal title.

123. Syr. adds "Magog."

124. On *hălô'* as an emphatic particle, see Brown, *Maarav* 4/2 (1987) 201-19, esp. 216.

125. Although MT *tēda'* offers a tolerable sense and is supported by Syr., Vulg., and Targ., many emend to *tē'ōr,* "you will be roused," with LXX on the assumption that MT misreads *r* as *d* and transposes the last two letters. Cf. REB, NRSV, Allen (*Ezekiel 20–48,* p. 200). It is equally possible the error was committed by the LXX translators.

126. Targ.'s paraphrase, "they will know the punishment of my might," may have recognized the anomalous form of the recognition formula, *lĕma'an da'at haggôyim 'ōtî.* The common deletion of this statement as a non-Ezekielian insertion (cf. Zimmerli, *Ezekiel 1,* p. 39; Allen, *Ezekiel 20–49,* p. 201) neutralizes its rhetorical force.

127. The vocative is rhetorical, reflecting the heightening of the speaker's emotion as the oracle progresses. The Syr. omission of the vocative and LXX attachment of it to v. 17 are insufficient grounds for deleting the name.

While the formulaic opening signals the commencement of the third frame,[128] the introductory particle, *lākēn,* "Therefore," intentionally draws a logical connection between this frame and the preceding: the arrogance of Gog has provoked the ire of Yahweh. But this frame serves a second purpose in offering a clue regarding Yahweh's motives in bringing the forces of Gog and his allies against the land of Israel. The message proper divides into two parts, the first (vv. 14b-16a) highlighting the initiative of Gog, and the second (v. 16b) Yahweh's involvement. By bringing together the divine and human dimensions of the campaign, the emphases of frames 1 and 2 have been conjoined.

14-16a The most striking feature of this brief scene is the manner in which Gog's target is identified. Apart from "the people which have been gathered from many nations to the mountains of Israel" (v. 8), prior to this they have been only vaguely hinted at. Twice the objects of attack, the people dwelling securely are explicitly identified as *ʿammî yiśrāʾēl,* "my people Israel" (vv. 14, 16). Furthermore, the land against which Yahweh brings Gog is *ʾarṣî,* "my land." Since the normal deity-nation-land relationships are operative, for Gog to attack this people and invade this land is to challenge their/its divine patron.

Verses 14b-16a highlight the opportunism of the invader. Precisely when Yahweh's people are enjoying their security in his land, Gog will pounce on the unsuspecting victim. The description of the military action summarizes vv. 4-9: he will emerge from his homeland in the far reaches of the north country; he and his vast host will sweep down on Yahweh's people riding their horses; and they will cover the land like a cloud.

16b The climax is signaled by the shift in attention to Yahweh's involvement. His control over all these events is described by means of an expanded version of the recognition formula. Three factors in the divine action are cited. First, Gog's invasion is planned according to Yahweh's timetable, *in the distant future* (*bĕʾaḥărît hayyāmîm,* lit. "at the end of the days"). The expression assumes knowledge of v. 8, and reaffirms that the invasion of the land of Israel is not imminent. It is pushed off into the distant future, after Yahweh's people have been regathered from the diaspora, have settled in their homeland, the signs of his blessing have become evident, and

---

128. Contra Zimmerli (*Ezekiel 2,* pp. 311-12), the diction of this frame is typically Ezekielian, and displays numerous semantic links with the foregoing: *yāšab lābeṭaḥ,* "to live securely" (v. 14; cf. vv. 8, 11); *yarkĕtê ṣāpôn,* "the remotest parts of the north" (v. 15; cf. v. 6); *ʾattâ wĕʿammîm rabbîm,* "you and many peoples with you" (v. 15; cf. vv. 6, 9); *qāhāl gādôl,* "a great assembly" (v. 15; cf. v. 4, *qāhāl rāb,* "a numerous assembly"); *ḥayil rāb,* "a numerous army" (v. 15; cf. v. 4, *kol-ḥêlekā,* "your army"); *ʿālâ kĕʿānān,* "to come up like a cloud" (v. 16; cf. v. 9); *bĕʾaḥărît hayyāmîm,* "in the latter days" (v. 16, perhaps a conflation of *mîyyāmîm rabbîm,* "after many days," and *bĕʾaḥărît hašānîm,* "in the latter years," in v. 8).

they have begun to enjoy their peaceful and tranquil state. Second, Gog's
invasion occurs at the overt instigation of Yahweh. He comes not merely
with Yahweh's permissive will, but as his agent. The formulaic declaration[129]
suggests to Ezekiel's audience that Yahweh is again carrying out his covenant
threats against his people. Third, Yahweh's purpose in bringing on the hordes
of Gog is to convince the nations of his presence and his person. He is not
satisfied with his own people drawing this conclusion from their full restoration as his people; as the sovereign of all nations he desires that all know
him, specifically his holiness.[130] The unique form of the statement represents
a deliberate rhetorical ploy, drawing attention to the fact that Gog is not
actually the agent through whom his holiness is manifested; he is the locus
of the revelation![131] The recognition formula provides the first concrete
indication since the opening challenge that the real antagonists in this oracle
are not Yahweh and Israel, but Yahweh and Gog. In an ironical twist, Gog's
opportunism vis-à-vis Israel is seized as an occasion to achieve Yahweh's
own goals. In the meantime, this frame has also provided the answer to the
first question raised by the first frame (vv. 3-9): Why would Yahweh bring
Gog against his own people after the covenant relationships had been fully
restored? Because an element in the divine agenda, the universal recognition
of his person, remains unfulfilled.

129. The pronouncement *wahăbi'ôtîkā 'al-'arṣî* follows a conventional prophetic
form, "I will bring A against B." Seven times in Kings the divine threat is announced by
the prophets with *hinĕnî mēbî' rā'â 'al,* "I will bring disaster on B": 1 K. 9:9 (on Israel);
14:10 (on Jeroboam); 21:21 (on Ahab), 29 (on Ahab's house); 2 K. 21:12 (on Jerusalem
and Judah); 22:16, 20 (on this place, viz., Jerusalem). This form is also characteristic of
Jeremiah's preaching (4:6; 5:15; 6:19; 11:8, 11, 23; 15:8; 19:3, 15; 23:12; 25:9, 13; 35:17;
36:31; 39:16; 42:17; 44:2; 45:5; 49:5, 8, 37; 51:64. Cf. the reversal in 31:8 and 32:42;
even as Yahweh had inflicted the curses, so he would bring blessing. The formula occurs
14 times in Ezekiel. However, the influence of the covenantal threat (Lev. 26:25) is evident
in the sixfold replacement of the general term for disaster *(rā'â)* with *ḥereb,* "sword" (5:17;
6:3; 11:8; 14:17; 29:8; 33:2), which also accounts for the use of *ḥereb* in v. 8 above. 14:21
lists "my four severe judgments: sword, famine, wild animals, plague." 14:22 has *hārā'â.*
Ezekiel's historicizing tendency is evident in his substitution of real agents for "sword"
(7:24 [the most barbaric of nations]; 23:22 [Jerusalem's lovers]; 26:7 [Nebuchadrezzar on
Tyre]; 28:7 [strangers on Tyre]), a rhetorical device to demonstrate that current events do
in fact represent the fulfillment of Yahweh's covenant threats. See also Odell, "Ezekiel
38–39," pp. 116-21.

130. Each previous reference to Yahweh displaying his holiness in the sight of the
nations (*lĕ'ênê haggôyim,* 20:41, 28:25; 36:23) had occurred in the context of regathering
his people, a theme that returns in 39:27. In 28:22 Yahweh's holiness is demonstrated by
his judgment of Tyre.

131. A conclusion confirmed by the observation that wherever the concern is the
revelation of Yahweh's holiness, it occurs in the midst of a people. So also Odell, "Ezekiel
38–39," p. 132.

(4) Frame 4: Yahweh's Counterplan: His Strategy (38:17-23)

17 *"Thus has the Lord Yahweh declared: Are you the one[132] of whom I have spoken in the past[133] through my servants, the prophets of Israel, who prophesied in those days that after many years[134] I would bring you against them?*

18 *Now on that day, the day Gog invades the land of Israel — the declaration of the Lord Yahweh — my fury will be aroused.[135] In my anger* 19 *and in my passion,[136] in my blazing wrath I have spoken. Assuredly, on that day, a great earthquake will occur on the land of Israel.* 20 *The fish of the sea, the birds of the sky, the animals of the field, every creature that crawls along the ground, and the entire human race on the face of the earth will quake before me. The mountains will be hurled down, the cliffs[137] will collapse, and every wall will crumble to the ground.* 21 *Then I will summon the sword against him, throughout all my mountains[138] — the declaration of the Lord Yahweh — every man's sword will be turned against his brother.* 22 *And I will punish him with pestilence and bloodshed; I will pour out torrential rain, hailstones, fire, and burning sulfur on him and his hordes and the many peoples accompanying him.*

23 *So I will display my greatness and my holiness;[139] I will make*

---

132. Many follow LXX, Syr., and Vulg. in reading an affirmative statement, assuming the *hē* on *ha'attâ* is a dittography (*BHS*, followed by NJPS, NAB, NIV, REB, Allen, *Ezekiel 20–48*, p. 210; etc.). But haplography in the versions is more likely. See the commentary.

133. *běyāmîm qadmônîm*, lit. "in former days," answers to *bě'aḥărît hayyāmîm*, "in the latter days" (v. 16).

134. LXX and Syr. smooth out MT's awkward asyndetic construction of *bayyāmîm hāhēm šānîm* by adding the copula to *šānîm*. Talmon (*Textus* 1 [1960] 171) plausibly proposes a conflation of two synonymous readings: *bymym hhm* and *[b]šnym*. Cooke (*Ezekiel*, p. 417) suggests that *šānîm* functions as a temporal accusative, answering the question, "How long?" Cf. GKC, §118k.

135. MT *ta'ălâ ḥămātî bě'appî*, lit. "my wrath shall go up in my nostrils," but *bě'appî* is best taken with v. 19.

136. LXX interprets "my passion" as a second subject of *ta'ăleh* in v. 18.

137. *BHS* suggests emending *hammadrēgôt* to *hammigdālôt*, "towers," with Syr. and Targ. Cf. the pairing of *ḥômâ* and *migdāl* in Isa. 2:15.

138. MT *wěqārā'tî 'ālāyw lěkol-hāray ḥereb*, lit. "And I will summon against him to all my mountains a sword," is difficult. LXX φόβον, "fear," seems to presuppose *ḥărādâ ḥereb* for *hāray ḥereb*. Cf. REB. Allen (*Ezekiel 20–48*, p. 201) views *hāray* as an adapted torso, *hr* having been written for *ḥr* under the influence of *wnhrsw hhrym* in v. 20, and then made more sensible by adding the suffix.

139. LXX intensifies the reading by adding ἐνδοξασθήσομαι, "and my glory," viz., "I will magnify myself, sanctify myself, and glorify myself."

myself known in the sight of many nations. Then they will know that I am Yahweh."

The new citation formula signals the commencement of the fourth literary frame. This frame consists of two unequal parts, clearly distinguished in style and purpose (v. 17, vv. 18-23).

17 Reminiscent of John the Baptizer's query of Jesus, "Are you the one who is to come, or are we to wait for another?" (Matt. 11:3; cf. Luke 7:19-20), Yahweh opens by asking Gog whether he considers himself the fulfillment of earlier prophecies. The question raises several of its own. Which prophecies does he have in mind, and what is Ezekiel's perception of his own position within Israel's prophetic tradition?[140] Several clues to the answers are provided within this text.

First, Yahweh claims the prophets as his own servants. The designation of Ezekiel's professional predecessors as *'abdî nĕbî'ê yiśrā'ēl,* "my servants, the prophets of Israel," sounds Deuteronomistic or Jeremianic.[141] This phrase distinguishes these prophets from false prophets, who claimed to speak for Yahweh but whom God himself disowned (see Ezek. 12:21–13:23). Yahweh affirms the authenticity and authority of their messages by referring to them as agents through whom he had spoken.[142] The idiom apparently derives from the practice of an officially authorized messenger recording his superior's message or delivering by hand the written copy of a message.[143] Second, the designation identifies these prophets as Israelite. In the ancient world, rulers would regularly appeal to prophets or diviners for a divine determination, especially prior to battles such as the one envi-

---

140. This text is overlooked by Carley, *Ezekiel Among the Prophets.* For a detailed discussion of this text see D. I. Block, "Gog in Prophetic Tradition: A New Look at Ezekiel XXXVIII 17," *VT* 42 (1992) 152-72.

141. Variations of *'abdî/'abdāyw hannĕbî'îm* occur in 2 K. 9:7; 17:13, 23; 21:10; 24:2; Jer. 7:25; 25:4; 26:5; 29:19; 35:15; 44:4. See also Amos 3:7; Zech. 1:6; Ezra 9:11; Dan. 9:6, 10. See Weinfeld, *Deuteronomy and the Deuteronomic School,* p. 351.

142. The clause *'ăšer dibbartî bĕyad 'abdî,* "of whom I spoke by the hand of my servants," seems odd, but this is a common Hebrew (cf. 2 K. 17:13, 23, etc.; BDB, p. 391) and extra-Israelite idiom for "by the agency of." See the almost exact parallel in the Aramaic Zakkur Inscription A:12, *w'nny b'lšmy[n wyml]l b'lšmyn 'ly [b]yd ḥzyn wbyd 'ddn,* "And Baalshamayn answered me, and Baalshamayn [spoke] to me by the hand of seers and messengers" (*KAI,* 202.11-12). Remarkably, *dibbēr bĕpeh,* "to speak by the mouth of," never occurs in the OT. For a similar use of *'ăšer,* "of whom," before a verb of speech see Gen. 3:17.

143. Cf. Saul's nonverbal gesture of sending pieces of the dismembered ox throughout the country by the agency of messengers *(bĕyad mal'ākîm),* along with the oral interpretation of the gesture, in 1 Sam. 11:7. For a discussion of this use of *bĕyad* see P. R. Ackroyd, *TDOT,* 5:410.

sioned here.[144] But the addition "of Israel" rules out any prophecy that might have been given in Gog's homeland or at another oracular site. The issue here is that Yahweh's Israelite prophets have made pronouncements, ostensibly about Gog. Third, they are former prophets, who prophesied *in the past* (lit. "in former days") and *in those days after many years* (lit. "in those days years"). Like *hannĕbî'îm hāri'šōnîm* in Zech. 1:4, both expressions represent "a stage of distanced reflection on past prophecy," and carry a sense of antiquity, which rules out any of Ezekiel's contemporaries.[145] Regardless of the textual history of *bayyāmîm hāhēm šānîm*, "in those days years," this phrase implies the continuous or repeated delivery of the same message.[146]

This comment seems to reflect the existence of an authoritative prophetic tradition alongside the Mosaic covenant Torah.[147] But did such a tradition exist in Ezekiel's time? If so, did he have access to it? In principle, if the prophetic experience is taken seriously, to ask the question is to answer it. Since it is Yahweh himself who speaks here about the messages of former prophets, the only conclusion required is that Yahweh was aware of this stream of tradition with which Gog is now associated. But this answer will satisfy few, and the question remains: could Ezekiel have been this self-conscious about the relationship of his utterances to previous prophecies? The question may be answered in the affirmative for at least four reasons.[148] (1) It is reasonable to suppose and it is explicitly attested that prophetic sayings were recorded and collected during or shortly after a prophet's lifetime.[149] (2) As

144. Cf. Nebuchadrezzar's use of divination to determine the direction of his Palestinian campaign in Ezek. 21:26-29 (Eng. 21-23). For a discussion of the role of oracular/prophetic revelation in waging war in the ancient Near East see M. Weippert, " 'Heiliger Krieg' in Israel und Assyrien: Kritische Anmerkungen zu Gerhard von Rads Konzept des 'Heiligen Krieges im alten Israel,' " *ZAW* 84 (1972) 460-93.

145. Cf. *měšal haqqadmōnî,* "a proverb of the ancients" (1 Sam. 24:14). The quotation is from Zimmerli (*Ezekiel 2,* p. 312), who deletes this verse since Ezekiel was dependent on the direct experience of the prophetic word. Hossfeld (*Untersuchungen,* p. 450) speaks of "einer theologischen Systematik" ("a theological systematic"), which is able to skim off present prophecy from earlier prophets whose pronouncements have already found historical fulfillment.

146. So Odell, "Ezekiel 38–39," p. 121; cf. Davidson, *Ezekiel,* p. 280. See also n. 134 above.

147. Cf. Cody, *Ezekiel,* p. 186.

148. For a detailed development of these arguments see Block, *VT* 42 (1992) 164-66.

149. J. Blenkinsopp cites as evidence Jer. 36:1-4; 45:12; and perhaps Isa. 8:16 (*A History of Prophecy in Israel* [Philadelphia: Westminster, 1983], p. 23). A remarkable analogue to Jer. 36:1-4 is found in a recently published document from Mari (*ARM* 26/2, no. 414). For discussion see A. Malamat, "New Light from Mari (ARM XXVI) on Biblical Prophecy (III-IV)," in *Storia e tradizioni di Israele,* Fest. J. A. Soggin, ed. D. Garrone and

Amos 3:7 suggests, Israelite prophets were well aware of their place in the history of the Israelite prophetic movement (see 2 K. 17:13, 23). (3) Jeremiah's and Ezekiel's vigorous confrontations with false prophets indicate that both men were reflective about the nature of prophecy and their own standing within the tradition.[150] (4) Ezekiel's prophecies give ample evidence of Jeremianic influence.[151] Accordingly, the present verse portrays a sophisticated and self-conscious reflection on the history of the Israelite prophetic tradition.

Regardless of their stance on the authenticity of v. 17, scholars generally agree that this rhetorical question expected an affirmative response. But the absence of any reference to Gog elsewhere in the prophets raises the question of which prophecies this text had in mind. Three possibilities have been proposed: (1) oracles that have been lost; (2) general pronouncements of the destruction of Yahweh's people; (3) a combination of Isaiah's announcement of the defeat of Israel's enemy "on the mountain of Israel" (Isa. 14:24-25) and Jeremiah's reference to "the foe from the north."[152] Since the Isaianic prophecy concerned the Assyrians, and Jeremiah understood his predictions to have been fulfilled by Nebuchadrezzar, Ezekiel is said to have adapted old oracles to new realities.[153]

As Odell has observed,[154] however, the third interpretation (Zimmerli's) flies in the face of the way in which Ezekiel's contemporaries would have interpreted Jeremiah's predictions. There can be little doubt they would have identified Babylon under Nebuchadrezzar as Jeremiah's foe "from the north," especially since Jeremiah had explicitly made this identification himself (Jer. 25:9). Ezekiel could only have appealed to such texts by drastically altering their meaning. M. Fishbane maintains that that is exactly what has transpired. "Presumably, Ezekiel (or a pseudo-Ezekiel) believed the advent of Gog to be the true fulfillment of this ancient prediction. In the process, a national oracle has been expanded and has assumed apocalyptic significance."[155]

F. Israel (Brescia: Paideia, 1992), pp. 185-88. For a consideration of a neo-Assyrian analogue to the present military context, see Millard, *RHR* 202 (1985) 137.

150. See Odell, "Ezekiel 38–39," p. 228 n. 78.

151. Cf. Ezek. 23 and Jer. 3:6-11; Ezek. 34 and Jer. 23:1-6; 36:24-28 and Jer. 31:31-34. Cf. Carley, *Ezekiel among the Prophets,* pp. 51-57.

152. For the first, see Hitzig, *Ezechiel,* p. 294; Herrmann, *Ezechiel,* p. 248. For the second, see, e.g., Skinner, "Ezekiel," p. 316; more recently Alexander, "Ezekiel," p. 933. For the third, see Jer. 4–6, esp. 6:22; and Zimmerli, *Ezekiel 2,* pp. 299-304. For fuller treatment of these possibilities see Block, *VT* 42 (1992) 166-70.

153. Zimmerli, *Ezekiel 2,* p. 303; similarly Fishbane, *Biblical Interpretation,* p. 477.

154. Odell, "Ezekiel 38–39," p. 36.

155. Fishbane, *Biblical Interpretation,* p. 477.

But such explanations are quite unnecessary. Now it may well be that if Yahweh had actually directed this question to Gog himself, and if Gog had been aware of the earlier pronouncements concerning the "foe from the north" by Israelite prophets, he would have answered in the affirmative. It would certainly have bolstered his ego if, apart from his personal greed, he could have claimed the role of Yahweh's agent, like Nebuchadrezzar before him, sent in to punish the Israelites. The question then feeds right in to Gog's egomaniacal ambitions.

Gog's self-understanding and Yahweh's perception of him are quite different, however, as the earlier frames have already demonstrated. According to the first frame (vv. 2-9) Yahweh alone brings Gog and his hordes on. Like a conqueror himself, Yahweh will lead Gog in, dragging in his captives with hooks in their jaws. According to the second frame (vv. 10-13), however, Gog is totally oblivious to the fact he is but a puppet on Yahweh's strings. He imagines he is campaigning against Israel of his own free will. Correspondingly, even if Gog would have answered this question positively, the correct answer is negative.[156] Gog is in fact not "the foe from the north" of whom Jeremiah had spoken. His role is entirely different. He is not commissioned by Yahweh to serve as his agent of judgment; he and his troops are brought down from the mountains for a single purpose: that the holiness of Yahweh might be displayed in the sight of the nations (cf. vv. 16, 23; 39:6-7; also 39:22, 28). Whatever havoc they wreak on Yahweh's people they do of their own volition, not at the command of God. This oracle, therefore, is not about unfulfilled prophecy, but about earlier prophecies illegitimately appropriated. Otherwise vv. 18-23 become nonsensical. How could Yahweh announce in one breath that Gog is his agent, and in the next vent his wrath on Gog with such fury?[157]

18-23 The literary style and tone change dramatically, and the second person of direct address, used throughout the preceding frames, gives way to the third person. For the first time the intensity of the opposition between Yahweh and Gog announced in the opening challenge formula (v. 3) becomes apparent as Yahweh vents his fury toward Gog without restraint. The cause of the provocation is declared to be Gog's invasion of the land of Israel,[158] an action that is now portrayed as his very own (cf. 39:2). But with the

---

156. So also Odell, "Ezekiel 38–39," p. 122. There is no reason syntactically why this could not be the case. For a precise parallel to the present question see 2 Sam. 7:5, with which compare its unequivocal declarative counterpart in 1 Chr. 17:4.

157. The problem is not solved by ascribing v. 17 and vv. 18-23 to different editorial hands. This situation would surely have been as intolerable to later editors as it would have been to the prophet himself.

158. 'admat yiśrā'ēl recurs in v. 19. On this expression see my *Ezekiel: Chapters 1–24*, p. 248.

covenant relationship between Yahweh and his people fully restored, Yahweh cannot stand idly by. The divine patron of Israel must act.

Yahweh's emotional reaction to Gog's invasion is obvious as he explodes, heaping up expressions for anger unparalleled in the book, if not in the entire OT.[159] Fortunately for Israel, the wrath previously poured out on them will now fall on their enemy. The firmness of Yahweh's resolve is reflected not only in the signatory formula, which interrupts the outburst, but also in the expressed motive for his utterance: "I have spoken in my passion," in v. 19a leaves no doubt that the following threats arise out of his anger.[160]

19b-20   These verses describe the effects of the divine wrath, first on the invaded territory itself, and then on the cosmos. Yahweh begins by warning of a massive earthquake that will rock the land on which Gog has his sights.[161] Although Ezekiel has associated other cosmic events with divine judgmental activity, for the first time Yahweh's fury is expressed in an earthquake.[162] But v. 20 declares that the reverberations of the quake will be felt throughout the earth, indiscriminately, causing all living things to quake *(rā'āš)*[163] and leveling the landscape. With its epicenter in the land of Israel, the quake will bring down mountains and cliffs,[164] symbols of divinely grounded stability, and crumble walls, symbols of strength fabricated by human hands. The force behind this cosmic upheaval is obliquely hinted at in the divine passive,

159. All these expressions have appeared earlier in the book. See *hēmâ*, "fury, rage" (33 times in Ezekiel; see esp. 24:8, where it also occurs with the verb *'ālâ*, "to rise"), *'ap*, "anger" (see Ps. 18:9 [Eng. 8], which speaks of smoke rising from Yahweh's nostrils), and *qin'â*, "zeal, passion" (see Ezek. 5:13). On *'ēš 'ebrātî*, "the fire of my overflow," see 21:36; 22:21, 31. Cf. *'ebrâ* alone in 7:19.

160. On *dibbartî běqin'ātî* see 5:13 and 36:6. Cf. the expansion, *bě'ēš qin'ātî dibbartî*, "in the fire of my passion I have spoken," in 36:5.

161. No explicit reference is made to direct divine causation, but this is implied by the strong asseveration, *'im-lō'*, "assuredly." This is the first time Ezekiel has used *rā'aš* of an earthquake. Cf. 3:12-13 (rumbling noise); 12:18 (trembling body); 37:7 (rattling of dry bones); 26:10, 15 (the din of the armies attacking Tyre); 27:28 (the sound of her fall); 31:16 (the collapse of the giant tree).

162. Other events include cloudburst, 13:11, 13; the drying up of the Nile, 30:12; the darkening of the stars, 32:7-8; the surging of the waves, 26:3, 19; the storm at sea, 27:26. On the motif in other prophets see Isa. 24:17-20; Joel 2:10; 3:3-4; 4:15-16 (Eng. 3:15-16). According to Hag. 2:6-7 and Zech. 14:4-5 the earthquake precedes Yahweh's eschatological acts of salvation. Cf. also Matt. 24:29-30; Mark 13:24-27.

163. The catalogue of creatures resembles Gen. 1:26, 28, and 9:2, though by virtue of their special status humans are excluded. Similar catalogues of animals occur in Gen. 7:14, 21, 23; 8:17; 1 K. 5:13. Analogous effects of divine fury are described in Zeph. 1:3 and Jer. 4:24-26.

164. In Cant. 2:14, the only other occurrence of *hammadrēgôt*, it is paired with *hehārîm*, "mountains." The word is cognate to Aram. *drg*, "staircase" (*DISO*, p. 60; *DNWSI*, pp. 259-60), and Akk. *durgu*, "mountain gully" (*AHW*, pp. 177-78).

wĕnehersû, "they will be hurled down," and the addition of *mippānay*, "before me," earlier in the verse. The latter enhances the theophanic flavor of this frame, reminiscent of the quaking of the earth beneath the feet of the Israelites when Yahweh stepped down on Mount Sinai.[165]

Ezekiel's imagery in vv. 19-20 is generally associated with Hebrew apocalyptic, and treated as a sign of the relative lateness of this composition.[166] But the correlation between divine anger and cosmic collapse was widely recognized in Mesopotamia long before the exile of Judah. After listing a series of evils committed by the Babylonians, the annals of Esarhaddon describe the result:

> Enlil [i.e., Marduk] observed these. His heart fumed; his liver raged. The Enlil of the gods, the lord of the lands, plotted evil in order to annihilate land and people. In the fury of his heart he determined to destroy the land and to bring the people to ruin. An evil curse was found upon his mouth. In the heavens and on the earth evil "forces" persisted. The symmetry (*mit-ḫur-tim*) [of the universe] collapsed. The courses of the stars of Enlil, Anu, and Ea were disrupted and augured evil. Their "forces" were constantly changing. The Araḫtu canal, a raging torrent, an angry stream, a swollen high tide like the deluge itself, flooded the city, its residences, and its temples, and transformed it into a wasteland.[167]

21-22 Whereas vv. 19-20 allude only obliquely to Yahweh's involvement in the earthquake, and the effects of his fury appear to fall indiscriminately on all inhabitants of the globe, the impression changes in v. 21 as Yahweh announces specifically the summoning of the sword against Gog. The MT is difficult but not impossible,[168] and the positioning of *ḥereb* at the end may serve an emphatic rhetorical purpose. The designation of the target as "my mountains" is unprecedented in Ezekiel, but it does occur in Isa. 14:25 and Zech. 14:5. Like our text, Isaiah portrays Yahweh defeating a foreign invader within his land (cf. also Isa. 49:11; 65:9), whereas Zechariah conjoins motifs of earthquake and foreigners fighting in the land of Israel. Unlike the

---

165. Exod. 19. See also Judg. 5:4-5; Isa. 30:27-28; Hab. 3:3-7; Ps. 68:8-9 (Eng. 7-8); 114.

166. Zimmerli (*Ezekiel 2*, p. 313) comments, "In comparison with the original Ezekiel oracle, the later apocalyptic style of vv 18-23 is unmistakable." Similarly, Fuhs, *Ezechiel 25–48*, p. 219.

167. The various recensions of the account are gathered by Borger, *Asarhaddon*, pp. 13-14, episodes 5-6. Cf. also *ARAB*, 2:250, §658.

168. See n. 138 above. Even if *ḥărādâ* occurs in 26:16 (on the textual uncertainties of that occurrence see the commentary on it), it is difficult to imagine how scribes could have mistakenly reproduced it as *hāray ḥereb*. The LXX reading may itself reflect the translator's uncertainty regarding the meaning of the word.

pre-586 B.C. situation, in the future, when Israel, Yahweh's people, is established in his land, alien invasion will excite the passions of Yahweh. He is the divine protector of both the land of Israel and its people.

Unlike the sword Yahweh had wielded against Israel (viz., Nebuchadrezzar), the sword he sends against Gog is in his own hands. Reminiscent of Gideon's war against the Midianites (Judg. 7:22), and Jehoshaphat's battle with the Transjordanian nations (2 Chr. 20:23), the troops in the armies of Gog and his allies will turn their weapons against each other.[169] But Yahweh's punishment of Gog is not limited to the sword. V. 22 lists the agents through which his punitive work is executed. The catalogue consists of three pairs of calamities, the first two being familiar from previous oracles, but the pairing of fire *('ēš)* and burning sulfur *(goprît)* is new.[170] Often rendered "brimstone," *goprît* is a yellow crystalline substance that ignites readily in air, giving off suffocating fumes. Since it is often found in regions of volcanic activity, Ezekiel may have envisioned a volcanic eruption, with the hot lava gushing forth and igniting anything combustible in its path.

The purpose of these calamities is announced with a single word, *wĕnišpaṭṭî*. The Niphal form normally denotes "to enter into judgment," or "to commit to trial" (cf. 17:20; 20:35-36), but since the guilt has already been established in this case, it must mean the carrying out of the sentence. The totality of the punishment is highlighted by casting the list of victims after the triad of forces named in vv. 6 and 9, and cataloguing seven punitive agents. The latter in particular declares that Yahweh will marshall all the forces of destruction at his disposal against this enemy that has dared to invade his land and attack his people

23 The first panel of the Gog oracle climaxes with a powerful interpretive statement, highlighting Yahweh's threefold revelatory purpose: to display his greatness *(hitgaddēl),* his holiness *(hitqaddēš),* and his person *(nôdaʿ).* The first two involve the only occurrences of these roots in the Hithpael stem in the book.[171] The Niphal of *yādaʿ,* "to make oneself known," has occurred in earlier affirmations of Yahweh's self-disclosure (20:5, 9; 35:11). While this declaration relates most directly to the fourth frame, it summarizes Yahweh's intentions for all the events of "that day" (cf. v. 18), beginning with Yahweh's conscription of Gog and ending with his annihilation. By rocking the earth

---

169. Cf. the adaptation of the motif of the enemies of God's people destroying themselves in Zechariah's eschatological battle (14:13).

170. The conjunction of these terms in Gen. 19:24 suggests that they may have constituted a standardized pair. Plague *(deber)* and bloodshed *(dām)* were juxtaposed with the sword in 5:17 and 28:23; torrents of rain *(gešem šôṭēp)* with hailstones *('abnê 'elgābîš)* in 13:13.

171. These are examples par excellence of the estimative-declarative reflexive use of the Hithpael stem. Cf. Waltke-O'Connor, *Syntax,* §26.2f.

and bringing down this far-flung military alliance in the full view of the nations, they will all acknowledge the truth that Israel had gained from her own judgment and subsequent restoration.

c. The Disposal of Gog (39:1-29)

(1) Frame 5: The Slaughter of Gog (39:1-8)

1 *"As for you, human, prophesy against Gog, and say: 'Thus has the Lord Yahweh declared:*

Look, I am against you, O Gog, prince, chief of Meshech and Tubal! 2 *I will turn you around,[1] drive you on,[2] lead you up from the remotest parts of the north, bring you to[3] the mountains of Israel,* 3 *only to strike your bow from your left hand, and knock your arrows out of your right hand.* 4 *On the mountains of Israel you will fall — you and all your hordes and the peoples accompanying you — I will hand you over as food to every kind of scavenging bird[4] and wild animal.* 5 *On the open field you will fall, for I have spoken — the declaration of the Lord Yahweh.* 6 *And I will send fire against Magog,[5] and on those who live[6] securely on the coastal lands. Then they will know that I am Yahweh.* 7 *And I will make my holy name known among my people Israel. Never again will I let my holy name be desecrated. Even the nations[7] will know that I am Yahweh, the Holy One in Israel.[8]* 8 *Look! It is coming!*

1. On *wĕšōbabtîkā* see 38:4.
2. *wĕšiššētîkā* is an inexplicable hapax form. See Greenspahn, *Hapax Legomena,* p. 166. Many relate the word to Ethiopic *sōsawa,* "to proceed, walk along" (Cooke, *Ezekiel,* p. 423; Zimmerli, *Ezekiel 2,* p. 290). BDB (p. 1058) and GKC (§55f) explain the form as an abbreviated Pilpel from a root *š".* A similar sense is achieved by emending *wšštyk* to *whš'tyk,* on the basis of Targ. *w't'ynk,* "and I will lead you astray" (*BHS; HALAT,* p. 1534). Others derive the word from *nāśā',* "to lift." M. Dahood ("Hebrew-Ugaritic Lexicography XI," *Bib* 54 [1973] 365) sees here a Shaphel form of this verb. Less likely is F. Schulthess's suggestion ("Noch einige Zurufe an Tiere," *Zeitschrift für Semitistik* 2 [1924] 16) of an onomatopoeic *ša'ša'a,* "to call a horse." AV "to leave the sixth part" follows the medieval derivation of the word from *šiššâ.* The context favors something like "to lead" or "to drive." Cf. LXX "to lead, show the way."
3. *'al* may also be interpreted as "against."
4. *ṣippôr kol-kānāp* is appositional to *lĕ'ēṭ.* On this use of the construct relation see GKC, §130e.
5. LXX mistakenly reads "Gog," but cf. Gen. 10:2.
6. LXX transforms the declaration of judgment into a promise of salvation for the coastal lands by reading *wbyšby* as *wyšbw,* "and they will return."
7. LXX reads "all the nations."
8. Under the influence of the book of Isaiah, LXX (except LXX[B]), Syr., and Vulg.

It will happen! — the declaration of the Lord Yahweh — that is the day that I have decreed.'"

Except for the absence of a command to Ezekiel to set his face toward his hypothetical audience, the introduction to the second half of the oracle against Gog echoes 38:2. Although a major break occurs at v. 17, the introduction applies to the entire chapter. But this panel is more fragmented than ch. 38, being broken up six times by the signatory formula and four times by the recognition formula.[9] These intrusions in the literary product preserve some of the prophet's increasing excitement in the oral stage of delivery.

The present frame recapitulates some of the action of 38:19-23, but the tone and emphasis have changed. Like 38:1-9, the description is more objective and focused. There is no reference to divine emotion; instead the attention shifts to the *actions* of Yahweh against Gog. Except for two references to Gog's forces falling (vv. 4, 5) and two recognition formulae (vv. 6, 7), Yahweh is the subject of every verb in the frame. In spite of the recapitulation the plot advances, moving from the defeat of Gog to the disposal of the vanquished enemy.

1-6b   As in 38:2, the challenge formula in 39:1b draws the lines in the conflict: Yahweh has set himself in opposition to Gog. By a series of eight sharp, hard-hitting declarations, Yahweh outlines his strategy against the foe: He will turn Gog around, drive him on, lead him up *(heʿĕlâ)* from the remotest part of the north,[10] bring him *(hēbîʾ)* to the mountains of Israel, knock *(hikkâ)* his bow out of his left hand, force him to drop *(hippîl)* his arrows from his right hand, deliver *(nātan)* his corpse as food *(lĕʾoklâ)* for all the beasts and birds of prey, and torch the lands from which Gog and his allies have come.

The last four statements represent advances over 38:1-9. Whereas previously the invaders had been described simply as riding on horses, now they appear as mounted archers, with bows in hand. This image is culturally sensitive, inasmuch as Scythian warriors were among the first people of antiquity to use bows and arrows on horseback. Their renowned skill with the bow is attested by Xenophon, who reports that they were able to shoot

---

read "the Holy One of Israel." Targ. gives an expanded reading, "that I am Yahweh, the Holy One, I have made my Shekinah dwell in Israel."

9. The signatory formula occurs in vv. 5, 8, 10, 13, 20, 29, which compares with only two occurrences in ch. 38. The recognition formula occurs in vv. 6, 7, 22, 28, which compares with only two occurrences in ch. 38.

10. As elsewhere (1:4; 26:7; 32:30) *ṣāpôn*, "north," is used in its normal directional sense, without mythological overtones, contra Hossfeld (*Untersuchungen*, p. 463, following B. Margulis, "Weltbaum und Weltberg in Ugaritic Literature," *ZAW* 86 [1974] 15 n. 45).

backwards while riding full speed, and by Lucian, who says they could hit a moving animal or bird while in full gallop.[11] The picture of archers holding their bows in their left hands and their arrows in the right is also realistic, since the majority of warriors would have been right-handed.[12] The effect of Yahweh's action is to neutralize Gog's offensive power completely.

4-5 Yahweh will perform the ultimate indignity upon the corpses of Gog and his forces[13] by handing them over to scavenging animals, through exposure on the mountains and on the open field. Two kinds of carrion-devouring animals are mentioned. Scavenging birds are referred to by 'êṭ, which occurs elsewhere only five times. While the etymology of the term is uncertain,[14] its usage is suggestive. Three texts explicitly describe this class of bird as eating slain carcasses, supporting the view that Ezekiel's birds are vultures, though the Hebrews did not always distinguish between vultures and eagles.[15] The rarity of 'ayiṭ probably accounts for the explanatory comment, ṣippôr kol-kānāp (lit. "bird of every wing").[16] ṣippôr is a generic term for fowl, though it most often refers to a small bird, suitable for human consumption.[17] Since the Israelites had strict taboos on eating birds of prey,[18] the phrase 'êṭ ṣippôr kol-kānāp appears oxymoronic. Ezekiel's intent is probably to include a wide range of carrion-eating birds, including vultures, ravens, and crows. The inclusive language hints at the magnitude of the debacle; there will be enough food for all kinds of scavengers. The mammalian scavengers are referred to generically as ḥayyat haśśādeh (lit. "creatures of the field"). Jackals and hyenas are obviously in

---

11. Xenophon, *Anabasis* 3.3.10; Lucian, *Hermotimos* 33. For further discussion see Yamauchi, *Foes*, pp. 91-95. See the illustration of mounted archers on p. 71.

12. Cf. Plato, *Laws* 795A, who observed that Scythians were equally skillful in shooting with their right or left hands.

13. The triadic expression 'attâ wěkol-'ăgappêkā wě'ammîm 'ăšer 'ittāk, "you and all your hordes and the forces accompanying you," recalls 38:9.

14. In the past scholars have generally derived it from a root meaning "to scream," cognate to Arab. 'ayyaṭā (BDB, p. 743; Cansdale, *Animals of the Bible Lands*, p. 147), but this sense does not suit any of the contexts in which the verb occurs in the OT. In at least two of these "to pounce on" is a more appropriate rendering (1 Sam. 14:32; 15:19; cf. also 25:14). Thus F. Zorell, *Lexikon Hebraicum*, 2nd ed. (Leiden: Brill, 1962), p. 510; W. von Soden, *Bibel und alter Orient: Altorientalische Beiträge zum Alten Testament von Wolfram von Soden*, ed. H.-P. Müller, BZAW 162 (Berlin and New York: de Gruyter, 1985), p. 214 n. 4; *HALOT*, p. 816.

15. See Gen. 15:11; Isa. 18:6; Jer. 12:9. Isa. 46:11 and Job 28:7 are less specific. *nešer* is used for both eagles and vultures. So also von Soden, *Bibel und alter Orient*, p. 214.

16. See n. 4 above. ṣippôr kol-kānāp substitutes for the more common 'ôp haššāmayim, "birds of the sky." Cf. Ezek. 17:23; 39:17; also Gen. 7:14; Deut. 4:17; etc.

17. Cansdale, *Animals of Bible Lands*, pp. 161-63, 188.

18. Ibid., pp. 140-41.

mind, but by not naming the species he allows other animals like wolves and lions to join in on the feast.[19]

6a-b Yahweh will send fire against the lands from which Gog and his allies have come. Fire had been used earlier as a symbol of judgment, but this is the first occurrence of *šillaḥ 'ēš bĕ,* "to send a fire in," in the book.[20] Amos's application of the idiom to the burning of city walls and other fortifications suggests an offensive tactic on Yahweh's part. Not satisfied with the destruction of the armies of Gog, he attacks their home territories, Magog, Gog's place of origin (cf. 38:2), and *yōšĕbê hā'iyyîm,* "the inhabitants of the coastal lands," a reference to the Mediterranean shores and island regions represented by Tarshish in 38:13,[21] referring to the maritime forces allied with the land armies headed by the Anatolian hordes. In 38:13 the prophet had created the impression that these and other merchant nations were only envious spectators to Gog's adventures, but now it becomes apparent that they have actually taken their stand with Gog against Yahweh. The description of the inhabitants as "secure" *(lābeṭaḥ)* highlights the irony of the situation. The long arm of Yahweh extends far beyond the borders of his own land to the ends of the earth.

6c-8 The last line of v. 6 summarizes the effect of Yahweh's punitive actions: the recognition of himself by the targets of his attack. The frame might have ended here, but vv. 7-8 are added as explanatory commentary to emphasize that the recognition of Yahweh was not an incidental result of his defeat of Gog; this had been his goal from the outset. His objective for the nations was a general recognition not simply of his person, however, but of his holy character. The strength of his determination is reflected in the threefold occurrence of the root *qdš.* Twice he refers specifically to his holy name *(šēm qodšî),* recalling 20:39 and 36:20-23.[22] The first reference (v. 7a) highlights Israel as the locus of the revelation; the second the permanence of this newfound awareness (v. 7b). Never again would he tolerate the desecration of his name. This revelation was necessary because it was precisely "in Israel" that his reputation had previously been defiled, leading to the nation's

---

19. Ezekiel's description recalls Jeremiah's word concerning the fate of Jerusalem (12:9): "Is my inheritance a vulture *('ayiṭ)* or a hyena *(ṣābûaʿ)?* Is it surrounded by vultures *('ayiṭ)?* Go! Gather all the wild animals *(ḥayyat haśśādeh)!* Bring them to devour *(lĕ'oklâ)!*"

20. Cf. 10:2, 6-7; 15:1-8; and the idiom *hiṣṣît 'ēš bĕ,* "to kindle a fire in," in 21:3 (Eng. 20:47). Amos uses both idioms: *šillaḥ 'ēš bĕ* (1:4, 7, 10, 12; 2:2, 5; cf. Hos. 8:14), and *hiṣṣît 'ēš bĕ* (1:14). Jeremiah employs only the latter (Jer. 17:27; 21:14; 43:12; 49:27; 50:32).

21. Cf. *'iyyîm* in Ezek. 26:15, 18; 27:3, 6-7, 15, 35. According to Gen. 10:4 Tarshish was a son of Javan, i.e., the Greeks.

22. See also the end of this oracle (39:29) and 43:7-8.

exile and creating misimpressions in the foreigners' minds concerning his character. But those days are long past. The Gog debacle will demonstrate once and for all the holiness of Yahweh, not as a theological abstraction but in action, as he stands to defend his people against the universal conspiracy of evil. The third reference to Yahweh's holiness occurs in v. 7c as Yahweh assumes a new title, *qādôš běyiśrā'ēl,* "the Holy One in Israel." While the form recalls Isaiah's genitival expression, *qědôš yiśrā'ēl,* "the Holy One of Israel" (Isa. 12:6; 43:3; 55:5; 60:9, 14), the locative variation is characteristically Ezekielian.

The frame concludes with an emotional declaration of the inevitability of the coming event. The opening exclamation, *hinnēh bā'â wěnihyātâ,* takes up a familiar call from Yahweh's earlier announcements of judgment for his own people. But this announcement is good news for Israel. Like "the day of Midian" in Isa. 9:3 (Eng. 4), "the day [of Gog]" represents the moment of Yahweh's decisive intervention on his people's behalf against this enemy. Contrary to a common opinion,[23] "the day of which I have spoken" does not pick up on 38:17, which had referred to an earlier prophecy by Ezekiel's predecessors. The antecedent pronouncements are Ezekiel's own declaration of the coming of Gog and his demise at the hands of Yahweh. Interpreted this way, the last line enhances the force of the otherwise interruptive signatory formula not only by providing an appropriate conclusion to this frame but also by signaling the end of Gog. In the next frame the residents of the land will take over, disposing of the spoils of the war.

(2) Frame 6: The Spoiling of Gog (39:9-10)

9 *"Then the residents of Israel's cities will go out and burn up the weapons completely:*[24] *hand shields and body shields,*[25] *bows and arrows, clubs and spears. For seven years they will fuel their fires with them.*[26] 10 *They will have no need to carry wood in from the field nor cut down any in the forests, because they will use the weapons as fuel for fires. They will seize the spoil of those who despoiled them, and plunder those who plundered them. The declaration of the Lord Yahweh."*

23. Cf. Zimmerli, *Ezekiel 2,* p. 315; Odell, "Ezekiel 38–39," p. 135.

24. MT *ûbi'ărû wěhîśśiqû,* lit. "and they will burn and kindle." LXX telescopes the pair into a single term.

25. The preposition *bě* should be prefixed to *māgēn* and *ṣinnâ* (cf. the preceding *běnešeq* and the following *běqešet*). Allen (*Ezekiel 20–48,* p. 201) and others interpret its absence as a sign of a gloss. But the pair is attested in the versions, though LXX reads the second term as "lance."

26. Lit. "they will burn them as fire for seven years."

The attention shifts from Ezekiel's radical theocentric portrayal of Gog's demise to a graphic and earthy picture of human survivors mopping up after an enormous battle. Gog and God have had their day; for the first time the Israelites enter the picture. This frame may be the shortest of the series, but the imagery is vivid. The scene opens with the sight of the inhabitants of the cities of Israel (yōšĕbê 'ārê yiśrā'ēl) emerging (yāṣĕ'û) from their homes to dispose of the weapons of the annihilated foe. But where have the people been during the conflict? Were they holed up behind the walls of their towns?[27] This would seem to contradict the picture of a nation without any defensive structures painted in 38:10-13, but this may be forcing undue realism on a figurative portrayal of events. In any case, the people of the land appear to have been untouched by Gog's invading forces.

Ezekiel highlights the magnitude and intensity of the mopping-up operations with four special rhetorical techniques. First, he constructs a hendiadys, ûbi'ărû wĕhiśśîqû, "they will burn and set on fire."[28] This description of burning the accoutrements of a vanquished foe recalls the burning of boots and blood-stained cloaks of enemy warriors after their yoke and rod have been broken in Isa. 9:4 (Eng. 5). Similarly Ps. 46:10 (Eng. 9) envisions breaking the bow, shattering the spear, and burning chariots as a sign of Yahweh's ultimate termination of all wars on earth. Ezekiel's pyric image compares typologically with Isaiah's eschatological vision of swords beaten into ploughshares and spears into pruning hooks (Isa. 2:4; Mic. 4:3), though without the eschatological dimension.

Second, Ezekiel presents a list of seven kinds of weapons to be burned.[29] The catalogue begins with the relatively rare but general term for armor, nešeq,[30] which is followed by six specific items arranged logically in

27. A "city" ('îr) is by definition a settlement surrounded by defensive walls.

28. G. R. Driver (Bib 19 [1938] 183-84) recognized the logical contradiction: fuel must be kindled *before* it is burned. But the second term may be too rare to draw firm conclusions regarding its meaning. wĕhiśśîqû, "they will kindle," has traditionally been derived from śālaq, which is related etymologically to sālāq, "to go up" (cf. Bauer-Leander, *Grammatik*, §52u; GKC, §66e; BDB, p. 969), perhaps as an Aramaized form (BDB, p. 701). The Hebrew form of the latter appears in the OT only in Ps. 139:8, whereas the Aramaic form is attested in Ezra 4:12; Dan. 2:29; 3:22; 6:24; 7:3, 8, 20. But a derivation from nāśaq, "to burn," is more likely (cf. HALOT, p. 728; Zimmerli, *Ezekiel 2*, p. 291). The Hiphil form occurs elsewhere only in Isa. 44:15, where it also appears as the second element in a word pair involving bi'ēr. Cf. also the marginal note of Sir. 43:4 (LXX^B), and the Masada Scroll reading of 43:21, on which see P. Skehan and A. A. di Lella, *The Wisdom of Ben Sira*, AB 39 (Garden City, N.Y.: Doubleday, 1987), pp. 488, 490. The Niphal occurs in Ps. 78:21.

29. On the use of seven to denote completeness see Ahroni, *HAR* 1 (1977) 17.

30. See also v. 10. Elsewhere the word occurs in 1 K. 10:25; 2 K. 10:2; 1 Chr. 9:24; Neh. 3:19; Isa. 22:8; Ps. 140:8; Job 20:24; 39:21.

three pairs: small shields *(māgēn)* and body shields *(ṣinnâ);* bows *(qešet)* and arrows *(ḥiṣṣîm);* clubs *(maqqēl yād)* and spears *(rōmaḥ).* Only the last two require comment. *maqqēl yād* (lit. "rod of a hand") may denote a simple club, but the contextual need for a parallel to *rōmāḥ* suggests a "javelin."[31] *rōmaḥ* is a common OT term for spear or lance, an instrument much larger and heavier than the javelin, used as a thrusting rather than throwing weapon.[32]

Third, he cites the practical benefit that the pile of weapons offered the Israelites. Rather than being burned in one gigantic bonfire, the armaments provided the land with seven years' worth of firewood, relieving the inhabitants of the task of scrounging for fuel in the fields, or cutting down the forests. This had the added benefit of providing the environment with a sabbatical week of years to recover from the devastation the invading army had wreaked.

Fourth, Ezekiel recognizes the irony in the event: the plunderers (cf. 38:12-13) have become the plundered, and vice versa. How the tables have turned! Those who had not raised a finger in their own defense may now divide the booty that has been delivered to their doorstep (cf. Judg. 5:30; 8:24-26; 2 K. 7:16; Isa. 9:2 [Eng. 3]).

These four elements combine to create a picture of utter and total destruction of the enemies' military hardware. Never again would these foes from the distant regions of the earth threaten God's people. As if a guarantee of the divine pronouncement is needed, Yahweh seals the frame with his aural signature, *nĕ'um 'ădōnāy yhwh,* "the declaration of the Lord Yahweh."

(3) Frame 7: The Burial of Gog in Hamonah (39:11-16)

11 *"On that day I will assign a burial site*[33] *for Gog right within Israel — the valley*[34] *of those who have passed on,*[35] *east of the sea.*

---

31. P. Joüon suggested that *yād* derives from *yādâ,* "to throw," hence a "throwing stick," perhaps iron-tipped ("*yād = jet* (Nombres 35:17-18; Ez 39:9)," *Mélanges de la faculté orientale de l'université Saint Joseph, Beyrouth* 6 [1913] 166-67). See Zimmerli, *Ezekiel 2,* p. 316.

32. See Num. 25:7; Judg. 5:8; 1 K. 18:28; 1 Chr. 12:8, 24 (Eng. 9, 25); 2 Chr. 11:12; 14:7; 25:5; 26:14; Neh. 4:7, 10, 15; Jer. 46:4; Joel 4:10 (Eng. 3:10). See also Yadin, *Art of Warfare,* 1:10.

33. LXX and Vulg. misread *mĕqôm šām* as *mĕqôm šēm,* "a famous place." Cf. Targ. *'tr kšr,* "a proper place." On MT's asyndetically crafted dependent clause, in place of the expected *māqôm 'ăšer šām,* "a place where there is . . ." (cf. 21:35), see GKC, §130c, d.

34. *gê* is defectively written for *gê'.* Cf. Bauer-Leander, *Grammatik,* §72v'.

35. *BHS* and many commentators (e.g., Allen, *Ezekiel 24–48,* p. 201) repoint the participle *hā'ōbĕrîm,* lit. "those who pass by," to *hā'ăbārîm,* "Abarim," though Zimmerli (*Ezekiel 2,* p. 292) agrees with P. Wernberg-Møller ("Observations on the Hebrew Participle," *ZAW* 71 [1959] 59) that since the participle and segholate forms may appear as variants of the same expression, emendation is unnecessary. See further the commentary.

It will block off those who pass on.[36] *There they shall bury Gog and all his hordes, and they shall name the place, 'the Valley of Hamon-Gog.'*[37] 12 *Then the house of Israel shall spend seven months burying them, so the land may be cleansed.* 13 *All the people of the land shall join in burying them,*[38] *and their fame will spread*[39] *on the day that I display my glory — the declaration of the Lord Yahweh.* 14 *And they shall set apart a standing commission of men*[40] *who shall pass through the land and bury*[41] *any who have passed on,*[42] *who[se corpses]*[43] *remain on the surface of the ground, in order to cleanse it. They shall conduct their search for a period of seven complete months.* 15 *As the commissioners tour the land, if anyone spots a human bone, he shall erect a marker beside it, until those responsible for the burials have buried it in the Valley of Hamon-Gog.* 16 *(Hamonah is actually a city name.) Thus they shall cleanse the land."*

The opening date notice not only signals a new frame; it also reminds the audience of the chronological distance between the present and the events of the Gog oracle. An intrusive signatory formula at the end of v. 13 appears to divide this frame into two parts, but the repetitive style[44] and the common burial theme

36. MT *wĕḥōsemet hî' 'et-hā'ōbĕrîm* is rendered freely by Targ., "and it is near the two mountain cliffs." *BHS* follows J. Bewer ("Textual and Exegetical Notes on the Book of Ezekiel," *JBL* 72 [1953] 165) in deleting *'et-hā'ōbĕrîm* as a gloss, and restoring the text with LXX and Syr.: *wĕḥāsĕmû 'et-gay'*, "and they will dam up the valley." So also Allen, *Ezekiel 20–48*, p. 201. But LXX may also have misread the Hebrew. See the commentary.

37. LXX "the common grave of Gog" transliterates *gê'* as τὸ γαι. Cf. Syr. "Gog's valley of death."

38. Adding the object to *wĕqābĕrû*, with LXX.

39. *wĕhāyâ lāhem lĕšēm*, lit. "and it will become a name for them."

40. The form of MT *'anšê tāmîd*, lit. "men of perpetuity," resembles *'ôlām tāmîd*, "continuous burnt offering," in 46:15.

41. G. R. Driver (*Bib* 19 [1938] 184) emends *mqbrym* to *mbqrym*, "those who search for." The asyndetic combination of two participles may refer to two groups (Hossfeld, *Untersuchungen*, p. 475).

42. *BHS* and many commentators (e.g., Allen, *Ezekiel 24–48*, p. 201) delete *'et-hā'ōbĕrîm* with LXX* and Syr. But the latter may have intentionally tried to smooth out an awkward reading, or omitted it by homoioteleuton. Targ.'s "with those who pass by" changes the sense but does support MT.

43. *hanôtārim*, "those who remain," which in context refers to the unburied coprses.

44. The following lexical items are repeated (in various forms): *qbr*, "to bury," 7 times; *'br*, "to pass over," 6 times; *hā'āreṣ*, "the land," 6 times; *hmwn*, "horde, tumult," 4 times; *gê'*, "valley," 3 times; *ṭhr*, "to cleanse," 3 times. The combination of *qbr* and *hmwn* provides a close link with the earlier description of Pharaoh's descent into the netherworld (32:17-22). Hossfeld (*Untersuchungen*, p. 472) notes the correspondence be-

carry across the entire paragraph. Vv. 14-16 represent an expansion of the theme mentioned in passing in v. 12. The signatory formula functions rhetorically, providing an emphatic pause after the reference to the manifestation of Yahweh's glory.[45] Vv. 11-13 focus the attention on the activity of the Israelites, who go out en masse to bury the remains of Gog's armies. Even so, the opening and closing references to the "day" remind the hearer/reader that for all this human activity, Yahweh's agenda is ultimately being served. In the first instance, Yahweh assigns *(nātan)* Gog his burial place (v. 11). In the second, though the events will result in the spread of Israel's fame, the divine objective is the revelation of Yahweh's own glory (v. 13).

The corpses of the enemy strewn about "the mountains of Israel" present the Israelites with a series of problems. First, since these are the bodies of Yahweh's enemies and the foes of his people, shall they be dignified with a proper burial, or be left out in the open, exposed to scavenging animals and the elements, as 37:1-10 had portrayed the bones of Israel? Israelite law required that all dead, including criminals, be given a prompt burial (Deut. 21:22-23). Second, given the vast numbers of slain, which burial ground has room for all these bodies? Third, since the victims are all foreigners, shall they be buried within the land of Israel, or be deposited outside its borders to preserve the sanctity of the land? The aim of vv. 11-13 is to answer these questions. Formally these verses resemble an edict, issued by a superior to his servants, containing precise instructions for carrying out a mission. Each verse deals with a different aspect of the enterprise.

11 The answer to the first question is obvious immediately: yes, the remains of Yahweh's enemies must be buried. The burden of v. 11 is to address the second question. Instead of solving it directly, however, the answer is cast in extremely enigmatic language, almost as if the prophet is posing another riddle to his audience, inviting them to figure out the spot Yahweh has in mind. The alert hearer/reader will recognize several important clues. First, the site is appointed by Yahweh. Second, in answer also to the third question, the corpses are to be buried "in Israel." Third, the specific site is identified as *gê hāʿōběrîm*. Scholars have interpreted this expression in several different ways, most notably as "Valley of Travelers," or as a variant spelling of Abarim.[46]

---

tween *gôg wĕʾet-kol-hămônâ,* "Gog and all [his] hordes" (v. 11), and "Pharaoh/Egypt and all his hordes" in 31:2, 18; 32:16 (24, 26), 31, 32.

45. So also Zimmerli, *Ezekiel 2,* p. 317.

46. NRSV and NJPS translate "Valley of the Travelers," treating *hāʿōběrîm* as a participle from *ʿābar,* "to pass over." For possible locations of the valley see Zimmerli, *Ezekiel 2,* p. 317. On Abarim cf. *HALOT,* p. 783; Allen, *Ezekiel 20–48,* p. 201. Although the OT knows of sites called Abarim, one east of Galilee (Jer. 22:20) and another in the Moabite highlands (Num. 27:12), both identifications are ruled out by the present emphasis on burial "in Israel."

With support from the Ugaritic text *KTU* 1.22.I.12-17, however, it seems best to treat *hā'ōbĕrîm* as a designation for "those who have passed on," that is, deceased heroes, referred to elsewhere as *rĕpā'îm.*[47] This netherworldly connection may hold the key to this frame as a whole. Gog and his warriors have imagined themselves to be like the nobles of old, but Yahweh hereby declares their doom. They are sentenced to death just as Egypt and all his companions in ch. 32. Fourth, the burial ground is located "east of the sea," presumably the Mediterranean.[48] Fifth, it is the site of mass burial. A common burial ground was suggested by the awkwardly singular form of *mĕqôm šam qeber* (lit. "a place where there is a grave"). When the corpses of Gog and his horde are gathered, the pile in the "valley of those who have passed on" will be completely blocked off, that is, filled, so it will hold no more bodies.[49] Sixth, because of its new usage, the site will receive a new name, *gê' hămôn gôg,* "the Valley of Hamon-Gog," which appears to play on *gê' hinnōm,* "the valley of Hinnom." Earlier this was the site of Molech worship and child sacrifice (e.g., Jer. 2:23), and the place where the bodies of animals and criminals were burned.[50] In any case, the place will serve as a permanent memorial to the destruction of the enemies of Yahweh and Israel. To utter the name is to recall the event. But where is this place? Each of these clues is vague, but their

47. This Ugaritic document associates *'brm* with *mlkm,* departed kings who are identified elsewhere as *rpim,* on which see B. Levine and J.-M. de Tarragon, "Dead Kings and Rephaim: The Patrons of the Ugaritic Dynasty," *JAOS* 104 (1984) 649-59; J. F. Healey, "*MLKM/RP'UM* and the *KISPUM,*" *UF* 10 (1978) 89-91. M. H. Pope describes the *'ōbĕrîm* as "those who cross over the boundary separating them from the living so that from the viewpoint of the living they 'go over' rather than 'come over'" (*UF* 19 [1987] 462). For the connection with the *rĕpā'îm* see also S. Ribichini and P. Xella, "'La valle dei passanti' (Ezechiele 39:11)," *UF* 12 (1980) 434-47; Spronk, *Beatific Afterlife,* pp. 229-30; M. H. Pope, "Notes on the Rephaim Texts from Ugarit," in *Essays on the Ancient Near East in Memory of Jacob Joel Finkelstein,* ed. M. de Jong Ellis (Hamden, Conn.: Archon, 1977), pp. 173-75. Although Ezekiel is not averse to speaking about the residents of the netherworld (cf. *haggibbôrîm,* "the mighty men, 32:27), for reasons unknown he avoids the term *rĕpā'îm.* Perhaps it bore too many pagan associations or was too closely tied to the cult of the dead.

48. East of "the Dead Sea" contradicts "in Israel." Furthermore, in the oracles against the nations "the sea" designates the Mediterranean (25:16; 26:5, 16, 17, 18; 27:3, 4, et passim in the chapter; cf. 47:8), though Ezekiel also identifies the Mediterranean as "the Great Sea" (47:10, 15, 19).

49. The word *ḥāsam* occurs elsewhere in the OT only in Deut. 25:4, where it describes the muzzling of an ox. The present usage may be illuminated by Sir. 48:17, which refers to Hezekiah creating a reservoir by damming up a stream. Given Ezekiel's penchant for using words with more than one sense in a given context, the second occurrence of *hā'ōbĕrîm* could also refer to travelers who would traverse the valley but are prevented by the huge mound of corpses blocking the valley.

50. Cf. Zimmerli, *Ezekiel 2,* pp. 316-17.

cumulative weight places it within the vicinity of Jerusalem, on which see further below.

12-13 These verses describe the effects of the burial of Gog's remains. First, their disposal results in the cultic purification of the land. This theme will receive fuller treatment in vv. 14-16, but for the moment the statement recalls Num. 19:11-22, which explains not only the contaminating effects of a corpse but also the process whereby a person so defiled may be ceremonially cleansed. The present pollution is of a different order than the defilement of the land brought on by the crimes of the Israelites,[51] a problem that Yahweh had resolved himself by purging the land of its population (exile) and allowing it time to rest and recuperate. After it had fulfilled its Sabbath years[52] and Yahweh had cleansed the people (36:24-25), they return to make a fresh start — a sacred people inhabiting a sacred land. The present pollution derives from two causes — an alien nation has invaded the sacred space, and now its corpses litter the land.[53] Unlike the former condition, since this contamination is not brought on by Israel's sin, and there is no demand to "bear their guilt" *(nāśā' 'āwōn),* this problem may be resolved by human (rather than divine) action, ritual rites of purification, in this case the burial of the dead. The present observation that the process will take a full week of months, rather than the week of days prescribed in Num. 19, speaks not only of the magnitude of the task but also of the concern to render the land absolutely holy.

Second, the impact of the Israelites' action will be felt far beyond the borders of their own country. The enthusiasm of the people for the task, reflected in the involvement of "all the people of the land,"[54] will make them famous. Ezekiel has previously shown great interest in the "name," viz., reputation, of Yahweh. For the first time he expresses concern for Israel's "name." The scrupulous burial of the enemy testifies to her passion for the purity of the land and to her newfound security in Yahweh.

Third, and most importantly, her actions will result in the public glorification of Yahweh. While Ezekiel has frequently employed the substantive *kābôd,* "glory," with reference to Yahweh's transcendent splendor and majesty, for only the second time Yahweh is the subject of a verb from this root:

51. Cf. 23:17 (whoredom of the nation as female); 36:17-18 (their ways and wanton deeds, bloodshed and idolatry). Cf Frymer-Kensky, in *The Word of the Lord Shall Go Forth,* pp. 406-9.

52. 2 Chr 36:21; cf. Lev. 26:32-45, on which see P. R. Ackroyd, *Exile and Restoration,* OTL (Philadelphia: Westminster, 1968), p. 242.

53. For a combination of these motifs see Ps. 79:1.

54. The expression *'am hā'āreṣ* has less to do with everyone owning his own property (cf. E. Würthwein, *Der 'amm ha'arez im Alten Testament,* BWANT 4/17 [Stuttgart: Kohlhammer, 1936], pp. 48-49, who argues that in the future no class distinctions will exist in the nation) than with the house of Israel being the rightful occupants of the land.

I display my glory. The present Niphal may be interpreted as a simple passive, with Yahweh being the one affected by the action, viz., he will "be glorified," but, as in 28:22, it is better interpreted reflexively: Yahweh effects his own glorification,[55] and finally receives the recognition he deserves. After all, the day of Gog is Yahweh's day.

14-16 Whereas 36:16-32 had concentrated on the purification of the population of Israel by Yahweh for his own glory, 39:14-16 expands on the theme raised in v. 12 — the cleansing of the land by his people. The process whereby the absolute purification of the land is achieved will involve four steps. (1) A standing commission shall be appointed to supervise the burial of Gog's remains. (2) These men shall pass up and down the length of the land, inspecting every corner for remnants of the vanquished foes' warriors. Ezekiel returns to his play on *'ābar*, "to pass through": the inspectors, referred to as *'ōběrîm*, "those who pass through," were to see to the burial of *hā'ōběrîm*, "those who have passed on," viz., the deceased "heroes."[56] Accompanying the inspectors would be another group, *měqabběrîm*, "buriers, sextons," charged with the responsibility of disposing of the discovered remains.[57] The reconnaissance team is to conduct their search for seven months, presumably concurrently with the heptad of months referred to in v. 12. (3) Whenever the inspectors discover so much as a bone of the enemy on the surface of the ground, the spot is to be marked with a signpost.[58] (4) The sextons shall follow the supervisors, transport the bones to the appointed site, and bury them in the Valley of Hamon-Gog.

The explanatory note in v. 16 constitutes a crux for the interpretation of this passage.[59] While scholars have generally either deleted *wěgam šem 'îr hămônâ* as a gloss[60] or emended it to yield a better sense, such changes rob the text of its punch line. Literarily the introductory particle flags this clause as an independent comment,[61] but rhetorically it performs an emphatic func-

---

55. On this use of the Niphal see C. Westermann, *THAT*, 1:801; Waltke-O'Connor, *Syntax*, §23.4h. The Niphal functions as a virtual equivalent to the Hithpael forms in 38:23.

56. On this meaning of the word see v. 11.

57. On the differentiation of function see Zimmerli, *Ezekiel 2*, p. 318; Hossfeld, *Untersuchungen*, p. 475.

58. Jer. 31:21 uses *ṣîyôn* of a road sign; 2 K. 23:17, of a grave marker.

59. See M. S. Odell, "The City of Hamonah in Ezekiel 39:11-16: The Tumultuous City of Jerusalem," *CBQ* 56 (1994) 479-89.

60. Those who delete it include *BHS;* Zimmerli, *Ezekiel 2*, p. 293; even generally conservative Barthélemy et al., *Preliminary and Interim Report*, 5:130. For an explanation of how the gloss might have appeared in the text see Allen, *Ezekiel 20–48*, p. 202. REB "no more will be heard of that great horde" is based on G. R. Driver's proposed emendation (*Bib* 19 [1938] 184): *wěgāmar šema' hămônô*.

61. Cf. Andersen, *Hebrew Verbless Clause*, p. 45; Muraoka, *Emphatic Words*, pp. 143-46.

tion. Whether the clause was added at the oral stage or at the time of transcription, it offers an additional clue to the riddle: Where are all these bodies to be buried? The answer, in a city called Hamonah.[62] But this answers one riddle with another. Where is this city called Hamonah? The answer is to be found in Ezekiel's use of *hāmôn* elsewhere.[63] In this context, the "Valley of Hamon-Gog" speaks of the tumultuous pomp of Gog and his hordes, which recalls the usage of the term in previous oracles against foreign nations, especially the final oracle against Egypt.[64] But the association of the term with Jerusalem in three earlier judgment oracles is especially instructive. The present form is linked assonantally with 7:12-14, where *hămônāh* had functioned as a shorthand expression for all of Jerusalem's riotous and rebellious behavior.[65] According to 5:7, Jerusalem's *hāmôn*, expressed in a refusal to follow the covenant demands and all kinds of abominations, had exceeded the tumult of all the surrounding nations. Some of these nations appear in 23:40-42, bringing their own base and boisterous ways right into the city of Jerusalem, at her invitation.

Ezekiel's present assertion that "Hamonah is a city name" should have solved the riddle for his audience. As in 23:4 and 48:35, however, instead of identifying the city by name, he uses a symbolic name, highlighting a particular characteristic of the place. In the present context *Hamonah*'s primary function is to memorialize the demise of Israel's last and greatest enemy, but by association it also memorializes the transformation of the city, and with it the nation. The people that had once superseded the pagan nations with their tumultuous arrogance and rebellion now impress the world with their scrupulous adherence to the will of Yahweh. Once the city (and the entire land) has been purged of every vestige of defilement, the stage is set for Yahweh to return (43:1-7) and to replace the retrospective name with a new, forward-looking *(mîyyôm)* one. Hamonah is gone, Yahweh is there!

---

62. Syntactically the predicate-subject structure, *wĕgam šem-ʿîr hămônâ*, with predicate indefinite relative to subject, signals a noncircumstantial verbless clause of classification (cf. Andersen, *Hebrew Verbless Clause,* pp. 42-46). Gen. 28:19 reverses the sequence of common and proper nouns: *wĕʾûlām lûz šēm-hāʿîr lāriʾšōnâ,* "but actually the name of the city was Luz previously." The addition of the adverbial modifier, *mîyyôm,* in 48:35 is neither the only nor even the most important difference between the final declaration of this book and the present statement. The absence of *gam* and the presence of the article in *wĕšēm-hāʿîr* call for a different interpretation.

63. Thus also Odell, "City of Hamonah," whose discussion has inspired many of the following observations.

64. Cf. Hossfeld, *Untersuchungen,* pp. 472-73; Bodi, *Ezekiel and the Poem of Erra,* pp. 119-20.

65. While the oracle is directed against the land as a whole, the activities described in the text are basically urban, and the city is specifically mentioned in vv. 15 and 23.

The seventh frame concludes by reiterating that the primary concern in all this human activity is the cleansing of the land. Yahweh is not satisfied with having defeated Gog and his allies; so long as their corpses are visible, the land remains unclean. A totally restored covenant relationship demands a God with a holy name, a holy people, and a holy land.

(4) Frame 8: The Victory Banquet (39:17-20)

> 17 *"As for you, human, thus has the Lord Yahweh declared:*[66] *'Proclaim to every kind of scavenging bird and to every wild animal:*
>
> *Assemble and come! Gather from all around to my sacrificial feast which I am preparing for you — a huge sacrificial feast — on the mountains of Israel. You may eat flesh and drink blood.* 18 *The flesh of valiant men you may devour, and the blood of the princes of the earth you may drink: rams, lambs, and male goats; bulls and fatlings of Bashan, all of them.* 19 *You may devour fat until you are satisfied and drink blood until you are intoxicated, at the sacrificial feast that I have prepared for you.* 20 *You may gorge yourself at my table with horses and charioteers,*[67] *valiant men and all the men of war.*
>
> *The declaration of the Lord Yahweh.' "*

The final frame in this sequence of literary caricatures commences with Yahweh's direct address of the prophet, followed by the citation formula. Thereafter the paragraph picks up an idea announced in passing in 39:4b and develops it in graphic detail. The placement of this frame after the scene involving the burial of Gog creates some logical and logistical problems, but the reader is reminded that this is a literary cartoon, and realism may be sacrificed for rhetorical effect. Indeed, as the oracle has progressed the scenes have become increasingly bizarre, climaxing here in a scene more fantastic than all. Comparable to political cartoons, this frame is to be interpreted not as prophetic literary photography but as an impressionistic literary sketch.

Like 38:1-9 and 39:1-5, the pronouncement proper is cast in the second person of direct address, but the audience has changed. The entire frame is cast in the form of an official invitation to special guests to attend a grand banquet hosted by Yahweh. Its structure may be sketched as follows:

---

66. The position of the citation formula after "the wild animals" in Syr. is more conventional. Cf. 21:33.

67. *rekeb*, lit. "chariot," but with LXX, Vulg., and Syr. read *rōkēb*, "rider" (collective). The present pair occurs also in 26:7.

Address of the herald:	*As for you, human,*
Notice of superior's message:	*Thus has the Lord Yahweh declared:*
Commissioning of the herald:	*Proclaim to every kind of scavenging bird and to every wild animal:*
Text of the invitation:	*Assemble and come! Gather from all around to my sacrificial feast, which I am preparing for you — a huge sacrificial feast — on the mountains of Israel. You may eat flesh and drink blood. The flesh of valiant men you may devour, and the blood of the princes of the earth you may drink: rams, lambs, and male goats; bulls and fatlings of Bashan, all of them. You may devour fat until you are satisfied and drink blood until you are intoxicated, at the sacrificial feast that I have prepared for you. You may gorge yourself at my table, with horses and charioteers, valiant men and all the men of war.*
Signature of the host:	*The declaration of the Lord Yahweh.*

The style may be formal, almost poetic, but the imagery is grotesque. The prophet's hypothetical addressees represent all kinds of carnivorous and scavenging creatures. In 39:4 Yahweh had announced to Gog that he was giving him as food to the wild creatures,[68] but now he dispatches the prophet with an official invitation to these very creatures to come and attend an enormous banquet that he has prepared for them. Following the custom of a conscientious host, the invitation presents the invitees with sufficient information to make an intelligent response.

First, they learn the identity of the host. Not only does he sign his name to the invitation; twice Yahweh affirms that he is the one preparing the feast for them (vv. 17b, 19b). Furthermore, the banquet is identified as *my sacrificial feast* (*zebaḥ*, v. 17b), and the spread referred to as *my table* (*šulḥān*, v. 20a). While most ancient Near Easterners could speak of sacrifices as food prepared by humans for the deity or for deceased royal ancestors, seldom, if ever, were humans invited to participate in communion meals with deity.[69] At

---

68. On *ṣippôr kol-kānāp* and *ḥayyat haśśādeh* see above on 39:4.
69. On sacrifices in the ancient world see G. A. Anderson, *ABD*, 5:871-73. The view that sacrifices in essence represented food for the gods (cf. Oppenheim, *Ancient Mesopotamia*, pp. 183-93) is probably an overstatement. For an illustration of a deity and

most, the king would eat of the food presented in sacrifice, but this is a far cry from Ezekiel's imagery of an indiscriminate host of animals dining at Yahweh's table.[70] By contrast, the biblical writers expressed remarkable freedom in their portrayal of Yahweh hosting banquets for earthly guests.[71]

Ezekiel's picture recalls several other prophetic texts, in which Yahweh's overwhelming victory is followed by a zebaḥ meal. Isa. 34:6-8 celebrates his day of vengeance upon Edom; Zeph. 1:7 displays even closer affinities to our text:

> Be silent before the Lord Yahweh,
>   For the day of Yahweh is at hand.
> Yahweh has prepared a sacrificial feast (zebaḥ);
> He has consecrated his invited guests.
> On the day of Yahweh's sacrificial feast,
> I shall punish the officials and the king's sons,
>   And all those dressed in foreign clothes.

Each of these banquets is designated a zebaḥ, which derives from a root meaning "to slaughter," and seems to have had reference to any sacrifices that were burned on an altar (mizbēaḥ).[72] More than one kind of zebaḥ was celebrated in Israel,[73] but it was generally assumed that this meal was eaten

---

a worshiper drinking through a long reed from a common jar, see *ANEP,* no. 158. See Oppenheim, *Ancient Mesopotamia,* p. 191.

70. See Oppenheim, *Ancient Mesopotamia,* pp. 189-91. The 12th-century-B.C. Ugaritic texts describe several banquets of the gods, but the participants are all divinities. See esp. the banquet of El and Asherah and their seventy children upon the completion of Baal's palace (*CTA,* 4.6.35-59; *ANET,* p. 134), and the celebration of Baal's victory over Yamm-Nahar (*CTA,* 3.1.1-25; *ANET,* pp. 135-36).

71. See esp. the covenant meal at Sinai in the presence of Yahweh (Exod. 24:11), and the psalmist's portrayal in Ps. 23:5-6.

72. Cf. the use of the Ugaritic cognate *dbḥ* in the following texts:

For two kinds of banquets (dbḥm) Baal hates,
Three the Rider of the clouds:
A banquet (dbḥ) of shamefulness,
A banquet (dbḥ) of baseness,
And a banquet (dbḥ) of a handmaid's lewdness. (*CTA,* 4.3.17-22; *ANET,* p. 132)

Go up to the top of the tower;
Climb to the top of the wall;
Lift up your hands to heaven,
Sacrifice (dbḥ) to Bull, your father El;
Cause Baal to come down with your sacrifice (dbḥ);
The son of Dagan with your game. (*CTA,* 14.2.73-79; *ANET,* p. 143)

73. The word may apply to burnt ('ôlâ), peace (šĕlāmîm), grain (minḥâ), purification (ḥaṭṭā't), and reparation ('āšām) offerings.

in the presence of Yahweh *(lipnê yhwh)*, that is, as his guest. The ritual varied, depending on whether it was a family or clan celebration on the one hand, or supervised by the priests at the tabernacle/temple on the other. But a common feature was the mood of rejoicing in communion and fellowship with Yahweh.[74] Ezekiel's designation of this banquet as a *zebaḥ* classifies it as a ritual event. But by altering all the roles he grossly caricatures the normal image of a *zebaḥ*. In place of a human worshiper slaughtering animals in the presence of Yahweh, Yahweh slaughters humans for the sake of animals, who gather from all over the world *(missābîb)* for this gigantic celebration *(zebaḥ gādôl)* on the mountains of Israel. The battlefield has been transformed into a huge sacrificial table.

Second, the invitation describes the menu. The last statement of v. 17 is thematic, calling on the participants to partake of flesh and blood, a merismic expression for carcasses as wholes.[75] V. 18 specifies these as the flesh of heroic figures *(gibbôrîm)* and the blood of the princes of the earth *(nĕśî'ê hā'āreṣ)*, which are to be devoured like fare normally served at a *zebaḥ* table: rams *('êlîm)*, lambs *(kārîm)*, male goats *('attûdîm)*, bulls *(pārîm)*, and the fatlings of Bashan *(mĕrî'ê bāšān)*.[76] These terms are obviously not used literally, but as animal designations for nobility.[77]

Third, the invitation emphasizes the abundance of food that has been prepared. *kullām*, "all of them," at the end of v. 18, prepares the reader for the lavish description in vv. 19-20. Meanwhile the caricaturing of the *zebaḥ* continues with the invitation to the animal guests to enjoy the "fat *(ḥēleb)* and

---

74. The full designation of the sacrifice was *zebaḥ šĕlāmîm,* "peace offering." See H. Ringgren, *TDOT,* 4:12-13; On the idea of communion in the peace offering see idem, *Israelite Religion,* pp. 170-71. For a fuller discussion of the *zebaḥ* in Israel see B. Lang, *TDOT,* 4:17-29.

75. The standardized word pair *bāśār* and *dām* is common in Hebrew (Gen. 9:4; 32:5-6; Lev. 6:20; 15:19; 17:11, 14; Deut. 12:23, 27; 32:42; Isa. 49:26; Ps. 50:13; 79:2-3; cf. Sir. 14:18); it also occurs in Ugaritic *(CTA,* 24.9) and Aramaic (Amherst Egyptian 63:6). See R. C. Steiner and C. F. Nims, "You can't offer your sacrifice and eat it too: A Polemical Poem from the Aramaic Text in Demotic Script," *JNES* 43 (1984) 95, and the comments on pp. 101-2.

76. Cf. 27:21, where lambs, rams, and he-goats occur in the list of trade goods provided by Arabia and the princes of Qedar for Tyre. In chs. 40–48 both rams (43:23, 25; 45:23-24; 46:4-7, 11) and bulls (e.g., 43:25-26) will appear as sacrificial animals. Cf. the metaphorical use of *'êlîm,* "rams," in 17:13; 30:13; 31:11, 14; but esp. *'êlê gibbôrîm,* "heroic rams." The phrase *mĕrî'ê bāšān* occurs only here in the OT, but references to *mĕrî'îm* as desirable sacrificial animals occur in 2 Sam. 6:13; Isa. 1:11; and Amos 5:22.

77. Cf. the metaphorical use of *'attûdîm* and *'êlîm* in 34:17. This verse provides the most comprehensive list of animal names used as designations for nobility in the entire OT. See Miller, *UF* 2 (1970) 177-86. Targ. interprets rather than translates each of these animal names: "kings, rulers, and governors, all of them mighty men, rich in possessions."

blood," which, in a normal sacrificial meal, would have been reserved for Yahweh (cf. 44:7, 15; Lev. 3:16-17; etc.). The remainder of this frame paints a picture of unrestrained gluttony at Yahweh's table.[78] Yahweh encourages the beasts and birds to gorge themselves with the flesh until they are full *('ākal lĕśābĕ'â)*, and to drink the blood until they are drunk *(šātâ lĕšikkārôn).*[79] The text of the invitation concludes with a reminder of the true sacrificial victims: all the participants in the previous battle against Yahweh, including the horses. Yahweh's signature closes both the invitation and this frame.

The literary image sketched here must have been shocking for a person as sensitive to cultic matters as Ezekiel. Even worse than the lack of restraint is the skewing of roles. Yahweh, the sovereign Lord, hosts foul scavenging creatures. Instead of serving clean, edible food, the divine host offers his guests human flesh, thereby violating the most serious taboo of all: the desecration of human life. Gen. 9:1-7 sanctions animal flesh as food for humans, but no one, neither human nor animal, was to shed human blood, let alone consume it! How the priestly prophet reacted to this horrifying image one may only speculate.

d. The Final Word (39:21-29)

21 *"Thus I will establish my glory among the nations, and all the nations will see my justice that I have executed, and my power*[80] *that I have imposed on them.* 22 *Then the house of Israel will know that I am Yahweh their God from that day onward.* 23 *And the nations will recognize that the house of Israel went off into exile on account of their own iniquity. Because they had acted faithlessly against me I hid my face*[81] *from them. When I delivered them into the power of their*

---

78. *šulḥānî,* "my table," denotes the table Yahweh has spread, rather than the table spread in Yahweh's honor, as in Mal. 1:7, 12.

79. The stereotypical nature of this description is evident from the Isaiah and Zephaniah texts cited above, as well as the following 2nd-century-B.C. Aramaic text from Egypt (Amherst Egyptian 63:5-7):

Let our teeth feel/chew tidbits;
Bring (them) that we may become fat and corpulent.
Let us eat flesh and become fat;
Let us cause blood to flow and drink to saturation.

For the complete text in transliteration, translation, and commentary see Steiner and Nims, *JNES* 43 (1984) 89-114.

80. *yādî,* lit. "my hand," but see Targ. *gbwrty,* "my strength." The idiomatic phrase *śîm yād bĕ,* lit. "to lay the hand on" someone, occurs only here in Ezekiel.

81. Targ. interprets the treachery as "against my Memra," and the hiding of Yahweh's face as removing his Shekinah.

adversaries,[82] *they fell to the sword, all of them.* 24 *I dealt with them according to their defilement and according to their treachery. Therefore I hid my face from them.*

25 *Assuredly, thus has the Lord Yahweh declared: 'Now I will restore the fortunes*[83] *of Jacob; I will have compassion on the whole house of Israel, and demonstrate passion for my holy name.* 26 *They will bear*[84] *their disgrace and all their acts of infidelity that they have perpetrated against me, when they dwell securely on their own land, with no one frightening them.* 27 *When I bring them back from the peoples, and regather them from the countries of their enemies, then I will display my holiness among them, in the sight of many nations.*[85] 28 *And they will know that I am Yahweh their God in that, having sent them off into exile*[86] *to the nations, I will gather them to their own land. I will never again leave any of them out there.*[87] 29 *Nor will I ever again hide my face from them, for*[88] *I will have poured out my Spirit*[89] *on the house of Israel. The declaration of the Lord Yahweh.' "*

82. The designation for enemy, *ṣār*, which occurs elsewhere in the book only in 30:16, is often deleted as secondary. Cf. Zimmerli, *Ezekiel 2*, p. 320.

83. Kethib *šbyt;* Qere *šbwt.* On the variation see my *Ezekiel: Chapters 1–24*, pp. 512-14.

84. MT *wĕnāśû* is pointed as if from *nāśā',* "to bear." Most read *wĕnāšû,* however, as if from *nāšâ,* "to forget" (*BHS,* NRSV, REB, NAS, NIV; J. Lust, "The Final Text and Textual Criticism. Ez 39,28," in *Ezekiel and His Book,* p. 53; etc.). But Zimmerli (*Ezekiel 2,* p. 295) has defended MT, noting: (1) the versions all follow MT; (2) *nāšâ* is absent from Ezekiel; (3) the Qal form of *nāšâ* is rare even outside Ezekiel; (4) the idiom *nāśā' kĕlimmâ,* "to bear shame," is common in Ezekiel (16:52, 54; 32:24-25, 30; 34:29; 36:6-7, 15; 44:13); (5) both here and in 16:54 the phrase follows *šûb šĕbût.* On III-*aleph* verbs appearing like III-*hē* verbs see GKC, §75qq; Bauer-Leander, *Grammatik,* §59c. Cf. *mlw* in 28:16.

85. *haggôyim rabbîm* is odd not only because these two words are rarely conjoined (cf. the more common *'ammîm rabbîm*), but also for the article on *gôyim.* Since LXX* lacks *rabbîm,* it is usually deleted as a gloss incompletely integrated into the text. But on the definite article on a noun but absent from its modifier see Davidson, *Syntax,* §32, Rem. 2.

86. MT *bĕhaglôtî 'ōtām.* LXX treats the infinitive as a Niphal of *gālâ,* "to reveal." Targ. supports MT, expanding the text with a justification for each of Yahweh's actions: (1) he exiled them "because they sinned against me"; (2) he restored them "because they repented."

87. These last two clauses are missing in LXX. Lust (in *Ezekiel and His Book,* pp. 48-54) argues that the *Vorlage* underlying LXX differed from the *Vorlage* of MT.

88. Treating *'ăšer* causally, in the sense of *ya'an 'ăšer,* with LXX and Vulg. (cf. Cooke, *Ezekiel,* p. 424; and 12:12), against Zimmerli (*Ezekiel 2,* p. 295), who interprets the particle temporally.

89. LXX reads τὸν θυμόν μου, "my wrath," in place of *rûḥî.* Against Lust (in *Ezekiel and His Book,* pp. 52-53), who argues that MT represents a deliberate change in the text at a time when ch. 39 was still followed by ch. 37 (as in Papyrus 967), LXX

♦ *Nature and Design*

Because of shifts in chronological perspective, the disappearance of Gog from the scene, the presence of three variations of the recognition formula, and a series of novel features, scholars are virtually unanimous in deleting some or all of these verses as late expansionistic modifications.[90] Nevertheless, this segment displays strong signs of authenticity, including numerous echoes of earlier prophecies of Ezekiel.[91] In response to those who would dissect vv. 21-29 into two or more segments, one may note that these verses contain no sharp formal divisions. All the material between the two signatory formulae at the ends of vv. 20 and 29, respectively, represents a single unit. The particle *lākēn,* "therefore," in v. 25 does function as a weak divider, but it also provides a sign of coherence in that the succeeding material is connected logically to the preceding.[92] Even the threefold occurrence of the recognition formula serves as a unifying factor, highlighting the prophet's central thesis. Indeed, the exact parallelism of the beginnings of vv. 22 and 23 immediately juxtaposed argues strongly against dividing them too sharply. But v. 23 is not cast in the usual shape of the recognition formula in Ezekiel, since it is not the person of Yahweh that is being acknowledged but the rationale for his treatment of his people.

On the other hand, one may view vv. 21-24 and 25-29 as two panels of a whole, displaying remarkable structural balance and symmetry, as the following synopsis illustrates:

Topic		Vv. 21-24	Vv. 25-29
A	The actions of Yahweh	21a	25
B	The response of the objects of his actions	21b	26-27
B′	The recognition formula (tied to Israel's exile)	22-23a	28
A′	The hiding of Yahweh's face	23b-24	29

In addition to their parallel structures, each segment is organized internally after a chiastic pattern. Both begin and end with descriptions of the divine action, between which are sandwiched the humans' responses,[93] arguing for

---

probably represents a harmonization with Ezekiel's stereotypical phrase *šāpak ḥēmâ,* "to pour out wrath." Targ.'s *rwḥ qdšy,* "my holy spirit," is more specific than MT.

90. For a summary of recent approaches and a more detailed analysis of this text see D. I. Block, "Gog and the Pouring Out of the Spirit: Reflections on Ezekiel XXXIX 21-9," *VT* 37 (1987) 257-61.

91. Cf. Cooke, *Ezekiel,* pp. 422-23.

92. Hossfeld (*Untersuchungen,* pp. 406-7) observes that *lākēn* may also function rhetorically to draw attention to the resumption of an idea.

93. Parunak (*Structural Studies,* p. 506) recognizes the following pattern: A (vv. 22-24) B (vv. 25-27) A′ (vv. 28-29).

a deliberateness of composition. This conclusion is supported by the fact that each ends with a reference to Yahweh hiding his face, a notion that is otherwise foreign to the book. By recognizing these divisions we discover another example of Ezekiel's "halving" of oracular pronouncements.[94]

But in content the two parts diverge, exhibiting a relationship to each other as that of "a dialectic of action and response."[95] The first describes Yahweh's action of judgment in response to Israel's rebellion; the second his salvific activity on her behalf, and the response this evokes in the nation. Furthermore, in the first recognition formula it is the nations primarily who recognize Yahweh; in the second it is Israel. In effect, even if not in style, vv. 20-29 perform the same function in relation to ch. 39 as 38:23 had served in relation to ch. 38. Each represents a summary statement of Yahweh's designs in his handling of his people.

(a) The Impact of Yahweh's Judgmental Activity (39:21-24)

21-22 These verses are transitional. Their backward look to Yahweh's war with Gog is reflected in the references to "the judgments that I have executed," "my hand that I have laid on them" (i.e., Gog and his hordes), and "from that day and onward" (viz., the day of Yahweh's victory). But the prophet's gaze also begins to turn toward the future, as evidenced in the consecutive perfects: "I will set my glory among the nations," "all the nations will experience my judgments," and "the house of Israel will know that I am Yahweh." This statement reaffirms that, as with most of Ezekiel's prophecies, the primary concern of the Gog oracle is revelatory: to make known the person and character of Yahweh, particularly his transcendent qualities: his greatness (*gādôl*) in 38:23; his holiness (*qādôš*) in 38:23; and his glory (*kābôd*) in 39:13. The last of this triad of motivations resurfaces in the opening announcement of Yahweh's intention in v. 21.

The employment of *nātan bě* (lit. "to put in place") with the substantive *kābôd,* "glory," treats the latter almost as if it were an objective, concrete reality, like the Shekinah glory that went before the Israelites during their wilderness wanderings and rested over the tabernacle (Exod. 40:34-38), and that later took up residence in Solomon's temple (1 K. 8:10-12). Ezekiel had witnessed the departure of this glory in visionary form himself (Ezek. 8–11), and he will announce its return to the rebuilt temple (43:1-5). As the glorious Shekinah had symbolized the presence of Yahweh among his people in the past, so the new vision of his glory would declare his presence among the

94. Cf. Greenberg, *Ezekiel 1–20,* pp. 25-27, 137-38; Odell, "Ezekiel 38–39," pp. 150-51.

95. Thus Odell, "Ezekiel 38–39," p. 151.

nations.[96] If the prophet initially had the sight of Yahweh's Shekinah glory in mind, however, he quickly moves from the visual image to the experience of his interfering presence in human history. But the actions by which Yahweh had intruded into earthly affairs to manifest his glory are not specified. Nor need they be, in the light of the immediately preceding account of the defeat of Gog.

The comments in v. 21b are interpretive, describing the significance of that event. Two unusual expressions are used. First, the nations will experience *(rā'â)* the justice of Yahweh. The translation of *mišpātî* as "my justice," rather than the usual "my judgment," is justified on several grounds.[97] (1) In 18:8 the phrase *'āśâ mišpāt* requires the translation "to execute justice." (2) When Ezekiel speaks of the execution of judgment he typically uses *'āśâ* with the plural form of *šepet*.[98] The preference for *mišpāt* here seems intentional. (3) In the Gog oracle, "to execute judgment" (or "to enter into judgment") is rendered with the verb *šāpat* (Niphal; cf. *nišpattî*, 38:22). (4) The present context demands that the greed and opportunism of Gog against innocent and unsuspecting Israel be met with justice (cf. 38:10-13). (5) Elsewhere in the OT the execution of *mišpāt* always involves the defense of the exploited in the face of those who run roughshod over their basic rights.[99] By contrast, *'āśâ šĕpātîm* has to do with punitive execution of divine judgment on those who rebel against him.[100]

Especially instructive for this discussion is 23:24, according to which Yahweh commits justice *(mišpāt)* into the hands of Oholibah's lovers, who are then authorized to judge *(šāpat)* her according to their *mišpātîm*, viz., the standards of conduct specified in the stipulations of suzerainty treaties. Here *mišpātî*, "my justice," interprets Yahweh's victory as an expression of sovereignty even over Gog. Yahweh had acted for the sake of his holy name, but he must also defend his rights as sovereign Lord. Therefore, in this case the purpose of the execution of divine justice is to defend not the violated rights of Israel but Yahweh's own position.[101]

Second, the nations will experience the power of Yahweh. As in 28:23, everything Yahweh does is public. In his exercise of justice and power his

---

96. This probably explains the replacement of the usual verb in the recognition formula, *yāda'*, "to know," with *rā'â*, "to see."

97. Contra Zimmerli (*Ezekiel 2*, p. 319), who finds a parallel in *wĕ'āśîtî bĕtôkēk mišpātîm* in 5:8.

98. The execution of judgments against Israel: 5:10, 15; 11:9; 14:21; 16:41. Against the nations: 25:11; 28:22, 26; 30:14, 19.

99. So also Odell, "Ezekiel 38–39," p. 157. Cf. 1 K. 8:45, 49, 59; Ps. 99:4; 119:84.

100. Exod. 12:12; Num. 33:4; 2 Chr. 24:24. In addition to the citations in n. 97, cf. also Ezek. 16:41; 23:10.

101. Cf. Odell, "Ezekiel 38–39," p. 157.

glory will be manifest among the nations. But Ezekiel had not delivered the message concerning the defeat of Gog for Gog's or the nations' sake. His primary audience consists of fellow exiles, and it is their transformation that he seeks. For this reason, his observation concerning the nations is interrupted by a statement announcing the implications for Israel of the victory over the military hordes. Repeating the recognition formula, now with "the house of Israel" as the subject, he adds the phrase *min-hayyôm hahû' wĕhālĕ'â,* "from that day onward." This addition focuses attention on the defeat of Gog as the event by which Yahweh's glory had been demonstrated through his execution of justice and his demonstration of power. This was a turning point in the nation's history. But the expression also indicates that even though the Gog debacle is considered an eschatological event (cf. 38:8, 16), it does not occur at the end of time. Rather, it marks the beginning of a new era, which will be characterized by Israel's recognition of Yahweh, that is, the full realization of covenant relationship.

23-24 The syntax of v. 23 links vv. 23-24 directly to the foregoing. Gog now fades out of view, however, being replaced in a new and greatly expanded version of the recognition formula by *haggôyim,* "the nations," over whom he had served as head. But this time the formula does not speak directly of the knowledge of God; rather, it dwells on his actions toward his people, which had been executed not in some far-off corner of the world but in the forum of the nations. When they reflect on the manner in which Yahweh has dealt with them, they will recognize another dimension of his justice; he has handled his people in accordance with what they have deserved.

From the perspective of the battle of Gog, the events described in vv. 23-24 are in the distant past. The people of Israel have returned to their land and have lived securely in it for many years, enjoying to the full their renewed covenant relationship with Yahweh. Now, after the defeat of Gog, the nations will realize that all the events preceding this restoration had in fact fulfilled the laws of divine justice. The dimensions of the guilt that had precipitated Israel's going into exile[102] are highlighted by four expressions: (1) *'āwōn,* "perversion," in Ezekiel particularly the twisting of the privileges of covenant relationship into a right; (2) *ma'al,* infidelity in covenant relationships, specifically treachery against Yahweh, the divine patron (*bî*);[103] (3) *ṭum'â,* "uncleanness, defilement," the same quality that their idolatry and bloodshed had

---

102. *gālâ,* "to go into exile," occurs elsewhere in Ezekiel only in v. 28 and 12:3. But cf. the nouns *gālût,* "exile" (1:2; 33:21; 40:1), and *gôlâ,* used of "exiles" (1:1; 3:11, 15; 11:24, 25) and as the abstraction, "exile" (12:3, 4, 7, 11; 25:3).

103. The verb reappears with its cognate accusative in v. 26. Cf. *ma'al ma'al* in 14:13; 15:8; 17:20; 18:24; 20:27.

imposed on the land (36:17-18); (4) *peša'*, the betrayal of Yahweh through the willful breaking of his covenant stipulations.

For all these reasons the Israelites had been exiled from their land. The nations, who had observed these events and puzzled over Yahweh's harsh treatment of his own people (36:20), had concluded that Yahweh was either incompetent to defend his people against Nebuchadrezzar, or he had gone back on his own covenant commitment to them. In either case, his reputation had been seriously profaned, because neither of these explanations was true. Rather, Israel had brought this fate on herself. The people had provoked the exile by treating the covenant relationship with contempt and treachery.

Verses 23-24 do not deny or evade the involvement of Yahweh in Israel's fate. On the contrary, they heighten it. The nation's disaster was the result of his direct action against them. First, Yahweh had *hid his face* from them. The twofold occurrence of the declaration in vv. 23 and 24 (and later in v. 29) provides a framework within which to interpret the divine response. The anthropomorphic notion of Yahweh "hiding his face" finds positive antitheses in expressions like "to cause the face to shine toward someone" *(hēʾîr pānîm ʾel)* and "to lift up the face toward someone" *(nāśāʾ pānîm ʾel)*, both of which occur in the Aaronic blessing (Num. 6:25-26) and represent ancient Near Eastern court language for looking favorably on someone.[104] For a king or prince to turn his face from a subject spelled disaster.[105] But the idea of the hidden face most commonly described the disposition of a deity, as in the following excerpt from "A Prayer of Lamentation to Ishtar":

> Accept the abasement of my countenance;
> Hear my prayers.
> Faithfully look upon me and accept my supplication.
> How long, O my Lady, wilt thou be angered
>   so that thy face is turned away?
> How long, O my Lady, wilt thou be infuriated,
>   so that thy spirit is enraged?
> Turn thy neck which thou hast set against me;
> Set thy face [toward] good favor.

---

104. *histîr pānîm*, "to hide the face," occurs 30 times in the OT. Cf. the related Akkadian idioms *pāna šākānu* and *pāna nadānu*, "to give the face," as well as *pāna wabālu*, "to bring the face (near)," on which see A. L. Oppenheim, "Idiomatic Akkadian," *JAOS* 61 (1941) 256-57; S. E. Balentine, *The Hiding of the Face of God in the Old Testament* (New York: Oxford University Press, 1983), pp. 22-28.

105. Cf. the following quotation from R. F. Harper, *Assyrian and Babylonian Letters* (Chicago: University of Chicago Press, 1892-1914), 885:25: "I shall turn (and) die if the crown prince my lord turns away his face from me." For the text see L. Waterman, *Royal Correspondence of the Assyrian Empire,* part II: *Translation and Transliteration* (Ann Arbor: University of Michigan Press, 1930-36), pp. 114-15.

> Like the water of the opening up of a canal
> > let thy emotions be released.
> My foes like the ground let me trample;
> Subdue my haters, and cause them to crouch down under me.
> Let my prayers and my supplications come to thee.
> Let thy great mercy be upon me.[106]

Except for Job 13:14 and 34:29, in every occurrence of this idiom in the OT this response is explicitly or implicitly portrayed as God's reaction to covenant betrayal.[107]

Although this is Ezekiel's only reference to Yahweh hiding his face, this is insufficient reason for deleting these verses as non-Ezekielian. Deut. 31:16-18 indicates that the idea of the hidden face of God is closely associated with the notion of divine abandonment, a prominent motif in Ezekiel's temple vision, and is given verbal expression by the people themselves, who rationalize their treacherous behavior with the excuse, "Yahweh does not see us; Yahweh has abandoned his land" (8:12; 9:9). Now the nations will learn that the hidden face of Yahweh was the natural and predicted response to the people's covenantal infidelity.

The last part of v. 23 describes the evidence for the hidden face of Yahweh: he had handed them over to the effects of their enemies. The devastation of Jerusalem and the exile of Judah's population was neither a function of the superior military strength of the Babylonian forces nor a reflection of Marduk's superiority over Yahweh. This was the result of Yahweh's own deliberate action against his people.

Verse 24 reiterates that Yahweh's actions toward his people were precisely what they had bargained for.[108] But divine justice is served not only by imposing a punishment suitable for the crime; the penalty also adheres to the warnings that Yahweh had built into his covenant (cf. Lev. 26:27-43; Deut. 28:49-68). Accordingly the glory of Yahweh will be established when the nations recognize the justice of Yahweh in the way he has handled his own people in the past, as well as his dealings with them in the present.

---

106. *ANET*, p. 385. Cf. the complaint of the afflicted in *Ludlul bêl nêmeqi* ("The Babylonian Job"), "I cried to the god (Marduk), but he did not look at me" (Lambert, *Babylonian Wisdom*, p. 38, line 4), which resembles the reaction of Job to God in the face of a similar plight in Job 13:14: "Why do you hide your face and count me as your enemy?"

107. See esp. Deut. 31:16-18. On the subject see R. E. Friedman, "The Biblical Expression *mastîr pānîm*," *HAR* 1 (1977) 4; and in greater detail Balentine, *Hiding of the Face of God*. See n. 104.

108. *ʿāśâ kĕ*, "to act in accordance with," recalls 24:14 and 36:19.

(b) The Impact of Yahweh's Saving Activity (39:25-29)

Fortunately for Israel, the judgment of Yahweh was not the final word. On the surface, the opening *lākēn* suggests that what follows is to be interpreted as a consequence of what has gone before, which is true in a sense. Since the threatened punishment of Israel for infidelity to the covenant was written into the constitution, crime and punishment were logically connected in a cause-effect association. However, that same covenant document had also declared that Yahweh would not abandon his people forever; on the contrary, Yahweh had promised he would not forget his covenant with his people (Lev. 26:44-46; cf. Deut. 4:30-31). Therefore, true to his word and in the interests of his own reputation, after he had punished his people by sending them off into exile, he was duty bound to restore them. This would represent but another phase of his administration of justice. But before the citation formula, *lākēn* also serves as a rhetorical attention getter, preparing the hearer for the final climactic announcement,[109] forbidding the hearers from closing their ears prematurely, and inviting them to hear the speech to the end. In content and style, the last segment of the Gog oracle differs significantly from the previous verses. The connection with Gog has disappeared completely. This is a message for Israel — the Israel of Ezekiel's own day.

The divine speech itself opens abruptly with *'attâ,* "Now," snatching the hearers' attention away from the distant utopian future, and returning them to the very real needs of the present. The interest is no longer in "the latter years" (38:8), or "the latter days" (38:16), but on today; not in "that day" (38:10, 14, 18, 19; 39:8, 11), or "from that day and onward" (39:22), but now. Ezekiel will end this remarkable oracle with a glorious promise for the exiles — a word of grace for a despairing people, wondering how and when all the events described in the previous six chapters might be fulfilled. These are the people who are asking, "In the light of Yahweh's abandonment of us in 586 and our present hopeless condition, what basis for hope is left?" The prophet's response is clear and unequivocal.

25 This verse is thematic, summarizing first Yahweh's action toward his people, then his motivation. In the first instance, Yahweh will restore the fortunes of Jacob. The idiom *hēšîb šĕbût/šĕbît,* encountered earlier in 16:53-58 (with reference to Israel) and 29:14 (with reference to Egypt), functions as a technical reference "to a model of restoration most frequently characterized by Yahweh's reversal of his judgment — *restitution integrum.*"[110] In his vision

---

109. Cf. March, in *Rhetorical Criticism,* pp. 259-62. On this use of *lākēn* in previous oracles see 5:7-8; 11:7; 13:13, 20; etc.

110. Thus Bracke, *ZAW* 97 (1985) 244. The same expression occurs in the Aramaic Sefire Stele III inscription: *hšbw 'lhn šybt by[t 'by],* "The gods have restored the fortunes of my father's house" (*KAI,* 224.24-25; *TSSI,* 2:9.24-25).

of the restoration, Ezekiel anticipates a complete reversal of the judgment that he had predicted in his earlier pronouncements and that his people had indeed experienced.

Ezekiel recognizes two motivational factors underlying Yahweh's restorative actions, the first relating to the need of his people, and the second to concern for his name. Within the context of the book, the present announcement of mercy is almost shocking. Apart from 20:26, where the root *rḥm* is used in its literal sense, "womb," this word is absent from the prophecies of Ezekiel. He has used terms like *ḥāmal,* "to have compassion," and *ḥûs,* "to pity," but except for 36:21, always in a negative sense.[111] The present reference to divine compassion is novel, celebrative of the new reality. Finally Yahweh's fury, provoked by Israel's rebellion and covenantal infidelity, will give way to grace.[112] But Yahweh's new disposition toward his people is driven by a second concern — passion for his holy name. While the association of *qin'â,* "zeal, passion," with the holy name provides obvious links with the preceding,[113] the present combination of zeal and mercy recalls Joel 2:18: "Yahweh was zealous for his land; Yahweh had compassion on his people."

26-27 Ezekiel expands on the two ideas expressed in v. 25b. First he observes the response of the house of Israel to the new outpouring of divine mercy. Far from being a source of pride at having been selected as the objects of divine compassion, the experience of grace will lead to a recognition of their own unworthiness. By the comment *nāśā' 'et-kĕlimmâ wĕ'et-kol-ma'al,* Ezekiel affirms that they will own or assume responsibility for the disgrace and the covenantal treachery that they have perpetrated. There is no excusing the rebellion, no passing off responsibility, no charge of injustice against Yahweh, no blame at having abandoned them. As predicted earlier in 16:61-63 and 36:31, far from causing them to forget their history, the experience of divine grace sensitizes them to their guilt. Furthermore, the nation need no longer be cowed into this sense of shame; precisely when they enjoy the benefits of the renewed favor, defined in terms of security within their own land (cf. 34:28), they will be filled with an intense sense of unworthiness. If divine mercy were a summons to blind forgetfulness,[114] the benefactor would lose sight of what grace in essence is — sheer unmerited favor!

---

111. Cf. 5:11; 7:4, 9; 8:18; 9:5, 10; 16:5.

112. S. D. Sperling translates *wĕriḥamtî* as "I will take back," from *rḥm* II, "to love," which he claims is distinct from *rḥm* I, "to be compassionate, show mercy" ("Biblical *rḥm* I and *rḥm* II," *JANES* 19 [1989] 156).

113. In 38:19 divine zeal and wrath (*'ebrâ*) combine to destroy the enemy forces; in 39:7 Yahweh announced his commitment to making his holy name (*šēm qodšî*) known among the nations.

114. Zimmerli, *Ezekiel 2,* p. 320.

Verse 27 elaborates on the notion of publicly vindicating Yahweh's holy reputation, an idea raised in v. 25b. The order of verbs is illogical, but the phraseology of restoration borrows heavily from previous pronouncements (cf. 28:25; 34:13; 36:24; 37:21). As has been observed often in the book, Yahweh's actions toward his people, both punitive and salvific, are played out before the worldwide audience.

28 The effect of this action on the nations is described in one final recognition formula, greatly elaborated to highlight the covenantal aspect of this new day of grace. Several themes from the previous six chapters return.[115] But at the heart of the international awareness this time is not only the knowledge of Yahweh but the recognition of Israel as his covenant people. They will realize that it was as their covenant Lord that he had sent them off into exile among them. This event is not to be attributed to any earthly military power nor to any superiority of Marduk over Yahweh. Accordingly, it is also as covenant Lord that Yahweh brings them back to their own land. Indeed, his commitment to his people is so complete and so precise that not a single one of them will be left out there among the nations.

On the surface there is nothing remarkable about the last two statements in v. 28, except, as noted above, that they are missing in LXX. On closer examination, however, these lines contain several stylistic surprises. First, Ezekiel's customary word for "gather," *qibbēṣ,* is replaced with a neologism, *kinnēs.*[116] Second, Ezekiel speaks of stragglers who remain behind in the diaspora as "leftovers."[117] Ezekiel's declaration that not a single individual will be left behind when Yahweh restores his people is without parallel in the OT.[118] Yahweh's restoration is not only total, however; it is permanent. He promises never again to hide his face from his people.

---

115. Some see here a formal conclusion to chs. 1–39 as a whole. Cf. Lust, in *Ezekiel and His Book,* p. 49.

116. Ezekiel has used this root earlier in 22:21, but elsewhere both Qal and Piel forms of the verb are restricted to writings generally thought to be late (Neh. 12:44; Est. 4:16; 1 Chr. 22:2), or texts that are difficult to date (Eccl. 2:8; 3:5; Ps. 33:7; 147:2). The Hithpael form in Isa. 28:20, like the noun *miknās* (Exod. 28:42; 39:28; Lev. 6:3; 16:4; Ezek. 44:18), derives from a different root. Cf. Hurvitz, *Linguistic Study,* p. 124 n. 201. While some see in the present occurrence evidence of a late editorial layer (Lust, in *Ezekiel and His Book,* pp. 49-50), with Hurvitz (*Linguistic Study,* pp. 122-24), it is preferable to recognize the transitional significance of Ezekiel's style. So also Rooker, *Biblical Hebrew in Transition,* pp. 156-58.

117. Elsewhere, in oracles of doom, the Hiphil form of *ytr* had been used of survivors of Yahweh's judgment (6:8; 12:16).

118. But cf. the LXX version of Zech. 10:10, "And none of them will be left behind," in place of MT, "Till there is no room for them." Contra Lust (in *Ezekiel and His Book,* pp. 50-51), to attribute this statement to a late compositional redaction is to rob this most creative of all prophets of his forte.

487

29 The oracle concludes with one more surprising twist, as Ezekiel transforms what had been for him a stereotypical threat of judgment, *šāpak ḥămātî,* "I will pour out my wrath,"[119] into a glorious gospel message, *šāpak rûḥî,* "I will pour out my Spirit." While there is some question concerning the significance of the conjunction *'ăšer,* it clearly links the permanence of the new relationship described in v. 29a with the pouring out of the Spirit upon the house of Israel in v. 29b.

One should not overlook the significance of the present statement within the book. This, the only occurrence of the notion of "pouring the divine Spirit on" someone in Ezekiel, is to be distinguished from the giving *(nātan)* of the Spirit in 36:27. While the earlier idiom had associated the divine action with the rebirth of the nation, her revitalization,[120] the divine Spirit poured out on the nation serves as a sign and seal of the covenant. The poured-out Spirit represents Yahweh's mark of ownership,[121] which accounts for his intervention against Gog on behalf of his people, before Gog may so much as touch them. The notion of "pouring" the Spirit is rooted in the perception of the *rûaḥ* as a sort of divine fluid that covers the object.[122] In each of the five occurrences of the idea in the OT,[123] the pouring out of Yahweh's Spirit signifies the ratification and sealing of the covenant relationship with his people. This act provides Israel the guarantee of new life, peace, and prosperity. It serves as the definitive event by which Yahweh claims and seals the newly gathered nation as his own. In the present context the causal clause, "For I will have poured out my Spirit on the house of Israel," explains why Yahweh has stood up for his people in the face of Gog's threat. The poured-out Spirit of Yahweh serves as a permanent seal of the "covenant of peace" *(běrît šālôm)* and the "eternal covenant" *(běrît 'ôlām)* mentioned in 37:26. In the present context, however, the promise of a permanent new relationship between deity and nation remains just that, a promise, a word. The function of the Gog oracle is to provide specific and concrete proof for the prophet and his audience that Yahweh meant exactly what he said.

The oracle foresees Israel as prosperous and secure in her land for a considerable period of time. In fact, in contrast to the immediacy of the prophetic utterance, the Gog episode is set in the latter days (38:6, 16), when

119. Cf. 7:8; 9:8; 20:8, 13, 21, 33, 34; 30:15; 36:18; also 21:36 and 22:31, which have *šāpak za'am.*

120. Cf. Ezekiel's fuller exposition of this notion in 37:1-14. For discussion of the Spirit as divine animating agency see Block, *JETS* 32 (1989) 34-41.

121. Cf. ibid., pp. 46-48.

122. Cf. D. J. A. Clines, "The Image of God in Man," *TynBul* 19 (1968) 82.

123. Cf. elsewhere Isa. 32:15 (with a different verb, *'ārâ*); 44:1-5; Joel 3:1 (Eng. 2:28); Zech. 12:10.

Yahweh's people will be enjoying all the blessings attendant to the revival of the nation and her relationship with her deity (38:8, 11, 14). Into this pacific and tranquil land Yahweh deliberately brings these hordes from the north (38:4-9), who imagine themselves to be operating of their own free will (38:10-13). Like Pharaoh of Egypt (Exod. 7–14), however, Gog is an agent of the revelatory purposes of Yahweh. That purpose has two dimensions: to declare the greatness, holiness, and glory of Yahweh's person, and to declare the firmness of his commitment to his people.[124] The defense of this people, who did not need so much as to lift a sword, vindicates his great name while at the same time confirming his word. The presence of the Spirit of Yahweh poured out on the returned exiles guarantees that he would never leave any of the house of Israel at the mercy of their enemies, and that he would never again hide his face from them, as the contemporaries of Ezekiel had just witnessed. In short, Gog becomes the agent through whom Yahweh declares concretely that the events of 586 B.C. will never be repeated.

EXCURSUS:
GOG IN JEWISH AND CHRISTIAN TRADITION

Among Ezekiel's many prophecies, the Gog oracle has enjoyed a special fascination in both Jewish and Christian tradition. It is tempting to see an allusion to Gog in the "king of the north" who figures so prominently in Dan. 11, but the fact that his conflict is with the king of the south precludes any direct connection. Later Jewish writings are more explicit in their references to Gog. Targ. Pseudo-Jonathan on Num. 11:26 has Eldad and Medad prophesying as follows:

> Behold, a king shall go up from the land of Magog at the end of the days. He shall assemble kings wearing crowns and lieutenants wearing armor, and all the nations shall obey him. They shall array battle in the land of Israel against the children of the Dispersion, but the Lord shall be ready for them by burning the breath of life out of them with the flame of fire that issues from beneath the throne of glory. Their dead bodies shall fall upon the mountains of the land of Israel, and the wild beasts of the field and the birds of heaven shall come and consume them. After that, all the dead of Israel shall be resurrected, and shall enjoy the good things which were secretly set aside for them from the beginning, and they shall receive the reward of their labor.[125]

---

124. For the first see Ezek. 38:16, 23; 39:7, 13, 21, 25, 27. For the second see 38:14-16; 39:7, 22-29.

125. As cited by Levey, *Messiah,* pp. 17-18.

While the treatment of this verse as eschatological and the ascription of the victory over Gog to God himself accords with Ezekiel's prophecy, the Fragment Targ. interprets it messianically:

> At the end, the very end of days Gog and Magog and their armies shall go up against Jerusalem, but they shall fall by the hand of the King Messiah. For seven full years the children of Israel shall use their weapons of war for kindling, without having to go into the forest to cut down the trees.[126]

This passage compares with Targ. Pseudo-Jonathan to Exod. 40:11:

> And you shall anoint the laver and its base, and consecrate it for Joshua your servant, chief of the Sanhedrin of his people, by whose hand the land of Israel is to be divided, and from whom is to descend the Messiah son of Ephraim, by whose hand the house of Israel is to vanquish Gog and his confederates at the end of the days.[127]

This division of the messianic personality occurs within a single context in the 5th-6th century *3 Enoch* 45:5, which significantly also deals with the Gog and Magog conflict:

> And I saw:
>   the Messiah the son of Joseph and his generation, and all that they will do to the gentiles.
> And I saw:
>   the Messiah the son of David and his generation, and all the battles and wars, and all that they will do to Israel whether for good or bad.
> And I saw:
>   all the battles and wars which Gog and Magog will fight with Israel in the days of the Messiah, and all that the Holy One, blessed be he, will do to them in the time to come.[128]

Allusions to the Gog oracle also appear in Christian apocalyptic tradition, probably as a result of Jewish influence.[129] Most notable is John's portrayal of the eschatological conflicts in Rev. 19–20. The scene of the birds

126. Ibid., p. 17; cf. idem, *Ezekiel*, pp. 105-6 n. 1.

127. Levey, *Messiah*, p. 15.

128. Translation of P. Alexander, *OTP*, 1:298. Gog and Magog also appear in *Sib. Or.* 3:319-20, 512. See ibid., pp. 369, 373. On the messianic figure as a descendant of Joseph/Ephraim as well as a Davidic king see Levey, *Messiah*, p. 16.

129. So M. McNamara, *The New Testament and the Palestinian Targum to the Pentateuch*, rev. ed., AnBib 27 (Rome: Pontifical Biblical Institute, 1978), pp. 233-37.

gathered for the great supper of God in 19:17-21 is clearly borrowed from Ezekiel's last frame (39:17-20):

> Then I saw an angel standing in the sun, and with a loud voice he called to all the birds that fly in mid-heaven, "Come, gather for the great supper of God, to eat the flesh of kings, the flesh of captains, the flesh of the mighty, the flesh of horses and their riders — flesh of all, both free and slave, both small and great." Then I saw the beast and the kings of the earth with their armies gathered to make war against the rider on the horse and against his army. And the beast was captured, and with it the false prophet who had performed in its presence the signs by which he deceived those who had received the mark of the beast and those who worshiped its image. These two were thrown alive into the lake of fire that burns with sulfur. And the rest were slain by the sword of the rider on the horse, the sword that came from his mouth; and all the birds were gorged with their flesh. (NRSV)

Although this passage never mentions Gog by name, the beast (θηρίον) certainly represents him. In the prophecy John fills in several details missing from Ezekiel's prophecy. The person through whom the invitation to the birds is extended is explicitly referred to as an authorized messenger.[130] The agent through whom God wins the victory over the beast rides a horse and is accompanied by a great army. The previous paragraph (vv. 11-16) proves his messianic character, and that his armies are heavenly hosts, not earthly. Ezekiel had made no reference to either the Messiah's or auxiliary forces' involvement in the defeat of Gog. John also adds a clue concerning the way the beast (Gog) had achieved hegemony over this worldwide alliance of forces arrayed against God. He had been accompanied by a false prophet who had charmed the other nations with (miraculous?) signs.[131] Acknowledgment of the beast's overlordship is expressed by receiving his mark of ownership (cf. 13:16-17) and prostration before his image. The beast and his prophet do not themselves land on God's table; they are cast directly into the lake of fire. From the beginning of the chapter it appears that these earthly events are occurring while preparations are being made for the celebration of the (restored) marriage covenant with the Lamb.

In a style characteristic of Ezekiel, John resumes the Gog-Magog motif in the following chapter, expounding on the defeat of the beast as follows (20:7-10):

130. In LXX ἄγγελος translates Heb. mal'āk, "messenger." Cf. G. von Rad, *TDNT*, 1:76-80.

131. Cf. Moses' signs of authentication in Exod. 3–4.

When the thousand years are ended, Satan will be released from his prison and will come out to deceive the nations at the four corners of the earth, Gog and Magog, in order to gather them for battle; they are as numerous as the sands of the sea. They marched up over the breadth of the earth and surrounded the camp of the saints and the beloved city. And fire came down from heaven and consumed them. And the devil who had deceived them was thrown into the lake of fire and sulfur, where the beast and the false prophet were, and they will be tormented day and night forever and ever. (NRSV)

This description opens with a chronological note, fixing the conflict after the protracted period of time, here referred to in idealistic terms as one thousand years. The previous verses had characterized this period as a time in which the saints, who had been slain by the beast previously for refusing to join his alliance, had been resurrected and had been enjoying the reign of the Messiah. The description of their state as "blessed" alludes to the security and well-being mentioned by Ezekiel.

This passage also provides further information on the schemes of the enemy. He is referred to specifically as ὁ Σατανᾶς, "the Adversary," Satan.[132] Yahweh's turning Gog around, putting hooks in his jaws, and bringing him out from the remotest parts of the north (Ezek. 38:4-6) is now interpreted as the release of the Adversary from prison. Ezekiel's merismic reference to allies from the distant north and the distant south (and traders from east and west?) is interpreted as from the four corners of the earth. Whereas Ezekiel had studiously avoided any reference to Jerusalem/Zion, John has the enemy forces surrounding "the beloved city" where the saints have sought refuge. The reference to the "camp" of the saints seems to contradict Ezekiel's picture of unwalled and undefended towns, but one should not necessarily impose consistency on these texts. The agent of the deceit of the nations, who is now identified as the devil (ὁ διάβολος), is captured and thrown into the fiery lake to join the beast and his prophet.

John's use of Ezekiel's oracle against Gog represents a remarkable adaptation of an OT tradition for a Christian theme. An event whose timing in the original prophecy is only vaguely set "in the latter days" is now identified as the penultimate event in human history; the picture of national peace and tranquility is transformed into a portrait of universal peace; the foreign foe becomes a satanic and diabolical force; the divine victory is placed in the hands of the Messiah. The message that had originally been presented

---

132. In Rev. 20:8 the phrase "Gog and Magog" functions appositionally to Satan. Cf. R. A. Alexander, "A Fresh Look at Ezekiel 38 and 39," *JETS* 17 (1974) 167 n. 6, for bibliography on this text.

to the Jewish exiles to bolster their sagging hopes has been transformed into a message of hope for all Christians.

♦ *Theological Implications*

In adapting Ezekiel's oracle of Gog for the Christians of his day John has invited the faithful in any age to hear the theological lessons of the passage, all of which have been presented in previous oracles.

First, Yahweh is the unrivaled lord of human history. He raises up nations; he puts them down. Their activities are always subservient to his agenda.

Second, Yahweh's reputation is linked to the status and welfare of his people. So long as they are mired in bondage and subservience to alien powers his holiness and glory stand in question. The ultimate vindication of his name is assured, however, and his people will be preserved in accordance with his promise.

Third, Yahweh keeps his covenant. He does not forget the commitments he has made to his people and will not abandon the faithful in their hour of need. As a seal of his commitment he pours out his Spirit on them. The implications that this covenantal interpretation of the pouring out of the Spirit has for the progress of the Holy Spirit's activity in the book of Acts are tantalizing and deserve further comment. It is remarkable that with every stage of the advance of the gospel, and the incorporation of new groups of people into the church, reference is made to the extraordinary manifestation of the Spirit's presence: (1) the Jews in Jerusalem (Acts 2:4, 33, 38); (2) the Samaritans (8:14-17); (3) Gentile proselytes of Judea (10:44-48; cf. 9:16); (4) Gentiles of Asia Minor (19:1-6). Each event signals a new phase and scope in the breadth of the embrace of the new covenant instituted in Christ. Furthermore, when Paul speaks of being sealed with the Spirit (2 Cor. 1:22; Eph. 1:13; 4:30), he is speaking of the possession of the Holy Spirit as the divine confirmation of the covenant. This alone is the basis of the believer's security.

Fourth, above all else Yahweh is a God of grace and mercy. He reaches out to those who have rebelled against him and offers not only forgiveness but the full benefits of covenant relationship.

Fifth, for the believer, the experience of divine grace is a humbling experience. Far from feeding egotistical ambitions and a misguided thirst for self-esteem, or from blinding one to one's sinful past, it evokes in the recipient intense feelings of unworthiness.

493

B. ENVISIONING THE GOOD NEWS: "STAND BY AND SEE THE RETURN OF YAHWEH!" (40:1–48:35)

♦ *Nature and Design*

The book of Ezekiel concludes on a glorious note, with a vision of Yahweh returning to his temple and establishing his residence in his city in the midst of his people. The new date notice, followed by the divine arrest of the prophet and his transportation to a new site, signals the beginning of a new literary unit. But this unit is larger and more complex than any other, extending until the end of the book, 48:35. An envelope structure is created by framing this entire block with an initial notice of the city near the high mountain (40:2) and a concluding reference to the city, now identified as *Yahweh Shammah*, "Yahweh is there." While the style and substance of the intervening materials display considerable variety, the entire unit is held together by the figure of a man, who, in tour guide fashion, escorts the prophet around the temple complex.

The genre of this section is described as a vision report (40:1). But few sections of the book have yielded such a wide range of interpretations, causing the reader to wonder whether this block of material should be classified as a visual riddle *(ḥîdâ)* or visual metaphorical speech *(māšāl)*.[1] While any proposed solution to the riddle must be deemed provisional, to unlock its meaning one needs to employ several different hermeneutical keys. The importance attributed to any one of these keys determines the outcome. I offer the following as a preliminary list of factors that one must consider in solving the riddle of Ezekiel's final vision.

1. The Nature of the Text. The text of many sections of chs. 40–48, particularly chs. 41 and 42, has suffered greatly in transcription and transmission. Many readings are uncertain, but the way one resolves textual problems occasionally has a critical bearing on one's approach to the material as a whole.[2] Sometimes the lack of sense in MT forces the textual critic to appeal to the LXX and other versions for a plausible resolution, but in such cases one is left with the suspicion that the versional renderings represent simply educated guesses at the meaning of the Hebrew *Vorlage*.

2. The Literary History of the Text. Whereas an earlier generation of Ezekiel scholars was hesitant to recognize Ezekiel's hand anywhere in chs. 40–48,[3] recent students of the prophet have tended to be more generous.

---

1. On *ḥîdâ* see 17:2; on *māšāl* see 17:2; 21:5 (Eng. 20:49); 24:3.
2. E.g., *bāmôtām/běmôtām* in 43:7, and *toknît/tabnît* in 43:10.
3. This includes those who denied any of the book to the exilic prophet (e.g., Torrey, *Pseudo-Ezekiel and the Original Prophecy;* idem, *HTR* 19 [1931] 123-30; cf. the

Especially influential has been the work of H. Gese, who argues for a complex multiphased evolution for the text, but credits Ezekiel with large portions.[4] Others, following a holistic approach, have been even more conservative in attributing virtually all of chs. 40–48 to the exilic prophet.[5] A related problem is the relationship of this section to the Priestly material in the Pentateuch, on which see below, pp. 498-501.

3. The Historical Context of the Vision. The opening notice dates the present visionary experience on the tenth day of the first month, twenty-five years after the deportation of Jehoiachin, and fourteen years after the fall of Jerusalem (40:1). If the preceding salvation oracles are to be dated shortly after the fall of the city (cf. 33:21-22), more than a decade separates this prophetic experience from the preceding oracles. One may only speculate about what historical circumstances provoked the present vision, but two features of the date notice deserve consideration. First, the vision occurs in the "twenty-fifth year" of the exile. The number is significant not only for its correspondence with multiples of twenty-five that dominate the temple vision; but as one-half of fifty it invites linkage with the Israelite Jubilee, "the year of release."[6] The midpoint of the Jubilee cycle marked a turning of the

---

recent attempt to revive the late pseudepigraphic interpretation of the book by Becker, *Künder des Wortes,* pp. 137-49), who insisted that the historical Ezekiel communicated his messages only in poetic form, that he was only a prophet of doom, or that he functioned in Jerusalem rather than in Babylon. For representatives of these approaches see M. Haran, who evaluates the results as "somewhat frivolous" and the methodology "for the most part, far from sound" ("The Law-Code of Ezekiel XL–XLVIII and Its Relation to the Priestly School," *HUCA* 50 [1979] 46 n. 2).

4. Apart from numerous glosses, Gese (whom Zimmerli tends to follow) recognizes as secondary the *nāśî'* (44:1-3; 45:21-25; 46:1-10, 12), Zadok (44:6-16; 44:17-31 [with insertions]; 45:13-15), and land division (48:1-29) strata. See *Der Verfassungsentwurf des Ezechiel (Kap. 40–48) traditionsgeschichtlich untersucht,* BHT 25 (Tübingen: Mohr, 1957), pp. 109-15, for a summary. More recently Laato (*Josiah and David Redivivus,* pp. 189-96), who follows Gese's basic thesis, has argued that the Zadokite layer dates to the early Persian period, while the *nāśî'* layer is exilic. S. S. Tuell has found an Ezekielian core (with minor insertions) in 40:1–43:7a; 44:1-2; 47:1-12; 48:30-35 (*The Law of the Temple in Ezekiel 40–48,* HSM 49 [Atlanta: Scholars Press, 1992]). Most of the remainder, which he calls "the Law of the Temple," represents later (Persian period) additions.

5. See M. Greenberg, "The Design and Themes of Ezekiel's Program of Restoration," *Int* 38 (1984) 81-208; Hals, *Ezekiel,* pp. 285-89; J. G. McConville, "Priests and Levites in Ezekiel: A Crux in the Interpretation of Israel's History," *TynBul* 34 (1983) 3-31. D. L. Stevenson follows a holistic approach, but she attributes the text to an exilic rhetor, without committing herself to the prophet Ezekiel (*The Vision of Transformation: The Territorial Rhetoric of Ezekiel* [Ph.D. diss.; Ann Arbor: University Microfilms, 1992]). For a convincing rejection of Gese's methodology and conclusions see Duguid (*Ezekiel and the Leaders,* pp. 27-31, 87-90), who dismisses the notion of so-called *nāśî'* and Zadokite strata as myth.

6. See Lev. 25. Ezekiel's familiarity with the Jubilee is evident in 46:17.

corner, turning the sights away from the tragedy of exile in the direction of renewal. Because Yahweh is the true owner of the land, it cannot be forever out of the possession of those to whom he had granted it; it must be returned on schedule, despite historical realities.[7]

Second, the vision occurs on the tenth day of the first month, which invites association with Exod. 12:2, according to which the beginning of the year commemorated Israel's release from Egyptian bondage.[8] However, Ezekiel's present location in Babylon also stimulates linkage with the annual Babylonian *akītu,* an elaborate eleven-day festival in the month of Nisan, celebrating the supremacy and enthronement of Marduk and ensuring the success of the enterprises of the coming year. The climax of the celebrations involved the king of Babylon "seizing" the hand of Marduk and conducting his image in procession to the *akītu* temple outside the city, where the *akītu* rituals were performed.[9] Like the inaugural vision, and the earlier vision of the departure of the *kābôd,* this vision strikes at the heart of paganized perspectives of Ezekiel's compatriots, who interpreted their exile as a sign of Marduk's supremacy over Yahweh. But just as in the earlier contexts Yahweh had demonstrated his sovereign freedom to appear to Ezekiel *in Babylon,* the heart of "Marduk-land," and to abandon the temple in Jerusalem of his own free will, so now he proclaims in visionary form his kingship not only in Jerusalem (the city is not named) but also over the entire world. He will not wait for any human king to lead him in procession; he comes of his own free will and in his own time (43:1-9). Accordingly, this vision serves a polemical purpose: to celebrate the kingship of Yahweh, and to inspire new hope and faith in the exiles.

4. The Declared Genre of the Material. Ezek. 40:2 identifies the genre of chs. 40–48 as *mar'ôt 'ĕlōhîm,* "divine visions," which links this block most directly with Ezekiel's inaugural vision (1:1) and the earlier temple vision (8:1).[10] The substantive parallels among these texts require that the same

---

7. So also J. A. Fager, *Land Tenure and the Biblical Jubilee: Uncovering Hebrew Ethics through the Sociology of Knowledge,* JSOTSup 155 (Sheffield: JSOT Press, 1993), p. 76; cf. Zimmerli, *Ezekiel 2,* pp. 346-47. Less likely is J. van Goudoever's suggestion that the twenty-fifth year marks the end of the Jubilee cycle ("Ezekiel Sees in Exile a New Temple-City at the Beginning of a Jobel Year," in *Ezekiel and His Book,* pp. 344-49).

8. On the meaning of the special expression *rō'š haššānâ* see the commentary below.

9. See J. Klein, *ABD,* 1:138-39; J. A. Black, "The New Year Ceremonies in Ancient Babylon: 'Taking Bel by the Hand' and a Cultic Picnic," *Religion* 11 (1981) 39-59; B. Halpern, *The Constitution of the Monarchy in Israel,* HSM 25 (Chico, Calif.: Scholars Press, 1981), pp. 51-61.

10. The divine seizure ("the hand of Yahweh was upon me") and transportation of the prophet by the Spirit of Yahweh also link this text with 37:1.

hermeneutical principles employed in the interpretation of the previous prophecies apply here, and that one interpret this block in the light of the previous visions of God. Here Ezekiel is offered a glimpse of spiritual possibilities for Israel based on the reality revealed in ch. 1 and answering the abuses exposed in chs. 8–11 and the inadequacy of the *miqdāš mĕʿaṭ,* "sanctuary in small measure" (11:16), of the exilic situation.

5. Precursors to This New Temple Vision. In the commentary on 36:16-38 I noted the links between this restoration oracle and the multiphased judgment oracle found in ch. 20. The links between ch. 20 and Ezekiel's final vision are even stronger. Indeed, since the agenda is set in historical phases VI (20:32-38) and VII (20:44-45), the present block of material represents another case of typically Ezekielian resumptive exposition. Preceding the announcement of the renewal of the covenant and the restoration of the exiles to the land of Israel (20:37-38),[11] Yahweh had declared, *ʾemlôk ʿălêkem,* "I shall be king over you" (20:33). The notion of Yahweh's renewed kingship over Israel had been suggested by the "divine shepherd" vocabulary in 34:7-22, but explicit references to him as "king" over his people have been lacking — until 43:7, where Ezekiel witness the "enthronement of Yahweh" and hears his declaration of kingship over Israel. Phase VII, which describes Israel's final historical state, anticipates several other features in the present complex: (1) The adverb *ʾaḥar* (20:39) points to the climax of Israel's history. The word is missing in chs. 40–48, but the placement of the latter after the Gog oracle, which is fixed chronologically *bĕʾaḥărît haššānîm,* "in the latter years" (38:8), is suggestive. (2) While the meaning shifts slightly, the term *mattĕnôt,* "gifts" (20:39), is not picked up again in the book until 46:16-17. (3) *har qodšî, har mĕrôm yiśrāʾēl,* "my holy mountain, the high mountain of Israel," anticipates *har gābōah mĕʿōd,* "an extremely high mountain," in the land of Israel *(ʾereṣ yiśrāʾēl)* in 40:2. (4) The offerings prescribed in 46:1-15 answer to the gifts Yahweh says he will receive in 20:40-42 as a sign of Israel's acceptance. (5) The spiritual geography reflected in the design of the temple complex and the strict control of access to the temple in chs. 40–43 fulfill Yahweh's stated objective in 20:41: *wĕniqdaštî bākem,* "I will manifest my holiness among you." (6) The promise of return to the land of Israel (20:42) is fulfilled concretely in the division of the land among the twelve tribes (chs. 47–48). In the light of these connections, Ezek. 40–48 may justifiably be interpreted as an exposition of the theme, "the restored kingship of Yahweh," earlier raised in ch. 20.[12]

But this section also resumes a topic raised only for a moment in

11. The fulfillment is described in 36:18-38 and 37:15-28.
12. This connection is also drawn by Stevenson, *Vision,* pp. 179-80.

37:26-28: the establishment of Yahweh's permanent residence, his sanctuary, among his people. Indeed, it is not totally surprising that at least one LXX manuscript, Papyrus 967, places this vision immediately after ch. 37, which leads to a further consideration.

6. The Literary Structure of the Vision. While some despair of finding a coherent program in Ezekiel's final vision,[13] at the macroscopic level at least, following the opening preamble (40:1-4) the text divides into three major units: 40:3–43:27, 44:1–46:24, and 47:1–48:35, which deal, respectively, with Yahweh's establishment of his residence in the temple, Israel's response to his presence in their midst, and the apportionment of the healed land to the twelve tribes. The significance of this arrangement goes beyond its sheer logic; its parallels to the Mosaic Torah are obvious. The latter also begins with the provision for Yahweh's residence in the midst of Israel (Exod. 25:1-40), then prescribes Israel's response to his presence (all of Leviticus and much of Numbers), and concludes with arrangements for the apportionment of the land to the twelve tribes (Num. 34–35). These parallels provide an early clue that Ezekiel is functioning as a second Moses.

7. The Literary Context of This Vision. Since chs. 40–48 come after the Gog oracle, some have interpreted them cosmologically, as the culmination of an ancient mythic pattern in which a deity overcomes a challenge from the forces of chaos in a fierce battle, which is followed by a victory procession, the enthronement of the deity, and a feast of celebration.[14] But one also needs to consider the broader context. The parallels between Ezek. 40–48 and the Mosaic Torah can hardly be coincidental in view of the remarkable correspondences between the broad structure of Ezekiel's restoration oracles in chs. 40–48 and the Exodus narratives as a whole, as table 15 (p. 499) illustrates. These correspondences strengthen the impression that Ezekiel is perceived as a second Moses. Is he the prophet predicted in Deut. 18:14-22, whom Yahweh would raise up from Israel and who would be like Moses?

8. The Relationship Between the Priestly Prescriptions in the Mosaic Torah and Ezekiel 40–48. Perhaps the most significant issue in the interpretation of Ezek. 40–48 is the relationship of this vision to the Mosaic Torah. Since this is the only corpus of legislation in the OT that does not come from

---

13. Note the pessimistic evaluation of S. Tuell ("The Temple Vision of Ezekiel 40–48: A Program for Restoration?" *Proceedings, Eastern Great Lakes Biblical Society* 2 [1982] 98): "the legislation of these chapters is a crazy-quilt, affixed to the core vision in a nearly random fashion. No attempt to find here a coherent 'program' can succeed, for there is no such program to be found. If we would hear Ezekiel's voice from among this babble, we need to reclaim the core vision."

14. Thus S. Niditch, "Ezekiel 40–48 in a Visionary Context," *CBQ* 48 (1986) 208-24, esp. 220-23.

Table 15. Ezekiel 40–48 and the Exodus Narratives

Feature	Exodus Narrative	Ezekiel's Restoration Oracles
Yahweh commissions a human agent.	Exod. 3–4	Ezek. 33
Yahweh separates Israel from the nations and delivers her from bondage.	Exod. 5–13	Ezek. 34–37
Enemy forces challenge Yahweh's salvific work on his people's behalf.	Exod. 14–15	Ezek. 38–39
Yahweh appears on a high mountain.	Exod. 19	Ezek. 40:1-4
Yahweh provides for his residence among his people.	Exod. 25–40	Ezek. 40:5–43:27
Yahweh prescribes the appropriate response to his grace.	Lev. 1:1ff. Num. 21 (?)	Ezek. 44:1–46:24
Yahweh provides for the apportionment of his land to his people.	Num. 34–35	Ezek. 47–48

the mouth of Moses,[15] a comparison with the Mosaic Torah is in order. Numerous parallels may be cited.

a. The Torahs have virtually identical linguistic textures.[16] Both are pre-occupied with Priestly concerns: the sanctuary and its furnishings, the offices of the cult personnel, the sacrificial system with its sin and guilt offerings, the relationship of the tribes of Israel to the cult and its center.

b. Both recognize the Levites as religious functionaries, but restrict the office of priesthood to a specific line within the tribe.

c. Both Torahs were directly revealed by Yahweh to his intermediary to be passed on to the people (cf. Exod. 19:3; 24:12; et passim; and Ezek. 40:4; 44:6).

d. Both Torahs were revealed on a high mountain, the first on Mount Sinai, referred to as "the mountain of God" (Exod. 24:12-18); the second on an initially unnamed mountain (Ezek. 40:2), but later identified as "Yahweh is there" (48:35).

e. In both, the revelation of the plans of the sanctuary follow the establishment of the covenant between Yahweh and his people.[17]

---

15. A fact noted by J. Levenson, *Theology of the Program of Restoration of Ezekiel 40–48*, HSM 10 (Missoula, Mont.: Scholars Press, 1976), p. 39.

16. So also Haran, *HUCA* 50 (1979) 59.

17. In the former, it follows immediately after the ratification of the covenant (Exod. 24:1-11; cf. 25:1ff.); in the latter the two events are separated by the Gog oracle.

f. In both the presence of Yahweh is visibly demonstrated by the entrance of his *kābôd* into the sanctuary (Exod. 40:34-38; cf. Ezek. 43:1-9).

g. Neither human mediator is permitted to enter the land he envisions. Moses is permitted to view it from Mount Abarim (Num. 27:12-13; Deut. 32:48-52); Ezekiel observes the land from the mountain of revelation, but when the vision is over he returns to Babylon to share it with his fellow exiles.[18]

Levenson is certainly correct in viewing Ezekiel's mountaintop prophetic experience as a programmatic revelation, and the prophet himself as a second Moses. But these links should not blind the reader to the substantial discrepancies in detail that exist between Ezekiel's and Moses' Torahs. These will be noted in greater detail in the commentary, but for the moment some of the more obvious examples may be highlighted, as in table 16 (p. 501).

These and other differences challenge the fundamental prophetic law of noncontradiction; true prophecy must agree with Mosaic revelation (Deut. 18:15-18).[19] Explanations for these discrepancies have varied. Some argue that Ezekiel's Torah antedates that of Moses (P). Or do these sets of regulations reflect competing exilic priestly traditions, with the "Mosaic" tradition winning the day? Does Ezekiel, viewed by some as "the spiritual father of Judaism,"[20] lay the foundation for postexilic Judaism of which P was regarded as the salient expression? Or does Ezekiel's Torah represent a deliberate departure from Moses?[21] Was the exilic prophet offering a purified liturgy to replace the Priestly tradition, which he views as fundamentally and intentionally flawed from the beginning, and which he characterized earlier as "no good laws" (*ḥuqqîm lōʾ ṭôbîm*, 20:25)?[22]

The heavy influence of the Mosaic Torah on Ezekiel is evident in the judgment oracles. Indeed, this prophet attributed Israel's demise to their infidelity

18. See Levenson, *Theology,* pp. 42-44.

19. The herculean efforts of an otherwise obscure scribe to answer the questions raised by these discrepancies are reflected in the following citation from *b. Shabbat* 13b: "Rabbi Judah quoted the statement of Rab: A certain man has been remembered for a blessing, and Hananiah ben Hezekiah is his name. For were it not for him, the Book of Ezekiel would have been suppressed, since its words contradict those of the Torah. What did he do? He brought up three hundred barrels of oil and stayed in the upper room until he had explained away everything."

20. Haran (*HUCA* 50 [1979] 63 n. 30) credits B. Duhm and R. Smend with this notion.

21. Haran (ibid.) observes that "P" is much more carefully crafted and displays many more signs of authenticity and originality than Ezekiel's Torah, which he characterizes as an "impoverished offshoot of the former."

22. See Levenson, *Theology,* p. 39.

Table 16. Mosaic Torah and Ezekielian Torah

Feature	Mosaic Torah		Ezekielian Torah	
Priestly line	Aaronic	Exod. 28	Zadokite	40:46; 43:19; 44:15
Vestment materials	Gold Dyed wool Luxury linen (*šēš māšmār*)	Exod. 28	Plain linen (*pištîm*)	44:17-19
Sanctuary Furnishings	Ark Lampstand Anointing oil Table of bread of the Presence	Exod. 25	Missing Missing Missing Missing	
New moon offering	Two bulls One ram Seven male lambs	Num. 28:11	One bull Six sheep One ram	46:6-7

to the covenant, and understood the judgment of 586 B.C. as the precise fulfillment of the covenant curses. To be sure, for rhetorical and polemical purposes he is not above radically revisionist reconstructions of the nation's past (cf. chs. 16, 20, 23), but never does he lose respect for the Mosaic tradition. Nor should we expect him to, since he is, after all, of the traditional priestly line himself.

9. Fantastic and Stylized Elements in the Vision. While some elements of Ezekiel's vision of the future derive from well-known physical realities, others are quite idealistic and even unimaginable. The high mountain on which he observes the new city is reminiscent of the high and holy mountain of Yahweh encountered earlier in 17:22 and 20:40,[23] but also has affinities with the mythical Mount Zaphon on which dwelt Baal, the storm deity of the Canaanites, and with Mount Olympus, the home of the Greek gods. The river, whose source lies within the temple complex itself, flows through the Judean desert increasing dramatically in size, and turning the wasteland into an Edenic paradise, even healing (*rāpā'*) the Dead Sea (47:1-12). The plan of the city is idealized as a perfect square with three gates punctuating each side to provide admittance for the twelve tribes. The emphasis on the twelve tribes itself reverses five centuries of history. The apportionment of the land of Israel

23. Cf. earlier prophets' references to Zion as the mountain of the house of Yahweh, established as the highest of all the mountains and raised above the hills (Isa. 2:2; Mic. 4:1), a description that hardly fits the ridge on which Jerusalem is built, a mere 2,500 feet above sea level.

among the tribes to a large extent disregards topographic and historical realities. The dimensions of the temple and the city are dominated by multiples of five, with twenty-five being a particularly common number. All in all Ezekiel's scheme appears highly contrived, casting doubt on any interpretation that expects a literal fulfillment of his plan.

10. The Influence of Ezekiel's Design on Later Writers. Some have interpreted Ezekiel's Torah as a program for the postexilic restoration of the nation of Israel in its own homeland.[24] If this was the case, however, had he lived to see the actual return, he would have found the religious and political scene in Judah extremely disappointing. To be sure, many exiles would return to Jerusalem, a *nāśî'* would be recognized among them (Sheshbazzar, Ezra 1:8), and the temple would be rebuilt. Nonetheless, not only were the returnees but a handful of Judeans; the land was never divided among the tribes, no figure like Ezekiel's *nāśî'* emerged in the community, the reconstructed temple fell far short of Ezekiel's plan, and most seriously of all, the *kābôd* of Yahweh failed to return (cf. Hag. 2:3-9).

This does not mean, however, that Ezekiel's vision was forgotten. The massive Temple Scroll composed by the Dead Sea covenanters several centuries before Christ displays numerous connections with Ezekiel. But the blueprint for the temple and the city of Jerusalem envisioned there go their own ways for the most part.[25] Closer adherence to Ezekiel is evident in early Christian writings, most notably Rev. 21–22, which displays a series of important links with our text:

a. A visionary transport of the prophet to a high mountain (21:10).
b. The sight of a new world with Jerusalem at the center (21:1-2, 10).
c. The dwelling of God in the midst of his people, which produces a state of perfect well-being (21:3-4).
d. The presence of the glory of God in the city (21:11).
e. A heavenly interpreter with a measuring rod with which he measures the city (21:15-17).
f. A symmetrical plan of the city complete with high walls and twelve gates, one for each of the tribes (21:11-21).

24. Zimmerli (*Ezekiel 2*, pp. 328-29) speaks of a "draft constitution," which envisions "the complete fulfillment of the future which Yahweh had promised for Israel." Cf. Clements, *God and Temple*, p. 106.

25. For the *editio princeps* see Y. Yadin, ed., *The Temple Scroll*, 3 vols. in 4 (Jerusalem: Israel Exploration Society, 1983). See also J. Maier, *The Temple Scroll: An Introduction, Translation and Commentary*, JSOTSup 34, tr. R. T. White (Sheffield: JSOT Press, 1985). For a study of the influence of Ezek. 40–48 on the Qumran community see F. García Martinez, "L'interprétation de la Torah d'Ézéchiel dans les mss. de Qumran," *RevQ* 13 (1988) 441-52.

g. An emphasis on the purity and holiness of those within (21:27).

h. The presence of the river of life (22:1).

Although the skeletal parallels are impressive, the major divergences in detail point to two different fulfillments.[26] As with the Gog oracle, John appears to have taken an earlier motif and adapted it for his own purposes.

With at least these ten factors to consider in interpreting Ezek. 40–48, it is no wonder scholars have arrived at such widely divergent conclusions. The shape of one's work will depend on how one juggles these elements and how they are ranked. Since the postexilic community appears not to have made any effort to implement Ezekiel's program, many interpret the vision eschatologically, in keeping with its present literary location after the Gog oracle. Accordingly, the high mountain of Ezekiel's vision is none other than

26. Note the following discrepancies:

Element	The Ezekielian Perspective	John's Perspective
Identity of the holy city	unnamed in 40:2 renamed "Yahweh Shammah" (48:35)	the new Jerusalem (21:2)
Nature of the city	square apparently constructed of ordinary stones	cubical (21:16) constructed of precious materials, stones, and metals
Role of the temple	at the center of everything	its existence emphatically denied (21:22)
Role of sacrifices	at heart of the ritual	the (sacrificial) Lamb lives among the people
Nature of the residents	continuing need to distinguish between the pure and impure	absolute purity of all (21:26-27)
Scope of the vision	parochially Israelite	universal (21:24-27)

Alexander ("Ezekiel," pp. 945-46) sees in Ezekiel a portrait of the millennium and in Revelation the eternal state, the former representing a kind of "firstfruits," a microcosm, a beginning, of the latter. Ezekiel's sacrifices provide the basis for dispensationalist insistence on a role for sacrifices in the millennium. In response to the NT rejection of any and all sacrifices after the final sacrifice of Christ, the function of sacrifices is redefined. Rather than perceiving them as efficacious, since only Christ's sacrifice actually atones for sin, the Mosaic offerings represent "picture lessons" looking forward to the Messiah's work. Since Ezekiel's millennial sacrifices look back on the same event, they are regarded as memorial "picture lessons." See Alexander, "Ezekiel," pp. 946-52. But J. C. Whitcomb rejects the memorial interpretation, preferring a ceremonial understanding ("Christ's Atonement and Animal Sacrifices in Israel," *GTJ* 6 [1985] 201-17). At the quasi-physical level they offer temporal cleansing and forgiveness to the offerer (hence guaranteed protection from physical and temporal punishment), and reminding the Gentiles outside of the continued presence of sin. Similarly M. Rooker, "Evidence from Ezekiel," in *A Case for Premillennialism: A New Consensus,* ed. D. J. Campbell and J. L. Townsend (Chicago: Moody, 1992), pp. 132-33.

Zion, the place of security and divine revelation, and the source of life and blessing, which figures so prominently in other eschatological texts.[27] But the mountain is also a new Sinai on which the Torah of Yahweh is revealed to his special mediator (Ezekiel as a new Moses), and the *nāśî'* is a messianic figure, in whom are combined monarchic and priestly functions.[28] Accordingly, chs. 40–48 present a picture of the reconstituted nation finally functioning as a genuine theocracy. Levenson speaks of "a liturgical manifesto," a constitution for "the kingdom of priests and a holy people," and the present era as an in-between period, sandwiched between two temple epochs.[29] Levenson frequently offers what is essentially a theological interpretation of elements of the vision, but a more literalist millenarian understanding has had a long history in Christian circles.[30] Since Israel's prophets tended not to distinguish between near and distant aspects of the great events of which they spoke, it is not always easy to distinguish between millennial and eternal realities.

While many features of chs. 40–48 commend an eschatological interpretation, this view is weakened considerably by the absence of eschatological language. Expressions like "on that day," "in the latter days," and "after many years," common in the Gog oracle, are lacking entirely. *'ôlām,* "forever, eternal," occurs three times, but in none of these does it carry a distinctly eschatological sense.[31] Nor is it clear that the "prince" should be interpreted

27. See Isa. 2:1-4 (= Mic. 4:1-5); 33:20-24; Joel 4:17-18 (Eng. 3:17-18); Zech. 14:8; Ps. 48. See Levenson, *Theology,* pp. 7-24.

28. A view reflected in the rabbinic commentaries of Kimchi and Mezudat David. Cf. Levey, *Ezekiel,* pp. 5, 119. See the discussion by Levenson, *Theology,* pp. 57-107; and Caquot, *Semitica* 14 (1964) 21-22.

29. See Levenson, *Theology,* pp. 129, 150. Cf. his comment on p. 45: "The highly specific nature of the description of the Temple, its liturgy and community bespeaks a practical program, not a vision of pure grace. For example, when the text says that eight steps led up to the vestibule of the inner court (Ezek. 40:31), can this be other than a demand that the new Temple be constructed just so? Can this be only description? The fact that God has already constructed the Temple does not mean that man has no role in its construction. On the contrary, what Ezekiel was shown is the divinely constructed model, the *tabnît* like the one David showed Solomon (1 Chr. 28:11-19)."

30. The history of millenarian movements in Christendom is explored by N. Cohn, *The Pursuit of the Millennium,* rev. ed. (New York: Oxford University Press, 1970). Cf. the recent anthology of essays, *A Case for Premillennialism: A New Consensus,* ed. D. J. Campbell and J. L. Townsend (Chicago: Moody, 1992). For millenarian interpretations of these chapters see Feinberg, *Prophecy of Ezekiel,* pp. 233-39; Alexander, "Ezekiel," pp. 942-52.

31. The language of 43:7, 9, "I will dwell among the descendants of Israel forever," is formulaic and traditional, as is the reference to the *huqqôt 'ôlām tāmîd,* "a continual ordinance for all time," in 46:14. Cf. *huqqat 'ôlām* (Exod. 12:14, 17; 28:43; 29:9; Lev. 3:17; 7:36; 10:9; 17:7, 29, 31, 34; 23:14, 21, 31, 41; 24:3; Num. 10:8; 15:15; 18:23; 19:10,

messianically. In Ezekiel's Torah he functions primarily, if not exclusively, as a liturgical personage, without a hint of a Davidic connection.[32] Furthermore, contrary to popular opinion, the description of the temple is not presented as a blueprint for some future building to be constructed with human hands.[33] Nowhere is anyone commanded to build it. The man with the measuring line takes Ezekiel on a tour of an existing structure already made. Indeed, were it not for the present literary location of the temple vision, it is doubtful that the eschatological interpretation would ever have arisen.

Ezekiel's salvation oracles have looked forward to the day when the twelve tribes of Israel would be regathered and returned to their hereditary homeland, the Davidic dynasty would be restored, Yahweh's covenant of peace with Israel would be renewed, and he would establish his permanent residence in their midst. It would have been inconceivable for Ezekiel to envision a full restoration of his people without a literal fulfillment of each of these elements. Nevertheless, in view of the considerations cited above, it seems best to interpret chs. 40–48 ideationally.[34] The issue for the prophet is not physical geography but spiritual realities. As in his earlier vision, historical events are described from a theological plane, and the interpreter's focus must remain on the ideational value of that which is envisioned. At the time of Ezekiel's prophetic inauguration, the sight of Yahweh enthroned above the cherubim had reassured him of his presence even in Babylon among the exiles (1:1-28a). His visionary ingestion of the scroll spoke of the importance of accepting the divine message and its incorporation into his own experience (1:28b–3:15). The observation of the abominations in the temple and the consequent departure of the divine *kābôd* provide theological justification and rationalization for Nebuchadrezzar's razing of Jerusalem (8:1–11:25). The vision of the revivified dry bones is not a prophecy of literal individual resurrection, but a declaration of the certainty of the eventual resuscitation of Israel by a new infusion of breath from Yahweh.

While more complex and extensive than any of these, Ezek. 40–48 should be interpreted along similar lines. The prophet is hereby introduced to the theological realities awaiting his own people. Whereas 37:26-27 had spoken of the establishment of Yahweh's permanent residence among his people, following their homecoming, the present vision picks up the theolog-

---

21) and *hoq 'ôlām*, "permanent statute" (Exod. 29:28; 30:21; Lev. 6:11, 15; 7:34; 10:15; 24:9; Num. 18:8, 11, 19; also Jer. 5:22) in the Mosaic Torah.

32. According to Alexander ("Ezekiel," p. 974), a messianic interpretation is excluded by the facts that natural children are envisaged for the prince (Ezek. 46:16) and, even more important, that he must make a sin offering for himself (45:22). Cf. the sinlessness of Christ (Heb. 4:15).

33. This point is argued convincingly by Stevenson, *Vision,* pp. 14-21.

34. The expression is more readily understood and more accurate than Stevenson's "territoriality."

ical theme and describes the spiritual reality in concrete terms, employing the familiar cultural idioms of temple, altar, sacrifices, *nāśî'*, and land. In presenting this theological constitution for the new Israel, Yahweh announces the righting of all the old wrongs, and the establishment of permanent, healthy deity-nation-land relationships. Ezekiel's final vision presents a lofty spiritual ideal: Where God is, there is Zion.[35] Where God is, there is order and the fulfillment of all his promises. Furthermore, where the presence of God is recognized, there is purity and holiness. Ezekiel hereby lays the foundation for the Pauline spiritualization of the temple. Under the new covenant, even Gentiles' communities may be transformed into the living temple of God (1 Cor. 3:16-17). Moreover, through the indwelling presence of the Spirit of God, individual Christians become temples, residences of deity (1 Cor. 6:19).

1. The New Temple (40:1–43:11)

♦ *Nature and Design*

While the date notice of 40:1 formally opens Ezekiel's entire Torah (chs. 40–48), one may treat 40:1–43:11 as a distinct redactional subunit with its own formal introduction (40:2-4) and its own special interest.[36] Although some include 43:12, and even the consecration of the altar (43:13-27), within the first major section,[37] it is preferable to end with 43:10-11, whose charge to the prophet to describe the temple to his people forms an impressive *inclusio* with 40:3-4. This conclusion is reinforced by the form of 43:12, which functions as a heading for the next section.[38] The genre of the intervening material is classified as *mar'ôt 'ĕlōhîm,* "divine visions," in 40:2a, a conclusion supported by numerous occurrences of *hinnēh* (lit. "Behold") and the nature of the narrative. As in ch. 8 the prophet is led around the temple complex by a supernatural tour guide, who draws Ezekiel's attention to significant details along the way (see fig. 1, p. 508). All the while he is taking precise measurements of the complex, which the prophet conscientiously notes.

The introduction and conclusion to the description of the temple com-

---

35. This is preferable to Tuell's "Wherever the people of the Lord are, there is Zion" (*Proceedings* 2 [1982] 102).

36. Many view 43:1-11 as the first segment of the next major section, chs. 43–46. Cf. Parunak, *Structural Studies,* pp. 506-9; Gese, *Verfassungsentwurf,* pp. 2, 6, 36, 54; Zimmerli, *Ezekiel 2,* p. 406; Vogt, *Untersuchungen,* pp. 132, 146, 165; more recently Allen, *Ezekiel 20–48,* pp. 249-50.

37. On including 43:12 see Greenberg, *Int* 38 (1984) 189-94. For further discussion of the structure of 40:1–43:12 see Talmon and Fishbane, *ASTI* 10 (1976) 138-53. For including 43:13-27 see Stevenson, *Vision,* pp. 159-61.

38. So also Tuell, *Law of the Temple,* pp. 45-46.

plex (40:4–43:11) are deliberately crafted so that the latter answers to the former. In both the guide addresses the prophet by the characteristically Ezekielian phrase, *ben-'ādām,* "human," and both contain a command to the prophet to report back to his people, albeit in slightly different form.[39]

The vision proper divides into two unequal parts: a lengthy account of the tour of the temple complex (40:5–42:20),[40] and a description of the return of the glory of Yahweh to his residence (43:1-9). This account displays several affinities with other divine residence accounts in the OT. First, like the descriptions of the tabernacle (Exod. 25–31; 36–40) and the temple of Solomon (1 K. 6–8; 2 Chr. 2–3), the description is composite, focusing on various aspects of the complex. Except for the altar, however, Ezekiel seems unconcerned about the accoutrements and furniture of the temple. His interest is in the design of sacred space, not the objects that fill up that space. Second, in divine residence accounts, the description of the sanctuary comes to a dramatic conclusion with the arrival of Yahweh's *kābôd* in the temple, symbolic of his imprimatur on the sanctuary itself, but also a visible demonstration of Yahweh's presence in the building and among his people. This event highlights the primary function of the temple in ancient Israel and in the ancient Near Eastern world in general: to serve as the residence of deity.

The motif of temple building plays a prominent role in ancient Near Eastern literature. In mythological texts, the construction of a temple often follows the victory of the god over his enemies.[41] But temple building was

---

39. See the following synopsis:

40:4	43:10
ben-'ādām	*'attâ ben-'ādām*
haggēd 'et-kol-'ĕšer-'attâ rō'eh	*haggēd 'et-bêt-yiśrā'ēl*
lĕbêt yiśrā'l	*'et-habbayit*
Human,	You, human,
Describe everything you see	describe for the house of Israel
to the house of Israel.	the house.

40. To assist the reader in comprehending the complex and at times bewildering report of Ezekiel's tour around the temple complex, fig. 2 (p. 509) traces the movements of the prophet.

41. In the Babylonian *Enuma Elish,* Marduk's victory over Tiamat, by which he earned his kingship among the gods, is followed up with the creation of the universe and humans, whose role would be to serve the gods. The latter is followed almost immediately by the construction of Marduk's temple, Esagila, in Babylon, as a suitable place for him to reside (*ANET,* p. 68). According to Canaanite mythology, Baal earned the right to his own palace on Mount Zaphon by his victory over Mot (*ANET,* pp. 129ff.). For discussion of these texts see V. Hurowitz, *I Have Built You an Exalted House: Temple Building in the Bible in the Light of Mesopotamian and Northwest Semitic Writings,* JSOTSup 115 (Sheffield: JSOT Press, 1992), pp. 93-96 and 100-105, respectively.

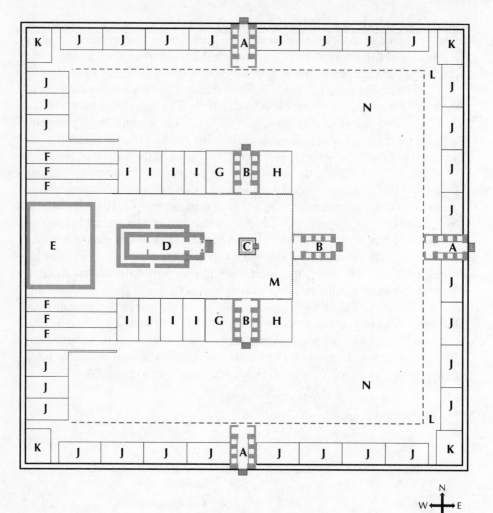

N
W ← → E
S

Key

A Outer gates (40:5-16, 20-27)
B Inner gates (40:28-37)
C Altar (43:13-17)
D Temple (40:48–41:11, 15-26)
E Binyān (41:12-14)
F Priestly sacristies (42:1-14)
G Priestly chambers (40:44-46)
H Chamber of offerings (40:38)
I Outer chambers (41:9b-10)
J Worshiper's chambers (40:17)
K Kitchens (46:19-24)
L Lower pavement (40:18)
M Inner court (40:44)
N Outer court (40:17-19)

Figure 1. The Temple Compound

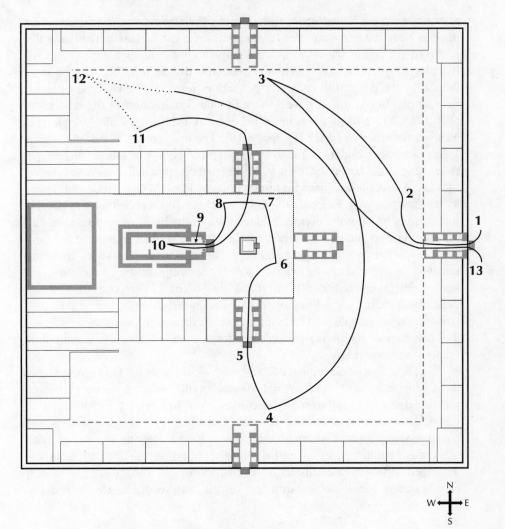

Key

1	40:1-16	**6**	40:32-34	**10**	41:1-4
2	40:17-19	**7**	40:35-37	**11**	42:1-14
3	40:20-23	**8**	40:44-46	**12**	46:19-24
4	40:24-27	**9**	40:48-49	**13**	42:15-20
5	40:28-31				

Figure 2. Ezekiel's Temple Tour

not only the concern of gods. Among the officially recognized functions of ancient Near Eastern kings was the maintenance of the cult, which naturally involved providing the state or local deity with a residence appropriate for his divine splendor. Typically, however, the divine host had the right to determine the nature of his dwelling, a fact reflected in the OT in the precise instructions that Yahweh gave Moses for the construction of the tabernacle (Exod. 25:40), and in the transcribed plan of the (Solomonic) temple that Yahweh provided to David (1 Chr. 28:19). The best-known extrabiblical analogue to these accounts is found in the Temple Hymn of Gudea of Lagash. According to the account, Gudea had a dream through which Ningursu ordered him to construct a sanctuary for him in Lagash. For two days Gudea withdrew to the sanctuary of Eninnu, where he received further visions and precise instructions on how the divine residence was to be built. In response, he had his city purified and gathered the materials for the project. When the building was completed and the temple had been blessed, he was rewarded by being received in the assembly of the gods.[42] Underlying the care taken to build sanctuaries precisely according to the deities' plans was the conviction that a defective building would not stand.[43] An offended divinity would refuse to smile upon his people, and without that smile their welfare was jeopardized. The presence of the divine patron's residence therefore stood as a symbol of security and prosperity.

The editorial placement of Ezek. 40:5–43:11 after the Gog oracle aligns these prophecies with the Baal and Marduk myths, which have the residence for the deity built after major victories over the enemy.[44] Nonetheless, Ezekiel's account should not be interpreted as a blueprint to follow in an actual construction project.[45] Although the analytic tone has a ring of realism, with numerous reminiscences of earlier plans, explicit instructions to build the described structure are missing.[46] Furthermore, not only does the design display many idealistic features; the dimensions recorded are exclusively

42. For discussion of this account see Hurowitz, *Exalted House*, pp. 33-57. Hurowitz discusses numerous other texts of this genre.

43. Thus J. J. M. Roberts, "Yahweh's Foundations in Zion (Isa. 28:16)," *JBL* 106 (1987) 41.

44. M. Nobile (in *Ezekiel and His Book*, p. 255 n. 6) sees in the Gog oracle the radicalization of the oracles against the foreign nations, who must be disposed of before the salvation oracles can begin.

45. Cf. the Temple Scroll from Qumran, which contrasts the temple to be built by the Israelites with the eschatological temple that Yahweh would construct himself (29:8-10). For discussion see Yadin, *Temple Scroll*, 1:182-87.

46. Contrary to Hurowitz's mistaken comment, "An explicit and detailed command to build a temple at some unspecified date in the future concludes the book of Ezekiel (chs. 40–48)" (*Exalted House*, p. 138).

horizontal measurements, apparently without regard for the vertical distances required by architectural plans. Accordingly, the purpose for this temple tour account must be sought elsewhere.

Haran has recognized "the absolute absence of any rhetorical trait" in Ezekiel's Torah,[47] but this does not mean the present description lacks a rhetorical purpose. On the contrary, the twofold command to the prophet to declare to the house of Israel all that he observes (40:4; 43:10) demands a rhetorical interpretation. The precision in the measurements, the presence and size of the gateways, the emphasis on purity, the centrality of the altar, and the strict regulations controlling access to the inner court are designed to shame *(klm)* Ezekiel's exilic audience for past abuses (43:10). Expressed positively, Ezekiel envisions a day when abominations in the sanctuary cease (cf. 8:1-18), and all Israel worships Yahweh in spirit and in truth (cf. John 4:23).

a. Preamble (40:1-4)

1 *In*[48] *the twenty-fifth year of our exile, at the beginning*[49] *of the year, on the tenth [day]*[50] *of the month, in the fourteenth year after*[51] *the city had been conquered, on that very day*[52] *the hand of Yahweh came upon me,*[53] *and he brought me there.*[54] 2 *In divine visions*[55] *he brought me to the land of Israel and set me down*[56] *on an extremely high mountain, on which was a structure*[57] *resembling a city, to the*

47. Haran, *HUCA* 50 (1979) 51.

48. Syr. adds the superscription *bnyn' dbyt'*, "the plan of the house."

49. LXX ἐν τῷ πρώτῳ μηνὶ, "in the first month," harmonizes the date notice with others in the book.

50. The rare cardinal form *'āśôr* (cf. *'ăśirî* in 29:1; 33:21) has been encountered earlier in 20:1 and 24:1. The word for day is missing.

51. *'aḥar 'ăšer*, in place of the conventional *'aḥărê 'ăšer*, occurs elsewhere only in Ruth 2:2.

52. On the construction of *bĕ'eṣem hayyôm hazzeh*, see my *Ezekiel: Chapters 1-24*, p. 774.

53. On the masc. verb after *yad yhwh* see above on 37:1.

54. The emphatic function of *šāmmâ* is missed by LXX, which omits the word. Many delete it with LXX (cf. Gese, *Verfassungsentwurf*, p. 10 n. 2).

55. As in 8:3, LXX reads sg.

56. *wayĕnîḥēnî*, vocalized as in 37:1. Wernberg-Møller (*VT* 8 [1958] 305-6) proposes a Samaritanized form of *nḥh*, "to lead, guide."

57. *mibneh*, from *bānâ*, "to build," is a biblical hapax, but its meaning is illuminated by a late Phoenician inscription found at Piraeus (*KAI*, 60.2; *TSSI*, 3:148-50), which contains the phrase *mbnt ḥṣr bt 'lm*, "the buildings of the court of the temple."

south.[58] 3 *When he brought me there, I noticed*[59] *standing at the gate a man whose form had the luster of copper. In his hand he held a linen cord*[60] *and a measuring stick.*

4 *The man said to me, "Human, look carefully*[61] *and listen closely.*[62] *Pay attention*[63] *to all that I am about to show you — for you have been brought*[64] *here expressly for the showing — and describe everything you see to the house of Israel."*

1a The preamble to the temple vision opens with a complex date notice containing three distinct elements. First, *the twenty-fifth year of our exile* relates the vision to Ezekiel's own deportation to Babylon in 597 B.C. As noted earlier, the number twenty-five (multiples of which appear repeatedly in the vision) alludes to the midpoint of the Jubilee cycle. According to Israelite tradition, every fiftieth year on the Day of Atonement the horn *(yōbēl)* was to be blown throughout the land proclaiming release *(děrôr)* to all enslaved Israelites.[65] The application of the term *děrôr* to the return from exile in Isa. 61:1 indicates that after the Babylonian captivity Jubilee language was appropriated for this event. The possibility that Ezekiel looked on the return from captivity as a Jubilee kind of experience finds support in his own reference to the year of liberty *(šěnat hadděrôr)* in 46:17. Accordingly, the twenty-fifth year may signal a turning of the corner in their bondage to the Babylonians. Instead of looking back on the moment of their enslavement, the exiles may from here on look forward to their release.[66]

Second, the vision came to Ezekiel on *the tenth day of the month* at the *beginning of the year.* Unlike other date notices in the book, which at this point identify the month by number,[67] here the time within the year is specified

---

58. LXX "opposite me" smooths out MT's awkward *minnegeb.* Elsewhere in chs. 40–45, "south" is always referred to as *dārôm.* Many (e.g., *BHS*) delete the word as a gloss.

59. *hinnēh,* lit. "Behold."

60. *pětîl,* from *pātal,* "to twist," is used elsewhere of decorative cords in the priest's ephod (Exod. 28:28, 37; 39:3, 21, 31; cf. Num. 15:38). In Judg. 16:2 it denotes a rope used to tie up Samson.

61. Lit. "Look with your eyes."

62. Lit. "and with your ears hear."

63. Lit. "Set your mind/heart."

64. This is the only attested occurrence of the Hophal form of *bô',* on which see Bauer-Leander, *Grammatik,* §53a; and GKC, §74d. Syr. reads, "I have come"; LXX "you have come." Targ. renders the verb impersonally, "they have brought you."

65. See Lev. 25, esp. vv. 9-10. Cf. Jer. 34:8, 15, 17. For a detailed study of the ethics of the custom see Fager, *Land Tenure.*

66. Cf. Zimmerli, *Ezekiel 2,* pp. 346-47.

67. Cf. 1:1; 8:1; 20:1; 24:1; 29:1; 29:17; 30:20; 31:1; 32:1; 32:17; 33:21.

as *bĕrō'š haššānâ* (lit. "at the head of the year"). This is the only occurrence of the expression in the OT, but it finds an Akkadian counterpart in *re-eš šatti,*[68] presumably a reference to the first month. Appealing to Lev. 25:9, which prescribes that the ram's horn proclaiming release to all slaves be blown on the tenth of Tishri, some have argued for an autumnal date,[69] supposedly following the civil/royal Jerusalemite calendar. But Ezekiel's priestly heritage and the overtly cultic nature of chs. 40–48 render adherence to a civil, rather than religious, calendar extremely unlikely.[70] Furthermore, not only has Ezekiel consistently based his date notices on a Nisan New Year; the cultic rituals he prescribes in 45:18-25 presuppose the same. *rō'š haššānâ* should therefore be understood as the beginning of the year, which, according to the traditional Israelite calendar fell in the spring in the month of Nisan. The present vision may therefore be dated 10 Nisan, in the 25th year of the exile, which computes to April 28, 573 B.C.,[71] making this the second latest of Ezekiel's recorded prophecies. Only the oracle against Egypt in 29:1 is later.

Why the tenth day of the first month should have triggered this prophetic experience one may only speculate. Exod. 12:3 prescribes the tenth day of the first month as the beginning of the Passover festival. But Ezekiel's Torah shows no interest in the Passover at all. As suggested in the introductory comments above, the annual Babylonian New Year festival may provide the most likely solution. This vision functions polemically against pagan notions of the supremacy of Marduk as celebrated in the *akītu* festival. Many in Ezekiel's audience had undoubtedly been enamored by these festivities, especially in the wake of Yahweh's failure to defend them. For these and all who despaired of Yahweh's ability or willingness to save, this prophecy proclaims anew the reign and rule of Yahweh.

Third, the prophecy is dated in the *fourteenth year after the city had been conquered,* that is, after the fall of Jerusalem to Nebuchadrezzar's forces. This date agrees with the twenty-fifth year of exile and confirms 573 B.C. as the year in which this revelation occurred. The addition of "on that very day" underlines the importance of the event recorded in 2 Chr. 36:10: "At the turn of the year, King Nebuchadrezzar sent for him [Jehoiachin] and brought him to Babylon." On the anniversary of this tragedy, Ezekiel may have been contemplating not only the deportation of Jehoiachin and the second wave of exiles, but also the razing of Jerusalem, when he is suddenly overwhelmed by the power of Yahweh.

---

68. *AHW,* p. 975.

69. Zimmerli, *Ezekiel 2,* pp. 346-47; Gese, *Verfassungsentwurf,* pp. 9-10.

70. On the problem of the New Year in Israel see Block, "New Year," *ISBE,* 3:529-32.

71. So also Lang, *Ezechiel,* pp. 40-41; Thiele, *Mysterious Numbers,* pp. 186-91.

1b-2 The triad of expressions used to describe Ezekiel's prophetic experience, all familiar from previous contexts,[72] invite the reader to interpret the following prophecy as the third and final member in a triad of visionary experiences. Why the prophet's destination should be identified as *'ereṣ yiśrā'ēl,* "the land of Israel,"[73] rather than Ezekiel's generally preferred *'admat yiśrā'ēl* is not clear. Whether intentional or not, it orients the reader toward the territorial interests that will characterize later chapters. In any case, whereas others may have despaired at the divorce between nation and hereditary homeland effected by Nebuchadrezzar's deportation, for Ezekiel Judah and the rest of the land once occupied by Israel represent much more than simply a Babylonian province; this land belongs to his people.

More specifically, Ezekiel is deposited on *an extremely high mountain (har gābōah mĕ'ōd),* on the southern slope of which he notices an impressive citylike structure. The prophet's refusal to name either mountain or city reflects his continuing polemic against official Jerusalem theology, even though it had been discredited fourteen years earlier. At the same time he invites the reader to associate this mountain with the world mountain from which peace and prosperity emanate forth to all the world,[74] or Sinai, where the divine King had first revealed himself to his people (Exod. 19). The characterization of the structure by *'îr,* "city," is intentional, as the following description will show. Here the designation applies not to the city Jerusalem as a whole, but to the temple complex, conceived as "a walled enclosure."[75]

3-4 Arriving at the temple complex, the prophet's attention was drawn to the figure of a man, whose form glowed like copper, holding a measuring line in his hand. The former detail identifies him as a supernatural figure, though it is also reminiscent of the bronze figures that were seen supporting the throne of Yahweh in Ezek. 1:7. From vv. 3-4 it is apparent that here he has two functions. On the one hand, like the guide in the old

---

72. The hand of Yahweh coming upon him, which echoes 1:3, is less forceful than the hand falling on him, seizing him by the hair, and carrying him off in 8:1. His conveyance *(hēbî')* to the site where Jerusalem had once stood, compares with 37:1, where he is carried off *(hōṣî')* to the valley of dry bones. On *mar'ōt 'ĕlōhîm,* "divine visions" or "visions of God," see 1:1 and 8:3.

73. The expression occurs elsewhere only in 27:17 and 47:18.

74. Cf. Levenson, *Theology,* pp. 7-36.

75. So also B. Levine, "The Temple Scroll: Aspects of Its Historical Provenance and Literary Character," *BASOR* 232 (1978) 16. The influence of the present text on the Temple Scroll from Qumran is evident in the designation of that temple as *'yr hmqdš,* "city of the sanctuary" (*Temple Scroll* 40:12), on which see J. Milgrom, " 'Sabbath' and 'Temple City' in the Temple Scroll," *BASOR* 232 (1978) 6-27.

temple vision in ch. 8, he will escort Ezekiel around the temple complex. His opening words suggest that he is expecting the prophet. He instructs him to pay close attention to all that he will see and hear because he is to relay everything back to his people. The instruction to observe and listen carefully alerts the reader also to mark well both the guide's actions and his speech. On the other hand, like the man with the writing case in 9:2, the instruments in his hand point to a second role: he is also a surveyor. The first device, a cord made of flax fibers *(pĕtîl-pištîm),* would be used like a modern carpenter's tape to measure longer distances, such as the lengths of buildings.[76] The second tool is a measuring reed *(qĕnēh hammiddâ),* which would be used like a carpenter's yardstick to measure shorter distances. The instruments hint at the importance of what is to follow. The design of that which is about to be measured is intentional and significant. Ezekiel is to concentrate on what the guide is about to show him. After all, he is not simply a tourist visiting an historical site, or even a worshiper on a pilgrimage to a shrine. He is a mediator of divine revelation. Twenty years after his call to prophetic ministry he is still functioning as a spokesman for God to the exiles in Babylon.

The instruments in the surveyor's hands prepare the reader for the detail with which the prophet's observations will be recorded. But they also raise questions concerning the source of and inspiration for this vision. On the one hand, some have seen in the architectonic delineation and analytic-descriptive tone evidence for an actual temple ground plan that the prophet discovered in the archives.[77] Since Ezekiel was of priestly stock, however, the present detail may simply reflect his familiarity with the Solomonic temple that was still standing when he was exiled. On the other hand, the reference to "divine visions" and the prophet's location on the top of the mountain invite comparison with Moses' experience on Mount Sinai described in Exod. 25:1–31:18. Twenty years earlier (Ezek. 1:1-28) the doors of heaven had been thrust open, and the King of Israel, robed in his transcendent glory, had come down to Ezekiel by the Chebar canal. Now, two decades later, the prophet will be given a tour of the heavenly residence of God, of which the tabernacle and the Jerusalem temple had been but replicas.[78]

---

76. Cf. the measuring line *(ḥebel middâ)* used by another angelic interpreter to determine the dimensions of Jerusalem (Zech. 2:5).

77. Talmon and Fishbane, *ASTI* 10 (1976) 139.

78. Cf. also Isaiah's vision in Isa. 6:1-4.

b. The Design of Sacred Space (40:5-46)

(1) The Exterior Features of the Temple Compound (40:5-19)

(a) The Outer Wall (40:5)

5 *I noticed[1] a wall running all around[2] the temple compound.[3] The measuring rod in the man's hand was six cubits long, according to the long cubit.[4] When he measured the structure,[5] its thickness turned out to be one rod[6] and its height was also one rod.*

After being introduced to the man with the measuring rod standing at the gate in vv. 3-4, the reader expects the survey of the temple compound to begin there, immediately. Instead the prophet's attention is drawn to a wall surrounding the entire precinct. What is more, he notices the height of the wall, which is remarkable because nowhere in the following description will he be interested in vertical dimensions. Not surprisingly, some wonder whether this verse is a secondary addition, prematurely anticipating 42:15-20.[7] As one approaches a complex such as this from the outside, however, the wall is naturally the first object to catch one's eye. Furthermore, by opening and closing this lengthy description of the temple with a reference to the city wall the author has created an effective *inclusio*.

This verse provides several pieces of information that will assist the reader in recreating in her or his mind the images described in the following chapters. First, this wall defines the sacred compound as a *city* (*'îr*). The designation is normally reserved for walled settlements, but this wall validates the present designation of a temple compound. Second, the definition of the cubit as "a cubit plus a span" clarifies the standard of measurement to be employed

---

1. Here and elsewhere in this visionary account, "I noticed" translates *hinnēh*, lit. "Behold."

2. On the duplicated phrase *sābîb sābîb*, a linguistic mark of relative lateness esp. common in chs. 40–42, see above on 37:2.

3. Throughout this text *bayit*, "house," refers to the entire temple complex.

4. Heb. *bā'ammâ wāṭōpaḥ*, "according to the [normal] cubit plus a span." S. J. DeVries suggests that the form *bā'ammâ* derives from an antique Semitic idiom (*1 Kings*, WBC 12 [Waco: Word, 1985], pp. 90-93).

5. *binyān*, an Ezekielian neologism under Aramaic influence, was misunderstood by LXX as "outer work." The form recurs in 41:12, 15; 42:1, 5, 10 (cf. *binyâ* in 41:13). For discussions of the word see Hurvitz, *Linguistic Study*, pp. 132-35; Wagner, *Aramaismen*, p. 36, §44.

6. Ezekiel's tendency to follow the order, measurement dimension plus measurement, is typical of Late Biblical Hebrew, probably under Aramaic influence. Cf. Rooker, *Biblical Hebrew in Transition*, pp. 113-14.

7. See Zimmerli, *Ezekiel 2*, p. 348.

in the description. The Israelites knew of three different kinds of cubits, whose sizes varied according to the number of handbreadths that made up the cubit — five, six, or seven. The Chronicler's reference to the cubit "according to the first standard" (1 Chr. 3:3) suggests that the unit of measurement employed in building Solomon's temple differed from the cubit used by this man.[8] On the basis of the Siloam inscription, which indicates that Hezekiah's tunnel was 1,200 cubits long,[9] the normal cubit (six handbreadths) has been estimated at 17.6 in. (44.6 cm). Since the ratio of the normal to the long cubit was 6:7, the cubit used here approximated 20.5 in. (52 cm.), which is remarkably close to the Egyptian long or royal cubit of 52.3 cm.[10] Third, the verse provides the dimensions of the wall. A crosscut would have appeared as a square 6 cubits by 6 cubits, which translates into a wall about 10 ft. high and 10 ft. thick! Like most of the account to follow, the materials used to construct the item are not specified.

(b) The Outer East Gate (40:6-16)

6 *Then he approached the gateway[11] facing east[12] and climbed its steps.[13] He measured the threshold[14] of the gate; it was one rod deep.[15]* 7 *Each recess was one rod wide and one rod deep. The wall between[16] the recesses measured five cubits,[17] and the threshold of*

---

8. Rabbinic sources refer to the "cubit of Moses," the traditional cubit to be used in building sacred structures. See Cf. A. S. Kaufman, "Determining the Length of the Medium Cubit," *PEQ* 116 (1984) 120-22.

9. *ANET,* p. 321.

10. Cf. R. B. Y. Scott, "The Hebrew Cubit," *JBL* 77 (1958) 205-14; idem, "Weights and Measures of the Bible," *BA* 22 (1959) 22-40; M. A. Powell, *ABD,* 6:899-90. On the royal cubit see Herodotus, *Hist.* 1.178.

11. The versions recognize the implicit definiteness of the anarthrous form *ša'ar* (cf. 43:4). Definite forms occur in 40:20, 22; 42:15; 43:1.

12. *ša'ar 'ăšer pānāyw derek haqqādîmâ,* lit. "the gate whose face was in the direction of the east."

13. Instead of translating the verb *wayya'al,* LXX harmonizes the text with vv. 22 and 26 by reading "seven steps." Qere correctly reads Kethib's *bm'lwtw* as pl. According to Andersen and Forbes (*Spelling in the Hebrew Bible,* pp. 323-28), the defective spelling *w* for *yw,* which occurs frequently in this vision, represents an archaic convention.

14. LXX renders *sap* as αιλαμ, apparently confusing this structural feature with the *'êlim,* "vestibule," in vv. 9-10.

15. NJPS notes correctly that *rōḥab,* usually rendered "width," may represent the measurement from an outer surface inward, hence "depth" here. LXX drops the word. *wĕ'ēt sap 'eḥād qāneh 'eḥād rōḥab* in MT (and Targ.) is incomprehensible and looks like dittography.

16. *ûbên* functions substantivally for "the space between two recesses."

17. After *ḥāmēš 'ammôt* LXX adds a lengthy insertion, on which see Gese, *Verfassungsentwurf,* pp. 130-32.

*the gate, next to the vestibule of the gate, on the inside, was one rod.
8 Then he measured the vestibule of the gate [on the inside; it was
one rod. 9 Next he measured the vestibule of the gate];[18] it was eight
cubits, and its jambs were two cubits. Now the vestibule of the gate
was on the inside. 10 The recesses of the gate facing east numbered
three on either side.[19] They were all the same size, and the jambs on
either side were the same size as well. 11 Then he measured the width
of the opening of the gate; it was ten cubits. The total width[20] of the
gateway was thirteen cubits. 12 In front of the recesses was a boundary
line one cubit wide. There was a boundary line one cubit wide on
either side. The recesses on either side were six cubits deep. 13 Next
he measured the gateway from the ceiling of one recess to the ceiling
[opposite it];[21] the total distance was twenty-five cubits. The openings
[of the recesses] were opposite each other.[22] 14 Then he measured[23]
the vestibule;[24] it was sixty[25] cubits. [Toward the jamb of the court
the gate was round about.][26] 15 The distance from the front of the*

18. The repetitious bracketed material is missing in numerous Hebrew mss., LXX,
Syr., and Vulg., and should probably be deleted as dittography.

19. The idiom *mippōh . . . mippōh,* "from here . . . from here," is unique to Ezek.
40–41 (cf. vv. 12, 21, 26, 41, 48).

20. *'ōrek* usually denotes length, but here the full width of the gateway, inclusive
of the jambs and the sockets, seems intended.

21. *miggag hattā' lĕgaggô,* lit. "from the roof of the recess to its roof." NRSV
and REB follow the common emendation of *miggag* to *miggaw,* "back wall," based on
LXX τοῖχος, which frequently translates *qîr,* "wall." But the other major versions reflect
MT. Since each recess is 6 cubits deep and the gateway is 13 cubits wide, yielding a total
of 25 cubits, the measurements were apparently taken from the points at which the roof
and the walls met.

22. *petaḥ neged petaḥ,* "opening next to opening," is an explanatory comment on
the relationships of the recesses, but it need not be deleted as a late gloss, as proposed by
Zimmerli, *Ezekiel 2,* p. 335.

23. Interpreting *wayya'aś* as loosely equivalent to *wayyāmād,* which the context
clearly requires. Perhaps the expression is an abbreviation for "and he did/performed the
measurement." The translation "And he made the supports," though supported by Targ.,
makes no sense.

24. *'ēlîm* looks like a pl. of *'ēl,* "supports" (cf. vv. 9-10), but this is difficult in
the context. Emendation to *'ulām,* "vestibule" (NRSV, REB) requires a simple orthographic
adjustment, but is admittedly provisional. Zimmerli (*Ezekiel 2,* p. 335) follows Gese
(*Verfassungsentwurf,* pp. 140-48) in deleting the entire verse as a corrupt combination of
elements from vv. 15-16. For a complex explanation of how v. 14 might have arisen see
Allen, *Ezekiel 20–48,* p. 220.

25. *šiššîm,* "sixty," is difficult, if not impossible. REB reads "fifty" with *BHS.*
Cf. v. 15.

26. Any reconstruction of MT's meaningless *wĕ'el 'ēl heḥāṣēr haššaʿar sābîb sābîb*
is speculative. The translation offered is quite literal.

gate,[27] *that is, the facade,*[28] *to the front of the interior*[29] *vestibule was fifty cubits.* 16 *The recesses and their jambs*[30] *had closed niches on the interior of the gateway on all sides. The vestibules also had niches*[31] *all around on the inside, and each jamb*[32] *was adorned with palm decorations.*

6-7 Given the east orientation of the temple and the role it will play in subsequent scenes, the tour commences appropriately at the east gate. The luminous man pulls out his rod and begins taking measurements. It is obvious from archeological excavations of numerous Levantine city gate structures in the past century that the prophet's portrayal reflects familiarity with architectural convention.[33] Without reference to their measurements or number, the prophet observes the man approaching the gate from the outside by a series of steps (*maʿălôt*, #1).[34] According to vv. 22 and 26, there were seven steps. Having reached the top of the steps the guide measures the threshold (*sap,*

---

27. Neither MT *wĕʿal pĕnî haššaʿar,* "and against the face of the gate," nor LXX "and the open place of the gate" is meaningful. Zimmerli (*Ezekiel 2,* p. 335) suggests that *ʿal pĕnî* is a corruption from *millipĕnê.* Perhaps *ʿal* should be treated as a substantive like *bên* in v. 7.

28. The hapax *yiʾtôn* is an architectural term of unknown meaning. The context (and LXX ἔξωθεν) suggests a reference to the outer side of the east gate, perhaps the molding or the decorative frame, which represented the point of reference for the measurement of the gateway.

29. *happĕnîmî* is equivalent to *lipnîmâ,* though Gese (*Verfassungsentwurf,* p. 143) deletes the word as an erroneous insertion from v. 19, intended to provide an interpretation for the incomprehensible *hāyiʾtôn.*

30. This 3rd masc. sg. suffix form on *ʾēlêhēmâ* occurs only here, but it compares with fem. *-êhenâ* in 1:11. On the form see GKC, §91l; Joüon-Muraoka, *Grammar,* §94i. On the present form in Qumran writings see M. Burrows, "Orthography, Morphology, and Syntax of the St. Mark's Isaiah Manuscript," *JBL* 68 (1949) 209; Gese, *Verfassungsentwurf,* p. 148. Although LXX supports MT, *BHS* and many commentators delete *wĕʾel ʾēlêhēmâ* as a gloss. See T. A. Busink, *Der Tempel von Jerusalem von Salomo bis Herodes,* vol. 2, *Von Ezechiel bis Middot* (Leiden: Brill, 1980), p. 719.

31. MT *lāʾēlammôt wĕhallônôt.* From here to v. 30 the spelling *ʾ[y]lm* replaces *ʾwlm.* Allen (*Ezekiel 20–48,* p. 221) reads *hallônôt lĕʾēlammô,* "belonging to its porch (were) windows." Cf. *lĕʾēlammô hallônôt,* proposed by Gese (*Verfassungsentwurf,* p. 149), with support from LXX. Since *wĕkēn* introduces the second half of the verse, the *ʾathnach* on *lāʾēlammôt* should be transferred to the second *sābîb.*

32. While LXX erroneously reads *ʾêlām* for *ʾayil,* it correctly reflects a pl. original (*ʾēlāyw?*). The rendering of Targ. translates, "and on top of each support was a crown." An architectural capital seems to be in mind.

33. For a study and diagrams of such gates in the Solomonic era see A. Mazar, *Archaeology of the Land of the Bible 10,000-586 B.C.E.* (Garden City, N.Y.: Doubleday, 1990), pp. 384-87, 465-70.

34. The number identifies the location of the feature in fig. 3 (p. 520).

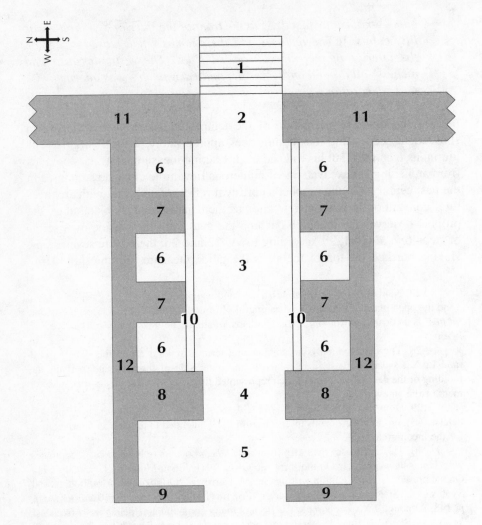

**Figure 3. The Outer East Gate
of Ezekiel's Temple (40:5-16)**

#2), which turns out to be one rod deep (6 long cubits, about 10 ft.), the same width as the wall itself (*hômâ*, #11, v. 5). Entering the gateway, attention is drawn to the square recesses (*tā'*, #6) on each side. V. 7 notes that they were square, one rod wide and one rod deep, converted in v. 12b to 6 cubits. V. 10 indicates there were six of these recesses, identical in size, three on each side, a pattern well attested in Iron Age II structures. The recesses were separated by walls (*bên*, #7) 5 cubits (about 8.5 ft.) thick (v. 7b). According to v. 12, definition was given to the space in each recess by a boundary marker (*gĕbûl*, #10) one cubit (about 20.5 in.) wide (or high?) running across the front.[35] Nothing is said of the function of these recesses, but it is clear they were to serve as guardrooms where security personnel would be posted to defend against intruders.[36]

8-10 Continuing the tour, the guide reaches another threshold (*sap*, #4) which separates the guardroom area from the vestibule (*'ûlām/'ulām*),[37] a larger room just inside the gate (#5). The dimensions of this threshold matched the outer counterpart (#2), suggesting that the wall (#8) between the vestibule and the recess area was thicker than those between the recesses. Although traffic moved through the area, the vestibule was perceived as a rectangular room, 8 cubits (about 13.5 ft.) deep and running the entire width of the gate.[38] At the front it was supported by two jambs (*'êlîm*, #9, v. 9), which functioned as the west wall of the structure.

11-15 The guide returns to the front of the gate. He measures the gate opening (#2) and establishes it to be 10 cubits (about 17 ft.) wide. But the gateway itself (#3) is 13 cubits (about 22 ft.) wide. According to v. 13 he also took the measurement of the roof of the structure, from the back side of one recess to the back side of the other. The height of the ceiling is not indicated, but the horizontal distance is established as 25 cubits (about 43 ft.), which agrees with previous measurements according to which each recess was 6 cubits deep and the gateway was 13 cubits. The architectural term *gag* usually refers to a roof, but since the inside of the structure is being measured, "ceiling" makes more sense. The outside measurements, like the width of the back walls (#12), are undetermined. In v. 15 the guide measures the length of the gateway from the front entrance to the vestibule at the back. This time

---

35. In 43:13 *gĕbûl* denotes a low ledge.

36. In real life these recesses often had a bench running all the way around, providing a place for city officials to sit and conduct legal and administrative business (cf. Job 29:7; 31:21).

37. M. Görg relates *'ulām* to Egyp. *wmr.t*, "roof," extant in Coptic *oualme/ouolme* ("Weiteres zur Gestalt des Tempelbaus," *BN* 13 [1980] 22-25). *'wlm* is a variant spelling of *'ylm*. See v. 16. The word denotes "a (roofed) antechamber or hall."

38. Although it is difficult to picture, v. 14 (MT) suggests that somewhere in the complex there were 60-cubit supports. Or should "vestibule" be read? See n. 24 above.

the total, 50 cubits (about 86 ft.), is obviously based on an exterior measurement, as a cross section of the gateway demonstrates:

$$\#13 + \#6 + \#7 + \#6 + \#7 + \#6 + \#8 + \#11 + \#9$$
$$6 + 6 + 5 + 6 + 5 + 6 + 6 + 8 + 2 = 50$$

The 25 × 50 spatial dimensions give this gateway a perfectly proportioned rectangular shape.[39]

16 This verse provides a description of the walls of the gateway, all of which were punctuated by *ḥallônôt 'ăṭumôt,* whose meaning is unclear. The versions assume a derivation of *'ăṭumôt* from *'ṭm,* "to shut, close," suggesting "closed windows/apertures."[40] Peshitta's expansion, "windows open on the inside, narrow on the outside," and Vulgate's *fenestra obliquas,* "slanting windows," envisage the kind of aperture common in defensive towers through which archers would shoot their arrows.[41] Accordingly these were probably openings through which the temple guards could observe the activities inside the court around the gates.[42]

But the use of a semantic cognate in the Temple Scroll may point in another direction. In the context of the description of the building in which the altar utensils were to be stored, the phrase *ḥlwnym pnymh 'šwmym,* "blocked windows in their inner faces" (35:11), identifies niches (viz., blocked windows) in which vessels were placed.[43] This interpretation is confirmed in 30:12, according to which the niches were to be two cubits wide by four cubits high by two cubits deep (cf. Ezek. 35:12). If one assumes that

---

39. Cf. the geometric design of the Shechem gate discussed by D. Milson, "The Design of the Temples and Gates at Shechem," *PEQ* 119 (1987) 97-105.

40. The verb is used of closing the lips in Prov. 17:28; of stopping the ears in Prov. 21:13 and Isa. 33:15. Levey (*Ezekiel,* p. 111) translates Targ. as "windows which narrowed," but adds a footnote, "Or 'closed,' 'shuttered.' "

41. G. R. Driver (*Bib* 35 [1954] 305) associates the word with Arab. *'atama,* "contracted, narrowed," hence "loopholes." LXX "secret doors" seems not to have known what to do with the expression. More likely is the rendering "latticed" in 41:16. Others see here a reference to "framed windows" (Galling, in Fohrer-Galling, *Ezechiel,* p. 226; Zimmerli, *Ezekiel 2,* p. 336), perhaps like the one illustrated by the famed "Woman at the Window" ivory carving from Nimrud (*ANEP,* no. 131; Barnett, *Ancient Ivories,* p. 50 and plate 50b; Mallowan, *Nimrud and Its Remains,* 2:522 and fig. 429). The carving appears to portray a window framed in diminishing recesses, which would be appropriate for walls as thick as those making up this gate structure. Cf. also *ḥallônê šĕqupîm 'ăṭumîm,* in 1 K. 6:4, which M. Noth translates "framed windows with bars" (*Könige,* BKAT 9 [Neukirchen-Vluyn: Neukirchener, 1968], p. 95).

42. For fuller discussion of this technical expression see G. Molin, "Ḥalonoth 'ăṭumoth bei Ezechiel," *BZ* 15 (1971) 250-53; J. Ouellette, "'Aṭumîm in 1 Kings VI:4: A Dravidian Origin," *Bulletin of the Institute of Jewish Studies* 2 (1974) 99-102.

43. Yadin (*Temple Scroll,* 2:142) translates "niches in their inner faces."

the walls of the building were three cubits thick like the building housing the laver (33:11), this would leave a one-foot wall behind the niche. Since these niches all had doors, they functioned as cupboards for storing the utensils.[44] Accordingly, Ezekiel's *hallônôt 'ăṭumôt* must also have been niches that broke up the flat surfaces of the walls. Concerning their function one may only speculate. Perhaps they held the instruments used by the temple guards to maintain order in the sacred area.

The second detail of the walls is clearer. The jambs were decorated with palm fronds, adding an aesthetically pleasing touch to the entire sight.[45]

The information offered by the narrative is insufficient to construct the gates. We do not know how high they were or the material used to build them. Stevenson notes correctly that the important issue is not what the boundary structures look like, but the spaces within those boundaries.[46] It is these spaces that are defined, spaces whose overall dimensions (25 × 50 cubits) constitute a perfectly proportioned rectangle. The physical structures serve those spaces. The enormous size of the gate and its design with six recessed guardrooms reflect the sanctity of the territory within and the seriousness with which access to sacred space must be controlled. Subsequent revelations will clarify why this is so.

While the size and design of the gateway reflect its importance in the temple complex, structures like this were seldom if ever associated with temple courts. Such installations were normally built to protect human settlements against invaders.[47] But the Gog oracle had declared in no uncertain terms that Israel's last enemy had been defeated by Yahweh, the one who would reside in this city. Surely he needed no protection! What then was the purpose of these structures? The question is left unanswered for the moment, but subsequent chapters will indicate the function of these gates. They are to be manned by Levites to guard the sacred space within the walls against the kind of desecration witnessed in ch. 8.

44. For a full discussion of the "house of utensils" see Yadin, *Temple Scroll*, 1:224-27. This interpretation is accepted by J. Maier, "Die Hofanlagen im Tempel-Entwurf des Ezechiel im Licht der 'Tempelrolle' von Qumran," in *Prophecy*, Fest. G. Fohrer, ed. J. A. Emerton, BZAW 150 (Berlin: de Gruyter, 1980), p. 62; and Fuhs, *Ezechiel 25–48*, p. 229.

45. Cf. the palmette carvings decorating Solomon's temple (1 K. 6:29-36). Proto-Aeolic architectural supports with capitals decorated with stylized palmettes are well attested in Israelite archeological remains from the Iron Age. See Mazar, *Archaeology*, pp. 474-75.

46. Stevenson, *Vision*, p. 24.

47. See Yadin, *Art of Warfare*, 2:322-25, 368-74.

(c) The Outer Court (40:17-19)

17 *Then he brought me into the outer court. I noticed there were chambers, as well as a pavement,*[48] *laid out*[49] *around the entire court. There were thirty chambers facing the pavement.* 18 *The pavement, which flanked the gates, ran their entire length.*[50] *This was the lower pavement.* 19 *Then he measured the dimensions of the court*[51] *from the interior*[52] *front of the gateway to the court facing the outside;*[53] *it measured one hundred cubits. So far the eastern [gate]; now to the northern [gate].*[54]

Before moving to the north gate the guide leads Ezekiel through this east gate for a quick look around the outer court. What he sees is not entirely clear because he employs technical architectural terms whose meanings are disputed. The first, *lĕšākôt*, must refer to some kind of chambers. For the moment not much is said about them, except that they appear opposite the prophet, facing the paved courtyard, and that he is able to count thirty of them. From 42:6 one may assume that these rooms were pillared porticoes, used by worshipers as eating and meeting places during religious events. It

48. The spirantized *p* is regular in *riṣĕpâ*, "pavement" (cf. v. 18; 42:3; 2 Chr. 7:3; Est. 1:6), distinguishing this expression from *rišpâ*, "glowing coal." On the form see Bauer-Leander, *Grammatik*, §75f; Rooker, *Biblical Hebrew in Transition*, p. 162.

49. Since *'āśûy* (masc.) clashes with the fem. antecedent *riṣĕpâ*, and is dropped by LXX, the passive participle is commonly dropped or emended to *'ăśûyâ (BHS)*. But the form recurs in 41:18, again in disagreement with its subject (cf. 41:20, 25, where the expected *'ăśûyim* occurs). Gese (*Verfassungsentwurf*, p. 152) cautions against improving distinctive grammatical features on the basis of classical grammar. Zimmerli (*Ezekiel 2*, p. 337) retains MT, suggesting that the form be treated as a technical term used as a noun (like *mĕḥuqqeh* in 8:10 and 23:14).

50. Lit. "the pavement alongside the wing of the gates, close by the length of the gates."

51. MT reads simply *rōḥab*, "width," but the required sense is reflected in LXX, which adds "the court."

52. Like *'ōrek* and *rōḥab*, *hattaḥtônâ* is used imprecisely, and the fem. form clashes with the antecedent, *ša'ar*. In the present context it seems to refer not to relative elevation but to the interior side of the gateway. Based on LXX, many emend to *hthṭwn 'l pny*. Cf. *BHS*; Gese, *Verfassungsentwurf*, p. 153.

53. MT *lipnê heḥāṣer happĕnîmî miḥûṣ*, "to the front of the court that faces outward," is awkward. LXX reads *haššāʿar*, "the gate," instead of "the court," which makes more sense. Allen (*Ezekiel 20–48*, p. 221) suggests that MT was corrupted under the influence of vv. 23 and 27.

54. An attempt to make sense out of *haqqādîm wĕhaṣṣāpôn*, which is awkward in the context, and usually deleted as a marginal gloss. LXX harmonizes the fragment with v. 24 by reading the guidance formula, "and he brought me to the gate."

is not clear how they were arranged, but it is reasonable to suppose there were eight along each of the north, south, and east outer walls, four on each side of the respective gates, and six on the west side, next to the priestly sacristies (42:1-14). Their size and shape are not given, but if those on the north, south, and east sides were broad rooms each 50 cubits wide, and those on the west long rooms 25 cubits wide, ample provision would be made for the walls between the chambers.

The second feature, represented by the rare word *riṣĕpâ*, receives more attention. The word, a late equivalent of *qarqaʿ*,[55] occurs only five times in the entire OT, three of which are in these chapters. In 2 Chr. 7:3 it is used of the pavement to which the people bow down with their faces in homage to Yahweh after they see his glory enter the Solomonic temple. In Est. 1:6 *riṣĕpâ* denotes a mosaic floor in the palace of the king of Persia inlaid with porphyry, marble, mother of pearl, and precious stones.[56] Accordingly, it appears that when the prophet emerges from the gate complex, he stands before a raised pavement. Indeed, the reference to *hāriṣĕpâ hattaḥtônâ*, "the lower pavement," at the end of v. 18, suggests at least two levels to this court. The first flanked the gate structure and ran the entire perimeter of the outer wall, in front of the chambers; the second was farther to the inside, presumably at the same level as the base of the walls of the inner court. This clarifies v. 34, which notes that eight steps led up to the gateway to the inner court. In any case, the space between the front of the gateway of the outer wall and the court on the next level was paved and measured 100 cubits (about 170 ft.; v. 19; cf. v. 34).

(d) The Outer North Gate (40:20-23)

20 *As for the gate of the outer court facing north,*[57] *he measured*[58] *its length and breadth.* 21 *It had three recesses on either side, as well*

---

55. On which see Rooker, *Biblical Hebrew in Transition,* pp. 162-63.

56. Although LXX translates λιθόστρωτος, "pavement of stones," in both these contexts, in v. 17 of our text, as well as in 42:3, LXX reads περίστυλα, "peristyle." In v. 18, however, it has στοαί, "stoa," which usually refers to a roofed colonnade. Yadin (*Temple Scroll,* 1:263) suggests that the Greek translators must have envisaged a series of columns along the gates. He also notes that *prwr* [ʾmwdym], "stoa" (of standing columns), replaces Ezekiel's *riṣĕpâ* in the Scroll. J. Maier (in *Prophecy,* p. 60) finds in *riṣĕpâ* an Akkadian loanword, cognate to *raṣāpu,* "to pile up, to arrange in layers" (*AHW,* pp. 959-60), *riṣpu,* "construction," and *riṣiptu,* "erection" (*AHW,* p. 989). A possible Palmyrene cognate has been recognized in *rṣp,* "to establish" (*DISO,* p. 282; *DNWSI,* p. 1082).

57. LXX begins the verse with the guidance formula.

58. The use of the perfect and *wĕqāṭal* forms instead of conventional consecutive imperfects, evident also in vv. 24 and 35 as well as 41:13-15 and 42:15-20, is a matter of style. Contra *BHS,* there is no need to emend *mādad* to *wayyāmād.*

as its own jambs and vestibule.[59] *Its measurements were the same as the first gate:*[60] *fifty cubits long and twenty-five cubits wide.* 22 *The niches of its vestibule*[61] *and its palm decorations were the same size*[62] *as those of the gate facing east. [People] would go up*[63] *to it by means of seven steps, and find its vestibule in front of them.*[64] 23 *Like the eastern [gate],*[65] *the north gate faced a gate leading to an inner*[66] *court. He measured the distance from one gate to the other; it was one hundred cubits.*

Omitting the visionary guidance formula, v. 20 moves directly into a sketch of the northern gate of the outer wall. Having provided a detailed description of the eastern gate, a summary statement is adequate. This gate contains all the features of the former: three recesses on either side of the walkway, jambs, a vestibule, niches, and palm decorations. Its measurements were also identical. One new detail is recorded: the number of steps leading up to the gate was seven. Since the gates were identical in every other respect, one may assume that the same number of steps led up to the eastern gate. While the account tends not to be concerned with vertical measurements, this observation hints at the lay of the land. Not surprisingly, the entire temple complex was elevated above the surrounding landscape. V. 23 also notes that, as was the case with the eastern gate, anyone passing through the gate would wind up standing immediately opposite another gate of an assumed inner wall. The space between the gates again measures 100 cubits (about 170 ft.). Reference to the pavement is missing, but one may assume

---

59. The defective form *'lm* for *'ylm* (a variant spelling of *'wlm;* cf. vv. 29, 31, 33, 36) recurs in v. 24 (cf. vv. 29, 31, 33, 36). The sg. verb *hāyâ* was determined by the nearest subject.

60. LXX removes the ambiguity by reading "the gate facing east."

61. MT *wĕḥallônāw wĕ'ēlammô,* "its windows and its vestibules," is difficult because *ḥallôn/ḥallômîm(ôt)* is never construed with a pronominal suffix and the copula is inappropriate on *'ēlām,* which has already been mentioned. Emendation to *wĕḥallônôt/îm 'ēlammô* is recommended. On the first word see S. Talmon, "Emendation of Biblical Texts on the Basis of Ugaritic Parallels," in *Studies in Bible,* ScrHier 31, ed. S. Japhet (Jerusalem: Magnes and Hebrew University Press, 1986), p. 299 n. 56.

62. It is unnecessary to drop MT *kĕmiddat* or emend it to *kĕmô,* since the stress throughout is on corresponding size and proportion.

63. Interpreting the pl. verb *ya'ălû* impersonally. Hebrew translates literally, "and by seven steps they would go up."

64. Contra Zimmerli (*Ezekiel 2,* p. 339), the antecedent of *lipnêhem* is not *ma'ălôt,* but the "people" understood as the subject of the verb. Emendation to *lipnîmâ,* "on the inside," on the basis of LXX is unnecessary.

65. LXX "like the gate that faced toward the east" captures the intended sense.

66. *ḥāṣēr* may be construed as either masc. (also vv. 27-28, 44; 43:5) or fem. (vv. 17, 20; 8:16; 10:3-5).

that the two- (or more) tiered pavement covered the area between these gates as well.

(e) The Outer South Gate (40:24-27)

24 *Then he brought me to the south side. I noticed a gate on the south side. When he measured its jambs*[67] *and its vestibule, the measurements were the same as the previous ones had been.* 25 *It [the gate] and its vestibule had niches*[68] *all around just like the previous niches. Its length was fifty cubits and its breadth twenty-five cubits.* 26 *A stairway of seven steps led up to it;*[69] *its vestibule was before them.*[70] *It had palm decorations on its jambs on either side.* 27 *The inner court also had a gate facing toward the south. He measured the distance from one gate to the other on the south side; it was one hundred cubits.*

The visionary guidance formula, which was missing from the previous paragraph, opens the description of the southern gate. The order and manner in which the details are presented differ slightly from the foregoing, but this gate is clearly a duplicate copy of the eastern and northern gates.

(2) The Interior Features of the Temple Compound (40:28-46)

(a) The Gates of the Inner Wall (40:28-31)

28 *Then he brought me through the south gate to the inner court.*[71] *He measured the south*[72] *gate; its dimensions were the same as the previous [gates].* 29 *Its recesses, jambs, and vestibule were also the same size as the others. Both it [the gate] and its vestibule had niches all around. It was fifty cubits long and twenty-five cubits wide.* 30 *There*

67. LXX harmonizes the text with the preceding, adding "and the recesses."

68. Like *ḥāṣēr, ḥallôn* could be construed as either masc. (cf. v. 22; 41:16, 26) or fem. (vv. 16, 29, 33, 36; 41:16). See also 1 K. 6:4; Jer. 9:20; 22:14; Joel 2:9, all masc.; Cant. 2:9, fem. On the reduced vowel in a closed syllable (*kĕhaḥăllōnôt,* also Cant. 2:9) see E. A. Knauf, "Ḥatef Pataḥ in geschlossener Silbe im Codex Leningradensis," *BN* 19 (1982) 57-58.

69. *ûma'ălôt šib'â 'ōlôtāw* is difficult, construing a fem. numerical adjective with a fem. noun (cf. Waltke-O'Connor, *Syntax,* §15.2.2); *'ōlâ* is never used this way elsewhere. Zimmerli's suggestion (*Ezekiel 2,* p. 340) of a mistaken *hē/mem* interchange is plausible.

70. As in v. 22, the masc. suffix on *lipnêhem* assumes the people who climb the stairs.

71. The versions and numerous Hebrew mss. correctly treat *ḥāṣēr* as definite. On the anarthrous form of a definite noun see GKC, §126w.

72. LXX drops MT's superfluous *haddārôm,* probably the result of dittography.

were vestibules on all sides, twenty-five cubits long and five cubits wide.[73] 31 *Its vestibule faced the outer court,*[74] *and palms decorated its jambs. Its stairway*[75] *had eight steps.*

32 *Then he brought me into the inner court on the east side. He measured the gate; its dimensions were the same as the previous [gates]. 33 Its recesses, jambs, and vestibule were also the same size as the previous ones. It [the gate] and its vestibule had niches all around. It was fifty cubits long and twenty-five cubits wide. 34 Its vestibule faced the outer court,*[76] *and palms decorated its jambs on either side. Its stairway had eight steps.*

35 *Then he brought me to the north gate. He measured it; its dimensions were the same as the previous [gates], 36 as were its recesses, jambs, and vestibule. It also had niches*[77] *all around. It was fifty cubits long and twenty-five cubits wide. 37 Its vestibule*[78] *faced the outer court, and palms decorated its jambs on either side. Its stairway had eight steps.*

Leaving the outer gates the guide directs the prophet through a series of gateways that provide passage to an inner court. An inner wall apparently separated the inner court from the outer, but the absence of any reference to it at least raises the possibility that these gates were symbolic. The symmetry of the temple complex becomes even more obvious when the descriptions of the three gates are juxtaposed as in table 17 (p. 529).

The guide continues the tour by moving from the southern gate of the outer wall to the nearest counterpart on the inner wall. The prophet discovers that this gate opens to an inner court. He also observes that these gateways have the same component features and dimensions. But he cites two significant differences. First, whereas the gates on the outer wall projected inward, with the vestibule to the outer court, these project outward, and represent mirror

73. V. 30 is suspect for several reasons: (1) It is missing in LXX; (2) a counterpart is lacking in the descriptions of the other two gates; (3) the pl. "vestibules" is inappropriate for the context; (4) the dimensions of the vestibule(s) are inconsistent with previous statements. I suspect dittography.

74. As in v. 28, *ḥāṣēr* is implicitly definite, though Zimmerli (*Ezekiel 2,* p. 341) suggests that the article has dropped off by haplography.

75. Both Kethib and Qere mistakenly vocalize *m'lw* as pl., here as well as in vv. 34, 37. On the suffixed form see Bauer-Leander, *Grammatik,* §73l; GKC, §93ss.

76. *leḥāṣēr* is equivalent to *'el-ḥāṣēr* in v. 31. On the implicit definiteness of *ḥāṣēr* see n. 74 above.

77. LXX harmonizes the wording with vv. 29 and 33 by adding "and its vestibule."

78. The context requires emending MT *wě'êlāw* to *wě'ēlammô* with LXX. Cf. vv. 31 and 34. MT may be defended as the *lectio difficilior,* but it makes little sense here.

Table 17. The Three Gates[79]

The South Gate	The East Gate	The North Gate
28 *wayĕbî'ēnî*	32 *wayĕbî'ēnî*	35 *wayĕbî'ēnî*
'el-ḥāṣēr happĕnîmî	*'el-heḥāṣēr happĕnîmî*	*'el-ša'ar haṣṣāpôn*
bĕša'ar haddārôm	*derek haqqādîm*	
wayyāmād 'et-haššaʿar	*wayyāmād 'et-haššaʿar*	*ûmādad*
haddārôm		
kammiddôt hā'ēlleh	*kammiddôt hā'ēlleh*	*kammiddôt hā'ēlleh*
29 *wĕtā'āw wĕ'êlāw*	33 *wĕtā'āw wĕ'êlāw*	36 *tā'āw 'ēlāw*
wĕ'ēlammāw	*wĕ'ēlammāw*	*wĕ'ēlammāw*
kammiddôt hā'ēlleh	*kammiddôt hā'ēlleh*	
wĕḥallônôt lô	*wĕḥallônôt lô*	*wĕḥallônôt lô*
ûlĕ'ēlammāw sābîb sābîb	*ûlĕ'ēlammô sābîb sābîb*	*sābîb sābîb*
ḥămiššîm 'ammâ 'ōrek	*'ōrek ḥămiššîm 'ammâ*	*'ōrek ḥămiššîm 'ammâ*
wĕrōḥab	*wĕrōḥab*	*wĕrōḥab*
'eśrîm wĕḥāmēš 'ammôt	*ḥāmēš wĕ'eśrîm 'ammâ*	*ḥāmēš wĕ'eśrîm 'ammâ*
30 *wĕ'ēlammôt sābîb sābîb*		
'ōrek ḥāmēš wĕ'eśrîm 'ammâ		
wĕrōḥab ḥāmēš 'ammôt		
31 *wĕ'ēlammāw 'el-ḥāṣēr*	34 *wĕ'ēlammāw leḥāṣēr*	37 *wĕ'ēlammāw leḥāṣēr*
haḥîṣônâ	*haḥîṣônâ*	*haḥîṣônâ*
wĕtimōrîm 'el-'êlāw	*wĕtimōrîm 'el-'êlāw*	*wĕtimōrîm 'el-'êlāw*
	mippô ûmippô	*mippô ûmippô*
ûma'ălôt šĕmôneh ma'ălô	*ûšĕmôneh ma'ălôt ma'ălô*	*ûšĕmôneh ma'ălôt ma'ălô*
28 And he brought me	32 And he brought me	35 And he brought me
to the inner court	to the inner court	to the north gate.
by the south gate.	toward the east.	
And he measured	And he measured	And he measured;
the south gate;	the gate;	
the measurement	the measurement	the measurement
was like these.	was like these.	was like these.
29 And its recesses	33 And its recesses	36 And its recesses
and its jambs	and its jambs	and its jambs
and its vestibule;	and its vestibule;	and its vestibule;
the measurement	the measurement	
was like these.	was like these.	
And its vestibule	And its vestibule	And its vestibule
had niches all around.	had niches all around.	had niches all around.
Fifty cubits was its length	Its length was fifty cubits	Its length was fifty cubits
and its width was	and its width was	and its width was
twenty and five cubits.	five and twenty cubits.	five and twenty cubits.
30 Its vestibules were		
all around.		
Its length was		
five and twenty cubits		
and its width		
was five cubits.		
31 Its vestibule faced	34 Its vestibule faced	37 Its vestibule faced
the outer court,	the outer court,	the outer court,
and palm decorations	and palm decorations	and palm decorations
were on its jambs.	were on its jambs	were on its jambs
	on either side.	on either side.
Its stairway	Its stairway	Its stairway
had eight steps.	had eight steps.	had eight steps.

79. The translation in the table is more literal than that offered above to facilitate more concise comparisons.

images of the former.[80] Both face the pavement. Since both are 50 cubits long, the distance between them (100 cubits) is equal to the combined length of the gate structures. Second, v. 31 notes that the second gate was reached by eight steps, which probably represented a pavement of eight terraces, though a stairway between two levels is also possible. Either way, the topography reflects the ascending importance of the sacred space, and increasing degree of sanctity, as one nears the center of the temple complex, a fact reinforced by the need for two sets of gates, each with its own set of gates and guardrooms.

Several features are glaringly absent from the description. The temple complex lacks western gates.[81] Ezekiel will discover that this area was taken up with other structures (chs. 41–42). The narrative records no vertical dimensions, suggesting again that the focus is on the space within the structures, rather than the structures themselves. Furthermore, it gives no linear dimensions for the walls. For this the reader must wait until 42:15-20.

(b) The Chamber of Offerings at the Northern Gate (40:38-43)

38 *There was a chamber whose door opened into the vestibule of the gate*[82] *where they wash the burnt offering.* 39 *In the vestibule of the gate, on either side,*[83] *were two tables on which to slaughter the burnt offering,*[84] *the purification offering, and the reparation offering.* 40 *Off to the side, on the outside, as one goes up*[85] *to the entrance of the gate facing north,*[86] *were two tables. Off to the other side of the vestibule of the gate were two more tables.* 41 *Four tables flanked the gate on either side — eight tables in all — on which to slaughter [the sacrifi-*

80. Contra Busink (*Tempel*, 2:710), who has the gateways of the inner court projecting inward as well, but this creates difficulties in visualizing the chambers.

81. In stark contrast to the temple laid out in the Temple Scroll. For diagrams see Yadin, *Temple Scroll*, 1:252; Maier, *Temple Scroll*, fig. 3.

82. The requirements of the context (cf. v. 39) and the sg. *liškâ* demand that MT *bĕ'êlîm haššĕʿārîm*, "into the jambs, the gates," be emended to *bĕ'ulām haššaʿar.* On the basis of the pl. some apply the present description to all the gates (see Keil, *Ezekiel,* pp. 215-16).

83. LXX omits the last clause of v. 38 and v. 39 to this point, probably by parablepsis.

84. For LXX's omission of *hā'ôlâ wĕ* . . . see Zimmerli, *Ezekiel 2,* p. 367.

85. Interpreting *lāʿôleh* as *lamed* plus participle. Zimmerli (*Ezekiel 2,* p. 363) argues that the parallel in v. 40b points to a scribal error for *lĕ'ulā m/lĕ'ēlām.* LXX and Syr. read *lĕ'ōlâ,* "for the burnt offering."

86. Twice in this verse LXX has these tables facing the east, probably to retain a connection with the eastern gate.

cial animals]. 42 *The four tables*[87] *used for the burnt offerings were [made of] hewn stone. They were one and one-half cubits long, one and one-half cubits wide, and one cubit high.*[88] *On them they place*[89] *the utensils with which they slaughter the burnt offering and the sacrificial offerings.*[90] 43 *Shelves,*[91] *one handbreadth wide, were fastened on the inside, all around. The flesh of the offering*[92] *was to be laid on the tables.*[93]

The tour of the temple grounds is temporarily suspended as two particular features are singled out for more careful scrutiny. Indeed, these paragraphs lack all the elements that have characterized the account so far. Although the dimensions of the table are given, there is no reference to the guide, let alone his measuring activity. The general symmetry of the narrative to this point is abandoned as the focus shifts from structural features of the complex to a particular piece of furniture, to a series of rooms occupied by cult personnel, and then to the role of a special class of priests. Indeed, if vv. 38-46 were deleted the account of the tour would read like a continuous narrative. Nevertheless, this segment should not be discounted as inauthentic or the work of later hands. From v. 45 it is evident that these observations were made during the course of the tour. Indeed, the insertion lends realism to the account. As anyone who has been led around a new site by a tour guide knows, the leader often pauses along the way to describe a particular feature with greater detail, thereby adding both understanding and interest to what could otherwise become routine.[94]

38 Nevertheless, the tour around the temple complex, which has been proceeding methodically, appears to halt momentarily at the north gate of the

---

87. The article has been dropped from *šulḥānôt*, probably by haplography.

88. The LXX order is width, length, height. LXX also has the table 2½ cubits long.

89. With all the major versions, I delete the conjunction on *wĕyannîḥû*, probably as a pseudo-dittography before *yod*.

90. *wĕhazzebaḥ* is commonly deleted as a gloss. Since the last clause makes better sense after v. 43a, many transpose these statements. Cf. NJPS note; Allen, *Ezekiel 20–48*, p. 222.

91. LXX γεῖσος, "projection," Vulg. *labia,* and Syr. *spwthwn* assume a derivation of *haššĕpātayim* from *śāpâ,* "lip." Most translations follow Targ. *'wnqlyn,* "hooks," envisioning a series of hooks attached to the pillars of the slaughtering room on which the carcasses were hung while being skinned. See Levey, *Ezekiel,* p. 113 n. 19. MT points the word as a dual, but a pl. sense is preferred.

92. On the spirantized *bet* in *haqqorbān* see GKC, §9v.

93. LXX rewrites this sentence, "above the tables were roofs to give protection from the rain and the heat."

94. Cf. Hals, *Ezekiel,* p. 298.

inner wall. For the first time the author adds observations concerning consistency and function. Here the prophet's attention is drawn to a chamber *(liškâ)* adjacent to and apparently entered from the vestibule, presumably also on the eighth terrace at the top of the pavement. The function of this room is clear: to provide a place for washing sacrificial animals prior to slaughter.[95] According to 1 K. 7:38, the furniture in Solomon's temple included ten basins of bronze, whose function is explained by the Chronicler: "He also made ten basins in which to wash, and set five on the right side, and five on the left. In these they were to rinse what was used for the burnt offering."[96] But the procedure for washing sacrificial animals is spelled out already in the Mosaic Torah. In Lev. 1:9 and 13 the entrails *(qereb)* and the lower legs *(kĕrā'îm)* of the burnt offering victim are singled out for washing. Since these parts are the most likely to be soiled in the first place, it appears the procedure is as concerned about physical cleanliness as ceremonial.[97]

39 Ezekiel's gaze returns to the vestibule of the gate complex, where he notices a pair of tables *(šulḥānôt)* on each side of the room on which the burnt, purification, and reparation offerings were to be slaughtered. A comment on each is in order.

the burnt offering (holocaust). The noun *'ôlâ* derives from the verb *'ālâ,* "to go up," presumably a reference to the smoke/scent rising to the sky. The ritual of the burnt offering involved the total consumption of the offering by fire; no portion was ever eaten by humans.[98] The primary function of the holocaust was propitiatory, to turn away divine wrath, and expiatory, to atone for sin.[99]

the purification offering. The designation for purification offering, *ḥaṭṭā't* (traditionally rendered "sin offering"), derives from the privative Piel form of the verb meaning "de-sin," viz., "to cleanse, decontaminate, purify." Six stages in the ritual have been identified: (1) the sacrificial animal is brought to the sanctuary; (2) the offerer lays his hands on the animal; (3) the animal is slain; (4) the blood of the victim is daubed on sacred places and objects (cf. 43:19-27); (5) the remains of the animal are disposed of by burning

---

95. *dûaḥ* (always in Hiphil) is a Late Biblical Hebrew technical term for cultic washing of a sacrifice, replacing the earlier verb *rāḥaṣ,* on which see Rooker, *Biblical Hebrew in Transition,* pp. 164-66.

96. 2 Chr. 4:6. Gese (*Verfassungsentwurf,* p. 154) suggests that the Chronicler was dependent on Ezek. 40:37.

97. So also Zimmerli, *Ezekiel 2,* p. 367.

98. Exod. 29:18 describes its nature and significance: "Turn the whole ram into smoke upon the altar; it is an *'ôlâ* to Yahweh as a pleasing odor; it is a fire [offering] to Yahweh."

99. Cf. 45:15, 17. For a study of the *'ôlâ* see J. Milgrom, *Leviticus 1–16,* AB 3 (New York: Doubleday, 1991), pp. 172-77; G. A. Anderson, *ABD,* 5:877-78.

or eating; (6) the purification formula is pronounced (cf. Lev. 12:8). While Milgrom has argued that purification offerings functioned only to decontaminate sacred objects and places (cf. 43:19-27), some texts associate the ritual with forgiveness (cf. Lev. 4:20, 26, 31). When purifications offerings are associated with other sacrifices, which they often are, they are always presented first to cleanse the sacrificial appurtenances that other offerings may be received.[100]

the reparation offering. The noun *'āšām,* usually rendered "guilt offering," derives from a root *'āšēm,* which often means "to feel guilty." But the sense "reparation" is suggested by the verbs associated with the offering: *šillēm,* "to pay," and *hēšîb,* "to bring."[101] Furthermore, the *'āšām* may be converted into a monetary equivalent. Specific occasions mentioned in the OT for the offering include misappropriating or misusing sacred objects, inadvertent or unknown sin, false oaths involving damage to others, the rite of purification for a leper, renewing a Nazirite vow, and engaging in sexual relations with a slave girl betrothed to another. In principle the offering is perceived as restitution, reparation, for sullying a sacred object or person.[102]

40-43 Verse 40 suggests that anyone approaching the northern gate from the outside could see two more pairs of tables on each side of the vestibule entrance.[103] If Haak's understanding of *kātēp* as the facade of the gate perpendicular to the passageway is correct,[104] these tables were situated against the wall on the outside. As one proceeds to v. 41, the arrangement of furniture becomes increasingly difficult to visualize. Are the eight tables referred to now additional tables? Or have only four more entered the picture? The language appears phenomenological. As one enters the vestibule one notices four additional tables, two on each side of the doorway, positioned against the inside of the vestibule wall *(kātēp)* opposite those visible from the outside. The outside four were probably intended for the actual slaughter of the sacrificial animal (v. 41) and the inside ones for washing. V. 42 describes four of the tables, apparently those visible to the prophet outside. These tables consisted of ashlars, that is, rectangular hand-sawn stones, as opposed to natural rock.[105] The tables were square, one and one-half cubits

100. On the purification offering see Milgrom, *Leviticus,* pp. 253-64; Anderson, *ABD,* 5:879-80.

101. Cf. *hiqrîb,* "to present," used of other sacrifices.

102. On the reparation offering see Milgrom, *Leviticus,* pp. 339-45; Anderson, *ABD,* 5:880-81.

103. Thus Busink's portrayal of the inner gates (*Tempel,* p. 710) with their vestibules in line with the wall itself is unlikely.

104. R. Haak, "The 'Shoulder' of the Temple," *VT* 33 (1983) 274-75.

105. A definition of ashlars is provided by 1 K. 7:9 (with reference to the stones

in length and width (about 31 in.), and one cubit high (about 20.5 in.), a comfortable height for those involved in the slaughter of the sacrificial victims.

As it stands, the last half of v. 42 is confusing. Are the tables on which the utensils used in the slaughter of the animals are to be laid the same ones as the slaughtering tables themselves? If so, the issue seems to be protecting the sanctity of the tools by not letting them be defiled through contact with the ground in the process of the slaughter. Taken by itself, however, the last comment seems to refer to tables on which the instruments are placed while not in use. This certainly suits v. 43a, which speaks of special appurtenances all around the wall (of the vestibule?), presumably for storing such utensils. These "storage" tables are probably the four located on the inside of the vestibule wall. But v. 43b appears to reserve these for the flesh of the sacrificial animal *(běśar haqqorbān)*[106] as it awaits formal presentation as an offering inside the court. Much better sense could be made of the passage if v. 43b were located after the dimensions of the tables are given in v. 42, and v. 43a and 42b were transposed. Then the focus in v. 42 could remain on the tables as places of slaughter and holding the flesh, and in v. 43 on the storage of the utensils used in the process. The present literary arrangement may reflect shifts in the prophet's focus as he toured the precinct.

The nature of the appurtenances *(šěpatayim)* on the walls used to store the utensils is disputed. These have traditionally been understood as hooks or pegs on which to hang the utensils.[107] However, a slight repointing yields "lips," and in a derived sense "ledges, shelves,"[108] which probably refers to small niches in the walls, one handbreadth deep. Analogues may be recognized in the "receptacles for the altar utensils" *(btym lkly hmzbḥ)* on the walls of the "house of the laver" referred to in the Temple Scroll.[109]

---

used in Solomon's palace): stones "cut according to measure, sawed with saws, back and front" (NRSV). On the use of ashlars in Israelite construction see Mazar, *Archaeology,* pp. 471-75.

106. *qorbān,* which refers to any gift presented to Yahweh, occurs elsewhere in the book only in 20:28. On the expression see Milgrom, *Leviticus,* p. 145.

107. NRSV, NASB. Based on the dual form, NIV reads "double-pronged hooks."

108. Thus NJPS. REB "rims" is a modification from NEB "ledges." Zimmerli (*Ezekiel 2,* p. 367) reads "storage trays."

109. See Temple Scroll 30:13. According to Yadin's reconstruction of 32:9, these depositories were one cubit square. See *Temple Scroll,* 1:220-21.

(c) The Priestly Chambers (40:44-46)

44 *Outside*[110] *the inner gate,*[111] *in the inner court were two chambers,*[112] *one*[113] *located at the side of the north gate, facing*[114] *southward, and the other*[115] *at the side of the south*[116] *gate facing*[117] *north.* 45 *Then he said to me, "This chamber*[118] *that faces southward is [reserved] for the priests responsible for guarding*[119] *the temple.* 46 *And the chamber that faces northward is [reserved] for the priests responsible for guarding the altar — they are the descendants of Zadok, who alone of the descendants of Levi may approach Yahweh in his official service."*

44 Although many delete this paragraph as a secondary insertion,[120] there is no compelling reason to deny the prophet these observations. Nevertheless, the opening phrase of v. 44 suggests a change in point of view. The prophet has now passed through the northern gateway of the inner wall into the inner court, from where he notices several additional chambers opposite one another on either side of the gate. It is difficult to visualize the scene the author describes. But even before this issue is resolved, the original text must be established: MT reads *liškôt šārîm,* "chambers of singers"; LXX presupposes *lĕšākôt šĕtayim,* "two chambers." Although most translations follow LXX,

110. REB and RSV follow LXX in beginning this paragraph with a new visionary guidance formula. NRSV drops it.

111. LXX reads "inner court."

112. Reading *liškôt šĕtayim,* "two chambers," with LXX, rather than MT *liškôt šārîm* (*BHS,* REB, RSV, NJPS, NIV, NAB, JB), though Vulg. *gazofilacia cantorum,* Syr. *drwrbn',* and even Targ. "chambers of the Levites" all reflect MT. NRSV has returned to MT. See further the commentary.

113. Reading *'ăšer* as *'aḥat* with LXX and Vulg.

114. The contextual need for a singular suffix suggests emending MT *ûpnêhem,* "and their face," to *ûpānêhā,* "and its face."

115. The association with *liškôt* requires the fem. form *'aḥat* in place of MT *'eḥād.*

116. Reading *haddārôm* with LXX in place of MT *haqqādîm,* "east."

117. Like *ûpnêhem* earlier, *pĕnê* calls for *pĕnêhā.*

118. *zōh hallíškâ,* normally "this is the chamber," is awkward. *hallíškâ* should be understood as appositional to *zeh.* On *zōh,* a late dialectical variation of the fem. demonstrative *zō't,* see Cooke, *Ezekiel,* p. 445.

119. *šāmar mišmeret,* lit. "guarded the guardianship." See the commentary.

120. Zimmerli (*Ezekiel 2,* pp. 365-66) is offended by (1) the absence of the visionary guidance formula and references to the measurement of the architectural structures; (2) the premature explanation of the guide, which detracts from the climactic announcement in 41:4; (3) the use of *wayĕdabbēr* instead of *wayyō'mer* in v. 45; (4) the nominative sentence (v. 45), which reflects the influence of 41:4; (5) the explicit naming of the Zadokites. For a rejoinder see McConville, *TynBul* 34 (1983) 20-21 n. 42.

Hurvitz has found in MT further evidence of the transitional nature of Ezekielian Hebrew. He observes that the first references to official temple musicians occur in Chronicles and Ezra-Nehemiah,[121] but that these are designated *měšōrărîm* rather than *šārîm*. Where the latter expression occurs, these are either court musicians,[122] or musicians in a popular procession, who may appear in religious contexts (Ps. 68:26 [Eng. 25]; 87:7) but never as official temple musicians, let alone priestly functionaries.[123] Accordingly, the present reference to a special room reserved for temple musicians suggests a relatively late historical context in which the role of music had been established in official worship. Nonetheless, the absence of the postexilic designation, *měšōrărîm,* indicates that Ezek. 40:44 antedates the second temple period.[124]

One may question this interpretation, however, for several reasons. First, while Hurvitz's lexical arguments and his observation that at this point Ezekiel's temple service shows no evidence of borrowing from the tabernacle service are convincing, his treatment of the Chronicler's evidence as anachronistic is less satisfactory. Not only does it discredit the Chronicler unnecessarily; its diminution of the role of music in the Solomonic temple service is improbable, especially in the light of the prominence of music in the religious service of Israel's neighbors.[125] Second, a reference to temple musicians at this point catches the reader off guard, because it ill suits the literary context. Although Ezekiel often raises a subject only to drop it immediately, in this instance the intrusiveness is intolerable. The explanation offered by the guide in v. 45 is linked syntactically and logically with the sight described in v. 44.[126] Third, this interpretation overestimates the status of the singers in the cult hierarchy. Since these quarters are located "in the inner court," their occupants must have been of the priestly order. However, Israelite tradition consistently distinguishes temple musicians from the officiating priesthood. "The singing Levites" (*halěwîyim hamměšōrărîm,* 2 Chr. 5:12) are always grouped with the supporting cast of Levites, who were responsible for maintaining the temple service but were excluded from officiating in the cult.[127] Fourth, the

---

121. *šārîm* does occur in later writings, but always in noncultic contexts: 2 Chr. 9:11 (taken over from 1 K. 10:12); 35:25 (taken over from a Jeremianic source?); Eccl. 2:8 (or is this evidence of an early date?).

122. See 2 Sam. 19:35 (Eng. 36); 1 K. 10:12; Eccl. 2:8. The musicians carried off from Jerusalem by Sennacherib (*ANET,* p. 288) were probably court musicians.

123. Information on David as the founder and organizer of the musical aspects of the temple service derives exclusively from the Chronicler (1 Chr. 15:26-27 [cf. 2 Sam. 6:13-14]; 2 Chr. 5:11-14 [cf. 1 K. 8:10-11]; 23:12-13 [cf. 2 K. 11:13-14]).

124. A. Hurvitz, "The Term *lškwt šrym* (Ezek 40:44) and Its Place in the Cultic Terminology of the Temple," in *Studies in Bible,* ed. Japhet, pp. 49-62, esp. 56-59.

125. See D. A. Foxvog and A. D. Kilmer, *ISBE,* 3:436-37.

126. If these are singers' quarters, *zōh,* "This," in v. 45 lacks an antecedent.

127. Cf. 1 Chr. 6:1-33 (Eng. 31-48); 9:1-44. Cf. Ezra 2:70; Neh. 7:73. The foun-

reading of LXX makes perfect sense, and the rendering in MT is readily explained as a spelling error, a *taw* having been misread as a *resh*.

45-46 Fortunately, neither Ezekiel nor the reader is left to wonder about the purpose of these two chambers, located at the north and south gates, respectively.[128] In a rare moment, the guide interrupts Ezekiel's gaze by verbally clarifying their function. The first part of the interpreter's comment is cast in the form of two perfectly parallel sentences, reflecting the structural symmetry of the temple compound (literally translated):

zōh hallîškâ 'ăšer pānêhā derek haddārôm	*lakkōhănîm šōmĕrê mišmeret habbāyit*
wĕhallîškâ 'ăšer pānêhā derek haṣṣāpôn	*lakkōhănîm šōmĕrê mišmeret hammizbēaḥ*

This is the chamber that faces south for the priests who perform guard duty for the temple.
and the chamber that faces north for the priests who perform guard duty for the altar.

But what service do these priests perform? The answer depends on the meaning of the idiom *šāmar mišmeret*. While scholars commonly assume that cultic service is involved,[129] this is probably incorrect. The verb *šāmar* is primarily a military term, "to keep, to guard, to watch," from which derives *mišmeret*, which refers fundamentally to military guard duty.[130] The common understanding of the idiom is reflected in 2 K. 11:4-7, where Joash's Carite guards are identified as *šōmĕrê mišmeret bêt hammelek*, "those who perform guard duty for the house of the king."[131] These men are to accompany the king wherever he goes, and are authorized to kill anyone who threatens him. This is the interpretation required in our text.[132] The priests here are not primarily functionaries in the cult, but defenders of the sanctity of temple space and altar.[133] This understanding clarifies the function of these chambers,

---

dation for the distinction between supporting Levites and officiating priests is laid in Num. 18:1-7.

128. Assuming LXX is correct; see n. 116 above.

129. See BDB, p. 1038, "perform the service imposed by." Zimmerli (*Ezekiel 2,* p. 358) interprets the roles of these priests as "seeing to the service of the house" and "performing the service at the altar," respectively. This interpretation would have been more likely if the guide had said *šōmĕrê haššārēt*, "guarding the service."

130. In 2 Sam. 20:3 *bêt mišmeret,* "guardhouse," reverses the elements found in Ezek. 40:45.

131. In 2 K. 11:6 temple guards are called *šōmĕrê mišmeret bêt-yhwh*, "those who perform guard duty for the house of Yahweh."

132. Cf. the description of temple gatekeepers' duties in 1 Chr. 9:17-27, esp. v. 23: "They and their sons were in charge of the gates (*'al haššĕ'ārîm*) of the house of Yahweh, that is, the house of the tent as guards (*lĕmišmārôt*)."

133. So also Greenberg, *Int* 38 (1984) 193. Regarding the use of the idiom in P, Milgrom (*Leviticus,* p. 7) concludes, "In connection with the Tabernacle it means 'guard duty' *and nothing else.*" Cf. idem, "The Levites: Guards of the Tabernacle," in *Numbers,*

particularly their location next to the gateways to the inner court. These *lĕšākôt* are houses of the guards, probably the sleeping quarters of the units on duty, to ensure the uninterrupted presence of officers to prevent the kinds of abuses described in ch. 8. Since they are located inside the temple compound, the guards must be of the priestly order.[134]

Many recognize in the guide's explanation a division of labor among the priests, an assertion of Zadokite power (they have access to the altar) over the rest of the priests (they have access to the temple).[135] But this understanding is doubtful for several reasons. First, it is based on a faulty understanding of Num. 18:5, which, by specifically referring to "performing guard duty for the sanctuary" *(šāmar mišmeret haqqōdeš)* and "guard duty for the altar" *(mišmeret hammizbēaḥ),* differentiates between priestly responsibilities. But the distinctions drawn in Num. 18:1-7 are not between two groups of priests, but between the Aaronid priests and other Levitical functionaries. Second, it is based on a faulty distinction between *bayit,* "house," and *mizbēaḥ,* "altar." But the strict parallelism of the guide's statements suggests relative synonymity of meaning in the lines, with "altar" serving as a nearer definition and concretization of "house,"[136] a usage inspired by Num. 18:5, where the identical phenomenon occurs. Accordingly, *zōh* at the beginning of line one does double duty, and the *waw* at the beginning of line two functions epexegetically. Both chambers are for priestly officers.[137] Third, it fails to recognize the full force of the clarifying comment regarding the Zadokites, which applies to both parallel lines.[138] The priests who guard the temple and those who guard the altar must all be Zadokites, of Levitical descent, authorized to approach *(haqqĕrēbîm)* Yahweh to officiate for him *(lĕšārĕtô).*[139] In 44:15-31 Ezekiel will learn

---

JPS Torah Commentary (Philadelphia: Jewish Publication Society, 1990), pp. 341-42; idem, *Studies in Levitical Terminology: The Encroacher and the Levite: The Term ʿAboda* (Berkeley: University of California Press, 1970), pp. 8-10. Ezekiel will have much more to say about *šōmĕrê mišmeret* in ch. 44.

134. Similarly Stevenson, *Vision,* p. 69.

135. Zimmerli, *Ezekiel 2,* p. 368; Stevenson, *Vision,* pp. 68-69.

136. In contrast to 44:14, where *bayit* carries the broad sense of "temple compound."

137. R. K. Duke recognizes a distinction in roles, but no differentiation in rank ("Punishment of Restoration? Another Look at the Levites of Ezekiel 44.6-16," *JSOT* 40 [1988] 74-75).

138. Prevailing scholarly opinion treats v. 46b as a late editorial insertion, a fragment of the Zadokite stratum that includes 43:19; 44:6-31; 45:4-5; 46:19-21, 24; and 48:11. See Gese, *Verfassungsentwurf,* pp. 21-22, 49, 57-65, 106-7, 89, 102, respectively, but esp. pp. 64-67. For a defense of 40:44-46 as part of Ezekiel's original vision see Tuell, *Law of the Temple,* pp. 31-33.

139. Similarly Duke, *JSOT* 40 (1988) 74-75.

more about the nature of these officiating duties,[140] but in the context the issue is not cultic service but maintaining the sanctity of sacred space. These priests are stationed at the gates to prevent a recurrence of the abominations witnessed in chs. 8–11.

c. The Dimensions of Sacred Space (40:47–42:20)

(1) The Interior Measurements (40:47–41:4)

47 *Then he measured the court. It was a square,[1] one hundred cubits long by one hundred cubits wide; and the altar was located in front of the temple building.* 48 *Then he brought me to the vestibule of the temple. He measured the jambs of the vestibule;[2] they were five cubits on either side. The width of the gateway was fourteen cubits,[3] and the sidewalls were three cubits wide on either side.* 49 *The vestibule was twenty cubits wide[4] and twelve[5] cubits long. [People][6] would approach it by climbing up ten[7] steps. There were pillars on either side of the jambs.*

41:1 *Then he brought me to the great hall. He measured the jambs; they were six cubits wide on either side. This was the width of each jamb.[8]* 2 *The entrance was ten cubits wide, and the side walls on either side of the entrance were each five cubits wide. Next he measured its [the great hall's] depth, forty cubits, and its width, twenty cubits.* 3 *Then he entered[9] the inner room and measured the jamb of the [next]*

---

140. Accordingly, clarification of these terms and the Zadokites' cultic role is delayed until the commentary on 44:15-31.

1. *mĕrubbā'at* is a Late Biblical Hebrew *mĕquṭṭal* form that displaces *rĕbûaʿ* completely in Mishnaic Hebrew. Cf. Hurvitz, *Linguistic Study,* pp. 27-30.

2. LXX points to *'êl hā'ulām* in place of MT's defectively written *'ēl 'ulām.*

3. Following LXX. MT seems to have dropped *'arbaʿ 'eśrê 'ammâ wĕkitĕpôt haššaʿar* by homoioteleuton.

4. Again the terms *'ōrek* and *rōḥab* are being used loosely. The former refers to the width from the standpoint of the observer (the longer side); the latter to the distance to the wall in front of him. Cf. Gese, *Verfassungsentwurf,* pp. 124-26.

5. Following LXX; MT *'aštê 'eśrēh,* "eleven," is impossible in the light of 41:13.

6. See n. 63 on v. 22 above.

7. Reading *'eśer* with LXX instead of MT's meaningless *'ăšer.*

8. Reading *rōḥab hā'lāyim* with LXX, though Targ., Syr., and Vulg. attest to *rōḥab hā'ōhel,* "width of the tent," apparently linking it with the *'ōhel mô'ēd,* "tent of meeting," in Exodus–Leviticus. But this is meaningless in the context. Allen (*Ezekiel 20–48,* p. 223) deletes the phrase as a comparative gloss on v. 2.

9. There is no need to read *wayyābō' (BHS)* in place of *ûbā'.* See analogous perfects in 40:24, 35; 41:13, 15; 42:15. On the use of the conjunction on the perfect see on 13:8; 17:18; 37:2.

entrance; it was two cubits. But the entrance itself was six cubits wide,
and the sidewalls[10] *on either side*[11] *of the entrance were each seven*
cubits deep. 4 *Then he measured its depth; it was twenty cubits. The*
breadth at the front of the great hall was also twenty cubits, and its
breadth was twenty cubits. Then he explained to me, "This is the holy
of holies."

47 The man with the measuring rod turns his attention to the inner court,
which had apparently been entered through the northern gate of the inner wall.
The description of this court is even briefer than the account of the outer court
in vv. 17-18. No reference is made to a boundary wall or to a pavement
between the inner wall and the temple building, but both may be assumed.
What is important is that the man is measuring the court. He establishes that
it is a perfect square, both its width and length being 100 cubits (about 170
ft.). He also notices an altar, situated in front of the temple building, but says
nothing more about it.[12] The narrator appears eager to move on to the temple
building, his primary focus of interest. On the basis of the description of
Solomon's temple (cf. 1 K. 8:64) and the general symmetry of the present
plan, one may assume that this altar was situated in the center of the inner
court, equidistant from the north and south walls of this court,[13] and visible
through the inner and outer gates from outside the temple complex.

48-49 Having completed the measurement of the courtyard, the guide
makes his way into the foreroom of the temple, taking Ezekiel with him (see
fig. 4, p. 541). This vestibule *('ulām)* is rectangular in shape, 20 cubits (about
34 ft.) wide and 12 cubits (about 20 ft.) long. As a whole the temple conforms
to the "long room" architectural design with the entrance on one of the short
ends, but since the entrance of this part is located on the longer side, the *'ulām*
itself is a "broad room." Even so, since the 14-cubit (about 24 ft.) doorway
(ša'ar) takes up more than two-thirds of the long wall, this vestibule is
obviously not to be visualized as an enclosed room.

The entrance is defined on either side by jambs, 5 cubits wide (about

10. Reading *wĕkitĕpôt* with LXX and the analogue in v. 2 (and 40:48). The word
seems to have mistakenly dropped out of MT. Perhaps the scribe's eye skipped to *happetah*.

11. Reading *mippōh wĕšeba' 'ammôt moppōh* with LXX. The segment may have
dropped out of MT at the same time as *kitĕpôt*.

12. A full description is found later in 43:13-17. O. Procksch maintained that
43:13-17 originally came immediately after 40:47 ("Fürst und Priester bei Ezechiel," *ZAW*
58 [1940-41] 102). Cf. also Galling-Fohrer, *Ezechiel*, p. 238 n. 1, "Ursprünglich hinter
40,47?" But Zimmerli observes correctly (*Ezekiel 2*, p. 355) that the present brevity is
intentional.

13. Zimmerli (*Ezekiel 2*, p. 355) locates it nearer the temple, leaving the center
open space.

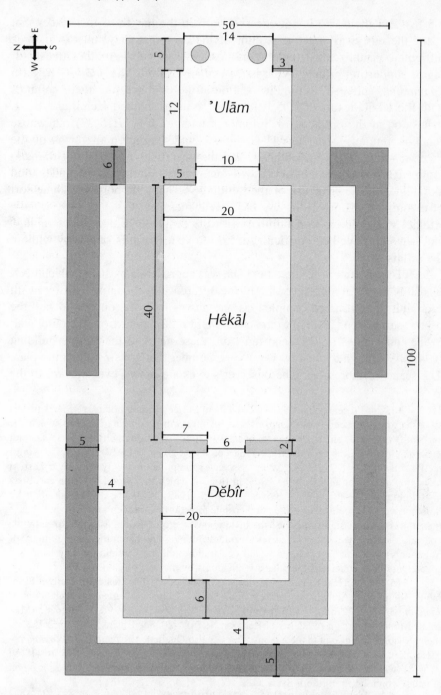

Figure 4. The Design of the Temple (40:47–41:11)

8.5 ft.). But their size is not excessive, given the length of the header that spans the entryway and the weight of the roof that they must bear. It is difficult to visualize the two columns next to the supports. Are they freestanding or supporting pillars? What is their relationship to the *'ulām?* The term *'ammudîm,* "pillars," and their location at the entrance link these columns with the 18-cubit (about 30.5 ft.) bronze columns, named Jachin and Boaz, that stood at the entrance of Solomon's temple (1 K. 7:15-22) but whose function remains a mystery.[14] Given the wide variation in forms of the "freestanding pillars" hypothesis, and the unconvincing nature of the analogic Near Eastern iconographic evidence, these pillars are best understood as integral to the structure of the building, perhaps supports for some sort of awning or canopy.[15] In any case, as a member of the priestly family, Ezekiel would have been familiar with the design of Solomon's temple,[16] and it would have been difficult for him to visualize this sanctuary without the pillars.

The narrator notes that the *'ulām* was approached by steps, which LXX plausibly numbers ten. Accordingly, the difference in elevation increases with each unit in this sacred complex, as one moves from the outside toward the center: seven steps lead up to the outer wall (v. 22), eight from the outer wall to the inner gates (v. 31), and ten from these gates to the temple building (v. 49), yielding a total of twenty-five, a number that governs the entire plan. The scene is impressive. The observer's eyes are drawn ever upward to the

14. Until recently most have viewed them as freestanding pillars, variously understood as lofty cressets, fire altars, obelisks, phalli, twin mountains between which the sun(-god) appeared, pillars of heaven, or trees of life. For bibliography see R. B. Dillard, *2 Chronicles,* WBC 15 (Waco: Word, 1988), p. 30 (on 2 Chr. 3:15-17); DeVries, *1 Kings,* p. 104 (on 1 K. 7:15-22). C. L. Myers associates the pillars not only with Near Eastern iconographic art but also with the *'ulām* in front of which they stood ("Jachin and Boaz in Religious and Political Perspective," *CBQ* 45 [1983] 178). She argues the *'ulām* of Solomon's temple represented "the microcosmic forecourt of Yahweh's microcosmic house *(hêkal* plus *dĕbîr),"* signifying the "the historic passage of Yahweh, as symbolized by the ark, into the earthly counterpart of his cosmic dwelling," and heralding the legitimacy of Solomon's rule. They provided a visual declaration that the Davidic dynasty exercised sovereignty over Israel and the adjacent kingdoms by the will of God.

15. On the Near Eastern evidence see J. Ouellette, "The Basic Structure of Solomon's Temple and Archaeological Research," in *The Temple of Solomon: Archaeological Fact and Medieval Tradition in Christian, Islamic, and Jewish Art,* ed. J. Gutmann (Missoula, Mont.: American Academy of Religion, 1976) 1-20. See Busink, *Tempel,* 2:752, on their structural integrity. On the canopy idea see also Ouellette (in *Temple of Solomon,* pp. 7-11; idem, "Le vestibule du temple de Salomon était-il un *bit ḫilâni?" RB* 76 [1969] 375-78), who argues that the vestibule of Solomon's temple conformed to the *bît ḫilâni* structure common in northern Syria.

16. According to 2 K. 25:13, 16-17 and Jer. 52:20-23, the Babylonians had hauled off these columns as booty.

top of this temple mount where stands the magnificent and utterly holy residence of Yahweh.

41:1-2   The tour of the temple continues as the guide leads Ezekiel into the next room, the *hêkāl*. This is the first occurrence of the term in the present vision, and only the third in the book (twice in 8:16). The word, found also in Canaanite and Ugaritic, is cognate to Akk. *êkallu,* but derives ultimately from Sumerian É.GAL, "big house." The Hebrew term is fundamentally a nonsacral expression, signifying any large, luxurious house, especially a king's palace.[17] When used of the Israelite sanctuary, *hêkāl* highlights the building's role as the palace of Yahweh.[18] In this context the term denotes not the temple as a whole but the great hall, the nave between the vestibule and the holy of holies. According to the guide's measurements, the jambs (*'ulām*) of the entryway to the *hêkāl* were 6 cubits wide (about 10 ft.),[19] even larger than the 5-cubit jambs of the *'ulām* (40:48). The doorway was 10 cubits (about 17 ft.) wide.[20] The great hall itself was a perfectly proportioned rectangle, 40 cubits (about 68 ft.) long and 20 cubits (about 34 ft.) wide. Since entrance was gained at the narrow end, this room is classified as a "long room." The absence of any reference to its decoration, furnishings, or function reflects the primary rhetorical concern to define sacred space, not to provide a blueprint for a construction project.[21]

3-4   Having measured the great hall, the guide proceeded into the inner sanctum. Appropriately, there is no mention of him taking the prophet inside with him, but Ezekiel is able to observe the man taking more measurements. This room was a perfect square of 20 cubits (about 34 ft.), exactly one-half the size of the *hêkāl*. But other dimensions have also been reduced. The side jambs are only 2 cubits (3.4 ft.) wide, and the width of the entryway *(petaḥ)* is only 7 cubits (about 12 ft.). For the first time a vertical dimension is given: the entrance is 6 cubits (about 10 ft.) high. As if the priestly prophet needed an explanation, when the man had completed the measurement of the room he announced verbally that this was the holy of holies (*qōdeš haqqŏdāšîm*). But nothing more is said.

The similarities between Ezekiel's and Solomon's temples (1 K. 6–7) are obvious. Both have two pillars of unknown function in the front. Both consist of three rooms. The dimensions of the supremely holy room (*qōdeš haqqŏdāšîm*) and the great hall (*hêkāl*) are identical.

---

17. Cf. 1 K. 21:1; 2 K. 20:18; Isa. 13:22; 66:6; Amos 8:3; Hos. 8:14; etc. For discussion see Haran, *Temples and Temple-Service,* pp. 13-14.

18. Note the expression *hêkal yhwh* in 8:16. Also 2 K. 6:5, 17; 7:21; Isa. 6:1, and elsewhere.

19. Cf. the 5-cubit supports of the entrance to the *'ulām* (40:48).

20. Cf. the 14-cubit (about 24 ft.) doorway of the *'ulām* (40:48).

21. For a general discussion of the rites performed within the *hêkāl* of the Israelite temple see Haran, *Temples and Temple-Service,* pp. 208-20.

But the differences are equally striking. Most obvious is the absence of detail in Ezekiel (though some of these will be filled in later); his description is reduced to the definitions of sacred space. Ezekiel's *'ulām* is 2 cubits deeper than Solomon's, resulting in a 2-cubit increase in the overall length of the temple (without making allowance for the width of the walls). Finally, the inner sanctum is identified as the *qōdeš haqqŏdāšîm,* rather than a *dĕbîr* (this term does not occur in Ezekiel).

Despite these differences, whereas Ezekiel's earlier visions of Yahweh and his temple incorporated numerous pagan motifs, the present vision of the temple is inspired only by authentic Yahwistic traditions. The Solomonic connection invites the reader to associate the significance of this temple as the residence of Yahweh with the function of the original. Although Ezekiel makes no explicit reference to the Davidic house, the present echo of the original invites reflection on the relationship between the *nāśî',* who will appear later, and the Davidic ruler. Nonetheless, the nature of the structure, and the narrative itself, reflect a continued concern to guard the sanctity of the temple (cf. 40:45). (1) The building is raised ten steps above the surrounding courtyard. (2) The entryways shrink in size as one moves from the fore-room to the supremely holy room at the back: the entry to the *'ulām* is 14 cubits (about 24 ft.), to the *hêkāl* 10 cubits (about 17 ft.), to the *qōdeš haqqŏdāšîm* 6 cubits (about 10 ft.). (3) The jambs at the entrances to the larger rooms increase in thickness as one approaches the *dĕbîr:* before the *'ulām* it is 5 cubits (about 8.5 ft.), before the *hêkāl* 6 cubits (about 10 ft.), though the jamb before the *dĕbîr* is only 2 cubits (about 3.4 ft.). (4) The prophet is escorted through the first two rooms, but not invited into the inner sanctum.[22] (5) The guide verbally announces the name of the inner sanctum: *qōdeš haqqŏdāšîm,* "the most holy place of all." Like the seraphim in Isa. 6:1-2, the threefold division of the temple proclaims Yahweh as the thrice holy one.

(2) The Auxiliary Structures of the Temple (41:5-12)

5 *Next he measured the wall of the temple; it was six cubits thick. The side chambers located all around the temple*[23] *were four cubits wide.* 6 *The side chambers were constructed one above the other, thirty units in three stories.*[24] *There were ledges on the wall of the temple*

---

22. In the original this room was closed to all, except for the high priest, who was permitted to enter once a year on the Day of Atonement. Cf. Lev. 16.

23. Targ. *shwr shwr mqp lbyt' shwr shwr* is even more cumbersome than MT *sābîb sābîb labbayit sābîb.*

24. MT *sēlāʿ 'el-sēlāʿ šālôš ûšĕlōšîm pĕʿāmîm,* lit. "side room over side room, thirty-three times," is difficult. A reversal of the numbers and omission of the copula yields the most likely sense: "thirty (side rooms), three times." Cf. LXX "chamber over chamber,

for the side chambers all around, to serve as supports, without the supports being integral to the temple wall itself. 7 A widening[25] *ramp spiraled*[26] *up to the side chambers, because the temple was surrounded*[27] *upward all around the building [with side chambers].*[28] *Therefore, the temple had a broad [passageway]*[29] *leading upward, allowing [traffic] at the bottom to pass through the middle story*[30] *to the top. 8 Then I noticed that the temple*[31] *had a raised platform*[32] *all around — the foundations*[33] *of the side chambers. Its elevation*[34]

---

thirty and three twice," which suggests two stories, each with thirty-three diminutive cells (cf. Vulg. *bis triaginta tria*). Targ. *tltyn wtlt ḥd' 'sry bsydr'* reflects a three-story construction with eleven per story. Many (e.g., Zimmerli, *Ezekiel 2*, p. 370; Gese, *Verfassungsentwurf*, p. 165) delete *ûšělōšîm* as a gloss. ·

25. MT vocalizes *wěrāḥăbâ* as a verb, "to be/become wide," but a subject is lacking. Many follow Targ. and read a noun, *rōḥab*, "width, widening," with support from LXX and Vulg.

26. The absence of the *dagesh* in *wěnāsăbâ* (from *sbb*, "to surround, turn") reflects Aramaizing influence. Cf. GKC, §67dd; Joüon-Muraoka, *Grammar*, §82j. Whereas LXX drops the word, Targ. reads a noun *msybt'*, "winding staircase." Perhaps an initial *mem* was mistakenly read as *wn*, which is not difficult to imagine. See further Gese, *Verfassungsentwurf*, p. 166.

27. Repointing *mûsab* as a Hophal participle, *mûsāb*. Gese (*Verfassungsentwurf*, p. 167) suggests that this clause functions as a closer definition of *msbh* in the previous line.

28. The verb *mûsāb* requires an adverbial accusative

29. According to NJPS and NRSV, *kēn rōḥab labbayit lěmā'lâ* suggests that the higher one ascended the wider the temple wall became. But this is architecturally improbable and syntactically unlikely. The adjective "broad" requires a referent.

30. On the basis of Targ. *b'wrḥ* and Vulg. *in medium*, Gese (*Verfassungsentwurf*, p. 168) proposes *btykwnh* instead of *ltykwnh*.

31. Although *wěrā'îtî labbayit* is attested in Targ., Vulg., and Syr., with support from LXX καὶ τὸ θραελ τοῦ οἴκου, many read the verb as *wtr'l*, an otherwise unknown technical architectural term (cf. LXX αἰλαμ for *'ylm* and θεε for *t'w*). Zimmerli (*Ezekiel 2*, p. 372) suggests that MT has arisen as a result of the transposition of consonants and the loss of the final consonant by haplography. But since MT conveys a tolerable sense, such operations may not be necessary.

32. Elsewhere *gōbah* denotes "height" (1:18; 19:11; 31:10, 14; 40:42; 43:13). *BHS* and many commentators repoint as *gabbâ*, "back, elevation, convex" (cf. 10:12; 16:24, 31, 39).

33. Reading *mwsdwt* with Qere in place of Kethib *mysdwt*. The measurement that follows is not "from the foundation" to some unspecified point, but the foundations themselves.

34. *'aṣṣîlâ* is apparently another technical building term of unknown meaning. LXX translates the term διάστημα, "intervening space," the same term used to render *mysdwt* earlier in the verse. Cf. Vulg. *spatio* and Targ. *rwḥ*, "space." Following K. Elliger ("Die grossen Tempelsakristeien im Verfassungsentwurf des Ezechiel (42,1ff.)," in *Geschichte und Altes Testament*, Fest. A. Alt, BHT 16 [Tübingen: Mohr, 1953], p. 92), Zimmerli reads "its top terrace" (*Ezekiel 2*, p. 372).

measured a full[35] rod, six cubits. 9 The outer wall belonging to the side chambers was five cubits thick. The open space[36] between the side chambers[37] belonging to the temple 10 and the other chambers, surrounding the entire temple, was twenty cubits wide. 11 The side chambers opened[38] to the open space, with one entrance on the north side, and another entrance on the south. This open area[39] was five cubits wide all the way around. 12 And the structure that was in front of the open space[40] on the western side [of the temple] was seventy cubits wide. The wall of the structure was five cubits thick all the way around, and it was ninety cubits long.

The boundaries of this subsection are marked by the twofold occurrence of the verb *mādad*, "to measure," at the beginning of v. 5 and again at the beginning of v. 13. The style of the intervening material differs from the preceding vision account in several respects. First, though the description obviously derives from firsthand observation, it lacks a visionary guidance formula. It is not clear at which point in the tour this part of the temple complex was visited. It would have been logical to climax the tour with the visit to the inner sanctum, in which case the area dealt with here would have been surveyed before the events described in 40:47–41:4. The present editorial arrangement may have been determined by a desire to take the reader quickly to the heart of the complex. Second, the narrative style reinforces the apparent lack of movement. Except for a few subordinate verbal clauses in vv. 6b-7, the description is made up entirely of verbless clauses by which the reader is introduced to a whole series of technical architectural expressions: *qîr* (wall), *ṣēlā'* (side chamber), *bā'ôt* (ledges), *'ăḥûzîm* (supports), *měsibbâ* (staircase), *gōbah* (raised platform), *môsĕdôt* (foundations), *'aṣṣîlâ* (elevation), *munnāḥ* (open space), *lěšākôt* (chambers), *petaḥ* (entrance), *binyān* (structure), *gizrâ* (open space). The plethora of textual notes above reflects how uncertain their

---

35. On *mlw*, defectively spelled for *mlw'*, "full," see GKC, §23f. Cf. the measurement expressions *ml' qwmtw*, 1 Sam. 28:20; *nl' hḥbl*, 2 Sam. 8:2; *ml' rḥb*, Isa. 8:8.

36. *wa'ăšer munnāḥ*, lit. "that which is left to rest," viz., left alone, here used in the sense of "free space." So NRSV.

37. *bêt ṣĕlā'ôt* is suspicious. On the analogy of v. 10 and LXX, "in the middle of the sides," *byt* is probably a corruption of *byn*. Zimmerli (*Ezekiel 2*, p. 373) finds a remnant of an original article on *ṣĕlā'ôt* in the down stroke of the *taw*.

38. Many read pl. *wptḥy*, "entrances," instead of MT *wptḥ*, "entrance."

39. In place of *měqôm hammunnāḥ*, lit. "place of the open space," LXX reads τοῦ φωτός, "window," which in 42:7, 10, 12 translates *gādēr*, "wall." Allen (*Ezekiel 20–48*, p. 224) suggests that a gloss, *mqwm hmnḥ*, intended to explain v. 9b, has mistakenly displaced *gdr hmnḥ*.

40. *gizrâ*, a synonym for *munnāḥ*.

meanings are. But the cataloguing of architectural features contributes to the static stylistic tone. Third, regarding subject, the narrative departs from the spatial concerns and from those features of a temple compound that would have been of greatest interest to a worshiper. Fourth, echoes of the description of the Solomonic temple in 1 K. 6:5-8[41] are clearly heard, as the synopsis in table 18 (p. 548) demonstrates.

While the distinctive vocabulary, style, and arrangement of Ezekiel's description demonstrate stylistic freedom, his presentation reflects a general familiarity with the 1 Kings text or with the Solomonic temple structure itself. The enigmatic nature of the narrative, particularly its technical vocabulary, make it difficult to visualize these chambers. Nevertheless, a tentative reconstruction may be proposed.

5 The paragraph opens by noting the thickness of the temple wall — 6 cubits (about 10 ft.). This means these walls are not only as thick as the jambs of the doorway between the 'ulām and the hêkāl (cf. 41:1), but just as thick as the wall around the temple compound (40:5). Ezekiel's concern here is not the wall itself, however, but a series of auxiliary structures that appear to run all the way around the temple (with the obvious exception of the front, and perhaps the foreroom). The designation for these structures, ṣĕlāʿôt, from the noun ṣēlāʿ, "rib" (cf. Gen. 2:21-22), points to "side chambers."[42] In any case, when they were measured, the (bottom) chambers were found to be 4 cubits wide, being bounded on one side by the temple wall itself, and on the other side by a second wall 5 cubits thick (v. 9a). The massiveness of the walls is remarkable; both inside and outside walls are thicker than the width of the rooms.

6 This verse indicates that there were three ṣĕlāʿôt. The text is far from clear, but the parallel in 1 K. 6:6 suggests that three stories are envisioned. Unlike the 1 Kings text, which had failed to give the number of side rooms in Solomon's temple, the phrase šĕlōšîm pĕʿāmîm, "thirty times," offers a clue for this structure. While the sentence structure is difficult, the figure seems to identify the number of cells in each story,[43] yielding a total of ninety rooms. Since these auxiliary structures went to the top of the building (v. 7), the entire temple was boxed in.

41. For a discussion of textual and interpretive matters see DeVries, *1 Kings*, pp. 87-96.

42. In the description of the Solomonic temple the same word denotes the cedar planks lining the inside of the building (1 K. 6:15-16), perhaps because of the resulting "ribbed" appearance.

43. Busink (*Tempel*, 1:213-14; 2:759) reconstructs Solomon's auxiliary rooms on the basis of Ezekiel's number, arguing that this figure must be borrowed from the earlier structure. If Ezekiel's structure had been totally original, he would have used some multiple of twenty-five.

Table 18: A Synopsis of Ezekiel 41:5-9a and 1 Kings 6:5-6, 8

Ezekiel 41:5-9a	1 Kings 6:5-6, 8
5 *wayyāmād qîr-habbayit šēš 'ammôt wĕrōḥab haṣṣēlā' 'arba' 'ammôt sābîb sābîb labbayit sābîb.* 6 *wĕhaṣṣĕlā'ôt ṣēlā' 'el-ṣēlā' šālôš ûšĕlōšîm pĕ'āmîm ûbā'ôt baqqîr 'ăšer-labbayit laṣṣĕlā'ôt sābîb sābîb lihyôt 'ăḥûzîm wĕlō'-yihyû 'ăḥûzîm bĕqîr habbāyit.* 7 *wĕrāḥăbâ wĕnāsĕbâ lĕma'ĕlâ lĕma'ĕlâ laṣṣĕlā'ôt kî mûsab-habbayit lĕma'ĕlâ lĕma'ĕlâ sābîb sābîb labbayit 'al-kēn rōḥab-labbayit lĕmā'ĕlâ wĕkēn hattaḥtônâ ya'ăleh 'al-hā'elyônâ lattîkûnâ.* 8 *wĕrā'îtî labbayit gōbah sābîb sābîb môsĕdôt haṣṣĕlā'ôt mĕlô haqqāneh šēš 'ammôt 'aṣṣîlâ.* 9a *rōḥab haqqîr 'ăšer-laṣṣēlā' 'el-haḥûṣ ḥāmēš 'ammôt.*	5 *wayyiben 'al-qîr habbayit yāṣiwa' sābîb 'et-qîrôt habbayit sābîb lahêkāl wĕladdĕbîr wayya'āś ṣĕlā'ôt sābîb.* 6 *hayyāṣiwa' hattaḥtōnâ ḥāmēš bā'ammâ roḥbāh wĕhattîkōnâ šēš bā'ammâ roḥbāh wĕhaššĕlîšît šeba' bā'ammâ roḥbāh kî migrā'ôt nātan labbayit sābîb ḥûṣâ lĕbiltî 'āḥōz bĕqîrôt habbāyit.* 8 *petaḥ haṣṣēlā' hattîkōnâ 'el-ketep habbayit hayĕmānît ûbĕlûlîm ya'ălû 'al-hattîkōnâ ûmin-hattîkōnâ 'el-haŝĕlišîm.*
5 Next he measured the wall of the temple; it was six cubits thick. The side chambers located all around the temple were four cubits wide. 6 The side chambers were constructed one above the other, thirty units in three stories. There were ledges on the wall of the temple for the side chambers all around, to serve as supports, without the supports being integral to the temple wall itself. 7 A widening ramp spiraled up to the side chambers, because the temple was surrounded to the top all around the building [with side chambers]. Therefore, the temple had a broad [passageway] leading upward, allowing [traffic] at the bottom to pass through the middle story to the top. 8 Then I noticed that the temple had a raised platform all around — the foundations of the side chambers. Its elevation measured a full rod, six cubits. 9a The outer wall belonging to the side chambers was five cubits thick.	5 And he built a platform alongside the wall of the temple, all around the walls of the temple including the nave and the inner sanctum. And he built side chambers all around. 6 The bottom story was five cubits wide; the middle story was six cubits wide; the third story was seven cubits wide, for he allowed offsets for the temple all around the outside to prevent them from being attached to the walls of the temple. 8 The entryway of the bottom story was on the south side of the temple, and by flights of stairs one would go up to the middle story, and from the middle to the third [story].

548

The second half of v. 6 is difficult to visualize. Although the wording differs from 1 K. 6:6b, some dependence on this text[44] justifies interpreting the present statement in its light. The meaning of Ezekiel's *bā'ôt* is uncertain, but this technical building term corresponds to the *migrā'ôt* referred to in 1 K. 6:6.[45] Used architecturally, the word describes the terraced form of Solomon's temple wall. Derived from the common root *bô'*, "to go, come," Ezekiel's expression suggests a terraced ledge large enough to walk along, an image supported by the width of each story along Solomon's temple wall: 5, 6, and 7 cubits, respectively. Since the outer wall of Ezekiel's buildings was apparently uniformly 5 cubits (about 8.5 ft.) thick from bottom to top (v. 9a), the size of the cells must have increased from the bottom to the top floors.[46] The joists that held up the respective stories rested on the ledges *(bā'ôt)* in the temple wall that served as *'ăḥûzîm*, "supports" (v. 6), rather than being embedded in the temple wall itself, perhaps to prevent a threat to the sanctity of the temple by damage to the walls.[47]

7 This verse is extremely difficult to interpret. At issue seems to be the architectural feature that provides access to the top story of side chambers. Drawing support from the rabbinic use of *msbh* for "gallery," some recognize a single large exterior ramp or stairway running around the north, west, and south sides of the building.[48] But this interpretation yields a physically impossible reconstruction. To have a ramp like this all around the building would have made it impossible to provide light for the chambers.[49] Moreover, the links between Ezekiel's and Solomon's temples prove a much better basis for interpretation than a late and often speculative rabbinic tractate. Rather than using an exterior ramp, 1 K. 6:8 states specifically that access to the upper stories was gained through *lûlîm*, probably to be understood as interior spiral

---

44. Hurvitz (*Linguistic Study*, pp. 121-23) argues that Ezekiel's *lō'* plus finite verb (*wĕlō'-yihyû 'ăḥûzîm bĕqîr habbāyit*, "The brackets were not in the wall of the temple itself") functions as a later equivalent of the more ancient pattern involving *lĕbiltî* plus infinitive (*lĕbiltî 'ăḥōz bĕqîrôt habbāyit*, "that they [the supports] should not take hold of the walls of the temple themselves").

45. So G. R. Driver, *Bib* 35 (1954) 305. *migrā'ôt* is a hapax noun from a root *gr'*, "to diminish" (Ezek. 16:27), "to withdraw" (5:11).

46. See fig. 5 (p. 550). For a similar interpretation, though with a different understanding of the outer walls, see M. Haran, *Encyclopaedia Olam Ha-Tanakh*, vol. 12, *Yehezkel* (Hebrew), ed. G. Brin (Ramat Gan: Revivim, 1984), p. 212. For a popular and illustrated discussion see V. Hurowitz, "Inside Solomon's Temple," *BR* 10/2 (1994) 26-27, 31. A slightly different construction is proposed by J. Ouellette, "The *Yaṣia'* and *Ṣela'ot*," *JNES* 31 (1972) 187-91.

47. Zimmerli, *Ezekiel 2*, p. 377.

48. See *b. Middot* 4:5. Cf. Gese, *Verfassungsentwurf*, p. 167; Zimmerli, *Ezekiel 2*, p. 377.

49. Thus Busink, *Tempel*, 2:762.

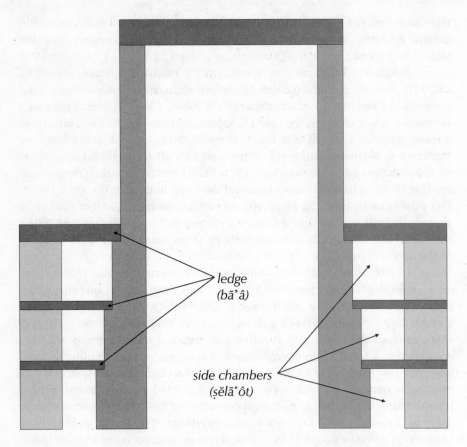

Estimated height based on proportional requirements,
assuming the height is the same as the width (50 cubits)
and the auxiliary structures are one-half the height.

Figure 5. Ezekiel's Auxiliary Structures (41:5-12)

staircases (i.e., progressing upward with 90 degree turns).[50] Furthermore, this picture conforms better to extrabiblical analogues, in which access to upper stories was gained by interior stairways.[51]

8-9a The interpretation of v. 8, which is equally difficult, is complicated by the absence of a parallel element in 1 K. 6. The prophet notes that the temple stands on a *gōbah,* apparently a raised platform, functioning as a foundation *(môsĕdôt)* for the side chambers, and raising the elevation of an already imposing structure a full 6 cubits (about 10 ft.). V. 9a gives the thickness of the outer walls — 5 cubits (about 8.5 ft.). Considering the width of these walls (5 cubits, doubled), the cells (4 cubits, doubled), the temple walls at the base (6 cubits, doubled), and the interior dimensions of the temple (20 cubits), the overall width of the structure is exactly 50 cubits (about 85 ft.). Adding the interior dimensions of the temple, 85 cubits (cf. 40:48–41:4), and the width of the rear cells inclusive of the walls yields a total length of 100 cubits (about 170 ft.). Not only does this create a perfectly proportioned rectangle (100 × 50 cubits); it continues the use of multiples of twenty-five.

9b-11 Here the prophet describes a new detail: the space between the side cells *(ṣĕlā'ôt)* and another set of chambers, referred to as *lĕšākôt.* Nothing more is said about these structures in the vision, but they are obviously to be distinguished from the priests' quarters in 40:44 or the priestly vestries described in 42:1-9. The prophet's interest is in the size of the open space *(munnāḥ)* between the sets of rooms, measured at 20 cubits wide. This figure appears to clash with v. 11b, which knows of a 5-cubit space around the side chambers. Whether something has fallen out of the text or it has been corrupted in transmission,[52] v. 11 continues the description of the relationship of the side chambers to the surrounding area. Two gates, one on the north side and the other on the south, open out onto the surrounding open space. The perspective of *petaḥ haṣṣēlā' lammunnāḥ,* "the opening of the side chamber to the open space," is that of an observer on the inside looking out, but how this observer got inside is not indicated. It is doubtful he would have entered from the *hêkāl.*[53] On the contrary, the presence of exterior doors is designed to

---

50. Cf. K. A. Kitchen, "Two Notes on the Subsidiary Rooms of Solomon's Temple," *ErIsr* 20 (Yigael Yadin Memorial Volume) (1989) 108*; DeVries, *1 Kings,* p. 94; contra Noth *(Könige,* p. 99), who interpreted these as trap doors.

51. Cf. the Egyptian temples of Sahure (ca. 2500 B.C.) and the great temple of Amun at Karnak built by Thutmose III (ca. 1479-1425 B.C.). For description and discussion see Kitchen, *ErIsr* 20 (1989) 107*-12*. This interior reconstruction had been proposed also by Galling (in Fohrer-Galling, *Ezechiel,* pp. 229-30). After discussing various proposals, Busink *(Tempel,* 2:763) deletes all but the last clause of v. 7 as secondary.

52. The reading in LXX either attests an early corruption or reflects the Greek translators' efforts with a difficult passage. See n. 37 above.

53. Contra Busink, *Tempel,* 2:760.

protect the sanctity of the nave. In any case, when this observer exits the side chambers he enters an open area, 5 cubits wide. Whether this was a raised platform, perhaps an extension of the foundation of the entire structure (cf. v. 8),[54] or a specially paved area surrounding the building, is unclear. According to the latter, it would have been included within the previously mentioned 20-cubit open area; according to the former, probably not.

Having sketched the auxiliary chambers around the temple, the reader is left wondering what function they were intended to serve. 1 Kings 6 offers no clues either. Analogous single and multistoried rooms from Egyptian cult centers[55] suggest that their significance was well known to Ezekiel and his original readership. They probably served as storehouses for temple treasures. In temples built by Merneptah and Ramsses III the amount of storage space is three or four times the area of the temple itself.[56] Although different in design, Mesopotamian temples often had storage rooms within and adjacent to the temple buildings whose areas surpassed that of the temple proper. Such storage space housed ritual equipment, votive gifts, and the revenue taken in by the temple. Since revenue was not in money but in kind, enormous space was required for sacks of grain, amphorae of oil, and the kegs of wine, not to mention other kinds of goods that found their way into the priests' hands. But the author is obviously not concerned about these structures' practical use. What matters to him are spatial relationships. These annexes are designed so that, while abutting the temple, they maintain the sense of proportion without threatening its sanctity. They are built upward and outward, without intruding on the architectural space of the sanctuary itself.[57]

12 Here the prophet introduces another exterior structure, the *binyān*, a large building located behind the temple (fig. 5). The neologism *binyān*, which occurs outside Ezekiel only seven times, functions as a late alternative to *bayit*.[58] Only the barest details concerning this nondescript edifice are given: (1) It was located west of the temple building. (2) It was separated from the temple by a *gizrâ*, "restricted space."[59] (3) Its walls were 5 cubits thick (about 8.5 ft.), like the side chambers. (4) The building was imposing for its size. Internally it measured 90 cubits long by 70 cubits wide (about 150 ft. by 120 ft.), which

---

54. So Taylor, *Ezekiel*, p. 261.

55. Cf. Kitchen, *ErIsr* 20 (1989) 108*-9*.

56. Ibid., p. 109*.

57. Cf. Stevenson, *Vision*, pp. 30-31.

58. Cf. the discussion by Hurvitz, *Linguistic Study*, pp. 132-35.

59. In the context the expression appears to function as a variant of *munnāḥ*, but its derivation from *gāzar*, "to cut, divide," yields different connotations. This is not merely leftover space (*munnāḥ*, on which n. 36 above) but a "restricted space," presumably because it is off limits to common folk, or perhaps even to the priest. V. 14 employs the same word for space in front of the temple.

means that its external dimensions were 100 by 80 cubits, exceeding the area of the temple itself! Again nothing is said of its function, but its presence here represents an intentional reaction to excesses of the Judean monarchy, whose claims for space tended to encroach upon sacred temple territory.[60]

(3) The General Dimensions of the Temple Complex (41:13-15a)

13 *Then he measured*[61] *the temple. It was one hundred cubits long. The restricted area and the structure*[62] *including its walls was also one hundred cubits long.* 14 *The width of the front of the temple including the restricted area on the east side was also one hundred cubits.* 15a *He also measured the length of the structure facing the restricted area at the back,*[63] *along with its balconies*[64] *on either side; it was one hundred cubits long.*

The opening verb and the shift in subject point to a new phase in the temple tour and a new literary subsection. This short paragraph ties together several loose ends, making explicit several details that could have been recognized in 40:47–41:12: (1) The exterior of the temple is measured, confirming the building to be 100 cubits long. (2) The depth of the restricted space *(gizrâ)* at the rear of the temple, including the area taken up by the *binyān,* is identical, 100 cubits (about 170 ft.),[65] which means the "restricted area" at the rear of the temple is the same as on the north and south sides (v. 10). (3) The north-south direction of the *binyān* is measured and established as 100 cubits.[66] The fourth detail, the *'attîqêhā'* on the outside of the *binyān,* is more difficult. *'attîqêhā',* which occurs only here and in 42:3, 5, has been rendered "ledges" or "corridors."[67]

---

60. See below on 43:7-8.
61. On the weak *waw* with the perfect see 40:24, 35; 41:15; 42:15.
62. *binyâ* is a fem. variation of *binyān,* encountered earlier and recurring in v. 15.
63. MT *'aḥărêhā* should probably be repointed *'ăḥôrêhā.* See Targ. on 8:16.
64. The Masoretes recognized the irregularity of Kethib *w'twqyh'* pointing the *taw* with a *hireq* (cf. Qere *'tyqyh'*). On the Aramaic influence reflected in the final *aleph* see Hurvitz, *Linguistic Study,* p. 88 n. 105; Howie, *Date and Composition,* p. 65. Cf. *kl'* in 36:5 and *gb'* in 31:5. Many treat *wě'attiwqêhā' mippô ûmippô* as a secondary gloss. See Allen, *Ezekiel 20–48,* p. 224.
65. This is the figure arrived at by adding the interior dimensions of the building (70 cubits), east and west walls (twice 5 cubits, v. 12), and the width of the "open areas" *(munnāh)* on the north and south sides of the building (20 cubits, v. 10).
66. This matches the figure arrived at by adding its interior width (90 cubits) and two walls, each 5 cubits thick (v. 12).
67. For the former see NJPS, apparently following Elliger (in *Geschichte und Altes Testament,* p. 85), who explains the form as a noun derived from *nātaq,* "to tear off, cut

Any solution to the riddle of the *'attîqîm* must consider a series of factors. (1) These items are associated with the *binyān* itself, apparently appearing on the outside. (2) V. 16 has *'attîqîm* inside the great hall as well; these either came in threes or consisted of three levels *(lišloštām)*. (3) According to 42:3-5 *'attîqîm* were visible from both inner and outer courts, again associated with the number three,[68] with the upper exemplars taking up more space than the lower ones. No firm conclusions about these structures are possible at the present time, but some sort of galleries or balconies may be imagined. This interpretation has the added advantage of matching both etymologies suggested above. "Balconies" are at the same time "ledges" and "walkways."[69] But their function remains a mystery.

(4) The Interior Decorations and Furnishings (41:15b-26)

15b *Now the interior*[70] *of the great hall and the vestibules of the court*[71] 16 *the thresholds*[72] *and the closed niches,*[73] *as well as the balconies all around on all three sides,*[74] *opposite the threshold,*[75] *were paneled*[76] *with wood all around, from the ground*[77] *to the niches,*

---

off," with proclitic *aleph*. He draws attention to the well-known ivory carving, "The Woman at the Window," which portrays a window whose frames recede by steps (*ANEP*, no. 131; cf. Barnett, *Ancient Ivories*, p. 51 and plate 50b). Accordingly, the long wall of the *binyān* was punctuated by framed windows or ledges of some sort. For the latter see REB, following G. R. Driver, "Studies in the Vocabulary of the Old Testament III," *JTS* 32 (1930/31) 363; idem, *Bib* 19 (1938) 185. Cf. *AHW*, pp. 260-63; *CAD*, 4:384-95 (on *etēqu*); 10/2:297-98 (on *mūtaqu*).

68. Cf. n. 124 below.

69. Similarly Maier, *Prophecy*, p. 64 n. 18.

70. LXX reads *hpnymy* as *hpnwt*, "and the corners." NRSV and RSV follow LXX, wrongly assuming the decoration of the inner sanctum will also be dealt with. But see Wevers, *Ezekiel*, p. 307.

71. Although Targ. and Vulg. follow MT's pl. *w'lmy hḥṣr*, LXX correctly reads sg. in keeping with the requirements of the context. Perhaps we should read *w'lmw hḥṣr*. LXX assumes *wh'lm hḥswn*, "and the outer vestibule."

72. LXX reads *sĕpunîm*, "paneled," in place of MT *hassippîm*.

73. On *haḥallônîm hā'ăṭumôt* see n. 41 above on 40:16. LXX translates "closed off with netting."

74. The antecedent of *lišloštām* is unclear. Based on the fem. form of the numeral following the masc. noun, the most likely guess is that the *'ăṭumîm* (themselves obscure) had either three parts or three sides.

75. LXX and Syr. omit *neged hassap*, perhaps because it was not understood. Many delete the phrase as a gloss. See *BHS;* Gese, *Verfassungsentwurf*, p. 175.

76. The hapax *śĕḥîp* is cognate to Akk. *siḥpu*, "overlay," and describes a veneering technique using wood. On its etymology see Garfinkel, *Akkadian Influences*, pp. 133-34.

77. Reading *wmh'rṣ* with LXX in place of MT *wh'rṣ*.

including the covered niches,[78] 17 *and extending to*[79] *the top of the entrance,*[80] *both in*[81] *the inner temple and on the outside. And on all the walls round about, inside and out were carefully designed*[82] 18 *and carved*[83] *cherubim and palm decorations, with a palm between each pair of cherubim.*[84] *Each cherub had two faces:* 19 *a human face was turned toward the palm on one side, and the face of a lion was turned to the palm on the other side. They [the figures] were carved all over the entire temple.* 20 *The cherubim and palms were carved*[85] *from the ground to the tops of the entrances; similarly the wall of the great hall.*[86]

21 *As for the great hall,*[87] *its doorposts*[88] *were squared.*[89] *In front*

78. Although *wĕhahallōnôt mĕkussôt* is attested in all the versions, many delete the first word as a dittograph, and see in the second a reference to covering with wood or reliefing of wooden walls. Cf. Allen, *Ezekiel 20–48,* p. 224. LXX's paraphrastic "and the doors opened three times to peep through" carries the opposite sense of Targ.'s "and the narrowing windows" (so Levey, *Ezekiel,* p. 114).

79. Reading *'ad* instead of *'al* with Targ. and on the analogy of v. 20.

80. Although many follow LXX in dropping *'al-mē'al happetaḥ,* as per the emendation in n. 79 above, the phrase provides a sensible conclusion to v. 16. The area between the ground and the tops of the entrances is referred to again in v. 20.

81. Either *wĕ'al* was miswritten as *wĕ'ad,* or the latter was exchanged with *'al* at the beginning of the verse.

82. Again LXX appears to have dropped a word (*middôt,* "measurements"; cf. Vulg. and Syr., which read a verb, "and he measured") because it was not understood. Some emend *mdwt* to *dmwt,* "likeness," and place the word before *kĕrûbîm* (Allen, *Ezekiel 20–48,* p. 225). Unlike the vision of 1:1-28, however, *dĕmût* is unsuitable here where objects observed are precisely described. An original *middôt* probably refers to a measured off area on the walls where the reliefs occur (Zimmerli, *Ezekiel 2,* p. 384), or to the carefully designed nature of the reliefs themselves. Everything about this temple is planned.

83. Both here and in v. 19 MT *wĕ'āśûy* is awkward, but it has been encountered earlier in 40:17. Targ. reads a noun, *glyp krwbyn,* "engraving of cherubs."

84. Lit. "and the palm was between cherub and cherub." On the Late Biblical Hebrew construction *bên . . . lĕ . . .* in place of *bên . . . ûbên . . . ,* see Rooker, *Biblical Hebrew in Transition,* pp. 117-19.

85. Finally, the form *'ăśûyim* agrees with the subject, which precedes, as in 40:17.

86. The *puncta extraordinaria* over *hahêkāl,* which is repeated in v. 21, recognizes the textual difficulty. Cf. Bauer-Leander, *Grammatik,* §79. If this word were a dittograph, then *wĕqîr* should have been written *baqqîr,* "on the wall." LXX drops one *hahêkāl* and apparently reads *wĕqōdeš* for *wĕqîr.* BHS proposes *laqqîr* on the analogy of v. 25.

87. *hahêkāl* is missing in LXX, Vulg., Syr.; see n. 84 above.

88. Repointing *mĕzûzat* as a pl., *mĕzûzōt.* Neither Syr., which omits the word, nor LXX, which treats it as a synonym for *mĕkussôt* in v. 16, understood *mzwzt.*

89. On the form *rĕbu'â* (cf. *mĕrubbā'â* in 40:47), see Hurvitz, *Linguistic Study,* pp. 27-30.

of the holy place[90] *there was an object resembling* 22 *a wooden altar.*[91]
It was three cubits high,[92] *two cubits*[93] *deep, and two cubits wide.*[94] *It
had corners,*[95] *and its base*[96] *and sides were made of wood. Then he
told me, "This is the table that stands before Yahweh."*

23 *The great hall and the holy place each had double doors.* 24 *The
double doors consisted of two swinging leaves;*[97] *two leaves belonged
to one door and two leaves belonged to the other.* 25 *Carved*[98] *on these,
that is, on the doors of the great hall, were cherubim and palm decorations, similar to those carved on the walls.*

And there was a wooden railing[99] *in front of the vestibule.* 26 *There
were closed niches and palms on either side, on the side walls of the
vestibule, the side chambers, and the railings.*

The interpretive problems of Ezekiel's final vision intensify in 41:15b-26. (1) In
scarcely one of these dozen verses is the text clear. My translation is suggestive
only, and may be challenged at virtually every turn. (2) The passage lacks
stylistic coherence and flow, as it moves from one topic to another without
offering adequate treatment of any. (3) In regard to context, the text is intrusive.
After leading the prophet through the temple and taking measurements of the
sacred space, the guide almost disappears from the narrative. For the moment
attention is focused on internal decoration. But this description of the interior of
the *hêkāl* would not only have been more natural at an earlier juncture (after

90. Targ. interprets *haqqōdeš* as *byt kpwry,* "place of atonement," viz., the holy
of holies.

91. Joüon-Muraoka, *Grammar,* §131a, treats *hammizbēaḥ 'ēṣ* as appositional, viz.,
"the altar (is) wood." See further Andersen, *Hebrew Verbless Clause,* p. 20. However, the
article on *hammizbēaḥ* appears suspect, perhaps the result of faulty verse division and
dittography.

92. Reading *gbhw* with LXX, Targ., and Syr. The absence of the *waw* on MT *gbh*
is due to haplography.

93. Whereas Early Biblical Hebrew expressed "two cubits" with the dual form
'ammātayim, Ezekiel prefers *šĕtayim 'ammôt.* For discussion see Hurvitz, *Linguistic Study,*
pp. 30-32.

94. Reading *wĕrāḥĕbô šĕtayim 'ammôt* with LXX. The phrase seems to have
dropped out of MT by homoioteleuton.

95. The suffix on *ûmiqṣō'ôtāw,* which is not reflected in the versions, is probably
influenced by the following nouns.

96. Reading *wa'ădānāyw* with LXX καὶ ἡ βάσις αὐτοῦ, in place of MT *wĕ'orkô,*
"and its length," which is awkward. *wa'ădānāyw* occurs more than 50 times in the
instructions for the tabernacle in Exod. 25–40.

97. The fem. gerundive participle, *mûsabbôt,* "that can be turned," is equivalent
to *gĕlîlîm,* "revolving," in 1 K. 6:34.

98. Fem. sg. *wa'ăśûyâ* ill suits the context, unless the form carries a neuter sense.

99. Following Allen, *Ezekiel 20–48,* p. 218.

41:2?), when the guide and the prophet were still inside; there is little connection with the sequel in ch. 42. Indeed, the latter would fit much better immediately after 41:11. (4) As for form, vv. 15b-26 defy a clear pattern. The visionary guidance formula is absent, leaving the reader to wonder how the prophet got back into the temple to make the present observations. The announcement by the hitherto absent guide in v. 22b catches one completely by surprise. Formally and stylistically this announcement would have been more at home nearer to v. 4. (5) The passage is internally inconsistent in its vocabulary. The great hall and the porch are referred to as *hahêkāl happĕnîmî*, "the inner temple room," and *'ulammê heḥāṣēr*, "the vestibules of the court," respectively, in v. 15b, but they are *habbayit happĕnîmî*, "the inner room of the temple," and *laḥûṣ*, "the outside," or simply *pĕnîmî wĕhaḥîṣôn*, "the inner and the outer," in v. 17. Whereas v. 4 had identified the inner sanctum as *qōdeš haqqŏdāšîm*, "the holy of holies," now it is simply *qōdeš*, "the holy place."

Not surprisingly, scholars have attributed this material to a hand different from the one responsible for the surrounding narrative of the tour of the temple grounds.[100] Whether or not this description was inspired by the description of Solomon's temple, and even if these verses were inserted in the present context secondarily, nothing is here that one could not attribute to Ezekiel himself, and no signs point unequivocally to a date later than the surrounding tour reports.[101] While intrusive, the announcement in v. 22 provides a stylistic link with v. 4. The ornamentational links with the Solomonic temple suggest some authorial familiarity with the original. The differences arise because Ezekiel receives this vision more than three decades after his last visit to the temple in Jerusalem. The lexical inconsistency reflects the richness of the Hebrew vocabulary. The placement of this material is not entirely illogical. Having completed the general survey of the temple, the editor deemed it appropriate to insert this passage before moving on to another area of the temple complex (42:1-20). The incompleteness of the description and the syntactical lapses may suggest that these verses preserve only fragments of originally longer descriptions. In any case, the present collection ties together a series of loose ends.

15b-20 The first half of this description concerns the interior decoration of the temple, beginning with a survey of the inner walls of the *hêkāl*, the great hall of the temple.[102] Many of the details of vv. 16-17 are obscure.

---

100. Zimmerli, *Ezekiel 2*, pp. 386-87; Wevers, *Ezekiel*, p. 297; Galling, in Fohrer-Galling, *Ezechiel*, pp. 233-34.

101. So also Hals, *Ezekiel*, p. 298. Zimmerli (*Ezekiel 2*, p. 387) derives this section from priestly circles planning to rebuild the temple during the exile, but he allows that it may also have been inspired by the reality of the second temple.

102. *happĕnîmî* reflects the perspective of the observer, who views the nave toward the inside. *'ulammê heḥāṣēr* refers to the front vestibule (cf. 40:48-49).

Passing reference is made to three features that ran all around the room: "thresholds" *(hassippîm)*, "closed niches" *(haḥallônîm hāʾăṭumôt)*, and "balconies" *(hāʾattîqîm)*. One is probably correct in understanding the *threshold* as a wooden beam that jutted out underneath the niches.[103] The expression for *closed niches* has been encountered earlier in 40:16, and the term for *balconies* has occurred in the previous verse, where it referred to some exterior feature of the *binyān*. The interpretation of this feature is frustrated by the absence of a counterpart in either the Mosaic tabernacle or the Solomonic temple. Since there is no hint in the OT that the cultic proceedings inside the temple were ever open to lay observers, the reference cannot be to public galleries.[104] The word, used in a derived sense, may identify a decorative or architectural feature, perhaps a prominent sill that ran all around the room beneath the niches.[105] The following modifier, *lišloštām*, suggests a three-tiered sill around the room. The description implies that every inch of wall space was paneled with wood, from the thresholds below at the entrances to the closed niches above. The vestibule *(laḥûṣ)* was paneled similarly.

According to vv. 17b-20, from the floor to ceiling (v. 20), all over the entire temple the walls were decorated with beautiful carvings of cherubim and palm trees, motifs obviously borrowed from Solomon's temple (1 K. 6:29-36). Unlike the four-headed creatures of Ezekiel's earlier visions (chs. 1, 10) these cherubim have only two heads, one human, the other like a lion. This form may have been necessitated by their context: they were not freestanding figures but carved and incorporated into the walls. No mention is made of "open flowers" *(pĕṭûrê ṣiṣṣîm)* or of gold overlay, which had figured prominently in Solomon's ornamentation. Nor is the significance of the winged sphinxes and palms explained, though these skillfully carved sculptures will have certainly enhanced the beauty of the interior. The present arrangement of palmette trees flanked by a pair of animals facing each other is attested not only on ancient ivories; the design was common in other art forms as well.[106] But more than aesthetics is involved in this design. In these figures aspirations of life and prosperity (palm) and security (cherubim) coalesce. In Israelite thought, the divine resident of this house was the source of both.

---

103. Cf. Busink, *Tempel*, 2:755.

104. Though these balconies may have provided a vantage point for junior priests to observe the high priest perform the ritual acts, the OT is silent on such allowances.

105. Busink *(Tempel, 2:755)* interprets *šḥyp ʿṣ sbyb sbyb* as a reference to this wooden beam.

106. Cf. the ivory carving from Arslan Tash portraying a tree between two ram sphinxes facing each other (Barnett, *Ancient Ivories*, plate 47b). For further discussion see Busink, *Tempel*, 1:267-86. From within Israel itself see the scene painted on one of the large ʿAjrud storage jars published by P. Beck, "The Drawings from Ḥorvat Teiman (Kuntillet ʿAjrud)," *TA* 9 (1982) 13-16 and fig. 4.

21-22 The prophet shifts the reader's attention to the entryway to the great hall. The phrase *mĕzûzat rĕbuʿâ* is obscure. It may refer to a "fourfold graded door-frame," which narrows toward the rear of the door casing.[107] But *rĕbuʿâ* is better interpreted as a variant form of *rābûaʿ*, the common word for "square."[108] The passing reference to the doorposts is followed by a more detailed description of a special table in front of the entrance to the inner sanctum. Resorting to analogical description,[109] for the first time the narrator seems lost for words to describe a feature of the temple complex. What it was about this object that reminded him of an altar is not certain. It cannot have been its wooden constitution, since altars of wood would themselves be consumed with the offerings burnt upon them. Perhaps a combination of the proportion[110] and the special corners reminded the observer of an altar. While it is self-evident that a 2-cubit square altar would have four corners, the mere mention of the *miqṣōʿôt* points to a special design, probably like the "horned" altar referred to in 43:15, and like numerous exemplars that have been discovered in Levantine cult sites.

Ezekiel's puzzlement over an object shaped like an altar but made of wood may have prompted the guide's otherwise intrusive interpretation. The form of *zeh haššulḥān ʾăšer lipnê yhwh*, "This is the table that [stands] before Yahweh," resembles the announcement concerning the inner sanctum in v. 4: *zeh qōdeš haqqŏdāšîm*, "This is the holy of holies," and may suggest that the present observations were made during the same tour of the interior of the temple. The term *šulḥān* and the reference to its position "before Yahweh" link the object to the table perpetually set with the bread of the Presence in the tabernacle (Exod. 25:23-30). But that table was made of acacia wood and overlaid completely with gold (in the present table the wood is exposed), and its proportions were different. Whereas the height of Ezekiel's table exceeds its width and length, the original had been rectangular, and its length (2 cubits) was greater than its height (1½ cubits). No wonder Ezekiel needs an explanation. Either the table represents an altar with the bread of the Presence functioning as a type of nonburnt offering presented to Yahweh (1 Sam. 21:3-6), or its structure resembled an altar.

23-25a These verses describe the temple doors. As in Solomon's

---

107. Thus Zimmerli (*Ezekiel,* p. 388), following Noth (*Könige,* p. 127).

108. Cf. the five-sided doorposts at the entrance to the holy of holies of Solomon's temple (1 K. 6:31).

109. The form of *hammar'eh kammar'eh hammizbēaḥ ʿēṣ*, "something like an altar made of wood," recalls descriptions of theophanic sights. See chs. 1 and 10. The double expression *hammar'eh kammar'eh* occurs above in 40:3, and again below in 43:3.

110. A 2-cubit square object with a height of 3 cubits is not dissimilar from stone altars that have been discovered in Arad, Megiddo, and Dan. For description and illustration see T. C. Mitchell, *IBD,* 1:34-37; also R. D. Haak, *ABD,* 1:164-67.

temple (1 K. 6:34), entrance to both the great hall and the inner sanctum was gained by double doors consisting of two swinging leaves *(šĕtayim mûsabbôt dĕlātôt),* each of which was set in its own pivot hole next to the jamb. Like the rest of the interior, the doors were decorated with palm and cherub carvings.

25b-26 Finally the attention turns from the great hall *(hêkāl)* to the vestibule *('ûlām),* perhaps reflecting the outward movement of guide and tourist. The opening line is almost totally obscure, since the meaning of the technical architectural term *'āb* is unknown. Many explanations for the expression have been offered, but all are equally speculative.[111] According to v. 26b, whatever function the *'āb* had in the vestibule, it also had in the auxiliary storage rooms *(sĕlā'ôt)* off to the side. Perhaps the original context from which these literary fragments have been excerpted contained more information on these technical architectural elements. A final note on the decoration of the vestibule is inserted between these two notes concerning the "railings(?)." Like the great hall, the porch was decorated with covered niches and palmette carvings. Nothing is said about cherubim.

(5) The Great Priestly Sacristies (42:1-14)

1 *Then he led me out northward*[112] *to the outer*[113] *court. He brought me to the set of chambers*[114] *that were adjacent to the restricted area and adjacent to the structure to the north.* 2 *The length of the façade,*[115] *— [the side of] the north entrance —* [116] *was one hundred*

---

111. RSV and NRSV "canopy"; NEB and REB "cornice"; NJPS and NAB "lattice"; JB "screen"; NASB "threshold"; NIV "overhang." Elsewhere the word denotes some feature in the porch of Solomon's House (Palace) of the Forest of Lebanon (1 K. 7:6).

112. *hadderek* is redundant before *derek haṣṣāpôn* and should be deleted as dittography. Targ. offers a plausible interpretation of the movement: "by way of the gate that faces north." LXX replaces *hadderek* with εἰς τὴν αὐλὴν, "to the gate," which is only implicit in MT, and adds "to the east in front of," before "the court."

113. LXX misreads *haḥîṣônâ* as "inner."

114. MT reads a collective sg.; LXX specifies "five chambers."

115. So NJPS. MT *'el-pĕnê,* "before," is meaningless at the beginning of v. 2. This is probably either a corrupted dittograph of the previous two words *(BHS)* or a fragment of a further detail that has dropped out (K. Elliger, "Die Grossen Tempelsakristeien im Verfassungsentwurf des Ezechiel (42,1ff.)," in *Geschichte und Altes Testament,* Fest. A. Alt, BHT 16 [Tübingen: Mohr, 1953], p. 84). Targ. paraphrases: "Along the length, which was one hundred cubits, there was a door that faced north."

116. *petaḥ haṣṣāpôn,* lit. "the entrance of the north," is often deleted as a gloss, perhaps an explanatory note on *petaḥ* in 41:11 (Allen, *Ezekiel 20–48,* p. 225). Others emend *petaḥ* to *pĕ'at,* "in the direction of," following LXX πρὸς βορρᾶν, and on the analogy of 41:12. Zimmerli *(Ezekiel 2,* p. 392) cites also 47:17-20; 48:1.

cubits,[117] *and its width was fifty cubits.* 3 *Opposite the twenty [cubit space]*[118] *belonging to the inner court and the pavement belonging to the outer court was a set of balconies,*[119] *arranged one on top of the other in three levels.*[120] 4 *In front of the chambers was a walkway ten cubits wide on the inside [of the courtyard?]*[121] *— a passage one cubit wide —* [122] *but their entrances were on the north side.* 5 *The upper chambers were narrowed*[123] *because the balconies took more space away from them*[124] *than from the bottom and middle levels of the structure.*[125] 6 *For they were arranged in three stories,*[126] *and they had no pillars like those in the courts.*[127] *For this reason they [the upper chambers] were terraced back*[128] *from the bottom more than*

117. The unusual word order of '*ōrek 'ammôt hammē'â* (cf. 40:27) seems to have occurred in two stages: (1) the final *hē* was detached from '*orkâ* and attached to the following *mē'â;* (2) *hammē'â* and '*ammôt* were transposed. On the dimension preceding measure in Ezekiel see Rooker, *Biblical Hebrew in Transition,* pp. 113-14.

118. MT reads simply *hā'eśrîm,* "the twenty"; "cubits" is understood. So also Targ.

119. '*attîq* is a collective sg.

120. MT *baššĕlišîm,* "in thirds," is a stylistic variant of *mĕšillāšîm* in v. 6.

121. '*el-happĕnîmît* is reflected but not understood by LXX, which treats the phrase like '*el-pĕnê* in v. 2. The question raised by MT is, inside what — the *binyān* or the courtyard? I follow REB.

122. *derek 'ammâ 'eḥāt* is obscure. LXX and Syr. point to an original *wĕ'ōrek mē'â 'ammâ,* "and its length was one hundred cubits," which appropriately envisions a walkway running the entire length of the building. Allen (*Ezekiel 20–48,* p. 226) treats *derek* as a comparative gloss (cf. *derek* in place of *mahălak* in v. 11) that displaced an original *wĕgādēr,* "and a wall."

123. MT *qĕṣurôt,* lit. "cut short"; Targ. renders *dḥyqn,* "pressed, narrowed" (also used of *ne'ĕṣal* in v. 6); Syr. *z'wryn,* "reduced, diminished." LXX ὡσαύτως, "similar," misses the point.

124. The sense of MT's obscure *kî yôkĕlû 'attîqîm* seems to be captured by Targ., "the balconies took space away from them" (Levey, *Ezekiel,* p. 115). *yākōl,* normally "to be able," must carry the sense of "to prevail" (cf. Gen. 32:26, 29 [Eng. 25, 28]), but this calls for a revocalization, *yākĕlū (BHS).* Several Hebrew mss. have a Qere reading, *y'klw,* "they ate up," lending a much more forceful picture. LXX "the pillars projected out from them" is an unlikely guess.

125. LXX "from underneath the pillars and the intervals" misunderstands MT *mēhattaḥtōnôt ûmēhattikōnôt binyān;* Syr. omits the phrase entirely. Except for treating *binyān* as definite, Targ. follows MT. Zimmerli (*Ezekiel 2,* pp. 394-95) construes these words as a separate sentence: "From the lower and middle (stories) upwards the building was constructed."

126. On the Pual form meaning "to be done three times" see Waltke-O'Connor, *Syntax,* §25.4c.

127. NRSV follows LXX in reading *haḥăṣērôt haḥîṣônôt,* "the outer courts."

128. *ne'ĕṣal,* a Niphal participle of '*āṣal,* "to withdraw, take away," is probably

*the lower and middle stories. 7 There was also a wall[129] there, which
ran outside parallel to the chambers, on the side toward the outer
court in front of the chambers. It was fifty cubits long, 8 since the
chambers of the outer court were fifty cubits deep, whereas [the wall]
in front of the great hall[130] was one hundred cubits long. 9 At the base
of these chambers[131] was an entryway[132] from the east, if one entered
them [the chambers][133] from the outer court, 10 at the beginning[134]
of the wall of the court. On the south side,[135] adjacent to[136] the
restricted area and adjacent to the structure, were additional chambers 11 with a walkway in front of them as well. They looked just like
the chambers that were on the north side; the length and width,[137]
as well as all their exits,[138] their design, and their entrances, were
identical to 12 the chambers[139] on the south side. There was an en-*

---

a technical building term. "Terrace" follows Elliger, in *Geschichte und Altes Testament*,
p. 92; and Zimmerli, *Ezekiel 2*, p. 394.

129. As in 41:11, LXX misconstrues *gādēr* as *'ôr*, "light."

130. While Syr., Vulg., and Targ. omit *wěhinnēh*, LXX καὶ αὖται suggests a
repointed original, *wěhēnnâ*. It is generally assumed that the chambers are being measured,
but since the subject of the preceding principal clause is *gādēr*, attention seems to be drawn
to a second wall. In spite of its attestation in Vulg., Targ., and Syr., *'al-pěnê hahêkāl* is
generally emended on the basis of LXX to *'al-pěnêhā hakkōl*, and together with *wěhēnnâ*
read something like, "and they were facing it; the whole [measured] one hundred cubits."
See Allen, *Ezekiel 20–48*, p. 226.

131. Reading *wmtḥt hlškwt* with Qere in place of Kethib *wmtḥth lškwt*. Zimmerli
(*Ezekiel 2*, p. 395) follows LXX in reading *wěpithê hallěšākôt*, "and the doors of the
chambers." Syr. *tr'' d'kdr'* compares with MT *ûkěpithê hallěšākôt* in v. 12. MT is seen to
be the result of miswriting two letters and dividing the words in the wrong place. But Allen
(*Ezekiel 20–48*, p. 226) suggests plausibly that LXX is due to assimilation.

132. Reading *hmbw'* with Kethib.

133. The form *lāhēnnâ* occurs elsewhere only in 1:5, 23; and Zech. 5:9.

134. Reading *běrō'š* with v. 12 and LXX ἐν ἀρχῇ, in place of MT's meaningless
běrōḥab (so *BHS* and many commentators).

135. The context demands reading *derek haddārôm* with LXX, in place of MT
haqqādîm, "east."

136. Here *'el-pěnê* is equivalent to *neged* in v. 1.

137. MT reads *kě'orkān kēn roḥbān*, lit. "like their length so their width," but
LXX probably reflects the original *ûkěroḥbān*.

138. Although the versions support MT *wěkōl môṣā'êhen*, most emend to
ûkěmôṣā'hen, "and like their exits." LXX harmonizes the form with the following by
adding the comparative particle, "and like all. . . ."

139. Hebrew *ûkěpithê hallěšākôt* is missing in LXX and looks like dittography
from the previous word. Most commentators emend MT to *ûmittaḥat* on the basis of the
corrected form in v. 9 (cf. *BHS*; Elliger, in *Geschichte und Altes Testament*, p. 98 n. 4).
Assuming the series of comparisons has concluded at the end of v. 11, Zimmerli deletes
the particle of comparison.

trance at the beginning of the passageway[140] *along the protective*[141] *wall,*[142] *permitting entrance on the east side.*[143]

13 *Then he said to me, "The northern and*[144] *southern chambers that are in front of the restricted area are the sacred chambers in which the priests*[145] *who come before Yahweh shall eat the most sacred offerings. There they shall deposit the most sacred offerings — the grain offerings, sin offering, and reparation offering — for the place is holy.* 14 *Once the priests have entered,*[146] *they shall not proceed out of the holy place to the outer court, without first depositing*[147] *the vestments in which*[148] *they have ministered, because they are holy. Instead they shall don other garments before approaching the area where the people are."*[149]

The boundaries of this literary subunit are marked by the visionary guidance formula in 42:1 and the end of the guide's announcement in v. 14.[150] The latter is confirmed by the summary statement of the entire tour, especially the guide's

140. The second *derek* is commonly deleted with LXX as a dittograph *(BHS)*.

141. The variation in renderings of *hăgînâ* in the versions indicates that the meaning of this technical architectural term was lost early in the history of the text. On the term see Elliger, in *Geschichte und Altes Testament,* pp. 99-101.

142. The translation of *haggĕderet hăgînâ* follows NJPS and NRSV. The versions offer a variety of guesses at the meaning of this hapax: LXX "interval"; Vulg. *vestibulum separatum;* Syr. "the course of the ravine"; Targ. "the platform of the Levites." The meaning of this technical term was lost early in the history of the text. On the term see Elliger, ibid.

143. *derek haqqādîm bĕbô'ān* corresponds to *mēhaqqādîm bĕbō'ô lāhēnnâ*. Since the narrative does not attempt to harmonize the descriptions of the north and south chambers, emendation on the basis of v. 9 is unnecessary.

144. The versions recognize the need for the copula.

145. LXX harmonizes the reading with 40:46 and 44:15 by adding "the sons of Zadok."

146. *bĕbō'ām hakkōhănîm,* "when they enter, the priests." On the infinitive construct with proleptic pronominal suffix see Joüon-Muraoka, *Grammar,* §146e; GKC, §131n; Rooker, *Biblical Hebrew in Transition,* pp. 92-93.

147. MT translates lit. "and there they shall deposit their vestments."

148. Zimmerli (*Ezekiel 2,* p. 397) considers the fem. suffix on *bāhen* and the independent pronoun *hēnnâ* corruptions, but inconsistencies of gender (and number) are common in these chapters.

149. LXX reads "before touching the people"; Targ., "and then mingle with the people."

150. Despite, or perhaps because of, the many problems posed by this text, scholars have not taken it seriously enough. Eichrodt (*Ezekiel,* p. 548) devotes less than half a page to it. The most comprehensive treatment is provided by Elliger, in *Geschichte und Altes Testament,* pp. 79-103, but this study is over forty years old and in need of revision, esp. in the light of the publication of the Temple Scroll from Qumran.

measuring activities in v. 15. Structurally the passage divides into two parts: a description of a new complex of buildings (vv. 1-12), followed by the guide's explanation of the function of these buildings (vv. 13-14). The first subdivides further into two uneven parts: a detailed description of the structures around the north gate of the temple complex (vv. 1-10a), and a summary declaration of the similarity of the southern installations (vv. 10b-12). The visionary guidance formula ties this account to the basic narrative, reconvening the prophet's tour of the temple complex (cf. 40:1-37, 47-49; 41:1-4). This time, however, although measurements of certain features are given, references to the guide actually taking measurements are lacking; only the results of his work are given. Accordingly, after v. 1, there is no further mention of the prophet being led from place to place, though it is obvious from the account that this must have transpired. The guide's explanatory speech provides the most striking departure from previous descriptions. Unlike 41:4 and 41:22, 42:13-14 are not limited to declaratory identification of an object; for the first time the narrative offers an expanded statement concerning the significance of the items observed. While many see in these departures evidence of a second hand,[151] nothing in the passage precludes the prophet's own literary involvement. Like the foregoing, this report, which derives from another phase of Ezekiel's visionary guided tour of the temple complex, maintains the distinction between priesthood and laity, and guards the sanctity of the sacred space.

1-2 The account opens with a report of the completion of the tour of the inner court and its buildings. Being led by the guide through the north gate, the prophet arrives in the outer court, the region between the two walls surrounding the temple mount. Turning westward, he notices a complex of chambers (lĕšākôt), designated by Elliger as the temple "sacristy." The lexical links between vv. 1-12 and 40:17-19 invite comparison with the thirty chambers facing the pavement (riṣĕpâ) north and south of the temple building, but these structures are located farther back, opposite (neged) the restricted area and the large building (binyān) at the rear of the temple, apparently separated from them by a narrow space. The length of the building was 100 cubits, identical to the length of the binyān (80 cubits) plus the restricted area behind the temple (20 cubits), and its width was 50 cubits.

3-6 Virtually every detail concerning the design and appearance of the chambers is open to debate, and any reconstruction is tentative (see figs. 6A and 6B, p. 565). The structure was complex, apparently consisting of three parts, with the roof of each part a different level. In the absence of pillars (v. 6) these were designed like terraces, the upper balconies being set progressively farther back than those beneath them (vv. 5-6), and creating the

151. Zimmerli (*Ezekiel 2*, pp. 397-98) attributes this section to a priestly circle in the exile who must have had access to the prophet's own plan of the sanctuary.

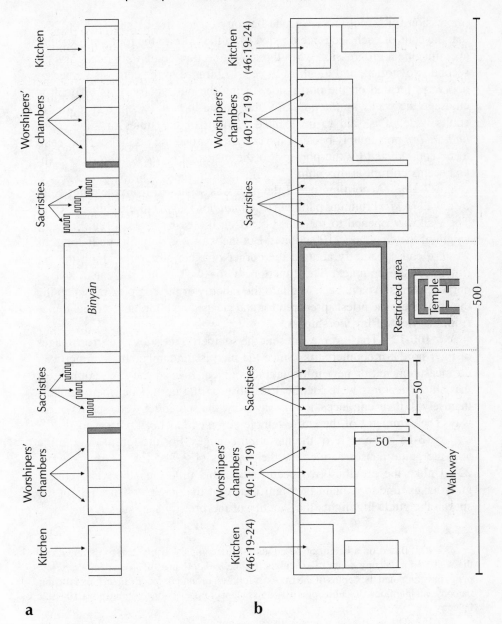

Figure 6. Frontal View (a) and Top View (b) of the West Wall of the Temple Complex (42:1-12)

impression for the observer of one balcony on top of another. It is possible that the cells of each section extended from the floor to the roof, but one may also imagine a progression, with the lowest section being only one story, the second two-storied, and the third three.[152] Entrance to the cell was gained by doorways located on the north side, facing the outer court. It is difficult to envisage the walkway (mahǎlāk)[153] mentioned in v. 4, except that it was 10 cubits wide. It is said to be located in front of the suites of cells (lipnê hallěšākôt), presumably because the entrances are to the north, but this seems to be contradicted by the phrase "to the inside" ('el-happěnîmît, v. 4). The text seems corrupt at this point.

7-10a According to v. 7 the path was separated from the outer court by a wall (gādēr) running parallel (lě'ummat hallěšākôt) to the suites of cells. The walkway opened to the outer court on the east side (v. 9) and ran the length of the chambers (100 cubits). But the wall was only 50 cubits long. Its western end apparently abutted the corner of other structures along the perimeter of the complex. The function of the wall is not indicated, but its purpose seems to have been to guard the sanctity of the complex by screening the area where the priests prepared for and cleaned up after their official duties from the view of lay worshipers.

10b-12 These verses present the southern sacristies as mirror images of their northern counterparts. Since the plan is fundamentally symmetrical, no measurements or new information is given. Instead the text emphasizes that all the features were identical to those on the north side: the chambers themselves, their entrances, the passageway, the screening wall, and its doorway. The symmetry of the entire temple complex has been preserved.

13-14 The style of the narration changes. For the fourth time in the tour the guide pauses to identify the features observed (cf. 40:45-46; 41:4, 22). Unlike the previous two occurrences, this time the otherwise reticent guide takes time to explain the significance of the object.[154] Throughout the speech the guide highlights the sanctity of the priestly sacristies.

---

152. Based on a height of 50 cubits for the complex, equivalent to the height of the wall, and a balcony depth of 10 cubits (cf. the mahǎlāk in v. 4), Maier (in *Prophecy*, p. 66) has computed the depths of the floors as follows: ground floor, 40 cubits plus 10-cubit balcony; middle floor, 30 cubits plus 10-cubit balcony; upper floor, 20 cubits plus 10-cubit balcony.

153. The word, which occurs elsewhere only in Jon. 3:3, 4; Zech. 3:7; and Neh. 2:6, is a Late Biblical Hebrew alternative for *derek*, "way," probably developed under Aramaic influence. Cf. Rooker, *Biblical Hebrew in Transition*, pp. 167-69.

154. Whereas the previous identifying statements had been structured after the pronominal subject plus nominal predicate pattern, this one begins with a suspended subject, followed by pronominal subject. Their structures may be compared by juxtaposing the statements as follows:

First, he locates the chambers in relation to the temple itself: opposite the restricted area *(haggizrâ)* behind the temple.

Second, they are explicitly described as holy: *hēnnâ liškôt haqqōdeš,* "They are holy chambers."

Third, they are reserved for the highest order of priests — those who have access to Yahweh *('ăšer qĕrôbîm layhwh).*

Fourth, they represent a place where only the most sacred portions of the offerings may be consumed. The expression *qodšê haqqŏdāšîm,* "the holiest of holy gifts," is to be distinguished from *qōdeš haqqŏdāšîm,* "the holy of holies," in 41:4.[155]

Fifth, they provide a place for the storage of the most sacred gifts: the grain offering *(hamminhâ),* the sin offering *(hahaṭṭā't),* and the reparation offering *(hā'āšām).* The triad of offerings recalls 40:39, except that here the grain offering replaces the whole burnt offering *('ôlâ).* But this list of sacrifices, portions which are reserved for priestly consumption, is also traditional. Lev. 6:10 (Eng. 17) identifies these three as "most holy" *(qōdeš qādāšîm).* For explanations of the sin and reparation offerings see the commentary on 40:39 above. The *grain offering (minhâ)* represented a gift or tribute to deity, consisting of grain or flour. Either the offering could be burned up entirely on an altar or portions of it could be reserved for the priests. Grain offerings were acceptable as substitutes for animals for the burnt offering if the offerer could not afford the more expensive gifts. They were often presented with oil and frankincense and in association with other gifts. While the grain offerings tended to function as gifts expressive of gratitude to God, an expiatory connection is suggested by 45:15, 17.[156]

Sixth, the chambers provided a place to store the priestly garments worn when performing cultic service (v. 14).[157] On the assumption that holiness is contagious,[158] special regulations are prescribed for the care of priestly garments. When the priests arrive at the sacred precinct to perform their rituals,

---

40:45   *zōh halliškâ 'ăšer pānêhā derek haddārôm . . .*
41:4   *zeh qōdeš haqqŏdāšîm*
41:22   *zeh haššulḥān 'ăšer lipnê yhwh*
42:13   *liškôt haṣṣāpôn liškôt haddārôm 'ăšer 'el-pĕnê haggizrâ hēnnâ liškôt
         haqqōdeš 'ăšer . . .*

155. Cf. Lev. 6:9 (Eng. 16), which prescribes that the most holy offerings must be eaten "in the holy place" *(bĕmāqôm qādōš).*

156. On the grain offering see Milgrom, *Leviticus,* pp. 195-202; Anderson, *ABD,* 5:874-75.

157. On the emphatic threefold repetition of *šām,* "there," in vv. 13-14 see Stevenson, *Vision,* pp. 69-70.

158. On the contagion and dynamism of holiness see Milgrom, *Leviticus,* pp. 45, 443-56.

they are to enter the doorway of the wall, head straight for the sacristies, and don the sacred vestries. Before they return to the people they are to doff them and leave them in the chambers.

Although one may try to translate the narrative description of these priestly sacristies into visual form (fig. 6, p. 565), any portrayal is provisional. In fact, the text lacks the necessary information for a building plan. Some dimensions are imprecise; most are missing. The burden of the present account is to show that the holiness of sacred space extends beyond the concentric design of the temple complex to the form of the auxiliary structures and the conduct of humans within those structures. Again the proportions of sacred space are more important than the appearance of the buildings. These structures are perfect rectangles, 100 × 50 cubits, located next to a perfect square (the *binyān* plus restricted area), 100 × 100 cubits. But the former are separated from the latter by an intervening space. The boundaries between the outer court and the priestly chambers are defined by the 50-cubit wall. Access to the sacristies is controlled by these walls, the walkway between them and the chambers, and the entrances on the north and south sides, respectively. Strict rules are prescribed for maintaining their sanctity, and preventing the contagion of holiness infecting the people.

(6) The Concluding Temple Measurements (42:15-20)

15 *When he had finished measuring the interior temple area, he led me out through the gate that faced east. Then he measured the perimeter [of the temple].* 16 *Using the measuring rod*[159] *he measured the east side; it was five hundred cubits*[160] *— in rods,*[161] *using the measuring rod. Then he turned around*[162] 17 *and measured*[163] *the north*

159. LXX omits *biqnēh hammiddâ*.

160. Reading *ḥmš m'wt* with Qere and the versions in place of Kethib's *ḥmš 'mwt*, "five cubits," undoubtedly an error of metathesis. Cf. vv. 17-19.

161. Most follow LXX in deleting *qānîm* as a redundant gloss. Its presence creates inordinate interpretive problems. Since one rod was 6 cubits (40:5), vv. 16-20 define a 3000 (500 × 6) cubit square temple precinct, which is incompatible with the 500 × 500 cubit square envisioned by 40:15–41:13. Either *qānîm* is to be deleted here and throughout vv. 16-17 as an erroneous gloss on *biqnēh hammiddâ* (thus Allen, *Ezekiel 20–48*, p. 227). However, MT may be defended as the *lectio difficilior,* and it is unlikely that this error would have been made four times. If the word is to be retained (as I have done), it probably identifies an instrument rather than a unit of measurement. To delete the word leaves the description without a unit of measurement, but such ellipses are common. Cf. v. 20; 43:16-17; 45:1; 46:22.

162. Reading *sābab* with support from v. 19 and LXX, rather than MT *sābîb,* which Targ. and Vulg. support. Syr. drops the word.

163. Adding the copula with LXX and Syr. to smooth the reading.

side; it was five hundred cubits — in rods, using the measuring rod. Then he turned around 18 *and measured the*[164] *south side; it was five hundred cubits — in rods, using the measuring rod.* 19 *He turned to the west side [and] measured it; it was five hundred cubits — in rods, using the measuring rod.* 20 *Thus he measured it [the temple complex] on the four sides. It was surrounded by a wall five hundred cubits long and five hundred cubits wide, designed to separate the holy area from the common.*[165]

The visionary guidance formula in v. 15 signals a new subunit and ties this segment in with the preceding narrative. Structurally this paragraph divides into three parts, an opening statement (v. 15), the detailed description (vv. 16-19), and a concluding statement (v. 20). Stylistically this paragraph is distinguished from much of the preceding in several ways. First, after opening with three syndetic perfects (*wěkillâ . . . wěhôṣî'anî . . . ûmědādô*), the text shifts to a series of asyndetic perfects.[166] Second, the narrative is repetitious and formulaic,[167] reflecting the balance and symmetry in the design of the entire temple complex. V. 20 performs double literary duty, creating an *inclusio* with 40:5 (note the reference to the wall), and forming a conclusion to the tour narrative with 43:12, with which it seems to have been linked prior to the editorial insertion of the *kābôd* pericope (43:1-9).[168]

164. Many read *'el* with LXX, in place of MT's object marker *'et,* but LXX may reflect a secondary harmonization with v. 19. Cf. v. 17.

165. On the Late Biblical Hebrew construction *bên . . . lě . . . ,* in place of the earlier *bên . . . bên,* see Rooker, *Biblical Hebrew in Transition,* pp. 117-19; Hurvitz, *Linguistic Study,* p. 113. Cf. 22:26; 44:23.

166. *mādad* (4 times), *sābab* (3 times), if the emendations in vv. 17-18 suggested in the textual notes are adopted. The presence of this feature in earlier texts (40:24, 35; 41:3, 13, 15) has a cohesive effect on the overall narrative.

167. The repetition may be highlighted by juxtaposing the key statements as follows (assuming the emendations suggested in the textual notes):

v. 16	*mādad rûaḥ haqqādîm biqnēh hammiddâ*		*ḥămēš mē'ôt qānîm biqnēh hammiddâ*
v. 17	*sābab mādad rûaḥ haṣṣāpôn*		*ḥămēš mē'ôt qānîm biqnēh hammiddâ*
v. 18	*sābab 'ēt*	*rûaḥ haddārôm mādad*	*ḥămēš mē'ôt qānîm biqnēh hammiddâ*
v. 19	*sābab 'el-*	*rûaḥ hayyām mādad*	*ḥămēš mē'ôt qānîm biqnēh hammiddâ*

v. 16   he measured the east side using a measuring rod;
    it was five hundred cubits — in rods, using the measuring rod.
v. 17   he turned and he measured the north side;
    it was five hundred cubits — in rods, using the measuring rod.
v. 18   he turned and the south side he measured;
    it was five hundred cubits — in rods, using the measuring rod.
v. 19   he turned to the west side and he measured;
    it was five hundred cubits — in rods, using the measuring rod.

168. Cf. Talmon, and Fishbane, *ASTI* 10 (1976) 142-46.

15-20 According to v. 15, the measurement of the perimeter of the temple complex occurred after the interior tour had been completed.[169] To witness this the guide leads the prophet outside through the east gate. According to MT the order in which the sides are measured is east, north, south, west, a sequence that Rev. 21:13 also follows.[170] Ezekiel's reference to the four directions as "the four winds" (*'arba' rûḥôt*) represents a rare use of the Heb. *rûaḥ,* "spirit, wind, breath."[171] The guide's measurements confirm the shape of the temple complex as one large square, 500 cubits by 500 cubits (ca. 850 ft.).[172] The shape and size of the entire complex reflect a lofty theological and spiritual ideal, according to which the residence of Yahweh must be perfectly proportioned.[173]

Verse 20 concludes with a note explaining the function of the outside walls. They are not constructed to keep enemy forces out, if by these forces one means human foes of Israel, but to protect the sanctity of the sacred area from the pollution of common touch and to prevent the contagion of holiness from touching the people. They guarantee that the violence done to Yahweh's Torah and the profanation of things sacred described in 22:26 never occurs again. In the past priests had failed to maintain the distinction between the

169. The report of the interior priestly kitchens is delayed until 46:19-24.

170. LXX creates a counterclockwise sequence by reversing vv. 18 and 19.

171. For a discussion of this passage in the context of Ezekiel's usage of *rûaḥ* see Block, *JETS* 32 (1989) 33. J. T. Milik recognizes a similar construction in a Phoenician inscription ("Notes d'épigraphie et de topographie palestiniennes," *RB* 66 [1959] 557).

172. The east-west distance agrees with length computed from the respective dimensions of the internal structures described earlier:

Depth of the eastern exterior gate	50 cubits
Distance between exterior and inner gates	100 cubits
Depth of the inner east gate	50 cubits
Depth of the inner temple court	100 cubits
Length of the temple with auxiliary structures	100 cubits
Depth of the restricted area at rear of temple	20 cubits
Depth of the *binyān* (inclusive of the walls)	80 cubits
Total distance, east to west,	500 cubits

173. Cf. *m. Middot* 2:1. According to Josephus (*Ant.* 15.11.3, §400), Herod's temple acropolis had a perimeter of 4 stades, each side being one stade long. Archeological explorations have confirmed that the postexilic temple acropolis, constructed over the ruins of the preexilic acropolis, was designed after this ideal model. The present-day platform of the temple mount consists of a square 262.5 m. per side, which computes remarkably to 500 cubits per side (assuming Ezekiel employs the great cubit of 525 mm.). My thanks to Randall Younker for drawing my attention to this detail and to the discussion by B. Mazar, "The Temple Mount," in *Biblical Archaeology Today: Proceedings of the International Congress on Biblical Archaeology, Jerusalem, April 1984,* ed. J. Amitai (Jerusalem: Israel Exploration Society, 1985), pp. 465-66.

holy and profane, but the present structures guard against such abominations under the new order. Later, in 44:23, Ezekiel will emphasize the role of the priests in indoctrinating the laity on the issue and their own modeling of respect for these distinctions.

Thus ends the tour of the temple grounds. The prophet has been prepared for the climactic moment, the arrival of its divine resident, which will become the issue in ch. 43. Before considering that event, however, we may reflect on the significance of the overall design of the temple complex and the way in which sacred/profane distinctions are guarded. First, from a bird's-eye view of the precinct, one recognizes modified concentric gradations of sanctity (fig. 7, p. 572). At the center of sacred space is the holy of holies, which only Yahweh may enter. The next ring, incorporating the remainder of the temple building and apparently the sacristies, are open to the Zadokites, "who have access to Yahweh" (42:13). The third ring, around the central altar and within the inner gates, is the sphere of the Levites. The outer court, open to lay worshipers, constitutes the fourth ring. Fifth, sixth, and seventh rings may be recognized in the temple mount, the surrounding territory of Israel, and the rest of the world (38:12), respectively. Relative to the holy of holies, the sphere of the Zadokites is profane; relative to the sphere of the Zadokites, the area of the Levites is profane, and so on. This concentric hierarchy of sanctity is reinforced by their verticality. Rather than lines drawn on a flat plane, these rings function as altitude markers on a relief map.[174] Each unit represents a terrace spatially higher than the one relatively more profane. Thus from a distance an observer would see the temple mount, with seven steps leading up to the outer court (40:22, 26), eight steps ascending to the inner court (40:31, 34, 37), and ten steps going up to the vestibule of the temple building (40:49). The boundaries of sacred space are marked by walls, and access to the respective levels is controlled by a series of gates.

Second, a bird's-eye view also recognizes a central spine of sacrality, increasing as one moves horizontally from east to west (fig. 8, p. 573).[175] The prophet's description recognizes eleven elements along this central spine: the eastern steps (1) lead up to the eastern outer court gate (2), which opens to inner court steps (3), which lead up to the inner court gate (4), which opens to the altar (5), which stands before ten steps (6), leading up to the vestibule (7), which leads to the Great Hall (8) and the holy of holies (9). Behind the temple proper one finds the *gizrâ*, "restricted area" (10), and the *binyān* (11). Increasing restrictions on access to the respective areas are reflected in the sequential narrowing of entryways and the placement of guards at strategic

174. Cf. J. Z. Smith, *To Take Place: Toward Theory in Ritual* (Chicago: University of Chicago Press, 1987), pp. 56-57.
175. Cf. ibid., pp. 57-58.

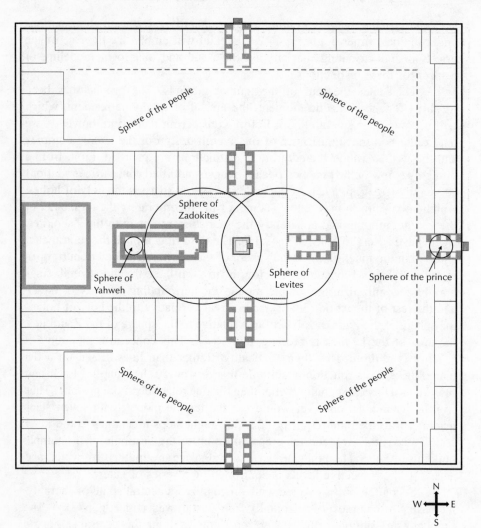

Figure 7. The Spheres of Sacred Space

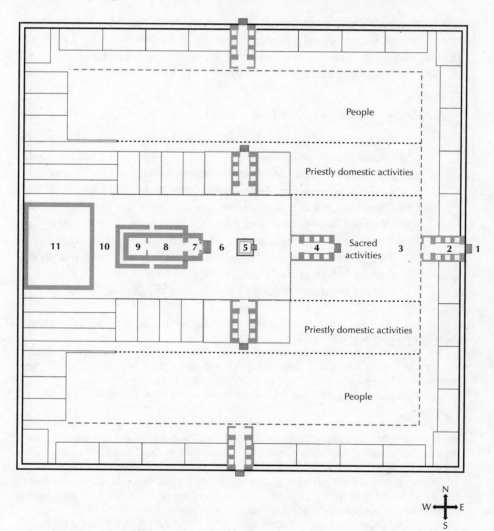

Figure 8. The Spine of Sacred Space

points. Accordingly, one may recognize increasingly sacred spheres along this spine accessible respectively to the following: the *nāśî'* (44:1-3), Levitical priests, Zadokites, Yahweh. Significantly, lay worshipers will enter and exit through the north and south gates (46:9).

c. The Return of Yahweh to His Temple (43:1-9)

1 *Then he led me to the gate, the gate[1] that faces[2] toward the east.* 2 *I noticed[3] the glory of the God of Israel approaching from the east. The noise it made sounded like the rumble of mighty waters, and the landscape lit up with his glory.* 3 *The vision I saw was like the vision I had seen[4] when I came[5] to destroy the city, and like the vision[6] that I saw by the Chebar River, and I fell down on my face.* 4 *The glory of Yahweh entered the temple by way of the gate[7] facing the east.* 5 *Then the Spirit picked me up and brought me into the inner court, and look, the glory of Yahweh filled the temple!*

6 *I heard someone speaking[8] to me from the temple,[9] even as the*

1. LXX, Vulg., and Syr. drop the second *ša'ar.* The absence of the article increases the suspicion of dittography.

2. *'ăšer pōneh* occurs only here in the book, but the reading is not ungrammatical, and Ezekiel's style varies. Cf. *'ăšer pānāyw* (40:6, 20), *'ăšer mopneh* (9:2), and the participle *happōneh* alone (8:3; 11:1; 44:1; 46:1, 12; 47:2).

3. *wĕhinnēh,* lit. "And behold," which expresses surprise, is common in visionary contexts.

4. MT *ûkĕmar'ē' hammar'eh 'ăšer rā'îtî kammar'eh 'ăšer rā'îtî,* "And like the sight of the sight that I saw, like the sight that I saw," is cumbersome in translation, but the construction *kě... kě...* is normal. Cf. Gen. 18:25; 44:18; Lev. 7:7; 24:22; 25:40; Num. 15:15; Judg. 8:18; 1 K. 22:4; Isa. 24:2; Hos. 4:9; Hag. 2:3; Ps. 139:12; and in Ezekiel, 16:44 (see Andersen and Freedman, *Hosea,* pp. 359-61). Emendation to *hammar'eh kammar'eh* with LXX and 41:21 (cf. 8:4) is unnecessary (contra *BHS*). The correspondence of the visions is heightened by the fourfold repetition of *mar'eh.*

5. Although MT *bĕbō'î,* "when I came," is supported by LXX and Syr., since Ezekiel had no part in the destruction of Jerusalem, the final *yod* is probably an error for *waw,* viz., *bĕbō'ô,* "when he came" (thus several Hebrew mss., Theodotion, Vulg.). Alternatively, MT may preserve a miswritten abbreviation, *bb' y[hwh],* "when Yahweh came" (Galling in Fohrer-Galling, *Ezechiel,* p. 241). Targ. *b'tnbywty,* "when I prophesied," offers a different solution.

6. MT's addition, *mar'ôt,* "visions," which LXX and Targ. read as sg., may have been influenced by 1:1 and 8:3. Syr. probably correctly omits the word.

7. With the anarthrous form of *ša'ar* cf. 9:2; 40:6.

8. MT's Hithpael *middabbēr* contrasts with the usual Piel *mĕdabbēr.* According to Rashi, the Piel is used in conversation between humans, but the Hithpael occurs when the issue is the internal speech of the Shekinah overheard by a messenger (so Gese, *Verfassungsentwurf,* p. 34). Cf. 2:2.

9. On the form *mēhabbāyit* see Bauer-Leander, *Grammatik,* §81p'.

man[10] *was standing*[11] *next to me.* 7 *He said to me, "Human, as for the place*[12] *of my throne, and the place for the soles of my feet, where I will dwell*[13] *in the midst of the descendants of Israel*[14] *forever — never again will they defile my holy name, neither they nor their kings, with their harlotry and the funerary offerings of their kings at their deaths.*[15] 8 *Whenever they placed their threshold next to my threshold, and their doorposts next to my doorposts, with only a wall between me and them, they would defile*[16] *my holy name with the abominable practices that they committed. Therefore I consumed them in my fury.* 9 *Now*[17] *let them remove their harlotry and the funerary offerings of their kings far from me, and I will dwell among them forever."*

♦ *Nature and Design*

The survey of the outside dimensions of the temple complex in 42:15-20 concludes the description of sacred space. But this does not mean that the story is over. The prophet is brought back to the east gate to observe an event, the significance of which cannot be overestimated (43:1-9). But before I

10. With the versions one expects *wĕhā'îš* instead of *wĕ'îš*.

11. According to Rooker (*Biblical Hebrew in Transition,* p. 108), the Late Biblical Hebrew and Mishnaic Hebrew construction *hāyâ* plus participle "connotes the durative and iterative aspect." Cf. 34:2.

12. Most English translations follow the lead of Targ. in interpreting *'et* as "This" (NJPS, NRSV, NIV, NASB, NAB, JB), but Targ.'s reading may have been influenced by Isa. 66:1. REB "Do you see the place of my throne" is based on LXX, which inserts Ἑόρακας (= *hărā'itā*) before *ben-'ādām*. Some scholars treat *'et* as an emphatic particle, equivalent to a demonstrative pronoun, as in Mishnaic Hebrew (Gese, *Verfassungsentwurf,* p. 34; Zimmerli, *Ezekiel 2,* p. 409; Joüon-Muraoka, *Grammar,* §125j), but this is better recognized as an anacoluthon, with the objects of the verb *lō' yĕṭammĕ'û* having been brought forward to the beginning of the sentence (Muraoka, *Emphatic Particles,* p. 155; Barthélemy, et al., *Preliminary and Interim Report,* p. 170).

13. LXX softens the anthropomorphism of MT by reading *šĕmî,* "my name," as the subject of the verb, perhaps under the influence of Deut. 12:11. Predictably, Targ. expands with "for I will make my Shekinah dwell there."

14. LXX reads *bêt yiśrā'ēl,* "house of Israel," a harmonization with prevailing Ezekielian usage. But MT *bĕnê yiśrā'ēl,* which occurs elsewhere in 2:3; 12:23; 35:5, may be deliberately archaizing. Cf. Block, *SR* 13 (1984) 301-2, 320-22.

15. Vulg., Syr., and Targ. (Sperber) interpret MT *bāmôtām,* "on their high places," viz., from *bāmâ.* LXX reads *bĕtôkām,* "in their midst." Most modern translations repoint *bĕmôtām,* "in their deaths," with numerous Hebrew mss., Theodotion, and several rabbinic editions of Targ. See Gese, *Verfassungsentwurf,* p. 34.

16. On the customary consecutive plus perfect see GKC, §112i.

17. Numerous Hebrew mss., LXX, and Vulg. smooth out the reading by adding the copula, *wĕ'attâ.*

comment on the text in detail, its place in the present context must be examined.

The isolation of vv. 1-9 as a semi-independent unit has long been recognized.[18] Gese has demonstrated convincingly, however, that the stylistic and thematic links between 43:1-9 and 43:10-11 are too strong to lead to an absolute break between the two.[19] In the past scholars have tended to treat 43:1-9 as the first part of the next major literary unit.[20] But one may question this approach on two counts. First, it fails to recognize the function of vv. 10-11. While these verses continue the divine speech begun in v. 7, in their present literary context they also serve as a conclusion to the temple tour. Indeed, the charges to the prophet to describe the temple to his people in 40:3-4 and 43:10-11 create an impressive *inclusio*.

Second, this approach violates the integral unity of the prophetic experience and the account of the temple tour by removing the climactic event.[21] The present pattern — the description of the sanctuary followed by the entrance of the divine *kābôd* into the building — follows the pattern of two previous biblical parallels, the construction of the tabernacle (Exod. 25–40) and Solomon's temple (1 K. 6–8). In both instances, the arrival of the glory served as a visible seal of Yahweh's approval on the construction project. God had taken up residence in his palace. But this pattern is also witnessed in extrabiblical parallels.[22] Neo-Assyrian kings tended to take great pains, not only to rebuild ruined temples for the gods, but also to record their achievements. Accordingly, the climax of these reconstruction projects occurred when the king would bring the restored images of deities home to their temples.

Among the best-known accounts is the following report by Esarhaddon of the events that followed the completion of the rebuilding of Esagila, the temple of Marduk, the divine patron of Babylon: "The gods and goddesses

18. Fohrer-Galling (*Ezechiel*, pp. 237-45) remove this text from its present literary context and treat 42:15-20 and 43:13-27 as a continuous narrative, with 43:10-12 having been added by a later hand. 43:1-9 is to be joined with 44:1-2 and 47:1-12.

19. Gese, *Verfassungsentwurf*, pp. 39-43. Zimmerli (*Ezekiel 2*, p. 412) concurs, viewing "the unity of authorship as an entirely possible assumption." Tuell (*Law of the Temple*, pp. 38-44) dissents, treating vv. 7b-9 and 10-11 as redactional additions from the Persian era.

20. Parunak, *Structural Studies*, pp. 506-9; Gese, *Verfassungsentwurf*, pp. 2, 6, 36, 54; Zimmerli, *Ezekiel 2*, p. 406; Vogt, *Untersuchungen*, pp. 132, 146, 165; more recently Allen, *Ezekiel 20–48*, pp. 249-50.

21. This is recognized also by Stevenson (*Vision*, pp. 55-61) and Tuell (*Law of the Temple*, pp. 35-42).

22. Cf. Block, *Gods of the Nations*, pp. 147, 157; Bodi, *Ezekiel*, pp. 217-18; Tuell, *Law of the Temple*, pp. 37-38. Stevenson (*Vision*, pp. 59-61) compares the return of Yahweh with Marduk's taking up residence in the *akītu* temple, the climactic moment in the annual New Year's festival.

who lived therein, who had caused the flood and the downpour, whose visage had become sad, I raised up out of their miserable condition; I had their dusty trains polished; I cleaned their dirty garments; and I caused them to dwell in their holy places forever."[23]

Ashurbanipal's excitement at having completed the rebuilding of Eḫulḫul, the temple of Sin at Harran, is evident in his comment, "I grasped the hands of [Sin(?)] and caused him to enter amid rejoicing and caused him to take up his abode."[24] This declaration is reminiscent of the neo-Babylonian Nabonidus's report of having rebuilt the same sanctuary: "I carefully executed the command of his (Sin's) great godhead. . . . I built anew the Ehulhul, the temple of Sin, and completed this work. I (then) led in procession Sin, Ningal, Nusku and Sadarnunna, from Shuanna (in Babylon), my royal city, and brought (them) in joy and happiness (into the temple), installing them on a permanent dais. I made abundant offerings before them and lavished gifts (on them). I filled Ehulhul with happiness and made its personnel rejoice."[25]

Since these accounts view the return of the deity as the necessary and climactic events of temple-building projects, Ezekiel's description of the return of Yahweh's kābôd provides a natural conclusion to the temple tour. But the present placement of this segment creates some tensions within the broader context. After the statistical description of the perimeter wall of the temple in 42:15-20, the present narration of an event is unexpected. Furthermore, the sketch of the temple provided in 40:2–42:20 appears incomplete. Several items undoubtedly observed during the visit to the inner court, specifically the altar (43:13-17) and the priestly kitchens (46:19-24), have yet to be described. Finally, the notice in 43:1 that Ezekiel was led by the guide to the (outer) eastern gate clashes with 42:15, the most recent occurrence of the guidance formula, which had found him at the same spot. The following verses suggest that the measurement of the circumference of the temple complex had brought tour guide and prophet back to their starting point. How then could Ezekiel be brought again to the east gate? But this is probably a literary problem. The vision of the return of the kābôd would logically have occurred at the end of the temple tour, when it has been confirmed in the prophet's mind that all is in readiness for the entrance of the divine resident. The awkwardness of the transition between 42:20 and 43:1 suggests the beginning of a semi-independent unit.

Although the archival nature of the temple description is abandoned,

---

23. Cf. Borger, *Asarhaddon*, p. 23, episode 32. Elsewhere he reports rebuilding the temples of other gods and bringing their images home. See *ARAB*, 2:262, 282, 284, §§674, 738, 748.

24. *ARAB*, 2:353-54, §§914-15.

25. *ANET*, p. 563.

and the subject matter may catch the reader unfamiliar with ancient traditions off guard, the present pericope is integrated stylistically with its broader literary context. First, it begins with the visionary guidance formula.[26] Second, the reference to "a man standing nearby" requires an antecedent, which is supplied by the tour guide, who has led the prophet all around the temple complex in the preceding narrative. Third, the charge to Ezekiel in vv. 10-11 to relay the information about the temple to his compatriots and to record it for their sakes assumes a vital connection between the present vision and the revelation of the temple plans.

1-2, 4 Having been led back to the east gate by the tour guide (v. 1), Ezekiel has his attention arrested by a remarkable phenomenon: the return of Yahweh's *kĕbôd*. His eyes followed the movement of the *kābôd* as it appeared in the east, made its way into the temple complex through the east gate, and finally entered the temple *(habbayit)* itself. Meanwhile the whole earth seemed to light up with the emanating radiance of the divine majesty. The optical spectacle was accompanied by an acoustic sensation: the sound of a mighty rumbling, like the sound of ocean waves.

The words used to describe the event are all carefully chosen. The phenomenon itself is identified as *kĕbôd 'ĕlōhê yiśrā'ēl,* "the glory of the God of Israel." The initial preference for the long form of the expression[27] reflects the significance of the event: the divine patron of the nation is returning; one of the central themes of the salvation oracles of chs. 34–37 is being fulfilled. As in the exodus, Sinai, and tabernacle narratives, the glory is the visible manifestation of the divine presence,[28] a fact reinforced by Yahweh's own interpretive comment in 44:2. Although Yahweh could have entered the temple area through the northern or southern gate, the choice of the east gate is deliberate, leading in a straight line along the central spine of concentrated sacrality to the holy of holies. The singular form, "gate," in v. 4 is a shorthand expression for this entire passageway. Furthermore, the present course signifies a reversal of the tragedy described in chs. 10–11. The last time the prophet had encountered the divine glory the latter hovered over the east gate and then disappeared over the mountain east of the city (11:19, 23), symbolic of Yahweh's abandonment of his people. The present movement affirms that the

---

26. The form of the formula, with *wayyôlikēnî,* "and he led me," is familiar from 40:24 (cf. also 47:6), but less common than *wayĕbî'ēnî,* "and he brought me" (40:17, 28, 32, 35, 48; 41:1; 42:1; 44:4; 46:19; cf. 40:2), or *wayyôṣî'ēnî,* "and he took me out" (42:1; 46:21; 47:2; cf. 42:15).

27. Cf. *kĕbôd yhwh,* "the glory of Yahweh," vv. 4, 5; also 1:28; 3:12, 23; 10:4a, 4b, 18; 11:23; 44:4. The present form has been encountered earlier in 8:4; 9:3; 10:19; 11:22.

28. H. Schmid ("Jahwe und die Kulttradition von Jerusalem," *ZAW* 67 [1955] 191) finds in the present account elements of the Sinai and divine mountain traditions.

nation's period of separation from him is past; Yahweh has taken up residence in his temple in their midst.

While the accompanying noise reminded the landlubber prophet of the sound of roaring ocean waves, the expression *kĕqôl mayim rabbîm* also links this theophany with Ezekiel's inaugural vision (1:24). The earlier comparison with the tumult of an army camp is not drawn explicitly, but one may recognize in the sound an allusion to the triumphant procession of a conqueror returning from war. The light and fire motif had also been present in the opening vision (1:4, 13), but here the radiance of the divine *kābôd* seems even more intense, lighting up the earth and announcing to all the arrival of Yahweh.[29] The account of progress of the divine procession continues in v. 4. Yahweh has only one goal in mind: to reestablish his residence in the temple. For the moment, the narrative is satisfied to announce simply the arrival of the *kābôd* at its goal. The narrator will return to the subject in 44:1-4.

3 This verse interrupts the narrative with a notice of the prophet's reaction. The links with earlier visions implied by the expressions used in vv. 2 and 4 are now explicitly expressed, albeit in reverse order of the prophet's experience. First, this theophany reminds him of the vision of Yahweh's departure from his temple in chs. 8–11. In an ironical twist, however, the prophet now interprets the earlier vision in terms, not of divine abandonment, but of his arrival to destroy Jerusalem. The purposive infinitive *šaḥēt,* "to destroy," provides a specific link with the appalled response of the prophet in 9:8: "Ah, Lord Yahweh! Are you destroying *(mahšît)* the entire remnant of Israel by pouring your fury out on Jerusalem?" Additional echoes of this earlier vision appear in the following verses.[30] Second, the appearance of the *kābôd* sends Ezekiel's mind back even farther to his first theophanic encounter with Yahweh (1:4-28) on the banks of the Chebar canal. While the heavenly chariot and its cherubimic attendants had dominated the earlier account, here the focus is on the *kābôd* itself. The prophet's physical response, falling down on his face, indicates that neither years of reflection nor decades of divine service have dulled his sense of awe and terror at the sight of the glory of God.

5-6 The parallels with the inaugural experience continue as the prophet is picked up by the divine Spirit *(rûaḥ)* and set on his feet (cf. 2:2). But this time, rather than rejuvenating him to hear the divine speech, the Spirit conveys him into the inner court.[31] From this vantage point he expresses

---

29. Cf. the effect of the theophany in Isaiah's vision: *mĕlō᾽ kol-hā᾽āreṣ kĕbôdô,* "the whole earth is full of his glory" (Isa. 6:3).

30. The allusion confirms that ch. 9 is integral to the earlier vision account (chs. 8–11).

31. Cf. 3:12, 14; 8:3; 11:1, 24; 37:1. On the Spirit of Yahweh as "agency of conveyance" see Block, *JETS* 32 (1989) 33-34.

surprise (cf. *hinnēh*) at the sight of the building filling with the divine *kābôd*.[32] However, all this is preparatory to the divine speech that the prophet is about to hear (vv. 6-9).[33] But the record of the divine speech is delayed again by an enigmatic circumstantial clause reporting the presence of a man beside Ezekiel. Who is he? How did he get there? What is his function? While some have suggested that "the man" is Yahweh,[34] he is better identified with the guide who has been dutifully measuring and orienting the prophet to the temple area. After being suddenly arrested by the Spirit and wafted into the temple court, Ezekiel would have been reassured by the guide's presence. Apparently he had free access to the grounds even after the divine *kābôd* had arrived; he did not need the transportation or authority of the Spirit. Nothing more is said about him. He disappears mysteriously from view, leaving the prophet to concentrate on the message he is about to receive from the newly arrived divine king, who now begins to speak.

7-11 The divine speech divides into two major parts: an explanation for Ezekiel (vv. 7-9), and a charge to the prophet (vv. 10-11). In addition to the change in subject matter, the bifurcation of Yahweh's address is also reflected formally. On the one hand, each section opens with the familiar direct address of the prophet: *ben-'ādām*, "Human." On the other, the twofold declaration "I will dwell among the descendants of Israel/them forever," in vv. 7 and 9, creates an effective *inclusio* around the first part, highlighting this section as a declaration of Yahweh's intentions in entering the temple.

The opening of the speech, *wayyō'mer 'ēlay ben-'ādām*, "And he said to me, 'Human,'" is not only typically Ezekielian; this is precisely how Yahweh's first speech to Ezekiel had been introduced in 2:1. The address proper begins with a formal announcement, "This is the place of my throne, the place for the soles of my feet." The language is obviously royal; Yahweh is hereby declaring that the temple is his palace and asserting his claims to kingship over Israel. While the tradition of the temple as the palace of Yahweh has a long history,[35] Ezekiel's portrayal of the temple itself rather than the ark

---

32. The description is much more restrained than Isaiah's in Isa. 6.

33. V. 6a echoes 2:2, as this synopsis shows:

2:2	*wā'ešma' 'ēt mĕdabbēr 'ēlay,*	"And I heard one speaking to me."
43:6	*wā'ešma' middabbēr 'ēlay mēhabbāyit,*	"And I heard one speaking to me from the temple."

34. J. Herrmann, *Ezechielstudien*, BWANT 2 (Leipzig: Hinrichs, 1908), cited by Zimmerli, *Ezekiel 2*, p. 415.

35. The tabernacle narratives portray the holy of holies as the divine throne room, separated from the great hall by the veil (Exod. 26:31-35), with the ark and its special cover *(kappōret)* thought of as Yahweh's throne. As the representative of the people, Moses would meet with Yahweh before the ark (cf. Exod. 25:22; 30:6; Lev. 16:2; Num. 7:89). This function of the ark is reflected in Yahweh's title *yōšēb hakkĕrubîm*, "who sits upon

of the covenant as the throne of Yahweh is striking. In the prophet's inaugural vision cherubim were observed carrying the throne of God (1:24-28), but the present speech is silent concerning the role of the ark or the cherubim, suggesting perhaps the fulfillment of Jeremiah's prediction in 3:16-17: "in those days . . . they shall no longer say, 'The ark of the covenant of the Lord.' It shall not come to mind or be remembered, or missed; nor shall another one be made. At that time Jerusalem shall be called the throne of the Lord, and all nations shall gather to it, to the presence of the Lord in Jerusalem." Unless one assumes the presence of the ark in the temple, Ezekiel apparently sees no need for such symbols of the divine rule. The existence of the city itself will be evidence of Yahweh's eternal presence (cf. Ezek. 48:35).[36]

The image of divine kingship is concretized with the description of the temple as "the place for the soles of my feet" *(mĕqôm kappôt raglay).* This phrase is a variation of *hădōm raglāyw,* "his footstool," which identifies literally the object on which a person rests one's feet, and by extension functions as an expression of dominion.[37] Ezekiel's conjunction of Yahweh's throne and his footstool in the temple reminds one of 1 Chr. 28:2, where David explicitly associates the *hădōm* with the ark of the covenant, and several additional texts identifying Zion/the temple as Yahweh's footstool (Ps. 99:5; 132:7; Lam. 2:1), especially Isa. 60:13, which pairs *mĕqôm miqdāšî,* "the place of my sanctuary," with *mĕqôm raglay,* "the place of my feet."[38]

The austerity of this assertion of divine kingship is deliberately tempered by the twofold reference to Yahweh's eternal *(lĕ'ôlām)* residence in the midst of the descendants of Israel (vv. 7, 9). The verb *šākan* alludes to the tabernacle/temple as the *miškān,* "dwelling place," of Yahweh, and the locative modifier, *bĕtôk bĕnê yiśrā'ēl,* "in the midst of the descendants of Israel," offers hope to those who had experienced the catastrophic effects of

---

the cherubs" (1 Sam. 4:4; 2 Sam. 6:2; 2 K. 19:15; 1 Chr. 13:5; Isa. 37:16; Ps. 80:2; 99:1). The ark provided a visual answer to the question: How can Yahweh, who is enthroned in the heavens (Ps. 2:4; 11:4; 113:5; 123:1), exercise his kingship on earth? See Solomon's dedicatory prayer in 1 K. 8.

36. Cf. 48:35. For a discussion of the ark as the throne of Yahweh see M. Metzger, *Königsthron und Gottesthron,* 2 vols., AOAT 15 (Neukirchen-Vluyn: Neukirchener, 1985), 1:352-58.

37. As in Ps. 110:1, where Yahweh promises to David that he will make his enemies his *hădōm,* and Isa. 66:1, where the heavens, portrayed as Yahweh's throne, are contrasted with the earth, his footstool. This sense is reflected in another designation for footstool, *kebeš,* which derives from *kābaš,* "to subdue, subjugate"; see 2 Chr. 9:18. For pictorial representations of ancient footstools see *ANEP,* nos. 332, 371, 415-17, 456-60, 463, 493, 537, 545, 604, 631.

38. For further discussion see Metzger, *Königsthron und Gottesthron,* pp. 358-59. Metzger interprets the mountain on the Hammurabi Stele as the footstool of Shamash.

his departure, as portrayed in chs. 8–11. This declaration is intended to answer the people's bewilderment over their future, particularly their questions regarding their relationship with Yahweh. The vision of the return of the *kābôd* offers optical reinforcement of verbal pronouncements in earlier salvation oracles (chs. 34–37) that Yahweh will come back and establish his residence among them, never again to leave. Ezekiel's temple represents a symbol of his recommitment.

Unlike a Babylonian account of the return of Marduk to his shrine, in this account of Yahweh's reappearance in the temple Yahweh expresses no sentimentality or homesickness for his city,[39] nor a softening of ethical and spiritual demands on his people. On the contrary, vv. 7b-9 emphasize that while with God nothing has changed, Israel cannot carry on as she had prior to Yahweh's departure in 586 B.C. In the first instance, Yahweh stands by previous assertions of concern for the sanctity of his name.[40] The one who resides in this holy temple on this holy mountain demands a holy reputation. He will not tolerate an unholy people misrepresenting him before the nations. Yahweh's general demand for the cessation[41] of name-defiling behavior is concretized by citing a series of specific offenses that had provoked the furious outpouring of his wrath in an earlier era: spiritual harlotry of nation and king, and the veneration of the deceased.

The first charge is summed up in one word, *zĕnûtām*, "their harlotry," which occurs twice in vv. 7b-9. While the word may denote spiritual infidelity in general (Num. 14:33), in Ezekiel this unfaithfulness is expressed in illicit affairs with other gods and political powers.[42] By framing vv. 7-9 with general accusations of "harlotry" of "the house of Israel" and referring to the funerary offerings of "*their* kings," Ezekiel maintains a primary focus on the sins of the people. The specific offenses of the kings are described parenthetically.

Many scholars recognize in the guide's explanation a division of labor among the priests and an assertion of Zadokite power (they have access to

39. According to a prophetic speech of Marduk, dated in the reign of Nebuchadrezzar I (1127-1105 B.C.), when Marduk had fulfilled *his* days in exile, he yearned for his city and called all of the gods and goddesses back home. For the text in transliteration and commentary see Borger, *BO* 28 (1971) 3-24. English translations are provided by Block, *Gods of the Nations*, pp. 169-76; and Longman, *Fictional Akkadian Autobiography*, pp. 233-35.

40. The expression *ṭimmē 'et-šēm qodšî*, "to defile my holy name" (a variation of *ḥillēl šēm qodšî*, found earlier in 20:39; 36:20, 23; 39:7), appears twice.

41. On the Piel form *killâ*, "to bring to an end, exterminate," in connection with Yahweh's "pouring out of his wrath on them," see 20:13 (with *ḥămātî*) and 22:31 (with *za'mî*).

42. *zĕnût* occurred previously in 23:27, where it served as a stylistic variant of *taznût* and *zĕnûnîm*. The spiritual meaning of the root *znh*, "to commit harlotry," has been graphically explained in the extended word pictures of chs. 16 and 23.

the altar) over the rest of the priests (they have access only to the temple).[43] However, this understanding is doubtful for several reasons. First, it is based on a faulty understanding of Num. 18:5, which, by specifically referring to "performing guard duty for the sanctuary" *(šāmar mišmeret haqqōdeš)* and "guard duty for the altar" *(mišmeret hammizbēaḥ)* differentiates between priestly responsibilities. But the distinctions drawn in Num. 18:1-7 are not between two groups of priests but between Aaronid priests and other Levitical functionaries. Second, it is based on a faulty distinction between *bayit,* "house," and *mizbēaḥ,* "altar." The strict parallelism of the guide's statements suggests relative synonymity of meaning in the lines, with "altar" serving as a nearer definition and concretization of "house."[44] This usage is inspired by Num. 18:5, where the identical phenomenon occurs. Accordingly, *zōh* at the beginning of line one does double duty, and the *waw* at the beginning of line two functions epexegetically. Both chambers are for priestly officers.[45] Third, elsewhere in Numbers, guarding the sanctuary *(mišmeret haqqōdeš)* is defined as the duty of the Levites and Aaronids.[46] Fourth, this interpretation fails to recognize the full force of the clarifying comment regarding the Zadokites, a comment that applies to both parallel lines. The priests who guard the temple and those who guard the altar must all be Zadokites, of Levitical descent, officially authorized to approach *(haqqĕrēbîm)* Yahweh to officiate for him *(lĕšārĕtô).*[47] In 44:15-31 Ezekiel will learn more about the nature of these duties;[48] in this context, however, the issue is not cultic service but maintaining the sanctity of sacred space. These priests are stationed at the gates to prevent a recurrence of the abominations witnessed in chs. 8–11.[49]

The second name-defiling activity is less clear, because the meanings of all three words in *pigrê malkêhem bĕmôtām* are debated. In 6:5 the first

43. Zimmerli, *Ezekiel 2,* p. 368; Stevenson, *Vision,* pp. 68-69.

44. In contrast to 44:14, where *bayit* carries the broad sense of "temple compound."

45. R. K. Duke recognizes a distinction in roles but no differentiation in rank ("Punishment or Restoration? Another Look at the Levites of Ezekiel 44.6-16," *JSOT* 40 [1988] 74-75).

46. Num. 3:32, 38. Thus also Duguid, *Ezekiel and the Leaders,* pp. 88-89. Cf. the translation of B. Levine, *Numbers,* AB 4 (New York: Doubleday, 1993), p. 153.

47. Similarly Duke, *JSOT* 40 (1988) 74-75; Duguid, *Ezekiel and the Leaders,* pp. 89.

48. Accordingly, clarification of these terms and the Zadokites' cultic role is delayed until the commentary on 44:15-31.

49. Prevailing scholarly opinion treats v. 46b as a late editorial insertion, a fragment of the Zadokite stratum that includes 43:19; 44:6-31; 45:4-5; 46:19-21, 24; and 48:11. See Gese, *Verfassungsentwurf,* pp. 21-22, 49, 57-65, 106-7, 89, 102, respectively, but esp. pp. 64-67. For a defense of 40:44-46 as part of Ezekiel's original vision see Tuell, *Law of the Temple,* pp. 31-33.

lexeme, *pĕgārîm,* had denoted the corpses of idolaters strewn about their idols, a sense familiar from other occurrences in the OT, and corresponding to the common meaning of the Akkadian cognate, *pagrum.*[50] Assuming consistency of usage, many interpreters recognize in the present context an allusion to royal graves located in the vicinity of the temple precinct.[51] But no such tombs have been discovered near enough to the Solomonic temple grounds to be considered defiling to the temple; moreover, most of the kings were buried "in the city of David," some distance removed from the temple area.[52] In the light of recent research, *pĕgārîm* should be interpreted not as corpses themselves but as some aspect of a cult of the dead. The present usage relates to the pagan practices cited in Lev. 26:30, where *pigrê gillûlîm* seems to refer not to "the corpses/carcasses of idols," as in the usual understanding, but to some element of the cult of the dead. Whether this involved memorial stelae to the gods erected in honor of kings, or special offerings to the deceased, akin to Akk. *pagru*-offerings,[53] the issue is some sort of ancestor cult.

But one's understanding of *pĕgārîm* is affected by the meaning attached to the following *mĕlākîm.*[54] Most commentators treat the expression according to its common usage, "kings," that is, the past kings of Israel who had not only failed to separate the temple physically from the palace but had also set up memorial stelae for themselves. But there may be more to it. Some see here an alternative designation for *rĕpā'îm,* a term used by Canaanites to refer to deceased and divinized kings. This usage of *mĕlākîm* is admittedly rare in

---

50. Cf. *AHW,* p. 809.

51. Taylor, *Ezekiel,* p. 265; Wevers, *Ezekiel,* p. 312; Cody, *Ezekiel,* p. 219; Alexander, "Ezekiel," p. 969. So also Spronk, *Beatific Afterlife,* p. 250.

52. Cf. Bloch-Smith, *Judahite Burial Practices,* pp. 116-19; J. Simons, *Jerusalem in the Old Testament: Researches and Theories* (Leiden: Brill, 1952), pp. 194-225; K. Galling, "Die Nekropole von Jerusalem," *PJ* 32 (1936) 73-101. Two exceptions were the apostate kings Manasseh (2 K. 21:18; 2 Chr. 33:20) and Amon (2 K. 21:26), who were interred in "the garden of Uzza," which appears to have been on the grounds of the palace.

53. For the former see D. Neiman (*JBL* 67 [1948] 55-60), who appeals to the Ugaritic usage of *pgr;* cf. K. Galling, "Erwägungen zum Stelenheiligtum von Hazor," *ZDPV* 75 (1959) 11. For fuller discussion see Lewis, *Cults of the Dead,* pp. 72-79. Cf. also the pillar Absalom set up for himself in the King's Valley in 2 Sam. 18:18. For the latter see J. H. Ebach, *"Pgr* = (Toten-) Opfer? Ein Vorschlag zum Verständnis von Ez. 43,7.9," *UF* 3 (1971) 365-68; G. C. Heider, *The Cult of Molek: A Reassessment,* JSOTSup 43 (Sheffield: JSOT Press, 1985), pp. 392-94; *HALOT,* p. 911. Cf. the identification of Dagan as *bēl pagrê* in the Mari texts, on which see J. F. Healey, "The Underworld Character of the God Dagan," *JNSL* 5 (1977) 43-51.

54. The term *melek* occurs three times in vv. 7-9, but nowhere else in chs. 40–48. The preference for *melek* over *nāśî'* in this context may be due to the long-standing nature of the problem. Not only the last reigning monarchs, but even earlier kings who may have deserved the title *melek* failed to respect the gradations of sanctity. Cf. Duguid, *Ezekiel and the Leaders,* pp. 41-42.

the OT, but it accords with the special use of *mlkm* in Ugaritic texts.[55] Accordingly Ezekiel has in mind the veneration of the deified spirits of Israel's royal ancestors, analogous to the cult of the dead at Ugarit.[56] Such cults were based on the assumption that the dead had power over the living, and that proper attention to them by cultic means would ensure a positive influence.[57] While somewhat problematic textually, the third word, *bĕmôtām,* "in their deaths," reaffirms the mortuary nature of the activity.[58] With this statement Ezekiel indicts the former kings for cultic abominations, in addition to the moral sins noted earlier.

The third name-defiling activity is equally obscure. The reference to threshold butting up against threshold and doorpost next to doorpost with only a wall separating the structures looks like an infringement of sacred space. Texts like 2 K. 11 reflect the close proximity of the divine and royal palaces,[59] but the narratives nowhere hint at Yahweh's displeasure with this situation. The comment alludes to the violation of sacred space by illicit palace-sponsored construction activity within the temple courtyard.[60] Unless

55. For the OT Heider (*Cult of Molek,* p. 392) points to Isa. 24:21. For the Ugaritic material see M. Dietrich and O. Loretz ("Neue Studien zu den Ritualtexten aus Ugarit," *UF* 13 [1981] 69-74), who understand the *mlkm,* like *rp'ym,* as beneficent spirits of the dead worshiped by the living. Cf. also Healey, *UF* 10 (1978) 89-91; Heider, *Cult of Molek,* pp. 391-95. P. Xella ("Aspekte religiöser Vorstellungen in Syrien nach den Ebla- und Ugarit-Texten," *UF* 15 [1983] 288) finds a sg. counterpart in Eblaite *ilib.*

56. On which see M. H. Pope, "The Cult of the Dead at Ugarit," in *Ugarit in Retrospect: Fifty Years of Ugarit and Ugaritic,* ed. G. D. Young (Winona Lake, Ind.: Eisenbrauns, 1981), pp. 159-79.

57. Although orthodox Yahwism forbade the veneration of the dead (e.g., Deut. 14:1; 26:14; on the proscriptions see Bloch-Smith, *Judahite Burial Practices,* pp. 126-30), the persistence of the practice in Israel is evident in several texts. Ps. 106:28 refers to "sacrificial meals for the dead" (*zibḥê mētîm,* cf. vv. 37-38); Isa. 65:3-5a describes people spending the night in the rock-cut tombs; Amos 6:7 and Jer. 16:5 speak of the *marzeaḥ,* a funerary feast; 2 Chr. 16:12 has the diseased Asa seeking aid from the *rĕpā'îm* instead of Yahweh (so also Pope, *UF* 19 [1987] 461). Ps. 16:3-4 mentions pouring out libations of blood to the "saints who are in the earth" (*qĕdôšîm 'ăšer bā'āreṣ*) and the "mighty ones" (*'addîrîm*). Thus Pope (*UF* 19 [1987] 462-63), approving of Spronk, *Beatific Afterlife,* p. 249. On the cult of the dead in Israel see further Block, *BBR* 2 (1992) 129-31; Lewis, *Cults of the Dead* (1989); Bloch-Smith, *Judahite Burial Practices,* pp. 109-32.

58. This sense is not ruled out by the traditional rendering, "on their high places," since all kinds of pagan cultic activities were performed on the high places. W. F. Albright suggests that the *bāmôt* functioned primarily as mortuary shrines (*Archaeology and the Religion of Israel,* 5th ed. [Garden City, N.Y.: Doubleday, 1969], pp. 102-4).

59. See the relationship of palace and temple as portrayed by Beitzel, *Moody Atlas,* p. 159; and *The Harper Atlas of the Bible,* ed. J. B. Pritchard (New York: Harper & Row, 1987), pp. 86-87.

60. "Threshold to threshold" and "doorpost to doorpost" are probably hyperbolic figures of speech highlighting this encroachment.

this also involved royal tombs,[61] the most likely culprit is Manasseh. According to 2 K. 21:4, this ruler built altars for all the hosts of heaven in both courts of the temple, but one may reasonably suppose that he also constructed chapels to house the pagan images in this area.[62]

The fourth charge accuses the Israelites of *abominable practices*. As in 36:31, where the term also appears in a context concerned with the sanctity of the divine name, *tôʿēbâ* serves as a catchall for all disgusting and scandalous pagan activities. The last clause of v. 8 reaffirms that Yahweh refuses to minimize the severity with which he has treated his own people.

The first part of Yahweh's speech (vv. 7-9) concludes with an exhortation and a promise. First the Israelites are challenged (in the jussive) to remove their spiritual harlotry and their pagan funerary practices. In a context concerned with the sanctity of sacred space, the word *yĕrahăqû*, "let them put far away," is well chosen. Whereas the priests were authorized to come near (*qārab*) to Yahweh (40:46; 42:13; 43:19), and offerings were to "be brought near" (*hiqrîb*) to him (see 43:24), the evils cited here were to be banished. The challenge is issued to guard the sanctity not only of the people but also of the temple and the reputation of God. The divine approval will be expressed by Yahweh returning and establishing his permanent residence within the midst of his people.

d. Epilogue to the Temple Vision (43:10-11)

> 10 "As for you,[63] human, describe the temple[64] to the family of Israel so they may be humiliated[65] for their crimes. Let them measure the perfection,[66] 11 and they themselves will be humiliated[67] for everything

---

61. Bloch-Smith (*Judahite Burial Practices*, p. 116 n. 1) finds a reference to tomb doorposts in Isa. 57:8.

62. While the function of Ezekiel's *binyān* is nowhere defined, it appears to have been intended to fill up the space behind the temple, presumably to prevent the recurrence of this problem.

63. LXX, Vulg., Syr., and many Hebrew mss. smooth out the reading by adding the copula.

64. Hebrew *habbayit*, "the house."

65. On the Niphal form *niklam*, see 36:32. Cf. also the noun *kĕlimmâ* in 16:27, 54, 61.

66. Appealing to LXX, Syr., and Targ., Zimmerli (*Ezekiel 2*, p. 410) emends MT *tknyt* to *tkntw*, "its layout," assuming either the haplographic omission of *waw* before *w'm* or the transposition of *tw* to *wt* (miswritten as *yt*), but this involves an unnecessary switch from the root *tkn* to *kwn* (Stevenson, *Vision*, pp. 20-21). The present form occurs elsewhere only in 28:12, and Targ. and Vulg. support an identical rendering here. RSV and NEB follow LXX in reading the previous verb, *ûmādĕdû*, as *wĕmarăʾēhô*, "and its appearance." REB drops the entire clause.

67. Reading *wĕhēm yikkālĕmû*, with LXX and Vulg. The unconditionality of the

they have done. As for the design[68] *of the temple — its layout,*[69] *exits, and entrances,*[70] *as well as all its laws and instructions — make known. Write them down in their sight so they may observe all my rulings and all my ordinances by executing them."*[71]

Having presented this charge for the people and the promise of his presence, in vv. 10-11 Yahweh concludes his speech with a command to Ezekiel to transmit the measurements of the temple complex to his fellow exiles.[72] The prophetic charge consists of a series of clauses whose sense is not always clear and whose arrangement is certainly not logical by Western standards. Direct commands to the prophet are interspersed with motive clauses and invitations to the people to consider the significance of the revelation. The series of nouns in this list is irregular and overloaded. The following synopsis compares the entries in MT and LXX:

------

foregoing renders a conditional clause at this point improbable. Cf. Gese, *Verfassungsentwurf,* p. 40.

68. NRSV and REB read *wṣrt,* "and you shall describe," with LXX, assuming a metathesis in MT's *ṣwrt.* The following sequence of nouns supports the latter.

69. LXX omits *ûtĕkûnātô.*

70. The influence of the preceding verb, *ûmôṣāʾayw,* is evident in the pronunciation of *ûmôbāʾayw.* Cf. *ûmĕbôʾayw* in 26:10; 27:3; 33:31; 42:9; 44:5; 46:19. LXX omits the word.

71. This verse is difficult in MT. LXX presupposes a different text, and many scholars emend accordingly. See Cooke, *Ezekiel,* pp. 474-75; Allen, *Ezekiel: 20–48,* p. 243; Tuell, *Law of the Temple,* p. 43 n. 64; Zimmerli, *Ezekiel 2,* pp. 410-11. See further below.

72. The strategic positioning of these verses transforms the entire visionary experience (40:2–43:11) into a (re)commissioning experience, similar in structure and details to Ezekiel's inaugural vision and call in 1:4–3:11. Note the following parallels:

1. Yahweh encounters Ezekiel in a theophanic vision, followed by a direct charge to communicate with his compatriots.
2. The vision itself climaxes in the appearance of the *kābôd* of Yahweh.
3. The vision is accompanied by a sound like the rumbling of waters.
4. The vision is connected with the Chebar River.
5. The prophet responds to the *kābôd* by falling on his face.
6. The divine Spirit picks him up and prepares him for further interaction.
7. Specific reference is made to a throne.
8. Yahweh speaks to Ezekiel directly, in both instances addressing him as *ben-ʾādām,* "Human."
9. The spiritual condition of the Israelites is described, albeit in different terms.
10. The prophet is commanded to pass on to his compatriots a divine message.
11. The commissioning involves a written document: in the first instance, a scroll with the message already transcribed; in the present the prophet is instructed to record the message himself.

MT	LXX
1 the design of the temple	the design of the temple
2 and its layout	and its exits
3 and its exits	and its structure
4 and its entrances	
5 and its entire design	
6 and all its ordinances	and all its ordinances
7 and its entire design	
8 and all its instructions	and all its instructions
9 its entire design	all my laws
10 and all its ordinances	and all my ordinances

The original reading is difficult to establish, but I propose the following:

#1-4   Retain MT. LXX reversed the order of 2 and 3 and dropped #4.
#5   Delete from MT with LXX.
#6   Retain with MT and LXX.
#7   Delete from MT with LXX.
#8   Retain with MT and LXX.
#9   Read *wěkol-mišpāṭay* with LXX (τὰ δικαιώματά μου) in place of MT *kol-ṣûrātô*.
#10   Retain but read first common sg. suffix of LXX in place of MT third masc. pl. suffix.[73]

10 The style of the opening announcement is striking not only for its economy but also for the choice of words: *haggēd 'et-bêt-yiśrā'ēl 'et-habbayit* (lit. "Proclaim [to] the house of Israel the house"). One may recognize a deliberate echo of 40:3, except that the vague expression "all that you see" is replaced with specific content, "the house." The message of "the house" should have been music to the exiles' ears, for it embodied all their hopes and aspirations. Having witnessed the destruction of the temple in 586, and having lived for two decades hundreds of miles away from the sacred site, they must have wondered what had become of Yahweh's ancient promise to dwell among his people. In this context, no news could have been more welcome than the announcement of "the house."

11 This verse offers an expansion of the charge, which the prophet now learns involves three elements: the shape of the temple, its exits and entrances, and its cultic procedures. The first, *ṣûrat habbayit*, "the layout of the temple," concerns the overall design of this sacred space, paying particular attention to the boundaries defining the gradations of sanctity. The

73. For alternative reconstructions see Zimmerli, *Ezekiel 2*, pp. 410-11; Gese, *Verfassungsentwurf*, pp. 39-43.

second concerns access to the sanctuary. The function of these doorways is to regulate access to the respective levels of sacred space by offering entrance to authorized personnel and prohibiting access to unauthorized persons. The addition of the third element, represented by the terms *ḥuqqôt* ("prescriptions, ordinances"), *tôrôt* ("instructions"), and *mišpāṭîm* ("laws"), emphasizes Yahweh's desire for his people to grasp the significance of Ezekiel's scheme. While little has been said so far about the temple ritual, this addition recognizes that knowledge of the lay of sacred space and of the principles of access is insufficient for the maintenance of its holiness. Its sanctity is also affected by the manner in which cultic activities are performed within its borders.[74]

But what has been revealed to Ezekiel is not just an oracle to be announced to the people as an oral word. The proclamation is to be accompanied by written documentation. The verb *kātab* is often interpreted as "to draw, sketch," that is, produce a ground plan for the people to study[75] and take measurements of its layout (v. 10). But to limit the verb to "drawing" is certainly too restrictive. Yahweh is hereby calling for a written transcript of the revelation, which is to serve as a means of persuasion.[76] Accordingly the verb *mādad,* "to measure," calls for a mastery of the internal and external boundaries of sacred space. However, the intended emotional response, captured by the verb *niklam,* "to be humiliated," is comprehensible only if the verb also involves the recognition of the spiritual and theological significance of those boundaries.

The intended effect of the vision on the people is striking: *so that they may be humiliated.* There is no thought of celebrating the return of Yahweh to their midst, any more than there had been in the establishment of the everlasting covenant in 36:32. On the contrary, the purpose clause in v. 10b, involving the Niphal of *klm,* introduces a homiletical dimension to the vision. In challenging the people to consider their role in the desecration of the divine name through their iniquitous behavior *('ăwônôt),* the word *niklam* shatters assumptions of worthiness and forces the audience to accept responsibility for the failure of divine-human relations.[77] This spiritual map of holiness puts them in their place: they are sinners visited by God, and invited to his presence by grace alone. Even in the new order, they do not earn the right to divine favor. Yahweh returns on his own initiative and for his own purposes.

---

74. The juxtaposing of the verbs *šāmar,* "to keep, guard," and *'āśâ,* "to do, perform," in the last line of v. 11 is deliberate.

75. Thus Zimmerli, *Ezekiel 2,* p. 419. Cf. *lĕ'ênêhem* (v. 11).

76. See Davis, *Swallowing the Scroll,* p. 123; Stevenson, *Vision,* p. 15.

77. Cf. M. S. Odell, "The Inversion of Shame and Forgiveness in Ezekiel 16.59-63," *JSOT* 56 (1992) 111-12.

♦ *Theological Implications*

Before turning to the next major part of the final vision, I offer a summary of the key theological lessons of 40:1–43:11.

First, this vision proclaims the ineffable holiness of God, which may be communicated only through the medium of analogy. Not only is he enthroned above the heavens, removed from all "gods"; he dwells in absolute splendor in his house, separate from his people.

Second, this vision proclaims the glorious mercy of God, who invites sinners into a relationship with himself and provides the means whereby that relationship can be expressed, though without contaminating his own holiness or endangering the life of his devotees. Because he longs for fellowship with humans he comes to dwell among them, though without sacrificing any of his glory. Ezekiel and his audience were privileged to learn this lesson through visionary revelation, but Christians recognize the ultimate expression of the divine desire in Jesus, who is not only the restored temple (John 2:19-22) but the physical manifestation of divine glory — full of grace and truth (John 1:14).

Third, the vision exposes the sinfulness of human beings, even those who pride themselves in being the people of God. Against the backdrop of divine holiness, penitent sinners rightly feel shame because of their rebellious ways. The glorious news of the gospel is not that we are worthy of access to him, but that he receives us in spite of our sin. However, that God invites us as we are does not mean that he accepts our condition as satisfactory. He calls on his people to put away their idolatrous ways and to sanctify his name through righteous living.

2. The New Torah (43:12–46:24)

a. Preamble (43:12)

> 12 *"This is the Torah of the temple. All its surrounding territory at the top of the mountain shall be absolutely holy. Look! This is the Torah of the temple."*[1]

Appealing to texts like Lev. 14:54-57 and Num. 7:84-88, some argue that this verse represents the conclusion to the account of the temple tour.[2] Supposedly v. 12 was originally attached to 42:20, before the account of the return of Yahweh was inserted. But this interpretation is questionable on several

---

1. Many delete *hinnēh zō't tôrat habbāyit* as a superfluous gloss. See Allen, *Ezekiel 20–48*, p. 243.
2. Talmon and Fishbane, *ASTI* 10 (1976) 140-41. So also Zimmerli, *Ezekiel 2*, p. 420.

counts.[3] First, whereas Lev. 14:54-57 is preceded by prescriptive legislation, the present statement follows a lengthy descriptive section. Second, while formulae like the present *zō't tôrat habbayit,* "This is the Torah of the temple," often occur at the end of legislation, their presence at the beginning is not uncommon in the Mosaic Torah.[4] Third, whereas the classification of the following material as *tôrâ* is confirmed in 44:5, nowhere is the preceding descriptive material so designated. Admittedly, the term *tôrōt* occurs in v. 11, but as we have noted, in association with *ḥuqqôt* (and *mišpāṭîm*) it is best understood as a designation for cultic (and moral) behavior, a category that suits most of the material in 43:13–46:24. Indeed, the present placement of this large section immediately after v. 11 invites the reader to interpret it as an exposition of *tôrâ, ḥuqqôt,* and *mišpāṭîm.* Accordingly, "This is the Torah of the temple" functions not as a colophonic conclusion to the description of sacred space in 40:5–43:11, but as a heading for the following ritual regulations governing access to and activities within that space.

Although this is not the first time the word *tôrâ* has occurred in Ezekiel,[5] its meaning calls for further comment. Whereas most translations understand the word legally, and render *tôrâ* as "law,"[6] the noun is derived from the Hiphil form of *yrh* III, "to teach, instruct." Accordingly, "instruction" is more precise etymologically.[7] Ezekiel reflects long-standing Israelite tradition in associating "instruction" with the priests (7:26), particularly instruction in cultic and ceremonial matters. He had earlier accused the cult officials of profaning Yahweh among the people by doing violence *(ḥāmas)* to Yahweh's Torah, profaning his sacred rituals and objects *(qŏdāšîm),* failing to distinguish the holy from the profane, failing to teach *(hôdîaʿ)* the difference between clean and unclean, and disregarding Yahweh's Sabbaths (22:26). Not only does most of the content of 43:13–46:24 fall within these categories; 44:23-24 represent an intentional righting of the wrongs listed in 22:26 by recharging the priests with responsibility in these very areas.

The need for a clear understanding of Torah arises out of the utter sanctity of the temple mountain and its environs, thereby highlighting the inviolability of sacred space.[8] The term *gĕbûl* normally denotes a border

---

3. So also Tuell, *Law of the Temple,* pp. 45-46.

4. At the end, Lev. 7:31; 13:59; 14:32, 54-57; cf. also 11:46; 12:7; Num. 2:29-31; 6:21; 30:17. At the beginning, Talmon and Fishbane (*ASTI* 10 [1976] 140) acknowledge Lev. 6:2, 7, 18 [Eng. 9, 14, 25]; 7:2, 11; Num. 19:2; 31:21; etc.

5. The word occurs elsewhere in Ezek. 7:26; 22:26; 43:11, 12 (bis); 44:5.

6. AV, RSV, NRSV, NAB, NIV; cf. JB "charter." NEB and REB "plan" appears to follow LXX.

7. Thus NJPS; cf. Targ. *'wryt',* "instruction, lesson." On the verb see S. Wagner, *TDOT,* 6:339-47. On *tôrâ* see G. Liedke and C. Petersen, *THAT,* 2:1031-43.

8. Hence the association of Torah with controlling access to the temple in 44:5.

(43:13, 17, 20), a concrete barrier (40:12), or territorial boundary (cf. 47:16-17); but as in 11:10-11, here the word refers to the area within defined borders, viz., within the walls of the sacred precinct. The expression *qōdeš qodšîm*, "distinctively holy," not to be confused with *qōdeš haqqŏdāšîm*, "the holy of holies" (41:4), speaks of the separation of the entire area from profane and secular touch. Even though God's people and his land were declared to be holy, that is, set apart for him, it was impossible to keep them in a perpetual state of sanctity corresponding to the holiness of Yahweh himself.[9] Elevated above the realm of the common and surrounded by massive walls, the absolute holiness of this area, established by the residence of the deity himself, was to be strictly guarded. Only the priests, specially consecrated, could enter here, and only the sacred gifts could be brought inside. While Yahweh may have condescended to dwell among his people, extreme measures will be prescribed to prevent the contagion of impurity inside and the contagion of holiness outside.

b. The New Altar of Burnt Offerings (43:13-27)

13 *Now these are the dimensions of the altar in cubits (a cubit being one normal cubit[10] plus a handbreadth). Its gutter was one cubit [deep][11] and one cubit wide, with a curb of one span[12] around its edge.[13] This is the base[14] of the altar. 14 From the bottom gutter[15] to the [top of] the lower wall was two cubits, and its width was one cubit. From the lower[16] wall to the [top of] the higher one[17] was four cubits,*

9. Cf. Skinner, "Ezekiel," p. 328.
10. Several Kennicott mss., LXX, and Syr. drop one member of MT *'ammâ 'ammâ*, but Targ. and Vulg. retain the redundancy.
11. Vulg. and Syr. read a more natural *wḥyqh 'mh* than MT *wḥyq h'mh*, which arose from incorrect word division. Here and in the rest of this translation bracketed words fill in ellipses to clarify the sense for modern readers. See the commentary.
12. *hā'eḥād* is missing in LXX and Syr. The indefinite fem. antecedent *zeret* leads one to expect *'aḥat*.
13. *šĕpātāh*, lit. "its lip," but *śāpâ* is often used in the derived sense of "brim, edge." Zimmerli (*Ezekiel 2*, p. 423) correctly observes that the fem. suffixes on *ûgĕbûlāh* and *šĕpātāh* refer to the gutter, not the altar.
14. Many read *gōbah*, "height," with LXX τὸ ὕψος (NRSV, REB, NAB, NJPS, NIV, JB), but the final *hē* reflects a dittography from the previous *hammizbēaḥ*. Targ. reads *ṭqws*, "measurement."
15. *ûmēḥêq hā'āreṣ*, lit. "and from the gutter of the ground." With LXX one should probably drop the copula, which was probably added because of an incorrect connection of the previous clause with v. 13, rather than v. 14.
16. *haqqĕṭannâ*, lit. "smaller."
17. *haggĕdôlâ*, lit. "bigger."

and its width was one cubit.[18] *15 The altar hearth*[19] *was four cubits [high]; and from the hearth four horns projected upward.*[20] *16 The hearth was twelve cubits long by*[21] *twelve cubits wide, a four-sided square.*[22] *17 The wall*[23] *consisted of four equal sides; it was fourteen cubits long and fourteen cubits wide. The curb running around it*[24] *was one-half cubit*[25] *[high],*[26] *and together with its gutter*[27] *one cubit wide all around, and its stairway*[28] *faced*[29] *toward the east.*

18 *Then he said to me, "Human, this is what the Lord Yahweh*[30] *has declared: These are the ordinances concerning the altar [to be observed] on the day when it is constructed, for offering up whole burnt offerings on it*[31] *and for dashing blood upon it.* 19 *For a purification offering you shall deliver a young bull to the Levitical priests who are from the line of Zadok, and thus may approach me*[32] *— the declaration*

18. Read *wrḥbh 'mh* for MT *wrḥb h'mh*, which may have arisen from faulty word division.

19. Qere reads *h'ry'l*, "the lion of God" (cf. Isa. 29:1-2) for Kethib's *hhr'l*, which translates lit. "the mountain of God." The *plene* spelling *h'r'yl* also occurs in the context (v. 16). While Vulg. and LXX transliterate rather than translate the word, Targ. reads *mdbḥ'*, "altar," throughout. On the etymology see the commentary.

20. Following LXX, REB adds "one cubit," presupposing Heb. *'ammâ*.

21. On the preposition *beth* in the sense of "by," see v. 17; 45:2; 48:20.

22. Cf. *rābûa'*, "square," with the neologistic form *mĕrubbā'*, encountered earlier in 40:47, and recurring in 45:1-2. On the forms see Hurvitz, *Linguistic Study*, pp. 27-30.

23. BHS inserts *haggĕdôlâ*, which is assumed to have dropped out, perhaps by homoioteleuton. Cf. v. 14. But the description is cryptic throughout, and the primary interest is in the upper part of the altar.

24. Consonantal *sbyb 'wth* should either be read *swbb 'wth* (G. R. Driver, *Bib* 35 [1954] 308) or *sbybwth*, "around it." Allen (*Ezekiel 20–48*, p. 244) suggests that the duplication in LXX κυκλόθεν κυκλούμενον αὐτῷ and Targ. *sḥwr sḥwr* may reflect an original *swbb 'wth sbyb*.

25. As in v. 14, the article on *h'mh* is awkward.

26. "Wide" is also possible, but this interpretation of the *gĕbûlâ* is consistent with v. 13.

27. On *wĕhaḥēq lāh* as an abbreviation for *wĕhaḥēq 'ăšer lāh* (cf. 41:9; 42:3) see Cooke, *Ezekiel*, p. 476.

28. *ûma'ălōtēhû* is ambiguous, and may be translated either sg., "its step" (Targ.), or pl., "its steps" (LXX, Vulg., Syr.). On the form of the suffix see GKC, §91l; Andersen and Forbes, *Spelling*, pp. 137-38.

29. MT infinitive construct *(pĕnôt)* should be repointed as a participle *(pōnôt)*.

30. The LXX mss. are inconsistent in their rendering of the divine name, ranging from LXX⁹⁶⁷ which omits *'ădōnāy*, to LXXᴼ(Arm) which reads κύριος κύριος, and LXXᴮ which expands to κύριος ὁ Θεὸς Ισραηλ.

31. Note the assonance of *lĕha'ălôt 'ālāyw 'ôlâ*.

32. With *haqqĕrōbîm 'ēlay* cf. *haqqĕrēbîm . . . 'el-yhwh* in 40:46.

of the Lord Yahweh — to render priestly service to me. 20 *You shall take*[33] *some of its blood and smear it on its four horns, the four sides of the [upper] ledge, and the surrounding curb. Thus you shall decontaminate*[34] *it and purge it.*[35] 21 *Then you shall take the bull [chosen for] the purification offering,*[36] *and have them burn it*[37] *by the temple guard*[38] *outside the sanctuary.* 22 *On the second day you shall present an unblemished young goat as a purification offering. They shall decontaminate the altar just as they had done with the bull.* 23 *When you have completed the decontamination ritual, you shall offer an unblemished young bull of the herd as well as an unblemished ram of the flock.* 24 *When you present them*[39] *before Yahweh, the priest shall sprinkle salt on them and offer them as a whole burnt offering to Yahweh.* 25 *Each day, for seven days, you shall prepare a goat as a sin offering. They shall also prepare a young bull of the herd and a ram of the flock, both unblemished.* 26 *For seven days*[40] *they shall make atonement for the altar, thereby purifying it and ordaining it for divine service.*[41] 27 *Thus they are to complete the period.*[42] *Then from the eighth day onward, the priests may sacrifice your whole burnt offerings and your peace offerings on the altar, and I will accept*[43] *you.*

The declaration of the Lord Yahweh."

33. LXX renders this and the following verbs in the 3rd person.

34. For a discussion of the privative use of Piel see the commentary.

35. *wĕkippartāhû* is missing in LXX. On the form of the suffix see Joüon-Muraoka, *Grammar,* §62e.

36. *haḥaṭṭā't* functions appositionally to *ḥappār,* perhaps having been added to distinguish this bull from the animal used as the burnt offering in vv. 23-24 (Allen, *Ezekiel 20–48,* p. 244).

37. Allen (*Ezekiel 20–48,* p. 238) proposes an indefinite subject for *śĕrāpô.* Cf. Zimmerli's (*Ezekiel 2,* p. 434) comparison with Lev. 16:27-28.

38. The meaning of *mipqad* is unclear. Most translations follow the versions in treating it as a place. Cf. LXX ἐν τῷ ἀποκεχωρισμένῳ and Vulg. *in separato loco,* "in the separated place." Cf. Targ. *b'tr dḥzy,* "in its proper place" (thus Levey, *Ezekiel,* p. 118). See the commentary.

39. LXX reads MT *wĕhiqrabtām* as a pl. verb.

40. LXX considers this time notice a part of v. 25, and places a copula before *yĕkappĕrû.*

41. An interpretive rendering of the idiom *milĕ'û yādāw,* lit. "they shall fill its hand." See further the commentary. Qere reads pl. *ydyw,* "his hands," as if the priests are being dedicated. Cf. LXX "their hands."

42. This sentence is missing in LXX.

43. On *rāṣā',* an Aramaized variant of *rāṣâ,* see GKC, §75rr. Cf. 20:40-41.

♦ *Nature and Design*

In 40:47 Ezekiel had noted in passing the presence of an altar in front of the temple. But the subject had been dropped immediately. The present text may be interpreted as one more example of typically Ezekielian resumptive exposition. The centrality of the altar in the new order is reflected not only by its location in the inner court at the exact center of the 500-cubit-square temple complex,[44] but also by the pride of place its description enjoys within the Ezekielian Torah. The altar unit is framed by the formal announcement of the object's measurements in v. 13 and the signatory formula in v. 27. The differences in these two borders reflect the twofold division of the literary unit into semi-independent segments clearly distinguished by both content and style. The first (vv. 13-17) consists of a factual description of the altar that would have been at home in the preceding report of the temple tour after 40:47. With its prescriptions for the ritual consecration of the altar, the second (vv. 18-27) represents true Torah.

(1) The Nature of the Altar (43:13-17)

This section opens with a formal announcement, *wĕ'ēlleh middôt hammizbēaḥ,* "These are the measurements of the altar."[45] While this concern for measurements links this paragraph to the temple tour narrative, for the first time the description deals with cultic furnishings. Compared to the style of the previous accounts, the report of the altar is impersonal, devoid of any narrative framework or prophetic formulae.[46] The nearest analogue is found in 41:5-15, but even there the opening *wayyāmād* reflects at least a "rudimentary narrative framework."[47] Not only have both prophet and guide disappeared; there is no hint of any awareness of the return of the *kābôd,* so graphically described in the foregoing. Furthermore, the specification of the cubit used in the measurement of the altar seems oblivious to a similar note in 40:5, and the observations on the altar's height represent a significant departure from the preceding description, which has been satisfied to provide horizontal dimensions of the temple complex.

In the light of these and other observations, even scholars who credit the prophet Ezekiel with a large proportion of the prophecies contained in the

44. The precise location of the altar is never explicitly indicated, but based on the information Ezekiel provides with respect to the other items along the central spine, it must be located at the midpoint of the temple grounds. See fig. 9.

45. Verbless clauses of this type, with an initial *waw* plus *'ēlleh,* are common in headings. Cf. Gen. 10:1; 11:27; Exod. 1:1; 21:1; etc.

46. E.g., word-event, citation, signatory, visionary guidance formulae.

47. So Hals, *Ezekiel,* p. 308. Cf. Gese, *Verfassungsentwurf,* p. 45.

book deny him this altar description.[48] While I do not deny the involvement of editors or disciples of Ezekiel in the formation of the book, none of these considerations eliminates the prophet himself as a candidate for the authorship of the present text. They merely highlight how out of place this description would have been in the earlier tour account.[49] The isolation of this object for such detailed description reflects its centrality in the cultus, particularly its importance in purifying the temple grounds from pollution caused by territorial violation.[50]

In the past it has been fashionable to find inspiration for this altar design in the Babylonian ziggurat (terraced temple towers).[51] Although some of the technical vocabulary may be illuminated by Akkadian cognates, the resemblances with the Solomonic altar are much more striking. The total length of the sides, 18 × 18 cubits, compares with the 20-cubit square of the first temple altar (2 Chr. 4:1); the horns, familiar from 1 K. 2:28, were a common feature of Palestinian altars; its height, measured from the bottom of the gutter to the top of the horns (9 cubits?), is similar to Solomon's 10 cubits. Accordingly, the details of Ezekiel's altar reflect either firsthand familiarity with the preexilic altar, or an ancient document or tradition describing it.[52] At the same time, contrary to the opinion of some,[53] one should not construe Ezekiel's description as a blueprint for constructing an altar, any more than chs. 40–42 represent a plan for a building project. The absence of visionary formulae should not blind the reader to the fact that the divine

48. E.g., Fohrer in Fohrer-Galling, *Ezechiel,* p. 153. Hals (*Ezekiel,* p. 308) finds here a doubtlessly "later, secondary elaboration intended largely to satisfy curiosity." Even Craigie (*Ezekiel,* p. 291) opens the door for an addition by editors and disciples.

49. Contra May ("Ezekiel," p. 54), who proposed that 43:13-17 originally followed 40:47. This conclusion is reinforced by the contrast between the realism of the altar's dimensions and the ideal nature of the temple design.

50. Cf. Stevenson, *Vision,* p. 160.

51. W. F. Albright, "The Babylonian Temple-Tower and the Altar of Burnt-Offering," *JBL* 39 (1920) 137-42; idem, *Archaeology and the Religion of Israel,* pp. 146-48; Fohrer, in Fohrer-Galling, *Ezechiel,* p. 238; R. de Vaux, *Ancient Israel,* p. 412; more recently Fishbane, *Biblical Interpretation,* p. 370 n. 132. See the reconstruction by Busink, *Tempel,* 2:731.

52. The latter is preferred by Tuell, *Law of the Temple,* p. 50. M. Dijkstra concludes, "It is . . . possible that the text in Ezekiel is not a fictional design, but realistically describes the construction of the altar of the second temple and predecessor of the altar of M. Middoth III 1ff. . . . On the other hand, the conservatism with which temples and altars were renovated in the ancient Near East (cf. e.g. Ezra iii 3, and 1 Macc. iv 47) is support enough for the supposition that the stone altar of the second temple continued the tradition of the first temple, so that the original building instruction of the altar of Ezekiel may reliably reflect the traditional form of the altar in the temple of Jerusalem" ("The Altar of Ezekiel: Fact or Fiction?" *VT* 42 [1982] 36).

53. Note Dijkstra's repeated use of "building instruction."

revelation of the ideal new order continues. The text contains no orders to build; it assumes an existing structure in the middle of sacred space, which provides the key to correct intercourse with Yahweh.

On the surface, the editorial location of vv. 13-17 seems intrusive, especially if v. 12 is interpreted as a heading for the following chapters. After "This is the Torah of the temple" one anticipates the kind of priestly legislation found in vv. 18-27. But the placement of the present laws regarding the altar at the beginning of a legal corpus follows the pattern reflected in each of the major law codes of the Pentateuch: (1) Exod. 20:22-23, at the head of the so-called Book of the Covenant (Exod. 20:22–23:33); (2) Lev. 17:1-9, at the head of the Holiness Code (Lev. 17–26); Deut. 12:1-27, at the head of the Deuteronomic Code (Deut. 12:1–26:15).[54] Furthermore, deleting vv. 13-17 as an extraneous document creates a new series of problems, since vv. 18-27 obviously presuppose this description (see esp. v. 20). The differences in style between these parts are less a function of differing historical contexts, or even sources, than of the genres of the respective materials.

While the placement of this altar description is reminiscent of Exod. 20:22-26, its agenda differs radically. Unlike the earlier account, it contains no instructions on how to build the altar and reveals no interest in its composition (stone or earth). All that matters are its size and shape, the latter of which is seen to match the symmetry of the temple complex as a whole. To prevent misunderstanding, the author reminds the reader of the unit of measurement: the long cubit, which is one handbreadth longer than the normal cubit (i.e., about 20.5 in.).[55] Fig. 9 (p. 598) attempts to visualize the altar, but many details of the description are obscure, a problem created by the employment of numerous technical architectural expressions whose meanings have been lost.

13 Beginning at the bottom, v. 13b apparently describes a gutter all around the altar one cubit deep and one cubit wide. The problem of interpretation arises from the expression *ḥêq*, which normally means "bosom, lap."[56] But its meaning is clarified somewhat by *ḥêq hā'āreṣ* (lit. "bosom of the earth") in v. 14. Although this phrase lacks any mythic connotations, it may be modeled semantically on Akk. *irat erṣeti(m)/kigalli(m)*, the formal designation for the foundation platform of the divine palace and of Etemenanki, the temple-tower of Marduk.[57] However, the context calls for an

---

54. See further S. M. Paul, *Studies in the Book of the Covenant in the Light of Cuneiform and Biblical Law,* VTSup 18 (Leiden: Brill, 1970), p. 34.

55. See above on 40:5.

56. It could also denote a fold in a garment in which personal objects were held (Exod. 4:6-7; Prov. 16:13; 17:23).

57. See S. H. Langdon, *Die neubabylonische Königsinschriften,* VAB 4 (Leipzig: Hinrichs, 1912), 1.1.36 (Nabopolassar); 1.1.31 (Nebuchadrezzar). On the expressions see *AHW,* p. 386; *CAD,* 7:186; Garfinkel, *Akkadian Influences,* pp. 76-77.

HORIZONTAL VIEW

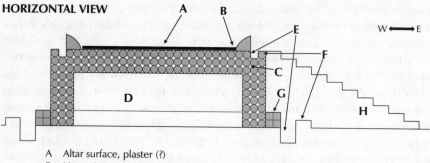

A   Altar surface, plaster (?)
B   Horns (qĕrānôt)
C   Upper wall, uncut stones (hā'ăzārâ haggĕdôlâ)
D   Inner base, soil
E   Gutter (hêq)
F   Curb (gĕbûl)
G   Lower wall, cut stones (hā'ăzārâ hattaḥtônâ)
H   Steps (ma'ălôt)

TOP VIEW

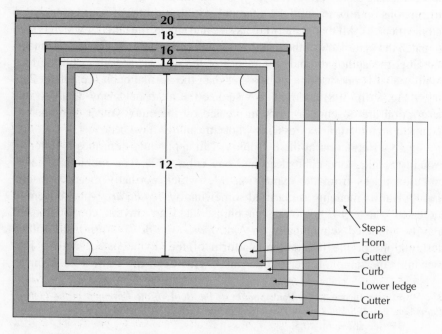

Figure 9. Ezekiel's Altar of Burnt Offerings

interpretation along the lines of 1 K. 22:35, where *ḥêq* refers to a depression or cavity of a chariot into which the blood of the slain King Ahab ran. Accordingly, the present *ḥêq hā'āreṣ* is best understood as a gutter sunk into the ground one cubit deep and one cubit wide at the bottom of the altar.[58] *hā'āreṣ,* "of the ground," distinguishes this trench from another one at the top of the altar (v. 17). This gutter functioned as a receptacle for the blood and gore of sacrificial animals, making it easier for the officiants to work, and prevented the defilement of the sacred ground by the spilled blood of the victims. Added insurance against this eventuality is provided by a curb *(gĕbûl),* one span in height (one-half cubit), that enhanced the edge of the gutter all around the altar.

The last line of v. 13 shifts attention from the gutter around the altar to the structure itself. The base *(gab hammizbēaḥ)* is mentioned first. *gab* denotes primarily "torso, back" (cf. 1:18; 10:12), and in a derived sense any convex form.[59] Here it refers to the substructure on which the altar is built.[60]

14 The altar's dimensions are given in v. 14a. The vertical measurement of the base, from the bottom of the gutter to the top, was 2 cubits (about 41 in.), and its width was 1 cubit (20.5 in.). Since the sides of the altar built on top of this *gab* were 2 cubits shorter than the base, to the observer it appeared as a ledge running all around the altar. This ledge is referred to by a special architectural term, *'ăzārâ,* whose etymology is obscure. The best clues to the meaning of the word are found in 2 Chr. 4:9, Sir. 50:2, and rabbinic writings, where it denotes the walled temple courtyard.[61] The present application suggests a row of stones, probably uncut, 1 cubit high, which supported the superstructure and prevented the altar walls from collapsing outward from the weight of the fill inside. This element is further characterized as *hā'ăzārâ hattaḥtônâ,* "the low wall," and *hā'ăzārâ haqqĕṭannâ,* "the small wall," which distinguishes it from a second wall, described as *hā'ăzārâ haggĕdôlâ,* "the large wall." Since the horizontal dimensions of the lower *'ăzārâ* were greater than those of the one above it, these designations obviously derive from the walls' relative elevations, rather than their real size. While nothing is said about the composition of the wall, one may imagine large stones carefully set to support the upper framework and the earth fill of the altar (cf.

---

58. So also Zimmerli, *Ezekiel 2,* pp. 425-26; G. André, *TDOT,* 4, 356; D. P. Wright, *The Disposal of Impurity: Elimination Rites in the Bible and in Hittite and Mesopotamian Literature,* SBLDS 101 (Atlanta: Scholars Press, 1987), pp. 151-52.

59. In 16:24, 31, 39 it had identified a raised platform for prostitution. Dijkstra (*VT* 42 [1992] 28) suggests that *ḥêq* is related to *gab* as breast is to back.

60. So also M. Haran, "Mizbeaḥ," *EM,* 4:774; Wright, *Disposal of Impurity,* p. 151; Zimmerli, *Ezekiel 2,* p. 426; contra Busink, *Tempel,* 2:732-33.

61. Jastrow, *Dictionary,* p. 1062. Cf. Arab. *ma'ḏar,* "dam, wall," as cited by Dijkstra, *VT* 42 (1992) 28 n. 25.

Exod. 20:25). The altar itself consisted of a 14-cubit square (v. 17), rising 4 cubits above the base (v. 14). The composition of the sides of this platform creates the impression of a second wall *(hāʿăzārâ haggĕdôlâ)* framing the altar proper. These walls were topped by a curb *(gĕbûl)* 1 cubit wide and one-half cubit high, which was set off from the main stage by another gutter all around (v. 17), an initial holding trench for the blood of the victims. A real altar would presumably have had one or more conduits draining the liquids from this gutter to the bottom trench, which would drain them away from the site.

15-16 The stage within these borders, where the sacrificial rites were performed, is identified by a special word, *harʾēl* (v. 15) or *hāʾărîʾēl* (v. 16). Ariel appears elsewhere as the personal name of two individuals in the OT (2 Sam. 23:20 = 1 Chr. 11:22; Ezra 8:16), and as a cryptic name for Jerusalem (Isa. 29:1-2, 7), but none of these occurrences sheds any light on the present usage. *ʾărîʾēl* translates literally "lion of El," but it is difficult to imagine why the top of an altar should have been so designated. A more likely explanation derives the word from a root *ʾārâ,* "to burn," cognate to Arab. *ʾry,* from which has developed *ʾirat,* "hearth, fireplace," in which case the final *lamed* represents an afformative element, comparable to the *lamed* on *karmel,* "Carmel."[62] This usage of the word is without parallel in the OT, but some have seen an altar hearth in the *ʾrʾl* of David, which Mesha dragged before his nation's divine patron, Chemosh,[63] after his victory over Israel.

The other spelling, *harʾēl,* is equally problematic. Albright proposed an etymological link between *ʾărîʾēl* and Akk. *arallû(m),* which supposedly carried the dual sense of "netherworld" and "mountain of the gods." But it has now been established that this word, borrowed from Sumerian, has nothing to do with a cosmic mountain.[64] It seems best, therefore, to treat *harʾēl* as an intentional theological play on an architectural designation for the flat surface of the altar on which the offerings were presented.

Nothing is said about the composition or design of the hearth, except that it had horns protruding upward at each of the corners. That this was no innovation is clear from written descriptions of the Mosaic altar (Exod. 29:12; Lev. 4:7, 18; etc.), and the one used by Solomon at the time of his accession (1 K. 1:50-53; 2:28-29), and from numerous exemplars that have been dis-

---

62. Cf. C. R. North, "Ariel," *IDB,* 1:218. Cognates have also been identified in Phoenician and Punic. Cf. *DNWSI,* p. 107; *DISO,* p. 24; *KAI,* 2:50-51. On the afformative *lamed* see GKC, §85s; Joüon-Muraoka, *Grammar,* §88Mm; BDB, p. 74a.

63. According to the Mesha Inscription, lines 12-13 (*ANET,* p. 320). Cf. *KAI,* 2:175; *TSSI,* 1:75-76, 80; S. Segert, "Die Sprache des moabitischen Königsinschrift," *ArOr* 29 (1961) 240; J. J. M. Roberts, "Ariel," *HBD,* p. 63.

64. Cf. *AHW,* p. 186; *CAD,* 1/2:226-27; Zimmerli, *Ezekiel 2,* p. 426.

covered by archeologists,[65] though none of these comes near to matching Ezekiel's altar in size. The function of these horns is unknown, but the fact that blood was to be smeared on them during the sacrifice (Lev. 4:7) attests to their importance in the ritual. Endangered persons seeking asylum in the sanctuary would seize the horns of the altar and expect divine protection (1 K. 2:28-34).

17 The text closes with a note that the hearth was approached by steps on the east side. This feature flies in the face of the Mosaic proscription on steps for an altar (Exod. 20:26). Either Ezekiel assumes that the Mosaic Torah will be superseded by his new constitution, or a literal fulfillment of the details of this vision is not anticipated. The stairs symbolize Yahweh's provision for an effective means of service. By locating them on the east side of the altar the priest may keep his face toward Yahweh in the temple as he approaches with the sacrificial victim.

But what kind of altar was this? The question may be answered by stepping back and taking a broad view of the installation, and by comparison with other exemplars. The most impressive feature of this altar is its massive size. Viewed from the top, inclusive of the bottom gutter and its lip, the outer perimeter measured 20 × 20 cubits (about 34 ft.), covering an area of 1,156 square ft.; the altar proper (*'ăzārâ gĕdôlâ*) was 14 × 14 cubits (about 24 ft.), an area of 576 square ft.; and the hearth (*'ărî'ēl*) was 12 × 12 cubits (about 20.5 ft.), 420 square ft. (see fig. 9). This means that the altar proper is as wide as the entryway to the temple, and the overall width is the same as its vestibule (40:49). From the bottom of the gutter to the top of the altar the structure measured 6 cubits (about 10 ft.). The imposing dimensions are matched by the impressive capacity of the trenches. If one assumes that the base of the altar was a 16 × 16 cubit square (v. 17), the gutter on each side must have been 17 cubits long by 1.5 cubits deep by 1 cubit wide, yielding a total volume of 102 cubic cubits (about 3,804 U.S. gallons).[66] This was sufficient capacity for the blood of hundreds of animals, and would probably have enabled the uninterrupted slaughter of sacrificial victims from morning till night.

This was obviously not the kind of altar described in Exod. 27:1-8, whose dimensions were a mere 5 × 5 × 3 cubits. Nor was it like the numerous horned altars discovered at Dan, Megiddo, Beer-sheba, and Ekron, now housed in the museums of Israel. The only biblical structure with which it compares is the Solomonic altar, which measured 20 cubits square × 10 cubits high

---

65. Cf. Y. Aharoni, "The Horned Altar of Beer-sheba," *BA* 37 (1974) 2-6; L. F. Devries, "Cult Stands: A Bewildering Variety of Shapes and Sizes," *BARev* 13/4 (1987) 31; etc.

66. $17 \times 1 \times 1.5 = 25.5 \times 4 = 102$ cubits^3 × 8,615 (in^3 per cubit^3) = 878,730 in^3 ÷ 231 (in^3 per gal.) = 3,804 gallons.

(using the smaller, 17.5 in. cubit). With these dimensions we may compare the large circular altar, 26 ft. in diameter and 4.5 ft. high, made of uncut boulders at Megiddo, which was used continuously by the Canaanites for centuries before and after the turn of the second millennium B.C., as well as the recently identified large rectangular structure, 24.5 ft. wide × 29.5 ft. long × 5 ft. high, on Mount Ebal.[67] Even if this interpretation of this installation, which consists of a framework of uncut stones and dirt fill, proves to be incorrect, the reasonableness of Ezekiel's proportions is beyond doubt,[68] and the question of the constitution of his altar may also have been solved. In accordance with Exod. 20:24-25, the frame for his altar was probably constructed of uncut stones, and then filled with soil. The horizontal surfaces would have been paved with flat stones and/or plastered with lime.

After Ezekiel's vision, the history of Israelite thinking on altar construction takes some interesting turns. While we have no information on the size and construction of the altar built by Zerubbabel and the returned exiles, Ezra 3:2 emphasizes that the design and function of this altar were determined by the written Torah of Moses, the man of God. Either the returned exiles were ignorant of Ezekiel's vision, or they rejected it as normative Torah for themselves. The next significant reference to the altar of burnt offerings is found in the Temple Scroll of the Qumran community. Unfortunately all that remains of the altar description are fragments of words. Nevertheless, the expression *pnh w'mh,* "face and a cubit," recalls the "faces" and one-cubit walls of Ezekiel's altar, and Yadin's reconstruction of 12:13, *bnwy kwlw* [']*bn*[*ym slmwt . . .*], "all built of [whole (unhewn)] stones," has links with Deut. 27:5-6.

The altar that stood in front of the temple in Jerusalem in Josephus's time (*J.W.* 5.5.6, §§222-26) provides an interesting comparison with Ezekiel's altar. The prophet's structure would have been dwarfed beside this 50 × 50 × 15 cubit installation. It had horns on each corner, and was constructed in its entirety without the use of iron tools. Josephus's reference to a "ramp" *(kbs)* reflects respect for the Mosaic taboo on steps and a repudiation of Ezekiel's design. But the talmudic tractate *m. Middot* 3:1 knows of a stepped altar with

---

67. Cf. Y. Yadin, "Megiddo," *EAEHL,* 3:837ff. A. Zertal speculates that this may have been the altar used by Joshua when he and the Israelites first entered Canaan (Josh. 8:30-35; cf. Deut. 27–28) ("An Early Iron Age Cultic Site on Mount Ebal: Excavation Seasons 1982-1987," *TA* 13-14 [1986-87] 105-65, esp. 157-61; idem, "Has Joshua's Altar Been Found on Mt. Ebal?" *BARev* 11/1 [1985] 26-43; idem, "How Can Kempinski Be So Wrong?" *BARev* 12/1 [1986] 43-53). Cf. A. Mazar's cautious acceptance of at least the cultic nature of the site (*Archaeology of the Land of the Bible,* p. 350). For a contrary interpretation see A. Kempinski, "Joshua's Altar — An Iron Age I Watchtower," *BARev* 12/1 (1986) 42-49.

68. For a diagrammatic comparison of these altars see fig. 10 (p. 603).

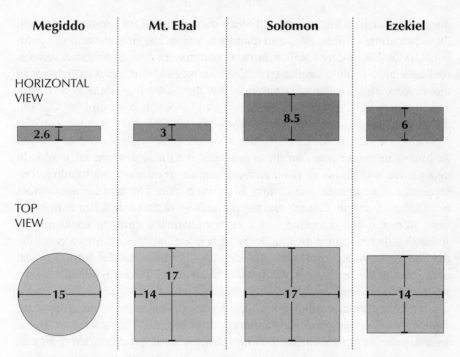

Figure 10. A Comparison of Ancient Altars (in long cubits)

a base *(hyswd)* and three pedestal blocks that measured 28 × 28, 26 × 26, and 24 × 24 cubits, respectively, moving upward from the bottom.[69]

This continuing fascination with the altar in Jewish tradition reflects its importance in the Israelite cult. The altar symbolized Yahweh's desire to commune with his people and provided the key to their acceptance with him.

(2) The Consecration of the Altar (43:18-27)

Although the prescription for the consecration of the altar in vv. 18-27 clearly depends on vv. 13-17, v. 18 marks the beginning of a new subsection. The legal and cultic agenda of this text is set by the introductory formula, *'ēlleh ḥuqqôt hammizbēaḥ,* "These are the ordinances of the altar." But considerations of genre are complicated by the prophetic framework, consisting of Yahweh's direct address of Ezekiel with *ben-'ādām,* "Human," followed by the citation formula, *kōh 'āmar 'ădōnāy yhwh,* "Thus has the Lord Yahweh declared," at the beginning (v. 18), and the signatory formula, *nĕ'um 'ădōnāy yhwh,* "the declaration of the Lord Yahweh," at the end (v. 27). This tone is reinforced by another interruptive occurrence of the latter formula in v. 19. Although *wayyō'mer* and *wayĕdabbēr,* "And he said," have marked divine speech previously in this final vision, in each case it has identified the utterances of the angelic guide.[70] For the first time in chs. 40–48 Yahweh speaks directly.[71] How he speaks is not clear, though the absence of an identified subject for *wayyō'mer* in v. 18 may point to the angelic figure as a relay for the following divine speech (cf. 43:6-11). In any case, these formulaic insertions have the effect of transforming a priestly cultic document into a prophetic oracle. In view of Ezekiel's priestly heritage and his long-standing role as prophet to the exiles, there is no need to take offense at this hybridization of the text.[72] On the contrary, it enhances the impression of Ezekiel as a second Moses, the recipient of direct divine revelation to be communicated to the people as Torah.

Apart from this prophetic overlayer, the text is cast in the standard

---

69. Rabbi Jose rationalizes these measurements, which are exactly double those of Ezekiel's altar, by noting that Ezekiel's measurements were taken from the midpoint of each side in either direction.

70. See 40:3-4, 46; 41:22, although 43:6-7 is ambiguous.

71. His words are introduced by *wayyō'mer,* "and he said" (44:2; 44:2, 5), the citation formula (43:18; 44:6, 9; 45:9, 18; 46:1, 16; 47:13), and the signatory formula (43:19, 27; 44:12, 15, 27; 45:9, 15; 47:23; 48:29). The "man" who speaks in 43:6-7 reappears in 47:6, 8, and presumably in 43:18; 46:20, 24. On this distribution of divine discourse markers see Maier, *Speaking of Speaking,* pp. 239-40.

72. Cf. F. Baumgärtel's doubts about the presence of the signatory formula in prescriptive texts ("Die Formel *nĕ'um Jahwe,*" ZAW 73 [1961] 285-86).

form of cultic ritual,[73] complete with (1) sacro-legal heading (v. 18b), which compares with v. 12 above and Exod. 12:43; (2) body (vv. 19-27a), which establishes the procedure for the consecration of the altar along the lines of Exod. 29:36-37, 40:9-11, and Lev. 16:18-19; and (3) postscript (v. 27b), which summarizes the use of the altar in the future. Unlike most ritual regulations, which tend to be cast in stereotypical language in the third person, after opening in the second person, the person and number of the subjects of the activity fluctuate as follows:

vv. 19-21a	second person singular
v. 21b	third person singular
v. 22a	second person singular
v. 22b	third person plural
vv. 23-24a	second person singular
v. 24b	third person plural
v. 25a	second person singular
vv. 25b-27b	third person plural
v. 27c	first person singular.

This inconsistency is complicated by the introduction of the priests as new subjects in vv. 24b and 27b. This leads some to conclude that the priests, not the prophet, were the primary agents in the original text; consequently the third person plural should be read throughout.[74] It is preferable, however, to assume a plurality of agents involving both the prophet and the priests.[75]

Although most scholars date this passage later than the lifetime of Ezekiel,[76] the prophet's own involvement in this passage is not out of the question. As a member of the priestly family he was surely acquainted with Mosaic regulations concerning the consecration of the altar. Having noticed the altar in the courtyard during his tour of the temple complex, he may have puzzled over the manner in which its ritual could be reinstituted. This

73. Cf. R. Rendtorff, *Die Gesetze in der Priesterschrift,* FRLANT 44 (Göttingen: Vandenhoeck & Ruprecht, 1954), p. 12.

74. Gese, *Verfassungsentwurf,* p. 48.

75. K. Koch, *Die Priesterschrift von Exodus 25 bis Leviticus 16: Eine überlieferungsgeschichtliche und literarkritische Untersuchung,* FRLANT 53 (Göttingen: Vandenhoeck & Ruprecht, 1959), pp. 104-8. For an attempt to restore a measure of literary smoothness by deleting contradictory segments see O. Procksch, *ZAW* 58 (1940-41) 105.

76. Zimmerli (*Ezekiel 2,* p. 431) dates it to the latter part of the exile, when people were beginning to anticipate the imminent restoration of the cult in Jerusalem and the rebuilding of the altar, though he isolates vv. 25-27 as a later expansion. Tuell (*Law of the Temple,* pp. 51-53) finds here the harmonization of two authoritative traditions by a single redactor in one sitting, composed as a necessary prerequisite for the cultic legislation to follow.

oracle/ritual prescription is presented as the divine response to this concern. But Yahweh's answer must have gone far beyond the prophet's wildest dreams. Not only does he hold out the prospect of accepting the Israelites' worship by revealing how the altar was to be consecrated; he elevates the stature of Ezekiel in the new constitution to that of a latter-day Moses. Typically, however, the stoic prophet offers no hint of his response to this promotion.

The opening formula classifies the regulations that follow as *huqqôt hammizbēaḥ*, "altar ordinances," the noun *ḥôq* deriving from *ḥāqaq*, "to engrave" (cf. 4:1). As in the Mosaic Torah, in Ezekiel the expression identifies a statute fixed by a superior, generally God. In cultic contexts it often denotes "prescribed ceremony."[77] The present text reflects the exilic situation, looking forward to the day when the altar rituals will be reinstituted. V. 18b specifies two functions of the altar: it provides a place for presenting whole burnt offerings to Yahweh and for performing the blood-sprinkling ritual *(lizrōq ʿālāyw dām)*.[78] From the form of the declaration the reader is led to expect regulations for these ceremonies, but this is not to be. Before acceptable rituals can be performed, the altar itself must be properly decontaminated and consecrated. This subject will occupy vv. 19-27.

(a) The Officials in the Decontamination Ceremony

Verse 19 identifies the personnel who are to participate in purification ceremony. Laypersons are predictably excluded.

The prophet Ezekiel. The prominent role prescribed for Ezekiel in the consecration of the altar is remarkable, especially since the previous narrative had left no hints that he was to participate in the future cultic activity. Although chs. 40–48 as a whole are cast in idealized visionary form, this revelation offers some compensation for the prophet's not having been able to minister in the Jerusalem temple.[79] His involvement may be summarized as follows: (1) Procure the young sacrificial bull and deliver it to the officiating priests (v. 19). (2) Perform the blood-sprinkling ceremony (v. 20). (3) Participate in

---

77. Cf. Exod. 12:14, 17, 43; 30:21; Lev. 16:29, 31; 17:7; 24:3; Num. 9:3, 12, 14; 10:8; 18:23; 19:10. For further discussion see H. Ringgren, *TDOT*, 5:139-45. Ezekiel uses *ḥuqqôt* more than any other prophet (22 times), usually pairing it with *mišpāṭîm*, "judgments, standards," to refer to Yahweh's covenant statutes, both ethical and cultic.

78. On the *ʿōlâ* see above on 40:39. The verb *zāraq* has occurred earlier in 10:2 and 36:25, but with a totally different significance. For the association of these two rites see Lev. 1:5, 11; 8:19; 9:12; 2 K. 16:15; 2 Chr. 29:22. The blood-sprinkling ritual was also part of the *zebaḥ šĕlāmîm*, "peace offering" (Exod. 24:6; Lev. 3:2, 8, 13; 9:18; 17:6), and the *ʾāšām*, "reparation offering" (Lev. 7:2). For a study of *zāraq* see G. André, *TDOT*, 4:162-65.

79. See my *Ezekiel: Chapters 1–24*, pp. 83-85.

offering the bull as a purification offering (v. 21). (4) Offer the male goat as a purification offering (v. 22). (5) Present an unblemished bull and ram before Yahweh (vv. 23-24). (6) Participate in this decontamination ritual for seven days (v. 25). A comparison with the altar purification ceremony in Exod. 29 suggests that Ezekiel is to take Moses' place. In receiving the instructions from Yahweh for the ritual in the form of a direct address and being charged to initiate the proceedings, his elevation to the status of cult founder — a second Moses — is confirmed.[80]

The Levitical priests of Zadokite descent. Like 40:46b, the reference in v. 19 anticipates the fuller discussion of the role of the Zadokites in 44:10-16.[81] Their status is defined by *haqqĕrōbîm 'ēlay lĕšārĕtî,* "those who approach me to serve me." Whereas the verb *'ābad* speaks of service to a deity in general, *qārab lĕšārēt,* "to approach to serve," is a technical expression for cultic service in particular.[82] In 44:12 *šērēt* denotes to take care of idols, which, on the analogy of pagan practice elsewhere, would have involved the feeding and clothing of cult statues. But since Yahweh tolerated no images of himself the expression could not be used in such a concrete sense by orthodox Yahwists.[83] Here this ministry will involve participation in the consecratory rituals. The following specifically priestly activities are cited: (1) Receive the young bull whose blood is to be used in the blood-sprinkling ceremony from Ezekiel (v. 19). (2) Burn the bull of the purification offering in the appointed place (? v. 21). (3) Decontaminate the altar using the bull offered as a purification offering (v. 22). (4) Offer the unblemished bull and ram as holocausts before Yahweh (v. 24). (5) Make atonement for, consecrate, and purify the altar for seven days (v. 26). (6) Offer the people's holocausts and peace offerings on the altar from the eighth day onward.

(b) The Rites of the Decontamination Ceremony

The balance between Ezekiel's duties and the priests' responsibilities reflects the cooperation required in the ceremony. The activities are to last for an entire week, preparing the way for the burnt and peace offerings on the eighth day. The text does not indicate on which day of the week they should start; the first day (Sunday) seems most likely. The specific rites may be best analyzed by examining them according to the respective days.

80. Levenson, (*Theology,* pp. 37-44) notes also that like Moses, Ezekiel does not enter the promised land; he only gazes at it from a distance.

81. Gese (*Verfassungsentwurf,* p. 115) identifies v. 19 as part of the Zadok stratum.

82. The phrase occurs five times in chs. 40–48: 40:46; 43:19; 44:15, 16; 45:4.

83. According to C. Westermann (*THAT,* 2:1020), the nearest OT analogue is provided by Samuel "serving Yahweh" (1 Sam. 2:11; 3:1), i.e., "the face of Yahweh" (1 Sam. 2:18), apparently a reference to service before the ark.

19-21 *Day one.* The first day's ritual involves three principal activities. First, Ezekiel is to initiate the week-long ritual by procuring a young bull and presenting it to the Zadokite priests, who will slaughter it, presumably on the altar. The candidate for the sacrifice is identified simply as a young male bovine.[84] Nothing is said about the nature of the animal, but the purgatory context and the description of the victims in v. 23 demand a specimen without blemish.

Second, blood is to be collected from the victim and daubed on the four horns of the altar, the four sides of the altar, and the curb (*gĕbûl*) surrounding the entire altar. Of the two curbs surrounding the altar, this involves the top one. Although *pĕnôt hā'ăzārâ* is usually translated "corners of the ledge," the four sides (lit. "faces") of the altar (referred to by the technical term *'ăzārâ*) are intended.[85]

Third, the carcass is to be removed outside the sacred precinct (*miḥûṣ lammiqdāš*) and burned. The location of the burning is specified by the phrase *bĕmipqad habbayit*. Since *mipqād,* from *pāqad,* "to number, appoint," is used in the sense of "census, muster," in 2 Sam. 24:9 and 1 Chr. 21:5, most interpret the word as a special "place of muster" within the temple grounds.[86] But the semantic range of *mipqād* is not limited to "census." Since derivatives of *pqd* are often substituted for derivatives of *šmr,*[87] the present context calls for a sense something like "temple guard," perhaps another designation for *šōmĕrê mišmeret habbayit,* "who perform guard duty for the temple," encountered earlier in 40:45.[88] Accordingly the remains of the sacrificial victim

---

84. The appositional expression *par ben-bāqār,* "a young bull, a son of the herd," recurs in 43:23, 25; 45:18; 46:6. It is borrowed from the Mosaic Torah, where it occurs in a variety of contexts: the consecration of the priest (Exod. 29:1), the purification offering for inadvertent sin (Lev. 4:3, 8, 14), as well as other offerings (cf., e.g., Num. 7, passim). *bāqār* distinguishes cattle from *ṣō'n,* smaller domesticated livestock, sheep and goats.

85. *'el-'arbā' pĕnôt hā'ăzārâ* answers to *'al-hammizbēaḥ sābîb,* "against the altar round about," in Exod. 29:16, 20; Lev. 1:5, 11; etc. See BDB, p. 284, for more references.

86. Zimmerli, *Ezekiel 2,* p. 434. Cf. W. Schottroff, *THAT,* 1:469; I. Beit-Arieh, "A First Temple Period Census Document," *PEQ* 115 (1983) 105-8.

87. Cf. *bêt mismeret* (2 Sam. 20:3; also *bêt mišmār,* Gen. 42:19), and *bêt happĕquddōt* (Jer. 52:11), both of which mean "prison"; *mišmeret miṣwat yhwh* (Josh. 22:3), *mišmeret yhwh* (1 K. 2:3) and *piqqûdê yhwh* (Ps. 19:9 [Eng. 8]; 119:4, 15), "the charge of Yahweh"; *mišmeret bĕnê gēršôn/'ahărōn* (Num. 3:32; 1 Chr. 23:32) and *pĕquddātām* (1 Chr. 24:3, 19), of priestly divisions; *mišmeret* (Exod. 16:23, 32) and *piqqādôn/hipqĕdû* (Lev. 5:21, 23; Jer. 36:20), "safekeeping." Cf. the discussion by Y. Garfinkel, "The Meaning of the Word *mpqd* in the Tel 'Ira Ostracon," *PEQ* 119 (1987) 19-23.

88. Cf. also 2 K. 11:7, as well as Neh. 3:31, where reference is made to *ša'ar hammipqād,* "the guard's gate." For *mpqd,* "guard," on a 6th-century Tel 'Ira ostracon see Garfinkel, *PEQ* 119 (1987) 22.

were to be disposed of by temple personnel, away from the sanctuary outside the inner court.[89]

Two verbs express the aim of the first day's actions: *ḥiṭṭē'* and *kippēr*. The first, the Piel verb underlying *ḥaṭṭā't*, "purification offering," is based on a common Semitic term for sin, an offense against deity of failing to measure up to his or her standards.[90] But how can an object such as an altar be "de-sinned" or decontaminated? Defilement is a contagion that prohibits sacred use and must be removed. This is achieved by performing privative rites, such as those described here.[91] The purpose of these procedures is not the forgiveness of sin but the purification of a place. This is a one-time ritual preparing the altar for the sacrifices that will ensure the well-being of the community.[92] This notion is reinforced by the second verb, which, though it usually means "to perform rites of expiation," that is, to pay a price to atone for a crime and avert death, in this context requires a purgative sense.[93]

The cause of the defilement is not indicated. Outside orthodox Yahwistic circles the source of the impurity was thought to be demonic, in which case the aim of the decontaminating ritual was to rid the precinct of the demons and to stave off their return.[94] While a residue of this notion may be reflected in the prohibition of Molech worship because it defiles *(ṭm')* the sanctuary (Lev. 20:3), the concern about defiling malevolent powers is largely expunged in Israelite

---

89. Cf. the "purification offering" for the individual, an offering that required the animal to be burned outside the camp (*miḥûṣ lammaḥăneh,* Lev. 4:12, 21; 8:17; 9:11; 16:27) and the disposal of the victim sacrificed on the Day of Atonement (Lev. 16:27-28).

90. In Hebrew thought, sin can be removed only by a divine act of forgiveness (Ps. 25:18; 32:5), blotting out (104:14), washing (51:4, 9 [Eng. 2, 7]), purging (*ḥiṭṭē',* Piel, 51:9 [Eng. 7]), and "not taking into account" (25:7). This is achieved by properly performed cultic acts of atonement (cf. 79:9), provided the person bringing the offering comes with a pure heart and sincere faith. For studies of the term see K. Koch, *TDOT,* 4:309-19; R. Knierim, *THAT,* 1:541-49.

91. On the privative significance of the Piel *ḥiṭṭē'* see Milgrom in a series of articles conveniently gathered in *Studies in Cultic Theology and Terminology,* SJLA 36 (Leiden: Brill, 1983), esp. pp. 67-95.

92. On the purification offering see Milgrom, *Leviticus,* pp. 253-64; Anderson, *ABD,* 5:879-80.

93. Its association with *ṭihar,* "to cleanse," in v. 26 supports the purgative sense. Milgrom (*Leviticus,* pp. 1079-84) argues that the word means primarily "rub off, wipe," and that "atone, expiate," represent the final abstract stage in its evolution. See my *Ezekiel: Chapters 1–24,* p. 520. For the expiatory sense see B. A. Levine, "Prolegomenon," in G. B. Gray, *Sacrifice in the Old Testament: Its Theory and Practice,* Library of Biblical Studies (repr. New York: Ktav, 1971), p. xxviii. For a full study of *kippēr* see Levine, *In the Presence of the Lord: A Study of Cult and Some Cultic Terms in Ancient Israel,* SJLA 5 (Leiden: Brill, 1974), pp. 55-76.

94. Cf. J. Milgrom, "Israel's Sanctuary: The Priestly 'Picture of Dorian Gray,'" *RB* 83 (1976) 392.

thinking.[95] Nonetheless, three other sources of pollution were recognized: (1) contact with a corpse prior to entry into the sanctuary (Num. 19:13, 20); (2) affliction with a pelvic discharge (Lev. 15:31-33) or leprosy (Num. 5:2); and (3) inadvertent sin by an individual (Lev. 4:1-7), a leader (4:22-30), or the community as a whole (4:13-21). The present ceremonies assume the fundamental profanity of the altar, if for no other reason than because of human contact.[96] Unlike other offerings (42:13; 44:29), the meat of the sacrificial victim was not eaten by the priests. Instead it was removed from the sacred area and destroyed by fire, presumably because it had absorbed the defilement.

But how did this occur? Unlike the Mosaic Torah, this text knows of no ritual laying on of hands, such as occurred in the purification offering for the individual (Lev. 4:4, 15, 24, 29), or the ritual of the Day of Atonement (Lev. 16:21).[97] The contamination may have been conveyed to the animal the moment the blood from the bull touched the hearth or as the blood was daubed on the altar. Either way, the perception is based on the close identification of blood with the *nepeš*, the very being of the creature.[98] For this reason, the final act in this ritual of purification involved not the blood smeared on the altar but the bull itself.

22-24 *Day two.* The rites of the second day were to begin with the ritual slaughter of a male goat, with the same stated purpose as the sacrifice of the bull the day before: as a purification offering *(lĕhaṭṭā't)* for cleansing the altar.[99] For the first time an animal without defect *(tāmîm)* is explicitly demanded. This sacrifice is to be followed by the slaughter of a second bull and a ram, again without defect (v. 23), as whole burnt offerings *('ôlâ)*. V. 24 adds a new element: while performing these rituals the priests are to throw salt onto them. This text offers no hint of its significance, but the act recalls the expression *melaḥ bĕrît 'ĕlōhêkā*, "the salt of the covenant of your God," in Lev. 2:13. The preservative qualities of salt apparently rendered it a perfect symbol of the permanence of covenant relationship.[100] The addition of salt to

---

95. Contra Levine, *In the Presence of the Lord,* pp. 79-91, who argues that the Israelite ritual of expiation involved the use of magic to eliminate evil forces.

96. On the contagion of defilement see Hag. 2:10-14.

97. This ritual of laying on of hands to transfer contamination is also attested in Hittite sources. See Milgrom, *Studies,* p. 81.

98. See N. Zohar, "Repentance and Purification: The Significance and Semantics of *ḥṭ't* in the Pentateuch," *JBL* 107 (1988) 609-18, esp. 612-13.

99. Cf. the consecration of the altar in Exod. 29:36-37, and the Day of Atonement (cf. Lev. 16:11, 15, 18). The verb *ḥiṭṭē'* occurs three times in Ezek. 43:22-23.

100. Cf. Num. 18:19 and 2 Chr. 13:5, in which a *bĕrît melaḥ*, "covenant of salt," denotes an eternal covenant. L. G. Herr ("Salt," *ISBE,* 4:286) notes the Arab idiom, "There is salt between us." Cf. also the expression "to eat the salt of the palace" in Ezra 4:14. See also Milgrom, *Leviticus,* pp. 191-92.

the ritual served as a reminder to Ezekiel and the priests of Yahweh's commitment to his people.

25-27 *Days three-seven.*[101] V. 25 prescribes that purgative rituals were to last a full week. Each day the prophet was to prepare a goat for a purification offering (v. 25a), and the priests were to prepare a bull and a ram, all without blemish of course. V. 26 explains that the entire series of sacrifices contributes to the decontamination of the altar. To the expressions *kippēr* and *ṭihar,* a third is added. *millē' yād* means literally "to fill the hands," but the expression was commonly used idiomatically for the ordination of a person, especially a priest.[102] The idiom seems originally to have involved the presentation either of a token payment for assuming an office or of the symbol of office. While Exod. 29:22, 26, 27, 31 and Lev. 8:22, 29 speak of an ordination ram *('êl hammillu'îm),* the present ordination of an inanimate sacred object is without parallel.

This prescription for the consecration of the altar concludes in v. 27 with a formal declaration of the goal of the ritual: to render the altar fit for regular sacrificial activity. Two offerings, which often appear together, are named as symbols of the new covenantal standing of the people before Yahweh: *'ôlâ,* "burnt offering," and *šĕlāmîm,* "peace offerings" (cf. Exod. 24:5). These two offerings reflect the two-sided nature of covenant relationship. The first, consisting of a sacrificial victim consumed entirely by fire, was a presentation for God; the second, eaten by the worshiper, provided nourishment for the human. The term *šĕlāmîm* applied to several different types of offerings (Lev. 7:11-18): thanksgiving sacrifices *(tôdâ),* vowed sacrifices *(neder),* freewill offerings *(nĕdābâ). šĕlāmîm* were joyful offerings, celebrating the well-being the worshiper experiences in relationship to the deity.[103]

---

101. Because of the overlap with the preceding and affinities to the Mosaic regulations in Exod. 29:36b-37 (cf. Lev. 8:33, 35), many regard these verses as secondary additions. Thus W. Rautenberg, "Zur Zukunftsthora des Hesekiel," *ZAW* 33 (1913) 102, followed by Zimmerli, *Ezekiel 2,* pp. 431, 435. But without v. 27b in particular this unit lacks a conclusion. Furthermore, as Allen observes (*Ezekiel 20–48,* p. 259), v. 27b creates a partial *inclusio* with v. 18b.

102. Cf. Exod. 28:41; 29:9, 33; Lev. 8:33; 16:32; 21:10; Num. 3:3; Judg. 17:5, 12; 1 K. 13:33; 2 Chr. 13:9. For other persons see Exod. 32:29 (Levites); 1 Chr. 29:5 (people); 2 Chr. 29:31 (whole congregation).

103. On the *šĕlāmîm* see Milgrom, *Leviticus,* pp. 217-25; Anderson, *ABD,* 5:878-79. Levine (*In the Presence of the Lord,* pp. 3-52) interprets this as "an efficacious gift of greeting, offered 'in the presence of the Lord' " (p. 52). These views contrast with traditional interpretations, which had viewed the *šĕlāmîm* variously as "communion offerings" (de Vaux, *Ancient Israel,* p. 427), "restitution payments" (Gray, *Sacrifice in the OT,* p. 7), "peace offerings" (Cooke, *Ezekiel,* p. 473), or "final offering" (Zimmerli, *Ezekiel 2,* p. 435, following R. Rendtorff, *Studien zur Geschichte des Opfers im alten Israel,* WMANT 24 (Neukirchen-Vluyn: Neukirchener, 1967], pp. 81-83).

Verse 27 represents a fitting climax for the present unit. After a week of consecratory rites, the temple doors could be opened for sacred business. The building has been restored, Yahweh has returned, the altar has been carefully constructed and dutifully consecrated; let the worship begin. The priests may now appear before Yahweh on behalf of the people with full assurance of being received by him. With Yahweh as subject, *rāṣâ*, "to accept," represents one of the most hopeful words in human language. This altar Torah provides for the fulfillment of the promise made long ago in 20:40-41, the only other occurrence of the word in the book. This promise is guaranteed by the divine signature in the form of the signatory formula *ně'um 'ădōnāy yhwh*, "the [firm] declaration of the Lord Yahweh."

♦ *Theological and Practical Implications*

For all its detail and formal obsolescence for Christians after Calvary, Ezekiel's altar Torah proclaims a glorious gospel of grace.

First, the altar symbolizes the delight Yahweh finds in the worship of his people. He has not returned to his temple to bask in the glory of his new surroundings. He has come to have fellowship with humans. The days of his wrath are far behind, and he reaches out to them, offering a smile and acceptance to those who appear in his divine court.

Second, Yahweh provides a way of acceptable worship. In a previous age, the Torah mediated by Moses provided a system of civil, moral, and cultic guidelines that were the envy of the world (Deut. 4:6-8). Unlike the nations around, Yahweh's people were not left experimenting and guessing what types of behavior and cultic expressions would be favorably received. The Mosaic revelation had informed the people clearly of divine expectations. It would be the same in the new order. Through Ezekiel, the new Moses, Yahweh declares his will, offering guidelines on acceptable approaches to him. The cultic system represented by this altar should not be interpreted as a human effort to reach God. On the contrary, it signifies God's condescension to sinners in need of his grace.

Third, as a corollary, even in the new order defilement threatens fellowship with God. Even the altar, at the heart of the sacred precinct, is polluted by the human touch and must be decontaminated. If the sacred precinct must experience cleansing *(ḥiṭṭē', ṭihar, kippēr)*, how much more fundamentally sinful mortals. This altar gives eloquent witness to the reality of the human heart, even under ideal conditions.

Fourth, interpreted in the light of the sacrifice of Christ, Christians may rejoice because: (a) they have a mediator superior in quality and effectiveness to Moses and Ezekiel (Heb. 3); (b) they have a permanent high priest who has direct access to the heavenly throne of God and who offers perpetual intercession on their behalf (Heb. 4:14–7:28); (c) the blood of a perfectly unblemished sacrifice has purchased favor with God, and eliminated the need for any further sacrifices (Heb. 9:1–10:31). God has provided a way!

c. Regulations Regarding the Outer East Gate (44:1-3)

1 *Then he brought me back to the outer gate of the sanctuary, the one that faces east; but it was closed.* 2 *Then Yahweh[1] said to me, "This gate must remain closed; it shall not be opened! And no human is to enter through it because Yahweh the God of Israel has entered by it. Therefore it must remain closed.[2]* 3 *But the prince,[3] and only the prince,[4] may sit in it to eat a meal before Yahweh. He shall enter through the vestibule of the gateway, and exit by the same way."*

The limits of this fragment of the temple tour report are set by two occurrences of the visionary guidance formula (vv. 1, 4).[5] On the basis of form and subject matter, the intervening material divides into two notes: an observation and prescription concerning the eastern gate (vv. 1-2) and a regulation for the prince (v. 3). The use of *hēšîb*, "he brought me back," links the prophet's present experience with a previous visit to the same gate (40:6-23), as well as to the spectacular event he had witnessed here — the return of Yahweh's *kābôd* through this gate (43:1-5). Indeed, the permanent closing of the gate is explicitly tied to this event. The use of *hēšîb* also cautions against dividing

1. The third person reference to Yahweh and the irregular word order (cf. 9:4; 23:36) lead many to delete the name as a gloss (Gese, *Verfassungsentwurf,* pp. 50-51; Zimmerli, *Ezekiel 2,* p. 437; Allen, *Ezekiel 20–48,* p. 244). But MT is not ungrammatical and the reading is attested in virtually all Hebrew mss. and the versions (except LXX[239]); on the principle of *lectio difficilior,* MT should be retained.

2. *hāyâ* plus participle *(sāgûr)* is a late construction, on which see Rooker, *Biblical Hebrew in Transition,* p. 108.

3. Although Muraoka (*Emphatic Words,* p. 157) dismisses *'et-hannāśî'* as "hopelessly corrupt," emendation of *'et* to *'ak* (BHS) or *'el* (G. J. Botterweck, "Textkritische Bemerkungen zu Ezechiel 44:3a," *VT* 1 [1951] 145-46) is unnecessary, if one allows an emphatic use of *'et.* See J. Blau, "Zum angeblichen Gebrauch von *'ēt* vor dem Nominativ," *VT* 4 (1954) 7 n. 3. Rooker (*Biblical Hebrew in Transition,* pp. 88-90) recognizes the increasing frequency of *'et* plus nominative construction (11 times in Ezekiel) in Mishnaic Hebrew.

4. On *'et* with the emphatically repeated subject used in a limiting sense see Boadt, *Ezekiel's Oracles,* p. 31. G. R. Driver's reading (*Bib* 35 [1954] 308-9) of MT as "*qua* prince," which underlay NEB "when he is here as prince," is dropped by REB. Most commentators follow LXX and Syr. and delete the second occurrence as a dittograph. Cf. *BHS;* Zimmerli, *Ezekiel 2,* p. 438.

5. The form of the formula in v. 1 is new: *wayyāšeb 'ōtî derek . . . .* Modifications will recur in 47:1, 6. Cf. the more common form in v. 4.

the literary units and subunits that constitute chs. 40–48 too sharply. While the account of the visionary tour of the temple appeared to have broken off at 43:12, there is evidently more. In fact, the report of the tour resumes in 46:19. The opening line adds a second new element by referring to the temple area as *hammiqdāš*, "the sanctuary." While the word had occurred frequently in chs. 1–39[6] and will dominate the remainder of this vision, since 40:1 the complex of structures at the top of this sacred hill had been consistently designated *habbayit*, "the house." The switch in terminology is well timed; the return of the glory of Yahweh in 43:1-5 and the consecration of the altar had transformed the temple mount into a holy place.

Ezekiel is impressed by the sight of the closed east gate.[7] But he is not left to wonder about this observation for long. By means of an animated divine speech he learns why it was shut. How the speech was delivered is not clear. The insertion of "Yahweh" as the subject of the verb of speaking may have been intentional to distinguish this divine speech from others that may have been relayed by the angelic guide (cf. 43:6-7). However, since the guide served as an authorized messenger of Yahweh, his words were considered divine speech, in which case "Yahweh" may have been deliberately inserted to focus attention on the divine resident of this temple. In any case, the tone of the speech itself is emphatic, an effect enhanced by the reference to Yahweh by the long form of his title: "Yahweh, the God of Israel."

The closing of the gate is significant for several reasons. First, as the text itself declares, because Yahweh has passed through this gate it is henceforth barred to all human traffic. The issue is access to the sacred precinct. Prior to Yahweh's arrival, there had apparently been no restrictions on passage through this gate. If the prophet had not passed through it himself, he had observed the guide walking about inside it, taking measurements of the gate's features. Once Yahweh has made his grand entrance into his temple, however, no one else may enter here. Priests must enter the inner court to perform their services, but not even they may follow in Yahweh's steps.

Second, by inference one may conclude that if the closed gate symbolizes the sanctity of the precinct, particularly the central spine, it also declares the permanence of Yahweh's residence within the temple.[8] The closing of the door presents the prophet with a visual affirmation of the promises expressed verbally in 43:7, 9. Yahweh hereby announces concretely that he would reside among the descendants of Israel forever. The tragedy of 11:23 will never be repeated.

---

6. Of Yahweh's temple in 5:11; 8:6; 9:6; 11:16; 21:7; 23:38-39; 24:21; 25:3; 37:26, 28; of Tyre in 28:18. In 43:21 *miqdāš* had denoted the temple itself.

7. The passive participle *sāgûr* occurs three times in vv. 1-2.

8. Cf. Zimmerli, *Ezekiel 2*, p. 440.

Third, the closed gate presents a veiled polemic against pagan notions. Among the many activities involved in the Babylonian New Year festival was the ritual "opening of the gate" *(pît bâbi)*.[9] The sacred gate *(bābu ellu)* apparently remained closed to all human traffic except on the great day of the festival when Marduk would exit and later return in procession through it. The closing of this gate declares on the one hand that Yahweh is not dependent on human arms for residence in the temple. No one, neither well-intentioned worshipers nor foreign conquerors like Nebuchadrezzar, may enter here. As the sovereign over Israel, and by extension over the earth, Yahweh opens gates that no one may close, and closes gates that no one may open. No enemy, either human or divine, will ever crash his sacred residence, remove him from his throne, and drag him off, according to the common treatment of the images of patron deities of conquered lands. Yahweh reigns supreme.

But there is more to this gate. The prophet is unexpectedly introduced to a new figure, the *nāśî*. The abruptness of the notice and the fact that v. 3b is largely repeated in 46:8 has raised many questions concerning the authenticity of the verse.[10] Nonetheless, the integration of the verse within its present context, as well as the pattern of zigzagging from topic to topic, common in the book, speak for its originality. Furthermore, the present passing reference to the *nāśî*, to be followed by a fuller treatment later (45:21–46:12), presents another example of resumptive exposition.

While detailed comments on this figure will be delayed until he returns for fuller treatment later in the book, several preliminary observations may be made. First, the *nāśî* occupies the gateway through which Yahweh had entered the temple, transforming an access vehicle into a place for cultic activity. Here he may eat his sacrificial meals[11] before Yahweh. Second, in this his first appearance in the Ezekielian Torah, he is a cultic figure, one singled out and authorized to eat before Yahweh in the sacred gate, a significant departure from the role of the *nāśî* in chs. 1–39, where he poses as a Davidic figure (cf. 34:24; 37:25). Third, this text places severe restrictions on the rights of the *nāśî*. Yahweh may authorize him, even invite him, to eat before him in this gate, but as a mortal he must enter by another way. V. 3b is somewhat ambiguous, but in context it prescribes that he must enter the court either by the north or south gate and then make his way inside this gateway through the vestibule *('ulām)*. Only Yahweh may enter from the outside.

---

9. Cf. *ANET*, p. 334, line 440. For references see *CAD*, 2:20. On Babylon as "the holy gate" of Marduk and the ritual "opening of the gate" see E. Unger, *Babylon: Die heilige Stadt nach der Beschreibung der Babylonier,* 2nd ed. (Berlin: de Gruyter, 1970), pp. 201-6.

10. Gese (*Verfassungsentwurf,* p. 86) treats v. 3 as the opening verse of the *nāśî* stratum of text. Cf. Zimmerli, *Ezekiel 2,* p. 439.

11. *leḥem,* lit. "bread," but here used in a broader cultic sense.

In the past, scholars have tended to interpret this text as an invitation to special status for the *nāśî*.[12] More recently some have recognized here an antimonarchic polemic.[13] Whereas under the old order kings had built temples, appointed cult officials, assigned ritual duties, offered sacrifices, and encroached on sacred space with their private buildings (43:7-8), this ordinance assigns the civil ruler a third rank — two or three rungs below deity. Zadokite priests have access to Yahweh, and the Levites may serve within the courts, but the *nāśî* is repulsed. He must eat his meals at the gate. Which of these alternatives one prefers will depend on one's interpretation of subsequent texts involving this enigmatic figure.

d. Regulations Regarding Temple Service (44:4-31)

♦ Nature and Design

The visionary guidance formula in v. 4 marks the beginning of a new unit which, on the basis of the next occurrence of the formula, carries on through 46:19. Since the epochal work of Julius Wellhausen,[14] scholars have generally treated this material as a series of later additions, uncharacteristic of the prophet Ezekiel, and reflective of the postexilic struggle for hegemony between Zadokite and Levite factions within the priesthood.[15] Admittedly the prescriptive style of the cultic ordinances contrasts sharply with the prophet's vision of an obedient people, responding to Yahweh out of hearts that have been transformed (chs. 34–37), and the judgmental nature of 44:6-14 is surprising in the broader context. But as Hals has noted, the vision of holiness that characterizes the new era cannot be divorced from the concrete expression of that quality. Indeed, the path to the future involves the undoing of past evil, and it is this conviction that underlies the shape of the present text.[16] Moreover, in the broad structure of chs. 40–48

12. Thus J. Wright comments: "The east gate legitimates the prince's power, equating him with the divine presence within the society" ("A Tale of Three Cities: Urban Gates, Squares, and Power in Iron Age II, Neo-Babylonian and Achaemenid Israel," paper presented to the Society of Biblical Literature Annual Meeting, New Orleans, November, 1990, p. 17). See also Levenson, *Theology,* pp. 69, 113-15.

13. Smith, *To Take Place,* pp. 61-62; Stevenson, *Vision,* pp. 139-43.

14. Wellhausen, *Prolegomena to the History of Ancient Israel,* tr. A. Menzies and J. Black (Edinburgh: A. & C. Black, 1885), pp. 151-61.

15. The evaluation of Eichrodt (*Ezekiel,* p. 563) is typical: "This, of course, cannot obscure the fact that the appendix has no connection whatsoever with what Ezekiel originally wrote, and that it betrays its totally different origin by its form and content." Tuell (*Law of the Temple,* pp. 54-152) treats this "law of the temple proper" as a post-Zerubbabel Jerusalemite insertion.

16. Hals, *Ezekiel,* p. 315.

one may recognize further indications of Ezekiel's neo-Mosaic status. We have already observed that the Mosaic Torah (Exod. 25–40), which concentrates on the provision of a residence for Yahweh and climaxes in the arrival of the glory of Yahweh in his residence as a sign of his presence among his people, finds an echo in Ezek. 40:1–43:11. Now we will discover that the concrete cultic prescriptions for the way of holiness in Leviticus and the legal portions of Num. 1:1–30:16 also have an answer in Ezek. 43:12–46:24. Furthermore, the instructions on the division of the land in chs. 47–48 answer to Num. 34–35. While evidence for the overall unity of Ezek. 40–48 does not necessarily argue for an Ezekielian hand in 44:4–46:18, the dismissal of this section as a late addition underestimates the contribution of the overall structure to the portraiture of the prophet as a second Moses.

With respect to form, vv. 6b-31 represent one of the most remarkably structured units in the book. The opening citation formula, "Thus has the Lord Yahweh declared," and the threefold occurrence of the signatory formula, "the declaration of the Lord Yahweh" (vv. 12, 15, 27), highlight the entire text as a divine speech. Scholars have generally interpreted this as a prophetic judgment speech, sentencing the Levites to a status inferior to that of the Zadokite priests on account of their past sins.[17] To be sure, vv. 6b-8, beginning with the emphatic idiom *rab lākem*, "Enough . . . ," function as a sort of accusation, and one may view vv. 9-14 as a divine sentence. But several considerations argue against this interpretation.[18]

First, some of the primary formal signs of typical judgment speeches are absent from this text. Not only is the *ya'an . . . lākēn . . .* , "Therefore . . . because . . . ," formulation missing;[19] the announcement of the sentence is not cast as divine action in the first person or as that of his agent in the third. Accordingly, one should recognize this text for what it purports to be — a series of directives issued by Yahweh regulating admission to the sacred precinct, analogous to Deut. 23:2-4. Second, this interpretation misconstrues the function of the present text within chs. 40–48. The Ezekielian Torah presents the exilic prophet's eschatological vision for Israel. He looks forward to the day when the old wrongs will all be righted and Israel will once again enjoy a harmonious relationship with Yahweh and with her environment. This passage does not gloss over the Levites' past sins, but the emphasis is on their role within the cult envisioned. The intention is constructive rather than punitive and destructive. Third, this judgmental interpretation treats this text

---

17. Zimmerli, *Ezekiel 2*, pp. 452-53. Tuell (*Law of the Temple*, pp. 54-59) limits the judgment oracle to vv. 1-14.

18. See also the critique by Stevenson, *Vision*, pp. 76-91.

19. In order to maintain his interpretation, Zimmerli (*Ezekiel 2*, p. 448) must emend *lākem* at the end of v. 8 to *lākēn*, and read it with v. 9.

as a polemical pro-Zadokite document reflective of their struggle with the Levites for hegemony within the Israelite priesthood after the exile. Space limitations preclude a fuller response to this theory, but one should note that the recognition of a political struggle between the two groups in this passage depends on the presuppositions that an interpreter brings to the text.

This is not to deny the obvious judgmental features of this text. But the attention to past ills is best interpreted as necessary background for the prescription of roles in the new order. The central issue is spelled out in the second pair of expressions in v. 5b: future access to sacred space.

(1) Preamble (44:4-6a)

4 *Then he brought me through the north gate to the front of the temple. I looked and look, the glory of Yahweh filled the temple of Yahweh!*[20] *Then I fell down on my face.* 5 *Yahweh said to me,*[21] *"Human, pay attention.*[22] *Look closely and listen carefully*[23] *to everything I have to say to you regarding*[24] *all the ordinances concerning the temple of Yahweh and regarding all its instructions.*[25] *Pay attention to the entrances*[26] *of the temple and all*[27] *the exits of the sanctuary.* 6 *You shall say to the rebellious family,*[28] *the family of Israel. . . ."*

Within chs. 40–48, 44:4-6a play a pivotal role, shifting the attention from the visual revelation of Yahweh, newly returned to his temple, to his aural rev-

---

20. The exclamation mark captures the note of surprise expressed by *hinnēh*.

21. As in v. 2, the subject *yhwh*, inserted after *wayyō'mer 'ēlay*, is generally treated as a mistaken addition. If so, the gloss was added early since it has unanimous manuscript and versional support.

22. Heb. *śîm libběkā*, lit. "set your heart/mind."

23. The Hebrew has a chiastic structure, lit. "Look with your eyes and with your ears hear."

24. On the *lamed* used to identify the topic of a verb of saying see Waltke-O'Connor, *Syntax*, §11.2.10g.

25. Reading pl. *twrtyw* with Qere in place of Kethib *twrtw*.

26. Reading pl. *lmbw'y hbyt* as Targ., Syr., and Vulg. suggest, in place of consonantal *lmbw' hbyt*. MT has either suffered from a metathetical corruption, with *yod* miswritten as *waw* (cf. 43:11), or the final vowel letter has been mistakenly omitted.

27. One expects *ûběkol*, if not *ûlěkol*, for MT *běkol*, though the *beth* may introduce a direct object. See Allen, *Ezekiel 20–48*, p. 244. Van Dijk (*Prophecy*, p. 83) treats the *beth* emphatically. Cf. 23:7; 33:5; Job 31:12.

28. Thus LXX πρὸς τὸν οἶκον τὸν παραπικραίνοντα; cf. Targ., "to the rebellious people, to the house of Israel." Unless MT's shortened form (without *bêt*), which occurs elsewhere only in 2:7 (also textually questionable), involves the concrete use of an abstract noun (GKC, §83b-c), one should probably recognize a homoioteleutonic error. Cf. *BHS*.

elation in the form of an extended series of ordinances communicated as divine speech. The *waw*-consecutive on *wĕ'āmartā* in v. 6 links the charge to the prophet to speak to Israel syntactically and logically the commands in v. 5, but the imitative character of vv. 4-5 ties this segment tightly to the foregoing. The verbal echoes of 43:3, 5 in v. 4 are obvious,[29] but the differences are significant enough to suppose a subsequent experience. Nevertheless, the prophet's reaction to the sight of the divine glory is the same — awed prostration. Increasing familiarity does not increase this mortal's right to stand in the presence of deity, even if he is God's commissioned prophet.

The correspondence between 44:5 and 40:4 is equally striking.[30]

29. These may be highlighted by juxtaposing the texts as follows:

44:4	43:3, 5
	5 *wattiśśā'ēnî rûaḥ*
wayĕbî'ēnî	*wattĕbî'ēnî*
derek ša'ar haṣṣāpôn	
'el-pĕnê habbayit	*'el-haḥāṣēr happĕnîmî*
wā'ēre'	
wĕhinnēh	*wĕhinnēh*
mālē' kĕbôd-yhwh 'et-bêt yhwh	*mālē' kĕbôd-yhwh habbayit*
wā'eppōl 'el-pānāy	3 *wā'eppōl 'el-pānāy*
	5 Then the Spirit picked me up
Then he brought me	and brought me
through the north gate	
to the front of the temple.	into the inner court,
I looked	
and look,	and look,
the glory of Yahweh	the glory of Yahweh
filled the temple of Yahweh!	filled the temple!
Then I fell down on my face.	3 And I fell down on my face.

30. The common features may be highlighted by juxtaposing the texts:

44:5	40:4
wayyō'mer 'ēlay yhwh	*wayĕdabbēr 'ēlay hā'îš*
ben-'ādām	*ben-'ādām*
śîm libbĕkā	
wĕrĕ'ēh bĕ'ênêkā	*rĕ'ēh bĕ'ênêkā*
ûbĕ'oznêkā šĕma'	*ûbĕ'oznêkā šĕma'*
	wĕśîm libbĕkā
'ēt kol-'ăšer 'ănî mĕdabbēr 'ōtāk	*lĕkol 'ăšer-'ănî mar'eh 'ōtāk*
Yahweh said to me,	And the man said to me,
"Human,	"Human,
set your heart.	
and look with your eyes	Look with your eyes
and with your ears hear	and with your ears hear
	and set your heart
everything that I tell you."	to all that I show you."

Yahweh's personal replacement of the guide as the subject of the verb highlights the divine authority behind the following ordinances, and the replacement of a verb of seeing with a verb of hearing reflects the change in the genre of the experience. Instead of concluding the list with the appeal to reflect on what his eyes and ears perceive, *śîm libběkā,* "pay attention," heads the list. V. 5b identifies the objects of the prophet's careful attention. The rare use of the Piel form *mědabbēr*[31] links the present text with 2:8, which contains the same command with virtually the same construction, suggesting that this event represents a recommissioning of the prophet. At the time of his original call the command to listen well had also been preceded by a vision of Yahweh's *kābôd.* But Ezekiel learns quickly that the content of this divine communication differs radically from the earlier speech. Whereas previously he had been sent out to proclaim judgment and woe, this message is defined by four expressions: *kol-ḥuqqôt bêt-yhwh, kol-tôrôtāyw, měbô'ê habbayit,* and *môṣā'ê hammiqdāš.* This series of phrases, which reverses the order found in 43:11,[32] divides into two pairs. The first refers to the procedures governing activity within the sacred area; the second to regulations governing access.

The charge in v. 6a supports my interpretation of 40:4-6a as a mini-recommissioning event. The description of the audience as [*bêt*] *měrî*[33] *bêt yiśrā'ēl,* "a house of rebellion, the house of Israel," occurs only here in chs. 40–48, but the allusion to the prophet's original call is obvious.[34] While the reference to Israel may seem odd in a context preoccupied with Levite and Zadokite affairs, national issues are clearly in view in vv. 6b-8, and they return in ch. 45. Furthermore, even within the priestly legislation, national concerns are just below the surface (cf. vv. 10, 15, 19). The world that Ezekiel envisions is still no utopia. Just as the sacrificial altar in front of the temple testifies to the continued need for cleansing (cf. v. 27), so the present reference to "the rebellious house" affirms the continuity with the old Israel. Indeed, it is this condition of the people that underlies the foregoing emphasis on maintaining the sanctity of the temple, and the following ordinances for the Zadokites (vv. 22-27).

Verses 4-6a enhance the image of Ezekiel as a new Moses. Not only is the vision of the entrance of the *kābôd* into the temple followed by an oral revelation (in the form of *tôrôt* and *ḥuqqôt*); Ezekiel is commissioned as the mediator of that revelation.

31. It occurs elsewhere only in 1:28 and 2:8; cf. the Hithpael in 2:2 and 43:6.

32. On this reversal of elements as a form of chiastic parallelism see S. Talmon, "The Textual Study of the Bible — A New Outlook," in *Qumran and the History of the Biblical Text,* ed. F. M. Cross and S. Talmon (Cambridge: Harvard University Press, 1975), pp. 359-62.

33. See textual n. 28 above.

34. See 2:5, 6, 8; 3:9, 26, 27; cf. also 17:12; 24:3.

*(2) The Problem of the Past: The Violation of Sacred Space
(44:6b-8)*

> 6b *"Thus has the Lord Yahweh declared: I have had enough of[35] all your abominations, O house of Israel, 7 ushering in foreigners, uncircumcised of heart and uncircumcised of body, allowing them to occupy[36] my sanctuary, and to desecrate my temple[37] when you presented food[38] — fat and blood — to me.[39] You[40] have violated my covenant with all[41] your abominations. 8 You have failed to guard my sacred rituals,[42] and appointed others[43] to guard my sanctuary for yourselves."[44]*

6b   Ezekiel provides perspective for his regulations concerning professional access to the temple by reviewing the problems of the past. The indictment opens solemnly with the citation formula, emphasizing that the following statements come with Yahweh's full authority. The form of the opening volley, *rab lākem,* reflects the serious tone in the divine voice.[45] The general expression *tôʿăbôtêkem,* "your abominable actions," expresses Yahweh's evaluation of the Israelites' past behavior.

7-8   These verses identify the specific charge: admission of foreigners to the sacred precinct. These foreigners are referred to as *běnê nēkār,* an

---

35. The idiom *rab lākem,* lit. "much to you," is filled out to yield the equivalent sense in English.

36. *lihyôt bě . . . ,* lit. "to be in."

37. Vulg., Targ., and Syr. smooth out the reading by dropping the suffix on *ʾet-bêtî.* The identification of the object renders the suffix on *lěhallělû,* "to desecrate it," superfluous. LXX drops it and also begins the verb with the conjunction rather than the preposition. Allen (*Ezekiel 20–28,* p. 245) treats *ʾet* as a sign of an exegetical gloss on *miqdāšî.*

38. Targ. *qwrbn,* "sacrifice," grasps the significance of *lehem.* LXX and Vulg. read more literally, "bread."

39. On the dative use of the suffix on *laḥmî* see Boadt, *Ezekiel's Oracles,* p. 30.

40. Reading second person pl. with LXX, Vulg., and Syr., in place of MT third person pl., *wayyāpērû.*

41. On *ʾel* in the sense of *ʿal* see my *Ezekiel: Chapters 1–24,* p. 99 n. 67.

42. LXX has omitted the first part of v. 8. Allen (*Ezekiel 20–48,* p. 245) suggests a 17-letter line may have been missing in the *Vorlage.*

43. The fem. suffix on MT *wattěśîmûn* probably confused a final *mem* for *nun* prior to the shift to the square script when *mem* and *nun* were sharply distinguished.

44. Many read *lākēn* with LXX (διὰ τοῦτο) in place of MT *lākem,* and connect it with the beginning of v. 9, but this is probably a harmonizing alteration.

45. Cf. the twofold occurrence of the expression in Num. 16:1-7, where it frames the dialogue between the Korahites and Moses, opening the formers' charges (v. 3) and Moses' response (v. 7). In Deut. 3:26 this phrase expresses Yahweh's frustration with Moses. The present construction, followed by partitive *min,* is most like 1 K. 12:28.

expression that occurs only here and in v. 9 in Ezekiel. Whereas the Akkadian cognate *nakrum,* "enemy," bears an overtly hostile sense, the basic sense of Hebrew *nēkār* is "unknown."[46] The choice of expression must be deliberate, since elsewhere Ezekiel has consistently referred to foreigners as *zārîm,* "strangers."[47] Two explanations may be considered. First, previous occurrences of *zār/zārîm* have always denoted either foreign nations functioning as Yahweh's agents of judgment or nations under divine judgment themselves. Here, however, the referents are not foreign political powers but individuals ritually unfit to participate in cultic activity. Second, the choice of expression reflects Ezekiel's priestly status and his familiarity with priestly tradition. Gen. 17:12 defines a *ben-nēkār* as *lō' mizzar'ăkā,* "not from your descendants." According to v. 27, the door to the covenant community would open if such outsiders would submit to the rite of circumcision (cf. Exod. 12:43).

The reasons for the exclusion of the *běnê nēkār* from the sanctuary are given in a motive clause in Lev. 22:25 (a text with other ties to our passage as well): they are intrinsically defective *(kî mošḥātām bāhem)* and fundamentally blemished *(mûm bām).* Although the Mosaic Torah rejected all gifts from the *běnê nēkār,* the Israelites of whom Ezekiel speaks had apparently admitted them into the temple and even assigned them to temple service. Ezekiel characterizes these foreigners as spiritually and physically uncircumcised (vv. 7, 9). The meaning of the latter expression, *'arělê bāśār,* "uncircumcised of flesh," is obvious, especially in the light of Gen. 17 and Exod. 12. The former, *'arělê lēb,* "uncircumcised of heart," is a Deuteronomic phrase,[48] but its origin may be traced to the Levitical covenant curses (Lev. 26:41). An identical version of the present form occurs in Jer. 9:25, where Ezekiel's senior contemporary indicts Israel for being "uncircumcised of heart" like all the nations.

Who these foreigners were and the context in which these offenses were committed one may only speculate. Candidates include the Gibeonites, who had made peace with Israel and then been assigned menial tasks in the Yahweh cult (Josh. 9:27); the people of Baal of Peor; the Nethinim, descendants of the slaves of Solomon; and Carians, members of the royal guard in Jerusalem who had originally come from Asia Minor but whose duties included guarding the temple on the king's behalf (2 K. 11:4-8).[49] The last

46. Ps. 18:45-46 (Eng. 44-45) describes the *běnê-nēkār* as "a people you do not know." For discussion of the Hebrew term see Block, *ISBE,* 4:561-63.

47. See Ezek. 7:21; 11:9; 28:7, 10; 30:12; 31:12.

48. Deuteronomy presents a two-sided picture of heart circumcision. Whereas 10:16 challenges the Israelites to circumcise their own hearts, 30:6 attributes this operation to Yahweh, resulting in a new and wholehearted covenant commitment (*'āhab,* lit. "love") to Yahweh.

49. On the Gibeonites cf. the discussion and bibliography provided by Levenson,

hypothesis finds support in v. 11 in Ezekiel's appointment of the Levites as "armed guards" *(pĕquddôt)* to replace these foreigners.[50] While guard duty could also be outside the gate, in v. 7 the prophet complains that these foreigners were brought right into the sanctuary. Whoever they were, the Israelite policy in the staffing the temple was lax. Finding little enthusiasm for the cult among their own ranks, instead of employing proper Levitical gatekeepers, the house of Israel (v. 6b) had turned to willing replacements from outside the covenant community. The primary offenders in this crime are not the Levites but the people as a whole.

According to v. 8, the role of the foreigners is defined as *šāmar mišmeret qodāšāy,* which, as we have seen, is cultic terminology for performing guard duty.[51] This duty involved primarily guarding the gates of the temple, but it may have extended to assisting the laity with their sacrifices, a responsibility that Num. 18:1-7 assigns to the Levites. This possibility accords with v. 7, which suggests that the foreigners were inside the temple, engaged in the sacrificial rituals. The reference to sacrifices as food *(leḥem)* for Yahweh comes disturbingly close to the pagan notion that offerings represented the victuals by which the appetites of the gods were satisfied.[52] Although orthodox Yahwists rejected a literal understanding of the notion, they apparently had no problem with using it as a figure of speech.[53] But in the crass form of Ezekiel's statement one should probably recognize deliberate cultural coloring, since that is how these foreigners and paganized Israelites perceived the blood and fat of the sacrificial victims (cf. v. 16) presented *(hiqrîb)* to a deity. While the guilt for encroachment of the sanctuary by ritually ineligible persons rested with the Levites, Ezekiel indicts the nation for failure to maintain the sanctity of the temple. The people could neither excuse themselves nor treat the Levites as scapegoats for their own offense.

Ezekiel identifies two consequences of this encroachment on sacred space: the sanctuary and all things sacred had been desecrated *(ḥillēl),* and

---

Theology, pp. 134-36. On Baal of Peor see Num. 25 (Levenson, ibid., pp. 136-38), but here Israel is said to have joined in Moabite celebrations, not the reverse. On the Nethinim see Ezra 2:43-58; J. B. Graybill, *ISBE,* 3:525. But according to Greenberg (*JAOS* 70 [1950] 44 n. 9), by the time of the exile these folk would have been thoroughly integrated in Yahwism. On the Carians see Allen (*Ezekiel 20–48,* p. 261), following Skinner ("Ezekiel," p. 330).

50. So also Duguid, *Ezekiel and the Leaders,* pp. 76-77.

51. Cf. above on 40:45. So also R. K. Duke, "Punishment or Restoration? Another Look at the Levites of Ezekiel 44:6-16," *JSOT* 40 (1988) 64.

52. Oppenheim, *Ancient Mesopotamia,* pp. 183-98.

53. See Lev. 3:11; 21:21-22; Num. 28:2. Haran (*Temples and Temple-Service,* p. 17) treats "God's food" as "fossilized routine terminology" rooted in pagan culture.

Yahweh's *covenant* is rendered null and void.[54] It is not clear which covenant Ezekiel has in mind. While some argue for Yahweh's covenant with Levi,[55] this interpretation not only focuses prematurely on the Levites, who are first named in vv. 9-14, but also overlooks that the present crimes involve the entire house of Israel. Ezekiel views the temple in the midst of the people as the visible sign of Yahweh's covenant. Israel's failure to respond to his gracious presence with ethical and cultic obedience[56] absolved Yahweh of responsibility toward his covenant partner. To the prophet, the admission of foreigners into the temple struck at the heart of Israel's relationship with God.

(3) The Solution for the Future: The Protection of Sacred Space (44:9-16)

9 *"Thus has the Lord Yahweh declared: No foreigner, uncircumcised of heart and uncircumcised of body, may enter my sanctuary — no foreigner at all[57] who is found among the descendants of Israel.[58]*

10 *But[59] the Levites [shall enter],[60] those who defected from me when Israel wandered away from me, who wandered away from me[61] after their idols, and they shall bear their guilt.* 11 *They shall be inside my sanctuary performing guard duty at the gates of the temple and ministering for the temple. They shall be the ones slaughtering the burnt*

---

54. The expression *qodāšāy,* "my holy things" (v. 8), is deliberately ambiguous, encompassing consecrated things in general, including the temple complex (41:4, 21, 23; 42:14; 44:27), its furniture and accoutrements (Exod. 29:37; 30:10, 29; etc.), and the sacred rituals (Ezek. 36:38; 42:13). On *hēpîr bĕrît,* "to break a covenant," see my *Ezekiel: Chapters 1-24,* p. 544 n. 117.

55. See Jer. 33:17-26; Mal. 2:4-9. See Levenson, *Theology,* pp. 146-47.

56. See Exod. 19-24; 34:10-27. The present voiding of the covenant through cultic disobedience compares with the moral failures that had the same effect in 16:58-59.

57. Most interpret the *lamed* on *lĕkol-ben-nēkār* emphatically (see Allen, *Ezekiel 20-48,* p. 245); it is better treated as an appositional marker. Cf. Waltke-O'Connor, *Syntax,* §11.2.10h.

58. LXX reads "house of Israel," a harmonization with prevailing Ezekielian style. But see the commentary.

59. On *kî 'im* as a strong adversative after negative sentences see GKC, §163a; Andersen, *Sentence,* p. 184; Waltke-O'Connor, *Syntax,* §39.3.5d.

60. The verbal idea of *kî 'im halĕwîyyim* is picked up from *bô'* in the previous verse, a phenomenon witnessed elsewhere in the book (33:11; 36:22; 44:22). Cf. Duke, *JSOT* 40 (1988) 65.

61. LXX's omission of *'ăšer tā'û* appears to be homoioteleuton, the scribe's eye having skipped from one *'ăšer* to the other, though most delete the phrase in MT as a gloss. In 48:11 the phrase appears in a more natural context.

offerings and the sacrifices for the people; and they shall attend to them[62] *by ministering to them.*[63]

12 *Because they used to minister*[64] *to them in front of their idols, which were iniquitous stumbling blocks for the house of Israel,*[65] *therefore I have sworn an oath against them*[66] *— the declaration of the Lord Yahweh — and they shall bear their guilt.*[67] 13 *But they shall not have access*[68] *to me to perform priestly duties for me, nor have access to any of my sacred areas or the most holy offerings.*[69] *They shall bear their shame and the abominations that they have perpetrated.* 14 *And I will appoint them as temple guards, responsible for all its maintenance and all the work that is done inside it.*

15 *As for the Levitical priests,*[70] *the descendants*[71] *of Zadok, who performed guard duty for my sanctuary while the descendants of Israel*[72] *were defecting from me, they are the ones who shall have access to me by ministering to me. They shall attend to me*[73] *by offering me fat and blood — the declaration of the Lord Yahweh.* 16 *They are the ones who shall enter my sanctuary, and they are the ones who shall have access to my table by ministering to me, and perform guard duty for me."*

The citation formula in v. 9a signals a new subsection of this divine speech. On the basis of subject matter and style this section continues until v. 16, but it breaks down into three uneven parts: (1) a theme statement, negatively

62. Lit. "they shall stand before them." LXX reads "the people."

63. The *lamed* plus infinitive construct has an adverbial function. Cf. GKC, §114o.

64. On the customary use of the imperfect see Cooke, *Ezekiel,* p. 481. *BHS,* Zimmerli (*Ezekiel 2,* p. 449), and others view *yĕšārĕtû* as a scribal error for the perfect *šērĕtû.*

65. Lit. "They became to the house of Israel a stumbling block of iniquity/guilt." On MT *wĕhāyû* (LXX καὶ ἐγένετο suggests *wayĕhî*) see A. Rubinstein, "The Anomalous Perfect with *Waw*-Conjunctive in Biblical Hebrew," *Bib* 44 (1963) 62-69.

66. *nāśā'tî yādî 'ălêhem,* lit. "I raised my hand against them."

67. LXX omits the last clause.

68. *nāgaš,* lit. "to touch."

69. *qodšê haqqĕdāšîm,* lit. "holy things of holy things."

70. The quotation of this text in the Covenant of Damascus (CD 3:21–4:2) document from Qumran omits the conjunction on *whkhnym,* but attaches it to *hlwym.* See Rabin, *Zadokite Documents,* pp. 30-31; P. R. Davies, *Damascus Covenant,* JSOTSup 25 (Sheffield: JSOT Press, 1982), pp. 240-41; Lust, in *Ezekiel and His Book,* p. 93.

71. CD 3:21–4:2 adds the conjunction to *bny.*

72. LXX reads *bêt yiśrā'ēl* in place of MT *bĕnê yiśrā'ēl.*

73. CD 3:21–4:2 drops *'ly lšrtny w'mdw lpny lhqryb,* probably by parablepsis, and replaces *yqrbw* with *ygšw.* Cf. v. 13.

expressed (v. 9b); (2) regulations governing the Levites' role in the temple service (vv. 10-14); and (3) regulations concerning the role of the Zadokites in temple service (vv. 15-16). Like the rest of Ezekiel's vision for the temple, this legislation is intended to guard the sanctity of the house of Yahweh by regulating access to the sacred site.

(a) The Role of the Levites (44:9-14)

9 After the opening citation formula reminding the audience (and reader) of the divine source of the following ordinances, Yahweh takes the first step to safeguard the holiness of the temple and its cult: he bars all who are outside the covenant community from the sacred precinct (v. 9). Obviously answering to the offenses described in vv. 7-8, Ezekiel reaffirms the Mosaic restrictions (Exod. 12:43-51) on access to the sanctuary. Resident foreigners who had not identified with Israel physically and spiritually were prohibited entry.

10-14 As a second step to protect the sanctity of the temple, Yahweh reassigns the Levites with guard duty for the sanctuary. The Levitical responsibilities are presented in two formulations, whose parallel structure may be highlighted by juxtaposing the two parts as in table 19 (p. 627). The first phrase in v. 10 functions as a heading for all five verses. Thereafter, the text bifurcates in characteristic Ezekielian fashion, each of the two parts reporting past sins by the Levites, a statement of the consequence of those actions, and an announcement of their reinstallation to temple service. Vv. 10-11 are sketchy in the first two parts, but expansive in the third; in vv. 12-14 this pattern is reversed.

The opening phrase introduces the Levites for the first time in the book. The name "Levite" derives from an eponymous ancestor, Levi, one of the twelve sons of Jacob (Gen. 34:25-30; 49:5). During the wilderness wanderings the Levites were assigned a substitute role for the firstborn in Israel, which otherwise belonged to Yahweh (Num. 3:40-43). They were specially appointed for tabernacle service, their duties including maintenance of the tabernacle, carrying the ark of the covenant,[74] and restricted cultic service. According to Num. 3–4 the last duty included assisting the priests in their temple service (Num. 3:6, 8; cf. 1 Chr. 23:28-32), though the nature of that service is not clear. When the land of Canaan was divided among the tribes, because of their spiritual role within Israel, the Levites did not receive a contiguous territory; rather, special cities, scattered throughout the land, were set aside for them (Num. 35:1-8; Josh. 14:14). Although the Levites are known to have distin-

---

74. See Num. 1:48-54; 8:24-26; Deut. 10:8-9. On ʿăbōdâ, "physical work," see J. Milgrom, *Studies*, pp. 18-46.

Table 19: A Synopsis of Ezekiel 44:10-11 and 44:12-14[75]

Heading	Ezekiel 44:10-11	Ezekiel 44:12-14
Introduction	But the Levites [shall enter],	
Past Sin of the Levites	those who defected from me when Israel wandered away from me, who wandered away from me after their idols,	Because they used to minister to them in front of their idols, which were iniquitous stumbling blocks for the house of Israel.
The Result	and they shall bear their guilt.	Therefore I have sworn an oath against them — the declaration of the Lord Yahweh — and they shall bear their guilt. But they shall not have access to me to perform priestly duties for me, nor have access to any of my sacred areas or the most holy offerings. They shall bear their shame and the abominations that they have perpetrated.
The New Charge	They shall be inside my sanctuary performing guard duty at the gates of the temple and officiating in the temple. They shall be the ones slaughtering the burnt offerings and the sacrifices for the people; and they shall attend to them by officiating for them.	And I will appoint them as temple guards, responsible for all its maintenance and all the work that is done inside it.

---

75. Cf. the Hebrew texts:

Ezekiel 44:10-11	Ezekiel 44:12-14
10 *kî 'im-halĕwiyyim*	
'ăšer rāḥăqû mē'ālay bĕtĕ'ôt yiśrā'ēl	12 *ya'an 'ăšer yĕšārĕtû 'ôtām lipnê gillûlêhem*
'ăšer tā'û mē'ālay 'aḥărê gillûlîm	*wĕhāyû lĕbêt yiśrā'ēl lĕmikšôl 'āwōn*
	'al-kēn nāśā'tî yādî 'ălêhem
	nĕ'um 'ădōnāy yhwh
wĕnāśĕ'û 'ăwōnām	*wĕnāś'û 'ăwōnām*
11 *wĕhāyû bĕmiqdāšî mĕšārĕtîm*	13 *wĕlō' yiggĕšû 'ēlay lĕkahēn lî*
pĕquddôt 'el-ša'ărê habbayit	*wĕlāgešet 'al-kol-qodāšay*
ûmĕšārĕtîm 'et-habbāyit	*'el-qodšê haqqĕdāšîm*
	wĕnāśĕ'û kĕlimmātām wĕtô'ăbôtām 'ăšer 'āśû
hēmâ yišḥăṭû 'et-hā'ōlâ	14 *wĕnātattî 'ôtām šōmĕrê mišmeret habbāyit*
wĕ'et-hazzebaḥ lā'ām	*lĕkōl 'ăbōdātô*
wĕhēmâ ya'amdû lipnêhem lĕšārĕtām	*ûlĕkōl 'ăšer yē'āśeh bô*

guished themselves for their loyalty to Yahweh on several occasions (Exod. 32:26-29; Deut. 10:8-9), our text does not remember those noble times. Instead the first formulation (vv. 10-11) accuses them of abandoning Yahweh at a critical time, when the Israelites were going astray.[76]

The nature of Israel's defection is defined in the first formulation as going "after their idols,"[77] but from v. 12 the Levites had apparently been more than accomplices in the crime; they seem to have led the way. The event to which Ezekiel is alluding cannot be determined, though scholars have made various suggestions: the golden calf incident; the assumption of cultic activities by the Gibeonites who were assigned menial tasks in the temple; the actions of the Mushites, a syncretistic clan singled out by the Aaronids for their idolatry; and the defection of an isolated group of priests (kĕrāmîm) of the high places, who officiated in the aberrant cult practices prior to the destruction of these centers under the reforms of Josiah.[78] Unfortunately, the vagueness of Ezekiel's comment renders any theory speculative.

One must interpret Ezekiel's accusations regarding the Levites against the background of Num. 18:21-23, which assigns them responsibility for guarding the sanctity of the sanctuary against encroachment by the laity. Ezekiel announces the consequences of failure to fulfill this charge: wĕnāśĕʾû ʿăwōnām, "they [the Levites] shall have bear their guilt/punishment." The expression is familiar from previous oracles (Ezek. 4:4; 14:10; etc.), but its meaning here is determined in large measure by Num. 18:1, 23, where the same idiom places responsibility for the welfare of Israel on the Aaronids and Levites. According to Num. 18:7 the Levite guards were authorized to kill anyone attempting to violate the holiness of the sanctuary by encroachment. If they failed in this charge, only the Levites would be punished. In Milgrom's

---

76. The expression for defection, rāḥaq mēʿal, lit. "to go far from," provides an intentional contrast with qārab, used in vv. 15-16 of the priestly approach to Yahweh. According to Num. 18:3, Aaron was to bring the Levites near (hiqrîb) so they could assist in the sanctuary service. On the links between this text and Num. 8:1-7, 22-23, see Fishbane, Biblical Interpretation, pp. 138-43. The term for apostasy, tāʿâ, is used primarily of animals wandering off course or away from the flock. Cf. Ezek. 14:11; Ps. 119:176.

77. On Ezekiel's favorite word for idols, gillûlîm, "dung pellets," see 6:3-4; 14:3-11; 16:18ff.

78. For the golden calf see Exod. 32; but as Levenson (Theology, p. 134) observes, the narrative actually highlights the fidelity of the Levites, while being critical of the Aaronids. For the Gibeonites see Josh. 9:27; Zimmerli, Ezekiel 2, p. 454. But the text is silent on Levitical involvement. Cf. Levenson, Theology, pp. 135-36. For the Mushites see Levenson, Theology, pp. 136-40, following F. M. Cross, Canaanite Myth and Hebrew Epic (Cambridge: Harvard University Press, 1973), pp. 198-215. But many of the assumptions are too conjectural to be convincing. For the priests of the high places see 2 K. 23:8-9; thus R. Abba, "Priests and Levites in Ezekiel," VT 28 (1978) 4.

words, the Levites function as a "lightning rod to attract God's wrath upon themselves" for Israel's sin.[79] Accordingly, in this context Ezekiel would be affirming that the Levites would be responsible for their people's guilt of encroachment.[80] But the phrase *wĕnāśĕʾû ʿăwōnām* is best interpreted in its normal sense: for their own failure to guard the house against encroachment, the Levites will experience Yahweh's punishment.[81] Because of their guilt they may not perform the most sacred aspects of the temple ritual. While Ezekiel's primary intention is to guarantee the future sanctity of the temple, not to demote the Levites,[82] he does not gloss over their past sins. The converted perfect construction does indeed thrust the fulfillment of the announcement into the future, but this does not mean that their future status is diminished because of past sin. Within the broader context of this statement,[83] Ezekiel envisions a new day when the past evil situation is undone, and normal relationships among deity, laity, and priesthood are restored. This means that the Levites will be reinstated as honorable guardians of the sanctuary, functioning faithfully as Yahweh's temple servants. Yahweh has not forgotten his ancient covenant with Levi.[84]

Accordingly, the final clauses of v. 10 and v. 11 represent two sides of the same coin. The first perceives the coin from the perspective of responsibility; the second highlights the renewed privilege: the Levites are reinstalled as guarantors of the sanctity of the temple.[85] The repetition, *wĕhāyû bĕmiqdāšî mĕšārĕtîm . . . ûmĕšārĕtîm ʾet-habbāyit*, "They shall be in my sanctuary serving . . . serving the temple," and the use of the verb

---

79. Milgrom, *Studies in Levitical Terminology*, p. 31. See his fuller discussion, pp. 22-33.

80. Cf. ibid., p. 27; Duke, *JSOT* 40 (1988) 66.

81. Thus Duguid, *Ezekiel and the Leaders*, p. 76. On the use of the expression in Num. 18 see Levine, *Numbers 1–20*, pp. 439-40.

82. Contra Wellhausen, *Prolegomena*, pp. 122-23; A. H. J. Gunneweg, *Leviten und Priester*, FRLANT 89 (Göttingen: Vandenhoeck & Ruprecht, 1965), pp. 188-203; A. Cody, *A History of Old Testament Priesthood*, AnBib 35 (Rome: Pontifical Biblical Institute, 1969), pp. 166-68; idem, *Ezekiel*, pp. 259-61; P. D. Hanson, *Dawn of Apocalyptic*, pp. 263-69; idem, "Israelite Religion in the Early Postexilic Period," in *Ancient Israelite Religion*, Fest. F. M. Cross, ed. P. D. Miller Jr., et al. (Philadelphia: Fortress, 1987), pp. 500-501; Fishbane, *Biblical Interpretation*, p. 140. For a refutation of the demotion hypothesis see Duguid, *Ezekiel and the Leaders*, pp. 75-80.

83. Cf. Abba, *VT* 28 (1978) 1-9; Stevenson, *Vision*, pp. 81-82.

84. References and allusions to this covenant occur in Deut. 10:8-9; Jer. 33:21; Mal. 2:4-5; Neh. 13:29. Although its terms are not spelled out, the covenant (to be distinguished from one made with the Aaronids, Num. 25:10-13) seems to have been the Levites' reward for an exceptional demonstration of loyalty (Exod. 32:25-29).

85. Fohrer's deletion of this verse as a secondary gloss (*Ezechiel*, p. 247) is to be rejected on form-critical and contextual grounds.

šērēt highlight their role.[86] While this must have included menial housekeeping and maintenance chores, analogous to the original Levite commission to take care of the portable tabernacle in the desert,[87] Ezekiel names two additional functions: the Levites are assigned to guard duty at the gates of the temple, and they are authorized to represent the people in the temple worship.

The former charge, expressed by *pĕquddôt 'el-ša'ărê habbayit,* which functions appositionally to *mĕšārĕtîm,* "serving," is a stylistic variant of *šōmĕrîm mišmeret habbayit,* "keepers of the guard of the temple."[88] Two dimensions of the latter charge are identified. First, the Levites shall slaughter *(šāḥat)* the sacrificial animals of the burnt offerings *('ôlâ)* and regular (peace) offerings *(zebaḥ)* for the people *(lā'ām).* This authorization actually represents a promotion over the Mosaic legislation, according to which the worshiper would kill the victim himself.[89] Under the old order the priest apparently performed the altar ritual, with the worshiper standing by inside the court in front of the tabernacle. Num. 16:9 suggests that the Levite guard may have accompanied the layperson into the court and perhaps assisted in the slaughter. With Yahweh's heightened concern to maintain the sanctity of the place, all laypersons are excluded from the inner court. Ezek. 46:24 prescribes that the Levites even boil the edible portions of the sacrifices in the outer court on behalf of the people. Second, the Levites shall stand before the people to serve them, *'āmad lipnê lĕšārĕtām,* "to stand before to serve them,"[90] being a technical expression for official service.

12-14 The second formulation of the Levites' assignment opens similarly with a notice of the Levites' past failures, though with a stronger emphasis on their perversion. Instead of standing before Yahweh to serve him and to bless his name (see Deut. 10:8), they had served *(šērēt)* the people in front of their idols *(gillûlîm).* Instead of guarding their spiritual welfare, they

86. The root occurs three times in this verse, functioning in these first two instances as a technical term for cultic service in general. Cf. C. Westermann, *THAT,* 2:1021-22; Milgrom, *Studies in Levitical Terminology,* p. 25. Cody *(History,* p. 74) acknowledges that the verb is not necessarily restricted to properly priestly activities.

87. See Num. 1:48-54; 4:3-15; 18:6 (cf. the use *'ăbōdâ* in v. 14), on which see Haran, *Temples and Temple-Service,* pp. 59-61.

88. See above on Ezek. 40:46. In 9:1 *pĕquddôt hā'îr,* "the inspectors of the city," functioning as Yahweh's agents of judgment, had begun executing the inhabitants of Jerusalem at the sanctuary. On the present usage see above on 43:21.

89. Cf. Lev. 1:5, 11; 3:2, 8, 13; 4:14, 15, 24, 29, 33; 17:3-4.

90. The use of the idiom with people as the object is influenced by Num. 16:9. When used of cultic officials elsewhere it always has Yahweh as the object of the preposition. Cf. v. 15. On the replacement of *'ēdâ* with *'am* as the designation for the congregation see Hurvitz, *Linguistic Studies,* pp. 65-67. Rooker *(Biblical Hebrew in Transition,* pp. 143-46) observes that the former falls out of use in Late Biblical Hebrew.

had promoted iniquitous stumbling blocks,[91] provoking Yahweh's ire. With *nāśā'tî yādî 'ălêhem,* "I raised my hand against them," the idiom of Yahweh's benevolent oath is transformed into a punitive gesture directed against a favored group.[92] The signatory formula after this reference to Yahweh's past action not only adds solemnity to the declaration but also brings closure to the previous phase of divine-Levite relations, permitting a redirection of attention toward more favorable days in the future. As in v. 10, the concluding clause in v. 12, "They shall bear their responsibility," also looks forward rather than back, highlighting the responsibility that Yahweh places on the Levites for the preservation of the temple's sanctity.

Nor should v. 13 be interpreted as punitive demotion of the Levites to an inferior status. Treating the conjunction at the beginning as a disjunctive *waw,* this statement reaffirms their status one rung below the priests. This is expressed negatively by denying them direct access to Yahweh and the most sacred aspects of his cult. The phrase *nāgaš 'el/'al* with Yahweh as object occurs elsewhere only in Jer. 30:21, a noncultic context. Here its meaning is elucidated by the following phrase, *lĕkahēn lî,* "to function as priest on my behalf." The Mosaic Torah had reserved the privilege reflected in the phrase exclusively for the Aaronic priests.[93] The sacred aspects of the cult are referred to by two expressions, *kol-qodāšay,* "all my holy things," and *qodšê haqqĕdāšîm,* "the holiest things."[94] If a distinction is to be drawn between these expressions, the second probably functions as a closer definition of the first. *qodāšîm* is a vague term, which may refer to those sacrifices considered absolutely and irreversibly holy, or to the most sacred objects in the inner court and temple.[95] Since the series of sacrifices listed in vv. 28-30 depends on Num. 18:9-20, where these same offerings are designated *qōdeš haqqŏdāšîm,* "the most holy things," the former is more likely, but not to the exclusion of *kĕlî haqqōdeš,* "all the holy furnishings," and *hammizbēaḥ,* "the altar," cited in Num. 18:3.[96] The intention is to exclude the Levites from

91. In keeping with his use of the idiom elsewhere (Ezek. 7:6; 14:3, 4, 7; 18:30), contra prevailing opinion (e.g., NASB, NRSV), Stevenson (*Vision,* p. 85) correctly applies *mikšôl 'āwōn* to the idols, with *gillûlîm* being the subject of *wĕhāyû.*

92. The use of *'al* with this oath formula occurs only here in the OT, in contrast to the inseparable preposition *lĕ* elsewhere: 20:5-6, 15, 23, 28, 42; 47:14; Exod. 6:8; Num. 14:30; Neh. 9:15. The perfect verb is rightly understood as a reference to past action, i.e., the exile. Cf. Duke, *JSOT* 40 (1988) 69.

93. See Exod. 28:1, 3, 4, 41; 29:1, 44; 30:30; 40:13, 15; Lev. 7:35. See also 1 Chr. 5:36; 24:2. Without *lî,* Exod. 31:10; 35:19; 39:41; Lev. 16:32; Num. 3:3, 4; Deut. 10:6.

94. The expression is not to be confused with *qōdeš haqqĕdāšîm,* "holy of holies," which refers to the inner sanctum of the temple.

95. Haran, *Temples and Temple-Service,* p. 16 n. 5.

96. Gunneweg, *Leviten und Priester,* pp. 199-200.

participating in the cultic rituals performed in the inner court of this temple, but not as a punitive demotion.

The converted perfect *wĕnāśĕû* in the last line of v. 13, which undoubtedly refers to a future state, does not contradict this understanding of the Levites' appointment. The clause announces two consequences of the Levites' past behavior. First, they will bear their shame for their actions. *kĕlimmâ*, "shame," is to be interpreted here as it had been used in the salvation oracles.[97] Elsewhere in Ezekiel the experience of shame occurs in the context not of judgment but of salvation. Intense shame and humiliation occurred after those who had sinned experienced forgiveness and the gracious restoration of God.[98] The word implies an intense sense of unworthiness in the light of one's past actions. Second, the Levites will bear their "abominations." The precise nature of the actions Ezekiel has in mind when he speaks of *tô'ăbôt* is not clear. The Levites, a lower class of temple cult personnel, had presumably also gone astray after idolatrous cults, along with the masses of the population (20:30ff.; 23:37ff.); they may even have participated actively in the aberrant cult rituals. Yahweh does indeed hold them accountable for these sins; they must bear their own punishment. But Ezekiel's assignment of the Levites' role in the new temple cult does not represent a demotion from a previous higher rank; this is a reinstatement to their original noble position. They may not function as priests, to be sure, but theirs is still a privileged role. On the analogy of previous references to the gracious work of God (after judgment for sin), far from causing the Levites to gloat with pride over their assignment, this act of divine grace will precipitate a sense of shame and intense unworthiness over their restoration within the cult of Yahweh.

The recommissioning of the Levites concludes in v. 14 with a positive reiteration of their responsibilities: (1) to be guards of the temple *(šōmĕrê mišmeret habbāyit);* (2) to maintain it in every respect;[99] (3) to supervise everything that transpires inside the temple grounds. The activities of the priests who ranked above them are obviously excluded, but it would have involved regulating access to the holy place and ensuring that all activities, at least in the outer court where they were stationed, were performed with the care and decorum the divine Resident deserved. In short, after experiencing the judgment of God for gross past failures, the Levites are hereby fully rehabilitated and repatriated.

97. See Ezek. 16:53-54, 60-63; 20:39-44; 36:31-32; 39:25-26; 43:10-11.

98. Cf. Duke, *JSOT* 40 (1988) 70. Stevenson (*Vision,* p. 83) follows Odell (*JSOT* 56 [1992] 104) in interpreting "shame" as the feeling evoked by a loss of status, rather than guilt.

99. While in Num. 4 *'ăbōdâ* refers to the mantling and dismantling of the tabernacle (Milgrom, *Numbers,* pp. 343-44), since the temple is a permanent structure, the word obviously denotes other chores involved in the care of the building and grounds.

(b) The Role of the Zadokites (44:15-16)

In vv. 15-16 Ezekiel's attention turns to another group of religious functionaries, the Levitical priests. The legislation for them intentionally echoes the
preceding regulations for the Levites both structurally and stylistically, as the
synopsis in table 20 (p. 634) indicates: the opening *wĕhakkōhănîm halĕwiyyim*
answers to *halĕwîyim* in v. 10; like the two formulations above, the first half
(v. 15) glances backward to past behavior, while the second half (v. 16) offers
a prescription for the future; the phraseology is deliberately imitative.

"Levitical priests" is a Deuteronomic phrase, identifying authorized cult
functionaries in Israel, in contrast to illegitimate counterfeits who surface
occasionally in the OT narratives.[100] The title assumes common tribal membership with the nonpriestly Levites just addressed, but they are distinguished by
their superior status: *kōhănîm* descended from Zadok. The Zadokites appeared
briefly in 40:46 as guardians of the altar *(šōmĕrê mišmeret hammizbēaḥ),*
distinguished from the rest of the Levites by their right to approach *(haqqĕrēbîm)*
Yahweh and to perform cultic service *(lĕšārĕtô)* for him. In 43:19 the Lord
assigns the Levitical priests, descendants of Zadok, a special role in the consecration of the altar. Later a special tract of land will be set aside for them. Ezekiel
says nothing about the original appointment of the Aaronic line to priestly duty,
nor of the ascendancy of the Zadokites over the Elide house.[101] Instead he notes
their past distinguished devotion to Yahweh. While the Israelites (and with them
the Levites, vv. 10, 12) had apostatized *(tāʿû mēʿālay)* from Yahweh, the
Zadokites had defended the sanctuary *(šāmĕrû ʾet-mišmartî),* for which they are
now rewarded with continued access to Yahweh.

In echoing and modifying the legislation for the Levites, Ezekiel
deliberately contrasts the roles of the Levites and the Zadokites in the new
order. (1) Where the Levites had been forbidden to approach Yahweh, the
Zadokites are authorized to do so freely.[102] (2) Where the Levites had to be
content with standing before the people and serving them, the Zadokites could
stand before Yahweh and present to him his food, the offerings of fat and
blood (cf. v. 7). (3) Where the Levites were authorized to perform guard duty
at the gates of the sanctuary, the Zadokites could go right inside. (4) Where
the Levites had to be satisfied with slaughtering the sacrificial animals on the

---

100. For the Deuteronomic phrase see Deut. 17:9, 18; 18:1; 24:8; 27:9; cf. the
variant "the priests the sons of Levi" in 21:5 and 31:9. For the counterfeits see, e.g.,
Micah's priest (Judg. 17:3), and the priesthood established by Jeroboam (1 K. 12:32).

101. For the original appointment see Exod. 28:1, 43; Lev. 9; Num. 3:10; etc. The
genealogical connection between Zadok and Aaron is drawn in 1 Chr. 6:3-12, 50-53. Cf.
also 24:3. On the ascendancy of the Zadokites see 1 K. 1:5-8; 2:26-27, 35; cf. 1 Sam.
3:11-14.

102. *nāgaš* (v. 13) is replaced by the more common *qārab* (v. 15).

Table 20: A Synopsis of Ezekiel 44:15-16 and 44:10-13

Ezekiel 44:15-16

Ezekiel 44:10-13

15 *wĕhakkōhǎnîm halĕwiyyim bĕnê ṣādôq*
   'ǎšer šāmĕrû mišmeret miqdāšî

   bitĕ'ôt bĕnê yiśrā'ēl mē'ālay

   hēmmâ yiqrĕbû 'ēlay lĕšārĕtēnî

   wĕ'āmĕdû lipānay lĕhaqrîb li ḥēleb
   wādām

   nĕ'um 'ǎdōnāy yhwh.

16 *hēmmâ yābō'û 'el-miqdāšî*

   wĕhēmmâ yiqrĕbû 'el-šulḥānî
   lĕšārĕtēnî

   wĕšāmĕrû 'et-mišmartî.

10 *kî 'im-halĕwiyyim*
   'ǎšer rāḥǎqû mē'ālay

   bitĕ'ôt yiśrā'ēl 'ǎšer tā'û mē'ālay

13 *wĕlō'-yiggĕšû 'ēlay lĕkahēn lî wĕlāgešet*
   'al-kol-qodāšay 'el-qodšê haqqĕdāšîm

11d *wĕhēmmâ ya'amĕdû lipnêhem*
    lĕšārĕtām.

11a *wĕhāyû bĕmiqdāšî mĕšārĕtîm*

11c *hēmmâ yišḥǎṭû 'et-hā'ōlâ wĕ'et-*
    hazzebaḥ lā'ām

11b *pĕquddôt 'el-ša'ǎrê habbayit*
    ûmĕšārĕtîm 'et-habbāyit

15 As for the priests,
   the Levites, the descendants of Zadok,
   who performed guard duty for my
   sanctuary

   while the descendants of Israel
   were defecting from me,

   they are the ones who shall have
   access to me
   by ministering to me.

   And they shall stand before me
   to present to me fat and blood

   — the declaration of the Lord
   Yahweh.

16 They shall come into my sanctuary,

   and they shall have access to my table

   to minister to me,

   and they shall perform guard duty
   for me.

10 But the Levites,
   those who defected from me

   when Israel
   wandered away from me,

13 But they shall not have
   access to me
   to perform priestly duties for me,
   nor have access to any of my sacred
   areas or the most holy offerings.

11d and they shall attend to them
    by ministering to them.

11a They shall be inside my sanctuary
    ministering.

11c They shall be the ones who slaughter
    the burnt offerings
    and the sacrifices for the people;

11b performing guard duty at the gates of
    the temple and ministering for the
    temple.

people's behalf, the Zadokites were invited to come right to Yahweh's table, viz., the altar.[103] (5) Where the Levites were assigned guard duty for the temple complex (habbayit), the Zadokites were guardians of Yahweh himself (miš-martî, v. 16).

Scholars have traditionally assumed that Ezekiel's hierarchical paradigm was based on the priestly model in Mosaic tradition, which separated the Levites for spiritual service, while the other tribes were being apportioned their territories. Their possession (naḥălâ) was a spiritual charge, not land (see Deut. 10:9; 18:2). Meanwhile the family of Aaron was specially chosen for the actual priestly service, with the Elide line eventually assuming the ascendancy within officialdom. Because of corruption within the Elide house (1 Sam. 3:11-15), under David and Solomon the Elides had been replaced by the Zadokites, who maintained their superior position until the exile, and probably beyond (cf. 1 Chr. 6:1-15). Ezekiel himself was probably a Zadokite (cf. Ezek. 1:3), as was Ezra, the leader of the spiritual revival among the returned exiles (Ezra 7:1-7).

Since Wellhausen, however, the scholarly reconstruction of the history of the priesthood looks quite different. Three periods in its evolution may be identified: (1) premonarchic Israel, without a hereditary priesthood; (2) monarchic Israel, when the Levites emerged as the dominant priestly class; (3) the postexilic period, when the Aaronids gained supremacy and the Levites were degraded to hierodules.[104] By advocating the demotion of the Levites for their past sin, Ezekiel supposedly provided the impetus for the ascendancy of the Zadokites.[105] Consequently, since the Aaronid-Levite distinction is fully operational in P, this source must postdate Ezekiel.

In the latter part of the 20th century the house of Wellhausen has come under increasing criticism, for a variety of reasons. Linguistic and conceptual considerations point to the chronological priority of P over Ezekiel, and the separation of the priests from the Levites as an Ezekielian innovation can no longer be maintained.[106] The hypotheses of a bitter feud between Aaronids/

---

103. Cf. Ezek. 41:22. Like the reference to Yahweh's food in v. 7, this is a figure of speech, borrowed from the surrounding cultures, but whose literal interpretation is to be repudiated. Cf. Haran, Temples and Temple-Service, p. 17.

104. For full expositions of this reconstruction see Wellhausen, Prolegomena, pp. 151-61; de Vaux, Ancient Israel, pp. 361-66; Cody, History, passim.

105. H. H. Rowley's theory of Zadok as a Jebusite priest of an old Canaanite shrine in Jerusalem, elevated to the priesthood over Israel by David, has been largely abandoned ("Zadok and Nehushtan," JBL 58 [1939] 113-41). Cross (Canaanite Myth, pp. 207-15) suggests that Zadok was an Aaronid priest at Hebron. See Levenson, Theology, pp. 139-40, for further discussion.

106. For linguistic critiques see Hurvitz (Linguistic Studies) and Rooker (Biblical Hebrew in Transition). For conceptual considerations cf. Abba, VT 28 (1978) 1-9; idem,

Zadokites and Levites in the history of Israel reads a great deal more into the texts of P and Ezekiel than is warranted. To be sure, the competition between the lines of Abiathar and Zadok was intense under the united monarchy, but to read a similar conflict into the rise of the Levite-Aaronid division is unwarranted. Exod. 32 does indeed portray Aaron in an extremely negative light while at the same time glorifying the Levites, but this does not justify treating this event as the background for all the prescriptive texts regulating the activities of the respective groups. One's approach to Ezek. 44:9-16 must be equally cautious. The realistic portrayal of the Levites presents a stark contrast to the idealistic picture of the Zadokites, but this does not necessarily translate into an anti-Levite polemic. Nor are hierarchical structures by definition adversarial or polarized. If Ezekiel was indeed a spokesman for the Zadokite faction, the book's failure to identify him as a Zadokite anywhere in the book is extraordinary. On the contrary, the citation of his descent from Buzi in 1:3 may represent an intentional attempt to diffuse any suggestion of personal partisanship.

In any case, one should interpret the faithfulness of the Zadokites in relative rather than absolute terms. Ezekiel himself mentions that in the past the priests have done violence to Yahweh's Torah and disregarded the sanctity of the Sabbath (22:26), problems whose resolution the prophet will explicitly announce (44:24). But they have been relatively more faithful than the rest of the Levites who led the people into apostasy. Their past fidelity in this regard was not to become a source of pride, but it was rewarded with greater privilege, which in turn would be accompanied by greater responsibility and the expectation of higher standards. As in the cases of Abraham (Gen. 26:5) and David (1 K. 3:6; 9:4), the righteousness of the Zadokites was rewarded with what may be termed the "covenant of grant."[107]

The present legislation is remarkable because, despite their past sin, the Levites are totally rehabilitated and recommissioned to take their place in the new cultic order. This reality is rendered all the more impressive by the masterful manner in which Ezekiel adapts an ancient Mosaic *traditum* (Num. 18:17, 22-23) to create a new *traditio*.[108] Although the contrast between past

---

"Priests and Levites," *IDB*, 3:876-89. See also R. Abba, "Priests and Levites in Deuteronomy," *VT* 27 (1977) 257-67; J. G. McConville, *Law and Theology in Deuteronomy*, JSOTSup 23 (Sheffield: JSOT Press, 1984), pp. 135-53; M. D. Rehm, "Levites and Priests," *ABD*, 4:297-310.

107. This type of covenant, which appears to have been common throughout the ancient Near East, is characterized by distinctive vocabulary to describe the ancestor's faithfulness: "keeping my charge," "walking before me," having "a perfect heart." Cf. Duguid, *Ezekiel and the Leaders*, p. 82; M. Weinfeld, "The Covenant of Grant in the Old Testament and in the Ancient Near East," *JAOS* 90 (1970) 184-205.

108. The expressions used by Fishbane, *Biblical Interpretation*, p. 143.

Levitical failures and the fidelity of the Zadokites has introduced new factors into the equation, the old hierarchical paradigm for cultic functionaries provides the foundation for the new order. After centuries of Zadokite service, the reaffirmation of their status as heirs of the Aaronid privileges as outlined in the Mosaic Torah is to be expected. Nonetheless, while the role of the Levites is refined, the essential *traditum* of Moses also remains normative for them in the new order.

The central concern of Ezekiel's priestly legislation is obvious: to guard the sanctity of the temple and its cult. Indeed, the prophet's structuring of the citizens conforms to the hierarchical territorial design of sacred space. Foreigners are out of the picture all together; lay worshipers may bring their burnt and regular offerings, but the animals shall be slaughtered by the Levites; the latter control access by guarding the gates, and physically maintain the sanctuary and its cult; in the inner court Zadokites offer Yahweh his food on the altar. Remarkably, not a word is said about the high priest or the most sacred space of all — the holy of holies, the throne room of Yahweh himself. Did any human ever have access to this room? Did Ezekiel envision an annual Day of Atonement, when the high priest would enter this most sacred space of all? Such questions cannot be answered.

(4) The New Zadokite Order (44:17-31)

17 *"And when they enter the gates of the inner court they shall be clothed with linen garments; they shall not be wearing anything woolen while they minister in the gates of the inner court or on the inside.* 18 *Linen turbans shall be on their heads, and linen breeches shall be on their loins. They shall not be dressed in any clothing that causes one to perspire.* 19 *When they go out to the outer gate[109] to the people, they shall take off the garments in which they have been ministering. They shall leave them in the sacred chambers and put on different clothing to prevent them from transmitting holiness to the people by contact with the clothes.[110]* 20 *They shall neither shave their heads, nor let their hair grow long; they shall keep [the hair of] their heads trimmed.[111]* 21 *And no priest shall drink[112] wine when he enters the inner court.* 22 *They shall*

109. MT's repetition of *'el-heḥāṣēr haḥîṣônâ* is dittography; the second occurrence is absent from LXX, Vulg., Syr.

110. Lit. "They shall not sanctify the people with their clothes."

111. LXX "They shall keep their heads covered" has probably misread the root *ksh* for MT *ksm*. On the possible connection of this word with Akk. *kasāmu*, "to cut," see Garfinkel, *Akkadian Influences*, pp. 92-93.

112. *yištû* and *běbô'ām* are pl. in form, in keeping with the collective sense of *kol-kōhēn*.

not marry widows or divorcees;[113] *they may marry only*[114] *virgins of truly Israelite descent*[115] *or widows who are widows of priests.* 23 *They shall instruct my people on the distinction between the sacred and the profane, and they shall inform them of the difference between what is clean and what is unclean.* 24 *In the context of formal disputes*[116] *they shall officiate as judges;*[117] *they shall render judgment*[118] *according to my laws.*[119] *They shall observe my instructions and my decrees relating to all my appointed festivals, and they shall maintain the sanctity of my Sabbaths.* 25 *They shall not defile themselves by going near*[120] *a dead person. Only*[121] *in the case of a father or mother, or a son or daughter, or a brother*[122] *or unmarried sister*[123] *may they defile themselves.*[124] 26 *But after he has purified himself,*[125] *he shall count off*[126] *seven days.* 27 *And on the day he enters the sanctuary,*[127] *to the inner court to minister in the sanctuary, he shall present*[128] *his own sin offering. The declaration of the Lord Yahweh.*

28 *They will not have title to any grant;*[129] *I am their grant. You shall not give*[130] *them a possession in Israel; I am their possession.*

113. The verbs in Hebrew are pl. in form, but the objects are sg.

114. On the adversative use of *kî ʾim* see above on v. 10.

115. *bĕtûlat mizzeraʿ bêt yiśrāʾēl,* lit. "virgins from the seed of the house of Israel." LXX and Syr. omit *bêt,* but see 20:5 for support for MT.

116. LXX κρίσιν αἵματος interprets *rîb* narrowly as "a case of blood."

117. Kethib *yʿmdw lšpṭ,* "they shall stand to judge," is supported by LXX, Syr., and Targ., against Qere *yʿmdw lmšpṭ,* "they shall stand for judgment."

118. LXX and Targ. rightly support Qere *yšpṭhw,* in place of Kethib *wšpṭhw,* though the suffix is not attested in the versions. On the Late Biblical Hebrew practice of attaching the third masc. suffix directly to a verb ending in *u/û,* see Rooker, *Biblical Hebrew in Transition,* pp. 86-87.

119. MT *bĕmišpāṭay,* "by my judgment." On *bet* introducing standard of measurement see BDB, p. 90c.

120. Lit. "They shall not go near for defilement." MT *ybwʾ* is a metathetical scribal error for *wybʾw.* Cf. 10:3; 36:20; etc.

121. On the adversative use of *kî ʾim* see n. 59 above.

122. Adding the copula to MT with many Hebrew mss., LXX, Vulg., and Syr.

123. Syr. adds *btwltʾ,* perhaps under the influence of Lev. 21:3 (Zimmerli, *Ezekiel 2,* p. 451).

124. LXX reads sg.

125. MT *wĕʾaḥărê ṭāhŏrātô,* "after he is clean." Syr. reads "after his pollution."

126. Following LXX, Syr., and one Hebrew ms., which assume *yispôr.* Kethib (followed by Vulg. and Targ.) reads pl. *ysprw,* either in harmony with v. 25 or as an error of metathesis for *yspwr.*

127. Zimmerli (*Ezekiel 2,* p. 451) deletes *ʾel-haqqōdeš* as a superfluous gloss with LXX, but see Allen, *Ezekiel 28–40,* p. 246.

128. LXX reads the verbs as pl., probably under the influence of v. 25.

129. MT *wĕhāyĕtā lāhem lĕnaḥălâ,* lit. "And she shall become their special possession," makes no sense in the context, since it lacks a fem. antecedent. The construc-

29 *As for the grain, purification, and reparation offerings, they shall eat them. Every devoted thing in Israel shall belong to them.* 30 *The first of all the first ripened produce of all kinds, and every gift of whatever kind from all your gifts shall belong to the priests.*[131] *And the first of your dough you shall give to the priest to cause a blessing to rest over your homes.*[132]

31 *The priests shall not eat any bird or animal that has died naturally or been torn by a predator."*

♦ *Nature and Design*

Verses 17-31 are clearly distinguished from vv. 6-16 in style and form, as prophetic speech gives way to a catalogue of regulations governing the conduct of the priests. Remarkably, no subjects for the verbs appear in the composition until v. 21, from which one may conclude that, whatever their origin, an attempt has been made to integrate these ordinances, and that the list is intended as a continuation of the foregoing. The smooth transition from v. 16 to v. 17 suggests that the antecedents to the verbs, with their third masculine forms, must be the sons of Zadok, named in v. 15, a conclusion confirmed by the absence of the Levites from this text. The goal of this legislation, therefore, is to define in detail how the priests were to guard the sanctity of sacred space and demonstrate their own special holiness through their conduct.

Nevertheless, this section is not stylistically uniform. The second person of direct address is used in vv. 6-9 and resumed in vv. 28-30, leading some to conclude that these verses represent the original conclusion to the regulations for the priests in vv. 6-16.[133] Moreover, the plural forms in vv. 17-25 and 28-31 are interrupted by two verses that prefer the singular, suggesting to some scholars evidence of further editorial stages. But such con-

---

tion resembles *wĕhāyîtā lāhem lĕnaḥălâ*, where the land is the subject of the verb, but the land has not been mentioned previously in the context. Allen (*Ezekiel 20–48*, p. 246) suggests that the sentence originated as a comparative gloss on 45:18, which was then erroneously placed in the present column. The correct reading is suggested by Vulg. *non erit autem eis hereditas* and LXX[967] καὶ οὐκ ἔσται αὐτοῖς κληρονομία = *wĕlō' tihyeh lāhem naḥălâ*, which also suits the needs of the parallelism. Cf. *BHS*. NJPS and NRSV assume *zō't tihyeh lāhem naḥălâ*.

130. LXX reflects *lō' tuttan*, "It shall not be given."

131. Under the influence of the key word *kōl*, *yihyeh* is masc. instead of the expected fem. after *tĕrûmâ*.

132. LXX and Syr. read pl. *bāttêkem* (?) for MT sg. *bêtekā*, which disagrees with the verb *tittĕnû*.

133. Gese, *Verfassungsentwurf*, pp. 62-63; Zimmerli, *Ezekiel 2*, p. 453.

clusions regarding the evolution of the text are speculative, being based on modern standards of literary consistency.

(a) Practical Instructions for the Zadokites (44:17-27)

The shift in style in v. 17 is determined by the source of vv. 17-27. Most of these ordinances are lifted out of the Mosaic Torah, highlighting again the continuity between Yahweh's past relationships with his people and his designs for the future, though with some tightening of the rules. The sanctity of the priests, which must reflect the sanctity of the God whom they serve, is to be evident in all their actions, professional and private.

17-19 *Rule one:* the priestly clothing. Beginning the priestly regulations with the subject of clothing, Ezekiel emphasizes that when priests enter into the inner court to perform the rituals, they are to wear linen clothing.[134] The entire priestly uniform was to be made of linen, from the turban (*pĕʾēr*) to the undergarments *(miknāsîm)*. But these garments were to be worn only while the priests were functioning in an official capacity. Prior to their entrance into the inner court they were to exchange their regular clothing for priestly vestments in the *sacred chambers (liškôt haqqōdeš)*, a reference to the special rooms encountered earlier during the temple tour (42:1-14). After the rituals had been completed, but before leaving the inner court the priests were to return to the chambers to change back into their everyday clothes.

Ezekiel also spells out the rationale for these ordinances. Garments made of wool *(ṣemer)* are forbidden because this material causes the wearer to perspire, and like other bodily excretions, sweat was considered defiling (Deut. 23:12-14 [Eng. 11-13]).[135] The reason for banning the wearing of priestly vestments among the people is the obverse of the rationale for the prohibition of wool. Whereas wearing wool would violate sacred space through defilement, wearing sacred vestments out among the people would violate the holiness of the temple by distributing its sanctity, a notion that will return in 46:10. There is no need for Ezekiel to elaborate on the contagion of holiness because the idea was commonly accepted. Just as communicable diseases are spread by germs or viruses, so holiness may attach itself to a person. While the people were charged to live ethically holy lives, contact

---

134. *pištîm,* "flax plant." In 40:3 the word identifies a flax rope. Cf. Ezekiel's earlier reference to ordinary linen with *baddîm* (9:2, 11; 10:2, 6, 7), which is also common in the Mosaic Torah (Exod. 28:42; 39:28; Lev. 6:3; 16:4; etc.), and fine luxury linen as *šēš* (Ezek. 16:10, 13; 27:7).

135. With *yezaʿ*, a hapax, cf. *zēʿâ* in Gen. 3:19. The root is related to Akk. *izūtu/zūtu,* "sweat." Cf. *AHW,* p. 1539; Garfinkel, *Akkadian Influences,* p. 87. Cf. Herodotus's description of the scrupulosity of the Egyptian cult officials, who were continually washing their linen garments (*Hist.* 2.37).

with holy objects was a strict taboo.[136] In extending this ordinance to priestly garments Ezekiel adopts a stricter stance than the Mosaic Torah, which, in warning about the contagion of holiness, prohibits lay contact with the sanctuary, its furnishings and objects, but avoids any reference to the priest's clothing.[137] While Ezekiel was undoubtedly aware of the lethal consequences of holy contagion, his present concern is not the potential victims but protecting the sanctity of the sanctuary.

20 *Rule two:* the priestly hair. Ezekiel's ordinance demands that priests neither shave *(gilleaḥ)* their heads completely, nor let their locks *(pera')* grow long and hang loosely *(šilleaḥ)* on their shoulders. This requirement is obviously inspired by Lev. 21:5, 10, which adds the taboo of shaving the edges of the beards and cutting the flesh to the prohibition on shaving the head. While neither context offers a rationale for the regulation given, one could interpret the association of these practices with grief and mourning rites[138] as a prohibition on mourning by the priest. But shaving the head was also associated with the cult of the dead. If the ordinary Israelites were to abstain from any practices that might be interpreted as pagan, how much more the priests? But the fact that Ezekiel transforms a custom associated with mourning to a general regulation for the priesthood suggests a third consideration. Like scarred skin, both the shaved head and long, unkempt hair were considered signs of disfigurement (cf. Lev. 19:27). If the sacrificial animals were to be without defect or blemish, how much more those functionaries who stand before the holy God in service?

21 *Rule three:* the priestly drink. Ezekiel's prohibition of wine prior to entrance into the inner court is inspired by Lev. 10:9. While it is tempting to recognize here a taboo on pagan cultic intoxication, it is preferable to see in this ordinance a recognition of the numbing and deluding effects of alcohol on the mind.[139] When he entered the court, the priest was to be focused on

---

136. The lethal effects of such contact are explicitly declared in Num. 4:15 and illustrated in 1 Sam. 6:19 (more than 50,000 men of Beth-shemesh were struck down because some had looked inside the ark of the covenant) and 2 Sam. 6:6-9 (Uzzah was struck dead for touching the ark, despite his noble intention of protecting it). On the contagion of holiness see Haran, *Temples and Temple-Service,* pp. 175-77; Milgrom, *Leviticus,* pp. 443-56.

137. See Exod. 29:37; 30:26-30. According to Milgrom (*Leviticus,* p. 447) the placement of "Whatever touches them will become holy" at the end of v. 29 intentionally excludes the priests (and their garments) from the taboo.

138. Cf. Job 1:20; Jer. 7:29; Mic. 1:16. See my *Ezekiel: Chapters 1–24,* pp. 261-62, and above on 27:31.

139. On pagan cultic intoxication cf. *Enuma Elish* 3.134-38 (*ANET,* p. 66). On the numbing effects cf. Gen. 9:21; Hos. 4:11; Prov. 20:1; 23:29-35. On the deluding effects see esp. Isa. 28:7.

his task and in total control of his faculties. Inebriation opens the door to desecration of sacred space.

22 *Rule four:* the priestly marriage. Ezekiel's ordinance demands the same scrupulosity in the priests' choice of wives as in all other aspects of their lives. Widows of deceased laymen and divorcees were disqualified; only virgins of Israelite descent or widows of priests were permitted. This regulation is briefer than the Mosaic antecedent in Lev. 21:7, 14-15, which also forbids the marrying of a harlot. No justification for the regulation is offered, though Ezekiel undoubtedly assumed that the traditional reasons still applied. According to the Mosaic ordinance, the exclusions arose from a concern for sacred "seed" *(zera')*, the dilution of the purity of the priestly line. But Ezekiel's ordinance is less restrictive; he allows marriage with virgins outside the priestly clan — any Israelite virgin is a candidate — and for widows, provided their previous husbands were priests, since her previous contact with a priest had not compromised her holiness.

23-24 *Rule five:* the priest's public roles. These verses are distinguished from the preceding in both style and substance as the focus shifts from the priests' cultic service before Yahweh to their function in Israelite society, referred to by Yahweh affectionately as "my people." Three dimensions of their public role are specified. First, the priests are commanded to educate the people in matters holy *(qōdeš)* and profane *(ḥōl)*, unclean *(ṭāmē')* and clean *(ṭāhôr)*. The verb *hôrâ*, "to instruct," echoes the substantive *tôrâ*, "instruction," in 43:12; and although the word never occurs in Ezekiel, underlying *hôdîa'* is the noun *da'at*, "knowledge."[140] This verse conflates Lev. 10:10-11, which first highlights the necessity of the priest to make these same distinctions, and then speaks of the priest's responsibility to teach *(hôrâ)* Israel all the statutes *(ḥuqqîm)* that Yahweh had communicated to Moses.

Second, the priests are charged with responsibility for the administration of justice. In disputes *(rîb)* they are to *officiate as judges* (*'āmad lišpōṭ*, lit. "stand to judge"). The verb "to stand" is not to be taken literally, but in the sense of "to take their official place," since in judicial proceedings judges customarily sat (cf. Exod. 18:13), while the disputants stood before him (Num. 35:12). According to Exod. 18:19-22, Moses retained the responsibility for teaching the statutes *(ḥuqqîm)* and the instructions *(tôrôt)*, but he assigned to appointed elders the task of settling disputes within the community. Nevertheless, the judicial role of the religious functionaries in Israel has a long history. Deut. 33:10 perceives this role as a natural corollary to the Levites' teaching

---

140. So Zimmerli, *Ezekiel 2*, p. 460. On the priestly role in imparting/guarding *tôrâ* and *da'at* see Hos. 4:6 and Mal. 2:7. On the didactic function of the Levites see the Blessing of Moses, Deut. 33:10.

responsibilities.[141] But Ezekiel's placement of this charge specifically in the hands of the priests appears to follow Deut. 17:8-13 and 19:15-21, the latter of which speaks of litigants standing before Yahweh while the judicial priests[142] hear the case. The expression *according to my laws (běmišpāṭay)* identifies the standard of judgment by which the priests are to render decisions.[143] Ezekiel's reference to *mišpāṭay* may allude to a specific record of divine decisions in legal cases, such as those found in Exod. 21–23,[144] or he may simply be referring to the divine standards in general. Obviously no record of past decisions could foresee every possible future case. As the representative of Yahweh, the priest was expected to be able to discern the will of Yahweh and to apply it in each new situation.

Third, the priests were to be models of obedience to the will of God. The expressions *tôrōtay,* "my instructions," *ḥuqqōtay,* "my decrees," *kol-mô'ăday,* "all my appointed feasts," and *šabbôtay,* "my Sabbaths," cover the entire range of divine expectations: civil, moral, religious, and cultic. Under the assumption "like people, like priest" (Hos. 4:9), the burden of resolving the earlier problems (cf. Ezek. 22:26) rests on the shoulders of the priestly class. The call for a holy people begins at the top.

25-27   *Rule six:* the priestly responsibilities toward the dead. Resuming the style of vv. 17-22,[145] these verses continue the concern for priestly purity by regulating the priests' contact with the dead. Specifically, they were permitted to make funeral arrangements only for their immediate relatives: father, mother, son, daughter, brother, unmarried sister. In eliminating the opportunities for ritual defilement through contact with the corpses of laypeople, Ezekiel's ordinance agrees with the Mosaic Torah (Lev. 21:1-3). Whether Ezekiel would have followed the Mosaic Torah in prohibiting all contact with the dead by the high priest (Lev. 21:11) is unknown, since the high priest is never mentioned in chs. 40–48.[146] The cryptic prescription for purification following defilement (v. 26) assumes familiarity with the rituals spelled out in detail in the Mosaic Torah (Num. 19). The defiled person is to

141. With the establishment of the monarchy most of the judicial responsibility appears to have been assumed by the king and his appointed judges (cf. 1 Sam. 8:5-6, 20).

142. *hakkōhănîm wěhaššōpěṭîm,* lit. "the priests and the judges," is either a hendiadys or a word pair linked by the epexegetical *waw.*

143. Similar constructions occur in 7:27 and 23:24, though both passages have in view human rather than divine standards.

144. So Zimmerli, *Ezekiel 2,* p. 461.

145. Zimmerli's suggestion (ibid.) that these verses originally followed v. 22 is appealing, though overly reliant on modern standards of stylistic consistency.

146. Why Ezekiel's Torah omits any reference to the high priest is unclear. Does he envision a more democratized priesthood? Or does the *nāśî',* "prince," as patron of the cult render a high priest superfluous?

be washed with specially prepared purification water on the third and seventh days after the defilement. At the end of the week he shall be considered cleansed from his impurity and fit again to resume his spiritual duties. Upon his return to the temple his first act must be the presentation of his purification offering (ḥaṭṭā't).

The concluding signatory formula (v. 27) not only brings Ezekiel's regulations for the priests to an end; it adds solemnity to these ordinances and places them on a par with the Mosaic Torah: this too is divine torah.

(b) The Special Status of the Zadokites (44:28-31)

Verses 28-30 introduce a new theme, the priests' titled property, that will be picked up and developed more fully in ch. 45. The allusions to Num. 18:8-20 and the return to the second person plural forms in vv. 28b and 30a (cf. vv. 6-8) suggest that vv. 28-30 may have originally followed immediately after vv. 6-16.[147] By contrast, v. 31 continues the list of regulations for the priests in vv. 17-28. How or why vv. 28-30 were separated from their original context is a mystery. The aim of vv. 28-30 is to define the special status of the priests. This is achieved in two ways.

28 First, Yahweh offers the priests special title to himself. Whereas grants of land will later be bestowed on the rest of the Israelites (chs. 47–48), here Yahweh gives himself to the priests. Ezekiel uses two traditional designations for these awards: naḥălâ and 'ăḥuzzâ. The first is usually translated with inheritance terminology, on the assumption that Yahweh is the divine father and Israel his firstborn son.[148] The patrimonial overtones often recede into the background, however, and feudal nuances come to the fore.[149] Accordingly, Yahweh is perceived as the divine overlord who divides his land among his vassals and gives it to them as a grant. The second, which derives from 'āḥaz, "to seize, grasp," is more general and juristic than naḥălâ,[150] referring to a legal holding. In the present context the two terms should not be distinguished too finely. Both refer to property granted to a subject by the divine Lord.

Yahweh's offer of himself to the priests is announced with an emphatic twofold declaration:

147. So also Cooke, *Ezekiel*, p. 488; Gese, *Verfassungsentwurf*, p. 64; Zimmerli, *Ezekiel 2*, p. 461.

148. C. J. H. Wright, *God's People in God's Land*, pp. 18-20.

149. Cf. Block, *Gods of the Nations*, pp. 76-79.

150. Thus F. Horst, "Zwei Begriffe für Eigentum (Besitz): naḥălâ und 'ăḥuzzâ," in *Verbannung und Heimkehr: Beiträge zur Geschichte und Theologie Israels im 6. und 5. Jahrhundert v. Chr.*, Fest. W. Rudolph, ed. A. Kuschke (Tübingen: Mohr, 1961), pp. 153-56.

'ănî naḥălātām   **"I am their grant."**
'ănî 'ăḥuzzātām   **"I am their possession."**

The statements are remarkable not only for the divine condescension they express but also for the manner in which they adapt ancient traditions. The notion of Yahweh as the portion of his people has a long history. According to the ancient Song of Moses, whereas Yahweh divided the nations among their respective "sons of God"[151] and gave to them their *naḥălâ,* he reserved his people (*'ammô*) as his own portion (*ḥēleq/naḥălâ*). The precedent for Ezekiel's reversal of these roles is found in Num. 18:20, where Yahweh declares to Aaron: "You shall have no [land] grant (*lō' tinḥāl*); you shall have no portion (*ḥēleq*); I am your portion (*ḥēleq*) and your grant (*naḥălâ*) in the midst of the descendants of Israel."[152] As in the original context, the statement in our text highlights the spiritual charge of the Zadokites. They are not granted access to real estate, but to Yahweh himself.

29-30   Second, Yahweh admits the priests to his table. On first sight, these verses appear simply to provide for the physical well-being of the priests. In the absence of land of their own they are dependent for their welfare on the gifts of the rest of the Israelites. But this interpretation misses the point. Whereas in v. 16 Yahweh had authorized the Zadokites to approach his table, otherwise known as the altar (40:46), now they are invited to eat Yahweh's food. Seven items are listed in the priests' menu: (1) grain offerings (*minḥâ*), (2) purification offerings (*ḥaṭṭā't*), (3) reparation offerings ('*āšām*), (4) every irredeemable devoted thing (*ḥērem*), (5) the best of the firstfruits of every kind (*rē'šît kol-bikkûrê kōl*), (6) every single contribution (*kol-tĕrûmat kōl mikkōl tĕrûmôtêkem*), (7) even the best of the Israelites' dough (*rē'šît 'ări-sôtêkem*). These seven entries highlight the comprehensiveness of the priests' access to Yahweh's table. With the notable exception of the '*ôlâ,* "burnt offering," all that the Israelites bring to him they may enjoy.

The first three items have appeared together earlier in 42:13 and require no further comment. The fourth, *ḥērem,* which occurs only here in Ezekiel, may carry two different meanings. On the one hand, in both biblical and extrabiblical sources the noun may denote that which is totally devoted to Yahweh and condemned for destruction under the terms of the holy war.[153] This may include humans, animals, fields, cities, and metal objects. On the

151. *bny 'lm,* according to 4QDt and LXX ἀγγέλων Θεοῦ. MT reads *bny yśr'l,* "sons of Israel." For a discussion of this text see Block, *Gods of the Nations,* pp. 13-22.
152. Elsewhere the grant is extended to the entire tribe of Levi: Deut. 10:9; 18:2; Josh. 13:33. Cf. Josh. 18:7, which identifies the grant of the Levites as *kĕhunnat yhwh,* "the priesthood of Yahweh."
153. Cf. Deut. 7:26; 13:16-18; Josh. 6:13, 17-18; 7:1-2, 13, 15; 22:20; 1 Sam. 15:21; 1 K. 20:42; cf. the Mesha Inscription, line 17 (*KAI,* 181.17).

other hand, *ḥērem* also designates items proscribed for any use, except that which was prescribed for the cult.[154] The present context, which authorizes the priests to eat the *ḥērem,* obviously demands the latter interpretation. The fourth category of offering denotes the choice produce of the first cutting of grain, and the first picking of grapes and olives and any other kind of crop.[155] The designation for the fifth, *těrûmâ,* which has been encountered earlier in 20:40 and will figure prominently again in chs. 45 and 48, derives from *rûm,* "to be high," and denotes a gift set aside by its owner and transferred to God's possession.[156] Although most understand *'ărisôt* in the seventh item as coarse meal, this interpretation is uncertain. The problem is compounded by the fact that the word *'ărîsâ* occurs only here, in Num. 15:20, 21, and in Neh. 10:38, always with *rē'šît* and always as a gift for the priests. My translation follows LXX, though the targumic rendering and rabbinic usage of *'ărîsâ* suggest a link with the kneading trough.

There is nothing creative about Ezekiel's list of offerings. Except for the last item, which derives from Num. 15:20, 21, every entry is mentioned in Num. 18:8-20, under the title of *těrûmōtāy* and *kol-qōdeš haqqodāšîm,* "my gifts, all the most holy things" (cf. the latter in Ezek. 45:13). Aaron and his priestly clan are given full authorization to eat from all of Yahweh's offerings, which are holy for them (v. 10) and set aside as sacred meals for priestly use.[157] The present legislation recognizes the Zadokites as the true heirs of the Aaronids.

The list of gifts for the priests concludes with a final motivation: to ensure the divine blessing on the Israelites' houses. This correlation between scrupulosity in offering gifts to Yahweh, that is, to the priests, is reminiscent of Deut. 24:19, but as Num. 6:22-27 asserts, one of the priests' special roles within the community was to pronounce the blessing of Yahweh on the people. Accordingly, the people's own well-being was ultimately dependent on their generosity.

31 *Rule seven:* the priestly proscription on unclean food. An unexpected prohibition, with stylistic links to vv. 17-27, brings this subunit to a

154. Cf. Lev. 27:21, 28-29; Num. 18:14. See further Levine, *In the Presence of the Lord,* pp. 129-30.

155. Milgrom (*Leviticus,* pp. 190-91) distinguishes *rē'šît* from *bikkûrîm* as "first-processed" and "first-ripened" produce, respectively.

156. The term finds Akkadian cognates in *tarīmtu* and *rīmūtu.* For discussions of the term see Milgrom, *Studies in Cultic Theology,* pp. 159-72; idem, *Numbers,* pp. 226-27; idem, *Leviticus,* pp. 473-85.

157. According to vv. 25-29, the Israelites were commanded to present one-tenth of their produce to the Levites. But of this tithe the best, i.e., Yahweh's portion, was to be set aside for Aaron the priest and his clan. See further O. Eissfeldt, *Erstlinge und Zehnten im Alten Testament: Ein Beitrag zur Geschichte des israelitisch-jüdischen Kultus,* BWANT 22 (Leipzig: Hinrichs, 1917), pp. 65-67.

close. The proscription on eating carrion of any kind, whether it has died a natural death or been killed by a predator, presents a stark contrast with the preceding menu for the priests. This proscription echoes the general ban on eating carrion for all Israelites in Exod. 22:30 (Eng. 31), but seems to have been inspired by Lev. 22:8, in which the regulation is specifically applied to the Aaronids. In any case, Ezek. 4:14 demonstrates that the prophet was familiar with these proscriptions. As under the Mosaic constitution, so in Ezekiel's new order, everything about the life and conduct of the Levitical priests was designed to maintain their sanctity, and with this the sanctity of the temple.

♦ *Theological Implications*

In the light of the abolition of the Levitical/Aaronic priesthood in Christ (Heb. 7) and the democratization, or, more properly, the expansion of the priesthood to the corporate body of Christ (1 Pet. 2:5, 9), the theological and practical relevance of this text may escape the Christian reader. On reflection, however, several extremely important theological lessons emerge.

First, from a pastoral theological perspective, this passage reminds the reader that the call to spiritual leadership comes from God alone. The isolation of the Levites as guardians of Ezekiel's temple has its roots many centuries earlier, not only in the separation of the Levites under Moses; seeds can be recognized much earlier in Jacob's blessing of the eponymous ancestor (Gen. 49:5-7). While this pronouncement looks more like a curse than a blessing, the prediction of the dispersal of Levi among the Israelites will later find its fulfillment in an incredibly positive light, as Yahweh appoints them as his own special agents of grace to the nation. The calls of the Levites (Mal. 2:4-5), Aaronids, and Zadokites were all rooted in his sovereign choice. Similarly in the church, ministers of God are not self-appointed; theirs is a vocation (rather than a profession) resting entirely on the sovereign calling of God.

Second, the privilege of ministry in the kingdom of God carries with it the awesome burden of responsibility for the welfare of God's people. Vv. 23-24 are illuminating in suggesting how this charge is fulfilled: (1) by instructing the community of faith in the divine standards of holiness and purity; (2) by settling disputes among God's people using divine standards as a basis of judgment; (3) by scrupulously modeling obedience to the will of God.[158]

Third, the extension of the priesthood to all believers in the NT heightens, rather than lessens, the spiritual demands placed on lay members of the community of faith. Under the old order maintaining the sanctity of the temple

---

158. For a telling analysis of this responsibility see K. Menninger, *Whatever Became of Sin?* (New York: Hawthorn, 1973), pp. 192-205.

was the charge of a special class. Under the new all believers are called to a life of purity and holiness, for the praise of him who has called them out of darkness into his marvelous light (1 Pet. 2:10).

Fourth, in Christ believers find not only the perfect and final sacrifice for their sins, but also the perfect example of priestly responsibility. The sinless one has provided a pattern for all who follow in his spiritual lineage.

e. Regulations Regarding Priestly and Princely Lands (45:1-8a)

1 *"When you subdivide[1] the land as a grant, from the land you shall reserve a gift for Yahweh. It shall be a holy district, twenty-five thousand cubits long,[2] and twenty thousand[3] cubits wide. It shall be holy throughout its entire area.* 2 *Of this[4] area a full square five hundred cubits by five hundred cubits shall be reserved[5] for the sanctuary. The sanctuary in turn shall be surrounded by an open space fifty cubits deep.* 3 *And from this measured-off area you shall measure[6] off [an area] twenty-five thousand[7] cubits long and ten thousand cubits wide, in which shall stand the sanctuary, the most holy place of all.* 4 *It is sacred,[8] set off from[9] the land. It shall be designated for the priests who serve in the sanctuary, and who approach Yahweh to serve him. It shall be a place for their houses, as well as the holy area for the sanctuary.*[10] 5 *An additional property twenty-five thousand cubits long*

1. *ûbĕhappîlĕkem,* lit. "When you cast [lots]."

2. The duplication of *'ōrek* before and after the number represents a conflated reading. Either position is possible (cf. vv. 3, 5), but Ezekiel generally prefers the measurement dimension before the number, in keeping with a trend in Late Biblical Hebrew. See Rooker, *Biblical Hebrew in Transition,* pp. 113-14.

3. With LXX, assuming an original *'eśrîm 'elep,* as in vv. 3, 5, contra MT and Targ. *'ăśārâ 'elep,* "ten thousand."

4. Contra Zimmerli (*Ezekiel 2,* p. 465), the antecedent of masc. *mizzeh* is *gĕbûl,* not distant fem. *tĕrûmâ.*

5. LXX adds the copula, which might reflect *wĕhāyâ 'el* in the *Vorlage.* On this use of *'el* see 40:16.

6. Since the pl. form suits the context better, *BHS* and most commentators treat *tmwd* as an error of metathesis for *tmdw.*

7. Reading *ḥmšh* with Qere instead of Kethib's *ḥmš.*

8. Most delete *qōdeš* with LXX*, linking the last part of v. 3 to v. 4, which yields "It will be the most sacred part of the country" (cf. Allen, *Ezekiel 20–48,* pp. 240, 246). But MT is not ungrammatical.

9. Treating the *min* as partitive.

10. LXX ἀφωρισμένους τῷ ἁγιασμῷ αὐτῶν and Targ. *wkbš' lmqdš'* reflect an original *wmgrš lmqdš,* suggesting that MT *wmqdš lmqdš* is dittography. But the former may just as well have been the result of careless readings of the original. The proposed emendation *(BHS)* of *lmqdš* to *lmqnh* after Josh. 14:4 and 21:2 is speculative.

and ten thousand cubits wide shall belong[11] to the Levites who take care of the temple. It shall belong to them as their possession, their cities to live in.[12]

6 Alongside the sacred reserve, you shall set aside the city property, five thousand cubits wide and twenty-five thousand cubits long.[13] It shall belong to the entire house of Israel.

7 And [you shall set aside space][14] for the prince, on each side of the holy reserve and the city property, in front of the holy reserve on the west and east sides.[15] Its length shall correspond[16] to the [tribal] territories from the western[17] border to the eastern border 8a of the land.[18] And it shall be his possession in Israel."

♦ *Nature and Design*

Chapter 45 opens abruptly without formal introduction and with a jarring change of subject: the territorial *tĕrûmâ* for Yahweh. On first sight the citation formula in v. 9 appears to signal the beginning of the next subunit, but the singular suffix on *lô* in v. 8a points back to *nāśî'*, "prince," in v. 7, suggesting that the first clause in the verse closes this section. With regard to its genre, 45:1-8a finds its closest analogue in 48:8-22, where the allocation of the priestly and princely properties is described in even greater detail. While these two texts are linked by numerous lexical and stylistic features and a parallel sequence of topics (sanctuary, priests, Levites, city, prince), the relationship between the two is uncertain. Most interpret 45:1-8a as an excerpt from the

11. Retaining Kethib's *yhyh* rather than Qere's erroneous *whyh*. Cf. vv. 4, 6.

12. MT *'eśrîm lĕšākōt* is attested in Targ., Vulg., and Syr., but it makes little sense in the context. Emendation to *'rym lšbt*, "cities to live in," following LXX πόλεις τοῦ κατοικεῖν, is preferable. Cf. Barthélemy, et al., eds., *Preliminary and Interim Report*, 5:178-79. Presumably at an early date a *kaph* was mistakenly written for *beth* in the second word, and a *śin* mistakenly inserted in the first word, perhaps under the influence of the surrounding text.

13. Except for here and 48:8 (as well as Zech. 2:6 [Eng. 2]), elsewhere *'ōrek*, "length," always precedes *rōḥab*, "width."

14. The verb *tittĕnû* in v. 6 serves v. 7 as well.

15. *mippĕ'at yām yāmmâ ûmippĕ'at qēdmâ qādîmâ*, lit. "to the west westward and to the east eastward." The *hē* directive on *qēdmâ* should probably be dropped to correspond with the previous *yām*, and the word repointed as *qādîm*.

16. The pl. form *lĕ'ummôt* is unprecedented and is generally read as sg. *lĕ'ummat*. However, Rooker (*Biblical Hebrew in Transition*, p. 77) observes that the form agrees with the pluralizing tendency found in Late Biblical Hebrew.

17. LXX πρὸς θάλασσαν and the parallel *qādîmâ* support *yāmmâ* in place of MT *yām*.

18. Linking *lā'āreṣ* to v. 7 with LXX, and reading *yhyh* as *wyhy*. Cf. v. 5.

later statement.[19] It is preferable, however, to view the later text as an expansion of the present passage. First, 45:1-8a is intentionally integrated into the Torah of the temple (44:4–46:18). Its hinge position is apparent in its placement at the midpoint of this unit and in its relationship to its literary environment, as the following chart demonstrates:[20]

Priestly Concerns		Princely Concerns
(44:5-31)		(45:8b–46:18)
44:5-8	Description of Past Offenses	45:8b-12
44:9-27	The New Responsibilities	45:13–46:15
44:28-31	Inheritance and Possession	46:16-18

Priestly and Princely Concerns:

The Allotment of Land 45:1-8a

The switch from priestly to princely concerns occurs within vv. 1-8a, with vv. 1-5 dealing with the priestly real estate allotments *('ăhuzzâ),* v. 6 with the whole house of Israel, and vv. 7-8a with the prince. Second, the strategy of resumptive exposition, dealing briefly with a subject only to drop it, but then returning to it later for fuller development, is characteristic of the book. This feature may be purely editorial, but it seems to reflect authentic Ezekielian style. Indeed, the seeds of vv. 1-8a were sown in 44:28-30. *'ăhuzzâ,* which appears in 44:28 with Yahweh's self-introduction as the special grant *(nahălâ)* and "possession" *('ăhuzzâ)* of the priests, reappears five times in 45:5-8. *těrûmâ,* a special designation for people's gifts for the priests, which occurs twice in 44:30a, reappears four times in 45:1, 6-7, albeit with a different nuance. The reference to priestly property in 44:28 may have triggered the present elaboration and adaptation. Combining these three texts, a three-stage evolution of Ezekiel's thinking on the priestly patrimony emerges:

I. The priests have no land that they may call their own; their patrimony *('ăhuzzâ)* is Yahweh himself (44:28).
II. The priests may build their houses on the property reserved for Yahweh *(těrûmâ layhwh),* the area set apart as sacred *(qōdeš min-hā'āreṣ,* 45:1-5).
III. The priests' allotments shall surround the allotment on which the sanctuary is located, and the Levites' allotments shall surround these. But the ownership of all by Yahweh stands (48:8-20).

---

19. Zimmerli, *Ezekiel 2,* p. 467; Hals, *Ezekiel,* p. 323; Allen, *Ezekiel 20–48,* p. 264. Wevers (*Ezekiel,* p. 324) suggests that this summary version was placed here as a corrective to 44:28.

20. Cf. Parunak, *Structural Studies,* pp. 522-23.

1-4 This section opens with a temporal clause, anticipating the apportionment of the land of Israel among its residents. The expression *ûběhappîlěkem 'et-hā'āreṣ,* "when you cast the land," represents an elliptical variant for the fuller "when you cast the lot *(gôrāl)*" for the land.[21] Although Ezekiel employs different verbs,[22] the image of dividing up territory by means of the lot is inspired by two OT texts. Num. 26:53-56 prescribes the division of the land of Canaan among the twelve tribes of Israel as territorial spoils of holy war against the inhabitants (cf. also 33:54; 34:13; 36:2-3); Josh. 18:6-10 describes the fulfillment of these prescriptions. The use of the lot reflects the conviction that Yahweh owns the land and has authority to distribute it to whomever he pleases.[23] Ezekiel envisions the present prescriptions regarding Yahweh's *těrûmâ* transpiring in the context of the reapportionment of the land among the tribes of Israel. However, the divine allotment would not be identified by lot. The area described here was reserved in advance by Yahweh himself.

Two expressions highlight the significance of the land set apart for Yahweh. First, *reserve a gift for Yahweh.* Whereas the cultic expression *hērîm těrûmâ layhwh* (lit. "raised as a contribution for Yahweh") is used elsewhere of movable property of different kinds presented as gifts to Yahweh,[24] Ezekiel's application of the phrase to real estate here and later in 48:8-10 is unique. By designating this donation a *těrûmâ,* Ezekiel portrays the land as a gift that may be handed back to the gracious divine benefactor. On the analogy of the first loaf of bread offered to Yahweh in Num. 15:19-20, one may assume that this territory was to be set apart for Yahweh prior to the allocation of the tribal lands. Although Yahweh identifies the land to be set aside for himself, the use of the second person implies the involvement of the Israelites in the process. When the divine patron brings his people back home he assumes that they will administer it on his behalf. Second, the land is characterized as "a holy district separate from the rest of the land" *(qōdeš min-hā'reṣ).* The end of v. 1 declares that this sanctity extends to the entire area within its borders *(gěbûlāh).*

---

21. The abbreviated form recurs in 47:22 and 48:29. Cf. also 47:14b.

22. *ḥālaq běgôrāl* in Num. 26:55-56; *yārâ gôrāl* in Josh. 18:6; *hišlîk gôrāl* in Josh. 18:8; *hitnaḥēl běgôrāl* in Num. 33:54. Ezekiel's *nāpal* plus *gôrāl* had occurred earlier in 24:6. For other references to the Ezekielian variant of the idiom see Even-Shoshan, *Concordance,* pp. 231-32.

23. Yahweh's role in the original division of the land was highlighted further by having the lot cast *lipnê yhwh,* "before Yahweh" (Josh. 18:6, 8, 10). For a formal expression of divine sovereignty over the lot see Prov. 16:33.

24. Materials for the tabernacle (Exod. 35:24), bread dough (Num. 15:19-20), sacred gifts (18:19, 29), the tithe (18:24, 26, 28), gold acquired as booty (31:52). Cf. Milgrom, *Leviticus,* p. 473.

While the location of Yahweh's *tĕrûmâ* will not be disclosed until ch. 48, here Ezekiel focuses on its dimensions and layout.[25] According to v. 1b, the larger consecrated area is to be 25,000 cubits long and 20,000 cubits wide. Assuming the continued use of the long cubit as the unit of measurement,[26] the length computes to slightly more than 8 mi., and the width to almost 6½ mi., covering an area over 50 square mi. or 33,500 acres. According to v. 3 this tract is cut in half lengthwise, creating two strips 25,000 cubits long by 10,000 cubits wide. One of these strips was reserved for the sanctuary *(miqdāš)*, characterized as *qōdeš qodāšîm*, "the most holy place," and the homes of the priests. Rather than designating the priests by name as Zadokites (cf. 48:11), the instructions identify them by function as *mĕšārĕtê hammiqdāš*, "the ministers of the sanctuary," and *haqqĕrēbîm lĕšārēt 'et-yhwh*, "those who come near to minister to Yahweh."

Perhaps sensing the inappropriateness of mortals sharing a residential area with Yahweh, and filling in a detail necessary for understanding v. 3, Ezekiel/Yahweh interrupts the description in v. 2 to isolate the plot of land on which the sanctuary itself was to stand.[27] Ezekiel envisioned a 500-cubit square, surrounded by a protective no-man's-land, 50 cubits (about 85 ft.) wide, which would serve as a buffer protecting the absolute holiness of the sanctuary itself.[28] These dimensions agree with the measurements of the temple compound in 42:20.

5 Reflecting the distinctions drawn in ch. 44, the second 25,000-by-10,000 cubit strip of land was allocated for the second-rank cult personnel, the Levites, who are described professionally as *mĕšārĕtê habbayit*, "ministers of the temple complex."[29] In this context only the priests' portion is referred to by *naḥălâ;* the land of the Levites (and the people) is designated their *'ăḥuzzâ*. With this distinction, Ezekiel has drawn another literary wedge between the two classes of priests. The prophet anticipates the Levitical tract to be dotted by cities where they would live.[30]

25. For a sketch of the allotments described in this text see below, p. 733.

26. The long cubit was approximately 20.5 inches. See above on 40:5.

27. Because of its intrusiveness and the designation of the sanctuary as *haqqōdeš* (cf. *himmiqdāš* elsewhere in this context), most interpret this either as a secondary accretion under the influence of 42:15-20 (Zimmerli, *Ezekiel 2*, p. 468; Allen refers to it as an "afterthought," *Ezekiel 20–48*, p. 265), though some have proposed that v. 2 originally followed v. 4 (Cooke, *Ezekiel*, p. 493).

28. As noted above on 27:28, the term *migrāš* often refers to the common pastureland outside a walled settlement (Num. 35:2ff.; Josh. 21:11ff.). Cf. J. Barr, "*Migraš* in the Old Testament," *JSS* 29 (1984) 15-31, esp. p. 23 on Ezekiel's usage of the term.

29. Cf. the designation of the priests as *mĕšārĕtê hammiqdāš* in v. 4.

30. According to Haran (*Temples and Temple-Service*, p. 127), he undoubtedly also expects them to cultivate this land and to live off the produce (cf. 48:18).

The designation of the Levite settlements as *ʿārîm* recalls the Levitical cities prescribed in Num. 35:1-8. Instead of being scattered throughout the land of Israel, however, the Levitical cities shall be concentrated in the sacred area next to the property of the priests and the sanctuary itself. This is a practical arrangement, since their commission involves sanctuary ministry. Ezekiel is also silent on the pasturelands *(migrāš)* for the Levites' livestock. Perhaps the prophet envisioned the people sustaining them through their contributions *(těrûmâ)* as they would the priests (cf. 44:30). But it appears from this legislation that the Levites must be satisfied with real estate.

6-8a   These verses move on to the next level of land holdings, referred to enigmatically as *ʾăhazzat hāʿîr*. This tract is to be 5,000 cubits (about 1.6 mi.) wide and 25,000 cubits (about 8 mi.) long, and is to be situated adjacent to the sacred reserve. It is accessible to the whole house of Israel, perhaps offering dormitory space for worshipers making their annual pilgrimages to the temple. To learn whether this strip was north or south of the sanctuary the reader must await ch. 48.

Verses 7-8a refocus on the *nāśîʾ*, who is to receive a special grant, two large tracts of land on either side, east and west, of the sacred reserve. While the dimensions of these properties are not specified (cf. 48:21-22), v. 7 suggests that the north-south distance of each plot equals the combined widths of the two strips set aside for the Levites and the priests (viz., 2 × 10,000 cubits) and the width of tract allocated for the city (5,000 cubits), yielding a combined width of 25,000 cubits. Given the special status of the *nāśîʾ* under Ezekiel's constitution (cf. 44:3), this allocation of a special *ʾăhuzzâ* within the nation of Israel is not surprising.

♦ *Theological Implications*

The cold tone and statistical nature of 45:1-8a should not blind the reader to the theological significance of Ezekiel's territorial design.

First, Yahweh remains the true landowner of the territory of Israel, retaining authority over its administration. This is reflected in the guidelines he provides for the distribution of properties among its inhabitants. The *těrûmâ layhwh* at the heart of the country symbolizes the locus of power.

Second, the sanctity of Yahweh and his temple is the driving force behind this territorial legislation. The central tract, 500 cubits square, is reserved for the sanctuary, the most holy place (vv. 3-4). This property is protected from defiling touch by a 50-cubit buffer *(migrāš, v. 2)*. Outside this open space, the priests who have access to Yahweh have their homes, though they do not possess the land on which their houses are built. The next level is set aside for the Levites, who maintain the temple but are prohibited from officiating in the rituals. Beyond this, one finds the area set apart for citizens coming to worship at the central shrine, and finally the land set aside for the head of state. Like the sanctuary itself, the properties are deliberately designed and assigned to reflect decreasing spheres of holiness as one moves outward from the core. Accordingly, as one moves inward from the outside, these more or less concentric rectangles reflect increasing restrictions on access, culminating in the sanctuary, where Yahweh alone dwells.

Third, the territorial scheme reflects the relative importance of the officials of state within the new constitution. The priests may not own land, but they have Yahweh as their possession, and they have access to him. The relatively inferior status of the Levites is reflected in their portion being farther removed from the core. While the role of the *nāśî'* has yet to be spelled out in detail, the location of his grant outside the sacred reserve reflects his relatively secular, nonpriestly role. Nevertheless, the size of his allotment provides a hint of his status within the nation. This is the one who is authorized to sit in the gate of the sanctuary as *nāśî'* (44:2).

f. Miscellaneous Regulations (45:8b-17)

(1) A Challenge for Princes (45:8b-9)

8b *"No longer shall my princes*[31] *oppress my people, but they shall permit*[32] *the house of Israel to have the land according to their tribes.* 9 *This is what the Lord*[33] *Yahweh has declared: You have gone far enough,*[34] *O princes of Israel! Put a stop to your violence*[35] *and abuse.*[36] *Practice what is just and right. Put an end*[37] *to your evictions of my people. The declaration of the Lord Yahweh."*

Framed by citation and signatory formulae, v. 9 looks like a fragment of a separate oracle, to which has been added v. 8b. Together vv. 8b-9 are transitional. While the content and tone change, the interest in *nĕśî'îm*, "princes,"

---

31. LXX reads *nĕśî'ê yiśrā'ēl,* "the princes of Israel."

32. On this use of *nātan* see Bertholet, *Hesekiel,* p. 159.

33. *'ădōnāy* is missing in most LXX mss., but LXX[B] reads κύριος Θεος.

34. On *rab lākem* see 44:6.

35. On *ḥāmās* see my *Ezekiel: Chapters 1–24,* pp. 255-56.

36. *šōd* occurs only here in Ezekiel, but it appears to have been a standard correlative for *ḥāmās* (Hab. 1:3; in reverse order, Jer. 6:7; 20:8; Amos 3:10). *ḥāmās wāšōd* may be interpreted as a hendiadys, "the violence of oppression," i.e., lawless behavior. Cf. Andersen and Freedman, *Amos,* p. 407.

37. Ezekiel's use of *hērîm* for "put an end to" or "stop," which is rare (cf. Dan. 8:11), may have been determined by the need for a correlative to the more common *hēsîr,* which occurs in v. 9a. See this use of the latter in Isa. 1:16; Ps. 66:20; Dan. 11:31.

and land links this segment to the preceding territorial legislation involving the *nāśî'*. In the verb *hārîmû* (v. 9) one may also hear an echo of *těrûmâ* (v. 1), which derives from the same root. However, the concern of this fragment with justice, specifically the catchword *ṣědāqâ/ṣedeq,* anticipates vv. 10-12.

The abrupt change from statistical legislation to accusation and appeal here catches the reader by surprise. Yahweh opens by announcing an end to oppressive rule by the princes of Israel. The plural form *něśî'îm* proves he is thinking not of *the nāśî'* of the future, but of the haunting figures of kings of the past.[38] Ezekiel had used the term *hônâ,* "oppress," earlier in 18:7, 12, 16, of a wicked man exploiting the poor and the needy, and in 22:7, 29, of wronging the fatherless and the widow. Here *hônâ* refers to a political leader's confiscation of commoners' real estate (see further 46:18). The best-known example in the OT involves the seizure of Naboth's land by Ahab and Jezebel, king and queen of the northern kingdom (1 K. 21). But Samuel's warning to the people of the "ways of kings" in 1 Sam. 8:14 suggests that this kind of behavior was widespread in the ancient world. In his vision of the future, however, Ezekiel consistently looks forward to righting all past wrongs. Here he declares that instead of confiscating the property of subjects, rulers are to protect the rights of all Israelites to their tribal allotments. The reference to the nation as *'ammî,* "my people," reflects the concord between deity and nation that should characterize the relationship between rulers and their inferiors as well.

The firmness of Yahweh's resolve to right past wrongs is reflected in the prophetic formulae bordering v. 9. His exasperation with the rulers of the past and his burden for the present are expressed in the opening line of his speech, *rab lākem něśî'ê yiśrā'ēl.*[39] Ezekiel's new order promises no utopia; the potential for exploitative rule still exists. In v. 9 Yahweh appeals to the princes directly, in the second person, to stop their abusive behavior, specified as violence *(ḥāmās),* oppression *(šōd),* and expulsion of the people from their land *(gāraš).* He calls for a new commitment to justice *(mišpāṭ)* and righteousness *(ṣědāqâ),* viz., the maintenance of Yahweh's covenant standards, especially the protection of the rights of the weak. To the cultic offenses of 44:6 have been added these moral sins. Yahweh has had enough of both.

---

38. For the future *nāśî'* see 44:3; 45:16-17; 46:1-18; 48:21-22. The pl. *něśî'îm,* which occurs only here in chs. 40–48, answers to *mělākîm* of 43:7-9, that is, the succession of Israelite monarchs, rather than a contemporaneous class. Cf. also 19:1ff.

39. Cf. 44:6. On *rab lākem* as an opening exclamation see Haran, *HUCA* 50 (1979) 49 n. 9.

(2) A Business Ordinance (45:10-12)

10 *"You shall maintain*[40] *honest weights,*[41] *and an honest ephah, and an honest bath.* 11 *The ephah and the bath shall be the same size, with the bath holding one-tenth of a homer, and the ephah holding one-tenth of a homer. Their capacities shall be based on the size of the homer.* 12 *The shekel shall weigh twenty gerahs. Twenty shekels plus twenty-five shekels plus fifteen shekels shall make up the minah for you."*[42]

The word order and jussive form of this fragmentary ordinance resemble similar regulations in the Holiness Code of the Mosaic Torah (Lev. 19:36).[43] This legislation may have circulated as an independent ordinance for all Israelites, like the Mosaic injunctions, but by placing it immediately after the appeal in v. 9, it has special relevance for the leaders of the nation. In an economic environment lacking official norms for weights and measures, merchants were particularly tempted to cheat their customers by falsifying balances and measurements. The former was achieved by using improper weights (shekels);[44] the latter by false bottoms and other means of altering the sizes of vessels. How prevalent such corruption was in the marketplace is evident from the frequency with which the prophets rail against the practice (e.g., Amos 8:5-6; Hos. 12:8 [Eng. 7]; Mic. 6:10-11). Reminiscent of the Mosaic Torah, which based the appeal for honest weights and measures on the character of Yahweh (Lev. 19:36), the wise man wrote, "A false weight (*mō'znê mirmâ*) is an abomination to Yahweh, but a just weight (*'eben šĕlēmâ*) is his delight" (Prov. 11:1; cf. 16:11; 20:10).

The balances, ephahs, and baths referred to represent the standard instruments of measurement with which any Israelite would have been familiar. The dual form of *mō'znayim* reflects the two-armed design of the balances, in which the weight of produce to be exchanged was determined by counterweights on the opposite side. The ephah was the dry standard used to measure

---

40. *yĕhî lākem*, lit. "let there be for you."

41. On *mō'znayim*, "balance, scale," see my *Ezekiel: Chapters 1–24*, p. 193.

42. The MT is difficult: the form for "fifteen," *'ăśārâ waḥămiššâ*, occurs only here (cf. GKC, §97d, e; Bauer-Leander, *Grammatik*, §79m, q), and the final *šeqel* is sg. when pl. is expected. Allen (*Ezekiel 20–48*, p. 247) conjectures that *ḥămiššâ wĕ'eśrîm*, "five and twenty," is a marginal note that found its way into the text, displacing *ḥămiššâ wĕ'eśrâ*, "five and ten." As for the other numbers, *'eśrîm*, "twenty," and *ḥămiššâ*, "five," were added to the text later under the influence of the numbers in the context. Most follow LXX.

43. Cf. an alternate form in Deut. 25:13-16.

44. Lev. 19:36 speaks of *'abnê ṣedeq*, "just stones."

grain.[45] Zech. 5:5-11 envisages an ephah as a basket large enough to hold a person, but the term was probably applied loosely to a large container. Ezekiel decrees that an ephah was to be one-tenth of a homer. Estimations of the size of a homer vary.[46] Most would accept a 220-liter homer, in which case the ephah would be approximately 22 liters (about 5.8 U.S. gal.). While the origin of *bat,* "bath," is unknown, texts like the present one suggest that it was a liquid measure.[47] Our text equates the size of the bath with that of the ephah, both fixed at one-tenth of a homer.

Verse 12 regulates the weights used with the balances. Whereas in 4:10 *šeqel* had denoted simply "weight," here it is used technically of a stone whose weight was to be fixed at 20 gerahs. The gerah was Israel's smallest unit of weight, equivalent to approximately 0.57 grams. By this calculation Ezekiel's standardized shekel would have weighed about 11.4 grams (0.4 oz.). Ezekiel's minah was to be the sum of 20 + 25 + 15 = 60 shekels. The evidence is not conclusive, but the standard Israelite minah is generally estimated at 50 shekels.[48] If MT is correct, Ezekiel's 60-shekel minah constitutes a metrological innovation, probably inspired by the sexagesimal Babylonian system.

(3) The *těrûmâ* Ordinance (45:13-17)

13 *"This is the offering you shall raise: one-sixth of an ephah from a homer*[49] *of wheat, and one-sixth*[50] *of an ephah from a homer of barley. 14 The prescribed amount of oil — measured in baths —* [51] *shall*

---

45. *'êpâ,* from Egyp. *ypt.* See *HALOT,* p. 43.

46. *ḥōmer* is related to Akk. *imēr,* "donkey load," a unit of measure attested in the 2nd-millennium Ugaritic texts *(ḥmr)* and widespread in Mesopotamia and among western Semites. The Hebrew homer ranged from a low of 134 liters (3.8 bushels) to a high of 230 liters (6.5 bushels). For discussion of these weights and measures see O. R. Sellers, *IDB,* 4:834-35; E. M. Cook, *ISBE,* 4:1048-51; M. A. Powell, *ABD,* 6:897-908.

47. Used for measuring oil, here and in Ezra 7:22; wine in 2 Chr. 2:10 (Eng. 9); wine and water in 1 K. 7:26.

48. Primarily because, where weights are given in the OT, they tend to be multiples of 50. Cf. Gen. 23:15; Exod. 30:24; Num. 31:52; 1 Sam. 15:5. *māneh* occurs four other times: 1 K. 10:17; Ezra 2:69; Neh. 7:71-72.

49. Targ., Vulg., and Syr. render *ḥōmer* as *kôr.* LXX reads γομορ here but κόρου in v. 13b.

50. In *wěšiššîtem* MT has created a new denominative Piel verb, "and you shall give one-sixth part," out of the ordinal *šiššît* (cf. Waltke-O'Connor, *Syntax,* §24.4h). The versions and the parallelism of the previous phrase argue for deletion of the final *mem,* which is probably due to wrong word division.

51. Most delete the appositional phrase *habbat haššemen,* lit. "the bath the oil," as a gloss, in spite of support from the versions. See Allen, *Ezekiel 20–48,* p. 247.

be one-tenth of a bath from each kor[52] *(ten baths equal one homer, because ten baths equal one homer).*[53] 15 *[The prescribed offering] from the flock shall be one sheep for every two hundred.*[54] *[These are the products] from the watered areas*[55] *of Israel that shall serve as grain offerings, whole burnt offerings, and peace offerings to make atonement for them*[56] — *the declaration of the Lord Yahweh.*

16 *All the people of the land*[57] *are obligated to*[58] *the prince in Israel in presenting this offering.* 17 *But the prince shall be responsible for the whole burnt offerings,*[59] *the grain offerings, and the libations at the festivals, the new moon celebrations, the Sabbaths, and all the other appointed convocations of the house of Israel. He shall provide the purification offerings, the grain offerings, the whole burnt offerings, and the peace offerings, to make atonement on behalf of the house of Israel.*"

zō't hattĕrûmâ 'ăšer tārîmû, "This is the *tĕrûmâ* offering that you shall present," functions as a formal heading for vv. 13-17, though vv. 10-12 provide necessary background, especially for vv. 13-15. In vv. 16-17, which shift stylistically to the third person of indirect address, the aim is to specify the role of the *nāśî'* in relation to the previous *tĕrûmâ* ordinance. However, this interest in the prince is immediately abandoned in favor of the annual pilgrimage festivals (vv. 18-25).

52. *min hakkōr* is mistakenly dropped in LXX.

53. A literal reading of MT. The first occurrence of this phrase is missing in LXX and usually deleted as dittography. Perhaps Vulg., which reads *kōr* in place of the second *ḥōmer,* points to an original that has been lost by assimilation. If so, the parenthetical comment equates the volumes of these two units of measurement. The present context, involving liquids, also supports *kōr; ḥōmer* is used to measure dry products.

54. LXX increases the demand by reading *hammā'tayim* as "ten."

55. *mimmišqēh,* from *šāqâ,* "to drink," is used in Gen. 13:10 of irrigation ditches, hence NRSV "pastures." Targ. *mptym',* "from the fatlings," treats the term metonymically. REB "clan" follows LXX in reading *mimmišpĕḥôt. BHS* follows Gese (*Verfassungsentwurf,* p. 70 n. 1) in emending to *mimmiqnēh,* "from the cattle."

56. LXX reads "for you."

57. *hā'āreṣ* is ungrammatical after *hā'ām* and is dropped by LXX. Gese (*Verfassungsentwurf,* p. 72) suggests that it entered the text under the influence of *'am hā'āreṣ* in v. 22 and 46:3. It is preferable, however, to read *kol 'am hā'āreṣ,* dropping the article on *hā'ām.*

58. On *hāyâ 'el,* "be obligated to," see Gese, *Verfassungsentwurf,* p. 71 n. 2.

59. Most emend *hā'ōlôt* to sg. *hā'ōlâ,* on the strength of numerous Hebrew mss. and the following entries in this list. The pl. is appropriate in the context, however, and many translations (including LXX) render the following sg. forms as pl. forms.

13-15 The actual *tĕrûmâ* instructions break down into three parts, regulating the taxing of grain, olive oil, and sheep, respectively, for the regular ritual sacrifices. The difference between the present use of *tĕrûmâ* and v. 1, where it identified a tract of land set apart for Yahweh, is obvious. But it is also distinguished from the *tĕrûmâ* mentioned in 44:30, where the word denoted the choice offerings of the first products of the harvest. Now *tĕrûmâ* is used nontechnically of those gifts that are donated for the regular sacrifices.[60] To provide for these offerings wheat and barley are to be taxed at the rate of ⅙ of an ephah for every homer of grain, which amounts to a ⅟60 levy, or 1.6 percent. The rate for olive oil is ⅟10 of a bath for every homer, or 1 percent.[61] Sheep are to be taxed at one animal per 200, that is, at the rate of 0.5 percent. The concluding statement indicates that these contributions are to be used for the grain *(minḥâ),* whole burnt *('ôlâ),* and peace *(šĕlāmîm)* offerings through which expiation *(kippēr)* could be achieved for the people. The divine signatory formula brings these instructions to a close.

16-17 These verses represent an added note clarifying the role of the *nāśî'* in these *tĕrûmâ* offerings. While active participation in the ritual of the cult is excluded, here he is presented as its patron and guardian. The citizens of the land[62] are accountable to him for the manner in which they respond to these obligations. As for the prince, he must make them available to the priests at the national festivals *(ḥaggîm):* the new moon festivities *(ḥŏdāšîm),* the sabbaths *(šabbātôt),* and all the other appointed celebrations. Furthermore, he must provide the victims/produce for all the sacrifices, which are listed in one of the most comprehensive catalogues in the OT: purification offering *(ḥaṭṭā't),* grain offering *(minḥâ),* burnt offering *('ôlâ),* peace offering *(šĕlāmîm),* and libations *(nēsek).*[63] Conspicuous for its absence is the reparation offering *('āšām),* but this list is not intended to be exhaustive; the frequency with which Ezekiel's Torah refers to the *'āšām* (40:39; 42:13; 44:29; 46:20) leaves no doubt about its inclusion in the regular cult ritual.

It is evident from these lists that in Ezekiel's new order sin will continue to be a problem for the nation. As he had done through Moses, however, through this prophet Yahweh reveals his magnanimous provision

---

60. For Mosaic analogues see Exod. 30:11-16 and Deut. 12:6, 11, 17 (*tĕrûmat yādĕkā,* "the gift of your hand").

61. At this point Ezekiel introduces a new measure, the *kōr,* described in an explanatory note as equivalent to a homer. The term derives from Sumerian GUR, and seems to have found its way into West Semitic via Akk. *kurru. kōr* occurs nine times in the OT, both as a liquid and a dry measure. Cf. Cook, *ISBE,* 4:1049.

62. As in 7:27, *'am hā'āreṣ,* "people of the land," refers to all full citizens.

63. These consisted of liquids, primarily olive oil and wine, poured out to Yahweh, usually in association with other sacrifices (Num. 28–29).

for forgiveness and fellowship with him. Under this constitution, the *nāśî'* plays a critical part; he is guardian and patron of the cult. The size of the tracts of land allocated for him reflect the importance of his role. These territories provided him with land where flocks presented to him could graze and the grain and oil could be stored, until they were required for presentation in the sanctuary.

g. Regulations Regarding the National Festivals (45:18–46:15)

♦ Nature and Design

Verse 17 concludes with a reference to the annual festivals *(haggîm)* in Israel's cultic calendar. In 45:18–46:15 the prophet picks up on this theme with instructions regarding some of Israel's major national celebrations. These ordinances consist of two segments, each being introduced by the citation formula (45:18; 46:1). Beyond this, they share with the preceding a concern for purgation, first of the temple (cf. v. 20), then for the worshipers themselves. 45:18-25 subdivides into two parts, each of which begins with its own date notice (vv. 18, 21). As in vv. 15 and 17, this division is reinforced by the concluding purpose statement in v. 20 announcing the reason for the preceding ritual: to purge the temple *(wĕkippartem 'et-habbāyit).*[1] The first part concentrates on the observances themselves; the second reintroduces the *nāśî'.* The literary style throughout is stiff, if not monotonous, but this is characteristic of formal ritual prescriptions.

(1) The New Passover (45:18-25)

18 *"Thus has the Lord*[2] *Yahweh declared: In the first month, on the first day of the month, you shall take*[3] *a young bull without defect and purify the sanctuary.* 19 *Then the priest shall take some of the blood from the purification offering and smear it on the doorposts*[4] *of the temple, and on the four sides*[5] *of the ledge of the altar, and on the gate*[6] *of the inner court.* 20 *You shall do the same on the seventh day of the*

---

1. On this interpretation of *kippēr* see above on 43:20.
2. *'ădōnāy* is missing in most LXX mss.; LXX[B] reads κύριος Θεός.
3. MT uses second person sg. in vv. 18-20a, but pl. in vv. 20b-21. LXX reads pl. here.
4. MT points *mĕzûzat* as sg., but as LXX, Vulg., and Syr. indicate, the pl. is to be read.
5. On *pĕnôt* meaning "sides" see above on 43:20.
6. The versions support the sg. reading.

month[7] on behalf of[8] anybody who sins inadvertently or out of ig-norance.[9] Thus you[10] shall purge the temple.[11]

21 On the fourteenth day of the first month you shall celebrate the Passover. The festival[12] shall last for seven[13] days, during which time bread made without yeast shall be eaten.[14] 22 On that day the prince shall provide a bull for a purification offering on his own behalf and on behalf of all the people of the land. 23 During the seven days of the festival he shall offer a whole burnt offering to Yahweh consisting of seven bulls and seven rams without defect, every day for seven days. Each day he shall also offer a male goat as a sin offering. 24 He shall also provide as a grain offering an ephah for each bull, an ephah for each ram, and a hin of oil for each ephah. 25 In[15] the seventh month, beginning on the fifteenth day of the month, in a similar seven-day festival, he shall provide for the same purification, whole burnt,[16] grain, and oil offerings."

18-20 Following the opening citation formula, the first segment of this ordinance is framed by a date notice at the beginning and a purpose clause at the end. The prescribed ritual may be summarized as follows. On the first day of the year the prophet is to procure an unblemished young bull to be sacrificed for the ritual decontamination (ḥiṭṭēʾ) of the temple. The officiating priest is to collect the blood and smear some of it on the doorposts (mĕzûzôt) of the

7. LXX ἐν τῷ ἑβδόμῳ μηνὶ μιᾷ τοῦ μηνός (= baššĕbîʿî bĕʾeḥad laḥōdeš), "in the seventh month on the first day of the month," assumes another purificatory performance at the beginning of the second half of the year. Several Hebrew mss. read laḥōdeš in place of baḥōdeš, as one would expect.

8. On this use of min cf. BDB, p. 580a.

9. LXX seems to have misread MT mēʾîš šōgeh ûmippetî as mēʾîš lōqēaḥ pat, "for anyone who takes a portion."

10. The consecutive perfect suggests a conclusion to the series begun in v. 18. Cf. GKC, §111k.

11. This statement, opening with a consecutive perfect, functions as a purpose clause.

12. The order of happāsaḥ ḥāg is unusual (cf. ḥāg happāsaḥ in Exod. 34:25), but supported by the major versions. If MT's separation of the two words is accepted, the missing article (hē) may have been lost by pseudo-haplography. Allen (Ezekiel 20–48, pp. 247-48) suggests that ḥāg represents an inserted note paving the way for the Feast of Unleavened Bread in v. 23.

13. šibʿat appears appropriately as sg. in several Hebrew mss. and the versions.

14. LXX ἔσεσθε and Syr. tʾklwn read active voice in place of MT's impersonal passive. On the latter see GKC, §121a, b.

15. LXX and Syr. smooth out the text by adding the copula.

16. MT omits the copula before kāʿōlâ, but it should probably be added, with Syr. and LXX.

temple and the gates, as well as on the sides of the altar. This procedure is to be repeated on the seventh day of the month for the benefit of the population and the purgation of the temple. There is some debate whether the present ordinance involves an annual ritual or a one-time affair. Some see here Ezekiel's answer to the annual Day of Atonement in the Mosaic Torah, the rituals of which were intended to effect the cleansing of both the sanctuary and the community.[17] However, several considerations argue against this interpretation.

First, the date notice[18] prescribes that the rituals in vv. 18-20 be performed on New Year's Day. But neither the Mosaic Torah nor any other part of the OT envisions a regular New Year's festival in Israel. The Israelites must surely have welcomed the arrival of the New Year with special festivities, but the customs that might have marked the occasion have been so overshadowed by other celebrations of the religious calendar that not a trace remains.[19] According to Exod. 40:2, the nearest counterpart to the present text, the tabernacle was erected on the first day of the year, which may suggest that Ezekiel also has in mind some inaugural activity.

Second, Ezekiel's role compares with that of Moses in the inauguration of the tabernacle worship. The vacillation between singular and plural verbs creates some tension, but one may assume that singular forms in vv. 18 and 20a prescribe activities for the prophet himself, whereas the plural in v. 20b associates him with the priest (mentioned in v. 19) and with the Israelites as a whole. Accordingly, an annual event involving Ezekiel would have limited the applicability of this ordinance to the lifetime of the prophet. But the annual celebrations within the sanctuary were priestly affairs. Indeed, on the Day of Atonement only the high priest entered the tabernacle to perform the purification rites. Ezekiel's Torah provides no hints that he is to function as the high priest. On the contrary, texts such as 43:18-27 carefully distinguish the prophet's role from those of the priests. Moreover, chs. 40–48 consistently present him as a new Moses, rather than a new Aaron.

Third, this text exhibits numerous links with the prescriptions for the initiatory purification of the altar in 43:18-27. In addition to the aforementioned involvement of the prophet, one may note the following:

17. Cf. Allen, *Ezekiel 20–48*, p. 266; Zimmerli, *Ezekiel 2*, p. 482; Wevers, *Ezekiel*, pp. 327-28.

18. The date notice is truncated, lacking a modifier for *bāri'šôn*, "on the first." But this omission, as well as the following *bĕ'eḥād laḥōdeš*, "on the first [day] of the month," are characteristically Ezekielian. With the former cf. 29:17; 30:20; 48:18, 21; with the latter 26:1; 29:17; 31:1; 32:1.

19. Cf. Block, *ISBE*, 3:529-32.

a. The statements concerning the purpose of the ritual. V. 18 announces the goal of this ritual as the decontamination of the sanctuary. The use of the Piel verbs, *ḥiṭṭē'* and *kippēr,* recall two of the key words in 23:20, 22, 23, 26. Indeed, the clause *wěkippartem 'et-habbāyit,* "you shall purge the temple," answers exactly to *yěkappěrû 'et-hammizbēaḥ,* "they shall purge the altar."

b. The activity of the prophet. In 45:18 Ezekiel is ordered to take *(lāqaḥ)* a sacrificial animal and cleanse the sanctuary *(miqdāš),* which summarizes the kinds of actions described in detail in 43:19-24.

c. The nature of the victim. The phraseology of v. 18, which requires the sacrifice of a perfect young bull *(par-ben-bāqār tāmîm),* derives directly from 43:23, 25 (cf. v. 19).

d. The nature of the ritual. Some of the blood is to be collected from the victim and applied to the sacred objects. The statement in v. 19, "He shall take from the blood of the decontamination offering and smear it on" echoes "and you shall take from the blood of it [the decontamination offering] and smear it on" in 43:20.[20]

e. The involvement of the ledges of the altar. While the decontamination of the temple proper calls for the smearing of the blood on the doorposts of the house and on the posts of the gates, the reference to smearing it on "the four sides of the ledge" *('el-'arba' pěnôt hā'ǎzārâ)* of the altar catches the reader by surprise. What has smearing the altar to do with purifying the temple? The verbatim insertion of a phrase lifted from another context reflects a deliberate effort to link these ordinances.

f. The seven-day framework. The charge to perform this ritual on the seventh day of the month (v. 20) raises the question of what has happened in the intervening week. The answer is provided by 43:25-27, which calls for a daily repetition of the decontamination ritual for an entire week.

g. The reference to the popular benefits of the ritual. 45:20 observes that the benefactors of the decontamination procedure are "those who go astray" *(šāgâ)* and "the simple-minded" *(petî).* The former expression refers primarily to livestock, such as sheep, going astray (cf. Ezek. 34:6), but it is used in a derived sense of sin committed in ignorance in Lev. 4:13 and Num. 15:22. The latter, common in the wisdom writings, identifies the naive, gullible person. The present combination holds out the possibility of atonement for all unwitting sin. While there is no direct counterpart to this phrase in 43:18-27, the plural object of

---

20. Cf. *wělāqaḥ . . . middam haḥaṭṭā't wěnātan 'el* (45:19) with *wělāqaḥtā middāmô wěnātattâ 'al* (43:20).

the verb *wěrāṣîtî,* "and I will accept you," indicates that for all the attention to the ritual decontamination of the altar, Yahweh's ultimate concern is the restoration of his relationship with the people.

The combination of all these factors provides convincing evidence that the ritual described here is not intended as an annual purificatory rite, but a one-time event, analogous to, if not associated with, the inaugural decontamination of the altar described in 43:18-27. Whether or not these two accounts were ever more closely connected, the abbreviated style of the present ordinance assumes familiarity with the earlier account.

21 This verse introduces a more familiar subject, the type of material anticipated by v. 17. The word *ḥag,* which appears for the first time, functions as a *Leitwort,* tying the celebration in the seventh month (v. 25) to the preceding Passover ordinance. The etymology of *ḥag* is obscure, but the root is familiar through Arab. *ḥaǧǧ,* "festival, pilgrimage," and the verb *ḥaǧǧa,* "to undertake a pilgrimage." In the OT *ḥag* denotes an annual community festival celebrated by the Israelites. *ḥaggîm* were typically characterized by rejoicing and singing in the context of processions to the sanctuary, where the sacrificial offerings would be presented to Yahweh.[21]

The first *ḥag* dealt with here is the Passover. The etymology of *pesaḥ* remains a mystery. The narrative of the original Passover event and instructions for its celebration, along with the associated Feast of Unleavened Bread, are provided in Exod. 12:1-28.[22] The Passover was a *zebaḥ,* an animal sacrifice to be eaten by the sacrificer. Exod. 12 indicates that the festival originated in Egypt, on the night Yahweh slaughtered the firstborn of the land. The Israelites avoided this fate by having the head of each household procure an unblemished lamb, slaughter it, and smear its blood on the doorposts. The meat of the lamb was to be eaten in haste, with traveling clothes donned and walking stick in hand. The blood on the door served an apotropaic function — to turn away Yahweh. Later Passover celebrations served two purposes: to commemorate Yahweh's deliverance of Israel from Egypt, and to link the participants with that original event, actualizing that deliverance for each generation of Israelites.

Only in Exod. 34:25 is the Passover celebration proper identified as a *ḥag,* "a pilgrim feast." This term is applied elsewhere to the associated Feast of Unleavened Bread,[23] but never to the Passover itself. Nonetheless,

---

21. For further discussion see Haran, *Temples and Temple-Service,* pp. 290-303; B. Kedar-Kopfstein, *TDOT,* 4:201-13.

22. Further instructions on paschal observances occur in Exod. 34:25; Lev. 23:5; Num. 9:1-14; 28:16; Deut. 16:1-8, on which see Haran, *Temples and Temple-Service,* pp. 317-48.

23. On the seventh day of which the Israelites were to appear before Yahweh (Exod. 13:3-7; Deut. 16:2-4).

that the Passover was celebrated as a pilgrim feast is likely not only because it is associated with the Feast of Unleavened Bread,[24] but also because Deut. 16:1-8 anticipates a centralized celebration, at the place where Yahweh would choose to establish his residence. Furthermore, historically the three mandatory pilgrimage festivals were celebrated in Jerusalem.[25] Ezekiel's classification of the Passover as a *ḥag,* therefore, does not break with the common understanding.

22-24 The opening lines of Ezekiel's Passover ordinance (v. 21) resemble the Mosaic prescriptions. The *ḥag* was to take place on the fourteenth day of the first month, and to last for seven days. During that week no unleavened bread was to be eaten. In vv. 22-24, however, the form of the ordinance adheres more closely to custom than to statutory law. Several customary features may be noted.

First, the *nāśî'* is to play a leading role. Whereas Exod. 12–13 presents the original Passover as a family affair, led by the head of the household, Ezekiel charges the national head of state with responsibility for the celebration. The requirement that he provide the sacrificial animals codifies what seems to have been the custom for some time.[26]

Second, the sacrificial victim has changed from an unblemished lamb to a bull for the purification offering on the first day, and to bulls, rams, and goats on the following seven days. The original instructions on the Passover do not mention these animals (Exod. 12–13), but later Mosaic legislation called for the slaughter of bulls and rams and male goats during the seven-day festival following the Passover proper (Num. 28:16-25). The Chronicler identifies the Passover victims in the Hezekian celebration simply as the *pesaḥ* (2 Chr. 30:15-17), which may be interpreted as the prescribed unblemished lambs. In keeping with Num. 28:16-25, however, the animals slain during the following seven days involved vast numbers of bulls and sheep as well. The issue becomes more complicated in the feast sponsored by Josiah. 2 Chr. 35:7-9 has the king and his nobles providing thousands of bulls and lambs and sheep for the Passover *(pĕsāḥîm).* Ezekiel's legislation may thus represent

---

24. This was one of the three occasions when all male Israelites were required to appear before Yahweh (Exod. 23:14-18).

25. Solomon appears to have inaugurated this custom (2 Chr. 8:13); later texts speak of its long-standing neglect (2 K. 23:22). Reforming kings specifically invite all Israel and Judah to Jerusalem to celebrate the Passover (Hezekiah, 2 Chr. 30:1-27; Josiah, 35:1-19; cf. 2 K. 23:21-23). This tradition of gathering in Jerusalem for the Passover continued after the exile (Ezra 6:19-22).

26. As royal patron of the Passover, Hezekiah had initiated the celebration, resolved problems of timing, issued the decree for national participation and spiritual renewal, interceded on behalf of the people, encouraged the Levites, and provided the animals (2 Chr. 30). Cf. Josiah's similar role decades later (2 Chr. 35:1-19).

the culmination of an internal evolution of the Passover, the phases of which one may trace as follows:

1. *pesaḥ* as lamb alone (Exod. 12:1-28)
2. *pesaḥ* as lamb alone with attendant sacrifices of bulls and goats (Num. 28:16-25; 2 Chr. 30:15-17)
3. *pesaḥ* as lamb and bulls and goats (2 Chr. 35:7-9)
4. *pesaḥ* as bulls and goats, without mention of lambs (Ezek. 45:21-24).

Significantly, when the Passover is reinstituted after the exile, the community appears to return to the original pattern (Ezra 6:19-22).

In addition to the animal sacrifices, Ezekiel introduces grain offerings to the Passover *ḥag*. The impetus for this modification may have come from Num. 28:20-21, which prescribes that animal sacrifices be accompanied by grain offerings: 3⁄10 measure (presumably of an ephah) of fine flour for a bull, and 2⁄10 for a ram. No mention is made of oil. Ezekiel adjusts the amount of the grain offering to one ephah of grain for each bull and ram, and one hin of oil for the same.

Third, the focus of the celebration has changed. On the day of the Passover, the prince is to provide for himself and the people a bull for a purification offering *(ḥaṭṭā't)*. This shift parallels the change in the nature of the sacrificial victims. Whereas the function of the original Passover was apotropaic, to ward off Yahweh's lethal actions, and subsequent celebrations provided annual reminders of that original event,[27] in the Ezekielian ordinance the memorial purposes of the Passover are overshadowed by the purgative concern. Thus, while the Passover, the most fundamental of all Israelite celebrations, is retained in Ezekiel's new religious order, its nature and significance have been changed.

25 Chapter 45 closes with a brief note on a third cultic event, a seven-day pilgrim feast *(ḥag)* on the fifteenth day of the seventh month. Ezekiel again prescribes purification, whole burnt offerings, and grain offerings, along with oil libations, with the *nāśî'* playing the leading role. The autumnal festivals prescribed in the Mosaic Torah are referred to as the Feast of Booths (Lev. 23:39-44; Deut. 16:13, 16) and the Feast of Ingathering (Exod. 23:16; 34:22), but Ezekiel makes no effort to identify these observances with his.[28] However, Ezekiel's autumnal *ḥag* divides the Israelite cultic calendar

---

27. Num. 28:16-25 introduces purification offerings to the seven-day feast following the Passover, but they are still absent from the Passover itself.

28. To link this festival with ancient Canaanite autumnal celebrations, Solomon's festivities (1 K. 8:2), or the fall event prescribed by Jeroboam in his aberrant cult (2 K. 12:32) is speculative. Cf. Zimmerli, *Ezekiel 2*, p. 484.

into two halves, each of which begins with a pilgrim feast before Yahweh and a series of offerings.

Although Ezekiel retains the label of the ancient rite of Passover, his ordinance calls for a dramatic transformation of the festival. Like the original Passover (Exod. 12–13), Ezekiel's celebration has inaugural significance. Through this celebration the nation of Israel becomes the people of God. Whereas the function of the original Passover sacrifice was apotropaic (to ward off Yahweh), however, Ezekiel's is purgative. Like the rest of this prophet's Torah, the cult of the new order is preoccupied with holiness: maintaining the sanctity of the temple (v. 20) and of the worshiper (v. 22). Before the rituals can be performed, viz., before the new spiritual relationship between Yahweh and his people can be celebrated, the defilement of the building and the people must be purged. Through the Passover celebration, the temple complex becomes sacred space and the Israelites become a holy people. In this newly constituted theocracy the role of the *nāśî'* is pivotal. As the patron and guardian of cult, he bears the responsibility for the sanctification of the temple and the nation, a subject that ch. 46 will address in greater detail.

(2) Other Festivals (46:1-15)

1 *"Thus has the Lord*[29] *Yahweh declared:*
The gate of the inner court that faces east shall remain closed[30] *during the six working days.*[31] *But on the Sabbath day it shall be opened, and on the day of the new moon it shall be opened.* 2 *The prince shall enter from the outside*[32] *by way of the vestibule of the gateway, and he shall stop*[33] *next to the doorpost of the gate, while the priests present his whole burnt offering and his peace offerings. Then he shall prostrate himself on the threshold*[34] *of the gate, and make his exit. But the gate shall not be closed until the evening.* 3 *The people of the land shall prostrate themselves*[35] *before Yahweh at the entrance*

29. *'ădōnāy* is missing in most LXX mss., but LXX[B] reads κύριος Θεός.

30. The expression *yihyeh sāgûr,* "it shall be closed," echoes *sāgûr yihyeh* and *wĕhāyâ sāgûr* in 44:2-3. The *hāyâ* plus participle construction has been observed also in 34:2; 43:6. See Rooker, *Biblical Hebrew in Transition,* pp. 108-9.

31. The expression *yĕmê hamma'ăśeh* "the days of work," occurs only here in the OT. Targ. reads *ywmy ḥwl',* "profane days."

32. The principal LXX witnesses mistakenly relate *miḥûṣ* to the gate.

33. *wĕ'āmad,* lit. "stand."

34. The versions fail to distinguish *miptān* from *mĕzûzâ.*

35. On the pl. verb with a collective noun as characteristically Ezekielian see Rooker, *Biblical Hebrew in Transition,* pp. 94-96.

of that gate on the Sabbaths and the new moon festivals. 4 *And the whole burnt offering which the prince presents to Yahweh on the Sabbath day shall consist of six lambs without defect and a ram without defect.* 5 *A grain offering of one ephah shall accompany the ram, whereas the grain offering accompanying the lambs shall be as much as he can afford.*[36] *A hin of oil shall accompany each ephah.* 6 *On the day of the new moon the offering shall consist of a young bull without defect,*[37] *six lambs, and a ram without defect.* 7 *As a grain offering he shall present an ephah for the bull and an ephah for the ram, whereas for the lambs he shall bring whatever he can afford.*[38] *A hin of oil shall accompany each ephah.* 8 *When the prince enters,*[39] *he shall come in by way of the vestibule of the gateway; and he shall exit by the same way.* 9 *When the people of the land come before Yahweh at the appointed celebrations, anyone who enters by way of the north gate to worship shall leave by way of the south*[40] *gate. And whoever enters by way of the south gate shall leave by way of the north gate. They shall go back through the same gate by which they entered. They shall indeed*[41] *exit*[42] *through the opposite gate.*[43] 10 *And the prince shall come in among them when they enter, and he shall exit among them when they leave.*[44]

36. "Whatever he can afford" is an idiomatic rendering of *mattat yādô*, "gift of his hand." While some translate it more optatively, "as much as he wishes" (NJPS; NRSV; NIV; Fuhs, *Ezechiel 24–48*, p. 254; Allen, *Ezekiel 20–48*, p. 241), my interpretation assumes equivalence to *ka'ăšer taššîg yādô*, "whatever his hand can secure" (v. 7). *taššîg* is a Hiphil form of *nāšag*, "to reach, overtake." Ezekiel's style is influenced by the Mosaic Torah (Lev. 5:11; 14:21-32; 25:26, 49; 27:8; Num. 6:27).

37. The context and the versions (which read sg.) suggest that the pl. *těmîmim* represents a dittographic error.

38. On the difference in idiom from that found in vv. 5 and 11, see n. 36 above.

39. On the temporal clause with *bě* plus infinitive construct without *wěhāyâ* or *wayěhî*, see Rooker, *Biblical Hebrew in Transition*, pp. 103-5. Zimmerli (*Ezekiel 2*, p. 491) observes correctly that the opening *ûběbô' hannāśî'*, "and when the *nāśî'* enters," introduces a more precise explication of *ûbā' hannāśî'*, "and the prince shall enter," in v. 2.

40. Here and in chs. 47–48 "south" is referred to by *negeb*, instead of *dārôm*, which had been used in chs. 40–42.

41. On the emphatic use of *kî* see above on 30:3.

42. Whereas the previous verbs were construed as sg., the pl. occurs after the collective subject *'am*. Ezekiel is notoriously inconsistent in the treatment of collectives (cf. Rooker, *Biblical Hebrew in Transition*, pp. 94-96). Contra Zimmerli (*Ezekiel 2*, p. 488), it is preferable to view the versional sg. forms as harmonistic, rather than MT as dittographic.

43. Assuming the suffix on *nikěḥô* refers to the gate rather than the person.

44. On the pl. *yēṣē'û* see n. 42 above.

11 *At the pilgrim festivals and at the appointed celebrations the grain offering accompanying the bull shall be an ephah, and for the ram it shall be an ephah. But for the lambs it shall be whatever he can afford.*[45] *A hin of oil shall accompany each ephah.*

12 *Whenever the prince presents a voluntary whole burnt offering or voluntary peace offerings to Yahweh, the gate that faces east shall be opened*[46] *for him. Then he shall present his whole burnt offering and his peace offerings exactly as he does on the Sabbath day. Afterward he shall leave, and when he has made his exit the gate shall be closed behind him.*

13 *You shall provide*[47] *a one-year-old lamb without defect for the whole burnt offering to Yahweh daily. You shall provide it every morning.*[48] 14 *And every morning you shall provide with it a grain offering, consisting of one-sixth of an ephah and one-third of a hin of oil to moisten*[49] *the flour. It is a grain offering for Yahweh, a permanent decree.*[50] 15 *Thus they shall present*[51] *the lamb and the grain offering, and the oil every morning as a regular whole burnt offering.*"

♦ Nature and Design

The citation formula in 46:1 signals a new subunit that continues until the next occurrence of the formula in v. 16. Although vv. 16-18 share an interest in the *nāśî'* with vv. 1-15, the subject matter is quite different. The first and larger segment deals with the great religious festivals of Ezekiel's new order; the second with real estate matters. For the purpose of analyzing the substance of the material it is helpful to link these two parts with 44:3, 45:7-9, 21-25, 46:1-12, and 16-18, but the theory of an original *nāśî'* stratum should allow for the possibility of the prophet Ezekiel himself being responsible for this

---

45. See n. 36 above.

46. Treating the subject of the *ûpātaḥ* impersonally.

47. LXX and Vulg. fail to recognize the beginning of a new subsection when they harmonize the second person of MT with the preceding third person. NRSV reflects an emended text.

48. LXX renders MT's duplicated *babbōqer babbōqer* with a single word.

49. *rōs,* from *rāsas,* is a hapax form (cf. *rāsîs,* "to moisten," parallel to "dew," *ṭal,* in Cant. 5:2), answering to *bālal,* "to mix," in Num. 28.

50. MT *ḥuqqôt 'ôlām* should be read sg., *ḥuqqat 'ôlām,* with many Hebrew mss. and the versions. That LXX πρόσταγμα διὰ παντός is an abbreviation of MT *ḥuqqôt 'ôlām tāmîd* is suggested by Targ., Vulg., and Syr., all of which reflect MT. *tāmîd* is superfluous here, and may represent a marginal gloss that has found its way into the text, perhaps under the influence of v. 15 (so Gese, *Verfassungsentwurf,* p. 85 n. 2) or Num. 28:6.

51. Reading *w'św* with Kethib, Syr., Targ., against Qere *y'św.* The pl. form assumes the involvement of the priests.

stratum.[52] The interweaving of themes is probably editorial, but it reflects at most the staged development of the literary composition.[53]

With respect to genre, the opening formula invites the reader to interpret vv. 1-15 as a divine speech. However, the variation in literary style complicates the picture. The predominantly third person form is interrupted in vv. 13-14 by the second person of direct address. With regard to content, vv. 1-12, which may be classified as cultic ordinances, weave together regulations pertaining to the proper functioning of the gate to the temple (vv. 1-3, 8-10, 12) and additional sacrificial regulations (vv. 4-7, 11), and are cast in a ritual style.[54] One recognizes in this material another example of characteristically Ezekielian resumptive exposition. The gate regulations build on 44:1-3, and the sacrificial ordinances clarify 45:17. The combination of gate and festival ordinances enhances the role of the *nāśî'* in Ezekiel's new order as patron and guardian of the cult.

1 In 44:3 Ezekiel observed that after Yahweh's *kābôd* had entered the temple, the eastern gate of the outer wall was shut. Since this gate was reserved for Yahweh, and since he had entered the temple never to leave again, it was to remain closed. But this did not mean that there was to be no more activity within the gate structure. On the contrary, v. 3 had specified that within this gateway the prince was to eat bread before Yahweh, having entered from the inside, via the vestibule (*'ulām*). Now we learn that some activity is to transpire in the gate structure of the inner court as well.[55] Yahweh's instructions begin with a statement of principle: on workdays the eastern gate of the inner court is to remain shut. Only on the Sabbath day and on the new moon is it to be opened. Although gates of the type described in ch. 40 were designed primarily for defensive purposes, this prescription is intended to secure the temple not militarily but spiritually, by controlling access to the temple. It is assumed that the sanctity of the place would be violated if people would enter the courts on days other than those declared

52. Based on the sg. form of *nāśî'* and the juxtapositioning of *nāśî'* with *'am hā'āreṣ,* "people of the land," Gese (*Verfassungsentwurf,* pp. 85-87) limits the *nāśî'* stratum to 44:1-3, 44:21a, 22-25, and 46:1-10, 12. Zimmerli (*Ezekiel 2,* p. 552) deletes 44:1-2 from this stratum; Allen (*Ezekiel 20–48,* p. 253) suggests that 45:8, 9, 16-17, and 46:16-18 would have been attracted to this stratum at an early date. Tuell (*Law of the Temple,* pp. 12-13) observes correctly that the so-called Zadok stratum (44:6-16; 44:17-31 [inserted]; 44:28-30a; 45:13-15) is closely interwoven and deals with the same issues of calendar and cult, but his attribution of this material to the Persian period leaves as many questions as Gese's thesis.

53. Cf. Greenberg, *Int* 38 (1984) 199.

54. The use the consecutive perfect in vv. 2-3 and the opening *kî* in v. 12 create a casuistic flavor. Cf. Koch, *Priesterschrift,* pp. 107-8.

55. *ša'ar heḥāṣēr happĕnîmît* (v. 1) compares with *ša'ar hammiqdāš haḥîṣôn* in 44:1.

holy. While this ordinance also assumes the continued relevance of the Decalogue (Exod. 20:8-11; Deut. 5:12-15), here the concern is the sanctity not so much of the day but of the place where Yahweh is to be worshiped. Yahweh's name is not to be profaned by people coming in from the fields and appearing before him. More will be said about the Sabbath and the new moon later.

2-3 Even though the eastern gate to the inner court was to be opened on the Sabbath and the new moon, this did not grant general admittance to the inner court on these occasions. On the contrary, the gate regulations clearly reflect and reinforce the stratification of society. However, this ordinance focuses on the *nāśî'*.

Ezekiel prescribes four specific actions for the prince. First, the prince shall enter the gate structure from the outer court through the vestibule (*'ûlām*).[56] Second, the prince is to stand by the post of the gate, that is, the jamb between the vestibule and the series of guard recesses, since the inner gates were mirror images of the outer.[57] This vantage point enables him, as guardian and patron of the cult, to observe the cultic activity of the priests. But the prince himself is not to move any closer, let alone step out onto this most sacred space of the inner court. Third, while the priests present his whole burnt offerings and peace offerings to Yahweh on the altar in the inner court, the prince shall prostrate himself on the threshold of the gate, an appropriate response of a mortal in the presence of deity.[58] Fourth, the prince is to leave the gate structure. The duration of his stay in the gate is unspecified, but v. 2b suggests that his time is limited, since after he has left, the gate must remain open the rest of the day.

As in 45:22 (and Lev. 4:27), the expression *people of the land* (*'am hā'āreṣ*) denotes more than simply the residents of the territory. These are citizens, members of the cultic community (exclusive of the *nāśî'* and temple officials) at worship. On these Sabbaths and new moon festivals the citizens of the restored community of faith shall gather and pay homage to Yahweh by prostrating themselves at the entrance of the inner gate.[59]

---

56. See the description of the gate in 40:5-16.

57. The architectural vocabulary changes from ch. 40, *mĕzûzâ*, "doorpost," replacing *'ayil*, though *mĕzûzâ* had been used of the doorposts of the temple (41:21; 43:8; 45:19) and the inner gate (*mĕzûzat ša'ar*, 45:19). See above on 40:28-37.

58. On *hištaḥăwâ* as a nonverbal gesture of homage see my *Ezekiel: Chapters 1-24*, pp. 297-98. Note the change in architectural terminology, with *sap* (40:6) being replaced by *miptān*, which earlier had designated the threshold of the temple (9:3; 10:4, 18; cf. also 47:1).

59. *lipnê yhwh*, "before Yahweh," links their activity with the prince's meal in the gateway of the outer wall in 44:3. The phrase assumes that any activity inside the temple complex is an expression of worship before Yahweh.

4-8 Further description of the activities in the outer court is delayed momentarily to provide details of the sacrifices to be presented on the Sabbaths and new moon festivals. The absence of the purification *(ḥaṭṭā't)* and peace *(šĕlāmîm)* offerings from the discussion suggests either that the present text represents an abbreviation of a longer original, which may have included at least the peace offering (v. 2), or that the author expects readers to fill in corresponding information for the peace offering.[60] In keeping with the *nāśî*"s role as patron of the cult, he is to provide the materials for the Sabbath and new moon festivals.

4-5 Undoubtedly with an eye to the abuses of the past,[61] Ezekiel begins with instructions for the Sabbath offerings. Yahweh's sacrificial requirements for these celebrations are relatively modest in comparison with those for the other major feasts: six lambs and a ram (all without defect), along with an ephah of grain to go with the ram, and as much as the person can afford with the lambs. Despite the obvious influence of the Mosaic Torah in these prescriptions (Num. 28:9-10),[62] the differences in detail are striking, as table 21 (p. 673) illustrates. It is not clear why the amount of grain required to accompany the lamb is left open-ended, but the specification of the amount of oil required repeats verbatim the amount called for in 45:24b.

6-7 These verses prescribe the offerings for the new moon festivals. Elsewhere in the book, particularly in the date notices, *ḥōdeš* has denoted "month,"[63] but as in 45:17, here it refers to a religious festival celebrated at the appearance of the new moon. The cult of the moon was widespread in the ancient Near East, and the moon god figures prominently in the mythologies.[64] Orthodox Yahwism strictly forbade the worship of the moon, as it did the veneration of any other heavenly body.[65] However, the Mosaic Torah invites

---

60. Cf. 45:17-25, which includes the peace offering in the list of offerings (v. 17) but provides no details for this sacrifice.

61. See 20:12-24; 22:8, 26; 23:38. Cf. 44:24, where the priests in particular had been charged to sanctify these days, along with the other appointed festivals.

62. While Num. 28:9 prescribes two male lambs, accompanied by two-tenths (of an ephah) of fine flour mixed with oil, these are in addition to the *tāmîd*, the regular daily offerings, and the whole burnt offerings (v. 10).

63. See Ezek. 1:8; 8:1; 20:1; 24:1; 26:1; 29:1, 17; 30:20; 31:1; 32:1, 17; 33:21. Cf. also 45:18, 20, 21, 25.

64. Cf. Nanna-Sin in Mesopotamia, Yeraḥ at Ugarit and Karatepe, Sachar ("crescent") in Old South Arabic, and Sahar in Aramaic inscriptions, paired with Shamash (e.g., in the inscription of Zakkur [Zakir] of Hamath; see *KAI*, 202B.24; *TSSI*, 2:12-13). These names appear frequently as the theophoric element in personal names. On the moon cult in the ancient Near East see R. North, *TDOT*, 4:233-34; A. Jirku, "Der Kult des Mondgottes im altorientalischen Palästina-Syrien," *ZDMG* 100 (1950) 202-4; T. H. Gaster, *IDB*, 3:436.

65. The OT usually refers to the lunar cult by *yārēaḥ* (Deut. 4:19; 17:2-5; 2 K.

Table 21: A Comparison of the Mosaic and
Ezekielian Sabbath Sacrifices

Element	Mosaic Torah	Ezekielian Torah
Number of lambs	2	6
Number of rams	—	1
Amount of grain per lamb	²⁄₁₀ ephah flour	according to means
Amount of grain per ram	—	1 ephah
Amount of oil	unspecified — mixed with the flour	1 hin/ephah

Israel to celebrate the first days of the months *(rā'šê ḥŏdāšîm)*, along with the appointed festivals *(mô'ădîm)* with gladness and trumpet blasts, and whole burnt offerings.[66] Indeed, the great eschatological vision of Isa. 66:23 foresees a day when all flesh will be engaged in the perpetual worship of Yahweh, from one *ḥōdeš* to another, and from one Sabbath to another. Like the Sabbaths, with which the new moon festivals are often associated, the new moon celebrations in Israel tended to become routine and perfunctory, leading to the scathing indictments of the prophets (Hos. 2:13 [Eng. 11]; 5:7; Isa. 1:13-14). The Ezekielian Torah calls for a reinstitution of the Mosaic monthly festivals, but again with significant modifications, as table 22 (p. 674) indicates. In calling for a hin of oil with "one ephah," the latter must refer to flour, though Ezekiel does not specify it. Nor does he prescribe any wine to mix with the oil, or a purification offering to go with the new moon festival. His Torah is obviously going its own way.

    8-10   The focus returns to the *nāśî'*, specifically the manner in which he is to enter and leave the outer court. He must enter the gateway by way of the vestibule *('ûlām)* and leave the same way. Thus he is prohibited from passing through the gateway into the inner court and exiting via another gate. How he got into the outer court in the first place will be explained in

---

23:5; Jer. 8:2; Job 31:27-28), though Cant. 6:10; Isa. 24:23; 30:26 speak of the moon as *lĕbānâ*, "white one." The moon is included in *ṣĕbā' haššāmayim*, "the host of heaven" (Jer. 19:13; Zeph. 1:5).

    66. For the former see Num. 10:10; cf. Ps. 81:4 (Eng. 3). For the latter see Num. 28:11-15: two bulls, one ram, and seven male lambs, along with specified amounts of grain, fine flour, oil, and wine. In Samuel's day, everyone was expected to participate in the new moon festivals (1 Sam. 20:5, 18, 24; cf. 2 K. 4:23), and Israel's/Judah's kings sponsored such cultic activities; see David (1 Chr. 23:31), Solomon (2 Chr. 2:4 [Eng. 3]; 8:13), and Hezekiah (2 Chr. 31:3). Cf. also Ezra 3:5. Prophetic support is reflected in Amos's apparent prohibition of commerce on the day of the new moon (8:5).

Table 22: A Comparison of the Mosaic and
Ezekielian New Moon Sacrifices

Element	Mosaic Torah	Ezekielian Torah
Number of bulls	2	1
Number of rams	1	1
Number of lambs	7	6
Amount of grain per bull	3/10 ephah flour	1 ephah
Amount of grain per ram	2/10 ephah flour	1 ephah
Amount of grain per lamb	1/10 ephah flour	according to means
Amount of oil	unspecified — mixed with the flour	1 hin/ephah
Amount of wine per bull	1/2 hin	
Amount of wine per ram	1/3 hin	
Amount of wine per lamb	1/4 hin	

---

vv. 9-10. The *nāśî'*'s entry into the sacred precinct at the appointed festivals[67] is to coincide with the arrival before Yahweh of the people, whose movement is also strictly regulated. They are permitted to enter the outer court through either the northern or the southern gate, but, unlike the *nāśî'*, they may not turn around inside the precinct and exit via the gate through which they entered. Although the reason for this regulation is not specified, it seems best to interpret this pragmatically, as a means of crowd control. Ezekiel's vision of hundreds of thousands of people thronging the temple courts "before Yahweh" on the prescribed festival days would have been a logistical nightmare, which this ordinance sought to manage. However, the prescription may perceive turning around in the sacred precinct as inappropriate and offensive to God, or simply as another means of ensuring that every detail in the worship of Yahweh was ordered, like the order and symmetry inherent in the design of sacred space itself. V. 10 requires that the *nāśî'* enter and leave the court in the midst of the worshiping throng *(bĕtôkām)*. The ordinance prohibiting him from rushing in ahead of the citizens or loitering after they have left has profound communal implications. To be sure, as patron and sponsor of the cult, the *nāśî'* is elevated functionally above the populace. However, this regulation is designed to reinforce his (corporate) solidarity with the people, in contrast and as a complement to the priests' identification with Yahweh.

11 This verse seems stylistically disruptive and redundant after vv.

67. *mô'ădîm* refers to the Sabbaths and new moon festivals, as well as the New Year, Passover, and autumnal celebrations described in Ezek. 45:18-25.

4-7, but the addition links the *ḥaggîm* (of 45:18-25?) with the *mô'ădîm* (of 46:1-10). Furthermore, it highlights the standardization of all the offerings accompanying the animal sacrifices: one ephah of grain for each bull and ram, and as much as the worshiper is able to bring with each lamb, and with each ephah of flour, an ephah of oil as well. The worship of Yahweh in Ezekiel's new cultic structure is to be ordered and symmetrical in every respect.

12 This subunit concludes with one more ordinance for the *nāśî'*, regulating his freewill offerings to Yahweh within the context of the prescribed festivals and community celebrations. The term *nĕdābâ*, from *nādab*, "to incite," in Qal, but "volunteer," viz., "incite oneself," in Hithpael,[68] is a general designation for spontaneous sacrificial expressions of happiness, without regard to kind. According to Ezekiel, like the prescribed Sabbath offerings, these may take the form of whole burnt offerings (*'ôlâ*) or peace offerings (*šĕlāmîm*) or both.[69] Both the manner and timing of this offering are striking. As on the prescribed sabbaths and new moon festivals, whenever the *nāśî'* is inspired to bring a freewill offering, the east gate is to be opened, enabling him to observe the priests presenting his sacrifices to Yahweh. Upon completion of the ritual, he is to exit the precinct, and the eastern gate of the inner wall is to be closed once more.

13-14 Although these verses are commonly treated as a late addition, the association of legislation involving the *tāmîd* with Sabbath and new moon offerings finds a precedent in the Mosaic Torah.[70] The present use of the second person, reminiscent of 45:18-20, suggests that this section is addressed to the prophet himself, a fact recognized by the reversion to the third person in v. 15. This ordinance makes two demands. First, a one-year-old lamb without defect is to be provided for a whole burnt offering (*'ôlâ*) to Yahweh every morning. Second, each morning the *'ôlâ* is to be accompanied by a grain offering consisting of ⅙ ephah of flour moistened with a hin of oil. The

---

68. See the Hithpael for military duty (Judg. 5:2, 9) or other service (2 Chr. 17:16; Neh. 11:2), but esp. for free will offerings (1 Chr. 29:5, 6, 9, 14, 17; Ezra 1:6; 2:68; 3:5). The abstract noun occurs impressively in narratives concerning sanctuary constructions: the tabernacle (Exod. 35:29; 36:3), Solomon's temple (2 Chr. 31:14), the second temple (Ezra 1:4; 8:28). Elsewhere *nĕdābâ* is frequently linked with *neder,* an offering brought out of a sense of duty in fulfillment of a vow, rather than spontaneously, from the freedom of one's own heart (cf. Lev. 7:16; Num. 15:3; 29:39; etc.).

69. According to Milgrom (*Leviticus,* pp. 218-19, 419-20), *nĕdābâ* may serve as a surrogate for *šĕlāmîm.* Cf. Num. 15:3, 8.

70. Scholars treating it as an addition note (1) a shift from the second to the third person; (2) an intrusive concern with *tāmîd,* which has been out of the picture in 45:17–46:12; (3) the precise prescription of ⅙ ephah of grain in the *minḥâ,* instead of being left to the discretion of the offerer. The Mosaic precedent, Num. 28:1-15, describes the *'ôlat tāmîd,* incorporating the Sabbath and new moon offerings, in detail. *tāmîd* denotes "regular, routine," rather than "perpetual." Cf. on 39:14.

Table 23: A Comparison of the Mosaic and
Ezekielian *tāmîd* Sacrifices

Element	Mosaic Torah	Ezekielian Torah
Time of day	every morning and every evening	every morning
Number of lambs	2 (one in A.M.; one in P.M.)	1
Amount of grain per lamb	⅒ ephah flour	⅙ ephah flour
Amount of oil per lamb	¼ hin	⅓ hin to moisten flour
Amount of wine per lamb	¼ hin	—

references to the fine flour *(sōlet)* and its moistening with oil are mentioned for the first time in this context. The permanence of the present ordinance is emphasized with *ḥuqqat ʿôlām,* "eternal decree," a stereotypical expression borrowed from the Mosaic Torah (cf. Exod. 12:14). The influence of the Mosaic Torah on the Ezekielian ordinance is obvious, but the differences are significant, as the comparison with Num. 28:1-8 in table 23 (above) demonstrates. Apart from differences in specifications, especially striking are Ezekiel's omission of any reference to wine libations and the demand for an offering every evening (Num. 28:4-5, 8). Either Ezekiel expects his audience to assume the morning offerings will be answered by counterparts at the end of each day, based on the Mosaic Torah, or he is once more cutting his own path.[71]

15   This verse offers a summary of vv. 13-14, except that the third person form transfers responsibility for the *tāmîd* from Ezekiel to the priests.

♦ *Theological Implications*

Like its Mosaic predecessor, Ezekiel's cultic calendar envisioned an elaborate sacrificial pattern, complete with annual festivals, weekly Sabbaths, and daily sacrificial rituals. As mediator of the new cultic order the prophet continues to function as a new Moses, mediating a new constitution for the community of faith as revealed and established by Yahweh. Apart from modifications in the order of the presentation, however, Ezekiel's departures from the traditional calendar are dramatic. First, the most obvious differences involve the number of sacrificial animals and the amounts of accompanying flour, oil, and wine (see the tables above). Second, whereas Num. 29:1-15 says

71. 2 K. 16:15 suggests that under Ahaz the *tāmîd* offerings had been split, with the *ʿôlâ* being offered as the morning *tāmîd* and the *minḥâ* as the evening *tāmîd*.

nothing about Moses' involvement in the rituals, the second person singular in Ezek. 46:13-14 at least hints at the participation of Ezekiel. Third, while Num. 28:1-15 does not envision the involvement of anyone in the ritual except the worshipers themselves and by implication the priests, Ezekiel's ordinance has a new figure, the *nāśî*', playing a prominent role, as the one who provides the sacrificial animals and materials.

Ezekiel's audience must have noticed these discrepancies, for they challenge the age-old notion that the Mosaic revelation functioned as the standard by which the veracity of all subsequent prophecy was to be evaluated (see Deut. 18:15-22). Either Ezekiel anticipates the actual fulfillment of his prophecies with his own literal supersession of Moses, or the present rituals represent an ideational cultic calendar for the new age. The former is unlikely in the light of Ezekiel's own conflict with the false prophets (chs. 12–13); the latter accords well with the prophet's ideological portrayal of sacred space in chs. 40–43. In any case, to posit a reinstitution of millennial sacrifices on the basis of Ezekiel's cultic ordinances is unwarranted.[72]

At the same time, this passage adds several significant details to Ezekiel's portrait of the *nāśî*'. This ordinance reinforces the impression of a fundamentally religious (though not cultic), rather than civil/political, role. The *nāśî*' alone may enter the eastern gateway of the inner wall and observe the rituals performed in the inner court. Indeed, the gate will open up for him (v. 12), and he will be the first to bow before Yahweh in worship. Furthermore, as the patron of the cult, the prince is responsible for providing the sacrificial animals and other resources needed in the rituals. Even so, his primary identification is with the laypeople rather than the cult functionaries. The community at worship may look to him as their leader.

But this ordinance makes its own contribution to Ezekiel's theological vision. On the one hand, it reaffirms that Yahweh will not become common or familiar even with his people. Enthroned in his glory, he resides inside his temple, where only those whom he authorizes may enter. Neither people nor prince may view him directly; they may not even enter the inner court. The degrees of holiness inherent in sacred space are reflected in concentric walls of accessibility. But the glorious fact remains: in his grace Yahweh not only invites the worship of mortals; he reveals to them activities that guarantee acceptance with him and appoints officials whom he will receive on their behalf. The alienation of the distant past is over. Ezekiel's vision of daily, weekly, and monthly rituals proclaims the continuing grace of a deity at peace with his people.

72. Contra Rooker, in *Case for Premillennialism,* pp. 131-34.

h. Regulations Regarding Management of Royal Lands (46:16-18)

16 *"Thus has the Lord[1] Yahweh declared: If the prince presents a gift to each of his sons as an inheritance,[2] it shall belong to his sons.[3] It shall be their possession by inheritance.* 17 *And if he presents a gift from his inheritance to one of his servants, it shall belong[4] to him until the year of liberation,[5] when it shall return[6] to the prince. His sons shall by all means[7] keep their inheritance.* 18 *The prince shall not seize any of the people's inheritance by evicting[8] them from their property. He must grant the inheritance to his sons from his own property in order that none of my people are dispossessed of their property."*

This fragment represents a relatively independent unit, with its own opening citation formula in v. 16. It divides into two parts, the first (vv. 16-17) being cast in the form of a bifurcated casuistic regulation, and the second (v. 18) consisting of a prohibition, followed by a positive announcement of proper procedure. Several details link this fragment with 45:1-9: the primary interest in the *nāśî'* (though 45:8 had dealt with "princes"); the concern for real estate (*'ăhuzzâ);* the possibility of exploitation of the citizenry by the rulers, employing the verb *hônâ* (cf. 45:8); and the reference to Israel as "my people" (*'ammî).* While some have concluded from these ties that 45:10–46:15 was inserted secondarily between sections that were originally linked, one may also argue that this section belonged originally after 48:21-22, which also deals with the prince's property.[9] Any reconstruction of the editorial process

---

1. *'ădōnāy* is missing in most LXX mss.; LXX[B] reads κύριος Θεός.

2. Most commentators emend MT *nahălātô* to *minnahălātô* on the basis of LXX and v. 17. But not only is MT sensible; LXX may reflect dittography, the *mem* at the beginning of the previous word having been mistakenly duplicated. The same lack of care may have caused LXX translators to drop the *minnahălātô* in the next verse.

3. This conditional sentence follows the Late Biblical Hebrew pattern: asyndetic apodosis plus imperfect verb. Cf. Rooker, *Biblical Hebrew in Transition,* pp. 120-22.

4. This is the only occurrence in Ezekiel of the Early Biblical Hebrew pattern of conditional clauses: syndetic apodosis plus converted perfect verb.

5. Targ. interprets *šěnat hadděrôr* as *št' dywbyl',* "year of the Jubilee."

6. Since *wěšābat* appears to be a primitive *qatalat* form, replacing expected *wěšābâ, BHS*'s proposed emendation is unnecessary. In Lev. 22:13 and Isa. 23:17 the two forms appear together. On the form cf. GKC, §72o; Joüon-Muraoka, *Grammar,* §42f.

7. Treating *'ak* asseveratively. See Waltke-O'Connor, *Syntax,* §35.3.5d; GKC, §143b.

8. As in Lev. 25:14 and Ezek. 45:8, *hônâ* refers to the forced expulsion of a landowner and the confiscation of his property.

9. Cf. Hals, *Ezekiel,* p. 334. Zimmerli (*Ezekiel 2,* p. 496) credits these sections to the same editorial hand.

is conjectural, but this fragment's present location on the heels of a longer section (45:1-15) highlights the role of the prince.

Ezekiel's ordinance governing the administration of "crown" lands finds no counterpart in the Mosaic Torah. Where Mosaic materials deal with royal abuses, they focus on exploitation of the office of kingship for personal advantage by building up the military, establishing a harem, and accumulating wealth (Deut. 17:14-20). Ezekiel's present concern arises out of abuses common to the Israelite and Judean monarchies. When the monarchy was first established in the 11th century B.C., Samuel had warned the Israelites that a king would conscript their sons to work his land, expropriate the best of their fields, vineyards, and olive groves, and offer them as royal grants to his servants.[10] Such properties ended up in the king's possession through conquest or legal means: purchase, inheritance, or gift.[11] With the enhancement of royal power, however, kings were often tempted to exploit their subjects by the forced confiscation of private property, a tendency graphically illustrated in Ahab's seizure of Naboth's land (1 K. 21).[12] Foundational to Israel's real estate laws was the conviction that Yahweh was the owner of the land. He had divided the land among the tribes and given specific areas to the clans and families of Israel as inalienable property.[13] While some such transfers were almost inevitable, to ensure the permanent connection of particular families with particular lands, and thereby to prevent extreme social stratification through exploitation by the economically powerful, the Mosaic Torah established the Jubilee ordinance. According to this institution, at the end of every fifty-year period land that had fallen into outsiders' hands would return to the proper family.[14] In any case, over the centuries not only did the amount of land in royal hands increase; the rulers tended to accumulate the best land as well.[15]

---

10. See 1 Sam. 8:12-14. For discussions of Ugaritic parallels to this text see I. Mendelsohn, "Samuel's Denunciation of Kingship in the Light of the Akkadian Documents from Ugarit," *BASOR* 143 (1956) 19-20; A. F. Rainey, *RSP,* 2:97-98.

11. For purchase see 2 Sam. 24:24; 1 K. 16:24; cf. 1 K. 21:1-2. As inheritance see 2 Sam. 9:7ff.; 16:4; 19:30. As gifts see 1 K. 9:16.

12. As a foreigner Ahab's Tyrian wife, Jezebel, naturally lacked any sensitivity to the distinctive Israelite disposition toward the issue. K. Baltzer, "Naboths Weinberg (1 Kön 21): Der Konflikt zwischen israelitischem und kanaanäischem Bodenrecht," *Wort und Dienst* 8 (1965) 73-88. Fager's contention (*Land Tenure,* p. 102) that Israel's Jubilee laws represent an exilic priestly reaction to these abuses is not convincing.

13. Cf. Fager, *Land Tenure,* pp. 116-18.

14. See Lev. 25. For a full discussion of the ordinance see Fager, *Land Tenure.* See also Levine, *Leviticus,* pp. 270-74; Wright, *God's People in God's Land,* pp. 152-59; idem, *ABD,* 3:1025-30; F. I. Andersen, "The Socio-Juridical Background of the Naboth Incident," *JBL* 85 (1966) 46-57.

15. The OT lacks any evidence of a nationally observed Jubilee. Cf. C. J. H. Wright, *ABD,* 3:1027-28; Fager, *Land Tenure,* pp. 34-35.

Ezekiel addresses the issue from two sides. First, he secures the permanent ownership of crown lands for the *nāśî'* and his family by presenting two scenarios, both in casuistic form. On the one hand, he authorizes the prince to present portions of his property to his sons as a gift,[16] thereafter to be considered the sons' property *('ăḥuzzâ)*. This transfer presents no problems since the inheritance *(naḥălâ)* remains in the prince's family. On the other hand, should the *nāśî'* wish to award some of his land to his servants *('ăbādāyw)*, such transfers of ownership are to be temporary. Because the land has passed into the hands of one outside the family, in the year of liberation *(šĕnat haddĕrôr)* it must return to the prince. Whereas Ezekiel's contemporary, Jeremiah, applied the term *dĕrôr* to the "release" of persons (Jer. 34:8, 15, 17), the present usage is inspired by Lev. 25, which established the Israelite custom of "proclaiming release" *(qārā' dĕrôr)* every fiftieth year. In this "Year of Jubilee" all enslaved Israelites were to return *(šûb)* to their patrimonial holdings *('ăḥuzzâ)*. Ezekiel modifies the Mosaic ordinance by prescribing the return *(šûb)* of the land to the original owners' hands. Thus the divinely established link between family and property will be maintained.

In v. 18 Ezekiel secures the possession of the commoners' land holdings by prohibiting the *nāśî'* from exploitatively confiscating their divinely granted properties. If he wishes to grant his sons an inheritance *(naḥălâ)*, he may give them some of his own land, but he may not seize the property of his subjects. This prohibition affirms that while Yahweh assigns special roles to some (the *nāśî'* and the priests), he is concerned about the welfare of all Israelites, here affectionately referred to as *'ammî*, "my people."[17] As patron of the entire nation and owner of the entire land of Israel, he has established inviolable links between specific families and specific lands. The aim of this regulation, as expressed in the final purpose clause, is to right past wrongs, warning the *nāśî'* and his sons not to misbehave like the *nĕśî'îm* described in Ezek. 34:5-6, 21, exploiting their subjects and scattering *(pûṣ)* them from their lands. The verb *pûṣ* also links this ordinance with earlier references to the scattering of Israel among the nations (11:17; 20:34, 41; 28:25), suggesting that Ezekiel perceives the relationship between family and property as a microcosm of the link between the nation and the land of Israel as a whole.

Whether or not Ezekiel envisions this *nāśî'* as a messianic figure, the realism of this portrait is remarkable. As patron of the cult the prince enjoys a privileged position, but he stands in the shadow of the priesthood, barred from the inner court and subject to clearly defined restrictions. Furthermore, like the rulers of Israel in the past, he is vulnerable to temptations of self-

16. Cf. the present use of generic *mattānâ* with 20:26, 31, 39, where the word had denoted sacrificial gifts.

17. Cf. *'am hā'āreṣ*, "the people of the land," in v. 3.

aggrandizement, and ever in danger of exploiting his office at the expense his subjects.[18] In regulating the activity of the *nāśî*', this fragment reminds those who occupy positions of leadership in the community of faith that theirs is a service vocation, not a profession of privilege. Responsible leaders exercise authority within the bounds set by God, resisting the temptation to use the office for personal advantage and mindful of the rights of the inferiors. After all, the call to leadership is a gift of God, to be used for the benefit of all his people. At the same time, this legislation places firm strictures on other classes among the nobility (*śārîm* and *zĕqēnîm*), since they would stand to gain the most from a king's sweeping powers to confiscate and redistribute land. In Ezekiel's plan Israel is reconstituted a nation of free citizens, all of whom have equal rights regarding the ownership and occupation of land.[19]

i. The Temple Kitchens (46:19-24)

19 *Then he brought me through the passage at the side of the gateway, to the sacred chambers[20] of the priests,[21] which faced north. And there I noticed[22] an area at the far side to the west.[23]* 20 *He said to me, "This is the place where the priests shall boil the reparation offering and the purification offering, and where[24] they shall bake the grain offering, to prevent them from bringing them [the offerings] out into the outer court, thereby rendering the people holy.*

21 *Then he took me out to the outer court, and led me past the four*

18. Cf. J. Becker, *Messianic Expectation in the Old Testament,* tr. D. E. Green (Philadelphia: Fortress, 1980), pp. 62-63.

19. Cf. Duguid, *Ezekiel and the Leaders,* p. 130.

20. Since nouns in construct relation do not tolerate the article, the prefixed *hē* in *halliškôt haqqōdeš* was probably added inadvertently under the influence of the following '*el-hakkōhănîm*. Cf. *liškôt haqqōdeš* in 42:13.

21. MT '*el-hakkōhănîm* would have the prophet visiting the priests inside, even though he never encounters anyone other than the guide in the vision. With LXX, Targ., and Syr., which understand the priests as owners of the rooms, and *happōnôt ṣāpônâ*, "north-facing," as a reference to the chambers, an original *lakkōhănîm* or '*ăšer lakkōhănîm* may be proposed, '*l* functioning as an abbreviation for '*šr l*. Cf. Cooke, *Ezekiel,* p. 516; G. R. Driver, *Textus* 1 (1960) 123.

22. MT *wĕhinnēh,* lit. "and behold," expresses surprise.

23. LXX omits *yāmmâ,* "to the west," probably by haplography. Targ. and Syr. support Kethib in reading the ending of the preceding *byrktym* as a suffix, "at their far side" (cf. Gen. 49:13 for a similar form), but the dual absolute form represented by Qere, *yrktym,* followed by *ymh* (familiar from Exod. 26:27; 36:32; cf. 26:23; 36:28), is preferable.

24. '*ăšer . . . šām* earlier in the verse leads one to expect the adverb *šām* after the second '*ăšer.* Cf. LXX καὶ ἐκεῖ, "and there." Wevers's deletion of this admittedly awkward phrase as secondary (*Ezekiel,* p. 228) imposes unnecessarily rigid stylistic standards on the ancient writer.

corners of the court. In each corner of the court[25] I noticed[26] an enclosure. 22 The fenced-in enclosures[27] in the four corners were all the same size — each one measuring forty cubits long and thirty cubits wide.[28] 23 Inside each,[29] all around was a row [of masonry].[30] Beneath the rows hearths were constructed[31] all the way around. 24 Then he said to me, "These are the kitchens[32] where those who minister in the temple shall boil the sacrifices presented by the people."

♦ *Nature and Design*

After more than two chapters of oracles introduced by the prophetic citation formula (44:9–46:18), the threefold visionary guidance formula (46:19, 21; 47:1) signals a return to the visionary reporting style of 40:1–44:8. With regard to genre, therefore, 46:19-24 would have been more at home earlier, perhaps after 42:14.[33] While the unit appears dependent stylistically on 42:1-14, especially v. 13,[34] the designation of the Levites as *mĕšārĕtê habbayit*, "those who serve the temple" (v. 24), links it with 45:5, where the expression appears for the first time. The dimensions of these kitchens impose an additional complication in establishing the place of this text within chs. 40–48. On the one hand, measurements of the 40-by-30 cubit order occur nowhere else in the

25. On distributive repetition in Hebrew see Waltke-O'Connor, *Syntax*, §12.5; GKC, §123d.

26. MT reads *wĕhinnēh*, lit. "and behold."

27. Many emend MT's seemingly incomprehensible *qṭrwt* to *qṭnwt*, "small" (Zimmerli, *Ezekiel 2*, p. 499; NRSV, etc.), on the basis of LXX μιχρά and Syr. *dqdqt'*. But MT (supported by Targ.) is preferable on the basis of *lectio difficilior*. See further the commentary.

28. MT adds a denominative Hophal fem. participle, *mĕhuqṣāʿôt*, "corner rooms," at the end of the verse. The absence of the word in LXX, Vulg., and Syr., as well as the suspicions expressed by the Masoretes (note the *puncta extraordinaria*, on which see GKC, §5n), suggest that it may have originated as a marginal gloss on the masc. form *miqṣôʿôt* in v. 21 (cf. Allen, *Ezekiel 20–48*, p. 249).

29. MT *wĕṭûr sābîb bāhem*, lit. "around in each was a row." Zimmerli (*Ezekiel 2*, p. 499) defends MT against *BHS*'s proposed *lāhem*.

30. *ṭîrâ* replaces *ṭûr* in v. 23b. See also 25:4. On the significance of the word see the commentary.

31. Uninflected *ʿāśûy* in 40:17 and 41:18 argues against *BHS*'s emendation to *ʿăśûyôt taḥat*.

32. Although Targ., Syr., and Vulg. read sg., *bêt hamĕbaššĕlôt* should be construed as pl. with LXX. For this rare construction of the pl. see GKC, §124r; Joüon-Muraoka, *Grammar*, §136n.

33. Thus Ewald, *Prophets*, pp. 205-6. For a response see Keil, *Ezekiel*, pp. 348-49.

34. Cf. lexical links between 42:13 and 46:19-20: *minḥâ*, *ḥaṭṭāʾt*, *ʾāšām*, and esp. *liškôt haqqōdeš*.

temple plan.[35] On the other hand, the lexical links with earlier texts may just as well point to common authorship as to literary borrowing by a second hand. Furthermore, the present unit exhibits the common Ezekielian practice of "halving" (vv. 19-20, 21-24), each segment being introduced by its own guidance formula.[36] These two parts belong together and must be interpreted in the light of each other.[37] They have essentially the same shape, and both involve an area of the temple complex relating to the cooking of sacrificial meals. Both subdivide into two parts, an identification of the location of the structures described, followed by an explanation of their function.

To delete this passage as a secondarily inserted *Nachtrag* on the basis of novelty not only imposes stifling restrictions on any author but fails to respect the significance of the paragraph in the present context. Unlike Ezekiel's earlier accounts of the temple grounds, the primary concern here is not to describe the temple kitchens. The issue is the distinctive functions of two groups of kitchens: those in the inner court and those in the outer court. In keeping with the overall plan of the temple, the descriptions of these kitchens accentuate the increasing sanctity of the entire complex as one moves from the outer fringes to the inside. At the same time they highlight the professional distinctions between priests and Levites, as outlined in the Torah of the temple, 43:12–46:18. Finally, the problems created by deleting or moving this text are as serious as those intended to be solved. This operation would have left 47:1 following immediately on 46:18. However, the form of the visionary guidance formula here depends on 46:19 and 21.

In view of the stylistic and substantive links with the surrounding Ezekielian material, the importance of sacrificial meals in ancient cultic systems, and the explicit provision for the same in the Mosaic Torah (Exod. 29:32-33; Lev. 10:12-13; etc.), there is no compelling reason for denying the prophet a visit to the temple kitchens, or even a written report thereof.[38] This is not to deny the tensions created by the present arrangement, but to allow the possibility of theological agendas overriding logical considerations in the editorial process. Inasmuch as this text returns to a narration of the temple tour, it functions as a sort of appendix, tying up loose ends. Since its primary concern is to show that even the culinary arrangements of the new order were designed to guard the

35. These considerations lead many to delete 46:19-24 as inauthentic and non-Ezekielian. See Gese, *Verfassungsentwurf,* p. 89; Zimmerli, *Ezekiel 2,* p. 501.

36. This need not mean they were originally distinct messages, as argued by Cooke (*Ezekiel,* p. 513), who locates vv. 19-20 originally after 42:14 and vv. 21-24 after 40:17.

37. So also Zimmerli, *Ezekiel 2,* p. 500. Rautenburg (*Zukunftsthora,* p. 97) rearranges the respective parts in the following order: 42:14; 40:38-43; 46:19-24.

38. Greenberg comments: "There is no evidence for dissociating arranger from author (Ezekiel), but the complex associative linkage of this division especially indicates that its composition was in stages" (*Int* 38 [1984] 199).

graded levels of holiness within the temple complex, however, it advances notions that have been of more recent concern within the book.

19-20 According to the existing sequence of visionary guidance notices, Ezekiel and his guide had last been seen entering the north gate into the inner court to the front of the temple to witness the return of the glory of Yahweh (44:4). Now the prophet is led back through the north gate into the outer court. Turning left (west), he arrives at the northern priestly quarters, "the sacred chambers" *(liškôt haqqōdeš),* which he enters apparently via the passageway *(hammābô')* referred to in 42:9. While these rooms were visible to worshipers and entrance to this area was gained from the outer court, they were considered an extension of the inner court. Although only the northern kitchen is reported, the symmetry of the overall structure suggests that a counterpart also existed on the south side.

At the far end of the passage he notices a special area *(māqôm),* which the guide immediately identifies as an outdoor kitchen. The reader is left to wonder about the design of the kitchen, but its function is clearly stated. This is where the priests prepare their sacred meals: their portions of the "reparation" *('āšām),* "purification" *(ḥaṭṭā't),* and "grain" *(minḥâ)* offerings. How these meals were to be prepared is not indicated, except that the meat portions are to be boiled *(bāšal)* and the cereal portions baked *('āpâ).* From the final clause in v. 20 it is evident that the purpose of these arrangements was more important than the actual recipe for the meals. The prohibition on removing sacred portions from the sacristies reinforces the point made in 42:13, that the priests were to eat their most holy meals *there.* One may assume they are also to be prepared there to protect the priestly meals from profane touch (cf. 1 Sam. 2:12-17). Like the regulation regarding the priestly vestries (44:19), however, this prohibition is explicitly based on the contagious quality of holiness and intended to guard the people from harmful and perhaps lethal exposure to these objects (cf. Lev. 10:1-2; 2 Sam. 6:6-7).

21-22 The new guidance formula signals a new phase in the tour of the kitchens. Returning to the outer court, Ezekiel is led from corner to corner all the way around the complex. He notices in each corner a discreet but identical 40-by-30-cubit (about 68×51 ft.) area. Apart from their dimensions, the reader is again left guessing about the nature of these enclosures. The details provided are described with enigmatic technical architectural expressions. While the first word in the designation for the enclosures, *ḥăṣērôt qěṭurôt,* is clear ("court"), the second defies explanation. One's immediate response is to propose an Aramaism, cognate to Arab. *qaṭara,* "to couple together, to line up,"[39] but this

---

39. Which may explain Symmachus's συνημμένη. Cf. G. R. Driver, *Bib* 35 (1954) 311; Kopf, *VT* 8 (1958) 199; *HALOT,* p. 1095. This interpretation is followed by Allen, "integrated(?) enclosures" *(Ezekiel 20–48,* p. 248), and Busink *(Tempel,* 2:723), who envisages the courts abutting the wall surrounding the temple precinct.

association provides little help in reconstructing what the prophet saw. NJPS "unroofed" follows *m. Middot* 2:5, where the same root is understood as "without a roof."[40] However, the Aramaic rendering of Targ., *mqṭrn,* "fenced in,"[41] makes better sense in the present context.

23 The meaning of *ṭûr,* and its feminine variant, *ṭîrâ,* is also uncertain. The term usually denotes "row," on the basis of which some recognize in *ṭîrôt* stone walls fencing in the courts.[42] But these rows appear to be associated directly with the structures used to prepare the food. In fact, here the hearths *(mĕbaššĕlîm)* are constructed underneath *(taḥat)* the "rows." Accordingly, one should probably imagine a series of ovens made of tiered stones, or a stone ledge around the inside of the enclosure under which the fireplaces were located.

24 Although many questions regarding the design of these kitchens remain, the guide leaves no doubts concerning their function. The corner installations of the outer court provided facilities for lay worshipers to prepare their sacred meals. While the priests' meals were identified according to the offerings from which their portions were drawn, these are referred to more generally as *zebaḥ hā'ām,* "the sacrificial meals of the people." The cooks are identified as *mĕšārĕtê habbayit,* "those who serve the temple," evidently a reference to the Levites, whose duties had been spelled out in 44:11-14, as opposed to the Zadokite priests.

No counterparts to Ezekiel's temple kitchens are found in either the accounts of the tabernacle ritual or the description of Solomon's temple. Deut. 16:7 prescribes that Passover meals be cooked and eaten at the place *(māqôm)* that Yahweh chooses, but in the larger context's concern with annual pilgrimage festivals, "the place that Yahweh chooses" suggests no more than the site of the anticipated central shrine. According to 2 Chr. 35:11-13, at the time of Josiah's Passover, the Levites and priests slaughtered the sacrificial animals, cooked them "according to the custom" *(kammišpāṭ),* and distributed the portions to the people. Temple kitchens were obviously involved. 1 Sam. 2:12-17 describes how regulations like those outlined by Ezekiel could be violated, but the account assumes the reader's familiarity with the culinary arrangements.[43]

40. Yadin (*Temple Scroll,* 2:159) renders *ḥṣrwt qṭrwt* as "open courts." By this interpretation, however, the modifier *qṭrwt* seems superfluous since, as Busink (*Tempel,* 2:723) observes, *ḥāṣērôt* were by definition roofless.

41. Thus Levey, *Ezekiel,* p. 125; cf. Jastrow, *Dictionary,* p. 1353.

42. So Zimmerli, *Ezekiel 2,* p. 501; Busink, *Tempel,* 2:723. It is used of rows of gemstones (Exod. 28:17-20; 39:10-13), ornaments (1 K. 7:20, 24, 42), window frames (1 K. 7:4), and pillars (1 K. 7:2-3, 18). In 1 K. 6:36 and 7:12 *ṭûr* refers to a row of decorated cut stones, overlaid with beams.

43. Samuel's meal with Saul (1 Sam. 9:19-27) takes place away from the central shrine and is of a different order than the regular sacrificial meals envisioned in our text.

♦ Theological Implications

In bringing Ezekiel's Torah of the temple to a close, this short appendix reaffirms several important principles.

First, the Lord's business must be conducted in a manner respectful of his holiness. In Ezekiel's blueprint for the future every detail is determined by Yahweh. Even seemingly inconsequential matters like the temple kitchens and the activities conducted therein are designed to reflect the gradations of holiness that govern the shape of the entire complex. The priests' unique responsibilities in the service of Yahweh were accompanied by special privileges, like eating portions of the reparation, purification, and grain offerings. While lay participation in these meals was prohibited to prevent the contagion of holiness, the special kitchens in the outer court offered them the privilege of eating in the courts of Yahweh.

Second, these kitchens affirm Yahweh's determination to commune with them. In dramatic contrast to Mesopotamian observances, where the table of the deity was set primarily for the deity's benefit,[44] Yahweh invited his people to eat at his table. Thus Ezekiel's kitchens symbolize paradoxically both the transcendence and the immanence of Yahweh. The concern for the sanctity of the divine residence and all that transpires therein accords perfectly with the radiance of the divine glory. However, by eating at Yahweh's table, the Israelites celebrated their covenantal peace with God and delighted in fellowship with him. Herein lies the relevance of this text for the modern believer. True worshipers fall down before the transcendent majesty of God, and with the seraphim of Isa. 6 proclaim his holiness, but with joyful hearts they accept his gracious invitation to eat the communion meal, the Eucharist, in his presence.

3. The New Land (47:1–48:29)

The visionary guidance formula in v. 1 signals the beginning of a new literary unit. Although both form and genre set off 47:1-12 from 47:13–48:35, this segment shares with the remainder of the book a common vocabulary and interest in the land.[1] Its function at the head of the literary map of Israel compares with the role of 43:13-27 in relation to Ezekiel's "Torah of the temple." Just as the altar needed to be cleansed of its defilement before the

---

44. On which see Oppenheim, *Ancient Mesopotamia*, pp. 183-98.

1. Regarding form, see the citation formula, followed by a formal heading in v. 13. As for genre, 47:1-12 is cast as another episode in Ezekiel's guided tour; the remainder is prescriptive, fashioned as a divine speech addressed directly to Israel. On the vocabulary see Allen, *Ezekiel 20–48,* p. 276.

temple worship system could be established, so the land must be renewed before it can play its intended role in the deity-nation-land relationship.[2]

a. The Healing of the Land (47:1-12)

1 *Then he brought me back to the entrance of the temple. I was struck by the sight of[3] water issuing from underneath the temple threshold and flowing eastward — after all, the temple faced east. The water flowed down below[4] from the right side of the facade of the temple on the south side of the altar. 2 Then he led me out through the north gate[5] and took me around the outside to the outer[6] gate that faces eastward.[7] I noticed[8] the water[9] trickling[10] out from the south side. 3 Meanwhile the man continued eastward, with the measuring line in his hand. He measured off one thousand cubits[11] and led me through the water. It was ankle deep.[12] 4 Then he measured off one thousand cubits, and led me through the water. It was knee deep.[13] Then he measured off one thousand cubits, and led me through [it]. It was waist deep. 5 Then he measured off one thousand cubits. Now it was a stream,[14] which I was unable to cross[15] on account of the water level.[16] The stream was deep enough to swim[17] in,*

2. Cf. Stevenson, *Vision,* p. 164.

3. *wĕhinnēh,* lit. "And behold."

4. Somewhat awkward here, *mittaḥat* is missing in LXX, Syr., and Vulg., suggesting to many that it was erroneously copied from v. 1a (Toy, *Ezekiel,* p. 201; Cooke, *Ezekiel,* p. 522; Fuhs, *Ezechiel 25–48,* p. 257). But the omission may also reflect an attempt by early translators to smooth the text.

5. On *derek šaʿar ṣāpônâ,* without the article on the last word, see 46:9; 47:15.

6. LXX reads *heḥāṣēr* for *haḥûṣ.*

7. On the analogy of 43:1, many assume a transposition of *derek* and *happôneh* (see *BHS*).

8. *wĕhinnēh,* lit. "and behold."

9. The article on *mayim* was probably dropped by haplography. Cf. LXX.

10. On the onomatopoeic hapax *mĕpakkîm* see the commentary.

11. *ʾelep bāʾammâ,* lit. "a thousand with the cubit." On the idiom see 40:5.

12. MT *mê ʾopsāyim,* "waters of the ankles," involves an accusative of measure. See Joüon-Muraoka, *Grammar,* §127b; GKC, §128n. LXX ἀφέσεως simply transliterates *ʾopsāyim.*

13. *mayim birkāyim.* Contextual consistency calls for *mê birkāyim.* Thus many Hebrew mss., Targ., LXX.

14. *naḥal* is missing in LXX.

15. LXX and Syr. read third person, but the focus is on the prophet himself.

16. *kî gāʾû hammayim,* lit., "because the waters had risen up."

17. *śāḥû,* "swimming," is a hapax form, on which see W. von Soden, "Ist im Alten Testament schon vom Schwimmen de Rede?" *ZAH* 4 (1991) 165-70; GKC, §§24d, 93x. The verb *śāḥâ* occurs in Ps. 6:7 (Eng. 6) and possibly Isa. 25:11, though von Soden doubts the latter.

but impossible to wade across. 6 *Then he said to me, "You have been staring, human!"*[18] *Then he led me back*[19] *to the bank of the stream.*[20] 7 *When I got back*[21] *I was struck by the sight of a vast number of trees*[22] *on both banks of the stream.*

8 *Then he explained to me, "This water flows*[23] *out to the eastern region,*[24] *descends to the Arabah,*[25] *and enters the sea, the sea of stagnant waters.*[26] *Then the waters are healed,* 9 *and every living creature that swarms thrives*[27] *wherever the stream*[28] *flows. There are vast numbers of fish because these waters have arrived there, bringing healing and life wherever the stream flows.*[29] 10 *And*[30] *fishermen*

18. With Joüon-Muraoka, *Grammar,* §161b, ascribing exclamatory force to the prefixed *hă* on *hărā'îtā.* Most read a question.

19. MT has two verbs, *wayyôlikēnî wayĕšibēnî,* lit. "and he led me and took me back."

20. On *śĕpat hannahal* as an accusative of direction see Brockelmann, *Syntax,* §89.

21. MT *bĕšûbēnî* is odd, and should be read either *wayĕšibēnî,* "Then he brought me back" (but this would be redundant), or *bĕšûbî.* See G. R. Driver, *Bib* 35 (1954) 312.

22. *'ēṣ rab mĕ'ōd* may also translate "a gigantic tree," but in the light of v. 12, the collective sense is preferable.

23. The opening participle determines the continuous present tense of the verbs that follow.

24. LXX Γαλιλαίαν misunderstands *haggĕlîlâ* as a proper name. Vulg. *ad tumulos sabuli* relates the term to *gal,* "heap of stones."

25. LXX Ἀραβίαν; Vulg. *ad plana deserti.*

26. MT *'el-hayyāmmâ hammûṣā'îm,* "to the sea which have been brought out," is difficult. LXX τὸ ὕδωρ τῆς διεκβολῆς, "the waters of the breakthrough," assumes *hammayim* for *hayyāmâ,* which has the advantage of numerical agreement between noun and adjective. Vulg. deletes *'el-hayyāmmâ,* apparently recognizing the redundancy. REB "noxious" and NJPS "foul" follow G. R. Driver's (*Bib* 19 [1938] 186-87) explanation of *hammûṣā'îm* as a Hophal participle of *ṣû',* "to be polluted, filthy." Zimmerli (*Ezekiel 2,* p. 507) and BHS read *hahămûṣîm,* "salted." Cf. *hāmîṣ* in Isa. 30:24. The intended sense is undoubtedly caught by Syr. *sry',* "stagnant" (so NRSV).

27. Lit. "live."

28. The versions read MT's problematic dual *nahălayim* as sg.; Ehrlich (*Randglossen,* p. 158) emended it to *nahălām,* "their [viz., the waters'] stream." The dual form may have been influenced by the reference to two rivers in Zech. 14:8. The Ugaritic texts locate the home of El at the source of the two rivers *(mbk nhrm).* For references see Gordon, *UT,* p. 442. On this connection see Clements, *God and Temple,* p. 107 n. 2.

29. This sentence is both redundant and difficult in Hebrew. It assumes the subject of the pl. verb *wĕyērāpĕ'û* is the stagnant waters of the sea (cf. v. 8b). The following sg. *wāhāy* may be shorthand for "and teeming with life." While the final clause, *kol 'ăšer-yābô' šammâ hannahal,* "everywhere where the stream flows," is commonly deleted as a dittographic variant of *kol-'ăšer yābô' šam nahălayim* in v. 9a (cf. Allen, *Ezekiel 20–48,* pp. 271, 274), it is better retained as emphatic repetition.

30. LXX reads *wĕhāyâ* as *wĕhāyâ,* "and it will live," and places it at the end of v. 9. Syr. and Vulg. omit the word.

stand[31] *beside it,*[32] *all the way from En-gedi to En-eglaim. It is*[33] *a place where nets are spread out to dry. The variety*[34] *and abundance of its fish*[35] *are comparable to those of the fish in the Mediterranean Sea.*[36] 11 *As for its swamps*[37] *and marshes*[38] *— they are not healed; they are reserved as sources*[39] *of salt.*[40] 12 *All kinds of trees providing food*[41] *grow up along the stream, on both banks. Their leaves never wither, nor does their fruit ever cease. Every month they produce fresh fruit*[42] *because its [the stream's] waters flow out from the sanctuary. Their fruit provides*[43] *food and their leaves healing.*"[44]

♦ *Nature and Design*

Because of its uncharacteristic lexical forms, doublets, repetitions, grammatical anomalies, substantive infelicities, and awkward interruptions, critical scholarship has not taken kindly to the text of 47:1-12.[45] Apart from several

31. Reading *wĕʿāmĕdû* with the versions. Cf. Kethib *yʿmdw* and Qere *ʿmdw.* For a discussion see Gese, *Verfassungsentwurf,* p. 90 n. 1.
32. Allen (*Ezekiel 20–48,* p. 274) correctly identifies the antecedent as the stream, not the sea.
33. The pl. *yihyû* is determined by the presence of two place-names.
34. Reading *lĕmînāh* in place of MT *lĕmînâ.* On the form of the suffix, without mappiq, see GKC, §91e; Joüon-Muraoka, *Grammar,* §94h.
35. On the pl. suffix on *dĕgātām* see n. 28 above. The versions read sg.
36. *hayyām haggādôl,* lit. "the great sea" (cf. vv. 15, 19, 20; 48:28).
37. *biṣṣōʾt,* which occurs elsewhere only in Job 8:11 and 40:21 (as a place where reeds grow), is related to *bōṣ,* "mud," in Jer. 38:21. *bṣʾtyw* is an Aramaized pl. form of *biṣṣâ* and need not be corrected to *bṣwtyw* (contra Zimmerli, *Ezekiel 2,* p. 508).
38. LXX καὶ ἐν τῇ ὑπεράρσει αὐτοῦ incorrectly derives *gĕbaʾāyw* from *gābah,* not *gebeʾ,* "cistern, pool," which occurs elsewhere only in Isa. 30:14.
39. *nittānû,* lit. "they shall be given."
40. Targ. expands to "salt pits."
41. *kol-ʿēṣ-maʾăkāl,* lit. "all food trees."
42. *yĕbakkēr* is a denominative Piel from *bĕkôr,* "firstborn," meaning "to bear early or new fruit." Cf. J. Milgrom, "Hittite *ḫuelpi,*" *JAOS* 96 (1976) 575-76.
43. The idiom is *hāyâ* plus *lĕ.* With Qere and LXX read sg. *whyh* rather than Kethib pl. *whyw.*
44. *tĕrûpâ* is a hapax from *rûp,* a by-form of *rāpāʾ,* "to heal." Cf. also Sir. 38:4.
45. Lexical forms: *negeb,* "south" (v. 1; cf. *dārôm* in 40:24, 27-28, 44-45; 41:11; 42:12-13, 18); *qāw,* "measuring line" (v. 3; cf. *pĕtîl pištîm* in 40:3); *miptān,* "threshold" (v. 1; cf. *sap* in 40:7-8; 41:16[?]; 43:9). Doublets: e.g., *derek happôneh* (v. 2), both terms of which mean "in the direction of." See n. 7 above. Repetitions: note esp. *naḥal ʾăšer lōʾ-ʾûkal laʿăbōr* and *naḥal ʾăšer lōʾ-yēʿābēr* (v. 5); *kol-ʾăšer yābôʾ šām naḥălayim* and *kol ʾăšer-yābôʾ šāmmâ hannāḥal* (v. 9); *haddāgâ rabbâ mĕʾōd* (v. 9) and *dĕgātām . . . rabbâ mĕʾōd* (v. 10); *hammayim hāʾelleh wĕyērāpĕʾû* (v. 9) and *wĕnirpĕʾû hammayim* (v. 8). Grammatical anomalies: e.g., *bĕṣēʾt hāʾîš* without a preceding *wĕhāyâ* or *wayĕhî* in v. 3;

text-critical problems, however, nothing in the subunit is unbecoming of the prophet himself. Scholars agree on the fantastic nature of the renewal of the land portrayed here, which brings to a fitting climax not only the final vision but the prophecy of Ezekiel as a whole. It seems that by the time the prophet reached this phase of the tour, the sights he had witnessed had so gripped him that his excitement affected the literary quality of the report (cf. chs. 1, 7). His amazement is reflected in the threefold occurrence of *wĕhinnēh* (vv. 1, 2, 7),[46] and recognized by the interruptive comment of the guide in v. 6. This marvelous picture of renewal would have stirred the heart of any true Israelite, especially one who had lived through the desolation of Judah and spent many years in exile.

Structurally Ezek. 47:1-12 divides into two parts: vv. 1-7 and 8-12. The pattern of verse division in Hebrew and English Bibles obscures the remarkable symmetry of these two panels. In *BHS* they are virtually identical in length, the first consisting of 100 words, the second 102 words. This result may be purely accidental, but it suggests that the final form represents a deliberate literary composition, rather than the product of a series of editorial supplementations and mistaken insertions of marginal glosses. But the two panels are distinguished in genre. Vv. 1-7 are essentially narrative in form, while vv. 8-12 are taken up entirely with divine speech, formally introduced with *wayyō'mer 'ēlay*, "And he said to me," in v. 8. As a whole 47:1-12 may be classified as a vision report, complete with an account of the sight itself and its interpretation. But it is more. Yahweh's interpretation transforms the vision into a "prophecy of salvation."[47] However, the staged nature of the proceedings (including vision and interpretation), combined with the fantastic nature of the images, suggests another literary cartoon, which, like the Gog oracle (chs. 38–39), consists of eight frames, four in each part.

---

but on this construction see Rooker, *BHT,* pp. 103-5. Infelicities: the guidance formula in v. 1; the appearance of the man measuring the depth of the stream in vv. 3-5. Interruptions: the question/exclamation in v. 6a is separated from its answer in v. 8 by another guidance formula and prophetic observation in vv. 6b-7. On the basis of these considerations Fuhs (*Ezechiel 25–48,* pp. 256-60) reduces the basic text to vv. 1aβ, b, 2b, 6a, 8, 9aβ, b2, 12, which was originally attached to 43:7a. Wevers (*Ezekiel,* p. 333) maintains that this segment has been so heavily touched up by later scribal apocalypticists that it is impossible to recover its original form.

46. In vision reports *wĕhinnēh* not only introduces new scenes; it often expresses "excited perception." See D. J. McCarthy, "The Uses of wᵉhinnēh in Biblical Hebrew," *Bib* 61 (1980) 332-33.

47. So also Hals, *Ezekiel,* p. 338.

(1) The Vision of the River of Life (47:1-7)

1 *The first frame.* The opening scene of this literary cartoon finds the prophet being brought back to the entrance of the temple *(habbayit)* by the heavenly guide. If this text originally followed 44:1-2, as some maintain, the point of origin will have been the exterior east gate. According to the present arrangement, however, Ezekiel was last seen inspecting the sacrificial kitchens (46:21-24). Now he is amazed by the sight of a small stream of water gushing out from under the *miptān,* "threshold," an architectural designation for the slab of stone at the base of a doorway visible to an observer outside.[48] The last line of v. 1 identifies the place where the water emerges more precisely: *mikketep habbayit hayĕmānît,* "from the right side of the facade of the temple." *ketep* is also an architectural term, referring to the part of the gate structure that extends horizontally from the opening itself to the next corner, and vertically from the ground up at least as far as the top of the door. Each gate/door would have four *kĕtāpôt,* two on the inside and two outside.[49] But how are we to imagine the stream emerging from the right side of the facade and then flowing south of the altar, which according to 40:47 stands east of the temple? On the one hand, if the prophet as observer is the point of reference, "right" must mean the north side of the door opening, in which case the water would need to flow south along the wall and then turn toward the altar. On the other hand, the layout of the temple and the stream's direction of flow point to an east orientation, in which case *hayĕmānît* means both "right" and "south."

2 *The second frame.* Having allowed Ezekiel to observe the stream issuing from the threshold of the sanctuary, the guide leads him out of the temple complex by way of the north gate to the outside of the east gate. The most direct route to this spot would have led through the eastern gate itself, but it was barred to human traffic (44:1-2). Arriving outside the gate, Ezekiel notices water trickling out under the wall on the south side of the gate structure.[50] He describes the trickling action of the water with a hapax, *mĕpak-kîm,* an onomatopoeic formation from *pak,* "bottle," conveying the sound of liquid gurgling out of a flask. The choice of expression is intentional, highlighting the modest size of the stream at its source — no larger than the flow of water from the mouth of a small vessel.[51]

48. See above on 46:2.

49. Cf. Haak, *VT* 33 (1983) 276-77.

50. Zimmerli (*Ezekiel 2,* p. 511) observes correctly that the present alternation of *negeb* and *yĕmānît* to denote "south" and "right," respectively, rather than *dārôm* (cf. 40-42), need not suggest a secondary editorial hand. In 21:2 (Eng. 20:46) Ezekiel uses three different words for south: *negeb, dārôm, têmān.*

51. In its only other occurrences (1 Sam. 10:1; 2 K. 9:1, 3), *pak* refers to a vessel

3-5 *The third frame.* In the third scene the tour guide assumes a now thoroughly familiar role, symbolized by the measuring instrument in his hand.[52] Whether or not he has picked up a different instrument, the use of a new term, *qaw,*[53] alerts the reader to a possible shift in significance. The man's earlier measurement of the temple and its environs had highlighted its symmetrical plan and the gradations of holiness as one moved inward toward the sacred residence of Yahweh. But now the guide's intentions have changed. Ezekiel observes him wading downstream, measuring his distance from the temple as he goes. The third frame is actually subdivided into four stages, which portray in vivid visual terms the increasing volume of the stream as it flows eastward. The repetitive style of the first three stages reflects the guide's methodical manner, but the departure from the pattern in the fourth signals the climactic phase.[54]

With the east gate as his starting point, the guide measures his movement away from the temple, pausing at 1,000-cubit (about 1700 ft.) intervals to bring the prophet along. At each interval Ezekiel notes the depth of the water in which he is wading. The results are quite fantastic. Having begun as a mere trickle, the stream reaches his ankles at 1,000 cubits, his knees at 2,000 cubits, and his waist at 3,000 cubits. At the 4,000-cubit mark the trickle *(mĕpakkîm)* has swelled to a stream *(naḥal),* too deep to wade through and deep enough for swimming. At this point the measurement stops, leaving prophet and reader to extrapolate a geometric increase in volume of water every 1,000 cubits as it flows toward the sea. That this effect is achieved without apparent contributions from tributaries heightens the magnitude of the miracle.

---

used in anointing. The rabbinic tradition (*b. Yoma* 77b) has Rabbi Phinehas explaining on behalf of Rabbi Huna that the water emerges from the holy of holies (cf. Rev. 22:1) as a liquid thread the size of a locust's antenna, grows to the thread of a warp by the time it reaches the entrance to the sanctuary, and the thread of the woof once it reaches the entrance to the temple court. By the time it "bubbles forth" under the threshold of the sanctuary the flow has increased to the size of the mouth of a small flask. Here the word for "bubble forth," *pākak,* also plays on *pak,* "flask, pitcher."

52. In chs. 40–42 Ezekiel had watched him measuring the temple compound.

53. *qaw* is more common outside Ezekiel than either *qĕnēh hammiddâ,* "measuring reed," or *pĕtîl pištîm,* "line of flax" (40:3). Note *qaw middâ,* "measuring line," in Jer. 31:39; cf. 1 K. 7:23 = 2 Chr. 4:2; 2 K. 21:13; Isa. 34:11, 17; 44:13; Lam. 2:8; Job 38:5; Zech. 1:16.

54. Compare the structures of vv. 3-5 as follows:

v. 3   *wayyāmād 'elep bā'ammâ wayya'ăbirēnî bammayim mê 'opsāyim*

v. 4a *wayyāmād 'elep bā'ammâ wayya'ăbirēnî bammayim mê birkāyim*

v. 4b *wayyāmād 'elep bā'ammâ wayya'ăbirēnî   mê motnāyim*

v. 5   *wayyāmād 'elep naḥal 'ăšer lō'-'ûkal la'ăbōr*

           kî gā'û hammayim mê śāḥû naḥal 'ăšer lō'-yē'ābēr

6-7 *The fourth frame.* The sight has left Ezekiel staring in amazement. He is brought back to his senses by the guide's comment, which, though generally understood as a question, makes more sense in this context as an exclamation.[55] Obviously the prophet has been looking! The guide then leads him out of the water back to the bank. The third *wĕhinnēh* expresses his surprise at a new sight he had not noticed before. Both sides of the stream were lined with dense groves of trees. What conclusions the prophet drew from this observation one may only speculate, though now he must have recognized that he had been witnessing more than a lesson on Yahweh's miraculous power to increase a stream's volume of water. Did he begin to "see" the symbolic significance of the waters?

(2) The Interpretation of the River of Life (47:8-12)

8a, bα *The fifth frame.* However Ezekiel may have interpreted the stream and the trees on its bank, the interpretation offered by the guide leaves no doubts concerning its intended meaning. The first frame of the interpretive panel of this cartoon is essentially geographical in nature. Ezekiel learns that this stream, which disappears over the eastern horizon, eventually enters the sea. The number four figures again in four discrete expressions used to describe the stream's course.

First, the stream flows *'el-haggĕlîlâ haqqadmônâ* (lit. "the eastern circuit"),[56] a vague reference to the region between Jerusalem and the Jordan River. Second, the stream descends into the *Arabah*. Today the name usually identifies the depression south of the Dead Sea that terminates in the Gulf of Aqabah, but in the OT the name was also used more generally of the rift valley that runs from Lake Tiberias (Galilee) in the north to the Gulf of Aqabah in the south.[57] Ezekiel has in mind the south end of the Jordan Valley. Third, the water is said to flow into *the sea (hayyāmmâ)*. Although *yām* had earlier referred to the western sea, viz., the Mediterranean, here it obviously means the Dead Sea. Fourth, the destination is defined more precisely as *hayyāmmâ*

---

55. Joüon-Muraoka, *Grammar,* §161b, claims emphatic force for the prefixed *hă* in all occurrences of *hărā'îtā.* Cf. 8:12, 15, 17; 1 K. 20:13; 21:29; Jer. 3:6. See also BDB, p. 210. The verb *rā'â* is capable of a wide range of meanings: to see, observe, gaze, discover, become aware, perceive, experience; etc. See D. Vetter, *THAT,* 2:693-701.

56. Cf. *kol gĕlîlôt happĕlištîm,* "all the regions of the Philistines" (Josh. 13:2; Joel 4:4 [Eng. 3:4]), and *gĕlîlôt hayyardēn,* "the regions of the Jordan" (Josh. 22:10-11).

57. Cf. C. G. Rasmussen, *Zondervan NIV Atlas of the Bible* (Grand Rapids: Zondervan, 1989), p. 51. Today the valley running from Lake Tiberias to the Dead Sea is known as the Ghor, "the depression." Arabah is associated with Tiberias in Deut. 3:17; Josh. 11:2; 12:3; with the Red Sea and Elath in Deut. 1:1; 2:8. The Dead Sea is occasionally called the Sea of Arabah (Deut. 4:49; Josh. 3:16; 12:3; 2 K. 14:25).

hammûṣā'îm, the sea of stagnant waters. The expression is problematic textually, but the context supports a reference to the stagnant nature of the Dead Sea.

hammûṣā'îm is an appropriate description for the Dead Sea. The surface of this remarkable body of water is 1300 ft. (about 400 m.) below sea level, making it not only the lowest point in the rift valley but the lowest on the surface of the earth. With a salinity today of 26-35 percent, this body of water is also justly known as "the Salt Sea."[58] Three factors contribute to this special quality: the unusually saline feeder streams that emerge from sulfurous springs and flow through nitrous soil; the absence of an outlet, which means that all its minerals are trapped; the hot, dry atmosphere, which produces an evaporation rate equal to if not greater than the inflow of water from feeder streams and rivers. After millennia of accumulation, the high amounts of sodium, magnesium, calcium, potassium, and other chemicals have left the Dead Sea virtually devoid of life. With the exception of a few oases, the vegetation along its shores is limited to a few halophytic (salt-loving) species.[59]

The messenger seems oblivious to the geographic problems this course of the stream presents. In order for water to flow from Jerusalem to the Jordan Valley it must flow down into the Kidron, up over the Mount of Olives, and then cross a series of valleys and mountain ranges before it reaches its destination. Whether or not he envisions a cleavage of the barriers like that foreseen in Zech. 14:4, the scene calls for a miraculous act, the converse of that experienced by the Israelites at the Red Sea. Instead of creating a dry path through the sea, this holy stream produces a watercourse through the desert.

8bβ-10 *The sixth frame.* The last clause of v. 8 introduces a new literary picture, in which the focus is no longer topographic but biological. The moment the stream from the temple reaches the "Salt Sea" its waters are miraculously *healed.* *rāpā'* normally refers to the healing of a diseased body, but in this case the miracle involves neutralizing the baneful chemicals in the water, so it becomes fresh and life is no longer inhibited.[60] The fourfold *kol,* "all," and the repetition of an entire clause, *kol-'ăšer yābô' šām[mâ] naḥălayim,* "wherever the stream flowed," in v. 9 emphasize the thoroughness of the "healing." In language reminiscent of Gen. 1:20-21, the sea "swarms" *(šāraṣ)* with "every living creature" *(kol-nepeš ḥāyâ)* in "every place where

---

58. The salinity of the Great Salt Lake (Utah) is 18 percent; the ocean is 3.5-5 percent. On the expression "Salt Sea" see Gen. 14:3; Num. 34:3, 12; Deut. 3:17; Josh. 3:16; 12:3; 15:2, 5; 18:19. Cf. also *gê' [ham]melaḥ,* "Valley of Salt," in 2 Sam. 8:13; 2 K. 14:7; 1 Chr. 18:12; 2 Chr. 25:11; Ps. 60:2.

59. See further Rasmussen, *NIV Atlas,* pp. 44-45; Beitzel, *Moody Atlas,* pp. 40-42.

60. Cf. Elisha's "healing" of "poisonous water" *(hammayim rā'îm)* by throwing salt(!) into it (2 K. 2:19-22), and Moses' "sweetening" *(mātaq)* of bitter *(mārîm)* water at Marah by tossing in a piece of wood (Exod. 15:25). Cf. H. J. Stoebe, *THAT,* 2:803-9.

the stream flows." The causal clause, *kî bā'û šāmmâ hammayim hā'ēlleh,* "because these waters have arrived there," leaves no doubt about the source of the healing. The arrival of the living water from the temple revives the Dead Sea, which results in the profuse multiplication of fish *(wĕhāyâ haddāgâ rabbâ mĕ'ōd).*

Verse 10 concretizes the literary picture. All around the Dead Sea, from En-gedi to En-eglaim, fishermen are at work, spreading their nets and hauling in their catches. *En-gedi* (modern 'Ain Jidi) is a flourishing oasis on the western shore of the Dead Sea, opposite the Arnon River in Moab, whose waters emerge from a permanent spring on top of an escarpment 600 ft. above the lake and produce a ribbon of green along the stream to the sea. *En-eglaim* is more difficult to locate, but an identification with Eglath-shelishiyah, mentioned in Isa. 15:5 and Jer. 48:34 in association with Zoar, points to a spot on the east side of the Dead Sea.[61] Accordingly, En-gedi and En-eglaim, located on opposite sides of the Dead Sea, represent a topographical *merismus,* highlighting the totality of the "healing" of the waters. From west to east, all around the lake, fishermen will spread their nets to catch their fish. The present expression, *mištôah lahărāmîm,* "a spreading place for nets," carries a different sense than *mištah hărāmîm* in 26:5, 14. In the earlier text the image of nets spread out had served as a warning of judgment for Tyre; the city will be reduced to a bare rock where fishermen dry their nets. Here the figure symbolizes blessing. But these revived waters are renowned not only for the abundance of life they support but for the variety of their species. Indeed, the number of "their kinds" *(mînāh)* will rival the Great Sea *(hayyām haggādôl),* that is, the Mediterranean. One can scarcely imagine a greater contrast than between the Dead and Mediterranean Seas.

11 *The seventh frame.* But the guide informs Ezekiel of exceptions to this remarkable picture of life. According to v. 11, the water in the swamps *(biṣṣō'tāw)* and marshes *(gĕbā'āyw)* is not freshened. The shallow region of the tongue-shaped *Lashon* (Arab. *Lisan*), the peninsula jutting into the sea from the eastern shore, where the water is too shallow for fish, presents the most likely candidate for such murky pools of water. The preservation of some pockets of saltiness is intentional, recognizing the economic benefit of the minerals found in and around the Dead Sea. *salt (melah)* is not only a valuable seasoning and preserving agent; the word functions generically for a wide range of chemicals extracted from the sea.

12 *The eighth frame.* The guide's exposition on the revitalizing power of the temple stream concludes by returning briefly to the fourth scene, specifically the trees that flourish on both banks. This time the focus will be on the abundance of their growth and their benefits for human use. This image

61. See G. A. Herion, *ABD,* 2:501; A. F. Rainey, *ISBE,* 2:80-81.

is achieved with a few impressive strokes of the literary brush. First, both banks are filled with *kol-'ēṣ* (lit. "every tree"), which suggests both profusion and variety, answering to the species of fish mentioned in v. 10. Second, like the trees in Eden (Gen. 2:15-17), these will remain perpetually green and provide an endless supply of food *(ma'ăkāl)*. The impression of regularity and reliability, reflected in *lō'-yittōm piryô*, "its fruit will not fail," is rendered more concrete with *loḥŏdāšāyw yĕbakkēr*, "according to their months they will yield fresh fruit." This picture of abundance contrasts with the mediocrity that characterizes produce at the end of a harvest season. Third, in addition to satisfying aesthetic sensitivities, the never-withering leaves *(lō'-yibbôl)* serve a medicinal function, offering healing to sickly and wounded bodies. As in the case of the revitalized Dead Sea (v. 9), a causal clause removes all doubts about the source of this fruitfulness and healing: because their nourishing waters originate *(yāṣā')* in the sanctuary.[62]

With this comment, the interpretation of the vision comes to an abrupt halt. Both prophet and reader are left marveling at the life-giving power of the stream that flows from the house of Yahweh.

EXCURSUS:
THE AFTERLIFE OF EZEKIEL'S LIFE-GIVING RIVER

Few doubt that Ezekiel's vision of a life-giving stream has been influenced, at least in part, by Gen. 2:10-14, which portrays paradise as a garden, rendered fruitful by a river flowing out of Eden and dividing into four branches, and which Yahweh visits daily (3:8). However, Ezekiel offers this ancient Edenic tradition a special twist by merging it with official Zion theology, according to which the temple in Jerusalem is the source of blessing and nourishment to a dry and thirsty land.[63] If there is any cosmic symbolism at all behind or

---

62. Like *bayit* in v. 1, *miqdāš* is used in the general sense of the temple compound, rather than the temple building itself.

63. This Zion-river connection recalls Ps. 46:5 (Eng. 4), which speaks of "a river whose streams *(pĕlāgîm)* make glad the city of God, the holy habitation of the Most High" (NRSV). See also Ps. 36:9-10 (Eng. 8-9), where those who take refuge under Yahweh's wings drink "of the abundance of his house" *(yirwĕyun middešen bêtekā)*, "the river of his delights" *(naḥal 'ădānêkā tašqēm)*, since with him is "the fountain of life" *(mĕqôr ḥayyim)*. Ezekiel was undoubtedly familiar with the Gihon spring in the Kidron Valley, a vital source of water for Jerusalem from the 2nd millennium; it may have been considered sacred (cf. 1 K. 1:38), but nowhere is it associated with the temple. Zimmerli (*Ezekiel 2,* p. 511) also links the stream from the temple with the "gently flowing waters of Shiloah" (Isa. 8:6-7), but the connection is remote.

inherent in 47:1-12,[64] it is subordinated completely to Ezekiel's national agenda. Like his oracles against the nations and his promises of restoration, Ezekiel's vision for the future is focused on his own people and his own native land. That fishermen harvest their catches on the east side of the Dead Sea has no bearing on the nations; it simply enhances the image of this stream which vitalizes the stagnant waters wherever it flows. But what became of this vision?

The nearest analogue to Ezek. 47:1-12 is found in Joel 4:17-18 (Eng. 3:17-18). While agreement on the date of this prophet's ministry is lacking, the weight of the evidence favors an early exilic date,[65] in which case Ezekiel's motifs, if not his prophecy, would have been alive in the prophetic consciousness. Having compared the restored land of Israel to Eden earlier (2:3), in this oracle Joel describes the nation's glorious future:

> And you will know that I am Yahweh your God,
> Who dwells in Zion, my holy mountain.
> And Jerusalem will be holy;
> Never again will strangers pass through it.
> In that day the mountains will drip with wine,
> And the hills will flow with milk.
> All the gullies (*'ăpîqîm*) of Judah will flow with water;
> A spring (*'ayin*) will issue from the temple (*bayit*) of Yahweh,
> And water the Wadi of the Acacias.

The opening recognition formula, the specific vocabulary, and the focus on the nation of Israel are all strongly reminiscent of Ezekiel. Later Zechariah painted the eschatological scene with even bolder strokes. Although his interest is still narrowly nationalistic, in Zech. 14:5b-11 he links Yahweh's transformation of Jerusalem with universal sovereignty and cosmic restructuring. Speaking of Jerusalem, he predicts: "In that day living waters (*mayim ḥayyîm*) will flow from Jerusalem, one-half of them toward the Eastern (Dead) Sea, the other half to the Western (Mediterranean) Sea. This will happen in the summer time as well as in the winter" (v. 8). He says nothing

---

64. Thus Stevenson, *Vision*, p. 164; Fishbane, *Biblical Interpretation*, pp. 370-71; Batto, *Slaying the Dragon*, pp. 157-59, 176-77. Some have identified extrabiblical analogues to Ezekiel's association of temple and stream:'Gudea Cylinder B, 14.19-24 (Tuell, *Law of the Temple*, pp. 69-70); the Canaanite myth of El the high god living "at the source of the two rivers, the meeting place of the two deeps" (*'il mbk nhrm b'dt thmt; Ugaritica*, V, 7.3, on which see Clifford, *Cosmic Mountain*, pp. 48-51). On this connection see P. C. Craigie, *Psalms 1–50*, WBC (Waco: Word, 1983), pp. 343-44.

65. So H. G. M. Williamson, "Joel," *ISBE*, 2:1077-78; L. C. Allen, *The Book of Joel*, NICOT (Grand Rapids: Eerdmans, 1976), pp. 19-25.

about the source of the waters, though the Ezekielian image may be assumed.[66]

Later Jewish believers continued to find inspiration in Ezekiel's vision of the temple stream. The motif is not referred to directly in the Temple Scroll, but Yadin finds in 47:1-3 the stimulus for a conduit that conducts the water away from the house of the laver.[67] The imaginary account in the *Letter of Aristeas* of "an uninterrupted supply not only of water, just as if there were a plentiful spring rising naturally from within, but also of indescribably wonderful underground reservoirs," must have been inspired by Ezekiel.[68] According to a rabbinic midrash, Ezekiel's (and Zechariah's) stream will divide into three branches, which flow into the Sea of Tiberias (Galilee), the Sea of Sodom (Dead Sea), and the ultimate destination, the Great Sea (Mediterranean), respectively, and eventually encompass the whole world.[69]

Ezekiel's vision of the stream also lives on in the NT. One may recognize a veiled allusion in Jesus' words in John 7:38: "As the scripture has said, 'Out of the believer's heart shall flow rivers of living water,' " presumably as a life-giving agent of divine grace and blessing. The expression ὕδατος ζῶντος, "living waters," points immediately to Zechariah's *mayim ḥayyîm,* but secondarily to Ezekiel. Some have seen a connection with Ezekiel's En-eglaim in the 153 fish caught in John 21:11.[70] B. Grigsby has carried this interpretation still further, suggesting that the evangelist sees the resurrected Christ as fulfilling the role of Ezekiel's temple, dispensing living water to a barren world.[71] Whereas these interpretations are far from certain, the Ezekielian connection in Rev. 22:1-2 is obvious: "Then he [the interpreting

---

66. The image of Yahweh as a source of "living," viz., fructifying, waters appears also in Isa. 44:3-4; 55:1; 58:11.

67. Temple Scroll 30:12-14; see Yadin, *Temple Scroll,* p. 223.

68. *Aristeas* 89. Cf. Simons, *Jerusalem,* p. 48 n. 3. For the text see *OTP,* 2:18.

69. *T. Suk.* 3:3ff.; *Pirqe de Rabbi Eliezer* 51; *Yalqut Šim'oni* on Ezekiel no. 383 (47). See Levey, *Ezekiel,* p. 127 n. 2.

70. According to J. A. Emerton ("The Hundred and Fifty-three Fishes in John XXI.11," *JTS* 9 [1958] 86-89; idem, "Some New Testament Notes," *JTS* 11 [1960] 335-36), the figure is arrived at by a rabbinic interpretive device, known as *gematria,* by which the numerical values of words are totaled. The sum of the numerical value of letters involved in Eglaim may be computed as follows: ' (= 70) + *g* (= 3) + *l* (= 30) + *y* (= 10) + *m* (= 40), hence Eglaim = 153. The numerical value of Gedi is 17 (*g* = 3, *d* = 4, *y* = 10), which, when multiplied by 9, yields 153. The number 9 derives from the sum of the digits of 153. Recognizing this interpretation would be more convincing if it were based on Greek forms of the names, P. R. Ackroyd combined the spellings of several mss., arriving at the following result: Ηγγαδι value 33 + Αγαλλειμ value 120 = 153 ("The 153 Fishes in John XXI.11 — A Further Note," *JTS* 10 [1959] 94).

71. B. Grigsby, "Gematria and John 21[11] — Another Look at Ezekiel 47[10]," *Exp-Tim* 95 (1984) 177-78.

angel] showed me a river of the water of life, as clear as crystal, coming from the throne of God and of the Lamb through the middle of the street of the city. On either side of the river was the tree of life, with its twelve kinds of fruit, which it produces every month, and the leaves of the tree, which offer healing for the nations." The following verses demonstrate that John found in Ezekiel's vision the supreme imagery for the lifting of the curse from the earth.

Fascination with Ezek 12:1-12 is evident also in the writings of the early church. Even the Antiochian interpreters abandoned the literal for the allegorical interpretation. For example, Bishop Theodoret of Antioch (A.D. 393-458) drew the following connections:

Detail	Significance
River	The grace of Christ, who according to the flesh derives from the threshold of the Davidic line
River's increase	The growth of the church
Fourfold measurement	The four evangelists
Depth of the last sounding	The relative depth of the last gospel
Fruit of the trees	Good works
Foliage	The inner joy that accompanies good works
Course from Jerusalem through Galilee to the desert and on to the Dead Sea	The course of the gospel across Galilee to civilized pagans and barbarians
The freshening power of the stream's water	The sanctification of the myths and fables of pagans
The fish and fishermen	Souls and those who go after them
The salt pools	Lukewarm Christians whose punishment is a useful warning to others.[72]

Similar approaches are found in Polychronius, the brother of Theodore of Mopsuestia, Ephraem the Syrian (A.D. 306-73), and Jerome (A.D. 345-419).[73]

72. Cf. Neuss, *Ezechiel in Theologie und Kunst,* p. 59.
73. For Theodore the temple stream is a picture of the saving grace of Christ and baptism through which that grace is received (Neuss, ibid., p. 60). For Ephraem the stream initially represents the revitalized Jewish people after their return, but esp. the growing numbers of Christians who respond to the call of the Lord at the third, ninth, and eleventh hours. The life-giving power represents the power of the apostolic teaching which trans-

More recent Christian interpretation of Ezek 47:1-12 has tended to follow the lead of the early church, seeking to discover its meaning through a spiritualizing, if not allegorical, hermeneutic.[74] Reacting against spiritualizing excesses, literalist millenarians maintain that Ezekiel's vision foresees a future temple built on Mount Zion, with waters actually issuing forth from the building. These waters will make their way across the desert to the Dead Sea, freshen up its water, and fructify the land. The required contravention of natural and physical laws is no obstacle, since this is presented as a gloriously miraculous act of God.[75]

The question arises whether Ezekiel would have approved of either approach. Would he accept the dissolution of his own people into some sort of spiritual ideal, or did he really expect a literal fulfillment of his oracle? Respectful consideration of the genre of this prophetic experience, the details of the passage, and the broader context all point in another direction. First, the prophecy of the life-giving stream came to Ezekiel in visionary form, as part of the large revelation encompassing chs. 40–48. As we have frequently observed, this vision is characterized by idealistic and symbolic imagery, qualities that it shares with other visions in the book (chs. 1, 8–11, 37). None of the previous visions has called for a literal interpretation. But neither has the prophet been consciously proclaiming mystico-spiritual messages whose meaning was hidden until the coming of Christ. His was a profoundly theological message, intended for his immediate audience and designed to answer the utter despair and cynicism under which his people languished. Their shock at divine abandonment and expulsion from the homeland called for a message of reversal. Where the vision of the dry bones had announced the lifting of the curse of death, this vision proclaimed the renewal of all aspects of the deity, nation, and land relationships.

Second, virtually every detail of the vision is unrealistic and caricatured. Streams do not issue forth from temple thresholds, nor do they increase geometrically in size and volume, from a mere trickle to an unfordable stream in the desert, without benefit of tributaries. Waters do not flow over or through

---

forms the pagans (Neuss, ibid., p. 63). For Jerome the stream is a picture of the teaching of the church and the grace of baptism. The farther one progresses in one's Christian life, the deeper one enters into the life-giving waters. The river flows between two rows of trees, the books of the OT and NT, renders everything fruitful, and refreshes even the Dead Sea found in the souls of those who have died in sin (Neuss, ibid., p. 75).

74. After surveying a series of opinions, Greenhill commented, "We may take the gospel, with the gifts and graces of the Spirit, to be these waters; for the gospel is the ministration of the Spirit, as the Apostle saith, 2 Cor. iii.8" (*Ezekiel,* p. 815). His commentary proceeds accordingly.

75. See Feinberg, *Ezekiel,* pp. 271-73; cf. the more moderate statement of Alexander, "Ezekiel," pp. 988-90.

hills. When fresh water contacts putrid water, particularly the most fouled body on earth, the influence is from foul to fresh, not the reverse. A body of water as lifeless as the Dead Sea cannot match the Mediterranean in the number and variety of its fish, nor do marsh waters differ generically from water of the larger body. Trees do not break the seasonal patterns and produce fruit every month of the year, nor do the leaves of these trees have medicinal value. All these features suggest an impressionistic literary cartoon with an intentional ideological aim.

♦ *Theological Implications*

What then is the permanent message of Ezek. 47:1-12 for the people of God? The following lessons are suggestive. First, the prerequisite to renew the environment is to restore a people's relationship with God. That Ezekiel's portrayal of the land of Israel's physical revitalization comes at the end of this elaborate vision is no accident. This may happen only after Yahweh has returned to his people, and his people have accepted his presence with authentic faith and humble worship. Nor is it coincidental that before the stream flows out over the desert and down to the Arabah to rejuvenate land and sea, it passes by the altar. This structure, standing in the very center of the temple complex, symbolizes God's desire to receive sinful humans and his delight in their worship.

Second, conversely, the renewal of the environment represents the natural and logical concomitant of spiritual renewal. In the beginning God had pronounced the world he had made good (Gen. 1:31). At the cosmic level, the rebellion of humanity had brought his curse upon that good earth, and its only hope is in the lifting of the curse. This vision presents this same truth at the national level. Like his ancient Near Eastern neighbors, and in keeping with Yahweh's original covenant (Lev. 26:1-13; Deut. 28:1-14), Ezekiel expected the spiritual renewal of his people to be accompanied by the lifting of the curse from the land, demonstrated materially in numerous progeny, abundant crops, and large herds of livestock. In Ezek. 34:26-27 and 36:8-11 God had given his verbal promise of renewal and blessing; now that promise is concretized in visual form: Judean desert and Dead Sea, the most inhospitable of land and marine environments, respectively, serve as dramatic symbols of renewal.[76] Rev. 22:3 offers an interpretation of the river of life that is in perfect keeping with the historical interpretation of this text: "No longer will there be any curse" (NIV).

Third, the renewal of God's people is from start to finish a miraculous work of divine grace. The revitalization of the landscape is not achieved

76. Cf. Greenberg, *Int* 38 (1984) 199.

through human ingenuity, technology, or effort; it is the result of Yahweh's lifting of the curse and replacing it with his blessing. This river of life does not originate in the palace of the earthly king, but in the house of God. Wherever it flows, it produces life, even in the Dead Sea, the ultimate symbol of the curse (cf. Gen. 18). At the same time, the manner in which God produces life out of death is most remarkable. From small and often imperceptible beginnings and with little promise, God's grace transforms a hostile world.[77] Such is the mystery of divine power, miraculously bringing life out of death.

Fourth, Yahweh's concern for his holiness is matched by his desire to bless his people. Prior to ch. 47, everything about the design and ritual of the temple had reflected Yahweh's determination to protect his holiness. But this agenda has now been almost totally eclipsed.[78] Here the issue is not divine holiness but earthly well-being, abundant life that God offers to those among whom he resides and whom he rules. This passage declares that divine sanctity and grace are not antithetical notions but perfect correlatives of the divine character. Illegitimate contact with divine holiness by humans may be lethal, but not because Yahweh delights in death. On the contrary, the stream that flows from his temple symbolizes Yahweh's firm and enthusiastic vote for life (cf. 18:32).

But where does all this leave the believer on this side of the cross? If one cannot spiritualize the stream as the Messiah, or the water as the water of baptism, or the four measurements as pictures of the four Gospels, what then is left? Everything. First, believers may rejoice in knowing that their well-being is the passion of God, and that when one's relationship with him is right, then the rest of life will be as well (Matt. 6:33). Second, the work of renewal in an individual's life and in the church is from start to finish a divine work. Third, the Lord retains his interest in the physical environment. "This is my Father's world," and when the human race is finally reconciled to him, all of creation will reap the benefits (Rom. 8:18-25). Fourth, as the new temple of God, the church serves as the agent of life and renewal to a world that languishes under the curse of sin and death (cf. 1 Cor. 3:16; 2 Cor. 6:16-18). Fifth, the abundant life is offered to all who worship the Lord in spirit and in truth, for whoever believes in him will overflow with rivers of living water (John 7:38).

---

77. This stream offers an OT antecedent to Jesus' parabolic mustard seed, which, as a symbol of the kingdom of God, begins as a mere speck, but grows into a huge tree where birds may dwell and nest (Matt. 13:31-32).

78. The only remaining hint is found in the final reference to the temple as *hammiqdāš,* "the holy place" (v. 12).

My old songs sprang up from a bitter well,
And were contrived to channel off the flow
Into a guarded land, a distant hell
Which I could view apart, and then let go.
But now before me seems a river sweet
And clear, which runs into a land unknown.
The only songs I know are for retreat,
For stepping back, aloof, afraid, alone.
I shall not force this new geography
Into old paths of pain, but tentative
Let this bright stream create new songs in me
Whose forms I do not know, yet form must give.
I will not make the music: I will be
The song itself, while so you flow through me.[79]

b. The Reapportionment of the Land of Israel (47:13–48:29)

♦ Nature and Design

The material from 47:13 to 48:29 constitutes a single literary unit, formally framed by the last occurrences of the citation and signatory formulae in the book, which also mark the intervening section off as divine speech. The latter impression is strengthened by Yahweh's self-reference in the first person in 47:14 and 48:11, as well as the use of the second person of direct address in 47:13-14, 21-23 (which also concludes with the signatory formula), 48:8-9, 29. But the address proper has its own formal boundaries: "This is the boundary according to which you shall divide up the land as a special grant among the twelve tribes of Israel" (47:13aβ-bα), and "This is the land that you shall apportion by lot as a special grant for the tribes of Israel. These are their respective allotments" (48:29a-bα). However, the address is not uniform, either in style or content. Indeed, the bulk of the unit has a different flavor, and variations in expression and tone point to a rather complex structure. First, the material that actually answers the agenda set by the framework is limited to two relatively small segments, 48:1-7 and 48:23-27. That these may originally have been combined as an uninterrupted document finds support in their common style and subject matter. Even so, the cold and impersonal style sounds less like a speech than a tribal boundary list, derived perhaps from a preexistent map. The boundary list is interrupted by a more detailed and less stilted description of the property set aside for the priests (48:8-14), the "city" for all Israelites (vv. 15-20), and the allotment of the prince (vv. 21-22). With

79. A poem by my student, Alison Bucklin (1983); used by permission.

the exception of vv. 8-9, these subsections are all cast in the third person of indirect address. The only part of the speech still unaccounted for, 47:15-20, reports the boundaries of the land of Israel as a whole. Like the tribal lists, the style is deliberate and formal, again presented in the third person.

Scholars have traditionally attributed these variations in style and content to different hands that have taken the preexisting material and added their own interpretations.[1] Zimmerli insists on an exilic origin at least for the basic text, since hints of the period of restoration are absent. Since the roles of the Levites and priests in the sanctuary service are differentiated, the situation later than 40:45-46a seems to be envisioned, but the devaluation of the Levites called for in 44:10ff. is not reflected in the basic text (he deletes 48:11 as a secondary addition). At the same time, the picture of the prince *(nāśî')* is becoming more concrete, suggesting a Davidic figure at the head of a community with the temple at the center. Thus ch. 48 is given priority over 45:1-8a, and the basic text of 47:13–48:29 is seen as the product of reflection in the priestly "school" of Ezekiel.[2]

But such a late date for the text seems unnecessary. Allen observes rightly that rather than correcting 47:14, vv. 22-23 provide an effective parallel and climactic advancement of vv. 13-14.[3] The unexpected reminder of the distinctions between priests and Levites in 48:11-12 (cf. 44:4-16) is probably a late redactional addition, but this does not rule out an Ezekielian origin. Indeed, questions of authorship and redaction may overlap. Given Ezekiel's priestly status and the concern for cultic affairs expressed elsewhere, inserted comments on the sanctuary service and the gradations of holiness are not as unusual as they appear at first. The portrait of the *nāśî'* in 48:21-22 (as in previous portions of chs. 40–48) is admittedly less idealistic than the person with the same title in 34:24 and 37:25, but the images are not incompatible. Apart from textually problematic readings, there is nothing in this text that could not come from Ezekiel's mouth, if not his pen.

---

1. According to Fohrer (*Ezechiel*, pp. 257-62) 47:13-23 belongs before 45:1-8, which presupposes it, though vv. 14 and 21-23 are deleted as later glosses. 48:1-8 and 23-29 are later elaborations on the division of the land among the tribes, referred to only in passing in 45:8. 48:9-22, which is dependent on 45:1-8, was composed at an even later date and inserted in its present position. Gese (*Verfassungsentwurf,* pp. 99-100) claims that, except for 47:13b and 47:22-23, all of 47:13–48:29 derives from a single hand, the apparent disjunctions being attributable to tradition-historical rather than compositional factors. In the light of "the unmistakable framing of 47:13–48:29," Zimmerli (*Ezekiel 2,* p. 526) also advises against dissecting the larger unit into a series of independent units, but his original basic text is slightly less generous than Gese's. In addition to 47:13b and 47:22-23, he deletes 48:11-12, 21b-22, as secondary amplifications.

2. Zimmerli, *Ezekiel 2,* p. 542.

3. Allen, *Ezekiel 20–48,* p. 278.

This does not mean this prophecy was originally delivered in the present written form. On the contrary, signs of redaction are as evident here as anywhere else in the book. Ezekiel may have received the revelation reflected in the boundary list (47:15-21), the apportionment of the tribal territories (48:1-7, 23-28), and the Levitical (48:8-10, 13-14), common (48:15-20), and princely (48:21-22) allotments on separate occasions. Even though the form of 47:15-21 is traditional (see below), the larger literary unit begins logically with an overview of the national boundaries. At an earlier stage, 48:1 may have followed 47:21, and 48:1-7 and 23-28 probably constituted a single unit, now broken up by the lengthy insertion, 48:8-10, 13-22. The placement of the interruption between the accounts of the Judahite and Benjamite allotments seems intentional, reflecting the relative geographic positions of the respective territories. The framework (47:13-14; 48:29), the expressed concern for the aliens (47:22-23), and the Zadokite insertion (48:11-12) represent the latest stages in the redactional process. But these smaller segments have been intentionally integrated into the text to create a more or less coherent whole.[4] These insertions determine the tone of the entire unit, transforming otherwise cold and formal descriptions into a forceful prophetic document. The message proclaimed here is not merely the work of a human cartographer drawn up in some office. The literary unit comes with the same divine authority as the previous seven chapters, and indeed the entire book.

(1) The New Boundaries for the Land (47:13-23)

13 *Thus has the Lord Yahweh declared:*
"This is the boundary[5] according to which[6] you shall divide up the land as a special grant among[7] the twelve tribes of Israel. [Joseph shall receive two allotments.][8] 14 *The land that I swore to give to your*

---

4. The *Leitwort* of 47:15-20, *gĕbûl*, "boundary," occurs in the formal introduction in vv. 13-14, and is assumed by the retrospective pronoun in v. 22 (*'ôtāh*), as well as the fem. verb in 48:12 *(wĕhāyĕyâ)*, whose subject is identified in v. 10. The *Leitwort* in 48:12, *tĕrûmâ*, is borrowed from the preceding paragraph.

5. Even Barthélemy, et al., eds. (*Preliminary Report*, 5:188) treat *gēh gĕbûl* as an error for *zeh haggĕbûl*, the first *gimel* probably having been written in anticipation of the second, and the article dropped by haplography. This conclusion is supported by LXX, Vulg., and Targ., as well as the form of the colophon in 48:29. MT points *gēh* like *gēy[']*, "valley," which is the reading of Syr.

6. The conjunction *'ăšer* introduces an adverbial accusative. Cf. Keil, *Ezekiel*, p. 362.

7. On *lamed* after *hitnaḥēl* introducing the beneficiaries of the action see Lev. 25:46 and Num. 33:54.

8. Although *yôsēp ḥăbālîm* (though rendered dual in Targ., Vulg.) is attested in all the versions, it is intrusive and ungrammatical. If anything, *lĕyôsēp ḥablāyim* (dual) is required. Allen (*Ezekiel 20–48*, p. 274) suggests a harmonizing gloss.

ancestors, you shall receive as a special grant, equally apportioned.[9]
This land shall fall to you as a special grant.

15 *This shall be the border of the land: In the north*[10] *it shall run
from the Mediterranean Sea*[11] *through*[12] *Hethlon and Lebo-hamath*[13]
16 *to Zedad, Beruthah, and Sibraim*[14] *(which is located between the
territories of Damascus and Hamath) as far as Hazer-hatticon,*[15]
which is on the border of Hauran. 17 *So the border*[16] *shall run from
the sea to Hazer-enon,*[17] *that is, the northern border of Damascus,
with the territory of Hamath to the north.*[18] *This*[19] *shall be the north
side.*

18 *On the east side [the border shall run] from a point*[20] *between
Hauran and Damascus, between*[21] *Gilead and the land of Israel, with
the Jordan forming the border*[22] *as far as the eastern sea, to Tamar.*[23]
This shall be the east side.

19 *On the south side*[24] *[the border shall run] from Tamar as far as*

9. *'îš kĕ'āḥîw,* lit. "each like his brother" (cf. Lev. 7:10).

10. The *hē* directive on *ṣāpônâ* has lost its force after *lip'at.*

11. *hayyām haggādôl,* lit. "the great sea."

12. The article on *hadderek* is ungrammatical. Cf. 48:1.

13. MT reads simply *lĕbô'; ṣĕdādâ* and *ḥāmāt,* the first word in v. 16, were
apparently transposed. Cf. LXX and 48:1.

14. LXX adds Ηλιαμ after Sibraim. Cf. 2 Sam. 10:16.

15. The versions cannot agree on the meaning of *ḥāṣēr hattîkôn:* Targ. *brykt 'gyb'y,*
"pond of the Agibites"; Vulg. *domus Tichon.* BHS emends to *ḥāṣērâ 'ênôn* on the basis
of LXX αὐλὴ τοῦ Σαυναν (LXX^A Ευναν), "the court of Saunan (Eunan)," as well as
v. 17, 48:1, and Num. 34:9-10. But the location of Hazer-hatticon cited renders this
emendation unlikely. See the commentary.

16. The article has dropped from *gĕbûl* by haplography. See the versions and
BHS.

17. After *min-hayyām, ḥāṣēr 'ênôn* should either be preceded by a preposition, *'ad*
or *lĕ,* or have a *hē* directive attached.

18. *gĕbûl dammeśeq wĕṣāpôn ṣāpônâ ûgĕbûl ḥ'māt,* lit. "the border of Damascus
and north northward and the border of Hamath," is confusing. Though *wĕṣāpôn* is attested
in the versions, it is probably an early dittographic gloss. Cf. 48:1.

19. *w't* is an error for *zō't* that is repeated in vv. 18 and 19. Cf. v. 20.

20. This is the sense of *mibbên.* Many insert Hazar-enon (*BHS,* RSV), though
NRSV has deleted it.

21. *ûmibbên,* lit. "from between."

22. *miggĕbûl* may be a scribal error for *magbîl.* Cf. LXX (διορίζει), Vulg., Syr.

23. The verb *tmdw,* pointed by MT as "you shall measure," is out of place.
Emendation to *tmrh,* "date palm," viz., Jericho, is supported by LXX Φοινικῶνος and
Syr. *'l ym' mdnḥy' dtmr,* as well as v. 19 and 48:28. Cf. Zimmerli, *Ezekiel 2,* p. 520;
Barthélemy, et al., eds., *Preliminary Report,* 5:192-93; NRSV. *tmr* reappears in v. 19.

24. The redundancy, *negeb têmānâ,* is supported by LXX (joined with the copula)
and 48:28. 21:2 uses three designations for south, *negeb, dārôm,* and *têmān.*

the waters of Meribath-kadesh,[25] *to the brook*[26] *and the Mediterranean Sea. This shall be the south side.*

20 *On the west side the Mediterranean Sea shall form the boundary*[27] *as far as a point opposite Lebo-hamath. This shall be the west side.*

21 *You shall apportion this land among yourselves according to the tribes of Israel.* 22 *You shall allot it*[28] *as a special grant for yourselves and for the proselytes who reside among you, who have fathered children among you. You shall treat them the same as you do the ethnic Israelites. They shall share the allotment*[29] *[of land] as a special grant among the tribes of Israel.* 23 *His special grant is to be awarded to him within whatever tribe the proselyte resides. The declaration of the Lord Yahweh.*"

Although the opening citation formula actually applies to all of 47:13–49:29, the signatory formula at the end of v. 23, which invites the reader to interpret the preceding as divine speech, also signals the end of a discreet literary segment. Vv. 15-20, which delineate the boundaries of the land of Israel, constitute the heart of the speech. In keeping with the content, the style is formal and cast in the third person. The conclusion that vv. 13-14 and 21-23 were deliberately composed to provide the boundary description with a literary framework is supported by a series of stylistic and lexical features.[30] The vesting of aliens with full landholding rights in vv. 22-23 admittedly introduces a new element, but this array of links points to a single hand and a deliberately

---

25. MT pl. *mĕrîbôt qādeš* is reflected in LXX Μαριμωθ and Targ. *mṣwt rqm.* On the rendering of Kadesh as Reqam in Targ. see Gen. 16:14; 20:1. The sg. rendering is supported by 48:28, as well as Num. 27:14 and Deut. 32:51.

26. Targ. *'ḥsn'* and Syr. *ywrtn'* read *nḥlh* as "inheritance."

27. With LXX διορίζει and Syr. *mtḥm* read *magbîl.*

28. *wĕhāyâ* before *tappilû* is dropped by LXX and Vulg. That *tappilû* is shorthand for *tappilû gôrāl* is recognized by LXX βαλεῖτε αὐτήν ἐν κλήρῳ and Vulg. *mittetis . . . in hereditatem.*

29. MT's pointing of *yippĕlû,* "they shall be allotted," makes no sense; people are never divided this way. With *BHS* the word should be repointed as a Hiphil, *yappilû.* See Zimmerli, *Ezekiel 2,* p. 521.

30. (a) Both are cast in the second person of direct address (cf. the third person in vv. 15-20); (b) they share the same key root, *nḥl,* with the three occurrences in vv. 13-14 being matched by three counterparts in vv. 21-23 (the two occurrences in v. 14 are verbal; the remainder nominal); (c) the clause *wĕnāpĕlâ hā'āreṣ hazzō't lākem bĕnaḥălâ,* "And this land shall fall to you as a special grant," in v. 14, is answered by *tappilû 'ôtāh bĕnaḥălâ lākem,* "you shall drop it [the land] as a special grant," in v. 22; (d) the reference to "the twelve tribes of Israel" *(šĕnê 'āśār šibṭê yiśrā'ēl)* in v. 13 is matched by "the tribes of Israel" *(šibṭê yiśrā'ēl)* in v. 21; (e) the comparative phrase *'îš kĕ'āḥîw,* "each like his brother," corresponds roughly to *wĕhāyû lākem kĕ'ezrāh bibnê yiśrā'ēl,* "And they shall be to you like the native born among the sons of Israel." Cf. Allen, *Ezekiel 20–48,* p. 278.

composed subunit. Although the center section offers an objective description of Israel's territorial limits, the emphasis on *naḥălâ,* "special grant," in the framework gives it a theological spin.

(a) Preamble (47:13-14)

13 The opening announcement, *zeh haggĕbûl,* "This is the boundary/territory," introduces the key word of this subunit and links the opening statement formally with the boundary description that follows. The singular form of *gĕbûl,* which occurs nine times in vv. 15-20, functions collectively for the entire area to be apportioned. According to the modifier, the territory delimited by the *gĕbûl* is to be apportioned as Yahweh's grant of land[31] to the twelve tribes of Israel. Since inheritance terminology is inevitably associated with passing down property or privilege from parent to child, as in 45:1, the root *nḥl* should be interpreted feudally, rather than hereditarily. Biblical accounts of land distribution among the Israelites never speak of Yahweh, the donor, as father; they portray him as suzerain.[32] Thus *naḥălâ* denotes property, in this case land, specially granted by a superior to his inferiors as a reward for services rendered, or in anticipation of services yet to be performed. Ezekiel is undoubtedly aware of Yahweh's claims to ownership of the land (cf. Lev. 25:23),[33] now to be redistributed among the tribes of the vassal nation. The choice of *šibṭê yiśrā'ēl,* rather than *bêt yiśrā'ēl,* Ezekiel's favorite collective designation for the nation, is deliberate. The phrase occurs eight times in this final unit,[34] but elsewhere only in 37:19, where by his sign-action the prophet had highlighted the eventual reunion of all "the tribes of Israel." However, the present text had been foreshadowed by a passing reference to the granting *(nātan)* of land to "the house of Israel" *lĕšibṭêhem,* "according to their tribes."

In 37:19 Ezekiel had not specified how many "tribes of Israel" would participate in the national restoration. The present announcement that the land is to be distributed among *twelve (šĕnê 'āśār)* answers the question.[35] Although

---

31. The Hithpael form of *nḥl* occurs only here in Ezekiel (cf. v. 14b, Qal), and elsewhere only six times (Lev. 25:46; Num. 32:18; 33:54 [bis]; 34:13; Isa. 14:2). The verb is a denominative derived from the noun *naḥălâ,* "special land grant." Since the act of distributing the grant is expressed by the Piel and Hiphil, a reflexive sense, "to apportion among yourselves," is suggested, which suits the present context well, even though the beneficiaries of the action are identified as "the tribes of Israel." See n. 7 above.

32. Contra C. J. H. Wright (*God's People in God's Land,* pp. 15-23), who acknowledges Deut. 14:1 as the sole direct reference to Israel as Yahweh's son.

33. On which see ibid., pp. 1-13; Block, *Gods of the Nations,* pp. 74-84; Fager, *Land Tenure,* pp. 31-34.

34. Cf. vv. 21, 22; 48:1, 19, 23, 29, 31.

35. Their names will be listed in 48:1-7, 23-28.

the nation had been divided politically for nearly four hundred years, as in the case of all his prophetic colleagues Ezekiel's vision of Israel's future is based on the tradition of a united nation consisting of twelve tribes of Israel descended from Jacob's twelve sons. By the time of this prophecy, the northern tribes, referred to as Ephraim and his associates in 37:19, had been scattered throughout the former Assyrian Empire for two and one-half centuries, and now the people of Judah had joined them. From a human standpoint, the future of the nation was hopeless (cf. 37:11). But in this divine word Ezekiel hears a promise that the curse of intertribal alienation, separation from Yahweh, and exile from the land would be reversed. The command to apportion the land symbolizes the culmination of Israel's rehabilitation and declares concretely that *shalom* among deity, nation, and land has been fully restored.

Verse 13 ends with an unexpected note, reminding the readers that in this twelve-tribe system Joseph has a double portion *(ḥablāyim).*[36] The literal usage of *ḥebel,* "a cord, rope," has been encountered earlier in 27:4, but the word may also denote "measuring rod," from which is derived the sense "surveyed and allotted tract of land," and "region, territory."[37] The present usage abbreviates the fuller expression *ḥebel naḥălâ,* "specially granted tract," which describes the land of Israel in Deut. 32:9 and 1 Chr. 16:18 (= Ps. 105:11). While the note does not explain the double portion, it reflects a vision of the future that is rooted in the traditions of the past, specifically Jacob's pronouncement of a special blessing on Joseph's two sons, Ephraim and Manasseh (Gen. 48:8-22), by which he conferred on them status equal to his immediate sons and gave Joseph an extra share in his inheritance. With the removal of Levi from the territorial allotments, this bifurcation of the line of Joseph enabled a retention of the twelve-tribe system.

14 In its reiteration of the command to divide the land as a special grant,[38] v. 14 establishes the standard for the distribution: each of the ancestral brothers *('āḥ)* is to receive an equal share. The declaration also asserts that this apportionment represents the fulfillment of the oath that Yahweh had

---

36. The preference for *ḥebel* over *ḥēleq* (45:7; 48:8, 21) as a designation for "tribal allotment" is insufficient reason to deny Ezekiel this note. As a priest, he was sensitive to Levi's special status and its implications for the twelve-tribe system. This note alerts the reader to the irregularity in the twelve-tribe tradition and signals its continuation in the new order.

37. On the meaning "cord" see the synonym *'ăbōt* in 3:25 and 4:8. For measuring rod cf. *ḥebel middâ* in Zech. 2:5 (Eng. 1), and *ḥebel* alone in 2 Sam. 8:2; Amos 7:17; Mic. 2:5; Ps. 78:55. For "surveyed land" see H.-J. Fabry, *TDOT,* 4:177. On "region " cf. *ḥebel 'argōb,* "the region of Argob," Deut. 3:4, 13, 14; *ḥebel 'akzîb,* "the region of Achzib," Josh. 19:29; *ḥebel hayyām,* "the region of the sea," Zeph. 2:5. The term is used in an abstract sense of one's "lot, fortune," in Job 21:17; Ps. 16:5.

38. Note the switch from the Hithpael to the Qal of the denominative verb *nḥl.*

made to the patriarchal ancestors more than a millennium earlier.[39] Ezekiel's people should have welcomed the news that Yahweh had not forgotten his oath. In the face of long-standing national apostasy, resulting in exile from the land, this command to reapportion the land provides concrete proof that Yahweh's word remains firm. He is Yahweh; he has spoken; he will perform.

Verse 14b reiterates the burden of this passage with an unusual active construction. Since land does not actually fall to anyone, the phrase *nāpal/hippîl lākem běnahǎlâ,* "to fall/cast as a grant," should be interpreted figuratively.[40] The idiom derives from the practice of casting lots *(gôrāl)* to select or distribute property.[41] While this method had been used originally to apportion the Canaanite territory among the tribes (Num. 33:54; 34:13), the lot will apparently play no part in this distribution. In addition to the present principle of equality among the tribes, the following chapter has Yahweh dictating the allotments.

The vocabulary and style of vv. 13-14 send an early signal to the reader to associate this unit with 45:1-8. Indeed, the key motifs (the land falling as a special grant, the beneficiaries being the tribes of Israel) are borrowed from the opening and concluding statements of the earlier text. Although most scholars view 45:1-8 as a late insertion under the influence of 47:13–48:29, this passage offers another example of typically Ezekielian resumptive exposition.

(b) The Boundary List (47:15-20)

The reader expects the territorial distribution to occur immediately after vv. 13-14. Instead, vv. 15-20 define Israel's exterior frontiers (see map 2, p. 710). The transition from preamble to boundary description is signaled formally by the superscription, *wězeh gěbûl hā'āreṣ,* "This is the boundary of the land."[42] Thereafter Ezekiel describes successively the northern, eastern, southern, and western borders. Each definition is framed by *lip'at/ûp'at* plus compass point ("As for the north side," etc.) in the beginning, and *zō't pě'at* plus compass point ("This is the north side," etc.) at the end. Several features of this boundary list suggest that it has been intentionally patterned after the Mosaic counterpart in Num. 34:1-12:[43] an opening preamble referring to "the land falling as a special grant"; a clockwise order, though with different starting points (south in Num-

---

39. See Gen. 13:14-17, etc. Ezekiel refers to the patriarchal promise of land twice in 20:28 and 42, both involving Yahweh's oath.

40. The expression occurred earlier in 45:1, and returns in v. 22. For variations of the same see Num. 34:2; Josh. 13:6; 23:4; Judg. 18:1.

41. See my *Ezekiel: Chapters 1–24,* p. 778.

42. The form is similar to *zō't tôrat habbāyit* in 43:12.

43. In turn Num. 34 has numerous links with Josh. 13–19, on which see A. G. Auld, *Joshua, Moses and the Land: Tetrateuch-Pentateuch-Hexateuch in a Generation since 1938* (Edinburgh: T. & T. Clark, 1980), pp. 75-76.

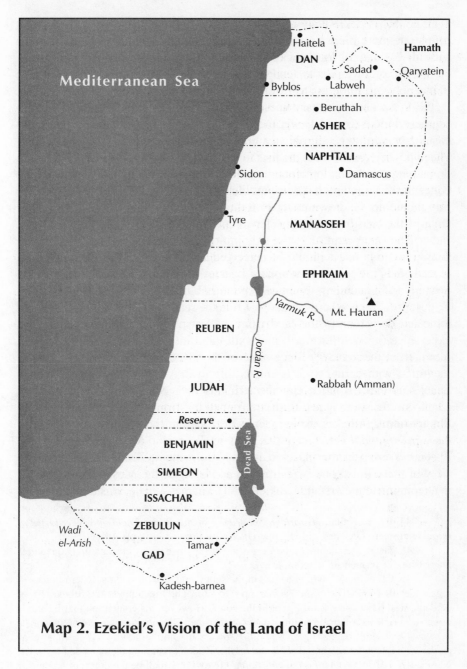

Map 2. Ezekiel's Vision of the Land of Israel

bers; north in Ezekiel); stylistic and lexical echoes. This document, therefore, offers one more piece of evidence that Ezekiel is deliberately portrayed as a second Moses, drafting a new constitution for the reconstituted nation of Israel.

Although moderns tend to interpret a "border" primarily as a line drawn between adjoining territories, *gĕbûl* denotes principally "territory," that is, the area within boundary lines. Z. Kallai has observed that detailed boundary descriptions generally list the outermost territories of the allotment, occasionally naming geographic features on the border line proper, while abbreviated descriptions restrict the lists to territorial designations. Furthermore, on the assumption that allotments were described from the inside out toward the edges, if the boundary list does not identify a specific geographic feature, the line should not be drawn exactly on the settlements named, but at the outside edge of the territory under the jurisdiction of the settlement.[44] Accordingly, rather than interpreting Ezekiel's definition of Israel's *gĕbûl* as a line drawn from point to point, it should be perceived as a chain of peripheral territories.

15-17 *The northern border.* Ezekiel's northern orientation is reflected not only in his compass point of departure, but also in the detail with which he describes the northern border.[45] While the reason for this orientation is not indicated, it perceives the land from the perspective of the prophet's own experience (he was led north into exile) and his aspirations (the exiles will return from the north).[46] Since none of the places named in this list can be identified with certainty, it is impossible to draw a firm boundary line on Israel's northern frontier. But the affinities with Num. 34:7-9 that this text displays offer some clues. Both are framed by formal statements identifying the northern border as the subject.[47] Both define the starting point as *min-hayyām haggādôl* (lit. "from the great sea," i.e., the Mediterranean). There is some overlap in the places named: Lebo-hamath, Zedad, Hazer-enon. In view of these links, one is justified in appealing to the Mosaic boundary list in attempting to understand Ezekiel's.[48] The names will be considered in order.

44. Cf. Z. Kallai, *Historical Geography of the Bible: The Tribal Territories of Israel* (Jerusalem: Magnes and Hebrew University Press, 1986), pp. 100-101 n. 5.

45. The rugged nature of the terrain and the absence of any clear natural boundaries may also have influenced its complexity.

46. Cf. Num. 34, which begins in the south, and describes the southern border in greater detail. Tuell (*Law of the Temple,* pp. 155-56) rightly recognizes the perspective of a people who have come from Egypt to the south. However, his contention that Ezekiel's orientation reflects a Persian point of view (rather than Babylonian) is not convincing.

47. Ezekiel begins *lip'at ṣāpônâ,* "Toward the northern side" (v. 15), and concludes with *zō't pē'at ṣāpôn,* "This is the northern side" (assuming the emended text). Cf. Num. 34:7, *wĕzeh yihyeh lākem gĕbûl ṣāpôn,* "[Now] this shall be the northern border for you."

48. Apart from the toponymic deviations, the most obvious difference is Ezekiel's failure to refer to marking out the borderline *(tā'â).*

Hethlon. The name occurs only here in the OT. If this site is to be identified with modern Heitela northeast of Tripoli, at the foot of Jebel Akkar, south of the El-Kebir River, then Ezekiel's *derek ḥetlōn,* "the way of Hethlon," might have followed the Eleutheros road.[49] But this interpretation is far from certain. Where Ezekiel has Hethlon Num. 34:7 cites Mount Hor. This is obviously not the Edomite Mount Hor where Aaron died (Num. 20:22-29; 33:38), but probably one of the peaks of the Lebanese range north of Byblos, perhaps Jebel Akkar or Ras Shaqqah.[50]

Lebo-hamath. Some have rendered *lĕbô' ḥămat* as "the Pass of Hamath," but it is more likely to be identified with a specific place, modern Lebweh, near the spring of Naba' Labweh, one of the principal sources of the Orontes River in the Beqa', and some 45 mi. north of Damascus.[51] The name appears as Lab'u in the Egyptian texts and Laba'û in Assyrian inscriptions.[52] In earlier times Lebo-hamath had constituted the northern border of Solomon's kingdom (1 K. 8:65), and later of Jeroboam II's northern kingdom of Israel (2 K. 14:25).

Zedad appears to be preserved in the name of modern-day Sedad, a village situated east of Sirion (Anti-Lebanon Range), near the Damascus-Ohms road, 35 mi. northeast of Lebweh.[53]

Beruthah is probably to be associated with a city of Hadadezer, king of Aram-Zobah, located in the Beqa' (2 Sam. 8:8). It is usually equated with Bereitan, situated south of Ba'albek,[54] and 30 mi. north-northwest of Damascus.

Sibraim is completely unknown, and must have been relatively unfamiliar even in Ezekiel's time, which would account for the explanatory phrase that follows: "which is located between the territories of Damascus and Hamath." This comment rules out any identification with Sepharvaim, which was located in Babylonia.[55]

Hazer-hatticon also defies identification, but it must have been obscure

---

49. Cf. Y. Aharoni, *The Land of the Bible: A Historical Geography,* rev. ed., tr. A. F. Rainey (Philadelphia: Westminster, 1979), p. 80 n. 40; R. de Vaux, "Le pays de Canaan," *JAOS* 83 (1968) 29; Simons, *Geographical and Topographical Texts,* p. 102.

50. Cf. Milgrom, *Numbers,* p. 286; Rasmussen, *NIV Atlas,* p. 238.

51. For the former see JB; cf. J. Gray, *I & II Kings,* rev. ed., OTL (Philadelphia: Westminster, 1970), p. 615. For the latter cf. B. Mazar, *Cities and Districts in Eretz Israel* (Jerusalem: Mosad Bailik, 1975), pp. 167-81.

52. Cf. S. Aḥituv, *Canaanite Toponyms in Ancient Egyptian Documents* (Jerusalem: Magnes and Hebrew University Press, 1984), p. 131; Aharoni, *Land of the Bible,* pp. 72-73.

53. Aharoni, *Land of the Bible,* p. 73.

54. Ibid., p. 73; Simons, *Geographical and Topographical Texts,* p. 333.

55. Cf. 2 K. 17:24, 31; 18:34; 19:13. Thus J. A. Montgomery, *A Critical and Exegetical Commentary on the Books of Kings,* ICC (Edinburgh: T. & T. Clark, 1951), p. 472. R. Zadok locates Sepharvaim in the vicinity of Nippur ("Geographical and Onomastic Notes," *JANES* 8 [1976] 115).

even in Ezekiel's time, calling for the explanatory comment: "which is on the border of Hauran."[56] A position somewhere between Hauran and Damascus, perhaps parallel with Tyre and Dan, may be proposed.[57]

Hauran. The name occurs only here and in v. 18 in the Bible. But it appears in Nineteenth Dynasty Egyptian texts as *Ḫu-ru-na,* and in 9th-century Assyrian annals as *Ḫa-u-ra-ni.*[58] Under Assyrian rule Hauran constituted one of a series of administrative districts in this region.[59] Hauran, modern Jebel Druze, identified the high mountainous region east of Galilee, which separates Bashan from the desert.[60] Some equate Ziphron in Num. 34:9 with Ezekiel's Sibraim, but the literary structure favors a Ziphron-Hauron equation. Ziphron, perhaps the name of an oasis in the Hauran region, has not been positively identified.

Hazer-enon. Although Hazer-enon appears in both boundary lists, it has not been positively identified. Scholars tend to equate it with modern Qaryatein, 70 mi. northeast of Damascus toward Palmyra.[61]

Damascus. Until its fall to the Assyrians in 732 B.C., Damascus was the base of the strongest Aramaean kingdom to Israel's north and northeast. Known to the Arabs as the "pearl of the east," this commercial and political center east of the Anti-Lebanon range on the Abana River has been occupied continuously until the present day.[62]

Hamath was a major city-state on the middle Orontes River, 100 mi. north of Damascus. During the first centuries of the 1st millennium B.C. the state was ruled by Hittite (Anatolian) kings, but with the accession of Zakkur in the 8th century, the power shifted to Aramaean control. Like the other states in the area, Hamath lost its political independence to the Assyrians, Tiglath-pileser III having subdivided its territory among his generals. Isa. 11:11 notes that captive Israelites were brought to Hamath by the Assyrians, and according

56. This addition renders the emendation to Hazer-Enon unnecessary, since the latter is too far north of Hauran.

57. This would correspond with the northwest border of the Assyrian province of Hauran. Cf. J. M. Miller and J. H. Hayes, *A History of Ancient Israel and Judah* (Philadelphia: Westminster, 1986), p. 333, map 24.

58. Cf. *ARAB,* 1:261, §672; *ANET,* p. 280, which reports that Shalmaneser III advanced as far as "the mountains of Hauran" *(šadê mātḫa-ú-ra-ni).*

59. Cf. *ARAB,* 2:314, §818; *ANET,* p. 298; on which see Aharoni, *Land of the Bible,* p. 376. Hauran was probably included in Tiglath-pileser III's "sixteen districts of Aram" (*ARAB,* 2:314, §818).

60. Aharoni, *Land of the Bible,* pp. 37-38. It was known in Hellenistic times as Auranitis.

61. Simons, *Geographical and Topographical Texts,* p. 102; Aharoni, *Land of the Bible,* p. 73.

62. *ARAB,* 1:279, §777; *ANET,* p. 283. Cf. Aharoni, *Land of the Bible,* p. 376. See further on 27:18 above.

to 2 K. 17:24 Esarhaddon resettled people from this place in Israel. The city fell eventually to Babylon (Jer. 39:5), under whose control it remained during the ministry of Ezekiel.[63] Neither Damascus nor Hamath is mentioned in Num. 34:7-9.

While locating the places named is difficult, Ezekiel's boundary poses several additional problems. First, whereas a border chain (summarized in v. 17, "So the border shall run from the sea to Hazer-enon") consisting of Hethlon (Heitela), Lebo-hamath (Lebweh), Zedad (Sadad), Sibraim (?), and Hazer-enon is sensible, Beruthah (Bereitan), located more than 15 mi. south of Lebo-Hamath, is out of place. Second, since Mount Hauran is due east of the Sea of Galilee, a boundary line running through Hazer-hatticon, "which is on the border of Hauran," is no longer a northern border, but an eastern frontier. Third, what is Hamath, which was situated far to the north of the line drawn from Hethlon to Hazer-enon, doing in this list?

While no completely satisfactory solution has been proposed, several observations may be made. First, Ezekiel's use of *gĕbûl* should be interpreted broadly as "territory, area," rather than narrowly as "boundary line." Accordingly, instead of drawing the border through the town of Beruthah, it should be traced along the northern edge of the region within its orbit, perhaps as far north as the headwaters of the Litani River, almost due west of Lebo-hamath. Second, Ezekiel seems to use the term *ṣāpôn* loosely. Hauran is actually east of Galilee, but from Ezekiel's Judahite perspective, all these regions were generally to the north. Third, the text of v. 17 is somewhat problematic, but Ezekiel does not appear to view Hamath as within Israelite territory. A border running from the sea to Hazer-enon would probably have coincided with the ancient boundary separating the kingdoms of Damascus and Hamath.[64]

It is commonly accepted that the border defined in Num. 34:7-9 coincided with the northern limits of "the land of Canaan," the designation of Syria-Palestine under Egyptian control, beyond which lay the lands of the Hittites.[65] Only twice in Israel's history did the political borders of Israel extend as far north as Lebo-hamath: under David[66] and under Jeroboam II

---

63. On the state of Hamath see J. D. Hawkins, *RLA*, 3:66-70; M.-L. Buhl, *ABD*, 3:33-36.

64. Note the roles of Hamathite and Damascene rulers in revolts against Shalmaneser III (858-824 B.C.; *ARAB*, 1:223, §611; *ANET*, pp. 278-79) and Sargon II (721-705 B.C.; *ARAB*, 2:3, §5; *ANET*, p. 285).

65. Aharoni, *Land of the Bible*, pp. 67-77; de Vaux, *JAOS* 88 (1968) 23-30; G. Wenham, *Numbers: An Introduction and Commentary*, TOTC (Downers Grove, Ill.: InterVarsity Press, 1981), p. 117. The Egyptian definition also underlies Josh. 15:1-4.

66. David received the voluntary submisssion of Toi king of Hamath (2 Sam. 8:1-12), but the northern frontier of "the kingdom of David," apparently "the land of Israel," seems to have been considered Lebo-hamath (1 K. 8:65; 1 Chr. 13:5; 2 Chr. 7:8).

(2 K. 14:25). Harking back to the ancient Mosaic boundary is one more way Ezekiel finds to highlight the complete restoration of his people.[67]

18 *The eastern border.* Ezekiel's dependence on the Mosaic definition of the "land of Israel" is not as evident in his eastern border. Like Num. 34:10-12, v. 18 is framed by formal opening and closing statements, but this is where the similarities end. Not only is Ezekiel's definition much more economical, using as few words as possible to make the same point; his point of departure is Hauran rather than Hazer-enon. Unlike the Numbers text, which cites specific place-names, Ezekiel describes the boundary in terms of regional designation (Hauran, Damascus, Gilead). He omits any reference to Chinereth (Sea of Galilee), and changes the name of the Dead Sea from *yām hammelaḥ,* "Salt Sea," to *hayyām haqqadmônî,* "eastern sea."[68]

Following the opening title, *ûpĕ'at qādîm,* "As for the east side," Ezekiel's delineation of the eastern border begins naturally where the northern boundary had left off — at some spot (Hazer-hatticon?) on the border between the Mount Hauran and Damascene territories. Running southwestward the boundary skirts the southern limits of land in Damascus's orbit (Karnaim),[69] due east of the Sea of Galilee, probably following the Yarmuk tributary to the Jordan River. From here the Jordan River serves as the border, until it enters the Dead Sea. The southern limit of the eastern boundary is fixed at Tamar. Some have identified this site with modern ʿAin Ḥoṣob, an important intersection of the east-west road from Bozrah to Kadesh-barnea and the north-south roadway along the Arabah, some 20 mi. southwest of the Dead Sea.[70] Although the passage is also problematic textually, 1 K. 9:18 seems to include among Solomon's fortified cities a "Tamar in the desert of the land."[71]

Remarkably, like Num. 34:10-12, Ezekiel's definition of the land of Israel excludes the Transjordanian regions previously occupied by the tribes of Gad, Reuben, and one-half of Manasseh. At the time of the conquest Yahweh had conceded this land to these tribes, but it was never recognized as integral to the promised land.[72] For Ezekiel, as for Moses, "the holy land" stops at the Jordan River; beyond this the land is unclean.

19 *The southern border.* Ezekiel's description of the southern frontier continues his abbreviated style. The boundary line begins at Tamar, the final point of the eastern boundary, and runs southwestward through the valley

---

67. Tuell's claim of a Persian derivation of the northern border (*Law of the Temple,* pp. 156-60) fails to recognize the significance of this correspondence.

68. The designation occurs elsewhere only in Joel 2:20 and Zech. 14:8.

69. On which see Aharoni, *Land of the Bible,* p. 376.

70. Ibid., p. 70; J. T. Butler, *ISBE,* 4:724-25.

71. See Butler, *ISBE,* 4:725; J. K. Lott, *ABD,* 6:315-16.

72. For a telling illustration of the problematic position of the Transjordan in relation to the rest of the land of Israel see Josh. 22.

south of Mount Halak to Meribath-kadesh, an alternate name for Kadesh-barnea.[73] This site (modern ʿAin el-Qudeirat) was the richest and most centrally located oasis on the southern border of the Desert of Zin.[74] From Kadesh the border follows the *brook* (of Egypt), Wadi el-Arish, to the Mediterranean Sea, identified here as *the Great Sea*. The Brook of Egypt, not to be confused with the Nile, "the River of Egypt," drained the northern Sinai Desert and formed a natural boundary between Egypt and the land of Canaan.

20 *The western border.* As in Num. 34:6, the Mediterranean forms the western boundary of the land of Israel. By following the coast from the mouth of the Brook of Egypt to a point opposite Lebo-hamath the borderline has been brought full circle.

(c) Epilogue (47:21-23)

The epilogue to Ezekiel's boundary list opens with a summary reiteration (v. 21) of the preamble (vv. 13-14). Vv. 22-23 represent Ezekiel's answer to Num. 34:13-15, but with a creative new twist. Whereas the earlier boundary list had been followed by a note on a fringe *territory,* the Transjordanian region occupied by the two and one-half tribes, Ezekiel concludes his description with a comment on fringe *people* within the Israelite community, the *gērîm,* "resident aliens," actually "proselytes,"[75] since they are participating in the life of the community. In 14:7 Ezekiel had applied the term to syncretistic proselytes who, like the apostate Israelites, have distanced themselves from Yahweh through their idolatry. Later, in 22:7, 29, Ezekiel classifies these non-Israelites ethnically with widows, orphans, the poor and needy, persons within the community who are vulnerable to oppression and exploitation, those whom the Mosaic legislation had been careful to protect. Whatever the historical reality in Israel, the traditional ideal is summarized in Lev. 19:33-34: "When a *gēr* resides *(yāgûr)* with you in your land, you shall not oppress him. The *gēr* who resides *(haggār)* with you shall be to you like the native *(ʾezrāḥ)* among you; you shall love the *gēr* as yourself, for you were *gērîm* in the land of Egypt. I am Yahweh your God."

But such consideration from native Israelites must have been an empty dream for aliens throughout most of the nation's history (cf. 1 Chr. 22:2; 2 Chr. 2:16 [Eng. 17]). However free they might have been to join the community of faith through the rite of circumcision (Exod. 12:43-48), the apparent

---

73. Mount Halak was the southern limit of Joshua's conquest. Cf. Josh. 11:17; 12:7. This form of the name, Meribath-kadesh, which plays on the verb *rîb,* "to contend," occurs elsewhere only in Ezek. 48:28; Num. 27:14; Deut. 32:15.

74. Aharoni, *Land of the Bible,* p. 70.

75. On Ezekiel's use of *gēr* see my *Ezekiel: Chapters 1–24,* pp. 429, 708-10.

prohibition on land ownership prevented full integration into the community and kept them in a perpetual state of dependence.[76] Recognizing the theological significance of landholding in Israel, Ezekiel insists that in the new order, all distinctions between *gērîm* and ethnic Israelites (*'ezraḥ*) will be eliminated. Proselytes are to receive their allotted portions as well.[77]

Ezekiel does not promise landholding rights to all foreigners. The *gēr*'s identification with Israel must be demonstrated by residing, and fathering children while residing, among the Israelites. These qualifications are intended to distinguish between other foreigners residing temporarily in Israel and proselytes, and to guard the sanctity of the holy community now resident in the holy land. Even so, Ezekiel's guarantee of full citizenship for all foreigners who marry and raise their children within the family of Israel is "more radical than anything else in all the legal corpora of the Hebrew Bible."[78] No longer will they be second class, dependent on charity or at the mercy of the native citizens.

But the right to receive a land grant symbolizes more than social equality within the community; it guarantees for the *gēr* all the spiritual rights and privileges associated with membership in the people of Yahweh.[79] With this ordinance Ezekiel has given concrete expression to the glorious ideal celebrated in Isa. 56:3-8:

> Do not let the foreigner *(ben hannēkār)* joined to Yahweh say,
>   "Yahweh will keep me apart from his people";
> And do not let the eunuch say,
>   "I am just a dried up tree."
> For thus has Yahweh declared:
> "As for the eunuchs who keep my Sabbaths,
> who choose the things that please me
> And hold fast to my covenant,
> In my house and within my walls

---

76. Cf. Deut. 24:17-22. On the *gēr*'s position see C. J. H. Wright, *God's People in God's Land,* pp. 99-103.

77. This is the only occurrence of *'ezraḥ* in Ezekiel. The derivation of the word is uncertain, though it seems to be cognate to Akk. *um/nzarḫu,* which in middle and neo-Assyrian denoted "aboriginal, homeborn, homebred, indigenous," in contrast to "foreigner, alien, immigrant." K. Deller proposes a derivation from 6th-century Bab. **uzzaraḥ,* the self-designation of Babylon's native population ("Assyrisch *um/nzarḫu* und Hebräisch *'äzraḥ,*" *ZA* 74 [1984] 235-39). Whatever its etymology, the meaning of Heb. *'ezraḥ,* "native born, full citizen," is clear, since, except for Lev. 23:42 and Ps 37:35, it always occurs opposite *gēr.* In Deut. 1:16 *gēr* is contrasted with *'āḥ,* "brother." Cf. Punic *mzrḥ,* "clan" (*KAI,* 69.16).

78. Levenson, *Theology,* p. 123.

79. Cf. Maier, *Temple Scroll,* pp. 171-72; D. Kellermann, *TDOT,* 2:448.

I will give them a monument and a name
Better than sons and daughters.
I will give them an everlasting name
That shall never be cut off.
As for the foreigners (*běnê hannēkār*)
Who attach themselves to Yahweh,
To minister to him,
And to love the name of Yahweh,
To be his servants —
All those who keep the Sabbath
And do not profane it,
And who hold fast to my covenant —
These I will bring to my holy mountain,
And let them celebrate in my house of prayer.
Their burnt offerings and sacrifices
Shall be welcome on my altar;
Because my house shall be called
A house of prayer for all the peoples."
The declaration of the Lord Yahweh,
Who gathers those rejected by Israel:
"I will add more to the company of those already gathered."

(2) New Tribal Allotments (48:1-7, 23-29)

1 *"These are the names of the tribes:*
First,[80] *beginning*[81] *at the northern extreme, adjacent to*[82] *the Heth-*
lon road, Lebo-hamath and Hazar-enan (which is the border of Damas-
cus, with Hamath to the north), running[83] *from east*[84] *to west,*[85] *[the*
tribe of][86] *Dan.*

2 *Second, adjacent to the territory of Dan, from east to west, [the*
tribe of] Asher.

80. Each of the tribal allotments ends with the numeral *'eḥād*, "one," an ancient way of checking off individual items in a series. Cf. Josh. 12:9-24. English convention places the numeral at the beginning.
81. The preposition *min* on *miqṣēh* is a *min* of source.
82. On *'el* in the sense of *'al* see 1:17. Zimmerli (*Ezekiel 2*, p. 521) correctly rejects BHS's emendation to *min-hayyām*.
83. With LXX and Vulg. I read *wěhāyû lô*, "and they shall be for him," as *wěhāyâ*, "and it shall be." Cf. 47:10, 22. The pl. verb has anticipated the series of subjects.
84. The context and following forms support emending *pě'at* to *mippě'at*.
85. *ymh* has been miswritten as *hym*. Cf. LXX.
86. Here and throughout the following list "the tribe of" has been inserted for the sake of clarity in accordance with 47:21-23 and 48:1.

3 *Third, adjacent to the territory of Asher, from east to west, [the tribe of] Naphtali.*

4 *Fourth, adjacent to the territory of Naphtali, from east to west, [the tribe of] Manasseh.*

5 *Fifth, adjacent to the territory of Manasseh, from east to west, [the tribe of] Ephraim.*

6 *Sixth, adjacent to the territory of Ephraim, from east to west, [the tribe of] Reuben.*

7 *Seventh, adjacent to the territory of Reuben, from east to west, [the tribe of] Judah.*

. . . .

23 *As for the rest of the tribes, eighth, from east to west, [the tribe of] Benjamin.*

24 *Ninth, adjacent to the territory of Benjamin, from east to west, [the tribe of] Simeon.*

25 *Tenth, adjacent to the territory of Simeon, from east to west, [the tribe of] Issachar.*

26 *Eleventh, adjacent to the territory of Issachar, from east to west, [the tribe of] Zebulun.*

27 *Twelfth, adjacent to the territory of Zebulun, from east to west, [the tribe of] Gad.*

28 *And adjacent to the territory of Gad at the southern end,[87] the border[88] shall run from Tamar, as far as[89] the waters of Meribath-kadesh, to the Wadi [of Egypt],[90] and the Mediterranean Sea.[91]*

29 *This is the land that you shall apportion by lot as a special grant[92] for the tribes of Israel. These are their respective allotments. The declaration of the Lord Yahweh."*

◆ *Nature and Design*

Following the pattern of Num. 34, after a digressionary description of national borders (47:15-20), ch. 48 satisfies the anticipation created by 47:13-14, 21.

87. *'el-pĕ'at negeb têmānâ*, "at the side of the south southward." On the redundancy see above on 47:19.

88. LXX, Targ., and Syr. support restoring the article on *gĕbûl*, which seems to have dropped off by haplography.

89. Vulg. and Syr. correct the reading by assuming an inserted *'ad*. Cf. 47:19.

90. Vulg. mistakenly translates *naḥălâ* as *hereditas*. Cf. 47:19. "Of Egypt" has been added for the sake of clarity.

91. Lit. "the great sea."

92. Emending *minnaḥălâ* to *bĕnaḥălâ*, with support from several Hebrew mss., LXX, Vulg., and Targ. Cf. 45:1; 47:22.

Although the bulk of the chapter (vv. 1-29) is taken up with territorial allocations, only vv. 1-7 and 23-29 involve the tribal allotments. The heart of the chapter (vv. 8-22) deals with tangential allocations, the grants of the priests (vv. 9-14), the city (vv. 15-20), and the prince (vv. 21-22). These segments have undoubtedly been inserted into what was originally a unitary survey of the tribal apportionments for rhetorical reasons, which will be explored later. Meanwhile, for the sake of convenience, vv. 1-7 and 23-29 may be analyzed as if they were a single document.

The limits of the territorial document are formally set by the title, *wě'ēlleh šěmôt haššěbāṭîm,* "Now these are the names of the tribes" (v. 1), and the colophon, *"zō't hā'āreṣ 'ăšer tappîlû běnaḥălâ lěšibṭê yiśrā'ēl wě'ēlleh maḥlěqôtām,* "This is the land that you shall apportion by lot as a special grant for the tribes of Israel (v. 29). These are their respective allotments." The form of the former is influenced by Num. 34:17, 19, even though the content of the list follows its own course.[93] The latter displays stylistic links with 47:13-14, 21. The references to "the tribes of Israel" in both introduction and conclusion highlight the intrusive nature of vv. 8-22. The entire territorial allotment list is sealed with the signatory formula, *ně'um 'ădōnāy yhwh,* "the declaration of the Lord Yahweh," which reminds the reader that these allocations are divinely prescribed.

The list itself is appropriately framed by summary descriptions of the northern and southern national frontiers. The former draws the boundary line along the Hethlon road *(derek ḥetlôn),* through Lebo-hamath and Hazer-enan, on the border between Damascene and Hamathite territories. The latter (v. 28) represents a virtual quotation of 47:19, drawing the southern border from Tamar to the Meribath-kadesh oasis, down the Brook of Egypt to the Mediterranean Sea.[94]

The entries in the list are monotonously formal. With three exceptions, all allocations are described identically: *wě'al gěbûl* [tribal name, henceforth TN][1] *mippě'at qādîmâ 'ad pě'at yāmmâ* TN[2] *'eḥād,* "And adjacent to the territory of TN[1], from east to west, TN[2], one [territory]." The first (Danite, v. 1) and last (Gadite, v. 28) distributions have been modified to link with the summaries of the northern and southern borders, respec-

---

93. Cf. also Josh. 14:1, *wě'ēlleh 'ăšer nāḥălû běnê yiśrā'ēl bě'ereṣ kěnā'an,* "Now these are [the grants] that the sons of Israel claimed in the land of Canaan," at the head of the actual allotments after the land had been conquered.

94. Note the similarities (assuming the textual corrections):

47:19	48:28
ûpě'at negeb têmānâ	*'el-pě'at negeb têmānâ wěhāyâ*
mittāmār 'ad-mê měrîbat qādeš	*mittāmār 'ad-mê měrîbat qādeš*
naḥălâ 'el-hayyām haggādôl	*naḥălâ 'el-hayyām haggādôl*

tively. The first two words of the eighth (Benjamite, v. 23), *wĕyeter haššĕbāṭîm,* "As for the remainder of the tribes," are resumptive, being required after the secondary insertion of vv. 8-22.

Rather than analyzing each entry in this list, I offer a series of synthetic observations on the document as a whole.

First, Ezekiel's understanding of Israel's tribal structure follows the traditional premonarchical order: (a) The land is divided into twelve tribal allotments (cf. Josh. 13–19). (b) The tribe of Levi is excluded from the allocations. (c) The twelve-tribe system is maintained by elevating Joseph's sons, Manasseh and Ephraim, to full tribal status and assigning a separate territory to each (cf. 47:13). Accordingly, this literary map expresses concretely the prophetic hope for reunion of all the tribes of Israel as foretold in 37:16-23. In appealing to these ancient tribal structures Ezekiel repudiates the pragmatically centralized administration of the monarchy (1 K. 7–19).[95]

Second, Ezekiel's tribal allocations display little concern for historical realities. In accordance with 47:15-20, the territory east of the Jordan is completely overlooked, Reuben, Gad, and one-half of Manasseh having rejoined their compatriots. Formerly northern Issachar, Zebulun, and Gad are located at the south end of the country, and Judah is north of Benjamin. Dan's position at the extreme north clashes with Joshua's original assignment (Josh. 19:40-48), but accords with the historical reality of the Danite seizure of land from the Laishites, even if without divine sanction (Judg. 18). But any correspondences to historical reality in the list seem purely coincidental.

Third, Ezekiel's tribal boundaries run against the grain of natural topography. Whereas the physical landscape of the land of Israel is defined by north-south lines (the coastal plain, the central spinal region, the Jordan rift valley), Ezekiel's borders all run in an east-west direction. The effect is highly artificial. Insofar as communication is easier within rather than across topographic regions, however, this arrangement facilitates intertribal exchange and access for all to the sacred *tĕrûmâ.*

Fourth, Ezekiel's allocations are based on a paradigm of tribal parity and designed to neutralize the inequities of the past.[96] The ideal expressed in the earlier reference to *ʾîš kĕʾāḥîw,* "each like his brother" (47:14), is demonstrated by (a) the deliberately repetitive style of each entry; (b) shifting the center of gravity northward, thereby replacing the grossly asymmetrical 2:10 monarchic structure (1 K. 11:30-31) with a more balanced 5:7 tribal arrangement; (c) assigning east-west strips of land, thereby distributing desirable and

---

95. Cf. R. W. Klein, *Israel in Exile,* OBT (Philadelphia: Fortress, 1979), pp. 90-91.
96. Josh. 17:14-18 provides an illustration of the problems created by the original allotment.

undesirable zones more equitably among the tribes and avoiding monopolistic control over the best lands by any tribe.[97]

But this does not mean that Ezekiel has achieved a utopia, completely devoid of stratification. The present modified concentric design is by definition hierarchical. An ideal map, in which all tribes have identical sociopolitical status, and all enjoy equal access to the temple, would be designed like a wheel, with spokes for boundaries and the apex of each territory abutting the sacred area. In Ezekiel's plan distances alone create inequalities. Most obviously the outlying tribes must travel farther to worship in the sacred *tĕrûmâ* than those nearer by. Furthermore, if we assume the strips of territory were all the same width (about 25 mi.),[98] differences in east-west distances create great inequities. Whereas the distance from the Mediterranean to the Jordan River at the south end of the Sea of Galilee is only 40 mi., the tip of the Dead Sea is 70 mi. from the Mediterranean. Even more problematic is the massive eastward bulge of the border north of the Sea of Galilee, where the strips could have been 100 mi. long. Nonetheless, any attempt to interpret all these details literally is futile. Either Ezekiel was unfamiliar with the actual distances between these points,[99] or, more likely, his map represents an artificial ideal, in keeping with the rest of chs. 40–48. In any case, one should construe this document not as a literary photograph of the land of Israel but as a cartographic painting by an artist with a particular theological agenda.[100]

Fifth, Ezekiel's territorial allocations respect the traditional genealogical relationships among the tribes, distinguishing between the descendants of Jacob's wives (Leah and Rachel) and their handmaidens (Bilhah and Zilpah).[101] This discrimination, reflected in the tribes' respective proximity to the *tĕrûmâ*, may be highlighted by listing them in geographic order and noting their ancestress as follows:

Dan	(Bilhah [Rachel])
Asher	(Zilpah [Leah])
Naphtali	(Bilhah)
Manasseh	(Rachel)
Ephraim	(Rachel)
Reuben	(Leah)

97. See further M. Greenberg, "Idealism and Practicality in Numbers 35:4-5 and Ezekiel 48," *JAOS* 88 (1966) 63-66.

98. The distance between northern and southern boundaries is approximately 300 miles.

99. Cf. Zimmerli, *Ezekiel 2,* p. 541.

100. G. C. Macholz speaks of a "theological geography" ("Noch Einmal: Planungen für den Wiederaufbau nach der Katastrophe von 587," *VT* 19 [1969] 331).

101. Cf. Gen. 29–30. This has long been recognized. See Cooke, *Ezekiel,* pp. 531-32; Fohrer, *Ezechiel,* p. 262.

Judah	(Leah)
... *hattĕrûmâ* ...	
Benjamin	(Rachel)
Simeon	(Leah)
Issachar	(Leah)
Zebulun	(Leah)
Gad	(Zilpah)

The tribes descended from Jacob's primary wives enjoy pride of place, nearest the sanctuary, the eight Leah and Rachel tribes being distributed equally, four on each side of the *tĕrûmâ*. The tribes descended from the handmaidens are placed at the extremities, farthest from the sacred reserve. Appropriately, Ephraimite and Manassite allotments are side by side, intentionally (?) reflecting their status as two branches of the Josephite line.

Sixth, while Judah and Benjamin retain their historical positions near the sanctuary, perhaps reflective of their royal past,[102] their positions are reversed. Benjamin's position may have been influenced by the name (Benjamin = "son of the right hand, viz., south").[103] But the placement of Judah is striking. There is some ambiguity in Judah's position, next to the *tĕrûmâ*.[104] Although the dualities of the monarchic period remain in the north-south grouping, the disruptive regional loyalties are neutralized by assigning Judah's territory with the northern tribes and denying any tribe the religio-political center.[105] This is reserved for the sacred *tĕrûmâ* between Benjamin and Judah.

Seventh, the manner in which the tribal territories are allotted signals a return to an ancient theocratic ideal. The present plan may be interpreted as a criticism of increasing "feudalism" in Israel.[106] It is not feudalism per se that is criticized, however, but the exploitative nature of Israel's past monarchic feudalism. Ezekiel does not call for the abolition of "feudal" structures; his plan proposes a restoration of the kind of theocratic feudalism that had been intended for the nation from the beginning. Yahweh is Israel's true king; the land is his, not an earthly monarch's, to distribute among the tribes as he sees fit. In fact, each tribe is to view its territory as its *naḥălâ*, its special grant, received from the divine overlord as an act of grace to be sure, but also as an honorarium for services (to be) rendered.

102. According to Josh. 18:28, Jerusalem was originally allotted to Benjamin, but the city was captured by David, a Judahite, and made the capital of his tribally based kingdom (2 Sam. 5:5-6). Judah's royal status is well known (cf. Gen. 49:10), but Saul, the first king of Israel, was a Benjamite (1 Sam. 9).

103. Cf. Zimmerli, *Ezekiel 2,* p. 541.

104. Macholz (*VT* 19 [1969] 335) interprets this as pride of place.

105. Cf. Smith, *To Take Place,* pp. 65-66.

106. Macholz, *VT* 19 (1969) 340.

(3) The Sacred "Reserve" (48:8-22)

♦ *Nature and Design*

The earlier observation that vv. 8-22 constitute an insertion into what was originally a unitary document requires a slight adjustment. Not only does the absence of v. 8a leave the tribal allotments of Judah and Benjamin abutting each other; the opening line is identical in form to the lists of territories in vv. 2-7 and 24-27: *wĕ'al gĕbûl yĕhûdâ mippĕ'at qādîmâ 'ad-pĕ'at-yāmmâ*, "And adjacent to the territory of Judah, from east to west."[107] Instead of ending the statement with the standard tribal name plus *'eḥād*, however, the text reads *tihyeh hattĕrûmâ*, "the reserve shall be." This statement must be original to the territory list, but the mention of the *tĕrûmâ* provides the occasion for a lengthy aside in the literary proceedings. In the end, the insertion takes on a life of its own and becomes the most important part of the chapter. The reader now learns that the geographic north-south arrangement has been intentionally mirrored in the shape of the text. In context the tribal allotments function primarily as a framework for the description of the *tĕrûmâ;* literary and geographic centers coalesce.

The key word in this entire subunit is *tĕrûmâ*, which occurs no fewer than a dozen times. But the expression is not new. The present text offers another example of resumptive exposition, picking up and developing a theme introduced earlier in 45:1-8.[108] Some have argued that vv. 9-22 come from a different hand than v. 8 because the meaning of *tĕrûmâ* shifts from a strip of land stretching across the entire breadth of Israel (corresponding to the tribal allotments) to the sacred square at the center,[109] but this explanation fails to recognize the fluidity with which Ezekiel often uses words. Both the larger portion of land, including that allocated for the prince, and the smaller sacred core represent portions excluded from the tribal allocation and reserved for Yahweh's direct control.[110] This approach also misses the significance of the expression *hannôtār*, "the remainder," that is, of the *tĕrûmâ*, which introduces the treatments of the common city property and that set aside for its personnel (vv. 15, 18), as well as the portion of the *nāśî'* (v. 21). To remove v. 8 robs *hannôtār* of an antecedent, and vv. 8-22 of a thesis statement. Indeed, the relationship between v. 8 and *hannôtār* provides the key to the structure of

107. Vv. 1b, 23, and 28 have been adjusted as the context requires.
108. While questioning the Ezekielian authorship of both, many (e.g., Cooke, *Ezekiel*, pp. 493, 532) assume the present text to be chronologically prior to 45:1-8.
109. Cf. Cooke, *Ezekiel*, p. 532.
110. Cf. Yahweh's reservation of Israel for himself when the nations were allocated to the "sons of God" (Deut. 32:8-9).

725

vv. 8-22. Following the opening statement (v. 8), the text divides into three panels dealing successively with the sacred reserve (*tĕrûmâ haqqōdeš*, vv. 9-14), the common city property (*'ăhuzzat hāʿîr*), vv. 15-20), and the allotment of the prince (vv. 21-22). The first panel subdivides further into descriptions of the priestly and Levitical reservations.

(a) The Sanctuary Allotment (48:8-14)

8 *"And adjacent to the territory of Judah, running from east to west shall be the reserve that you shall devote [to Yahweh].*[111] *Its width shall be twenty-five thousand cubits, and its length equal to that of the [tribal]*[112] *allotments, running from east to west. Within it*[113] *shall be the sanctuary.*

9 *The reserve that you devote for Yahweh shall be twenty-five thousand cubits long and twenty thousand cubits*[114] *wide.* 10 *The sacred reserve shall be set apart for the following [orders]: For the priests there shall be [an area] twenty-five thousand cubits*[115] *on the northern side, ten thousand cubits in width on the western side, ten thousand cubits in width on the eastern side, and twenty-five thousand cubits in length*[116] *on the southern side. The sanctuary of Yahweh shall be within it.*[117] 11 *[It shall be reserved] for the consecrated priests, from the descendants*[118] *of Zadok, who perform guard duty for me,*[119] *and who, unlike the Levites, refused to wander away when the descendants of*

---

111. Hebrew *tārîmû*, lit. "to raise," that is "dedicate, devote," is elliptical. An object is added for the sake of clarity. See v. 9.

112. See n. 86 above.

113. The masc. suffix on *bĕtôkô* has been influenced by *ḥēleq*, rather than its actual antecedent, fem. *tĕrûmâ*. Cf. Kethib *btwkh* in v. 21.

114. As in 45:1, the context requires that *'ăśeret 'ălāpîm*, "10,000," be read as *ʿeśrîm 'ālep*. Thus LXX[967], εἴκοσι χιλιάδες, in contrast to the other LXX witnesses, most of which read erroneously "25,000."

115. Vulg. harmonizes with the other three sides by presupposing an inserted *'ōrek*, "in length."

116. MT *rōḥab . . . rōḥab . . . 'ōrek*. The words are missing in LXX[B] and inconsistently attested in other LXX mss. In fact, LXX[B] omits the east side completely. Cf. Ziegler, *Ezekiel*, p. 326. While Targ. follows MT, Syr. presupposes only the first *rōḥab*.

117. LXX assumes an original *bĕtôkām*, "in their [the priests'] midst," for MT *bĕtôkô*. See n. 113 above.

118. Redividing MT *lkhnym hmqdš mbny* as *lkhnym hmqdšym bny*, with support from LXX, Targ., Syr. Cf. 44:15 and 2 Chr. 26:18. Hurvitz (*Linguistic Study*, p. 36 n. 36) suggests that MT may be retained if *mqdš* refers to the "allotted portion" rather than the priests. The Pual passive of *qdš* occurs elsewhere only in Isa. 13:3, a noncultic context.

119. *'ăšer šāmĕrû mišmartî*, lit. "who kept my guard." See 44:16.

Israel wandered away. 12 *It shall be their own special reserve,*[120] *distinguished from the land reserve*[121] *as especially holy, adjacent to the territory of the Levites.*

13 *For the Levites*[122] *there shall be an area alongside the territory of the priests twenty-five thousand cubits in length and ten thousand cubits in width. The entire length*[123] *shall be twenty-five thousand cubits and the width twenty thousand*[124] *cubits.* 14 *None of this prime land shall be for sale;*[125] *nor shall it ever be traded*[126] *or transferred,*[127] *because it is sacred to Yahweh."*

8   As indicated, v. 8 sets the agenda for vv. 8-22. Parallel to the twelve tribal territorial grants *(naḥălôt)* is a thirteenth strip of land, identified as the *tĕrûmâ,* a technical sacrificial expression for a "gift" dedicated *(hērîm)* to Yahweh.[128] There is irony in Ezekiel's unique usage of the term inasmuch as the command to dedicate the *tĕrûmâ* occurs in a context where Yahweh is giving his land to his people. But cast in the second person plural of direct address (like v. 9), v. 8 calls for action by the Israelites: they are to raise *(hērîm)* the territorial reserve as if it were an offering presented to deity.[129] This tract of land shall measure 25,000 cubits wide (about 8 mi.) and run from the eastern border (the Jordan) to the western border (the Mediterranean), parallel to the tribal allotments. For the first time these allotments *(naḥălôt)* are referred to as *ḥălāqîm,* "portions" (cf. 45:7), which link this text with Joshua's division of

120. *tĕrûmiyyâ* is a hapax form, on which see Bauer-Leander, *Grammatik,* §61; BDB, p. 929a; Zimmerli, *Ezekiel 2,* pp. 522-23.

121. *mittĕrûmat hāʾāreṣ,* lit. "from the reserve of the land," with the prefixed *min* on *mittĕrûmat* interpreted partitively.

122. Recognizing the parallel with v. 11, LXX and Vulg. rightly read *wĕlallĕwîyim* rather than *wĕhalĕwîyim.*

123. Targ. and LXX assume *kl h'rk,* which must be a mistake for original *klh 'rk* (Syr.). MT reads *kl 'rk.*

124. As in v. 9, *'śr[y]m* (reflected by LXX) has been miswritten as *'śrt.*

125. *yimkĕrû,* lit. "they shall not sell." LXX οὐ πραθήσεται may presuppose either an original passive *yimmākēr* or impersonal *yimkĕrû.* Targ., Syr., and Vulg. support MT.

126. LXX καταμετρηθήσεται reads *ymr* as *ymd,* "one shall measure." Both LXX and Targ. *yḥlp* support the sg. reading of MT against Syr. and Vulg.

127. Reading *y'byr* with Qere in place of Kethib *y'bwr.*

128. See Milgrom, *Leviticus,* pp. 473-81. Greenberg (*Int* 38 [1984] 202) suggests that this land is so designated because each tribe had to surrender a little so the strip might be available for national and administrative purposes.

129. Cf. the use of the verb *hērîm* plus cognate accusative *tĕrûmâ* in cultic contexts: 45:13 (grain offerings); Exod. 35:24 (silver and bronze offerings for the tabernacle); Num. 15:19-20 (meal offerings); 18:19 (*ḥŏdāšîm,* holy offerings); 18:24, 26, 28, 29 (the tithe).

the territorial spoils of holy war against the Canaanites.[130] Situated between Judah and Benjamin, the *těrûmâ* splits the *ḥǎlāqîm* into two unequal groups, seven in the north and five in the south. This tract not only represents the theological center of gravity (not the geographic middle!) of the nation; it has its own nucleus, the sanctuary *(miqdāš)* "in its midst" *(bětôkô)*.

9-12 The wording of the call to "lift up" *(hērîm)* the *těrûmâ* for Yahweh *(layhwh)* in vv. 9-10a echoes 45:1, with the phrase *těrûmat haqqōdeš*, "the reserve of the consecrated area," answering to *qōdeš min-hā'āreṣ*, "consecrated area from the land." The dependence of vv. 10b-12 on 45:3-4 for the description of the reserve becomes obvious when the two texts are placed side by side, as in table 24 (p. 729).

The common elements are obvious: (1) identical dimensions, 25,000 cubits by 10,000 cubits; (2) the sanctuary *(miqdāš)* within the priestly territory; (3) assignment to the priests who serve Yahweh; (4) emphasis on the sanctuary and the sanctity of the place.[131]

But the differences are much more striking: (1) the absence of the command to measure the area in the second text; (2) expansion of the length and breadth of the property in the first to a description of the measurements of each of the four sides in the second; (3) specific identification of the sanctuary *(miqdāš)* as Yahweh's sanctuary *(miqdāš yhwh);* (4) expansion of the priests' role, though with echoes from other earlier texts;[132] (5) reference to their *těrûmâ* separated from the larger *těrûmâ* stretching across the breadth of the land *(těrûmat hā'āreṣ);* (6) failure to mention the residential function of the priests' allotment; (7) explicit location of the priestly and Levitical reserves next to each other. In view of the links with 44:6-16, especially the interest in the Levites' problematic past, Ezekiel appears to be pulling together threads from several earlier contexts.

13a The links with 45:1-8 continue in the description of the Levites' allotment in v. 13a, especially its external dimensions. The shrinking descrip-

---

130. The verb *ḥālaq,* "to divide, to share" (cf. 5:1), is often used of dividing "spoil" (cf. Josh. 22:8 [Qal]; Exod. 15:9; etc. [Piel]). On the root see M. Tsevat, *TDOT,* 4:447-51.

131. *miqdāš,* "sanctuary, sacred place," occurs four times in 45:3-4 and once in 48:10b-12; both characterize the priestly allotment as *qōdeš qodāšîm,* "the most holy [place]."

132. Whereas previously they had been identified as the ones "who serve the sanctuary" *(měšārětê hammiqdāš)* and "who approach to serve Yahweh" *(haqqěrēbîm lěšārēt yhwh),* now they are (a) "consecrated ones" *(haměquddāšîm);* (b) the sons of Zadok (cf. 40:46; 44:15); (c) the ones who perform guard duty for Yahweh *('ǎšer šāměrû miš-martî;* cf. 44:8, 15, 16); (d) the ones who did not go astray when the rest of the Israelites and the Levites became apostate *(lō'-tā'û;* cf. 44:10, 15). The perspective accords with 44:4-16, but the language is different.

Table 24: A Synopsis of Ezekiel 45:3-4 and 48:10b-12[133]

Ezekiel 45:3-4

ûmin-hammiddâ hazzō't tāmôd
'ōrek ḥămiššâ wĕ'eśrîm 'elep
wĕrōḥab 'ăśeret 'ălāpîm

ûbô-yihyeh hammiqdāš
qōdeš qodāšîm
qōdeš min-hā'āreṣ
hû' lakkōhănîm
mĕšārĕtê hammiqdāš yihyeh
haqqĕrēbîm lĕšārēt 'et-yhwh

wĕhāyâ lāhem māqôm lĕbottîm

ûmiqdāš lammiqdāš

And from this measured-off area
you shall measure off [an area]
25,000 cubits long
and 10,000 cubits wide,

and in it the sanctuary shall be,
the most holy place.
It is sacred, set off from the land.
It shall be for the priests
who serve the sanctuary,
who approach to serve Yahweh.

It shall be a place for their houses,

and the holy area for the sanctuary.

Ezekiel 48:10b-12

lakkōhănîm
ṣāpônâ ḥămiššâ wĕ'eśrîm 'elep
wĕyāmmâ rōḥab 'ăśeret 'ălāpîm
wĕqādîmâ rōḥab 'ăśeret 'ălāpîm
wĕnegbâ 'ōrek ḥămiššâ wĕ'eśrîm 'ālep
wĕhāyâ miqdāš-yhwh bĕtôkô

lakkōhănîm hamĕquddāš mibbĕnê ṣādôq
'ăšer šāmĕrû mišmartî

'ăšer lō'-tā'û
bit'ôt bĕnê yiśrā'ēl
ka'ăšer tā'û halĕwîyim
wĕhāyĕtā lāhem tĕrûmîyâ mittĕrûmat
hā'āreṣ
qōdeš qodāšîm
'el-gĕbûl halĕwîyim

For the priests
there shall be [an area]
25,000 cubits on the northern side,
10,000 cubits wide on the western side,
10,000 cubits wide on the eastern side,
and 25,000 cubits long on the southern side.
The sanctuary of Yahweh shall be within it.

[It shall be] for the consecrated priests,
consecrated from the descendants of Zadok,
who perform guard duty for me,
and who did not go astray,
when the Israelites went astray,
like the Levites went astray.

It shall be their own reserve,
distinguished from the land reserve,
the most holy place,
adjacent to the territory of the Levites.

tion of the Levites' preserve reflects their relative subordination. There is no mention of their duties, nor of the function this piece of land is to serve for them. The only new element is the notice that their property abuts the priestly land.

13b-14 The prophet returns to common priestly and Levitical issues. The 25,000-by-20,000-cubit measurements are arrived at by adding the width of the two strips of land. Introducing a feature missing in 45:1-8, v. 14 highlights the inalienability of these holdings with a prohibition on selling, trading, or transferring the property into anyone else's hands. Although Yahweh is sovereign over the entire land of Israel in a general sense, as a *tĕrûmâ* presented by the people, he has a special claim to this property. That claim must be strictly guarded by those authorized to live on it, his officially consecrated cult functionaries. This injunction recalls the regulations governing the prince's allotment (45:16-18), though here the emphasis on the land as Yahweh's sacred property is much stronger. Remarkably, however, this text is silent on the 500-cubit-square holy place referred to in 45:2.

(b) The Public Allotment (48:15-20)

15 *"The remaining five thousand cubits wide area alongside the twenty-five thousand cubits shall be open to the public.*[134] *It shall belong to the city, providing residential and open space. The city itself shall be located in the center.* 16 *These are its [the city's] dimensions: the north side forty-five hundred cubits; the south side forty-five hundred cubits;*[135] *the east side*[136] *forty-five hundred cubits; the west side forty-five hundred cubits.* 17 *The open space belonging to the city shall extend two hundred fifty cubits to the north, two hundred fifty cubits to the south, two hundred fifty cubits to the east, and two hundred fifty cubits to the west.* 18 *The remaining area that runs lengthwise alongside the sacred reserve shall measure ten thousand cubits on the east side and ten thousand cubits on the west.*[137] *Its produce shall*

133. For the sake of comparison, the translation in the synopsis is necessarily more literal than that offered with the commentary.

134. *ḥōl hû'*, lit. "it shall be profane/unconsecrated." As in 2 Sam. 20:15, 1 K. 21:23, and Lam. 2:8, LXX προτείχισμα has misread *ḥōl* as *ḥēl* (*hyl*), "rampart."

135. The dittography represented by the second *ḥmš* was recognized already by the Masoretes, who deliberately failed to add vowel points.

136. *ûpĕ'at* is mistakenly written *ûmippĕ'at* in MT.

137. MT adds *wĕhāyâ lĕ'ummat tĕrûmat haqqōdeš*, "and it will be alongside the sacred reserve." This is a case of vertical dittography from the identical phrase in the previous line that must have occurred early since it is supported by the versions.

provide food for the city's laborers. 19 *The city's workforce,*[138] *coming from all the tribes of Israel, shall farm it.*[139] 20 *The entire reserve shall be a square*[140] *twenty-five thousand cubits by twenty-five thousand cubits. You shall set apart the sacred reserve along with the property of the city."*

In 45:6 Ezekiel had introduced "the city possession" *('ăḥuzzat hā'îr)* as a 5,000-cubit wide strip of land adjacent to the sacred reserve *(tĕrûmat haq-qōdeš)* belonging to the entire house of Israel *(lĕkol-bêt yiśrā'ēl).* Now he returns to this theme for fuller exposition.

15-17 Verse 15 opens with a reference to "the remainder" *(han-nôtār),* that is, the 5,000-cubit wide rectangle that remains of the 25,000-cubit square in the center of the greater *tĕrûmâ,* once the priestly and Levitical allotments have been isolated. The description of the city, located in the center *(bĕtôkōh)* of this rectangle, opens with a formal superscription: *wĕ'ēlleh mid-dôtêhā,* "Now these are its measurements." Although the city is square in shape, the length of each side *(pē'â)* is mentioned separately;[141] north, south, east, and west sides are all 4,500 cubits (about 1.5 mi.). This interest in specifics continues in v. 17, which announces in the identical north-south-east-west order that the city is framed on each side by a 250-cubit (about 430 ft.) open area *(migrāš).* Together the city and its open space constitute a 5,000-cubit square, extending from one side of the 5,000-cubit rectangle of land to the other. The remainder *(hannôtār)* consists of two 10,000 × 5,000 cubit rectangles east and west of the city, adjacent to the sacred reserve *(tĕrûmat haqqōdeš).* So far the description of the city and its lands.

But what was the purpose of these allotments so carefully surveyed and mapped? The text offers several clues. First, the earlier notice that the city belonged to the entire house of Israel (45:6) is now formally confirmed: *it shall be open to the public* here *(ḥōl-hû',* lit. "it is profane/unconsecrated," v. 15). Unlike 7:21-24, 22:16, and elsewhere, *ḥōl* does not carry negative defiling connotations. In this context, as in 22:26, 42:20, and 44:23, the word expressed the antithesis of sanctity, in the sense of unconsecrated, ordinary, common.[142] In contrast to the priests' and Levitical allotments to the north,

138. MT construes *hā'ōbēd* as a collective; LXX renders the word as a pl.

139. The masc. suffix on *ya'abĕdûhû* refers to *nôtār,* and no emendation is necessary. On the attachment of the suffix directly to the verb in later Hebrew see Rooker, *Biblical Hebrew in Transition,* pp. 86-87.

140. *rĕbî'ît* usually denotes "fourth." Unless the word may also mean "square," an emendation to *rĕbû'â* or *mĕrubba'at* is suggested.

141. Cf. the simpler description of the holy place *(haqqōdeš)* in 45:2 as a 500 × 500 cubit square *(mĕrubbā').*

142. Cf. W. Dommershausen, *TDOT,* 4:416-17.

the city was open to the public. The construction of v. 15bα is awkward, but the expression *lĕmôšāb,* "for dwelling," suggests that the city was designed to provide pilgrims from the tribal lands with housing whenever they came to the sanctuary to worship.

Second, the city is surrounded by *migrāš,* a word that generally identifies a demarcated zone outside the walls of a city. In an earlier period the *migrāš* around Levitical cities had been set apart as pastureland for the Levites' livestock (Num. 35:4-5). Here the term represents an unoccupied strip of agricultural land around the city core,[143] apparently set apart to provide board and sustenance for worshipers temporarily residing in the city.

18-19   Third, vv. 18-19 designate the larger tracts of land on either side of the city as a source of food for the city's workers *('ōbĕdê hā'îr).* The latter are apparently to be distinguished from the worshipers, who would spend a few days in the city and then return to their homes. Providing accommodation for all these pilgrims required a permanent administrative and manual labor force. To ensure parity, and to provide equal access to the privilege, the workers were to be drawn from all the tribes. These 10,000 × 5,000–cubit zones east and west of the city presumably served the practical purpose of compensating for land within the workers' own tribal allotments that had to be given up whenever they were appointed for city service.

20   This verse summarizes the content of vv. 8-19. Taken together, the sacred reserve, consisting of the priestly and Levitical allotment, and the city property form a 25,000-cubit square.

The design of this area reflects three levels of increasing sanctity: profane city, moderately sacred Levitical tract, most sacred priestly land. The text is frustratingly vague, however, on the spatial relationships among these three, especially the relative positions of the priests' and the Levites' allotments. The traditional interpretation of *bĕtôkô/ōh* in vv. 8 and 10 would have the sanctuary located in the "center" of the 10,000-cubit wide priestly *tĕrûmâ* (v. 10), which is positioned between the Levitical allotment to the north and the city property to the south (vv. 15-20).[144] But one should probably understand *bĕtôk* more loosely as "in the midst," rather than "in the center," and the three east-west strips of land belonging to the priests, the Levites, and the city should be taken together as a 25,000-cubit square in the midst of the broader *tĕrûmâ,* with the crown lands on either side. If one assumes with medieval commentators that the general north-south orientation of chs. 47–48 extends to 48:8-22, then the present order of

---

143. Cf. Barr, *JSS* 29 (1984) 15-31.

144. See the sketches by Cooke, *Ezekiel,* p. 532; Fuhs, *Ezechiel 25–48,* p. 271; Allen, *Ezekiel 20–48,* p. 282. Zimmerli (*Ezekiel 2,* p. 535) moves the sanctuary northward nearer to the border of the Levites' allotment so it is in the center of the larger *tĕrûmâ.*

descriptions of the priestly, Levitical, and city properties also reflects their geographic arrangements. Accordingly, the priestly strip is the most northerly, abutting the territory of Judah, with the Levitical allotment sandwiched between it and the city property, which abuts the land of Benjamin (fig. 11).[145] Further observations on the significance of this arrangement will be offered below.

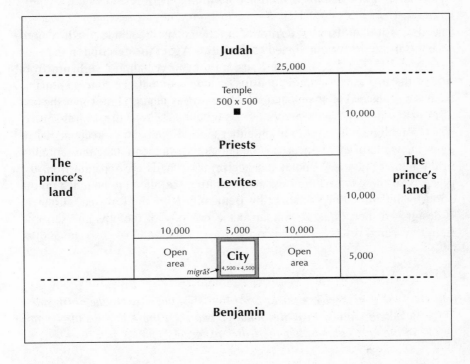

Figure 11. The Sacred Reserve

(3) The Allotments of the Prince (48:21-22)

21 *"The remaining areas on either side of the sacred reserve and the city property shall belong to the prince. The prince shall own [the land] parallel to the [tribal] portions[146] from the twenty-five thousand*

145. Thus Macholz, *VT* 19 (1969) 335; Greenberg, *Int* 38 (1984) 202; Klein, *Ezekiel*, p. 186.
146. The article seems to have dropped off *ḥĕlāqîm* by haplography.

cubit reserve[147] *as far as the eastern frontier, and westward from the twenty-five thousand [cubit reserve] as far as*[148] *the western frontier. The sacred reserve and the sanctuary of the temple shall be located in its center.*[149] 22 *It shall be separate from the property of the Levites and the city property*[150] *located in the midst of the area belonging to the prince. [The area lying] between the territory of Judah and the territory of Benjamin shall belong to the prince."*[151]

The discussion of Israel's territorial arrangements concludes with a brief account of the property assigned to the *nāśî'*. Again the description depends heavily on 45:7-8. The opening lines are taken over almost verbatim from 45:7. After that the description goes its own way, though the concern remains the dimensions and relative locations of the prince's land. Three times the text affirms that the *nāśî'*'s property is to lie on either side of the central square. V. 21a highlights their position on either side of the central precinct; v. 21b gives the width of these tracts (25,000 cubits), again mentioning the centrality of the temple; and v. 22 notes that the prince's lands are separate from the property of the city and the Levites, reiterating that they are bounded on the north by Judah and on the south by Benjamin. Now the Levitical allotment is designated their *'ăhuzzâ*, similar to the property of the city, and separate from the sacred reserve.

4. The New City (48:30-35)

> 30 *"And these are the exterior limits*[1] *of the city: On the north side,*[2] *which measures*[3] *forty-five hundred cubits,* 31 *there shall be three gates of the city, named after the tribes of Israel:*[4]

147. Thus MT, supported by Targ., but *tĕrûmâ* is missing in LXX and Syr. On the basis of the parallel in the next line many emend to *qādîmâ* (Zimmerli, *Ezekiel 2*, p. 525; Allen, *Ezekiel 20–48*, p. 275).

148. On *'al* in the sense of *'el* see my *Ezekiel: Chapters 1–24*, p. 99 n. 67. Emendation to *'ad (BHS)* to preserve the parallelism is unnecessary.

149. The suffix on Kethib *btkh* refers to the sacred precinct, not to the rest of the area as suggested by Qere *btkw*.

150. Though attested in the versions, the preposition *min* prefixed to *'ăhuzzat* in both instances is often deleted as a scribal error; but see Allen, *Ezekiel 2*, p. 276.

151. Many follow Syr. in dropping *lannāśî' yihyeh* as a dittograph (Allen, *Ezekiel 20–48*, p. 276), but the versional omission may be the result of haplography.

1. *tôṣĕ'ôt*, lit. "exits." So the versions, but see the commentary.

2. The preposition *min* on *mippĕ'at* is used locatively.

3. *middâ*, lit. "measurement," occurs in connection with the north and south sides only. There is no need to impose stylistic conformity on vv. 30-34 (cf. Syr.).

4. The Hebrew, which is rather clumsy at this point, translates lit., "And the gates

    Gate 1:[5] *Reuben;*   *Gate 2: Judah;*   *Gate 3: Levi.*

32 *On*[6] *the forty-five-hundred-cubit east side there shall be three gates:*

    Gate[7] *1: Joseph;*   *Gate 2: Benjamin;*   *Gate 3: Dan.*

33 *On the south side, which measures forty-five hundred cubits, there shall be three gates:*

    Gate 1: Simeon;   *Gate 2: Issachar;*   *Gate 3: Zebulun.*

34 *On*[8] *the forty-five-hundred-cubit west side there shall be three gates:*[9]

    Gate 1: Gad;   *Gate 2: Asher;*   *Gate 3: Naphtali.*

35 *The perimeter shall be 18 thousand cubits. And from that time*[10] *on the name of the city shall be 'Yahweh Shammah.'*"[11]

The section 48:30-35 is a supplement to the chapter and the book, set off formally by the title, *wĕʾelleh tôṣĕʾōt hāʿîr,* "Now these are the exterior limits of the city." However, the geographic focus and the use of *ʾeḥād,* "one," to identify items in the list (cf. 48:1) link this text with the foregoing. Indeed, one may interpret it as an expansion of v. 16. The form of the title is familiar, but the vocabulary is not; this is the only occurrence of *tôṣĕʾōt* in the book.[12] The traditional rendering of the word, "exits," is based on the normal use of

---

of the city [shall be named] after the names of the tribes of Israel, three gates facing north. . . ." Contra Zimmerli (*Ezekiel 2,* p. 544), however, reconstruction of the verse is unnecessary.

    5. On the significance of the numeral *ʾeḥād,* "one," which follows each name, see above on v. 1.

    6. On *ʾel* in the sense of *ʿal* see my *Ezekiel: Chapters 1–24,* p. 99 n. 67. Vv. 33-34 drop the preposition.

    7. Dropping the conjunction on *šaʿar,* with numerous Hebrew mss. and the versions.

    8. The parallels and the versional evidence suggest restoring the copula to MT *pĕʾat.*

    9. The lack of an antecedent and the parallels suggest restoring MT *šaʿărêhem* to *ûšĕʿārîm* with Syr. and one LXX*.

    10. On the use of *yôm,* "day," in the sense of "time" see R. Althann, "*Yôm,* 'Time' and Some Texts in Isaiah," *JNSL* 11 (1983) 3-8.

    11. LXX either misread *yhwh šāmmâ* as *yhwh šĕmâ,* "Yahweh is its name," or is based on a different *Vorlage.* Cf. Syr. *mryʾ šmmh,* "Lord is his name," and Targ.'s expansive, *wšmh dqrtʾ ytprš mywmʾ dyšry škyntyh ywy tymn,* "And the name of the city, designated from the day that the Lord makes His Shekinah rest upon it, shall be: The Lord is there." Thus Levey, *Ezekiel,* p. 129. Y. Qoler suggests the final *hē* on *šāmmâ* functions as an abbreviation for the tetragrammaton ("Biblical Symbols, Abbreviations, and Acronyms," *Beth Mikra* 35 [1989-90] 317-24 [Hebrew]).

    12. Cf. *môṣāʾîm* in 42:11; 43:11; 44:5.

the root *yṣ'*, "to go out."[13] But this meaning ill suits the present context, which describes city walls, each according to its measurements and the gates that punctuate it.[14] It is preferable to recognize here the influence of Num. 34, where the word is used of geographical "extremities, outskirts."[15] Why this word should have been preferred over the normal expression for walls, *ḥômâ* (26:4, 9, 10, 12; 38:20), is not clear, but it may provide a hint at their anomalous function. Normally walls are designed to restrict access, to keep unwanted people out, but the multiplicity of gates and the idyllic nature of the present vision suggest the opposite function.[16]

The manner in which the measurement of each side is given echoes v. 16.[17] But the modification in sequence, from north-south-east-west to clockwise north-east-south-west, follows the survey of the boundaries of the land (47:15-20), suggesting that the city is being perceived as a microcosm of the land.[18] The image of a city with twelve gates *(šĕʿārîm)* distributed equally among the four sides and named after the twelve tribes of Israel is strikingly unconventional. City walls were usually designed intentionally with only one gate, though the Jerusalem Ezekiel knew had at least six.[19] A remarkable extrabiblical analogue to the present design is found in the Babylonian temple tower of Marduk, Etemenanki, whose sacred precinct was also laid out as a square, accessible through twelve gates.[20] Unlike Ezekiel's city, however, these were not distributed equally among the four sides. Whether or not Ezekiel was familiar with Etemenanki, his twelve gates offered unrestricted access to Israelite worshipers from all points of the

---

13. Thus the versions and most modern translations (NJPS, NRSV, NIV, NASB, etc.).

14. M. R. Hauge, "Some Aspects of the Motif 'The City Facing Death' of Ps 68,21," *SJOT* 1 (1988) 5-6.

15. So also Allen, *Ezekiel 20–48*, p. 276, following Cook, *Ezekiel*, p. 537. This usage occurs also in Josh. 17:18; 1 Chr. 5:16; Ps. 68:21 (Eng. 20).

16. The walls of the temple complex were also to restrict access; see 40:5; 42:20. Cf. the reference to cities without walls in 38:11.

17. Note the term for measurement, *middâ* (vv. 30, 33; cf. pl. *middôt* in v. 16), and the length of the walls (4,500 cubits), which yield a perimeter of 18,000 cubits.

18. Cf. Allen, *Ezekiel 20–28*, p. 284.

19. For illustrations see Pritchard, ed., *Harper Atlas*, pp. 120-21. Jeremiah mentions the following: Potsherd Gate (19:2, perhaps known as the Dung Gate in Nehemiah's time; cf. Neh. 2:13; 3:13-14; 12:31), Corner Gate (31:38), Horse Gate (31:40), Benjamin Gate (20:2; 37:13; 38:7), People's Gate (17:19), Middle Gate (39:3, perhaps to be identified with the Ephraim Gate of 2 K. 14:13 = 2 Chr. 25:23), Gate Between the Walls (52:7). On Jerusalem in the preexilic period see D. Bahat, *The Illustrated Atlas of Jerusalem*, tr. S. Ketko (New York: Simon and Schuster, 1990), pp. 24-31; W. S. LaSor, *ISBE*, 2:1013-16.

20. For the temple plan see Wiseman, *Nebuchadrezzar*, p. 69; Unger, *Babylon*, plate 24, fig. 36.

compass, a point emphasized explicitly by naming the gates after the twelve tribes of Israel.

The notion of gates named after Israelite tribes is not new, but Ezekiel's rationale is not entirely clear. The preexilic pattern of naming gates after tribal territories toward which they open is followed in the names of the northern and southern gates,[21] with the remainder (except for Levi) distributed between the eastern and western sides. Whereas the entries in the territorial list had been based on past history and geography, the names of the city gates adhere more closely to Israel's genealogical traditions. Levi now finds his rightful place among the tribes, forcing the subsumption of Ephraim and Manasseh under Joseph to preserve the quota of twelve names. Unlike the reasoned order of the tribal territories, the arrangement of the gate names is uncertain. There is no doubt about which names are on which side, but their order depends on whether the clockwise sequence of compass points extends to the sequence of names as well. The options may be illustrated as follows:

Revision of the description of the four gates

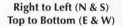
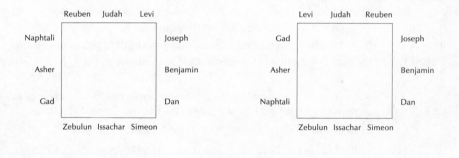

21. Note the Ephraim (2 K. 14:13 = 2 Chr. 25:23) and Benjamin (Jer. 37:13; 38:7; Zech. 14:10) gates. Cf. LaSor, *ISBE,* 2:1014-15. The Judah and Reuben gates open northward, and the Simeon, Issachar, and Zebulun gates open southward, all toward their territorial namesakes.

22. Based on the east-west orientation of the tribal allotments. Cf. vv. 1-7, 23-27.

The boundary descriptions of the land of Israel (47:15-20) provide a precedent for the clockwise arrangement,[23] but the second option adheres more closely to the tribal territorial allotments, the closer antecedent. Nonetheless, the groupings of names, which again reflect an awareness of the genealogical tradition, are more important than their sequence. The names of the three most important Leah tribes are on the north side, with Judah in the center (nearest the temple); the remaining three Leah names are opposite them to the south. Joseph and Benjamin, the two sons of Rachel, are appropriately linked on the east side, and the two Zilpah tribes are together in the west, leaving only the Bilhah tribes, Naphtali and Dan, which are split up to fill the gaps in the east and west sides, but positioned opposite each other (according to the second option).

If the square layout of the city and the twelve-gate system resemble the sacred precinct of Marduk in Babylon, Ezekiel's naming of the gates after the names of the tribes of Israel compares with the naming of the nine gates of Babylon after Babylonian deities.[24] Named after the patron deities of the cities to which the roads that passed through them led, they also designated the processional point of entrance of each of these gods in the annual New Year's celebration in honor of Marduk.[25] Ezekiel may have passed through Babylon some time during his exile, and/or been familiar with the city plan, including the sequence of gates in the wall. If so, one may recognize in his naming of the city gates a profound ideological message. If the naming of Babylon's gates after divinities reflects a perception of the sanctity of the city,[26] by ascribing tribal names to this city Ezekiel gives concrete witness to this as "the people's city," accessible to citizens from every part of the nation.[27] At the same time, he has repudiated the notion of a political capital, linked with any particular tribe, as Jerusalem, the Judahite capital, had been.

23. This arrangement is assumed by Wise (*Temple Scroll,* pp. 78-79), who makes the following comparison with the gates of the city in the Qumran Temple Scroll:

	Ezekiel	**Temple Scroll**
North	Reuben, Judah, Levi	Dan, Naphtali, Asher
East	Joseph, Benjamin, Dan,	Simeon, Levi, Judah
South	Simeon, Issachar, Zebulun,	Reuben, Joseph, Benjamin
West	Gad, Asher, Naphtali	Issachar, Zebulun, Gad

24. Cf. the north side: Lugalgirra (= Nergal) Gate, Ishtar Gate, Sin Gate; the east side: Marduk Gate, Zababa (= Ninurta) Gate; the south side: Enlil Gate, Urash Gate, Shamash Gate; the west Side: Adad Gate. For maps see Wiseman, *Nebuchadrezzar,* pp. 46-47; Unger, *Babylon,* plate 57.

25. On the nature and significance of these gates see Unger, *Babylon,* pp. 65-75.

26. Cf. the title of Unger's book, *Babylon: Die heilige Stadt nach der Beschreibung der Babylonier.*

27. Cf. the characterization of the city as *ḥōl,* "common," in v. 15.

Nor is this the city of a king, as the city of David had been. The *nāśî'* has no claim to it; it belongs to everybody (cf. 45:6).

Characterizing the city as *ḥōl,* "common" (v. 15), and opening it to the masses of Israel's population, however, does not mean that it is perceived as secular, sterilized of theological and spiritual significance. On the contrary, from the time of its founding, or at least the naming of the gates, the city will bear a new name, *yhwh šāmmâ,* "Yahweh is there." Like Ezekiel's restoration oracles, this name announces the undoing of a past evil situation. The sound of *yhwh šāmmâ* may remind some of *yĕrûšālayim,* "Jerusalem,"[28] but the city's past bloodshed *(dāmîm),* abominations *(tô'ăbôt),* and idolatry *(gillûlîm)* had so polluted the name[29] that Ezekiel (Yahweh) could not name this place after the old city. With its Canaanite origins, the name Jerusalem symbolized the city's degenerate and faithless past; but Ezekiel looks forward to a new day when the city will bear the name of Yahweh with honor.[30] At the same time, he announces a reversal of the city's most recent past. The crisis precipitated by Yahweh's abandonment of the city, so graphically portrayed in chs. 8–11, is over; Yahweh has returned!

But there is something else remarkable about this city bearing this new name. The center of gravity in Ezekiel's cartography of power is obviously the temple, the place where Yahweh resides in the midst of the most sacred *tĕrûmâ* several miles north of the city.[31] In comparison the city is for human habitation; it is "profane, common" *(ḥōl);* it is located in the geographic residue, the leftover *(hannôtār,* v. 15). Like the temple, however, the city is located in the center of the (civic) band; it also is square, and surrounded by open space *(migrāš).* But with this new name the implicit symbolism of the design is made explicit: the city reflects the presence of Yahweh! With this renaming, a place of "secular" work and agricultural production, with a mixed

---

28. Cf. McConville, *Jerusalem,* p. 43; Greenberg, *Int* 38 (1984) 202.

29. Note *ṭĕmē'at haššēm,* "defiled of name," in 22:5.

30. The name, which means something like "foundation of [the god] Shalem," is first attested in the 19th/18th-century Egyptian Execration Texts as (U)rušalimum (Aḥituv, *Canaanite Toponyms,* p. 122; *ANET,* p. 329), and appears again as Urušalim in Akkadian Amarna Letters from the 14th century B.C. Cf. appellations for Jerusalem/Zion elsewhere in the OT: *'îr hā'ĕlōhîm,* "the city of God" (Ps. 46:5 [Eng. 4]; 48:2, 9 [Eng. 1, 8]), *qiryat melek rāb,* "the city of the great king" (Ps. 48:3 [Eng. 2]), and *'îr yhwh,* "the city of Yahweh" (Isa. 60:14; Ps. 48:9 [Eng. 8]; 101:8), as well as Jeremiah's anticipatory *yhwh ṣisqēnû,* "Yahweh is our righteousness" (33:16).

31. Depending on where one locates the priestly *tĕrûmâ* and the temple within it, the distance could be (1) under 2 mi., if the temple is located in the center of the priestly *tĕrûmâ,* which in turn is between the Levitical allotment and the "common" remainder (Allen, *Ezekiel 20–48,* p. 283); (2) about 2½ mi. if the temple is in the center of the reserve as a whole (Zimmerli, *Ezekiel 2,* p. 535); (3) 4-5 mi. if (as I prefer) the temple is in the center of the priestly *tĕrûmâ,* which is adjacent to the allotment of Judah.

lay population, is converted into a civic counterbalance to the gravity of the temple within the sacred realm.[32] The aura of the divine presence will emanate forth beyond the sacred residence, pervading the entire reserve, and transforming a symbol of mere social and civic egalitarianism into a portent of the new spiritual reality. The name celebrates the healing of relationships among deity, people, and land. Under the new order, where the people are, there is Yahweh. He does not only invite them to himself in the temple; he has come to them!

The stylization and idealism evident in Ezekiel's description of temple and Torah continues in Ezekiel's territorial vision. This is evident in at least six cartographic features. First, undergirded by egalitarian convictions, and designed to correct the injustices of the past, the tribal territories appear as strips of land running across the land from east to west without respect to — nay, in defiance of — the geographic grain. Second, the territorial allocations, with the secondary tribes assigned the outer territories and Judah and Benjamin at the center, are governed more by ideal than historical reality. Third, the centrifugal Mosaic arrangement for extending the influence of the cult to all parts of the nation through Levitical cities is replaced by a centripetal paradigm in which all cultic and administrative personnel live near the central shrine, and all Israel must come to it for worship. Fourth, the land set aside for the prince and the religious functionaries displays the same concern for balance and symmetry evident in the temple complex itself. While the reserve as a whole consists of a strip of land 25,000 cubits wide running all the way across the land, parallel to the tribal allotments, it is divided into three parts. The religious properties in the center are flanked by the *nāśî'* lands on each side. Fifth, the sacred heartland consists of identical priestly and Levitical allotments (25,000 × 10,000 cubits), but the addition of the city property yields a perfect square, 25,000 × 25,000 cubits. Sixth, the city's design transcends topography, history, and custom. It is laid out as a perfect 4,500-cubit square, with twelve gates, named after the tribes of Israel and distributed equally among the four walls (for an era of peace!). Furthermore, this "capital" belongs to the people; it is not the private property of the king or the preserve of one tribe. In the light of all these considerations, a literal fulfillment of these conditions is obviously not anticipated.

For all its surreality and stylization, the earthiness of Ezekiel's vision of the city of the redeemed contrasts sharply with that of Isa. 54:12. The latter text captivates the imagination with images of gates made of crystal and walls decorated throughout with precious stones. Centuries later, the Christian apostle John combined these two models in a glorious apocalyptic

32. Cf. Smith, *To Take Place,* pp. 68-69.

vision of the holy city, the new Jerusalem (Rev. 21:10-17). The images of splendor are borrowed from Isa. 54, but the basic design derives from Ezekiel. This new Jerusalem, which descends out of heaven from God, is also laid out as a square, surrounded by a great wall. While the foundation stones are named after the twelve apostles, the twelve magnificent gates[33] (three on each side) are named after the tribes of Israel. But John's creativity is as impressive as his appreciation for the prophetic tradition. His heavenly Jerusalem needs no temple for God to reside in and from which his glory could emanate; the Lord God the Almighty and the Lamb are its temple, and the glory of the Lord radiates forth from him (Rev. 21:22-23). Furthermore, while John has no reservations about the name Jerusalem, his city has taken on a universal character. All the nations will walk by the light of the divine *kābôd* (δόξα τοῦ Θεοῦ, Rev. 21:24), and the kings of the earth will bring their tribute (δόξα) to it (21:24-27), which contrasts sharply with Ezekiel's parochialism.

Contrary to the opinion of many, Ezekiel's cartographic vision is extremely narrow.[34] It appears sometimes that he deliberately reins in universalistic tendencies of the so-called Zion-tradition (cf. Isa. 2:1-4; Mic. 4:1-4). Not only does the river that flows from Jerusalem affect only the land of Israel (Ezek. 47:1-12); Ezekiel gives no hint anywhere of expanding his horizons. He is concerned exclusively with the salvation of his people. Aliens are welcome in the community of faith (cf. 47:22-23), but only as they integrate into the physical people of Yahweh. Ezekiel's city is open to the twelve tribes of Israel; he is silent on admission to anyone else. But for John the boundaries of the covenant have been burst wide open. Entrance to the city is gained through the gates of the twelve tribes, but the kingdom of God rests on the foundation of the twelve apostles.

♦ *Theological Implications*

In spite of the overt parochialism of this, the last in the collection of Ezekiel's prophecies, the theological implications for the modern reader are compelling.

First, Ezekiel's vision of Israel's territorial arrangement offers a profound theology of land. Most obviously, the land belongs to God. As sovereign he has authority to distribute it among his people; he is entitled to "royal lands"; his residence constitutes the geographic center of gravity. His call for a *těrûmâ* invites his subjects to acknowledge his sovereignty and celebrate the receipt of the national territory as a gift from him. Just as in the cult,

33. In v. 21 he notes that the gates were made of twelve pearls.
34. So also K. P. Darr, "The Wall Around Paradise: Ezekielian Ideas about the Future," *VT* 37 (1987) 271-79.

where the *tĕrûmâ* offered worshipers an opportunity to return a gift of produce to Yahweh in recognition of his ownership over all things, so this territorial *tĕrûmâ* reminds Israel that Yahweh is the real owner of the land.

Second, Ezekiel's territorial vision extends the concentric rectangles of graded sanctity beyond the temple walls. The concentricity is admittedly not exact, but the sanctuary represents the center of gravity for the priestly share of the *tĕrûmâ,* which is the center of gravity of the central square of the reserve, which in turn is the center of gravity for the nation as a whole. Whereas the temple design carefully regulated access to the different gradations of holiness in cultic worship, the territorial allotments regulated daily life. Priests and Levites did not occupy tribal property, but they, and only they, could live in land set aside for Yahweh. Citizens of the twelve tribes could own their land, but access to the *tĕrûmâ* would not only be temporary; they entered through the filter of the city. To the smallest and largest detail Ezekiel's final vision proclaims the holiness of Yahweh, and the sanctity of his land. God may condescend to reside among his own people, but he does so without any sacrifice to his holiness.

Third, Ezekiel's territorial vision proclaims a new understanding of the community of faith. If the allocation of land to each of the tribes, with special allotments for the religious functionaries, recognizes structure within the people of God, the nature of the distributions also affirms divine concerns for justice. The allotment of land "each like his brother" is based on egalitarian foundations designed to prevent the social injustices of the past. Without equitable distribution Yahweh's ancient promises to the nation cannot be fully realized by all. Even the design and function of the city reflect Ezekiel's fundamental social premise, that all citizens have equal rights to his worship, as well as to his benefits. This city is for the entire household of faith, irrespective of tribe and social standing. Furthermore, and despite the prophet's exclusivistic vision, aliens are welcome here. They must come on Yahweh's terms, through the existing community of faith, to be sure, but if they identify with the faith of his people they are entitled to all the rights and privileges extended to the heirs of the traditions.

Fourth, this vision proclaims a new understanding of civil leadership. The *nāśî'* in Ezekiel's concluding vision is an enigmatic figure. On the one hand, the title links him with the person described in 34:24 and 37:25. But the portrait of this person is less than ideal, and in the narrative of the vision the prophet avoids any Davidic connection, the basis of all messianic hopes. On the other hand, he does play an extremely important role in the new society. Having commented on each of the fragments in which the *nāśî'*'s position in Ezekiel's new order is defined (44:3, 45:7-8 and its echo in 48:21, and 45:21–46:12), I may synthesize and summarize his privileges and responsibilities as follows.

1. Although the outer eastern gateway is forever closed to human traffic, the *nāśî'* alone may sit in the gateway and eat his sacrificial meals there (44:1-3).
2. The *nāśî'* is assigned a special territorial grant, separate from the tribal allotments, consisting of two large tracts of land on either side, east and west, of the sacred reserve (45:7-9; 48:21).
3. The *nāśî'* must provide the prescribed animals, grain and oil for the purification *(haṭṭā't),* whole burnt *('ôlâ)* offerings, and grain *(minḥâ)* offerings, which are to be offered on his and the people's behalf (45:21-25).
4. On weekly Sabbaths and new moon celebrations the *nāśî'* shall enter the eastern gateway of the inner court through the vestibule, stand by the post of the gate,[35] that is, the jamb between the vestibule and the series of guard recesses (see 40:28-37), to observe the priests presenting the offerings on his behalf. Forbidden to step out onto the most sacred space of the inner court, he must prostrate himself on the threshold of the gate (46:1-7, 12).
5. At the appointed festivals the *nāśî'* must enter the sacred precinct with the rest of the lay worshipers, who are permitted to enter the outer court through either the northern or the southern gate. Unlike the *nāśî',* however, the common folk may not turn around inside the precinct and exit via the gate through which they entered (46:8-10).
6. The *nāśî'* may present additional voluntary offerings to Yahweh, but they must be presented in the same way as the Sabbath and new moon offerings, with him observing from the inner east gate. After the offerings are completed, he must leave this gate and it shall be shut behind him (46:12).
7. The *nāśî'* may present portions of his property to his sons as their permanent possessions, but should he wish to award any of his land to his servants, in the year of liberation *(šĕnat haddĕrôr)* it must return to the prince (46:17).
8. The *nāśî'* is forbidden from confiscating property of the people and giving them to his sons as their own territorial grants (46:18).

What then is to be made of all these regulations? Some have recently recognized in the Ezekielian Torah a fundamentally antimonarchic polemic.[36] Whereas under the old order kings had built temples, appointed cult officials,

35. The architectural vocabulary changes from ch. 40, *mĕzûzâ,* "doorpost," replacing *'ayil,* though *mĕzûzâ* had been used of the doorposts of the temple (41:21; 43:8; 45:19) and the inner gate (*mĕzûzat ša'ar,* 45:19).

36. Smith, *To Take Place,* pp. 61-62; Stevenson, *Vision,* pp. 139-43.

assigned ritual duties, offered sacrifices, and encroached on sacred space with their private buildings (43:7-8), this ordinance assigns the civil ruler a third rank — two or three rungs below deity. Zadokite priests have access to Yahweh, and the Levitical priests may serve within the courts, but the *nāśî'* is repulsed. He must eat his meals at the gate.[37] Furthermore, in this vision the temple is deliberately separated from the royal palace complex (43:8; 48:19), the capital "city" is not the king's private preserve but belongs to the entire house of Israel, and severe restrictions are placed on the prince's management of land.

But these details do not necessarily reflect a basic antimonarchic stance in Ezekiel's final vision. One must distinguish between the monarchy in principle and the conduct of Israel's monarchs in history. In the face of the general ancient Near Eastern association of mature nationhood with kingship structures, specific traditional monarchic expectations, and the eternality of the Davidic covenant (2 Sam. 7), it is inconceivable that Ezekiel would have opposed the monarchy per se. On the contrary, as we have seen, in Ezek. 37:16-28 (cf. 34:23-24) the prophet combines ancient tribal and Davidic covenantal traditions to promise specifically the return of David as *melek* over all the tribes of Israel. Furthermore, reconfiguring power structures is no guarantee that the abuses of the past will be resolved. Ezekiel's final vision does not eliminate hierarchical institutions; it redefines how existing structures will work in his new order.

Scholars have correctly recognized the special status of the *nāśî'* in Ezekiel's final vision.[38] He is clearly an exalted figure, far more important than the "princes" of the premonarchic period. But does this mean that Ezekiel identifies this *nāśî'* with the messianic figure described in 34:23-25 and 37:21-25? According to some, to deny this link appears to drive a wedge between the *nāśî'* in chs. 40–48 and the *nāśî'* in earlier chapters.[39] However, this conclusion is not as certain as it seems. First, Israelite messianic expec-

37. Tuell (*The Law of the Temple,* p. 119) interprets *nāśî'* as equivalent to *phh,* "governor," as "a title descriptive of the cultic task of the *nśy'*." According to Tuell, for the postexilic priestly establishment this "was of paramount concern and reminiscent of Israel's ancient and honorable past, yet lacking dynastic or imperial overtones," hence unoffensive to the Persian overlords.

38. J. Wright comments: "The east gate legitimates the prince's power, equating him with the divine presence within the society" ("A Tale of Three Cities: Urban Gates, Squares, and Power in Iron Age II, Neo-Babylonian and Achaemenid Israel," paper presented to the Society of Biblical Literature Annual Meeting, New Orleans, November, 1990, p. 17).

39. Levenson, *Theology,* pp. 75-101. Laato (*Josiah and David Redivivus,* p. 196) recognizes the temple mountain, the restoration of the temple, and the important role of the Messiah in this restoration, as links between the pro-*nāśî'* traditions of chs. 40–48 and chs. 34 and 37.

tations were by definition monarchic in flavor, and immutably based on Yahweh's dynastic covenant with David.[40] But why are chs. 40–48 silent on the Davidic connection? They seem indeed to portray the *nāśî'* as an honorable figure, but without apparent political power. Second, Israelite messianism insisted on a close link between the Messiah and Jerusalem/Zion. But why does Jerusalem seem to be out of the picture in Ezekiel's final vision? The prince and his land are deliberately separated from the city bearing the name "Yahweh is there" (48:35) and the temple, Yahweh's true residence. Third, Israelite messianism perceives the Messiah as sovereign over the entire universe. But why does this vision both tie him down to the land of Israel and place severe restrictions on the rights of the *nāśî'*? Yahweh may authorize him, even invite him to eat before him in this gate, but as a mortal he must enter by another way. Only Yahweh may enter through the eastern gate. Fourth, and perhaps most seriously, elsewhere (including Ezekiel's own statements in 34:23-24 and 37:21-25) Israel's Messiah is always portrayed in glorious idealistic terms elsewhere. But why is the portrait of the *nāśî'* in the Ezekielian Torah so shockingly realistic? Not only must offerings be presented on his behalf; specific ordinances warn him not to exploit and abuse his subjects like Israel's kings had done in the past (46:18).

These questions may be answered from several directions. First, although one might expect a consistent use of a technical term like *nāśî'* throughout the book, Ezekiel has a habit of using the same expressions with different nuances.

Second, a dramatic shift in genre is evident between the earlier restoration oracles (chs. 34–39) and the idealistic final vision. Whereas the former are closely tied to history, anticipating a wholesale reversal of the events surrounding the fall of Jerusalem in 586 B.C., the latter is contrived, ideational, symbolic, and many of its features are unimaginable. Contrary to common popular opinion, the description of the temple is not presented as a blueprint for some future building to be constructed with human hands.[41] This vision picks up the theme of divine presence announced in 37:26-27 and describes the spiritual reality in concrete terms, employing the familiar cultural idioms of temple, altar, sacrifices, *nāśî'*, and land. In presenting this theological constitution for the new Israel, Yahweh announces the righting of all old wrongs and the establishment of permanent healthy deity-nation-land relationships. Ezekiel's final vision presents a lofty ideal: Where God

---

40. For a study of Ezekiel's messianic vision as a whole and the relationship of the *nāśî'* to the Messiah, see D. I. Block, "Bringing Back David: Ezekiel's Messianic Hope," in *The Lord's Anointed: Interpretation of Old Testament Messianic Texts,* eds. P. E. Satterthwaite, et al. (Grand Rapids: Baker, 1995), pp. 167-88.

41 A point convincingly argued by Stevenson, *Vision,* pp. 14-21.

is, there is Zion. Where God is, there is also order and the fulfillment of all his promises.

Third, the primary concern in this vision is not political but cultic. The issue is not the return of David but the presence of Yahweh. Accordingly, the *nāśî'*'s role is facilitative, not regally symbolic. Unlike past kings, who perverted the worship of Yahweh for selfish ends or sponsored the worship of other gods, this *nāśî'*'s charge is to promote the worship of Yahweh in spirit and in truth. In this vision (and only here), with its radically theocentric portrayal of Israel's future, the *nāśî'* emerges as a religious functionary, serving the holy community of faith, which itself is focused on the worship of the God who dwells in their midst. Where the presence of God is recognized, there is purity and holiness. Ezekiel's *nāśî'* is not responsible for the administration of the cult, he does not participate actively in the ritual, and he does not build the temple, design the worship, or appoint the priests. These prerogatives belong to Yahweh. This agrees with the image of the *nāśî'* in 34:23-24, who is installed as undershepherd by Yahweh only after the latter has personally rescued Israel.[42] In this ideological presentation the *nāśî'* functions as Yahweh's appointed lay patron and sponsor of the cult, whose activity ensures the continuance of *shalom* between deity and subjects. The God of Israel has fulfilled his covenant promises, regathering the people and restoring them to their/his land. More important, he has recalled the people to himself and established his residence in their midst. Now let them celebrate, and let the *nāśî'* lead the way!

Herein lies the hope of Ezekiel's message for Christians. In Jesus the Messiah, the glory of Yahweh, has descended and dwells among us, full of grace and truth (John 1:14). He is Immanuel, "God with us!" Where two or three are gathered in Jesus' name, there he is (Matt. 18:20).

---

42. Cf. Duguid, *Ezekiel and the Leaders,* pp. 50-55.

INDEX OF SELECTED SUBJECTS

INDEX OF AUTHORS

757

INDEX OF SCRIPTURE REFERENCES

Note: All references are to the Masoretic text.

INDEX OF EXTRACANONICAL
LITERATURE

INDEX OF SELECTED HEBREW
WORDS AND PHRASES

808